Criminal Procedure and Sentencing

Seventh Edition

Criminal Procedure and Sentencing provides a comprehensive, analytical and up-to-date guide to each step of the criminal process, from the arrest of the suspect through to trial, sentencing and appeals. Full account is taken of both statutory and case law developments.

Key aspects of criminal procedure and sentencing are analyzed in the light of sources such as Government consultation papers and academic commentary.

This seventh edition:

- has been completely re-written and includes new flowcharts and glossaries
- highlights areas of particular controversy or debate
- is supported by a Companion Website which provides regular updates on developments in this fast-moving area.

This book provides an excellent introduction to criminal procedure and sentencing for anyone studying the criminal process as part of an LLB or LLM degree, for students on the Bar Vocational Course or Legal Practice Course, and anyone who is involved in the operation of the criminal justice system or who is interested in how the system works.

The Companion Website is available at: http://www.routledgecavendish.com/textbooks/9780415442923

Peter Hungerford-Welch, LLB, PGC (TLHE), FHEA, Barrister (Inner Temple), is Associate Dean at The City Law School, City University, London.

Criminal Procedure and Sentencing

Seventh Edition

Peter Hungerford-Welch

Routledge·Cavendish
Taylor & Francis Group
LONDON AND NEW YORK

Seventh Edition published 2009
by Routledge-Cavendish
2 Park Square, Milton Park, Abingdon, Oxon, OX14 4RN

Simultaneously published in the USA and Canada
by Routledge-Cavendish
270 Madison Ave, New York, NY 10016

Previous editions published by Cavendish Publishing Limited

*Routledge-Cavendish is an imprint of the Taylor and Francis Group,
an informa business*

© 2009 Hungerford-Welch, P.

First edition   1994
Second edition   1995
Third edition   1996
Fourth edition   1998
Fifth edition   2000
Sixth edition   2004
Seventh edition   2009

Typeset in Times by RefineCatch Ltd, Bungay, Suffolk
Printed and bound in Great Britain by
TJ International Ltd, Padstow, Cornwall

British Library Cataloguing in Publication Data
A catalogue record for this book is available from the British Library

Library of Congress Cataloging in Publication Data
Hungerford-Welch, Peter.
   Criminal procedure and sentencing / Peter Hungerford-Welch. – 7th ed.
      p. cm.
   Rev. ed. of: Criminal litigation and sentencing / Peter Hungerford-Welch.
6th ed. 2004.

ISBN13: 978–0–415–44292–3 (pbk)
ISBN10: 0–415–44292–3 (pbk)

1. Criminal procedure – Great Britain. 2. Sentences (Criminal procedure) –
Great Britain. I. Hungerford-Welch, Peter. Criminal litigation and sentencing.
II. Title.
   KD8329.3.H86 2008
   345.42'05–dc22   2008003501

Dedicated to Jane Hungerford-Welch

Preface

This book started life as Lecture Notes on Criminal Litigation and Sentencing, a comparatively slim volume based on lectures given to students on the Bar Vocational Course at the Inns of Court School of Law (now fully incorporated into The City Law School at City University, London). After three editions under the Lecture Notes banner, it was felt that the book should be expanded to make it more useful for practitioners (barristers, solicitors and legal executives), for pupil barristers and trainee solicitors, and for students pursuing the academic study of criminal procedure as part of an LLB or LLM programme. Indeed, I hope that this book will be of interest to anyone who is interested in how our system of criminal justice operates.

As well as setting out the rules governing procedure and sentencing (based on statute law and on case law), there are also contextual materials to help the reader understand how the rules have come into existence and to evaluate those rules.

My thanks go to Routledge-Cavendish, and to the production company RefineCatch, for their hard work in putting this book together (and their patience with last-minute amendments). I owe a special debt of gratitude to my wife Jane, without whose help, encouragement and support this book would never have seen the light of day.

I have endeavoured to state the law as at June 2008.

Criminal justice is a fast-moving area, with a seemingly endless flow of statutes and case law. To keep this book up-to-date, there is a companion website at <http://www.routledgecavendish.com/textbooks/9780415442923/> where updated material will be placed regularly.

Peter Hungerford-Welch, LLB, PGC(TLHE), FHEA, Barrister
Associate Dean
The City Law School, City University, London
June 2008

Contents

Table of cases

Table of statutes

Table of statutory instruments

Table of European legislation

Chapter 1

Theoretical perspectives in criminal litigation

ABOUT THIS BOOK

This book offers a fairly detailed description of the system of criminal procedure in England and Wales. It also endeavours to explain how the system has come to be as it is. The book also provides some tools for critical analysis of the system, identifying possible shortcomings in the system.

In this first chapter, we look at some of the further reading that is available (both practitioner textbooks and texts and journals that are written from a more theoretical perspective) and at some websites that are of use to those interested in criminal justice. We then examine some of the theoretical perspectives that enable us to evaluate our criminal justice system.

1.1 SOURCES

First, we look at some of the sources that are available to those who want to find out more about the criminal justice system.

1.1.1 Practitioner texts

The main sources used by criminal practitioners are:

- *Blackstone's Criminal Practice*: a one-volume book published annually by Oxford University Press, with supplements issued during the course of the year. It contains substantive criminal law as well as procedure, evidence and sentencing, and covers both the Crown Court and magistrates' courts. There is a companion website at <http://www.oup.com/uk/>.
- *Archbold: Criminal Pleading Evidence and Practice*: a one-volume book published annually by Sweet & Maxwell, with supplements issued during the course of the year. It contains substantive criminal law as well as procedure, evidence and sentencing, but it only covers the Crown Court. There is also *Archbold Magistrates' Courts Criminal Practice*, a one-volume work (again published annually), covering magistrates' courts.
- *Stone's Justices Manual*: a three-volume annual publication. It contains substantive

law (both criminal and civil) as well as procedure, evidence and sentencing, but it covers only the magistrates' courts.

- Thomas, D, *Current Sentencing Practice* (Sweet and Maxwell, looseleaf).

1.1.2 Academic textbooks

Academic textbooks which offer critical analysis of some of the issues raised by the English Criminal Justice System include:

- Ashworth, A, *Sentencing and Criminal Justice* (Cambridge University Press, 2005).
- Ashworth, A and Redmayne, M, *The Criminal Process* (OUP, 2005).
- Easton, S and Piper, C, *Sentencing and Punishment: The Quest for Justice* (OUP, 2005).
- McConville, M and Wilson, G, *Handbook of the Criminal Justice Process* (OUP, 2002).
- Sanders, A and Young R, *Criminal Justice* (OUP, 2007).
- Uglow, S et al, *Criminal Justice* (Sweet & Maxwell, 2002).

1.1.3 Journals

Useful journals include:

- The *Criminal Law Review* (a very good source of articles, and commentaries on case law, on both substantive criminal law and evidence, procedure and sentencing, published by Sweet & Maxwell).
- The *Justice of the Peace* (which covers matters of interest to those who practice in the magistrates' courts, published by LexisNexis Butterworths).
- The *Journal of Criminal Law* (published by Vathek Publishing Ltd).

1.1.4 Law reports

Cases of relevance to the criminal justice system often appear in the mainstream law reports, such as the official Law Reports and the Weekly Law Reports published by the Incorporated Council of Law Reporting, and the All England Law Reports published by LexisNexis Butterworths. However, there are also some law reports that cover specifically criminal cases, including:

- Criminal Appeal Reports (Cr App R).
- Criminal Appeal Reports (Sentencing) (Cr App R(S)).
- Justice of the Peace Reports (JP).

1.1.5 Websites

The internet contains a vast array of resources of interest to students of criminal justice. Some of the most useful websites of particular interest to anyone with an interest in the criminal justice system include the following:

- Many of the rules on criminal procedure can be found in the *Criminal Procedure Rules* and the *Consolidated Criminal Practice Direction* (the later is referred to in this book as the *Consolidated Practice Direction*). Both these sources are available at: <http://www.justice.gov.uk/criminal/procrules_fin//index.htm>.
- The Ministry of Justice is responsible for the courts, prisons, probation, criminal law and sentencing. It was created on 9 May 2007 and took over its responsibilities from the Department for Constitutional Affairs. Its home page is: <http://www.justice.gov.uk/index.htm>.
- The general Government website for matters relating to criminal justice is, aimed at people who are appearing in court (as defendants or witnesses) or who have been called for jury service, is: <http://www.cjsonline.gov.uk/index.html>.
- Office for Criminal Justice Reform: <http://www.cjsonline.gov.uk/the_cjs/departments_of_the_cjs/ocjr/index.html>.
- The Home Office (responsible for 'leading a national effort to protect the public from terror, crime and anti-social behaviour'): <http://www.homeoffice.gov.uk/>.
- The section devoted to Crime and Victims is: <http://www.homeoffice.gov.uk/crime-victims/>
- The Criminal Procedure Rules and the Consolidated Practice Direction: <http://www.justice.gov.uk/criminal/procrules_fin/index.htm>.
- Her Majesty's Courts Service: <http://www.hmcourts-service.gov.uk/>.
- Crown Prosecution Service: <http://www.cps.gov.uk/>.
- Sentencing Guidelines Council: <http://www.sentencing-guidelines.gov.uk/>.
- Judicial Studies Board: <http://www.jsboard.co.uk/>.
- British and Irish Legal Information Institute (very useful for case law): <http://www.bailii.org/>
- Andrew Keogh's 'CrimeLine' (for practitioner-focussed updates on statutory and case law developments): <http://www.crimeline.info/>

In this book reference will be made to two major reviews of criminal litigation that were published in 2001:

- The *Review of the Criminal Courts of England and Wales* by the Right Honourable Lord Justice Auld (September 2001)(the *Auld Review*), available at <http://www.criminal-courts-review.org.uk/>; and
- The *Halliday Report (Making Punishments Work: Review of the Sentencing Framework for England and Wales)* (July 2001), available at <http://www.homeoffice.gov.uk/documents/halliday-report-sppu/>.

Useful 'portal'/'gateway' sites (containing links to useful web-based resources) include:

- Delia Venables: <http://www.venables.co.uk/> (for Crime, Police, Prisons, Magistrates see <http://www.venables.co.uk/sitesc.htm#crime>).
- Intute (formerly SOSIG): <http://www.intute.ac.uk/socialsciences/law> (for Criminal Justice, see <http://www.intute.ac.uk/socialsciences/cgi-bin/browse.pl?id=120527>; for Criminal Law and Procedure, see <http://www.intute.ac.uk/socialsciences/cgi-bin/browse.pl?id=120862>, and for Criminology, see <http://www.intute.ac.uk/socialsciences/cgi-bin/browse.pl?id=120855>).

1.2 EVALUATING THE CRIMINAL JUSTICE SYSTEM – AN INTRODUCTION TO THEORETICAL PERSPECTIVES

What should our criminal justice system be trying to achieve? In para 7 of Chapter 1 of his *Review of the Criminal Courts in England and Wales*, Lord Justice Auld refers to the two key 'aims' identified in the Government's Paper, *Criminal Justice System: Strategic Plan 1999–2002*. Those aims are:

a   reducing crime and the fear of crime and their social and economic costs; and
b   dispensing justice fairly and efficiently to promote confidence in the law.

The second of those aims was said to give rise to a series of objectives:

- to ensure just processes and just and effective outcomes;
- to deal with cases throughout the criminal justice process with appropriate speed;
- to meet the needs of victims, witnesses and jurors within the system;
- to respect the rights of defendants and to treat them fairly;
- to promote confidence in the criminal justice system.

It is interesting to note that the third of these objectives refers to jurors but does not make any reference to the lay magistrates who deal with the vast majority (over 90 per cent) of criminal cases in England and Wales; these unpaid lay people are crucial to the functioning of our criminal justice system.

A similar set of priorities was put forward in *A Fairer Deal for Legal Aid* (Department for Constitutional Affairs, 2005). Paragraph 4.1 says that:

> The Criminal Justice System (CJS) must be fair. It is based on the principle that the guilty must be convicted and the innocent acquitted. This requires:
>
> - good investigation
> - accurate charging
> - effective prosecutions
> - robust case management and
> - effective defence services.

1.2.1 Devising theoretical models

How do we assess whether our system of criminal justice is 'fit for purpose'? How do we decide whether proposals for reform are 'good' or 'bad' suggestions? One way is to devise a theoretical model (setting out what the system should be striving to achieve and how it should be going about it).

Herbert Packer, an American jurist, in 'Two models of the criminal process' ((1964) 113 U PAL Rev 1) and *The Limits of the Criminal Sanction* (Stanford University Press, 1968) proposed two models of criminal justice:

a   the 'crime control' model: this has as its primary objective the repression of crime (in other words, the lowering of crime rates), achieved by the efficient apprehension and punishment of criminals; and b   the 'due process' model: this has as its primary objective procedural fairness (in other words, the protection of the rights of the accused), achieved by presenting formidable impediments to carrying the prosecution past each step in the legal process.

Packer makes it clear that neither model is presented as corresponding to reality or as representing the ideal criminal justice system. Rather, the two models offer a basis for examining how a criminal justice system might take account of the competing demands of different value systems which have differing (and inconsistent) priorities. In other words, these models offer a framework for examining the tensions between competing claims within a criminal justice system. Packer suggests that it may be worthwhile examining where, on the spectrum between the extremes represented by the two models, our present practices seem to fall, and what appears to be the direction and thrust of current trends within our system. Moreover, we can compare our own values with the values which underlie the two models.

1.2.1.1 'Crime control'

Packer (1968: 158) says of the 'crime control' model that the:

> . . . value system that underlies the Crime Control model is based on the proposition that the repression of criminal conduct is by far the most important function to be performed by the criminal process. The failure of law enforcement to bring criminal conduct under tight control is viewed as leading to the breakdown of public order and thence to the disappearance of an important condition of human freedom. If the laws go unenforced – which is to say, if it is perceived that there is a high percentage of failure to apprehend and convict in the criminal process – a general disregard for legal controls tends to develop . . . the crime control model requires that primary attention be paid to the efficiency with which the criminal process operates to screen suspects, determine guilt, and secure appropriate dispositions of persons convicted of crime.

The two risks inherent in the failure to repress crime are:

a   the risk that people will take the law into their own hands (in other words, becoming vigilantes), leading to public disorder (mob rule); and
b   the risk that crime rates will increase further because people believe they will be able to get away with offending.

This model seeks a system that is efficient, in the sense of being able to apprehend, try, convict and sentence a high proportion of offenders whose offences become known. The system will thus be operating successfully (according to the values underpinning crime control) if there is a high rate of apprehension and conviction of offenders.

The crime control model places great emphasis on the investigative stage of the criminal process. To achieve a high rate of detection and convictions, speed is important (and this requires that the hands of the investigators and prosecutors are not unduly tied), as is finality (in the sense of minimising the occasions for challenge).

Packer suggests that the criminal process according to this model is seen as a 'screening process', in which each successive stage (investigation, arrest, subsequent investigation, preparation for trial, trial or plea, conviction, sentence) involves 'a series of routinised operations whose success is gauged primarily by their tendency to pass the case along to a successful conclusion'. For these purposes, Packer defines a successful conclusion as one that:

> throws off at an early stage those cases in which it appears unlikely that the person apprehended is an offender and then secures, as expeditiously as possible, the conviction of the rest, with a minimum of occasions for challenge.

This requires that, at the stage of the police investigation (and perhaps at the charge review and the evidence review by the prosecuting authority), those who are probably innocent are 'screened out' and those who are probably guilty are 'passed quickly through the remaining stages of the process'.

Packer notes that this approach requires what he terms 'a presumption of guilt'. This is because 'the screening processes operated by police and prosecutors are reliable indicators of probable guilt': once the police (and the prosecution) have determined to their own satisfaction that there is enough evidence of guilt to justify taking the case forward, 'all subsequent activity directed toward him is based on the view that he is probably guilty'. However, it should be pointed out that the reliability of the view of the police officer or prosecutor may well be open to question: the instinct of the police officer or prosecutor may well be to look for further evidence that the suspect is guilty, rather than evidence that would exonerate the suspect. This is one of the tensions in the law relating to the disclosure of unused prosecution material (where the law requires the prosecution to retain, and then disclose to the defence, material which weakens the prosecution case or strengthens the defence case).

This 'presumption of guilt' stems from (possibly misplaced) confidence in the reliability of the fact-finding that takes place at the investigative stage (and the subsequent evidential review stage). According to the crime control model, if we can be confident in the accuracy of those initial stages, the remaining stages of the process can be relatively perfunctory. Indeed, the crime control model would suggest that the trial process is likely to be less capable of producing reliable fact-finding than the earlier investigative stages. On this basis, the criminal process must put special weight on the quality of that earlier fact-finding. This, in turn, makes it important to place as few restrictions as possible on the investigative process. If the early fact-finding stages are the most important, the corollary is that the subsequent stages are relatively unimportant and should therefore be truncated as much as possible. An effective investigation would ideally lead either to the exoneration of the suspect or the suspect confessing to the offence and then promptly entering a guilty plea (cf Sanders and Young (2007: 20).

Packer contrasts this *de facto* presumption of guilt with the (legal) presumption of innocence, which he defines as a direction to those involved in the process to 'ignore the presumption of guilt in their treatment of the suspect. It tells them, in effect, to close their eyes to what will frequently seem to be factual probabilities' or, put another way, to close their eyes to 'the probability that, in the run of cases, the preliminary screening process operated by the police and the prosecuting officials contains adequate guarantees of reliable fact-finding'.

It might be thought that the crime control model would tolerate the conviction of the innocent in a way that the due process model would not. However, if the system makes so many mistakes that public confidence is eroded, it would cease to be an effective system. The difference between crime control and due process (which we consider next) is that accuracy of outcome is a lower priority for crime control than it is for due process.

1.2.1.2 'Due process'

In contrast to the values of crime control, Packer says that according to 'due process' values, each successive stage of the criminal process 'is designed to present formidable impediments to carrying the accused any further along in the process'. He makes it clear, however, that those who subscribe to due process values will not necessarily reject all of the foundations of crime control. Proponents of due process do not, for example, have to argue that it is not desirable to repress crime. However, the due process approach does aim to give maximum protection to the innocent, and so emphasises the importance of putting in place safeguards against errors.

The due process approach places much less faith in the reliability of the initial investigative stages of the process. It points out that witnesses can make mistakes, that confessions may be induced by various forms of coercion (whether intentional or not), and that the police are looking for evidence of guilt, not innocence. The due process model would argue additionally that the trial process itself may not lead to reliable fact-finding, and so there must be the possibility of further scrutiny (by ways of appeals) open to the accused (with the result that finality has a low priority in the due process model).

This takes us to questions of efficiency and resources; as Packer puts it: 'how much reliability is compatible with efficiency?' In other words: 'how much weight is to be given to the competing demands of reliability (a high degree of probability in each case that factual guilt has been accurately determined) and efficiency (expeditious handling of the large numbers of cases that the process ingests)?' The safeguards required by due process are expensive (for example in terms of court time) and there has to be a limit on what the State can afford to expend on criminal justice.

A good illustration of the conflict between crime control and due process is in the use (or exclusion) of evidence that was obtained improperly. The crime control would allow evidence to be used in a trial so long as it is relevant, because it has probative value; it does not matter how the evidence was obtained (even if it was obtained illegally). Due process, however, would exclude from the trial evidence that was not obtained properly, even if that evidence is highly relevant. Adherents of due process would justify this approach on the basis of the need to uphold the integrity, or moral legitimacy, of the system. This example perhaps also shows that the reality lies between the two extremes – in the UK, evidence that was obtained illegally may be admissible, but only if its probative value exceeds its prejudicial effect on the fairness of the trial of the accused.

The crime control model is not only more optimistic about the improbability of error in a significant number of cases, but is also, at least to an extent, more tolerant about the number of errors that it will put up with. The due process model insists on the prevention and elimination of mistakes to the greatest extent possible, whereas the crime control model accepts the probability of mistakes up to the level at which those mistakes interfere with the goal of repressing crime (either because too many guilty people are escaping justice or because a general lack of confidence in the process leads to a decrease in the deterrent efficacy of the criminal law). As Packer says (1968: 165), the aim of due process 'is at least as much to protect the factually innocent as it is to convict the factually guilty'.

The combination of stigma and loss of liberty that can result from conviction of a criminal offence is viewed by the due process model as very serious. For this reason, the due process model is prepared to accept a substantial diminution in the efficiency with which the criminal process operates in the interest of preventing oppression of the individual by the State. Packer (1968:166) highlights the importance of the concept of 'legal guilt'. He writes that:

> According to this doctrine, a person is not to be held guilty of a crime merely on a showing that in all probability, based upon reliable evidence, he did factually what he is said to have done. Instead, he is to be held guilty if and only if these factual determinations are made in procedurally regular fashion and by authorities acting within competences duly allocated to them. Furthermore, he is not to be held guilty, even though the factual determination is or might be adverse to him, if various rules designed to protect him and to safeguard the integrity of the process are not given effect.

This requires, for example, that there must not be unacceptable delay (a concept that is given full expression in the European Convention on Human Rights: see, for example, *Attorney General's Reference (No 2 of 2001)* [2003] UKHL 68; [2004] 2 AC 72); moreover, only an impartial tribunal can be trusted to make determinations of legal, as opposed to factual, guilt.

Packer goes on to note that by 'forcing the state to prove its case against the accused in an adjudicative context, the presumption of innocence serves to force into play all the qualifying and disabling doctrines that limit the use of the criminal sanction against the individual, thereby enhancing his opportunity to secure a favourable outcome'. The key point is the proposition that 'the factually guilty may nonetheless be legally innocent and should therefore be given a chance to qualify for that kind of treatment'. This is exemplified by the fact that a conviction may be unsafe even if there is clear evidence showing the guilt of the accused (see the discussion in Chapter 13, when we examine the role of the Criminal Division of the Court of Appeal).

Packer notes that one of the hallmarks of due process is the notion that 'there can be no equal justice where the kind of trial a man gets depends on the amount of money he has'. This concept is what the European Court of Human Rights refers to as 'equality of arms', and is seen as a fundamental characteristic of a fair trial under Art 6 of the European Convention. It follows that the State must institute a system of legal aid, and that a defendant whose defence is publicly funded should be in no worse a position than a defendant who is paying for his own defence.

As Sanders and Young (2007: 19) point out, neither of Packer's models corresponds with reality, and neither was intended by Packer to be taken as an ideal. Rather they represent 'extremes on a spectrum of possible ways of doing criminal justice'. They go on to observe (2007: 23) that the difference between the models is that they represent different points of view about what the limits of the powers of the State should be in upholding law and order. Or, as Ashworth and Redmayne put it (2005: 38), these two models 'help in interpreting trends in criminal procedure ... They are designed as interpretive tools, to enable us to tell (for example) how far in a particular direction a given criminal justice system tends'.

The two models essentially represent extremes but are marked by a very important difference. The due process model requires individual liberties to be protected even at the cost of guilty people sometimes going free, whereas the crime control model can tolerate innocent people occasionally being mistakenly convicted. Of course, the crime control model could not accept a large number of mistaken convictions (since that would reduce confidence in the system, thereby diminishing its effectiveness).

1.2.1.3 A 'rights-based' approach

Ashworth and Redmayne summarise the two main goals of the criminal justice system as 'regulating the processes for bringing suspected offenders to trial so as to produce accurate determinations, and . . . ensuring that fundamental rights are protected in those processes' (2005: 48, 55). It is worth noting that over 90 per cent of defendants plead guilty, and so there is no trial. It may be, therefore, that the first of these two goals needs to be re-worded to make it clear that it is an important goal of the system that only those who are in fact guilty of an offence plead guilty to it if they forgo their right to a trial to determine their guilt or innocence.

Ashworth and Redmayne adopt a 'rights-based' approach when evaluating the criminal justice system. They would evaluate a justice system according to the extent to which that system respects the rights of those involved in the system. They accept that this approach requires more than simply devising a list of such rights, since 'rights may conflict with each other or with other social values. Some rights may also seem to be more important, or weightier, than others' (2005: 35). However, they make it clear that they are not advocating a 'balancing' process in which some rights can be traded off against others. What they advocate is carefully structured reasoning in order to justify interference with rights (2005: 46). They commend what they describe as a 'principled approach' to criminal justice. They say that the 'purpose of the criminal process is to bring about accurate determinations through fair procedures. The approach therefore emphasises various rights and principles that ought to be safeguarded' (2005: 375).

There are several international documents that attempt to set out key rights. In Chapter 6 we examine, amongst other things, the United Nations Convention on the Rights of the Child; this is an important document that is highly relevant to cases involving young defendants (or young witnesses). There is also the 2000 EU Charter of Fundamental Rights. However, the most important instrument has to be the European Convention on Human Rights, which became fully part of our law through the Human Rights Act 1998. The provisions of the European Convention on Human Rights that have effect under the Human Rights Act 1998 are set out in Sched 1. Those that are relevant to criminal litigation and sentencing are:

Article 2: Right to life

1   Everyone's right to life shall be protected by law. No one shall be deprived of his life intentionally save in the execution of a sentence of a court following his conviction of a crime for which this penalty is provided by law.

2   Deprivation of life shall not be regarded as inflicted in contravention of this Article when it results from the use of force which is no more than absolutely necessary:

(a)   in defence of any person from unlawful violence;

(b)   in order to effect a lawful arrest or to prevent the escape of a person lawfully detained;

(c)   in action lawfully taken for the purpose of quelling a riot or insurrection.

Article 3: Prohibition of torture

No one shall be subjected to torture or to inhuman or degrading treatment or punishment.

Article 4: Prohibition of slavery and forced labour

1   No one shall be held in slavery or servitude.

2   No one shall be required to perform forced or compulsory labour.

3   For the purpose of this Article the term 'forced or compulsory labour' shall not include:

(a)   any work required to be done in the ordinary course of detention imposed according to the provisions of Article 5 of this Convention or during conditional release from such detention;

(b)   any service of a military character or, in case of conscientious objectors in countries where they are recognised, service exacted instead of compulsory military service;

(c)   any service exacted in case of an emergency or calamity threatening the life or well-being of the community;

(d)   any work or service which forms part of normal civic obligations.

Article 5: Right to liberty and security

1   Everyone has the right to liberty and security of person. No one shall be deprived of his liberty save in the following cases and in accordance with a procedure prescribed by law:

(a)   the lawful detention of a person after conviction by a competent court;

(b)   the lawful arrest or detention of a person for non-compliance with the lawful order of a court or in order to secure the fulfilment of any obligation prescribed by law;

(c)   the lawful arrest or detention of a person effected for the purpose of bringing him before the competent legal authority on reasonable suspicion of having committed an offence or when it is reasonably considered necessary to prevent his committing an offence or fleeing after having done so;

(d)   the detention of a minor by lawful order for the purpose of educational supervision or his lawful detention for the purpose of bringing him before the competent legal authority;

(e)   the lawful detention of persons for the prevention of the spreading of infectious diseases, of persons of unsound mind, alcoholics or drug addicts or vagrants;

(f)   the lawful arrest or detention of a person to prevent his effecting an unauthorised entry into the country or of a person against whom action is being taken with a view to deportation or extradition.

2   Everyone who is arrested shall be informed promptly, in a language which he understands, of the reasons for his arrest and of any charge against him.

3   Everyone arrested or detained in accordance with the provisions of paragraph 1(c) of

this Article shall be brought promptly before a judge or other officer authorised by law to exercise judicial power and shall be entitled to trial within a reasonable time or to release pending trial. Release may be conditioned by guarantees to appear for trial.

4   Everyone who is deprived of his liberty by arrest or detention shall be entitled to take proceedings by which the lawfulness of his detention shall be decided speedily by a court and his release ordered if the detention is not lawful.

5   Everyone who has been the victim of arrest or detention in contravention of the provisions of this Article shall have an enforceable right to compensation.

Article 6: Right to a fair trial

1   In the determination of his civil rights and obligations or of any criminal charge against him, everyone is entitled to a fair and public hearing within a reasonable time by an independent and impartial tribunal established by law. Judgment shall be pronounced publicly but the press and public may be excluded from all or part of the trial in the interest of morals, public order or national security in a democratic society, where the interests of juveniles or the protection of the private life of the parties so require, or to the extent strictly necessary in the opinion of the court in special circumstances where publicity would prejudice the interests of justice.

2   Everyone charged with a criminal offence shall be presumed innocent until proved guilty according to law.

3   Everyone charged with a criminal offence has the following minimum rights:

(a)   to be informed promptly, in a language which he understands and in detail, of the nature and cause of the accusation against him;

(b)   to have adequate time and facilities for the preparation of his defence;

(c)   to defend himself in person or through legal assistance of his own choosing or, if he has not sufficient means to pay for legal assistance, to be given it free when the interests of justice so require;

(d)   to examine or have examined witnesses against him and to obtain the attendance and examination of witnesses on his behalf under the same conditions as witnesses against him;

(e)   to have the free assistance of an interpreter if he cannot understand or speak the language used in court.

Article 7: No punishment without law

1   No one shall be held guilty of any criminal offence on account of any act or omission which did not constitute a criminal offence under national or international law at the time when it was committed. Nor shall a heavier penalty be imposed than the one that was applicable at the time the criminal offence was committed.

2   This Article shall not prejudice the trial and punishment of any person for any act or omission which, at the time when it was committed, was criminal according to the general principles of law recognised by civilised nations.

Article 8: Right to respect for private and family life

1   Everyone has the right to respect for his private and family life, his home and his correspondence.

2   There shall be no interference by a public authority with the exercise of this right
except such as is in accordance with the law and is necessary in a democratic society
in the interests of national security, public safety or the economic well being of the
country, for the prevention of disorder or crime, for the protection of health or morals,
or for the protection of the rights and freedoms of others.

Article 14: Prohibition of discrimination

The enjoyment of the rights and freedoms set forth in this Convention shall be secured
without discrimination on any ground such as sex, race, colour, language, religion, political
or other opinion, national or social origin, association with a national minority, property,
birth or other status.

Article 18: Limitation on use of restrictions on rights

The restrictions permitted under this Convention to the said rights and freedoms shall not
be applied for any purpose other than those for which they have been prescribed.

It is to be noted that much of the language is quite archaic. Moreover, the Convention is
to be regarded as a 'living instrument'. The decisions of the European Court of Human
Rights (based in Strasbourg) are therefore very important in interpreting the Convention in today's world. One of the challenges faced by the European Court is that the
provisions of the Convention have to be applied both to 'accusatorial' systems such as
ours and to 'inquisitorial' systems adopted elsewhere. In the inquisitorial system, the
court takes an active role in fact-finding (and may, to a greater or lesser extent, even
direct the conduct of the investigation); in the accusatorial system, the court essentially
acts as a neutral umpire as the prosecutor presents the case against the accused and the
defence advocate tries to highlight reasonable doubt in that case. It could be said that
the accusatorial approach is not actually a quest for the truth: the court is not concerned with what actually happened, but whether it is satisfied so that it is sure that
the case against the accused is proven. So far as the due process model is concerned, the
defence advocate plays a role of central importance in protecting the interests of the
accused; similarly, the court plays a vital role in excluding evidence that has been
obtained improperly.

The European Court has emphasised the importance that there should be 'equality
of arms' as between the prosecution and defence (see, for example, *Foucher v France*
(1997) 25 EHRR 234) – in other words, there should be what might be called 'a level
playing field'.

The right to have a criminal charge adjudicated upon without undue delay is also an
important one: delay is a common ground for seeking the dismissal of charges on the
basis of abuse of process (see below).

Another significant document is the Charter of Fundamental Rights of the European Union (2000/C 364/01) (<http://www.europarl.europa.eu/charter/pdf/text_
en.pdf>), which contains the following provisions in Chapter VI ('Justice'):

Article 47: Right to an effective remedy and to a fair trial

Everyone whose rights and freedoms guaranteed by the law of the Union are violated has
the right to an effective remedy before a tribunal in compliance with the conditions laid
down in this Article.

Everyone is entitled to a fair and public hearing within a reasonable time by an independent and impartial tribunal previously established by law. Everyone shall have the possibility of being advised, defended and represented.

Legal aid shall be made available to those who lack sufficient resources in so far as such aid is necessary to ensure effective access to justice.

Article 48: Presumption of innocence and right of defence

1   Everyone who has been charged shall be presumed innocent until proved guilty according to law.
2   Respect for the rights of the defence of anyone who has been charged shall be guaranteed.

Article 49: Principles of legality and proportionality of criminal offences and penalties

1   No one shall be held guilty of any criminal offence on account of any act or omission which did not constitute a criminal offence under national law or international law at the time when it was committed. Nor shall a heavier penalty be imposed than that which was applicable at the time the criminal offence was committed. If, subsequent to the commission of a criminal offence, the law provides for a lighter penalty, that penalty shall be applicable.
2   This Article shall not prejudice the trial and punishment of any person for any act or omission which, at the time when it was committed, was criminal according to the general principles recognized by the community of nations.
3   The severity of penalties must not be disproportionate to the criminal offence.

Article 50: Right not to be tried or punished twice in criminal proceedings for the same criminal offence
No one shall be liable to be tried or punished again in criminal proceedings for an offence for which he or she has already been finally acquitted or convicted within the Union in accordance with the law.

It will be noted that there is considerable overlap with some of the provisions of the European Convention on Human Rights.

Ashworth and Redmayne make it clear that they are not suggesting that the European Convention on Human Rights is to be regarded as providing a complete solution. They note a number of omissions from the rights it creates – for example, 'victims' rights, protection for witnesses, special rights for young people and for women (whether as defendants, victims or witnesses), fault requirements for criminal convictions and so on' (2005: 376). Thus, they note the need to go beyond the rights enshrined in the Convention (which focus very much on the rights of the defendant) and they write about the needs for the rights of the victim to be part of the equation (2005: 48ff). They are essentially suggesting that adherence (or non-adherence) to human rights provides a useful measure for judging whether or not a criminal justice system is achieving what it ought to achieve and is doing so by legitimate means.

1.2.1.4 A 'freedom-based' approach

Sanders and Young propose an alternative framework for evaluating criminal justice, namely 'the enhancement of freedom'. They identify the key aims as follows (2007: 43):

- convicting the guilty;
- protecting the innocent from wrongful conviction;
- protecting victims;
- maintaining human rights: the protection of everyone (innocent and guilty) from arbitrary or oppressive treatment;
- maintaining order;
- securing public confidence in, and co-operation with, policing and prosecution;
- pursuing these goals efficiently and effectively without disproportionate cost and consequent harm to other public services.

They rightly note that few people would disagree with any of these aims, but people will differ on their relative priority.

They take as their starting point in devising a way to critique criminal justice the premise that the primary purpose of the system is 'to protect and enhance freedom' (2007: 44). They 'see none of these objectives as goals in themselves' but rather as 'means to achieving the overriding goal of freedom'; allocating priority to conflicting goals is then achieved by prioritising 'the goal that is likely to enhance freedom the most' (ibid). Lest this approach be mis-used, they are at pains to emphasise that they 'reject outright' the simplistic utilitarian approach whereby 'the freedom of the majority could "trump" the basic freedoms, or human rights, of an unpopular minority' (2007: 45). The freedom model can thus be used as a basis for appraising proposals for reform, at least where those proposals include some extension of the coercive powers of the State – such enhancement of State powers should, they say, only be granted 'if it is likely to enhance more freedom than it erodes' (2007: 46).

1.2.1.5 Competing interests in the criminal justice system: stakeholders

We have seen that Packer's two models are in some ways best regarded as descriptive rather than evaluative. In order to evaluate the efficacy of a criminal justice system, it is also necessary to examine the interests of all those with a stake in that system. Those 'stakeholders' include:

- the State itself, acting on behalf of society as a whole: a key purpose of the criminal law is to ensure that retribution for criminal conduct is meted out by the State, making it less likely that individuals, or their friends and family, will seek their own revenge against the perpetrator (in other words, reducing the risk of vigilantism);
- the victim (whose interests are now formally recognised through victim impact statements and who may want to see the perpetrator punished and may want to receive some sort of compensation for the harm suffered);
- the accused (whether an individual or a corporate body): the accused enjoys the right not to be wrongly convicted. This in turn encompasses three key rights:

  a   the right not to be convicted if he is, in fact, innocent;

b   the right not to be convicted (irrespective of whether or not he is, in fact, guilty) if the prosecution cannot prove their case against the accused beyond reasonable doubt; and

c   the right not to be convicted through an unfair process (one aspect of which is the concept in the jurisprudence of the European Court of Human Rights that there should be 'equality of arms' between the accused and the prosecution);

- the family and friends of the accused (who will suffer wrongly if the accused is wrongly convicted);
- the family and friends of the victim (who want to 'see justice done');
- the police and prosecuting authorities (whose task could be made impossible by too many rules and regulations limiting what they can do in the investigation and prosecution of crime);
- the prosecuting lawyers (who, in the UK, are meant to be independent from the police but who must have a very close working relationship with the police if they are to perform their role effectively, and who are supposed to be 'ministers of justice', putting the facts fairly before the court rather than striving for a conviction at all costs);
- the defence lawyers (who have to represent clients whom they may well believe to be guilty);
- witnesses (some of whom run the risk of intimidation);
- the courts – the judges, magistrates and court staff (who cannot administer the law if cases are not disposed of efficiently and so take an excessive time to be resolved, leading to intolerable backlogs);
- jurors;
- the taxpayer, who ultimately pays for the criminal justice system (the police, the courts, the prosecuting authorities and publicly-funded defence work);
- the media (whose pronouncements often shape public opinion rather than report on public opinion);
- politicians (criminal justice has become a political issue, with the main parties eager to show that they are, to use an often-quoted phrase, 'tough on crime and tough on the causes of crime').

It is, of course, somewhat misleading to assess criminal justice issues through the eyes of groups of stakeholders, since all stakeholders in a particular group will not in fact all take the same view. For example, the taxpayer, who effectively funds the criminal justice system, may well want to have a system which is as cost-effective as possible, but different taxpayers would be willing to see different proportions of the State's income through taxation being spent on criminal justice. Indeed, people may be in more than one category of stakeholder. An individual may, for example, be both a victim of crime and a (suspected) perpetrator of crime during the course of their lifetime. However, some generalisations are possible (and legitimate). For instance, it is not only the (innocent) suspect who has an interest in having a system that protects the innocent from wrongful conviction: the victim of an offence has an interest in the right person being convicted of that offence (if the wrong person is convicted, that means that the real perpetrator has gone unpunished).

1.2.1.6 Resolving the conflict

As Sanders and Young point out (2007: 8), 'a compromise has to be struck between procedures which allow the effective prosecution of suspected offenders whilst reducing the risk of wrongful conviction to an acceptable level'. This does, however, beg the question what level of wrongful convictions is to be regarded as acceptable. It is sometimes said to be a founding maxim of English law that 'it is better that ten guilty persons escape, than that one innocent suffer'. This is based on a dictum from William Blackstone's *Commentaries on the Laws of England* 1765–69 (Book 4, Chapter 27). What level of error *should* be regarded as acceptable?

The question becomes even harder to answer when we extend it to take account not just of wrongful conviction (the conviction of someone who is in fact innocent) but also of the right not be convicted by unfair means. As Taylor and Ormerod put it in 'Mind the gaps: safety, fairness and moral legitimacy' [2004] Crim LR 266:

> The criminal justice system is not merely about convicting the guilty and ensuring the protection of the innocent from conviction. There is an additional and onerous responsibility to maintain the moral integrity of the criminal process.

The tensions between the interests of particular stakeholders sometimes become even more apparent in the case of serious offences. The more serious the offence, the more important it is that the perpetrator is caught and punished (to deter that person – and others – from committing such offences and to give the public confidence that they are being protected by the law). However, the consequences of a wrongful conviction in such a case are particularly dire for the person suspected of the offence if he is innocent (given the likely sentence for a really serious offence and the effect on the reputation of the accused).

In *R v Ward* (1993) 96 Cr App R 1 at 52, Glidewell LJ, giving the judgment of the court, said that the trial process should be:

> . . . developed so as to reduce the risk of conviction of the innocent to an absolute minimum. At the same time we are very much alive to the fact that, although the avoidance of the conviction of the innocent must unquestionably be the primary consideration, the public interest would not be served by a multiplicity of rules which merely impede effective law enforcement.

It follows, as was said by Lord Bingham in *Brown v Stott* [2003] 1 AC 681 at 704, that 'a fair balance [has to be struck] between the general interest of the community and the personal rights of the individual'.

One of the leading concepts in the jurisprudence of the European Court of Human Rights is that of 'proportionality': it is a legitimate aim to prevent crime, but measures to achieve this objective must be proportionate (in other words, no more than necessary to achieve the legitimate objective).

But what is proportionate? There are tensions or competing interests within the criminal justice system. On the one hand, the system should ensure that the guilty are convicted and the innocent are protected from wrongful conviction. However, if there are too many protections in place to make the conviction of the accused more difficult, it becomes more difficult to convict those who are guilty. These tensions are equally present when the concept of human rights is applied: the accused (whether in fact innocent or guilty) should enjoy protection from arbitrary or oppressive treatment; on the other hand, the victim has rights too. This ambivalence also appears when one looks at the interests of the State. On the one hand, it is not in the interests of society to have a criminal justice system that allows improper treatment of those suspected of crime; on the other hand, if there are so many barriers to convicting defendants, more people who are in fact guilty will go free (reducing public confidence in the effectiveness of the criminal justice system to protect its members, leading to people being less willing to co-operate with the police and the prosecuting authorities, and increasing the risk of people taking the law into their own hands).

It also has to be borne in mind that criminal justice comes at a price. On one reading of the crime control model, the investigation by the police would be so effective that there would be little need for trials, since all of those (or virtually all of those) brought before the courts would be guilty. However, such thorough investigation would place an intolerable demand on the resources of the police. Likewise, if one were to go to the extreme version of the due process model, trials would take an inordinate length of time (because of the procedural protections which could be invoked) and could result in the cost of investigations being wasted because so many cases are thrown out on the basis of technicalities. Inevitably, there has to be compromise, since the goals of the criminal justice system have to be achieved without disproportionate cost. There is a finite amount of money available for public services: the more that is spent on the justice system, the less there is available for other important public services (education, health, etc.). It is for this reason that there has been a major drive for efficiency and cost effectiveness (for example, Martin Narey's *Review of Delay in the Criminal Justice System* (Home Office, 1997) and the moves to curb the ever-growing cost of the criminal defence service contained in the Criminal Defence Service Act 2006).

1.2.1.7 *Trying to achieve the balance: the Criminal Procedure Rules*

Section 69 of the Courts Act 2003 makes provision for the creation of Criminal Procedure Rules (mirroring the Civil Procedure Rules). These rules govern the practice and procedure to be followed in the criminal courts. The Rules are made by a committee known as the Criminal Procedure Rules Committee. The membership of the Criminal Procedure Rules Committee is governed by s 70 of the 2003 Act. It comprises the Lord Chief Justice and a number of members appointed by the Lord Chancellor. Under s 70(2), the Committee must include judges of all levels (including High Court/ Court of Appeal judges, Circuit Judges, a District Judge (magistrates' courts), a lay justice, a justices' clerk, criminal practitioners, a police representative, and representatives of voluntary organisations with a direct interest in the work of criminal courts).

Under s 69(4) of the Courts Act 2003, the power to make or alter Criminal Procedure Rules is to be exercised with a view to securing that:

a   the criminal justice system is accessible, fair and efficient; and
b   the rules are both simple and simply expressed.

The Rules apply to both the Crown Court and the magistrates' courts, with the intention of promoting greater integration of the courts and greater consistency of practice.

The Rules begin with an 'overriding objective', expressed in the following terms:

1.1 The overriding objective

(1) The overriding objective of this new code is that criminal cases be dealt with justly.

(2) Dealing with a criminal case justly includes–

    (a) acquitting the innocent and convicting the guilty;

    (b) dealing with the prosecution and the defence fairly;

    (c) recognising the rights of a defendant, particularly those under Article 6 of the European Convention on Human Rights;

    (d) respecting the interests of witnesses, victims and jurors and keeping them informed of the progress of the case;

    (e) dealing with the case efficiently and expeditiously;

    (f) ensuring that appropriate information is available to the court when bail and sentence are considered; and

    (g) dealing with the case in ways that take into account–

        (i)   the gravity of the offence alleged,

        (ii) the complexity of what is in issue,

        (iii) the severity of the consequences for the defendant and others affected, and

        (iv) the needs of other cases.

1.2 The duty of the participants in a criminal case

(1) Each participant, in the conduct of each case, must–

    (a) prepare and conduct the case in accordance with the overriding objective;

    (b) comply with these Rules, practice directions and directions made by the court; and

    (c) at once inform the court and all parties of any significant failure (whether or not that participant is responsible for that failure) to take any procedural step required by these Rules, any practice direction or any direction of the court. A failure is significant if it might hinder the court in furthering the overriding objective.

(2) Anyone involved in any way with a criminal case is a participant in its conduct for the purposes of this rule.

1.3 The application by the court of the overriding objective

The court must further the overriding objective in particular when–

    (a) exercising any power given to it by legislation (including these Rules);

    (b) applying any practice direction; or

    (c) interpreting any rule or practice direction.

Philip Plowden in 'Make do and mend, or a cultural evolution?' (2005) 155 NLJ 328, makes the point that it is a matter of regret that the presumption of innocence is not made more explicit in the overriding objective. He also expresses concern at rule 1.1(2)(b), saying that this proposition seems to propose an equality of interest between defence and prosecution that is alarming. In contrast to civil proceedings, the criminal justice system does not represent the state holding an arena between disputing parties, but is a context where the state and all its resources are ranged against the individual defendant.

It is also to be noted that rule 1.1(2)(d) is selective in the people listed. For example, it fails to include magistrates, despite the fact that the overwhelming majority of cases are dealt with in the magistrates' court.

Plowden (ibid) expresses most concern at r 1.1(2)(g). He comments:

> Even if the proposition is no more sinister than to suggest that the resources allocated to a matter may need to be greater where it is more complex or more serious, it is not drafted in this way. In its present wording it can equally be interpreted as permitting 'justice on the cheap' for matters where the penalty is low, or where courts are struggling to deal with many other cases, without taking into account the fundamental principle that the trial must be fair. This would have sat more happily as a separate principle, clearly subject to the overriding objective of dealing with cases justly. It is unattractive that this proposition should be enshrined as part of the overriding objective.

It is of course the case that there has to be some degree of proportionality, since it is not possible – given limited resources – to have an elaborate trial process for even the most minor of offences. However, it is important to underline that the basic requirements of fairness should apply to all trials, whatever the seriousness of the offence.

In March 2008, the Law Society issued a Practice Note, *Criminal Procedure Rules: impact on solicitors' duties to the client* (<http://www.lawsociety.org.uk/documents/downloads/practicenote_criminalprocedurerules.pdf>). The Note says of rule 1.2(1)(c):

> It is essential to appreciate that the purpose of Rule 1.2(1)(c) is to enable the court to control the preparation process and avoid ineffective and wasted hearings. When something goes wrong because of a failure of a defendant to co-operate with his or her solicitors the court should be aware of this and if the solicitor fails to keep the court informed, he or she risks breaching their duty to the court under the provisions of the Rules.

The Note goes on to state that:

> . . . if a solicitor is aware of any significant failure (whether or not the defendant is responsible for that failure) to take any procedural step required by the CPR or any practice direction or any direction of the court, it is neither a breach of the defendant's right to silence, nor legal professional privilege, for the solicitor to reveal that he or she has been unable to comply with the court's order.
>
> It would not involve a breach of legal professional privilege for the court to ask the defendant or his or her lawyer to reveal whether instructions have been given, for the purpose of allowing the court to ensure that the case is ready to proceed. It would be a breach, of course, for the court to ask what has been said between them. Courts should be aware that there are difficulties in asking a solicitor to confirm any more than this, for example, whether or not the solicitor has prepared a proof of evidence.

> Particular difficulties will arise if a client changes his or her instructions in circumstances where it is proper for the solicitor to continue acting. If the change in instructions will cause delay, whilst the solicitor must inform the court of the likelihood of delay, privilege will prevent disclosure of the reason for it.

This Practice Note highlights the 'divided loyalty' faced by the advocate who owes duties both to the client and to the court.

In any event, it is clear that the courts are sometimes prepared to take a different approach to the interpretation of the rules of criminal procedure in light of the overriding objective. In *R v Ashton* [2006] EWCA Crim 794; [2007] 1 WLR 181, for example, the Court of Appeal held that, whenever a court is confronted by failure to take a required step, properly or at all, before a power is exercised ('a procedural failure'), the court should first ask itself whether the intention of the legislature was that any act done following that procedural failure should be invalid. If the answer to that question is 'no', then the court should go on to consider the interests of justice generally, and particularly whether there is a real possibility that either the prosecution or the defence may suffer prejudice on account of the procedural failure. If there is such a risk, the court must decide whether it is just to allow the proceedings to continue. The prevailing approach to litigation is to avoid determining cases on technicalities (when they do not result in real prejudice and injustice) but instead to ensure that they are decided fairly on their merits. This approach is reflected in the Criminal Procedure Rules and, in particular, the overriding objective. Accordingly, in the absence of a clear indication that Parliament intended jurisdiction automatically to be removed following procedural failure, the decision of the court should be based on a wide assessment of the interests of justice, with particular focus on whether there was a real possibility that the prosecution or the defendant may suffer prejudice. If that risk is present, the court should then decide whether it is just to permit the proceedings to continue (per Fulford J, giving the judgment of the court, at paras 4 and 9). The consequence of this is that a number of earlier authorities had to re-visited, since they would be decided differently using the approach laid down in *Ashton* (see paras 67–69 and 75–78).

The approach taken in *Ashton* was based on two earlier decisions: *R v Sekhon* [2002] EWCA Crim 2954, [2003] 1 WLR 1655 and *R v Soneji* [2005] UKHL 49, [2006] 1 AC 340. However, the impact of *Ashton* should not be over-estimated. In *R v Clarke* [2008] UKHL 8; [2008] 1 WLR 338, Lord Bingham of Cornhill (at para 20) said that the effect of the 'sea-change' brought about by that line of authority had been exaggerated, and that cases such as *Ashton* 'do not warrant a wholesale jettisoning of all rules affecting procedure irrespective of their legal effect'. In all such cases, the key question is whether Parliament intended a particular procedural failure to nullify the subsequent proceedings.

1.2.1.8 Case management

One of the ways in which it is intended that effect should be given to the overriding objective is through proactive case management. Part 3 of the Criminal Procedure Rules provides as follows:

3.2 The duty of the court

(1) The court must further the overriding objective by actively managing the case.

(2) Active case management includes—

(a) the early identification of the real issues;

(b) the early identification of the needs of witnesses;

(c) achieving certainty as to what must be done, by whom, and when, in particular by the early setting of a timetable for the progress of the case;

(d) monitoring the progress of the case and compliance with directions;

(e) ensuring that evidence, whether disputed or not, is presented in the shortest and clearest way;

(f) discouraging delay, dealing with as many aspects of the case as possible on the same occasion, and avoiding unnecessary hearings;

(g) encouraging the participants to co-operate in the progression of the case; and

(h) making use of technology.

(3) The court must actively manage the case by giving any direction appropriate to the needs of that case as early as possible.

3.3 The duty of the parties

Each party must—

(a) actively assist the court in fulfilling its duty under rule 3.2, without or if necessary with a direction; and

(b) apply for a direction if needed to further the overriding objective.

3.4 Case progression officers and their duties

(1) At the beginning of the case each party must, unless the court otherwise directs—

(a) nominate an individual responsible for progressing that case; and

(b) tell other parties and the court who he is and how to contact him.

(2) In fulfilling its duty under rule 3.2, the court must where appropriate—

(a) nominate a court officer responsible for progressing the case; and

(b) make sure the parties know who he is and how to contact him.

(3) In this Part a person nominated under this rule is called a case progression officer.

(4) A case progression officer must—

(a) monitor compliance with directions;

(b) make sure that the court is kept informed of events that may affect the progress of that case;

(c) make sure that he can be contacted promptly about the case during ordinary business hours;

(d) act promptly and reasonably in response to communications about the case; and

(e) if he will be unavailable, appoint a substitute to fulfil his duties and inform the other case progression officers.

3.5 The court's case management powers

(1) In fulfilling its duty under rule 3.2 the court may give any direction and take any step actively to manage a case unless that direction or step would be inconsistent with legislation, including these Rules.

(2) In particular, the court may—

   (a) nominate a judge, magistrate, justices' clerk or assistant to a justices' clerk to manage the case;

   (b) give a direction on its own initiative or on application by a party;

   (c) ask or allow a party to propose a direction;

   (d) for the purpose of giving directions, receive applications and representations by letter, by telephone or by any other means of electronic communication, and conduct a hearing by such means;

   (e) give a direction without a hearing;

   (f) fix, postpone, bring forward, extend or cancel a hearing;

   (g) shorten or extend (even after it has expired) a time limit fixed by a direction;

   (h) require that issues in the case should be determined separately, and decide in what order they will be determined; and

   (i) specify the consequences of failing to comply with a direction.

(3) A magistrates' court may give a direction that will apply in the Crown Court if the case is to continue there.

(4) The Crown Court may give a direction that will apply in a magistrates' court if the case is to continue there.

(5) Any power to give a direction under this Part includes a power to vary or revoke that direction.

(6) If a party fails to comply with a rule or a direction, the court may –

   (a) fix, postpone, bring forward, extend, cancel or adjourn a hearing;

   (b) exercise its powers to make a costs order; and

   (c) impose such other sanction as may be appropriate.

[Rules 3.6 and 3.7 deal with applications to vary directions and agreement to vary time limits fixed by directions respectively.]

3.8 Case preparation and progression

(1) At every hearing, if a case cannot be concluded there and then the court must give directions so that it can be concluded at the next hearing or as soon as possible after that.

(2) At every hearing the court must, where relevant—

   (a) if the defendant is absent, decide whether to proceed nonetheless;

   (b) take the defendant's plea (unless already done) or if no plea can be taken then find out whether the defendant is likely to plead guilty or not guilty;

   (c) set, follow or revise a timetable for the progress of the case, which may include a timetable for any hearing including the trial or (in the Crown Court) the appeal;

   (d) in giving directions, ensure continuity in relation to the court and to the parties' representatives where that is appropriate and practicable; and

(e)   where a direction has not been complied with, find out why, identify who was responsible, and take appropriate action.

(3)   In order to prepare for a trial in the Crown Court, the court must conduct a plea and case management hearing unless the circumstances make that unnecessary.

3.9 Readiness for trial or appeal

(1)   This rule applies to a party's preparation for trial or (in the Crown Court) appeal, and in this rule and rule 3.10 trial includes any hearing at which evidence will be introduced.

(2)   In fulfilling his duty under rule 3.3, each party must—

    (a)   comply with directions given by the court;

    (b)   take every reasonable step to make sure his witnesses will attend when they are needed;

    (c)   make appropriate arrangements to present any written or other material; and

    (d)   promptly inform the court and the other parties of anything that may—

        (i)   affect the date or duration of the trial or appeal, or

        (ii)   significantly affect the progress of the case in any other way.

(3)   The court may require a party to give a certificate of readiness.

3.10 Conduct of a trial or an appeal

In order to manage a trial or (in the Crown Court) an appeal –

    (a)   the court must establish, with the active assistance of the parties, what disputed issues they intend to explore; and

    (b)   the court may require a party to identify –

        (i)   which witnesses that party wants to give oral evidence,

        (ii)   the order in which that party wants those witnesses to give their evidence,

        (iii) whether that party requires an order compelling the attendance of a witness,

        (iv)   what arrangements are desirable to facilitate the giving of evidence by a witness,

        (v)   what arrangements are desirable to facilitate the participation of any other person, including the defendant,

        (vi)   what written evidence that party intends to introduce,

        (vii) what other material, if any, that person intends to make available to the court in the presentation of the case,

        (viii) whether that party intends to raise any point of law that could affect the conduct of the trial or appeal, and

        (ix)   what timetable that party proposes and expects to follow.

Rules 3.5 and 3.10 were amended by the Criminal Procedure Rules Committee following the case of *R (Kelly) v Warley Magistrates' Court* [2007] EWHC 1836 (Admin), in which the Administrative Court had held that the absence of any appropriate sanction within Pt 3, as it was then drafted, rendered ineffectual the particular case management direction that was in issue in that case. Pt 3 was amended to make explicit the court's powers to impose sanctions.

The concept of robust case management was not a new one. In *R v Jisl* [2004] EWCA Crim 696, Judge LJ said, at para 114:

> The starting point is simple. Justice must be done. The defendant is entitled to a fair trial: and, which is sometimes overlooked, the prosecution is equally entitled to a reasonable opportunity to present the evidence against the defendant. It is not however a concomitant of the entitlement to a fair trial that either or both sides are further entitled to take as much time as they like, or for that matter, as long as counsel and solicitors or the defendants themselves think appropriate. Resources are limited. The funding for courts and judges, for prosecuting and the vast majority of defence lawyers is dependent on public money, for which there are many competing demands. Time itself is a resource. Every day unnecessarily used, while the trial meanders sluggishly to its eventual conclusion, represents another day's stressful waiting for the remaining witnesses and the jurors in that particular trial, and no less important, continuing and increasing tension and worry for another defendant or defendants, some of whom are remanded in custody, and the witnesses in trials which are waiting their turn to be listed. It follows that the sensible use of time requires judicial management and control.

At para 116, his Lordship concludes that, 'Active, hands-on, case management, both pre-trial and throughout the trial itself, is now regarded as an essential part of the judge's duty'.

This was a point emphasised by Judge LJ in the earlier case of *R v Chaaban* [2003] EWCA Crim 1012, where his Lordship said:

> [35] . . . The trial judge has always been responsible for managing the trial. That is one of his most important functions. To perform it he has to be alert to the needs of everyone involved in the case. That obviously includes, but it is not limited to, the interests of the defendant. It extends to the prosecution, the complainant, to every witness (whichever side is to call the witness), to the jury, or if the jury has not been sworn, to jurors in waiting. Finally, the judge should not overlook the community's interest that justice should be done without unnecessary delay. A fair balance has to be struck between all these interests.
>
> [36] Virtually any adjournment produces inconvenience for someone. What used to be described as an adjournment culture, if it ever existed, is a thing of the past. Adjournments have to be justified. If at all possible, they must be avoided. Proper case preparation is required from both sides. When asked to consider an adjournment, the judge must closely scrutinise the application, and, unless satisfied that it is indeed necessary and justified, should refuse it. . . .
>
> [37] . . . as part of his responsibility for managing the trial, the judge is expected to control the timetable and to manage the available time. Time is not unlimited. No one should assume that trials can continue to take as long or use up as much time as either or both sides may wish, or think, or assert, they need. The entitlement to a fair trial is not inconsistent with proper judicial control over the use of time. At the risk of stating the obvious, every trial which takes longer than it reasonably should is wasteful of limited resources. It also results in delays to justice in cases still waiting to be tried, adding to the tension and distress of victims, defendants, particularly those in custody awaiting trial, and witnesses. Most important of all it does nothing to assist the jury to reach a true verdict on the evidence.

[38] In principle, the trial judge should exercise firm control over the timetable, where necessary, making clear in advance and throughout the trial that the timetable will be subject to appropriate constraints. With such necessary evenhandedness and flexibility as the interests of justice require as the case unfolds, the judge is entitled to direct that the trial is expected to conclude by a specific date and to exercise his powers to see that it does.

Philip Plowden in 'Case management and the Criminal Procedure Rules' (2005) 155 NLJ 416, says of the requirement that there should be an early identification of the issue in the case:

[M]any will find less palatable the proposition that a defendant can therefore be required to indicate, in advance, the detail of what he disputes about the prosecution case. It is true that the criminal trial is 'not a game under which a guilty defendant should be provided with a sporting chance', but if there is a meaningful presumption of innocence, it is hard to see why the defendant should be required to assist the prosecution to prepare their case and to convict him.

He concludes that 'there can be no principled objection to the efficient management of cases by the court, provided that the pressure to progress the case never undermines the need for a fair trial' but that 'if the case management provisions of the Criminal Procedure Rules are to succeed in their objective, they will need to show their requirements take account of the realities of criminal practice'. He points out that delay can arise because of parties other than the defence and prosecution – there may, for example, be delay in obtaining necessary evidence.

R (Robinson) v Sutton Coldfield Magistrates' Court [2006] EWHC 307 (Admin); [2006] 4 All ER 1029 concerned failure to comply with time limits under the Rules and the granting by the court of an extension of time. The court rejected the argument that the discretion to extend time should be fettered by a requirement that the time should only be extended in exceptional circumstances, but went on to rule that 'any application for an extension will be closely scrutinised by the court' (per Owen J at para 16).

1.2.1.9 Code of practice for victims

One of the themes of Government pronouncements on the criminal justice system in recent years has been the need to shift the balance so that the focus is not just on the rights of the accused but also the needs of others – most importantly, the victim – are taken properly into account.

Section 32 of the Domestic Violence, Crime and Victims Act 2004 makes provision for the publication of a Code of Practice for victims. It provides as follows:

(1) The Secretary of State must issue a code of practice as to the services to be provided to a victim of criminal conduct by persons appearing to him to have functions relating to—

(a) victims of criminal conduct, or

(b) any aspect of the criminal justice system.

. . .

(3) The code may include provision requiring or permitting the services which are to be provided to a victim to be provided to one or more others—

(a) instead of the victim (for example where the victim has died);
(b) as well as the victim.

(4) The code may make different provision for different purposes, including different provision for—

(a) different descriptions of victims;
(b) persons who have different functions or descriptions of functions;
(c) different areas.

(5) The code may not require anything to be done by—

(a) a person acting in a judicial capacity;
(b) a person acting in the discharge of a function of a member of the Crown Prosecution Service which involves the exercise of a discretion.

(6) In determining whether a person is a victim of criminal conduct for the purposes of this section, it is immaterial that no person has been charged with or convicted of an offence in respect of the conduct.

. . .

Under s 34(2):

> . . . the code is admissible in evidence in criminal or civil proceedings and a court may take into account a failure to comply with the code in determining a question in the proceedings.

The Code was duly published in 2005 and is available at <http://www.home-office.gov.uk/documents/victims-code-of-practice>

1.3 ABUSE OF PROCESS

The values of the criminal justice system come into sharp focus in any consideration of 'abuse of process'. Where proceedings would amount to an abuse of process, the court may order that those proceedings be stayed, the effect of which is that the case against the accused is stopped.

In *R v Beckford* [1996] 1 Cr App R 94, Neill LJ said (at 100) that the constitutional principle which underlies the jurisdiction to stay proceedings is that 'the courts have the power and the duty to protect the law by protecting its own purposes and functions'. His Lordship quoted the words of Lord Devlin in *Connelly v DPP* [1964] AC 1254 at 1354, that the courts have 'an inescapable duty to secure fair treatment for those who come or are brought before them'.

In *Horseferry Road Magistrates' Court, ex p Bennett* [1994] 1 AC 42, there was no suggestion that the accused could not have a fair trial. However, it was held that the court nonetheless had power to stay the proceedings. Lord Griffiths (at 61–2) said:

If the court is to have the power to interfere with the prosecution in the present circumstances it must be because the judiciary accept a responsibility for the maintenance of the rule of law that embraces a willingness to oversee executive action and to refuse to countenance behaviour that threatens either basic human rights or the rule of law . . . I have no doubt that the judiciary should accept this responsibility in the field of criminal law.

In *DPP v Humphreys* [1977] AC 1, Lord Salmon (at 46) commented that a judge does not have:

any power to refuse to allow a prosecution to proceed merely because he considers that, as a matter of policy, it ought not to have been brought. It is only if the prosecution amounts to an abuse of the process of the court and is oppressive and vexatious that the judge has the power to intervene. Fortunately, such prosecutions are hardly ever brought but the power of the court to prevent them is . . . of great constitutional importance and should be jealously preserved.

In *Beckford*, Neill LJ (at 101) identified two types of case which are likely to amount to an abuse of process:

a   cases where the court concludes that the defendant cannot receive a fair trial; and
b   cases where the court concludes that it would be unfair for the defendant to be tried.

In *Derby Crown Court, ex p Brooks* (1985) 80 Cr App R 164, Sir Roger Ormrod said (at 168–9) that:

The power to stop a prosecution arises only when it is an abuse of the process of the court. It may be an abuse of process if either:

(a)   the prosecution have manipulated or misused the process of the court so as to deprive the defendant of a protection provided by the law or to take unfair advantage of a technicality; or
(b)   on the balance of probability the defendant has been, or will be, prejudiced in the preparation or conduct of his defence by delay on the part of the prosecution which is unjustifiable . . . The ultimate objective of this discretionary power is to ensure that there should be a fair trial according to law, which involves fairness both to the defendant and the prosecution . . .

The first of these categories focuses on the trial process; the latter is applicable where the accused should not be standing trial at all (irrespective of the fairness of the actual trial).

In abuse of process cases, two key questions usually have to be addressed:

1   to what extent is the accused prejudiced?
2   to what degree are the rule of law and the administration of justice undermined by the behaviour of the investigators or the prosecution?

There is no exhaustive list of matters which are capable of amounting to abuse of process but it is possible to derive some broad categories from the case law. Important examples include:

- lengthy delay which causes prejudice to the accused;
- failure to honour an undertaking given to the accused;
- failing to secure evidence or destroying evidence;
- tactical manipulation or misuse of procedures in order to deprive the accused of some protection provided by the law, or taking unfair advantage of a technicality;
- entrapment;
- abuse of executive power.

It should be noted that it is not an abuse of process to prosecute someone where the evidence against them is weak, and so a judge has no power to prevent the prosecution from presenting their evidence merely on the basis that he considers a conviction unlikely (*Attorney General's Ref (No 2 of 2000)* [2001] 1 Cr App R 36).

It should also be borne in mind that, although much of the case law on abuse of process comes from cases tried in the Crown Court, abuse of process arguments can also be raised in a magistrates' court. However, in *Horseferry Road Magistrates' Court, ex p Bennett* [1994] 1 AC 42, the House of Lords ruled that the jurisdiction exercised by magistrates to protect the court's process from abuse is confined strictly to matters directly affecting the fairness of the trial of the particular accused with whom they are dealing (such as delay or unfair manipulation of court procedures). It does not extend to a wider supervisory jurisdiction to uphold the rule of law. The rationale behind this distinction is that supervision of the use of executive power is a responsibility that is properly vested in the High Court. It follows that where such an issue arises in a magistrates' court, the proper course is for the magistrates to adjourn the matter so that an application can be made to the Divisional Court (or at least to send the case to the Crown Court for trial if the offence is not triable only in the magistrates' court). In *R (Salubi) v Bow Street Magistrates' Court* [2002] 1 WLR 3073, the Divisional Court reiterated that a magistrates' court's power to stay criminal proceedings for abuse of process is strictly confined to matters directly affecting the fairness of a trial before it and that this power should be exercised sparingly.

Where the defence argue that the prosecution is an abuse of process, they bear the burden of establishing abuse, on the balance of probabilities (*Telford Justices ex p Badhan* [1991] 2 QB 78). It should be noted, however, that in *R v S* [2006] EWCA Crim 756, Rose LJ observed (at para 20) that:

> the discretionary decision whether or not to grant a stay as an abuse of process, because of delay, is an exercise in judicial assessment dependent on judgment rather than on any conclusion as to fact based on evidence. It is, therefore, potentially misleading to apply to the exercise of that discretion the language of burden and standard of proof, which is more apt to an evidence-based fact-finding process.

It is submitted that this comment should be taken as applying to abuse of process applications generally (i.e. it should not be limited to those where delay is an issue), since the balancing of competing interests is at the heart of abuse claims. Nonetheless, it is clear that there is, in effect, a presumption that the trial should go ahead unless there is a compelling reason for stopping it from taking place.

In very rare cases, the court may intervene to prevent an abuse of process before a suspect has been formally charged. However, the court will order that a police investigation be discontinued, on the basis that there is no prospect of an eventual prosecution, only in the most exceptional cases. Where there were unquestionably reasonable grounds initially to suspect a person under investigation, the Court should be very slow to second-guess the police in deciding at what point he can be dismissed from the enquiry; to hold otherwise would involve an unwelcome blurring of the separate roles of Court and prosecutor/investigator (*R (C) v Chief Constable of 'A'* [2006] EWHC 2352 (Admin), per Underhill J at para 32).

We will now look in a little more detail at some of the broad categories of abuse of process, so that we can consider the themes that emerge from the case law.

1.3.1 Delay

Deliberate delay is likely to be held to amount to an abuse of process. For example, in *Brentford Justices, ex p Wong* [1981] QB 445, proceedings (for careless driving) were commenced (just) within the six-month period permitted for summary offences by s 127 of the Magistrates' Courts Act 1980 but the summons was not served until three months later. The prosecutor accepted that the delay was because he had not then reached a firm decision on whether to take proceedings, and he was trying to keep his options open. The Divisional Court held that the case could properly be regarded as one where the proceedings should be stayed.

Where the delay is inadvertent, the proceedings may nevertheless be stayed if there has been inordinate or unconscionable delay due to the prosecution's inefficiency, and prejudice to the defence from the delay is either proved or to be inferred (per Lloyd LJ in *Gateshead Justices ex p Smith* (1985) 149 JP 681). In *Grays Justices, ex p Graham* [1982] QB 1239, it was held that, although delay alone could be sufficient to justify a stay of proceedings, if sufficiently prolonged, some other impropriety is generally required. The test to be applied is whether the delay in bringing the proceedings is of such magnitude as to render them vexatious and an abuse of the court's process. At p 1248, May LJ said, 'we do not think that this court should create any form of artificial limitation period for criminal proceedings where it cannot truly be said that the due process of the criminal courts is being used improperly to harass a defendant'. In summary, then, the delay must cause prejudice to the accused, and the delay must be unjustified.

In *Bow Street Stipendiary Magistrate, ex p DPP* (1990) 91 Cr App R 283 at 296–7, Watkins LJ made it clear that, to amount to an abuse of process, delay has to produce 'genuine prejudice and unfairness'. In some cases, however, prejudice would be presumed from substantial delay and the prosecution will have to rebut that inference of prejudice. At p 300, his Lordship reiterated that it is 'perfectly proper, according to circumstances, to infer prejudice from the mere passage of time', and added that such an 'inference is more easily drawn when dealing with a single brief but confused event which must depend on the recollections of those involved'. Similarly, in *Telford Justices, ex p Badhan* [1991] 2 QB 78, the Court of Appeal said that, whilst it is for the accused to show on the balance of probabilities that a fair trial is now impossible, where the period of delay is long, it can be legitimate for the court to infer prejudice without proof of specific prejudice.

In *Bell v DPP of Jamaica* [1985] AC 937, the Privy Council laid down guidelines for determining whether delay would deprive the accused of a fair trial. The relevant factors were said to be:

a the length of delay;
b the prosecution's reasons to justify the delay;
c the accused's efforts to assert his rights; and
d the prejudice caused to the accused.

In *Attorney General's Ref (No 1 of 1990)* [1992] QB 630, Lord Lane CJ said (at 643):

> Stays imposed on the grounds of delay or for any other reason should only be employed in exceptional circumstances . . . In principle, therefore, even where the delay can be said to be unjustifiable, the imposition of a permanent stay should be the exception rather than the rule. Still more rare should be cases where a stay can properly be imposed in the absence of any fault on the part of the complainant or prosecution. Delay due merely to the complexity of the case or contributed to by the actions of the defendant himself should never be the foundation for a stay.
> . . . no stay should be imposed unless the defendant shows on the balance of probabilities that owing to the delay he will suffer serious prejudice to the extent that no fair trial can be held: in other words, that the continuance of the prosecution amounts to a misuse of the process of the court. In assessing whether there is likely to be prejudice and if so whether it can properly be described as serious, the following matters should be borne in mind: first, the power of the judge at common law and under the Police and Criminal Evidence Act 1984 to regulate the admissibility of evidence; secondly, the trial process itself, which should ensure that all relevant factual issues arising from delay will be placed before the jury as part of the evidence for their consideration, together with the powers of the judge to give appropriate directions to the jury before they consider their verdict.

The same approach was adopted by the House of Lords in *Attorney General's Ref (No 2 of 2001)* [2004] 2 AC 72. In that case, their Lordships had to consider (*inter alia*) whether criminal proceedings might be stayed on the ground that there had been a breach of the reasonable time requirement imposed by Art 6(1) of the European Convention on Human Rights in circumstances where the accused could not demonstrate that any prejudice had arisen from the delay. Lord Bingham, at para 24, said:

> If, through the action or inaction of a public authority, a criminal charge is not determined at a hearing within a reasonable time, there is necessarily a breach of the defendant's Convention right under article 6(1). For such breach there must be afforded such remedy as may (Article 8(1)) be just and appropriate or (in Convention terms) effective, just and proportionate. The appropriate remedy will depend on the nature of the breach and all the circumstances, including particularly the stage of the proceedings at which the breach is established. If the breach is established before the hearing, the appropriate remedy may be a public acknowledgement of the breach, action to expedite the hearing to the greatest extent practicable and perhaps, if the defendant is in custody, his release on bail. It will not be

appropriate to stay or dismiss the proceedings unless (a) there can no longer be a fair hearing or (b) it would otherwise be unfair to try the defendant. The public interest in the final determination of criminal charges requires that such a charge should not be stayed or dismissed if any lesser remedy will be just and proportionate in all the circumstances. The prosecutor and the court do not act incompatibly with the defendant's Convention right in continuing to prosecute or entertain proceedings after a breach is established in a case where neither of conditions (a) or (b) is met, since the breach consists in the delay which has accrued and not in the prospective hearing. If the breach of the reasonable time requirement is established retrospectively, after there has been a hearing, the appropriate remedy may be a public acknowledgement of the breach, a reduction in the penalty imposed on a convicted defendant or the payment of compensation to an acquitted defendant. Unless (a) the hearing was unfair or (b) it was unfair to try the defendant at all, it will not be appropriate to quash any conviction. Again, in any case where neither of conditions (a) or (b) applies, the prosecutor and the court do not act incompatibly with the defendant's Convention right in prosecuting or entertaining the proceedings but only in failing to procure a hearing within a reasonable time.

It follows that a stay should not be ordered if the defendant's right to a fair trial can be protected in some other way, such as excluding particular items of evidence, or directing the jury about the problems caused to the defence by the delay.

In *Dyer v Watson* [2004] 1 AC 379, Lord Bingham said that the 'threshold of proving a breach of the reasonable time requirement is a high one, not easily crossed' (para 52). His Lordship went on to say that, if the period which has elapsed is one which, on its face and without more, gives ground for real concern, it is necessary for the court to look into the detailed facts and circumstances of the particular case (ibid). His Lordship then listed the factors to be taken into account:

- the complexity of the case (the more complex a case, the longer the time which must necessarily be taken to prepare it adequately for trial and for any appellate hearing);
- the conduct of the defendant (a defendant cannot properly complain of delay which he has caused);
- the manner in which the case has been dealt with by the administrative and judicial authorities (i.e. the prosecution and the court).

There is no general obligation on a prosecutor to act with all due expedition and diligence, but a marked lack of expedition, if unjustified, would point towards a breach of the reasonable time requirement (para 55).

More recently, the Court of Appeal, in *R v S* [2006] EWCA Crim 756; (2006) 170 JP 434, Rose LJ (at para 21) summarised the position as follows:

(i) Even where delay is unjustifiable, a permanent stay should be the exception rather than the rule;
(ii) where there is no fault on the part of the complainant or the prosecution, it will be very rare for a stay to be granted;
(iii) no stay should be granted in the absence of serious prejudice to the defence so that no fair trial can be held;

(iv) when assessing possible serious prejudice, the judge should bear in mind his or her power to regulate the admissibility of evidence and that the trial process itself should ensure that all relevant factual issues arising from delay will be placed before the jury for their consideration in accordance with appropriate direction from the judge;

(v) if, having considered all these factors, a judge's assessment is that a fair trial will be possible, a stay should not be granted.

The possibility of giving the defendant some other redress for the delay must not be overlooked. In *Spiers (Prosecutor Fiscal) v Ruddy* [2007] UKPC D2, Lord Bingham of Cornhill said (at para 16) that in cases where there has, or may have been

> such delay in the conduct of proceedings as to breach a party's right to trial within a reasonable time but where the fairness of the trial has not been or will not be compromised . . . such delay does not give rise to a continuing breach which cannot be cured save by a discontinuation of proceedings. It gives rise to a breach which can be cured, even where it cannot be prevented, by expedition, reduction of sentence or compensation, provided always that the breach, where it occurs, is publicly acknowledged and addressed.

In the Crown Court, where there has been delay in bringing the prosecution, specimen direction number 37 (issued by the Judicial Studies Board) suggests that the trial judge should point out to the jury that, because they are concerned with events which are said to have taken place a long time ago, they must appreciate that there may be a danger of real prejudice to the accused and this possibility must be borne in mind when considering whether the case against him has been proved. The jury should be directed that they should 'make allowances for the fact that, from the defendant's point of view, the longer the time since an alleged incident, the more difficult it may be for him to answer it' and that (even if they believe that the delay is understandable) if they decide that, because of the delay, the accused has been placed at a real disadvantage in putting forward his case, they must take that into account in his favour when deciding if the prosecution has made them sure of his guilt. An important question is therefore whether, in the particular circumstances of the case, such a warning is adequate to negate the prejudice that the accused would otherwise suffer because of the delay.

Cases involving sexual offences, such as child abuse cases, may be regarded as an exceptional category in their own right. It is often the case that such allegations emerge a long time after the alleged abuse took place. The view generally taken by the courts is that the unfairness can be minimised by a direction to the jury to take proper account of the fact that the accused was handicapped in defending the case because of the length of time which has elapsed since the alleged offence was committed. Any residual prejudice is regarded as outweighed by the importance of prosecuting such serious offences. See, for example, *R v E* [2004] 2 Cr App R 621, where the Court of Appeal dismissed an appeal against conviction on the basis that the appellant was not put in an impossible position to defend himself; the Court said that juries should be trusted to make allowances not only for the lapse of time but also for the difficulties faced by the accused.

In *R v Smolinski* [2004] EWCA Crim 1270; [2004] 2 Cr App R 40, Lord Woolf CJ (at paras 8 and 9) pointed out that in cases of alleged sexual offences, it is sometimes very difficult for young children to speak about such matters and therefore it is only many years later that the offences come to light. However, when a long time has elapsed, careful consideration must be given by the prosecution as to whether it is right to bring the prosecution at all. If, having considered the evidence to be called, and the witnesses having been interviewed on behalf of the prosecution, a decision is reached by the prosecuting authorities that the case should proceed, then unless the case is exceptional, an abuse of process application will be unsuccessful. If an application is to be made to a judge, the best time for doing so is after any evidence has been called and for the judge then, having scrutinised the evidence with particular care, to come to a conclusion whether or not it is safe for the matter to be left to the jury. A similar point about the timing of applications based on abuse of process was made by Hooper LJ in *R v Burke* [2005] EWCA Crim 29 (at para 32):

> Prior to the start of the case it will often be difficult, if not impossible, to determine whether a defendant can have a fair trial because of the delay coupled with the destruction of documents and the unavailability of witnesses. Issues which might seem very important before the trial may become unimportant or of less importance as a result of developments during the trial, including the evidence of the complainant and of other witnesses including the defendant should he choose to give evidence. Issues which seemed unimportant before the trial may become very important.

John Jackson and Jenny Johnstone, in 'The reasonable time requirement: an independent and meaningful right?' [2005] Crim LR 3 argue that the House of Lords in *Attorney General's Reference (No 2 of 2001)* was too restrictive in its ruling that it would only be appropriate in very exceptional cases to grant a stay of proceedings after a breach of the Convention right to be brought to trial within a reasonable time. They argue that, in the absence of any other readily available remedy, this means that the right is not as meaningful as it should be. Their criticisms are based on three principal grounds:

i   although their Lordships conceded that there could be exceptional situations where the sheer length of the proceedings may justify a stay, they did not place enough emphasis on the fact that an unreasonable delay may cause such prejudice to the accused that the only appropriate response in this situation is to stay the proceedings;

ii the need for criminal proceedings to be brought to final determination cannot be separated from the need to bring about this finality within a reasonable time, since there will be circumstances when delay will make it impossible to achieve finality; and

iii there is also a case for not holding a trial where it is no longer fair on the participants to require them to recount events and account for actions so far in the past.

1.3.2 Failing to obtain, losing or destroying evidence

The leading authority on such cases is *R (Ebrahim) v Feltham Magistrates' Court* [2001] EWHC Admin 130; [2001] 1 WLR 1293. Brooke LJ said (at para 74) that the starting point must be whether there was a duty on the investigator to obtain or retain the material in question. If there was a duty, and that duty has been breached, a stay will be granted only if the accused has suffered 'serious prejudice' as a result of the failure to obtain the evidence, or by its loss or destruction. Brooke LJ said that there has to be either an element of bad faith, or at the very least some serious fault, on the part of the police or the prosecution authorities, for this ground of challenge to succeed (para 23). It follows that a stay will, unless there has been bad faith on the part of the prosecution, only be granted where the accused could not have a fair trial. At para 25 Brooke LJ said:

> Two well-known principles are frequently invoked in this context when a court is invited to stay proceedings for abuse of process:
>
> (i)   The ultimate objective of this discretionary power is to ensure that there should be a fair trial according to law, which involves fairness both to the defendant and the prosecution, because the fairness of a trial is not all one sided; it requires that those who are undoubtedly guilty should be convicted as well as that those about whose guilt there is any reasonable doubt should be acquitted.
> (ii) The trial process itself is equipped to deal with the bulk of the complaints on which applications for a stay are founded.

At para 27, his Lordship went on:

> It must be remembered that it is a commonplace in criminal trials for a defendant to rely on 'holes' in the prosecution case, for example, a failure to take fingerprints or a failure to submit evidential material to forensic examination. If, in such a case, there is sufficient credible evidence, apart from the missing evidence, which, if believed, would justify a safe conviction, then a trial should proceed, leaving the defendant to seek to persuade the jury or justices not to convict because evidence which might otherwise have been available was not before the court through no fault of his. Often the absence of a video film or fingerprints or DNA material is likely to hamper the prosecution as much as the defence.

Other cases illustrate how the courts apply these principles. For example, in *R v Medway* [2000] 1 Cr App R (S) 191, the accused was convicted of robbery. It was alleged that he robbed an elderly lady of her handbag. A closed-circuit television camera was operating in the area, but the police, having looked at the film, decided that it contained nothing of value. The tape was destroyed. The trial judge refused to stay the trial as an abuse of process. The Court of Appeal dismissed the appeal, saying that there was nothing to show that the absence of the tape made the conviction unsafe. An accused could be disadvantaged in a case where evidence had been tampered with, lost or destroyed, but it was only in exceptional circumstances (for example, where such interference was malicious) that a stay was justified. The clear implication is that a defendant is disadvantaged only if the absence of the evidence might have made a difference to the outcome of the trial.

In *R v Dobson* [2001] EWCA Crim 1606, the Court of Appeal considered the position where police had failed to obtain CCTV footage which might have been relevant to the accused's defence of alibi. Potter LJ (at para 34) said that, in determining whether there was an abuse of process, it was appropriate to consider:

(1) What was the duty of police in the circumstances?

(2) Did the police fail in their duty in not obtaining and retaining the relevant video tape footage?

(3) If so, was the prejudice suffered 'serious prejudice to the extent that no fair trial could be held' in the light of such failure?

(4) Separately from (3), did the police failure constitute such bad behaviour, in the sense of bad faith or serious fault, as to render it unfair that the defendant should be tried at all?

In the present case, the police should have looked at the CCTV footage, and had failed in their duty to do so. However, the prejudice was not serious because it was uncertain whether the footage would have assisted the defence, and the accused could have requested it or sought other evidence to support his alibi. There was no question of malice or intentional omission, as opposed to oversight, on behalf of the police. The judge was therefore right to conclude that a fair trial was possible.

In *Khalid Ali v Crown Prosecution Service, West Midlands* [2007] EWCA Crim 691, the Court of Appeal emphasised that, in such cases, the mere fact that missing material might have assisted the defence will not necessarily lead to a stay. In considering whether or not to order a stay, the court will have regard to whether there is sufficiently credible evidence, apart from the missing evidence, leaving the defence to exploit the gaps left by the missing evidence. Moses LJ (at para 30) said that the 'rationale for refusing a stay is the existence of credible evidence, itself untainted by what has gone missing'.

A similar approach was taken in *DPP v Cooper* [2008] EWHC 507 (Admin), where the prosecution case was that bank notes in the accused's possession had tested positive for the presence of heroin. The forensic test had been video-taped. However, the video had been lost. Moreover, the defence were unable to carry out their own independent tests on the bank notes because they had been tested using a spray that would make subsequent testing impossible. The defence therefore submitted that they had been denied access to material which was clearly relevant to the issues in the case, and that a fair trial could not take place as they had been denied the ability to rebut the expert evidence of the prosecution as a result of a failure on the part of the police to preserve evidence until the conclusion of the proceedings. The Administrative Court held that the proceedings did not constitute an abuse of process. At para 9, Silber J pointed out that the defendant still had adequate means to challenge the prosecution case, since the forensic scientist who conducted the tests on the bank notes could have been questioned about the way she conducted those tests and how she had reached her results; moreover, the magistrates or jury would have been able to make adequate allowance for the fact that the defendant had not been able to see a video of the tests being carried out or to carry out their own tests.

1.3.3 Going back on a promise

In *R v Croydon Justices, ex p Dean* [1993] QB 769, the Divisional Court held that, where the police give a person an undertaking, promise or representation that he will not be charged in exchange for his co-operation, it may amount to an abuse of process if he is subsequently prosecuted. In such circumstances, it is not necessary for the accused to show that there was bad faith on the part of the police.

An example of a prosecution change of mind amounting to an abuse of process is *R v Bloomfield* [1997] 1 Cr App R 135. The defendant was charged with possession of a Class A controlled drug. At a preliminary hearing, prosecuting counsel indicated to the defence that the Crown wished to offer no evidence because it was accepted that the accused had been the victim of a set-up. Owing to the presence in court of certain people, it would have been embarrassing to the police and prosecution if no evidence had been offered that day, so counsel spoke to the judge in his room. An order was then made in open court to adjourn the case and re-list it 'for mention'. The Crown Prosecution Service (CPS) subsequently arranged a conference with new prosecuting counsel and informed the defence that there had been a change of plan and that the Crown intended to continue the prosecution against the defendant. An application at the trial to stay the proceedings as an abuse of process failed. However, it was held by the Court of Appeal that allowing the prosecution to go ahead amounted to an abuse of process since, whether or not there was prejudice to the accused, it would bring the administration of justice into disrepute if the Crown were permitted to revoke its original decision. The concept of 'bringing the administration of justice' into disrepute is an important one in the field of abuse of process.

Similarly, *R (H) v Guildford Youth Court* [2008] EWHC 506 (Admin) concerned a juvenile accused of assault. Before he was interviewed by the police, it was intimated to his solicitor that it was possible that the case would be dealt with by way of a final warning as a way of resolving the matter. The juvenile admitted the offence and was bailed to an 'intervention clinic', when it was indicated that the matter would be dealt with by way of a final warning. The CPS subsequently decided that a prosecution would be appropriate, and the juvenile was charged. Silber J, at para 16, ruled that 'the fact that a promise was made by an officer of the State, namely the police officer who was in charge at that stage deciding whether or not to prosecute, is something that there is a clear public interest in upholding'. The proceedings should therefore have been stayed as an abuse of process.

Another example is *Jones v Whalley* [2006] UKHL 41; [2007] 1 AC 63, where a private prosecution was held to be an abuse of process because the accused had previously been cautioned by the police for the offence in question, and the terms of the caution had said, expressly, that he would not have to go before a criminal court in connection with the matter. The House of Lords observed that allowing private prosecutions to proceed, despite an assurance that the offender would not have to go to court, would tend to undermine the system of cautions. It should be noted that the abuse complained of in this case was not abuse going to the fairness of the trial (since evidence of the accused's admission to the offence, and of the caution administered by the police, could have been excluded), but went to the fairness of trying the accused at all.

Giving an indication that the case will be dropped does not necessarily mean that it will be an abuse of process for the prosecution to have a change of mind. In *R v Mulla* [2003] EWCA Crim 1881; [2004] 1 Cr App R 6, the defendant was charged with causing death by dangerous driving. On the first day of the trial, the prosecution indicated that they would be willing to accept a plea of guilty to the lesser charge of careless driving. The judge was unhappy with this and invited the prosecutor to reconsider. Later that day, having reconsidered the matter, the prosecution indicated that they had decided to proceed with the original charge of causing death by dangerous driving. The Court of

Appeal held that this did not amount to an abuse of process. This was not a case in which the accused's hopes were raised, later to be dashed, since he knew from the beginning of the proceedings in court that the judge did not approve of the course which the prosecution were proposing to take. The court said that factors to be considered include what view is expressed by the judge when the prosecution gives its indication, the period of time over which the prosecution reconsiders the matter before they change their mind, whether or not the accused's hopes have been inappropriately raised, and whether there has been, by reason of the change of course by the prosecution, any prejudice to the defence (per Rose LJ at para 22).

In *R v Abu Hamza* [2006] EWCA Crim 2918; [2007] QB 659, Lord Phillips CJ (at para 54) said that where a person has been told he will not be prosecuted for an offence:

> it is not likely to constitute an abuse of process to proceed with a prosecution unless (i) there has been an unequivocal representation by those with the conduct of the investigation or prosecution of a case that the defendant will not be prosecuted and (ii) that the defendant has acted on that representation to his detriment. Even then, if facts come to light which were not known when the representation was made, these may justify proceeding with the prosecution despite the representation.

Lord Phillips added (at para 50) that:

> it is usually in the public interest that those who are reasonably suspected of criminal conduct should be brought to trial. Only in rare circumstances will it be offensive to justice to give effect to this public interest.

A similar approach was taken in *DPP v B* [2008] EWHC 201 (Admin), where the accused was originally charged with a single charge of sexual assault. However, when he appeared before the Crown Court, the judge considered that the single count failed to reflect the criminality which was alleged against the accused, the complainant having alleged that she had been sexually abused by the accused over a period of years. The prosecution subsequently sought to bring 17 charges of sexual assault against the accused, to reflect the years over which the sexual abuse had allegedly occurred. The Divisional Court held that this did not amount to an abuse of process. Latham LJ pointed out (at para 10) that proceedings should be stayed for abuse of process only 'in very exceptional circumstances, where it can properly be said that the consequence would be injustice, or where the circumstances giving rise to the proceedings in respect of which the application is made offend one's sense of justice overall'. His Lordship (at para 12) accepted that the accused was clearly at risk of a substantially greater sentence than he would have been under the original charge, but said that this was not unjust, since the accused was not going to be exposed to any sentence other than the proper sentence that should be imposed for the offences which were established (whether through guilty pleas or following trial) against him.

1.3.4 Manipulation of procedure

An example of manipulation of procedure is where a charge alleging a summary offence is replaced with one alleging an indictable offence, or vice versa. Paragraph 7.3

of the Code for Crown Prosecutors (see below) makes it clear that the charge should not be changed simply because of the decision made as to trial venue. In *R v Canterbury and St Augustine Justices, ex p Klisiak* [1982] QB 398, it was said that the court should interfere with the prosecution decision as to what offences to proceed with only 'in the most obvious circumstances which disclose blatant injustice' (per Lord Lane CJ at p 411). Thus, it has to be clear that the change in the charge is not a bona fide result of a re-assessment of the appropriateness of the original charge. As it was put in *R v Sheffield Justices, ex p DPP* [1993] Crim LR 136, it is only appropriate to interfere where the court concludes that the prosecution were acting in bad faith (deliberately manipulating the system to deprive an accused of his rights).

1.3.5 Entrapment

The leading authority on entrapment is *R v Looseley* [2001] UKHL 53; [2001] 1 WLR 2060. The House of Lords held that, although entrapment is not a substantive defence in English law, where an accused can show entrapment, the court should normally stay the proceedings, since a prosecution founded on entrapment would be an abuse of the court's process. Lord Nicholls of Birkenhead (at para 19) said:

> Police conduct which brings about, to use the catchphrase, state-created crime is unacceptable and improper. To prosecute in such circumstances would be an affront to the public conscience . . . In a very broad sense of the word, such a prosecution would not be fair.

However, his Lordship continued (at para 21):

> If the defendant already had the intent to commit a crime of the same or a similar kind, then the police did no more than give him the opportunity to fulfil his existing intent. This is unobjectionable. If the defendant was already presently disposed to commit such a crime, should opportunity arise, that is not entrapment. That is not state-created crime. The matter stands differently if the defendant lacked such a predisposition, and the police were responsible for implanting the necessary intent.

At para 23, his Lordship says that:

> a useful guide is to consider whether the police did no more than present the defendant with an unexceptional opportunity to commit a crime . . . The yardstick for the purpose of this test is, in general, whether the police conduct preceding the commission of the offence was no more than might have been expected from others in the circumstances. Police conduct of this nature is not to be regarded as inciting or instigating crime, or luring a person into committing a crime.

As Lord Hutton put it, at para 101, particular emphasis is placed on the need:

> to consider whether a person has been persuaded or pressurised by a law enforcement officer into committing a crime which he would not otherwise have committed, or whether the officer did not go beyond giving the person an opportunity to break the law, when he would have behaved in the same way if some other person had offered him the opportunity

to commit a similar crime, and when he freely took advantage of the opportunity presented to him by the officer.

It follows that if a person freely takes advantage of an opportunity to break the law given to him by a police officer, the police officer is not to be regarded as inciting or instigating the crime.

Ultimately, however, as Lord Nicholls points out at para 25:

> . . . the overall consideration is always whether the conduct of the police or other law enforcement agency was so seriously improper as to bring the administration of justice into disrepute.

His Lordship goes on to enumerate some of the factors to which the court must have regard when applying this test (paras 26–29):

> *The nature of the offence.* The use of pro-active techniques is more needed and, hence, more appropriate, in some circumstances than others. The secrecy and difficulty of detection, and the manner in which the particular criminal activity is carried on, are relevant considerations.
>
> *The reason for the particular police operation.* It goes without saying that the police must act in good faith and not, for example, as part of a malicious vendetta against an individual or group of individuals. Having reasonable grounds for suspicion is one way good faith may be established, but having grounds for suspicion of a particular individual is not always essential. Sometimes suspicion may be centred on a particular place, such as a particular public house. Sometimes random testing may be the only practicable way of policing a particular trading activity.
>
> *The nature and extent of police participation in the crime.* The greater the inducement held out by the police, and the more forceful or persistent the police overtures, the more readily may a court conclude that the police overstepped the boundary: their conduct might well have brought about commission of a crime by a person who would normally avoid crime of that kind. In assessing the weight to be attached to the police inducement, regard is to be had to the defendant's circumstances, including his vulnerability. This is not because the standards of acceptable behaviour are variable. Rather, this is a recognition that what may be a significant inducement to one person may not be so to another. For the police to behave as would an ordinary customer of a trade, whether lawful or unlawful, being carried on by the defendant will not normally be regarded as objectionable.
>
> *The defendant's criminal record.* The defendant's criminal record is unlikely to be relevant unless it can be linked to other factors grounding reasonable suspicion that the defendant is currently engaged in criminal activity . . .

The House of Lords also noted that there is no appreciable difference between the requirements of Art 6 of the European Convention on Human Rights (having regard to relevant decisions of the European Court of Human Rights, such as *Teixeira de Castro v Portugal* (1999) 28 EHRR 101) and English law.

1.3.6 Abuse of executive power

Abuse of executive power is a further (indeed extreme) example of matters which may bring the administration of justice into disrepute. In *R v Horseferry Road Magistrates' Court, ex p Bennett* [1994] 1 AC 42, the accused had been brought back forcibly to the UK in disregard of the extradition procedures that were available. This was held to amount to an abuse of process even though a fair trial was possible. The point was that the accused should not have been before the court in the first place. Similarly, in *R v Mullen* [2000] QB 520, the security services and police had procured the defendant's unlawful deportation from Zimbabwe. The Court of Appeal ruled that, even if no complaint can be made as to the fairness of the trial itself, unconscionable conduct on the part of the authorities in bringing the accused before the court may amount to an abuse of process. This will be the case 'where it would be offensive to justice and propriety to try the defendant at all' (per Rose LJ at p 537). Thus, a conviction may be regarded as unsafe on the basis that the trial on which it was founded was an abuse of process.

The same approach had been adopted by the House of Lords in *R v Latif* [1996] 1 WLR 104. The defendant was convicted of being knowingly concerned in the importation into the UK of heroin which had been brought into the country by an undercover customs officer. The House of Lords held that whether the proceedings should have been stayed on the ground of abuse was a matter of discretion for the judge, who had to decide whether the matters said to constitute abuse of process amounted to what Lord Steyn described (at p 112) as an 'affront to the public conscience'. His Lordship added (at p 113) that this requires the judge to:

> balance the public interest in ensuring that those that are charged with grave crimes should be tried and the competing public interest in not conveying the impression that the court will adopt the approach that the end justifies any means.

Closely related to abuse of executive power are cases where the investigators have behaved in a way that is wholly improper. A good example is *R v Grant* [2005] EWCA Crim 1089; [2006] QB 60, where the police unlawfully intercepted and recorded privileged conversations between the suspect and his legal advisor. No useful evidence was gathered in this way, and so there was nothing to exclude under s 78 of the Police and Criminal Evidence Act 1984. Laws LJ (at para 54) said that the court was:

> . . . in no doubt but that in general unlawful acts of the kind done in this case, amounting to a deliberate violation of a suspected person's right to legal professional privilege, are so great an affront to the integrity of the justice system, and therefore the rule of law, that the associated prosecution is rendered abusive and ought not to be countenanced by the court.

His Lordship concluded (at para 57) that the deliberate interference with the suspect's right to the confidence of privileged communications with his solicitor 'seriously undermines the rule of law and justifies a stay on grounds of abuse of process, notwithstanding the absence of prejudice consisting in evidence gathered by the Crown as the fruit of police officers' unlawful conduct'.

1.4 ETHICS AND CRIMINAL JUSTICE: A SELECTION OF MATERIALS

For a discussion of ethical issues that arise in criminal cases, see:

- Boon, A and Levin, J, *The ethics and conduct of lawyers in the UK*, 1999, Oxford: Hart Publishing.
- Blake, M and Ashworth, A, 'Some ethical issues in prosecuting and defending' [1998] Crim LR 16–34.

The journal *Legal Ethics* (Hart Publishing <http://www.hartjournals.co.uk/le/>) contains interesting articles on the ethical dimensions of the practice of law. For example, see:

- John Jackson, 'The Ethical Implications of the Enhanced Role of the Public Prosecutor' (2006) 9 *Legal Ethics* 35 (exploring the ethical implications that arise from the enhanced role being given to public prosecutors in England and Wales in advising on criminal investigation, directing charges and in diversion and advocacy. Jackson argues that in order to develop ethical principles that take full account of these expanding activities, there is a need for a clearer delineation of their professional role within the criminal justice system. It is argued that as part of their prime concern to protect the well-being of the community, prosecutors should play a greater role in fostering restorative justice).
- Ed Cape, 'Rebalancing the Criminal Justice Process: Ethical Challenges for Criminal Defence Lawyers' (2006) 9 *Legal Ethics* 56 (considering the ethical obligations of criminal defence lawyers in the context of significant change to the criminal process in England and Wales. Cape argues that since coming to power in 1997 the Labour Government has been engaged in a programme of changing the criminal justice system from one based upon the principle of fair trial rights to one based on 'managerialist' values. He argues that defence lawyers are increasingly being prevented from acting in the best interests of their clients and that professional conduct rules fail adequately to articulate and prioritise the relationship between the lawyer's obligation to the client and to the court, with the result that lawyers are left to resolve ethical dilemmas created or exacerbated by the transformation of the criminal process without adequate ethical guidance. He proposes that the legal professions should challenge the Government's plans to transform the criminal process, and re-fashion professional conduct rules around human rights values).
- Lee Bridges, 'The Ethics of Representation on Guilty Pleas' (2006) 9 *Legal Ethics* 80 (addressing what should be the ethical stance of criminal defence lawyers when representing clients on guilty pleas. Bridges considers whether there are circumstances in which a defence lawyer should withdraw from representation rather than continue to act for a client who intends to plead guilty. He notes that ethical discussion tend to focus on two issues which arise in relation to the client who intends to plead not guilty: how far the lawyer can go ethically in advising such a client to change his plea to guilty, especially where the prospects of acquittal are poor and in a situation where conviction following trial is likely to result in a more

severe sentence; and what ethical limitations are placed on the lawyer in continuing to represent a client where that client tells the lawyer that he is in fact guilty but wishes to proceed on the basis of a not guilty plea. Bridges addresses what should be the ethical stance of the defence lawyer in the opposite situation, where the client privately claims to be innocent (and the lawyer may well believe that he or she is innocent and that there is a good chance of acquittal) but states an intention to plead guilty, possibly because of pressure from within the criminal justice system (e.g. in order to be eligible for a lesser sentence than if convicted following a not guilty plea) or from external factors).

It is also instructive to look at s 3 of the Bar's Code of Conduct (available on the website of the Bar Standards Board at <http://www.barstandardsboard.org.uk/stand-ardsandguidance/codeofconduct/>), part of which deals with criminal cases. It deals with the duties of prosecuting and defence counsel, and so far as the latter is concerned addresses such issues as what to do if a client says that he is innocent but wants to plead guilty anyway, and what counsel should do if a client confesses his guilt to counsel (see ss 11.5 and 12). The Code provides as follows:

Standards Applicable in Criminal Cases
10 Responsibilities of Prosecuting Counsel

. . .

10.1 Prosecuting counsel should not attempt to obtain a conviction by all means at his command. He should not regard himself as appearing for a party. He should lay before the Court fairly and impartially the whole of the facts which comprise the case for the prosecution and should assist the Court on all matters of law applicable to the case.

10.2 Prosecuting counsel should bear in mind at all times whilst he is instructed:

(i)   that he is responsible for the presentation and general conduct of the case;
(ii) that he should use his best endeavours to ensure that all evidence or material that ought properly to be made available is either presented by the prosecution or disclosed to the defence.

10.3 Prosecuting counsel should, when instructions are delivered to him, read them exped-itiously and, where instructed to do so, advise or confer on all aspects of the case well before its commencement.

10.4 In relation to cases tried in the Crown Court, prosecuting counsel:

(a) should ensure, if he is instructed to settle an indictment, that he does so promptly and within due time, and should bear in mind the desirability of not overloading an indictment with either too many defendants or too many counts, in order to present the prosecution case as simply and as concisely as possible;
(b) should ask, if the indictment is being settled by some other person, to see a copy of the indictment and should then check it;
(c) should decide whether any additional evidence is required and, if it is, should advise in writing and set out precisely what additional evidence is required with a view to serving it on the defence as soon as possible;
(d) should consider whether all witness statements in the possession of the

prosecution have been properly served on the defendant in accordance with the Attorney General's Guidelines;

(e)   should eliminate all unnecessary material in the case so as to ensure an efficient and fair trial, and in particular should consider the need for particular witnesses and exhibits and draft appropriate admissions for service on the defence;

. . .

10.6 Prosecuting counsel should . . . have regard to the following recommendations of the Farquharson Committee [*The Farquharson Guidelines, The Role and Responsibilities of the Prosecution Advocate* <http://www.cps.gov.uk/Publications/prosecution/farqbooklet.html>]:

(a)   Where counsel has taken a decision on a matter of policy with which his professional client has not agreed, it would be appropriate for him to submit to the Attorney General a written report of all the circumstances, including his reasons for disagreeing with those who instructed him;

(b)   When counsel has had an opportunity to prepare his brief and to confer with those instructing him, but at the last moment before trial unexpectedly advises that the case should not proceed or that pleas to lesser offences should be accepted, and his professional client does not accept such advice, counsel should apply for an adjournment if instructed to do so;

(c)   Subject to the above, it is for prosecuting counsel to decide whether to offer no evidence on a particular count or on the indictment as a whole and whether to accept pleas to a lesser count or counts.

10.7 It is the duty of prosecuting counsel to assist the Court at the conclusion of the summing-up by drawing attention to any apparent errors or omissions of fact or law.

10.8 In relation to sentence, prosecuting counsel:

(a)   should not attempt by advocacy to influence the Court with regard to sentence: if, however, a defendant is unrepresented it is proper to inform the Court of any mitigating circumstances about which counsel is instructed;

(b)   should be in a position to assist the Court if requested as to any statutory provisions relevant to the offence or the offender and as to any relevant guidelines as to sentence laid down by the Court of Appeal;

(c)   should bring any such matters as are referred to in (b) above to the attention of the Court if in the opinion of prosecuting counsel the Court has erred;

(d)   should bring to the attention of the Court any appropriate compensation, forfeiture and restitution matters which may arise on conviction, for example pursuant to sections 35–42 of the Powers of Criminal Courts Act 1973 and the Drug Trafficking Offences Act 1986;

(e)   should draw the attention of the defence to any assertion of material fact made in mitigation which the prosecution believes to be untrue: if the defence persist in that assertion, prosecuting counsel should invite the Court to consider requiring the issue to be determined by the calling of evidence in accordance with the decision of the Court of Appeal in *R v Newton* (1983) 77 Crim App R 13.

11 Responsibilities of Defence Counsel

11.1 When defending a client on a criminal charge, a barrister must endeavour to protect his client from conviction except by a competent tribunal and upon legally admissible evidence sufficient to support a conviction for the offence charged.

11.2 A barrister acting for the defence:

(a) should satisfy himself, if he is briefed to represent more than one defendant, that no conflict of interest is likely to arise;

(b) should arrange a conference and if necessary a series of conferences with his professional and lay clients;

(c) should consider whether any enquiries or further enquiries are necessary and, if so, should advise in writing as soon as possible;

(d) should consider whether any witnesses for the defence are required and, if so, which;

(e) should consider whether a Notice of Alibi is required and, if so, should draft an appropriate notice;

(f) should consider whether it would be appropriate to call expert evidence for the defence and, if so, have regard to the rules of the Crown Court in relation to notifying the prosecution of the contents of the evidence to be given;

(g) should ensure that he has sufficient instructions for the purpose of deciding which prosecution witnesses should be cross-examined, and should then ensure that no other witnesses remain fully bound at the request of the defendant and request his professional client to inform the Crown Prosecution Service of those who can be conditionally bound;

(h) should consider whether any admissions can be made with a view to saving time and expense at trial, with the aim of admitting as much evidence as can properly be admitted in accordance with the barrister's duty to his client;

(i) should consider what admissions can properly be requested from the prosecution;

(j) should decide what exhibits, if any, which have not been or cannot be copied he wishes to examine, and should ensure that appropriate arrangements are made to examine them as promptly as possible so that there is no undue delay in the trial;

(k) should as to anything which he is instructed to submit in mitigation which casts aspersions on the conduct or character of a victim or witness in the case, notify the prosecution in advance so as to give prosecuting Counsel sufficient opportunity to consider his position under paragraph 10.8(e).

11.3 A barrister acting for a defendant should advise his lay client generally about his plea. In doing so he may, if necessary, express his advice in strong terms. He must, however, make it clear that the client has complete freedom of choice and that the responsibility for the plea is the client's.

11.4 A barrister acting for a defendant should advise his client as to whether or not to give evidence in his own defence but the decision must be taken by the client himself.

11.5

11.5.1 Where a defendant tells his counsel that he did not commit the offence with which he is charged but nevertheless insists on pleading guilty to it for reasons of his own, counsel should:

(a) advise the defendant that, if he is not guilty, he should plead not guilty but that the decision is one for the defendant; counsel must continue to represent him but only after he has advised what the consequences will be and that what can be submitted in mitigation can only be on the basis that the client is guilty.

(b) explore with the defendant why he wishes to plead guilty to a charge which he says he did not commit and whether any steps could be taken which would enable him to enter a plea of not guilty in accordance with his profession of innocence.

11.5.2 If the client maintains his wish to plead guilty, he should be further advised:

(a) what the consequences will be, in particular in gaining or adding to a criminal record and that it is unlikely that a conviction based on such a plea would be overturned on appeal;

(b) that what can be submitted on his behalf in mitigation can only be on the basis that he is guilty and will otherwise be strictly limited so that, for instance, counsel will not be able to assert that the defendant has shown remorse through his guilty plea.

11.5.3 If, following all of the above advice, the defendant persists in his decision to plead guilty:

(a) counsel may continue to represent him if he is satisfied that it is proper to do so;

(b) before a plea of guilty is entered counsel or a representative of his professional client who is present should record in writing the reasons for the plea;

(c) the defendant should be invited to endorse a declaration that he has given unequivocal instructions of his own free will that he intends to plead guilty even though he maintains that he did not commit the offence(s) and that he understands the advice given by counsel and in particular the restrictions placed on counsel in mitigating and the consequences to himself; the defendant should also be advised that he is under no obligation to sign; and

(d) if no such declaration is signed, counsel should make a contemporaneous note of his advice.

12 Confessions of Guilt

12.1 In considering the duty of counsel retained to defend a person charged with an offence who confesses to his counsel that he did commit the offence charged, it is essential to bear the following points clearly in mind:

(a) that every punishable crime is a breach of common or statute law committed by a person of sound mind and understanding;

(b) that the issue in a criminal trial is always whether the defendant is guilty of the offence charged, never whether he is innocent;

(c) that the burden of proof rests on the prosecution.

12.2 It follows that the mere fact that a person charged with a crime has confessed to his counsel that he did commit the offence charged is no bar to that barrister appearing or continuing to appear in his defence, nor indeed does such a confession release the barrister from his imperative duty to do all that he honourably can for his client.

12.3 Such a confession, however, imposes very strict limitations on the conduct of the defence. [A] barrister must not assert as true that which he knows to be false. He must not connive at, much less attempt to substantiate, a fraud.

12.4 While, therefore, it would be right to take any objections to the competency of the

Court, to the form of the indictment, to the admissibility of any evidence or to the evidence admitted, it would be wrong to suggest that some other person had committed the offence charged, or to call any evidence which the barrister must know to be false having regard to the confession, such, for instance, as evidence in support of an alibi. In other words, a barrister must not (whether by calling the defendant or otherwise) set up an affirmative case inconsistent with the confession made to him.

12.5 A more difficult question is within what limits may counsel attack the evidence for the prosecution either by cross-examination or in his speech to the tribunal charged with the decision of the facts. No clearer rule can be laid down than this, that he is entitled to test the evidence given by each individual witness and to argue that the evidence taken as a whole is insufficient to amount to proof that the defendant is guilty of the offence charged. Further than this he ought not to go.

12.6 The foregoing is based on the assumption that the defendant has made a clear confession that he did commit the offence charged, and does not profess to deal with the very difficult questions which may present themselves to a barrister when a series of inconsistent statements are made to him by the defendant before or during the proceedings; nor does it deal with the questions which may arise where statements are made by the defendant which point almost irresistibly to the conclusion that the defendant is guilty but do not amount to a clear confession. Statements of this kind may inhibit the defence, but questions arising on them can only be answered after careful consideration of the actual circumstances of the particular case.

13 General

13.1 Both prosecuting and defence counsel:

(a) should ensure that the listing officer receives in good time their best estimate of the likely length of the trial (including whether or not there is to be a plea of guilty) and should ensure that the listing officer is given early notice of any change of such estimate or possible adjournment;

(b) should take all reasonable and practicable steps to ensure that the case is properly prepared and ready for trial by the time that it is first listed;

(c) should ensure that arrangements have been made in adequate time for witnesses to attend Court as and when required and should plan, so far as possible, for sufficient witnesses to be available to occupy the full Court day;

(d) should, if a witness (for example a doctor) can only attend Court at a certain time during the trial without great inconvenience to himself, try to arrange for that witness to be accommodated by raising the matter with the trial Judge and with his opponent;

. . .

13.2 If properly remunerated . . ., the barrister originally briefed in a case should attend all plea and directions hearings. If this is not possible, he must take all reasonable steps to ensure that the barrister who does appear is conversant with the case and is prepared to make informed decisions affecting the trial.

. . .

15 Attendance of Counsel at Court

. . .

15.3.1 If during the course of a criminal trial and prior to final sentence the defendant voluntarily absconds and the barrister's professional client, in accordance with the ruling of the Law Society, withdraws from the case, then the barrister too should withdraw. If the trial judge requests the barrister to remain to assist the Court, the barrister has an absolute discretion whether to do so or not. If he does remain, he should act on the basis that his instructions are withdrawn and he will not be entitled to use any material contained in his brief save for such part as has already been established in evidence before the Court. He should request the trial judge to instruct the jury that this is the basis on which he is prepared to assist the Court.

15.3.2 If for any reason the barrister's professional client does not withdraw from the case, the barrister retains an absolute discretion whether to continue to act. If he does continue, he should conduct the case as if his client were still present in Court but had decided not to give evidence and on the basis of any instruction he has received. He will be free to use any material contained in his brief and may cross-examine witnesses called for the prosecution and call witnesses for the defence.

16 Appeals

. . .

16.2 If his client pleads guilty or is convicted, defence counsel should see his client after he has been sentenced in the presence of his professional client or his representative. He should then proceed as follows:

(a) if he is satisfied that there are no reasonable grounds of appeal he should so advise orally and certify in writing . . . No further advice is necessary unless it is reasonable for a written advice to be given because the client reasonably requires it or because it is necessary e.g. in the light of the circumstances of the conviction, any particular difficulties at trial, the length and nature of the sentence passed, the effect thereof on the defendant or the lack of impact which oral advice given immediately after the trial may have on the particular defendant's mind.

(b) if he is satisfied that there are more reasonable grounds of appeal or if his view is a provisional one or if he requires more time to consider the prospects of a successful appeal he should so advise orally and certify in writing . . . Counsel should then furnish written advice to the professional client as soon as he can and in any event within 14 days.

16.3 Counsel should not settle grounds of appeal unless he considers that such grounds are properly arguable, and in that event he should provide a reasoned written opinion in support of such grounds.

16.4 In certain cases counsel may not be able to perfect grounds of appeal without a transcript or other further information. In this event the grounds of appeal should be accompanied by a note to the Registrar setting out the matters on which assistance is required. Once such transcript or other information is available, counsel should ensure that the grounds of appeal are perfected by the inclusion of all necessary references.

16.5 Grounds of Appeal must be settled with sufficient particularity to enable the Registrar and subsequently the Court to identify clearly the matters relied upon.

16.6 If at any stage counsel is of the view that the appeal should be abandoned, he should at once set out his reasons in writing and send them to his professional client.

So far as solicitors are concerned, it is worth noting the 'core duties' identified in the Solicitors' Code of Conduct:

1.01 Justice and the rule of law
You must uphold the rule of law and the proper administration of justice.

1.02 Integrity
You must act with integrity.

1.03 Independence
You must not allow your independence to be compromised.

1.04 Best interests of clients
You must act in the best interests of each client.

1.05 Standard of service
You must provide a good standard of service to your clients.

1.06 Public confidence
You must not behave in a way that is likely to diminish the trust the public places in you or the profession.

In March 2008, the Law Society issued a Practice Note, *Criminal Procedure Rules: impact on solicitors' duties to the client*. The Note observed that:

The role of the solicitor when acting on behalf of a client who is actually or potentially the subject of criminal proceedings can be a complex one. As a lawyer the solicitor owes professional duties to his or her client, as well as – as one of its officers – to the court. On occasions these various duties may conflict with each other.

Whilst the court is entitled to expect the solicitor to act towards it with integrity, neither misleading nor deceiving it, the court should not demand that the solicitor in so acting should breach professional duties owed by the solicitor towards his or her client(s). Indeed, as explained below, the solicitor's proper discharge of the duty to their client should not cause him or her to be accused of being in breach of their duty to the court.

Reference should also be made to the Code for Crown Prosecutors, which is available on the CPS website (<http://www.cps.gov.uk/publications/docs/code2004english.pdf>). Paragraph 1.1 of the Code makes the point that 'fair and effective prosecution is essential to the maintenance of law and order' and notes that 'even in a small case a prosecution has serious implications for all involved – victims, witnesses and defendants. It goes on to explain that the purpose of the Code is to enable Crown Prosecutors to make 'fair and consistent decisions about prosecutions'. The main provisions of the Code are as follows:

2 GENERAL PRINCIPLES

. . .

2.2 Crown Prosecutors must be fair, independent and objective. They must not let any personal views about ethnic or national origin, disability, sex, religious beliefs, political views or the sexual orientation of the suspect, victim or witness influence their decisions. They must not be affected by improper or undue pressure from any source.

2.3 It is the duty of Crown Prosecutors to make sure that the right person is prosecuted for the right offence. In doing so, Crown Prosecutors must always act in the interests of justice and not solely for the purpose of obtaining a conviction.

2.4 Crown Prosecutors should provide guidance and advice to investigators throughout the investigative and prosecuting process. This may include lines of inquiry, evidential requirements and assistance in any pre-charge procedures. Crown Prosecutors will be proactive in identifying and, where possible, rectifying evidential deficiencies and in bringing to an early conclusion those cases that cannot be strengthened by further investigation.

2.5 It is the duty of Crown Prosecutors to review, advise on and prosecute cases, ensuring that the law is properly applied, that all relevant evidence is put before the court and that obligations of disclosure are complied with, in accordance with the principles set out in this Code.

. . .

3 THE DECISION TO PROSECUTE

3.1 In most cases, Crown Prosecutors are responsible for deciding whether a person should be charged with a criminal offence, and if so, what that offence should be. Crown Prosecutors make these decisions in accordance with this Code and the Director's Guidance on Charging. In those cases where the police determine the charge, which are usually more minor and routine cases, they apply the same provisions.

3.2 Crown Prosecutors make charging decisions in accordance with the Full Code Test (see section 5 below), other than in those limited circumstances where the Threshold Test applies (see section 6 below).

3.3 The Threshold Test applies where the case is one in which it is proposed to keep the suspect in custody after charge, but the evidence required to apply the Full Code Test is not yet available.

3.4 Where a Crown Prosecutor makes a charging decision in accordance with the Threshold Test, the case must be reviewed in accordance with the Full Code Test as soon as reasonably practicable, taking into account the progress of the investigation.

4 REVIEW

4.1 Each case the Crown Prosecution Service receives from the police is reviewed to make sure that it is right to proceed with a prosecution. Unless the Threshold Test applies, the Crown Prosecution Service will only start or continue with a prosecution when the case has passed both stages of the Full Code Test.

4.2 Review is a continuing process and Crown Prosecutors must take account of any change in circumstances. Wherever possible, they should talk to the police first if they are thinking about changing the charges or stopping the case. Crown Prosecutors should also tell the police if they believe that some additional evidence may strengthen the case. This gives the police the chance to provide more information that may affect the decision.

4.3 The Crown Prosecution Service and the police work closely together, but the final responsibility for the decision whether or not a charge or a case should go ahead rests with the Crown Prosecution Service.

5 THE FULL CODE TEST

5.1 The Full Code Test has two stages. The first stage is consideration of the evidence. If the case does not pass the evidential stage it must not go ahead no matter how important or serious it may be. If the case does pass the evidential stage, Crown Prosecutors must proceed to the second stage and decide if a prosecution is needed in the public interest . . .

THE EVIDENTIAL STAGE

5.2 Crown Prosecutors must be satisfied that there is enough evidence to provide a 'realistic prospect of conviction' against each defendant on each charge. They must consider what the defence case may be, and how that is likely to affect the prosecution case.

5.3 A realistic prospect of conviction is an objective test. It means that a jury or bench of magistrates or judge hearing a case alone, properly directed in accordance with the law, is more likely than not to convict the defendant of the charge alleged. This is a separate test from the one that the criminal courts themselves must apply. A court should only convict if satisfied so that it is sure of a defendant's guilt.

5.4 When deciding whether there is enough evidence to prosecute, Crown Prosecutors must consider whether the evidence can be used and is reliable. There will be many cases in which the evidence does not give any cause for concern. But there will also be cases in which the evidence may not be as strong as it first appears. Crown Prosecutors must ask themselves the following questions:

Can the evidence be used in court?
Is the evidence reliable?

a   Is it likely that the evidence will be excluded by the court? There are certain legal rules which might mean that evidence which seems relevant cannot be given at a trial.
    For example, is it likely that the evidence will be excluded because of the way in which it was gathered? If so, is there enough other evidence for a realistic prospect of conviction?

b   Is there evidence which might support or detract from the reliability of a confession? Is the reliability affected by factors such as the defendant's age, intelligence or level of understanding?

c   What explanation has the defendant given? Is a court likely to find it credible in the light of the evidence as a whole? Does it support an innocent explanation?

d   If the identity of the defendant is likely to be questioned, is the evidence about this strong enough?

e   Is the witness's background likely to weaken the prosecution case? For example, does the witness have any motive that may affect his or her attitude to the case, or a relevant previous conviction?

f   Are there concerns over the accuracy or credibility of a witness? Are these concerns based on evidence or simply information with nothing to support it? Is there further evidence which the police should be asked to seek out which may support or detract from the account of the witness?

5.5 Crown Prosecutors should not ignore evidence because they are not sure that it can be used or is reliable. But they should look closely at it when deciding if there is a realistic prospect of conviction.

THE PUBLIC INTEREST STAGE

5.6 In 1951, Lord Shawcross, who was Attorney General, made the classic statement on public interest, which has been supported by Attorneys General ever since: 'It has never been the rule in this country – I hope it never will be – that suspected criminal offences must automatically be the subject of prosecution.' (House of Commons Debates, volume 483, column 681, 29 January 1951.)

5.7 The public interest must be considered in each case where there is enough evidence to provide a realistic prospect of conviction. Although there may be public interest factors against prosecution in a particular case, often the prosecution should go ahead and those factors should be put to the court for consideration when sentence is being passed. A prosecution will usually take place unless there are public interest factors tending against prosecution which clearly outweigh those tending in favour, or it appears more appropriate in all the circumstances of the case to divert the person from prosecution (see section 8 below).

5.8 Crown Prosecutors must balance factors for and against prosecution carefully and fairly. Public interest factors that can affect the decision to prosecute usually depend on the seriousness of the offence or the circumstances of the suspect. Some factors may increase the need to prosecute but others may suggest that another course of action would be better.

The following lists of some common public interest factors, both for and against prosecution, are not exhaustive. The factors that apply will depend on the facts in each case.

Some common public interest factors in favour of prosecution

5.9 The more serious the offence, the more likely it is that a prosecution will be needed in the public interest. A prosecution is likely to be needed if:

a   a conviction is likely to result in a significant sentence;

b   a conviction is likely to result in a confiscation or any other order;

c   a weapon was used or violence was threatened during the commission of the offence;

d   the offence was committed against a person serving the public (for example, a police or prison officer, or a nurse);

e   the defendant was in a position of authority or trust;

f   the evidence shows that the defendant was a ringleader or an organiser of the offence;

g   there is evidence that the offence was premeditated;

h   there is evidence that the offence was carried out by a group;

i   the victim of the offence was vulnerable, has been put in considerable fear, or suffered personal attack, damage or disturbance;

j   the offence was committed in the presence of, or in close proximity to, a child;

k   the offence was motivated by any form of discrimination against the victim's ethnic or national origin, disability, sex, religious beliefs, political views or sexual orientation, or the suspect demonstrated hostility towards the victim based on any of those characteristics;

l   there is a marked difference between the actual or mental ages of the defendant and the victim, or if there is any element of corruption;

m   the defendant's previous convictions or cautions are relevant to the present offence;

n   the defendant is alleged to have committed the offence while under an order of the court;

o   there are grounds for believing that the offence is likely to be continued or repeated, for example, by a history of recurring conduct;

p   the offence, although not serious in itself, is widespread in the area where it was committed; or

q   a prosecution would have a significant positive impact on maintaining community confidence.

Some common public interest factors against prosecution

5.10 A prosecution is less likely to be needed if:

a   the court is likely to impose a nominal penalty;

b   the defendant has already been made the subject of a sentence and any further conviction would be unlikely to result in the imposition of an additional sentence or order, unless the nature of the particular offence requires a prosecution or the defendant withdraws consent to have an offence taken into consideration during sentencing;

c   the offence was committed as a result of a genuine mistake or misunderstanding (these factors must be balanced against the seriousness of the offence);

d   the loss or harm can be described as minor and was the result of a single incident, particularly if it was caused by a misjudgement;

e   there has been a long delay between the offence taking place and the date of the trial, unless:

• the offence is serious;

• the delay has been caused in part by the defendant;

• the offence has only recently come to light; or

• the complexity of the offence has meant that there has been a long investigation;

f   a prosecution is likely to have a bad effect on the victim's physical or mental health, always bearing in mind the seriousness of the offence;

g   the defendant is elderly or is, or was at the time of the offence, suffering from significant mental or physical ill health, unless the offence is serious or there is a real possibility that it may be repeated. The Crown Prosecution Service, where necessary, applies Home Office guidelines about how to deal with mentally disordered offenders. Crown Prosecutors must balance the desirability of diverting a defendant who is suffering from significant mental or physical ill health with the need to safeguard the general public;

h   the defendant has put right the loss or harm that was caused (but defendants must not avoid prosecution or diversion solely because they pay compensation); or

i   details may be made public that could harm sources of information, international relations or national security.

5.11 Deciding on the public interest is not simply a matter of adding up the number of factors on each side. Crown Prosecutors must decide how important each factor is in the circumstances of each case and go on to make an overall assessment.

The relationship between the victim and the public interest

5.12 The Crown Prosecution Service does not act for victims or the families of victims in the same way as solicitors act for their clients. Crown Prosecutors act on behalf of the public and not just in the interests of any particular individual. However, when considering the public interest, Crown Prosecutors should always take into account the consequences for the victim of whether or not to prosecute, and any views expressed by the victim or the victim's family.

5.13 It is important that a victim is told about a decision which makes a significant difference to the case in which they are involved. Crown Prosecutors should ensure that they follow any agreed procedures.

6 THE THRESHOLD TEST

6.1 The Threshold Test requires Crown Prosecutors to decide whether there is at least a reasonable suspicion that the suspect has committed an offence, and if there is, whether it is in the public interest to charge that suspect.

6.2 The Threshold Test is applied to those cases in which it would not be appropriate to release a suspect on bail after charge, but the evidence to apply the Full Code Test is not yet available.

6.3 There are statutory limits that restrict the time a suspect may remain in police custody before a decision has to be made whether to charge or release the suspect. There will be cases where the suspect in custody presents a substantial bail risk if released, but much of the evidence may not be available at the time the charging decision has to be made. Crown Prosecutors will apply the Threshold Test to such cases for a limited period.

6.4 The evidential decision in each case will require consideration of a number of factors including:

- the evidence available at the time;
- the likelihood and nature of further evidence being obtained;
- the reasonableness for believing that evidence will become available;
- the time it will take to gather that evidence and the steps being taken to do so;
- the impact the expected evidence will have on the case;
- the charges that the evidence will support.

6.5 The public interest means the same as under the Full Code Test, but will be based on the information available at the time of charge which will often be limited.

6.6 A decision to charge and withhold bail must be kept under review. The evidence gathered must be regularly assessed to ensure the charge is still appropriate and that continued objection to bail is justified. The Full Code Test must be applied as soon as reasonably practicable.

7 SELECTION OF CHARGES

7.1 Crown Prosecutors should select charges which:

a   reflect the seriousness and extent of the offending;

b   give the court adequate powers to sentence and impose appropriate post-conviction orders; and

c   enable the case to be presented in a clear and simple way.
    This means that Crown Prosecutors may not always choose or continue with the most serious charge where there is a choice.

7.2 Crown Prosecutors should never go ahead with more charges than are necessary just to encourage a defendant to plead guilty to a few. In the same way, they should never go ahead with a more serious charge just to encourage a defendant to plead guilty to a less serious one.

7.3 Crown Prosecutors should not change the charge simply because of the decision made by the court or the defendant about where the case will be heard.

8 DIVERSION FROM PROSECUTION ADULTS

8.1 When deciding whether a case should be prosecuted in the courts, Crown Prosecutors should consider the alternatives to prosecution. Where appropriate, the availability of suitable rehabilitative, reparative or restorative justice processes can be considered.

8.2 Alternatives to prosecution for adult suspects include a simple caution and a conditional caution.

Simple caution

8.3 A simple caution should only be given if the public interest justifies it and in accordance with Home Office guidelines. Where it is felt that such a caution is appropriate, Crown Prosecutors must inform the police so they can caution the suspect. If the caution is not administered, because the suspect refuses to accept it, a Crown Prosecutor may review the case again.

Conditional caution

8.4 A conditional caution may be appropriate where a Crown Prosecutor considers that while the public interest justifies a prosecution, the interests of the suspect, victim and community may be better served by the suspect complying with suitable conditions aimed at rehabilitation or reparation. These may include restorative processes.

8.5 Crown Prosecutors must be satisfied that there is sufficient evidence for a realistic prospect of conviction and that the public interest would justify a prosecution should the offer of a conditional caution be refused or the offender fail to comply with the agreed conditions of the caution.

8.6 In reaching their decision, Crown Prosecutors should follow the Conditional Cautions Code of Practice and any guidance on conditional cautioning issued or approved by the Director of Public Prosecutions.

8.7 Where Crown Prosecutors consider a conditional caution to be appropriate, they must inform the police, or other authority responsible for administering the conditional caution, as well as providing an indication of the appropriate conditions so that the conditional caution can be administered.

YOUTHS

8.8 Crown Prosecutors must consider the interests of a youth when deciding whether it is in the public interest to prosecute. However Crown Prosecutors should not avoid prosecuting simply because of the defendant's age. The seriousness of the offence or the youth's past behaviour is very important.

8.9 Cases involving youths are usually only referred to the Crown Prosecution Service for prosecution if the youth has already received a reprimand and final warning, unless the offence is so serious that neither of these were appropriate or the youth does not admit committing the offence. Reprimands and final warnings are intended to prevent re-offending and the fact that a further offence has occurred indicates that attempts to divert the youth from the court system have not been effective. So the public interest will usually require a prosecution in such cases, unless there are clear public interest factors against prosecution.

9 MODE OF TRIAL

9.1 The Crown Prosecution Service applies the current guidelines for magistrates who have to decide whether cases should be tried in the Crown Court when the offence gives the option and the defendant does not indicate a guilty plea. Crown Prosecutors should recommend Crown Court trial when they are satisfied that the guidelines require them to do so.

9.2 Speed must never be the only reason for asking for a case to stay in the magistrates' courts. But Crown Prosecutors should consider the effect of any likely delay if they send a case to the Crown Court, and any possible stress on victims and witnesses if the case is delayed.

10 ACCEPTING GUILTY PLEAS

10.1 Defendants may want to plead guilty to some, but not all, of the charges. Alternatively, they may want to plead guilty to a different, possibly less serious, charge because they are admitting only part of the crime. Crown Prosecutors should only accept the defendant's plea if they think the court is able to pass a sentence that matches the seriousness of the offending, particularly where there are aggravating features.
Crown Prosecutors must never accept a guilty plea just because it is convenient.

10.2 In considering whether the pleas offered are acceptable, Crown Prosecutors should ensure that the interests of the victim and, where possible, any views expressed by the victim or victim's family, are taken into account when deciding whether it is in the public interest to accept the plea. However, the decision rests with the Crown Prosecutor.

10.3 It must be made clear to the court on what basis any plea is advanced and accepted. In cases where a defendant pleads guilty to the charges but on the basis of facts that are different from the prosecution case, and where this may significantly affect sentence, the court should be invited to hear evidence to determine what happened, and then sentence on that basis.

10.4 Where a defendant has previously indicated that he or she will ask the court to take an offence into consideration when sentencing, but then declines to admit that offence at court, Crown Prosecutors will consider whether a prosecution is required for that offence. Crown Prosecutors should explain to the defence advocate and the court that the prosecution of that offence may be subject to further review.

10.5 Particular care must be taken when considering pleas which would enable the defendant to avoid the imposition of a mandatory minimum sentence. When pleas are offered, Crown Prosecutors must bear in mind the fact that ancillary orders can be made with some offences but not with others.

11 PROSECUTORS' ROLE IN SENTENCING

11.1 Crown Prosecutors should draw the court's attention to:

- any aggravating or mitigating factors disclosed by the prosecution case;
- any victim personal statement;
- where appropriate, evidence of the impact of the offending on a community;
- any statutory provisions or sentencing guidelines which may assist;
- any relevant statutory provisions relating to ancillary orders (such as anti-social behaviour orders).

11.2 The Crown Prosecutor should challenge any assertion made by the defence in mitigation that is inaccurate, misleading or derogatory. If the defence persist in the assertion, and it appears relevant to the sentence, the court should be invited to hear evidence to determine the facts and sentence accordingly.

12 RE-STARTING A PROSECUTION

12.1 People should be able to rely on decisions taken by the Crown Prosecution Service. Normally, if the Crown Prosecution Service tells a suspect or defendant that there will not be a prosecution, or that the prosecution has been stopped, that is the end of the matter and the case will not start again. But occasionally there are special reasons why the Crown Prosecution Service will re-start the prosecution, particularly if the case is serious.

12.2 These reasons include:

a rare cases where a new look at the original decision shows that it was clearly wrong and should not be allowed to stand;

b cases which are stopped so that more evidence which is likely to become available in the fairly near future can be collected and prepared. In these cases, the Crown Prosecutor will tell the defendant that the prosecution may well start again; and

c cases which are stopped because of a lack of evidence but where more significant evidence is discovered later.

. . .

Chapter 2

Preliminaries

2.1 INTRODUCTION

In this chapter, we examine how a defendant is brought before the criminal courts; we consider what happens when a suspect is taken to a police station for questioning; we see how the decision to prosecute a suspect is taken; and we look at the structure and personnel of the criminal courts, and at the advocates who appear before them. However, we begin with a short introduction to some basic terminology and to the structure of the criminal courts and the criminal process.

2.1.1 Some basic terminology and the structure of the criminal courts

An adult defendant in a criminal case always makes his first appearance in a magistrates' court. Some cases are tried in the magistrates' court (comprising a bench of lay justices or a District Judge); others are tried by a judge (a Circuit judge, a recorder, or a High Court judge) and jury in the Crown Court. An offence is a 'summary offence' if it must be tried in a magistrates' court. An offence is an 'indictable offence' if it may or must be tried in the Crown Court; where an indictable offence may be tried by a magistrates' court instead of the Crown Court, it is known as an 'either-way' offence.

The Crown Court can also hear appeals from magistrates' court, as can the High Court. Appeals following Crown Court trials are heard by the Court of Appeal (Criminal Division).

2.1.2 The magistrates' court

The magistrates' court usually comprises three lay justices and a legally qualified clerk (often referred to as the court legal adviser). The lay justices are ordinary members of the public who have put themselves forward to sit as justices of the peace (JPs). They are unpaid, although they can claim reimbursement for travel expenses and loss of earnings. They receive basic training in the law, the evidence and the procedure which they are likely to encounter. Because they have only very elementary legal training, the lay justices need the help of their clerk, sometimes called the court legal adviser. Under s 27(2) of the Courts Act 2003, a person may be designated as a justices' clerk if he has a five-year magistrates' court qualification (in other words, if he has had the right to appear as an advocate in the magistrates' court for at least five years), or is a barrister or solicitor who has served for not less than five years as an assistant to a justices' clerk, or has previously served as a justices' clerk. Section 27(6) of the 2003 Act empowers the Lord Chancellor to appoint assistant justices' clerks. When a lay bench is sitting, submissions are addressed to the chairman, who is addressed as 'sir' or 'madam', as the case may be.

In some magistrates' courts, especially those in cities, there may be a District Judge (Magistrates' Court), formerly known as a 'stipendiary magistrate'. District Judges are appointed from amongst barristers and solicitors of at least seven years' standing (to be replaced by a five-year judicial-appointment eligibility condition as defined by s 50 of the Tribunals, Courts and Enforcement Act 2007). A District Judge can try a case sitting alone (by virtue of s 26(1) of the Courts Act 2003), whereas at least two lay justices must be sitting for a summary trial to take place. Because a District Judge is legally qualified and sits alone, cases in front of such magistrates tend to be disposed of more quickly than those that are heard by lay justices. The Courts Act 2003 also empowers District Judges to exercise some of the powers of Crown Court judges (Sched 4 sets out a number of specific interlocutory proceedings and rulings that fall within the jurisdiction of a district judge before a case is ready to go before a Crown Court judge). A district judge is addressed as 'sir' or 'madam', as the case may be.

Solicitors and barristers both have complete rights of audience in the magistrates' court.

2.1.3 The Crown Court

The Crown Court is always presided over by a judge. Where the Crown Court is trying a case, the judge sits with a jury. Very serious offences are usually tried by a High Court judge; most cases, however, will be tried by a Circuit judge or a part-time judge called a Recorder. A Circuit judge or Recorder is addressed as 'your Honour'; a High Court judge (or any judge sitting at the Central Criminal Court in London) is addressed as 'my Lord' or 'my Lady' as the case may be.

An applicant for appointment as a High Court judge must have had a right of audience (i.e. the right to appear as an advocate) in High Court proceedings for at least ten years, or must have been a Circuit judge for at least two years. An applicant for appointment as a Circuit judge must have had a right of audience for at least ten years, and must also have served either part-time as a Recorder on criminal cases or full-time as a District Judge hearing civil cases.

A solicitor or barrister with at least ten years' practice before the Crown or county courts, may be appointed a Recorder. They are required to sit for between 15 and 30 days each year with at least one continuous period of 10 days. The appointment is for an initial period of five years, extendible for further successive five-year terms up to the retirement age of 65.

For High Court and Circuit Judges, and Recorders, the 10-year qualifying period is to be replaced by a seven-year judicial-appointment eligibility condition as defined by s 50 of the Tribunals, Courts and Enforcement Act 2007.

The allocation of work in the Crown Court is governed by para III.21.1 of the Consolidated Practice Direction. Class 1 offences, which include murder and manslaughter, must be tried by a High Court judge or a Circuit judge authorised by the Lord Chief Justice to try such cases; class 2 offences, which include rape and serious sexual assaults, must be tried by a judge authorised to try such cases; class 3 offences (all offences not listed in class 1 or 2) may be tried by any Circuit judge or Recorder.

Recommendation 68.1 of Lord Justice Auld's *Review of the Criminal Courts of England and Wales* (the *Auld Review*) was that 'all work within the jurisdiction of the Crown Court should be triable by a Circuit Judge unless, on referral to a presiding judge, he specially reserves it for trial by a High Court judge' but this recommendation has not so far been taken up.

When the Crown Court is sitting as an appellate court from the magistrates' court, it comprises a Circuit judge or Recorder and two lay justices (though up to four lay justices may sit).

Barristers and solicitors with rights of audience in the higher courts have rights of audience for trials on indictment. However, where the Crown Court is hearing an appeal from the magistrates' court (see Chapter 7), or a committal for sentence from the magistrates' court (see Chapter 5), all barristers and solicitors have rights of audience.

For more information on the judiciary in the criminal courts, see <http://www.judiciary.gov.uk/about_judiciary/roles_types_jurisdiction/criminal_justice/index.htm>.

2.1.4 Open court

Both the magistrates' court and the Crown Court normally sit in open court and there is a strong presumption that they should do. However, any court does have a discretion to sit *in camera* (that is, to exclude the public) if this is necessary for the administration of justice. Decisions to sit *in camera* are, therefore, very rare (see, generally, *Attorney General v Leveller Magazine Ltd* [1979] AC 440).

Rule 16.10 of the Criminal Procedure Rules deals with the procedure for applying for evidence to be heard *in camera*. In *R v Yam* [2008] EWCA Crim 269, Lord Phillips CJ said (at para 6) that the court has 'an inherent power to exclude the press and the public where the interests of justice require it' but 'the interests of justice could never justify excluding the press and the public if the consequence would be that the trial would not be fair'.

2.1.5 Crown Prosecutors

Crown Prosecutors have to be either barristers or solicitors (s 1(3) of the Prosecution of Offences Act 1985). They have all the powers of the Director of Public Prosecutions (DPP) as regards 'the institution and conduct of proceedings' (s 1(6)). Thus, a Crown Prosecutor can authorise the commencement of proceedings where the consent of the DPP is required (s 1(7)). Similarly, a Crown Prosecutor can discontinue proceedings under s 23 or s 23A of the Prosecution of Offences Act 1985.

Crown Prosecutors, whether barristers or solicitors, may conduct trials in the magistrates' court. If the Crown Prosecutor is a barrister, or a solicitor with the Higher Rights of Audience qualification, he or she is able to appear in the Crown Court. However, in most cases, the Crown Prosecution Service (CPS) will brief counsel to prosecute in Crown Court trials.

The CPS also employ 'associate prosecutors', formerly known as 'designated caseworkers', under s 7A of the Prosecution of Offences Act 1985. These associate

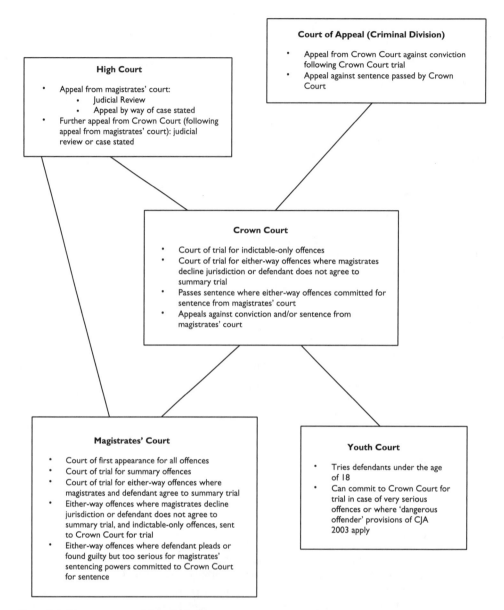

Figure 2.1 The structure of the criminal courts.

prosecutors are not legally qualified, but can exercise some of the powers normally exercised by Crown Prosecutors. They may, for example, represent CPS on bail applications and on other pre-trial applications, such as requests for adjournments. Importantly, however, the conduct of trials was excluded from their remit in the original version of s 7A. However, s 55(2)(a) of the Criminal Justice and Immigration Act 2008 removes this restriction by amending s 7A(2)(a)(ii) of the 1985 Act, so that trials are excluded from the remit of associate prosecutors only if they relate to either-way offences or offences which are punishable with imprisonment. The effect of this provision is that associate prosecutors may conduct trials only where the offence in question is a non-imprisonable summary offence; associate prosecutors are not allowed to conduct trials of either-way offences, or of summary offences that carry imprisonment as a potential penalty. Section 7A of the 1985 Act, as amended by the 2008 Act, also empowers associate prosecutors to represent CPS in proceedings in respect of 'preventative civil orders' (including ASBOs – see Chapter 22).

The fact that the 2008 Act, through its amendments to s 7A of the 1985 Act, enables associate prosecutors to conduct trials is very controversial (hence the restriction of that power to non-imprisonable summary offences). However, it should be borne in mind that, prior to the inception of the CPS, many prosecutions in the magistrates' courts were conducted by police officers, and that the relative informality of the magistrates' court should facilitate the work of such 'lay' prosecutors. Much depends on the level of training received by associate prosecutors (for example in the art of cross-examination), and whether that training is sufficient to bring them to a similar level to people who have qualified as solicitors or barristers.

2.2 COMMENCING PROCEEDINGS

There are a number of ways of bringing someone before the criminal courts:

- the issue of a 'written charge', followed by the issue of a 'requisition';
- the laying of an 'information', followed by the issue of a 'summons';
- arrest without warrant, followed by charge;
- arrest pursuant to a warrant, followed by charge.

We will now look in greater detail at each of these methods.

2.2.1 Written charge and requisition

Until the creation of this method of starting a criminal case, the only alternative to arresting a suspect was for the prosecutor to 'lay an information' and for the court to issue a summons based on that 'information' (this method of commencing a case is considered in the next section). In his *Review of the Criminal Courts of England and Wales*, Lord Justice Auld noted that magistrates' courts provided very little scrutiny of an information before issuing a summons. In para 55 of Chapter 10, he described it as an 'anomaly' that, in the more serious cases, the police arrest and charge the suspect without the intervention of the court. He therefore made these recommendations:

> 162 All public prosecutions should take the form of a charge, issued without reference to the courts, which should remain the basis of the accusation against the defendant throughout all stages of the case, irrespective of the level of court in which it is tried.

164 ... the charge should specify the date of first attendance at court on pain of arrest on warrant.

166 The same regime for commencing proceedings should apply to private prosecutions, save that: 1) the charge should only be administered in writing; 2) it should be subject to the prior permission of the court; 3) the permission should be endorsed on the charge sheet by an officer of the court; and 4) the court, before listing the matter, should notify the Director of Public Prosecutions.

...

168 The form of charge should be common to summary and indictable offences.

Section 29 of the Criminal Justice Act 2003 gave effect to some of these proposals by creating a new method of commencing criminal proceedings to replace the laying of informations and issuing of summonses in the case of 'public' prosecutions. Section 29 provides as follows:

(1)   A public prosecutor may institute criminal proceedings against a person by issuing a document (a 'written charge') which charges the person with an offence.
(2)   Where a public prosecutor issues a written charge, it must at the same time issue a document (a 'requisition') which requires the person to appear before a magistrates' court to answer the written charge.
(3)   The written charge and requisition must be served on the person concerned and a copy of both must be served on the court named in the requisition.
(4)   In consequence of sub-sections (1) to (3), a public prosecutor is not to have the power to lay an information for the purpose of obtaining the issue of a summons under section 1 of the Magistrates' Courts Act 1980.

For these purposes, a 'public prosecutor' is defined (in s 29(5)) as including the police, the Director of Public Prosecutions, the Attorney General, the Serious Fraud Office, the Serious Organised Crime Agency, HM Revenue and Customs.

The effect of s 29 is that notification of the requirement to attend court will be communicated to the accused by the prosecutor, not by the magistrates' court. Indeed, the magistrates' court has no involvement whatsoever until the accused makes his first appearance before the court.

Section 29(4) makes it clear that, for 'public' prosecutions, the new procedure is intended to replace the former procedure of laying an information (by removing the power of a public prosecutor to commence a case by laying an information). Section 30(4) further clarifies the ambit of the new procedure. It provides that:

Nothing in section 29 affects—

(a)   the power of a public prosecutor to lay an information for the purpose of obtaining the issue of a warrant under section 1 of the Magistrates' Courts Act 1980,
(b)   the power of a person who is not a public prosecutor to lay an information for the purpose of obtaining the issue of a summons or warrant under section 1 of that Act, or
(c)   any power to charge a person with an offence whilst he is in custody.

Thus, an information still has to be laid in order to secure the grant of an arrest warrant (see below); where a person is arrested, the case against them will still be commenced by way of a charge; and the new procedure is not available in the case of private prosecutions (which will have to be commenced by laying an information).

At the time of writing, s 29 had been brought into force in certain areas only (in that it applies only to magistrates' courts sitting in specified locations) by the Criminal Justice Act 2003 (Commencement No 16) Order 2007 (SI 2007 No 1999).

2.2.2 Laying an information and issuing a summons

This is a two-stage process: the laying of an information by the prosecutor, followed by the issue and service of a summons by the magistrates' court. It applies to private prosecutions (and to public prosecution where s 29 of the 2003 Act (see above) is not in force).

2.2.2.1 Laying an information

Before a summons can be issued to require the suspect to attend court an 'information' has to be laid at a magistrates' court. The information may be laid before a magistrate or a magistrates' clerk, and it may be done orally (in which case, the informant attends the magistrates' court) or in writing. A written information is 'laid' as soon as it is received in the clerk's office, even if it is not considered by a clerk or a magistrate until later (*R v Manchester Justices ex p Hill* [1983] 1 AC 328). No standard form has to be used; all that matters is that the document sent to the magistrates' court contains the essential elements of an information (*R v Kennet Justices ex p Humphrey and Wyatt* [1993] Crim LR 787).

2.2.2.2 Issuing a summons

Once an information has been laid, a summons may then be issued by a magistrate or clerk (usually the latter). The original version of ss 1 and 2 of the Magistrates' Courts Act 1980 contained detailed provisions regarding the territorial jurisdiction of magistrates' courts to issue a summons; however, those complexities were swept away by the Courts Act 2003, which gives magistrates national jurisdiction (see Chapter 4). In deciding whether or not to issue a summons, the magistrate or clerk should ensure that:

i   an offence known to law is alleged;
ii   it is not out of time (proceedings in respect of a summary offence must be started within six months of the alleged commission of the offence, by virtue of s 127 of the Magistrates' Courts Act 1980 (see Chapter 5));
iii the court has jurisdiction; and
iv   the informant has any necessary authority to prosecute (*R v Gateshead Justices ex p Tesco Stores Ltd* [1981] QB 470 at 478).

In *R v Bradford Justices ex p Sykes* (1999) 163 JP 224, it was held that there is no obligation upon a magistrate or clerk to make any inquiries before issuing a summons. The protection for an individual, against whom a summons is issued, is the right to apply to the magistrates' court to dismiss it, or to stay it, on the ground that the proceedings are an abuse of process (see Chapter 1); it is therefore unnecessary to provide that there should be, at an earlier stage, an obligation to investigate before the summons is issued. Indeed, it is submitted that it would, in most cases, be impracticable to expect the court to investigate the background to the case before issuing the summons. Given the inevitable lack of judicial scrutiny prior to the issue of a summons, it is perhaps not surprising that the new method of instituting proceedings established by the Criminal Justice Act 2003 (see above) enables proceedings to be commenced without reference to the court.

2.2.3 Contents of the written charge or information and summons

Rule 7.2 of the Criminal Procedure Rules provides as follows:

7.2 Statement of offence

(1) Every written charge issued by a public prosecutor and every information, summons or warrant laid in or issued by a magistrates' court shall be sufficient if it—

  (a) describes the offence with which the accused is charged, or of which he is convicted, in ordinary language avoiding as far as possible the use of technical terms; and
  (b) gives such particulars as may be necessary to provide reasonable information about the nature of the charge.

(2) It shall not be necessary for any of those documents to—

  (a) state all the elements of the offence; or
  (b) negative any matter upon which the accused may rely.

(3) If the offence charged is one created by or under any Act, the description of the offence shall contain a reference to the section of the Act, or, as the case may be, the rule, order, regulation, bylaw or other instrument creating the offence.

Thus, the documentation must set out the substance of the allegation against the accused. It will set out the statutory provision contravened (assuming the offence is a statutory one, as most are), together with a short summary of the facts of the case.

An allegation of careless driving, for example, would be set out as follows:

On 26 December 2008, driving a mechanically propelled vehicle, namely, a Ford Focus motor car registration number YZ 08 ABC, on a road, namely, Warmington High Street, without due care and attention, contrary to s 3 of the Road Traffic Act 1988.

In *Nash v RSPCA* [2005] EWHC Admin 338; (2005) 169 JP 157, it was held that, under what is now r 7.2 of the Criminal Procedure Rules, the accused is entitled to know what act or omission is alleged against him. However, if the documentation fails to give sufficient information to the accused as to the nature of the charge he faces, that of itself does not render the proceedings a nullity or any resulting conviction unsafe, provided that the requisite information was given to the accused in good time for him to be able fairly to meet the case against him.

Rule 7.7(2) of the Criminal Procedure Rules governs the contents of the summons (issued following the laying of an information) or requisition (issued along with a written charge). It stipulates that:

> A summons or requisition requiring a person to appear before a magistrates' court to answer to an information, written charge or complaint shall state shortly the matter of the information, written charge or complaint and shall state the time and place at which the defendant is required by the summons or requisition to appear.

Rule 7.3 of the Criminal Procedure Rules stipulates that an information or written charge may be for one offence only. It provides as follows:

> (1) ... a magistrates' court shall not proceed to the trial of an information or written charge that charges more than one offence.
> (2) Nothing in this rule shall prohibit two or more informations or written charges being set out in one document.

The summons or requisition will also show the address of the court which the defendant is to attend, and the date and time of the first court appearance which the accused has to make in respect of this offence (r. 7.7(2)).

Rule 7.7(3) provides that:

> A single summons or requisition may be issued against a person in respect of several informations, written charges or complaints; but the summons or requisition shall state the matter of each information, written charge or complaint separately and shall have effect as several summonses or requisitions, each issued in respect of one information, written charge or complaint.

The combined effect of these provisions is that each written charge (or information) may allege only one offence but a number of written charges (or informations) may be included in the same document (this is discussed in more detail in Chapter 5).

2.2.4 Service of the requisition or summons

Service of the requisition or summons is governed by Pt 4 of the Criminal Procedure Rules. Rule 4.7 provides that a summons or requisition may be served only in the following ways. If the accused is an individual, the documents must be served by:

- handing it to him, or
- leaving it at an address where it is reasonably believed that he will receive it, or
- sending it to him by first class post to an address where it is reasonably believed that he will receive it.

If the accused is a company, the documents must be served by:

- handing it to a person holding a senior position in that company, or

- leaving it at its principal office in England and Wales (or, if there is no readily identifiable principal office, then any place in England and Wales where it carries on its activities or business), or
- sending it by first class post to its principal office or where it carries on its business.

2.2.5 Arrest without warrant

Arrest without warrant is governed by s 24 of the Police and Criminal Evidence Act 1984 (PACE), which provides as follows:

(1) A constable may arrest without a warrant—

  (a) anyone who is about to commit an offence;
  (b) anyone who is in the act of committing an offence;
  (c) anyone whom he has reasonable grounds for suspecting to be about to commit an offence;
  (d) anyone whom he has reasonable grounds for suspecting to be committing an offence.

(2) If a constable has reasonable grounds for suspecting that an offence has been committed, he may arrest without a warrant anyone whom he has reasonable grounds to suspect of being guilty of it.

(3) If an offence has been committed, a constable may arrest without a warrant—

  (a) anyone who is guilty of the offence;
  (b) anyone whom he has reasonable grounds for suspecting to be guilty of it.

(4) But the power of summary arrest conferred by subsection (1), (2) or (3) is exercisable only if the constable has reasonable grounds for believing that for any of the reasons mentioned in subsection (5) it is necessary to arrest the person in question.

(5) The reasons are—

  (a) to enable the name of the person in question to be ascertained (in the case where the constable does not know, and cannot readily ascertain, the person's name, or has reasonable grounds for doubting whether a name given by the person as his name is his real name);
  (b) correspondingly as regards the person's address;
  (c) to prevent the person in question—
    (i)   causing physical injury to himself or any other person;
    (ii) suffering physical injury;
    (iii) causing loss of or damage to property;
    (iv) committing an offence against public decency (subject to subsection (6)); or
    (v)   causing an unlawful obstruction of the highway;
  (d) to protect a child or other vulnerable person from the person in question;
  (e) to allow the prompt and effective investigation of the offence or of the conduct of the person in question;
  (f) to prevent any prosecution for the offence from being hindered by the disappearance of the person in question.

(6) Subsection (5)(c)(iv) applies only where members of the public going about their normal business cannot reasonably be expected to avoid the person in question.

In the original version of s 24, a distinction was drawn between 'arrestable' offences and 'non-arrestable' offences. The current version of s 24 (as amended by s 110 of the Serious Organised Crime and Police Act 2005) abandons that distinction, with the effect that a police officer may arrest someone for *any* offence, provided that:

a   the person in question is suspected of involvement or attempted involvement in the commission of a criminal offence, in that:

- the person is committing (or the officer has reasonable grounds to believe that he is committing) the offence; or
- the officer has reasonable grounds to believe that the offence has been committed and also has reasonable grounds to believe that the person to be arrested has committed that offence; or
- the person is about to commit (or the officer has reasonable grounds to believe that the person is about to commit) the offence.

and

b   there are reasonable grounds for believing that the arrest is *necessary* on one or more of the grounds set out in s 24(5).

Code G of the Codes of Practice issued pursuant to the Police and Criminal Evidence Act provides additional guidance on these powers of arrest. Paragraph 2.9 of the Code suggests that condition (e) ('to allow the prompt and effective investigation of the offence or of the conduct of the person in question') may include cases such as:

(i)   Where there are reasonable grounds to believe that the person:

- has made false statements;
- has made statements which cannot be readily verified;
- has presented false evidence;
- may steal or destroy evidence;
- may make contact with co-suspects or conspirators;
- may intimidate or threaten or make contact with witnesses;
- where it is necessary to obtain evidence by questioning; or

(ii)   when considering arrest in connection with an indictable offence, there is a need to:

- enter and search any premises occupied or controlled by a person;
- search the person;
- prevent contact with others;
- take fingerprints, footwear impressions, samples or photographs of the suspect.

(iii)   ensuring compliance with statutory drug testing requirements.

The Code suggests that condition (f) ('to prevent any prosecution for the offence from being hindered by the disappearance of the person in question') may arise if there are reasonable grounds for believing that:

- if the person is not arrested he or she will fail to attend court;
- street bail after arrest would be insufficient to deter the suspect from trying to evade prosecution.

For a critical discussion of the new arrest powers, see R.C. Austin, 'The new powers of arrest: plus ca change: more of the same or major change?' [2007] Crim LR 459.

2.2.5.1 Meaning of 'reasonable grounds'

In *O'Hara v Chief Constable of the RUC* [1997] AC 286, the House of Lords considered the meaning of 'reasonable grounds' in the context of anti-terrorism legislation, which applied the same test as s 24 of PACE. It was held that, for a police officer to have reasonable grounds to effect an arrest, the question is whether a reasonable person would be of that opinion, having regard to the information which was in the mind of the arresting officer. In other words, the test is partly subjective (the officer must have formed a 'genuine suspicion' in his own mind that the suspect has committed the offence in question) and partly objective (there must be reasonable grounds for that suspicion). The House of Lords went on to hold that the information acted on by the officer need not be based on his own observations: he is entitled to form a suspicion on the basis of what he has been told. It is not necessary to prove what was known to the person who gave the information to the police officer or to prove that any facts on which the officer based his suspicion were actually true.

This test is compatible with the requirements of Art 5 of the European Convention on Human Rights (the right to liberty). In *O'Hara v UK* (2002) 34 EHRR 32 (following *Fox, Campbell and Hartley v UK* (1990) 13 EHRR 157), the European Court of Human Rights emphasised that the 'reasonableness' of the suspicion on which an arrest must be based forms an essential part of the safeguard against arbitrary arrest and detention laid down in Art 5(1)(c) of the Convention. The Court held (at para 34) that this requires the existence of some facts or information which would satisfy an objective observer that the person concerned may have committed the offence, though what may be regarded as reasonable will depend on all the circumstances of the particular case. The Court went on to observe (at para 36), that the standard imposed by Art 5 does not presuppose that the police have sufficient evidence to bring charges at the time of arrest. The object of questioning during detention is to further the criminal investigation by way of confirming or dispelling the suspicion that gave rise to the arrest. Thus facts which raise a suspicion need not be of the same level as those necessary to justify a conviction, or even the bringing of a charge.

The application of this test is illustrated by a civil case, *Hough v Chief Constable of Staffordshire* [2001] EWCA Civ 39; (2001) *The Times*, 14 February. The claimant was a passenger in a vehicle stopped by police. A routine check on the police computer said that the owner of the vehicle might be armed. The claimant was arrested but no weapon was found in his possession. He brought an action for damages. The Court of Appeal held that, where the arresting officer's suspicion is formed on the basis of a national police computer entry, the entry itself is capable of providing the necessary objective justification to afford the arresting officer the required reasonable suspicion. The court said that whether the computer entry in question sufficed to provide the necessary objective justification depended on the circumstances of the individual case. If the situation lacked urgency, and some further inquiry was clearly called for before the suspicion could properly be said to crystallise, then the computer entry alone would not suffice. In the present case, however, the entry itself provided ample justification for an arrest and the claim for wrongful arrest was defeated.

2.2.5.2 Information to be given on arrest

Section 28 of PACE sets out what the accused must be told when he is arrested:

(1) Subject to sub-section (5) below, where a person is arrested, otherwise than by being informed that he is under arrest, the arrest is not lawful unless the person arrested is informed that he is under arrest as soon as is practicable after his arrest.

(2) Where a person is arrested by a constable, sub-section (1) above applies regardless of whether the fact of the arrest is obvious.

(3) Subject to sub-section (5) below, no arrest is lawful unless the person arrested is informed of the ground for the arrest at the time of, or as soon as is practicable after, the arrest.

(4) Where a person is arrested by a constable, sub-section (3) above applies regardless of whether the ground for the arrest is obvious.

(5) Nothing in this section is to be taken to require a person to be informed—

  (a) that he is under arrest; or
  (b) of the ground for the arrest,

  if it was not reasonably practicable for him to be so informed by reason of his having escaped from arrest before the information could be given.

Article 5(2) of the European Convention on Human Rights requires that everyone who is arrested shall be informed promptly, in a language which he understands, of the reasons for his arrest and of any charge against him. This means that the suspect must be told 'in simple, non-technical language that he can understand, the essential legal and factual grounds for his arrest so as to be able, if he sees fit, to apply to a court to challenge its lawfulness' (*Fox, Campbell and Hartley v UK* (1990) 13 EHRR 157 (at para 40) and *Taylor v Chief Constable of Thames Valley Police* [2004] EWCA Civ 858).

Thus, when someone is arrested, they should, at the time of the arrest, be informed in non-technical language of the reason for the arrest. This is so even if the reason is obvious (*Abbassy v Metropolitan Police Commissioner* [1990] 1 WLR 385).

The information is normally given by the officer making the arrest, but s 28 of PACE is satisfied if an officer other than the arresting officer informs the person arrested of the reason for the arrest (*Dhesi v Chief Constable of West Midlands Police* (2000) *The Times*, 9 May).

Code C of the PACE Codes of Practice provides that:

10.3 A person who is arrested, or further arrested, must be informed at the time, or as soon as practicable thereafter, that they are under arrest and the grounds for their arrest . . .

10.4 . . . a person who is arrested, or further arrested, must also be cautioned unless:

    (a) it is impracticable to do so by reason of their condition or behaviour at the time;

    (b) they have already been cautioned immediately prior to arrest . . .

Note 10B supplements para 10.3 of the Code and provides that:

An arrested person must be given sufficient information to enable them to understand that they have been deprived of their liberty and the reason they have been arrested, e.g. when a person is arrested on suspicion of committing an offence they must be informed of the suspected offence's nature, when and where it was committed. The suspect must also be informed of the reason or reasons why the arrest is considered necessary. Vague or technical language should be avoided.

The terms of the caution to be administered on arrest are set out in para 10.5:

You do not have to say anything. But it may harm your defence if you do not mention when questioned something which you later rely on in Court. Anything you do say may be given in evidence.

2.2.5.3 'Citizen's arrest'

Arrest by people other than police officers is governed by s 24A of PACE. This provides as follows:

(1) A person other than a constable may arrest without a warrant—

    (a) anyone who is in the act of committing an indictable offence;

    (b) anyone whom he has reasonable grounds for suspecting to be committing an indictable offence.

(2) Where an indictable offence has been committed, a person other than a constable may arrest without a warrant—

    (a) anyone who is guilty of the offence;

    (b) anyone whom he has reasonable grounds for suspecting to be guilty of it.

(3) But the power of summary arrest conferred by sub-section (1) or (2) is exercisable only if—

    (a) the person making the arrest has reasonable grounds for believing that for any of the reasons mentioned in sub-section (4) it is necessary to arrest the person in question; and

    (b) it appears to the person making the arrest that it is not reasonably practicable for a constable to make it instead.

(4) The reasons are to prevent the person in question—

    (a) causing physical injury to himself or any other person;

    (b) suffering physical injury;

    (c) causing loss of or damage to property; or

    (d) making off before a constable can assume responsibility for him.

(5)   This section does not apply in relation to an offence under Part 3 or 3A of the Public Order Act 1986.

Thus, a member of the public may arrest someone who is in the act of committing (or whom he has reasonable grounds to suspect is committing) an indictable offence (that is, an offence which may or must be tried in the Crown Court). Where an indictable offence has already been committed, a member of the public can arrest someone who is (or whom he has reasonable grounds for suspecting to be) guilty of that offence.

The police powers of arrest are wider, in that a police officer can arrest for any offence (not just an indictable offence) and only has to have reasonable grounds for suspecting that an offence has been committed before he can arrest anyone whom he reasonably suspects of committing it. The practical effect of this difference is that if a member of the public (for example, a store detective) arrests someone whom he reasonably suspects of committing an indictable offence, the arrest will not be valid if an indictable offence has not in fact been committed (in *R v Self* [1992] 1 WLR 657, for example, the defendant was arrested by a store detective, with the help of a member of the public, on suspicion of shoplifting. There was a struggle in which the member of the public was kicked and punched by the defendant. The defendant was charged with theft and assault. He was acquitted of the theft but convicted of assault. The Court of Appeal held that the conviction for the assault could not be upheld. The store detective and the person assisting him had no right to detain the defendant, since the defendant had not committed the offence of theft and so there was no right to effect a 'citizen's arrest').

Furthermore, a member of the public cannot arrest someone who is apparently about to commit an arrestable offence, whereas a police officer can.

A member of the public who makes an arrest should deliver the person arrested into the hands of the police as soon as practicable: s 30(1)(b) of PACE. The police and the Crown Prosecution Service will then be responsible for charging the suspect if they decide to proceed with the case.

2.2.6 Voluntary attendance at a police station

Sometimes, a person will agree to go to a police station to be interviewed by the police without first being arrested. Someone who has not been arrested but who is 'helping the police with their inquiries' is free to leave at any time unless and until he is arrested. Section 29 of PACE provides that:

> Where for the purpose of assisting with an investigation a person attends voluntarily at a police station or at any other place where a constable is present or accompanies a constable to a police station or any such other place without having been arrested—
>
> (a)   he shall be entitled to leave at will unless he is placed under arrest;
> (b)   he shall be informed at once that he is under arrest if a decision is taken by a constable to prevent him from leaving at will.

Paragraph 3.21 of Code C provides that:

Anybody attending a police station voluntarily to assist with an investigation may leave at will unless arrested. If it is decided they shall not be allowed to leave, they must be informed at once that they are under arrest and brought before the custody officer, who is responsible for making sure they are notified of their rights in the same way as other detainees . . .

2.3 PROCEDURE AFTER ARREST

After the suspect has been arrested, he will (unless granted 'street bail' – see below) be taken to a 'designated police station' (that is, under s 35, one with facilities for the detention of suspects) as soon as practicable after arrest: s 30(1A) of PACE. The suspect will not be taken immediately to the police station if the case is one where the presence of the suspect elsewhere 'is necessary in order to carry out such investigations as it is reasonable to carry out immediately' (s 30(10A)); it may be necessary, for example, to search the suspect's home.

The time of the suspect's arrival at the police station is called the 'relevant time'. This is the moment from which the length of the suspect's detention starts to be measured. On arrival at the police station, the suspect is taken to the custody officer, defined by s 36 as an officer of the rank of a Sergeant or above (s 36(3)(a)) who is unconnected with the investigation of the case (s 36(5)) or else a 'staff custody officer' (s 36(3)(b)), who is a civilian employee.

2.3.1 'Street bail'

The requirement that the person must be taken to a police station as soon as practicable after the arrest (s 30(1A)) is (under s 30(1B)) made subject to s 30A. Sections 30A–30D provide for what has been termed 'street bail'. This empowers police officers to grant bail to persons following their arrest without the need to take them to a police station first. Section 30A provides that a constable may release on bail a person who has been arrested 'at any time before he arrives at a police station' (s 30A(2)). It requires that the person released on bail 'must be required to attend a police station' (s 30A(3)) and that any police station may be specified for that purpose (s 30A(5)). Under s 30A(4), conditions may be imposed on the grant of street bail only as permitted by s 30A(3A) and (3B). Section 30A(3A) specifically excludes requiring the person to provide security or a surety to guarantee his surrender to custody (see Chapter 3) and also forbids the imposition of a condition of residence in a bail hostel. Section 30A(3B) provides that, subject to the exclusions in sub-s (3A), the constable may impose any condition which appears necessary to secure that the person surrenders to custody, does not commit an offence while on bail, does not interfere with witnesses or otherwise obstruct the course of justice, or for the person's own protection (or, if he is under 17, his own welfare) or in the person's own interests.

Under s 30B, the police officer must give the person bailed, before he is released, a written notice setting out (a) the offence for which he was arrested, (b) the ground on which he was arrested (s 30B(2)), and informing him that he is required to attend a police station (s 30B(3)). Where conditions have been imposed, those conditions must be specified, and the notice must inform the person of his right to seek variation of those conditions (s 30B(4A)). The notice may also specify the police station and the time at which he is required to attend; if these details are not included in the notice, they must be supplied in a further written notice provided to the person later (s 30B(4) and (5)). The police can specify a different police station or a different time by giving the person written notice to that effect (s 30B(6), (7)). Under s 30C(1), the police can give the person a written notice that his attendance at the police station is no longer required.

Section 30C(4) provides that a person who has been released on bail under s 30A can be re-arrested if new evidence justifying a further arrest has come to light since his release.

Section 30D deals with failure to answer to bail granted under s 30A. Where the person fails to attend the police station at the specified time, he may be arrested without warrant (s 30D(1)). Under s 30D(2A), a person who has been released on conditional street bail may be arrested without warrant by a police officer if the officer has reasonable grounds for suspecting that the person has broken any of the conditions of bail.

Section 30CA(1) enables the person arrested to seek a variation of any conditions imposed on his street bail. The request is made to a custody officer at the police station which the suspect is required to attend.

Under s 30CB(1), if the request for a variation of conditions is refused by the police, the suspect may seek variation of the conditions by a magistrates' court. Under sub-s (2), the application to the court must be based on the ground that was relied upon when the request was made to the police; however, the court may also consider different grounds provided that they arise out of a change in circumstances that has occurred since the making of the application.

Home Office Circular 61/2003 (<http://www.knowledgenetwork.gov.uk/HO/circular. nsf/79755433dd36a66980256d4f004d1514/48b952fe7728f60980256df6005c91df?Open-Document>) gives guidance on 'street bail'. The Circular sets out the key aims of 'street bail':

- to enable officers to remain on patrol for longer periods and raise visibility;
- to give officers greater flexibility to decide how best to use their time and organise their casework; and
- to remove the need for suspects to be taken to a police station only to be bailed on arrival.

The Circular goes on to identify the benefits of this new power:

Who does it benefit?

- The police:

  - reduce the amount of time travelling to and from the station
  - better plan the investigation and work caseload
  - spend less time waiting at the police station to progress the investigation
  - ensure appropriate representation on answering bail

- The suspect:

- reduce the need to travel to a police station
- avoid spending time in detention whilst awaiting representation etc
- ensure that time spent in detention is focused on the investigation and not awaiting representation

- Legal representatives, parents, appropriate adults:

  - ability to plan and prepare for attendance

- The community:

  - increased police presence on the street
  - more officer time spent patrolling than dealing with 'bureaucratic' delays.

Part A (para 3) of the Circular goes on to identify the key matters to be taken into account by the police, noting that street bail enables front-line officers to apply their discretion at the point of arrest. The Circular identifies four key considerations:

- the nature of the offence;
- the ability to progress the investigation at the station;
- confidence in the suspect answering bail;
- the level of awareness and understanding of the procedure by the suspect.

It may be a source of some confusion that Pt F of the Circular (namely 'pocket-sized guide') provides guidance in slightly different terms. It states that:

> It is a matter for the discretion of the constable when street bail should be given. The primary considerations are:
>
> - the nature and seriousness of the offence;
> - fitness, vulnerability and awareness of the detainee;
> - potential for further offences to be committed;
> - preservation of evidence.

Part A of the Circular adds (paras 5 and 6) that:

> Officers must ensure that street bail is used fairly, objectively and without any bias against ethnic or other groups within the community. Supervising officers must monitor the use of street bail and consider whether officers under their supervision are making appropriate use of the power.
>
> Supervising officers should satisfy themselves that the decision to use or decline use of street bail is not on the basis of stereotyped image or inappropriate generalisations. Appropriate action should be taken by supervising officers if examination of the records reveals any trends or patterns which give cause for concern.

Part C contains more detailed guidance on the considerations to be applied when deciding whether or not to grant street bail:

> **What type of offence has been committed?** There is no definitive list of offences to

which street bail can be granted. It is a matter for the officer's discretion. However, it is unlikely that street bail would be granted in relation to a serious arrestable offence.

What impact has the offence had? How has the offence impacted on the victim and any bystanders – what impact has it had on the offender – how serious is the offence?

Would a delay in dealing with the offender result in loss of vital evidence? It might be necessary to take an arrested person to a police station to preserve and examine forensic evidence, which could be lost if the suspect is released.

Is the arrested person fit to be released back on to the streets? A drunken driver, or those with mental health problems, for example, may not be in a fit state to be returned to the streets. In the case of a juvenile, consideration must be given to the welfare of the child . . .

Does the arrested person understand what is happening? This particularly applies to vulnerable people who would normally require the assistance of an appropriate adult (i.e. mentally disordered or mentally vulnerable people and juveniles) but may also include those suspected to be under the influence of drink and/or drugs.

If released on bail is the arrested person likely to commit a further offence? The arresting officer must/should not grant street bail if there are reasonable grounds to believe that the arrested person might continue to commit that or another offence if released e.g. where fighting is involved.

Am I satisfied that the arrested person has provided a correct name and address? The bailing officer must not grant bail if he is not satisfied that the identification and address details provided are correct.

What about juveniles and other vulnerable people? You should assess the level of risk to the safety and welfare of a juvenile or vulnerable person.

Anthea Hucklesby in 'Not Necessarily a Trip to the Police Station: the Introduction of Street Bail' [2004] Crim LR 803 expresses the trenchant view that:

> The new street bail provisions are ill-thought out and misconceived. Bail decisions are some of the most difficult decisions which are made in the criminal justice process. They require decision makers to balance probabilities about the future behaviour of legally innocent people while protecting the liberty of suspects/defendants and ensuring public safety. The potential for making the wrong decisions in such circumstances is enormous and wrong decisions may have damaging consequences. It is difficult to see how informed and pro-portionate decisions will be made by police officers in the environment of the street where the situation may be heated, the circumstances of the offence unclear and/or disputed, victims may be present and information is likely to be limited . . . [S]treet bail may be used where there is little or no evidence, as an instrument of police authority and control or simply as a way of keeping tabs on known offenders.

Hucklesby also points out the risk of a disparity in the use of street bail between different police forces, and the risk (or likelihood, as she sees it) of street bail being used in a way that discriminates against certain groups (in particular, minority ethnic groups). She is also concerned that street bail, being considered outside a police station, is being granted or withheld in an environment where the protections of PACE (includ-ing the supervision of the custody officer) are absent; moreover, the exchanges which happen between the investigating officer and the suspect during the granting of street bail will be largely unregulated (providing the opportunity for informal interviewing to take place, which may result in incriminating evidence being provided by the suspect or being attributed to the suspect without the means of checking the authenticity or admissibility of the statements). She also expresses concern at a risk of 'net-widening': street bail may result in some suspects being bailed when they would otherwise have not been arrested, or who would have been arrested and then released (unconditionally) after they have attended the police station. Her ultimate conclusion is that:

> [T]here are significant issues raised by the introduction of street bail. These include the by-passing of suspects' rights at the police station, the possibility that the power will be used in a discriminatory way, the potential for net-widening and abuse of the powers by the police. Some of these issues have been highlighted in official documentation but they have not been adequately addressed in the legislation or in the guidance which has been issued to-date. Furthermore, the introduction of street bail erodes the separation of personnel involved in the investigation of offences and/or offenders and those who make bail/detention decisions and the safeguards for the rights of suspects which were introduced by PACE 1984 to prevent miscarriages of justice. Whilst any measure to reduce bureaucracy and increase the time police officers spend on the street is to be welcomed, this should not be at the expense of safeguarding suspects' rights and ensuring that appropriate and proportional remand decisions are made. The introduction of this significant police power requires careful monitoring and evaluation in order to assess its impact in terms of the extent of its use, reducing the time the police spend processing suspects and the broader issues.

It is certainly the case that the use of 'street bail' needs careful monitoring to ensure that it is not abused.

2.3.2 Arrival at the police station: duties of the custody officer

The main duties of the custody officer include:

- deciding whether there is sufficient evidence for the suspect to be charged or whether to authorise detention without charge (see s 37 of PACE);
- informing the suspect of his rights (for example, the right under s 56 to have someone informed of his arrest and the right under s 58 to consult in private with a solicitor); and
- keeping a 'custody record' documenting all that occurs during the suspect's detention, for example, meal breaks and interviews.

2.3.2.1 The right to have someone informed of the arrest

Under s 56 of PACE, the suspect has the right to have someone informed of their arrest. However, the exercise of this right can be delayed for up to 36 hours on the authority of an officer of the rank of Inspector or above. Section 56 provides as follows:

(1) Where a person has been arrested and is being held in custody in a police station or other premises, he shall be entitled, if he so requests, to have one friend or relative or other person who is known to him or who is likely to take an interest in his welfare told, as soon as is practicable except to the extent that delay is permitted by this section, that he has been arrested and is being detained there.

(2) Delay is only permitted—

    (a) in the case of a person who is in police detention for an indictable offence; and

    (b) if an officer of at least the rank of inspector authorises it.

(3) In any case the person in custody must be permitted to exercise the right conferred by sub-section (1) above within 36 hours from the relevant time, as defined in section 41(2) above.

. . .

(5) Subject to sub-section (5A) below an officer may only authorise delay where he has reasonable grounds for believing that telling the named person of the arrest—

    (a) will lead to interference with or harm to evidence connected with an indictable offence or interference with or physical injury to other persons; or

    (b) will lead to the alerting of other persons suspected of having committed such an offence but not yet arrested for it; or

    (c) will hinder the recovery of any property obtained as a result of such an offence.

(5A) An officer may also authorise delay where he has reasonable grounds for believing that—

    (a) the person detained for the indictable offence has benefited from his criminal conduct, and

    (b) the recovery of the value of the property constituting the benefit will be hindered by telling the named person of the arrest.

. . .

(10) Nothing in this section applies to a person arrested or detained under the terrorism provisions.

2.3.3 Detention without charge

Section 37 of PACE covers the situation where the custody officer decides that there is insufficient evidence to charge the suspect:

(2) If the custody officer determines that he does not have such evidence before him, the person arrested shall be released either on bail or without bail, unless the custody officer has reasonable grounds for believing that his detention without being charged is necessary to secure or preserve evidence relating to an offence for which he is under arrest or to obtain such evidence by questioning him.

(3) If the custody officer has reasonable grounds for so believing, he may authorise the person arrested to be kept in police detention.

Ed Cape, in 'Detention without charge: what does "sufficient evidence to charge" mean?' [1999] Crim LR 874, points out (drawing on research including D Brown, *PACE*

Ten Years On: A Review of the Research (Home Office Research Study 155, 1997)) that the examination by the custody officer of the need for the suspect's detention rarely amounts to a searching scrutiny, with the effect that almost all of those who are arrested are detained. Custody officers who were observed during the research did not ask arresting officers for much information at all about the evidence against the suspect before authorising the detention of the suspect. Cape's main concern in this article is to address the question whether the 'sufficient evidence to charge' test in s 37 'leaves unanswered the question of whether the police must decide upon charge once satisfied there is a prima facie case against the suspect, or whether they can delay charge until some higher threshold is met, such as whether there is sufficient evidence to give a realistic prospect of conviction'. Cape takes the view that the test applied by the police ('sufficient evidence to charge') and that applied by the CPS ('realistic prospect of conviction') are necessarily different. However, it seems logical that – in practice, if not in theory – the two tests should amount to the same thing, since the police are sending to the CPS a case with sufficient evidence, they hope, for that case to be taken forward by the CPS. Perhaps the key difference between the two tests is their mode of application – the decision of the custody officer is taken by a non-lawyer (in the potentially chaotic atmosphere of the police station custody area), whereas when the case is reviewed by the CPS, the review is carried out by a qualified lawyer. Given that, as a result of the reforms brought about by the Criminal Justice Act 2003, the charging decision ultimately rests with the CPS (and not the police), it seems inevitable that the two tests should be interpreted to mean the same thing.

2.3.3.1 Detention without charge: reviews

If the suspect is detained without charge, the detention is subject to periodic reviews according to the timetable set out in ss 40–44 of PACE.

Under s 40(3), reviews take place as follows:

(a)   the first review shall be not later than six hours after the detention was first authorised;
(b)   the second review shall be not later than nine hours after the first;
(c)   subsequent reviews shall be at intervals of not more than nine hours.

Thus, the first review takes place six hours after detention was first authorised; the second review at 15 hours after detention was first authorised; and the third review at 24 hours after detention was first authorised. Under s 40(1)(b), the reviews must be carried out by an officer of at least the rank of Inspector who has not been directly involved in the investigation. At each of these reviews, the review officer has to be satisfied that the conditions of continued detention (as set out in s 37(2)) continue to be satisfied.

Before deciding whether to authorise the continued detention of the suspect, the review officer must give the suspect (unless he is asleep or otherwise unfit by reason of his condition or behaviour), or any solicitor who is representing him and who is available at the time of the review, the opportunity to make representations about the continued detention (s 40(12)–(14)).

A review may be postponed if, having regard to the circumstances prevailing at the latest time when that review should take place, it is not practicable to carry out the review then (for example, because the suspect is then being interviewed and it would wreck the interview if it were to be suspended for a review to take place, or because no review officer is readily available at that time). Where a review is postponed, it must take place as soon as practicable after the time it should have taken place, and a reason for the delay must be noted on the custody record (s 40(4), (5), (7)). Importantly, a postponement of one review does not affect the time when subsequent reviews have to take place (s 40(6)).

Section 40A of PACE enables reviews of detention to be conducted by telephone rather than in person at the police station. The review officer will usually speak to the custody officer, and to the detained person (or their legal representative) if he wishes to exercise the right to make representations about the continuing need for detention. Under s 40A(2) of the 1984 Act, telephone reviews must not be conducted where it is reasonably practicable to carry out the review using video-conferencing facilities.

Home Office Circular 60/2003 (<http://www.knowledgenetwork.gov.uk/HO/circular. nsf/79755433dd36a66980256d4f004d1514/ff423f4013d2202780256df8003036fc?Open-Document>) contains the following guidance:

3.3 The review officer must consider each case individually and decide whether a telephone review is sufficient, or whether a review in person is most appropriate in the circumstances.

3.4 It will enable operational flexibility and provide scope to save the review officer's time by minimising effort that would otherwise be used up in travelling to conduct reviews.

3.5 But, importantly, the decision on the type of review must always take full account of the needs of the person in custody. The benefits of carrying out a review in person should always be considered, based on the individual circumstances of each case with specific additional consideration if the person is:

   – a juvenile (and the age of the juvenile); or
   – mentally vulnerable; or
   – has been subject to medical attention for other than routine minor ailments; or
   – there are presentational or community issues around the person's detention.

3.6 Should a telephone review be undertaken, the officer responsible for authorising continued detention shall ensure that the opportunity to make representations is given to the detainee (unless asleep), the detainee's solicitor if available at the time; and the appropriate adult if available at the time.

3.7 The review officer can decide at any stage that a telephone review should be terminated and that the review will be conducted in person. The reasons for doing so should be noted in the custody record.

2.3.3.2 Detention beyond 24 hours

After 24 hours from the time when detention was first authorised have elapsed, the suspect can only be detained without charge if the provisions of s 42ff apply (s 41(1)). Otherwise he must be released (with or without bail): s 41(7).

If the suspect is released because 24 hours have elapsed, he cannot be re-arrested without a warrant for the offence for which he was previously arrested 'unless new evidence justifying a further arrest has come to light after his release' (s 41(9)). This does not, however, prevent the arrest of the suspect under s 46A of PACE (arrest for failure to answer police bail).

Section 42(1) of PACE enables a suspect to be detained after 24 hours have expired. It provides that:

> Where a police officer of the rank of superintendent or above who is responsible for the police station at which a person is detained has reasonable grounds for believing that—
>
> (a) the detention of that person without charge is necessary to secure or preserve evidence relating to an offence for which he is under arrest or to obtain such evidence by questioning him;
> (b) an offence for which he is under arrest is an indictable offence; and
> (c) the investigation is being conducted diligently and expeditiously,
>
> he may authorise the keeping of that person in police detention for a period expiring at or before 36 hours after the relevant time.

In the original version of s 42, the power to authorise detention beyond 24 hours was confined to cases where the accused was suspected of a 'serious arrestable offence'. Under the Criminal Justice Act 2003, however, the restriction was amended to extend the power to detain beyond 24 hours to any indictable offence (i.e. one that may or must be tried in the Crown Court). Home Office Circular 60/2003 (see above) makes the point that this represents 'a significant additional power for the police' (para 4.3) and that it 'should be used sparingly and only where there is full justification' (para 4.4). The Circular also makes the point that detaining a juvenile or a mentally vulnerable person for longer than 24 hours without charge will only normally be justifiable where the offence is a serious one (para 4.8).

2.3.3.3 Detention beyond 36 hours

After 36 hours have elapsed since the 'relevant time', the suspect can be detained further without being charged only if this is permitted by a magistrates' court (s 43). The application for a warrant for continued detention is made *in camera* (that is, with the public excluded) before two or more lay justices (s 45(1)). The application has to be made on oath (s 43(1)). The suspect has a right to be present (s 43(2)) and, if he so wishes, to be legally represented at this hearing (s 43(3)).

Section 43(4) provides that:

> A person's further detention is only justified . . . if
>
> (a) his detention without charge is necessary to secure or preserve evidence relating to an offence for which he is under arrest or to obtain such evidence by questioning him;
> (b) an offence for which he is under arrest is an indictable offence; and
> (c) the investigation is being conducted diligently and expeditiously.

Section 43(14) stipulates that any information submitted in support of an application for a warrant of continued detention must state:

(a) the nature of the offence for which the person to whom the application relates has been arrested;

(b) the general nature of the evidence on which that person was arrested;

(c) what inquiries relating to the offence have been made by the police and what further inquiries are proposed by them;

(d) the reasons for believing the continued detention of that person to be necessary for the purposes of such further inquiries.

The police should apply for permission to detain the suspect before the initial 36-hour period has expired; if this is not practicable, then the application must be made to the magistrates not later than 42 hours after the initial detention (s 43(5)). In other words, there is a six-hour period of grace; thereafter, the suspect's continued detention can no longer be authorised and his continued detention is unlawful.

The magistrates can issue a warrant allowing a maximum period of no more than a further 36 hours' detention: s 43(12). If the police need even more time, they can make a further application to the magistrates, under s 44(1), for continued permission to detain the suspect without charge. However, the magistrates cannot authorise a period of detention which would mean that the suspect has been in custody for a total of more than 96 hours from the relevant time (s 44(3)).

Once 96 hours have elapsed from the relevant time, the suspect must either be charged or else released, either unconditionally or on bail to return to the police station (s 43(18)). Following his release, the suspect cannot be re-arrested without a warrant for the same offence unless new evidence has come to light (s 43(19)).

It should be noted that this timetable does not apply to suspects detained under the Prevention of Terrorism legislation (which permits a considerably longer period of detention without charge).

2.3.3.4 Non-compliance with review timetable

Where the suspect's detention is not reviewed in accordance with PACE (and none of the circumstances in s 40 which allow for postponement of the review are applicable), the detention is unlawful from the time when the review should have taken place, giving rise to a civil claim for damages for false imprisonment. It is immaterial in such a case that there were grounds to justify the continued detention, and so the suspect's continued detention would have been authorised had a review taken place. In *Roberts v Chief Constable of the Cheshire Constabulary* [1999] 1 WLR 662, it was said to be arguable that a late review may render lawful a person's detention from the time it takes place (leaving only the period immediately preceding the review as unlawful detention).

2.3.4 Interviewing suspects

Code of Practice C, issued to the police under PACE, sets out detailed rules for the detention and interviewing of suspects. It requires, for example, that suspects be given two light meals and a main meal each day and that they are given at least eight hours' rest per day: Code C 8 and Code C 12. In *R v Weerdesteyn* [1995] 1 Cr App R 405, the Court of Appeal confirmed that, where customs officers interview a suspect, the provisions of PACE and the Codes of Practice apply just as they do in the case of a police interview.

2.3.4.1 The caution

Code C 10.1 says that:

> 10.1 A person whom there are grounds to suspect of an offence must be cautioned before any questions about an offence, or further questions if the answers provide the grounds for suspicion, are put to them if either the suspect's answers or silence (i.e. failure or refusal to answer or answer satisfactorily), may be given in evidence to a court in a prosecution. A person need not be cautioned if questions are for other necessary purposes, e.g.:
>
> (a) solely to establish their identity or ownership of any vehicle;
> (b) to obtain information in accordance with any relevant statutory requirement . . .;
> (c) in furtherance of the proper and effective conduct of a search, e.g. to determine the need to search in the exercise of powers of stop and search or to seek co-operation while carrying out a search . . .

Note 10A provides that for there to be grounds to suspect someone of an offence:

> There must be some reasonable, objective grounds for the suspicion, based on known facts or information which are relevant to the likelihood the offence has been committed and the person to be questioned committed it.

Thus, a person whom there are grounds to suspect of an offence must be cautioned before any questions about it are put to him regarding his involvement or suspected involvement in that offence. This definition of when a caution must be administered excludes preliminary questions, for example, to establish the suspect's identity.

Code C, para 10.5, sets out the terms of the caution as follows:

> The caution which must be given on:
>
> (a) arrest;
> (b) all other occasions before a person is charged or informed they may be prosecuted,
>
> should, unless the restriction on drawing adverse inferences from silence applies, be in the following terms:
>
> 'You do not have to say anything. But it may harm your defence if you do not mention when questioned something which you later rely on in Court. Anything you do say may be given in evidence.'

Paragraph 10.8 stipulates that after any break in questioning under caution, the person being questioned must be made aware they remain under caution. If there is any doubt, the caution should be given again in full when the interview resumes. Thus, the caution has to be administered:

a upon arrest;
b before questioning commences; and
c where there is a break in the questioning, before the questioning resumes.

Paragraph 10.7 makes the point that minor deviations from the prescribed words of the caution do not constitute a breach of the Code, provided that the sense of the caution is preserved.

Paragraph 10.6 and Annex C (para 2) set out the alternative terms of the caution to be used when the restriction on drawing adverse inferences from silence applies because access to a solicitor has been denied under s 58 of PACE.

When the suspect is charged, the caution is repeated in the same terms except that the word 'now' replaces the words 'when questioned' (Code C 16.2).

2.3.4.2 The police interview

Code C 11.1A defines 'interview' in these terms:

> An interview is the questioning of a person regarding their involvement or suspected involvement in a criminal offence or offences which, under paragraph 10.1, must be carried out under caution . . .

It follows that if a person is being questioned only as a potential witness, there is no need to caution that person; however, if a person is about to be questioned as a potential suspect, a caution must be administered before that questioning begins.

Code C 11.1 provides that, except in emergencies, an interview may only take place at a police station.

The interview should be recorded (either a tape recording or a video recording). This of course means that there is a definitive record of what the suspect said and what was said to him. This protects the suspect from any risk that the police might be tempted to fabricate a confession, and it protects the police from allegations that they have fabricated any confession.

If the interview is not tape-recorded, a record must be made showing what is said; this should be done during or as soon as practicable after the interview. The record should be signed by the maker and the person interviewed should be given the opportunity to read and correct the record: see Code C 11.7–14.

Under Code C 11.6, the interview must cease once the police have enough evidence to provide a 'realistic prospect of conviction' (that is, the same test that is applied by the CPS when deciding whether or not to continue a prosecution):

> The interview or further interview of a person about an offence with which that person has not been charged or for which they have not been informed they may be prosecuted, must cease when:
>
> (a) the officer in charge of the investigation is satisfied all the questions they consider

relevant to obtaining accurate and reliable information about the offence have been put to the suspect, this includes allowing the suspect an opportunity to give an innocent explanation and asking questions to test if the explanation is accurate and reliable, e.g. to clear up ambiguities or clarify what the suspect said;

(b) the officer in charge of the investigation has taken account of any other available evidence; and

(c) the officer in charge of the investigation, or in the case of a detained suspect, the custody officer reasonably believes there is sufficient evidence to provide a realistic prospect of conviction for that offence . . .

2.3.4.3 Access to legal advice: s 58 of PACE

Under s 58(1) of the Police and Criminal Evidence Act 1984, a person who has been arrested and is being held in police custody is entitled, if he so requests, to consult a solicitor privately at any time. Under sub-s (4), if a person makes such a request, he must be permitted to consult a solicitor as soon as is practicable except to the extent that delay is permitted by s 58(6)–(8A). Even if those sub-sections apply, the suspect must be permitted to consult a solicitor within 36 hours (sub-s (5)). The provisions permitting delay in access to a solicitor are as follows:

(6) Delay in compliance with a request is only permitted—

(a) in the case of a person who is in police detention for an indictable offence; and
(b) if an officer of at least the rank of superintendent authorises it.

(7) An officer may give an authorisation under sub-section (6) above orally or in writing but, if he gives it orally, he shall confirm it in writing as soon as is practicable.

(8) Subject to sub-section (8A) below an officer may only authorise delay where he has reasonable grounds for believing that the exercise of the right conferred by sub-section (1) above at the time when the person detained desires to exercise it—

(a) will lead to interference with or harm to evidence connected with an indictable offence or interference with or physical injury to other persons; or
(b) will lead to the alerting of other persons suspected of having committed such an offence but not yet arrested for it; or
(c) will hinder the recovery of any property obtained as a result of such an offence.

(8A) An officer may also authorise delay where he has reasonable grounds for believing that—

(a) the person detained for the indictable offence has benefited from his criminal conduct, and
(b) the recovery of the value of the property constituting the benefit will be hindered by the exercise of the right conferred by sub-section (1) above.

Under sub-s (11), there may be no further delay in permitting the exercise of the right of access to a solicitor once the reason for authorising delay ceases to subsist. Nothing in s 58 applies to a person arrested or detained under the terrorism provisions (sub-s (12)).

In summary, the right of access to a solicitor can be denied by the police for up to 36 hours, but only if the following conditions are satisfied:

- denial is on the authority of a superintendent or more senior officer; and
- the offence is an indictable offence; and
- there are reasonable grounds for believing that allowing immediate access to a solicitor would lead to:

  a   interference with evidence connected with an indictable offence; or
  b   interference with or injury to other persons; or
  c   alerting of other persons suspected of committing an indictable offence (that is, other miscreants would be tipped off); or
  d   hindrance to the recovery of the proceeds of an indictable offence.

In *R v Samuel* [1988] QB 615, it was held that the suspicion must relate to the particular solicitor whom the suspect wishes to see. The police must therefore have grounds to suspect the honesty of that solicitor or else think him particularly naive. Similarly, in *R (Thompson) v Chief Constable of Northumbria* [2001] EWCA Civ 321; [2001] 1 WLR 1342, a chief constable had made a blanket order banning a probationary solicitor's representative from attending police stations in the force's area to advise persons in custody. The Court of Appeal held that such a blanket ban was unlawful. It is for the appropriate officer in the specific case to decide whether or not a particular person should in fact be excluded.

Given the importance of the right to legal advice while being detained (and questioned) by the police, and the risk that evidence will be excluded by the court if obtained where this right has been withheld, it is very rare for the police to invoke the power to delay access to a solicitor. There is a substantial risk that any evidence obtained from a suspect who is being denied access to a solicitor will be ruled inadmissible.

2.3.4.4 *Wrongful denial of access to legal advice*

Should there be wrongful exclusion of a solicitor, any confession obtained by the police may well be held inadmissible at trial under s 78 of PACE, which allows the court to exclude any prosecution evidence which would have an adverse effect on the fairness of the proceedings. The importance of legal advice was re-affirmed in *R v Mason* [1988] 1 WLR 139, where the police deceived a solicitor into thinking that the case against his client was stronger than it was and, because the legal advice was based on this fact, the police had effectively denied legal advice to the defendant. The Court of Appeal ruled that his subsequent confession should have been excluded.

In *Cullen v Chief Constable of the RUC* [2003] UKHL 39; [2004] 2 All ER 237, it was held (by a majority of 3:2) that the denial of a statutory right of access to a solicitor is incapable of causing loss or injury of a kind for which damages may be awarded. The appropriate remedy is the public law remedy of judicial review. This case was decided under Northern Ireland legislation but would be equally applicable to the right of access to a solicitor conferred by s 58 of PACE. With respect to the majority of their

Lordships, it is difficult to see how judicial review would provide an effective remedy, since the court would effectively be limited to granting a declaration that the police had acted unlawfully. It remains the case, therefore, that the main sanction where incriminating evidence is obtained in an interview following an improper denial of access to a solicitor is that the evidence is liable to be ruled inadmissible under s 78 of PACE. This would not have assisted Cullen, as he pleaded guilty to the charge and so the question of exclusion of evidence did not arise.

2.3.4.5 European Convention on Human Rights and the right to legal representation

Article 6 of the European Convention on Human Rights guarantees the right to legal representation. Denial of access to a solicitor during a police interview may violate this provision, especially if adverse inferences can be drawn from the defendant's failure to answer questions. It is for this reason that s 34(2A) of the Criminal Justice and Public Order Act 1994 provides that where the accused was not allowed an opportunity to consult a solicitor prior to being questioned or charged, as the case may be, no adverse inferences may be drawn from his failure to mention facts that he subsequently relies on in court.

In *Murray v UK* (1996) 22 EHRR 29 (which was followed in *Averill v UK* (2001) 31 EHRR 36), the European Court of Human Rights said (at para 45):

> Although not specifically mentioned in Article 6 of the Convention, there can be no doubt that the right to remain silent under police questioning and the privilege against self-incrimination are generally recognised international standards which lie at the heart of the notion of a fair procedure under Article 6. By providing the accused with protection against improper compulsion by the authorities these immunities contribute to avoiding miscarriages of justice and to securing the aim of Article 6.

The Court went on to say (at para 47):

> On the one hand, it is self-evident that it is incompatible with the immunities under consideration to base a conviction solely or mainly on the accused's silence or on a refusal to answer questions or to give evidence himself. On the other hand, the Court deems it equally obvious that these immunities cannot and should not prevent that the accused's silence, in situations which clearly call for an explanation from him, be taken into account in assessing the persuasiveness of the evidence adduced by the prosecution. Wherever the line between these two extremes is to be drawn, it follows from this understanding of 'the right to silence' that the question whether the right is absolute must be answered in the negative. It cannot be said therefore that an accused's decision to remain silent throughout criminal proceedings should necessarily have no implications when the trial court seeks to evaluate the evidence against him ... Whether the drawing of adverse inferences from an accused's silence infringes Article 6 is a matter to be determined in the light of all the circumstances of the case ...

The Court held that that there was no breach of the right to a fair trial under Art 6(1) or (2). However, there had been a violation of Art 6(3)(c), the right to defend oneself in person or through legal assistance of one's own choosing. The Court observed that:

> at the beginning of police interrogation, an accused is confronted with a fundamental dilemma relating to his defence. If he chooses to remain silent, adverse inferences may be drawn against him . . . On the other hand, if the accused opts to break his silence during the course of interrogation, he runs the risk of prejudicing his defence without necessarily removing the possibility of inferences being drawn against him. Under such conditions the concept of fairness enshrined in Article 6 requires that the accused has the benefit of the assistance of a lawyer already at the initial stages of police interrogation. To deny access to a lawyer for the first 48 hours of police questioning, in a situation where the rights of the defence may well be irretrievably prejudiced, is – whatever the justification for such denial – incompatible with the rights of the accused under Article 6.

In *Brennan v UK* (2002) 34 EHRR 18, the European Court had to consider the effect of the presence of a police officer during the defendant's consultation with his solicitor. The Court ruled (at para 58) that:

> an accused's right to communicate with his advocate out of hearing of a third person is part of the basic requirements of a fair trial and follows from Article 6(3)(c). If a lawyer were unable to confer with his client and receive confidential instructions from him without surveillance, his assistance would lose much of its usefulness, whereas the Convention is intended to guarantee rights that are practical and effective . . . However, the Court's case law indicates that the right of access to a solicitor may be subject to restrictions for good cause and the question in each case is whether the restriction, in the light of the entirety of the proceedings, has deprived the accused of a fair hearing. While it is not necessary for the applicant to prove, assuming such were possible, that the restriction had a prejudicial effect on the course of the trial, the applicant must be able to claim to have been directly affected by the restriction in the exercise of the rights of the defence.

The Court concluded that Art 6(3)(c) had been breached. The Court reasoned (at para 62):

> the Court cannot but conclude that the presence of the police officer would have inevitably prevented the applicant from speaking frankly to his solicitor and given him reason to hesitate before broaching questions of potential significance to the case against him . . . It is immaterial that it is not shown that there were particular matters which the applicant and his solicitor were thereby stopped from discussing. The ability of an accused to communicate freely with his defence lawyer . . . was subject to express limitation . . . It is indisputable that he was in need at that time of legal advice, and that his responses in subsequent interviews, which were to be carried out in the absence of his solicitor, would continue to be of potential relevance to his trial and could irretrievably prejudice his defence.

2.3.4.6 *The role of the solicitor during police interviews*

Since April 2001, publicly-funded advice at police stations is given (irrespective of the client's means) by solicitors or accredited representatives, acting under a contract with the Legal Services Commission known as the Criminal Defence Service General Criminal Contract.

Code C 6.1 provides that (except in those cases where delay in access to a solicitor is authorised under s 58 of PACE), all detainees must be informed that they may 'at any time consult and communicate privately with a solicitor, whether in person, in writing or by telephone, and that free independent legal advice is available from the duty solicitor'.

Paragraph 6.4 says that no police officer should, at any time, do or say anything with the intention of dissuading a detainee from obtaining legal advice. Paragraph 6.5 requires that the custody officer should act without delay to secure the provision of legal advice if it is sought. If the detainee does not wish to speak to a solicitor in person, he should be informed that the right to legal advice includes the right to speak with a solicitor on the telephone. If the detainee waives the right to legal advice, the officer should ask him why, and any reasons should be recorded on the custody record or the interview record.

Under para 6.6, a detainee who wants legal advice may not be interviewed (or continue to be interviewed) until they have received such advice unless the power to delay access to a solicitor under s 58 applies. If the suspect names a particular solicitor but that solicitor cannot be contacted or declines to attend, the detainee suspect must be advised of the Duty Solicitor Scheme. If he declines to ask for the duty solicitor, the interview may start (or continue) without further delay provided an officer of the rank of Inspector or above agrees.

Guidance Note 6B2 deals with the fact that, from April 2008, requests for publicly-funded legal advice have to go to a central call centre run by the Criminal Defence Service. The Note says that publicly funded legal advice has to be accessed by telephoning the Defence Solicitor Call Centre, which will determine whether legal advice should be limited to telephone advice or whether a solicitor should attend. Legal advice will be by telephone if a detainee is:

- detained for a non-imprisonable offence,
- arrested on a bench warrant for failing to appear and being held for production before the court (except where the solicitor has clear documentary evidence available that would result in the client being released from custody),
- arrested on suspicion of driving with excess alcohol (failure to provide a specimen, driving whilst unfit/drunk in charge of a motor vehicle), or
- detained in relation to breach of police or court bail conditions.

Attendance by a solicitor for an offence which would normally be suitable for telephone advice will depend on whether limited exceptions apply, such as:

- whether the police are going to carry out an interview or an identification parade,
- whether the detainee is eligible for assistance from an appropriate adult,
- whether the detainee is unable to communicate over the telephone,
- whether the detainee alleges serious maltreatment by the police.

Under para 6.8, a detainee who has been permitted to consult a solicitor in person is entitled to have the solicitor present when he is interviewed unless the power to delay access to a solicitor under s 58 applies. The solicitor may only be required to leave the interview if his conduct is such that the interviewer is unable properly to put questions to the suspect (para 6.9). If the interviewer considers a solicitor is acting in such a way, the interview will be stopped and the interviewing officer will consult a colleague not below rank of Superintendent if one is readily available (failing that, an officer not below the rank of Inspector and not connected with the investigation). After speaking to the solicitor, the officer consulted will decide if the interview should continue in the presence of that solicitor. If they decide it should not, the suspect will be given the opportunity to consult another solicitor before the interview continues and that solicitor given an opportunity to be present at the interview (para 6.10). Paragraph 6.11 makes the point that the removal of a solicitor from an interview is a serious step and, if it occurs, the officer of Superintendent rank or above who took the decision should consider if the incident should be reported to the Solicitors Regulations Authority.

Guidance Note 6D deals with the role of the solicitor during the interview:

> . . . The solicitor's only role in the police station is to protect and advance the legal rights of their client. On occasions this may require the solicitor to give advice which has the effect of the client avoiding giving evidence which strengthens a prosecution case. The solicitor may intervene in order to seek clarification, challenge an improper question to their client or the manner in which it is put, advise their client not to reply to particular questions, or if they wish to give their client further legal advice. Paragraph 6.9 only applies if the solicitor's approach or conduct prevents or unreasonably obstructs proper questions being put to the suspect or the suspect's response being recorded. Examples of unacceptable conduct include answering questions on a suspect's behalf or providing written replies for the suspect to quote.

Thus, a solicitor who is present when a suspect is being interviewed by the police should intervene if (for example) the police officers:

- ask unfair questions;
- ask questions which do not relate to the alleged offence(s);
- misrepresent the law;
- claim to know things but without having any factual basis for that knowledge;
- produce or refer to evidence which has not been shown to the suspect or the solicitor;
- misrepresent information;
- put pressure on the suspect by questioning him in a burdensome manner, by behaving abusively, or by attempting to influence the suspect's decision making.

In 'Incompetent police station advice and the exclusion of evidence' [2002] Crim LR 471, Ed Cape noted that there was a continuing cause for concern about the quality of advice given to suspects at police stations (despite the accreditation scheme for police station representatives, training materials produced by the Law Society, the quality targets incorporated into the General Criminal Contract (under which advice and assistance at police stations is given), and the description of the role of the lawyer contained in the Code of Practice). He argues that the European Court of Human

Rights has recognised that the fairness of a trial depends not only on what is done after charge, but may also be affected by what occurs at the police station stage. Accordingly, he concludes that the courts should exclude evidence which was obtained as a result of incompetence of the lawyer advising at the police station.

Concerns about the quality of police station advice were addressed to a very large extent through the system of accreditation, ensuring that only those who are competent to do so give such advice. However, there do remain some concerns. For example, a suspect may be entitled only to advice over the telephone for less serious offences, and so will not have a solicitor present if he is interviewed by the police.

The pressure of giving such advice should not be underestimated. The recording of interviews makes it much less likely that the police will ask grossly improper questions, or behave in a way that is unduly burdensome or oppressive. However, the risk of adverse inferences being drawn against a defendant who does not mention when questioned a fact that he later relies on in court, means that a decision about what facts to reveal (or not to reveal) can have serious repercussions. Even at this very early stage, the solicitor has to be thinking about trial strategy (for a trial that may be many months away) – is this fact going to be relied on in court as part of the defence case or not? It is also very important that the defence solicitor is able to find out what evidence the police already have (since this will affect the advice given to the client).

A defence solicitor might be a little reluctant to adopt too bullish an approach, as he may have to return to the same police station to represent another client and may well be seeking co-operation from the police. Although the police officers and the defence solicitor seem to be on opposite sides, there is a sense in which they have to work together as they are both working in the criminal justice system.

Given the fact that the police must have some evidence in order to effect an arrest, there must indeed be some likelihood that the suspect is guilty. On this basis, it has been said that some defence solicitors may not be as robust as they might be in representing their client's interests, as they may well believe that the client is guilty anyway.

2.3.4.7 Special rules for interviewing juveniles and persons at risk

Special rules apply to protect juveniles and other vulnerable groups. For example (under Code 11.15), a juvenile, or someone who is mentally disordered or otherwise mentally vulnerable, must not be interviewed regarding their involvement or suspected involvement in a criminal offence or offences, or asked to provide or sign a written statement under caution, unless an 'appropriate adult' (that is, a parent, guardian, or social worker) is present. Under para 11.17, the appropriate adult must be informed that they are not expected to act simply as an observer and that the purpose of their presence is to:

- advise the person being interviewed;
- observe whether the interview is being conducted properly and fairly;
- facilitate communication with the person being interviewed.

It is important that the adult understands their role. He or she may well seek to encourage the child (or vulnerable person) to answer police questions but care has to be taken to ensure that the adult does not exert undue pressure (or indeed become an additional interviewer!).

In *DPP v Blake* [1989] 1 WLR 432, it was held that a parent is not an appropriate adult if the juvenile and parent are estranged; in such a case, a social worker should be the appropriate adult. As Mann LJ put it (at p 440), 'the appropriate adult cannot . . . be a person with whom the juvenile has no empathy'. In *DPP v Cornish* (1997) *The Times*, 27 January, the Divisional Court held that evidence from an interview where an appropriate adult should have been present, but was not, should not be excluded automatically.

2.3.5 Charging the suspect

Section 37(7) provides that if the custody officer determines that there is sufficient evidence to charge the person arrested with the offence for which he was arrested, the person arrested shall be:

- released (without charge) on bail, or kept in police detention, for the purpose of enabling the DPP (in practice this means the CPS) to make a charging decision under s 37B; or
- released (without charge) on bail for a different purpose; or
- released (without charge) unconditionally; or
- charged.

To charge a suspect, the custody officer tells the suspect what offence(s) he is accused of. The suspect is cautioned that he does not have to say anything, that it may harm his defence if he does not mention now something he later relies on in court, and that anything he does say will be written down and may be given in evidence. The suspect is then asked if he has anything to say. Any reply must be noted down.

The second and third options are likely to be exercised only rarely. Release on bail without charge (despite there being sufficient evidence to charge) might be appropriate where further enquiries are still necessary (e.g. to check out an explanation given by the suspect which, if true, would exonerate him); unconditional release without charge may be appropriate if the public interest weighs against prosecuting the suspect (the case may, for example, be one that is best dealt with by an informal warning or by a caution).

2.3.5.1 Involvement of the CPS in the charging decision ('statutory charging')

The wording of s 37(7), which was amended by the Criminal Justice Act 2003, reflects the direct involvement of the CPS in the charging process. The prospect of the defendant pleading guilty, or being found guilty, depends in large measure on the defendant being charged with the right offence(s) on the basis of sufficient evidence. The *Auld Review* recommended early involvement of the CPS in charging decisions. The relevant Recommendations are as follows:

152 The Crown Prosecution Service should be given greater legal powers, in particular the

power to determine the initial charge, and sufficient resources to enable it to take full and effective control of cases from the charge or pre-charge stage, as appropriate.

. . .

154 The Crown Prosecution Service should determine the charge in all but minor, routine offences or where, because of the circumstances, there is a need for a holding charge before seeking the advice of the Service.

155 In minor, routine cases in which the police charge without first having sought the advice of the Service, they should apply the same evidential test as that governing the Service in the Code for Crown Prosecutors.

156 Where the police have preferred a holding charge, and in other than minor, routine offences, a prosecutor should review and, if necessary, reformulate the charge at the earliest possible opportunity.

These reforms are aimed at ensuring two key objectives:

a   that the defendant is charged with the appropriate offence (rather than, for example, one which is too serious); and

b   that the defendant is only charged if there is sufficient evidence, so that there is a realistic prospect of conviction.

According to the 3rd edition (February 2007) of the DPP's Guidance on Charging (<http://www.cps.gov.uk/publications/directors_guidance/dpp_guidance.html>), the police may charge or otherwise deal with a suspect without reference to the CPS, in the case of most road traffic offences and summary offences punishable with less than three months' imprisonment. In other cases, however, it will be appropriate for the police to refer the case to the CPS for a charging decision under s 37B (under a process which has come be known as 'statutory charging').

Section 37B(2) provides that where a suspect is released on bail without charge, or kept in police detention, for the purpose of enabling the CPS to make a charging decision, the CPS must decide whether there is sufficient evidence to charge the person with an offence. Under sub-s (3), if the Crown Prosecutor decides that there is sufficient evidence to charge the person with an offence, he shall decide:

a   whether or not the person should be charged and, if so, the offence with which he should be charged, and

b   whether or not the person should be given a caution and, if so, the offence in respect of which he should be given a caution.

Under sub-s (6), if the Crown Prosecutor decides that the person should be charged with an offence, or given a caution in respect of an offence, the person 'shall' (i.e. must) be charged or cautioned accordingly. However, if the decision is that the person should be given a caution but it proves not to be possible to give the person such a caution (as would be the case where the suspect denies the offence), he shall instead be charged with the offence (sub-s (7)).

Under sub-s (8), the charging will be done by a custody officer at the police station if the suspect is in police detention; if not, he will be charged using the written charge and requisition procedure established by s 29 of the Criminal Justice Act 2003 (see above).

The effect of this is that if the offence is one where the police think there is enough evidence to charge, and they do not wish to release the suspect on police bail, he will be held in custody pending a charging decision by the CPS (and if the decision is in favour of charging the suspect, the charging will be carried out by a custody officer). If, on the other hand, the police are content for the suspect to be on bail pending the charging decision, he will be released on bail when the police believe that there is sufficient evidence to charge him, and the CPS will then take the charging decision and (if they agree that there is sufficient evidence) issue a written charge and requisition.

The DPP's Guidance says, in s 2 (*Key Provisions and Principles of this Guidance*):

- Crown Prosecutors will determine whether a person is to be charged in all indictable only, either way or summary offences subject to those cases specified in this Guidance which the police may continue to charge.
- Charging decisions by Crown Prosecutors will be made following a review of evidence in cases and will be in accordance with this Guidance.
- Custody Officers must comply with this Guidance in deciding how a person is to be dealt with in accordance with s 37(7) PACE . . .
- Crown Prosecutors will seek to identify and resolve cases that are clearly not appropriate for prosecution at the earliest opportunity on consideration of whatever material is available.
- Crown Prosecutors will provide guidance and advice to investigators throughout the investigative and prosecuting process. This may include lines of enquiry, evidential requirements and assistance in any pre-charge procedures. Crown Prosecutors will be proactive in identifying, and where possible, rectifying evidential deficiencies and in bringing to an early conclusion those cases that cannot be strengthened by further investigation.
- Crown Prosecutors will only require 'evidential reports' where it is clear that the case will proceed to the Crown Court or is likely to be a contested summary trial or where it appears to the Crown Prosecutor that the case is so complex or sensitive that a decision to charge cannot be made without an evidential report.
- Where it is necessary, pre-charge bail arrangements will be utilised to facilitate the gathering of evidence, including, in appropriate cases, all the key evidence on which the prosecution will rely, prior to the charging decision being taken . . .

  . . .

- Persons may be charged whilst in police detention, or in accordance with s 29 of the Criminal Justice Act 2003 (charging by post) when it is brought into force. [The summons procedure may be used until that change in the process arrangements.]
- Where a Crown Prosecutor notifies a Custody Officer that there is insufficient evidence to charge, or that though there is sufficient evidence to charge, a person should not be charged or given a caution, the Custody Officer shall give notice in writing to that person that he is not to be prosecuted . . .
- Where Crown Prosecutors decide that a person should be charged with an offence or given a caution, conditional caution, a reprimand or final warning in respect of an offence, the person shall be charged or cautioned, or conditionally cautioned, or given a reprimand or final warning accordingly . . .
- Where Crown Prosecutors decide that a person should be cautioned but it proves not

to be possible to give the person such a caution, the person shall instead be charged with the offence . . .

- In order to facilitate efficient and effective early consultations and make charging decisions, Crown Prosecutors will be deployed as Duty Prosecutors for such hours as shall be agreed locally to provide guidance and make charging decisions. This service will be complemented by a centrally managed out of hours duty prosecutor arrangement to ensure a continuous 24 hour service.

In deciding whether the suspect should be charged and, if so, with what offence(s), the test set out in the Code for Crown Prosecutors (see Chapter 1) should normally be applied, namely (following a review of the evidential material provided) that there is enough evidence to provide a realistic prospect of conviction and that it is in the public interest to proceed. However, where the necessary information it not available, the Crown Prosecutor (or Custody Officer) will assess the case against the 'Threshold Test' set out in para 10, namely:

whether in all the circumstances of the case there is at least a reasonable suspicion against the person of having committed an offence (in accordance with Article 5 of the European Convention on Human Rights) and that at that stage it is in the public interest to proceed. The evidential decision in each case will require consideration of a number of factors including: the evidence available at the time and the likelihood and nature of further evidence being obtained; the reasonableness for believing that evidence will become available; the time that will take and the steps being taken to gather it; the impact of the expected evidence on the case, and the charges the totality of the evidence will support.

The use of Crown Prosecutors to decide whether the suspect should be charged and, if so, with what offence(s), was piloted during 2004 in a number of areas. The scheme was judged a success by the CPS and the Home Office. The benefits identified in the pilot areas included:

- increases in early guilty pleas and conviction rates;
- decreases in discontinued cases, ineffective trials and changed charges;
- improvements in the quality of prosecution files; and
- improved understanding and co-operation between the CPS and police.

The enhancement of the role of the CPS in the charging of suspects is discussed by Ian Brownlee in 'The Statutory Charging Scheme in England and Wales: Towards a Unified Prosecution System' [2004] Crim LR 896. He sets out the aims of the new arrangements in the following terms:

The specific aims of the new charging arrangements may be summarised as follows: the elimination at the earliest opportunity of hopeless cases, the production of more robust prosecution cases, the elimination of unnecessary or unwarranted delays in the period between charge and disposal and the reduction of the number of trials that 'crack' through the offering and acceptance of guilty pleas to reduced charges at a late stage in the process.

Brownlee notes that the genesis of the statutory charging scheme came from the fact that the *Auld Review* (at Chapter 10, para 35) identified as a 'significant contributor' to 'the prolonged and disjointed nature of many criminal proceedings' two closely connected matters: 'over-charging by the police and the failure of the Crown Prosecution Service to remedy it at an early stage'. Auld went on to say that, all too often the prosecutor did not 'review the case thoroughly, or with a sufficiently realistic eye, until late in the day'. This encouraged defendants who believed (whether rightly or wrongly) that they had been overcharged to maintain tactical pleas of not guilty until late in the process in the hope of securing last-minute reductions in the charge (and sometimes electing Crown Court trial in pursuit of that aim). Auld had concluded from this that an earlier determination of the correct charge (correct in the sense of reflecting accurately the true level of seriousness of the offending) would encourage the entering of guilty pleas at an earlier stage or, if not, at least help in identifying the real issues in contested cases, leading to more efficient case management within the court system.

Brownlee examines the criteria by which the success – or otherwise – of the scheme will be judged and the challenges that the scheme faces:

> ... statutory charging aims to eliminate hopeless cases at the earliest possible opportunity and to improve those cases that are to proceed by ensuring that all the evidence necessary to prove the case in court is obtained at an early rather than a later stage in the proceedings. Ideally, where a suspect is considered suitable for bail, the aim should be to acquire all the essential evidence and construct a coherent case before the suspect is even charged. Thereby, the prosecution would hope that the papers they serve as advance information at or before the first hearing is so compelling that a greater number of early guilty pleas will be encouraged. Even where cases are to be contested it is intended that any delay that is necessitated by the need to build effective cases will be located predominantly within the pre-charge stage rather than the court process. Success will be measured by the ability of the statutory charging scheme to reduce the number of discontinued charges and cracked trials, increase the proportion of early guilty pleas and contribute generally to the timeliness of the trial process by reducing the overall time from charge to disposal in cases where pre-charge advice has been taken.
>
> ... If the new scheme is to succeed and the wider ambitions of the CPS advanced, at least two practical problems will have to be addressed.
>
> ... The first of these is the mundane but essential issue of human resource management to ensure that there are sufficient prosecutors of adequate experience to deliver the sort of charging decisions that will have a positive impact on the system ... [The scheme depends] on the ability of duty prosecutors, often acting alone, in unfamiliar surroundings and in situations of some urgency and pressure, to come to the right decisions quickly. To identify key evidential and procedural issues and to anticipate potential problems at an early stage in an investigation is a task calling for considerable skill, experience and not a little self-confidence ... An even more fundamental challenge, perhaps, is to change the culture among police officers away from one in which the early charging of suspects is seen as a mark of completion and even success, towards an acceptance that suspects may have to remain on pre-charge bail longer while evidence is amassed and case files built ... [S]ome police officers may well view [statutory charging] as, at best, a frustrating intrusion by outsiders into well established working practices and, at worst, a diminution of their traditional constabulary independence ... [M]uch will depend again upon the ability of individual duty prosecutors to act effectively and, when necessary, robustly in establishing the new approach

to charging. The danger to be avoided is that of Crown Prosecutors exposed to police station culture 'going native', that is to say, adopting the 'machismo' sometimes associated with policing operations and becoming seduced by policing rather than prosecutorial priorities. Were that to happen to any appreciable extent, then the potential benefits to be gained from the early introduction of more rigorous standards of proof would be lost and one would be left with little more than a doubling up of the custody officer's role.

Having Crown Prosecutors in the police station may well result in more accurate charging, and in the decision whether or not to charge at all being based on a more careful and rigorous analysis of the evidence. Moreover, having CPS involvement during the course of the investigation may help to ensure that the evidence that is gathered is admissible in court. However, one possible disadvantage of this new system is that there might be a risk that, if Crown Prosecutors have more direct involvement at the charging stage (especially if they are based in police stations), some of the independence from the police which is supposed to be a hallmark of the CPS may be lost (reverting to the days before the institution of the CPS, when police forces instructed firms of solicitors to act for them and to prosecute cases on their behalf in court). One of the principles that underpinned the very creation of the CPS by the Prosecution of Offences Act 1985 was that there should be clear separation between the investigators and the prosecutor. Having Crown Prosecutors based in police stations might be regarded as running the risk that they will become infected by what some commentators term 'cop culture', and that they will lose the ability to remain objective and independent as they will be working alongside police colleagues in the fight against crime.

2.3.5.2 Police bail after charge

After a suspect has been charged, he must be released on police bail (with the condition that he must attend a specified magistrates' court on a specified date and at a specified time) unless any of the exceptions contained in s 38 of PACE apply. Under s 38(1)(a), bail may be withheld from a person who has been charged only if:

(i)   his name or address cannot be ascertained or the custody officer has reasonable grounds for doubting whether a name or address furnished by him as his name or address is his real name or address;

(ii) the custody officer has reasonable grounds for believing that the person arrested will fail to appear in court to answer to bail;

(iii) in the case of a person arrested for an imprisonable offence, the custody officer has reasonable grounds for believing that the detention of the person arrested is necessary to prevent him from committing an offence;

. . .

(iv) in the case of a person arrested for an offence which is not an imprisonable offence, the custody officer has reasonable grounds for believing that the detention of the person arrested is necessary to prevent him from causing physical injury to any other person or from causing loss of or damage to property;

(v)   the custody officer has reasonable grounds for believing that the detention of the person arrested is necessary to prevent him from interfering with the administration of justice or with the investigation of offences or of a particular offence; or

(vi) the custody officer has reasonable grounds for believing that the detention of the person arrested is necessary for his own protection.

In deciding whether there is a risk that the defendant will abscond, or commit a further offence, or interfere with witnesses, the custody officer must apply the same criteria as a magistrates' court (s 38(2A) of PACE). These criteria are considered in Chapter 3.

If the suspect is not granted bail under s 38 of PACE, he must be taken before the magistrates' court 'as soon as is practicable and in any event not later than the first sitting after he is charged with the offence' (s 46(2)). For these purposes, Sundays, Christmas Day and Good Friday are disregarded (s 46(8)). The magistrates will then decide whether or not to grant bail, using the criteria laid down in the Bail Act 1976 (set out in Chapter 3).

Section 47(3A) provides that, where a custody officer grants bail to someone who has been charged with an offence, he must specify the date of the person's appearance in the magistrates' court; that date should normally 'be not later than the first sitting of the court after the person is charged with the offence'. This has the effect that the first court appearance of the accused should take place at the next available sitting of the magistrates whether the suspect is released on police bail or not.

2.3.5.3 Imposition of conditions on police bail

Where a person is released on police bail under s 38 of PACE having been charged with an offence, the custody officer has power (under s 3A of the Bail Act 1976) to impose any condition on the grant of bail which a court could impose (with certain exceptions, such as a requirement of residence in a bail hostel). These conditions are considered in Chapter 3.

Section 3A(5) of the Bail Act 1976 says that:

> Where a constable grants bail to a person no conditions shall be imposed . . . unless it appears to the constable that it is necessary to do so—
>
> (a) for the purpose of preventing that person from failing to surrender to custody, or
> (b) for the purpose of preventing that person from committing an offence while on bail, or
> (c) for the purpose of preventing that person from interfering with witnesses or otherwise obstructing the course of justice, whether in relation to himself or any other person, or
> (d) for that person's own protection or, if he is a child or young person, for his own welfare or in his own interests.

Section 3A(4) of the Bail Act 1976 allows a custody officer, at the request of the accused, to vary the conditions of bail which were imposed when the defendant was charged, and adds that 'in doing so he may impose conditions or more onerous conditions'.

Where conditions are attached to police bail, reasons have to be given and recorded (s 5A(2) of the Bail Act 1976). Furthermore, where conditions have been attached to police bail, the defendant may apply to a magistrates' court to vary those conditions (under s 43B(1) of the Magistrates' Courts Act 1980), although it should be borne in mind that the court also has the power to withhold bail altogether or to 'impose more onerous conditions' (s 43B(2)).

2.3.5.4 *Further questioning*

Code C 16.5 provides that, once the suspect has been charged, he cannot be asked any further questions about the offence(s) with which he has been charged unless further questions are necessary:

- to prevent or minimise harm or loss to some other person, or the public;
- to clear up an ambiguity in a previous answer or statement;
- in the interests of justice for the detainee to have put to them, and have an opportunity to comment on, information concerning the offence which has come to light since they were charged or informed they might be prosecuted.

2.3.6 Release without charge on police bail

Sometimes police release a suspect without charge but require him to return to the police station at a later date (for example, for further questioning or to give the police or CPS further time in which to decide whether or not to charge him). In such a case, the suspect is usually released on police bail. Under s 47(1A) of PACE conditions may be imposed where a person is released on bail pending consultation with the CPS.

Where a suspect has been released on police bail with the condition that he should return to the police station on a specified date, he may be arrested without a warrant if he fails to attend the police station at the appointed time: s 46A(1) of PACE. He may also be arrested if the police have reasonable grounds for suspecting that he has broken any conditions of bail (s 46A(1A)).

Section 34(7) of PACE provides that, where a person returns to the police station to answer police bail, including 'street bail' (see above), or is arrested for failing to do so, he is to be regarded as having been arrested for the original offence at that moment. It follows that the suspect is in the same position as a person who is being detained without charge and so the custody timetable (set out below) applies.

2.3.7 Arrest with a warrant

Under s 1 of the Magistrates' Courts Act 1980, a warrant for the suspect's arrest may only be issued following the laying of an information if:

a   the information is in writing (s 1(3)); and
b   either:

  i   the offence to which the warrant relates is an indictable offence or is punishable with imprisonment; or
  ii the person's address is not sufficiently established for a summons or written charge and requisition to be served on him (s 1(4)).

Whereas a magistrate or a justices' clerk may issue a summons, only a magistrate is empowered to issue an arrest warrant. The warrant requires the police to arrest the suspect and take him before the magistrates' court named on the warrant (usually the issuing court).

Where the offence charged is an indictable offence, a warrant may be issued even if a summons or a written charge and requisition have previously been issued (s 1(6)); this would be appropriate if, for example, the documents had been returned by the Royal Mail undelivered.

In practice, it is quite rare for an arrest warrant to be sought as a means of commencing criminal proceedings. The police are able to arrest a suspect for any offence where the criteria in s 24 of PACE are satisfied (so a warrant is unnecessary in the vast majority of cases). In many cases it is preferable to issue a summons or (where it is a public prosecution) to adopt the written charge procedure established by the Criminal Justice Act 2003. If the summons or written charge and requisition cannot be served, the police can then apply to the magistrates' court for an arrest warrant. Indeed, under s 1(6A), where the offence charged is an indictable offence and a written charge and requisition have already been issued, an arrest warrant may be issued by a justice of the peace upon a copy of the written charge (rather than an information) being laid before the justice by a public prosecutor.

2.4 POLICE POWERS OF SEARCH

PACE also contains provisions governing the conduct of police searches of people, vehicles and premises.

2.4.1 Power to stop and search

The power to stop and search is contained in s 1 of PACE. Section 1(1) empowers a police officer to exercise the powers conferred by s 1:

(a) in any place to which at the time when he proposes to exercise the power the public or any section of the public has access, on payment or otherwise, as of right or by virtue of express or implied permission; or

(b) in any other place to which people have ready access at the time when he proposes to exercise the power but which is not a dwelling.

Section 1(2) defines the powers conferred by s 1:

. . . a constable—

(a) may search—

(i) any person or vehicle;
(ii) anything which is in or on a vehicle,

for stolen or prohibited articles, any article to which sub-section (8A) below applies or any firework to which sub-section (8B) below applies; and

(b) may detain a person or vehicle for the purpose of such a search.

The power to search a person or vehicle, or anything in or on a vehicle, arises only if the officer has 'reasonable grounds for suspecting that he will find stolen or prohibited articles', or articles to which sub-ss (8A) or (8B) apply (s 1(3)).

Section 1(6) confers a power of seizure if, in the course of the search, the officer discovers an article which he has reasonable grounds for suspecting to be a stolen or prohibited article, or an article to which sub-ss (8A) or (8B) applies.

The term 'prohibited article' is defined, by s 1(7). It encompasses offensive weapons (defined in sub-s (9) as articles made or adapted for use for causing injury to persons, or intended by the person having it with him for such use by him or by some other person) and articles which are made or adapted for use in the course of or in connection with (or intended by the person having it with him for such use by him or by some other person) the offences listed in sub-s (8), namely burglary, theft, taking a motor vehicle without authority, fraud, criminal damage. Sub-section (8A) extends the ambit of s 1 to articles related to offences under s 139 of the Criminal Justice Act 1988 (bladed articles), and sub-s (8B) extends it to fireworks which a person possesses in contravention of a prohibition imposed by fireworks regulations.

Sections 2 and 3 of PACE set out detailed rules regarding the procedure to be followed by a police officer when exercising the powers conferred by s 1 and the details that have to be recorded. Failure to comply with these provisions may make an otherwise lawful search unlawful, and thereby deprive police officers who face resistance of the protection afforded by the offence of assaulting a constable acting in the execution of his duty. Section 2(3), for example, requires a constable conducting a search to inform the person to be searched (before the search commences) of his name and police station, the object of the proposed search, and the grounds for making it. Failure to do so renders the search unlawful, and the illegality is not cured either by the fact that the search was reasonable (*Osman v DPP* (1999) 163 JP 725).

Home Office circular 60/2003 (<http://www.knowledgenetwork.gov.uk/HO/circular.nsf/79755433dd36a66980256d4f004d1514/FF423F4013D2202780256DF8003036FC/$file/CJ%20Act%20Guidance%2010-12-03.doc>) emphasises that the stop and search powers must be used 'fairly, objectively, and without any bias against ethnic or other groups within the community' (para 1.5).

Code of Practice A (issued under PACE), sets out detailed rules regulating the exercise of these powers of stop and search. It includes the following:

1.1 Powers to stop and search must be used fairly, responsibly, with respect for people being searched and without unlawful discrimination. The Race Relations (Amendment) Act 2000 makes it unlawful for police officers to discriminate on the grounds of race, colour, ethnic origin, nationality or national origins when using their powers.

...

1.4 The primary purpose of stop and search powers is to enable officers to allay or confirm suspicions about individuals without exercising their power of arrest. Officers may be required to justify the use or authorisation of such powers, in relation both to individual searches and the overall pattern of their activity in this regard, to their supervisory officers or in court. Any misuse of the powers is likely to be harmful to policing and lead to mistrust of the police. Officers must also be able to explain their actions to the member of the public searched. The misuse of these powers can lead to disciplinary action.

1.5 An officer must not search a person, even with his or her consent, where no power to search is applicable. Even where a person is prepared to submit to a search voluntarily, the person must not be searched unless the necessary legal power exists, and the search must be in accordance with the relevant power and the provisions of this code . . .

2.2 Reasonable grounds for suspicion depend on the circumstances in each case. There must be an objective basis for that suspicion based on facts, information, and/or intelligence which are relevant to the likelihood of finding an article of a certain kind . . . Reasonable suspicion can never be supported on the basis of personal factors alone without reliable supporting intelligence or information or some specific behaviour by the person concerned. For example, a person's race, age, appearance, or the fact that the person is known to have a previous conviction, cannot be used alone or in combination with each other as the reason for searching that person. Reasonable suspicion cannot be based on generalisations or stereotypical images of certain groups or categories of people as more likely to be involved in criminal activity.

2.3 Reasonable suspicion can sometimes exist without specific information or intelligence and on the basis of some level of generalisation stemming from the behaviour of a person. For example, if an officer encounters someone on the street at night who is obviously trying to hide something, the officer may (depending on the other surrounding circumstances) base such suspicion on the fact that this kind of behaviour is often linked to stolen or prohibited articles being carried . . .

2.4 However, reasonable suspicion should normally be linked to accurate and current intelligence or information, such as information describing an article being carried, a suspected offender, or a person who has been seen carrying a type of article known to have been stolen recently from premises in the area. Searches based on accurate and current intelligence or information are more likely to be effective. Targeting searches in a particular area at specified crime problems increases their effectiveness and minimises inconvenience to law-abiding members of the public. It also helps in justifying the use of searches both to those who are searched and to the general public. This does not however prevent stop and search powers being exercised in other locations where such powers may be exercised and reasonable suspicion exists.

. . .

2.6 Where there is reliable information or intelligence that members of a group or gang habitually carry knives unlawfully or weapons or controlled drugs, and wear a distinctive item of clothing or other means of identification to indicate their membership of the group or gang, that distinctive item of clothing or other means of identification may provide reasonable grounds to stop and search a person.

. . .

2.10 If, as a result of questioning before a search, or other circumstances which come to the attention of the officer, there cease to be reasonable grounds for suspecting that an article is being carried of a kind for which there is a power to stop and search, no search may take place. In the absence of any other lawful power to detain, the person is free to leave at will and must be so informed.

2.11 There is no power to stop or detain a person in order to find grounds for a search. Police officers have many encounters with members of the public which do not involve detaining people against their will. If reasonable grounds for suspicion emerge during such an encounter, the officer may search the person, even though no grounds existed when the encounter began. If an officer is detaining someone for the purpose of a search, he or she should inform the person as soon as detention begins.

. . .

4.1 An officer who has carried out a search in the exercise of any power to which this code applies, must make a record of it at the time, unless there are exceptional circumstances which would make this wholly impracticable (e.g. in situations involving public disorder or when the officer's presence is urgently required elsewhere). If a record is not made at the time, the officer must do so as soon as practicable afterwards. There may be situations in which it is not practicable to obtain the information necessary to complete a record, but the officer should make every reasonable effort to do so.

4.2 A copy of a record made at the time must be given immediately to the person who has been searched . . .

4.6 The record of the grounds for making a search must, briefly but informatively, explain the reason for suspecting the person concerned, by reference to the person's behaviour and/or other circumstances.

. . .

5.1 Supervising officers must monitor the use of stop and search powers and should consider in particular whether there is any evidence that they are being exercised on the basis of stereotyped images or inappropriate generalisations. Supervising officers should satisfy themselves that the practice of officers under their supervision in stopping, searching and recording is fully in accordance with this code. Supervisors must also examine whether the records reveal any trends or patterns which give cause for concern, and if so take appropriate action to address this.

. . .

5.3 Supervision and monitoring must be supported by the compilation of comprehensive statistical records of stops and searches at force, area and local level. Any apparently disproportionate use of the powers by particular officers or groups of officers or in relation to specific sections of the community should be identified and investigated.

5.4 In order to promote public confidence in the use of the powers, forces in consultation with police authorities must make arrangements for the records to be scrutinised by representatives of the community, and to explain the use of the powers at a local level.

Ed Cape, in 'The Revised PACE Codes of Practice: a Further Step Towards Inquisitorialism' [2003] Crim LR 355, noted that much of the research on the PACE powers of stop and search (including Brown, D, *PACE Ten Years on: a Review of the Research*, Home Office Research Study 155, 1997, chapter 2) has questioned the efficacy of the provisions, and points out that the MacPherson Report concluded that the 'perception and experience of the minority communities that discrimination is a major element in the stop and search problem is correct' (*Report of the Stephen Lawrence Inquiry*, Cm 4262, para 45.8).

MacPherson recommended that all 'stops', as well as 'stops and searches', should be recorded; that the recording requirements be extended to 'voluntary' stops and searches; and that the records should be monitored and scrutinised and the results published (recommendations 61–63). These recommendations were accepted by the Government, and a new section was added to Code A (A4.11–4.20) to set out the procedures to be followed for recording encounters where a police officer requests a person in a public place to account for themselves (actions, behaviour, presence in the area, possession of anything). Recorded details must include the reason why the officer questioned the person, the person's ethnicity and the outcome of the encounter.

2.4.2 Searching premises

It may also be necessary for the police to enter and search premises. Usually a search warrant is required, but there are circumstances where the police can proceed without a warrant.

2.4.2.1 Entry with a warrant

Entry *with* a warrant is governed by s 8 of PACE. Section 8(1) enables a justice of the peace, following an application by a police officer, to grant a warrant authorising the police to enter and search premises if there are reasonable grounds for believing that:

- an indictable offence has been committed (this includes either-way offences);
- there is material on the premises which is likely to be of substantial value to the investigation of the offence;
- the material is likely to be relevant evidence (defined in sub-s (4) as 'anything that would be admissible in evidence at a trial for the offence');
- the material does not consist of or include items subject to 'legal privilege', 'excluded material' or 'special procedure material' (see below); and
- any of the conditions specified in sub-s (3) are satisfied, namely that it is not practicable to communicate with any person entitled to grant entry to the premises (or to grant access to the evidence), or entry to the premises will not be granted unless a warrant is produced, or the purpose of a search may be frustrated or seriously prejudiced unless the police can secure immediate entry to the premises. In *Redknapp v Metropolitan Police Commissioner* [2008] EWHC 1177 (Admin), it was held that if the application for the warrant does not identify which of the conditions in s 8(3) is being relied on, the issue of the warrant will be unlawful.

Under s 8(1A), the magistrate may grant a 'specific premises warrant' or an 'all premises warrant'. Section 8(1B) provides that where the application is for an 'all premises warrant', the magistrate must also be satisfied the nature of the offence under investigation is such that it is necessary to search premises occupied or controlled by the person in question which are not specified in the application and that it is not reasonably practicable to specify in the application all the premises which he occupies or controls and which might need to be searched. A single warrant may include both types, provided that the relevant information is given to the magistrate (*Redknapp*).

Under s 8(1C), the search warrant may authorise entry to, and search of, premises on more than one occasion if the magistrate is satisfied that it is necessary to authorise multiple entries in order to achieve the purpose for which the warrant is issued. If the warrant authorises multiple entries, the number of entries authorised may be unlimited, or limited to a maximum (sub-s (1D)). Under s 15(5), a warrant authorises entry on one occasion only unless it specifically authorises multiple entries; if it specifies that it authorises multiple entries, it must also specify whether the number of entries authorised is unlimited, or limited to a specified maximum (s 15(5A)).

Section 8(2) empowers the police to seize and retain anything for which a search has been authorised under sub-s (1).

Under s 15 of PACE, the police officer applying for the warrant has to set out the grounds on which he makes the application (sub-s (2)(a)(i)) and to identify, so far as is practicable, the material to be sought (sub-s (2)(c)). The application for such a search warrant is made *ex parte* and must be supported by an 'information' in writing (subs (3)). The officer must answer on oath any question that the magistrate hearing the application asks him (sub-s (4)).

Section 50 of the Criminal Justice and Police Act 2001 empowers a person who is lawfully on premises, and who is authorised to search for something, to seize anything which he has reasonable grounds for believing to be something for which he may search and which he is empowered to seize. This enables him to seize the article and remove it from the premises for the purpose of determining whether it falls within the ambit of the search. It is a condition of exercise of this power that it is not reasonably practicable to make this determination on the premises (s 50(1)).

Rules regarding the execution of the search warrant are set out in s 16 of PACE. Under s 16(4), entry and search under a warrant 'must be at a reasonable hour unless it appears to the constable executing it that the purpose of a search may be frustrated on an entry at a reasonable hour'. A search under a warrant 'may only be a search to the extent required for the purpose for which the warrant was issued' (sub-s (8)).

Section 16(2A) enables any person authorised in the warrant to accompany the police when executing the warrant to search for and seize property. This enables civilians to take an active role in search and seizure operations. However, civilians may only exercise those powers in the company, and under the supervision, of a police officer (s 16(2B)).

If the warrant is an 'all premises' warrant, premises which are not specified in it may be entered or searched only if an officer of at least the rank of Inspector has given written authorisation (sub-s (3A)). No premises may be entered or searched for a second or subsequent time under a warrant which authorises multiple entries unless an officer of at least the rank of Inspector has given written authorisation (sub-s (3B)).

2.4.2.2 Entry without a warrant

There are also statutory provisions which enable the police to enter premises *without* a warrant. These provisions include ss 17 and 18 of PACE.

Section 17 of PACE empowers the police to enter and search premises in order to:

- execute an arrest warrant,
- arrest someone for an indictable offence (this includes either-way offences),
- arrest someone for an offence specified in sub-s 1(c)),
- recapture a person who is unlawfully at large,
- save life or limb, or
- prevent serious damage to property.

Under s 17(4), the power of search conferred by s 17 is limited to a power 'to search to the extent that is reasonably required for the purpose for which the power of entry is exercised'.

Section 18(1) of PACE allows a police officer to enter and search any premises occupied or controlled by a person who is under arrest for an indictable offence, if the officer has reasonable grounds to suspect that there is on the premises evidence relating to the offence for which the suspect has been arrested or to some other indictable offence which is 'connected with, or similar to, that offence'. The officer may seize and retain anything for which he may search under sub-s (1), but the scope of the search must be restricted to whatever is 'reasonably required for the purpose of discovering such evidence' (s 18(2), (3)). Premises must be occupied or controlled by the person under arrest if a search under s 18 of the 1984 Act is to be lawful; a reasonable belief that the premises are so occupied or controlled is not sufficient (*Khan v Metropolitan Police Commissioner* (2008), Court of Appeal, June 4).

Normally, such a search should be authorised in writing by an officer of at least the rank of Inspector (s 18(4)). However, a search may take place without such authorisation and without taking the suspect to the police station first if his presence at some other place is 'necessary for the effective investigation of the offence' (s 18(5), (5A)).

Code of Practice B (issued under PACE), sets out detailed rules regulating the exercise of these powers of entry and search. Para 1.3 says that officers 'should consider if the necessary objectives can be met by less intrusive means', and para 1.4 says that the police should 'exercise their powers courteously and with respect for persons and property' and should 'only use reasonable force when this is considered necessary and proportionate to the circumstances'.

2.4.2.3 Legal privilege

Material which is subject to 'legal privilege' is protected from the search and seizure provisions of PACE. Such material is defined by s 10(1):

(a) communications between a professional legal adviser and his client or any person representing his client made in connection with the giving of legal advice to the client;

(b) communications between a professional legal adviser and his client or any person representing his client or between such an adviser or his client or any such representative and any other person made in connection with or in contemplation of legal proceedings and for the purposes of such proceedings; and

(c) items enclosed with or referred to in such communications and made:

(i) in connection with the giving of legal advice; or

(ii) in connection with or in contemplation of legal proceedings and for the purposes of such proceedings,

when they are in the possession of a person who is entitled to possession of them.

Sub-section (2) adds the proviso that items 'held with the intention of furthering a criminal purpose are not items subject to legal privilege'.

2.4.2.4 'Excluded' and 'special procedure' material

Section 9(2) excludes from the scope of search warrants items subject to legal privilege, 'excluded material', and 'special procedure material'. The police can only gain access to 'excluded material' or 'special procedure material' by obtaining a warrant from a judge (a circuit judge or a district judge) under s 9(1) of PACE.

'Excluded material' is defined by s 11(1) of PACE. It includes:

(a)   personal records which a person has acquired or created in the course of any trade, business, profession or other occupation or for the purposes of any paid or unpaid office and which he holds in confidence;

...

(c)   journalistic material which a person holds in confidence and which consists:

(i)   of documents; or
(ii)   of records other than documents.

'Special procedure' material is defined by s 14. Under s 14(1), it includes journalistic material, other than excluded material, and material described in sub-s (2), namely material, other than items subject to legal privilege and excluded material, in the possession of a person who 'acquired or created it in the course of any trade, business, profession or other occupation or for the purpose of any paid or unpaid office' and which he holds in confidence.

The procedure for applying to a judge for access to 'excluded' or 'special procedure' material under s 9 is set out in Sched 1. The judge may only make an access order (under para 4) if satisfied on the balance of probabilities that one of the sets of access conditions is fulfilled. The first set of access conditions (Sched 1, para 2) requires that:

(a)   there are reasonable grounds for believing—

(i)   that an indictable offence has been committed;
(ii)   that there is material which consists of special procedure material or also includes special procedure material and does not also include excluded material on premises specified in the application, or on premises occupied or controlled by a person specified in the application (including all such premises on which there are reasonable grounds for believing that there is such material as it is reasonably practicable so to specify);
(iii)   that the material is likely to be of substantial value (whether by itself or together with other material) to the investigation in connection with which the application is made; and
(iv)   that the material is likely to be relevant evidence;

(b)   other methods of obtaining the material—

(i)   have been tried without success; or
(ii)   have not been tried because it appeared that they were bound to fail; and

(c)   it is in the public interest, having regard—

(i)   to the benefit likely to accrue to the investigation if the material is obtained; and

(ii) to the circumstances under which the person in possession of the material holds it,

that the material should be produced or that access to it should be given.

The second set of access conditions (Sched 1, para 3) requires that there be reasonable grounds for believing that there is excluded or special procedure material on the premises, in respect of which a magistrate would have had power to grant a search warrant but for the removal of that power by s 9(2), and that the issue of such a warrant would have been appropriate.

A judge also has the power to issue a warrant authorising a constable to enter and search premises (Sched 1, para 12). The judge must be satisfied that the second set of access conditions (see previous paragraph) is fulfilled and that there has been a failure to comply with an access order (para 12(b)).

Under para 12(a), a judge may also issue a warrant to enter and search premises if satisfied that either set of access conditions is fulfilled and that any of the conditions set out in para 14 are also fulfilled; those conditions include the following:

(a) that it is not practicable to communicate with any person entitled to grant entry to the premises;
(b) that it is practicable to communicate with a person entitled to grant entry to the premises but it is not practicable to communicate with any person entitled to grant access to the material;

. . .

(d) that service of notice of an application for an order under paragraph 4 . . . may seriously prejudice the investigation.

2.4.2.5 Use of reasonable force

Section 117 of PACE confers upon the police the power to use reasonable force when exercising these powers. It provides that:

Where any provision of this Act

(a) confers a power on a constable; and
(b) does not provide that the power may only be exercised with the consent of some person, other than a police officer,

the officer may use reasonable force, if necessary, in the exercise of the power.

A police officer who is exercising a statutory power to enter someone's home by the use of the reasonable force should explain the reason for exercising that power of entry to any occupant unless it is impracticable to do so (*O'Loughlin v Chief Constable of Essex* [1998] 1 WLR 374). It is reasonable, for the purpose of s 117, that police officers executing a search warrant should seek, by no more force than necessary, to restrict the movement of those in occupation of premises while those premises are being searched (*DPP v Meaden* [2003] EWHC 3005; [2004] 1 WLR 945).

2.5 IDENTIFICATION EVIDENCE

The gathering of identification evidence is governed by Code D of the PACE Codes. Detailed discussion of these matters is outside the scope of the present work, but it may be useful to note some of the key provisions of Code D, which include the following:

(a) Cases when the suspect's identity is not known

3.2 In cases when the suspect's identity is not known, a witness may be taken to a particular neighbourhood or place to see whether they can identify the person they saw. Although the number, age, sex, race, general description and style of clothing of other people present at the location and the way in which any identification is made cannot be controlled, the principles applicable to the formal procedures under paragraphs 3.5 to 3.10 shall be followed as far as practicable. For example:

    (a) Where it is practicable to do so, a record should be made of the witness' description of the suspect, before asking the witness to make an identification;

    (b) Care must be taken not to direct the witness's attention to any individual unless, taking into account all the circumstances, this cannot be avoided. However, this does not prevent a witness being asked to look carefully at the people around at the time or to look towards a group or in a particular direction, if this appears necessary to make sure that the witness does not overlook a possible suspect simply because the witness is looking in the opposite direction and also to enable the witness to make comparisons between any suspect and others who are in the area;

    (c) Where there is more than one witness, every effort should be made to keep them separate and witnesses should be taken to see whether they can identify a person independently;

    (d) Once there is sufficient information to justify the arrest of a particular individual for suspected involvement in the offence, e.g., after a witness makes a positive identification, the provisions set out from paragraph 3.4 onwards shall apply for any other witnesses in relation to that individual. Subject to paragraphs 3.12 and 3.13, it is not necessary for the witness who makes such a positive identification to take part in a further procedure;

    (e) The officer or police staff accompanying the witness must record, in their pocket book, the action taken as soon as, and in as much detail, as possible. The record should include: the date, time and place of the relevant occasion the witness claims to have previously seen the suspect; where any identification was made; how it was made and the conditions at the time (e.g., the distance the witness was from the suspect, the weather and light); if the witness's attention was drawn to the suspect; the reason for this; and anything said by the witness or the suspect about the identification or the conduct of the procedure.

3.3 A witness must not be shown photographs, computerised or artist's composite likenesses or similar likenesses or pictures (including 'e-fit' images) if the identity of the suspect is known to the police and the suspect is available to take part in a video identification, an identification parade or a group identification . . .

(b) Cases when the suspect is known and available

3.4 If the suspect's identity is known to the police and they are available, the identification procedures set out in paragraphs 3.5 to 3.10 may be used. References in this section to a suspect being 'known' mean there is sufficient information known to the police to justify the arrest of a particular person for suspected involvement in the offence. A suspect being 'available' means they are immediately available or will be within a reasonably short time and willing to take an effective part in at least one of the following which it is practicable to arrange:

- video identification;
- identification parade; or
- group identification.

. . .

Video identification

3.5 A 'video identification' is when the witness is shown moving images of a known suspect, together with similar images of others who resemble the suspect. Moving images must be used unless:

- the suspect is known but not available; or
- . . . the identification officer does not consider that replication of a physical feature can be achieved or that it is not possible to conceal the location of the feature on the image of the suspect.

The identification officer may then decide to make use of video identification but using still images.

. . .

Identification parade

3.7 An 'identification parade' is when the witness sees the suspect in a line of others who resemble the suspect.

. . .

Group Identification

3.9 A 'group identification' is when the witness sees the suspect in an informal group of people.

. . .

Circumstances in which an identification procedure must be held

3.12 Whenever:

(i) a witness has identified a suspect or purported to have identified them prior to any identification procedure set out in paragraphs 3.5 to 3.10 having been held; or

(ii) there is a witness available, who expresses an ability to identify the suspect, or where there is a reasonable chance of the witness being able to do so, and they have not been given an opportunity to identify the suspect in any of the procedures set out in paragraphs 3.5 to 3.10, and the suspect disputes being the person the witness claims to have seen, an identification procedure shall be held unless it is not practicable or it would serve no useful purpose in proving or disproving whether the suspect was involved in committing the offence. For example, when it is not disputed that the suspect is already well known to the witness who claims to have seen them commit the crime.

3.13 Such a procedure may also be held if the officer in charge of the investigation considers it would be useful.

Selecting an identification procedure

3.14 If, because of paragraph 3.12, an identification procedure is to be held, the suspect shall initially be offered a video identification unless:

(a) a video identification is not practicable; or
(b) an identification parade is both practicable and more suitable than a video identification; or
(c) paragraph 3.16 applies.

The identification officer and the officer in charge of the investigation shall consult each other to determine which option is to be offered. An identification parade may not be practicable because of factors relating to the witnesses, such as their number, state of health, availability and travelling requirements. A video identification would normally be more suitable if it could be arranged and completed sooner than an identification parade.

3.15 A suspect who refuses the identification procedure first offered shall be asked to state their reason for refusing and may get advice from their solicitor and/or, if present, their appropriate adult. The suspect, solicitor and/or appropriate adult shall be allowed to make representations about why another procedure should be used. A record should be made of the reasons for refusal and any representations made. After considering any reasons given, and representations made, the identification officer shall, if appropriate, arrange for the suspect to be offered an alternative that the officer considers suitable and practicable. If the officer decides it is not suitable and practicable to offer an alternative identification procedure, the reasons for that decision shall be recorded.

3.16 A group identification may initially be offered if the officer in charge of the investigation considers it is more suitable than a video identification or an identification parade and the identification officer considers it practicable to arrange.

It is clear from the Code that 'video identification' (rather than the traditional identity parade) is now the preferred option. The set of images used must include the suspect and at least eight other persons who, so far as possible, resemble the suspect in age, height, general appearance and position in life (see Annex A, para 1).

Where an identification parade takes place, it should consist of at least eight people (in addition to the suspect) who so far as possible resemble the suspect in age, height, general appearance and position in life (see Annex B, para 9). The participants stand in line and each one must be clearly numbered. Witnesses are brought in one at a time (para 13); they are told that the person they saw may or may not be on the parade and that, if they cannot make a positive identification, they should say so (para 16). In *R v Quinn* [1995] 1 Cr App R 480, the Court of Appeal said that if the Code of Practice on identification procedures is not complied with, a conviction based on such evidence may well be quashed.

2.6 ALTERNATIVES TO PROSECUTION

The fact that the police or CPS believe that there is sufficient evidence to justify prosecuting someone for an offence does not necessarily mean that the person will be prosecuted. An adult offender may be cautioned instead (in the case of a juvenile, a reprimand or warning may be issued).

In *R (U) v Commissioner of Police of the Metropolis* [2002] EWHC 2486 (Admin) [2003] 1 WLR 897, Latham LJ (at para 37), said that alternatives to prosecution:

> provide significant advantages both to the public, and to the individual offender. They constitute a sensible means of ensuring that resources are not wasted on cases where the paraphernalia of the court appearance is unnecessary given the character of the individual and the nature of the charge . . . From the offender's point of view, it results in the matter being dealt with expeditiously and does not result in a conviction, which undoubtedly has more serious consequences than a caution, reprimand or final warning.

When the case went to the House of Lords ([2005] UKHL 21; [2005] 1 WLR 1184), no disagreement with this dictum was expressed.

2.6.1 Adults

In the case of an adult offender, a 'caution' may be administered instead of the case going to court. This caution is not to be confused with the warning given before questioning; rather, it is a warning that committing a further offence will result in court action.

The arrangements for cautions of adults are set out in Home Office Circular 30/2005 (<http://www.knowledgenetwork.gov.uk/HO/circular.nsf/79755433dd36a66980256d4f-004d1514/d820bbad9e5edd8680257013004d1ccf?OpenDocument>). This refers to cautions for adults as 'simple cautions' (to distinguish them from 'conditional cautions' under the CJA 2003). Paragraph 6 of the Circular sets out the aims of the simple caution, namely:

- to deal quickly and simply with less serious offences;
- to divert offenders where appropriate from appearing in the criminal courts; and
- to reduce the likelihood of re-offending.

Paragraph 7 of the Circular sets out the criteria for giving a simple caution:

> In considering whether a Simple Caution is appropriate, a police officer must consider the following facts:
>
> - Is there sufficient evidence of the suspect's guilt to meet the Threshold Test (as outlined in the Director's Guidance)?

- Is the offence indictable only (and the available evidence meets the Threshold Test)? If the answer is 'yes', this disposal option must be referred to a Crown Prosecutor.
- Has the suspect made a clear and reliable admission of the offence (either verbally or in writing)? An admission of the offence, corroborated by some other material and significant evidential fact will be sufficient evidence to provide a realistic prospect of conviction. This corroboration could be obtained from information in the crime report or obtained during the course of the investigation. A Simple Caution will not be appropriate where a person has not made a clear and reliable admission of the offence (for example if intent is denied or there are doubts about their mental health or intellectual capacity, or where a statutory defence is offered).
- Is it in the public interest to use a Simple Caution as the appropriate means of disposal? Officers should take into account the public interest principles set out in the Code for Crown Prosecutors . . .
- Is the suspect 18 years or over? Where a suspect is under 18, a reprimand or final warning would be the equivalent disposal.

If all the above requirements are met, the officer must consider whether the seriousness of the offence makes it appropriate for disposal by a Simple Caution.

Paragraphs 11 to 16 of the Circular address the role of the victim in this process. Paragraph 11 says:

Before a Simple Caution can be given, it is important to try to establish:

- the views of the victim about the offence;
- the nature and extent of any harm or loss, and its significance, relative to the victim's circumstances;
- whether the offender has made any form of reparation or paid compensation (although this would not be appropriate in some cases, such as offences of violence). Police officers should not become involved in negotiating or awarding reparation or compensation.

Paragraph 15 contains an important rider:

In all circumstances where the views of victims are sought, care should be taken to ensure they are aware that although their views will be taken into account, they will not necessarily be conclusive to the outcome, as the final decision is at the discretion of the police and/or the CPS.

The Circular then lists a number of other important considerations, including the following:

17. *Does the suspect have any other cautions for similar offences?*
If the suspect has previously received a caution, then a further Simple Caution should not normally be considered. However, if there has been a sufficient lapse of time to suggest that a previous caution has had a significant deterrent effect (two years or more) then a Simple Caution can be administered. A Simple Caution can also still be administered if the subsequent offence is trivial or unrelated, or as part of a mixed disposal . . . If the suspect has previously received a Reprimand or Final Warning [when a juvenile], a period of two years should also be allowed to elapse before administering a Simple Caution.

18. *Has the suspect been made aware of the significance of a Simple Caution?*
If a Simple Caution is being considered, then the full implications must be explained to the suspect ... Under no circumstances should suspects be pressed, or induced in any way to admit offences in order to receive a Simple Caution as an alternative to being charged.

19. *Has the suspect given informed consent to being cautioned?*
If the suspect does not consent, then police may choose to continue with a prosecution. Officers must avoid any suggestion that accepting a Simple Caution is an 'easy option'. Similarly, every effort must be made to avoid any suggestion of the suspect being coerced into accepting a Simple Caution.

Paragraphs 21–23 require the approval of a decision to administer a caution:

21. When considering the suitability of an offence for disposal by Simple Caution, the decision should be referred to an officer of at least Sergeant rank (who may or may not be a Custody Officer) for approval. This officer must be unrelated to the investigation of the offence.
22. Once the approving officer is satisfied that the requirements for administering a Simple Caution have been met, they should give further consideration to:

    • if a Simple Caution is appropriate to the offence and the offender; and
    • if it is in the public interest to deal with the offence in this way.

23. Officers should take into account the public interest principles set out in the Code for Crown Prosecutors. Officers should not opt to take no further action (NFA) in circumstances in which the requirements of a Simple Caution are met.

Paragraph 26 sets out the process for administering a simple caution:

After the Simple Caution has been approved, it should be administered by someone who is suitably trained for this purpose and to whom the relevant authority has been delegated. This should not delay a person's release from custody where a suitable person is not immediately available. In these circumstances an officer of Inspector rank or above may determine an appropriate person to deliver the Simple Caution.

• Wherever possible, Simple Cautions should be administered at the police station. In exceptional circumstances, they could be administered at another suitable place, for example at the home of an elderly or vulnerable offender in the presence of a friend, relative or other appropriate adult.
• The suspect should not be pressed to make an instant decision on whether to accept the Simple Caution. They should be allowed to consider the matter, and if need be, take independent advice. In order to facilitate this, a suspect may be required to attend at a later date to enable the Simple Caution to be administered. Cautions clinics/surgeries are held in some areas as a means of streamlining and ensuring adequate supervision of the cautioning process.
• Once the Simple Caution has been administered, the offender should sign a form accepting the terms of the caution and should be given a copy of a caution acceptance pro-forma to take away. The pro-forma should include the offender's personal details (including occupation) and should outline the details of the offence. It should also

include information on the consequences of accepting a caution, as below. The form must explain that the offender's details can be passed to the victim, should they wish to pursue civil proceedings. The offender should sign to say that the terms of the Simple Caution are agreed, and the person administering the Simple Caution should also sign.

A simple caution does not count as a conviction but it must be entered on the police national computer and, if given for a 'recordable' offence, may be cited in court in any subsequent court proceedings and should be quoted on a Standard or Enhanced Disclosure issued by the Criminal Records Bureau and thus can be made known to a prospective employer. Where the offence is listed in Sched 3 to the Sexual Offences Act 2003, accepting a simple caution results in the offender becoming a 'relevant offender' for the purposes of the notification and registration requirements of Pt 2 of that Act (the so-called 'sex offenders register').

If a formal caution is administered in breach of the Home Office guidelines, then judicial review may be sought to quash the caution and have it deleted from police records. In *R v Metropolitan Police Commissioner ex p Thompson* [1997] 1 WLR 1519, Schiemann LJ said (at p 1521) that:

> judicial review is available as a remedy in respect of a caution; that this court will not invariably interfere, even in the case of a clear breach of the guidelines relating to the administration of cautions, as the availability of a remedy is a matter for the discretion of the court; that police officers responsible for applying the Home Office Circular which sets out the guidelines 'must enjoy a wide margin of appreciation as to the nature of the case and whether the preconditions for a caution are satisfied'; and that it will be a rare case where a person who has been cautioned will succeed in showing that the decision was fatally flawed by a clear breach of the Guidelines.

Where the suspect makes a clear and unequivocal admission, it is acceptable to administer a formal caution (as an alternative to commencing a prosecution) even if the admission was not obtained in an interview complying with Code C of the Codes of Practice; however, as a matter of good practice, the police should ensure that a formal interview (complying with Code C) takes place (*R v Chief Constable of Lancashire Constabulary ex p Atkinson* (1998) 192 JP 275). In *R (Wyman) v Chief Constable of Hampshire Constabulary* [2006] EWHC 1904 (Admin), the Divisional Court held that there must be clear and reliable evidence of a voluntary admission before a caution can be given, and the admission must relate to all the ingredients of the offence.

Normally, where someone has been cautioned for an offence, they will not subsequently be prosecuted for that same offence. In *Jones v Whalley* [2006] UKHL 41; [2007] 1 AC 63, the House of Lords held that it is an abuse of the court's process for a private prosecution to be brought against a person after he has accepted a formal caution by the police on the express assurance that, if he agrees to be cautioned, he will not have to go before a criminal court in connection with the offence.

It should also be borne in mind that the DPP has power under the Prosecution of Offences Act 1985 to take over and terminate a private prosecution if it is in the public interest to do so.

A caution is a criminal matter within s 18(1) of the Supreme Court Act 1981 (which provides that no appeal lies to the Court of Appeal from any judgment of the High

Court in any criminal cause or matter), and so the Court of Appeal has no jurisdiction to entertain an appeal from the decision of the High Court in judicial review proceedings challenging the lawfulness of the caution; the only appeal, therefore, is to the House of Lords, provided that there is a question of law raising a point of public importance (*R (Aru) v Chief Constable of Merseyside* [2004] EWCA Civ 199; [2004] 1 WLR 1697).

2.6.2 Conditional cautions

Part 3 of the Criminal Justice Act 2003 introduced 'conditional cautions'. Section 22 of the act defines conditional cautions and says who can administer them. It states:

(1) An authorised person may give a conditional caution to a person aged 18 or over ('the offender') if each of the five requirements in section 23 is satisfied.

(2) In this Part 'conditional caution' means a caution which is given in respect of an offence committed by the offender and which has conditions attached to it with which the offender must comply.

(3) The conditions which may be attached to such a caution are those which have one or more of the following objects—

    (a) facilitating the rehabilitation of the offender;

    (b) ensuring that the offender makes reparation for the offence;

    (c) punishing the offender.

(3A) The conditions which may be attached to a conditional caution include—

    (a) (subject to section 23A) a condition that the offender pay a financial penalty;

    (b) a condition that the offender attend at a specified place at specified times.

    'Specified' means specified by a relevant prosecutor.

(3B) Conditions attached by virtue of sub-section (3A)(b) may not require the offender to attend for more than 20 hours in total, not including any attendance required by conditions attached for the purpose of facilitating the offender's rehabilitation.

. . .

(4) In this Part 'authorised person' means—

    (a) a constable,

    (b) an investigating officer, or

    (c) a person authorised by a relevant prosecutor for the purposes of this section.

The term 'relevant prosecutor' is defined as including the Attorney General, the Director of the Serious Fraud Office, the Director of Revenue and Customs Prosecutions, and the Director of Public Prosecutions (s 27). The inclusion of the DPP means that all Crown Prosecutors fall within the definition.

In 2004, a Code of Practice on conditional cautions was issued under s 25 of the Criminal Justice Act 2003 (<http://www.cps.gov.uk/Publications/others/conditional-cautioning04.html>). Paragraph 1.2 of the Code notes that the key to determining whether a conditional caution should be given, instead of prosecution or a simple caution, is whether the imposition of specified conditions will be an appropriate and effective means of addressing an offender's behaviour or making reparation for the effects of the offence on the victim or the community. Paragraph 2.2 of the Code goes on to note that:

> The simple caution will remain available as a disposal, and may be appropriate in cases where no suitable conditions readily suggest themselves, or where prosecution would not be in the public interest, or where the suspect has forestalled what would otherwise have been a suitable condition by (for example) paying compensation to the victim (and can establish that he has done so). For those offences for which there is the option of issuing a fixed penalty notice, that will generally be the appropriate disposal unless such a notice has previously been issued to the offender, in which case a Conditional Caution might be more suitable.

Before a conditional caution can be administered, each of five requirements must be satisfied (in addition to the requirement that the offender must have attained the age of 18). These requirements are set out in s 23 of the Act:

(1) The first requirement is that the authorised person has evidence that the offender has committed an offence.

(2) The second requirement is that a relevant prosecutor decides—

    (a) that there is sufficient evidence to charge the offender with the offence, and
    (b) that a conditional caution should be given to the offender in respect of the offence.

(3) The third requirement is that the offender admits to the authorised person that he committed the offence.

(4) The fourth requirement is that the authorised person explains the effect of the conditional caution to the offender and warns him that failure to comply with any of the conditions attached to the caution may result in his being prosecuted for the offence.

(5) The fifth requirement is that the offender signs a document which contains—

    (a) details of the offence,
    (b) an admission by him that he committed the offence,
    (c) his consent to being given the conditional caution, and
    (d) the conditions attached to the caution.

Paragraph 4.1 of the Code says that, in order to avoid any suggestion that an admission has been obtained by offering an inducement, the prospect of a conditional caution should not be mentioned until the suspect has made a clear and reliable admission, in an interview under caution, to all the elements of the offence. Paragraph 4.1.ii says that it is necessary that, at the time the conditional caution is administered, the offender admits to the authorised person that he committed the offence (in addition to having admitted it in interview). Offenders should be advised of their right to seek legal advice to ensure they give informed consent to both the caution and the conditions, whether or not they have availed themselves of legal advice at an earlier stage.

Paragraph 4.1.iii of the Code makes it clear that there should not be any bargaining with the offender over the conditions – if he does not accept them in full, he should be prosecuted – and that it should be made clear that the conditions are to be performed within the agreed time.

Paragraph 3.2 of the Code says that where the circumstances of a particular case or offender readily suggest conditions, and where such conditions will provide a proportionate response to the offence, bearing in mind the public interest, a conditional caution will usually be appropriate. However, a person who has recently received a simple caution for a similar offence should not be given a conditional caution unless, exceptionally, it is believed that the condition(s) might be effective in breaking the pattern of offending. Previous cautions (or even convictions) for dissimilar offences may, however, be disregarded, as may cautions or convictions which are more than five years old, although failure to complete a previous conditional caution would normally rule out the issue of another (para 3.3).

Paragraph 5 of the Code deals with the conditions that may be attached to a caution. Those conditions must be:

a   *proportionate* to the offence (regard should be had to the likely sentence that the court would impose in the event of a conviction);
b   *achievable* (the conditions must make it clear what the offender must do and within what period of time; they must be realistic and should take account of the offender's circumstances, including physical and mental capacity, so that he can reasonably be expected to achieve them within the time set); and
c   *appropriate* (i.e. relevant to the offence and/or the offender).

Paragraph 5.2 of the Code gives a number of examples of conditions aimed at rehabilitation (e.g., taking part in treatment for drug or alcohol dependency, anger management courses, driving rectification classes, or involvement in a restorative justice process) and reparation (e.g., repairing or otherwise making good any damage caused to property, such as by cleaning graffiti, restoring stolen goods, paying modest financial compensation, or even a simple apology to the victim); compensation may be paid to an individual or to the community in the form of an appropriate charity. The Code also notes that specific conditions, such as that the offender should avoid a particular street or public house, may be included, but consideration should also be given as to whether alternatives, such as an ASBO (see Chapter 22), would be more appropriate (para 5.4).

Section 23A of the Criminal Justice Act 2003 (not in force at time of writing) enables the imposition of a financial penalty as a condition of a conditional caution. This power applies only to offences specified by statutory instrument (s 23A(1)). Under s 23A(3), the maximum amount of such a financial penalty is one-quarter of the amount of the maximum fine for which a person is liable on summary conviction of the offence, or £250, whichever is the lower. It should be noted that the limit on the amount of the financial penalty applies only to a requirement to pay money that is imposed for the purpose of punishing an offender. It does not, for example, preclude offenders also being required to pay compensation to victims for the purpose of making reparation for the offence, or to pay a sum of money to a charity by way of indirect reparation to the community.

Paragraph 9.1 of the Code notes that conditional cautions will usually be given at the local police station, but there is the option of selecting a location appropriate to the offence (e.g., giving it at the place where vandalism has occurred). It will be for the authorised person to determine the venue for administering the caution. However, the Code adds that cautions should not be given on the street or in the offender's home.

Paragraph 7.1 considers the role to be played by the victim. It notes that where a caution (whether simple or conditional) is regarded as a possibility, that fact may be mentioned to the victim in order to ascertain their views, but that it is vital not to give the impression that the victim's views will be conclusive as to the outcome. The decision on disposal is for the prosecutor, and there will be cases where the prosecutor takes the view that, in order to be proportionate to the level of the offence, conditions should be more (or less) onerous than those the victim would be willing to accept.

The sanction for non-compliance with the conditions is set out in s 24(1) of the 2003 Act:

> If the offender fails, without reasonable excuse, to comply with any of the conditions attached to the conditional caution, criminal proceedings may be instituted against the person for the offence in question.

If proceedings are instituted, the conditional caution ceases to have effect (s 24(3)).

Under s 24A of the 2003 Act, where a police officer has reasonable grounds for believing that the offender has failed, without reasonable excuse, to comply with any of the conditions attached to the conditional caution, he may arrest him without warrant. Under s 24A(2), a person arrested under s 24A must be:

(a) charged with the offence in question,
(b) released without charge and on bail to enable a decision to be made as to whether he should be charged with the offence, or
(c) released without charge and without bail (with or without any variation in the conditions attached to the caution).

Paragraph 6.1 of the Code points out that the deadline for the completion of conditions should not be too long. This is particularly important in relation to summary offences, where there is a time-limit of six months within which a prosecution must commence (under s 127 of the Magistrates' Courts Act 1980); for such offences, the deadline set should leave enough time for a prosecution to proceed in the event of non-compliance.

Paragraph 10.1 of the Code says that the onus is on the offender to show that the conditions have been satisfied. At the end of the process he has to sign a form that includes a declaration that the conditions have been met. Paragraph 10.3 says that whether any excuse given is reasonable or not is a matter for the relevant prosecutor to determine on all the available evidence. Where the CPS are satisfied that there is a reasonable excuse for the offender's failure to meet the conditions, they will have to decide whether the case should be regarded as closed, or whether it would be appropriate to set a new time-limit for completing conditions or (exceptionally) to revise the conditions, although they should not be made more onerous. A refusal by the offender to agree to revised conditions will usually result in prosecution for the original offence. It will not usually be appropriate to revise conditions more than once.

Where conditions have been partially completed, it is for the prosecutor to decide whether the offender should be prosecuted, or whether the extent of the part-compliance is sufficient to regard the conditional caution as having been fulfilled (para 10.4).

It is a standard condition that the offender will not commit further offences (para 5.3). Where further offending is alleged, it is for the CPS to decide whether it is such as to require the conditional caution to be cancelled and the original offence prosecuted (para 12.8).

Where several related or similar offences are admitted, they may be dealt with by a single conditional caution; breach of any of the conditions would make the offender liable for prosecution for all of the offences (para 2.7).

Schedule 26 to the Criminal Justice and Immigration Act 2008 inserts a new section, s 23B, into the 2003 Act, to make express provision for the variation of the conditions. It states that a relevant prosecutor may, with the consent of the offender, vary the conditions attached to a conditional caution by (a) modifying or omitting any of the conditions, and/or (b) adding a condition.

Similar guidance on conditional cautions is contained in The Director's Guidance on Conditional Cautioning: Guidance to Police Officers and Crown Prosecutors (5th edition, October 2007 <http://www.cps.gov.uk/Publications/directors_guidance/conditional_cautioning.html>).

Section 2 of the Guidance notes that:

- Conditional Cautions are intended to be a swift and effective means of dealing with straightforward cases where the offender is willing to admit the offence and to agree to comply with specified conditions. The disposal should only be used where it provides an appropriate and proportionate response to the offending behaviour.
- Cases will always proceed to court unless a Crown Prosecutor concludes that, in the first instance, the public interest can be met by an appropriate out of court disposal.

   . . .

- Where an offender fails to comply with the conditions of a caution, it is for a Crown Prosecutor to determine whether to commence proceedings, whether any reasons for non-compliance amount to a reasonable excuse, or to impose new conditions.

There is detailed guidance in Section 3 on the factors that should be taken into account by a Crown Prosecutor when deciding whether or not a conditional caution is appropriate:

Sufficient evidence to charge the offender with the offence
Before a Conditional Caution can be given, a Crown Prosecutor must be satisfied that there is sufficient evidence available to meet the evidential requirements of the Full Code Test set out in the Code for Crown Prosecutors.

Public interest factors to determine whether a Conditional Caution should be offered
A Crown Prosecutor must be satisfied that while the public interest justifies a prosecution, in the first instance, the interests of the victim, community or offender may be better served by the offender complying with suitable conditions aimed at reparation or rehabilitation. The Crown Prosecutor must also be satisfied that a prosecution will continue to be necessary should the offer of a Conditional Caution be declined or the offender fail to comply with the conditions . . .

Seriousness of the offence
The Crown Prosecutor must carefully consider the seriousness of the offence(s). The more serious the circumstances of the offence(s), the less likely it will be that the case is suitable for out of court disposal . . .

The likely outcome at court
The Crown Prosecutor should consider the range of penalties likely to be considered if the case were to proceed to the magistrates' court. Where the Crown Prosecutor concludes that a custodial sentence or a significant community penalty would be under consideration, a Conditional Caution will not be appropriate . . .

The effect on the victim
The views of individual victims should be considered wherever possible when deciding whether a Conditional Caution is appropriate . . . The decision is one for the Crown Prosecutor who must determine what weight is to be given to the victim's views in all the circumstances of the case. Any views of the victim whether in favour of prosecution or otherwise should not be the overriding consideration but will be a matter for the Crown Prosecutor to take into account in determining the action to be taken.

Circumstances of the offender
The Crown Prosecutor should consider the circumstances of the offender including any antecedent history in determining suitability for a Conditional Caution.

A history of recent offending, especially offences of a similar nature, is likely to be an indication that a prosecution should be preferred, but each case should be considered on its own merits.

The offender's attitude to both the offending behaviour and the proposed conditions should be considered. An offender who has shown some remorse for the offending behaviour and who has demonstrated a willingness to comply with the conditions is more likely to be suitable for a Conditional Caution. A Conditional Caution will not be appropriate for an offender who fails to accept full responsibility for his actions or who has given any indication that he may not comply with the conditions . . .

The likelihood of further offending
Custody Officers and Crown Prosecutors must assess the likelihood of re-offending during the period of the Conditional Caution . . . [W]here the maximum sentence allowed for the offence under consideration is limited to a fine, the case should generally be referred to a Crown Prosecutor for consideration of a Conditional Caution.

This assessment should take place at an early stage. Cases in which there is a high likelihood of re-offending will not be appropriate for a Conditional Caution and such cases should not be referred to a Crown Prosecutor. Where the Custody Officer is uncertain whether to refer the case to a Crown Prosecutor, the case should first be discussed with a Crown Prosecutor to determine whether a Conditional Caution may be appropriate.

However, where the Custody Officer considers that appropriate conditions would assist in the rehabilitation of the offender and would minimise the likelihood of re-offending, the case should be referred to a Crown Prosecutor to determine whether a Conditional Caution is appropriate in all the circumstances . . . Where the Crown Prosecutor agrees with the Custody Officer's assessment, a Conditional Caution may be offered. Cases in which the likelihood of re-offending cannot be managed by the inclusion of suitable conditions or in which there is a high likelihood of re-offending should be charged and proceed to court.

Dealing with multiple offenders
The charging of one offender in a case does not prevent the offer of a Conditional Caution to a co-defendant. A Conditional Caution can still be considered where it is appropriate either due to the level of involvement in the criminality or the circumstances of the offender . . .

Dealing with multiple offences
An offender may be Conditionally Cautioned for more than one offence on the same cautioning occasion. Generally, it will be appropriate to offer a single Conditional Caution for the totality of the offending rather than prefer individual Conditional Cautions for each offence. The more offences committed, the less likely it will be that the case remains suitable for out of court disposal, even if individually the cases would be suitable for a Conditional Caution. However where the totality of the offending does not cause the case to become so serious that a prosecution must follow, the offer of a Conditional Caution may still be appropriate.

Alternative out of court disposal
When considering any case referred for a Conditional Caution, if a Crown Prosecutor determines that no conditions are appropriate or that it is not necessary, in the public interest for the offender to be charged to court, the Crown Prosecutor should, after discussing the options with the Custody Officer or an officer involved in the investigation, determine whether a simple caution, penalty notice or other disposal would be more proportionate or appropriate.

It is clear from this that, although the final decision on whether or not to offer a conditional caution to the suspect has to be taken by a Crown Prosecutor, the police have a key role in deciding whether or not to pass the case to a Prosecutor for this decision to be taken. Paragraph 4.3 of the Guidance states that a custody officer should not consider a conditional caution where:

- The offender was on bail to court at the time the offence was alleged to have been committed.
- The Custody Officer assesses that appropriate conditions would not reduce the likelihood of re-offending.
- The offender would, if convicted of the offence, be in breach of a court order making him liable to be re-sentenced.
- The offender would be liable to prison recall if convicted for the offence.
- The offender has denied the offence or put forward a full or partial defence.

Paragraph 4.4 notes that the risk of re-offending will involve consideration of:

- Any previous convictions, including their date, nature and frequency.
- The offender's response to previous court orders, including bail.

- All the circumstances of the current offence, including any reason for its commission, any mitigating or aggravating factors (ACPO gravity factors) that may suggest re-offending or repeat victimisation.
- The offender's response to his arrest and indication of a willingness to co-operate.

Annex B to the Guidance suggests a range of conditions that might be imposed. Suggested reparative conditions, to make good the loss sustained by the victim or community and to repair relationships, are:

- to pay compensation;
- to personally repair or make good the damage;
- to undertake unpaid work on community property directly related to the harm caused;
- to write a letter of apology;
- to participate in restorative justice mediation.

Suggested rehabilitative conditions, to stop or modify offending behaviour or reduce the risk of offending behaviour, are:

- not to commit further offences for a defined period of time;
- to attend at a referral programme specifically related to the nature or cause of the offending behaviour;
- not to contact a named person or go to a specified location.

Section 5 of the Guidance deals in detail with the choice of conditions. It provides:

Considering Individual Victims – Reparative Conditions
Priority consideration should be given to reparation or compensation for the victim of the crime in a manner that is acceptable to the victim. Individual victims should, where possible, be consulted and suitable conditions canvassed. Any conditions involving the participation of a victim, including receiving a letter of apology from the offender or making a claim for compensation, should not be required unless the victim has been consulted and agrees. Payment of financial reparation should only be included where the victim has requested this.

The payment of compensation may be coupled with other conditions so long as the overall requirements contained in the conditions remain proportionate to the offending behaviour. Payment of compensation must be commensurate with the means of the offender and if too large an amount is involved, this may indicate that the case is too serious for a Conditional Caution. Individual victims should be consulted where it is proposed that the sum to be paid by the offender as a condition falls significantly short of the totality of the compensation claimed to determine if agreement can be made for the payment of a lesser sum.

   . . .

Reparative work for the community must relate directly to the nature of the offending behaviour. This will be particularly appropriate where this has involved damage to the community's property. The period of reparative work should be proportionate to the offender's behaviour and should not exceed 20 hours in total.

Considering the offender – Rehabilitative Conditions
Next in priority will be conditions designed to tackle offending behaviour and rehabilitate the offender . . . A condition not to commit an offence within a specified period may be all that is required where the offending was isolated and out of character and the offender appears responsive to the intervention of the police and appropriately remorseful. Ordinarily, this specified period should not exceed 16 weeks.

Where it appears that offending behaviour is linked to an addiction to drugs or alcohol, or both, and a suitable scheme is operating locally which is able to take referrals and provide therapy and/or counselling, conditions designed to encourage attendance at such schemes should be considered . . .

Restrictive Conditions
Conditions that impose restrictions may be included as part of a package of measures designed to rehabilitate offenders or to make good harm caused. They should not be imposed for a period exceeding the life of any such reparative or other rehabilitative conditions and the objectives may be achievable in a shorter period. The conditions, taken as a whole, must be proportionate to the level of offending and not so burdensome so as to seem to offer a disadvantage as compared to a likely court outcome. Restrictive conditions must be clear and unambiguous . . .

Payment of compensation
An offender should be allowed a reasonable overall time to make payment. To determine the length of time to be allowed for payment of compensation, regard should be had to his disposable income . . .

Crown Prosecutors should seek, wherever possible, to recover compensation within 16 weeks and conditions should impose this specific requirement . . .

Where the compensation sum under consideration is substantial, or there are complex issues to be considered, or an offender is already making substantial financial payments to the court and/or any such payments are subject to enforcement proceedings, the Crown Prosecutor is more likely to decide that the case is more appropriate for prosecution.

Time limit for completion of conditions for summary only offences
The time for completion of any conditions must allow sufficient time for prosecution in the event of any non compliance and decision to prosecute. Prosecution for summary only offences must be commenced within 6 months from the date of the offence. The period allowable for completion of any conditions for any summary only offence should be limited to 16 weeks from the date of the offence, and not the date of the administration of the Conditional Caution. In any either-way offence the conditions should generally be capable of being complied with within 16 weeks, however this does not preclude longer periods where in all the circumstances this is justified and proportionate.

Assessing compliance
. . . Conditions which contain restrictions are likely to be enforced by the arrest of an offender (where this is necessary) if the offender is found not to be in compliance with the restriction.

Variation of Conditions

Crown Prosecutors may be asked to agree to vary any conditions or the time set for the completion of conditions. Where this is because of a change of circumstances to the offender, the Crown Prosecutor will consider all the circumstances of the case and may agree to a variation where such a decision would be fair and just in all the circumstances, but where the variation is to the time set for completion the prosecutor must always bear in mind the time restrictions on summary only offences . . .

Section 7 of the Guidance returns to the decision of the Crown Prosecutor and stipulates that:

A Conditional Caution may be appropriate where a Crown Prosecutor believes that while the public interest justifies a prosecution in the first instance, the interests of the victim, community or offender outweigh the seriousness of the offence and may be better served by the offender complying with suitable conditions aimed at reparation or rehabilitation. The Crown Prosecutor must also carefully assess the likelihood of further offending. The Crown Prosecutor should consider whether the expected out-come of the case at court could have an impact on future offending that could not be achieved by the conditional caution. Where this is so, the matter should proceed to court.

Where a person is arrested under s 24A(1) of the Criminal Justice Act 2003 for failure to comply with any conditions of a Conditional Caution, he must be taken to a police station. Paragraphs 11.7–11 set out what happens next:

Following any arrest under s 24A (1), the Custody Officer must ascertain as soon as possible whether the offender has any reasonable excuse for non-compliance. Where the Custody Officer is satisfied that a reasonable excuse exists and the offender is able and willing to comply with the conditions, the offender may be released without bail to comply with the same conditions. Where the Custody Officer is satisfied that there is no reasonable excuse for non-compliance, the case will be referred to a Crown Prosecutor for a decision.

Where the Custody Officer considers that an offender can no longer comply with any or all of the conditions or has indicated that he will not do so, the case will be referred to a Crown Prosecutor.

A Crown Prosecutor will then consider whether there has been a failure to comply and if so, whether there is a reasonable excuse for the non-compliance. Where it is determined that there is a reasonable excuse, the Crown Prosecutor will determine whether it is appropriate to extend the period of time for completion of the conditions or vary the original conditions.

Where it is determined that there is no reasonable excuse, the Crown Prosecutor will decide whether or not the offender is to be charged with the original offence and notify the Custody Officer or officer involved in the investigation accordingly.

The conditions may be altered in the light of any change of circumstances since the Conditional Caution was imposed although the Crown Prosecutor should be satisfied that the change in circumstances is genuine and impact directly on the ability of the offender to complete the original conditions. The Crown Prosecutor should consider the effect on the victim of any significant variation of conditions and should arrange for the victim to be notified where appropriate. Where the conditions have been partially completed, a Crown Prosecutor will decide whether the extent of part-compliance is sufficient to regard the Conditional Caution as having been fulfilled, whether a variation of the conditions will aid their completion or whether a prosecution should ensue . . .

For a discussion of the use of conditional cautions and the move to the imposition of punitive conditions (such as unpaid work in the community or paying financial penalties), see Ian Brownlee, 'Conditional cautions and fair trial rights in England and Wales: form versus substance in the diversionary agenda?' [2007] Crim LR 129. Concerns have been expressed that conditional cautioning requires Crown Prosecutors to usurp the function of the judiciary in imposing punishment for criminal conduct. Brownlee rightly makes the point that 'the prospect that in future the conditional caution will be a vehicle through which offenders can end up performing unpaid work in the community or paying financial penalties reinforces the need to ensure that the cautioning procedure involves substantive rather than purely formal protections which ensure that those who are offered the chance to be cautioned on these terms make informed and free decisions as to the waiver of their Art 6 rights [to a fair trial]'.

In December 2007, the Ministry of Justice published an evaluation of the early implementation of the scheme of conditional cautions (see <http://www.justice.gov.uk/docs/conditional-cautions.pdf>). Among the findings were:

- Take-up was very uneven, as areas varied in their use of conditional cautions, with the majority being administered by a small number of areas (it is unclear why this was the case, and it is an unsatisfactory aspect of the scheme if offenders are not being treated consistently across the country).
- Just under half (48 per cent) of conditional cautions were administered within 14 days of arrest (meaning that the administration of a conditional caution took 65 days less than a prosecution in a guilty plea case).
- For cases that were not given a conditional caution the most common disposal was a charge. However, 11 per cent of the total number of cases considered were dealt with using a disposal less than a charge, namely a simple caution or no further action (demonstrating the potential for what the report described as 'up-tariffing' to occur with the new disposal).
- Compensation was the most frequently used condition.
- 70 per cent of conditional cautions were completed successfully. Offenders failed to comply with some aspects of the conditional caution in 24 per cent of cases, the majority of whom were prosecuted for the original offence, most of them receiving a conditional discharge.
- Practitioners identified three main benefits of conditional cautions: addressing the causes of crime, increasing victim satisfaction, and contributing to efficiency savings in the courts.

2.6.3 Juveniles: reprimands and warnings

A slightly different system applies to young offenders. Section 65 of the Crime and Disorder Act 1998 applies (by virtue of s 65(1)) to cases where:

(a) a constable has evidence that a child or young person ('the offender') has committed an offence;

(b) the constable considers that the evidence is such that, if the offender were prosecuted for the offence, there would be a realistic prospect of his being convicted;

(c) the offender admits to the constable that he committed the offence;

(d) the offender has not previously been convicted of an offence; and

(e) the constable is satisfied that it would not be in the public interest for the offender to be prosecuted.

Schedule 9 to the Criminal Justice and Immigration Act 2008 amends s 65(1) to take account of the creation of 'youth conditional cautions' (see below). The amended text is:

(a) a constable has evidence that a child or young person ('the offender') has committed an offence;

(b) the constable considers that there is sufficient evidence to charge the offender with the offence;

(c) the offender admits to the constable that he committed the offence;

(d) the offender has not previously been convicted of an offence or given a youth conditional caution in respect of an offence; and

(e) the constable does not consider that the offender should be prosecuted or given a youth conditional caution.

Thus, a reprimand or warning cannot be given if the offender has previously received a youth conditional caution. Where the offender has not previously received a youth conditional caution, the officer should consider whether such a disposal would be appropriate.

In such a case, s 65(2) provides that the police may reprimand the youngster if he has not previously been reprimanded or warned. Under s 65(3), the police may warn a youngster who comes within s 65(1) if:

a   he has not previously been warned; or

b   where he has previously been warned, the present offence was committed more than two years after the date of the previous warning and the police consider that the present offence is not sufficiently serious to require a charge to be brought (or a youth conditional caution to be given).

Section 65(3) goes on to state that no person may be warned more than twice.

Under s 65, the usual sequence of events would be:

• first offence: reprimand;

• second offence: warning;

• third offence: prosecution (or a second warning if the present offence is more than two years after the first warning and is not so serious as to require prosecution).

However, s 65(4) states that where the youngster has not previously been reprimanded, a warning may be administered (rather than a reprimand) if the police consider that the offence is so serious as to require a warning. Similarly, there is nothing to stop the police from prosecuting a youngster for a first or second offence where the seriousness of the offence makes that an appropriate course of action.

Under s 65(5), where the offender is under the age of 17, a reprimand or warning must be administered in the presence of an appropriate adult. The effect of re-offending must be explained to the youngster and to the adult. Section 66(1) requires that, where a warning has been administered, a youth offending team (YOT) must be informed. Unless they consider it inappropriate to do so, the YOT must arrange for the youngster to participate in a rehabilitation programme, with the aim of preventing him from re-offending (sub-s (2)).

Where a person has been warned under s 65 and is subsequently convicted of an offence committed within two years of the warning, the court dealing with him for the later offence cannot impose a conditional discharge unless it takes the view that there are exceptional circumstances relating to the offence or to the offender which justify its doing so (s 66(4)).

Reprimands, warnings and failure to participate in a rehabilitation programme may be cited in criminal proceedings in the same way that previous convictions may be cited (s 66(5)).

Detailed guidance is given in *Final Warning Scheme: Guidance for Police and Youth Offending Teams* (<http://www.homeoffice.gov.uk/documents/final-warning-scheme.pdf?version=1>) with some updating in Home Office Circular 14/2006 (<http://www.knowledgenetwork.gov.uk/HO/circular.nsf/79755433dd36a66980256d4f004d1514/a9010dacf92f37ab8025716f00317b53?OpenDocument>).

Paragraph 1.3 of the Guidance notes that the final warning scheme 'aims to divert children and young people from their offending behaviour before they enter the court system'. Paragraph 1.4 says that the scheme was designed to do this by:

- ending repeat cautioning and providing a progressive and effective response to offending behaviour;
- providing appropriate and effective interventions to prevent re-offending; and
- ensuring that young people who do re-offend after being warned are dealt with quickly and effectively by the courts.

Paragraph 1.9 adds that 'research shows that effective intervention at the final warning stage significantly reduces the rate of re-offending'.

Paragraph 8 of the Circular notes that two key questions must be addressed:

- Is the evidence such that, if prosecuted for the offence, there would be a realistic prospect of a conviction?
- Does the young person make a clear and reliable admission to all elements of the offence?

The Circular emphasises that warnings should not be administered to an offender in circumstances where there can be no reasonable expectation that this will curb his offending (para 11).

Paragraph 5 of the Circular also makes it clear that a warning may be used for breach of an ASBO. The police, in consultation with the youth offending team, should make an assessment of both the seriousness of the breach and the young person's history of offending. Where the breach of an ASBO is effectively a first criminal offence by the young person, then a warning may be appropriate, unless the breach was a 'flagrant' one (in which case a prosecution is appropriate unless there are 'very unusual circumstances').

Several paragraphs in the Guidance refer to the need for speed in the operation of the scheme. If a young offender is to be dealt with by means of a reprimand or a final warning, it is important (in the public interest and for the effective operation of the scheme) that the reprimand or final warning should be administered swiftly, in order to maximise the impact of such reprimand or final warning upon the young offender. One consequence of this is that if the police decide against this course of action (for example, because – at that stage – the juvenile denies the offence), the court will not usually require the police or the CPS to reconsider the decision not to offer a reprimand or warning after the juvenile has been charged (see *R (F) v CPS* [2003] EWHC 3266; (2004) 168 JP 93).

In *R (R) v Durham Constabulary* [2005] UKHL 21; [2005] 1 WLR 1184, the House of Lords held that the giving of a warning under s 65 of the Crime and Disorder Act 1998 does not involve the determination of a criminal charge against the juvenile, and neither does the decision of the police to issue the warning. Therefore no human rights issues arise under the fair trial provisions of the European Convention on Human Rights.

For discussion of the decision-making process involved in diverting young offenders from the courts, see Field, S, *Early intervention and the 'new' youth justice: a study of initial decision-making* [2008] Crim LR 177. Field concludes that pre-charge decision-making in youth justice remains a highly discretionary process, rooted in personal judgement, and he questions whether the custody officer is the appropriate initial decision-maker for pre-charge decisions about most young people.

2.6.4 Juveniles: 'youth conditional cautions'

Section 48 of the Criminal Justice and Immigration Act 2008 gives effect to Sched 9 to the Act, which makes provision for 'youth conditional cautions'. Paragraph 3 inserts new sections, ss 66A to 66H, into the Crime and Disorder Act 1998. Under s 66A(1), a youth conditional caution may be given to a child or young person if (a) he has not previously been convicted of an offence and (b) each of the five requirements in s 66B is satisfied. Under s 66B, the five requirements applicable to adult conditional cautions (set out in s 23 of the Criminal Justice Act 2003 – see above) are applicable to youth conditional cautions. If the offender is aged 16 or under, the explanation of the effect of the caution, and warning that failure to comply with any of the conditions attached to it may result in his being prosecuted for the offence, must be given in the presence of an appropriate adult (s 66B(5)). As with adults, the conditions must have the object of facilitating the rehabilitation of the offender, ensuring that the offender makes reparation for the offence, and/or punishing the offender (s 66A(3)). The conditions that may be imposed include payment of a financial penalty (limited to £100 by s 66C) or that the offender must attend a place specified by the prosecutor for up to 20 hours. This 20-hour limit does not apply to an attendance requirement imposed for the purpose of facilitating the offender's rehabilitation; this is to permit rehabilitative conditions involving, for example, drug or alcohol treatment programmes that may take longer than 20 hours in total (s 66A(4) and (5)).

Section 66D makes provision for the variation of conditions, but only with the consent of the offender.

As with adults, s 66E(1) provides that if the offender fails, without reasonable excuse, to comply with any of the conditions, proceedings may be instituted against him for the offence in question. Where a person who has been given a youth conditional caution is convicted of an offence committed within two years of the giving of the caution, the court which deals with him may not impose a conditional discharge unless it is of the opinion that there are exceptional circumstances relating to the offence or the offender which justify its doing so (s 66F). Section 66G requires publication of a Code of Practice in respect of youth conditional cautions.

2.6.5 Fixed penalty notices

Fixed penalty notices are a familiar feature of road traffic law. Section 54 of the Road Traffic Offenders Act 1988 provides that where a uniformed police officer has reason to believe that a person is committing, or has on that occasion committed, a fixed penalty offence, the officer may give him a fixed penalty notice in respect of the offence. However, such notices are not confined to road traffic law. Sections 1 and 2 of the Criminal Justice and Police Act 2001 make provision for fixed penalty notices for a large number of offences related to public order, and ss 43 and 44 of the Anti-Social Behaviour Act 2003 make similar provision for a number of offences relating to damage to property. There are also a number of statutory provisions for fixed penalty notices in environment protection legislation (e.g. s 88 of the Environmental Protection Act 1990, fixed penalty for leaving litter).

2.6.6 Alternatives to prosecution – critical analysis

The use of cautions and fixed penalty notices has the advantage of keeping less serious offences out of the court system, thus enabling resources to be focused on more serious offences. However, the imposition of a penalty without involvement of a court is seen by some as objectionable (on the basis that only a court should be able to impose a penalty). This is mitigated to some extent by the fact that a person who contests their liability to pay a fixed penalty can opt to go to court instead of paying the penalty. Critics respond to this point by saying that people who may have good grounds for contesting a fixed penalty notice may simply pay up rather than expending the time and effort of challenging the penalty in court.

It is clear that the importance of these alternatives to prosecution is growing. For the purpose of Government statistics, an offence is considered to have been 'brought to justice' when an offender has been cautioned, convicted or had the offence taken into consideration. According to the Criminal Statistics published by the Ministry of Justice for the year 2006–07 (<http://www.justice.gov.uk/docs/crim-stats-2006-tag.pdf>), during 2006/07, 1.43 million offences were brought to justice compared with 1.33 million in 2005/06 (an increase of seven per cent). In 2006/07, 694,000 notifiable offences were brought to justice through conviction in the courts (a decrease of two per cent compared with 2005/06). During the same period notifiable cautions increased by 15 per cent and offences taken into consideration increased by three per cent. During 2006/07, there were 149,000 penalty notices given for notifiable offences and a further 83,000 cannabis warnings were given. Convictions by a court account for 49 per cent of the total; penalty notices and cannabis warnings account for 16 per cent of the total. Of the 201,200 fixed penalty notices for disorder issued in 2006/07, 52 per cent (104,500) were paid in full without any court action.

2.7 THE DECISION TO PROSECUTE

We have already seen that where a suspect is arrested by the police, the decision to prosecute will be taken by a Crown Prosecutor. In any event, under s 3(2)(a) of the Prosecution of Offences Act 1985, it is the duty of the DPP to take over the conduct of all criminal proceedings, other than specified proceedings, instituted on behalf of a police force. This means that the case will be taken forward by the CPS, and this will include a review of the evidence (by a Crown Prosecutor).

The decision to start, or continue, a prosecution is taken in accordance with the Code of Conduct for Crown Prosecutors (set out in Chapter 1), which states that a prosecution should only be started or continued if there is a 'realistic prospect of conviction'. This means that a court is 'more likely than not' to convict the defendant of the charge alleged. In deciding whether or not this 51 per cent test is satisfied, the Crown Prosecutor should consider both the admissibility and the likely reliability of the evidence against the defendant. Thus, the Crown Prosecutor must take account of any challenges which the defence may make to the admissibility of evidence and must also see if there are discrepancies between what the various prosecution witnesses have said to the police and whether a prosecution witness might have a motive for lying. The Prosecutor should also consider whether a prosecution is in the public interest. For example, if the offence is a trivial one, and so in the event of conviction the court would be likely to impose only a very small or nominal penalty, the CPS might take the view that it is not in the public interest to continue proceedings. Similarly, a prosecution may not be in the public interest if it is likely to have an adverse effect on the physical or mental health of the victim or the offender. However, the Code makes it clear that 'the more serious the offence, the more likely it is that a prosecution will be needed in the public interest'.

2.7.1 Challenging the decision to prosecute

In the absence of dishonesty or bad faith or other exceptional circumstances, the decision to prosecute is not amenable to judicial review; challenges to such proceedings should be made in the context of the criminal trial or by way of appeal against conviction following such trial (*R v DPP ex p Kebilene* [2000] 2 AC 326). *Kebilene* was followed in *R (Pepushi) v CPS* [2004] EWHC 798 (Admin); [2004] Imm AR 549, where the court reiterated that a decision to prosecute is amenable to judicial review only in exceptional circumstances. Thomas LJ said (at paras 49–50):

> In view of the frequency of applications seeking to challenge decisions to prosecute, we wish to make it clear and, in particular, clear to the legal services commission (which funds

applications of this kind which seek to challenge the bringing of criminal proceedings) that, save in wholly exceptional circumstances, applications in respect of pending prosecutions that seek to challenge the decision to prosecute should not be made to this court. The proper course to follow, as should have been followed in this case, is to take the point in accordance with the procedures of the criminal courts . . .

The circumstances in which a challenge is made to the bringing of a prosecution should be very rare indeed . . . we stress that the legal services commission and those advising prospective applicants for judicial review should always realise that judicial review is very rarely appropriate where an alternative remedy is available. If such a remedy is available, a judicial review application should not be pursued.

Sharma v Browne-Antoine [2006] UKPC 57; [2007] 1 WLR 780 confirms that judicial review of a prosecutorial decision, although available in principle, is a highly exceptional remedy.

In *R (A) v South Yorkshire Police and Crown Prosecution Service* [2007] EWHC 1261 (Admin); (2007) 171 JP 465, a number of juveniles sought to challenge the decision to charge them rather than give a warning under s 65 of the Crime and Disorder Act 1998. They argued that the decision contravened the relevant Home Office Circular (see above). Gray J at para 65 said that the court:

should not intervene unless it is clearly established by these claimants that the decision to prosecute them has come about as a result of a departure from the statutory guidance for which departure there is no rational explanation. Even then, any intervention by this Court would be of course discretionary.

His Lordship added (at para 94) that 'the ultimate question for decision . . . is whether the decision to prosecute is sustainable or whether it is not'.

2.7.2 Challenging the decision not to prosecute

In *R v DPP ex p C* [1995] 1 Cr App R 136, Kennedy LJ (at p 141) said that the court would interfere with a decision *not* to prosecute only if the decision was reached:

(1)   because of some unlawful policy [such as a decision never to prosecute where the value of goods stolen was below £100]; or
(2)   because the [Prosecutor] failed to act in accordance with . . . the Code; or
(3)   because the decision was perverse. It was a decision at which no reasonable prosecutor could have arrived.

Further guidance was given in *R v DPP ex p Manning* [2001] QB 330, where Lord Bingham CJ said (at para 23):

Authority makes clear that a decision by the Director not to prosecute is susceptible to judicial review . . . But, as the decided cases also make clear, the power of review is one to be sparingly exercised. The reasons for this are clear. The primary decision to prosecute or not to prosecute is entrusted by Parliament to the Director as head of an independent, professional prosecuting service, answerable to the Attorney General in his role as guardian of the public interest, and to no one else. It makes no difference that in practice the decision will ordinarily be taken by a senior member of the Crown Prosecution Service . . . and not by the Director personally. In any borderline case the decision may be one of acute difficulty, since while a defendant whom a jury would be likely to convict should properly be brought to justice and tried, a defendant whom a jury would be likely to acquit should not be subjected to the trauma inherent in a criminal trial. . . . In most cases the decision will turn . . . on the exercise of an informed judgment of how a case against a particular defendant, if brought, would be likely to fare in the context of a criminal trial before (in a serious case such as this) a jury. This exercise of judgment involves an assessment of the strength, by the end of the trial, of the evidence against the defendant and of the likely defences. It will often be impossible to stigmatise a judgment on such matters as wrong even if one disagrees with it. So the courts will not easily find that a decision not to prosecute is bad in law, on which basis alone the court is entitled to interfere. At the same time, the standard of review should not be set too high, since judicial review is the only means by which the citizen can seek redress against a decision not to prosecute and if the test were too exacting an effective remedy would be denied.

Lord Bingham added (at para 33) that there is no general obligation on the CPS to give reasons for a decision not to prosecute. However, in a case where one might reasonably expect there to be a prosecution (in this case, there had been a death in custody and a properly directed coroner's jury had returned a verdict of unlawful killing implicating a person who, although not named, was clearly identified and whose whereabouts were known), reasons for a decision not to prosecute should be given.

In *R (Dennis) v DPP* [2006] EWHC 3211, Waller LJ (at para 30) summarised the relevant principles as follows:

First, if it can be demonstrated on an objective appraisal of the case that a serious point or serious points supporting a prosecution have not been considered, that will give a ground for ordering reconsideration of the decision. Second, if it can be demonstrated that in a significant area a conclusion as to what the evidence is to support a prosecution is irrational, that will provide a ground. Third, the points have to be such as to make it seriously arguable that the decision would otherwise be different, but the decision is one for the prosecutor and not for this court. Indeed it is important to bear that fact in mind at all stages. Fourth, where an inquest jury has found unlawful killing the reasons why a prosecution should not follow need to be clearly expressed.

2.7.3 Discontinuing proceedings

The DPP (in practice, this means any Crown Prosecutor) may, at any 'preliminary stage' of the proceedings, discontinue those proceedings by serving a notice of discontinuance under s 23 of the Prosecution of Offences Act 1985. Section 23(2) of the 1985 Act defines the term 'preliminary stage'. In the case of a summary offence, it is too late to serve a notice under s 23 once the court has begun to hear evidence for the prosecution (i.e. after the trial has begun). In the case of an indictable offence, it is too late to serve a notice at any stage of the proceedings after the accused has been sent for trial for the offence.

Discontinuance may take place, for example, where it becomes apparent that the case against the defendant is not as strong as it first seemed (for example, new evidence comes to light or a prosecution witness changes his story). According to figures released by the CPS, in the period 2004–07, an average of 11.6 per cent of cases in the magistrates' court were discontinued each year.

There was some criticism of the fact that CPS could discontinue Crown Court proceedings only prior to the stage when the case was sent to the Crown Court, since the on-going review of the evidence in a case may well mean that CPS wish to discontinue the case after the 'preliminary' stages are over, and if they wish to drop the case after that stage, they have to offer no evidence at the plea and case management hearing or at the start of the trial (according to the CPS figures for 2004–07, an average of 13.5 per cent of cases in the Crown Court ended with a judge-ordered acquittal, where the prosecution chose to offer no evidence). However, the exclusion by s 23(2) of cases that have been sent for trial to the Crown Court is mitigated to a large extent by s 23A of the Act. This section enables the DPP to give a notice of discontinuance where CPS has conduct of the proceedings and the accused has been sent to the Crown Court for trial, provided that the indictment has not been 'preferred' (i.e. signed by an appropriate officer of the Crown Court).

To discontinue proceedings under s 23, the DPP simply serves a notice on the magistrates' court. The DPP must give reasons for the decision to discontinue the proceedings to the court (s 23(5)) and must inform the accused, but is not obliged to give reasons to the accused (sub-s (6)). As discontinuance does not prevent the institution of further proceedings in respect of the offence (s 23(9)), the defendant may serve a counter-notice requiring that the proceedings continue (sub-s (7)); this would be appropriate in a case where the defendant wishes to have his name cleared by an acquittal. Where the discontinuance is under s 23A, the DPP serves a notice on the Crown Court. He has to give reasons for the discontinuance to the court (sub-s (3)) but not to the accused (sub-s (4)). Section 23A(5) provides that the discontinuance of proceedings under s 23A does not prevent the institution of fresh proceedings in respect of the same offence, but there is no provision to enable the accused to require that the proceedings continue.

In *Cooke v DPP* (1992) 95 Cr App R 233, it was held that s 23 only provides an additional method of discontinuing proceedings. The other ways of discontinuing proceedings (such as withdrawing a summons or charge or offering no evidence) remain available.

In *R v Grafton* [1993] QB 101, it was held that the decision to discontinue proceedings is entirely a matter for the prosecution; the agreement of the court is not required. This applies both in the magistrates' court and the Crown Court.

The powers of the DPP to discontinue a prosecution under s 23 of the Prosecution of Offences Act may be contrasted with the power of the Attorney General to enter a *nolle prosequi*. This power enables the Attorney General to terminate a prosecution at any time after the draft indictment has been signed. This power is exercised only rarely but its exercise cannot be challenged in the courts (*Gouriet v Union of Post Office Workers* [1978] AC 435).

The Auld Review discusses the power to discontinue a prosecution (at paras 64–68 of chapter 10) and concludes that:

171 The law should be amended to provide a form of procedure common to all courts to enable a prosecutor, without the consent of the defendant or the approval of the

court, to discontinue proceedings at any stage before close of the prosecution case on trial.

172 In the event of the prosecution discontinuing at any time before pre-trial assessment or, where there is no pre-trial assessment, before a stage to be specified, the prosecution should be entitled to reinstate the prosecution, subject to the court's power to stay it as an abuse of process.

173 In the event of the prosecution discontinuing after that stage, the defendant should be entitled to an acquittal, save where the court for good reason permits the prosecution to 'lie on the file'.

174 There should be common provision for all courts, subject to their approval and the agreement of the parties, to give formal effect to such discontinuance and, where appropriate, acquittal in the absence of the parties.

The most important of these recommendations is that a discontinuance should result in a formal acquittal, which is plainly much more satisfactory from the point of view of the accused.

2.7.4 Prosecutions by public bodies other than the police

Where a public body, such as HM Revenue and Customs or a local authority, commences a prosecution, the written charge and requisition procedure established by the Criminal Justice Act 2003 (which replaces the laying of informations and issue of summonses in the case of public prosecutions) is used.

If the conditions in s 24A of PACE are satisfied, the suspect may be arrested by a representative of the public body. Representatives of such bodies are not police officers and so are, in effect, making a 'citizen's arrest'. The person arrested will have to be taken to a police station to be charged by the custody officer. In *R v Stafford Justices ex p Customs & Excise Commissioners* [1991] 2 QB 339, followed in *R v Croydon Justices ex p Holmberg* [1992] Crim LR 892, it was held that proceedings commenced in this way are not deemed to have been instituted on behalf of a police force merely because a custody officer at a police station charged the suspect, and so the prosecution is conducted by the relevant public body (not by CPS). Proceedings are instituted on behalf of a police force (and therefore have to be taken over by CPS, under s 3(2)(a) of the Prosecution of Offences Act 1985) if the police investigated the case and arrested the suspect and brought him before the custody officer.

2.7.5 Private prosecutions

Where a member of the public wishes to commence a 'private prosecution', they may do so by laying an information at a magistrates' court. A member of the public can bring a private prosecution for any offence unless the offence is one for which the consent of the Attorney General or the DPP is required before a prosecution can take place (s 6(1) of the Prosecution of Offences Act 1985); such consent is needed for a small number of offences. The only other way in which a member of the public can commence criminal proceedings is to effect a 'citizen's arrest' under s 24A of PACE. However, following the arrest, the suspect must be handed over to the police (and CPS will then decide whether or not to charge the suspect).

When magistrates are considering whether to issue a summons for a private prosecution where the CPS have already brought and discontinued a prosecution arising out of the same events, they should not require special circumstances before agreeing to the issue of the summons. They should consider:

a   whether the allegation is an offence known to the law and, if so, whether the ingredients of the offence are prima facie present;
b   whether the issue of the summonses is time-barred;
c   whether the court has jurisdiction;
d   whether the informant has the necessary authority to prosecute; and
e   any other relevant facts.

However, where magistrates are considering whether to issue a summons for a private prosecution where the CPS have already brought a prosecution which is still proceeding, they should, in the absence of special circumstances, be slow to issue a summons at the behest of a private prosecutor in respect of the same matter (*R (Charlson) v Guildford Magistrates' Court* [2006] EWHC 2318; [2006] 1 WLR 3494, per Silber J (at para 19), following *R v Tower Bridge Magistrates ex p Chaudhry* [1994] QB 340).

Section 6(2) of the Prosecution of Offences Act 1985 enables the DPP to take over the conduct of any criminal proceedings. Once the DPP has taken over the conduct of the proceedings, he is free to discontinue them if he thinks it appropriate to do so.

As regards private prosecutions, Lord Justice Auld in his *Review* recommended that:

158 The right of private prosecution should continue, subject to the power of the Director of Public Prosecutions, on learning of a private prosecution, to take it over and discontinue it.

159 Any court before which a private prosecution is initiated should be under a duty forthwith to notify the Director of it in writing.

160 The Director, in deciding whether to discontinue a private prosecution that he has taken over, should apply the public interest test as well as the evidential test set out in the Code for Crown Prosecutors.

The latter recommendation in fact reflects existing practice. However, it is an important point to emphasise, given that the Code does not apply to a private prosecutor.

In *R (Gladstone) v Manchester City Magistrates' Court* [2004] EWHC 2806 (Admin); [2005] 1 WLR 1987, it was held that, unless an information is required by statute to be laid by any particular person, any person may lay it where the offence is not an 'individual grievance', provided that the prosecutor can 'establish a public interest and benefit, as opposed to a purely private interest in criminal proceedings' (per Leveson J at para 11). However, in *Ewing v Davis* [2007] EWHC 1730 (Admin); (2007) 171 JP 645, Mitting J ruled (at para 21) that there is no requirement that a private prosecutor has to demonstrate that it is in the public interest that he should bring a prosecution for an offence against a provision of a public general Act. His Lordship concluded that Leveson J's words in *Gladstone* should not be taken as an invitation to magistrates to examine the circumstances of alleged offences and their relation to the private prosecutor.

In *Jones v Whalley* [2006] UKHL 41; [2007] 1 AC 63, the House of Lords held that it is an abuse of the court's process for a private prosecution to be brought against a person after he has accepted a formal caution by the police on the express assurance that, if he agrees to be cautioned, he will not have to go before a criminal court in connection with the offence.

2.7.6 What happens next?

As we shall see in Chapter 4, some offences have to be tried in the magistrates' court ('summary trial', which is dealt with in Chapter 5), while others may be tried in that court if both the defendant and the magistrates agree; the remaining offences have to be tried before a judge and jury in the Crown Court ('trial on indictment', dealt with in Chapters 11 and 12). Even if a case is ultimately tried in the Crown Court, it will nevertheless start in the magistrates' court:

- where proceedings are started by means of a written charge and requisition procedure, the requisition requires the accused to attend a magistrates' court;
- where a private prosecution is commenced by the laying of an information and the issue of a summons, it is the magistrates' court which issues the summons and the summons requires the defendant to attend the magistrates' court which issued it;
- if the suspect is arrested and charged by the police, he may be granted police bail under s 38 of PACE. In that case, he will be handed a charge sheet which tells him the date, time and place of his first court appearance, which will be in the magistrates' court.
- If, after charge, the suspect is not granted police bail, then he will be held in custody by the police until the next sitting of the magistrates' court. At that hearing, the magistrates will decide whether to grant him bail or not (see Chapter 3).

2.7.7 Early administrative hearings

Section 50 of the Crime and Disorder Act 1998 provides for 'early administrative hearings' in the magistrates' court. It provides that where the accused has been charged with an offence at a police station, the magistrates' court before which he appears for the first time may consist of a single magistrate (s 50(1)). At this hearing, the accused must be asked 'whether he wishes to be granted a right to representation funded by the Legal Services Commission as part of the Criminal Defence Service and, if he does, the Legal Services Commission has to decide whether or not to grant him such a right' (s 50(2)). The single justice may then remand the accused in custody or on bail (s 50(3)). Such a hearing may also be conducted by a justices' clerk, with the important proviso that the clerk is not empowered to remand the accused in custody and may only vary conditions of bail imposed by the police if the prosecution and accused both consent to the clerk doing so (s 50(4)).

2.8 THE PACE CODES OF PRACTICE

Several references have been made in this chapter to Codes of Practice issued under PACE.

2.8.1 Breaches of the Codes

Breaches of the provisions of the Codes do not mean that any evidence obtained in breach of the Code in question (for example, a confession) is automatically inadmissible, but if there have been breaches of the code, any evidence so obtained may well be ruled inadmissible as a result. For example, in *R v Senior* [2004] EWCA Crim 454; [2004] 3 All ER 9, where questions had been asked by customs officers to establish the ownership of suspicious baggage prior to administering a caution (even though the passengers were effectively suspects at that stage), the questioning amounted to a breach of para 10.1 of Code C, but the court held that this did not require the evidence to be excluded at the trial.

2.8.2 Revisions to the Codes

These Codes are subject to periodic revision (under s 67 of PACE). Before a Code can be revised, or a new Code issued, there has to be consultation of interested parties and Parliamentary approval.

The Codes are very detailed and very voluminous. In March 2007, there was a consultation exercise on a further revision to the Codes of Practice (<http://police-.homeoffice.gov.uk/news-and-publications/publication/operational-policing/PACE-review?view=Binary>). In his Foreword to the Consultation Paper, 'Modernising Police Powers: Review of the Police and Criminal Evidence Act (PACE) 1984', Tony McNulty MP, Minister of State for Crime Reduction, Policing, Community Safety and Counter Terrorism wrote:

> We are rightly proud of the safeguards and protections afforded to the individual when they encounter the criminal justice system. These are essential in a democratic and mature society which protects the individual from arbitrary interference.
>
> However, there are bureaucratic processes and over-complicated procedures in the application of these safeguards which do not serve the best interests of the police, or the criminal justice system or, importantly, those of the victim.
>
> My aim is to re-focus the investigation and evidence gathering processes on serving the needs of victims and witnesses and helping raise the efficiency and effectiveness of the police service in delivering the drive of the Police Reform programme to have 21st century policing powers to meet the demands of 21st century crime.

This was echoed in the Introduction to the Consultation Paper by Vic Hogg, Director of the Policing Policy and Operations Directorate at the Home Office:

> Our key aim is to maintain the framework approach to police powers. In doing so, we will look to provide greater clarity for partners, stakeholders and the public on the exercise of

those powers; improve police efficiency and effectiveness; and focus on best serving the needs of the victim and the interests of the criminal justice system.

One possible outcome of the consultation process will be a move towards Codes which contain much less detail, simply setting out key principles to govern the investigation of offences.

Chapter 3

Bail

3.1 INTRODUCTION

In this chapter, we see what happens at the defendant's first court appearance and the subsequent adjournments before the case is ready to proceed to its next stage. In particular, we examine the principles which govern whether the defendant should be held in custody or granted bail prior to the trial.

3.2 ADJOURNMENTS

Adjournments are often necessary to enable the prosecution or the defence to prepare their case for trial. At each adjournment, the defendant is told the next date upon which he must attend court. The granting of an adjournment is a matter for the court's discretion, but the rules of natural justice require that both sides should be allowed to prepare and present their cases properly (*R v Thames Magistrates' Court ex p Polemis* [1974] 1 WLR 1371).

In *R v Kingston-upon-Thames Justices ex p Martin* [1994] Imm AR 172, it was said that the following factors should be taken into account in deciding whether or not to grant an adjournment:

- the importance of the proceedings;
- the likely adverse consequences for the person seeking the adjournment;
- the risk of prejudice if the application is not granted;
- the convenience of the court;
- the interests of justice in ensuring that cases are dealt with efficiently; and
- the extent to which the applicant has been responsible for the circumstances which have led to the application for an adjournment.

In *R v Hereford Magistrates' Court ex p Rowlands* [1998] QB 110 at p 127, Lord Bingham of Cornhill CJ said:

> It is not possible or desirable to identify hard and fast rules as to when adjournments should or should not be granted. The guiding principle must be that justices should fully examine the circumstances leading to applications for delay, the reasons for those applications and the

consequences both to the prosecution and the defence. Ultimately, they must decide what is fair in the light of all those circumstances.

This court will only interfere with the exercise of the justices' discretion whether to grant an adjournment in cases where it is plain that a refusal will cause substantial unfairness to one of the parties. Such unfairness may arise when a defendant is denied a full opportunity to present his case. But neither defendants nor their legal advisers should be permitted to frustrate the objective of a speedy trial without substantial grounds.

Applications for adjournments must be subjected to rigorous scrutiny. Any defendant who is guilty of deliberately seeking to postpone a trial without good reason has no cause for complaint if his application for an adjournment is refused . . . In deciding whether to grant an adjournment justices will bear in mind that they have a responsibility for ensuring, so far as possible, that summary justice is speedy justice.

In *DPP v Picton* [2006] EWHC 1108 (Admin), Jack J, gave further guidance (at para 9) on the exercise of the justices' discretion to grant an adjournment:

(a) A decision whether to adjourn is a decision within the discretion of the trial court. An appellate court will interfere only if very clear grounds for doing so are shown.

(b) Magistrates should pay great attention to the need for expedition in the prosecution of criminal proceedings; delays are scandalous; they bring the law into disrepute; summary justice should be speedy justice; an application for an adjournment should be rigorously scrutinised.

(c) Where an adjournment is sought by the prosecution, magistrates must consider both the interest of the defendant in getting the matter dealt with, and the interest of the public that criminal charges should be adjudicated upon, and the guilty convicted as well as the innocent acquitted. With a more serious charge the public interest that there be a trial will carry greater weight.

(d) Where an adjournment is sought by the accused, the magistrates must consider whether, if it is not granted, he will be able fully to present his defence and, if he will not be able to do so, the degree to which his ability to do so is compromised.

(e) In considering the competing interests of the parties the magistrates should examine the likely consequences of the proposed adjournment, in particular its likely length, and the need to decide the facts while recollections are fresh.

(f) The reason that the adjournment is required should be examined and, if it arises through the fault of the party asking for the adjournment, that is a factor against granting the adjournment, carrying weight in accordance with the gravity of the fault. If that party was not at fault, that may favour an adjournment. Likewise if the party opposing the adjournment has been at fault, that will favour an adjournment.

(g) The magistrates should take appropriate account of the history of the case, and whether there have been earlier adjournments and at whose request and why.

(h) Lastly, of course, the factors to be considered cannot be comprehensively stated but depend upon the particular circumstances of each case, and they will often overlap. The court's duty is to do justice between the parties in the circumstances as they have arisen.

At the heart of the law relating to adjournments is the principle that the parties should be given every reasonable opportunity to prepare their cases. For example, in *R v*

Sunderland Justices ex p Dryden (1994) *The Times*, 18 May, it was held that whether or not to adjourn a case is supremely a matter for the discretion of the Court hearing the case, and that a claim that there has been a breach of natural justice can only succeed if it can sensibly be said that the party was, as a result of the refusal of an adjournment, prevented from presenting their case or deprived of an opportunity of preparing a proper case (per Buckley J). Similarly, in *S v DPP* [2006] EWHC 1207 (Admin); (2006) 170 JP 707, it was said that, if it is necessary to adjourn the case to enable justice to be done following a failure by the prosecution properly to disclose matters which ought to be disclosed, then the adjournment must be granted, unless the court is satisfied that no prejudice would be caused to the defendant by proceeding.

In *R (Costello) v North East Essex Magistrates* [2006] EWHC 3145 (Admin); (2007) 171 JP 153, Collins J said (at para 11) that if:

> through no fault of a defendant, witnesses do not attend who should have attended, or where a defendant does not attend because he is unfit to attend, the magistrates ought generally to grant adjournments . . . [T]he criteria which [are] relevant in adjournment cases [include] the importance of the proceedings and their adverse consequences for the party seeking the adjournment; the risk of prejudice to that party and to the other party in the case; the convenience of the court (which . . . is perhaps the least of the factors which weigh); and whether the party seeking the adjournment was responsible for the problem that led to the application.

The same principle applies where a prosecution witness fails to attend, since an adjournment should not be refused to punish the inefficiency of the CPS or the supposed default of one of their witnesses (*R (DPP) v North and East Hertfordshire Justices* [2008] EWHC 103 (Admin); (2008) 172 JP 193, per Cooke J at para 27).

In *Bolton Magistrates' Court ex p Merna* (1991) 155 JP 612, the Divisional Court considered the position where the accused is absent, and seeks an adjournment on medical grounds. Bingham LJ said that if the court suspects the grounds to be spurious or believes them to be inadequate, it should ordinarily express its doubts, giving the defendant an opportunity to seek to resolve them. The court may call for better evidence, require further inquiries to be made or adopt any other expedient that is fair to both parties. His Lordship added that a claim of illness with apparently responsible professional support should not be rejected without the court satisfying itself that it is proper to reject it and that no unfairness would result. McCullough J (at p 616) said:

> Plainly applications to adjourn will be necessitated when there are genuine reasons for an accused being unable to attend court. Equally plainly there will be occasions when unmeritorious applications are made on behalf of defendants who are in fact fit to attend court but have chosen not to do so. The circumstances in which such applications are made will vary widely and, for my part, I would find it impossibly difficult to try to lay down, other than in the most general terms, the principles upon which justices should act. I will say no more than this. The discretion should be exercised judicially. It should be exercised with proper regard to the principle that a defendant is entitled to a fair trial; this must include a fair opportunity to be present to hear the evidence given against him and, should he want to do so, to give evidence in his own defence and call witnesses . . . Inevitably, there will be

occasions when the justices are not satisfied with the [medical certificate] and may want to hear more. They may want somebody to get in touch with the doctor; they may even want to hear the doctor give evidence before them. I am not attempting to lay down any principles. In many cases it may be that the sensible course is to adjourn for long enough for a telephone call to be made to the doctor by a court official or perhaps a police officer and that this will provide confirmation that the accused is indeed unfit to attend. If the justices should, after such an adjournment, still not be satisfied it may be the only reasonable thing to do will be to adjourn again to enable some further approach to be made. It will always be necessary to bear in mind that it is a serious step to proceed with a man's (sic) trial for an allegation of a criminal offence in his absence.

The fact that a medical certificate has been received from the accused is not conclusive. In *R v Ealing Magistrates' Court ex p Burgess* (2001) 165 JP 82, the Divisional Court said that justices have a discretion to reject an accused's medical certificate, refuse an adjournment and proceed to hear the case in his absence. That discretion has to be exercised with proper regard to the principle that a defendant has a right to a fair trial and a fair opportunity to be present. However, the principle only extended to a fair opportunity to be present and not an unlimited one.

R v Taylor [2008] EWCA Crim 680 concerned a trial in the Crown Court, but it is submitted that the same principles apply equally to magistrates' courts. It was held that, in cases where the defendant is absent involuntarily, the court is obliged to consider how long the proposed adjournment is likely to be and the extent to which the legal representatives could, in the defendant's absence, receive and act on instructions. The court has to take into account the public interest in the pursuit of a continuous trial and the interest not only of victims but also of witnesses. There is a public interest in not allowing a trial to be put off for an indefinite period (per Moses LJ at para 16). Nevertheless, where a defendant is absent through ill-health, the court must be astute to see if an adjournment for a short period will allow the defendant to recover, and such an adjournment should not be refused unless the circumstances compel it (ibid para 17). If the court has doubts about the genuineness or gravity of the defendant's symptoms, the proper course is to adjourn the case for a medical report to be prepared (para 18).

Usually, the fact that there have been previous adjournments in a case will militate against further adjournments. However, in *R v Highbury Juvenile Court ex p DPP* [1993] COD 390, the case had been adjourned three times. On the next occasion the case was listed, a prosecution witness failed to attend. The defendant argued that his recollection of the events leading up to the charge was becoming dim and that the case should be dismissed. The magistrates refused a prosecution application for an adjournment and, as the prosecution was unable to call any evidence, dismissed the case. It was held by the Divisional Court that, because the adjournment which would have been necessary was for a very short time, and bearing in mind that there is a public interest in ensuring that charges which are properly brought should be the subject of a proper adjudication and that there had been no fault on the part of the prosecution, the magistrates should have granted a further adjournment. However, in view of the delay, the Divisional Court took no action and so the acquittal stood.

In practice, an adjournment is only refused if the court takes the view that the party requesting the adjournment should be in a position to proceed now.

In *R (F) v Knowsley Youth Court* [2006] EWHC 695 (Admin), the case was listed for trial. Shortly before the trial, the prosecution indicated that they would be applying to vacate the trial date because they had not received the full file from the police. The application for an adjournment was listed for the morning of the day of the trial; it was heard by a bench of lay justices and refused. In the afternoon, at the beginning of the trial (before a district judge), the prosecution made another application for an adjournment. The judge, who was made aware that a similar application had been made to a different bench that morning, allowed the application. The defendants sought judicial review of the district judge's decision. The prosecution conceded that the afternoon application was essentially the same application as the morning one, and that there had been no material change in circumstances between the making of the two applications. The court held that the District Judge should have refused the application. In the absence of a change of circumstances, he was not entitled to revisit the decision to refuse an adjournment.

Similarly, in *R (Watson) v Dartford Magistrates' Court* [2005] EWHC 905, prior to the date set for trial, the prosecution had sought an adjournment due to the non-availability of two witnesses. The magistrates refused the application. The parties returned to court on the trial date and the prosecution made a further application for an adjournment. The application was successful. The defendant applied for judicial review of the decision to allow the adjournment. It was held that the magistrates were wrong to allow the adjournment, since there had not been a change in circumstances since the first request to adjourn the trial. The defendant's case was remitted to the magistrates and the prosecution were to be prohibited from calling oral evidence of the two witnesses who were previously unavailable.

Reasons for granting, or refusing, an adjournment should be given, but they do not have to be elaborate, so long as the basis for the decision is clear (*Essen v DPP* [2005] EWHC 1077 (Admin)).

A cautionary note was sounded in *R (CPS) v Uxbridge Magistrates* [2007] EWHC 205 (Admin); (2007) 171 JP 279, where it was said that the Divisional Court should be 'particularly slow' to interfere with a decision of a magistrates' court to refuse an adjournment (per Clarke J at para 5).

3.3 REMANDS: PROCEDURE IN COURT

Where a defendant is before the court because he has been arrested and charged, an adjournment is called a 'remand'. The remand may be in custody or on bail. This decision is governed by the Bail Act 1976.

It is usually the prosecutor who makes the formal application for the adjournment (although there is no reason why it could not be the defence, if the prosecution are ready to proceed but the defence are not). The Crown Prosecution Service (CPS) representative is asked by the court if there are any objections to bail and, if so, to summarise them. The objections are based on a form in the CPS file which has been filled in by the police. A list of the defendant's previous convictions (if any) will also be handed to the court.

There is no requirement for formal evidence of the matters which give rise to the objections to bail to be given (*R v Mansfield Justices ex p Sharkey* [1985] QB 613). The objections to bail are simply given by the CPS representative in court; a police officer will not be called to give evidence in support of the objections.

The defendant may then make an application for bail. The defence will try to show that the prosecution objections are ill-founded or that the objections can be met by the imposition of appropriate conditions. The prosecution will not normally reply to the defence bail application. However, in *R v Isleworth Crown Court ex p Commissioner of Customs & Excise* [1990] Crim LR 859, it was said that the prosecution have a right to reply to the defence submissions if this is necessary to correct alleged mis-statements of fact in what the defence have said.

The court then comes to a decision. If bail is refused, the court must say why. The reason(s) must be based on the grounds for withholding bail set out in the Bail Act 1976 and must be recorded in a certificate which is handed to the defendant.

The Schedule to the Justices' Clerks Rules 2005 (SI 2005/545) empowers a justices' clerk (or a person appointed to assist a justices' clerk) to perform the following functions connected with bail:

8. The extending of bail on the same conditions as those (if any) previously imposed, or, with the consent of the prosecutor and the accused, the imposing or varying of conditions of bail.

9. The further adjournment of criminal proceedings with the consent of the prosecutor and the accused, if but only if,

    (a) the accused, not having been remanded on the previous adjournment, is not remanded on the further adjournment; or

    (b) the accused, having been remanded on bail on the previous adjournment, is remanded on bail on the like terms and conditions, or, with the consent of the prosecutor and the accused, on other terms and conditions.

10.

    (1) The further adjournment of criminal proceedings, where there has been no objection by the prosecutor, where the accused, having been remanded on bail on the previous adjournment, is remanded on bail on the like terms and conditions in his absence.

    (2) The remand of the accused on bail in his absence at the time of further adjourning the proceedings in pursuance of sub-paragraph (1) above.

Contested bail applications, however, have to be dealt with by the magistrates.

3.4 THE BAIL ACT 1976

Section 4(1) of the Bail Act 1976 provides that, 'a person to whom this section applies shall be granted bail except as provided in Sched 1 to this Act'. This is sometimes said to create a 'right to bail'. This description is, however, rather inaccurate. It would be better to say that s 4 creates a (rebuttable) presumption in favour of bail.

Section 4(2) sets out the scope of s 4. It applies to:

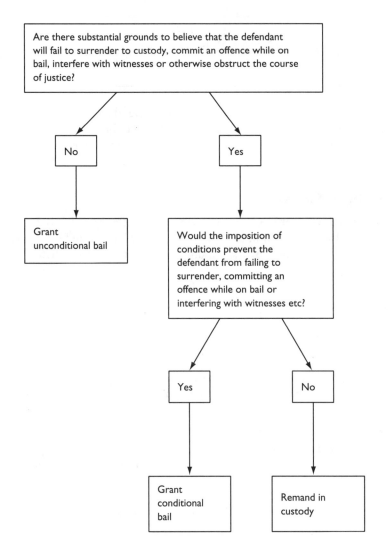

Figure 3.1 The decision-making process for bail.

... a person who is accused of an offence when—

(a) he appears or is brought before a magistrates' court or the Crown Court in the course of or in connection with proceedings for the offence, or
(b) he applies to a court for bail or for a variation of the conditions of bail in connection with the proceedings.

Section 4(4) provides that s 4 also applies:

... to a person who has been convicted of an offence and whose case is adjourned by the court for the purpose of enabling inquiries or a report to be made to assist the court in dealing with him for the offence.

> In summary, therefore, the presumption in favour of bail applies at all stages prior to conviction, and also after conviction, but only where the case is adjourned for a pre-sentence report.

Where s 4 does not apply (for example, when the defendant appeals against conviction and/or sentence, or where the defendant is committed for sentence following summary conviction of an either-way offence), the court nevertheless has a discretion to grant bail.

3.4.1 Imprisonable offences

If the defendant is charged with (or has been convicted of) an offence which is punishable with imprisonment, the presumption in favour of bail may be rebutted if the court finds that one or more of the grounds for withholding bail set out in Pt 1 of Sched 1 to the Bail Act applies.

3.4.1.1 Grounds for withholding bail

Those grounds are as follows.

Under para 2(1):
The defendant need not be granted bail if the court is satisfied that there are substantial grounds for believing that the defendant, if released on bail (whether subject to conditions or not) would:

(a) fail to surrender to custody; or
(b) commit an offence while on bail; or
(c) interfere with witnesses or otherwise obstruct the course of justice, whether in relation to himself or any other person.

These are the grounds that are most commonly invoked in practice.

Under para 2A:
The defendant need not be granted bail if (a) the offence with which he is charged is an indictable offence or an offence triable either way; and (b) it appears to the court that he was on bail in criminal proceedings on the date of the offence.

This exception to the presumption in favour of bail (that, at the time of the present offence, the defendant was already on bail in respect of earlier alleged offences) is amended by s 14(1) of the Criminal Justice Act 2003 to read as follows:

2A(1) If the defendant falls within this paragraph he may not be granted bail unless the court is satisfied that there is no significant risk of his committing an offence while on bail (whether subject to conditions or not).

(2) The defendant falls within this paragraph if—

(a) he is aged 18 or over, and

(b) it appears to the court that he was on bail in criminal proceedings on the date of the offence.

Section 14 of the Criminal Justice Act 2003 was brought into force from 1 January 2007 but only in relation to offences where the defendant is liable to a life sentence (see Criminal Justice Act 2003 (Commencement No 14 and Transitional Provision) Order 2006 (SI 2006/3217) and Home Office Circular 39/2006).

This amendment was made to ensure conformity with the Human Rights Act 1998. The Law Commission (Law Com No 269) had recommended that the Bail Act 1976 be amended to make it plain that the fact that the defendant was on bail at the time of the alleged offence is not an independent ground for the refusal of bail, as para 2A (as originally drafted) appeared to suggest, but is merely one of the considerations that the court should take into account when considering withholding bail on the ground that there is a real risk that the defendant will commit an offence while on bail. It is, of course, important in this context to remember the presumption of innocence: the accused is alleged to have committed an offence while on bail as a result of allegations of an earlier offence; at this stage, it cannot be assumed that he is guilty of either offence, since neither offence has been proved.

Under para 3:
The defendant need not be granted bail if the court is satisfied that the defendant should be kept in custody for his own protection or, if he is a child or young person, for his own welfare.

This provision may be invoked, for example, where the allegations against the defendant have resulted in a lot of publicity and ill-feeling against him.

Under para 4:
The defendant need not be granted bail if he is in custody in pursuance of the sentence of a court . . .

In other words, the accused is already in custody because he is serving a custodial sentence imposed for an earlier offence.

Under para 5:
The defendant need not be granted bail where the court is satisfied that it has not been practicable to obtain sufficient information for the purpose of taking the decisions required by this Part of this Schedule for want of time since the institution of the proceedings against him.

In other words, the court is satisfied that lack of time since the commencement of proceedings means that it has been impracticable to obtain the information needed to decide the question of bail properly.

Under para 6:
The defendant need not be granted bail if, having been released on bail in or in connection with the proceedings for the offence, he has been arrested in under s 7 of the Bail Act.

In other words, the accused has been arrested for absconding in connection with the present proceedings.

This paragraph is amended by s 15(1) of the Criminal Justice Act 2003 to read as follows:

(1) If the defendant falls within this paragraph, he may not be granted bail unless the court is satisfied that there is no significant risk that, if released on bail (whether subject to conditions or not), he would fail to surrender to custody.

(2) Subject to sub-paragraph (3) below, the defendant falls within this paragraph if—

  (a) he is aged 18 or over, and
  (b) it appears to the court that, having been released on bail in or in connection with the proceedings for the offence, he failed to surrender to custody.

(3) Where it appears to the court that the defendant had reasonable cause for his failure to surrender to custody, he does not fall within this paragraph unless it also appears to the court that he failed to surrender to custody at the appointed place as soon as reasonably practicable after the appointed time.

(4) For the purposes of sub-paragraph (3) above, a failure to give to the defendant a copy of the record of the decision to grant him bail shall not constitute a reasonable cause for his failure to surrender to custody.

Section 15 of the Criminal Justice Act 2003 was brought into force from 1 January 2007 but only in relation to offences where the defendant is liable to a life sentence (see Criminal Justice Act 2003 (Commencement No 14 and Transitional Provision) Order 2006 (SI 2006/3217) and Home Office Circular 39/2006).

The Law Commission (Law Com No 269) had recommended that para 6 be repealed altogether, on the basis that it is superfluous (in that the circumstances leading to the defendant being arrested under s 7 may properly be taken into account, under para 9(c) of Pt I of Sched 1 to the Bail Act 1976 (see below), as a possible reason for concluding that one of the Convention-compatible grounds for withholding bail is satisfied).

Under the revised version of para 6, the court is required to refuse bail to an adult defendant who has failed, without reasonable cause, to surrender to custody in answer to bail in the same proceedings, unless the court is satisfied that there is no significant risk that he would fail again to surrender if released.

In *R (Wiggins) v Harrow Crown Court* [2005] EWHC 882 (Admin), Collins J commented (at para 24) that, in the amendments made by the Criminal Justice Act 2003:

Parliament has added a number of paragraphs which indicate that if there have been particular actions by a defendant it may be in effect presumed that he should not have bail unless the court is satisfied that there is no significant risk that if released on bail he would fail to surrender to custody, or would commit an offence, or whatever the situation in question might be. That, in effect, reverses the usual burden whereby bail must be granted unless the court is satisfied of a particular situation. It then becomes necessary for the court to be persuaded, because of what has happened, that there is no significant risk that he would fail to surrender to custody, or not commit an offence, or whatever.

Under paras 6A to 6C:

Section 19(4) of the Criminal Justice Act 2003 added paras 6A–6C to Sched 1. These provide that a defendant aged 18 or over who has been charged with an imprisonable offence will not be granted bail (unless the court is satisfied that there is no significant risk of his committing an offence while on bail), where the three conditions set out in para 6B apply, namely:

(a) there is drug test evidence that the person has a specified Class A drug in his body (by way of a lawful test obtained under s 63B of the Police and Criminal Evidence Act 1984 or s 161 of the Criminal Justice Act 2003);

(b) either he is charged with an offence under s 5(2) or (3) of the Misuse of Drugs Act 1971 and the offence relates to a specified Class A drug; or the court is satisfied that there are substantial grounds for believing that the misuse of a specified Class A drug caused or contributed to the offence with which he is charged or that offence was motivated wholly or partly by his intended misuse of a specified Class A drug; and

(c) the person does not agree to undergo an assessment (carried out by a suitably qualified person) of whether he is dependent upon or has a propensity to misuse any specified Class A drugs, or he has undergone such an assessment but does not agree to participate in any relevant follow-up which has been offered.

If an assessment or follow-up is proposed and agreed to, it will be a condition of bail that they be undertaken (s 3(6E) of the Bail Act 1976).

Under para 7:

Where the defendant has been convicted and the case is adjourned for a pre-sentence report to be prepared:

the defendant need not be granted bail if it appears to the court that it would be impracticable to complete the inquiries or make the report without keeping the defendant in custody.

In other words, it would be impracticable to produce the pre-sentence report without keeping the defendant in custody.

3.4.1.2 *Factors to be taken into account*

The factors which have to be taken into account in deciding whether or not the grounds set out in Sched 1 have been established are listed in para 9 of that schedule, which provides that:

the court shall have regard to such of the following considerations as appear to it to be relevant, that is to say—

(a) the nature and seriousness of the offence or default (and the probable method of dealing with the defendant for it),

(b) the character, antecedents, associations and community ties of the defendant,

(c) the defendant's record as respects the fulfilment of his obligations under previous grants of bail in criminal proceedings,

(d) except in the case of a defendant whose case is adjourned for inquiries or a report, the strength of the evidence of his having committed the offence or having defaulted,

as well as to any others which appear to be relevant.

a   *Nature and seriousness of the offence*: this draws attention to the gravity of the offence. The main point is that if a custodial sentence is likely, that is an incentive to abscond.

b   *Character, antecedents, associations and community ties of the defendant*: the phrase 'character and antecedents' refers principally to any previous convictions. These may make a custodial sentence more likely (especially if the defendant, if convicted of the present offence, will be in breach of a suspended sentence of imprisonment). Section 42 of the Magistrates' Courts Act 1980 provides that, if a magistrate hears about a defendant's previous convictions in the course of a bail application, that magistrate is disqualified from trying the defendant if a summary trial takes place subsequently. However, this provision will be repealed when the repeals in Pt 4 of Sched 37 to the Criminal Justice Act 2003 come into effect.
The word 'associations' is generally taken to refer to undesirable friends with criminal records. Examining the defendant's 'community ties' involves looking at how easy it would be for the defendant to abscond and how much he has to lose by absconding. How long has the defendant lived at his present address? Is he single or married? Does he have dependant children? Is he in employment? How long has he had his present job? Does he have a mortgage or a protected tenancy?

c   *The defendant's bail record*: has he absconded or committed offences while on bail in the past? Absconding in earlier proceedings is regarded as evidence of a risk that he may do so again.

d   *The strength of the evidence against the defendant*: the strength of the prosecution case is relevant in that, if the defendant has a good chance of acquittal (for example, the prosecution case rests on uncorroborated identification evidence), it can be argued that there is no point in the defendant absconding. Conversely, if the prosecution case is strong, so that conviction is likely, the defendant may abscond rather than 'face the music' (especially if a custodial sentence is likely).

The concluding words of para 9 make it clear that the list of factors set out above is not exhaustive.

In particular, it should also be noted that s 4(9) of the Bail Act stipulates that, 'in taking any decisions required by Pt I or II of Sched 1 to this Act, the considerations to which the court is to have regard include, so far as relevant, any misuse of controlled drugs by the defendant'.

3.4.1.3 Juveniles

Section 14(2) of the Criminal Justice Act 2003 inserts a para 9AA (applicable to juvenile defendants), which reads as follows:

(1)   This paragraph applies if—

    (a)   the defendant is under the age of 18, and

    (b)   it appears to the court that he was on bail in criminal proceedings on the date of the offence.

(2)   In deciding for the purposes of paragraph 2(1) of this Part of this Schedule whether it is satisfied that there are substantial grounds for believing that the defendant, if released on bail (whether subject to conditions or not), would commit an offence while on bail, the court shall give particular weight to the fact that the defendant was on bail in criminal proceedings on the date of the offence.

Section 15(2) of the Criminal Justice Act 2003 also inserts a para 9AB (applicable to juvenile defendants), which provides as follows:

(1)   Subject to sub-paragraph (2) below, this paragraph applies if—

    (a)   the defendant is under the age of 18, and

    (b)   it appears to the court that, having been released on bail in or in connection with the proceedings for the offence, he failed to surrender to custody.

(2)   Where it appears to the court that the defendant had reasonable cause for his failure to surrender to custody, this paragraph does not apply unless it also appears to the court that he failed to surrender to custody at the appointed place as soon as reasonably practicable after the appointed time.

(3)   In deciding for the purposes of paragraph 2(1) of this Part of this Schedule whether it is satisfied that there are substantial grounds for believing that the defendant, if released on bail (whether subject to conditions or not), would fail to surrender to custody, the court shall give particular weight to—

    (a)   where the defendant did not have reasonable cause for his failure to surrender to custody, the fact that he failed to surrender to custody, or

    (b)   where he did have reasonable cause for his failure to surrender to custody, the fact that he failed to surrender to custody at the appointed place as soon as reasonably practicable after the appointed time.

Thus, the court is required, in assessing the risk of future absconding in the case of defendants under the age of 18, to give particular weight to the fact that they have failed to surrender to custody. At the time of writing, these provisions were in force only where the juvenile was charged with an offence carrying a life sentence.

3.4.2 Murder, manslaughter and rape

Section 25 of the Criminal Justice and Public Order Act 1994 (as amended by s 56 of the Crime and Disorder Act 1998) applies where the defendant is charged with murder, attempted murder, manslaughter, rape or attempted rape and has been convicted of one of these offences in the past. In a case to which s 25 applies, bail may only be granted if there are 'exceptional circumstances' which justify the grant of bail. In *R (O) v Harrow Crown Court* [2003] EWHC 868; [2003] 1 WLR 2756, the Divisional Court held that s

25 of the Criminal Justice and Public Order Act 1994 is compatible with the right to liberty guaranteed by Art 5 of the European Convention on Human Rights. However, the judges differed as to how s 25 actually operates, Kennedy LJ holding that s 25 effectively imposes a neutral burden (the court having to be 'satisfied' that there are exceptional circumstances), but Hooper J holding that s 25 should be regarded as placing an evidential burden on the defendant to produce or point to material which supports the existence of exceptional circumstances, so that it is then for the prosecution to satisfy the court that bail should not be granted. The case went to the House of Lords (*R (O) v Crown Court at Harrow* [2006] UKHL 42; [2007] 1 AC 249). Lord Carswell said (at para 6) that it is:

> plain from the ordinary meaning of the wording of s 25 that Parliament intended that if the judge deciding a bail application to which the section applies found the arguments for and against the existence of such exceptional circumstances evenly balanced and is left uncertain, he must refuse bail. I do not see how a judge could be 'satisfied' of the existence of exceptional circumstances justifying the grant of bail unless he came to the conclusion that the arguments in favour or the existence of such circumstances outweighed those in favour of it.

His Lordship concluded, at para 12, that:

> I have to agree with Hooper J that in its ordinary meaning the word 'satisfied' is less neutral and that to be satisfied requires more than a judgment or evaluation. As the court has to be satisfied that there are exceptional circumstances justifying the grant of bail, I conclude, in agreement with Hooper J, that the phrase connotes a burden or presumption. That being so, it is necessary to apply the technique of reading down s 25, so far as it is possible to do so, in order to avoid a breach of the appellant's Convention rights. It was agreed that this could be done, as Hooper J has set out in paragraph 99 of his judgment, by imposing an evidential burden on the defendant to point to or produce material which supports the existence of exceptional circumstances.

Lord Brown of Eaton-under-Heywood said, at para 35:

> ...I...have a mild preference for Hooper J's approach. Like him I read the section as placing a burden on the s 25 defendant. He has to rebut a presumption and if he fails to do so is to be denied bail...[I]n the vast majority of cases the court will reach a clear view one way or the other whether the conditions for withholding bail specified by Schedule 1 to the Bail Act 1976 are satisfied. But just occasionally the court will be left unsure as to whether the defendant should be released on bail - the only situation in which the burden of proof assumes any relevance - and in my judgment bail would then have to be granted. That must be the default position. Section 25 should in my judgment be read down to make that plain.

The House of Lords went on to hold that s 25 operates to dis-apply the ordinary requirement, under reg 6(6) of the Prosecution of Offences (Custody Time Limits) Regulations 1987: that bail should be granted automatically to anyone whose custody time limit has expired. Moreover, it was held that the continued detention in custody of a defendant awaiting trial after the court's refusal to extend the statutory custody time limit due to the prosecution's failure to act with due diligence and expedition, does not necessarily amount to a breach of the defendant's right to 'trial within a reasonable time' under Art 5(3) of the ECHR.

3.4.3 Summary offences

Section 52 and Sched 12 of the Criminal Justice and Immigration Act 2008 amend para 1 of Pt 1 of Sched 1 to the Bail Act 1976, so that where the imprisonable offence is a summary offence, or an offence to which s 22 of the Magistrates' Courts Act 1980 applies (criminal damage where the value involved is £5,000 or less), Pt 1 of the schedule to the 1976 Act does not apply. Schedule 12 to the 2008 Act goes on to insert a new Pt 1A into Sched 1 of the 1976 Act. Part 1A applies where the accused is charged with an imprisonable summary offence (or criminal damage where the value is £5,000 or less). It will provide that, in such cases, the exceptions to the presumption in favour of bail are as follows:

(a) where the accused has failed to surrender to custody and the court believes, in view of that failure, that he would (if released on bail) fail to surrender to custody (para 2);

(b) where the accused was on bail on the date of the current alleged offence and the court is satisfied that there are substantial grounds for believing that (if released on bail), he would commit an offence while on bail (para 3);

(c) where the court is satisfied that there are substantial grounds for believing that the defendant (if released on bail) would commit an offence while on bail by engaging in conduct that would, or would be likely to, cause physical or mental injury to someone else, or cause someone else to fear physical or mental injury (para 4);

(d) where the court is satisfied that the defendant should be kept in custody for his own protection or, if he is a child or young person, for his own welfare (para 5);

(e) where the accused is already serving a custodial sentence (para 6);

(f) where the accused has been arrested under s 7 of the Bail Act 1976, and the court is satisfied that there are substantial grounds for believing that (if released on bail) he would fail to surrender to custody, commit an offence while on bail or interfere with witnesses or otherwise obstruct the course of justice (whether in relation to himself or any other person) (para 7); and

(g) where the court is satisfied that it has not been practicable to obtain sufficient information for the purpose of taking the decision on whether or not to grant bail, due to lack of time since the institution of the proceedings against the accused (para 8).

Paragraph 3 of Sched 12 to the Criminal Justice and Immigration Act 2008 also inserts a new section, s 9A, into the Bail Act 1976. Under this provision, where an accused under the age of 18 is charged with an offence to which s 22 of the Magistrates' Courts Act 1980 applies (criminal damage where the value involved is £5,000 or less), and the trial of that offence has not begun, a magistrates' court (this term includes a youth court) which is deciding whether to withhold or grant bail must consider, having regard to any representations from the prosecution and the accused person, whether the value involved exceeds £5,000.

3.4.4 Non-imprisonable offences

The grounds for withholding bail where the offence, or every offence, of which the defendant is accused or convicted is one which is not punishable with imprisonment are contained in Pt 2 of Sched 1 to the Bail Act 1976. This provides that a defendant who is charged with (or convicted of) a non-imprisonable offence need not be granted bail in the following circumstances.

Under para 2:

The defendant need not be granted bail if—

(a) it appears to the court that, having been previously granted bail in criminal proceedings, he has failed to surrender to custody in accordance with his obligations under the grant of bail; and

(b) the court believes, in view of that failure, that the defendant, if released on bail (whether subject to conditions or not) would fail to surrender to custody.

Under para 3:

The defendant need not be granted bail if the court is satisfied that the defendant should be kept in custody for his own protection or, if he is a child or young person, for his own welfare.

Under para 4:

The defendant need not be granted bail if he is in custody in pursuance of the sentence of a court . . .

Under para 5:

The defendant need not be granted bail if—

(a) having been released on bail in or in connection with the proceedings for the offence, he has been arrested in pursuance of section 7 of this Act; and

(b) the court is satisfied that there are substantial grounds for believing that the defendant, if released on bail (whether subject to conditions or not) would fail to surrender to custody, commit an offence on bail or interfere with witnesses or otherwise obstruct the course of justice (whether in relation to himself or any other person).

This version of para 5 was substituted by s 13(4) of the Criminal Justice Act 2003 (in force since April 2004) to ensure conformity with the Human Rights Act 1998. The Law Commission (Law Com No 269) had recommended that the paragraph be amended by adding a requirement that (when considering the case of a defendant who has been arrested under s 7) the court must be satisfied that there are substantial grounds for believing that the defendant, if released on bail (whether subject to conditions or not) would fail to surrender to custody, commit an offence while on bail, or interfere with witnesses or otherwise obstruct the course of justice.

It is very rare for bail to be refused in the case of non-imprisonable offences. It should be noted that bail cannot be refused on the grounds that the defendant is likely to abscond or to commit offences while on bail.

3.5 CONDITIONS

If the magistrates grant unconditional bail, the defendant's only duty is to attend court on the date of the next hearing (s 3(1) of the Bail Act). It is, however, open to the court to attach conditions to the grant of bail. Section 3 of the Act provides as follows:

(4) He may be required, before release on bail, to provide a surety or sureties to secure his surrender to custody.

(5) He may be required, before release on bail, to give security for his surrender to custody. The security may be given by him or on his behalf.

(6) He may be required to comply, before release on bail or later, with such requirements as appear to the court to be necessary—

  (a) to secure that he surrenders to custody,

  (b) to secure that he does not commit an offence while on bail,

  (c) to secure that he does not interfere with witnesses or otherwise obstruct the course of justice whether in relation to himself or any other person,

  (ca) for his own protection or, if he is a child or young person, for his own welfare or in his own interests,

  (d) to secure that he makes himself available for the purpose of enabling inquiries or a report to be made to assist the court in dealing with him for the offence,

  (e) to secure that before the time appointed for him to surrender to custody, he attends an interview with an authorised advocate or authorised litigator, as defined by section 119(1) of the Courts and Legal Services Act 1990;

. . .

(6ZAA) Subject to section 3AA below, if he is a child or young person he may be required to comply with requirements imposed for the purpose of securing the electronic monitoring of his compliance with any other requirement imposed on him as a condition of bail.

(6ZA) Where he is required under sub-section (6) above to reside in a bail hostel or probation hostel, he may also be required to comply with the rules of the hostel.

. . .

Paragraph 3(6)(ca) was added by s 13 of the Criminal Justice Act 2003 in response to concern by the Law Commission that there was no power to impose a bail condition for the protection of the defendant even though one of the exceptions to the right to bail, in the Bail Act, is based on the need for protection of the defendant, and Convention case law recognises that, in certain circumstances, the protection of the defendant is capable of being a relevant and sufficient reason for detention.

Section 3 does not provide a comprehensive list of conditions that may be attached to the grant of bail, but it does set out, in sub-s (6), the basis on which conditions may be attached.

It should be noted that s 3(2) provides that 'No recognizance for his surrender to custody shall be taken from him'. In other words, an accused cannot act as surety for himself.

Sub-sections 3(6C)–(6E) of the Bail Act 1976 provide that, where:

a   the conditions set out in para 6B of Part 1 of Sched 1 are satisfied (namely, there is drug test evidence that the person has a specified Class A drug in his body, and either the offence is a drugs offence associated with a specified Class A drug or the court is satisfied that there are substantial grounds for believing that the misuse of a specified Class A drug caused or contributed to that offence or provided its motivation);

b   the person has been offered an assessment of whether he is dependent upon or has a propensity to misuse any specified Class A drugs (or such an assessment has been carried out and he has been offered follow-up); and

c   he has agreed to undergo that assessment and participate in any follow-up,

then the court, if it grants bail, shall impose as a condition of bail that the defendant both undergoes the relevant assessment and participates in any relevant follow-up proposed to him or, if a relevant assessment has been carried out, that the defendant participates in the relevant follow-up (s 3(6D)).

3.5.1 Examples of commonly imposed conditions

Sureties and security are the only conditions specifically mentioned in the Bail Act 1976. However, the court can impose any condition it thinks appropriate, provided that the condition is necessary on the grounds set out in the previous paragraph.

Commonly imposed conditions include the following:

- surety (where one or more persons, other than the defendant, promise to pay a specified sum to the court if the defendant absconds: see below for further details);
- security (where the defendant deposits money or one or more valuable items with the court). If the defendant absconds the court can order the forfeiture of some or all of the security;
- residence (that is, living and sleeping at a specified address);
- residence in a bail hostel (in which case, it is also a condition that the defendant must comply with the hostel rules (s 3(6ZA));
- reporting to a specified police station (on specified days and at specified times);
- curfew (requiring the defendant to stay indoors during specified hours at night);
- not to enter a particular building or to go to a specified place or to go within a specified distance of a certain address;
- not to contact, directly or indirectly, the victim or any named prosecution witnesses;
- surrender of defendant's passport to the police;
- before the time appointed for surrender to custody, to attend an interview with his solicitor (s 3(6)(e)).

In *McDonald v Procurator Fiscal, Elgin* (2003), *The Times*, 17 April (a case which came before the High Court of Justiciary in Scotland), the defendant had been granted bail subject to a condition that he remain in his dwelling at all times except between 10 am and 12 noon. The court held that this (rather onerous) requirement did not amount to detention or deprivation of his freedom and did not constitute an infringement of Art 5 of the European Convention on Human Rights.

In *R (CPS) v Chorley Justices* [2002] EWHC 2162; (2002) 166 JP 764, the question at issue was whether justices are empowered to attach a condition to the grant of bail, that the defendant would present himself at the door of his residence when required to do so by a police officer during the hours of curfew to which he was subject. It was held that there is power, under s 3(6) of the Bail Act, to impose such 'door-step' conditions, but it is a question of fact in each case whether such a condition would be necessary.

In *R (Stevens) v Truro Magistrates' Court* [2001] EWHC 558 (Admin); [2002] 1 WLR 144, it was held that it is permissible for a third party to make available an asset to a defendant in order to enable him to give it as security for his release on bail and the court can accept such an asset. As it is the defendant himself who gives the security, the arrangements the defendant might make with those who helped him put up the requisite security are not to be a matter for the court. There is no obligation for the third party to be notified before the security is forfeited on the defendant's non-attendance.

Under s 3AA of the Bail Act, where a juvenile is granted bail, compliance with any bail conditions can be enforced through electronic monitoring, provided that:

a he has attained the age of 12;
b either (i) he is charged with a violent or sexual offence, or an offence carrying at least 14 years' imprisonment, or (ii) he is charged with an imprisonable offence and he has a recent history of repeatedly committing imprisonable offences while on bail or to local authority accommodation; and
c a youth offending team has informed the court of its opinion that the imposition of the requirement is suitable for the juvenile.

Paragraph 2 of Sched 11 to the Criminal Justice and Immigration Act 2008 inserts a new sub-section, (6ZAA), into s 3 of the Bail Act 1976, to provide that the conditions which may be imposed under s 3(6) include electronic monitoring requirements for adults as well as juveniles. Moreover, para 4 of Sched 11 to the 2008 Act adds a new section, s 3AB, to the Bail Act 1976. When it is brought into force, this section will empower the court to impose electronic monitoring requirements on a person who has attained the age of 17, provided that the court is satisfied that, without the electronic monitoring requirement, the person would not be granted bail (s 3AB(2)). Where the person is aged 17 (and so a juvenile for most other purposes), a youth offending team must have informed the court that the imposition of electronic monitoring requirements will be suitable in his case (s 3AB(4)).

In the case of a juvenile, the court might also impose a condition of supervision by a Youth Offending Team (on a 'bail support and supervision programme').

3.5.2 When may conditions be imposed?

Paragraph 8(1) of Sched 1, Pt 1 (as amended by the Criminal Justice Act 2003) makes it clear that no conditions shall be imposed:

unless it appears to the court that it is necessary to do so—

(a) for the purpose of preventing the occurrence of any of the events mentioned in paragraph 2(1) of this Part of this Schedule [namely, fail to surrender to custody, commit an offence while on bail, or interfere with witnesses or otherwise obstruct the course of justice, whether in relation to himself or any other person], or

(b) for the defendant's own protection or, if he is a child or young person, for his own welfare or in his own interests.

In other words, conditions may be imposed only if the court regards them as 'necessary' to prevent the defendant from failing to surrender to custody, or committing offences while on bail, or interfering with witnesses or otherwise obstructing the course of justice, or where necessary for the defendant's own protection or welfare.

In *R v Mansfield Justices ex p Sharkey* [1985] QB 613, Lord Lane CJ said (at p 625) that whereas there have to be substantial grounds for believing that the defendant will abscond, commit further offences, etc., for bail to be withheld altogether, the test for the imposition of conditions is a lower one. To impose conditions on the grant of bail, it is enough if the justices 'perceive a real and not a fanciful risk' of the defendant absconding, committing further offences, etc. In *R (CPS) v Chorley Justices* [2002] EWHC 2162; (2002) 166 JP 764, the court noted that the only prerequisite for imposing conditions on bail under s 3(6) is that, in the circumstances of the particular case, imposition of the condition is 'necessary' to achieve the aims specified in the section.

3.5.3 Non-imprisonable offence

In *R v Bournemouth Magistrates ex p Cross* (1989) 89 Cr App R 90, it was held that conditions may be imposed when bail is granted to someone who is charged with a non-imprisonable offence.

3.5.4 Breaking conditions of bail

If the defendant is granted conditional bail but then breaches a condition of that bail, he is liable to be arrested under s 7(3) of the Bail Act 1976, which provides that:

A person who has been released on bail in criminal proceedings and is under a duty to surrender into the custody of a court may be arrested without warrant by a constable—

. . .

(b) if the constable has reasonable grounds for believing that that person is likely to break any of the conditions of his bail or has reasonable grounds for suspecting that that person has broken any of those conditions; or

(c) in a case where that person was released on bail with one or more surety or sureties, if a surety notifies a constable in writing that that person is unlikely to surrender to custody and that for that reason the surety wishes to be relieved of his obligations as a surety.

Under s 7(4), a person arrested under sub-s (3) must be 'brought as soon as practicable and in any event within 24 hours after his arrest before a justice of the peace', unless he was arrested within 24 hours of the time appointed for him to surrender to custody, in which case he must be brought before the court at which he was to have surrendered to custody. For these purposes Christmas Day, Good Friday and any Sunday are disregarded (s 7(7)).

In *R v Governor of Glen Parva Young Offender Institution ex p G* [1998] QB 877, the defendant was arrested for breach of bail conditions; he was taken to the cells of a magistrates' court within 24 hours of arrest but was not brought before a magistrate until two hours after the expiry of the 24-hour time limit. The Divisional Court held that the detention after 24 hours was unlawful: s 7(4) of the Bail Act 1976 requires the defendant to be brought before a justice of the peace (not merely brought within the court precincts) within 24 hours of arrest.

The importance of dealing with the accused within 24 hours was again emphasised in *R (Culley) v Crown Court sitting at Dorchester* [2007] EWHC 109 (Admin); (2007) 171 JP 373, where it was held that the time limit under s 7 is a strict one. It follows that the justice is required to complete his investigation and decision-making in relation to this matter within the 24-hour period. If the justice fails to do so, the continued custody of the accused becomes unlawful from the moment the 24-hour period has expired. If the justice purports to remand the accused in custody after that the time, the order is *ultra vires* and unlawful.

In *R v Liverpool Justices ex p DPP* [1993] QB 233, it was held that where the police arrest someone who is in breach of a bail condition or whom the police believe to be about to abscond, a single lay justice has the power to remand the defendant in custody or to grant bail subject to further conditions.

Section 7(5) of the Bail Act provides that:

> A justice of the peace before whom a person is brought under sub-section (4) . . . may . . . if of the opinion that that person—
>
> (a)   is not likely to surrender to custody, or
> (b)   has broken or is likely to break any condition of his bail,
>
> remand him in custody or commit him to custody, as the case may require or, alternatively, grant him bail subject to the same or to different conditions, but if not of that opinion shall grant him bail subject to the same conditions (if any) as were originally imposed.

In other words, the court has to decide whether the accused is indeed likely to fail to surrender to custody or has broken (or is likely to breach) any condition of his bail. It is likely that the defendant's bail will be withdrawn, so that he will be held in custody pending trial, or else bail will be granted again but subject to more stringent conditions.

The effect of the Human Rights Act 1998 on the procedure to be followed in such cases has been considered in several cases by the Divisional Court. In *R (Hussain) v Derby Magistrates' Court* [2001] EWCA Admin 507; [2001] 1 WLR 2454, the Divisional Court said that the s 7 procedure is not concerned with the trial of a criminal charge. Speed of determination is of the essence, and the defendant ought not to be kept waiting for a court to determine the matter any longer than is strictly necessary. This echoes the comments in *R v Liverpool City Justices ex p DPP* [1993] QB 233 at 241, that the 1976 Act requires the magistrate to conduct an 'informal inquiry' into the reasons for the defendant's arrest (per Roch, J).

In *R (DPP) v Havering Magistrates' Court* [2001] 1 WLR 805, the Divisional Court again considered s 7 in the context of Arts 5 and 6 of the Convention. The court confirmed that Art 6 has no direct relevance where justices are exercising their judgment whether or not to commit a person to custody following breach of bail conditions, since s 7 does not create any criminal offence. However, the court went on to hold that Art 5 is directly relevant, but said that the procedures applicable under domestic law are entirely compatible with the requirements of Art 5. The court went on to give detailed guidance on proceedings under s 7. Latham LJ, at para 38, said:

> Proceedings under s 7(5) are by their nature emergency proceedings to determine whether or not a person, who was not considered to present the risks which would have justified remanding in custody in the first instance, none the less does now present one or other of those risks. It is true that a literal reading of s 7(5) could lead to the conclusion that the mere fact of a breach of condition could justify detention. But it should be noted that such a finding only gives the justice the power to detain, and not the duty to detain . . . in exercising that power the justice would not be entitled to order detention by reason simply of the finding of a breach; that in itself is not a justification for the refusal of bail . . . The fact of a breach of a condition may be some evidence, even powerful evidence, of a relevant risk arising. But it is no more than one of the factors which a justice must consider in exercising his discretion under s 7(5).

At para 39, his Lordship went on to say that:

> the justice is simply required by the statute to come to an honest and rational opinion on the material put before him. In doing so he must bear in mind the consequences to the defendant, namely the fact that he is at risk of losing his liberty in the context of the presumption of innocence.

Having ruled that this is compatible with Art 5, his Lordship continued (at paras 40 and 41):

> [T]he material upon which a justice is entitled in domestic law to come to his opinion is not restricted to admissible evidence in the strict sense . . . I see nothing in . . . Art. 5 . . . which suggests that . . . reliance on material other than evidence which would be admissible at a criminal trial would be a breach of the protection required by Art. 5 . . .
>
> What undoubtedly is necessary is that the justice, when forming his opinion, takes proper account of the quality of the material upon which he is asked to adjudicate. This material is likely to range from mere assertion at the one end of the spectrum which is unlikely to have any probative effect, to documentary proof at the other end of the spectrum. The procedural task of the justice is to ensure that the defendant has a full and fair opportunity to comment on and answer that material. If that material includes evidence from a witness who gives oral testimony clearly the defendant must be given an opportunity to cross-examine. Likewise, if he wishes to give oral evidence he should be entitled to. The ultimate obligation of the justice is to evaluate that material in the light of the serious potential consequences to the defendant . . . and the particular nature of the material . . . taking into account, if hearsay is relied upon by either side, the fact that it is hearsay and has not been the subject of cross-examination, and form an honest and rational opinion. If his opinion is that the defendant has broken a condition of his bail, he must then go on to consider whether or not, in view of that

opinion, and in all the circumstances of the case, he should commit the defendant in custody or grant bail on the same or other conditions . . .

R (DPP) v Havering Magistrates' Court was followed in *R (Vickers) v West London Magistrates' Court* [2003] EWHC 1809; (2003) 167 JP 473. The defendant was arrested and brought before the justices for failing to comply with the bail conditions. Before the justices, he sought to raise a defence of reasonable excuse; however, the justices held that no such defence exists under s 7 of the Bail Act 1976. The defendant sought judicial review of that decision, contending that, when considering the matter under s 7(5), the justices were obliged to first decide whether a breach had occurred and, in reaching that decision, must have regard to any reasonable excuse which the accused put forward. The Divisional Court held that s 7(5) of the 1976 Act requires a two-stage approach. Gage J (at para 16) describes the two stages thus:

> First a decision must be made as to whether or not there has been a breach of a condition. If there has been no breach of a condition then the bailed person is entitled to be admitted to bail on precisely the same conditions – in other words, bail continues. If the justices are of the opinion that there has been a breach of the condition, then they must go on to consider whether or not the bailed person can be admitted again to bail or must be remanded in custody – that is the second stage.

At paras 17 and 18, his Lordship went on:

> In carrying out the first stage, the justices must obviously act fairly. The person alleged to have been in breach must be given the opportunity of answering the allegation . . . But in my judgment, that stage does not involve the justices in an inquiry as to whether the arrested person had a reasonable excuse for being in breach. Section 7 makes no mention of reasonable excuse in relation to a breach of condition. In addition . . . s 7 does not create an offence. It deals with a situation where a constable believes a person bailed has broken a condition of his bail. If the breach of bail is denied, then, obviously, the justices will have to consider any material put forward before them by both parties – the constable and the bailed person – before making a decision. In my judgment, in making that decision, the justices are not required to consider any reasonable excuse for a breach of a condition put forward by the bailed person . . .
>
> At the second stage, the justices will have to consider whether to grant bail or remand in custody assuming, of course, that they have been satisfied or are of the opinion that there has been a breach of condition. At that stage the question of why the bailed person breached his condition will be relevant. At that stage the justices will have to consider all the issues relating to reasonable excuse when deciding whether or not to grant bail. The breach of bail will be a factor, but . . . only one factor as to whether or not the bailed person is admitted to bail again.

His Lordship added that, if this procedure is followed, there will be no breach of Art 5 of the European Convention.

Where a defendant is granted conditional bail by the Crown Court following an appeal to that court against the refusal of bail by a magistrates' court, if the defendant is arrested under s 7 of the Bail Act 1976 for breach of a condition of his bail, he must be taken before a magistrate, not a judge of the Crown Court (*Re Marshall* (1994) 159

JP 688). The basis of this decision was simply that a Crown Court judge is not a 'justice of the peace' (as required by s 7(4)). However, under s 66 of the Courts Act 2003, every Crown Court judge is given the powers of a District Judge (Magistrates' Courts). It is submitted that a Crown Court judge could now deal with a person brought before him under s 7(4), but sitting as a District Judge, not a Crown Court judge.

In *R (Ellison) v Teeside Magistrates' Court* [2001] EWHC 12 (Admin); (2001) 165 JP 355, the defendant was arrested for breaking bail conditions imposed by the Crown Court. He was taken before a magistrates' court (under s 7). The magistrates remanded him in custody to appear at Crown Court to deal with the question of bail. It was held by the Divisional Court that, where a defendant is brought before a magistrates' court for breaching a condition of his bail, the magistrates must deal with the matter. They have no power to commit the defendant to the Crown Court to be dealt with for the breach.

Failure to comply with conditions of bail can also amount to contempt of court. However, that fact is of limited practical relevance. In *R v Ashley* [2003] EWCA Crim 2571; [2004] 1 WLR 2057, the defendant was convicted of contempt of court, arising out of breaches of bail conditions. He had been released on bail subject to conditions that required him to surrender his passport and not to leave the country. He broke both conditions but returned to face trial on the appointed day. The Divisional Court held that the purpose of placing restrictions on an individual's movements under the Bail Act 1976 is to ensure that he attends the trial. If the conduct breaching bail is known about at the time, that bail could be revoked. Furthermore, there may be cases where breach of a bail condition gives rise to a further offence (for example, where witnesses are intimidated). However, s 7 of the Bail Act 1976 does not create any offence. Although the defendant had breached bail conditions by leaving the country, he did return for his trial. It followed that the judge did not have power to deal with him by way of contempt of court.

Home Office Circular 34/1998 (para 11) discusses breach of the condition under s 3(6)(e) of the Bail Act 1976, namely that the defendant must attend an interview with his lawyer. The Circular emphasises that this condition carries the same sanctions as apply to breach of any other bail condition. Thus, the defendant is liable to arrest without a warrant and the court may vary his remand status. The Circular says that, as with any other condition, the consequences of failing to comply should be explained to the defendant at the time the requirement is imposed. However, the Circular does make the point that the defendant's solicitor should not be expected to report a breach if the defendant fails to attend an interview.

3.5.5 Application for variation of conditions

Section 3(8) of the Bail Act 1976 provides that where a court has granted bail in criminal proceedings, that court (or, where that court has sent the defendant to the Crown Court for trial or has committed him to the Crown Court for sentence, that court or the Crown Court) may:

on application—

(a) by or on behalf of the person to whom bail was granted, or

(b) by the prosecutor or a constable,

vary the conditions of bail or impose conditions in respect of bail which has been granted unconditionally.

In other words, where bail is granted subject to conditions, the defendant or the prosecution may apply to vary those conditions. Similarly, if unconditional bail was granted, the prosecution may apply to the court for conditions to be added.

During the period between the defendant being sent to the Crown Court for trial (or committed for sentence) and the defendant's surrender to custody at the Crown Court, the magistrates' court and the Crown Court have concurrent jurisdiction (so either may vary the conditions). Once the defendant has surrendered to the custody of the Crown Court, however, the magistrates no longer have any jurisdiction in relation to bail. So, in *R v Lincoln Justices ex p Mawer* (1996) 160 JP 219, the defendant was granted conditional bail by the Crown Court following her arraignment (i.e. the time when she was asked to enter a plea), the conditions being the same as those which the magistrates had originally imposed; the Divisional Court held that the magistrates' court could not entertain an application to vary the conditions imposed by the Crown Court.

3.6 SURETIES

In this section, we examine in greater detail one of the commonly imposed conditions of bail, namely sureties. Section 3(4) of the Bail Act 1976 provides that the accused 'may be required, before release on bail, to provide a surety or sureties to secure his surrender to custody'. A surety makes a formal promise to pay a fixed sum of money (known as the 'recognisance') if the defendant fails to surrender to custody. Section 8 of the 1976 Act sets out the procedure to be followed where the court grants bail subject to one or more sureties.

3.6.1 Granting of bail subject to surety

In deciding whether to grant bail subject to a surety, the court has to consider the suitability of the proposed surety. Section 8(2) provides that:

In considering the suitability for that purpose of a proposed surety, regard may be had (amongst other things) to—

(a) the surety's financial resources;
(b) his character and any previous convictions of his; and
(c) his proximity (whether in point of kinship, place of residence or otherwise) to the person for whom he is to be surety.

Thus, regard must be had to:

* the 'financial resources' of the proposed surety: could the surety pay the sum which he is promising to pay?;

- the 'character' of the proposed surety and whether he has 'any previous convictions': is the surety a trustworthy person?;
- the 'proximity' of the proposed surety to the person for whom he is to be surety: is the proposed surety a friend, relative or employer? How far away does he live from the defendant? The most important consideration under this heading is the relationship of proposed surety to the defendant: will the surety have the ability to control the defendant so as to ensure that he attends court when he should? Put another way, would the fact the surety stands to lose money if the defendant absconds operate on the mind of the defendant so as to deter him from absconding?

If the proposed surety is in court, he gives evidence of these matters and confirms that he understands the obligations he will be undertaking.

In fixing the amount of the surety, the court has regard to the seriousness of the offence, the degree of risk that the defendant will abscond, and to the means of the proposed surety. It is quite common to have two or more sureties. If the court will only grant bail subject to a recognisance of a certain amount and that amount is beyond the means of the proposed surety, then another person will have to be found. It should be noted that the defendant cannot stand as a surety for himself (s 3(2) of the Bail Act 1976).

The financial circumstances of the proposed surety are crucial. In *R v Birmingham Crown Court ex p Ali* (1999) 163 JP 145, Kennedy LJ (at p 147) said that:

> it is irresponsible (and possibly a matter for consideration by a professional disciplinary body) for a qualified lawyer . . . to tender anyone as a surety unless he or she has reasonable grounds for believing that the surety will, if necessary, be able to meet his or her financial undertaking . . . It should be borne in mind that a surety who genuinely believes that the defendant will surrender is liable to be cavalier about his or her own financial obligations. . .

If the defence are aware that someone has offered to act as a surety but that person is not in court, and the magistrates are satisfied that the person is a satisfactory surety, the court may grant bail subject to that named surety entering into the recognisance (that is, signing the formal document which sets out the agreement to act as surety) in front of a justice of the peace or a justices' clerk, or at a police station in front of an officer of the rank of Inspector or above (s 8(4)), or the governor of the prison where the accused is detained (r 19.5 of the Criminal Procedure Rules). The defendant remains in custody until this has been done.

If there is no one whom the defence can offer as a surety at the time of the hearing, the magistrates may grant bail subject to a surety who is acceptable to the police entering into a recognisance (for the amount fixed by the court) at a magistrates' court or a police station (s 8(3)). Again, the defendant stays in custody until a satisfactory surety has entered into a recognisance. If the potential surety is rejected by the magistrates' court clerk or police Inspector (as the case may be) because that person is not satisfied of the surety's suitability, the potential surety may apply to the magistrates' court to take his recognisance (s 8(5)).

3.6.2 Forfeiture of recognisance

If the defendant fails to surrender to custody when he should, there is a presumption that the full sum promised by the surety will be forfeited, unless it appears fair and just that a lesser sum (or none at all) should be forfeited. The burden of showing that the amount promised by the surety should not be forfeited (or that only part of that sum should be forfeited) lies on the surety (*R v Uxbridge Justices ex p Heward-Mills* [1983] 1 WLR 56).

The relevant factors have been considered in a number of cases, including *R v Southampton Justices ex p Green* [1976] QB 11, *R v Horseferry Road Justices ex p Pearson* [1976] 1 WLR 511, *R v Reading Crown Court ex p Bello* [1992] 3 All ER 353 and *R v Wood Green Crown Court ex p Howe* [1992] 1 WLR 702. Those factors include:

- The surety's means: has there been a change in financial circumstances since he agreed to act as surety which would make it unfair to order him to forfeit the sum promised?
- Culpability: did the surety take all reasonable steps to secure the defendant's attendance at court, again making it unfair to penalise the surety?

There is a strong presumption that the surety should forfeit the full recognisance. As it was put in *Pearson* by Lord Widgery CJ (at p 514):

> . . . the surety has seriously entered into a serious obligation and ought to pay the amount which he or she has promised unless there are circumstances in the case, either relating to . . . means or . . . culpability, which make it fair and just to pay a smaller sum.

The authorities in this topic were reviewed extensively by McCullough J in *R v Uxbridge Justices ex p Heward-Mills* [1983] 1 WLR 56. His Lordship summarised their effect thus (at p 62):

> . . . the more important principles to be derived from the authorities [are] as follows. (1) When a defendant for whose attendance a person has stood surety fails to appear, the full recognizance should be forfeited, unless it appears fair and just that a lesser sum should be forfeited or none at all. (2) The burden of satisfying the court that the full sum should not be forfeited rests on the surety and is a heavy one. It is for him to lay before the court the evidence of want of culpability and of means on which he relies. (3) Where a surety is unrepresented the court should assist him by explaining these principles in ordinary language, and giving him the opportunity to call evidence and advance argument in relation to them.

In both *R v Southampton Justices ex p Green* and *R v Uxbridge Justices ex p Heward-Mills*, the orders for forfeiture were quashed because the magistrates had failed properly to take into account the surety's want of means. Nevertheless, the cases emphasise that the burden is on the surety to show impecuniosity. If he wishes to put forward evidence on the matter, the court is under a duty to consider it, even if he had earlier claimed when being accepted as surety that he was worth the sum which he now states he cannot pay. However, there is no obligation on the court to initiate the inquiry. It is submitted that, if a proper inquiry was conducted into the surety's means at the time he stood, he should be relieved from his obligations on financial grounds only if something unforeseen has arisen between then and the consideration of forfeiture which prevents him meeting his obligation. Otherwise he benefits from having misled the court which accepted him as surety.

According to *R v Warwick Crown Court ex p Smalley* [1987] 1 WLR 237, there is no requirement of proof that any blame attached to the surety for the accused's failure to surrender. The court rejected the suggestion that there had to be some fault on the part of the surety for the recognisance to be forfeited. However, the authorities on this point were reviewed in *R v Reading Crown Court ex p Bello* [1992] 3 All ER 353, where Parker LJ summarised the position as follows (at p 363):

> The failure of the accused to surrender when required triggers the power to forfeit but the court, before deciding what should be done, must enquire into the question of fault. If it is satisfied that the surety was blameless throughout it would then be proper to remit the whole of the amount of the recognisance and in exceptional circumstances this would . . . be the only proper course.

Similarly, in *R v Harrow Crown Court ex p Lingard* [1998] EWHC 233 (Admin), Dyson J said (at para 20) that:

> in an exceptional case, where the surety is entirely blameless and the failure of the defendant to surrender to bail is wholly outside the control of, and unforeseeable by, the surety the court may in the exercise of its discretion remit the whole or a substantial part of the amount of the recognisance.

However, in *Howe* (at p 711), Watkins LJ said that there is no power for a surety to withdraw unless the defendant is before the court and appropriate application is made under s 3(8) of the Bail Act 1976 for a variation of the conditions of bail. However, if a surety has a change of mind (for example, he decides that the defendant is unlikely to attend court after all) and wishes to withdraw from the surety, he may give written notice to this effect to the police. The police can then arrest the defendant without a warrant, under s 7(3)(c) of the Act, which confers a power of arrest:

> . . . in a case where that person was released on bail with one or more surety or sureties, if a surety notifies a constable in writing that that person is unlikely to surrender to custody and that for that reason the surety wishes to be relieved of his obligations as a surety.

Even though the surety can formally withdraw from the recognisance only with the agreement of the court, a surety who has given written notice to the police may seek to argue that they should not forfeit the money promised if the defendant does indeed abscond. However, in *R v Maidstone Crown Court ex p Lever and Connell* [1995] 1 WLR 928, the Court of Appeal took quite a tough line. In that case, one of two sureties discovered that the defendant had not been home for two nights. That surety telephoned the other surety and the police. Attempts by the police to apprehend the defendant were unsuccessful. The judge ordered the first surety to forfeit £35,000 (out of a recognisance of £40,000) and the other £16,000 (out of a recognisance of

£19,000). The two sureties sought judicial review of this decision. The Court of Appeal upheld the judge's decision. Butler-Sloss LJ said (at p 930):

> It is for the surety to establish to the satisfaction of the trial court that there are grounds upon which the court may remit from forfeiture part or, wholly exceptionally, the whole recognisance. The presence or absence of culpability is a factor but the absence of culpability . . . is not in itself a reason to reduce or set aside the obligations entered into by the surety to pay in the event of a failure to bring the defendant to court. The court may, in the exercise of a wide discretion, decide it would be fair and just to estreat [i.e. forfeit] some or all of the recognisance.

The court added that judicial review will only be granted if the court's decision is perverse. In the instant case, a remission of about 15 per cent could not be said to be perverse.

The reason for the adoption of a fairly strict approach to the forfeiture of recognisances was set out by Butler-Sloss LJ at p 931, where her Ladyship quotes from Lord Widgery CJ in *R v Southampton Justices ex p Corker* (1976) 120 SJ 214 (also quoted by McCullough J in *R v Uxbridge Justices ex p Heward-Mills* [1983] 1 WLR 56 at p 59) where Lord Widgery refers to 'the real pull of bail':

> The real pull of bail, the real effective force that it exerts, is that it may cause the offender to attend his trial rather than subject his nearest and dearest who has gone surety for him to undue pain and discomfort.

Nonetheless, it is clear that there may be circumstances where the amount forfeited might be reduced because the surety has made considerable efforts to carry out his undertakings.

In *Choudhry v Birmingham Crown Court* [2007] EWHC 2764 (Admin); (2008) 172 JP 33, Gibbs J (at para 15) summarised the principles derived from *R v Maidstone Crown Court ex parte Lever and Connell*:

(a) The purpose of a recognizance is to bring the defendant to court for trial.
(b) The forfeiture of recognizance is not a penalty imposed on the surety for misconduct.
(c) It is for the surety to establish to the satisfaction of the court that there are grounds upon which the court may remit from forfeiture part or, wholly exceptionally, the whole recognizance.
(d) The absence of culpability on the part of the surety is not of itself a reason to set aside or reduce the obligation entered into.
(e) Absence of culpability is a factor to be considered. The court may, in the exercise of a wide discretion, decide it would be fair and just to estreat some or all of the recognizance.

His Lordship added (ibid) that 'the burden of satisfying the court that the full sum should not be forfeited rests upon the surety and is a heavy one: *R v Uxbridge Justices ex parte Heward Mills* [1983] 1 All ER 530'. Gibbs J concludes (at para 43) that the court may, in the exercise of its discretion, remit the whole or the substantial part of the amount of the recognizance in an exceptional case, but he added that 'there is no principle of law which requires it to do so'.

Section 120(1A) of the Magistrates' Courts Act 1980 provides that, where a person stands as a surety but the accused fails to attend court, the magistrates' court must:

a   declare the recognisance to be forfeited; and
b   issue a summons to the surety requiring him to appear before the court to show cause why he should not be ordered to pay the sum promised.

If the surety fails to attend that hearing, the court may proceed in his absence if satisfied that he was served with the summons.

Section 120(3) states that:

> The court which declares the recognizance to be forfeited may, instead of adjudging any person to pay the whole sum in which he is bound, adjudge him to pay part only of the sum or remit the sum.

The powers of the Crown Court as regards forfeiture of recognisances are contained in r 19.24 of the Criminal Procedure Rules. Rule 19.24 is in very similar terms to s 120(1A) of the 1980 Act. There is no express provision empowering the Crown Court to remit only part of the recognisance, but that power may be implied from r 19.24(2), which enables a surety 'to show cause why the Court should not order the recognizance to be estreated'.

In *Kaur v DPP* (2000) 164 JP 127, the Divisional Court held that the justices can only have regard to the assets of the surety; assets of third parties are irrelevant. Regard must be had to the surety's share in the equity of the matrimonial home; however, the impact on the surety and others, if the matrimonial home has to be sold to satisfy the recognisance, is a relevant factor in deciding whether to remit all or part of the recognisance. The court went on to confirm that lack of culpability on the part of the surety is not in itself a reason for not remitting the recognisance. Rose LJ summarised the relevant principles thus:

1.   Justices have a wide discretion under s 120 whether to remit in whole or in part;
2.   In exercising that discretion, they must plainly have regard only to the surety's assets. The assets of other persons are not assets which can properly be called upon to satisfy a surety's liability;
3.   Want of culpability by a surety in the accused's failure to appear is not in itself a reason for not forfeiting or for remitting a recognisance. But there may be circumstances . . . where the amount forfeited may be reduced because a culpable surety has made very considerable efforts to carry out his or her undertaking;
4.   Regard may properly be had to a surety's share in the equity of a matrimonial home when a recognizance is being entered into;
5.   When enforcement of a recognizance is being considered under s 120, the means of the surety at that time is one of the factors to be considered and, at that stage, the impact on both the surety and on others, if the matrimonial home has to be sold to satisfy the recognizance, is a relevant factor when deciding whether to remit a recognizance in whole or in part.

In *R v Birmingham Crown Court ex p Ali* (1999) 163 JP 145, it was held that where there has been no proper means inquiry and the surety then applies for a reduction in the amount of the recognisance to be forfeited under s 120, the sum should be reduced (if necessary) to a sum that the surety could be expected to pay in full within two, or at the most three, years.

The obligation entered into by the surety is a personal obligation. Under s 9 of the Bail Act 1976, if a person agrees with another to indemnify a surety against any liability under the recognisance, that person is guilty of an offence. This is so whether the agreement is made before or after the person to be indemnified becomes a surety, whether or not he in fact becomes a surety, and whether the agreement contemplates compensation in money or in money's worth (s 9(2)). The penalty (under sub-s (4)) is up to three months' imprisonment and/or a fine of up to £5,000 (or the offender can be committed to the Crown Court for sentence, where the maximum penalty is 12 months' imprisonment and/or a fine). Proceedings for an offence under s 9 can only be brought by (or with the consent of) the Director of Public Prosecutions (s 9(5)).

3.7 REPEATED BAIL APPLICATIONS

Schedule 1, Pt IIA to the Bail Act 1976 (inserted by s 154 of the Criminal Justice Act 1988) provides as follows:

(1) If the court decides not to grant the defendant bail, it is the court's duty to consider, at each subsequent hearing while the defendant is a person to whom section 4 above applies and remains in custody, whether he ought to be granted bail.

(2) At the first hearing after that at which the court decided not to grant the defendant bail he may support an application for bail with any argument as to fact or law that he desires (whether or not he has advanced that argument previously).

(3) At subsequent hearings the court need not hear arguments as to fact or law which it has heard previously.

Thus, at the first hearing after that at which bail was refused, the defendant can make a bail application whether or not it is based on arguments which were advanced on the first occasion. This means that the defendant may make bail applications on his first and second appearances before the court and may advance precisely the same arguments in each application if he so wishes. Or, if no application is made on the first appearance, the defendant may make an application on his second appearance. Thereafter, a material change of circumstances (that is, something relevant to bail) is required if a further bail application is to be made. So, in subsequent remands, the court should only consider whether the circumstances have changed since the last fully argued bail application was heard (for example, a possible surety comes forward or the defendant is offered employment).

This provision is based on *R v Nottingham Justices ex p Davies* [1981] 1 QB 38, in which the Divisional Court said the defendant should be allowed two fully argued applications. This was because the first application is often under-prepared due to lack of time, and so fairness demands that a second application be heard. Thereafter, however, the court would simply be hearing arguments that had been heard before;

hence, the requirement of a change in circumstances so that a third application for bail can only be made if there is some fresh material for the court to consider.

In *R v Dover and East Kent Justices ex p Dean* [1992] Crim LR 33, the defendant did not make a bail application on his first appearance at court and he consented to being remanded in his absence (under s 128 of the Magistrates' Courts Act 1980) for the next three weeks. On the occasion of his next appearance before the court (a month after his first appearance), the defendant sought to make a bail application. The magistrates would not let him do so, but the Divisional Court held that remands in the defendant's absence do not count as hearings for the purpose of determining whether a bail application can be made. The defendant's second appearance before the court was to be regarded as the second hearing (even though the case had been listed in the intervening weeks) and so he had a right to make a bail application.

In *R v Calder Justices ex p Kennedy* (1992) 156 JP 716, it was similarly held that if the magistrates remand the defendant in custody on the basis that there is insufficient information before the court to make a decision on bail (a permitted ground for refusing bail under Sched 1, Pt I, para 5 of the Bail Act 1976 – see above), this hearing does not count for these purposes. So, a full bail application may be made on the occasion of the defendant's next appearance and, if that application is unsuccessful, a second fully argued bail application can be made on his subsequent appearance before the court.

3.8 BAIL AND THE EUROPEAN CONVENTION ON HUMAN RIGHTS

Under Art 5 of the European Convention, which safeguards the right to liberty, a person charged with an offence must be released pending trial unless there are 'relevant and sufficient' reasons to justify continued detention (*Wemhoff v Germany* (1968) 1 EHRR 55). The case law of the European Court shows that this is interpreted in a way that is very similar to the UK's Bail Act 1976. The grounds accepted by the European Court of Human Rights for withholding bail include:

- the risk that the defendant will fail to appear at the trial. This has been defined as requiring 'a whole set of circumstances which give reason to suppose that the consequences and hazards of flight will seem to him to be a lesser evil than continued imprisonment' (*Stogmuller v Austria* (1969) 1 EHRR 155). The court can take account of 'the character of the person involved, his morals, his home, his occupation, his assets, his family ties, and all kinds of links with the country in which he is being prosecuted' (*Neumeister v Austria* (1979) 1 EHRR 91). The likely sentence is relevant but cannot of itself justify the refusal of bail (*Letellier v France* (1991) 14 EHRR 83);
- the risk that the defendant will interfere with the course of justice (for example, interfering with witnesses, warning other suspects, destroying relevant evidence). There must be an identifiable risk and there must be evidence in support (*Clooth v Belgium* (1992) 14 EHRR 717);
- preventing the commission of further offences; there must be good reason to believe that the defendant will commit offences while on bail (*Toth v Austria* (1991) 14 EHRR 551);

- the preservation of public order: bail may be withheld where the nature of the alleged crime and the likely public reaction to it are such that the release of the accused may give rise to public disorder (*Letellier v France* (1991) 14 EHRR 83).

Article 5 of the Convention also allows the imposition of conditions on the grant of bail.

It should be noted that the 'equality of arms' principle applies to bail applications (*Woukam Moudefo v France* (1991) 13 EHRR 549). This includes:

- the right to disclosure of prosecution evidence for purposes of making a bail application: *Lamy v Belgium* (1989) 11 EHRR 529 (the decision of the Divisional Court in *R v DPP ex p Lee* [1999] 2 Cr App R 304 largely accords with this);
- the requirement that the court should give reasons for the refusal of bail (*Tomasi v France* (1992) 15 EHRR 1) and should permit renewed applications for bail at reasonable intervals (*Bezicheri v Italy* (1990) 12 EHRR 210). Both these requirements are satisfied by the Bail Act 1976.

In *Hurnam v State of Mauritius* [2005] UKPC 49; [2006] 1 WLR 857, the Privy Council said that the seriousness of an offence cannot be treated as a conclusive reason for refusing bail to an unconvicted suspect: the right to personal liberty is an important constitutional right and a suspect should remain at large unless it is necessary to refuse bail in order to serve one of the ends for which detention before trial was permissible.

The Law Commission (<http://www.lawcom.gov.uk/docs/lc269.pdf>) considered the impact of the Human Rights Act 1998 on the law governing decisions taken by the police and the courts to grant or refuse bail in criminal proceedings. The Commission noted that Art 5 of the Convention states that, although reasonable suspicion that the detained person has committed an offence can be sufficient to justify pre-trial detention for a short time, the national authorities must thereafter show additional grounds for detention. They summarised the five additional grounds recognised under the Convention as follows, namely where the purpose of detention is to avoid a real risk that, were the defendant to be released:

1 he or she would:

  a fail to attend trial; or
  b interfere with evidence or witnesses, or otherwise obstruct the course of justice; or
  c commit an offence while on bail; or
  d be at risk of harm against which he or she would be inadequately protected; or

2 a disturbance to public order would result.

The Law Commission concluded that there are no provisions in the Bail Act which are incompatible with Convention rights. However, the Commission did identify some areas of the law which they believed would benefit from legislative reform. They also produced a Guide (*Guidance for Bail Decision-Takers and their Advisers*) to assist decision-makers to apply the Bail Act 1976 in a way that is compatible with the

Convention (a copy of the Guide can be accessed at <www.lawcom.gov.uk/docs/guide.pdf>). The Guide emphasises that a defendant should only be refused bail where detention is necessary for a purpose which Strasbourg jurisprudence has recognised as legitimate under Art 5(3). Thus, a domestic court exercising its powers in a way which is compatible with the Convention rights should refuse bail only where it can be justified both under the Convention, as interpreted in Strasbourg jurisprudence, and domestic legislation.

The Guide also points out that detention will only be necessary if the risk relied upon as the ground for withholding bail could not be adequately addressed by the imposition of appropriate bail conditions. Thus, the Commission concluded that conditional bail should be used in preference to detention where a bail condition could adequately address the risk that would otherwise justify detention.

Furthermore, the court refusing bail should give reasons for finding that detention is necessary. Those reasons should be closely related to the individual circumstances pertaining to the defendant, and be capable of supporting the conclusion of the court.

The guidance is important and worth quoting at length:

General principles applicable to the refusal of bail

. . .

3. Detention will only be necessary if the risk could not be adequately addressed by the imposition of appropriate bail conditions that would make detention unnecessary.
4. Any court refusing bail should give reasons that explain why detention is necessary. Those reasons should be closely related to the individual circumstances of the defendant.

. . .

The risk of offending on bail

7. The decision-taker must consider whether it may properly be inferred from any previous convictions and other circumstances relating to the defendant that there is a real risk that the defendant will commit an offence if granted bail, and that the defendant therefore falls within paragraph 2(b) of Part I of Schedule I to the Act. Provided that a decision to withhold bail is a necessary and proportionate response to a *real risk* that, if released, the defendant would commit an offence while on bail, such a decision will comply with the Convention.

Defendant on bail at the time of the alleged offence

8. The factor in paragraph 2A of Part I of Schedule I to the Act (a defendant who commits an indictable offence whilst on bail) does not, in itself, establish any Article 5(3) purpose.
9. Consequently, a court should not base a decision to withhold bail solely on paragraph 2A. To do so would infringe Article 5 and would be unlawful under sections 3 and 6 of the Human Rights Act 1998 (HRA).
10. That factor may, however, be *relevant* to a decision whether to withhold bail on the basis of another relevant exception, for example the risk that the defendant will commit an offence while on bail.

Detention for the defendant's own protection

11. A decision to refuse bail to a defendant under the exception in paragraph 3 of Part I of Schedule 1 to the Act, that is for the defendant's own protection (from self-harm or harm from others) would comply with the Convention, where:

    (1) detention is necessary to address a real risk that, if granted bail, the defendant would suffer harm, against which detention could provide protection; and

    (2) there are exceptional circumstances in the nature of the alleged offence and/or the conditions or context in which it is alleged to have been committed.

12. A decision of a court to order detention because of a risk of self-harm may be compatible with the ECHR even where the circumstances giving rise to the risk are unconnected with the alleged offence, provided that the court is satisfied that there is a real risk of self-harm, and that a proper medical examination will take place rapidly so that the court may then consider exercising its powers of detention under the Mental Health Act 1983.

Detention because of a lack of information

13. The refusal of bail under paragraph 5 of Part I of Schedule 1 to the Act, where it has not been practicable to obtain sufficient information for the taking of a full bail decision for want of time since the institution of proceedings against the defendant, would be compatible with Article 5 provided that:

    (1) detention is for a short period, which is no longer than necessary to enable the required information to be obtained, and

    (2) the lack of information is not due to a failure of the prosecution, the police, the court, or another state body to act with 'special diligence'.

14. There is no need in such a case for the court to be satisfied of any of the recognised purposes set out in paragraph 2 above.

15. After the initial short period of time has passed, a lack of information that is not due to a failure of a state body to act with 'special diligence' may be taken into account as a factor militating in favour of detention on another Convention-compliant ground for detention.

Detention following arrest under section 7
Paragraph 6 of Part I and paragraph 5 of Part II of Schedule 1

16. The broad provisions in paragraph 6 of Part I and paragraph 5 of Part II of Schedule 1 to the Act, that a defendant arrested pursuant to section 7 need not be granted bail, should be read subject to the narrower provisions governing bail following a section 7(3) arrest, set out in section 7(5) of the Act. That provision requires that bail should again be granted unless the justice is of the opinion that the defendant is not likely to surrender to custody, or has broken or is likely to break any condition of bail. Detention on one of these grounds will comply with the Convention only where this is necessary for one or more of the recognised purposes set out above in paragraph 2.

Section 7(5) hearings

17. At the hearing of section 7(5) proceedings there is no requirement that oral evidence should be heard in every case, but account should be taken of the quality of material presented. This may range from mere assertion to documentary proof. If the material includes oral evidence, the defendant must be given an opportunity to cross-examine. Likewise, a defendant should be permitted to give relevant oral evidence if he or she wishes to do so.

Section 25 of the Criminal Justice and Public Order Act 1994

18. The expression 'exceptional circumstances' in section 25 of the Criminal Justice and Public Order Act 1994 should be construed so that it encompasses a defendant who, if released on bail, would not pose a real risk of committing a serious offence. This construction achieves the purpose of Parliament to ensure that, when making bail decisions about defendants to whom section 25 applies, decision-takers focus on the risk the defendant may pose to the public by re-offending.

19. It is possible that some other circumstance might constitute 'exceptional circumstances'. Even if 'exceptional circumstances' do exist, bail may, nonetheless, be withheld on a Convention-compatible ground if this is deemed to be necessary in the individual case.

Conditional bail
Conditional bail as an alternative to custody

20. A defendant must be released, if need be subject to conditions, unless:

    (1) that would create a risk of the kind which can, in principle, justify pre-trial detention (set out above in paragraph 2), and
    (2) that risk cannot, by imposing suitable bail conditions, be averted, or reduced to a level at which it would not justify detention.

Conditional bail as an alternative to unconditional bail

21. A court should only impose bail conditions for one of the purposes which Strasbourg jurisprudence recognises as capable of justifying detention (set out above in paragraph 2).

22. A bail condition should only be imposed where, if the defendant were to break that condition or be reasonably thought likely to do so, it may be necessary to arrest the defendant in order to pursue the purpose for which the condition was imposed.

Reasons for imposing conditions

23. Decision-takers should state their reasons for imposing bail conditions and specify the purposes for which any conditions are imposed.

24. Decision-takers should also be alert to ensure that any bail conditions they impose do not violate the defendant's other Convention rights, such as those protected by Articles 8–11 of the Convention (the right to respect for family life, freedom of thought, conscience and religion, freedom of expression and freedom of assembly and association).

Giving reasons for bail decisions

25. It is of particular importance that decision-takers or their clerks make, and retain for the file, a note of the gist of the arguments for and against the grant of bail, and the oral reasons given by the tribunal for their decision.

. . .

Form of evidence

28. It is not necessary to hear sworn evidence in the great majority of cases. Courts should, in particular cases, consider whether fairness requires the calling of evidence on oath for the determination of the application, as a failure to call such evidence may cause a particular decision to fall foul of Article 5(4).

29. A court hearing bail proceedings should take account of the quality of the material presented. It may range from mere assertion to documentary proof. If the material includes sworn oral evidence, the defendant must be given an opportunity to cross-examine. Likewise, the defendant should be permitted to give relevant oral evidence if he or she wishes to do so.

Disclosure

30. *Ex parte Lee* [1999] Cr App R 304 recognises an ongoing duty of disclosure from the time of arrest. The Court of Appeal emphasised that at the stage before committal, there are continuing obligations on the prosecutor to make such disclosure as justice and fairness may require in the particular circumstances of the case, that is, where it could reasonably be expected to assist the defence when applying for bail. This will ensure that the defendant enjoys 'equality of arms' with the prosecution.

31. Compliance with this requirement, together with those imposed by the Attorney General's guidelines to prosecutors, should ensure compliance with the Convention. This will apply equally to hearings pursuant to s 7(5).

32. The duty of disclosure does not require that the whole of the prosecution file be disclosed to the defence prior to the hearing. It is sufficient if disclosure is provided of the material the defendant needs in order to enjoy 'equality of arms' with the prosecution in relation to the matter to be decided by the court.

Public hearing

33. Where normally the hearing would be in chambers, if the defendant requests that the bail hearing be held in public, it should be held in public unless there is a good reason not to do so.

The right to challenge pre-trial detention

34. The Convention gives a detained person the right to make further court challenges to the legality of his or her detention despite having already made one or more such challenges, where for example, with the passage of time, the circumstances which once were considered by a court to justify detention may have changed.

35. To ensure compliance with the Convention, Part IIA of Schedule 1 to the Act should be applied on the basis that courts should be willing, at intervals of 28 days, to consider arguments that the passage of time constitutes, in the particular case, a change in

circumstances relevant to the need to detain the defendant, so as to require the hearing of all the arguments on the question of bail. It may be, for example, that the time served on remand may have reduced the risk of the defendant absconding.

36. If the court finds that the passage of time does amount to a relevant change of circumstances then a full bail application should follow in which all the arguments, old and new, could be put forward and taken into account.

Lord Justice Auld, in his *Review of the Criminal Courts of England and Wales* (the *Auld Review*), notes the view of the Law Commission that the provisions of the Bail Act 1976 are compatible with the European Convention on Human Rights. However, he does note some shortcomings in the procedure by which bail decisions are taken (see paras 69–82 of Chapter 10) and recommends as follows:

175 Magistrates and judges in all courts should take more time to consider matters of bail.

176 Listing practices should reflect the necessity to devote due time to bail applications and allow the flexibility required for all parties to gather sufficient information for the court to make an appropriate decision.

177 Courts, the police, prosecutors and defence representatives should be provided with better information for the task than they are at present, in particular, complete and up to date information of the defendant's record held on the Police National Computer, relevant probation or other social service records, if any, verified information about home living conditions and employment, if any, and sufficient information about the alleged offence and its relationship, if any, to his record so as to indicate whether there is a pattern of offending.

178 Courts and all relevant agencies should be equipped with a common system of information technology . . . to facilitate the ready availability to all who need it of the above information.

179 There should be appropriate training for magistrates and judges in the making of bail decisions, with Article 5 ECHR and risk assessment particularly in mind, as the Law Commission has proposed.

. . .

181 Bail notices should be couched in plain English, printed and given to the defendant as a formal court order when the bail decision is made, so that he understands exactly what is required of him and appreciates the seriousness of the grant of bail and of any attached conditions.

182 All courts should be diligent in adopting the Law Commission's proposals for the recording of bail decisions in such a way as to indicate clearly how they have been reached.

The point about taking time is an important one. Bail applications tend to be dealt with very quickly by the courts, and it is questionable whether such speed is compatible with high-quality decision making.

3.9 CHALLENGING THE REFUSAL OF BAIL

In this section, we consider the various ways of challenging a refusal of bail. The starting point is the right of the defendant to know why bail was refused in the first place.

3.9.1 Record of reasons

Section 5 of the Bail Act 1976 provides as follows:

(3) Where a magistrates' court or the Crown Court—

    (a) withholds bail in criminal proceedings, or

    (b) imposes conditions in granting bail in criminal proceedings, or

    (c) varies any conditions of bail or imposes conditions in respect of bail in criminal proceedings,

    and does so in relation to a person to whom section 4 of this Act applies, then the court shall give reasons for withholding bail or for imposing or varying the conditions.

(4) A court which is by virtue of sub-section (3) above required to give reasons for its decision shall include a note of those reasons in the record of its decision and shall (except in a case where, by virtue of sub-section (5) below, this need not be done) give a copy of that note to the person in relation to whom the decision was taken.

(5) The Crown Court need not give a copy of the note of the reasons for its decision to the person in relation to whom the decision was taken where that person has legal representation unless his legal representative requests the court to do so.

Thus, the defendant receives a document setting out which ground(s) for withholding bail (from those specified in Sched 1 to the Act) were held to be applicable, and what factors were taken into account in deciding that the grounds were made out.

For example, the record of the decision might say that bail is being withheld because the court is satisfied that there are substantial grounds for believing that the accused will:

* *Fail to surrender to custody*
  Reasons: accused has two previous convictions for absconding; accused lacks community ties, being unemployed and of no fixed abode.
* *Commit an offence while on bail*
  Reasons: accused has three previous convictions for offences similar to that presently charged; accused has no apparent income; two of accused's previous convictions are for offences committed while on bail.

3.9.2 Certificate that full argument has been heard

Furthermore, s 5(6A) says that if a magistrates' court refuses bail after hearing a fully argued bail application, it must provide the defendant with a certificate that this is the case. If the magistrates allow a defendant to make a bail application because there has been a material change of circumstances (where the application could not be heard but for the change in circumstances as a result of Sched 1, Pt IIA of the Bail Act 1976 (see above)) but do not grant bail, they must state in the certificate what change of circumstances persuaded them to hear the application (sub-s (6B)).

Once the defendant has a certificate that full argument has been heard, he may apply for bail to the Crown Court in order to challenge the refusal of bail by the magistrates.

3.10 OPTIONS OPEN TO THE DEFENDANT WHEN BAIL HAS BEEN REFUSED OR CONDITIONS IMPOSED

In order to challenge the refusal of bail the defendant may:

- make a further application in the magistrates' court if this is permissible under Sched 1, Part IIA of the Bail Act 1976 (see above) – namely if this is only the defendant's second bail application or the defendant can show that there has been a material change of circumstances; or
- apply for bail to the Crown Court under s 81(1) of the Supreme Court Act 1981. (the procedure for which is set out below).

3.10.1 Crown Court bail application: procedure

An application may be made to the Crown Court if the defendant has a certificate (under s 5(6A) of the Bail Act 1976) from the magistrates' court that a fully argued bail application was made there (see above).

The defendant must give at least 24 hours' notice to the CPS (r 19.18(2) of the Criminal Procedure Rules). The defendant has no right to be present at the Crown Court hearing unless the Crown Court gives him leave to be present (r 19.18(5)); therefore, it is only in rare cases that the defendant will be present. The hearing is usually (though not invariably) in chambers (that is, the public are excluded and robes are not worn): r 16.11(2)(a) of the Criminal Procedure Rules. Otherwise, the procedure is the same as the magistrates' court, with the prosecution summarising the objections to bail and the defence replying.

It is perhaps questionable whether the practice of hearing bail appeals in private and in the absence of the accused fully accords with the European Convention. In *R (Malik) v Central Criminal Court* [2006] EWHC 1539 (Admin); [2007] 1 WLR 2455, the Court considered the practice of the Crown Court to hear bail applications in chambers. The court ruled that an application to hear a bail application in public must start from the 'fundamental presumption in favour of open justice' (per Gray J at para 40). The court has to consider whether it is necessary to depart from the ordinary rule of open justice in the interests of justice. This is not an exercise of discretion but of judgment as to whether a departure from the norm is justified (para 30). It may, for example, be appropriate for the court to sit in chambers if the delay involved in arranging a public hearing would defeat the purpose of the application (para 31). It may be in the interests of the accused for the application to be heard in private, for example where the prosecution need to rehearse a damaging case against the defendant or his co-accused; where the prosecution intend to give detailed reasons for fearing that the defendant will not surrender if given bail; where the defendant's previous convictions will be referred to;

where it will or may be necessary to reveal personal and confidential information about the defendant or about prosecution witnesses or others; and where the court may need to be told about information which has been provided to the prosecuting authorities by the defendant or by someone else connected with the case (para 33). Gray J added that it does not follow that bail applications have to be listed and called on in open court and then adjourned to chambers only if a case is made for doing so. There is nothing objectionable in listing bail applications on the provisional assumption that the interests of justice call for a closed hearing, so long as any application to sit in public is approached on the footing that it must be acceded to unless there is a sound reason for excluding the public. Such an application will ordinarily come from one or both of the parties, but it may also legitimately come from the media or some other third party (para 35). Where the accused defendant has legal representation, he has no right to be produced from prison for the purposes of a bail application. However, the increasing use of video links between the court and the prison where the defendant is detained effectively removes any disadvantage to the defendant by reason of his not being physically present when the application for bail is heard (para 38).

3.10.2 Jurisdiction of High Court

Section 22 of the Criminal Justice Act 1967 formerly empowered the High Court to grant bail in cases where bail has been refused by magistrates. However, under s 17 of the Criminal Justice Act 2003, s 22(1) of the 1967 Act was amended so that the High Court has power to grant bail only in cases 'where an application to the court to state a case for the opinion of the High Court is made'. Thus, it is only in the context of appeals by way of case stated (against conviction or, exceptionally, sentence) that the High Court has jurisdiction to grant bail in criminal cases. This amendment was based on Recommendation 183 of the *Auld Review*, that the right to make a bail application to a High Court judge after the matter had been determined by a criminal court exercising its original or appellate jurisdiction should be removed. This recommendation was made by Lord Justice Auld because the possibility of an application for bail to the High Court was felt to be unnecessary given the jurisdiction of the Crown Court to grant bail (see paras 84–86 of Chapter 10 of the Review).

For the sake of completeness, it should be noted that, under s 37 of the Criminal Justice Act 1948, the High Court may also grant bail where a person is appealing to the High Court by way of case stated from a decision of the Crown Court (in practice, this will be where a defendant appeals from the magistrates' court to the Crown Court and then seeks to appeal to the High Court from the decision of the Crown Court), where he is appealing from the Crown Court to the High Court by way of judicial review, seeking an order quashing the decision of the Crown Court (again this will be the case where the defendant is challenging a decision of the Crown Court in its appellate capacity), and where he has been convicted or sentenced by a magistrates' court and is appealing to the High Court by way of judicial review, seeking an order quashing the decision of the magistrates.

In summary, then, the High Court can no longer hear appeals against refusal of bail, but it can grant bail to those who are appealing to it against conviction or sentence.

Despite the amendment of s 22 of the 1967 Act, there remains the possibility of an application to the High Court for judicial review of the refusal of bail. Although

Stanley Burnton J, in *R (Lipinski and Johnson) v Wolverhampton Crown Court* [2005] EWHC 1950 (Admin) expressed doubts about the availability of judicial review to challenge the refusal of bail by a Crown Court judge because of the effect of s 29 of the Supreme Court Act 1981, which excludes judicial review in respect of 'matters relating to trial on indictment', the weight of authority seems to suggest that s 29 is not to be regarded as a bar on judicial review of such decisions. Moreover, under s 17(6)(b) of the 2003 Act, nothing in s 17 affects 'any right of a person to apply for a writ of habeas corpus or *any other prerogative remedy* (emphasis added)'.

In *R (M) v Isleworth Crown Court* [2005] EWHC 363, Maurice Kay LJ said (at para 7), that a decision as to bail at an early stage of criminal proceedings does not relate to trial on indictment. His Lordship referred to the case of *Cox* [1997] 1 Cr App R 20, where it had been held that a refusal of bail was not susceptible to judicial review, saying that the rationale of that decision was the availability of an alternative remedy, namely the possibility which then existed of an application to a High Court judge. However, that right has been abolished by s 17 of the Criminal Justice Act 2003. His Lordship went on to quote from s 17(6)(b) of the 2003 Act. He said that he had no doubt that 'prerogative remedies' in that context embraced those set out in s 29(1) of the Supreme Court Act 1981, namely mandatory orders, prohibiting orders and quashing orders. That meant, he said, that the Divisional Court now has jurisdiction to review a bail decision by the Crown Court. However, having ruled that judicial review was available in such cases, his Lordship went on to say (at paras 11 and 12):

> Although we have jurisdiction by reason of s 17(6)(b), I am in no doubt that it is a jurisdiction which we should exercise very sparingly indeed. It would be ironic and retrograde if, having abolished a relatively short and simple remedy on the basis that it amounted to wasteful duplication, Parliament has, by a side wind, created a more protracted and expensive remedy of common application . . . The test must be on *Wednesbury* principles, but robustly applied and with this court always keeping in mind that Parliament has understandably vested the decision in judges in the Crown Court who have everyday experience of, and feel for, bail applications. Of course if bail were to be refused on a basis such as 'I always refuse in this type of case', or some other unjudicial basis, then this court would and should interfere.

The exceptional nature of this jurisdiction was emphasised in *R (Galliano) v Crown Court at Manchester* [2005] EWHC 1125 (Admin), where the point was repeated that a defendant who has been refused bail by a Crown Court judge can only succeed on a claim for judicial review if he persuades the High Court judge that the decision made by the Crown Court judge was one which 'fell outside the bounds of what could be regarded as reasonable'. Nothing short of irrationality will entitle the High Court to interfere. Parliament has decided that the right to go to the High Court to seek bail should be abolished, and so the normal court of last resort in questions of bail is the Crown Court. The High Court will 'be reluctant to entertain claims for judicial review of a failure to grant bail and will only do so if satisfied that the decision of the Crown Court judge was an irrational one' (per Collins J at para 11).

In *R (Shergill) v Harrow Crown Court* [2005] EWHC 648, the court confirmed that s 29(3) of the 1981 Act does not preclude the Divisional Court from considering applications for judicial review of a decision to refuse bail, but made it clear that it was only in exceptional cases that the court would consider it right to review the decision of a

Crown Court judge in whom the relevant powers had been vested. Collins J went on to say that it is essential that reasons given by a Crown Court judge for refusing bail are recorded so that, if any application for judicial review is made, the Administrative Court has a record of the reasons for refusal.

Guidance on the procedure to be adopted was given in *R (Allwin) v Snaresbrook Crown Court* [2005] EWHC 742. Where a claimant brings an application for judicial review of the decision of a Crown Court judge to withhold bail, the prosecution and the Crown Court should be notified and the matter put before the Administrative Court as a matter for urgent consideration and an oral hearing on notice requested within as short a time as possible. Generally it will not be appropriate to grant bail on an interim application on the papers. The Administrative Court judge should direct an oral hearing within a day or two to effectively determine the issue. Such hearings will normally be dealt with by a single judge.

3.10.3 Appeal against conditions of bail

Section 16(1) of the Criminal Justice Act 2003 also enables the defendant to appeal to the Crown Court against the imposition of certain bail conditions (based on Recommendation 184 of the Auld Review, that defendants should have a right of appeal to the Crown Court in respect of conditions imposed by magistrates as to residence away from home and/or to the provision of a surety or sureties or the giving of security). This right of appeal may only be exercised in respect of certain conditions, set out in s 16(3):

(a) that the person concerned resides away from a particular place or area,
(b) that the person concerned resides at a particular place other than a bail hostel,
(c) for the provision of a surety or sureties or the giving of a security,
(d) that the person concerned remains indoors between certain hours,
(e) [a condition] imposed under section 3(6ZAA) of the 1976 Act (requirements with respect to electronic monitoring), or
(f) that the person concerned makes no contact with another person.

Furthermore, the right of appeal under s 16 can only be exercised if the defendant has previously made an application to the magistrates (under s 3(8)(a) of the Bail Act) for the conditions to be varied (s 16(5)) or where the prosecutor has previously made an application under s 3(8)(b) or 5B(1) (s 16(6)). On an appeal under s 16, the Crown Court may vary the conditions of bail (s 16(7)). Once the Crown Court has disposed of the appeal, no further appeal can be brought unless a further application has been made to the magistrates under s 3(8)(a) (see s 16(8)).

3.11 PROSECUTION CHALLENGES TO THE GRANT OF BAIL

3.11.1 Records of reasons for decision to grant bail

Section 5(2A) of the Bail Act provides that:

> Where a magistrates' court or the Crown Court grants bail in criminal proceedings to a person to whom section 4 of this Act applies after hearing representations from the prosecutor in favour of withholding bail, then the court shall give reasons for granting bail.

In a case where s 5(2A) applies, the court is required (by s 5(2B)) to include a note of those reasons in the record of its decision and, if requested to do so by the prosecutor, give him a copy of that record.

Two mechanisms exist to enable the prosecution to challenge the grant of bail to a defendant.

3.11.2 Prosecution appeals against grant of bail

The Bail (Amendment) Act 1993 allows the prosecution to appeal, in certain circumstances, against decisions by magistrates to grant bail.

Section 1 of the Bail (Amendment) Act 1993 provides that:

> Where a magistrates' court grants bail to a person who is charged with, or convicted of, an offence punishable by imprisonment, the prosecution may appeal to a judge of the Crown Court against the granting of bail.

The original version of the Act limited the right of appeal to cases where the offence was punishable with at least five years' imprisonment, but s 18 of the Criminal Justice Act 2003 extended the scope of the Act to cover all imprisonable offences. This followed Recommendation 185 of the Auld Review.

Under s 1(2) of the 1993 Act, the prosecution right of appeal applies only where the prosecution is conducted by or on behalf of the Director of Public Prosecutions (DPP) (this includes CPS prosecutions) or by a person 'who falls within such class or description of person as may be prescribed for the purposes of this section by order made by the Secretary of State'. Furthermore, for the Act to apply, the prosecution must have opposed the grant of bail in the magistrates' court (s 1(3)).

If the prosecution wish to exercise the right of appeal, oral notice of appeal is given to the magistrates 'at the conclusion of the proceedings in which bail has been granted and before the release from custody of the person concerned' (s 1(4)) and written notice of appeal must be served on the magistrates' court and on the defendant within two hours of the conclusion of the bail hearing (s 1(5)).

Where oral notice of appeal has been given, the court must remand the accused in custody until the appeal is determined (s 1(6)). If the prosecution serves written notice of appeal within the prescribed time, the accused is again formally remanded in custody (r 19.16(5) of the Criminal Procedure Rules). The defendant is then held in custody pending the Crown Court hearing, which must take place within 48 hours from the date on which oral notice of appeal is given (excluding weekends and public holidays): s 1(8) of the 1993 Act. If, having given oral notice of appeal, the prosecution fails to serve a written notice of appeal within the two-hour period specified in s 1(5) of the 1993 Act, 'the appeal shall be deemed to have been disposed of' (s 1(7) of the Act) and the clerk must direct the release of the accused (r 19.16(7) of the Rules).

The courts have accorded some latitude to prosecutors when interpreting the apparently strict time limitations in the Act. For example, in *R v Isleworth Crown Court ex p*

Clarke [1998] 1 Cr App R 257, the Divisional Court held that the requirement that the prosecutor must give oral notice of appeal against the decision to grant bail 'at the conclusion of the proceedings' was satisfied in a case where such notice was given to the magistrates' court clerk some five minutes after the court had risen. The court added that, because what is now r 19.16(1) of the Criminal Procedure Rules requires that oral notice of appeal had to be given to the clerk of the magistrates' court, there is no requirement that the justices themselves have to be in court before oral notice can properly be given to their clerk. Similarly, in *R (Jeffrey) v Warwick Crown Court* [2002] EWHC 2469, the prosecutor wished to appeal against the grant of bail to the accused but the written notice of appeal was served on the court three minutes late. The Divisional Court held that Parliament did not intend that the time limit for serving the notice of appeal should defeat an appeal if the prosecution had given itself ample time to serve the notice on the defendant within the two-hour period, had used due diligence to serve the notice within that period, and the failure to do so was not the fault of the prosecution, but was due to circumstances outside its control. Furthermore, the delay of three minutes had not caused the accused any prejudice (since he knew at the conclusion of the proceedings before the magistrates that the prosecution was exercising its right of appeal and he knew that he was being detained in custody as a result of the oral application for him to be remanded in custody until the appeal was disposed of).

In *R v Middlesex Guildhall Crown Court ex p Okoli* [2001] 1 Cr App R 1, the Divisional Court had to consider the effect of the 48-hour time limit (contained in s 1(8)). On 7 June 2000, the defendant was granted bail by a magistrates' court. The prosecution sought to appeal under the Bail (Amendment) Act 1993. The appeal was listed for 3 pm on 9 June. The defendant argued that, because this was more than 48 hours after the notice of appeal had been given, the Crown Court had no jurisdiction to hear the appeal. It was held that where an oral notice of appeal against a decision to grant bail has been given, the appeal hearing must commence within two working days of the date – not the time – on which notice of appeal was given. The Crown Court therefore had jurisdiction in the present case.

The need to have a written notice following the oral notice of appeal is to enable the question of whether or not to appeal to be considered by a Senior Crown Prosecutor. Guidance issued to Crown Prosecutors by the CPS (<http://www.cps.gov.uk/legal/section14/chapter_l.html#56>) says:

> The right of appeal under [the 1993 Act] should only be used in cases of grave concern where there are substantial grounds under the Bail Act 1976 which would allow the Court to refuse bail. The Prosecutor considering whether an appeal is appropriate should apply an overarching test of whether there is a serious risk of harm to any member of the public or any other significant risk of harm to any member of the public or any other significant public interest ground.
>
> . . .
>
> In considering whether an appeal is appropriate, the seriousness of the offence is a factor to be considered. The public interest ground should not be used to justify appeals in less serious cases. The nature of the offence which the defendant faces is relevant if it illustrates the risk created by granting bail. Examples might be extreme cases of personal violence such as murder, rape, robbery or aggravated burglary, particularly if it is alleged that weapons have been used in offences of violence or during the commission of sexual offences.

A serious risk of harm to public safety and property may give grounds to justify an appeal. Examples might be arson with intent to endanger life or being reckless as to whether life is endangered, terrorist offences or riot.

The risk to the individual victim or victims will be a factor. The following situations may justify the exercise of the right of appeal:–

- A record which discloses previous convictions, particularly of a similar kind against the same victim or victims with similar characteristics;
- Evidence of violence or threats of violence to the victim or his or her family; or
- Evidence of undue influence over the victim, for example where there are alleged sexual offences against young people or children.

A strong indication that the defendant may abscond may be relevant, particularly if he or she has no right to remain in Britain or has substantial assets or interests abroad. On the other hand the right of appeal should not be used simply because the defendant has no fixed address or settled way of life, particularly where this may be coupled with mental health problems (unless of course there are genuine indications of danger to the public).

The appeal takes the form of a re-hearing, and the judge may remand the defendant in custody or may grant bail subject to such conditions (if any) as he thinks fit (s 1(9) of the 1993 Act). The defendant is not entitled to be present at the hearing of the appeal unless he is acting in person or, in any other case of an exceptional nature, a Crown Court judge is of the opinion that the interests of justice require him to be present and gives him leave to be so (r 19.17(4)).

Where a Crown Court judge allows a prosecution appeal against the grant of bail by a magistrates' court under the 1993 Act, he must state the period for which the defendant is to be remanded in custody (in other words, the judge must specify the date on which the defendant is to appear in the magistrates' court), and that period must be in accordance with the periods specified in ss 128 or 128A of the Magistrates' Courts Act 1980 (see below). This is because the defendant is still under the jurisdiction of the magistrates' court (*R v Szakal* [2000] 1 Cr App R 248, followed in *Remice v Governor of Belmarsh* [2007] EWHC 936 (Admin)).

3.11.3 Prosecution application for reconsideration of grant of bail

Section 5B(1) of the Bail Act 1976 provides that where a magistrates' court has granted bail (or the defendant was granted police bail), the prosecution may apply to the magistrates' court for that decision to be reconsidered, asking the court to:

- vary the conditions of bail; or
- impose conditions in respect of bail which has been granted unconditionally; or
- withhold bail.

This provision only applies where the defendant is accused of an indictable (including triable either-way) offence (s 5B(2)).

Section 5B(5) clearly envisages the possibility of such an application being made in the absence of the defendant; however, r 19.2(3)(b) requires notice of the application to be given to the defendant and r 19.2(6) requires the court to consider any representations made by the defendant (whether in writing or orally) before taking a decision.

An application under s 5B is not, strictly speaking, an appeal, since it is not challenging the correctness of the original decision. Section 5B(3) provides:

> No application for the reconsideration of a decision under this section shall be made unless it is based on information which was not available to the court or constable when the decision was taken.

Thus, an application is only possible under s 5B if it is based on new information (in the sense of information which was not available when the original decision regarding bail was taken). The basis of the application is therefore not to impugn the original decision to grant bail but to draw to the court's attention a relevant change in circumstances.

3.11.4 The two procedures compared

It follows that the two main differences between the prosecution appeal against the grant of bail and the prosecution application for reconsideration of the grant of bail are:

* an application for reconsideration under s 5B depends on new information coming to light (and so is not impugning the original decision);
* an appeal under the 1993 Act is made to the Crown Court whereas an application for reconsideration is made to the magistrates' court.

3.12 WHAT HAPPENS IF THE DEFENDANT FAILS TO ATTEND COURT?

Section 2 of the Bail Act 1976 defines 'surrender to custody' to mean the accused 'surrendering himself into the custody of the court . . . at the time and place for the time being appointed for him to do so'. In other words, the defendant 'surrenders' to custody by attending the correct court, on the correct date and at the correct time, and by complying with that court's procedure for surrender, for example, reporting to a particular office or a particular person (*DPP v Richards* [1988] QB 701). As it was put in *R v Central Criminal Court ex p Guney* [1996] AC 616, a defendant surrenders to custody when he puts himself at the direction of the court or an officer of the court.

In the next sections, we consider what happens if the accused fails to surrender to custody in accordance with the terms of his bail.

3.12.1 The offence of absconding

Section 6(1) of the Bail Act 1976 states:

> If a person who has been released on bail in criminal proceedings fails without reasonable cause to surrender to custody he shall be guilty of an offence.

Under s 6(2):

> If a person who—
>
> (a)   has been released on bail in criminal proceedings, and
> (b)   having reasonable cause therefor, has failed to surrender to custody,
>
> fails to surrender to custody at the appointed place as soon after the appointed time as is reasonably practicable he shall be guilty of an offence.

It follows from s 6(2) that, if it is not reasonably practicable for the defendant to surrender to custody at the appointed time, he must do so as soon thereafter as it is reasonably practicable.

The burden of proof rests on the accused to prove (on the balance of probabilities) that he had reasonable cause for his failure to surrender to custody: s 6(3).

The procedure to be followed is set out in para I.13 of the *Consolidated Practice Direction*. This provides as follows:

> 13.2 The failure of defendants to comply with the terms of their bail by not surrendering can undermine the administration of justice. It can disrupt proceedings. The resulting delays impact on victims, witnesses and other court users and also waste costs. A defendant's failure to surrender affects not only the case with which he is concerned, but also the courts' ability to administer justice more generally by damaging the confidence of victims, witnesses and the public in the effectiveness of the court system and the judiciary. It is, therefore, most important that defendants who are granted bail appreciate the significance of the obligation to surrender to custody in accordance with the terms of their bail and that courts take appropriate action if they fail to do so.
>
> 13.3 There are at least three courses of action for the courts to consider taking: (a) imposing penalties for the failure to surrender; (b) revoking bail or imposing more stringent bail conditions; and (c) conducting trials in the absence of the defendant.

Penalties for failure to surrender

> 13.4 A defendant who commits a s 6(1) or s 6(2) Bail Act 1976 offence commits an offence that stands apart from the proceedings in respect of which bail was granted. The seriousness of the offence can be reflected by an appropriate penalty being imposed for the Bail Act offence.
>
> 13.5 The common practice at present of courts automatically deferring disposal of a s 6(1) or s 6(2) Bail Act 1976 offence (failure to surrender) until the conclusion of the proceedings in respect of which bail was granted should no longer be followed. Instead, courts should now deal with defendants as soon as is practicable. In deciding what is practicable, the court must take into account when the proceedings in respect of which bail was granted are expected to conclude, the seriousness of the offence for which the defendant is already being prosecuted, the type of penalty that might be imposed for the breach of bail and the original offence as well as any other relevant circumstances. If there is no good reason for postponing dealing with the breach until after the trial, the breach should be dealt with as soon as practicable. If the disposal of the breach

of bail is deferred, then it is still necessary to consider imposing a separate penalty at the trial and the sentence for the breach of the bail should usually be custodial and consecutive to any other custodial sentence (as to which see paragraph 13.13). In addition, bail should usually be revoked in the meantime (see paragraphs 13.14 to 13.16). In the case of offences which cannot, or are unlikely to, result in a custodial sentence, trial in the absence of the defendant may be a pragmatic and sensible response to the situation (see paragraphs 13.17 to 13.19). This was not a penalty for the Bail Act offence and a penalty might also be imposed for the Bail Act offence.

Initiating proceedings – bail granted by a police officer

13.6 When a person has been granted bail by a police officer to attend court and subsequently fails to surrender to custody, the decision whether to initiate proceedings for a s 6(1) or s 6(2) offence will be for the police/prosecutor.

13.7 The offence in this form is a summary offence and should be initiated as soon as practicable after the offence arises in view of the six months time limit running from the failure to surrender. It should be dealt with on the first appearance after arrest, unless an adjournment is necessary, as it will be relevant in considering whether to grant bail again.

Initiating proceedings – bail granted by a court

13.8 When a person has been granted bail by a court and subsequently fails to surrender to custody, on arrest that person should normally be brought as soon as appropriate before the court at which the proceedings in respect of which bail was granted are to be heard. (The six months time limit does not apply where bail was granted by the court.) Should the defendant commit another offence outside the jurisdiction of the bail court, the Bail Act offence should, where practicable, be dealt with by the new court at the same time as the new offence. If impracticable, the defendant may, if this is appropriate, be released formally on bail by the new court so that the warrant may be executed for his attendance before the first court in respect of the substantive and Bail Act offences.

13.9 Given that bail was granted by a court, it is more appropriate that the court itself should initiate the proceedings by its own motion. The court will be invited to take proceedings by the prosecutor, if the prosecutor considers proceedings are appropriate.

Conduct of proceedings

13.10 Proceedings under s 6 of the Bail Act 1976 may be conducted either as a summary offence or as a criminal contempt of court. Where the court is invited to take proceedings by the prosecutor, the prosecutor will conduct the proceedings and, if the matter is contested, call the evidence. Where the court initiates proceedings without such an invitation the same role can be played by the prosecutor at the request of the court, where this is practicable.

13.11 The burden of proof is on the defendant to prove that he had reasonable cause for his failure to surrender to custody (s 6(3) of the Bail Act 1976).

Proceedings to be progressed to disposal as soon as is practicable

13.12 If the court decides to proceed, the s 6 Bail Act offence should be concluded as soon as practicable.

Sentencing for a Bail Act offence

13.13 In principle, a custodial sentence for the offence of failing to surrender should be ordered to be served consecutively to any other sentence imposed at the same time for another offence unless there are circumstances that makes this inappropriate (see *R v White; R v McKinnon*).

Relationship between the Bail Act offence and further remands on bail or in custody

13.14 When a defendant has been convicted of a Bail Act offence, the court should review the remand status of the defendant, including the conditions of that bail, in respect of the main proceedings for which bail had been granted.

13.15 Failure by the defendant to surrender or a conviction for failing to surrender to bail in connection with the main proceedings will be a significant factor weighing against the re-granting of bail or, in the case of offences which do not normally give rise to a custodial sentence, in favour of trial in the absence of the offender.

13.16 Whether or not an immediate custodial sentence has been imposed for the Bail Act offence, the court may, having reviewed the defendant's remand status, also remand the defendant in custody in the main proceedings.

Trials in absence

13.17 A defendant has a right, in general, to be present and to be represented at his trial. However, a defendant may choose not to exercise those rights by voluntarily absenting himself and failing to instruct his lawyers adequately so that they can represent him and, in the case of proceedings before the magistrates' court, there is an express statutory power to hear trials in the defendant's absence (s 11 of the Magistrates' Courts Act 1980). In such circumstances, the court has a discretion whether the trial should take place in his/her absence.

13.18 The court must exercise its discretion to proceed in the absence of the defendant with the utmost care and caution. The overriding concern must be to ensure that such a trial is as fair as circumstances permit and leads to a just outcome.

13.19 Due regard should be had to the judgment of Lord Bingham of Cornhill in *R v Jones* [2003] AC 1 in which Lord Bingham identified circumstances to be taken into account before proceeding, which include: the conduct of the defendant, the disadvantage to the defendant, the public interest, the effect of any delay and whether the attendance of the defendant could be secured at a later hearing. Other relevant considerations are the seriousness of the offence and likely outcome if the defendant is found guilty. If the defendant is only likely to be fined for a summary offence this can be relevant since the costs that a defendant might otherwise be ordered to pay as a result of an adjournment could be disproportionate. In the case of summary proceedings the fact that there can be an appeal that is a complete rehearing is also relevant, as is the power to reopen the case under s 142 of the Magistrates' Court Act 1980.

In summary, if the defendant was granted bail by the court and then absconded, but is now before the court, it should be left to the prosecution to invite the court to take action if the prosecutor thinks it appropriate to do so. Section 6 does not require that the defendant be formally charged with an offence under s 6 (*Schiavo v Anderton* [1987] QB 20). Once the court has decided to proceed under s 6, there is then a hearing to determine whether or not the defendant is guilty of absconding.

The prosecution are generally quite keen for action to be taken where a defendant has absconded. This is because if the defendant is convicted of failing to answer his bail, this conviction can be used in any later proceedings against the defendant to show a risk that he will abscond again (Sched 1, Pt I, para 9(c) to the Bail Act 1976).

Failure to answer bail which was granted by a court (that is, rather than by the police) will be dealt with by the court at which the proceedings in respect of which bail was granted are to be heard. In other words, if the defendant is to be tried for the substantive offence in the magistrates' court, the Bail Act 1976 offence will be dealt with in that court. If the defendant is to be tried in the Crown Court, the Bail Act 1976 offence will be dealt with in that court (by a judge sitting alone, not by a jury). Paragraph 13.5 of the Practice Direction makes it clear that it is no longer appropriate to postpone consideration of the Bail Act 1976 offence until the conclusion of the substantive proceedings (as was formerly the practice).

Under s 6(5), an offence under s 6 is punishable 'either on summary conviction or as if it were a criminal contempt of court'. However, in *R v Lubega* (1999) 163 JP 221, the appellant arrived at the Crown Court 20 minutes late. The judge dealt with the matter as a contempt of court. The question for the Court of Appeal was whether the judge was entitled to treat the late arrival as a contempt of court. The court held that if the appellant had committed any offence, it was contrary to s 6(1) of the Bail Act 1976. The effect of s 6(5) is not to convert an offence under the Act into a contempt of court, but rather to provide a speedy method of disposing of the matter. The judge was therefore not entitled to deal with the matter as a contempt of court.

Section 6(7) of the Bail Act 1976 provides that a person convicted under s 6 is liable to up to three months' imprisonment and/or a fine of up to £5,000 in the magistrates' court or to 12 months' imprisonment and an unlimited fine in the Crown Court; the latter applies whether the defendant has been committed to the Crown Court for sentence (under s 6(6) of the Bail Act 1976) or if the offence is being dealt with by the Crown Court because the defendant had been sent for trial in the Crown Court before he absconded.

In contrast to failure to answer bail granted by a court, failure to answer police bail is dealt with by a formal charge. Section 15(3) of the Criminal Justice Act 2003 disapplies s 127 of the Magistrates' Court Act 1980, which prevents summary proceedings from being instituted more than six months after the commission of an offence, in respect of offences under s 6 of the Bail Act 1976, and instead provides that such an offence may not be tried unless proceedings are started within six months of the commission of the offence, or within three months of the date when the defendant surrenders to custody, is arrested in connection with the offence for which bail was granted, or appears in court in respect of that offence. This will ensure that a defendant cannot escape prosecution under s 6 of the Bail Act 1976 merely by succeeding in absconding for more than six months.

3.12.2 Reasonable cause

An offence is only committed under s 6 if the defendant has no reasonable cause for the failure to surrender. Section 6(3) makes it clear that it is for the accused to prove that he had reasonable cause for his failure to surrender to custody. As is always the case when a defendant bears a burden of proof, it is the civil standard that is the balance of probabilities.

In *R v Watson* (1990) 12 Cr App R(S) 227, *R v How* [1993] Crim LR 201, and *R v Boyle* [1993] Crim LR 40, the Court of Appeal has repeatedly emphasised that, when the court is dealing with an allegation of absconding, the defendant must be given an opportunity to explain the failure to surrender to custody, or (if the defendant admits the offence) to put forward any mitigation. Furthermore, where the defendant denies the offence, he should be given the chance to adduce evidence that he had good cause for the failure to surrender. Similarly, in *R v Hourigan* [2003] EWCA Crim 2306, where the defendant arrived late at the Crown Court (in breach of his bail), the Court of Appeal noted that, because the failure to surrender has to have been without reasonable cause, it is incumbent on the court, before deciding whether to impose a penalty, to decide whether the s 6(1) offence has been made out. The allegation that he has committed an offence under s 6(1) should be put to the defendant (either directly or through counsel). If the defendant admits the breach, the court can go on to consider the question of penalty. Where the defendant does not admit the breach, the court should make the necessary enquiries (for example, through questioning the defendant) and then make a formal announcement of whether the allegation is found to be proven or not, with reasons for that finding.

In *R v Liverpool City Justices ex p Santos* (1997) *The Times*, 23 January, it was held that a mistake by a solicitor may, depending on the circumstances, be a reasonable excuse for a defendant's failure to surrender to bail.

It must be emphasised that if reasonable cause exists at the time the defendant should have surrendered, then he should surrender as soon as reasonably practicable thereafter.

3.12.3 The penalty for absconding

Paragraph 13.13 of the *Practice Direction* refers to *R v White; R v McKinnon* [2002] EWCA Crim 2952; [2003] 2 Cr App R(S) 29, where the Court of Appeal said that a custodial sentence imposed for failure to surrender to custody under s 6 should normally be ordered to be served consecutively to any sentence of imprisonment imposed for the substantive offence for which the defendant was before the court. The court also made it clear that there is no principle of law that the sentence for failing to surrender to custody should be proportionate to the sentence for the substantive offence of which the defendant stands convicted. Indeed, the court pointed out that in *R v Neve* (1986) 8 Cr App R(S) 270, the Court of Appeal had upheld the imposition of a sentence of six months' imprisonment for failing to surrender to custody even though the defendant had been acquitted of the substantive offence.

In November 2007, the Sentencing Guidelines Council issued definitive guidance on sentencing for failure to surrender (<http://www.sentencing-guidelines.gov.uk/docs/Fail%20to%20Surrender%20to%20Bail.pdf>). This guidance identifies aggravating factors including:

- lengthy absence;
- serious attempts to evade justice;
- determined attempt seriously to undermine the course of justice;
- previous relevant convictions and/or repeated breach of court orders or police bail.

It also identifies mitigating factors, including:

- prompt voluntary surrender.

When not amounting to a defence:

- misunderstanding;
- a failure to comprehend bail significance or requirements;
- caring responsibilities.

So far as the latter is concerned, para 22 notes that:

> An offender's position as the sole or primary carer of dependant relatives may be personal mitigation when it is the reason why the offender has failed to surrender to custody.

Paragraph 13 reinforces the point that failure to surrender is a completely separate offence to the one in respect of which bail was granted:

> Seriousness is not reduced automatically by subsequent acquittal of the original offence. Whilst it may seem harsh that a defendant before the court for an offence of which he is not guilty should be punished for the ancillary offence of failure to surrender during the course of the prosecution of that offence, both the culpability and the likely harm – delay, distress and inconvenience to witnesses, and additional costs – are the same. Moreover, one of the most serious effects of a Bail Act offence can be that a trial cannot take place because of the failure to surrender and it will often be invidious to expect a court to identify genuinely innocent defendants.

The accused in *R v Scott* [2007] EWCA Crim 2757; (2008) 172 JP 149, arrived at court over an half-an-hour late, because he had overslept. The defence argued that this was 'de minimis', and that no Bail Act offence should be put to him. The court rejected this argument, holding that 'the mere fact that a defendant is only slightly late cannot afford him a defence' (per Toulson LJ at para 14). His Lordship added (at para 15) that, even accepting, for the sake of argument, the possibility that there could be circumstances where a defendant's late arrival at court was so truly marginal that it would be '*Wednesbury* unreasonable' (i.e. perverse) to pursue it, that would be a rare case. His Lordship explained this approach (at paras 16-17):

> Even if a delay is small it can still cause inconvenience and waste of time. If a culture of lateness is tolerated the results can be cumulative and bad for the administration of justice. If the message given to this appellant had been that being half-an-hour late did not really matter, it would have been the wrong message to him and to other people ... It was submitted that it was disproportionate and draconian that it should now be on his record

that he failed to surrender at the appointed time. Why so? It is a matter of fact he did fail to attend at the appointed time. It was submitted that this could have an unduly harsh effect in the future because another court might refuse him bail. If the message received by defendants is that a failure to answer to their bail on time may have an adverse effect on obtaining bail in future, we cannot see this as a cause for complaint.

The Sentencing Guidelines Council Guidelines make a similar point in para 15:

The period of time for which a defendant absconds is also likely to influence the court when considering sentence. Whilst being absent for a long period of time will aggravate an offence, the fact that a defendant arrives at court only a few days, or even only a few hours, late, is not a factor that will necessarily mitigate sentence; in many cases, the harm will already have been done (for example, the trial may have been put back, witnesses may have been inconvenienced and there may be an increased likelihood that witnesses will fail to attend at a future hearing).

Section E of the Guidelines makes a number of other important points:

6. A previous conviction that is likely to be 'relevant' for the purposes of this offence is one which demonstrates failure to comply with an order of a court.
7. Acquittal of the original offence does not automatically mitigate this offence.
8. The fact that an offender has a disorganised or chaotic lifestyle should not normally be treated as mitigation of the offence, but may be regarded as personal mitigation depending on the particular facts of a case.
    . . .
10. The sentence for this offence should normally be in addition to any sentence for the original offence. Where custodial sentences are being imposed for a Bail Act offence and the original offence at the same time, the normal approach should be for the sentences to be consecutive. The length of any custodial sentence imposed must be commensurate with the seriousness of the offence(s).

3.12.4 Bench warrant

If the defendant was originally arrested and charged, failing to attend court is not only an offence itself (s 6 of the Bail Act 1976) but also enables the court to grant a warrant for the defendant's arrest. Section 7(1) of the Bail Act 1976 provides that:

If a person who has been released on bail in criminal proceedings and is under a duty to surrender into the custody of a court fails to surrender to custody at the time appointed for him to do so the court may issue a warrant for his arrest.

Such a warrant is known as a 'bench warrant'.

If a defendant fails to attend court but there is a suggestion that he has a good reason for not doing so (but there is insufficient information to be sure of this), the court may issue a bench warrant 'backed for bail' (permitted by s 117 of the Magistrates' Courts Act 1980 and s 81(4) of the Supreme Court Act 1981 for magistrates and the Crown Court respectively). In other words, the warrant is endorsed with a direction to the police to release the defendant once he has been arrested and informed of the next date he must attend court. This serves to warn the defendant that failure to attend court may lead to his arrest. Such warrants are, however, sometimes viewed as consuming a disproportionate amount of police time and effort in return for little or no advantage. Guidance issued by Thomas LJ (the Senior Presiding Judge for England and Wales) in May 2006 (at <http://www.judiciary.gov.uk/docs/judgments_guidance/protocols/bail_trials_absence.pdf>) encourages the use of warning letters instead of warrants backed for bail: where the accused does not attend, and the court decides not to proceed in his absence and is considering the issue of a warrant backed for bail (described in the guidance as 'likely to be uncommon cases'), the court should consider whether it is better to send a letter to the accused 'directing him to attend and warning him of the consequences of non-attendance, instead of issuing a warrant backed for bail'. The guidance continues:

> if the defendant does not attend the rearranged hearing without good reason, the court should then consider proceeding in absence or issuing a warrant not backed for bail. Unless there were unusual circumstances, any other course of action would undermine the process. The letter to the defendant should make it clear that, if the defendant did not attend the rearranged hearing, a court might well proceed in absence or issue a warrant not backed for bail.

If the defendant clearly has a good reason for not attending court, the court should simply adjourn the case in the absence of the defendant, with the defendant being remanded on bail as before (s 129(3) of the Magistrates' Courts Act 1980). This is sometimes known as 'enlarging bail'.

The guidance issued by Thomas LJ also deals with the question of evidence of inability to attend court through sickness, and makes the point that:

> Proper evidence must be supplied if a defendant claims he is unwell and unable to attend court; the standard 'off-work' or 'unfit to work' sick note will generally not establish that a person is too ill to attend court. There should normally be a letter from a doctor expressly stating that the defendant is too ill to attend court; this should be provided to the court before the date the defendant is due to appear. A letter can be followed up by a phone call from the clerk or legal adviser to the surgery if the court has doubts about its validity. Unless there is such evidence, the court should consider proceeding in the defendant's absence.

If no good reason is apparent, an arrest warrant (not backed for bail) will be issued. The schedule to the Justices' Clerks Rules 2005 (SI 2005/545), para 3, empowers a clerk to issue a warrant of arrest, whether or not endorsed for bail, for failure to surrender to court, where there is no objection on behalf of the accused.

Having surrendered to the custody of the court, the defendant must remain within the precincts of the court unless and until the court grants him bail again. Section 7(2) of the Bail Act provides that:

> If a person who has been released on bail in criminal proceedings absents himself from the court at any time after he has surrendered into the custody of the court and before the court is ready to begin or to resume the hearing of the proceedings, the court may issue a

warrant for his arrest; but no warrant shall be issued under this sub-section where that person is absent in accordance with leave given to him by or on behalf of the court.

3.12.4.1 Failure to attend to answer requisition or summons

If the defendant was supposed to attend court to answer a requisition or summons (that is, he was not originally arrested and charged), a bench warrant can be issued under s 1(6) of the Magistrates' Courts Act 1980 provided that the offence charged is an indictable offence (i.e. one that may or must be tried in the Crown Court). A warrant may be issued by a single magistrate.

3.12.4.2 After arrest under a bench warrant

After arrest pursuant to a bench warrant not backed for bail, the defendant will be taken before the court which granted the warrant and the question of whether or not he should be released on bail (perhaps with more stringent conditions) or kept in custody will be decided by the court.

The guidance to judges and magistrates on the subject of bail from Thomas LJ, issued in May 2006, also deals with the action to be taken where the accused is arrested for breaching his bail. The guidance says that,

> when the offender is to be re-bailed, the court must always consider whether the conditions need strengthening and give reasons for its decision as to continuing the existing terms or strengthening the terms, such as by adding a tagging condition or requiring a surety or security. If a defendant has failed to surrender to bail, it will usually only be in the unusual case that a defendant will be re-bailed on the same terms.

As a result of absconding, the defendant's chance of being granted bail in the same proceedings are reduced because the court is entitled (under Sched 1, Pt I, para 6 to the Bail Act 1976) to give particular weight to the fact that the defendant has already absconded in connection with those proceedings.

3.12.5 Police powers

The police have the power to arrest without warrant a person who is on bail if there are reasonable grounds to believe that he will abscond. Section 7(3) of the Bail Act 1976 provides that:

> A person who has been released on bail in criminal proceedings and is under a duty to surrender into the custody of a court may be arrested without warrant by a constable—
>
> (a) if the constable has reasonable grounds for believing that that person is not likely to surrender to custody; . . .

After arrest, the defendant will be brought before the court.

3.12.6 Proceeding with the case in the defendant's absence

In some instances, it may be possible to continue with the case even though the defendant is not present in the courtroom. This is dealt with in the chapters which follow as we examine the various hearings that may take place in a criminal case.

3.13 PERIOD OF REMAND IN CUSTODY PRIOR TO CONVICTION

The maximum period of a remand in custody prior to conviction is 'eight clear days' unless s 128A of the Magistrates' Courts Act 1980 applies (s 128(6) of the Magistrates' Courts Act 1980). The term 'eight clear days' means that if a hearing takes place on Monday, the next hearing must take place no later than the following Wednesday. Section 128A(2) provides as follows:

> A magistrates' court may remand the accused in custody for a period exceeding 8 clear days if
>
> (a) it has previously remanded him in custody for the same offence; and
> (b) he is before the court,
>
> but only if, after affording the parties an opportunity to make representations, it has set a date on which it expects that it will be possible for the next stage in the proceedings, other than a hearing relating to a further remand in custody or on bail, to take place, and only
>
> (i)   for a period ending not later than that date; or
> (ii) for a period of 28 clear days,
>
> whichever is the less.

Thus, s 128A allows a remand in custody for up to 28 days but does not apply to the first remand hearing, as the defendant must have previously been remanded in custody for the same offence. Furthermore, for s 128A to apply, the next hearing must be 'effective', in the sense that (for example) the mode of trial hearing or summary trial will take place. Both the prosecution and the defendant must be allowed to make representations before a remand in excess of eight days is ordered, but the defendant's consent is not required. It should be noted that s 128A(3) provides that 'nothing in this section affects the right of the accused to apply for bail during the period of the remand'.

3.13.1 Remands in absence of the defendant

The provisions of s 128A of the 1980 Act should be contrasted with remands in the absence of the defendant which are possible, under s 128(3A)–(3E), provided that the defendant:

a   'has the assistance of a legal representative to represent him in the proceedings in that court' (s 128(1B)); and
b   consents to not being present at future remand hearings (s 128(1C)).

The defendant must be brought before the court on at least every fourth application for his remand (s 128(1A)(ii)). Thus, there can be a maximum of three remands *in absentia*, and so the defendant has to appear in court at least once a month.

It is open to the defendant to withdraw his consent to being remanded in his absence (s 128(3A)(d)). It follows that the defendant can still apply for bail during the 28-day period by giving notice to the court that he wishes to do so.

3.13.2 Remand after conviction

Following summary conviction, there may be a remand in custody of up to three weeks (four weeks if the offender is on bail) to enable the preparation of a pre-sentence report (s 10(3) of the Magistrates' Courts Act 1980).

3.13.3 Place of remand

Remand in custody means that the defendant is held in prison or (if aged 18–20) in a remand centre. However, s 128(7) of the Magistrates' Courts Act 1980 allows a remand to police custody for a maximum of three clear days; s 128(8) states that this is only possible if it is necessary for the purpose of making inquiries into offences other than those presently before court. The defendant must be brought back to the magistrates' court as soon as the need to question him ceases.

Where a defendant has been remanded in custody, he will have to be brought to the court from the place he is detained on the next date when he is due to appear in court (this is sometimes known as being 'produced'). The defendant will be kept in cells adjacent to the courtroom until his case is called on. At that point he will be escorted into the dock.

A juvenile may be remanded to Local Authority accommodation (which means that the young person will be looked after by the local authority; unless the type of accommodation is a condition of the remand, the local authority can choose what type of accommodation it provides for the young person), or may be subject to a 'secure remand' (used for young people whose offences are particularly serious or who have offended frequently). Young people subject to secure remand are usually placed in secure children's homes. Secure children's homes are run by local authority social services departments and focus on attending to the physical, emotional and behavioural needs of the young people they accommodate; they aim to provide young people with support tailored to their individual needs.

3.13.4 Use of live links

Section 57B of the Crime and Disorder Act 1998 applies to preliminary hearings in a magistrates' court or the Crown Court. The court may give a 'live link' direction requiring the accused, if he is being held in custody during the hearing, to attend it through a live link from the place at which he is being held (sub-s (3)). The court cannot give or rescind such a direction unless the parties to the proceedings have been given the opportunity to make representations (sub-s (5)). Where the court is a magistrates' court and it decides not to give a live link direction it must give reasons for not doing so (sub-s (6)). Section 57A(3) defines a 'live link' as 'an arrangement by which a person (when not in the place where the hearing is being held) is able to see and hear, and to be seen and heard by, the court during a hearing'.

3.14 CUSTODY TIME LIMITS

Section 22 of the Prosecution of Offences Act 1985 provides for 'custody time limits'. The custody time limits themselves are set out in the Prosecution of Offences (Custody Time Limits) Regulations 1987 (SI 1987/299). For either-way offences, the maximum period of custody between the accused's first appearance and the start of summary trial or the time when the court decides to send the accused to the Crown Court for trial is 70 days (reg 4(2)) unless, before the expiry of 56 days following the day of the accused's first appearance, the court decides to proceed to summary trial, in which case the maximum period of custody between the accused's first appearance and the start of the summary trial is 56 days (reg 4(3)). For indictable-only offences, the maximum period of custody between the accused's first appearance and the time when the court decides to send the accused to the Crown Court for trial is 70 days (reg 4(4)). For summary offences, the maximum period of custody beginning with the date of the accused's first appearance and ending with the date of the start of the summary trial is 56 days (reg 4(4A)). Where a case is sent for trial in the Crown Court, the maximum period of custody between the time when the accused is sent for trial and the start of the trial is 112 days (reg 5(3)).

These provisions apply to proceedings in the youth court even though the usual distinction between summary and indictable offences does not apply there (*R v Stratford Youth Court ex p S* [1998] 1 WLR 1758).

In *R v Leeds Crown Court ex p Whitehead* (2000) 164 JP 102, the custody time limit applicable to the defendant was due to expire on 15 October 1998. The trial commenced on 14 October 1998. On 26 January 1999, the trial was stopped and the jury discharged. A fresh trial date was set for 13 September 1999; the defendant was remanded in custody. The defendant argued that the custody time limit provisions were applicable to the period after the abandonment of the first trial. The Divisional Court held that, since the custody time limit provisions cease to apply at the start of the trial (that is, when a jury is sworn in: s 22(11A) of the 1985 Act), the time limit provisions did not apply to the period between when a trial is aborted in the Crown Court and the retrial. However, the court went on to say that if a trial is aborted and a retrial ordered, the judge should be vigilant to protect the interests of the accused by taking steps to fix a speedy retrial, or by considering the grant of bail, or even staying the proceedings as an abuse of process.

3.14.1 Expiry of the time limit

Under reg 8 of the Prosecution of Offences (Custody Time Limits) Regulations 1987, where a custody time limit has expired:

- the defendant has an absolute right to bail;
- the court cannot require sureties, or the giving of security as a condition of granting bail (but it can impose other conditions, such as conditions of residence, reporting to a police station, etc.); and

- following the grant of bail, the defendant may not be arrested without warrant (under s 7 of the Bail Act 1976) on the ground that a police officer believes he is unlikely to surrender to custody or that that he has, or is likely, to break a condition of bail.

If the defendant is granted bail because the custody time limit has expired, his right to bail continues only until he enters a plea. Thereafter, the court can withhold bail if any of the reasons for doing so under the Bail Act 1976 apply (*R v Croydon Crown Court ex p Lewis* (1994) 158 JP 886).

3.14.2 Extending the time limit

Section 22(3) of the 1985 Act provides that the 'appropriate court':

> may, at any time before the expiry of a time limit imposed by the regulations, extend, or further extend, that limit; but the court shall not do so unless it is satisfied—
>
> (a) that the need for the extension is due to—
>
> > (i) the illness or absence of the accused, a necessary witness, a judge or a magistrate;
> > (ii) a postponement which is occasioned by the ordering by the court of separate trials in the case of two or more accused or two or more offences; or
> > (iii) some other good and sufficient cause; and
>
> (b) that the prosecution has acted with all due diligence and expedition.

The 'appropriate court' to do so is the Crown Court if the defendant has been sent for trial to the Crown Court; otherwise the application should be made to the magistrates' court (sub-s (11)).

The application to extend the time limit must be made prior to the expiry of the limit: once the limit has expired, there is no power to extend it (*R v Sheffield Justices ex p Turner* [1991] 2 QB 472). The Auld Review considers the custody time limits contained in the Prosecution of Offences Act 1985 (see paras 262–70 of Chapter 10). Recommendation 226 says that s 22 should be amended to enable a court to consider and grant an extension of the custody time limit after its expiry, but only if such power is closely circumscribed, including a provision that the court should only grant an extension where it is satisfied that there is a compelling public interest in doing so. This proposal has not been acted on.

The court can decide whether or not to extend time on the basis of submissions from counsel; in other words, there is no need for evidence to be called if the court thinks that this would be unnecessary (*R v Norwich Crown Court ex p Parker and Ward* (1992) 96 Cr App R 68). In *Wildman v DPP* [2001] EWHC 14 (Admin); (2001) 165 JP 543, the Court said that the procedure for seeking an extension of a custody time limit may be more informal than a normal trial process, and so it is unnecessary to comply with the formal rules of evidence. The burden is on the prosecution to obtain an extension of time: they have to satisfy the court that it is a proper application and to enable the defendant to test the appropriateness of the application. In the majority of cases, it should be possible for the prosecution to make information available to the defendant, prior to the application, which will enable him to be satisfied as to the propriety of the application. In so far as it is necessary for a defendant to test any aspect of the application, the means must be provided to enable him to do that. However, the court said that formal disclosure of the sort which is appropriate prior to trial is not normally necessary for an application for bail or for an extension of custody time limits (per Lord Woolf CJ at para 24).

Guidance on extensions of custody time limits was given by the Court of Appeal in *R v Manchester Crown Court ex p McDonald* [1999] 1 WLR 841. Lord Bingham of Cornhill CJ said (at p 846) that the custody time limit provisions have:

> three overriding purposes: (1) to ensure that the periods for which unconvicted defendants are held in custody awaiting trial are as short as reasonably and practically possible; (2) to oblige the prosecution to prepare cases for trial with all due diligence and expedition; and (3) to invest the court with a power and duty to control any extension of the maximum period under the regulations for which any person may be held in custody awaiting trial. These are all very important objectives. Any judge making a decision on the extension of custody time limits must be careful to give full weight to all three.
>
> In any application to the court for an order extending custody time limits beyond the maximum period laid down in the regulations it is for the prosecution to satisfy the court on the balance of probabilities that both the statutory conditions in s 22(3) are met. If, but only if, the court is so satisfied does the court have a discretion to extend the custody time limit. If it is not satisfied it may not do so. If it is satisfied it may, but need not, do so.
>
> The requirement in s 22(3) that the court must be 'satisfied' means that the court can never abdicate its responsibility by making orders of extension on the nod, or simply because the parties agree or no objection is raised.

At p 847 his Lordship considered the condition in s 22(3)(b), that the prosecution should have acted with all due expedition:

> The condition looks to the conduct of the prosecuting authority (police, solicitors, counsel). To satisfy the court that this condition is met the prosecution need not show that every stage of preparation of the case has been accomplished as quickly and efficiently as humanly possible. That would be an impossible standard to meet . . . What the court must require is such diligence and expedition as would be shown by a competent prosecutor conscious of his duty to bring the case to trial as quickly as reasonably and fairly possible. In considering whether that standard is met, the court will of course have regard to the nature and complexity of the case, the extent of preparation necessary, the conduct (whether co-operative or obstructive) of the defence, the extent to which the prosecutor is dependent on the co-operation of others outside his control and other matters directly and genuinely bearing on the preparation of the case for trial . . .

His Lordship then addressed s 22(3)(a), which requires the court to be satisfied that there is good and sufficient cause for extending (or further extending) the maximum period of custody specified in the Regulations:

> The seriousness of the offence with which the defendant is charged cannot of itself be good and sufficient cause within the section . . . Nor can the need to protect the public . . . Nor . . . can it be a good cause that the extension is only for a short period . . .

His Lordship went on to note that the unavailability of a suitable judge or a suitable courtroom within the maximum period specified in the regulations may amount to good and sufficient cause for granting an extension of the custody time limit but only 'in special cases and on appropriate facts'.

In *R (Bannister) v Guildford Crown Court* [2004] EWHC 221, it was held that a routine case with no particular facts capable of constituting a good and sufficient cause will not qualify for an extension of custody time limits merely because of listing difficulties. The court pointed out that if the difficulty of providing judicial resources is too readily accepted as a good and sufficient reason for extending custody time limits, there is a danger that the purpose of the statutory provisions will be undermined. However, in *R (Gibson) v Crown Court at Winchester* [2004] EWHC 361; [2004] 1 WLR 1623, Lord Woolf CJ considered *Bannister* and held (at para 31) that the availability of resources (whether of courtrooms or of judges) is not an irrelevant consideration. Courts cannot ignore the fact that resources are limited and that at certain times the pressures on those resources would be greater than at other times. It is important that courts strive to overcome any difficulties that occurred; if they do not, that might debar them from extending the custody time limits. However, it is not correct that judges should ignore questions of the non-availability of resources.

In *Kalonji v Wood Green Crown Court* [2007] EWHC 2804 (Admin), Simon J (at para 22) provided a helpful summary of the relevant principles:

(1) A remand in custody involves a balancing of the interests of the public and of the defendant, who is presumed not to be guilty. Custody time limits exist as part of the protection of defendants for whom there is no redress if, at the end of the day, they are found not guilty . . .

(2) In any application to extend time limits in circumstances such as presently before the court it is for the prosecution to satisfy the court, on the balance of probabilities, that . . . the need for an extension is due to 'good and sufficient reason' and 'that the prosecution has acted with all due diligence and expedition'.

(3) In making that judgment, the court will have in mind that one of the three 'overriding purposes' of the legislation is to ensure that the periods for which unconvicted defendants are held in custody are as short as reasonably and practically possible.

(4) In special cases, and on appropriate facts, the unavailability of a suitable courtroom or a suitable judge within the maximum period may amount to a good and sufficient reason for extending time limits . . .

(5) In any application based on unavailability of a courtroom or judge, the judge should examine the circumstances rigorously to determine whether the cause is also 'sufficient' for any extension and, if so, for the length of extension . . .

(6) The absence of a courtroom or judge should not be too readily accepted as good and sufficient reason to extend time limits since that would subvert the purpose of the statutory provisions which are designed for the protection of the liberty of citizens. An example where reasons may be compelling is a case of murder which may require a High Court judge to preside or a case requiring a court with a secure dock which may not be available as promptly as other courts.

(7) The unavailability of appropriate courts or judges is unlikely to provide a good reason for extending custody time limits in a 'routine case' . . .

(8) Nevertheless 'the courts cannot ignore the fact that available resources are limited.

They cannot ignore the fact that occasions will occur when pressures on the court will be more intense than they usually are' . . .

(9)   Where the court under review has heard full argument and given its ruling, this court will be most reluctant to disturb that decision . . .

In *R v Leeds Crown Court ex p Bagoutie* (1999) *The Times*, 31 May (followed in *R (Bannister) v Guildford Crown Court*), the Court of Appeal held that, whilst it was plain that Parliament had intended to insist that prosecutors could not seek extensions where the need for the extension was attributable to their own failure to act with due expedition, the court was not obliged to refuse an extension because the prosecution was shown to have been guilty of avoidable delay where that delay had had no effect whatever on the ability of the prosecution and the defence to be ready for trial on a predetermined trial date.

What happens if the defendant is charged with another offence? In *R v Great Yarmouth Magistrates ex p Thomas* [1992] Crim LR 116, the defendant was charged with importing cannabis. The prosecution applied for an extension of the custody time limit, but the court refused to extend time. The defendant was released on bail but was immediately arrested by police for possessing cannabis with intent to supply. The Divisional Court held that there was nothing to stop the prosecution from bringing several charges against a defendant based on the same or similar facts, even if this results in there being several custody time limits in operation. However, the magistrates should ensure that the prosecution are not abusing the process of the court by doing so. Likewise, in *R v Stafford Crown Court ex p Uppal* (1995) 159 JP 86, where the defendant was charged with rape, at the expiry of the custody time limit (an application for an extension of time having been refused), the prosecution preferred an additional charge of false imprisonment arising out of the same facts as the rape. It was held that, where an additional charge is brought against a defendant who is already charged with an offence, the second offence has its own custody time limit and this is the case whether or not the second charge is based on additional evidence. It was also said that when the CPS are considering bringing further charges against a defendant, they should review the evidence at the earliest opportunity and, wherever possible, comply with the initial custody time limit. However, the CPS would not be guilty of abuse of process unless it was established that they brought further charges simply for the purpose of extending the time limit.

In *R (Wardle) v Leeds Crown Court* [2001] UKHL 12; [2002] 1 AC 754, the defendant was charged with murder. On the day that the custody time limit expired, the prosecution offered no evidence on the murder charge but charged the appellant with manslaughter arising out of the same facts. The question to be decided was whether the later charge caused a fresh custody time limit to start running. The House of Lords held that each separate offence attracts its own custody time limit; however, there would be no fresh custody time limit if the new charge is simply a re-statement of the other offence with different particulars. Thus, the new offence has to be a different offence in law if it is to attract a fresh custody time limit. The House of Lords went on to hold that the bringing of a new charge would be an abuse of process if the prosecution could not demonstrate, on the facts of the case, that the bringing of the new charge was justified, so that the court was satisfied that it had not been brought solely with a view to obtaining the substitution of a fresh custody time limit.

In *R (Thomas); R (Stubbs) v Central Criminal Court* [2006] EWHC 2138 (Admin); [2006] 1 WLR 3278, the court had to consider the approach to be taken to an application for a further extension of custody time limits. It was held that the court has to look at the matters giving rise to the need to grant that particular extension. Where a defendant asserts a lack of expedition or due diligence, and it appears that is the root cause of the application for the earlier extension of time, those matters are properly a matter for the earlier application, not the present application. However, that does not mean that delay prior to the earlier application cannot be relied on in a later application if it is the root cause of that later application.

Under s 22(7) of the Prosecution of Offences Act 1985, where a magistrates' court decides to extend, or further extend, a time limit, the accused may appeal against the decision to the Crown Court. Under sub-s (8), where a magistrates' court refuses to extend, or further extend, a time limit, the prosecution may similarly appeal against the refusal to the Crown Court. Sub-section (9) provides that an appeal under sub-s (8) may not be commenced after the expiry of the limit in question and also provides that where such an appeal is commenced before the expiry of the limit, the limit shall be deemed not to have expired before the determination or abandonment of the appeal.

Chapter 4

Classification and allocation of offences

4.1 INTRODUCTION

In this chapter, we examine how the decision is made as to which court (magistrates' court or Crown Court) the offence should be tried in, if that offence is one which can be tried in either court.

Mode of trial can be determined in any magistrates' court; it does not matter where in England and Wales the offence was allegedly committed (s 2 of the Magistrates' Courts Act 1980).

4.2 CLASSIFICATION OF OFFENCES

According to Sched 1 to the Interpretation Act 1978, there are three types of criminal offence:

a summary offences (offences which are triable only in the magistrates' court);
b indictable offences, which are either:

   i   triable only on indictment (triable only in the Crown Court); or
   ii   triable either way (triable either in the magistrates' court or the Crown Court).

To determine which category a particular offence falls into one should look at:

• Sched 1 to the Magistrates' Courts Act 1980, which lists a number of offences that are triable either way; or
• the statute which creates the offence: if the penalty refers both to summary conviction and to conviction on indictment, the offence is triable either way; if it refers only to conviction on indictment, the offence can be tried only in the Crown Court; if it refers only to summary conviction, the offence can be tried only in the magistrates' court.

Thus, if an offence is listed in Sched 1 to the 1980 Act or its penalty is expressed in a way which refers to both summary trial and trial on indictment, it is triable either way.

The rest of this chapter examines how it is decided where an either-way offence should be tried.

4.3 INDICATION AS TO A DEFENDANT'S INTENDED PLEA: THE 'PLEA BEFORE VENUE' HEARING

The 'mode of trial' procedure begins with the court seeking to find out the defendant's intended plea, a procedure known to practitioners as 'plea before venue'. This process is set out in ss 17A and 17B of the Magistrates' Courts Act 1980.

Section 17A applies where a defendant who has attained the age of 18 is charged with an offence that is triable either way (s 17A(1)). The s 17A procedure has to be carried out in the presence of the defendant (s 17A(2)). It begins with the charge being written down (if this has not already been done) and being read to the defendant (s 17A(3)). The court then explains to the defendant that he may indicate whether he intends to plead guilty or not guilty; the defendant must also be warned that if he indicates an intention to plead guilty, he will be regarded as having actually pleaded guilty and that the magistrates then have the power to commit him for sentence to the Crown Court (under ss 3 or 3A of the Powers of Criminal Courts (Sentencing) Act 2000 – see below) if they take the view that their sentencing powers are inadequate (s 17A(4)).

The defendant is then asked whether he intends to plead guilty or not guilty (s 17A(5)). If the defendant indicates that he intends to plead guilty, the magistrates must proceed as if the case were a summary trial at which the defendant had pleaded guilty (s 17A(6)). In other words, the indication of an intention to plead guilty is to be regarded as an actual plea of guilty.

If the defendant indicates that he intends to plead not guilty, the court goes through the mode of trial procedure set out in ss 18–21 of the Magistrates' Courts Act 1980 (described below): s 17A(7). Where the defendant declines to indicate how he intends to plead, the court must assume that he intends to plead not guilty and so must go through the mode of trial procedure (s 17A(8)).

The effect of these provisions is that where a defendant is charged with an either-way offence and indicates to the magistrates that he intends to plead guilty, he will be regarded as having agreed to summary trial and as having pleaded guilty. If the case is a serious one, in the sense that it calls for a sentence beyond the powers of the magistrates, the defendant will be committed for sentence to the Crown Court. The object of this reform was to ensure that defendants who intend to plead guilty do not end up in the Crown Court unless the case is a serious one.

Where the defendant indicates an intention to plead guilty to one or more either-way offences but is also sent to the Crown Court for trial in respect of an either-way offence to which he intends to plead not guilty, or in respect of an offence which is triable only on indictment, the magistrates may commit him to the Crown Court for sentence (under s 4 of the Powers of Criminal Courts (Sentencing) Act 2000) in respect of the offence(s) to which he had indicated a guilty plea (even if their sentencing powers would be adequate to deal with the offence(s)).

A Home Office Circular (45/1997) (available at www.nationalarchives.gov.uk) makes the point that some defendants, especially unrepresented defendants, may find the 'plea before venue' hearing difficult to understand. The Circular says (at para 15):

- the defendant will want to know whether his case will be dealt with that day in court. The court may wish to make this clear when explaining what will happen if the defendant indicates a plea of guilty or not guilty;
- the defendant must understand that an indication of a guilty plea will lead to conviction and sentence. But some defendants may be confused if the court tries to distinguish between plea indication and plea taking. It may be clearer to inform the defendant that if he tells the court that he intends to plead guilty, the outcome will be that he will be convicted of the offence, that the prosecutor will tell the court about the facts of the case, that the defence will have the opportunity to respond, and that the court will then proceed to consider sentence either on the same day or at a later date if the court requires more information about the case before deciding on the appropriate sentence;
- the defendant must also understand that the court has the discretion to commit him to Crown Court for sentence [under s 3 of the Powers of Criminal Courts (Sentencing) Act 2000] if it considers the offence to be so serious that its own sentencing powers are not sufficient to impose a great enough punishment;

. . .

- the defendant should be asked at the end of the explanation whether he understands and whether there is anything on which he would like further explanation.

The Home Office Circular contains an Annex with a suggested form of wording for the use of the magistrates' court when inviting the defendant to indicate his plea. It is as follows:

This/these offence(s) may be tried either by this court or by the Crown Court before a Judge and jury.

Whether or not this court can deal with your case today will depend upon your answers to the questions which I am going to put to you. Do you understand?

You will shortly be asked to tell the court whether you intend to plead guilty or not guilty to (certain of) the offence(s) [that is, only the offences which are triable either way] with which you are charged. Do you understand?

If you tell us that you intend to plead guilty, you will be convicted of the offence(s). We may then be able to deal with (part of) your case at this hearing. The prosecutor will tell us about the facts of the case, you (your representative) will have the opportunity to respond (on your behalf), and we shall then go on to consider how to sentence you. Do you understand?

We may be able to sentence you today, or we may need to adjourn the proceedings until a later date for the preparation of a pre-sentence report by the Probation Service. If we believe that you deserve a greater sentence than we have the power to give you in this court, we may decide to send you to the Crown Court, either on bail or in custody, and you will be sentenced by that court, which has greater sentencing powers. Do you understand?

[In cases where s 4 of the Powers of Criminal Courts (Sentencing) Act 2000 applies:]

If you indicate a guilty plea for this/these offence(s), even if we believe that our own sentencing powers are great enough to deal with you here, we may still send you to the Crown Court to be sentenced for this/these offence(s) because you have also been charged with [a] related offence(s) [for which you have already been committed for trial in that court [for which you will be committed for trial in that court]. Do you understand?

If, on the other hand, you tell us that you intend to plead not guilty, or if you do not tell us what you intend to do, we shall go on to consider whether you should be tried by this court or by the Crown Court on some future date. If we decide that it would be appropriate to deal with your case in this court, we shall ask you if you are content for us to do so or whether you wish to have your case tried in the Crown Court.

Before I ask you how you intend to plead, do you understand everything I have said or is there any part of what I have said which you would like me to repeat or explain?

Section 17B of the Magistrates' Courts Act 1980 deals with the situation where:

a   a person who has attained the age of 18 years appears before a magistrates' court charged with an offence triable either way;
b   the accused is represented by a legal representative;
c   the court considers that by reason of the accused's disorderly conduct before the court it is not practicable for proceedings under s 17A to be conducted in his presence; and
d   the court considers that it should proceed in the absence of the accused (s 17B(1)).

In such a case, the charge is written down (if not already done) and read to the lawyer; the lawyer is then asked whether the defendant intends to plead guilty or not guilty; if the lawyer indicates that the defendant intends to plead guilty, the case is regarded as a summary trial in which the defendant has pleaded guilty; if the lawyer indicates that the client intends to plead not guilty, or if the lawyer declines to indicate the defendant's intention regarding the plea, the court proceeds to the mode of trial hearing (s 17B(2), (3)).

In *R v Rafferty* [1999] 1 Cr App R 235, Thomas J (at p 237) considered the effect of plea before venue on bail, holding that:

> in most cases where a plea of guilty is made at the plea before venue, it will not be usual to alter the position as regards bail or custody. In the usual case, when a person who has been on bail pleads guilty at the plea before venue, the usual practice should be to continue bail, even if it is anticipated that a custodial sentence will be imposed by the Crown Court, unless there are good reasons for remanding the defendant in custody. If the defendant is in custody, then after entering a plea of guilty at the plea before venue, it would be unusual, if the reasons for remanding him in custody remained unchanged, to alter the position.

Where the defendant indicates a plea of guilty but the court does not pass sentence immediately, the magistrates must be careful not to create an expectation that the defendant will ultimately be sentenced in that court if they wish the option of committal for sentence to the Crown Court to remain open. In *R v Horseferry Road Magistrates' Court ex p Rugless* [2000] 1 Cr App R(S) 484, the defendant indicated a guilty plea at the 'plea before venue' hearing; the court accepted jurisdiction and ordered a pre-sentence report, stating that all sentencing options were to remain open, with the exception of committal to the Crown Court for sentence. At the next hearing, the magistrates committed the defendant to the Crown Court for sentence (under s 3 of the Powers of Criminal Courts (Sentencing) Act 2000). The Divisional Court held that the defendant had a legitimate expectation that he would be sentenced in the magistrates' court. The subsequent decision to commit him for sentence was in breach of this legitimate expectation; accordingly it was appropriate to quash the decision to commit for sentence. However, the expectation has to be a legitimate one. In *R (White) v Barking Magistrates' Court* [2004] EWHC 417, the defendant was charged with production of cannabis. The charges related to a large-scale production operation. When he appeared before the justices and pleaded guilty, they adjourned the matter. At the next hearing they committed him to the Crown Court for sentence. He applied for judicial review of the decision to commit, contending that, at the first hearing, the justices had created a legitimate expectation that they would deal with sentence themselves. It was held that although an expectation had been created by the justices at the earlier hearing that they would not commit the defendant to the Crown Court, that expectation would not be fulfilled, since it would have been an unreasonable decision by the justices. Given the severity of the offending, it would have been unreasonable, and therefore unlawful, for the justices not to have committed the defendant to be sentenced in the Crown Court.

4.4 MODE OF TRIAL HEARING: PROCEDURE

The procedure to be followed for the part of the mode of trial hearing after 'plea before venue', where the defendant indicates an intention to plead not guilty (or gives no indication of his intended plea) in respect of one or more offences, is set out in ss 18–21 of the Magistrates' Courts Act 1980.

This procedure applies where the defendant has attained the age of 18 and is charged with an either-way offence (s 18(1)). Under s 18(5), this procedure may take place before a single lay justice. However, if the accused is given the option of summary trial and accepts that option, a single justice cannot try the case (and so, where the preliminary hearing takes place before a single justice and the accused pleads not guilty, the case will have to be adjourned for hearing before a full bench (or a District Judge)). Similarly, although a single lay justice may take a guilty plea, sentence must be imposed by a full bench (or a District Judge).

The mode of trial procedure is as follows:

1 The court asks if the accused is aware of his right to receive advance information of the prosecution case (see below); if a request for disclosure has been made, the court will ask if the request has been complied with.
2 The prosecution make representations as to the appropriate mode of trial. This involves a brief summary of the facts of the alleged offence so that the magistrates can assess the seriousness of the offence. The prosecution will base their submissions on the criteria contained in s 19(3) of the 1980 Act and in the Mode of Trial Guidelines (discussed below).
3 The defence then have the chance of making representations as to the appropriate mode of trial. If the defendant wishes to be tried at the Crown Court, no representations will be made since, even if the magistrates decide that the case is suitable for summary trial, the defendant can nevertheless choose trial on indictment. If, on the other hand, the prosecution ask for trial on indictment but the defendant wishes to be tried summarily, the defendant will first have to persuade the magistrates to accept jurisdiction (that is, to rule that the case is suitable for summary trial).

4   Having heard the representations, the magistrates come to their decision whether or not to offer the defendant the option of summary trial (that decision being based on the criteria set out in s 19(3) of the 1980 Act and the Mode of Trial Guidelines).

5   If the magistrates decide that the case is *not* suitable for summary trial, the defendant will be sent to the Crown Court for trial.

6   If the magistrates decide that the case *is* suitable for summary trial, the defendant will be asked whether he wishes to be tried in the magistrates' court or by a judge and jury in the Crown Court. Before the defendant announces his choice, the court must first warn him that if he consents to a summary trial and is convicted, he may be sent to the Crown Court to be sentenced (under s 3 of the Powers of Criminal Courts (Sentencing) Act 2000). The defendant then announces his choice. In *R v Southampton Magistrates Court ex p Sansome* [1999] 1 Cr App R(S) 112, the court approved this form of wording:

> It appears to this court more suitable for you to be tried here. You may now consent to be tried by this court, but if you wish, you may choose to be tried by a jury instead. If you are tried by this court and are found guilty, this court may still send you to the Crown Court for sentence if it is of the opinion that greater punishment should be inflicted for the offence than it has power to impose. Do you wish to be tried by this court or do you wish to be tried by a jury?

If the defendant is charged with a 'specified offence' to which s 224 of the Criminal Justice Act 2003 applies, he should also be warned that, if he consents to be tried summarily and is convicted, he may also be committed to the Crown Court for sentence if he qualifies for a sentence of imprisonment for public protection or an extended sentence under the 'dangerous offender' provisions in the 2003 Act under s 3A of the Powers of Criminal Courts (Sentencing) Act 2000 (see Chapter 5).

The Criminal Justice Act 2003 (in provisions which had not been brought into force) was to have removed the possibility that the defendant might be committed for sentence to the Crown Court under s 3 of the 2000 Act if he was convicted by the magistrates following a trial after a 'not guilty' plea (and so committal for sentence under s 3 would have been possible only where the defendant had entered a guilty plea at the 'plea before venue' hearing). However, para 7 of Sched 13 to the Criminal Justice and Immigration Act 2008 cancels the amendment of s 3 of the 2000 Act, thus preserving the power of a magistrates' court to commit to the Crown Court for sentence an offender whom it has convicted after a summary trial, if it considers that a Crown Court sentence should be available (as well as having the power to commit an offender for sentence where he pleads guilty at the 'plea before venue' hearing).

7   The Criminal Justice Act 2003 also adds an additional step to the mode of trial procedure by amending s 20 of the Magistrates' Courts Act 1980 (this amendment is not in force at the time of writing) to give the defendant the opportunity to request an indication from the magistrates whether, if he were to plead guilty at that stage, the sentence would be custodial or not (new s 20(3)). The magistrates are given an unfettered discretion whether or not to give such an indication (new s 20(4)). Where an indication is given, the defendant is to be given the opportunity to reconsider his original indication as to plea (new s 20(5)). If he asks to reconsider his indication as to plea and indicates an intention to plead guilty, the magistrates'

court will proceed to pass sentence (new s 20(6) and (7)), if necessary adjourning for a pre-sentence report; in such a case, a custodial sentence will be available only if such a sentence was indicated by the court (new s 20A(1), which stipulates that where the magistrates give an indication as to sentence, no court (whether a magistrates' court or not) may impose a custodial sentence for the offence unless such a sentence was indicated in the indication of sentence given under s 20).

If the defendant declines to reconsider his plea indication, or if no sentence indication is given by the magistrates, the defendant will be given the choice of accepting summary trial or electing Crown Court trial (new s 20(8) and (9)). Where an indication of sentence is given and the defendant does not choose to plead guilty on the basis of it, the sentence indication is not binding on the magistrates who later try the case summarily, or on the Crown Court if the defendant elects trial on indictment (s 20A(3)).

8   Where the magistrates decline jurisdiction, or the accused elects trial on indictment, the case is currently sent to the Crown Court by way of committal proceedings. When the relevant provisions of the Criminal Justice Act 2003 come into force, the case will instead be sent to the Crown Court under s 51 of the Crime and Disorder Act 1998. For a fuller discussion, see Chapter 9.

9   Where the defendant is charged with several related either-way offences, pleads guilty to one or some, but not all, of them at the 'plea before venue' hearing and is sent to the Crown Court to be tried for the rest, s 4 of the Powers of Criminal Courts (Sentencing) Act 2000 empowers the magistrates to commit him to the Crown Court to be sentenced for the offence(s) to which he has pleaded guilty. For a fuller discussion, see Chapter 5.

The key point to emphasise about the mode of trial procedure is that summary trial of an either-way offence is possible only if the magistrates and the defendant both agree to it. If either the magistrates or the defendant want the case to be tried in the Crown Court, the case will have to be sent to the Crown Court for trial.

4.5 MODE OF TRIAL: RELEVANT FACTORS

Section 19(3) of the Magistrates' Courts Act 1980 currently states that in deciding whether or not a case is suitable for summary trial, the magistrates should have regard to:

- the nature of the case;
- whether the circumstances make the offence one of serious character;
- whether the punishment which a magistrates' court would have power to inflict for it would be adequate; and
- any other circumstances which appear to the court to make it more suitable for the offence to be tried in one way rather than the other.

Section 19(1) also requires the court to take account of any representations made by the prosecution and the defence.

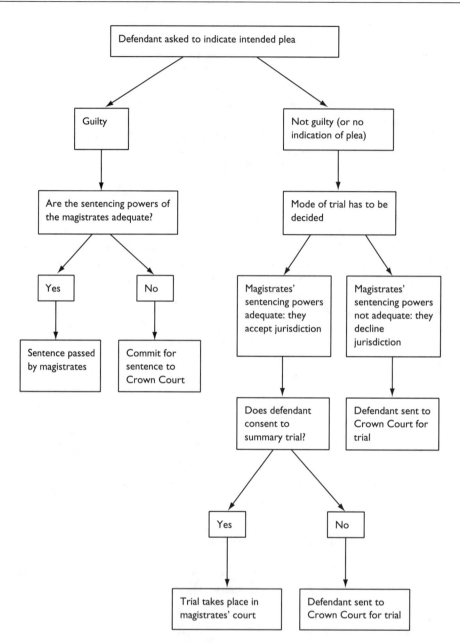

Figure 4.1 Determining mode of trial for either-way offences.

Section 19 is subject to amendment by the Criminal Justice Act 2003. When the amendments come into effect, s 19 will require the magistrates to consider:

a   whether the sentence which a magistrates' court would have power to impose for the offence would be adequate; and b   any representations made by the prosecution and/or the accused

Even prior to that amendment, the key question which the magistrates must ask themselves is whether their sentencing powers are sufficient to deal with the case. At the time of writing, the maximum sentence available in a magistrates' court is six months' imprisonment (12 months if the accused is charged with two or more offences which are triable either way). When the enhancement of those powers contained in the Criminal Justice Act 2003 comes into force, a magistrates' court will be able to impose 12 months for a single offence (and 65 weeks for two or more offences).

4.5.1 Guidelines

To help the magistrates decide which is the appropriate mode of trial for a particular case, para V.51 of the *Consolidated Practice Direction* contains Mode of Trial Guidelines:

> V.51.3 Certain general observations can be made:
>
> (a)   the court should never make its decision on the grounds of convenience or expedition;
>
> (b)   the court should assume for the purpose of deciding mode of trial that the prosecution version of the facts is correct;
>
> (c)   the fact that the offences are alleged to be specimens is a relevant consideration (although it has to be borne in mind that difficulties can arise in sentencing in relation to specimen counts, see *R v Clark* [1996] 2 Cr App R (S) 351 and *R v Canavan and others* [1998] 1 Cr App R (S) 243); the fact that the defendant will be asking for other offences to be taken into consideration, if convicted, is not;
>
> (d)   where cases involve complex questions of fact or difficult questions of law, including difficult issues of disclosure of sensitive material, the court should consider committal for trial;
>
> (e)   where two or more defendants are jointly charged with an offence each has an individual right to elect his mode of trial;
>
> (f)   in general, except where otherwise stated, either-way offences should be tried summarily unless the court considers that the particular case has one or more of the features set out in paragraphs V.51.4 to V.51.18 and that its sentencing powers are insufficient;
>
> (g)   the court should also consider its power to commit an offender for sentence under sections 3 and 4 of the Powers of Criminal Courts (Sentencing) Act 2000, if information emerges during the course of the hearing which leads it to conclude that the offence is so serious, or the offender such a risk to the public, that its powers to sentence him are inadequate. This means that committal for sentence is no longer determined by reference to the character and antecedents of the offender.
>
> Features relevant to individual offences
>
> V.51.4 Where reference is made in these guidelines to property or damage of 'high value' it means a figure equal to at least twice the amount of the limit (currently £5,000) imposed by statute on a magistrates' court when making a compensation order.

The fact that the court should assume for the purpose of deciding mode of trial that the prosecution version of the facts is correct means that there is little point in the defence making representations that the offence is not as serious as the prosecution allege.

It is a little strange that the guidelines say that it is not a relevant consideration that the defendant will be asking for other offences to be taken into consideration ('TICs' – see Chapter 16), as the presence of 'TICs' could affect the sentence that is passed. It should be borne in mind, however, that an offender will usually ask for offences to be taken into consideration only if he pleads guilty to the offence(s) with which he is actually charged (and mode of trial only has to be considered where the defendant indicates an intention to plead not guilty, or give no indication of intended plea). Moreover, it is a matter for the discretion of the sentencing court whether or not to accede to a request from the defendant to take additional offences into consideration.

Where the case involves complex questions of fact or difficult questions of law, the court should consider sending the defendant to the Crown Court for trial as the trial will be presided over by a professional judge. However, trial in a magistrates' court can be before a District Judge (and so listing the case for trial by a District Judge may be an alternative to sending the case to the Crown Court for trial).

According to the Mode of Trial Guidelines, where two or more defendants are jointly charged, the magistrates must consider each defendant separately; thus, it would be wrong to refuse to try a defendant summarily in a case which is suitable for summary trial merely because another defendant is to be tried in the Crown Court. This provision is based on the decision of the House of Lords in *R v Brentwood Justices ex p Nicholls* [1992] 1 AC 1 (followed in *R v Ipswich Justices ex p Callaghan* (1995) 159 JP 748 and *R v Wigan Justices ex p Layland* (1995) 160 JP 223), that s 19 of the Magistrates' Courts Act 1980 requires the justices to make a decision about mode of trial before the defendant(s) are put to their election; once that decision has been made, it should not be changed on the basis that one or more of the defendants elects Crown Court trial.

The original version of the Guidelines, issued in 1990, said that the magistrates, in determining mode of trial, should assume that the defendant has no previous convictions (indeed it was held in *R v Colchester Justices ex p NE Essex Building Co* [1977] 1 WLR 1109 that any previous convictions must not be revealed to the magistrates at this stage) and should not take account of any personal mitigating circumstances. However, the revised version of the Mode of Trial Guidelines omitted the principle that the defendant's antecedents are irrelevant. Similarly, the revised Guidelines omitted the principle stated in the original version that the magistrates should ignore any personal mitigating circumstances. Thus, it is submitted that, when determining mode of trial, the magistrates may take account of all the factors (except 'TICs') to which they would have regard if they were passing sentence.

When the amended version of s 19 of the Magistrates' Courts Act 1980 (see para 5 of Sched 3 to the Criminal Justice Act 2003) comes into effect, the relevance of previous convictions will be put beyond doubt, since s 19(2)(a) will specifically provide that the court 'shall give the prosecution an opportunity to inform the court of the accused's previous convictions (if any)'. This will settle once and for all the controversy over whether the magistrates should have regard to previous convictions when considering whether a case is suitable for summary trial. Bearing in mind that the magistrates are trying to predict whether the ultimate sentence will be one that is within their powers, it seems to make sense that they should be made aware of all the factors that would be relevant to that sentence.

The Guidelines make it clear that there is a presumption in favour of summary trial unless the case has aggravating features which render the magistrates' sentencing powers inadequate.

4.5.2 Sentencing Guidelines Council Allocation Guidelines

In 2006 the Sentencing Guidelines Council (a body established under the Criminal Justice Act 2003 and chaired by the Lord Chief Justice: see Chapter 16) issued draft guidelines on Mode of Trial (or 'allocation' as the process is termed in those Guidelines). When the version of s 19 of the 1980 Act substituted by the Criminal Justice Act 2003 comes into force, s 19(3) will require the court to 'have regard to any allocation guidelines (or revised allocation guidelines) issued as definitive guidelines under s 170 of the Criminal Justice Act 2003'.

Paragraph 3.1 of the current Draft Guidelines sets out the general considerations applicable to the mode of trial decision:

- The primary test is the adequacy of the sentencing powers of the court.
- A court will start with a general presumption towards trial in a magistrates' court.
- The features set out in the following guidelines will need to be considered in order to determine whether the sentencing powers of a magistrates' court are sufficient to deal with the case justly.
- In deciding whether the powers of a magistrates' court would be adequate, a court is required to have regard to the approach to the assessment of seriousness set out in the Council Guideline Overarching Principles: Seriousness.

Paragraph 3.3 notes that the question of the adequacy of the magistrates' sentencing powers is to be based on an assumption that the prosecution version of the facts is correct and goes on to say:

The issue for the court is the extent of its sentencing powers for the offence(s) charged following conviction based on the prosecution case at its highest.

3.3.1 Given that the allocation decision is only required where a guilty plea indication is not given, the court should allocate either-way cases according to the seriousness of the alleged offence, looking at the case at its worst from the point of view of the defendant. The reduction for a guilty plea principle should not influence the court in making an allocation decision.

3.3.2 The assessment of seriousness will be based upon representations from the prosecution and defence on the nature and circumstances of the offence. These will include factors that aggravate (legislative, general or offence-specific aggravating factors) or mitigate the seriousness of the offence, but will not extend to matters of personal mitigation.

3.3.3 The court will have regard to definitive guidelines issued by the Sentencing Guidelines Council relating both to principles of sentencing and to specific offences, and to relevant judgments of the Court of Appeal (Criminal Division).

3.3.4 In order to properly assess the seriousness of the offending conduct, courts should make efforts to consider together as many outstanding cases as possible where an allocation decision is yet to be made, unless this would result in significant delay or injustice to the prosecution or defence. Where appropriate, consideration may need to be given to transferring a case to another magistrates' court for this purpose, after consultation with that other court.

3.3.5 In assessing the seriousness of the current offence(s), the court must consider the existence and relevance of any previous convictions, taking into consideration the nature of the offence(s) to which the conviction(s) relate(s), the relevance of them to the current offence, and the time that has elapsed since the conviction(s).

3.3.6 Where a defendant has already been convicted of other matters but not yet sentenced, those convictions will be relevant to the assessment of seriousness of the offence(s) currently before the court.

3.3.7 The existence of a suspended sentence order will be relevant to the allocation decision as it will be a recorded conviction. The question of whether the defendant is liable to have the order implemented will be considered following conviction and so is not relevant to the allocation decision.

3.3.8 Where an offence is a specified offence, the issue of whether the offender should be made subject to a sentence for public protection under sections 224–236 of the Criminal Justice Act 2003 will be considered following conviction.

Paragraph 3.4 covers the possibility that the defendant might ask for offences to be taken into consideration. It says:

3.4.2 The possibility that, after conviction, an offender may ask for other matters to be taken into consideration will not be relevant to the seriousness of the offence before the court when considering allocation. A court could refuse to take additional offences into account when sentencing if they would render the powers of the court inadequate to deal with the case in an appropriate way.

Paragraph 3.5 addresses the argument that Crown Court trial is preferable in some cases because of the separation of the triers of law and fact (a separation that cannot be achieved in a magistrates' court). The Guidelines make it clear that this argument will rarely be relevant:

3.5.1 The procedures in a magistrates' court are generally likely to be adequate for all cases where sentencing is within the powers of that court. Accordingly, it will rarely be appropriate for a magistrates' court to decline summary trial for an offence within its sentencing range for reasons unconnected with the adequacy of sentence.

3.5.2 However, there may be a few rare and exceptional cases (for example where unusually complex disclosure issues regarding public interest immunity or sensitivity are to be decided) where it will be especially important to have the separation between Judge and jury that is possible in the Crown Court.

Paragraph 3.6 emphasises that there is a presumption in favour of summary trial, saying that 'as many cases as possible should be dealt with in the magistrates' court'. The paragraph goes on to say that any uncertainty as to the adequacy of the sentencing powers of the magistrates' court should be resolved in favour of the case being dealt with in the Crown Court. However, this is on the basis of the removal of the power to commit for sentence following conviction after a summary trial. The fact that, in the light of the effect of the Criminal Justice and Immigration Act 2008, this power of committal will remain in existence means that if the magistrates do retain jurisdiction in a case which is in fact too serious for their sentencing powers, the defendant may nonetheless be sent to the Crown Court to be sentenced.

Paragraph 3.7.2 deals with cases where there is more than one defendant:

> Where several defendants are contesting charges that are linked, the presumption is that a single trial will be in the interests of justice for the purpose of considering allocation.

This reverses the current situation, which requires that mode of trial should be considered for each defendant separately. It is submitted that the approach taken in the draft allocation guidelines is preferable, since having separate trials of different defendants in the Crown Court for those who elect trial on indictment and in the magistrates' court for those who do not is expensive so far as resources are concerned, causes inconvenience to witnesses (who have to testify twice) and runs the risk of inconsistent verdicts.

Paragraph 3.7.3 deals with cases where there is more than one defendant and one or more of the defendants is under 18:

> Where one or more of the defendants is a youth, any presumption in favour of sending the youth to the Crown Court to be tried jointly with an adult who is being sent must be balanced with the general presumption that young offenders should be dealt with in a youth court. In determining which is the appropriate court, examples of factors that should be considered when deciding whether to separate the youth and adult defendants include:
>
> * the young age of the offender, particularly where the age gap between the adult and youth offender is substantial;
> * the immaturity and intellect of the youth;
> * the relative culpability of the youth compared with the adult and whether or not the role played by the youth was minor;
> * lack of previous convictions on the part of the youth compared with the adult offender;
> * whether the trial of the adult and youth can be severed without inconvenience to witnesses or injustice to the case as a whole.

Paragraph 3.8 indicates what representations may appropriately be made by the prosecution or defence on the issue of allocation:

> 3.8.1 The assessment of offence seriousness for the purposes of the allocation decision is based on the prosecution case at its highest (see 3.1 above). Defence representations should normally be directed to identifying inaccuracies in the factual outline of the case, assessing the adequacy of the court's sentencing powers and determining the relevance of an offender's previous convictions.

4.5.3 Summary

The key question which the magistrates should ask themselves at a mode of trial hearing is: 'Assuming that what the prosecution say about the offence is correct and assuming the defendant has no previous convictions, are the powers of punishment available to this court [currently six months' imprisonment (or 12 months for two or more offences), to be increased to 12 months for one offence and 65 weeks for two or more] likely to be sufficient punishment?'

4.5.4 'Dangerous' offenders

It should be borne in mind that s 3A of the Powers of Criminal Courts (Sentencing) Act 2003 (inserted by the Criminal Justice Act 2003 but not in force at the time of writing) applies where an offender is convicted of a 'specified' either-way offence (as defined in s 224 of the 2003 Act) and it appears to the court that the criteria for the imposition of a sentence under ss 225(3) or 227(2) of the 2003 Act (dangerous offenders) are satisfied. In such a case, the court must commit the offender (in custody or on bail) to the Crown Court for sentence.

Section 3A(5) clarifies that nothing in s 3A prevents the court from committing the offender for sentence under s 3 if the provisions of that section are satisfied.

4.5.5 Powers of Crown Court following committal for sentence

Under s 5 of the Powers of Criminal Courts (Sentencing) Act 2000 (amended by the Criminal Justice Act 2003 – amendment not in force at the time of writing), where an offender has been committed for sentence under ss 3, 3A or 4, the Crown Court may deal with the offender in any way in which it could deal with him if he had just been convicted of the offence on indictment before the court.

4.6 PRESENCE OF THE DEFENDANT

The defendant must be present at the mode of trial hearing unless either of the following two exceptions applies.

- Under s 18(3) of the Magistrates' Courts Act:

    the court may proceed in the absence of the accused in accordance with such of the provisions of sections 19 to 22 below as are applicable in the circumstances if the court considers that by reason of his disorderly conduct before the court it is not practicable for the proceedings to be conducted in his presence;

- Under s 23(1) of the Magistrates' Courts Act, where:

    (a) the accused is represented by a legal representative who in his absence signifies to the court the accused's consent to the proceedings for determining how he is to be tried for the offence being conducted in his absence; and

(b)   the court is satisfied that there is good reason for proceeding in the absence of the accused.

the court may proceed in the absence of the accused, in which case the legal representative can speak on behalf of the absent defendant. It must be emphasised that this provision applies only where there is a good reason for the absence of the accused, such as illness; it does not apply if the accused simply fails to attend court.

4.7 WHERE SHOULD THE DEFENDANT CHOOSE TO BE TRIED?

If the magistrates do not offer the defendant the chance of summary trial, the defendant has no choice in the matter: the trial can only take place in the Crown Court. If the magistrates do accept jurisdiction, should the defendant agree to summary trial?

4.7.1 The advantages of summary trial

The main advantages of summary trial are as follows:

- The trial procedure is less formal. This means that the trial is less daunting, a fact which may be particularly relevant if the defendant is going to be unrepresented at trial, as will be the case if the defendant is not granted public funded representation and yet cannot afford legal representation.
- Summary trial takes a shorter time than a trial in the Crown Court. A case which would take half a day in the magistrates' court would take probably a whole day in the Crown Court. This means that summary trial is cheaper. This, too, is relevant if the defendant is not publicly funded but has chosen to pay for representation.
- It is sometimes said that an advantage of summary trial is that there is a limit on the sentence which the magistrates' court can pass (at the time of writing, six months' imprisonment for one either-way offence, 12 months for two or more). However, this advantage is largely nullified by the power of the magistrates to commit an offender for sentence (under s 3 of the Powers of Criminal Courts (Sentencing) Act 2000) if, having convicted him, they decide that their sentencing powers are inadequate to deal with him for the offence(s) of which they have convicted him. The Criminal Justice and Immigration Act 2008 cancels the planned removal of the power to commit for sentence an offender who is convicted following a summary trial, and so it will remain the case that agreeing to summary trial does not guarantee that, in the event of conviction, the sentence will ultimately be passed by the magistrates' court.

4.7.2 The advantages of trial on indictment

The advantages of trial on indictment are as follows:

- Jurors tend to be less 'case hardened' than magistrates. Magistrates, who sit regularly, may well have heard the same story before and therefore find it less convincing. Also, magistrates tend to be more trusting of police evidence than do jurors.

- In the magistrates' court, the justices are triers of law and fact whereas in the Crown Court, the judge is the trier of law and the jurors are the triers of fact. Two advantages of Crown Court trial flow from this fact:

  a   Where the admissibility of a piece of evidence is challenged in the Crown Court, the challenge is made in the absence of the jury and, if the judge rules the evidence inadmissible, the jury hear nothing of this evidence. In the magistrates' court, however, the justices themselves have to rule on any question concerning the admissibility of evidence. If they decide that a particular piece of evidence is inadmissible, they must then put it from their minds. It is difficult to be sure that the justices are able to ignore, for example, evidence that the defendant made a confession even where they have ruled that the confession is inadmissible. In *R v Ormskirk Justices ex p Davies* (1994) 158 JP 1145, it was held that one bench cannot delegate to another bench the duty of hearing and determining questions of admissibility; such decisions must be taken by the bench actually trying the case. However, under Sched 3 to the Courts Act 2003, a bench is empowered to able to give a pre-trial ruling on the admissibility of evidence and that ruling will bind the bench that eventually tries the case. This, to a large extent, negates the advantage of Crown Court trial where there is an issue over the admissibility of evidence, at least in cases where the admissibility point becomes apparent well before the start of the trial.

  b   If there is a point of law to be decided, it is easier to deal with that point in the Crown Court, presided over by a professional judge, than in the magistrates' court, where the justices (who have only elementary legal training) depend on their clerk for advice on questions of law (unless the trial takes place before a legally qualified District judge).

  c   Legal errors are also easier to detect in the Crown Court, as the judge has to set out the relevant law in the summing up to the jury.

- Another advantage of trial on indictment is said to be that the prosecution have to disclose copies of the statements made by the witnesses they will be calling at the Crown Court. This is because the witness statements of the people the prosecution propose to call as witnesses have to be served on the defence as an integral part of the process through which the case is transferred to the Crown Court. This advantage is less marked as a result of the advance information rules which have to be complied with before mode of trial is decided. This is especially so in light of para 57 of the Attorney General's Guidelines on disclosure, which provides that in the case of summary trial:

  > The prosecutor should, in addition to complying with the obligations under the Act, provide to the defence all evidence upon which the Crown proposes to rely in a summary trial. Such provision should allow the accused and their legal advisers sufficient time properly to consider the evidence before it is called.

The effect of this is to place a defendant who is being tried in the magistrates' court in the same position as a defendant who is being tried in the Crown Court as regards obtaining copies of the statements of the people to be called as prosecution witnesses.

- Another factor which might be relevant is the length of time the defendant will have to wait for a summary trial or a trial on indictment to take place. This depends very much on local conditions, as waiting lists vary considerably.
- It is a widely held belief that trial on indictment offers a more thorough examination of the issues in a case and a trial procedure that is fairer to the accused than summary trial. It may well be the case that this is more a matter of perception than reality. Nonetheless, in his Review of the Criminal Courts of England and Wales, Lord Justice Auld did recommend (Recommendation 8) that:

> Steps should be taken to provide benches of magistrates that reflect more broadly than at present the communities they serve by:
> . . .
> 8.5 equipping local Advisory Committees with the information to enable them to submit for consideration for appointment, candidates that will produce and maintain benches broadly reflective of the communities they serve, including the establishment and maintenance of national and local data-bases of information on the make-up of the local community and on the composition of the local magistracy;
> 8.6 instituting a review of the ways in which the role and terms of service of a magistrate might be made more attractive and manageable to a wider range of the community than is presently the case; and
> 8.7 persisting with the current search for occupational and/or social groupings as a substitute for political affiliations as a measure of local balance.

He also recommended that in order to strengthen the training of magistrates, the Judicial Studies Board should be made responsible for the content and manner of the training of magistrates. The Courts Act 2003 achieves this objective to a large extent by revising arrangements for training of justices (see s 19).

- Perhaps the most significant advantage of Crown Court trial is that the acquittal rate is higher in the Crown Court than in the magistrates' courts. However, the gap is much smaller than is often realised, as is shown by the statistics that follow:

4.7.3 Mode of trial: some statistics

Figures from the Crown Prosecution Service (CPS) Annual Reports show the following case results for CPS cases:

Magistrates' courts

Percentage of those pleading not guilty who were acquitted:

2006–07: 32%
2005–06: 29%
2004–05: 26.5%
2003–04: 27%

2002–03: 29%
2001–02: 30%
2000–01: 29%
1999–00: 28%
1998–99: 26%

Crown Court

(a) Case results:

Percentage of those pleading not guilty who were acquitted:

2006–07: 40%
2005–06: 38%
2004–05: 37%
2003–04: 38%
2002–03: 38%
2001–02: 42%
2000–01: 44%
1999–00: 43%
1998–99: 43%

(b) Either-way offences go to the Crown Court for trial either because the magistrates decline jurisdiction (holding that the case is too serious for trial in the magistrates' court) or because the defendant elects Crown Court trial.
Percentage of cases which went to Crown Court because of defendant's election:

2006–07: 10%
2005–06: 9%
2004–05: 9%
2003–04: 24%
2002–03: 27%
2001–02: 29%
2000–01: 30%
1999–00: 32%
1998–99: 29%

These figures can be compared with the official Judicial Statistics, which cover all prosecutions, not just those conducted by the CPS (and so they include, for example, prosecutions brought by HM Revenue and Customs). The Judicial Statistics show that during 2006, 59% of the defendants in the Crown Court who pleaded not guilty to all counts were acquitted (67% in both 2003 and 2004 and 66% in 2005).

It is clear from the figures that the proportion of acquittals in the Crown Court is higher than the acquittal rate in the magistrates' court (suggesting that defendants are, as is commonly supposed, more likely to be acquitted in the Crown Court). However, a number of points can be made about this conclusion:

- the gap between the acquittal rates of the two courts is not perhaps as high as some people might expect;
- national figures may well mask significant local variations (tough juries/lenient magistrates);
- it may well be that a number of cases which resulted in acquittal in the Crown Court would also have resulted in acquittal had they been tried in the magistrates' court; and
- considerably more either-way cases are tried in the Crown Court because the magistrates declined jurisdiction than are sent there because the defendant elected trial on indictment.

4.8 FAILURE TO FOLLOW THE CORRECT PROCEDURE IN DETERMINING MODE OF TRIAL

In *Kent Justices, ex p Machin* [1952] 2 QB 355, it was held that, because the jurisdiction of magistrates' courts to try either-way offences derives solely from statute, any failure to comply with the statutory procedure laid down for determining mode of trial renders any summary trial which follows that defective procedure *ultra vires* and therefore a nullity. However, *R v Ashton* [2006] EWCA Crim 794; [2007] 1 WLR 181 casts doubt on the authority of *Machin*. In *Ashton*, it was held that, in the absence of a clear indication that Parliament intended jurisdiction automatically to be removed following a procedural failure, the decision of the court should be based on an assessment of the interests of justice, with particular focus on whether there was a real possibility that the prosecution or the defendant may suffer prejudice. If that risk is present, the court should then decide whether it is just to permit the proceedings to continue. The Court of Appeal reached this conclusion largely through applying the overriding objective in Pt 1 of the Criminal Procedure Rules. This meant, said the court, that a number of authorities, including *Machin*, would have to be reconsidered (see paras 67–69).

4.8.1 Challenging a Decision to Accept Jurisdiction

It is difficult for the prosecution to mount a challenge against a decision in favour of summary trial, since it is essentially a matter within the magistrates' discretion. An application to quash a decision to accept jurisdiction will succeed only if the magistrates' decision was so obviously wrong that no reasonable magistrate could have arrived at it (*R v McLean ex p Metropolitan Police Commissioner* [1975] Crim LR 289). Nevertheless, in an appropriately clear-cut case, the Divisional Court will grant judicial review. In *R v Northampton Magistrates' Court ex p Commissioners of Customs and Excise* [1994] Crim LR 598, for example, the accused was charged with a VAT fraud which, on the prosecution case, had caused a loss of £193,000. The magistrates decided to try him summarily and the prosecution sought judicial review. The Divisional Court said that the correct approach was to ask whether the acceptance of jurisdiction was 'truly astonishing'. Here they must have concluded that it was, as they allowed the application and remitted the matter with a direction to the magistrates to reject jurisdiction.

4.9 CHANGING THE DECISION AS TO MODE OF TRIAL

Once the decision as to mode of trial has been taken, it is nonetheless possible for that decision to be altered. The circumstances when this is possible are set out in s 25 of the Magistrates' Courts Act 1980. This provision will be amended significantly when the relevant provisions of the Criminal Justice Act 2003 come into force. We will consider first the original wording of the section, and then the wording as amended by the 2003 Act.

4.9.1 Section 25: the original version

4.9.1.1 From summary trial to trial on indictment

Section 25(2) of the Magistrates' Courts Act 1980 says that, during a summary trial, the magistrates may terminate the trial at any time before the close of the prosecution case and send the case to the Crown Court for trial instead. In *R v Horseferry Road Magistrates' Court ex p K* [1997] QB 23, the Divisional Court held that the power to change from summary trial applies only once the trial has begun. The fact that the defendant has entered a plea of not guilty does not mean that the trial has begun. That only happens once the court has started to hear evidence or, for example, submissions on a preliminary point of law which has a direct bearing on the process of determining the guilt or innocence of the accused.

4.9.1.2 The magistrates have a change of mind

The magistrates may have a change of mind regarding mode of trial if, during a summary trial, they decide as they hear the prosecution evidence that the case is in fact more serious than the court had realised when they agreed to summary trial. However, in such a case, it should be noted that they could simply continue with the summary trial and, if they convict the defendant, commit him to the Crown Court to be sentenced.

If the defendant consents to summary trial and pleads guilty, it is then too late to send him to the Crown Court for trial (*R v Dudley Justices ex p Gillard* [1986] AC 442). In the case of a plea of guilty, the only course of action available to the magistrates, if (on hearing the facts of the case set out more fully by the prosecution) they decide that the case is too serious for them to deal with, is to commit the defendant to the Crown Court for sentence under s 3 of the Powers of Criminal Courts (Sentencing) Act 2000. If the defendant seeks to change his plea from guilty to not guilty, the magistrates should (if they allow him to do so) also reconsider mode of trial and send him for trial if they take the view that their sentencing powers are inadequate.

4.9.1.3 The defendant has a change of mind

The magistrates have a discretion to allow the defendant to withdraw his consent to summary trial. The test to be applied in deciding whether to exercise this discretion in the defendant's favour was set out in *R v Birmingham Justices ex p Hodgson* [1985] QB 1131, where the defendant did not realise that he had a defence to the charge, and

R v Highbury Corner Magistrates ex p Weekes [1985] QB 1147, where a 17-year-old defendant did not understand what a Crown Court was. The test to be applied in deciding whether to allow a defendant to withdraw his consent to summary trial is: did the defendant understand the 'nature and significance' of the choice which he had to make at the mode of trial hearing? In deciding this question, the magistrates should have regard to factors such as:

- whether the defendant knew that he had a possible defence to the charge;
- whether the defendant had access to legal advice before making his decision as to mode of trial;
- the defendant's age and apparent intelligence;
- possibly, whether the defendant has previous convictions (and so is likely to know something about criminal procedure).

It should be noted that the burden of proof lies on the defendant to show that he did not understand the nature and significance of the choice (*R v Forest Magistrates ex p Spicer* (1989) 153 JP 81).

4.9.1.4 The defendant successfully applies to change his plea

In *R v Bow Street Magistrates ex p Welcombe* (1992) 156 JP 609, it was held that if the defendant is allowed to change his plea from guilty to not guilty, he must also be given the opportunity to elect trial on indictment if he so wishes.

4.9.1.5 From trial on indictment to summary trial

Section 25(3) of the Magistrates' Courts Act 1980 provides that, at any time during committal proceedings, the justices may offer the defendant the chance of summary trial. This is the case whether it is the defendant or the justices who have a change of mind. It must be emphasised, however, that summary trial can only take place if both the defendant and the magistrates agree to it. It follows that if the magistrates decide that the case is not as serious as they thought when they declined jurisdiction, a summary trial still cannot take place without the defendant's consent. The defendant should be warned (or reminded if he was informed earlier) that he may be committed for sentence to the Crown Court if he is convicted by the magistrates.

4.9.2 Section 25 as amended by the Criminal Justice Act 2003

When s 25 of the 1980 Act is amended by the Criminal Justice Act 2003 (see para 11 of Sched 3 to the 2003 Act), the existing power to switch from summary trial to committal proceedings, or vice versa, will be abolished (partly to reflect the demise of committal proceedings for either-way offences). The amended version of s 25(2) provides that where the court is trying a case summarily (because the magistrates have ruled that the case is suitable for summary trial, and the accused has consented to summary trial), the prosecution may apply to the magistrates' court for the offence to be tried in the Crown Court instead.

This application must be made before the summary trial begins and must be dealt with by the court before any other application or issue in relation to the summary trial is dealt with (s 25(2A)). Under s 25(2B), the court may accede to the application only 'if it is satisfied that the sentence which a magistrates' court would have power to impose for the offence would be inadequate'.

Where the accused is charged with two or more offences that constitute, or form part of, a series of offences of the same or a similar character, the court has to consider adequacy of sentence in light of the maximum aggregate sentence which a magistrates' court would have power to impose for all of the offences taken together (s 25(2C)).

Where the magistrates accede to the prosecution application, the case is sent to the Crown Court for trial (s 25(2D)).

4.10 CRIMINAL DAMAGE: THE SPECIAL PROVISIONS

Section 22 of the Magistrates' Courts Act 1980 sets out a special procedure to be applied in cases of criminal damage (excluding arson) where the value involved is less than £5,000. Under s 22(2), if the amount involved does not exceed the 'relevant sum' (£5,000), the court must 'proceed as if the offence were triable only summarily' (and so there is no mode of trial hearing). So, where the value involved is £5,000 or less, the case must be tried summarily. Under s 33 of the Magistrates' Courts Act 1980, the maximum sentence in such a case is three months' imprisonment or a fine of up to £2,500 (that is, half the usual penalty); furthermore, there can be no committal for sentence to the Crown Court under s 3 of the Powers of Criminal Courts (Sentencing) Act 2000. However, when para 27 of Sched 32 to the Criminal Justice Act 2003 comes into force, the maximum sentence of imprisonment under s 33 will be increased to 51 weeks.

If 'it appears to the court clear that, for the offence charged, the value involved exceeds the relevant sum', the court will proceed to determine mode of trial in the usual way (sub-s (3)). Thus, where the value is more than £5,000, the usual mode of trial procedure applies. If the defendant consents to summary trial and is convicted, the usual penalties apply and a s 3 committal is possible.

Under s 22(4)–(6), if there is doubt as to whether the value involved is more or less than £5,000, the magistrates must offer the defendant the chance of summary trial. If he consents to summary trial, the trial will take place in the magistrates' court and, if he is convicted, the court will not be able to impose more than three months' imprisonment (under the Criminal Justice Act 2003, 51 weeks) or a fine greater than level 4 on the standard scale (currently £2,500) and there is no power to commit for sentence under s 3 of the Powers of Criminal Courts (Sentencing) Act 2000.

It follows that the first step in a case involving criminal damage is to ascertain the 'value involved'. This is defined (in Sched 2) as the cost of repair or, if the article is damaged beyond repair, replacement. The value may be ascertained on the basis of representations by the prosecution and defence. There is no obligation on the magistrates to hear evidence as to the value, though they have a discretion to do so (*R v Canterbury Justices ex p Klisiak* [1982] QB 398). Section 22(11) provides that where the accused is charged with two or more offences to which the section applies and which 'constitute or form part of a series of two or more offences of the same or a similar character', the court should take the value involved as being the aggregate of the values involved in each offence for the purpose of determining whether the special procedure applies.

Under s 22(8), where the defendant is convicted by a magistrates' court of an offence to which s 22 applies, he cannot appeal to the Crown Court against the conviction on the ground that the magistrates' decision as to the value involved was mistaken.

It must be emphasised that these special provisions apply only to criminal damage (and to offences under s 12A of the Theft Act 1968 – aggravated vehicle taking – but only where the only aggravating feature alleged is criminal damage). In the case of theft, for example, the defendant has an unfettered right to Crown Court trial no matter how small the value of the property stolen.

There are cases where ascertaining the value involved is far from straightforward. In *R (Abbott) v Colchester Justices* [2001] EWHC 136 (Admin); (2001) 165 JP 386, the defendant was charged with criminal damage to crops on a farm. The value of the damage itself was £750. However, there was also consequential loss of £5,000. The Divisional Court held that s 22 and Sched 2 are directed solely at identifying the value of the damage caused to the property itself and so are not concerned with determining the value of any consequential damage which may have resulted. The value involved in the present case therefore did not exceed the relevant sum and so the case had to be tried summarily. In *R (DPP) v Prestatyn Magistrates' Court* [2002] EWHC 1177; (2002) *The Times*, 17 October, the defendants were charged with causing criminal damage to genetically-modified crops. The District Judge was uncertain as to the value of the crops and so treated the offence as triable either way (under s 22(4)). It was held that, where there is no open market value, the magistrates have to find a market value of something in order to determine the value of the property damaged. In the instant case, the crop was being grown for research and not for sale. That gave it a real value but it was a different and probably greater value than maize grown for food. The District Judge was entitled to reach the conclusion that the crop was neither worthless nor limited in value to the price of ordinary maize but that he could not say whether the value was greater or less than £5,000, so that the case fell within s 22(4).

When s 17A ('plea before venue') was inserted into the Magistrates' Courts Act 1980 by the Criminal Procedure and Investigations Act 1996, there was no consequential amendment of s 22. As a result, it is unclear whether a court sentencing an accused who has indicated a plea of guilty to a charge of criminal damage where the value is below £5,000 is limited in its powers to a custodial sentence of three months and/or a fine of £2,500. It would clearly be more logical if the limit did apply. If it were not so, an accused pleading guilty would be at risk of heavier penalties than one found guilty after trial. Moreover, s 22(1) requires the court to determine the value involved in the offence before proceeding under s 19; the 'plea before venue' procedure set out in s 17A is effectively part of the mode of trial procedure under s 19.

4.11 THE ADVANCE INFORMATION RULES

Part 21.3 of the Criminal Procedure Rules provides that, in the case of offences which are triable either way, the prosecution must, if the defence so request, supply the defence with either.

(a) a copy of those parts of every written statement which contain information as to the facts and matters of which the prosecutor proposes to adduce evidence in the proceedings; or

(b) a summary of the facts and matters of which the prosecutor proposes to adduce evidence in the proceedings.

The purpose of this is to make it unnecessary for the defendant to elect Crown Court trial simply so that the prosecution case has to be revealed as part of the process of transferring the case to the Crown Court. The choice of whether to supply a summary or the witness statements lies with the prosecution.

The prosecution may only refuse to comply with a request for advance information, under r 21.4, if they think that compliance:

> might lead to any person on whose evidence he proposes to rely in the proceedings being intimidated, to an attempt to intimidate him being made or otherwise to the course of justice being interfered with.

At the mode of trial hearing, the court must ensure that the defendant is aware of the right to advance information and that, if advance information has been requested, the prosecution have complied with that request (r 21.5).

If the prosecution fail to comply with the request for advance disclosure, the magistrates' court has no power to order the prosecution to comply (*R v Dunmow Justices ex p Nash* (1993) 157 JP 1153). All the court can do is adjourn the mode of trial hearing, if necessary more than once, or, if satisfied that the defence have not been prejudiced by the prosecution's failure to comply with the Rules, proceed to determine mode of trial anyway (r 21.6(1)).

Moreover, the court cannot dismiss the charges brought by the prosecution because of non-compliance with the rules relating to advance information (*King v Kucharz* (1989) 153 JP 336). In *R (on the Application of AP, MD and JS) v Leeds Youth Court* [2001] EWHC 215 (Admin); (2001) 165 JP 684, the case against the defendants was adjourned for the prosecution to serve papers on the defence by a specified date; the youth court stated that failure to serve the papers would lead to dismissal of the case. On the adjourned hearing, the second bench refused to dismiss the charge even though the order for service of the papers had not been complied with. The Divisional Court held (following *King v Kucharz*) that, even taking account of Art 6 of the European Convention on Human Rights, the court does not have jurisdiction to dismiss proceedings for abuse of process simply on the basis of non-compliance with what is now Pt 21 of the Criminal Procedure Rules.

In *R v Stratford Justices ex p Imbert* [1999] 2 Cr App R 276, the Divisional Court held that Art 6 of the European Convention on Human Rights (which guarantees the right to a fair trial) does not require that prosecution witness statements should be disclosed to the defence before summary trial in the magistrates' court. The court held that disclosure of the witness statements is not necessary to achieve the 'equality of arms' required by the European Court of Human Rights in cases such as *Foucher v France* (1997) 25 EHRR 234.

In the case of summary offences, Pt 21 does not apply. However, para 57 of the Attorney General's Guidelines on Disclosure (<http://www.cps.gov.uk/legal/section20/chapter_c.html>) provides that in the case of summary trial:

> The prosecutor should, in addition to complying with the obligations under the [Criminal Procedure and Investigations Act 1996], provide to the defence all evidence upon which the Crown proposes to rely in a summary trial. Such provision should allow the accused and their legal advisers sufficient time properly to consider the evidence before it is called.

The effect of this is to put an accused who is being tried in the magistrates' court in the same position as an accused who is being tried in the Crown Court as regards obtaining copies of the statements of the people to be called as prosecution witnesses.

Paragraph 1.4 of Protocol for the Provision of Advance Information, Prosecution Evidence and Disclosure of Unused Material in the Magistrates' Courts (May 2006, <http://www.judiciary.gov.uk/docs/judgments_guidance/protocols/mags_courts_%20 disclosure.pdf>) says that:

> The prosecutor must ... be in a position to comply with any request for advance information either before or at the first hearing. The defence advocates should, save in exceptional circumstances, expect to be ready to go through that material with the defendant and advise on venue, plea and any ancillary matters there and then without the need for an adjournment. If necessary, cases can be put back in the list to allow the defence sufficient time to consider any material provided.

In a similar vein, para 1.7 says that:

> ... when faced with applications for adjournments to inspect documents referred to in advance information, courts should consider whether the information already provided is sufficient for the defendant to make an informed decision on venue and if so, whether any substantial prejudice will arise in refusing that application.

The desire to avoid delay is of course laudable, but it is important that the pursuit of that goal should not be allowed to inhibit the careful preparation of the defence case. To this end it is important that the defence are given sufficient time to prepare (indeed this is a right conferred expressly by Art 6(3)(b) of the European Convention on Human Rights).

4.12 SECTION 40 OF THE CRIMINAL JUSTICE ACT 1988

Section 40 of the Criminal Justice Act 1988 applies if the defendant is sent for trial in respect of an indictable (that is, indictable-only or triable either way) offence and the witness statements also disclose any one or more of the following summary offences:

- common assault;
- taking a conveyance without the owner's consent (s 12 of the Theft Act 1968);
- driving a motor vehicle while disqualified;
- criminal damage where the value involved is £5,000 or less;
- assaulting a prison custody officer or a secure training centre custody officer.

The summary offence(s) may then be included on the indictment if (under s 40(1)) it:

a   is founded on the same facts or evidence as a count charging an indictable offence; or

b   is part of a series of offences of the same or similar character as an indictable offence which is also charged.

This is the same test as that which applies to the joinder of counts on an indictment under r 14.2(3) of the Criminal Procedure Rules (see Chapter 10).

The effect of this provision is (for example) that the getaway driver at a robbery who has taken the car without the owner's consent can be indicted for robbery and for taking the vehicle (even though the latter is a summary offence) and the burglar who commits criminal damage in order to effect entry to the premises can be indicted for burglary and criminal damage (even if the value of the criminal damage is less than £5,000).

It is the prosecution who decide whether or not the linked summary offence(s) should appear on the indictment so that the Crown Court can try the summary offence(s) as well as the indictable offence.

Where s 40 applies, the summary offence(s) appear on the indictment and are tried as if indictable. Note, however, that if the defendant is convicted of a s 40 summary offence, the Crown Court cannot impose more than the maximum sentence which the magistrates' court could have imposed for that offence (at the time of writing, six months' imprisonment and/or a £5,000 fine, to be increased to 12 months' imprisonment under the Criminal Justice Act 2003). In *R v James* [2007] EWCA Crim 1906; [2008] 1 Cr App R (S) 44, the defendant pleaded guilty at the Crown Court to two counts of common assault, which had been put on the indictment by virtue of s 40, and not guilty to one count of actual bodily harm, but guilty to common assault in relation to that count. The Crown had accepted the plea. The judge imposed consecutive sentences of 4 months, 2 months and 3 months in respect of the offences (making a total of 9 months). The Court of Appeal ruled that the Crown Court could not impose a longer sentence than a magistrates' court could have imposed, and so the maximum aggregate sentence available in this case (given that the defendant was being sentenced only for summary offences) was 6 months.

Under s 40(4), the Secretary of State is empowered to specify additional summary offences to come within the ambit of s 40 (provided that any such offence is punishable with imprisonment or involves obligatory or discretionary disqualification from driving).

4.13 SECTION 41 OF THE CRIMINAL JUSTICE ACT 1988

Section 41 of the Criminal Justice Act 1988 provides as follows:

(1) Where a magistrates' court commits a person to the Crown Court for trial on indictment for an offence triable either way or a number of such offences, it may also commit him for trial for any summary offence with which he is charged and which—

(a) is punishable with imprisonment or involves obligatory or discretionary disqualification from driving; and

(b) arises out of circumstances which appear to the court to be the same as or connected with those giving rise to the offence, or one of the offences, triable either way,

whether or not evidence relating to that summary offence appears on the depositions or written statements in the case; and the trial of the information charging the summary offence shall then be treated as if the magistrates' court had adjourned it under section 10 of the Magistrates' Courts Act 1980 and had not fixed the time and place for its resumption.

(2) Where a magistrates' court commits a person to the Crown Court for trial on indictment for a number of offences triable either way and exercises the power conferred by sub-section (1) above in respect of a summary offence, the magistrates' court shall give the Crown Court and the person who is committed for trial a notice stating which of the offences triable either way appears to the court to arise out of circumstances which are the same as or connected with those giving rise to the summary offence.

(3) A magistrates' court's decision to exercise the power conferred by sub-section (1) above shall not be subject to appeal or liable to be questioned in any court.

(4) The committal of a person under this section in respect of an offence to which section 40 above applies shall not preclude the exercise in relation to the offence of the power conferred by that section; but where he is tried on indictment for such an offence, the functions of the Crown Court under this section in relation to the offence shall cease.

(4A) The committal of a person under this section in respect of an offence to which section 40 above applies shall not prevent him being found guilty of that offence under section 6(3) of the Criminal Law Act 1967 (alternative verdicts on trial on indictment); but where he is convicted under that provision of such an offence, the functions of the Crown Court under this section in relation to the offence shall cease.

(5) If he is convicted on the indictment, the Crown Court shall consider whether the conditions specified in sub-section (1) above were satisfied.

(6) If it considers that they were satisfied, it shall state to him the substance of the summary offence and ask him whether he pleads guilty or not guilty.

(7) If he pleads guilty, the Crown Court shall convict him, but may deal with him in respect of that offence only in a manner in which a magistrates' court could have dealt with him.

(8) If he does not plead guilty, the Crown Court may try him for the offence, but may deal with him only in a manner in which a magistrates' court could have dealt with him.

. . .

(11) Where the Court of Appeal allows an appeal against conviction of an offence triable either way which arose out of circumstances which were the same as or connected with those giving rise to a summary offence of which the appellant was convicted under this section—

(a) it shall set aside his conviction of the summary offence and give the designated officer for the magistrates' court notice that it has done so; and

(b) it may direct that no further proceedings in relation to the offence are to be undertaken;

and the proceedings before the Crown Court in relation to the offence shall thereafter be disregarded for all purposes.

...

In summary, s 41 of the Criminal Justice Act 1988 provides that if the magistrates send the defendant to the Crown Court for trial in respect of one or more offences which are triable either way, they may also send the defendant there for a plea to be taken in respect of any summary offence, provided that it:

- is punishable with imprisonment or with disqualification from driving; and
- arises out of circumstances which are the same as or connected with the either-way offence(s).

If, and only if, the defendant is convicted of the either-way offence (either pleading guilty or being found guilty by the jury), the summary offence(s) will be put to the defendant for plea. The summary offence(s) will thus not appear on the indictment and will not be tried by the jury.

It is the magistrates, rather than the prosecution, who decide whether or not to commit a summary offence to the Crown Court for the plea to be taken. Thereafter:

- if, having been convicted of the either way offence(s), the defendant pleads guilty to the summary offence(s), the Crown Court can pass any sentence which the magistrates could have imposed in respect of the summary offence(s) to which the defendant has pleaded guilty;
- if the defendant is acquitted of the either-way offence(s), he is not asked to enter a plea in respect of the summary offence(s);
- if, having been convicted of the either-way offence(s), the defendant pleads not guilty to the summary offence(s), the Crown Court (a judge sitting without a jury) may try him for the summary offence(s) or else may remit him to be tried in the magistrates' court for those offences.

In *R v Miall* [1992] QB 836, the defendant was sent for trial for perverting the course of justice. The magistrates tried also to send him, under s 41, for the plea to be taken in respect of a summary offence, driving with excess alcohol. It was held that s 41 could not be invoked, as the offence on the indictment (perverting the course of justice) was triable only on indictment, not triable either way.

In *R v Foote* (1992) 94 Cr App R 82, the defendant was sent for trial to the Crown Court in respect of a charge of reckless (now called dangerous) driving. The magistrates also sent him there under s 41 of the Criminal Justice Act 1988 for a plea to be taken in respect of a charge of careless driving arising out of the same incident. The defendant pleaded not guilty to the reckless driving and the prosecution decided to accept that plea; the court then tried to invoke s 41 to take a plea in respect of the charge of careless driving. This was held to be wrong, because s 41 could not apply where the defendant had not been convicted of the either-way offence.

In *R v Bird* [1995] Crim LR 745, the defendant was sent for trial in the Crown Court on charges of possession of an offensive weapon (an either-way offence) and driving while disqualified (a summary offence to which s 40 applies). By virtue of s 41, he was committed for plea in respect of a charge of driving without insurance. He was acquitted of the charge of possession of an offensive weapon but was convicted of driving while disqualified. The Court of Appeal held that, since the defendant had been convicted on indictment of driving while disqualified, that offence was to be treated as an indictable offence. It followed that the Crown Court was entitled to deal with the summary offence of no insurance under s 41.

Sub-section (8) is the corollary of the enactment of s 66 of the Courts Act 2003, which empowers Crown Court judges to exercise the powers of magistrates. This means that if the defendant is convicted of the either-way offence and then pleads not guilty to the linked summary offence, the Crown Court judge (sitting without a jury) is able to try the summary offence (following the procedure which would have been adopted had that offence been tried in the magistrates' court). If the judge decides not to try the summary offence, the case can be remitted to the magistrates for them to try it.

It should be noted that s 41 will be repealed when the repeals contained in Sched 3 (Pt 2) to the Criminal Justice Act 2003 come into effect. This is because s 51(3) of the Crime and Disorder Act 1998, as amended by Sched 3 to the Criminal Justice Act 2003, provides that where a defendant is sent to the Crown Court for trial in respect of an indictable-only or either-way offence, the justices may also send him for trial in respect of any related offence (provided that if the related offence is a summary one, it is punishable with imprisonment or disqualification from driving). Section 41 is thus rendered otiose.

4.14 ADJUSTING THE CHARGES TO DICTATE MODE OF TRIAL

It is possible for the prosecution to drop an existing charge and replace it with a new charge. Sometimes the effect of replacing one charge with another will be to replace an offence which is triable either way with one which is triable only summarily, thus depriving the accused of the possibility of Crown Court trial. In *R v Canterbury Justices ex p Klisiak* [1982] QB 398, it was held that the prosecution could only be prevented from doing this in 'the most obvious circumstances which disclose blatant injustice' (per Lord Lane CJ at p 411).

In *R v Sheffield Justices ex p DPP* [1993] Crim LR 136, the magistrates stayed proceedings against a defendant where the prosecution declined to proceed with a charge of assault occasioning actual bodily harm (triable either way) and substituted a charge of common assault (a summary offence). The Divisional Court granted a prosecution application for judicial review, holding that it is a matter for the prosecution to decide which charge to proceed with. The court would only intervene where there was evidence of bad faith (that is, deliberate manipulation of the system). In the present case, the charge of common assault was appropriate on the facts.

It is also possible for a charge which is triable either way to be replaced by an offence which is triable only on indictment. However, in *R v Brooks* [1985] Crim LR 385, the Court of Appeal warned that it would generally be unjust and wrong for the prosecution to do this if the magistrates have already accepted jurisdiction in respect of the either-way offence, since the prosecution would be frustrating that decision by changing the charge. Neill LJ summarised the position as follows (at p 337):

It is desirable that as far as possible the defendant should know from the outset the charge or charges that he has to meet. But in many cases it may be necessary to add additional charges or to substitute fresh charges for those previously preferred. New matters may come to light or the original case may appear on further consideration to be more or less serious than was first thought . . .

If the prosecution [after mode of trial has been determined] seek to prefer new charges or to substitute charges or to offer no evidence on certain charges the justices should consider the matter on its merits. The fact that the prosecution wish to add or substitute new charges either to ensure that the case is tried summarily or to ensure that it is tried in the Crown Court is not a ground for refusing the issue of a summons or other process provided that on the facts disclosed the justices are satisfied that the course proposed by the prosecution is proper and appropriate in the light of the facts put before them. Thus clearly the justices should not agree to the addition of a charge which is triable only on indictment if the facts are incapable of supporting such a charge and the fresh charge can be seen to be a device designed to deprive the justices of their jurisdiction to try the case themselves.

If the justices have already decided to try a matter summarily and the case is then adjourned, any later application by the prosecution to add an additional charge which would have the effect of making summary trial no longer possible should be scrutinised with particular care . . .

If the justices acting within their jurisdiction exercise their discretion bona fide and bring their minds to bear on the question whether they ought to grant a further summons or not, this Court is very unlikely to interfere except in an exceptional case where the decision satisfies the strict test of being unreasonable in a Wednesbury sense. The High Court is not a Court of Appeal from the justices in this regard.

Paragraph 7.1 of the Code for Crown Prosecutors says that charges should be chosen which reflect the seriousness of the offending, give the court adequate sentencing powers, and enable the case to be presented in a clear and simple way. Paragraph 7.2 goes on to say that Crown Prosecutors should never continue with more charges than necessary just to encourage a defendant to plead guilty to a few. In the same way, they should never go ahead with a more serious charge just to encourage a defendant to plead guilty to a less serious one. Finally, para 7.3 states that the charge should not be changed simply because of the decision made by the court or the defendant about where the case will be heard.

4.15 PROPOSALS TO REFORM THE MODE OF TRIAL PROCESS

In this section, we look at various proposals for reform of the mode of trial procedure and then examine in details the reforms brought about by the Criminal Justice Act 2003.

4.15.1 Proposals for reform

In Chapter 6 of his *Review of delay in the criminal justice system* ('Managing the distribution of cases between the courts'), published in 1997, Martin Narey recommended that defendants should no longer be able to veto the decision of magistrates to retain jurisdiction of cases. The Narey Review noted that:

> It is frequently claimed that the right of a defendant to elect trial by jury is an ancient one, enshrined in Magna Carta. In fact, there was no right to claim trial by jury until 1855. Up to that time, there were only two categories of offence: those triable only on indictment and those triable only summarily. Felonies (as opposed to misdemeanours) were always tried on indictment. But there was no element of defendant election.
>
> From the middle of the nineteenth century the simple distinction between cases triable on indictment and those triable summarily began to be eroded . . .
>
> The underlying principle that the defendant should consent to summary trial was preserved in these changes. But in the 1870s statutes began to introduce hybrid offences which could be tried either summarily or on indictment. The crucial point here was that some hybrid offences could be retained by magistrates without the defendant's consent.

The Review then considered the recommendations made in 1975 by the James Committee:

> By the time the James Committee reported ('The Distribution of Criminal Business between the Crown Court and Magistrates' Courts: Report of the Interdepartmental Committee 1975') the distinction between cases triable only on indictment, summary only cases and those indictable cases triable summarily with the defendant's consent was confused by three other types of case: hybrid cases carrying a right to elect trial by jury, hybrid cases without that right and summary cases which under certain circumstances could be tried on indictment. The James Committee concluded that this proliferation of categories had evolved as a result of largely unrelated developments in the summary jurisdiction of magistrates' courts which had not been considered as a whole. The Committee's recommendations led to the present threefold classification of offences as summary, either-way and indictable-only.
>
> The James Committee was clearly alive to the resource implications of jury trial. And they were conscious of the circumstances which made it important for some defendants more than others to be able to protect their reputation:
>
> > 'A professional person of good character, if convicted of a minor offence of dishonesty for example, will suffer in reputation and may lose his livelihood, whereas for a person with a long record of similar offences the only penalty will probably be the sentence actually imposed.'
>
> The committee also noted that few jurisdictions had found it necessary, or even regarded it as desirable, to build into their systems of criminal justice an element of personal choice by the defendant of the court in which he should be tried. But they concluded that, however anomalous the English system, account had to be taken of:
>
> > 'the regard in which the present right of election is held . . . There is a substantial body of opinion in favour of removing the defendant's right of election [but] this is almost entirely confined to those directly responsible for the administration of justice, whether as judges, court staff or prosecutors. Virtually all the organisations

> representing practitioners and almost every individual solicitor and barrister who wrote to us, together with most of the organisations representing a wider interest, took the contrary view.'

The Narey Review noted that those who argue in favour of preserving the defendant's right to elect trial rely on the seriousness of either-way offences: 'It is pointed out that, for example, the right to elect trial for theft is vital because of the effect of a conviction for dishonesty on a person's character.' However, Narey countered this by pointing out that 'there are a number of offences involving dishonesty including false representation for obtaining a benefit and fraudulent use of a telecommunications system, as well as offences such as soliciting, keeping a brothel, impersonation of a police officer, common assault and assault on a constable which have equally serious implications for a person's reputation and which are triable summarily only'.

The Review then examined the reasons defendants have for electing trial on indictment:

> There appear to be three objectives for defendants who elect trial. The first is to delay proceedings and therefore to put off conviction and sentence. (Some defence lawyers will admit that they will advise clients to do this in the hope of persuading the CPS to accept a plea to a less serious charge, or simply to make it more likely that prosecution witnesses will not attend the trial or will be vague in their recollections.) The second is to retain location in a local prison, close to family and friends (including friends in the prison) and with the additional visits available to unconvicted prisoners.
>
> The third objective is acquittal, the chances of which are higher at the Crown Court than at magistrates' courts (this does not imply that the Crown Court is fairer). Whatever the chances of acquittal at the Crown Court, a very large majority of defendants electing trial subsequently plead guilty. It is difficult to be precise, but it appears that about two thirds of defendants electing trial subsequently plead guilty and about three quarters of all defendants electing are subsequently convicted.

The Review noted the suggestion of reclassifying some either-way offences as summary-only and pointed out that it is 'frequently' suggested (for example, by the James Committee in 1975) that theft of a small monetary value should also be reclassified. However, Narey said that:

> I believe that reducing the number of cases going to the Crown Court through reclassifying minor theft would be an unsatisfactory solution, although I acknowledge that it might divert a significant number of cases from the Crown Court, perhaps in the region of two thousand (including cases committed by magistrates). Reclassification would mean that there would be no circumstances in which a theft of small monetary value could go to the Crown Court even where, because of the nature of the offence, magistrates considered that Crown Court trial was appropriate. (A minor theft from an elderly or other vulnerable person or a minor theft by a person in a position of trust are two examples.)
>
> There would also be circumstances, because of matters of reputation, or because a conviction for theft might lead to defendants losing their job, where it might be considered proper for a case to be heard in front of a jury. For those reasons, I recommend that the possibility of a defendant being tried at the Crown Court for any current either-way offence

should not be removed. But the final decision on venue should be one for the magistrates to make rather than the defendant.

Narey went on to discuss in more detail his recommendation that magistrates should decide venue in all either-way cases:

> Defendants should no longer be able to veto the decision of magistrates to retain jurisdiction of cases: instead, the decision should rest with magistrates, with the prosecutor making recommendations as to venue and the defence having the opportunity to make representations as well. Where the defence were able to produce convincing reasons for Crown Court trial, magistrates would be free to accept them and commit the case for trial.
>
> The 1993 Royal Commission made a similar recommendation and considered that in making their decision magistrates should consider a number of factors including the defendant's reputation and past record, the gravity of the offence, the complexity of the case and its likely effect on the defendant. (An alternative option would be to remove the right of election from defendants where they were being prosecuted for an offence similar in nature to an earlier conviction, since in those circumstances matters of reputation are not paramount. But this option, whilst initially attractive, would expose the Government to criticisms that it was offering a lower standard of justice to those with criminal convictions who, it might be argued, are most vulnerable to wrongful arrest and charge.)
>
> The Runciman Commission further suggested that in circumstances where prosecutor and defence agreed on venue, magistrates should not be involved in the decision. Presentationally this might be difficult. It is important that magistrates should take, and be seen to take, this decision. (It is true that in Scotland there is no role for the court in deciding venue – the decision being one for the prosecution alone, and with no right of appeal – and this appears to cause no controversy whatsoever; but any attempt to confer similar rights on the prosecution in England and Wales would be greeted with alarm.)

Narey went on to note that the Government's final response to the Royal Commission, published in June 1996, was that the removal of the right to elect trial on indictment 'should not be undertaken unless it is clear that it would be the only possible way of achieving the objective' and that the question should be reconsidered in the light of the effect of the 'plea before venue' procedure implemented by the Criminal Procedure and Investigations Act 1996. Narey commented that:

> This rather suggests that plea before venue provides an alternative to removing the defendant's veto on the mode of trial decision. In fact the two initiatives would be complementary: plea before venue is likely to reduce unnecessary committals by magistrates, whereas removing the right of election would remove unnecessary committals prompted by defendants. However successful the plea before venue initiative, it will not reduce defendant elections.

Narey was very conscious of the controversial nature of the proposal to remove the right to choose Crown Court trial. He tried to counter the arguments he expected to be raised against the proposal.

The first argument he anticipated is that the proposal amounts to erosion of a fundamental privilege. He answered this argument by saying:

The belief that the removal of the defendant's veto on the magistrates' decision on mode of trial would erode fundamental individual liberties established in the Middle Ages is widely shared but is not undisputed. At least one eminent historian regards the later interpretation of Magna Carta's 'lawful judgement of peers' to mean trial by jury as going far beyond the detailed intention and sense of the original charter; and the jury was not an independent tribunal but a group of local people selected because of their familiarity with the district and the accused, and certainly much less likely to be independent than a modern bench of magistrates.

The decision in the middle and late nineteenth century to allow cases to be tried summarily only with the consent of the accused has to be set in the context of a criminal justice process which extended very few of the protections currently afforded to defendants.

Narey concluded that:

If accepted, these recommendations would not rule out Crown Court trial for any defendant charged with an either-way offence, but it would stop an improper manipulation of the justice system. Magistrates would be well able to distinguish those defendants who, because of potential loss of reputation, or for other reasons, were justified in seeking a Crown Court hearing. Those cases would be a minority. The majority of cases in which the defendant elects trial result, eventually, in guilty pleas, but only after significantly increased inconvenience to victims and witnesses and at considerable extra cost.

In 1998, the Government published a *Consultation Paper, Determining Mode of Trial in Either Way Cases*, with the following purpose:

... to consider whether a defendant in an either-way case which the magistrates are willing to hear should continue to be able to decide where he should be tried; to consider whether some possible options for reform would be more consistent with the interests of justice and efficiency; and to invite comments on the alternatives. The paper is concerned not with the merits of jury trial, but only with the defendant's ability to choose it.

Given the fact that many defendants choose Crown Court trial because they perceive it as fairer and more thorough than summary trial, the exclusion of consideration of the merits of jury trial (as against trial in the magistrates' court) may perhaps be considered a little disingenuous.

The Consultation Paper started by putting the question of the defendant's right to elect Crown Court trial in its historical context, much as Narey had done. In para 6, the Paper noted that the proportion of cases where the magistrates decline jurisdiction exceeds, by a significant margin, those cases where the defendant elects Crown Court trial. The Paper suggested that a 'possible explanation is that some defendants have concluded that (as Home Office research has demonstrated) those who plead guilty having elected Crown Court trial are likely to receive a substantially heavier sentence than if they had pleaded guilty in the magistrates' court'.

The Paper went on to note (para 8) that:

... defendants in the Crown Court are more likely to plead not guilty than those who are tried in magistrates' courts: around one-third of defendants who go to the Crown Court plead not guilty to some or all charges, compared with fewer than one in ten in magistrates' courts. The percentage of defendants pleading not guilty in the Crown Court appears to be much the same whether they have elected to be tried there or have been directed there by the magistrates. At first sight this seems surprising since it might have been expected that defendants who elect would have a greater propensity to plead not guilty; but on the other hand, directed cases are likely to be relatively serious and possibly more likely to be contested for that reason.

In para 9, the Paper noted the disparity in acquittal rates between the Crown Court and the magistrates' court and said that:

> It is unclear . . . whether this is because juries are more inclined to acquit – rightly or wrongly – than magistrates, or because defendants with a good defence are more likely to be tried in the Crown Court, either as a result of having elected or (conceivably) by direction of the magistrates.

The Paper went on to summarise the arguments for and against (a) maintaining the status quo, (b) reclassifying some offences as summary offences, or (c) abolishing the right of the defendant to elect Crown Court trial. Dealing first with maintaining the status quo, the Paper first summarised the arguments in favour of preserving the status quo:

11. The fundamental argument in favour of the present arrangement is that allowing defendants charged with any non-summary offence to have access to trial by jury (which is the mode of trial which is considered appropriate for all serious cases) helps to promote confidence in the criminal justice system.

12. The considerations to which magistrates must have regard in deciding whether a case is suitable to be tried by them or should be tried by a jury, which are set out in the National Mode of Trial Guidelines, are broadly concerned with the seriousness of the case. The effect that conviction would have on the defendant's reputation is not one of these considerations. But reputation is widely perceived, at least in certain sorts of case, as a justification for continuing to allow the defendant to elect Crown Court trial. As the James Committee put it,

> A professional person of good character, if convicted of a minor offence of dishonesty for example, will suffer in reputation and may lose his livelihood, whereas for a person with a long record of similar offences the only penalty will probably be the sentence actually imposed.

13. When people who have never been accused of a criminal offence argue the case for the right to elect jury trial, it is usually on the basis that this is what they would want were they unfortunate enough to be charged with an offence which they had not committed.

14. Underlying the argument for allowing defendants to defend their reputation before a jury is the assumption that a jury is 'fairer' than a bench of magistrates. Home Office research has shown that defendants who elect Crown Court trial tend to do so mainly because they believe that their chances of acquittal are higher at the Crown Court than at magistrates' courts. Indeed that belief is borne out by the statistics, although the case in favour of election depends more on the existence of these perceptions that jury trial is advantageous than on whether they are well founded.

15. Some other arguments which are adduced in favour of election for trial – for example, the fact that a jury can acquit in the face of evidence which legally establishes the offence ('nullification') – go to the merits of trial by jury rather than to whether a defendant should be able to choose to be tried in this way.

Turning to the arguments that the present systems requires reform, the Paper said:

16. The fundamental argument against the present system is that it means that the additional delay and cost inseparable from Crown Court proceedings are incurred in cases which do not need to be tried there but which defendants have themselves chosen to take to the Crown Court because, rightly or wrongly, they see some advantage in doing so. Elected cases, by definition, are cases which the magistrates considered were suitable for them to deal with and which, but for the defendant's veto, they would have tried. The Royal Commission on Criminal Justice and the 'Review of Delay in the Criminal Justice System' (the Narey report) both considered that the court, and not the defendant, is best qualified to make the final decision where a case should be heard. That decision should be based on an objective assessment by the court of the gravity of the case, and not on defendants' own perception of what is advantageous for them (e.g. that there would be a better prospect of acquittal in the higher court).

17. It is open to question how many accused persons elect Crown Court trial out of a desire to defend their reputation. The Narey report quoted a senior and distinguished magistrate:

> 'In considering elections for trial I cannot remember the last time someone elected for reasons of reputation. Inevitably, the ones who elect are experienced defendants, the ones who know how to play the system.'

18. This assessment is borne out by Home Office research suggesting that only one in ten of the defendants who elect Crown Court trial are without previous convictions. Defendants who have a criminal record are less likely than those with none to be motivated primarily by a wish to clear their name. They may be attracted (especially where their previous record is such as to put them at risk, if convicted, of losing their liberty) by the better prospects for acquittal afforded by the Crown Court. But these prospects are insufficient to prevent two-thirds of defendants from eventually pleading guilty before the start of trial, and are irrelevant to the significant proportion of defendants who (according to the same research) intended to plead guilty from the outset.

19. For the great majority of defendants, the decision to elect Crown Court trial may be founded on a wish to delay the proceedings, for any of the following reasons:

    (i)   to apply pressure on the Crown to accept a plea to a less serious charge;
    (ii) to make it more likely that prosecution witnesses will fail to attend the trial or, if they do attend, will be vague in their recollections;
    (iii) to put off the evil day. If it achieves nothing else, electing Crown Court trial will at least postpone conviction and sentence and the consequent removal from a local prison, where defendants are close to family and friends and enjoy the additional visits and other privileges available to unconvicted prisoners.

20. The majority of cases in which the defendant elects trial result, eventually, in guilty pleas,

but only after significantly greater inconvenience and worry to victims and witnesses, and at considerable extra cost. This cost arises not only in court time and legal aid funds, but also in prison places, because defendants who are sentenced to imprisonment by the Crown Court having elected to be tried there tend to receive substantially longer terms than would have been imposed by the magistrates.

Turning to possible reforms of the system of allocating either-way offences, the Paper considered first reclassification of particular either-way offences as summary-only (as was done by the Criminal Justice Act 1988, when criminal damage (up to £5,000 in value), common assault, driving while disqualified, and taking a conveyance without authority became summary offences). The Paper (at para 22) cited simplicity as the main argument in favour of this approach:

Reclassification would be straightforward, and would have the potential to divert some of the more obviously minor cases from the Crown Court. The James Committee recommended in 1975 that theft involving a small monetary value should be reclassified. They suggested a cut-off point of £20, which would be rather more than £90 now; if this were adopted, it is estimated that reclassification of minor theft would enable the magistrates to deal with some 2,000 cases in which defendants now elect Crown Court trial.

However, the Paper went on (at para 23) to suggest that this sort of re-classification could well cause injustice:

The problem with reclassification is that it is a blunt instrument: it would deprive magistrates of the power to send cases in the reclassified categories to the Crown Court even where they considered the particular offence to be such that Crown Court trial was appropriate. For example, theft of even a small sum may be a serious matter where the victim is an elderly or other vulnerable person, or where the culprit is in a position of trust, or where a conviction for dishonesty might lead to the defendant losing his job.

The other disadvantage noted in the Paper is that the reclassification option would not affect the offences which are not reclassified and so defendants could still elect Crown Court trial of offences that the magistrates could deal with. The Paper therefore moved to what was plainly the Government's preferred option, namely the abolition of the right to elect Crown Court trial. Paragraph 25 introduced this section of the Paper by saying:

It is less obvious why the defendant should be allowed to insist on taking a case to the Crown Court which the magistrates have decided would be suitable for them to try. It is sometimes argued that no-one should be tried for a serious offence in a magistrates' court unless he is content to be tried there, but (as the James Committee noted in 1975) few other jurisdictions allow the defendant such an element of personal choice.

Paragraph 26 recalls that the 'Royal Commission on Criminal Justice recommended that venue in either-way cases should be decided by the parties where they were in agreement on the issue. Where they did not agree, it would be for the magistrates to decide where the case should be tried; they would have regard not only to any defence representations (as legislation already requires), but also to such factors as the gravity of the offence, the complexity of the case, the defendant's past record if any (which would be an innovation), and the effect of conviction (and the likely sentence) on the defendant's livelihood and reputation . . .'. Paragraph 27 recalls that the '*Review of Delay in the Criminal Justice System* recommended simply that the decision as to where either-way cases are heard should rest with the magistrates, having regard to recommendations as to venue from the prosecutor and from the defence, and that defendants should no longer be able to veto their decision'. On either basis, the defendant would no longer be able to veto summary trial.

Turning to the arguments for this approach, the Paper said:

> 28. The main argument for removing defendants' ability to choose jury trial is that it is not they, but the court, which is best qualified to determine where a case should be tried. Abolition would not automatically rule out Crown Court trial for any defendant charged with particular either-way offences (as reclassification would). It would prevent what some regard as manipulation of the justice system by defendants demanding Crown Court trial for no good reason.
>
> 29. The proposal that magistrates should be required to take account of those factors (such as harm to a hitherto unblemished reputation) which might justify a defendant in seeking a Crown Court hearing would go some way towards meeting the concerns of those who see election for trial primarily as a safeguard for defendants with a reputation to lose. It would mean that some of the cases in which the defendant now elects jury trial would go to the Crown Court by direction of the magistrates. But even on the assumption that this might happen in as many as a quarter of elected cases, there would still be a fall of some 15,000 in the number of committals for trial. By way of comparison, the implementation of the 'plea before venue' provision in s 49 of the Criminal Procedure and Investigations Act 1996 has led to a similar reduction in the number of cases committed to the Crown Court for trial.

Next, the arguments against the removal of the right to elect were set out:

> 30. The objection to the removal of election is essentially that it would result in defendants being tried summarily for indictable offences without their consent, and that the benefits of the present arrangement which are listed in paragraphs 11–14 above would be lost.
>
> 31. The system proposed by the Royal Commission is open to a particular objection in that it would admit of the possibility (albeit an unlikely one) that by agreeing on summary trial the Crown and the defence could together require magistrates to hear a case which they considered unsuitable for their jurisdiction.

Given the obviously controversial nature of the suggestion that the right to elect trial on indictment should be abolished, it is perhaps surprising that the arguments against were not set out in greater detail.

The Paper then considered a more limited proposal to limit the right to elect trial on indictment, namely that the right should be lost only where a defendant was prosecuted for an offence similar in nature to an earlier conviction. The basis for drawing a distinction between such offences and other accusations was that matters of reputation would not be paramount where the accused had previous convictions for similar offences.

Paragraph 33 set out the arguments in favour of this approach:

> A defendant who has already been convicted of the same sort of offence can hardly be said to have as strong a reason for defending his reputation as a defendant with an unblemished record, and is arguably less likely to have a genuine intention of doing so when electing Crown Court trial. The clearest examples of manipulation are where defendants with long criminal records elect Crown Court trial and then plead guilty at the last moment or are convicted after a trial. This option would enable the magistrates to deal with such cases.

The arguments against the proposal were set out in para 34:

> Not everyone would accept that those with criminal convictions should, for that reason alone, be denied a privilege accorded to other defendants. That a defendant has a criminal record does not imply that he or she is necessarily guilty of the offence charged; indeed it is arguable that it might be the existence of previous convictions which brought the defendant under suspicion. A defendant whose previous convictions were such as to put him at risk of a custodial sentence if convicted might even be regarded as having greater justification for seeking jury trial than those who were at no such risk.

The Government was determined to curtail the right of defendants to choose Crown Court trial for less serious charges. Two Bills were introduced in an attempt to achieve this objective.

4.15.2 Two Mode of Trial Bills

Two Criminal Justice (Mode of Trial) Bills were placed before Parliament in the late 1990s (<http://www.publications.parliament.uk/pa/ld199900/ldbills/003/2000003.htm> and <http://www.publications.parliament.uk/pa/cm199900/cmbills/073/2000073.htm>). The Government's intention was to remove the defendant's right to elect trial for either-way offences. Under both Bills, the choice of mode of trial would have been a matter for the magistrates. They would have heard representations from the prosecution and from the defence, and would then have decided whether the case was to be tried in the magistrates' court or the Crown Court.

The main impetus for reform was the fact that too much of the Crown Court's workload was felt to comprise cases that could have been dealt with in the magistrates' court, in the sense that they were not serious enough to justify the much more expensive form of trial. There was also a feeling that too many defendants were 'playing the system' by choosing Crown Court trial for offences that could have been tried in the magistrates' court (it was said that some defendants who had been remanded in custody until their trial, and who in fact intended to plead guilty, wanted to postpone pleading guilty as long as possible so that they were spending as much time as possible as remand prisoners, that time having to be deducted from any custodial sentence eventually passed; and it was suggested that some defendants who intended to contest the charges wanted to delay the trial as long as possible in the hope that the memories of the prosecution witnesses would have faded by the time of trial).

This proposal was intensely controversial, and many people argued that it was wrong to take away a person's right to choose trial by jury for any either-way offence.

The first version of the Bill required the magistrates to have regard to the likely effect of conviction on the defendant's livelihood and reputation. However, this was felt to discriminate unfairly against those with previous convictions. The second Bill went to the other extreme, and excluded all consideration of the circumstances of the offender. The accused would have had a right of appeal to the Crown Court (to a judge sitting alone, without lay justices) against a decision that he ought to be tried summarily. Both Bills, however, failed to complete their passage through Parliament.

It was perhaps strange that the Government should seek to retain more cases in the magistrates' court by targeting the right of the defendant to choose Crown Court trial, when in fact the majority of either-way offences that go to the Crown Court for trial do so because the magistrates ruled that the case was too serious for them to deal with.

4.15.3 The *Auld Review*

In Sir Robin Auld's *Review of the Criminal Courts of England and Wales* (the *Auld Review*), he argued that there should be a unified Criminal Court, with the Crown Court and magistrates' courts being replaced by a unified Criminal Court consisting of three Divisions: the 'Crown Division' (constituted as the Crown Court now is and exercising jurisdiction over all indictable-only matters and the more serious either-way offences allocated to it); the 'District Division' (consisting of a judge, normally a District Judge or Recorder, and at least two lay magistrates, and exercising jurisdiction over a range of either-way offences of sufficient seriousness to merit up to two years' custody); and the 'Magistrates' Division' (constituted as magistrates' courts now are, with either lay justices or a District Judge, and dealing with all summary matters and the less serious either-way cases allocated to them). Auld's plan was that the Magistrates' Division would allocate all either-way cases, according to the seriousness of the alleged offence and the circumstances of the defendant. In the event of a dispute as to venue, a District Judge would determine the matter after hearing representations from the prosecution and the defendant. The defendant would no longer have the right to choose trial by jury for an either-way offence. The main rationale for mixed tribunals was that they would 'combine the advantages of the legal knowledge and experience of the professional judge with community representation in the form of lay magistrates' (para 276). For a discussion of these proposals, see John Jackson, *Modes of trial: shifting the balance towards the professional judge* [2002] Crim LR 249.

The Government rejected the proposal to restructure the criminal courts in this way. However, the Courts Act 2003 does make provision for a much closer working relationship between the Crown Court and the magistrates' court, as well as a single committee to devise rules for both courts.

The *Auld Review* also tackled the highly controversial question of determining mode of trial for either-way offences. This topic is considered at length, in paras 119–72 of Chapter 5. The question was perhaps made all the more difficult by the failure of the two Mode of Trial Bills. Having reviewed all the arguments, Lord Justice Auld concludes that there is no good reason why a defendant should be able to choose the court in which he is tried (and he notes that this right is, in international terms, a rarity). Accordingly, the relevant recommendations are as follows:

32. In all 'either-way' cases, magistrates' courts, not defendants, should determine venue after representation from the parties.
33. In the event of a dispute on the issue, a District Judge should decide.
34. The defence and the prosecution should have a right of appeal on paper from any mode of trial decision on which they were at issue to a Circuit Judge nominated for the purpose, and provision should be made for the speedy hearing of such appeals.
   . . .
36. The procedure of committal for sentence should be abolished.

4.15.4 The Criminal Justice Act 2003

In the Criminal Justice Act 2003, the Government approached the concerns about the workload of the Crown Court from a different angle. Rather than seeking to restrict the defendant's right to elect Crown Court trial, the Act increases the sentencing powers of the magistrates. The effect of this is intended to be that the magistrates will find more cases suitable for summary trial; if more defendants are offered summary trial, the likelihood is that there will be an increase in the number of summary trials and a corresponding decrease in the number of Crown Court trials. This may seem to be a sensible approach given the fact that approximately two-thirds of either-way cases tried in the Crown Court are in that court because the magistrates declined jurisdiction (only one-third are there because the defendant, having been offered the option of summary trial, elected Crown Court trial). However, some commentators argue that it is inappropriate to increase the sentencing powers of the magistrates in this way, since:

a   the magistrates' courts could not cope with a significant increase in workload, and
b   many magistrates would regard themselves as ill-equipped to try more serious cases.

See, for example, Andrew Herbert, *Mode of trial and magistrates' sentencing powers: will increased powers inevitably lead to a reduction in the committal rate?* [2003] Crim LR 314 (an article based on a study which involved interviewing magistrates, clerks and defence solicitors). Herbert notes that the 'plea before venue' procedure met with only limited success in encouraging the entry of early guilty pleas. He says that the proportion of defendants who admit guilt at the 'plea before venue' hearing would appear to be lower than had been anticipated, and comments that:

> . . . [M]agistrates appear to view the decision to order reports as equating to an acceptance of jurisdiction and being virtually conclusive that they will finalise a case. The consequence of this practice is that they seem unwilling, or at the very least reluctant, to order reports in cases which might be outside their sentencing powers, opting instead to commit these defendants to the Crown Court at the PBV hearing.

On the increase in the sentencing powers of magistrates by the Criminal Justice Bill (or Act, as it now is), he says that these enhanced powers:

> might result in magistrates imposing longer prison sentences on offenders who currently

receive six months or less rather than lead to them accepting jurisdiction in a wider and more serious compass of cases.

He concludes as follows:

> . . . There can be little doubt that increased powers would have some effect on the committal rate. It is virtually inconceivable that magistrates would not retain any additional cases or that these cases would be completely offset by greater exercise of the right of election. It has been argued in this article, however, that the anticipated effect of increased powers on committal rates may well not be as significant as expected. The underlying reasons for this present as being the culture of the lay magistracy and the lack of impetus coming from within magistrates' courts to finalise more serious cases.
>
> The findings of this study suggest that attempts to change procedure cannot afford to underestimate the strength of the culture of the lay magistracy . . . Magistrates have traditionally viewed the purpose of a mode of trial hearing as being to provide a clearly defined path for a case. They have a belief that a decision to accept jurisdiction is essentially final. They adopt a cautious approach towards retaining cases in order to minimise the possibility of colleagues having to make an implicitly conflicting decision at the sentencing hearing. This conservative attitude provides one reason for the limited impact of plea before venue on committal rates. Magistrates view the decision to order reports as equating to an acceptance of jurisdiction and, therefore, tend to commit cases which might prove to be outside their sentencing powers.
>
> The effect of a cautious approach towards accepting jurisdiction is heightened by an apparent lack of impetus coming from within magistrates' courts to hear more serious cases. The objective of a reduced committal rate is, quite simply, seen by many court participants as being flawed. Almost all of the magistrates interviewed for this study believed that current mode of trial procedure was satisfactory and produced a fair and realistic division of business between the higher and lower courts in the interests of justice. Lawyers expressed the opinion that lay magistrates were already being asked to handle cases at the extreme of their ability. This view is crucial as magistrates are nearly always faced with an agreed or unchallenged application of the Crown and almost invariably endorse that recommendation. Increased sentencing powers may have the effect of net widening and lead to the imposition of longer custodial sentences. It may even be that a reduction in the committal rate would have the paradoxical consequence of the increased use of imprisonment as many defence solicitors believe that judges tend to be more lenient, and show greater faith in the efficacy of community orders, in some borderline categories of offence.
>
> . . . It is, however, possible to reach one positive and constructive conclusion. The prime implication of this study is that reform is more likely to be effected from within than imposed from without. Magistrates need to be made aware of the reasons why judges more often than not sentence either-way defendants within lower court powers. Their current knowledge of Crown Court sentences would appear to be largely confined to that gleaned from reading the local press . . . A significant reduction in the committal rate will only materialise when all magistrates' court participants believe that the objective of a lower rate equates with the interests of justice.

Steven Cammiss, in his article *'I will in a moment give you the full history': mode of trial, prosecutorial control and partial accounts* [2006] Crim LR 38, notes the factors which militate against the decision to commit for trial being based on an accurate prediction as to the sentence likely to be imposed in the event of the defendant being convicted: these include the perceived 'mundane' nature of the mode of trial hearing and the reluctance of all concerned to go into much detail about the nature of the offence and the background of the defendant. He also makes the point that the removal of the power to commit for sentence where the defendant is convicted following trial (as opposed to pleading guilty), as proposed by the Criminal Justice Act 2003 but reversed by the Criminal Justice and Immigration Act 2008, would have encouraged magistrates to 'play it safe' and so commit defendants to the Crown Court for trial if there was any doubt as to the adequacy of their sentencing powers.

Chapter 5

Summary trial

5.1 TERRITORIAL JURISDICTION

All criminal cases start life in the magistrates' court, in the sense that (however serious the alleged offence may be) the accused makes his first appearance in a magistrates' court. The basic jurisdictional rules for criminal cases are set out in ss 1 and 2 of the Magistrates' Courts Act 1980. Under the original version of these provisions, a magistrates' court could (subject to certain exceptions) only try summary offences which were alleged to have been committed in the county served by that court; on the other hand, a magistrates' court could try an offence which was triable either way, no matter where in England or Wales it was allegedly committed. Under Pt 2 of the Courts Act 2003, however, magistrates are given national jurisdiction, with lay justices being appointed for the whole of England and Wales (although each lay magistrate is assigned to a local justice area). The 2003 Act also amended ss 1 and 2 of the Magistrates' Courts Act 1980 so as to give magistrates the power to deal with cases no matter where the offence was committed, whether a summary offence or an either-way offence.

Consequently, under s 1 of the 1980 Act, any magistrate has jurisdiction to issue a summons or warrant (although it should be borne in mind that, under the Criminal Justice Act 2003, the issue of a summons following the laying of an information as a way of commencing criminal proceedings is not available to public prosecutors); under s 2 of the 1980 Act, any magistrates' court has to try any summary offence, irrespective of where that offence was committed, and any either-way offence, provided that the magistrates have accepted jurisdiction and the accused has consented to summary trial.

Even though the Courts Act 2003 gives magistrates a national jurisdiction, a local link (often seen as one of the great strengths of the magistracy) is retained at least to some extent, in that most cases are tried in the court that serves the area where the offence was committed, and most magistrates will be (fairly) local to that area. It should be borne in mind, however, that the closure in recent years of some smaller courts, and the centralisation of the magistrates' courts so they sit mainly in the larger centres of population, has tended to undermine the local nature of magisterial justice.

Section 30(3) of the Courts Act 2003 empowers the Lord Chancellor (with the concurrence of the Lord Chief Justice) to give directions as to the distribution and transfer of magistrates' courts business. Where a person is charged with an offence, the prosecution decide which court that person should appear before and this decision will have to take account of any such directions s 30(4). According to the *Directions Regarding Where Magistrates' Courts Can Sit and Criminal and Civil Jurisdiction and Procedure in*

Magistrates' Courts in England and Wales (<http://www.hmcourts-service.gov.uk/cms/files/Section_30_Direction_9_March_05.doc>), the 'guiding principle' governing which magistrates' court should hear a case is that it should be heard either at a magistrates' court for the local justice area in which (i) the offence is alleged to have been committed, or (ii) the person charged with the offence resides (para 5). However, this guiding principle may be departed from for good reason. Examples of potentially good reasons in individual cases are set out in para 6:

- the consolidation of similar complaints/offences against the same defendant or co-accused;
- the place in which the witnesses, or the majority of the witnesses, reside;
- the place where other cases raising similar issues are being dealt with;
- the need to prevent an appearance of bias on the part of the tribunal.

Paragraph 7 gives examples of potentially good reasons based on management issues unconnected with the individual case, such as:

- the consolidation of cases to be conducted by the same prosecutor;
- the efficient management of all court accommodation;
- the need to ensure an efficient distribution of cases between local justice areas;
- the place where other cases raising similar issues are being dealt with;
- the need to deal with cases of a specialist nature.

5.2 TIME LIMITS

There are no time limits applicable to indictable (including either-way) offences. However, proceedings in respect of a summary offence must be started within six months of the commission of the offence, unless the statute creating the offence provides otherwise (s 127 of the Magistrates' Courts Act 1980). Where a statute creates a continuing summary offence, a prosecution can be brought at any time until six months have elapsed from the date when the offence ceased to be committed: *British Telecommunications plc v Nottinghamshire CC* [1999] Crim LR 217 (here, the offence was that of failing to reinstate the highway after street works had been carried out; the last date when the offence ceased to be committed was when the reinstatement of the road was completed satisfactorily).

In *Atkinson v DPP* [2004] EWHC 1457; [2005] 1 WLR 96, it was held that where there is uncertainty as to whether proceedings have been commenced in time, the question should be determined according to the criminal burden and standard of proof and the magistrates should decline to hear the matter unless satisfied so that they are sure that the proceedings were started in time (following *Lloyd v Young* [1963] Crim LR 703).

In *Rockall v Department for Environment, Food and Rural Affairs* [2007] EWHC 614; [2007] 1 WLR 2666, it was held that the laying of the information is the act which should determine whether or not the time limit for bringing a prosecution for a summary offence has been met. The essential concept is that the information should be made available to the justices, or the clerk to the justices, within time. This will be so, in relation to postal delivery, when it can properly be inferred that it has been received, whether opened or not; and as far as transmissions by fax or other electronic means are concerned, it will be when it can properly be inferred that the information is retrievable, whether retrieved in fact or not. Where proceedings brought by public prosecutors are commenced by the method created by the Criminal Justice Act 2003, the written charge and requisition, it is unclear whether the proceedings will be regarded as having been commenced when the written charge and requisition are sent to the accused or when they are deemed to have been received by virtue of r 4.10 of the Criminal Procedure Rules. Given that, where a prosecution is commenced by the laying of an information, time stops running from the date of the laying of the information even though the accused is unaware that an information has been laid until he receives the summons subsequently issued by the court, it is submitted that time should stop running from the date of the sending of the written charge and requisition (not their receipt by the accused).

5.3 THE CONTENTS OF THE CHARGE/INFORMATION

The commencement of proceedings in the magistrates' court is governed by Pt 7 of the Criminal Procedure Rules.

5.3.1 Statement of offence

Rule 7.2(1) provides that:

> Every written charge issued by a public prosecutor and every information, summons or warrant laid in or issued by a magistrates' court shall be sufficient if it:
>
> (a) describes the offence with which the accused is charged, or of which he is convicted, in ordinary language avoiding as far as possible the use of technical terms; and
> (b) gives such particulars as may be necessary to provide reasonable information about the nature of the charge.

Under r 7.2(2), it is not necessary for the documents to state all the elements of the offence, or to negative any matter upon which the accused may rely by way of defence. Where the offence is a statutory one (as most are), the description of the offence must contain a reference to the section of the Act or Statutory Instrument which creates the offence (r 7.2(3)).

5.3.2 The rule against 'duplicity'

Rule 7.3(1) states that a magistrates' court 'shall not proceed to the trial of an information or written charge that charges more than one offence'. Thus, an information or charge should allege only one offence. This is sometimes known as the rule against 'duplicity'. Rule 7.3 sets out what happens where a single information or charge does allege more than one offence:

... the court shall call upon the prosecutor to elect on which offence he desires the court to proceed, whereupon the offence or offences on which the prosecutor does not wish to proceed shall be struck out of the information or written charge; and the court shall then proceed to try that information or written charge afresh.

Under r 7.4, if the information or charge is duplicitous, and the prosecution fail to choose between the offences, the court must dismiss the entire case.

In *Carrington Carr v Leicestershire County Council* (1994) 158 JP 570, it was held that there are five situations where an information or charge may be duplicitous:

- where two or more discrete offences are charged conjunctively in one charge/information, for example, a single charge/information alleges both dangerous driving *and* careless driving;
- where two offences are charged disjunctively (i.e. in the alternative) in one charge/information, for example, a single charge/information alleges dangerous driving *or* careless driving;
- where an offence was capable of being committed in more ways than one, for example, driving under the influence of drink or drugs, and both ways are referred to in one charge/information;
- where a single offence is charged in respect of an activity but the activity involved more than one act; and
- where a single activity is charged but a number of particulars are relied on by the prosecution to prove the offence, for example, a single act of obtaining by deception where the deception involved several misrepresentations.

In the latter two instances, it is submitted that a single charge may well be appropriate in some cases. However, if the defendant wishes to admit some but not other allegations, or wishes to raise different defences to different allegations, separate charges would be necessary.

An information or charge would be duplicitous if, for example, the defendant were charged with receiving stolen goods and another form of handling stolen goods in the same information or charge. However, a series of acts may amount to a single offence if those acts constitute a course of conduct; for example, stealing a number of items from a supermarket would be charged as a single allegation of theft, since it may fairly be described as comprising one single activity (*Heaton v Costello* (1984) 148 JP 688). In *DPP v McCabe* (1993) 157 JP 443, a single charge alleging theft of 76 library books over a period of a year was held not to be duplicitous. Similarly, in *Barton v DPP* [2001] EWHC Admin 223, the defendant was accused of taking sums of money, on 94 occasions, totalling of £1,338. The Divisional Court held that it was a 'continuous offence' and so the charge was not duplicitous. The court noted that this was not a case where the accused had put forward a specific answer to some of the alleged takings and not to others, requiring the specific answers to be considered separately.

Rule 7.3(2) makes it clear that r 7 does not prohibit two or more informations or written charges being set out in one document; it is simply the case that each individual information or charge may allege only one offence. Similarly, r 7.7(3) states that a single summons or requisition may be issued against a person in respect of several charges but must state the matter of each charge separately and shall have effect as if separate summonses or requisitions had been issued for each charge.

5.4 TRYING MORE THAN ONE OFFENCE OR MORE THAN ONE DEFENDANT

Where several defendants are charged with the same offence, they will be tried together. Where an accused faces more than one charge, or there are several defendants charged with separate (but linked) offences, a joint trial is possible.

More than one charge may be tried at the same time if the magistrates feel that there is a sufficient link between the offences. This is a matter for the discretion of the justices, who should ask themselves whether the interests of justice are best served by a joint trial or separate trials, balancing convenience for the prosecution against the risk of any prejudice to the defendant. As Lord Roskill put it in *Chief Constable of Norfolk v Clayton* [1983] 2 AC 473 at 492, 'The justices should always ask themselves whether it would be fair and just to the defendant or defendants to allow a joint trial'.

In *R (CPS) v Blaydon Youth Court* [2004] EWHC Admin 2296; (2004) 168 JP 638, the defendant faced two charges. One alleged a public order offence in the racially aggravated form; the other alleged the same offence in the non-aggravated form. The prosecution intended the second charge to be an alternative to the first and sought a joint trial of the two charges. The justices decided that to have both offences tried together would be 'duplicitous'. The prosecution sought judicial review of this decision. It was held (following *Clayton*) that a magistrates' court can conduct a joint trial of two charges against a defendant when the prosecution have brought those charges in the alternative. It was argued that this could mean that two convictions are recorded against the accused. The court answered this by saying that, if the magistrates convict the accused of the more serious offence, they can adjourn the less serious offence *sine die* (under s 10 of the 1980 Act) or else grant an absolute discharge (although the court emphasised that it would be 'unwise' to do the latter until the time for an appeal against the more serious conviction has expired; on this basis, it is submitted that it would generally be preferable for the less serious matter to be adjourned under s 10).

If the magistrates decide against a single trial where the defendant is accused of more than one offence, those justices should not hear any of the cases, as a magistrate trying a case should be unaware that the defendant faces other charges (*R v Liverpool Justices ex p Topping* [1983] 1 WLR 119). Each case would thus have to be heard by a different bench.

5.5 DISMISSING A CASE WITHOUT HEARING THE EVIDENCE

Section 15(1) of the Magistrates' Courts Act 1980 provides that if the prosecutor fails to attend the trial, the court may dismiss the case or, if evidence has been received on a previous occasion, proceed in the absence of the prosecutor. If, instead of dismissing the case or proceeding in the absence of the prosecutor, the court adjourns the trial, it can only remand the accused in custody if he was already in custody or cannot be remanded on bail by reason of his failure to find sureties (s 15(2)).

Where a magistrates' court dismisses a case under s 15 without consideration of the merits of the case because of the non-attendance of the prosecutor, there is no rule of law which prevents the court from dealing with an identical charge subsequently laid against the same defendant; the question to be decided is whether the new charge amounts to an abuse of process, and so the court must consider what prejudice would be caused to the defendant by the new charge (*Holmes v Campbell* (1998) 162 JP 655, where it was also held that because the accused was not at risk of conviction when the case was dismissed because of the absence of the prosecutor, it was not open to him to invoke the rule against 'double jeopardy' by claiming *autrefois acquit*).

A case can also be dismissed without a hearing if there has been significant delay causing prejudice to the accused. The circumstances where a case may be dismissed because of delay are considered in Chapter 1 (where abuse of process is discussed).

However, in *R v Watford Justices ex p DPP* [1990] RTR 374, it was held that the justices cannot dismiss a charge on the ground that the case is too trivial to justify the continuance of the proceedings. If the prosecution wish to adduce evidence, the magistrates must hear that evidence unless the prosecution are guilty of abuse of process.

In *DPP v Shuttleworth* [2002] EWHC 621 (Admin); (2002) 166 JP 417, a magistrates' court dismissed an information for want of prosecution. The prosecution were represented at the hearing but the prosecutor did not have the relevant file; the justices dismissed the charge without taking a plea. They relied on s 15(1) of the 1980 Act. It was held that, in the circumstances, the justices were not entitled to dismiss the charge when they did. Section 15 of the Act has to be read with the procedure on trial prescribed by s 9 of the Act. The first stage of that procedure is that the charge should be put to a defendant and a plea taken. In the instant case, there was enough information before the justices, notwithstanding the absence of the prosecution's file, to enable that to happen. The court said that, although the frustration of justices when faced with the absence of a prosecution file was understandable, s 15(1) of the Act is not a provision that should be used in a punitive or disciplinary fashion against the Crown Prosecution Service (CPS). Instead, where an additional hearing is required through the fault of one of the parties, the justices should consider making a costs order against the defaulting party.

In *R (O) v Stratford Youth Court* [2004] EWHC 1553 (Admin); (2004) 168 JP 469, key prosecution witnesses failed to attend. On the first occasion, the prosecution successfully applied for an adjournment; on the second occasion, the justices refused an adjournment; the prosecution thereupon offered no evidence and the justices dismissed the charge. The prosecutor then discovered that the complainant had by then arrived at court and made a request that the court be re-convened. The magistrates agreed to reconvene; they overturned their refusal to adjourn and rescinded their dismissal of the charge. It was held that where the prosecution have offered no evidence and the court has dismissed the charge, it is not open to the justices to reopen the case. In such a case, the justices are *functus officio*, and any further hearing against the defendant in relation to that matter will inevitably give rise to a successful plea of *autrefois acquit* on his behalf.

5.6 PLEADING GUILTY BY POST

Section 12 of the Magistrates' Courts Act 1980, which provides that the defendant may be offered the opportunity of pleading guilty by post, applies only to summary offences.

The defendant is sent a special form. On the form, the defendant can indicate a plea of guilty and can also draw to the court's attention any mitigating circumstances which may persuade the court to impose a more lenient sentence. At court, neither the prosecution nor the defence are represented. In open court, the clerk reads out the statement of facts which was sent to the defendant and whatever the defendant has written on the form or in an accompanying letter. The court then proceeds to pass sentence. However, a sentence of imprisonment or disqualification from driving cannot be imposed in the absence of the defendant. If the court is minded to impose such a sentence, the defendant will be summoned to attend on a later occasion (see s 11(3) and (4) of the Magistrates' Courts Act 1980).

Section 12A of the Magistrates' Courts Act 1980 makes provision for the application of s 12 where the defendant appears in court. If the accused has indicated that he wishes to plead guilty by post but nevertheless appears before the court, the court may (if the accused consents) proceed as if the defendant were absent. Similarly, if the accused has not indicated that he wishes to plead guilty by post but, when he attends court, indicates that he wishes to plead guilty, the court may (if the accused consents) proceed as if he were absent and he had indicated an intention to plead guilty by post. Where the court proceeds as if the defendant were absent, the prosecution summary of the facts of the case must not go beyond the statement served on the defendant when he was given the option of pleading guilty by post. However, if the accused is in fact present in court, he must be given the opportunity to make an oral submission with a view to mitigation of sentence.

Section 12 allows the police to serve witness statements (rather than just a statement of facts) with the summons/requisition. The witness statements are admissible as evidence unless the defendant objects. If the defendant fails to plead guilty by post or to attend court to plead not guilty, and so fails to object to the use of the witness statements as evidence, the court can proceed to try the defendant in his absence, the prosecution case being based upon the witness statements already served on the defendant.

5.7 PRESENCE OF THE DEFENDANT

Section 122(1) of the Magistrates' Courts Act 1980 provides that a party to any proceedings before a magistrates' court may be represented by a legal representative. Under sub-s (2), an absent party who is so represented is to be deemed present. Subsection (3), however, makes it clear that this does not apply where the accused is under a duty – for example under the Bail Act 1976 – to attend court.

It follows that where proceedings were commenced by summons or written charge and requisition (rather than by arrest and charge), the defendant is deemed to be present if his legal representative is in court (and the legal representative may enter a plea on behalf of the defendant if the latter is not in court). However, where the proceedings were started with the accused being arrested and charged by the police, the accused (if he is not in custody) will be at liberty because he has been granted bail (either by the police or by a magistrates' court) and so is under a duty to attend court; s 122 cannot excuse his non-attendance.

Section 13 of the Magistrates' Courts Act 1980 provides that where the accused fails to attend court and the magistrates decide not to proceed in his absence but to adjourn instead, they may issue a warrant for his arrest. However, s 13(2) provides that, where a summons/requisition was issued, a warrant may only be issued if the conditions set out in sub-s (2A) or (2B) are satisfied:

- it is proved the summons or requisition was served on the accused within what appears to the court to be a reasonable time before the trial; or
- the present adjournment is a second or subsequent adjournment of the trial, the accused was present on the last occasion when the trial was adjourned, and on that occasion the court determined the time for the hearing at which the adjournment is now being made.

In other words, it has to be proved that the defendant knew of the date of the present hearing.

Where the accused has attained the age of 18, a warrant may only be issued under s 13 if the offence with which he is charged is punishable with imprisonment, or the court, having convicted him of the offence, proposes to impose a disqualification on him (s 13(3) (adults)). The same applies to juveniles (s 13(3A)).

Where the defendant was originally arrested and charged, he must attend court personally or else he is in breach of his bail, entitling the court to issue a bench warrant for his arrest under s 7 of the Bail Act 1976 (see Chapter 3).

5.7.1 Trial in absence of the defendant

Under s 11(1) of the Magistrates' Courts Act 1980, a defendant may be tried in his absence in the magistrates' court (so long as service of the summons or requisition can be proved, or the accused was present in court when the case was last adjourned and the date of the present hearing fixed). However, if the offence charged is triable either way, the defendant can only be tried *in absentia* in the magistrates' court if, on an earlier occasion, he consented to summary trial.

According to CPS figures, in the period 2004–07, the prosecution secured a conviction in the absence of the defendant in an average of approximately 15 per cent of the cases brought by the CPS.

If a defendant claims he is ill it will rarely, if ever, be right for a court to exercise its discretion to refuse an application for an adjournment. If justices suspect that the excuse is spurious, they should express their doubts and give the defendant an opportunity to reply. If he has professional support (such as a medical certificate or doctor's letter) for his claim that he is ill, the justices should not refuse an application for an adjournment without properly satisfying themselves that the claim is spurious (*R v Bolton Justices ex p Merna* [1991] Crim LR 848).

In *R (R) v Thames Youth Court* [2002] EWHC 1670 (Admin); (2002) 166 JP 613, the defendant was a juvenile. On the day his trial was listed for hearing before the youth court, he was arrested in connection with an unrelated offence and so was unable to attend court. The District Judge decided to try the defendant in his absence. It was held that in cases where a defendant has plainly not absented himself from his trial voluntarily, the threshold of prejudice and fairness that the defendant has to demonstrate in order to establish that a guilty verdict might be unsafe is a comparatively low one, particularly where the defendant is a youth and where there is material about which counsel for the defendant would have wished to have taken instructions. It is an important consideration, said the court, that a juvenile might not have the same level of understanding as an adult. Even though the case concerned a juvenile, it is submitted that it would be wrong in principle for a defendant to be tried in his absence in any case where the court is aware that the absence is unavoidable and out of the defendant's control. Some support for this view may be derived from the decision in *R v Jones* [2002] UKHL 5; [2003] 1 AC 1, where the House of Lords held (in the context of Crown Court trial) that a judge has a discretion to commence a trial in the absence of the defendant, but this discretion should be exercised with great caution, and if the absence is attributable to involuntary illness or incapacity it would be very rarely, if ever, right to do so, at any rate unless the defendant was represented and asked that the trial should begin (per Lord Bingham, at para 13).

R (R) v Thames Youth Court was followed in *R (Davies) v Solihull Justices* [2008] EWHC 1157 (Admin). After his case had been called on, it was discovered that the defendant had been excluded from the court building by the court security staff because he was allegedly aggressive towards them and others. The justices ruled that the defendant had, by virtue of his conduct, voluntarily absented himself from the hearing of his case, and that he should be tried in his absence. The Divisional Court held that it is only in very rare circumstances that a criminal trial may proceed in the absence of the accused. In general, a trial may only proceed in his absence where either the accused was disturbing proceedings in court so that his removal was necessary, or where he had absconded or deliberately absented himself from the hearing. In the present case, the defendant's misbehaviour did not justify excluding him from his own trial. Moreover, the justices erred in treating him as being voluntarily absent, since he had wanted to be in court but was prevented by the exclusion. Whilst it could be said that the exclusion was his own fault, that was not the same as its being his own choice; the position was no different than if he had committed an offence and then been arrested on his way to trial. The court had taken no steps to see if the defendant's attendance could be secured. A pragmatic approach would have been for the court to issue a warning to the accused that if he misbehaved in court he would be removed and that his trial would proceed in his absence.

Section 54 of the Criminal Justice and Immigration Act 2008 amends s 11 of the Magistrates' Courts Act 1980. The original version of s 11 gave the court a discretion to proceed in the absence of the defendant if he did not appear. Section 54(2) of the 2008 Act amends s 11 so that s 11(1)(b) provides that, in those circumstances, where the accused is aged 18 or over, the court *must* proceed with a trial in the absence of the accused unless it would be contrary to the interests of justice; where the accused is under 18, the court *may* proceed in his absence (s 11(1)(a)). It is submitted that this creates a very strong presumption that the trial will take place in the absence of a defendant over the age of 18 who fails to attend court. However, this is subject to the proviso in s 11(2A), added by s 54(3) of the 2008 Act, that 'the court shall not proceed in the absence of the accused if it considers that there is an acceptable reason for his failure to appear'. Nonetheless, the new s 11(6), inserted by s 54(6) of the 2008 Act, makes it clear that the court is not required to enquire into the reasons for the absence of the accused before deciding whether to proceed in his absence. The court would, however, have to take account of facts known to it (for example, about the effect of severe weather on public transport, or if the accused has contacted the court to explain his absence) in deciding whether an acceptable reason for the accused's absence exists. Section 11(7) requires the court to state in open court its reasons for not proceeding in the absence of an accused who has attained the age of 18.

Sections 11(3) and (4) of the 1980 Act provide that a magistrates' court should not, in the absence of the defendant, pass a custodial sentence or impose any disqualification on him. However, under s 11(5) – added by s 54(6) of the 2008 Act – this restriction applies only where the proceedings were commenced by the laying of an information or by the issue of a written charge and requisition (and so do not apply to cases where the accused was arrested and charged).

Section 54(5) of the 2008 Act inserts a new sub-s (3A) into s 11 to provide that, where a court imposes a custodial sentence in the offender's absence, the person must be brought before the court before being taken to prison to start serving the sentence.

5.7.2 Setting aside conviction where the defendant did not know of proceedings (s 14 of the Magistrates' Courts Act 1980)

Under r 4.7 of the Criminal Procedure Rules, a summons or requisition may be served by posting it to an address where it is reasonably believed that the defendant will receive it, or by leaving it at such an address. There is therefore a risk that the summons or requisition will not, in fact, come to the attention of the defendant, and that the defendant will be tried and convicted in his absence under s 11 of the Magistrates' Courts Act 1980. The potential injustice of this is mitigated by s 14 of the Magistrates' Courts Act 1980, which provides that in these circumstances the conviction may be set aside.

Under s 14(1), the accused may, at any time during or after the trial, make a statutory declaration (i.e. a written statement under oath, similar to an affidavit) averring that he did not know of the summons/requisition, or the subsequent proceedings, until after the court had begun to try the case. The declaration must also state the date on which the defendant first became aware of the proceedings. The declaration must be served on the magistrates' court within 21 days of the date when the accused became aware of the proceedings. The effect of the service of the declaration is to render the summons or requisition, and all subsequent proceedings, void. However, the original information or written charge remains unaffected, and so a fresh summons or requisition can be served.

The defendant may attend the court in person to make the statutory declaration (in which case, it is sworn before a magistrate) or else he may swear the declaration before a solicitor or commissioner for oaths and then send it by post to the court. Under s 14(3), a magistrate may allow a declaration to take effect even if it was served after the 21-day time limit, if it was not reasonable to expect the defendant to effect service of the declaration within that time (for example, where the accused is out of the country at the time).

The problem of a defendant not knowing about proceedings never arises where proceedings are commenced by arrest and charge, since the charge sheet tells the defendant the date of his first court appearance.

5.8 SUMMARY TRIAL PROCEDURE

A magistrates' court conducting a summary trial will consist either of three lay justices or a District Judge; there will also be a clerk/court legal adviser to assist the court.

It is very rare for a District Judge to sit with lay justices. Indeed, the Lord Justice Auld's *Review of the Criminal Courts of England and Wales* (the *Auld Review*) recommended that:

- District Judges and magistrates should not routinely sit as mixed tribunals to deal with the general range or any particular type of case or form of proceeding, though there may be training and local 'cultural' advantages in their doing so from time to time depending on their respective availability and case loads (Recommendation 5.1).
- District Judges should concentrate on case allocation and management, cases of legal or factual complexity, cases of priority, such as those involving young offenders or offences of a sexual nature, and long cases (Recommendation 5.3).

The latter recommendation was perhaps largely unnecessary, as District Judges tend to be deployed in that way in any event.

Given the fact that District Judges are legally qualified, the *Auld Review* also recommends that they should normally sit without a court legal adviser (Recommendation 6). However, in practice, a court legal adviser will be present even where a District Judge is presiding.

Research carried out in 2000 for the Home Office by R Morgan and N Russell, *The Judiciary in the Magistrates' Courts* (<http://www.homeoffice.gov.uk/rds/pdfs/occ-judiciary.pdf>), noted that District Judges (stipendiary magistrates as they were then known) were around 30 per cent faster than lay magistrates in dealing with court business.

5.8.1 Outline of a summary trial

Section 9 of the Magistrates' Courts Act 1980 provides as follows:

(1) On the summary trial of an information, the court shall, if the accused appears, state to him the substance of the information and ask him whether he pleads guilty or not guilty.
(2) The court, after hearing the evidence and the parties, shall convict the accused or dismiss the information.
(3) If the accused pleads guilty, the court may convict him without hearing evidence.

The first stage in a summary trial is for the plea to be taken. The clerk/court legal adviser puts the allegation(s) to the defendant, who has to plead 'guilty' or 'not guilty'. A separate plea should be entered in respect of each charge faced by the defendant.

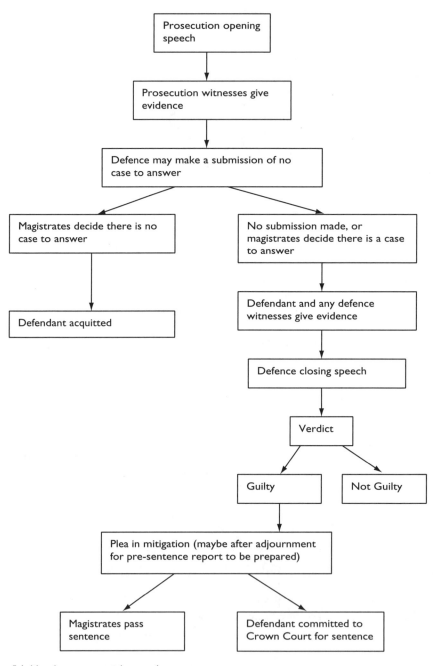

Figure 5.1 Usual summary trial procedure.

5.8.1.1 Procedure where the defendant pleads guilty

The procedure where the defendant pleads guilty is as follows:

1   The prosecution summarise the facts of the offence. It should be noted that if there is a significant difference between the prosecution version of the facts and the version to be put forward by the defence (for example, in the case of an offence of dishonesty, there is a dispute over the value involved in the offence), the court must either accept the defence version or else hear evidence on the question and then come to a decision on which version to believe (*R v Newton* (1983) 77 Cr App R 13).

2   The prosecutor hands the magistrates details of the defendant's previous convictions, if any. The prosecutor will have asked the defence to confirm that these details are correct. The magistrates will indicate which of the previous convictions they wish the prosecutor to read out loud on the basis that they are relevant to the sentence for the present offence; usually, it is only the most recent convictions that are read out. The prosecutor will also tell the court what is known about the personal circumstances of the defendant (employment, housing, etc); this is based on what the defendant told the police and will be very brief.

3   Once the prosecution have summarised the facts, the magistrates may decide to adjourn for a pre-sentence report. If not, the defence will make a plea in mitigation in order to try to persuade the court to impose a more lenient sentence. Having heard the plea in mitigation, the magistrates may pass sentence or may then decide to adjourn for a pre-sentence report. The adjournment cannot be for more than four weeks if the defendant is on bail, or three weeks if he is in custody (s 10(3) of the Magistrates' Courts Act 1980). If there has been an adjournment for a pre-sentence report, it is unlikely that the same magistrates will be sitting on the next occasion, so the prosecution will have to summarise the facts of the offence and the defence will have to do a full plea in mitigation. Sentence is then passed.

5.8.1.2 Procedure where the defendant pleads not guilty

Rule 37.1 of the Criminal Procedure Rules provides as follows:

(1)   On the summary trial of an information, where the accused does not plead guilty, the prosecutor shall call the evidence for the prosecution, and before doing so may address the court.

(2)   At the conclusion of the evidence for the prosecution, the accused may address the court, whether or not he afterwards calls evidence.

(3)   At the conclusion of the evidence, if any, for the defence, the prosecutor may call evidence to rebut that evidence.

(4)   At the conclusion of the evidence for the defence and the evidence, if any, in rebuttal, the accused may address the court if he has not already done so.

(5)   Either party may, with the leave of the court, address the court a second time, but where the court grants leave to one party it shall not refuse leave to the other.

(6)   Where both parties address the court twice the prosecutor shall address the court for the second time before the accused does so.

The procedure where the defendant pleads not guilty is usually as follows:

1   The prosecution may make an opening speech, briefly setting out what they hope to prove.

2   The prosecution witnesses give evidence (each one being examined-in-chief by the prosecution, cross-examined by the defence and, if necessary, re-examined by the prosecution).

3   The written statements of any prosecution witnesses may be read to the court (pursuant to s 9 of the Criminal Justice Act 1967) if the defence consent to this being done, as will be the case where the defence accept that the contents of the statement are true and so this evidence is not disputed.

4   After the close of the prosecution case, the defendant may make a submission that there is no case to answer. This submission is considered more closely below.

5   If the defence do not make a submission of no case to answer, or make a submission which is rejected by the magistrates, the defence may then call evidence.

6   If there are defence witnesses in addition to the defendant, the defendant should give evidence first. Each defence witness is examined-in-chief by the defence, cross-examined by the prosecution and, if necessary, re-examined by the defence.

7   After the defence witnesses have given evidence, the defence may make a closing speech.

8   The magistrates consider their verdict. A bench of lay magistrates usually retires to consider its decision, whereas a District Judge usually announces his decision immediately. Brief reasons for the verdict should be given (this is regarded as an important aspect of the right to a fair trial under Art 6 of the European Convention on Human Rights).

9   If the defendant is convicted, the prosecution supply the court with details of any previous convictions recorded against him, together with brief details of his personal circumstances. The court will either adjourn the case for a pre-sentence report or hear a plea in mitigation on behalf of the defendant and then pass sentence or at that stage adjourn for a pre-sentence report. The maximum period of the adjournment for reports to be prepared is four weeks if the defendant is on bail, three weeks if he is in custody (s 10(3) of the Magistrates' Courts Act 1980).

5.8.1.3 Sentencing powers

The sentencing powers of the magistrates are dealt with in more detail in later chapters. In summary, a magistrates' court cannot impose a custodial sentence of more than six months unless the offender has been convicted of two or more offences which are triable either way, in which case, the maximum is 12 months. These powers will be increased when the relevant provisions of the Criminal Justice Act 2003 come into force: the magistrates will then be empowered to impose up to 12 months' custody for a single offence (and a total of 65 weeks for two or more offences).

5.9 PRE-TRIAL HEARINGS

Paragraphs 204–35 of Chapter 10 of the *Auld Review* consider the practice and procedure relating to pre-trial hearings and pre-trial assessments. Recommendation 210 was that:

> In the preparation for trial in all criminal courts, there should be a move away from plea and direction hearings and other forms of pre-trial hearings to co-operation between the parties according to standard or adapted timetables, wherever necessary seeking written directions from the court.

The Review goes on to recommend that:

- there should be national standard timetables and lists of key actions for preparation for trial (Recommendation 211);
- the parties should be at liberty to seek leave from the trial court to vary the standard timetable (Recommendation 213);
- the parties should endeavour to prepare for trial in accordance with the timetable and list of key actions to resolve between themselves any issues of law, procedure or evidence that may shape and/or affect the length of the trial and when it can start (Recommendation 214);
- the timetable in each case should set a date for the 'pre-trial assessment' – i.e. an assessment by the parties and the court as to the state of readiness for trial (Recommendation 215);
- by the pre-trial assessment date, the parties should complete and send to the trial court a checklist showing progress in preparation and as to readiness for trial, and seeking, if appropriate, written directions (Recommendation 216);
- that there should only be a pre-trial hearing if the court or the parties consider it is necessary for the timely and otherwise efficient preparation for, and conduct of, the trial – for example, where one or other of the parties cannot comply with the timetable, or where there are unresolved issues affecting the efficient preparation for or conduct of the trial, or when the case is sufficiently serious or complex to require the guidance of the court (Recommendation 217);
- the judge or magistrates conducting an oral pre-trial hearing should be empowered to give binding directions or rulings subject to subsequent variation or discharge if justice requires it (Recommendation 219);
- where a pre-trial hearing is necessitated by one or other or both parties' failure without good cause to comply with the timetable or other directions of the court, or to resolve issues of procedure, law or fact between them, the court should have power:
  - to make such order as to payment of a publicly funded defence advocate for his attendance at the hearing as may be appropriate in the circumstances; and/or publicly to reprimand either party's advocate or those instructing them as appropriate; any such public reprimand to be communicated to and taken into account by the professional body of the person reprimanded and, where the person is franchised for publicly funded defence work, by the Legal Services Commission; and/or

– to make such order of costs against one or other or both sides as may be appropriate (Recommendation 220).

There is now a system of pre-trial hearings in the magistrates' courts.

5.9.1 Case management

Part V.56 of the *Consolidated Practice Direction* governs case management in magistrates' courts. Paragraph V.56.2 requires use of the case progression form set out in Annex E of the Practice Direction and makes the point that the form, together with the accompanying guidance notes, constitutes a case progression timetable for the effective preparation of a case. Moreover, the case progression forms to be used in magistrates' courts contain directions, all of which apply in every case unless the court orders otherwise (para V.56.6). The case progression form for the magistrates' court draws attention to a number of questions:

i   Has the accused been advised that the case may proceed in his absence?
ii   Has the accused been advised about credit for pleading guilty?
iii What are the 'trial issues' (e.g., identification – with details)?
iv   What applications are to be made (e.g., special measures, bad character, hearsay)?
v   What is the likely number of witnesses (both prosecution and defence) and, in the case of the former, will their statement be read under the CJA 1967, s 9)?
vi   What is the estimated length of trial?

The court will fix the trial date at (or shortly after) the hearing at which the accused pleads not guilty.

5.9.1.1 Standard directions

A number of standard directions are applicable to a summary trial unless the court orders otherwise. Time for compliance with the directions starts to run from the date of the hearing at which the trial date is fixed (unless the court orders otherwise). The standard directions include the following:

- *Prosecution case and disclosure.* The prosecution (if they have not done so already) must serve copies of the witness statements, along with any documentary exhibits, tapes of interview, and video or CCTV tapes within 28 days. The prosecution must also comply with its initial duty of disclosure under the Criminal Procedure and Investigations Act 1996 within 28 days.
- *Hearsay evidence.* The prosecution must serve any notice of intention to introduce hearsay evidence at the same time as it complies with its initial duty of disclosure, and the defence must serve any notice opposing the prosecution's notice within 14 days of receipt thereof. The defence must serve any notice of intention to introduce hearsay evidence within 14 days of the date on which the prosecution complied with its initial duty of disclosure, and the prosecution must serve any notice opposing the defence notice within 14 days of receipt thereof.
- *Bad character evidence.* The defence must serve any application to introduce the

bad character of a prosecution witness within 14 days of the date on which the prosecution complied with its initial duty of disclosure. The prosecution must serve any notice opposing the defence application within 14 days of receipt thereof. The prosecution must serve any notice to introduce the accused's bad character at the same time as it complies with its initial duty of disclosure, and the defence must serve any application to exclude evidence of the accused's bad character within seven days of receipt of the prosecution application.

- *Defence statement.* If a defence statement is to be given, the defence must serve it within 14 days of the prosecution complying with its initial duty of disclosure.
- *Witness statements.* If the defence wish a prosecution witness to give evidence in person at the trial (rather than allowing their statement to be read to the court under s 9 of the Criminal Justice Act 1967), the defence must notify the prosecution within seven days of receiving the prosecution case (i.e. the witness statements etc). The defence must serve any statements of defence witnesses who the defence propose not to give evidence in person at the trial within 14 days of receiving the prosecution case, and a party who wishes such a witness to give evidence in person at the trial must notify the prosecution within seven days of service of the statement.
- *Further disclosure.* The prosecution must complete any further disclosure at least 14 days before the trial.
- *Written admissions.* The parties must file any written admissions made under s 10 of the Criminal Justice Act 1967 within 56 days.
- *Expert evidence.* A party seeking to rely on expert evidence must serve the expert's report within 28 days. A party served with expert evidence must indicate whether the expert is required to attend at the trial, and either serve their own expert evidence in response, or indicate that they are not intending to rely on expert evidence, within 28 days of receipt of the other party's expert evidence. A meeting of experts to agree non-contentious matters and identify issues (if appropriate and if the parties agree) should take place within 28 days of service of both parties' expert evidence, and the parties must notify the court within 14 days of an experts' meeting whether the length of the trial is affected by the outcome of the meeting.
- *Points of law.* If any point of law is to be taken by a party and a skeleton argument would be helpful, it must be served, together with the relevant authorities, at least 21 days prior to the trial. The other party must serve a skeleton argument in reply, together with the relevant authorities, at least seven days prior to the trial.
- *Trial readiness.* The parties must certify readiness for trial, by filing a certificate of readiness, at least seven days prior to the trial.

The guidance notes point out that directions allow the parties eight weeks in which to prepare for trial (or 14 weeks where there is to be expert evidence). If the court fixes a trial date less than eight weeks after the date of the not guilty plea then directions relevant to the case will need to be modified.

The notes also make the point that not all the standard directions will be needed in every case where the defendant is pleading not guilty. If the accused intends to plead guilty but there is a dispute over the facts of the offence, and a Newton hearing is to be held, any reference to the trial in the standard directions should be read as a reference to the Newton hearing (with the timetable beginning on the date of the guilty plea).

The standard directions are described in the guidance notes as 'default directions', which will apply where the accused pleads not guilty unless the justices, a District Judge or a justices' clerk directs otherwise.

5.9.2 Power to make pre-trial rulings

Section 8A(4) of the Magistrates' Courts Act 1980 empowers magistrates to make binding rulings on:

(a) any question as to the admissibility of evidence;
(b) any other question of law relating to the case.

These provisions apply to summary offences, and either-way offences that are to be tried summarily, where the accused has pleaded not guilty; the power is exercisable at any stage up to the commencement of the trial once the accused has entered a not guilty plea (s 8A(1)). A ruling may be made following an application by a party to the case, or of the court's own motion (s 8A(6)). Under s 8A(3), a pre-trial ruling may only be given if it is in the interests of justice to do so and if the court has given the parties an opportunity to be heard. When the accused is unrepresented but wishes to be represented, the Legal Services Commission (through staff based at the court) must consider whether to grant legal representation at public expense (s 8A(5)).

A pre-trial ruling made by a magistrates' court remains binding until the case against the accused or, if there is more than one, against each of them, is disposed of (s 8B(1)). The case is disposed of when the accused is convicted or acquitted, or is sent to the Crown Court for trial (s 8B(2) and (6)). The magistrates' court may discharge or vary a pre-trial ruling on application by a party to the case or of its own motion, so long as the court has given the parties an opportunity to be heard and it is in the interests of justice to discharge or vary the ruling (s 8B(3) and (4)). An application for the discharge or variation of an order may be made only if there has been a material change of circumstances since the ruling was made or, if a previous application has been made, since the application (or last application) was made (sub-s (5)).

There is no separate right of appeal against a pre-trial ruling (if the accused is ultimately convicted, he can appeal to the Crown Court in the usual way; in the case of an acquittal, the prosecution could ask the magistrates to state a case to the Divisional Court).

Pre-trial reporting restrictions apply already under the 1980 Act, but s 8C extends the ambit of these restrictions to pre-trial rulings. Section 8C imposes restrictions on reporting of pre-trial hearings in order to avoid prejudicing the right to a fair trial (particularly important if the case is ultimately tried in the Crown Court). The publishing of anything other than basic factual information (defined in sub-s (7) as including the identity of the court and the names of the justices; the names, ages, home addresses and occupations of the accused and witnesses; the offence(s) with which the accused is accused; the names of counsel and solicitors in the proceedings; where the proceedings are adjourned; the date and place to which they are adjourned; any arrangements as to bail; whether legal aid was granted to the accused) is prohibited – unless the court orders that reporting restrictions should not apply – until such time as the case against the accused is disposed of. Breach of these reporting restrictions is a summary offence punishable (under s 8D of the 1980 Act) with a level 5 fine (currently £5,000). Under s 8D(6), proceedings for this offence may not be instituted otherwise than by or with the consent of the Attorney General.

The power to lift the reporting restrictions is conferred by sub-s (3). Where the court is minded to order that the reporting restrictions do not apply and the accused (or one of the accused) objects to the making of an order removing the restrictions, the court may make the order if (and only if) satisfied, after hearing representations from (each of) the accused, that it is in the interests of justice to do so (s 8C(4)(a) and (5)(a)).

The implementation of the power to make binding pre-trial rulings brought the powers of magistrates in pre-trial hearings heard in the magistrates' courts into line with those of the judges in the Crown Court (where the Criminal Procedure and Investigations Act 1996 empowers a judge to give binding rulings on matters of law and admissibility of evidence).

5.10 SUMMARY TRIAL IN MORE DETAIL

Several matters need to be considered in more detail.

5.10.1 Pre-trial disclosure

Under the Criminal Procedure and Investigations Act 1996, the prosecution have to disclose to the defence any material not previously disclosed which might undermine the prosecution case against the accused. The defendant then has the chance to make voluntary disclosure of the nature of the defence case (setting out the matters where the defence take issue with the prosecution and giving particulars of any alibi the defence will rely on at trial). If the defence provide voluntary disclosure of their case, the prosecution then has to reveal any previously undisclosed material which might reasonably be expected to assist the defence case. Full discussion of the rules relating to Disclosure may be found in Chapter 8.

Standard directions set out in the case progression forms used in magistrates' courts set a time-limit of 28 days from plea for the prosecution to provide the defence with the evidence required by para 57 of the Attorney General's Guidelines on Disclosure (April 2005), which requires the prosecution to provide the defendant with all the evidence upon which they intend to rely at trial (in so far as it has not already been provided as advance information, where that duty arises) to allow the defendant and his legal adviser sufficient time properly to consider the evidence before it is called. However, para 2.2 of the Protocol for the Provision of Advance Information, Prosecution Evidence and Disclosure of Unused Material in the Magistrates' Courts (May 2006, <http://www.judiciary.gov.uk/docs/judgments_guidance/protocols/mags_courts_%20 disclosure.pdf>) says that:

> late provision of such evidence should not automatically result in a trial being adjourned. The court must take into account the nature of the evidence being provided late and form a view as to how long is required to properly consider it. In the majority of cases, a competent advocate will be able to deal with the material then and there by the court allowing time before the trial commences, or even during the course of the trial.

However, it is submitted that the robust approach recommended by the Protocol should not be allowed to undermine the requirement in the Attorney General's Guidelines that the defence should have 'sufficient time properly to consider the evidence before it is called'.

5.10.2 Securing the attendance of witnesses

Section 97(1) of the Magistrates' Courts Act 1980 empowers a justice of the peace (or a clerk) to issue a witness summons if satisfied that a person is 'likely to be able to give material evidence' (or produce any document or other item of evidence that is likely to be material evidence) at a summary trial and that it is in the interests of justice to issue a witness summons to secure the attendance of the witness. 'Material evidence' means evidence of some value to the party seeking the order. In *R v Peterborough Magistrates' Court ex p Willis* (1987) 151 JP 785, it was held that a witness summons should not be issued to enable someone to find out whether the witness can give any material evidence, as there has to be material before the court on which it may be satisfied that the witness will be able to give material evidence. Similarly, before the magistrate (or clerk) can issue a summons requiring the production of documents or other items of evidence under s 97, he must be satisfied that the respondent is likely to be able to produce the requested documents, and that the documents contain material evidence (that is, evidence which is both relevant and admissible). It is for the party who seeks the production of the documents to adduce evidence which satisfies the justices that there is a real possibility that the documents are material. Documents which are requested merely for the purpose of possible cross-examination are not material (see *R v Reading Justices ex p Berkshire County Council* [1996] 1 Cr App R 239). Moreover, the applicant must be able to show that the item to be produced would be admissible evidence and not, for example, subject to legal professional privilege (*R v Derby Magistrates' Court ex p B* [1996] AC 487). In *R v Reading Justices ex p Berkshire County Council* Simon Brown LJ summarised the key principles governing such applications as follows (at p 246–47):

(i)   to be material evidence documents must be not only relevant to the issues arising in the criminal proceedings, but also documents admissible as such in evidence;

(ii) documents which are desired merely for the purpose of possible cross-examination are not admissible in evidence and, thus, are not material for the purposes of s 97;

(iii) whoever seeks production of documents must satisfy the justices with some material that the documents are 'likely to be material' in the sense indicated, likelihood for this purpose involving a real possibility, although not necessarily a probability;

(iv) it is not sufficient that the applicant merely wants to find out whether or not the third party has such material documents. This procedure must not be used as a disguised attempt to obtain discovery.

Where it has been established by evidence given on oath that the witness is likely to be able to give material evidence, and it is probable that a summons would not procure the attendance of the witness, the magistrate (but not a clerk) may, instead of issuing a summons, issue a warrant for the arrest of the witness (s 97(2)).

Under s 97(2B), the magistrate may refuse to issue a witness summons if he is not satisfied that an application for the summons has been made as soon as reasonably practicable after the accused pleaded not guilty.

The procedure for obtaining a witness summons may be found in Pt 28 of the Criminal Procedure Rules. Under r 28.3(1), a party seeking a witness summons must apply as soon as practicable after becoming aware of the grounds for doing so. Rule 28.3(2) requires the applicant to explain:

i   what evidence the proposed witness can give or produce,
ii why it is likely to be material evidence, and
iii why it would be in the interests of justice to issue a summons or warrant.

Section 97(3) deals with the situation where the witness fails to attend, despite the issue of a witness summons. If the court is satisfied by evidence given on oath that the witness is likely to be able to give material evidence (or produce any document likely to be material evidence), and it is proved that he has been served with the summons in the manner prescribed by Pt 4 of the Criminal Procedure Rules (the procedure for service of a witness summons is the same as that for service of any summons or requisition), and it appears to the court that there is no just excuse for the failure to attend, the court may issue a warrant for his arrest. Under s 97(4), a witness who attends or is brought before the court but refuses without just excuse to give evidence can be imprisoned for up to one month or until he gives evidence (if sooner), and/or he may be fined up to £2,500.

5.10.3 Defects in the information: amendment

Section 123 of the Magistrates' Courts Act 1980 provides that:

> (1) No objection shall be allowed to any information or complaint, or to any summons or warrant to procure the presence of the defendant, for any defect in it in substance or in form, or for any variance between it and the evidence adduced on behalf of the prosecutor or complainant at the hearing of the information or complaint.
>
> (2) If it appears to a magistrates' court that any variance between a summons or warrant and the evidence adduced on behalf of the prosecutor or complainant is such that the defendant has been misled by the variance, the court shall, on the application of the defendant, adjourn the hearing.

The effect of s 123 is that all but the gravest of errors can be ignored or cured by amendment. It appears from the case law that there are three categories of defect in the information.

5.10.3.1 Minor defects

First, there are minor defects which do not require amendment. This would include a minor misspelling or other inconsequential error that has misled no one. In *R v Sandwell Justices ex p West Midlands Passenger Transport Executive* [1979] RTR 17, for example, the charge alleged a defective rear nearside tyre, when in fact it was a rear offside tyre which was defective; a conviction based on this unamended charge was upheld.

5.10.3.2 Defects requiring amendment

Secondly, there are defects which require amendment (which is possible under s 123) but which are not so grave as to be incurable. If the defendant has been misled by the error, the court should remedy this by granting an adjournment to enable the defence to prepare their case in the light of the amendment. An example of this sort of defect is where the charge alleges an offence under a section of an Act which has been repealed and re-enacted in identical terms in a later statute (*Meek v Powell* [1952] 1 KB 164).

Similarly, in *Wright v Nicholson* [1970] 1 WLR 142, it was held that a charge can be amended to show a different date for the alleged commission of the offence, provided that an adjournment is granted if the defence need more time to prepare their case in the light of the amendment. This was so even though the defendant had an alibi for the date originally alleged. Indeed, in *R v Norwich Crown Court ex p Russell* [1993] Crim LR 518, the Divisional Court went even further. The information in that case alleged that the offence (criminal damage) had been committed on 19 February 1991. In fact, it was the prosecution's case that the offence was committed on 18 February. The discrepancy was not noticed until after the defendant had been convicted. The Divisional Court said that the justices had clearly ignored the confusion as to dates and there was no reason why the conviction could not stand, even though the information had not been amended.

In the case of summary offences, an important question is whether or not the six-month time limit for commencing a prosecution (see s 127 of the Magistrates' Courts Act 1980) has expired: if it has not, then there is nothing to stop the prosecution simply starting the proceedings again, and this is a strong factor in favour of allowing an amendment to the existing charge. However, the fact that the time-limit has expired is not necessarily fatal to an application to amend the existing charge. In *R v Scunthorpe Justices ex p McPhee and Gallagher* (1998) 162 JP 635, the defendant was charged with robbery; the prosecution sought to amend the charge to allege theft and common assault (a summary offence) instead. Dyson J said the charge can be amended under s 123 even if the amendment takes place more than six months after the commission of the alleged offence. This is so even if the amendment involves alleging a different offence, provided that (a) the new offence alleges the 'same misdoing' as the original offence (in other words, 'the new offence should arise out of the same (or substantially the same) facts as gave rise to the original offence'); and (b) the amendment can be made in the interests of justice. In considering whether it is in the interests of justice for the amendment to be made, the court should pay particular regard to the interests of the accused. If the amendment would result in the defendant facing a 'significantly more serious charge', it is likely to be against the interests of justice to allow such an amendment; similarly, the need for an adjournment would militate against the court granting leave for the amendment of the information.

The same approach had been taken in *R v Newcastle-upon-Tyne Justices ex p John Bryce (Contractors) Ltd* [1976] 1 WLR 517, where the prosecution were allowed to amend a charge which alleged 'use' rather than 'permitting use' of a vehicle, even though the effect was to charge a different summary offence and even though a new charge could not have been brought because more than six months had elapsed from the date of the alleged offence. It was said that the defence were not prejudiced by this amendment as the true nature of the offence was clear from the statement of facts on the original summons.

Another example is *DPP v Short* [2001] EWHC 885 (Admin); (2002) 166 JP 474, where the charge alleged that the defendant 'used' a vehicle with excess alcohol (rather than 'drove') under s 5 of the Road Traffic Act 1988. At the end of the evidence, the prosecution invited the justices to exercise their power under s 123 of the Magistrates' Courts Act 1980 to amend the information to substitute 'drove' for 'used', thus bringing the charge into line with the wording of s 5. The magistrates refused to allow the information to be amended. It was held by the Divisional Court that s 123 of the 1980 Act confers a wide discretion on justices to amend a charge, and that discretion should ordinarily be exercised in favour of amendment unless so amending would result in injustice to a defendant (per Owen J at para 22). In the present case, no injustice would have been caused to the defendant by the proposed amendment, since he was fully aware of the case against him. Accordingly, the justices had erred in refusing the prosecution amendment.

The very wide ambit of s 123 is shown by *James v DPP* [2004] EWHC 1663 (Admin); (2004) 168 JP 596. The defendant was charged with supplying a Class B drug. At the close of her case, it was submitted that the evidence, although demonstrating an attempt to supply the drug, did not demonstrate an actual supply. The prosecution, relying on s 123 of the 1980 Act, applied to amend the information to allege an offence of attempting to supply a Class B drug (contrary to the Criminal Attempts Act 1981). Issues arose as to whether the justices were right to allow the amendment after the close of the defendant's case and whether they were right not to hold fresh mode of trial proceedings after allowing the amendment. The Divisional Court held that there is no fetter on the justices relying on the very wide wording of s 123 to substitute a different offence, even where that offence arises under a different Act of Parliament, provided that no injustice is caused to the defendant in so doing. There is, said the court, no reason why magistrates' courts should apply different principles to the Crown Court, which has power to make such amendments. In the present case, the defendant had suffered no prejudice. The court went on to hold that, where there is no injustice to the defendant, there is no requirement on the magistrates to undertake the mode of trial procedure upon the amendment of the charge, even where one offence is substituted for another.

However, in *Shaw v DPP* [2007] EWHC 207 (Admin); (2007) 171 JP 254, the justices allowed an information to be amended to allege a different offence. The new offence carried imprisonment, whereas the original one did not. Significantly, the amendment had permitted the introduction of a new charge outside the six-month time limit imposed by s 127 of the 1980 Act. It was held that the substitution of a new offence with a significantly heavier penalty, especially one where the defendant faces the possibility of a custodial sentence, should have had led the justices to reach the conclusion that it was not in the interests of justice to allow such an amendment.

Where the effect of the amendment would be to replace one offence with a different one, a key question is how similar those offences are. In *R (Thornhill) v Uxbridge Magistrates' Court* [2008] EWHC 508 (Admin), the accused (who was suspected of a drink-driving offence) had been asked to provide a specimen of urine, it being accepted that a medical reason precluded him from providing a specimen of breath. He refused to comply and was charged with failing to provide a specimen of breath. The prosecution later sought to amend the charge to allege failure to provide a specimen of urine. The six-month time limit for commencing proceedings in respect of the failure to supply a specimen of urine had expired. Silber J held that there is a distinct difference between a failure to provide a specimen of urine and one of breath. In those circumstances the decision of the justices to permit the amendment of the charge had to be quashed. It was therefore unnecessary to consider whether the amendment was or was not in the interests of justice. This case may be contrasted with *Wyllie v CPS* [1988] Crim LR 753, where a charge of failure to provide a specimen of urine for analysis was amended to allege failure to provide a specimen of blood; the Divisional Court said the amendment was permissible, because, on the facts of the particular case, the evidence would have been the same whichever limb of the relevant section of the Road Traffic Act the case was prosecuted under.

5.10.3.3 Irremediable defects

Thirdly, there are fundamental errors which cannot be corrected by amendment (despite the wide wording of s 123 of the 1980 Act). This includes a charge which names the wrong person (for example, *Marco (Croydon) Ltd v Metropolitan Police* [1984] RTR 24; *R v Greater Manchester Justices ex p Aldi GmbH & Co KG* (1995) 159 JP 717). The only remedy for the prosecution in such a case is to start fresh proceedings (which, in the case of a summary offence, is only possible if less than six months have elapsed since the alleged commission of the offence). Similarly, in *R (J Sainsbury plc) v Plymouth Magistrates Court* [2006] EWHC 1749, for example, a charge was brought under food safety legislation naming the defendant as 'J Sainsbury plc (trading as Sainsburys Supermarket Ltd)'. It was argued that the charge did not name the proper defendant, since the relevant store was operated by J Sainsbury Supermarkets Ltd. The prosecution applied under s 123 to substitute J Sainsbury Supermarkets Ltd as defendant. The District Judge allowed the amendment notwithstanding that the time limit for bringing a prosecution had since expired. The Divisional Court ruled that the proper defendant had not been before the court and so the effect of the decision was improperly to prefer a charge against it out of time. Where the accused is misnamed but nonetheless appears before the court, this may have the effect of waiving the error and rendering amendment permissible (see *Allan v Wiseman* [1975] RTR 217, where the wrong surname was used but the right person was nonetheless before the court).

5.10.4 Withdrawal of summons/offering no evidence

If the defendant has not entered a plea, the prosecution can (with the agreement of the justices) withdraw the charge (*R v Redbridge Justices ex p Sainty* [1981] RTR 13). The prosecution may make such an application if one of their witnesses is not available but the court will not grant an adjournment because it takes the view that the prosecution should be in a position to proceed. Withdrawal of a charge in this way does not constitute an acquittal, so fresh proceedings may be brought unless it would amount to an abuse of process (*R v Grays Justices ex p Low* [1990] 1 QB 54).

If the defendant has entered a plea of not guilty, it is too late to withdraw the charge and so the prosecution must:

- proceed with the trial; or
- seek an adjournment; or
- offer no evidence.

The other situations where the prosecution offer no evidence are where:

- the defendant has pleaded guilty to one offence and the prosecution do not wish to proceed with another (closely related) charge; or
- where new evidence exonerating the defendant has come to light; or
- where the CPS have reviewed the evidence and decided that there is insufficient prospect of securing a conviction to merit continuing the proceedings.

If the prosecution offer no evidence, and an acquittal is recorded, fresh proceedings may be brought if (but only if) the defendant was never in jeopardy of conviction (*R v Dabhade* [1993] QB 329). For example, in *Holmes v Campbell* (1998) 162 JP 655, a magistrates' court dismissed the case against the defendants when the prosecutor failed to appear at the hearing. The prosecutor subsequently brought fresh proceedings (making the same allegations) but the magistrates' court declined to try the case on the ground that it would be an abuse of process. The Divisional Court held that, by virtue of s 15 of the 1980 Act, the defendants could not have been convicted at a hearing where the prosecutor was absent. They had therefore not been in jeopardy of conviction at that hearing and so the doctrine of *autrefois acquit* did not prevent the bringing of the fresh charge.

In *R (A) v South Staffordshire Youth Court* [2006] EWHC 1200 (Admin); (2007) 171 JP 36, the accused was charged with assault occasioning actual bodily harm (ABH). He pleaded not guilty. The prosecution subsequently preferred a charge of grievous bodily harm (GBH) and offered no evidence in respect of the ABH, which was formally dismissed by the court. During the trial of the GBH charge, the prosecutor concluded that he would not be able to establish that charge and offered the accused the opportunity to plead guilty to a charge of ABH. The question at issue was whether the court had jurisdiction to reopen the ABH charge. The court observed that in a case where a not guilty verdict is entered in the Crown Court under s 17 of the Criminal Justice Act 1967 (which provides that where the prosecutor offers no evidence, the court may order that a verdict of not guilty be recorded without the need for a verdict from a jury), a defendant is entitled to rely on the defence of *autrefois acquit* if charged again with that offence. This principle, said the court, applies equally where a magistrates' court dismisses a charge pursuant to s 27 of the Magistrates' Courts Act 1980 (which provides that where on the summary trial of an either-way offence the court dismisses the information, the dismissal shall have the same effect as an acquittal on indictment). The court was therefore *functus officio* (i.e. their jurisdiction was spent) and the decision to proceed on the ABH charge was therefore wrong.

5.10.5 Witnesses the prosecution must call

Where the prosecutor serves a bundle of witness statements on the defence prior to summary trial, the prosecution must call as witnesses all the people whose statements have been served, unless any of the exceptions which relate to Crown Court trials (set out in *R v Russell-Jones* [1995] 1 Cr App R 538 at 544–5, per Kennedy LJ) are applicable (*R v Haringey Justices ex p DPP* [1996] QB 351 at 357, per Stuart-Smith LJ).

5.10.6 Reading witness statements

Under s 9(2) of the Criminal Justice Act 1967, a written statement may be read aloud to the court as evidence (instead of the maker of the statement giving oral evidence) if:

- the statement is signed by its maker;
- the statement contains a declaration by the maker that it is true to the best of his knowledge and belief, and that he makes it knowing that he is liable to prosecution if he has wilfully stated in it anything which he knows to be false or does not believe to be true;
- a copy of the statement has been served on all the other parties to the proceedings; and
- none of the parties on whom the statement is served objects within seven days of service to the statement being used as evidence.

The last two requirements do not apply if the parties agree immediately before or during the hearing that the statement may be used as evidence rather than the witness giving 'live' testimony (see the proviso to s 9(2)). Where the conditions in sub-s (2) are satisfied, the statement is admissible as evidence to the same extent as oral evidence to the like effect by that person (s 9(1)).

Where the statement refers to a document or other object as an exhibit, a copy of that document must accompany the statement when it is served on the other parties or the other parties must be told how they can inspect a copy of that document or object (s 9(3)(c)). When the statement is read out at the trial, any document or exhibit referred to in it becomes an exhibit just as if it has been produced by a witness giving oral evidence (s 9(7)).

It is usually the statements of prosecution witnesses which are read out in this way, with the consent of the defence, on the basis that the defence concedes that the evidence of that witness is uncontroversial and so the defence do not wish to cross-examine that witness. However, there is no reason why the evidence of a defence witness cannot be given in this way (if the prosecution agree).

5.10.7 Objecting to prosecution evidence in a summary trial

Objections to prosecution evidence are made under ss 76 or 78 of the Police and Criminal Evidence Act 1984 (PACE).

The procedure to be followed where the defence object to prosecution evidence is made difficult because of the fact that the magistrates are the judges of both fact and law. There is a danger that the magistrates will learn the nature of the evidence in the course of the arguments about its admissibility: should they then rule the evidence inadmissible, they may have difficulty in ignoring it when reaching a verdict. This problem is mitigated to some extent by the availability of pre-trial rulings, but these will not avail where issues of admissibility are raised for the first time during the course of the trial itself.

The stage of the trial at which the magistrates rule upon a question of admissibility of evidence is a matter for their discretion (per Lord Lane CJ in *F v Chief Constable of Kent* [1982] Crim LR 682, followed in *R v Epping and Ongar Justices ex p Manby* [1986] Crim LR 555 and *A v DPP* (2000) 164 JP 317). In *F v Chief Constable of Kent*, Lord Lane said this:

> [It is] impossible to lay down any general rule as to when magistrates should announce their decision on this type of point, and indeed when the point itself should be taken. Every case will be different. Some sort of preliminary point, for instance with regard to the admissibility of a document or something like that, can plainly, with the assistance of the clerk, be decided straight away. Other points . . . may require a decision at a later stage of the case, possibly after further argument. It may be that in some cases the defendant will be entitled to know what the decision of the justices with regard to the admissibility of a confession is at the close of the prosecution case in order to enable him to know what proper course he should take with regard to giving evidence and calling evidence and so on. The object of the Justices is to ensure that what is done is just and fair to the defendant and just and fair to the prosecution . . .

It is submitted that where a confession is the main evidence against the accused, so that without it there might not be a case to answer, the interests of justice dictate that the admissibility of the confession, if disputed, should be determined as a preliminary issue. See the comments of Goff LJ in *ADC v Chief Constable of Greater Manchester* (Divisional Court, unreported, 14 March 1983), quoted in *Halawa v Federation against Copyright Theft* [1995] 1 Cr App R 21, at p 27), that:

> if the only evidence before magistrates is the evidence of a confession and nothing else, then as a matter of common justice, the magistrates ought to deal with the issue of the admissibility of that confession as a preliminary point, before the close of the prosecution case, so that the defendant can then decide whether to make a submission of no case to answer.

5.10.7.1 Section 76 of PACE

If the defence invoke s 76 and allege that a confession has been obtained by oppression or in circumstances where anything said by the defendant is likely to be unreliable, the magistrates have to hold a *voir dire* or 'trial within a trial' (*R v Liverpool Juvenile Court ex p R* [1988] QB 1). The terms in which s 76 is drafted stipulate that the court shall not admit the confession into evidence unless satisfied that it was not obtained by oppression or by words or conduct likely to render it unreliable. It follows that magistrates (just like the Crown Court) are obliged to hear evidence on the admissibility of the confession. The prosecution will generally have to call the police officers who were present when the defendant confessed and they can be cross-examined by the defence; the defendant may then give evidence (and be cross-examined by the prosecution). At this stage, it is only the admissibility of the confession, not its truth, which is in issue.

If the magistrates decide that the confession is inadmissible, the trial will continue (assuming there is other evidence against the accused), but no further mention may be made of the confession. If the confession is ruled admissible, the trial will resume with the police officer giving evidence of what the defendant said (unless this has already been done in the *voir dire*, in which case the evidence does not have to be repeated as the magistrates have already heard it).

At the conclusion of his judgment in *ex p R*, Russell LJ (at pp 10–11) summarised the position as follows:

1.   The effect of s 76(2) of the Police and Criminal Evidence Act 1984 is that in summary proceedings justices must now hold a trial within a trial if it is represented to them by the defence that a confession was or may have been obtained by either of the improper processes appearing in sub-paragraphs (a) or (b) of s 76(2).
2.   In such a trial within a trial the defendant may give evidence confined to the question of admissibility and the justices will not be concerned with the truth or otherwise of the confession.
3.   In consequence of paragraphs 1 and 2 above, the defendant is entitled to a ruling upon admissibility of a confession before, or at, the end of the prosecution case.
4.   There remains a discretion open to the defendant as to the stage at which an attack is to be made upon an alleged confession. A trial within a trial will only take place before the close of the prosecution case if it is represented to the court that the confession was, or may have been, obtained by one or other of the processes set out in sub-paragraphs (a) or (b) of s 76(2). If no such representation is made the defendant is at liberty to raise admissibility or weight of the confession at any subsequent stage of the trial. For the avoidance of doubt, I consider that 'representation' is not the same as, nor does it include, cross-examination. Thus the court is not required to embark upon, nor is the defence bound to proceed upon, a voir dire merely because of a suggestion in cross-examination that the alleged confession was obtained improperly.
5.   It should never be necessary to call the prosecution evidence relating to the obtaining of a confession twice.

In his fourth proposition, Russell LJ would seem to be encouraging defence advocates to delay formally objecting to a confession until their own case, at which stage the magistrates may still exclude the confession if the accused's evidence raises a reasonable possibility that there was a breach of s 76(2). However, with respect, this seems to be inconsistent with the case law on challenging confessions at trials on indictment (see *R v Sat-Bhambra* (1988) 88 Cr App R 55, where it was held that, once a confession had been adduced by the prosecution, it is too late for the defence to represent that it was obtained by oppression or in circumstances likely to render it unreliable).

5.10.7.2 Section 78 of PACE

Where the defence argue that a confession should be excluded under s 76 of PACE, the court is obliged to hear evidence about the obtaining of the confession (as the prosecution have to prove that the confession was not obtained in the manner forbidden by s 76); where, however, the admissibility of prosecution evidence falls to be considered under the general exclusionary discretion in s 78, the court has a discretion to hear evidence on the issue of admissibility but is not obliged to do so (and so may rule on the matter following submissions on behalf of the parties). In the latter type of case, it remains a matter for the justices' discretion when they determine admissibility (*Vel v Chief Constable of North Wales* (1987) 151 JP 510 and *Halawa v Federation Against Copyright Theft* [1995] 1 Cr App R 21). In *Vel*, it was held that magistrates may deal with an application to exclude evidence under s 78 when it arises or may leave the decision until the end of the hearing. The court declined to lay down any general rule, other than that the object should always be to secure a trial which is fair and just to both sides. In *Halawa*, Gibson LJ said (at p 34) that, in most cases, it is generally better for the magistrates to hear all the prosecution evidence (including the disputed evidence) before considering an application to exclude evidence under s 78. This does of course leave the justices with the very difficult (some might say impossible) task of putting from their minds prejudicial evidence that they have heard but then decide is inadmissible.

In *R v Bow Street Magistrates' Court ex p Proulx* [2001] 1 All ER 57, it was held that the approach to be adopted by the Divisional Court when exercising its supervisory jurisdiction over a decision of a magistrate who had rejected an application to exclude evidence of a confession under ss 76 and 78 of PACE is as follows: provided the magistrate has correctly directed himself on the law, the Divisional Court will only interfere with his findings of fact, and his assessment of their significance when ruling on the admissibility of evidence, if they are outside the range of conclusions open to a reasonable magistrate (that is, the Divisional Court will determine whether they could be interfered with on grounds of *Wednesbury* unreasonableness).

5.10.8 'Dock identifications'

Where the identity of the defendant as the person who committed the offence is in issue, the court will generally not allow a witness who has not previously identified the defendant at an identification procedure to be asked 'do you see the person who committed the offence in court today?' (a so-called 'dock identification'). The reason for not allowing this to be done is that the defendant is at a great disadvantage – the eyes of the witness are bound to go to the person sitting in the dock.

However, in *Barnes v DPP* [1997] 2 Cr App R 505, the defendant was charged with failing to provide a breath specimen. There had been no identity parade and the only evidence that the defendant was the person who refused to provide a specimen was a 'dock identification' by a police officer. The Divisional Court held that the justices had a discretion to allow a defendant to be identified in court even if there had not been a previous identification parade. In *Karia v DPP* [2002] EWHC 2175; (2002) 166 JP 753, the defendant appealed against conviction for a number of motoring offences on the ground that the magistrates should not have allowed the police officer who had stopped the vehicle to make a 'dock identification' of him, and that an identification parade should have been held. He argued that the decision in *Barnes v DPP* permitting dock identifications in such cases was incompatible with the Human Rights Act 1998. It was held that the aim of a dock identification in a case such as the present is usually to avoid an unmeritorious dismissal of a prosecution case resulting from a failure to make a purely formal identification of the defendant. In the present case, the defendant had not notified the prosecution that identity was in issue, and so the dock identification was not unfair. Since there had been no prior notification that identity was in issue, there was no basis on which the police could have considered that it would be useful to hold an identification parade. As far as the Human Rights Act point was concerned, a requirement that the issues should be made known to the court before or during the proceedings cannot infringe Art 6; a requirement that a defendant should indicate before or at his trial what are the issues in the trial does not infringe his right to silence. On this basis, it would appear that dock identifications are only to be ruled out where the defendant has already indicated that identity is in issue in the case.

In *North Yorkshire Trading Standards Department v Williams* (1994) 159 JP 383, Potts J said that it would be wrong to apply one approach to dock identifications for minor offences and another for more serious offences. However, Rose LJ said:

> First, although dock identifications are . . . generally undesirable they are admissible in law . . . Secondly, whether a dock identification should be admitted in the exercise of discretion is for the trial judge or justices to decide. There will clearly be circumstances, for example a proffered dock identification several years after the event, where the probative value will be nil or negligible and the prejudicial value so great that it should not be admitted. But each case must be considered on its own facts and in relation to its own circumstances in order to determine whether the prejudicial value of the evidence outweighs its probative value. Thirdly, if, in the exercise of that discretion, a dock identification is admitted in evidence, justices, like juries, will have to be reminded by their clerk of the dangers in identification evidence and of the potential weaknesses in it, in accordance with *R v Turnbull* [1977] QB 224 . . .

In *Holland v Her Majesty's Advocate* [2005] UKPC D1; [2005] HRLR 25, the Privy Council said that there is no basis, except perhaps in an extreme case, for regarding dock identifications as inadmissible *per se*. However, there will be cases where a dock identification may render the trial unfair. Where a dock identification does take place in a case where the witness has previously failed to identify the accused at an identification parade, the judge must warn the jury clearly of the particular risks of a dock identification. It is submitted that the same approach should apply in the magistrates' court. In *The State v Young* [2008] UKPC 27, Lord Carswell (at para 17) said that 'a dock identification, with all its weaknesses, may nevertheless be admitted in evidence with proper safeguards'. In the case of a Crown Court trial, the judge 'must give sufficient warnings about the dangers of identification without a parade and the potential advantage of an inconclusive parade to a defendant, and direct the jury with care about the weakness of a dock identification'. In a summary trial, it is submitted that the magistrates would have to direct themselves in similar terms.

See further T Watkin, 'In the dock – an overview of decisions of the High Court on dock identifications in the magistrates' court' [2003] Crim LR 463.

5.10.9 The submission of no case to answer

We have already seen that the defence may make a submission that there is no case to answer once the prosecution have called all their evidence. The principles to be applied to a submission of no case to answer in a magistrates' court were originally set out in *Practice Direction (Submission of No Case to Answer)* [1962] 1 WLR 227. This provided as follows:

> A submission that there is no case to answer may properly be made and upheld:
>
> (a)   when there has been no evidence to prove an essential element in the alleged offence;
> (b)   when the evidence adduced by the prosecution has been so discredited as a result of cross-examination or is so manifestly unreliable that no reasonable tribunal could safely convict upon it.
>
> Apart from these two situations a tribunal should not in general be called upon to reach a decision as to conviction or acquittal until the whole of the evidence which either side wishes to tender has been placed before it. If however a submission is made that there is no case to answer, the decision should depend not so much on whether the adjudicating tribunal (if compelled to do so) would at that stage convict or acquit but on whether the evidence is such that a reasonable tribunal might convict. If a reasonable tribunal might convict on the evidence so far laid before it, there is a case to answer.

However, this Practice Direction was revoked by the *Consolidated Practice Direction* and nothing was put in its place. This unfortunately leaves justices without clear guidance on the test to be applied when considering a submission of no case.

It is submitted that justices should continue to take the view that, if a submission of no case to answer is made, the decision should depend not so much on whether they would, at that stage, convict or acquit but on whether the evidence is such that a reasonable tribunal might convict. If a reasonable tribunal might convict on the evidence so far laid before it, there is a case to answer. Thus, the basic question to be answered is whether or not there is sufficient evidence on which a reasonable bench of magistrates could convict. In other words, the submission should succeed if a conviction would be perverse, in the sense that no reasonable bench could convict.

Where the justices are minded to dismiss a case prior to the start of the defence case (whether following a submission of no case to answer by the defence or of their own motion), the prosecution should be given the opportunity to address the court to show why the case should not be dismissed (*R v Barking and Dagenham Justices ex p DPP* (1995) 159 JP 373). This means that the prosecution have the right to reply to the defence submission that there is no case to answer unless, having heard the defence submission, the magistrates decide to rule against the defence and they indicate this fact to the prosecutor. If the submission is successful, the defendant is acquitted. If it is unsuccessful, the trial continues.

An important question that arises in the context of submissions of no case to answer in the magistrates' court is the extent to which the justices may have regard to the credibility of prosecution witnesses when considering such a submission. In the Crown Court, the judge has to be careful not to trespass on the territory of the jury. The test to be applied by the judge when ruling on a submission of no case to answer is set out in

R v Galbraith [1981] 1 WLR 1039: is the prosecution evidence so tenuous that, even taken at its highest, a jury properly directed could not properly convict on it? The requirement that the Crown Court judge should 'take the prosecution evidence at its highest' is intended to leave questions of credibility to the jury. Thus, submissions of no case to answer based on the credibility of the prosecution evidence should only succeed in the Crown Court where the prosecution evidence is clearly incredible. In *R v Barking and Dagenham Justices ex p DPP*, the Divisional Court said that questions of credibility should, except in the clearest of cases, not normally be taken into account by justices considering a submission of no case to answer in the magistrates' court.

Nonetheless, some justices may well take the pragmatic view that it would be inappropriate for them to go through the motions of hearing defence evidence if they have already formed the view that the prosecution evidence is so unconvincing that they will not convict on it in any event. However, the general principle remains that, so long as the necessary minimum amount of prosecution evidence has been adduced so as to raise a case on which a reasonable tribunal could convict, the justices should allow the trial to run its course rather than acquitting on a submission of no case to answer.

There is no legal obligation on magistrates to give reasons for rejecting a submission of no case to answer (*Moran v DPP* [2002] EWHC 89; (2002) 166 JP 467).

If a submission of no case to answer is made by the defence, it should be made clear to the magistrates that evidence will be called if the submission is unsuccessful. This avoids confusion, since the magistrates might otherwise think that the defence have simply chosen to make a closing speech without calling any evidence.

5.10.9.1 Re-opening the prosecution case

In some cases, the deficiency in the prosecution case which is highlighted by the defence submission of no case to answer may be cured by allowing the prosecution to reopen their case, rather than upholding the submission of no case to answer and acquitting the accused. In *Hughes v DPP* [2003] EWHC 2470; (2003) 167 JP 589, it was said that when, on a submission of no case to answer, a point is raised which has no bearing on the merits of the prosecution, and the defect in the prosecution case is one of omission (and probably oversight), the advocate acting for the prosecution should request leave to recall the relevant witness to supplement the prosecution evidence. Stanley Burnton J added that, in such a case, the magistrates should normally exercise their discretion to permit the prosecution to reopen their case so that such evidence can be given, particularly where the fact in question is likely to be uncontroversial. Indeed, if necessary, the magistrates should consider inviting the prosecution to recall the relevant witness (see para 16). It is submitted that it may well be appropriate for the justices to allow the prosecution to reopen their case, and thus adduce evidence that was inadvertently omitted, even if the missing evidence does have a more direct bearing on the merits of the prosecution case. If the defect in the prosecution case is one that could be cured simply and speedily by allowing them to reopen their case and recall a witness, it may well be that the interests of justice require that the prosecution be given the chance to remedy the defect. It is difficult to see how the defendant would be prejudiced by this decision. However, if the reopening of the prosecution case would require an adjournment, and thus cause delay in the disposal of the case, the balance of the interests of justice might require that the submission should be upheld and the defendant acquitted.

In *Hughes*, his Lordship deprecated the use of submissions of no case to answer to ambush the prosecution. At para 16, he said:

> An acquittal in the present case would have been a fortuitous and unmeritorious windfall. Ambushes of the kind attempted in this case are to be discouraged and discountenanced. Criminal proceedings are not a game: their object is to achieve a fair determination of the innocence or guilt of the defendant.

A similar point was made in *R (DPP) v Chorley Justices and Andrew Forrest* [2006] EWHC 1795, where Thomas LJ (at para 26), gave a warning that the defence must raise issues as early as possible in the case:

> It is . . . clear that what should have happened is that at the first hearing of a case of this kind, after the entry of the plea of not guilty, the defendant should have been asked first what was in issue. At that stage and at the first hearing, he should then have been asked what witnesses did he need . . . If a defendant refuses to identify what the issues are, one thing is clear: he can derive no advantage from that or seek, as appears to have happened in this case, to attempt an ambush at trial. The days of ambushing and taking last-minute technical points are gone. They are not consistent with the overriding objective of deciding cases justly, acquitting the innocent and convicting the guilty.

His Lordship added (at para 27):

> The duty of the court is to see that justice is done. That does not involve allowing people to escape on technical points or by attempting, as happened here, an ambush. It involves the courts in looking at the real justice of the case and seeing whether the rules have been complied with by 'cards being put on the table' at the outset and the issues being clearly identified.

In *Tuck v Vehicle Inspectorate* [2004] EWHC 728 (Admin), the Divisional Court considered another case in which magistrates had permitted the prosecution to repair omissions in their evidence after they had closed their case, following a submission of no case to answer. MacKay J summarised the principles applicable as follows (at para 15):

(1)   The discretion to allow the case to be reopened is not limited to matters arising *ex improviso* [i.e. unexpectedly] or mere technicalities, but is a more 'general discretion'.

(2)   The exercise of this discretion should not be interfered with by a higher court unless its exercise was wrong in principle or perverse.

(3)   The general rule remains that the prosecution must finish its case once and for all and the test to be applied is narrower than consideration of whether the additional evidence would be of value to the tribunal. The discretion will only be exercised on the rarest of occasions.

(4)   The discretion must be exercised carefully having regard to the need to be fair to the

defendant, and giving consideration to the question of whether any prejudice to the defendant will be caused.

(5)   The courts have in the past differed as to whether the mere loss of a tactical advantage can constitute such prejudice.

(6)   Criminal procedure while adversarial, is not a game, and the overall interests of justice include giving effect to the requirement that a prosecution should not fail through inefficiency, carelessness or oversight.

(7)   Of particular significance is the consideration of whether there is any risk of prejudice to the defendant.

A further example of the prosecution seeking to re-open their case may be found in *Smith v DPP* [2008] EWHC 771 (Admin), where (following a submission of no case to answer) a district judge permitted the prosecution to recall their main witness. Dyson LJ (at para 5) said that 'Prosecuting authorities should not be encouraged to believe that they can re-open a case to adduce evidence which was available to them but which they did not adduce before a case was closed. Sloppiness would result if it were thought that omissions could routinely be made good by the Crown at a later stage in the proceedings. On the other hand, the interests of the defendant must be balanced against the public interest in ensuring that those who have committed crimes should be convicted'. However, his Lordship went on to hold that the judge's decision to allow the Crown to re-open their case was not a plainly wrong exercise of his discretion. The witness had already given evidence that the person who committed the offence was the accused, and the judge was entitled to permit the prosecution to strengthen their case by allowing the witness to give evidence to meet a point made in the course of the submission of no case to answer.

In *Steward v DPP* [2003] EWHC 2251; [2004] 1 WLR 592, the justices acceded to a submission of no case to answer, and gave reasons why they had done so. The prosecutor then pointed out that the reasons given by the magistrates contained an error of fact. The justices reviewed their decision and concluded that there *was* a case to answer. The defendant, who was subsequently convicted, appealed by way of case stated on the basis that the justices had been acting *functus officio* by proceeding to hear the case after reaching a finding of no case to answer. The Divisional Court said that the justices were entitled to reopen a case, despite having acceded to a submission of no case to answer, where an error had been identified by the prosecution and it had been agreed by the defendant that there was an error in the reasons given by the justices. In those circumstances, the process of adjudication had not been completed and the justices were not *functus officio*. The present case was said to be distinguishable from *R v Essex Justices ex p Final* [1963] 2 QB 816 (where it was held that justices should not reopen a case once they have reached their decision), as that case had been reopened in order to hear further submissions on the evidence whereas, in the present case, the justices had identified their error straightaway, admitted it and rectified it; also, the earlier case was decided at a time when it was less common for justices to give reasons for accepting a submission of no case to answer (and so errors in their reasoning were less likely to be immediately apparent).

5.10.10 The defendant's evidence

If a submission of no case to answer is not made (or is unsuccessful), the defence then have the opportunity to present evidence to the court. If the defendant is going to call other witnesses as well as giving evidence himself, the defendant should give evidence first unless the court otherwise directs (see s 79 of PACE).

If the defendant decides not to give evidence, he runs the risk that the magistrates will be entitled to draw adverse inferences from his silence under s 35 of the Criminal Justice and Public Order Act 1994. The magistrates should warn the defendant of the possible consequences of not testifying (this warning is required by s 35(2) of the Act). However, in *Radford v Kent County Council* (1998) 162 JP 697, the magistrates failed to warn the defendant that adverse inferences could be drawn if he failed to testify. In their stated case, the justices said that 'we drew no inferences whatsoever from the failure of the appellant to give evidence, but simply were aware that the evidence for the prosecution was not rebutted by evidence from or on behalf of the appellant'. The Divisional Court held that, in the circumstances, although the warning of the consequences of not testifying is very important, the failure to give the warning in the present case did not render the appellant's conviction unsafe.

The adverse inference provisions of the CJPOA 1994, s 34, also apply to summary trials where the accused has failed to mention when questioned matters on which he subsequently relies his defence. In *T v DPP* [2007] EWHC 1793 (Admin); (2007) 171 JP 605, the Court summarised the approach to be taken in a case where a magistrates' court is considering whether to draw adverse inferences in such a case. The justices should ask themselves three questions (per Hughes LJ at para 26):

(1) Has the defendant relied in his defence on a fact which he could reasonably have been expected to mention in his interview, but did not? If so, what is it?
(2) What is his explanation for not having mentioned it?
(3) If that explanation is not a reasonable one, is the proper inference to be drawn that he is guilty?

At the conclusion of the defence evidence, a closing speech may be made on behalf of the defendant, unless an opening speech was made on behalf of the accused, in which case the permission of the court is necessary before the defence may address the court for a second time, in which case the prosecution must be allowed to make a closing speech first if they wish to do so (r 37.1(4) and (5)).

5.10.11 Reopening the prosecution case after defence evidence has been called

Rule 37.1(3) of the Criminal Procedure Rules provides that, 'at the conclusion of the evidence, if any, for the defence, the prosecutor may call evidence to rebut that evidence'. In practice, this provision is used quite sparingly (see *Price v Humphries* [1958] 2 QB 353; *Hammond v Wilkinson* (2001) 165 JP 786). It can be used, for example, to deal with something that has arisen *ex improviso* – that is, something that could not reasonably have been foreseen – during the course of the defence case. It can also be used where the prosecution seek to adduce evidence that is intended to remedy a 'technical deficiency' in their case. However, the power to allow the prosecution to reopen their case can go beyond such technical difficulties. For example, in *James v South Glamorgan County Council* [1994] 99 Cr App R 321, the main prosecution witness had not arrived but the trial proceeded nonetheless; after the prosecution case had been closed and while the defendant was giving evidence, the witness arrived. It was accepted by the magistrates that the witness had a good reason for being late and the prosecution were allowed to call him as a witness. It was held by the Divisional Court that, since the evidence had not been available at the proper time and there was no unfairness to the defendant (there was no suggestion that the defendant's case would have been differently conducted had the witness' evidence been given timeously), the decision of the magistrates was correct. Similarly, in *Khatibi v DPP* [2004] EWHC 83; (2004) 168 JP 361, Nelson J said (at para 17) that the discretion to admit evidence after the close of the prosecution case is not confined to the well-established exceptions of rebuttal and mere formality. The discretion must, however, be exercised with great caution. The magistrates should bear in mind the strictly adversarial nature of the English criminal process, whereby the cases for the prosecution and the defence are presented consecutively in their entirety. The normal order of events should not be departed from substantially unless justice really demands such a course of action. In deciding whether to exercise their discretion to permit the calling of evidence after the close of the prosecution case, the magistrates must look carefully at the interests of justice overall, and in particular at the risk of any prejudice to the defendant (see para 18).

In *R (Lawson) v Stafford Magistrates' Court* [2007] EWHC 2490 (Admin), the defendant was charged with driving in excess of the speed limit. During his closing submissions, defence counsel raised for the first time the issues that the prosecution had to satisfy the court that the signs indicating the limit complied with the relevant Regulations and that the speed measuring device should be tested. The justices invited the prosecution to apply for the case to be adjourned part-heard so that these evidential issues could be addressed. The defendant contended that the justices erred in encouraging an adjournment. The Divisional Court said that the accused had sought to ambush the prosecution and the magistrates were entitled to adjourn the case to receive further evidence. Aikens J (at para 32) pointed out that, in a pre-trial hearing before magistrates, a defendant or his lawyer should be specifically asked what issues are being taken by the defendant. His Lordship went on to say (at para 34) that 'magistrates have a jurisdiction to adjourn a trial to permit the prosecution to rectify a deficiency in evidence which is only identified by the defence at a very late stage, after the close of the prosecution case'. His Lordship explained (at para 39) that

> the courts' power to allow a case to be re-opened is a power which must be exercised rarely and having regard to the need to be fair to the defendant. A court must bear in mind the question of whether any prejudice to the defendant will be caused by a case being re-opened. However those points do not detract from the legal proposition that justices are entitled to hear evidence after the case has been closed where special circumstances exist.

5.10.12 Making speeches in a summary trial

The making of speeches in a summary trial is governed by r 37.1 of the Criminal Procedure Rules, quoted earlier in this chapter.

The trial will usually begin with an opening speech by the prosecutor (unless the prosecutor waives his right to make an opening speech). Such speeches are generally very brief. Unlike a trial in the Crown Court, however, the prosecutor has no entitlement to make a closing speech.

The defence are entitled to make only one speech, and so they may make either an opening speech or a closing speech. Most defence advocates would invariably choose to make a closing speech, since that is the last chance to address the magistrates before they consider their verdict and it is useful to be able to draw together the threads of the defence case and to highlight any reasonable doubt in the prosecution case.

Rule 37.1(5) enables the court to give permission to either party to make a second speech. Thus, if the prosecutor wishes to make a closing speech or the defence wish to make a closing speech as well as an opening speech, an application must be made to the magistrates. Where one party is allowed to make a second speech, the other party must also be allowed to make a second speech. Where the case is a complex one, the justices may well allow both parties to make two speeches. Rule 37.1(6) stipulates that, where both parties address the court twice, the closing speech for the accused takes place after the closing speech for the prosecution. Thus, the defence always have the last word.

5.10.13 Hearing further evidence after the justices have retired to consider their verdict

In *Khatibi v DPP* [2004] EWHC 83; (2004) 168 JP 361, Nelson J pointed out (at para 20) that it has generally been accepted that an application to call further evidence cannot succeed after the bench has retired to consider its verdict. It is only in the rarest of cases that further evidence may be adduced once the justices have retired to consider their verdict. In *Webb v Leadbetter* [1966] 1 WLR 245, one of two prosecution witnesses failed to arrive. The one available witness was called. The prosecution case closed. The defendant gave evidence and his case closed. The justices had retired to consider their decision when they were informed that the second prosecution witness, whose car had broken down, had arrived. They returned to court and allowed the prosecution to call him. His evidence corroborated that of the first prosecution witness. The defendant was convicted. The Divisional Court held that, although justices have a discretion to allow further evidence to be called in particular circumstances, the manner of the exercise of that discretion depends on the stage of the case. In the absence of 'special circumstances' (per Lord Parker CJ) or even 'very special circumstances' (per Sachs J), they should not allow evidence to be called after they have retired. In the instant case, such circumstances were absent and so the further evidence had been wrongly admitted. This decision was followed in *R (Traves) v DPP* [2005] EWHC 1482; (2005) 169 JP 421, where the accused was charged with driving whilst disqualified. At the trial, the prosecution failed to produce the memorandum of conviction which was necessary in order to prove that the accused had been disqualified. The defence made a submission of no case to answer. The justices retired to consider their decision but, before they returned to court to announce their decision, they were informed that the prosecution now had the evidence that had been lacking. The prosecution sought, and were granted, leave to reopen their case. The prosecution produced evidence of the disqualification and the defendant was convicted. Bean J said that the moment of retiring to consider the decision is a critical point, after which only very special circumstances could allow further evidence to be called. In the instant case, there existed no such very special circumstances and so the conviction was quashed.

However, in *Malcolm v DPP* [2007] EWHC 363 (Admin); [2007] 1 WLR 1230, the Divisional Court took a broader of view of what would amount to 'special circumstances' enabling the case to be reopened even after the justices had retired to consider their verdict. The accused had been charged with driving with excess alcohol. In her final speech, defence counsel submitted that there had been no warning, as required by the relevant legislation, that a failure to provide a specimen might render the accused liable to prosecution and that, accordingly, there was no admissible evidence of the analysis of alcohol in her breath. The magistrates retired to consider the submissions. They returned to court and gave their conclusions that the case would have to be dismissed because of the lack of admissible evidence of the proportion of alcohol in the appellant's breath. Before they formally dismissed the case, however, counsel for the prosecution requested leave to recall the officer in charge of the breath test procedure to establish that the required warning had been given. The Divisional Court reiterated the test established by *Webb v Leadbetter*, that special circumstances are required before they can receive further evidence after they have retired to consider their verdict. Stanley Burnton J said (at para 31):

> [Counsel for the appellant's] submissions, which emphasised the obligation of the prosecution to prove its case in its entirety before closing its case, and certainly before end of the final speech for the defence, had an anachronistic, and obsolete, ring. Criminal trials are no longer to be treated as a game, in which each move is final and any omission by the prosecution leads to its failure. It is the duty of the defence to make its defence and the issues it raises clear to the prosecution and to the court at an early stage ... Even in a relatively straightforward trial such as the present, in the magistrates' court (where there is not yet any requirement of a defence statement or a pre-trial review), it is the duty of the defence to make the real issues clear at the latest before the prosecution closes its case. In *R v Pydar Justices ex p Foster* [1995] 160 JP 87 at 90B Curtis J commented on the submission that a defending advocate was entitled to 'keep his powder dry'. He said:
>
> > 'Without any doubt whatsoever, it is the duty of a defending advocate properly to lay the ground for a submission, either by cross examination or, if appropriate, by calling evidence.'
>
> That was not done in this case.

The court concluded that there were, therefore, special circumstances entitling the magistrates to allow the case to be reopened. Moreover Stanley Burnton J added (at para 30) that 'I respectfully disagree with the decision of Bean J in *Traves*. In my judgment it was wrongly decided'. His Lordship appears to be saying that Bean J should have decided that the facts in that case did, in fact, disclose 'special circumstances'.

The position in magistrates' courts may be contrasted with the rule applicable in the Crown Court that, once a jury has retired to consider its verdict, no further evidence may be adduced before them (see *R v Owen* [1952] QB 362).

5.10.14 Change of plea

The magistrates have a discretion to allow a defendant to change his plea from guilty to not guilty at any stage before sentence is passed (*S (An Infant) v Recorder of Manchester* [1971] AC 481). Lord Upjohn, at p 507, observed that 'this discretionary power is one which should only be exercised in clear cases and very sparingly'. The question for the magistrates is whether the original plea was unequivocal and entered with a proper understanding of what the charge entailed. If the offence is triable either-way and the defendant is allowed to change his plea to one of not guilty, he should also be allowed to reconsider his consent to summary trial (*R v Bow Street Magistrates ex p Welcombe* (1992) 156 JP 609). Similarly, the magistrates can allow a defendant to change his plea from not guilty to guilty at any time before a verdict is returned.

In *Revitt v DPP* [2006] EWHC 2266 (Admin); [2006] 1 WLR 3172, the court observed that the onus lies on a party seeking to vacate a guilty plea to demonstrate that justice requires that this should be permitted. If, after an unequivocal plea of guilty, it becomes apparent that the defendant did not appreciate the elements of the offence to which he was pleading guilty, it is likely to be appropriate to permit him to withdraw his plea. Where the facts relied upon by the prosecution do not add up to the offence charged, justice will normally demand that the defendant be permitted to withdraw his plea.

The procedure for seeking to change plea from guilty to not guilty is set out in r 37.6 of the Criminal Procedure Rules, which provides as follows:

(1) The defendant must apply as soon as practicable after becoming aware of the grounds for making an application to change a plea of guilty, and may only do so before the final disposal of the case, by sentence or otherwise.

(2) Unless the court otherwise directs, the application must be in writing and it must—

  (a) set out the reasons why it would be unjust for the guilty plea to remain unchanged;
  (b) indicate what, if any, evidence the defendant wishes to call;
  (c) identify any proposed witness; and
  (d) indicate whether legal professional privilege is waived, specifying any material name and date.

(3) The defendant must serve the written application on—

  (a) the court officer; and
  (b) the prosecutor.

5.10.15 Seeing the magistrates in private

It is open to the justices to hear representations from the parties in private, but they should do so only in exceptional cases. Steps must be taken to ensure that all parties are aware of the private hearing and are represented at it. The clerk must take a contemporaneous note of the hearing (see *R v Nottingham Justices ex p Furnell* (1995) 160 JP 201).

5.10.16 The risk of bias

Unless there are special circumstances, making an interlocutory ruling on the admissibility of evidence does not deprive magistrates of the ability to continue the hearing of the trial (*R v Stipendiary Magistrate for Norfolk ex p Taylor* (1997) 161 JP 773). Therefore, magistrates should not normally disqualify themselves from hearing a trial merely because they have ruled in favour of an application by the prosecution for non-disclosure of material on the ground of public interest immunity (*R (DPP) v Acton Youth Court* [2001] EWHC 402 (Admin); [2001] 1 WLR 1828, expressly approved in *R v H* [2004] UKHL 3; [2004] 2 AC 134). Likewise in *KL and LK v DPP* [2001] EWHC 1112 (Admin); (2002) 166 JP 369, the prosecution made an application for the use of screens in relation to a prosecution witness, on the grounds that she would feel intimidated having to give evidence in the defendant's presence. The question to be decided was whether the justices should withdraw from the case after hearing the application. It was held that there is no objection in principle to justices hearing a case after having heard an application for the use of screens.

Section 42 of the Magistrates' Courts Act 1980 provides that a magistrate may not be a member of the court which tries an accused on a not guilty plea if he has, in the same proceedings, been informed (for the purpose of determining whether or not bail should be granted) that the accused has one or more previous convictions. This section is repealed by the Criminal Justice Act 2003, but this repeal has not yet been brought into effect and so s 42 remains in force. It is submitted that this must be an oversight. The fact that previous convictions may be admissible in the range of circumstances set out in ss 101 to 106 of the Criminal Justice Act 2003 makes it unlikely that knowledge of previous convictions should be sufficient to disqualify a magistrate from hearing a case. Moreover, it is arguable that a conviction would not necessarily be rendered invalid if a magistrate to whom s 42 applies was sitting. This argument would be strengthened by the approach taken in *R v Ashton* [2006] EWCA Crim 794; [2007] 1 WLR 181, where the key question in the case of procedural failures was held to be whether Parliament intended the proceedings to be invalidated by a procedural irregularity.

5.10.17 'Special measures' directions

An application can be made under s 19 of the Youth Justice and Criminal Evidence Act 1999 for special measures:

a   screening the witness from the defendant (s 23);
b   giving evidence by live link (s 24), although this provision will become less relevant as s 51 of the Criminal Justice Act 2003 (when in force), will enable a court to authorise witnesses, other than the defendant, to give evidence through a live link in criminal proceedings;
c   giving evidence in private, in a sexual case, or where there is a fear that the witness may be intimidated (s 25);
d   video recording of evidence-in-chief (s 27) – again, this provision will be made less relevant once s 137 of the Criminal Justice Act 2003 extends the circumstances in which evidence-in-chief can take the form of a video-recorded statement;

e   video recording of cross-examination and re-examination where the evidence-in-chief of the witness has been video recorded (s 28);

f   examination through an intermediary in the case of a young or incapacitated witness (s 29);

g   provision of aids to communication to enable the witness to testify despite any disability, disorder, or other impairment (s 30).

Part 8 of the Criminal Justice Act 2003 (not in force at the time of writing) extends the circumstances where 'live links' can be used to enable a witness other than a defendant to testify from a remote location.

These measures are also applicable in the Crown Court, and are dealt with fully in Chapter 11.

In *R (D) v Camberwell Green Youth Court* [2005] UKHL 4; [2005] 1 WLR 393, the House of Lords held that the use of live links, or video recording of testimony, is compliant with Art 6 of the ECHR. Their Lordships reasoned that the accused can see and hear all the evidence produced at the trial and has every opportunity to challenge and question the witnesses against him at the trial itself; the Convention does not guarantee a right to a face-to-face confrontation.

In *R (S) v Waltham Forest Youth Court* [2004] EWHC 715 (Admin); [2004] 2 Cr App R 21, the accused (who was aged 13) wanted to testify in her own defence but said that she was too scared to do so because of the physical presence in court of her co-defendants. The Divisional Court held that there is no power to make a special measures direction under the 1999 Act, or under the common law, in relation to the evidence of the accused. However, the effect of this case has been reversed to the extent that one special measure (namely, testifying via a 'live link') *is* now available for the accused under s 33A of the Youth Justice and Criminal Evidence Act 1999 (in force from January 2007).

5.10.18 Fitness to plead

In *R (P) v Barking Youth Court* [2002] EWHC 734; [2002] 2 Cr App R 19, the defendant was 16 years old and was to be tried in a youth court. His solicitor raised the issue of fitness to plead. It was held that, in the case of offences to be tried summarily, s 37(3) of the Mental Health Act 1983 (hospital orders and guardianship orders) and s 11(1) of the Powers of Criminal Courts (Sentencing) Act 2000 (which provides that if, on the trial of an offence punishable on summary conviction with imprisonment, the court is satisfied that the accused did the act or made the omission charged, but is of the opinion that an inquiry ought to be made into his physical or mental condition before the method of dealing with him is determined, the court must adjourn the case to enable a medical examination and report to be made) together provide a statutory framework for all the issues that arise in cases of defendants who are (or might be) mentally ill or suffering from severe mental impairment. In *R (Singh) v Stratford Magistrates' Court* [2007] EWHC 1582 (Admin); [2007] 1 WLR 3119, the Divisional Court observed that s 37(3) of the Mental Health Act 1983 provides the magistrates' court with the power, in an appropriate case, to abstain from either convicting or acquitting, but instead to make a hospital order. Rather than determining the issue of fitness to plead, as would happen in the Crown Court, the magistrates should first determine the factual question whether the defendant had done the act or made the omission charged, and then consider whether a s 37(3) order might be appropriate (adjourning for reports for that purpose).

Fitness to plead is dealt with more fully in the context of Crown Court trial.

5.11 THE ROLE OF THE CLERK/COURT LEGAL ADVISER

Whereas a lay justice receives only a very small amount of legal training, their clerk/court legal adviser is a qualified lawyer. The functions of the clerk are set out in s 28 of the Courts Act 2003 and in para V.55 of the *Consolidated Practice Direction*. Section 28 of the Courts Act 2003 says that:

(4)   The functions of a justices' clerk include giving advice to any or all of the justices of the peace to whom he is clerk about matters of law (including procedure and practice) on questions arising in connection with the discharge of their functions, including questions arising when the clerk is not personally attending on them.

(5)   The powers of a justices' clerk include, at any time when he thinks he should do so, bringing to the attention of any or all of the justices of the peace to whom he is clerk any point of law (including procedure and practice) that is or may be involved in any question so arising.

Paragraph V.55 of the *Practice Direction* states as follows:

V.55.1 A justices' clerk is responsible for:

(a)   the legal advice tendered to the justices within the area;
(b)   the performance of any of the functions set out below by any member of his staff acting as legal adviser;
(c)   ensuring that competent advice is available to justices when the justices' clerk is not personally present in court; and
(d)   the effective delivery of case management and the reduction of unnecessary delay.

V.55.2 Where a person other than the justices' clerk (a 'legal adviser'), who is authorised to do so, performs any of the functions referred to in this direction he will have the same responsibilities as the justices' clerk. The legal adviser may consult the justices' clerk or other person authorised by the justices' clerk for that purpose before tendering advice to the bench. If the justices' clerk or that person gives any advice directly to the bench, he should give the parties or their advocates an opportunity of repeating any relevant submissions prior to the advice being given.

V.55.3 It shall be the responsibility of the legal adviser to provide the justices with any advice they require properly to perform their functions, whether or not the justices have requested that advice, on:

(a)   questions of law (including European Court of Human Rights jurisprudence and those matters set out in section 2(1) of the Human Rights Act 1998);
(b)   questions of mixed law and fact;
(c)   matters of practice and procedure;

(d)   the range of penalties available;

(e)   any relevant decisions of the superior courts or other guidelines;

(f)   other issues relevant to the matter before the court; and

(g)   the appropriate decision-making structure to be applied in any given case.

In addition to advising the justices it shall be the legal adviser's responsibility to assist the court, where appropriate, as to the formulation of reasons and the recording of those reasons.

V.55.4 A justices' clerk or legal adviser must not play any part in making findings of fact, but may assist the bench by reminding them of the evidence, using any notes of the proceedings for this purpose.

V.55.5 A justices' clerk or legal adviser may ask questions of witnesses and the parties in order to clarify the evidence and any issues in the case. A legal adviser has a duty to ensure that every case is conducted fairly.

V.55.6 When advising the justices the justices' clerk or legal adviser, whether or not previously in court, should:

(a)   ensure that he is aware of the relevant facts; and

(b)   provide the parties with the information necessary to enable the parties to make any representations they wish as to the advice before it is given.

V.55.7 At any time justices are entitled to receive advice to assist them in discharging their responsibilities. If they are in any doubt as to the evidence which has been given, they should seek the aid of their legal adviser, referring to his notes as appropriate. This should ordinarily be done in open court. Where the justices request their adviser to join them in the retiring room, this request should be made in the presence of the parties in court. Any legal advice given to the justices other than in open court should be clearly stated to be provisional and the adviser should subsequently repeat the substance of the advice in open court and give the parties an opportunity to make any representations they wish on that provisional advice. The legal adviser should then state in open court whether the provisional advice is confirmed or if it is varied the nature of the variation.

V.55.8 The performance of a legal adviser may be appraised by a person authorised by the magistrates' courts committee to do so. For that purpose the appraiser may be present in the justices' retiring room. The content of the appraisal is confidential, but the fact that an appraisal has taken place, and the presence of the appraiser in the retiring room, should be briefly explained in open court.

V.55.9 The legal adviser is under a duty to assist unrepresented parties to present their case, but must do so without appearing to become an advocate for the party concerned.

V.55.10 The role of legal advisers in fine default proceedings or any other proceedings for the enforcement of financial orders, obligations or penalties is to assist the court. They must not act in an adversarial or partisan manner. With the agreement of the justices a legal adviser may ask questions of the defaulter to elicit information which the justices will require to make an adjudication, for example to facilitate his explanation for the default. A legal adviser may also advise the justices in the normal way as to the options open to them in dealing with the case. It would be inappropriate for the legal adviser to set out to establish wilful refusal or neglect or any other type of culpable behaviour, to offer an opinion on the facts, or to urge a particular course of action upon the justices. The duty of impartiality is the paramount consideration for the legal adviser at all times, and this takes precedence over any role he may have as a collecting officer. The appointment of other staff to 'prosecute' the case for the collecting officer is not essential to ensure compliance with the law, including the Human Rights Act 1998. Whether to make such appointments is a matter for the justices' chief executive.

The role of the clerk or court legal adviser is to advise on law, practice and procedure. Since the magistrates are the ultimate arbiters of both law and fact there is no obligation on them to adopt the clerk's advice on law, but it is accepted practice that they should in fact do so. Thus, in *Jones v Nicks* [1977] RTR 72 at 76, Lord Widgery CJ strongly criticised magistrates for rejecting the clerk's advice: 'Justices really must accept legal advice from their clerk in circumstances like this; if they do not, all that happens is that a great deal of time and money is wasted in bringing the matter up here to be put right.' If the clerk forms the view that the justices are wrong, however, he has no power to ignore their order and treat it as a nullity (*R v Liverpool Magistrates' Court ex p Abiaka* (1999) 163 JP 497). In those circumstances, he should put the matter before the same bench, or a different bench if the original bench is unavailable, so that they can consider his fresh legal advice and alter the original order, or he should arrange for the matter to go to the Crown Court or the High Court.

The importance of note-taking was emphasised in *L v CPS* [2007] EWHC 1843 (Admin); (2007) 171 JP 635. Collins J (at para 27) said that 'it is desirable that a note should be taken by someone – whether the clerk or someone deputised by the clerk – which is capable of being used as a formal note of the evidence if there is any later dispute as to what was or was not said in the course of evidence at the hearing'. Auld LJ (at para 37) echoed this, saying:

> It is clearly important that adequate notes are made, even in comparatively minor cases . . . going, albeit briefly, to the basis upon which the prosecution case is opened, the salient features of the evidence on both sides, and to any submissions as to law . . .

When a point of law arises during the course of proceedings, any advice given by the clerk to the magistrates should be given publicly in open court, so that the prosecution and defence can make submissions to the bench on that advice. In *R v Chichester Justices ex p DPP* [1994] RTR 175, it was said that, if the clerk who advises the justices is not the clerk who was present in court when the parties made their submissions on the point of law at issue, it is essential that the clerk should hear informal submissions on the relevant law from the parties before advising the justices.

Advice on law will include advice on the elements of the offence(s) charged and on questions of admissibility of evidence. So far as sentencing is concerned, the clerk should be careful not to go beyond advising on the range of penalties available and any relevant guidelines (whether from case law or from the Sentencing Guidelines Council); he should certainly not advocate a certain type of disposal, as this would be to interfere with a decision which is for the bench alone.

Paragraph V.55.4 of the *Consolidated Criminal Practice Direction* makes it clear the clerk or legal adviser must play no part in making findings of fact; such questions are solely for the magistrates. It follows that the clerk should not say whether or not he believes a particular witness. See, for example, *R v Stafford Justices ex p Ross* [1962] 1 WLR 456, where the conviction was quashed because, while the accused was giving evidence in his own defence, the clerk handed the bench a note which, in effect, suggested that the defendant's evidence ought not to be believed.

The clerk should not leave the court room with the justices when they retire to consider their verdict. If the magistrates require assistance from the clerk, he should join them only when asked to do so and should return to the court room once the advice has been given, so as to avoid giving the impression that he is participating improperly in the decision-making process. In *R v Eccles Justices ex p Farrelly* (1993) 157 JP 77, when the justices retired to consider their decision, the clerk left the courtroom and did not return until the justices had reassembled and were about to deliver their verdict; the clerk then spoke to the justices and went with them when they retired for a second time to reconsider their verdict. The Divisional Court said that the clerk's conduct had been such that a reasonable defendant or bystander might have concluded that the clerk had been participating in the decision-making process, and the convictions were quashed.

Where the justices request their adviser to join them in the retiring room, this request should be made in the presence of the parties in court. Paragraph V.55.7 of the *Consolidated Practice Direction* stipulates that any legal advice given to the justices in their retiring room should be regarded as provisional, and the adviser should then repeat the substance of the advice in open court and give the parties an opportunity to make representations on the correctness of that provisional advice; the legal adviser should state in open court whether the provisional advice is confirmed or if he has varied it (and, if so, how). The same point was made in *Clark v Kelly* [2004] 1 AC 681 (a case which concerned the role of the clerk to the justices in the district court (the Scottish equivalent of the magistrates' court)), where the Privy Council said that, subject to these safeguards, the role of the clerk is compatible with the defendant's right to a fair trial under Art 6 of the European Convention on Human Rights. However, it is submitted that this procedure may legitimately not be followed if the substance of the clerk's advice is simply repeating advice he has already given in open court, and on which the parties have already had the chance to make submissions. However, if the clerk advises the justices after they have retired to consider their decision and the clerk cites authority which was not cited in open court, he should inform the advocates in the case and give them the opportunity to make further submissions to the magistrates (*W v W* (1993) *The Times*, 4 June).

In *R (Murchison) v Southend Magistrates' Court* [2006] EWHC 569; (2006) 170 JP 230, the justices had retired to consider their verdict. They reached their decision and then invited the court legal adviser to assist in the compilation of reasons. After the legal adviser had done so, she informed the justices of the defendant's previous convictions. The justices then returned to court and gave their verdict. The defendant was convicted. Immediately afterwards, the justices announced that they had seen the defendant's previous convictions and were minded to adjourn sentence for a pre-sentence report. Judicial review of the conviction was sought on the ground that the justices had been made aware of the defendant's past before they had announced their decision in open court. The Divisional Court dismissed the appeal because the magistrates had not known of the defendant's previous convictions until after they had concluded their deliberations and had reached a reasoned decision. However, it was said that, as a matter of procedure, 'no advice should be offered by a legal adviser, provisional or otherwise, on sentence until the magistrates have returned to court, announced their decision on conviction, heard about the accused's antecedents and listened to counsel's submissions' (per Hallett LJ at para 20). The court added that 'legal advisers should only attend upon the bench . . . when called upon to do so; and then only to assist with matters arising at that stage' and that (given the possibility in the present case that the legal adviser went into the retiring room with a copy of the appellant's previous convictions in her hand) legal advisers should ensure that any such documentation is left elsewhere when they retire to give the justices legal advice (ibid at para 21).

Where the accused is unrepresented, the clerk may assist the defendant by asking any necessary questions of prosecution witnesses (although the clerk should not assume the role of defence counsel and cross-examine the prosecution witnesses). In *Simms v Moore* [1970] 2 QB 327 at 332, Lord Parker CJ gave the following guidance:

(1) In general neither the court nor the justices' clerk should take an active part in the proceedings except to clear up ambiguities in the evidence.

(2) So far as examining witnesses is concerned, this should never be done if the party concerned is legally represented . . . Nor . . . should this be done where a party, even though unrepresented, is competent to and desires to examine the witnesses himself.

(3) Where an unrepresented party is not competent, through a lack of knowledge of court procedure or rules of evidence or otherwise, to examine the witnesses properly, the court can at its discretion permit the clerk to do so.

(4) When this is permitted, there is no reason why the clerk should not do so by reference to a proof of evidence or statement handed in to him, provided always that an opportunity is given to the other side to see it or to have a copy.

(5) Where notes of evidence have to be or are taken, care should be taken not to use the proof or statement as the basis of the notes. The best course is for it to be arranged that someone else, possibly a member of the court itself, should take the note.

(6) Generally, the discretion in the court should be so exercised that examination of witnesses by the clerk should only be permitted when there are reasonable grounds for thinking that thereby the interests of justice would be best promoted, care being taken to see that nothing is done which conflicts with the rules of natural justice or the principle that justice must manifestly be seen to be done.

Thus, it is common practice for clerks to explain to an unrepresented defendant the purpose of cross-examination and, if the defendant himself still seems incapable of doing it properly, to frame suitable questions on his behalf. Moreover, under r 37.2 (1) of the Criminal Procedure Rules, the court must explain to an unrepresented defendant the substance of the charge in simple language. Rule 37.2(2) states that if the defendant, instead of asking questions in cross-examination, makes assertions, then the court should put any necessary questions to the witness on his behalf and may for this purpose question the defendant in order to bring out or clear up any point arising out of such assertions. Both of these functions are in practice usually discharged by the clerk. At the close of the prosecution case, the clerk will also inform the defendant of his right to give and call evidence if he so wishes.

5.12 THE DECISION OF THE JUSTICES

Usually, there are three lay magistrates. Their decision (whether to acquit or to convict) is by simple majority. The decision is announced in open court by the chairman. He does not state whether it is unanimous or by a majority. The chairman does not have a second or casting vote. If only two lay justices hear a case but cannot agree on a verdict, they have no option but to adjourn the case for retrial in front of a bench with three justices (*R v Redbridge Justices ex p Ram* [1992] QB 384).

In reaching their decision on a question of fact, it is open to magistrates to use their personal local knowledge, but they should inform the prosecution and the defence that they are doing so, so that those representing the parties have the opportunity of commenting upon the knowledge which the justices claim to have (*Bowman v DPP* [1991] RTR 263; *Norbrook Laboratories (GB) Ltd v Health and Safety Executive* [1998] EHLR 207). Thus, in *Gibbons v DPP* (2000, QBD, 12 December, unreported) the appellants were charged with assault. They said they had been acting in self-defence. An eye-witness gave evidence that she was 25 yards from the fight and that the appellants were responsible. After the closing speeches had been made, the District Judge had cause to visit the place where the alleged offence had occurred. While there, he checked the site of the assault, the distance the witness was located from the attack and whether her view would have been obstructed. The Divisional Court held that those were all critical issues at the trial. At the very least, the magistrate should have informed the parties of his intention of taking a view, so that they could have had the opportunity to make submissions as to where the witness had actually been located. It followed that, in the circumstances, there had been a defect in the trial process; the convictions were quashed and a retrial ordered.

Where the defendant is convicted the magistrates have to give brief reasons for their decision. In *McKerry v Teesdale & Wear Valley Justices* (2000) 164 JP 355, Lord Bingham said (at para 23):

> . . . justices are not obliged to state reasons in the form of a judgment or to give reasons in any elaborate form . . . It is not usual for magistrates to give detailed reasons . . . If an aggrieved party wishes to obtain more detailed reasons from a magistrates' court, then a request can be made to state a case . . .

In *R (McGowan) v Brent Justices* [2001] EWHC Admin 814; (2002) 166 JP 29, the Divisional Court confirmed that *McKerry v Teesdale & Wear Valley Justices* is still good law following the coming into force of the Human Rights Act 1998 and that, in a summary trial, it is enough for justices to indicate the basis of their decision without stating their reasons in the form of a judgment or giving reasons in any elaborate form. Tuckey LJ said (at para 18) that 'the essence of the exercise in a criminal case such as this is to inform the defendant why he has been found guilty. That can usually be done in a few simple sentences'.

5.12.1 Alternative verdicts

Whereas a jury can sometimes convict the defendant of a lesser offence even though that offence is not on the indictment (for example, theft instead of robbery) under s 3 of the Criminal Law Act 1967 (see Chapter 12), the magistrates have no such power (*Lawrence v Same* [1968] 2 QB 93). In that case, a conviction for common assault on a charge alleging unlawful wounding was set aside by the Divisional Court because it was in excess of jurisdiction.

However, there are certain statutory exceptions to this rule, such as the power to convict of careless driving instead of dangerous driving (see s 24 of the Road Traffic Offenders Act 1988) and the power to convict of taking a vehicle without the owner's consent instead of aggravated vehicle taking (see s 24A(5) of the Theft Act 1968). In *R (H) v Liverpool City Youth Court* [2001] Crim LR 487, the Divisional Court rejected the argument that the power to convict of the lesser offence under s 12A(5) was confined to the Crown Court.

Otherwise, if the prosecution wish the justices to consider alternative offences, those offences must be charged separately. The charges can then be tried together. If the defendant only faces one charge to begin with, but the prosecution want the court to have the power to convict the defendant of a different offence, the defendant has to be 'further charged' with the other offence. This course of action will be appropriate if the defendant is willing to plead guilty to an offence which is less serious than that originally charged and the prosecution are willing to accept that plea and drop the more serious charge. If the defendant is charged with alternative offences at the outset and pleads not guilty to both, and the magistrates convict the defendant of the more serious of the two offences, the magistrates should either adjourn the other charge *sine die* (that is, with no date being set, the understanding being that the defendant will hear no more of that charge) or else convict the defendant of the lesser offence too and impose only a nominal penalty in respect of it (*DPP v Gane* (1991) 155 JP 846 and *R (CPS) v Blaydon Youth Court* (2004) 168 JP 638).

5.12.2 Setting aside conviction or sentence

Section 142 of the Magistrates' Courts Act 1980 provides as follows:

(1) A magistrates' court may vary or rescind a sentence or other order imposed or made by it when dealing with an offender if it appears to the court to be in the interests of justice to do so; and it is hereby declared that this power extends to replacing a sentence or order which for any reason appears to be invalid by another which the court has power to impose or make.

. . .

(2) Where a person is convicted by a magistrates' court and it subsequently appears to the court that it would be in the interests of justice that the case should be heard again by different justices, the court may so direct.

. . .

(3) Where a court gives a direction under sub-section (2) above—

    (a) the conviction and any sentence or other order imposed or made in consequence thereof shall be of no effect;

. . .

> (5) Where a sentence or order is varied under sub-section (1) above, the sentence or other order, as so varied, shall take effect from the beginning of the day on which it was originally imposed or made, unless the court otherwise directs.

Section 142(2) of the Magistrates' Courts Act 1980 thus enables a defendant who was convicted in the magistrates' court (whether he pleaded guilty or was found guilty) to ask the magistrates to set the conviction aside. This application can be considered by the same magistrates who convicted the defendant or by a different bench. If the conviction is set aside, the case is reheard by different magistrates from those who convicted the defendant. An application under s 142(2) may be appropriate if, for example, the magistrates made an error of law or there was some defect in the procedure which led to the conviction. In *R v Croydon Youth Court ex p DPP* [1997] 2 Cr App R 411 (at p 416), McCowan LJ said that the purpose of s 142(2) is most accurately described as a 'power to rectify mistakes', and that it is generally and correctly regarded as a 'slip rule' (i.e. enabling the court to correct minor errors).

Section 142(1) of the Magistrates' Courts Act 1980 empowers a magistrates' court to vary or rescind a sentence if it is in the interests of justice to do so. Again, this power may be exercised by a different bench from that which passed the original sentence. The main use of this power is to remedy the situation where an illegal sentence is inadvertently passed on an offender.

The magistrates can reopen the case under s 142 regardless of whether the defendant pleaded guilty or was found guilty. However, s 142 cannot operate where the defendant was acquitted (see *Coles v East Penwith Justices* (1998) 162 JP 687, where the prosecution had withdrawn the charges and the Divisional Court held that there was no power under s 142(1) to rescind the defendant's costs order which had been made).

In *R v Dewsbury Magistrates ex p K* (1994) *The Times*, 16 March, the defendant (who was aware that the case was due to be heard) was convicted in his absence. His failure to attend court was not intentional. He sought a rehearing but the justices refused. This refusal was quashed by the Divisional Court, which said that any inconvenience to the court or to the prosecution should not outweigh the right of the defendant to have an opportunity of defending himself. Similarly in *R (Morsby) v Tower Bridge Magistrates' Court* [2007] EWHC 2766 (Admin); (2008) 172 JP 155, the defendant had been remanded in custody and so failed to attend his trial for another offence, of which he was convicted in his absence. He applied under s 142 to rescind his conviction and reopen the trial, but the magistrates' court refused. The Divisional Court held that the magistrates' court had placed substantially too much weight on the defendant's failure to communicate with the court from prison. The interests of justice clearly required the rescission of the claimant's conviction and a retrial in his presence.

However, in *R v Newport Magistrates' Court ex p Carey* (1996) 160 JP 613, the Divisional Court held that magistrates have a broad discretion in deciding whether or not to reopen a case under s 142. They are entitled to have regard to the fact that the defendant failed to attend the original hearing through his own fault and that witnesses would be inconvenienced if a retrial were to be ordered. Henry LJ also said that the magistrates were entitled to take account of the apparent strength of the prosecution case, although little weight should be given to it, since an apparently strong case can collapse during the course of a trial. His Lordship also pointed out that the magistrates, by refusing to reopen the case, were not 'finally shutting out the defendant from the judgment seat' because he still had his unfettered right of appeal to the Crown Court.

In *R (Holme) v Liverpool Justices* [2004] EWHC 3131 (Admin); (2005) 169 JP 306, the defendant pleaded guilty to dangerous driving; a pedestrian had sustained serious injuries. A community sentence was imposed. The CPS applied to reopen the case under s 142 on the basis the original counsel for the prosecution had not addressed the extent of the pedestrian's injuries and that the difference between the sentence imposed and the custodial sentence that it would probably have imposed had it known all the facts offended the principles of justice. On appeal to the Divisional Court, Collins J (at para 30) said that:

> the power under s 142 is to be used in a relatively limited situation, namely one which is akin to mistake or, as the court says, the slip rule. But there is no reason, on the face of it, to limit it further. It seems to me that if a court has been misled into imposing a particular sentence, and it is discovered that it has been so misled, then the sentence may properly be said to have been imposed because of a mistake; the mistake being the failure of the court to appreciate a relevant fact. That may well give power to the court to exercise the jurisdiction conferred by s 142, but it does not indicate that that power should necessarily be used.

At paras 42–43, his Lordship said that it is:

> possible to envisage circumstances where the failure of the court to be aware of such material factors could properly mean that there could be resort to s 142 [but] it would only be in very rare circumstances that it would be appropriate to resort to s 142 to consider an increase in sentence, particularly if that increase . . . brought the possibility of custody as opposed to another form of disposal.

The facts of the instant case, said the Court, did not come anywhere near justifying such a use of s 142.

There is no time limit within which applications for the setting aside of a conviction or sentence under s 142 must be made. However, where a defendant applies under s 142(2) for the trial to be reheard, delay in making the application is a relevant consideration for the magistrates in deciding whether or not to grant that application (*R v Ealing Magistrates' Court ex p Sahota* (1998) 162 JP 73).

5.13 COMMITTAL FOR SENTENCE

Even if a defendant is tried and convicted by a magistrates' court, he may still in certain circumstances be sentenced by the Crown Court.

5.13.1 Section 3 of the Powers of Criminal Courts (Sentencing) Act 2000

The first type of committal for sentence is under s 3 of the Powers of Criminal Courts (Sentencing) Act 2000, which applies where a defendant is convicted in a magistrates' court of an offence which is triable either way. The effect of a committal under s 3 is that the defendant will be sentenced by the Crown Court, whose sentencing powers are greater than those of the magistrates' court. Section 3 currently provides as follows:

(1) . . . this section applies where on the summary trial of an offence triable either way a person aged 18 or over is convicted of the offence.

(2) If the court is of the opinion—

  (a) that the offence or the combination of the offence and one or more offences associated with it was so serious that greater punishment should be inflicted for the offence than the court has power to impose, or

  . . .

  the court may commit the offender in custody or on bail to the Crown Court for sentence in accordance with section 5(1) below.

(3) Where the court commits a person under sub-section (2) above, section 6 below (which enables a magistrates' court, where it commits a person under this section in respect of an offence, also to commit him to the Crown Court to be dealt with in respect of certain other offences) shall apply accordingly.

  . . .

By virtue of para 8 of Sched 13 to the Criminal Justice and Immigration Act 2008, s 3(2)(a) of the 2000 Act will be re-worded so that it reads:

that the offence or the combination of the offence and one or more offences associated with it was so serious that the Crown Court should, in the court's opinion, have the power to deal with the offender in any way it could deal with him if he had been convicted on indictment.

This amendment does not alter the overall effect of s 3(2)(a) but relates the wording more closely to s 5 of the 2000 Act, which empowers the Crown Court (following a committal under s 3) to sentence the offender as if he had just been convicted following trial on indictment in the Crown Court.

Where the magistrates convict the defendant but take the view that their sentencing powers are inadequate, they can thus commit the defendant to the Crown Court to be sentenced (by virtue of s 3(2)(a)). Usually, this test is taken to mean that committal for sentence is appropriate where the justices think that more than six months' custody is appropriate (or 12 months if they are dealing with two or more either-way offences). However, in *R v Chelmsford Justices ex p Lloyd* [2001] 2 Cr App R(S) 15, the defendant pleaded guilty to an either-way offence. The justices decided that a custodial sentence was inappropriate. They wished to impose a fine, but felt that a fine in excess of their powers (limited to £5,000 per offence in the case of either-way offences) was appropriate. Accordingly, they committed the defendant to the Crown Court to be sentenced.

The Divisional Court held that there is no reason why justices cannot commit for sentence if they are of the opinion that, while imprisonment would not be appropriate, the offence merits a larger fine than they have the power to impose.

Where the defendant is committed for sentence, there is no presumption in favour of bail, as s 4 of the Bail Act 1976 does not apply. The committal may be on bail or in custody (s 3(1)); it is usually in custody, since the defendant faces a relatively long custodial sentence (*R v Coe* [1968] 1 WLR 1950 at 1954, per Lord Parker CJ).

However, *Coe* needs to be seen in the light of *R v Rafferty* [1999] 1 Cr App R 235, where the Court of Appeal considered the question whether a committal for sentence should be on bail or in custody where the accused indicates a plea of guilty in the 'plea before venue' procedure. Thomas J said (at p 237) that:

> in most cases where a plea of guilty is made at the plea before venue, it will not be usual to alter the position as regards bail or custody. In the usual case, when a person who has been on bail pleads guilty at the plea before venue, the usual practice should be to continue bail, even if it is anticipated that a custodial sentence will be imposed by the Crown Court, unless there are good reasons for remanding the defendant in custody. If the defendant is in custody, then after entering a plea of guilty at the plea before venue, it would be unusual, if the reasons for remanding him in custody remained unchanged, to alter the position.

It is submitted that *Rafferty* has effectively modified the principle stated in *Coe*.

5.13.1.1 Exercising the power to commit under s 3

In *R v Manchester Justices ex p Kaymanesh* (1994) 15 Cr App R(S) 838, the Divisional Court held that magistrates should normally exercise the power to commit the defendant for sentence under s 3 only if new information came to light which was not available to the magistrates when the decision to try the case summarily was reached. However, it was held in *R v Dover Justices ex p Pamment* (1994) 15 Cr App R(S) 778, that the exercise of the power to commit a defendant for sentence, despite having earlier accepted jurisdiction to try the case, is unfettered. Nonetheless, Kennedy LJ added (at p 782):

> I trust that magistrates will continue to think carefully when deciding to accept jurisdiction, because normally an accused should be able to conclude that once jurisdiction has been accepted, he or she will not on the same facts be committed to the Crown Court for sentence.

In *R v Sheffield Crown Court ex p DPP* (1994) 15 Cr App R(S) 768, it was held that where the magistrates commit a defendant for sentence under s 3, the Crown Court usually has no power to remit the case to the magistrates' court. If the order is plainly bad on its face (for example, s 3 is invoked by the magistrates in respect of an offence which is triable only summarily), the Crown Court could remit the case to the magistrates' court, but the proper course of action is usually for the defendant to apply to the Divisional Court for judicial review to quash the committal.

R v Sheffield Crown Court ex p DPP and *R v Dover Justices ex p Pamment* were followed and approved in *R v North Sefton Justices ex p Marsh* (1995) 16 Cr App R(S)

401. In that case, the Divisional Court held that the discretion to commit for sentence under s 3 is unfettered. It was said that *Kaymanesh* was wrongly decided and should not be followed. The decision to commit for sentence under s 3 does not have to be based on information received by the court after the decision to try the defendant summarily. In *R v Southampton Magistrates' Court ex p Sansome* [1999] 1 Cr App R(S) 112, the Divisional Court confirmed that the correct approach was that set out in *ex p Marsh*.

> Thus, in summary, magistrates should not normally commit a defendant for sentence under s 3 unless new information has come to light since the original mode of trial decision was taken. However, if magistrates do commit a defendant for sentence on the basis of information which was already known to the court when the decision to try the case was reached, judicial review will not be granted, since the magistrates have not acted beyond their powers.

The question of whether a s 3 committal can only be triggered by new information, or whether the magistrates can in effect simply change their minds about the adequacy of their sentencing powers, is now only relevant in those cases where the defendant indicates an intention to plead not guilty (or gives no indication as to plea) at the 'plea before venue' hearing. Where the defendant indicates an intention to plead guilty, he will do so in the magistrates' court, and so will be convicted by the magistrates, however serious the offence is and before the magistrates are given any information about the seriousness of the offence.

Guidance on the relationship between committal for sentence and the indication of plea (or 'plea before venue') procedure was given by the Divisional Court in *R v Warley Magistrates' Court ex p DPP* [1999] 1 WLR 216:

a Where a defendant indicates a guilty plea under the 'plea before venue' procedure in s 17A of the Magistrates' Courts Act 1980, the magistrates must take account of the discount to be granted for that guilty plea when deciding whether or not their sentencing powers are adequate to deal with the defendant.

b Where it is clear that the case is beyond the sentencing powers of the magistrates, they should be prepared to commit the defendant to the Crown Court for sentence without first seeking a pre-sentence report or hearing a full plea in mitigation (although they should warn the defence that they have this in mind so that the defence can make brief representations to oppose that course of action; if the magistrates are persuaded to change their minds, the prosecutor should be given a chance to reply). In other cases, the hearing should proceed as usual.

c Where there is a difference between the prosecution and defence versions of the facts of the offence:

  i if the magistrates think that their sentencing powers will be adequate however the dispute is resolved, they should adopt the procedure laid down in *R v Newton* (1983) 77 Cr App R 13 (either accepting the defence version or hearing evidence and making findings of fact);

ii   if they think that their sentencing powers will not be adequate however the dispute is resolved, they should simply commit for sentence, leaving the Crown Court to follow the *Newton* procedure;

iii   if the decision whether or not to commit turns, or may turn, on which version is found to be correct, the magistrates should follow the *Newton* procedure; if the offender is then committed for sentence, the Crown Court should adopt the findings of fact made by the magistrates at the *Newton* hearing unless the defendant can point to some significant development, such as the discovery of important new evidence in his favour.

If a defendant is aggrieved at a decision to commit him for sentence to the Crown Court, there is little that can be done about it. The decision to commit for sentence could be challenged by means of judicial review, but such a challenge would only succeed if the committal were perverse (in the sense that no reasonable bench of magistrates could have decided to commit the defendant for sentence). However, the defendant may derive some comfort from two points: firstly, it is by no means inevitable that the Crown Court will in fact impose a sentence which is more severe than the sentence which the magistrates' court could have imposed; secondly, the Court of Appeal has jurisdiction to entertain an appeal against the sentence that the Crown Court imposes if it is excessive.

One basis which has been accepted for challenging the decision to commit for sentence under s 3 of the 2000 Act is where the defendant had a legitimate expectation that he would be sentenced in the magistrates' court. To succeed, the defendant has to show that there was 'a clear and unequivocal representation' that sentence would be determined by the magistrates (*R v Sheffield Magistrates' Court ex p Ojo* (2000) 164 JP 659). In *R (Rees) v Feltham Justices* [2001] 2 Cr App R(S) 1, the magistrates invited the defendant's solicitor to mitigate before them and then adjourned the matter for the preparation of a pre-sentence report without stating that committal to the Crown Court was an option still open to them; this was held to be sufficient to give rise to a legitimate expectation that the justices themselves would pass sentence. Rose LJ (at para 12) said that, 'if justices have in mind that one of the options which is open to them is to commit for sentence, they should specifically say so'. Elias J said (at para 14):

> If the legitimate expectation is not to be created in those circumstances, it is incumbent on the justices to make it absolutely clear to the accused that the decision whether or not to commit for sentence has not been taken, and that he might yet be sent for sentence before the Crown Court.

The key question, however, is whether the original indication was a reasonable one, and therefore capable of creating a legitimate expectation. In *R (Harrington) v Bromley Magistrates Court* [2007] EWHC 2896 (Admin), the magistrates indicated that the defendant would not be committed to the Crown Court for sentence provided that the pre-sentence report did not disclose that he was a danger to the public. Although the report stated that he was not, he was nonetheless subsequently committed for sentence. He argued that his committal was unlawful, being contrary to a legitimate expectation engendered by the indication that had been given by the justices. Mitting J (at para 12) said that when the challenge is to the decision to commit, notwithstanding the indication given by the magistrates, the court is reviewing the reasonableness of the decision to commit for sentence, not the view taken by the original bench. However, it is impossible to conceive of circumstances in which a properly given indication could be gone back on by a subsequent decision without that decision itself being held to be irrational or unlawful. Whenever the challenge arises, whether it is to the original or subsequent decision, it is the rationality and lawfulness of the first decision which ultimately determines the issue.

The Divisional Court will interfere with the decision to retain jurisdiction rather than commit for sentence only if that decision is 'truly astonishing' (*R v Warley Magistrates' Court ex p DPP* [1999] 1 WLR 216 at 225, per Kennedy LJ; *R (DPP) v Devizes Magistrates' Court* [2006] EWHC 1072 (Admin) at para 25, per Maurice Kay LJ).

Paragraph 22 of Sched 3 to the Criminal Justice Act 2003 (which had not been brought into force) was to have amended s 3 of the 2000 Act so as to remove the possibility that the defendant might be committed for sentence to the Crown Court if he was convicted by the magistrates following a trial after a 'not guilty' plea (and so committal for sentence under s 3 would have been possible only where the defendant had entered a guilty plea at the 'plea before venue' hearing). However, s 53 of the Criminal Justice and Immigration Act 2008 gives effect to Sched 13 to the Act, which amends Sched 3 to the Criminal Justice Act 2003. Paragraph 7 of Sched 13 of the 2008 Act removes para 22 of Sched 3 to the 2003 Act, and so the amendment of s 3 to the 2000 Act is cancelled. The effect of this rather complicated legislative journey is to preserve the power of a magistrates' court to commit to the Crown Court for sentence an offender whom it has convicted after a summary trial, if it considers that a Crown Court sentence should be available (as well as having the power to commit an offender for sentence where he pleads guilty at the 'plea before venue' hearing).

5.13.1.2 Procedure in the Crown Court

The Crown Court, when hearing a committal pursuant to s 3, comprises a Circuit Judge or recorder (s 74 of the Supreme Court Act 1981).

The hearing takes the same form as the sentencing procedure in the magistrates' court, that is, the prosecution summarise the facts of the case and give details of the defendant's previous convictions (if any), followed by a defence plea in mitigation.

We have already seen that if there is a significant divergence between prosecution and defence versions, then there has to be a *Newton* hearing (unless the defence version of events is accepted). In the context of a s 3 committal, if a *Newton* hearing took place at the magistrates' court, the Crown Court should adopt the outcome. If the divergence between prosecution and defence versions becomes apparent for the first time at the Crown Court (or no *Newton* hearing was held at the magistrates' court), the Crown Court should hold a *Newton* hearing to determine the issue (see *Munroe v Crown Prosecution Service* [1988] Crim LR 823). A Crown Court judge has jurisdiction to allow a fresh *Newton* hearing to take place (even though one took place in the magistrates' court before the defendant was committed for sentence) if satisfied that it is in the interests of fairness and justice to do so. However, the judge should not ordinarily allow a defendant to reopen findings of fact determined by a magistrates' court unless the defendant can point to some significant development or matter, such as important further evidence discovered since the magistrates' court reached its conclusion on the facts (per Kennedy LJ in *R v Warley Magistrates' Court ex p DPP* [1999] 1 WLR 216 at 224). In *R (Gillan) v DPP* [2007] EWHC 380; (2007) 171 JP 330), Forbes J said, at paras 28–29:

> I am completely satisfied that the Crown Court does have jurisdiction to hold a further *Newton* hearing if it is in the interests of fairness and justice to do so . . . However, the fact that the Crown Court has jurisdiction or a power to hold a further *Newton* hearing does not mean, *ipso facto*, that it should accede to an application to do so in any case where it is apparent that the magistrates have already conducted such a hearing and made clear findings of fact as part of their perfectly proper decision-making with regard to committing the defendant to the Crown Court for sentence. Essentially, the matter is a question for the discretion of the judge, in the proper exercise of which he or she must be fully mindful of his or her obligation to carry out a proper inquiry into the circumstances of the case. . . . I would not expect the judge in the Crown Court to exercise his discretion in favour of allowing a defendant to reopen the magistrates' findings of fact unless the defendant was able to point to some significant development or matter, such as (but not confined to) the discovery of important further evidence having occurred since the Magistrates' Court reached its conclusion on the facts. In saying that, I would not wish it to be thought that I was laying down any absolute or strict formula as to how the judge should exercise his or her discretion in any particular case. Everything will depend upon the facts and circumstances of the particular case; each case must be considered individually.

Where the defendant is sentenced by the Crown Court following a s 3 committal, the maximum sentence which the Crown Court can impose is the same as if the defendant had just been convicted on indictment (s 5 of the Powers of Criminal Courts (Sentencing) Act 2000).

Some sentences depend on the age of the offender (for example, imprisonment is only possible if the defendant has attained the age of 21). In *R v Robson* [2006] EWCA Crim 1414; [2007] 1 All ER 506, the Court of Appeal considered the position where the offender has attained an age of relevance to sentencing powers during the period between the magistrates' court and Crown Court proceedings. The court had to decide whether the age of a defendant committed to the Crown Court for sentence is to be treated, for the purpose of sentence, differently from the age of a defendant convicted after trial (the latter has to be sentenced on the basis of his age at the date of his conviction), whether he is convicted following a guilty plea or a guilty verdict (*R v Danga* [1992] QB 476 and *R v Robinson* [1993] 1 WLR 168). The court held that the matter must be decided on the basis of the wording of the relevant statutory provisions. Where the statute refers to age at the date of conviction, the relevant date for sentencing purposes is the date of the conviction, not the date of the Crown Court appearance following committal for sentence.

5.13.2 Committal for breach of Crown Court order

The second form of committal for sentence is where a magistrates' court has convicted a defendant of any offence committed during the currency of a suspended sentence or a community order or conditional discharge imposed by the Crown Court. In such a case, the magistrates' court can commit the defendant to be dealt with by the Crown Court for the breach of the Crown Court order (which may mean the Crown Court re-sentencing the defendant for the offence originally dealt with by the Crown Court). The relevant provisions are: s 13(5) of the Powers of Criminal Courts (Sentencing) Act 2000 (breach of Crown Court conditional discharge); Sched 12, paras 8(6) and 11(2), of the Criminal Justice Act 2003 (breach of a requirement under a Crown Court suspended sentence and power to commit an offender convicted of an offence committed during the operational period of a Crown Court suspended sentence); Sched 8, para 9(6), of the 2003 Act (power to commit an offender who is in breach of a Crown Court community order). Where the offender is committed for sentence under these provisions, the Crown Court comprises a judge sitting alone.

Detailed guidance on the effect of some of the committal powers under the CJA 2003 was given by the Court of Appeal in *R v Majury* [2007] EWCA Crim 2968 (see Chapter 17).

5.13.3 Section 4 of the Powers of Criminal Courts (Sentencing) Act 2000

Section 4 of the Powers of Criminal Courts (Sentencing) Act 2000 provides that where the defendant has indicated that he will plead guilty to an either-way offence (and so is deemed to have pleaded guilty to it under the 'plea before venue procedure') and he is also sent for trial for one or more related offences, the magistrates may commit him to the Crown Court for sentence in respect of the either-way offence to which he has pleaded guilty. For the purposes of these provisions, one offence is related to another if the charges for them could be joined (under r 14.2(3) of the Criminal Procedure Rules) in the same indictment if both were to be tried in the Crown Court (s 4(7)), so the two charges must be founded on the same facts or must be a series (or part of a series) of offences of the same or similar character.

Section 4(4) provides that, where the justices have committed a defendant for sentence pursuant to s 4(2), the Crown Court can only exceed the sentencing powers of the magistrates' court in respect of the either-way offence to which the defendant indicated a plea of guilty if either:

a   the magistrates stated that they considered their sentencing powers were inadequate to deal with the defendant for that offence (and so they also had power to commit him for sentence under s 3); or

b   he is also convicted by the Crown Court of one or more of the related offences.

The relationship between ss 3 and 4 of the Powers of Criminal Courts (Sentencing) Act 2000 may seem rather confusing. The purpose of s 4 is to ensure that if the defendant is to be tried in the Crown Court for an offence which is related to an offence to which he has indicated a guilty plea at the 'plea before venue' hearing, then the magistrates can commit him to the Crown Court for sentence for that latter offence even if their sentencing powers are adequate to deal with that offence (and so a committal under s 3 would be inappropriate).

If the magistrates take the view that their sentencing powers are adequate to deal with the offence in respect of which the defendant has indicated a guilty plea, then only s 4 allows the justices to commit the defendant to the Crown Court for sentence for that offence. On the other hand, if the magistrates take the view that their sentencing powers are not adequate to deal with that offence, they have two options: they can either commit him for sentence for that offence under s 3, or they can commit him for sentence under s 4 but indicate that they took the view that their sentencing powers were inadequate and so could have invoked s 3. Obviously, the best practice will be to use s 3 where the magistrates' sentencing powers are not adequate and to use s 4 where their powers are adequate. In any event, when committing a defendant for sentence in these circumstances, the court should state whether it is doing so under s 3 or s 4. If the magistrates use s 4 but do not consider that their sentencing powers are adequate to deal with the offence, they should state (under s 4(4)) that they also had the power to commit the defendant for sentence under s 3, so as to avoid inadvertently fettering the powers of the Crown Court when dealing with the offence.

5.13.4 Section 6 of the Powers of Criminal Courts (Sentencing) Act 2000

Section 6 of the Powers of Criminal Courts (Sentencing) Act 2000 gives a power to commit for sentence which may be used to supplement a committal under any of the following provisions:

a   ss 3 to 4A of the 2000 Act (committal for sentence for either-way offences);
b   s 13(5) of the 2000 Act (conditionally discharged person convicted of further offence);
c   Sched 12, para 11(2) of the Criminal Justice Act 2003 (committal to Crown Court where offender convicted during operational period of suspended sentence).

These committal powers may be referred to as 'primary powers'.

Under s 6(2) of the 2000 Act, when a magistrates' court exercises a primary committal power in respect of an indictable offence, it may also commit the offender to the Crown Court to be dealt with in respect of any other offence of which he stands convicted (whether summary or indictable) that the magistrates' court has jurisdiction to deal with. Thus, to take the example of a magistrates' court which has decided to commit an offender (under s 3) for one either-way offence, a committal under s 6 may (for example) relate to:

a   another, less serious, either-way offence of which the magistrates have convicted the offender on the same occasion;
b   a summary offence of which they have convicted the offender on the same occasion.

Committal under s 3 for the secondary offence would not be appropriate in situation (a) because the offence is not sufficiently serious, and so the magistrates' powers of sentencing for it are adequate. In situation (b), a s 3 committal would be inappropriate because the section does not extend to summary offences.

The other use of s 6 is where a conviction in the magistrates' court puts the offender in breach of a suspended sentence passed by the Crown Court and the magistrates consider that, although the breach should be committed to the Crown Court under Sched 12, para 11(2)(a) of the Criminal Justice Act 2003, the offence giving rise to the breach is not in itself serious enough to warrant committal under s 3. The court should then commit the offender under para 11(2)(a), for possible activation of the suspended sentence, and under s 6, for sentence for the present offence.

Following a committal under s 6, the Crown Court may deal with the offender in any way the magistrates' court might have done had it not committed the offender to the Crown Court under s 6 (s 7(1)). The Crown Court's powers on a committal under s 6 are thus identical to the powers of the magistrates' court. This is because the purpose of a s 6 committal is to enable one court to deal with an offender for all matters outstanding against him, not to increase the sentence that may be imposed.

Two examples may help to illustrate the scope of s 6 of the 2000 Act:

a   The defendant is charged with theft (triable either way) and common assault (a summary offence) and the magistrates convict him of both charges. The magistrates decide that their sentencing powers are inadequate to deal with the theft and so they commit the defendant to the Crown Court in respect of that offence under s 3 of the 2000 Act. This section does not apply to summary offences and so cannot be used to enable the magistrates to commit the defendant to the Crown Court for the common assault. However, s 6 enables the magistrates to commit the defendant to the Crown Court for the common assault, and so the Crown Court can sentence him for both offences.

b   The defendant is charged with theft. The theft in question is a very minor offence and so the magistrates cannot invoke s 3 of the 2000 Act (since their sentencing powers are plainly adequate to deal with the theft). However, the defendant committed the theft while he was subject to a suspended sentence of imprisonment imposed by the Crown Court. If the magistrates want the Crown Court to deal with the defendant for the theft as well as dealing with him for the breach of the suspended sentence, they can commit him to the Crown Court to be dealt with for the breach of the suspended sentence and, under s 6, in respect of the theft.

5.13.5 Dangerous offenders: s 3A of the Powers of Criminal Courts (Sentencing) Act 2000

Section 3A of the 2000 Act is inserted by the Criminal Justice Act 2003 (but not in force at the time of writing). This provision enables a magistrates' court which convicts an adult defendant of a 'specified' either-way offence (as defined in s 224 of the 2003 Act) to commit him to the Crown Court for sentence when the criteria for an extended sentence or a sentence for public protection appear to be met under the 'dangerous offender' provisions in ss 225(3) or 227(2) of the 2003 Act. Where the magistrates' sentencing powers for the offence in question are inadequate, the option of committing under s 3 remains available (s 3A(5)).

Any other offences that the magistrates would otherwise be dealing with may be committed to the Crown Court for sentence under s 6 (s 3A(3)).

The 'dangerous offender' provisions are considered in more detail in Chapter 17.

5.14 TRANSFER OF CASES BETWEEN MAGISTRATES' COURTS

It sometimes proves necessary, or desirable, to transfer cases from one magistrates' court to another. Section 27A of the Magistrates' Courts Act 1980 facilitates the transfer of proceedings between magistrates' courts, providing as follows:

> (1) Where a person appears or is brought before a magistrates' court—
>
>> (a) to be tried by the court for an offence, or
>> (b) for the court to inquire into the offence as examining justices,
>
>> the court may transfer the matter to another magistrates' court.
>
> (2) The court may transfer the matter before or after beginning the trial or inquiry.
> (3) But if the court transfers the matter after it has begun to hear the evidence and the parties, the court to which the matter is transferred must begin hearing the evidence and the parties again.
>
> ...

Thus, s 27A enables magistrates' courts to transfer criminal cases to other magistrates' courts at any stage in the proceedings. This power may be exercised either on the application of the prosecution or the defence, or of the court's own motion (in the latter case the court should listen to representations from the parties before transferring the case to another court).

Furthermore, s 10 of the Powers of Criminal Courts (Sentencing) Act 2000 provides that, if one magistrates' court convicts a defendant and then discovers that he has been convicted of another offence at another magistrates' court but has not yet been sentenced, he may be remitted to that other court to be sentenced for both offences so long as the offence being remitted is imprisonable or carries disqualification from driving, and the other court consents to the transfer.

5.15 SPEEDY SUMMARY JUSTICE

In 2006, the Government published a paper entitled *Delivering Simple, Speedy, Summary Justice* (<http://www.dca.gov.uk/publications/reports_reviews/delivery-simple-speedy.pdf>). As well as reorganising the management of magistrates' courts, the proposals sought to streamline case management procedures in order to reduce the overall time between arrest and the conclusion of the case. To this end, the report focuses on four key areas:

a making the first hearing effective every time. This requires:

   i   the prosecution papers to be served on the defence and the court;
   ii the court to probe the parties to identify issues to be tried;
   iii directions and timescales to be set by the court and a date fixed for trial no later than six weeks; and
   iv where defendants plead guilty, that they are dealt with there and then.

b   ensuring that case progression is robustly managed by the judiciary without the need for a court hearing, supported by case progression officers, so that all unnecessary hearings are eliminated and cases proceed on the trial date as ordered;

c   bringing about a 'change in culture', so that orders are complied with to the right standard at the right time;

d   ensuring that the judiciary adopts a robust case management approach to adjournments in summary cases so that the expectation is that they will proceed on the day if one of the parties has simply failed to comply with directions or to be adequately prepared.

This report sends a clear signal to magistrates, and to the lawyers who practise in the magistrates' courts, that the case management powers contained in the Criminal Procedure Rules (see Chapter 1) will be applied robustly to ensure that delay is kept to a minimum.

The target of having summary trials within six weeks of the first appearance is an ambitious one. The Ministry of Justice published a 'Time Interval Study' for September 2007 (<http://www.justice.gov.uk/docs/tis0907.pdf>) showing results from a one-week survey of criminal cases completed in magistrates' courts to provide a snap-shot of how long it is taking to dispose of cases. The results show that for summary offences other than motoring offences, the average time between the offence and the completion of the case was 142 days (144 days for the snap-shot exercise carried out in the previous quarter).

The reintroduction of means testing for defendants seeking legal aid in the magistrates' court (see Chapter 14) can militate against achieving the objective that the first hearing should be effective. Moreover, in order for the first hearing to be effective, the prosecution must have served on the defendant (and on the court) all the necessary papers; this runs the risk of extending the time from arrest to first hearing to enable all that information to be collected and collated, with the result that the overall time taken to dispose of the case is not in fact improved.

Chapter 6

Young defendants and trial in the youth court

6.1 INTRODUCTION

In this chapter, we look at the way in which young defendants are dealt with by the courts. We examine the jurisdiction of the youth court and also what happens if the juvenile has committed a very serious offence or is jointly charged with an adult offender.

6.1.1 The importance of youth justice

The powers of the courts to deal with young offenders are a matter of considerable political importance. Juveniles commit a substantial proportion of criminal offences (for example, street violence, criminal damage, public disorder, drugs offences, car crime). Moreover, some of the worries that people have about crime are underpinned by fear of juvenile crime, a fear that is often fuelled by unruly juvenile behaviour. The sight of young people hanging around or behaving rowdily causes in many people a fear that things will get out hand.

In the 1997 Home Office Consultation Paper *Tackling Youth Justice* (<http://www.homeoffice.gov.uk/documents/cons-tackling-youth-justice-0997?view=Html>), it was pointed out that:

> Youth crime is one of the most serious problems facing England and Wales today. Young offenders can wreck their chances of leading worthwhile and fulfilled adult lives and they can wreck the lives of those whom they victimise.
>
> Involvement in offending and drug use amongst young people is widespread – one in two males and one in three females admitted to committing offences and the same number admitted using drugs at some time, though most offending is infrequent and minor. We know that a disproportionate amount of crime is committed by a hard core of persistent young offenders, with about 3% of offenders responsible for 25% of offences.

A detailed Consultation Paper was issued by the Home Office in November 1997. It was entitled *No More Excuses – A New Approach to Tackling Youth Crime in England and Wales* (Cmnd 3809) (<http://www.homeoffice.gov.uk/documents/jou-no-more-excuses?view=Html>). It begins by setting out the importance of youth crime, referring to Home Office research (*Young people and crime*, by John Graham and Ben Bowling. Home Office research study 145, 1995) that showed that, among 14–25-year-olds, one in two males and one in three females admitted to having committed an offence, and to statistics from 1996 (*Cautions, court proceedings and sentencing, England and Wales, 1996*, Home Office statistical bulletin 16/97) showing that, for offenders convicted or cautioned for an indictable offence, 10–15-year-olds account for around 14 per cent of known offenders, and 10–17-year-olds account for around 25 per cent (para 1.1). In other words, young people commit a disproportionate amount of crime. The Paper went on to note that it is a 'small hard core of persistent offenders' who are responsible for that disproportionate amount of crime. Paragraph 1.2 refers to Home Office research (Graham and Bowling, op cit) showing that about three per cent of young offenders commit 26 per cent of youth crime.

Paragraph 1.5 of the Consultation Paper sets out what are perceived to be the key factors related to youth criminality, namely:

- being male;
- being brought up by a criminal parent or parents;
- living in a family with multiple problems;
- experiencing poor parenting and lack of supervision;
- poor discipline in the family and at school;
- playing truant or being excluded from school;
- associating with delinquent friends; and
- having siblings who offend.

Paragraph 1.6 highlights 'two important influences', namely 'persistent school truancy and associating with offenders', but concludes that 'the single most important factor in explaining criminality is the quality of a young person's home life, including parental supervision'.

The Paper goes on to consider whether there is a need for active intervention, or whether juveniles will simply grow out of their offending behaviour. It says that:

> 1.9 A prevailing assumption behind youth justice policy has been the idea that youngsters will grow out of their offending behaviour. For many young offenders it is true that their first caution – or court appearance is enough to divert them from crime. But this assumption is wide of the mark when it comes to the hard core of persistent offenders who cause so much crime.
>
> 1.10 While many young offenders do grow out of their delinquent behaviour, research shows that this happens less markedly and far more slowly for young men than young women. For young men, the positive effects of personal and social development completing education, getting a job, leaving home, settling down with a partner – tend to be outweighed by the more powerful influences of the peer group and siblings. Desistance from offending is even less likely for young male offenders involved in regular drug or alcohol misuse.
>
> . . .
>
> 1.13 We know that those who start committing offences at an early age are more likely to become serious and persistent offenders. So the Government's youth justice reforms will focus efforts on preventing offending, on early and effective intervention to stop children and young people being drawn into crime and, if they are, to halt their offending before it escalates.

6.1.2 The aims of the youth justice system

It is doubtless because of concern over the level of youth crime that s 37(1) of the Crime and Disorder Act provides that it:

> shall be the principal aim of the youth justice system to prevent offending by children and young persons.

Section 37(2) goes on to require that:

> In addition to any other duty to which they are subject, it shall be the duty of all persons and bodies carrying out functions in relation to the youth justice system to have regard to that aim.

However, s 44(1) of the Children and Young Persons Act 1933 provides that:

> Every court in dealing with a child or young person who is brought before it, either as an offender or otherwise, shall have regard to the welfare of the child or young person and shall in a proper case take steps for removing him from undesirable surroundings, and for securing that proper provision is made for his education and training.

To reflect the creation of statutory objectives for sentencing young offenders, s 9(3) of the Criminal Justice and Immigration Act 2008 adds two additional sub-sections to s 44 of the 1933 Act:

> (1A) Sub-section (1) is to be read with paragraphs (a) and (c) of section 142A(2) of the Criminal Justice Act 2003 (which require a court dealing with an offender aged under 18 also to have regard to the principal aim of the youth justice system and the specified purposes of sentencing).
>
> (1B) Accordingly, in determining in the case of an offender whether it should take steps as mentioned in sub-s (1), the court shall also have regard to the matters mentioned in those paragraphs.

The provisions in s 142A of the 2003 Act are discussed in Chapter 16.

For an historical perspective on youth justice, see Caroline Ball, 'Youth justice? Half a century of responses to youth offending' [2004] Crim LR 167.

6.1.3 Youth offending teams

Pursuant to s 39 of the Crime and Disorder Act 1998, each local authority has to establish a youth offending team (YOT). The YOT has to comprise:

a   a probation officer;
b   a person with experience of social work in relation to children nominated by the director of children's services appointed by the local authority;
c   a social worker;
d   a police officer;

e   a person nominated by a Primary Care Trust or Local Health Board any part of whose area lies within the local authority's area; and

f   a person with experience in education nominated by the director of children's services.

Other people may be co-opted onto the YOT (for example, housing officers and people with experience of dealing with drugs and alcohol misuse). The functions of the YOT are to co-ordinate the provision of youth justice services for all those in the authority's area who need them, and to carry out such functions as are assigned to it in the local authority's 'youth justice plan'. The plan (made under s 40 of the Crime and Disorder Act 1998) sets out how youth justice services in the area are to be provided and funded, and the functions of the YOTs in that area. The YOT is able to ascertain the needs of each young offender, identifying the specific problems that make that young person offend and measuring the risk they pose to others. This enables the YOT to identify suitable programmes to address the needs of the young person in order to prevent further offending.

6.2 TERMINOLOGY

The 'youth court' has jurisdiction to deal with young defendants, namely those aged 10–17 years (inclusive); 10–13-year-olds are called 'children' and 14–17-year-olds are called 'young persons'. This distinction is relevant as sentencing powers differ to some extent according to whether the juvenile is a child or a young person.

The youth court thus has jurisdiction where the defendant is under the age of 18 (i.e. has not yet had their 18th birthday). The choice of the age of 17 as the cut-off point is in some senses arbitrary. In the *Review of Delay in the Criminal Justice System*, Martin Narey (in Chapter 8, 'Managing the Youth Court') suggests that 17-year-olds should be dealt with by the adult court (a recommendation that was not accepted by the Government). He points out that:

> When the youth court replaced juvenile courts in October 1992, the age limit was raised from 17 to 18 on the basis that 16 and 17 year olds ought to be treated in the same way as 'near adults'. Almost everyone I have spoken to has agreed that defendants of 17, who were previously dealt with by magistrates' courts, are unsuitable for the jurisdiction of the youth court, where they now account for a third of all cases. They tend to be experienced as offenders (about 60 per cent of 17 year olds before the youth court have previous convictions, compared with about 50 per cent of 16 year olds and 45 per cent of 15 year olds) and, I am told, they are often disruptive and unco-operative. There certainly are 17 year olds whose immaturity makes them suitable for the youth court, just as there are defendants of 16 for whom the adult court would be the proper forum. But a line has to be drawn, and in my view it should be the 17th rather than the 18th birthday. 17 year olds already count as adults at the police station, where they can be questioned without the presence of an adult; and they remain the responsibility of the Probation Service, who otherwise deal only with adult offenders. I therefore recommend that 17 year olds should be returned to the jurisdiction of the adult court ... The removal of this large group of relatively serious and troublesome offenders would enable

the youth court to concentrate on dealing more promptly and effectively with children up to school leaving age.

6.3 THE AGE OF CRIMINAL RESPONSIBILITY

There is an irrebuttable presumption that a person who is under the age of 10 cannot be guilty of a criminal offence.

There used to be a rebuttable presumption that a child aged between 10 and 14 was incapable of committing an offence. This presumption, sometimes called *doli incapax*, was that children under the age of 14 did not know the difference between right and wrong (and therefore were incapable of committing a crime) unless the prosecution were able to prove that they did have this understanding. Hence, a child aged under 14 could only be convicted of a criminal offence if the presumption of *doli incapax* was first rebutted. To rebut the presumption, the prosecution had to adduce evidence to prove that the child knew that what he was doing was seriously wrong, rather than simply naughty. This presumption was, however, abolished by s 34 of the Crime and Disorder Act 1998. Prior to this, Pt III of the Home Office Consultation Paper *No More Excuses: A New Approach to Tackling Youth Crime in England and Wales*, had expressed the view that the need to rebut the presumption could 'lead to real practical difficulties, delaying cases or even making it impossible for the prosecution to proceed' (para 4.3). Paragraph 4.4 went on:

> The Government believes that in presuming that children of this age generally do not know the difference between naughtiness and serious wrongdoing, the notion of *doli incapax* is contrary to common sense. The practical difficulties which the presumption presents for the prosecution can stop some children who should be prosecuted and punished for their offences from being convicted or from even coming to court. This is not in the interests of justice, of victims or of the young people themselves. If children are prosecuted where appropriate, interventions can be made to help prevent any further offending.

In *C v DPP* [1996] AC 1, the House of Lords had ruled that the doctrine of *doli incapax* remained part of English law (allowing an appeal from the Divisional Court, which held that it no longer formed part of the law). However, the House of Lords recommended that Parliament should review this presumption.

Three main arguments were put forward by the Government in favour of reform in Pt 1 of the Consultation Paper, *Tackling Youth Crime* (see para 7ff), namely that the presumption was:

- archaic;
- illogical; and
- unfair in practice.

It was believed to be *archaic* on the grounds that the notion that the average 10–13-year-old did not know right from wrong seemed contrary to common sense in an age of compulsory education from the age of five, and that the doctrine had developed at a time when punishments were much harsher (whereas now the emphasis is as much on preventing reoffending as on punishment for the crime).

The presumption was thought to be *illogical* since, in practice, the presumption could be rebutted if the prosecution produced evidence that the child was of normal mental development for his age. However, the doctrine itself presumed that children of that age normally did not know right from wrong, so to rebut the presumption by proving the child's normality was logically inconsistent.

The presumption was said to be *unfair* in practice, in that it placed a very heavy burden on the prosecution to provide the evidence necessary to show that a child knew his act was seriously wrong. To rebut the presumption, the prosecution had to produce evidence separate from the facts of the offence (for example, evidence of the child's response to police questioning, or reports from his teachers or from an educational psychologist).

The Consultation Paper also noted that discontinuance of a case because of insufficient evidence to rebut the presumption was not necessarily in the young offender's best interests, since it could mean that an opportunity to take appropriate action to prevent re-offending was missed.

The Paper considered two options for reform: outright abolition of the presumption (so that young defendants aged 10–17 would all be treated in the same way) or reversal of the presumption (so that the court would start with the presumption that a child aged 10–13 was capable of forming criminal intent but that child would be acquitted if the defence adduced evidence that the child did not know that what they did was seriously wrong and the prosecution were unable to show beyond reasonable doubt that the child did indeed know that the action was seriously wrong). The option taken by the Government in the Crime and Disorder Act 1998 was outright abolition of the presumption.

However, the concept of *doli incapax* reappeared in *CPS v P* [2007] EWHC 946 (Admin); (2007) 171 JP 349. This case is considered later in this chapter in the context of fitness to stand trial, but it is worth noting here that Smith LJ said (obiter) that in her view the effect of s 34 of the Crime and Disorder Act 1998 was 'to abolish the presumption that a child is *doli incapax* but not the defence itself' (para 46). In other words, there is no presumption that a child under the age of 14 is incapable of forming criminal intent, but it is open to the defence to argue that the particular child was incapable of doing so. Where the defence raise the issue, her Ladyship said that, as a 'matter of general principle the burden should remain on the Crown to prove that the child had the requisite understanding. Moreover, the standard of proof should be the usual criminal standard' (para 47). Gross J, in a short judgment concurring in the result, expressly declined to express a view, one way or the other, on the question of *doli incapax*, apart from underlining the importance of the point and the need for its resolution in due course.

The views of Smith LJ did not, however, find favour with the Court of Appeal. In *R v T* [2008] EWCA Crim 815, Latham LJ (at para 20) said that it was difficult to see how the abolition of the presumption was intended to result in anything other than the abolition of the concept of *doli incapax* as having any effect in law. The Court therefore upheld the ruling of the trial judge, that the accused (who was aged 12) was precluded by s 34 of the Crime and Disorder Act 1998, from raising the issue of *doli incapax*.

In any event, it remains the case that there is a conclusive presumption that a child under 10 cannot commit an offence and so is outside the jurisdiction of the criminal courts. However, if a child of that age is beyond the control of their parents and is therefore at risk of harm, a family proceedings court can make a care or supervision order under s 31 of the Children Act 1989.

6.4 JUVENILES AND BAIL

The Bail Act 1976 (with its presumption in favour of bail) applies to juveniles. The criteria for granting bail are virtually the same as for adults. The most important differences are that:

- a juvenile can be refused bail (or conditions imposed on the grant of bail) where this is necessary for his own welfare, not just if necessary for her own protection, as is the case with adults (Sched 1, Pt 1, paras 3 and 8 of the Bail Act 1976);
- a parent or guardian may be asked to act as a surety not only for the juvenile's attendance at court (the function of the surety in the case of adult defendants) but also for compliance with any other conditions of bail which the court may impose (s 3(7) of the Bail Act);
- where bail is withheld, whether before or after conviction, juveniles under the age of 17 are remanded to local authority accommodation unless the criteria laid down in s 23(5) of the Children and Young Persons Act 1969 (set out below) are satisfied.

6.4.1 Remands to local authority accommodation

Under s 23(1) of the Children and Young Persons Act 1969, where a court remands a child or young person in custody, the remand is to local authority accommodation. However, under s 23(4) the court may require the local authority to comply with a 'security requirement', namely that the accused 'be placed and kept in secure accommodation'. Before a security requirement can be imposed, the conditions set out in ss 23(5) and 23(5AA) have to be satisfied. In summary, those conditions are that:

a the accused has attained the age of 12 and is of a 'prescribed description' (see below); and

b the accused has been charged with, or has been convicted of, either (i) a violent or sexual offence, or an offence punishable in the case of an adult with imprisonment for a term of 14 years or more, or (ii) one or more imprisonable offences which amount (or would, if he were to be convicted of the offences with which he is charged, amount) to a 'recent history of repeatedly committing imprisonable offences while remanded on bail or to local authority accommodation'; and

c the court is of the opinion, after considering all the options for the remand of the accused, that 'only remanding him to local authority accommodation with a security requirement would be adequate (a) to protect the public from serious harm from him, or (b) to prevent the commission by him of imprisonable offences'.

The 'prescribed description' referred to in s 23(5) is supplied by the Secure Remands and Committals (Prescribed Description of Children and Young Persons) Order (SI 1999/1265). It applies the provision to girls and boys aged 12, 13 or 14 and to girls aged

15 or 16. However, the s 98(1) of the Crime and Disorder Act 1998 bring boys aged 15 or 16 within the scope of s 23(5).

In deciding whether the public needs to be protected from the juvenile, it is necessary for the court to assess the risk of serious harm to the public by reference to the nature of the offences in respect of which he has been charged or convicted, and the manner in which these offences were carried out (or are alleged to have been carried out if the defendant has not yet been convicted); it is not enough to consider only the risk that such offences might be repeated. In *R v Croydon Youth Court ex p Grinham* (1995) *The Times*, 3 May. Leggatt LJ ruled as follows:

> Even a dwelling-house burglary is not necessarily calculated to cause serious harm if, for example, the burglar is careful only to enter unoccupied houses in daylight and steal television sets. A series of such offences, if apprehended, could not be aggregated so as to render serious such harm as might be caused by them.
>
> In any particular case it might be proper to infer from the record of a young person that the public was liable to incur serious harm at his hands, having regard to the nature of the offences with which he had been charged, or of which he had been convicted, or the manner in which he had carried them out. Though it would not be necessary to conclude that there was a risk of death or serious personal injury being caused, the Court would have to be satisfied that the young person whom they were minded to remand was liable to cause harm that could sensibly be described as serious on account of the nature of the offence or offences that might be committed and not merely of the risk of repetition.

Section 23(7) provides that where a juvenile is remanded to local authority accommodation, the court can impose such conditions as it would be able to impose on an adult offender under s 3(6) of the Bail Act 1976. These conditions can include electronic monitoring under s 23AA of the Act. Section 23A(1) of the Children and Young Persons Act 1969 provides that where a juvenile has been remanded to local authority accommodation and conditions have been imposed under s 23(7), he may be arrested without a warrant if the police have reasonable grounds for suspecting that he has broken any of the conditions.

6.5 YOUTH COURTS

Section 50 of the Courts Act 2003 sets out a new framework under which lay magistrates and District Judges are authorised to hear youth court cases. By virtue of s 50(2), a lay justice or District Judge has to be authorised to sit in a youth court before he or she can do so. These personal authorisations are valid throughout England and Wales, reflecting the national jurisdiction of the magistracy. Magistrates (including District Judges) have to receive special training before being authorised to sit in the youth court. This is because of the sensitive nature of some youth court cases, and the specific knowledge and understanding that is required to deal with young defendants. Justices who have received the appropriate authorisation are known as 'youth justices' when they sit in the youth court.

The *Youth Courts (Constitution of Committees and Right to Preside) Rules* 2007 (SI 2007/1611) provide for the formation of a 'youth panel' for each local justice area, consisting of the youth justices for the local justice area. Rule 10(1) makes provision for the constitution of youth courts, requiring that a youth court must consist of either (a) a District Judge sitting alone, or (b) not more than three justices, including at least one man and one woman. A single-sex bench is permissible if a mixed gender bench is not available due to circumstances unforeseen when the justices to sit were chosen (or if the only man or the only woman present cannot properly sit as a member of the court) and the members of the youth court think it 'inexpedient in the interests of justice for there to be an adjournment' (r 10(2) and (3)). Rule 11 makes provision for the chairmanship of youth courts (requiring that a youth court other than one consisting of a District Judge sitting alone, should be chaired by a District Judge if he is sitting as a member of the court, or by a youth justice who is on the list of approved youth court chairmen).

Thus, where the youth court comprises a bench of lay magistrates, there should be no more than three justices and there should (unless a properly constituted court is not available and it is inexpedient to adjourn) be at least one male and one female. The importance of compliance with these rules was emphasised in *R v Birmingham Justices ex p F* (2000) 164 JP 523. Only two male magistrates were available to sit in the youth court. Both parties were legally represented and no issue was taken by the parties as to the constitution of the court. The Divisional Court granted judicial review, and ordered a re-trial, holding that what is now r 10(1) is mandatory unless the justices decide in their discretion to proceed under what is now r 10(2) and (3). Such discretion has to be exercised publicly and with submissions from the parties. In the present case, it had not been exercised in that way. This issue might, however, be re-opened in the light of *R v Ashton* [2007] 1 WLR 181, where it was held that, where there has been a procedural failure in the exercise of a statutory power, the court should first ask itself whether the intention of the legislature was that any act done following that procedural failure should be invalid. The decision in *Birmingham Justices ex p F* would, of course, stand if it were to be held that Parliament did intend the particular irregularity to be fatal (cf *R v Clarke* [2008] UKHL 8; [2008] 1 WLR 338).

The essential point to underline about the jurisdiction of the youth court is that the distinction between indictable, triable either way and summary offences does not apply to young defendants. Thus, a bench of justices in the youth court may try an offence which, in the case of an adult defendant, would be triable only in the Crown Court. Furthermore, a juvenile has no right to elect Crown Court trial in any case where an adult defendant would have such a right (although the justices in the youth court may decline jurisdiction in respect of certain indictable offences – see below).

The Courts Act 2003 also enables the higher judiciary (including Circuit Judges and Recorders) to hear youth court cases. This occurs as a result of the extension of their jurisdiction, by s 66 of the Act, to include that of a District Judge (Magistrates' Courts). Section 66(3) specifically provides that such judges can sit in as members of a youth court without any further authorisation. This means mean that, in particularly difficult or sensitive cases, a senior judge may sit (as a magistrate) in the youth court. However, the fact that long-term detention (under s 91 of the Powers of Criminal Courts (Sentencing) Act 2000) of offenders under the age of 18 may be imposed only by the Crown Court means that serious cases involving juveniles will, in any event, continue to be tried in the Crown Court.

6.6 DIFFERENCES BETWEEN THE YOUTH COURT AND ADULT MAGISTRATES' COURT

A youth court is simply a form of magistrates' court, albeit with slightly different procedures to make it more amenable to young defendants. The main difference between the youth court and the ordinary (adult) magistrates' court is that there is less formality in the youth court than in an adult magistrates' court. For example:

- the juvenile sits on a chair, not in a dock, and usually has a parent or guardian sitting nearby;
- the juvenile and any juvenile witnesses are addressed by their first names;
- the oath taken by witnesses is to promise (not swear) to tell the truth;
- the terminology differs slightly, for example, a 'finding of guilt' (not a 'conviction') and an 'order made upon a finding of guilt' (not a 'sentence'). Note, however, that the juvenile pleads 'guilty' or 'not guilty'.

Apart from the attempt to make the atmosphere less forbidding, the procedure for a trial in the youth court is the same as the procedure for summary trial in the adult magistrates' court (which is discussed in detail in Chapter 5).

6.6.1 Exclusion of the public

The public are excluded from the courtroom under s 47(2) of the Children and Young Persons Act 1933, which provides that:

> No person shall be present at any sitting of a youth court except—
>
> (a) members and officers of the court;
> (b) parties to the case before the court, their solicitors and counsel, and witnesses and other persons directly concerned in that case;
> (c) bona fide representatives of newspapers or news agencies [news gathering or reporting organisations];
> (d) such other persons as the court may specially authorise to be present.

Thus, the only people entitled to be present in the youth court apart from the accused, the parents and the justices and their clerk are:

- the lawyers representing the juvenile or the prosecution in the present case; the lawyers cannot enter the courtroom if a case they are appearing in is not yet being dealt with;
- court officials (for example, the usher);
- reporters (but note the reporting restrictions set out below);
- probation officers and social workers concerned in the case;
- witnesses giving evidence (they are allowed to remain in court once they have given evidence);
- anyone else directly concerned in the case;
- anyone whom the magistrates specifically allow to be present (for example, law students).

Note that if a juvenile is appearing as an accused, or as a witness, in the adult magistrates' court or the Crown Court, the public have the right to be present unless the court takes the exceptional step of sitting *in camera*.

6.7 REPORTING RESTRICTIONS

Section 49 of the Children and Young Persons Act 1933 imposes automatic reporting restrictions to protect the identity of any child or young person concerned in the proceedings (whether as a defendant or as a witness). This section applies to newspaper reports and to broadcast programmes (s 49(3)). Section 49(1) prevents the publication of material that is likely to lead members of the public to identify the juvenile as someone concerned in the proceedings (for example, his name, address, school). Publication of any picture of the juvenile is also banned. The wording of s 49 is due to be amended by the Youth Justice and Criminal Evidence Act 1999 (the amendments were not in force at the time of writing), but the effect of s 49 will remain the same. Breach of these reporting restrictions is punishable, on summary conviction, by a fine not exceeding level 5 (£5,000): s 49(9).

The reporting restrictions under s 49 last only while the person in question is under 18. In *DPP v Todd* [2003] EWHC 2408; (2004) 168 JP 194, during the course of proceedings in the youth court, the defendant attained the age of 18. The justices ruled that s 49 no longer applied. The Divisional Court agreed, holding that a defendant in proceedings before the youth court ceases to benefit from the reporting restrictions contained in s 49 as soon as he attains the age of 18. The specific purpose of s 49, said the court, is to protect children and young persons from the adverse consequences of publicity. Such restrictions are an exception to the general right to report proceedings, and so should be interpreted narrowly. The fact that a person had been a young person at the commencement of proceedings could not, said the court, justify such a person continuing to benefit from s 49 once he has ceased to be a young person.

The imposition of reporting restrictions brings into focus the potential conflict between, on the one hand, the juvenile's right to privacy and, on the other hand, the right to free speech and the freedom of the press. In *Re S (a child) (identification: restriction on publication)* [2004] UKHL 47; [2005] 1 AC 593, the House of Lords held that the press should not be restrained from publishing the identity of the defendant in a murder trial in order to protect the privacy of the defendant's child, who was not involved in the criminal proceedings. The House had to consider the interplay between Arts 8 (right to respect for private and family life) and 10 (freedom of expression) of the European Convention on Human Rights. Lord Steyn (at para 17) summarised the effect of the earlier decision of the House of Lords in *Campbell v MGN Ltd* [2004] UKHL 22; [2004] 2 AC 457:

> First, neither article has as such precedence over the other. Secondly, where the values under the two articles are in conflict, an intense focus on the comparative importance of the specific rights being claimed in the individual case is necessary. Thirdly, the justifications for interfering with or restricting each right must be taken into account. Finally, the proportionality test must be applied to each.

His Lordship goes on to say, at para 30:

> A criminal trial is a public event. The principle of open justice puts, as has often been said, the judge and all who participate in the trial under intense scrutiny. The glare of contemporaneous publicity ensures that trials are properly conducted. It is a valuable check on the criminal process. Moreover, the public interest may be as much involved in the circumstances of a remarkable acquittal as in a surprising conviction. Informed public debate is necessary about all such matters. Full contemporaneous reporting of criminal trials in progress promotes public confidence in the administration of justice. It promotes the values of the rule of law.

In *Re W (Children: Identification – restrictions on publications)* [2005] EWHC 1564 (Fam); [2006] 1 FLR 1, the court was again called upon to consider the relationship between Arts 8 and 10 of the European Convention on Human Rights. Sir Mark Potter P ruled (at para 53) that:

> each Article propounds a fundamental right which there is a pressing social need to protect. Equally, each Article qualifies the right it propounds so far as it may be lawful, necessary and proportionate to do so in order to accommodate the other. The exercise to be performed is one of parallel analysis in which the starting point is presumptive parity, in that neither Article has precedence over or 'trumps' the other. The exercise of parallel analysis requires the court to examine the justification for interfering with each right and the issue of proportionality is to be considered in respect of each. It is not a mechanical exercise to be decided upon the basis of rival generalities. An intense focus on the comparative importance of the specific rights being claimed in the individual case is necessary before the ultimate balancing test in terms of proportionality is carried out ... [The] interest in open justice [is] a factor to be accorded great weight in both the parallel analysis and the ultimate balancing test and stated that, at first instance, the judge had rightly so treated it ...

His Lordship went on to hold that the weight to be accorded to the right freely to report criminal proceedings will not invariably be determinative of the outcome. Although it is the 'ordinary' rule that the press, as public watchdog, may report everything that takes place in a criminal court, that rule might nonetheless be displaced in unusual or exceptional circumstances.

In *R v Croydon Crown Court ex p Trinity Mirror plc* [2008] EWCA Crim 50, a five-judge Court of Appeal (including the Presidents of the QBD and the Family Division) said that it is 'impossible to over-emphasise the importance to be attached to the ability of the media to report criminal trials ... this represents the embodiment of the principle of open justice in a free country. An important aspect of the public interest in the administration of criminal justice is that the identity of those convicted and sentenced for criminal offences should not be concealed' (per Sir Igor Judge P, at para 32). On this basis, the Court set aside an order protecting the identity of the children of the accused, saying (at para 33) that:

> Everyone appreciates the risk that innocent children may suffer prejudice and damage when a parent is convicted of a serious offence ... However ... if the court were to uphold this

ruling so as to protect the rights of the defendant's children under Article 8, it would be countenancing a substantial erosion of the principle of open justice, to the overwhelming disadvantage of public confidence in the criminal justice system, the free reporting of criminal trials and the proper identification of those convicted and sentenced in them. Such an order cannot begin to be contemplated unless the circumstances are indeed properly to be described as exceptional.

In *C v CPS* [2008] EWHC 854 (Admin); (2008) 172 JP 273, the Divisional Court said that great care must be taken when making orders restricting the reporting of criminal proceedings. Such orders should not to be made as a matter of routine. They require a careful balance of matters relating to the public interest. Before making such an order the court should generally ask members of the press whether they have any submissions.

6.7.1 Lifting the restrictions

Under s 49(5)(a), the court has a discretion to 'dispense to any specified extent' with the reporting restrictions if satisfied that it is 'appropriate to do so for the purpose of avoiding injustice' to the juvenile in question (for instance, where the defence wish to make an appeal for potential witnesses to come forward). The power to lift the reporting restrictions may be exercised by a single justice (s 49(8)).

Furthermore, s 49(5)(b) provides that the court may also lift (wholly or in part) the reporting restrictions in respect of a child or young person who is 'unlawfully at large' (for example, the juvenile was granted bail but has absconded), and the court is satisfied that it is necessary to dispense with those restrictions 'for the purpose of apprehending him'. This provision applies only to a child or young person who is charged with, or who has been convicted of, a violent or sexual offence, or an offence punishable (in the case of an adult) with imprisonment for 14 years or more. Moreover, this power can only be exercised following an application by or on behalf of the Director of Public Prosecutions, which includes applications by the Crown Prosecution Service (s 49(7)).

Perhaps more controversial, under s 49(4A) of the Children and Young Persons Act 1933, the court, if it is satisfied that it would be 'in the public interest to do so', may order that the reporting restrictions should be lifted where the child or young person has been convicted of an offence. The parties to the proceedings must be given an opportunity to make representations before such an order is made (s 49(4B)).

In *McKerry v Teesdale Justices* (2000) 164 JP 355, the Divisional Court noted that there was a tension between the need to protect the juvenile's right to privacy and the 'hallowed principle that justice is administered in public, open to full and fair reporting of the proceedings in court, so that the public may be informed about the justice administered in their name' (per Lord Bingham CJ at para 17). His Lordship stressed that the power to dispense with anonymity must be exercised with 'very great care, caution and circumspection' and added:

It would be wholly wrong for any court to dispense with a juvenile's prima facie right to anonymity as an additional punishment. It is also very difficult to see any place for 'naming and shaming'. The court must be satisfied that the statutory criterion that it is in the public interest to dispense with the reporting restriction is satisfied. This will very rarely be the case, and justices making an order under s 49(4A) must be clear in their minds why it is in the public interest to dispense with the restrictions.

The Divisional Court also held that, in weighing up the public interest, it is open to the court to hear representations from a representative of the press (even from a reporter present in court, who will of course have no formal right of audience).

6.7.2 Reporting restrictions where juveniles appear in an adult court

If a juvenile appears in the adult magistrates' court (or the Crown Court), there are no automatic reporting restrictions to prevent the reporting of the identity of the juvenile, since s 49 of the Children and Young Persons Act 1933 applies only to the youth court. However, reporting restrictions may be ordered by the court under s 39 of the Act.

Under s 39, the court may direct that no newspaper report of the proceedings shall reveal the name, address or school, or include any particulars calculated to lead to the identification of any child or young person concerned in the proceedings, either as defendant or witness; also, no picture of that person may be published in any newspaper.

In *R v Central Criminal Court ex p S* (1999) 163 JP 776, the Divisional Court held that there has to be a good reason for making an order under s 39 preventing identification of a juvenile who appears before an adult court. The court said that in deciding whether or not to make such an order, the weight which the court should attach to the various factors relevant to the decision might be different at differing stages of the proceedings. For example, after the juvenile has been convicted, it might be appropriate to place greater weight on the interest of the public in knowing the identity of those who have committed serious crimes.

In considering the range of factors that may be considered by a court when determining whether or not to make a direction under s 39, some useful guidance comes from the judgment of Simon Brown LJ in *R v Winchester Crown Court ex p B* [1999] 1 WLR 788 at 790 (that decision was not followed in *R v Manchester Crown Court ex p H and D* [2000] 1 WLR 760, but this was on a point that does not affect what is said below). His Lordship identified a set of principles which should be considered when determining whether or not to make a s 39 direction:

(i)   In deciding whether to impose or thereafter to lift reporting restrictions, the court will consider whether there are good reasons for naming the defendant.

(ii) In reaching that decision, the court will give considerable weight to the age of the offender and to the potential damage to any young person of public identification as a criminal before the offender has the benefit or burden of adulthood.

(iii) By virtue of s 44 of the Act of 1933, the court must 'have regard to the welfare of the child or young person'.)

(iv) The prospect of being named in court with the accompanying disgrace is a powerful deterrent and the naming of a defendant in the context of his punishment serves as a deterrent to others. These deterrents are proper objectives for the court to seek.

(v)   There is a strong public interest in open justice and in the public knowing as much as possible about what has happened in court, including the identity of those who have committed crime.

(vi) The weight to be attributed to the different factors may shift at different stages of the proceedings and, in particular, after the defendant has been found, or pleads, guilty and is sentenced. It may then be appropriate to place greater weight on the interest of the public in knowing the identity of those who have committed crimes, particularly serious and detestable crimes.

(vii) The fact that an appeal has been made may be a material consideration.

Under s 39(2), breach of an order under s 39 is punishable with a fine not exceeding level 5 (£5,000). In *R v Tyne Tees Television Ltd* (1997) *The Times*, 20 October, the defendant published material in breach of an order under s 39 of the Children and Young Persons Act 1933. The judge dealt with this as a contempt of court. The Court of Appeal said that the proper course would have been for the judge to report the matter so that proceedings for the offence created by s 39 could be taken, not to treat it as a contempt of court.

In *Briffet & Bradshaw v DPP* [2001] EWHC Admin 841; (2002) 166 JP 66, a newspaper editor appealed against his conviction for an offence under s 39 after publishing information about a juvenile, in breach of an order imposing reporting restrictions. It was held that a person would only be guilty of an offence under s 39 if the terms of the order imposing reporting restrictions are 'clear and unambiguous'. This means that 'the order must leave no doubt, in the mind of a reasonable reader or recipient, as to precisely what it is that is prohibited' (per Laws LJ at para 13). The court added that the making of a s 39 order is only justified if Art 10 of the European Convention on Human Rights is complied with, in the sense that the restriction of free expression is required to meet a 'pressing social need' (para 24).

After an order has been made under s 39, it is open to the court to discharge that order. In *R v Central Criminal Court ex p S* (above), the Divisional Court declined to follow *R v Leicester Crown Court ex p S* [1993] 1 WLR 111, holding that it is *not* the case that an order under s 39 should be discharged only in 'rare and exceptional circumstances'. In *R v Lee* [1993] 1 WLR 103 (CA), Lloyd LJ said at p 110:

> For our part, we would not wish to see the court's discretion fettered so strictly. There is nothing in s 39 about rare or exceptional cases. There must of course be a good reason for making an order under s 39, just as there must be a good reason for lifting the restriction on publicity of proceedings in the [youth] court under s 49, namely to avoid injustice to the child. The rule under s 49, as has been pointed out, is the reverse of the rule under s 39. The onus is . . . the other way round. If the discretion under s 39 is too narrowly confined, we will be in danger of blurring the distinction between proceedings in the [youth] courts and proceedings in the Crown Court, a distinction which Parliament clearly intended to preserve.

It should be noted that, rather anachronistically (and unlike s 49), s 39 applies only to newspapers. However, s 45 of the Youth Justice and Criminal Evidence Act (not in force at the time of writing) replaces s 39 of the 1933 Act. It provides that, in proceedings other than in the youth court, the court may direct that no matter relating to the accused or a witness shall, while he is under the age of 18, be included in any publication if it is likely to lead members of the public to identify him as a person concerned in the proceedings (s 45(3)). The court may make an 'excepting direction', which dispenses, to the extent specified in the direction, with the restrictions imposed by a direction under s 45(3) if it is satisfied that it is necessary in the interests of justice to do so (s 45(4)) or if satisfied that the effect of the restrictions is to impose a substantial and unreasonable restriction on the reporting of the proceedings, and that it is in the public interest to remove or relax that restriction (s 45(5)). The mere fact that the proceedings have been determined or abandoned is not sufficient in itself (ibid). In deciding whether to impose reporting restrictions, or to make an excepting direction, the court must have regard to the welfare of the juvenile in question (s 45(6)). The restrictions apply to any identifying details, but include (in particular) the juvenile's name and address, the identity of any school or other educational establishment attended by him, the identity of any place of work, and any still or moving picture of him (s 45(8)).

6.8 ATTENDANCE OF PARENT OR GUARDIAN

Section 34A(1) of the Children and Young Persons Act 1933 provides that if the juvenile is under 16, the court *must* (or, if the juvenile is 16 or 17, the court *may*) require a parent or guardian 'to attend at the court during all the stages of the proceedings, unless and to the extent that the court is satisfied that it would be unreasonable to require such attendance, having regard to the circumstances of the case'. This was intended by the Government, at least in part, to underline parental responsibility for the wrongdoings of their children. Where the child is in local authority care, he will be accompanied by a local authority social worker or foster parent (see s 34A(2)).

If the juvenile is not legally represented, the court must allow the parent or guardian to assist in the conduct of the defence (see r 38.2(1) of the Criminal Procedure Rules). So, the parent or guardian of an unrepresented juvenile might, for example, assist with the cross-examination of prosecution witnesses.

6.9 FITNESS TO STAND TRIAL

Fitness to plead in the context of adults is dealt with in Chapter 12. In *CPS v P* [2007] EWHC 946 (Admin); (2007) 171 JP 349, the Divisional Court had to consider the issues that arise where a youth court has to consider the question of the young defendant's capacity to stand trial. At para 48, Smith LJ said:

> The test for fitness to plead is that set out in *Pritchard* [1836] 7 C & P 303, namely 'whether the accused will be able to comprehend the course of the proceedings so as to make a proper defence'. Usually, a defendant will only be found unfit to plead when s/he has either mental illness or substantial impairment of intellectual capacity. A child might be *doli incapax* without any such impairment but simply on account of immaturity or the unusual nature of his upbringing. The test for deciding upon fitness to plead bears some resemblance to the criteria . . . relevant to the question of whether a defendant is capable of effective participation in the trial. The criteria are also similar, although not identical, to those . . . relating to the

essential elements of a fair trial ... Thus it appears to me that there is a large measure of overlap between the issues of 'sufficient understanding of right from wrong', 'fitness to plead', 'ability to participate effectively in a trial' and 'the fairness of the trial' ... A child who, due to immaturity or lack of understanding, does not know that what is alleged against him is seriously wrong may well also, for the same reasons, be unable to participate effectively in a trial.

Her Ladyship also emphasised (at paras 54–57) the need to keep the issue of capacity under review and, as part of that review process, to consider whether the case was one where the court should simply make a finding of fact whether the juvenile committed the *actus reus* of the offence (thus enabling a disposal under the Mental Health Act 1983 rather than convicting the accused):

[T]he court has a duty to keep under continuing review the question of whether the criminal trial ought to continue. If at any stage the court concludes that the child is unable to participate effectively in the trial, it may decide to call a halt. However, the court may consider that it is in the interests of the child that the trial should continue ... If the court decides that it should call a halt to the criminal trial on the ground that the child cannot take an effective part in the proceedings, it should then consider whether to switch to a consideration of whether the child has done the acts alleged ... The decision as to whether or not to switch to fact-finding is one for the discretion of the court ... I consider that proceedings should be stayed as an abuse of process before fact-finding only if no useful purpose at all could be served by finding the facts. If the court decides to find the facts and finds that the defendant did the acts alleged, it would then consider whether to seek further medical evidence with a view to making an order under the Mental Health Act 1983. If the court finds that the defendant did not do the acts alleged, the proceedings would be brought to an end by a finding of not guilty.

6.10 PROCEDURE FOR SENTENCING JUVENILES IN THE YOUTH COURT

Where a juvenile has been convicted following a trial in the youth court, he or she will be sentenced by that court: the youth court has no general power to commit the juvenile to the Crown Court for sentence (indeed, the Crown Court has no greater powers of sentence in respect of a juvenile convicted by the youth court). There are, however, two circumstances where committal for sentence is or may be possible: one is where the juvenile pleads guilty to an offence which carries a maximum sentence of at least 14 years' custody, and so falls within s 91 of the Powers of Criminal Courts (Sentencing) Act 2000 (this power of committal, under s 3B of the 2000 Act, was not in force at the time of writing); the other is where the offence falls within the 'dangerous offender' provisions of the Criminal Justice Act 2003, in which case committal for sentence is possible under s 3C of the 2000 Act.

Assuming the juvenile is to be sentenced in the youth court, the procedure to be followed is set out in Pt 44 of the Criminal Procedure Rules. Under r 44.1(2)(a) of the Criminal Procedure Rules, before passing sentence on a juvenile (whether he was found guilty or pleaded guilty), the court must give the juvenile and his parent or guardian the chance to address the court. Under r 44.1(2)(b), the court must consider all available information as to the juvenile's general conduct, home surroundings, school record and medical history. If such information is not available, the court should consider adjourning the case to enable such information to be produced (r 44.1(2)(c)).

There will usually be a pre-sentence report (written by a social worker, rather than a probation officer, as would be the case for an adult offender) and also a school report. Under r 44.1(2)(d), any written report may be received and considered by the court without being read aloud. If reports are read out and the court considers it necessary in the interests of the juvenile, it may require him or his parent or guardian, if present, to withdraw from the court (r 44.1(2)(e)).

However, under r 44.1(3), any written reports have to be made available to the legal representative (if any) of the juvenile, to his parent or guardian (if present at the hearings) and (unless the court otherwise directs on the ground that it appears to it impracticable to disclose the report having regard to his age and understanding, or undesirable to do so having regard to potential serious harm which might thereby be suffered by him) to the juvenile.

6.11 PLACE OF FIRST APPEARANCE

The juvenile's first court appearance in respect of an offence will be in the youth court unless the case is one of the exceptional ones where the first appearance is in the adult magistrates' court. Those exceptional cases are where:

a   the juvenile is jointly charged with an adult; or
b   the juvenile is charged with aiding and abetting an adult to commit an offence (or vice versa); or
c   the juvenile is charged with an offence which arises out of circumstances which are the same as (or connected with) those which resulted in the charge faced by an adult accused.

These exceptions exist because no one who is 18 or older at the time of their first court appearance should ever appear in the youth court, yet defendants who are jointly charged (or charged with closely connected offences) should appear together in court. The result is that a juvenile in such a case appears alongside the adult in the adult magistrates' court.

6.12 PLACE OF TRIAL

We have already seen that a juvenile may be tried in the youth court for an offence which is triable only on indictment in the case of an adult offender, and that a juvenile never has a right to elect trial on indictment.

In this section, we consider the circumstances in which a juvenile may be tried in the Crown Court or in an adult magistrates' court. The law in this area seems to be rather complicated, as it is to be found in a combination of statutory sources:

- s 46 of the Children and Young Persons Act 1933;
- s 18 of the Children and Young Persons Act 1963;
- s 24 of the Magistrates' Courts Act 1980;
- s 29 of the Magistrates' Courts Act 1980.

The key points may, however, be summarised quite briefly. There are five circumstances in which the trial of a juvenile may take place in the *Crown Court*. These are where the juvenile is charged with:

a   homicide (i.e. murder or manslaughter);
b   a firearms offence where there is a mandatory minimum sentence under s 51A of the Firearms Act 1968;
c   an offence to which s 91 of the Powers of Criminal Courts (Sentencing) Act 2000 applies (i.e. an offence which carries at least 14 years' imprisonment in the case of an adult or one that is specified in s 91 itself);
d   a 'specified' offence as defined by s 224 of the Criminal Justice Act 2003 (and so falling within the ambit of the 'dangerous offender' provisions of that Act); or
e   an offence where there is an adult co-accused.

There is only one situation where the trial of a juvenile may take place in an *adult magistrates' court*, namely where the juvenile is charged alongside an adult.

6.12.1 Crown Court trial of juveniles

We will look first at the situations in which a juvenile either may or must be tried in the Crown Court.

6.12.1.1 *Murder and manslaughter; certain firearms offences*

Where a juvenile is charged with homicide (that is, murder or manslaughter), or with offences covered by s 51A of the Firearms Act 1968 (mandatory minimum sentence for certain firearms offences), the trial *must* take place in the Crown Court (s 24(1) of the Magistrates' Courts Act 1980).

6.12.1.2 *Section 91 of the Powers of Criminal Courts (Sentencing) Act 2000*

The next situation where a juvenile may be tried in the Crown Court is where s 91 of the Powers of Criminal Courts (Sentencing) Act 2000 applies to the offence. Section 91 empowers the Crown Court to order that a juvenile be detained for a period not exceeding the maximum sentence of imprisonment which may be imposed on an adult offender for the offence in question. Under s 91(1), this power applies only where a juvenile who has attained the age of 10 is charged with:

a   an offence which carries at least 14 years' imprisonment in the case of an adult offender;

b   certain offences under the Sexual Offences Act 2003, including s 3 of that Act (sexual assault); or

c   a firearms offence to which the mandatory minimum sentence provisions in s 51A of the Firearms Act 1968 apply.

The power to send a juvenile for trial in the Crown Court if he is charged with one or more of these offences is currently contained in s 24(1)(a) of the Magistrates' Courts Act 1980, which empowers the magistrates to send the juvenile to the Crown Court for trial if:

a   s 91 of the 2000 Act applies to the offence; and

b   the court 'considers that if he is found guilty of the offence it ought to be possible to sentence him' to long-term detention under s 91.

These provisions are necessary because of the relatively limited ambit of the custodial sentence that would normally be applicable in the case of an offender under the age of 18, namely the detention and training order (DTO), discussed in Chapter 17. The DTO is limited to a total of 24 months (12 months' custody followed by 12 months' supervision); where the offender has not attained the age of 15, a DTO can only be made if he is a 'persistent offender'; and the DTO is not available at all where the offender is under 12. Section 91 of the 2000 Act enables the Crown Court to pass a longer term of detention than would otherwise be possible (given the 24 month limit on the duration of the DTO), and it enables the Crown Court to impose a term of detention where otherwise no detention would be possible (in the case of an offender under the age of 12, or an offender under the age of 15 who is not a persistent offender).

When s 51A of the Crime and Disorder Act 1998 (added to the 1998 Act by the Criminal Justice Act 2003) comes fully into force, the power to send a juvenile for trial where the offence falls within s 91, and the court takes the view that if he is found guilty of the offence it ought to be possible to sentence him under s 91, will be contained in s 51A(3)(b) of the Crime and Disorder Act 1998).

It should be noted that the Crown Court is not obliged to pass a sentence of detention under s 91 of the 2000 Act. The court retains the power to deal with the offender in any way that the youth court could have done. If the Crown Court decides not to sentence the juvenile under s 91, it is undesirable for the Crown Court to remit the case to the youth court for sentence (under s 8 of the 2000 Act), since the youth court will already have expressed the view that the case is too serious for its powers (see *R v Allen and Lambert* (1999) 163 JP 841).

6.12.1.3   The decision to commit in a s 91 case

Magistrates in the youth court should only commit a juvenile for trial in the Crown Court if, on its facts, the case is sufficiently serious to justify a sentence of detention under s 91 of the 2000 Act.

In *R v Inner London Youth Court ex p DPP* (1997) 161 JP 178, the Divisional Court said that the proper question for magistrates to ask themselves when deciding whether or not to commit a juvenile to the Crown Court for trial in a s 91 case is this: 'If this defendant were convicted of the offence with which he stands charged, would it be "proper" for a Crown Court when sentencing to exercise its powers under s 91?' If the answer is 'yes', the juvenile should be sent to the Crown Court for trial.

This question was revisited in *R (D) v Manchester City Youth Court* [2001] EWHC 860 (Admin); [2002] 1 Cr App R(S) 135. Gage J said that 'a magistrates' court should not decline jurisdiction unless the offence and the circumstances surrounding it and the offender are such as to make it more than a vague or theoretical possibility that a sentence of detention [under s 91] may be passed' (para 22). Of course, this means that the justices must take into account the sentencing practice of the Crown Court and the Court of Appeal in relation to s 91. As Stanley Burnton J observed in *R (C and D) v Sheffield Youth Court; R (N) v Sheffield Youth Court* [2003] EWHC 35 (Admin); (2003) 167 JP 159 (at para 39):

> In deciding whether it considers that it ought to be possible to sentence a defendant pursuant to s 91, the youth court must consider the sentencing powers of the Crown Court and the guidance that has been given as to their exercise. If, on the basis of that guidance, there is no real possibility of such a sentence, committal is inappropriate.

His Lordship added (at para 40) that, in making its decision, the youth court should take into account any undisputed facts put forward as mitigation (such as the good character of the accused). However, contentious mitigation should be ignored: if the case is sent to the Crown Court and the defendant is convicted, mitigation will be a matter for that court.

In *R (D) v Manchester City Youth Court*, Gage J noted that there is nothing in the statute to prevent the Crown Court using its powers under s 91 to impose a sentence of less than two years' detention (indeed, Lord Lane CJ in *R v Fairhurst* (1986) 8 Cr App R(S) 346 (at p 349) had said that a sentence of less than two years may well be appropriate in some cases). However, his Lordship said (at para 23) that:

> ... it will only be in very exceptional and restricted circumstances that it will be appropriate to do so, rather than make a detention and training order. The fact that an offender ... does not qualify for a detention and training order because he is not a persistent offender does not seem to me such an exceptional circumstance as to justify the passing of a period of detention of less than two years under s 91.

Gage J modified his view slightly in *R (W) v Thetford Youth Court* [2002] EWHC 1252; [2003] 1 Cr App R(S) 67, where he said that he remained of the opinion that, in respect of offenders under 15, if the court is prohibited from making a DTO, an order under s 91 will not generally be appropriate. His Lordship added (at para 29) that he also remained of the view that:

> where an offence or offences are likely to attract a sentence of less than two years' custody the appropriate sentence will be a detention and training order. In the case of an offender under 15, who is not a persistent offender or a child under 12, the most likely sentence will be a non-custodial sentence. It follows that in most cases the appropriate place of trial will be the youth court.

However, his Lordship went on to say (at para 30) that he accepted:

> that there may be cases where, despite the fact that the offender is under 15 and no
> detention and training order can be made, the only appropriate sentence is a custodial
> sentence pursuant to s 91 and possibly for a period of less than two years. But I remain of
> the opinion that the circumstances of the offence and offender will only rarely call for a
> sentence pursuant to s 91, particularly if the court is dealing with an offender under the age
> of 12. In expressing my views . . . *R (D) v Manchester City Youth Court*, my use of the expression
> 'very exceptional' may be more restrictive than was strictly necessary or justified. But, I
> remain of the view that the mere fact that a youth court, unable to make a short detention
> and training order, considers that the option to pass a short custodial sentence should be
> available, does not mean that it should decline jurisdiction. It seems to me that in such
> circumstances the fact that a detention and training order is not available indicates that
> Parliament intended that generally a non-custodial sentence should be passed. Perhaps it
> would be better to say that cases involving offenders under 15 for whom a detention and
> training order is not available will only rarely attract a period of detention under s 91; the
> more rarely if the offender is under 12.

An important issue is whether the magistrates are entitled to have regard to the fact that
the Crown Court is inherently a less suitable forum for the trial of younger defendants.
In *R v Devizes Youth Court ex p A* (2000) 164 JP 330, it was held that where a youth
court decides that a custodial sentence (where that is only available in the Crown Court)
or a longer period of custody than would be available (under a DTO) needed to be an
option available to the sentencing court, the youth court has no option but to send the
juvenile to the Crown Court for trial. The court specifically ruled out the argument that
the Crown Court is not a suitable place to deal with a case against a juvenile, holding
that the relevant provisions of international conventions (the United Nations' Standard
Minimum Rules for the Administration of Juvenile Justice, the United Nations' Convention on the Rights of the Child and the European Convention on Human Rights)
affect the way in which the trial is conducted and not the decision as to whether the case
is dealt with in the Crown Court or the youth court. As Brooke LJ put it, at para 15, if
the justices form the judgment that if the defendant is found guilty of the offence it
ought to be possible to sentence him to detention under s 91, then they are 'bound' to
send him to the Crown Court for trial. It follows from *Devizes* that if the defendant
before the youth court is charged with an offence to which s 91 applies, the only
question for a youth court is whether it considers that if he is found guilty of the
offence, it ought to be possible to sentence him pursuant to s 91. Once it so considers,
the youth court has no discretion in the matter. Questions of the suitability of the
Crown Court for the trial of the offender are irrelevant to the decision to be made by
the youth court.

However, in *R (W) v Southampton Youth Court* [2002] EWHC 1640 (Admin); [2003]
1 Cr App R(S) 87, Lord Woolf CJ said (at para 16):

> While the need to impose the appropriate sentence is important, so is the need to ensure
> that wherever possible the trial should take place in the appropriate settings. That is more
> satisfactorily achieved in a youth court than in a Crown Court.

His Lordship went on to say (at para 18) that the justices:

> should start off with a strong presumption against sending young offenders to the Crown Court unless they are satisfied that that is clearly required, notwithstanding the fact that the forum for trial will not be so appropriate as the Youth Court.

In *R (C and D) v Sheffield Youth Court; R (N) v Sheffield Youth Court* [2003] EWHC 35 (Admin); (2003) 167 JP 159, Stanley Burnton J said that he did not think that Lord Woolf had intended to suggest that a youth court which considers that it ought to be possible to sentence the defendant pursuant to s 91 nonetheless has a discretion whether or not to commit him to the Crown Court. His Lordship said (at para 38) that:

> If he did, his observation was inconsistent with the decision in *Devizes*, where the point was the basis of its decision, and I should follow *Devizes*. In any event, in my judgment, *Devizes* was correctly decided. Section 24(1) unambiguously requires the youth court to commit to the Crown Court if the conditions for the exercise of the power to commit are satisfied: the words are 'the Court shall commit the accused for trial'. Parliament has decided that the Crown Court is the suitable venue for the trial of persons under the age of 18 if the conditions expressly laid down by s 24(1) are satisfied.

In *R(C) v Balham Youth Court* [2003] EWHC 1332 (Admin); [2004] 1 Cr App R (S) 22, Scott Baker LJ (at para 33) said that:

> the fact that an offender . . . does not qualify for a detention and training order because he is only 14 and not a persistent offender is not an exceptional circumstance to justify passing a sentence of less than two years under s 91 of the 2000 Act.

At para 34 he said that the relevant question is whether the case is a serious one that detention above two years would or might realistically be required. In *R(M and W) v West London Youth Court* [2004] EWHC 1144 (Admin), Leveson J (at para 16) put the same question in slightly different terms:

> . . . whether there is a real prospect that a custodial sentence of, or in excess of, two years might be required, or is there any unusual feature of this case which might justify a sentence of less than two years, pursuant to s 91, for which purpose the absence of a power to impose a detention and training order because the offender is under the age of 15 is not an unusual feature.

In *R (H) v Southampton Youth Court* [2004] EWHC 2912 (Admin); [2005] 2 Cr App R (S) 30, it was emphasised that defendants under 18, and in particular those under 15, should be tried in the youth court, with Crown Court jurisdiction being reserved for the most serious crimes. It would, said the court, only be in exceptional cases that a defendant aged 12–14 would be sent for trial to the Crown Court. Leveson J summarised the relevant principles as follows (at paras 33–35):

> 33. The general policy of the legislature is that those who are under 18 years of age, and in

particular children of under 15 years of age, should, wherever possible, be tried in the youth court. It is that court which is best designed to meet their specific needs. A trial in the Crown Court with the inevitably greater formality and greatly increased number of people involved (including a jury and the public) should be reserved for the most serious cases.

34. It is a further policy of the legislature that, generally speaking, first-time offenders aged 12 to 14 and all offenders under 12 should not be detained in custody and decisions as to jurisdiction should have regard to the fact that the exceptional power to detain for grave offences should not be used to water down the general principle. Those under 15 will rarely attract a period of detention and, even more rarely, those who are under 12.

35. In each case the court should ask itself whether there is a real prospect, having regard to his or her age, that this defendant whose case they are considering might require a sentence of, or in excess of, two years or, alternatively, whether although the sentence might be less than two years, there is some unusual feature of the case which justifies declining jurisdiction, bearing in mind that the absence of a power to impose a detention and training order because the defendant is under 15 is not an unusual feature.

In *R (CPS) v Redbridge Youth Court* [2005] EWHC 1390; (2005) 169 JP 393, the court (at para 11) summarised the key principles as follows:

- Although it is not necessary, in order to invoke s 91 of the PCC(S)A 2000 that the crime be one of exceptional gravity, the power to make an order for detention is a long-stop reserved for very serious offences.
- In cases to which s 91 applies, the youth court should start with a strong presumption against sending a young defendant to the Crown Court unless it is satisfied that it is clearly required. The general policy of the legislature is that those under 18 years of age and, in particular, children under 15 years of age, should, wherever possible, be tried in the youth court. A trial in the Crown Court should be reserved for the most serious cases.
- Accordingly, the magistrates should not decline jurisdiction unless the offence and the circumstances surrounding it and the offender are such as to make it more than a vague or theoretical possibility that a sentence of detention for a long period might be passed under s 91.
- Given that the maximum period for which a magistrates' court might impose a detention and training order is 24 months, s 91 is primarily applicable to cases of such gravity that the court is or might be considering a sentence of at least two years. There must be a real possibility or a real prospect of such a sentence.

Further guidance was given by the Divisional Court in *R(CPS) v South East Surrey Youth Court* [2005] EWHC 2929 (Admin); [2006] 1 WLR 2543, where it was said (by Rose LJ at para 17) that, when deciding whether or not to send a juvenile for trial in the Crown Court, justices should bear in mind:

(i)   the policy of the legislature . . . that those who are under 18 should, wherever possible, be tried in a youth court, which is best designed for their specific needs . . .

(v)   when a youth under 18 is jointly charged with an adult, an exercise of judgment will be called for by the youth court when assessing the competing presumptions in favour of (a) joint trial of those jointly charged and (b) the trial of youths in the youth court. Factors relevant to that judgment will include the age and maturity of the youth, the comparative culpability in relation to the offence and the previous convictions of the two and whether the trial can be severed without either injustice or undue inconvenience to witnesses.

The decision to send a juvenile for trial under s 24 of the Magistrates' Courts Act 1980 (or s 51A of the Crime and Disorder Act, which will be the relevant authority when it comes into force) is based on representations made by the prosecution and the defence. No evidence is called (*R v South Hackney Juvenile Court ex p RB and CB* (1983) 77 Cr App R 294).

To make a sound decision, the magistrates need full and accurate information. In *R (W, S and B) v Brent, Enfield and Richmond Youth Courts* [2006] EWHC 95 (Admin); (2006) 170 JP 198, Smith LJ (at para 6) said:

> If the Youth Court is to make a satisfactory decision it must have all the necessary information before it. The facts of the case as alleged, which must be assumed to be true unless manifestly not, should be accurately put before the court. For that reason, the summary of the facts must be scrupulously fair and balanced, and it is the duty of both advocates to ensure that that is so. The court should be told of any undisputed mitigation that will be available to the defendant including, if one has already been made, an indication of an intention to plead guilty. Also the defendant's previous record must be accurately described . . .

It used to be the case that the youth court should not be told of any previous findings of guilt recorded against the juvenile (*R v Hammersmith Juvenile Court ex p O* (1987) 86 Cr App R 843). However, that rule is no longer applicable. When a youth court is deciding whether or not to commit a juvenile to stand trial in the Crown Court in a case where there is a possibility of a sentence of detention under s 91, the court is entitled to know about any previous findings of guilt recorded against the juvenile (*R (Tullet) v Medway Magistrates' Court* [2003] EWHC 2279 (Admin); (2003) 167 JP 541, where the court said that it would be illogical to ignore matters that would be relevant to the sentencing court).

6.12.1.4 Juveniles charged with several offences

Where a juvenile appears before a youth court charged with a number of offences and is sent to the Crown Court in respect of some (but not all) of them, the youth court is not required to adjourn proceedings in respect of the other offences (s 10(3A) of the Magistrates' Courts Act 1980).

Section 24(1A) of the Magistrates' Courts Act 1980 provides that where a magistrates' court sends a juvenile to the Crown Court in a case to which s 91 of the Powers of Criminal Courts (Sentencing) Act 2000 applies, the court may also send him for trial for any other indictable offence with which he is charged at the same time, even if the other indictable offence is not within the ambit of s 91, provided that the charges for both offences can properly be joined in the same indictment. This will be the case where

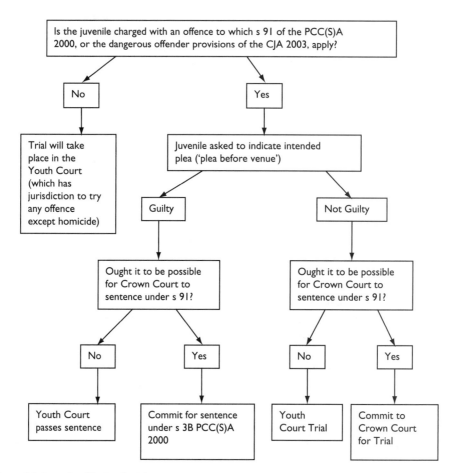

Figure 6.1 Juveniles: Mode of trial.

the offences are founded on the same facts or form (part of) a series of offences of the same (or a similar) character. Obviously, in the event of conviction, the Crown Court could only order long-term detention in respect of those offences to which s 91 applies.

When s 51A of the Crime and Disorder Act 1998 comes into force, sub-s (4) will empower the magistrates, if they send a juvenile for trial for an offence to which s 91 of the 2000 Act applies, to send him for trial for any indictable or summary offence with which he is also charged and which appears to the court to be related to the s 91 offence (if the offence is a summary one it must be punishable with imprisonment or involve disqualification from driving).

6.12.1.5 Revisiting the decision to try the case summarily where s 91 applies

Section 25(6) currently applies where the court is trying an offence to which s 91 applies and it appears to the court at any time before the conclusion of the evidence for the prosecution that the case is, after all, one which should have been sent to the Crown

Court for trial. It empowers the court to discontinue the summary trial and send the case to the Crown Court instead. Under s 25(7) if, during committal proceedings in respect of an offence to which s 91 applies, the court decides that it was in fact unnecessary to send the case to the Crown Court, it may proceed to try the case summarily instead.

In *R (H) v Balham Youth Court* [2003] EWHC 3267; (2004) 168 JP 177, the Divisional Court ruled that a youth court has the power under s 25 of the Magistrates' Courts Act 1980 to reopen its decision as to mode of trial in cases where there is a power to commit for trial with a view to the imposition of a sentence under s 91. Thus, if the youth court decides to try the case, it has power under s 25 to terminate the trial and send the case to the Crown Court for trial instead. However, the court ruled that, in light of earlier case law (including *R v Liverpool Justices ex p CPS* (1990) 90 Cr App R 261), the court cannot reopen its original decision concerning mode of trial until it actually embarks upon the summary trial (or, until committal proceedings have been abolished, the committal hearing). Once the court has embarked upon the hearing, it has at its disposal the various powers set out in s 25 of the 1980 Act.

In *R (on the Application of K) v Leeds Youth Court* [2001] EWHC 177 (Admin); (2001) 165 JP 694, it was held that the exercise of the discretion under s 25(6) has to be based on good, proper and relevant reasons, relating to the seriousness of the offence. The magistrates are entitled to keep the trial under review and to change their decision, if it becomes apparent that the original decision is no longer appropriate. Circumstances justifying such a decision are likely to vary from case to case, but include a change in circumstances and instances where new material emerges; also cases where, as the evidence unfolds, the manner in which it is presented would justify such a decision. In the present case, once it became clear to the justices that the oral testimony had put a different perspective on the bare statement of the offences, they were entitled to exercise their powers under s 25(6).

The position will change when the amendments to s 25 of the 1980 Act brought about by the Criminal Justice Act 2003 come into force. Those amendments are discussed in Chapter 5. The revised version of s 25 will apply only where the defendant has attained the age of 18, and so will not apply to the youth court.

6.12.1.6 Challenging refusal to commit for trial in a s 91 case

If the juvenile is charged with an offence which falls within the ambit of s 91 of the Powers of Criminal Courts (Sentencing) Act 2000 but the magistrates decide to try the case summarily, the prosecution may seek judicial review to quash that decision if it is unreasonable (*R v Inner London Youth Court ex p DPP* (1997) 161 JP 178). In *R (DPP) v Camberwell Youth Court; R (H) v Camberwell Youth Court* [2004] EWHC 1805 (Admin); [2005] 1 WLR 810, the Divisional Court said that such decisions should be challenged by means of an application for judicial review (and not the seeking of a voluntary bill of indictment, as to which see Chapter 9).

6.12.1.7 Challenging the decision to commit for trial in a s 91 case

Similarly, the appropriate procedure for challenging a decision to send a juvenile to the Crown Court for trial is to seek judicial review in the High Court. In *R v AH* [2002]

EWCA Crim 2938; (2003) 167 JP 30, the youth court sent the defendant to the Crown Court for trial. At the start of the trial in the Crown Court, an application to stay the proceedings as an abuse of process was made on the ground that the case should not have been sent for trial. It was held that the appropriate forum for challenging the decision to send for trial is the Divisional Court (by way of an application for judicial review) rather than by making an abuse of process application in the Crown Court.

It used to be thought that the Divisional Court would apply the well known *Wednesbury* 'perversity' test to any challenge to a decision to send for trial. However, in *R (W) v Thetford Youth Court* [2002] EWHC 1252; [2003] 1 Cr App R(S) 67, Sedley LJ (at para 40) said that, 'The question is . . . not whether the youth court's judgment has crossed the bounds of rationality but whether in our judgment it is wrong'. Similarly, in *R (W) v Southampton Youth Court* [2002] EWHC 1640 (Admin); [2003] 1 Cr App R(S) 87, Lord Woolf CJ (at para 21) said:

> The right test to apply is to ask the question: did the Youth Court come to a decision which I would regard as being wrong? It may not necessarily be the same decision to which I would have come. Before we interfere, we have to come to the conclusion that the decision is wrong.

The same approach was adopted in *R (C and D) v Sheffield Youth Court* [2003] EWHC 35 (Admin); (2003) 167 JP 159, where Stanley Burnton J (at para 41) said that the test to be applied by the High Court on judicial review of a decision of a Youth Court under s 24(1) of the 1980 Act is this:

> In the judgment of the High Court, was the decision of the Youth Court wrong? The test is one appropriate to a review court rather than one making the original decision. Parliament has clearly given the original decision to the Youth Court, and in terms that admit of some latitude . . . It is not sufficient for the High Court to consider that it would have made a different decision . . . to that of the Youth Court. Only if the High Court is satisfied that the original decision was wrong may it interfere.

Where a youth court intends to decline jurisdiction to hear a case and send a young defendant for trial at the Crown Court, the magistrates should give reasons for this decision (*R (C) v Balham Youth Court* [2003] EWHC 1332 (Admin); (2003) 167 JP 525 (per Scott Baker LJ at para 14)).

6.12.1.8 Joint charge with adult to be tried in the Crown Court

The next situation where a juvenile may be tried in the Crown Court is where the juvenile is jointly charged with an adult. Where a juvenile and an adult are jointly charged, their first court appearance will be in an adult magistrates' court (not a youth court, which would be an inappropriate forum for a case involving an adult defendant).

Where there is an adult co-accused, the first matter to be determined is whether he is going to plead guilty or not guilty; and, if he is going to plead not guilty, whether he is to be tried in the Crown Court or the magistrates' court. Section 24(1)(b) of the Magistrates' Courts Act 1980 provides that a juvenile may be sent to the Crown Court to be tried jointly with an adult if:

- the juvenile is jointly charged with the adult (in practice, this will include cases where one is alleged to have aided and abetted the other, since both will usually be charged as principal offenders); and
- the adult is going to be tried in the Crown Court (either because the offence is triable only on indictment in the case of an adult, or else the mode of trial hearing resulted in a decision in favour of trial on indictment rather than summary trial); and
- the justices decide that it is 'necessary in the interests of justice' that the juvenile and the adult should both be sent to the Crown Court for trial.

In deciding whether or not it is 'necessary in the interests of justice' to send the juvenile to the Crown Court under s 24(1)(b), the court has to balance what may well be conflicting interests. On the one hand, it is desirable that there should be a joint trial, to avoid the cost and inconvenience of having two trials (e.g. prosecution witnesses having to give their evidence twice), to avoid the risk of inconsistent verdicts, and to avoid the risk of disparity in the sentences which are passed in the event of conviction. On the other hand, a juvenile may well find appearing in the Crown Court an unduly traumatic experience.

Paragraph 3.7.3 of the Draft Guidelines on allocation issued by the Sentencing Guidelines Council (<http://www.sentencing-guidelines.gov.uk/docs/allocation_draft_guideline_160206.pdf>) make the point that, where one or more of the defendants is a juvenile, any presumption in favour of sending the juvenile to the Crown Court to be tried jointly with an adult who is being sent there must be balanced with the general presumption that young defendants should be dealt with in a youth court. The Draft Guidelines give examples of factors that should be considered when deciding whether to separate the youth and adult defendants:

- the young age of the offender, particularly where the age gap between the adult and youth offender is substantial;
- the immaturity and intellect of the youth;
- the relative culpability of the youth compared with the adult and whether or not the role played by the youth was minor;
- lack of previous convictions on the part of the youth compared with the adult offender;
- whether the trial of the adult and youth can be severed without inconvenience to witnesses or injustice to the case as a whole.

Similar points are made in the CPS guidance on 'youth offenders' (<http://www.cps.gov.uk/legal/section4/chapter_b.html>), where the relevant factors are said to include:

- the respective ages of the adult and youth;
- the respective roles of the youth and adult in the commission of the offence;
- the likely plea;
- whether there are existing charges against the youth before the youth court;
- the need to deal with the youth as expeditiously as possible consistent with the interests of justice; and
- the likely sentence upon conviction.

Generally speaking, the younger the juvenile and the less serious the charge, the more reluctant the justices should be to send the juvenile to the Crown Court. Also relevant is the likely plea of the juvenile and the degree of his involvement in the offence. If the juvenile is likely to plead guilty and it is accepted by the prosecution that he played only a minor role in the offence, it is likely to be more appropriate to deal with him separately.

It should also be noted that if a juvenile is sent for trial in the Crown Court because he is jointly charged with an adult, he may also be tried in the Crown Court for any other indictable offence which is charged at the same time, provided that it can validly be joined in the same indictment (s 24(2) of the Magistrates' Courts Act 1980).

Normally, s 24(1)(b) will be relevant where a juvenile and an adult appear together in an adult magistrates' court. However, in *R v Coventry City Magistrates ex p M* (1992) 156 JP 809, it was held that the power to send a juvenile for trial in the Crown Court under s 24(1)(b) is not confined to an adult magistrates' court in which the adult and the juvenile appear together. A youth court can also exercise this power in a case where a juvenile before it is to be jointly indicted with an adult who has already been sent for trial by an adult magistrates' court.

When it comes fully into force, s 51 of the Crime and Disorder Act 1998 will replace s 24(1)(b) of the 1980 Act. Where the juvenile is charged jointly with an adult who has been sent for trial for the same or a related offence, the court shall, if it considers it necessary in the interests of justice to do so, send the juvenile forthwith to the Crown Court for trial for the indictable offence and for any related offences, though if a related offence is a summary offence, this provision will apply only if it is punishable with imprisonment or involves obligatory or discretionary disqualification from driving (s 51(7)).

6.12.1.9 Special arrangements where a juvenile is tried in an adult court: treatment of vulnerable defendants

In *V v UK* (2000) 30 EHRR 121, the European Court of Human Rights scrutinised the procedure adopted for the murder trial of juveniles in the Crown Court. At the opening of the trial, the judge made an order (under s 39 of the Children and Young Persons Act 1933) that there should be no publication of the names, addresses or other identifying details of the accused, or publication of their photographs. Nevertheless, the trial took place in the full glare of national and international publicity. The Court held the right of the two accused to a fair trial under Art 6(1) had been violated. The Court stated that it is essential that a young child charged with a serious offence attracting high levels of media interest should be tried in such a way as to reduce as far as possible any feelings of intimidation. It considered that the formality and ritual of the Crown Court must at times have seemed incomprehensible and intimidating for a child aged 11. Moreover, there was evidence that certain of the modifications to the courtroom, in particular the raised dock (which was designed to enable the accused to see what was going on), had the adverse effect of increasing their sense of discomfort during the trial, since they felt exposed to the scrutiny of the press and public. Further, there was evidence that the post-traumatic stress disorder suffered by the accused, combined with the lack of any therapeutic work since the offence, had limited their ability to instruct lawyers or testify in their own defence. The Court found that they were unable to follow the trial or take decisions in their own best interests. They were therefore unable to participate effectively in the criminal proceedings against them and were, in consequence, denied a fair hearing in breach of Art 6(1).

It should be emphasised that the Court did not find that trial of juveniles in the Crown Court is necessarily unfair, only that appropriate adaptations to the procedure have to be made to accommodate the needs of the young defendant.

Paragraph III.30 of the *Consolidated Practice Direction* makes detailed provision for changes to the procedure of the court to accommodate the needs of vulnerable defendants, including young ones. It provides as follows:

III.30.1 This direction applies to proceedings in the Crown Court and in magistrates' courts on the trial, sentencing or (in the Crown Court) appeal of (a) children and young persons under 18 or (b) adults who suffer from a mental disorder within the meaning of the Mental Health Act 1983 or who have any other significant impairment of intelligence and social function. In this direction such defendants are referred to collectively as 'vulnerable defendants'. The purpose of this direction is to extend to proceedings in relation to such persons in the adult courts procedures analogous to those in use in youth courts.

III.30.2 The steps which should be taken to comply with paragraphs III.30.3 to III.30.17 should be judged, in any given case, taking account of the age, maturity and development (intellectual, social and emotional) of the defendant concerned and all other circumstances of the case.

The overriding principle

III.30.3 A defendant may be young and immature or may have a mental disorder within the meaning of the Mental Health Act 1983 or some other significant impairment of intelligence and social function such as to inhibit his understanding of and participation in the proceedings. The purpose of criminal proceedings is to determine guilt, if that is in issue, and decide on the appropriate sentence if the defendant pleads guilty or is convicted. All possible steps should be taken to assist a vulnerable defendant to understand and participate in those proceedings. The ordinary trial process should, so far as necessary, be adapted to meet those ends. Regard should be had to the welfare of a young defendant as required by section 44 of the Children and Young Persons Act 1933, and generally to Parts 1 and 3 of the Criminal Procedure Rules (the overriding objective and the court's powers of case management).

Before the trial, sentencing or appeal

III.30.4 If a vulnerable defendant, especially one who is young, is to be tried jointly with one who is not, the court should consider at the plea and case management hearing, or at a case management hearing in a magistrates' court, whether the vulnerable defendant should be tried on his own and should so order unless of the opinion that a joint trial would be in accordance with Part 1 of the Criminal Procedure Rules (the overriding objective) and in the interests of justice. If a vulnerable defendant is tried jointly with one who is not, the court should consider whether any of the modifications set out in this direction should apply in the circumstances of the joint trial and so far as practicable make orders to give effect to any such modifications.

III.30.5 At the plea and case management hearing, or at a case management hearing in a magistrates' court, the court should consider and so far as practicable give directions on the matters covered in paragraphs III.30.9 to III.30.17.

III.30.6 It may be appropriate to arrange that a vulnerable defendant should visit, out of court hours and before the trial, sentencing or appeal hearing, the courtroom in which that hearing is to take place so that he can familiarise himself with it.

III.30.7 If any case against a vulnerable defendant has attracted or may attract wide-spread public or media interest, the assistance of the police should be enlisted to try and ensure that the defendant is not, when attending the court, exposed to intimidation, vilification or abuse. Section 41 of the Criminal Justice Act 1925 prohibits the taking of photographs of defendants and witnesses (among others) in the court building or in its precincts, or when entering or leaving those precincts. A direction informing media representatives that the prohibition will be enforced may be appropriate.

III.30.8 The court should be ready at this stage, if it has not already done so, where relevant to make a reporting restriction under section 39 of the Children and Young Persons Act 1933 or, on an appeal to the Crown Court from a youth court, to remind media representatives of the application of section 49 of that Act. Any such order, once made, should be reduced to writing and copies should on request be made available to anyone affected or potentially affected by it.

The trial, sentencing or appeal hearing

III.30.9 Subject to the need for appropriate security arrangements the proceedings should, if practicable, be held in a courtroom in which all the participants are on the same or almost the same level.

III.30.10 A vulnerable defendant, especially if he is young, should normally, if he wishes, be free to sit with members of his family or others in a like relationship, and with some other suitable supporting adult such as a social worker, and in a place which permits easy, informal communication with his legal representatives. The court should ensure that a suitable supporting adult is available throughout the course of the proceedings.

III.30.11 At the beginning of the proceedings the court should ensure that what is to take place has been explained to a vulnerable defendant in terms he can understand, and at trial in the Crown Court it should ensure in particular that the role of the jury has been explained. It should remind those representing the vulnerable defendant and the supporting adult of their responsibility to explain each step as it takes place, and at trial to explain the possible consequences of a guilty verdict. Throughout the trial the court should continue to ensure, by any appropriate means, that the defendant understands what is happening and what has been said by those on the bench, the advocates and witnesses.

III.30.12 A trial should be conducted according to a timetable which takes full account of a vulnerable defendant's ability to concentrate. Frequent and regular breaks will often be appropriate. The court should ensure, so far as practicable, that the trial is conducted in simple, clear language that the defendant can understand and that cross-examination is conducted by questions that are short and clear.

III.30.13 A vulnerable defendant who wishes to give evidence by live link in accordance with section 33A of the Youth Justice and Criminal Evidence Act 1999 may apply for a direction to that effect. Before making such a direction the court must be satisfied that it is in the interests of justice to do so, and that the use of a live link would enable the defendant to participate more effectively as a witness in the proceedings. The direction will need to deal with the practical arrangements to be made, including the room from which the defendant will give evidence, the identity of the person or persons who will accompany him, and how it will be arranged for him to be seen and heard by the court.

III.30.14 In the Crown Court robes and wigs should not be worn unless the court for good reason orders that they should. It may be appropriate for the court to be robed for sentencing in a grave case even though it has sat without robes for trial. It is generally desirable that those responsible for the security of a vulnerable defendant who is in custody, especially if he is young, should not be in uniform, and that there should be no recognisable police presence in the courtroom save for good reason.

III.30.15 The court should be prepared to restrict attendance by members of the public in the courtroom to a small number, perhaps limited to those with an immediate and direct interest in the outcome. The court should rule on any challenged claim to attend.

III.30.16 Facilities for reporting the proceedings (subject to any restrictions under section 39 or 49 of the Children and Young Persons Act 1933) must be provided. But the court may restrict the number of reporters attending in the courtroom to such number as is judged practicable and desirable. In ruling on any challenged claim to attend in the court-room for the purpose of reporting the court should be mindful of the public's general right to be informed about the administration of justice.

III.30.17 Where it has been decided to limit access to the courtroom, whether by reporters or generally, arrangements should be made for the proceedings to be relayed, audibly and if possible visually, to another room in the same court complex to which the media and the public have access if it appears that there will be a need for such additional facilities. Those making use of such a facility should be reminded that it is to be treated as an extension of the courtroom and that they are required to conduct themselves accordingly.

III.30.18 Where the court is called upon to exercise its discretion in relation to any pro-cedural matter falling within the scope of this practice direction but not the subject of specific reference, such discretion should be exercised having regard to the principles in paragraph III.30.3.

Lord Justice Auld, in Chapter 5 of his *Review of the Criminal Courts of England and Wales*, considered (in paras 207–11) the trial of young defendants. He makes the point that youth court justices are specially trained to deal with juveniles, whereas a ran-domly selected jury has no such training; he also notes that the period of delay between arrest and disposal is much greater in the Crown Court than in the youth court (he quoted figures from 2001, where the period between arrest and sentence for young offenders was 197 days in the Crown Court as against 66 days in the youth court). In any event, there remains the question of whether Crown Court trial is really appropri-ate for young defendants, even if the trial process is modified. The Review recommends that:

48   All cases involving young defendants who are presently committed to the Crown Court for trial or for sentence should in future be put before the youth court consisting, as appropriate, of a High Court Judge, Circuit Judge or Recorder sitting with at least two

experienced magistrates and exercising the full jurisdiction of the present Crown Court for this purpose.

49 The only possible exception should be those cases in which the young defendant is charged jointly with an adult and it is considered necessary in the interests of justice for them to be tried together.

50 The youth court so constituted should be entitled, save where it considers that public interest demands otherwise, to hear such cases in private, as in the youth court exercising its present jurisdiction.

This proposal was only accepted to a limited extent in that, under the Courts Act 2003, all High Court and Crown Court judges are given the power to act as justices of the peace (and so are entitled to exercise the jurisdiction of justices); using this power, a senior judge could sit as a justice in a magistrates' court or youth court. Thus, the Courts Act 2003 in effect lays the foundation for the reform suggested by Lord Justice Auld.

The danger of Crown Court trial being inappropriate for some young defendants is highlighted by the decision of the European Court of Human Rights in *SC v UK* (2004) 40 EHRR 10. The applicant, who was aged 11 years at the time, challenged the fairness of his Crown Court trial. The European Court held that there had been a breach of the applicant's right to a fair trial. The Court said that the right of an accused to effective participation in the trial includes not only the right to be present, but also to hear and follow the proceedings (para 28). The Court went on (in the same paragraph) to say that:

In the case of a child, it is essential that he be dealt with in a manner which takes full account of his age, level of maturity and intellectual and emotional capacities, and that steps are taken to promote his ability to understand and participate in the proceedings . . . including conducting the hearing in such a way as to reduce as far as possible his feelings of intimidation and inhibition. . .

At para 29, the Court went on:

The defendant should be able to follow what is said by the prosecution witnesses and, if represented, to explain to his own lawyers his version of events, point out any statements with which he disagrees and make them aware of any facts which should be put forward in his defence.

In the present case, two experts had assessed the juvenile as having a very low intellectual level for his age. The Court said that it could not conclude that the juvenile was capable of participating effectively in his trial.

The Court concluded (in para 35) as follows:

The court considers that, when the decision is taken to deal with a child, such as the applicant, who risks not being able to participate effectively because of his young age and limited intellectual capacity, by way of criminal proceedings rather than some other form of disposal directed primarily at determining the child's best interests and those of the community, it is essential that he be tried in a specialist tribunal which is able to give full consideration to and make proper allowance for the handicaps under which he labours, and adapt its procedure accordingly.

The trial in this case took place before the measures set out in the *Consolidated Practice Direction* first came into effect, but it is unlikely that the measures in that Practice Direction would have brought about a different result. However, the effect of the decision of the European Court would seem to be confined to children whose intellectual level is unusually low.

In *R (TP) v West London Youth Court* [2005] EWHC 2583 (Admin), [2006] 1 WLR 1219, the main issue was whether the intellectual capacity of the accused (who was aged 15 but had a mental age of 8) was such that he could not effectively participate in the proceedings. It was held (considering *SC v UK* (above)), that neither youth nor limited intellectual capacity necessarily leads to a breach of Art 6. What is crucial is whether the tribunal hearing the case (whether a youth court or adult court) is able to adapt its procedures so that the defendant can participate effectively in the proceedings. At para 26, Scott Baker LJ suggested steps such as:

(i)   keeping the claimant's level of cognitive functioning in mind;

(ii)   using concise and simple language;

(iii)   having regular breaks;

(iv)   taking additional time to explain court proceedings;

(v)   being proactive in ensuring the claimant has access to support;

(vi)   explaining and ensuring the claimant understands the ingredients of the charge;

(vii)   explaining the possible outcomes and sentences;

(viii) ensuring that cross-examination is carefully controlled so that questions are short and clear and frustration is minimised.

6.12.1.10 *Accused testifying via live link*

Section 33A of the Youth Justice and Criminal Evidence Act 1999 allows the court (whether the Crown Court or a magistrates' court), on application by the accused, to direct that any evidence given by him should be given via a 'live link'. Section 33B defines 'live link' very broadly: it encompasses any technology that enables the accused to see and hear a person in the courtroom, and to be seen and heard by the persons listed in sub-s (2), namely the judge or justices (or both) and the jury (if there is one); where there are two or more accused in the proceedings, each of the other accused; the legal representatives acting in the proceedings, and any interpreter or other person appointed by the court to assist the accused.

Before giving a live link direction, the court must be satisfied that it would be in the interests of justice to do so, and:

a   if the accused is under the age of 18, that his ability to participate effectively as a witness giving oral evidence is compromised by his 'level of intellectual ability or social functioning', and that use of a live link would enable him to participate more effectively as a witness, whether by improving the quality of his evidence or otherwise (s 33A(4)); or

b   if the accused is aged 18 or over, that he is unable to participate effectively in the proceedings effectively as a witness giving oral evidence because he has a mental disorder (within the meaning of the Mental Health Act 1983) or a 'significant impairment of intelligence and social function', and that use of a live link would enable him to participate more effectively as a witness, whether by improving the quality of his evidence or otherwise (s 33A(5)).

The Explanatory Notes that accompany the Police and Justice Act 2006 (which inserted the relevant sections into the 1999 Act) make it clear that the presumption in the case of adult defendants is that they should give evidence in court. The criteria set out in s 33A(5) are intended to ensure that the use of live links is reserved for exceptional cases where the accused has a condition that prevents effective participation as a witness and so may prevent a fair trial from taking place. In the case of a juvenile accused, however, the test is less strict (in that there is no reference to a mental disorder or impairment); it is sufficient that the accused's ability to participate is compromised. The Notes make the point that this 'lower threshold recognises that it may be more common for juveniles to experience difficulties during the trial through limited intelligence and social development, than it would be for adults' but goes on the emphasise that s 33A(4) 'is aimed at juvenile defendants with a low level of intelligence or a particular problem in dealing with social situations, and is not intended to operate merely because an accused is a juvenile and is nervous, for example'.

Section 33A(6) provides that, where a live link direction has been given, the accused must give all his evidence in that way. It follows that any cross-examination of the accused also has to take place via a live link. However, the court may, in the exercise of its discretion, discharge a live link direction if it appears to the court to be in the interests of justice to do so (sub-s (7)). This may be appropriate where, for example, the accused finds that giving evidence over a live link is more difficult than expected and believes that giving evidence in open court would allow him to give better quality evidence.

This provision applies to all criminal courts, including the youth court, but it is submitted that orders are most likely to be appropriate under s 33A when the juvenile is being tried in the Crown Court or in an adult magistrates' court.

6.12.1.11 Sentencing juveniles after Crown Court trial alongside an adult

If a juvenile is convicted at the crown court following joint trial with an adult, the Crown Court should remit the juvenile to the youth court for sentence unless it is undesirable to do so (s 8 of the Powers of Criminal Courts (Sentencing) Act 2000). In *R v Lewis* (1984) 79 Cr App R 94, however, it was held that remission to the youth court would generally be undesirable because:

*   the Crown Court judge (having presided over the trial) will be better informed on the facts of the case;
*   there would otherwise be a risk of unacceptable disparity in the sentences if co-accused are to be sentenced in different courts on different occasions;
*   there would be unnecessary duplication of proceedings (causing unnecessary delay and fruitless expense).

6.12.1.12 Plea before venue in the youth court

Sections 24A–24D of the Magistrates' Courts Act 1980 (inserted by the Criminal Justice Act 2003 but not in force at the time of writing) apply a procedure similar to that contained in ss 17A–17C (the 'plea before venue' hearing – see Chapter 4) to cases involving a defendant who is under the age of 18 where the court has to decide whether to send him to the Crown Court for trial, either because he is charged alongside an adult co-accused or because he is charged with an offence to which s 91 of the Powers of Criminal Courts (Sentencing) Act 2000 applies.

Section 24A(1) of the Magistrates' Court Act 1980, will apply where:

a   the juvenile is charged with an offence to which s 91 of the 2000 Act applies, or
b   the court sends an adult for trial under s 51(1) and a juvenile appears before the court on the same or a subsequent occasion charged jointly with the adult with an indictable offence for which the adult is sent for trial (or with an indictable offence which appears to the court to be related to that offence).

Section 24A(1) specifically excludes the offences listed in s 51A(12): homicide and firearms offences where the mandatory minimum sentence provisions of s 51A of the Firearms Act 1968 apply. These offences have to be tried in the Crown Court.

In cases where s 24A applies, the juvenile will be asked to indicate how he intends to plead to the offence(s). If he indicates that he intends to plead guilty, he will be regarded as having entered a plea of guilty (sub-s (7)); if he indicates that he intends to plead not guilty (or gives no indication), the court proceeds to determine where the juvenile will be tried:

• In the case of offences to which s 91 of the 2000 Act applies, the youth court will send the juvenile to the Crown Court for trial if the court considers that, if he is found guilty of the offence, it 'ought to be possible to sentence him' under s 91 (s 51A(3)(b) of the Crime and Disorder Act 1998).
• Where the juvenile is charged alongside an adult, the court will send the juvenile to the Crown Court for trial if it considers it 'necessary in the interests of justice' to do so (s 51(7) of the 1998 Act).

Section 24B of the 1980 Act enables the 'plea before venue' procedure to take place in the absence of the juvenile where he is represented by a legal representative, the court considers that by reason of the accused's disorderly conduct before the court it is not practicable for proceedings under s 24A to be conducted in his presence, and the court considers that it should proceed in the absence of the accused. In such a case, the legal representative speaks on behalf of the accused.

6.12.1.13 Committal for sentence following plea before venue

At the time of writing, the power to pass a sentence of detention under s 91 of the Powers of Criminal Courts (Sentencing) Act 2000 can only be exercised by the Crown Court where the juvenile was convicted on indictment (i.e., where the juvenile either pleaded guilty in the Crown Court or was convicted in that court). However, under the new 'plea before venue' procedure for juveniles, if the offence is one to which the provisions of s 91 of the 2000 Act apply, the magistrates will be empowered by s 3B of the 2000 Act to commit the juvenile to the Crown Court for sentence.

The power to commit for sentence under s 3B is available where the juvenile indicates a guilty plea at the 'plea before venue' hearing and the court is of the opinion that the offence(s) are such that 'the Crown Court should, in the court's opinion, have power to deal with the offender' under s 91 (s 3B(2)). The committal may be in custody or on bail (ibid)). Section 3B(3) provides that where a juvenile is committed for sentence under s 3B, s 6 of the 2000 Act (which enables a magistrates' court to commit the offender to the Crown Court to be dealt with in respect of other offences for which the court would otherwise be passing sentence) is applicable. It should be noted that s 3B does not apply where the young defendant indicates an intention to plead not guilty (or gives no indication) and is convicted after summary trial; in such cases, the youth court must pass sentence itself.

Section 4A of the Powers of Criminal Courts (Sentencing) Act 2000 (also not in force at the time of writing) also applies where a juvenile is charged with an offence falling within the ambit of s 91 of the 2000 Act and, at the 'plea before venue' hearing, the juvenile indicates an intention to plead guilty to that offence. Under s 4A(2), if the court sends the juvenile to the Crown Court for trial for one or more offences that are related to the s 91 offence, it may commit him (in custody or on bail) to the Crown Court to be dealt with in respect of the s 91 offence. Under s 4A(4), if the magistrates commit the s 91 offence to the Crown Court for sentence but do not state that, in their opinion, the case is one where it ought to be possible to impose detention under s 91, the Crown Court cannot impose detention under s 91 for that offence (and so is limited to the sentences that could be imposed by the youth court). This provision thus mirrors s 4 of the 2000 Act, which is applicable to adult offenders.

Under s 5A(1) of the Powers of Criminal Courts (Sentencing) Act 2000, where an offender is committed for sentence under ss 3B or 4A of the 2000 Act, the Crown Court may deal with the offender in any way in which it could deal with him if he had just been convicted of the offence on indictment before the court.

6.12.1.14 Dangerous offenders

Section 3C of the Powers of Criminal Courts (Sentencing) Act 2000 (also added by the Criminal Justice Act 2003) came into force in April 2005. It enables committal for sentence of dangerous young offenders. Where a juvenile is convicted of a 'specified offence' (i.e. an offence specified in s 224 of the 2003 Act), and it appears to the court that the criteria for the imposition of a sentence under ss 226(3) or 228(2) of the 2003 Act (dangerous offenders) would be met, the court must commit the offender (in custody or on bail) to the Crown Court for sentence (s 3C(2)). Following committal under s 3C, the Crown Court can deal with the offender in any way in which it could deal with him if he had just been convicted of the offence on indictment before the court (s 5A(1)).

The offender can also be committed (under s 6 of the 2000 Act) to be sentenced for other offences that the magistrates would otherwise be dealing with (s 3C(3)).

The coming into force of s 3C of the Powers of Criminal Courts (Sentencing) Act

2000 necessitates a consideration of the relationship between s 91 of the 2000 Act and ss 226 and 228 of the 2003 Act.

Essentially, there are three types of offence:

a   offences which fall within s 91 but which are not 'specified offences' under s 224: the court follows the plea before venue procedure (under s 24A of the Magistrates' Courts Act 1980) and may commit the juvenile to the Crown Court, under s 3B of the 2000 Act, if he indicates a guilty plea;

b   offences which are 'specified offences' but which do not fall within s 91: the justices must decide whether it appears to them that the criteria for the imposition of a sentence under ss 226 or 228 of the Criminal Justice Act 2003 are satisfied. If the justices take the view that the criteria are satisfied, they must send the juvenile to the Crown Court for trial. If the justices take the view that the criteria are not satisfied, they will try the case summarily. If they try the case and convict the juvenile, and decide at that stage that the criteria are, in fact, satisfied (they will, of course, have much more information by that stage), they must commit the juvenile to the Crown Court for sentence under s 3C(2);

c   offences that are both 'specified' offences and fall within s 91: the justices will go through the plea before venue procedure. If the juvenile indicates a guilty plea, he may be committed for sentence either under s 3B, on the basis that the justices are of the opinion that the Crown Court ought to have power to impose detention under s 91 (a test that depends on the seriousness of the offence), or under s 3C, on the basis that it appears to the court that the criteria for the imposition of a sentence under s 226 or s 228 would be met (a test that depends largely on there being a significant risk of future serious harm). If the juvenile indicates an intention to plead not guilty (or gives no indication), the justices have to decide whether to try the case summarily or to send the juvenile for trial in the Crown Court. If the justices take the view that the Crown Court ought to be able to pass a sentence under s 91, or that the defendant is likely to satisfy the criteria for a sentence under s 226 or s 228, they must send the juvenile for trial in the Crown Court. If the justices decide to try the case themselves and they find the juvenile guilty, they will be able to commit him to the Crown Court for sentence under s 3C (if they decide, at that stage, that the criteria for a sentence under s 226 or s 228 are met) but not under s 3B (which applies only to guilty pleas). If the juvenile is committed for sentence under s 3C, the Crown Court has power (under s 5A) to impose a sentence under s 91 if it decides that the criteria for a sentence under s 226 or s 228 are not in fact met.

In *R (CPS) v South East Surrey Youth Court* [2005] EWHC 2929 (Admin); [2006] 1 WLR 2543, Rose LJ said (at para 17) that the justices should have regard to the following:

> . . . (ii) the guidance given by the Court of Appeal (Criminal Division), in particular in para 17 of the judgment in *R v Lang* [2006] 1 WLR 2509, particularly in (iv) in relation to non-serious specified offences;
>
> (iii) the need, in relation to those under 18, to be particularly rigorous before concluding that there is a significant risk of serious harm by the commission of further offences:

such a conclusion is unlikely to be appropriate in the absence of a pre-sentence report following assessment by a young offender team;

(iv) in most cases where a non-serious specified offence is charged, an assessment of dangerousness will not be appropriate until after conviction, when, if the dangerousness criteria are met, the defendant can be committed to the Crown Court for sentence – a procedure with which the Crown Court has, for many years, been familiar . . .

6.12.2 Summary trial of juveniles in adult magistrates' court

We now examine cases where a juvenile must, or may, be tried in an adult magistrates' court.

6.12.2.1 Procedure where juvenile is not to be tried in the Crown Court

If the juvenile is jointly charged with an adult, and the justices decide that it is not necessary in the interests of justice to send the juvenile to the Crown Court for trial, even though the adult co-accused is to be tried by the Crown Court, the charge will be put to the juvenile in the adult magistrates' court and a plea taken from him.

If the juvenile pleads guilty, the magistrates will consider whether their sentencing powers in respect of the juvenile are adequate. Those powers, which are contained in s 8(8) of the 2000 Act, are to make any one or more of the following orders:

- absolute discharge (that is, no action is taken against the juvenile);
- conditional discharge (that is, no action is taken against the juvenile unless he reoffends during the period specified by the court);
- a fine (up to £1,000 for a juvenile who has attained the age of 14; up to £250 for one who has not (s 135 of the Powers of Criminal Courts (Sentencing) Act 2000));
- requiring the juvenile's parents to enter into a recognisance to keep proper control of him.

In addition, the court may disqualify the offender from driving or holding a driving licence and make ancillary orders such as orders to pay compensation and costs.

If none of the powers listed in s 8(8) is appropriate, the adult magistrates' court will remit the offender to the youth court to be dealt with under s 8(6) of the 2000 Act.

Note that an adult magistrates' court dealing with a juvenile cannot impose a custodial sentence or a community sentence, nor can it commit the juvenile to the Crown Court for sentence.

If the juvenile pleads not guilty, the adult magistrates' court may try him (under s 29(2) of the Magistrates' Courts Act 1980). However, in the absence of a good reason to the contrary (for example, the prosecution wish to offer no evidence), he should normally be remitted to the youth court for trial (again under s 29(2)).

6.12.2.2 Trial of juvenile in adult magistrates' court – joint charge

Where the juvenile is jointly charged with an adult who is to be tried summarily (that is, it is a summary offence or else an either-way offence where the adult defendant and the justices agree to summary trial), the place of trial for the juvenile may differ depending on the plea entered by the adult and on whether the charge is a joint charge or merely a related charge:

- **If the adult pleads not guilty to the joint charge:** The adult magistrates' court will ask the juvenile to plead (guilty or not guilty). If the juvenile pleads not guilty, the adult court must try him (s 46(1)(a) of the Children and Young Persons Act 1933). If he pleads or is found guilty, the magistrates will remit him to the youth court for sentence if the sentences which the adult court can impose (see above) are inappropriate.
- **If the adult pleads guilty to the joint charge:** If the juvenile pleads not guilty, the adult magistrates' court may try him under s 29(2) of the Magistrates' Courts Act 1980 or else remit him to the youth court for trial. Although the magistrates could theoretically try the juvenile (even though the adult has pleaded guilty, so that there will be no trial of the adult), it is much more likely that they will remit him to the youth court for trial. If the juvenile pleads guilty (or the adult court does try him and he is found guilty), the adult court will remit him to the youth court for sentence if none of the sentences which the adult court can impose are appropriate.
- **Aiding and abetting, etc.:** If the juvenile is charged with aiding and abetting the adult, or the adult is charged with aiding and abetting the juvenile, the adult magistrates' court has a discretion to try them both if they both plead not guilty (s 46(1)(b) of the Children And Young Persons Act 1933; s 18(a) of the Children And Young Persons Act 1963). If the adult and juvenile are charged with offences which arise out of the same circumstances and both plead not guilty, the adult magistrates' court may either try the juvenile or remit him to the youth court for trial (s 18(b) of the Children and Young Persons Act 1963). If the adult pleads guilty and the juvenile not guilty, the magistrates are likely to remit the juvenile to the youth court for trial; if the adult magistrates' court tries the juvenile and convicts him, he will be remitted to the youth court for sentence if the magistrates' sentencing powers (see above) are inappropriate.

  Where one offender is charged with taking a conveyance without the owner's consent and another is charged with allowing himself to be carried in a conveyance which has been taken without the owner's consent, although these are in reality separate offences, they are to be regarded as jointly charged for these purposes (*R v Peterborough Justices ex p Allgood* (1995) 159 JP 627).

6.12.2.3 Mistake in age

If an adult magistrates' court starts to deal with a defendant believing him to be 18 or over and it then transpires that he is a juvenile, the court can either continue to hear the case or remit it to the youth court, whichever seems most appropriate in the circumstances (s 46(1)(c) of the Children and Young Persons Act 1933).

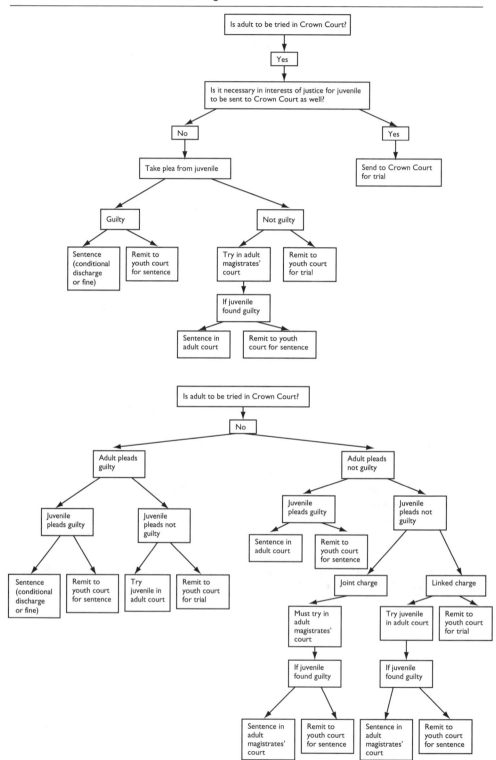

Figure 6.2 Juveniles: Jointly charged with adult.

6.13 RELEVANT DATE FOR DETERMINING AGE

Section 29(1) of the Children and Young Persons Act 1963 provides that:

> Where proceedings in respect of a young person are begun for an offence and he attains the age of eighteen before the conclusion of the proceedings, the court may continue to deal with the case and make any order which it could have made if he had not attained that age.

Thus, the youth court has jurisdiction if the accused is under 18 when the proceedings are begun. In *R v Uxbridge Youth Court ex p H* (1998) 162 JP 327, the defendant was 17 when arrested and charged but, by the time he made his first appearance at the youth court, he had turned 18. The Divisional Court held (construing s 29) that proceedings are begun when the defendant first appears before the justices; it followed that the youth court did not have jurisdiction to deal with this defendant.

What happens if a 17-year-old has his 18th birthday during the course of proceedings in the youth court? The House of Lords held in *R v Islington North Juvenile Court ex p Daley* [1983] 1 AC 347 at 364, per Lord Diplock, that:

> ... The only appropriate date at which to determine whether an accused person has attained an age which entitles him to elect to be tried by jury is the date of his appearance before the court on the occasion when the court makes its decision as to mode of trial.

In *Daley*, the accused was 16 when he made his first appearance in the youth court (when the case was simply adjourned). By the time he next appeared, he had attained the age of 17 and so had ceased to be a juvenile according to the law at the time. The effect of the decision of the House of Lords was that he was entitled to elect trial by jury, because he became an adult before mode of trial was determined. The reference by Lord Diplock in *Daley* to the moment when the youth court 'makes its decision as to the mode of trial' is unhelpful to the extent that the only situations in which the court has to choose between summary trial and trial on indictment are when either the juvenile is jointly charged with an adult who is being sent to the Crown Court for trial or when the juvenile is charged with an offence which falls within the ambit of s 91 of the Powers of Criminal Courts (Sentencing) Act 2000 or the 'dangerous offender' provisions of the CJA 2003. Thus, in the great majority of cases, there is no separate occasion on which mode of trial for a juvenile is determined. It is submitted that Lord Diplock must be taken as having meant that the right of a person who attains the relevant age during the currency of proceedings against him to be tried on indictment for an indictable offence depends either upon his age when mode of trial is determined, or – if there is no express determination of mode of trial – upon his age when the court is ready for the charge to be put. If he is under that age on the occasion of entering a plea, he has no right to elect trial on indictment, even if the matter is forthwith adjourned for trial at a later date and he attains the relevant age before any evidence is heard. The corollary is that, where the offence charged is triable only on indictment in the case of an adult, an erstwhile juvenile must go to the Crown Court for trial if he attains the age of 18 before a plea is taken (*Vale of Glamorgan Juvenile Justices, ex parte Beattie* (1986) 82 Cr App R 1).

Cases where the defendant attains the age of 18 between conviction and sentence are dealt with by s 9 of the Powers of Criminal Courts (Sentencing) Act 2000. Under s 9(1), the youth court is empowered, in such a case, to remit the defendant to the adult magistrates' court to be sentenced. The adult magistrates' court may then 'deal with the case in any way in which it would have power to deal with it if all proceedings relating to the offence which took place before the youth court had taken place before [the adult court]' (s 9(2)(b)). There is no right of appeal against the order of remission (s 9(4)).

In *R (Denny) v Acton Youth Court* [2004] EWHC 948 (admin); [2004] 1 WLR 3051, a 17-year-old was charged with attempted robbery. He entered a plea of not guilty at the youth court. By the time the matter came on for trial and he was found guilty, he was 18. The justices in the youth court adjourned sentence and remitted him to the adult court pursuant to s 9. The adult court remitted the case to the youth court for that court to reconsider (under s 142 of the Magistrates' Courts Act 1980) the decision to remit. The Divisional Court held that the order remitting the case to the adult magistrates' court under s 9 was defective by reason of illegality: youth courts should never remit a defendant to a magistrates' court for sentence in relation to an offence which, in the case of an adult, is triable only on indictment. The court went on to say that, provided the adult court has not reached the stage of considering sentence, it is possible for the youth court to rescind a remittal to an adult magistrates' court under s 142 of the 1980 Act, since a remittal under s 9 is an 'order made when dealing with an offender'.

It should be noted that the type of sentence is generally fixed by the offender's age at the date of conviction (*Danga* [1992] QB 476; *R v Robson* [2006] EWCA Crim 1414; [2007] 1 All ER 506). Nevertheless, the court should have regard to the offender's age at the date when the offence was committed when considering the severity of the penalty to impose. In *R v Ghafoor* [2002] EWCA Crim 1857; [2003] 1 Cr App R(S) 84, it was held that 'where a defendant crosses a relevant age threshold between the date of the commission of the offence and the date of conviction ... [the] starting point is the sentence that the defendant would have been likely to receive if he had been sentenced at the date of the commission of the offence' (per Dyson LJ at para 31). 'The sentence that would have been passed at the date of the commission of the offence is a "powerful factor". It is the starting point, and other factors may have to be considered. But ... there have to be good reasons for departing from the starting point' (para 32). In *R v Bowker* [2007] EWCA Crim 1608; [2008] 1 Cr App R (S) 72, the Court of Appeal again considered the approach to be taken where an offender who has attained the age of 18 is convicted of an offence committed whilst under the age of 18. The Court emphasised that the principle that his culpability should be judged by reference to his age at the time of the offence is only a starting point. The sentence that would have been imposed at the time of the commission of the offence is a 'powerful' factor, not the sole or determining factor. The sentencer also has to take account of the matters set out in s 142 of the CJA 2003, including deterrence.

6.14 APPEALS FROM THE YOUTH COURT

For discussion on appeals from the youth court, see Chapter 7, which deals with appeals from magistrates' courts.

6.15 ASSESSING THE EFFECTIVENESS OF THE YOUTH COURT

In the 1997 Consultation Paper issued by the Home Office, *No More Excuses – A New Approach to Tackling Youth Crime in England and Wales* (Cmnd 3809) (<http://www.homeoffice.gov.uk/documents/jou-no-more-excuses?view=Html>), chapter 2 considers the aims of the youth justice system and refers to the Crime and Disorder Bill (now Act) which sets out in statutory form the aim of the youth justice system, namely to prevent offending by young people.

Paragraph 2.9 refers to proposals made by the Home Secretary's Youth Justice Task Force (an advisory group comprising a range of people with varied experience of the youth justice system, including victim issues, plus representatives of relevant Government departments), which suggested that the aim of preventing offending by young people should be achieved through the following objectives:

- the swift administration of justice so that every young person accused of breaking the law has the matter resolved without delay;
- confronting young offenders with the consequences of their offending, for themselves and their family, their victims and their community;
- punishment proportionate to the seriousness and persistence of offending;
- encouraging reparation to victims by young offenders;
- reinforcing the responsibilities of parents; and
- helping young offenders to tackle problems associated with their offending and to develop a sense of personal responsibility.

Chapter 9 of the paper sets out the Government's vision for a youth court for the 21st century. Paragraph 9.2 notes that:

... A frank assessment of the current approach of the youth court must conclude that, all too often, inadequate attention is given to changing offending behaviour. This is not the fault of individuals working within the system. It is encouraged by the court's very structures and procedures ... the purpose of the youth court must change from simply deciding guilt or innocence and then issuing a sentence. In most cases, an offence should trigger a wider enquiry into the circumstances and nature of the offending behaviour, leading to action to change that behaviour. This requires in turn a fundamental change of approach within the youth court system.

Paragraph 9.3 lists some of the reforms needed to enable this to happen:

- speedier decisions on guilt or innocence, much closer to the date of the offence and with less tolerance of adjournments;
- a system which is more open, and which commands the confidence of victims and the public;
- processes which engage young offenders and their parents and focus on the nature of their offending behaviour and how to change it;
- a stronger emphasis on using sentencing to prevent future offending; and
- more efficient arrangements for the scheduling and management of cases.

An important aspect of the approach commended by the Government is engaging with the offender. Paragraph 9.6 notes that this requires:

- training magistrates so that they understand the value of talking directly to both the young defendant and his or her parents during court proceedings, even where the young person has legal representation;
- encouraging magistrates to question young defendants about the reasons for their behaviour, before reaching a final decision on sentencing; and
- encouraging youth courts to ensure that the physical environment of the courtroom promotes proceedings which involve the young person directly and which are less adversarial.

Paragraph 9.7 encourages 'opening up the youth court'. It says:

> There must also be more openness in youth court proceedings. In law, youth courts have some discretion over who can attend proceedings and over the lifting of reporting restrictions. But present practice places too much emphasis on protecting the identity of young offenders at the expense of the interests of victims and the community. Justice is best served in an open court where the criminal process can be scrutinised and the offender cannot hide behind a cloak of anonymity.

To achieve this, para 9.8 says that:

> The Government believes that the youth court should make full use of its discretion to lift reporting restrictions in the public interest following conviction. This is particularly important where the offence is a serious one; where the offending is persistent or where it has affected a number of people or the local community; and at the upper age range of the youth court. Occasions when it would not be in the best interests of the public, and others concerned with the case, to lift reporting restrictions might include cases where an early guilty plea was entered or where naming the young offender would result in revealing the identity of a vulnerable victim.

This part of the paper concludes (para 9.9):

> Though the Government does not want to make youth courts entirely open in the same way as adult courts, it believes that magistrates should make use of their existing discretion to admit victims and members of the public to youth courts. Victims, in particular, have a strong claim to be present during the trial to see justice being done, unless in the circumstances of the particular case this would be contrary to the interests of justice.

Of course, in the case of adult defendants, a trial in open court is seen as fundamental to the fairness guaranteed by Art 6 of the European Convention on Human Rights. However, this approach has to be modified in the case of young defendants, where trial in open court may be regarded as inimical to fairness (see *T and V v UK* (2000) 30 EHRR 121 and the provisions of the *Consolidated Practice Direction* that deal with vulnerable defendants (including young defendants)).

Turning to the sentencing process, the Government indicates in para 9.21 that it wants youth court sentencing to be built on the concept of restorative justice:

- Restoration: young offenders apologising to their victims and making amends for the harm they have done;
- Reintegration: young offenders paying their debt to society, putting their crime behind them and rejoining the law abiding community; and
- Responsibility: young offenders – and their parents – facing the consequences of their offending behaviour and taking responsibility for preventing further offending.

In para 9.22, it is said that this approach is intended to:

- ensure that the most serious offenders continue to be dealt with in a criminal court to provide punishment, protect the public and prevent reoffending;
- provide an opportunity for less serious offending to be dealt with in a new non-criminal panel, enforced by a criminal court;
- involve young people more effectively in decisions about them – encouraging them to admit their guilt and face up to the consequences of their behaviour;
- involve the victim in proceedings, but only with their active consent; and
- focus on preventing offending.

6.15.1 International obligations

A number of international instruments lay down principles to guide the administration of youth justice.

6.15.1.1 United Nations Standard Minimum Rules for the Administration of Juvenile Justice (the 'Beijing Rules'), November 1985

See <http://www.un.org/documents/ga/res/40/a40r033.htm>

PART ONE
GENERAL PRINCIPLES
1. Fundamental perspectives

1.1 Member States shall seek, in conformity with their respective general interests, to further the well-being of the juvenile and her or his family.

1.2 Member States shall endeavour to develop conditions that will ensure for the juvenile a meaningful life in the community, which, during that period in life when she or he is most susceptible to deviant behaviour, will foster a process of personal development and education that is as free from crime and delinquency as possible.

1.3 Sufficient attention shall be given to positive measures that involve the full mobilization of all possible resources, including the family, volunteers and other community groups, as well as schools and other community institutions, for the purpose of promoting the well-being of the juvenile, with a view to reducing the need for intervention under the law, and of effectively, fairly and humanely dealing with the juvenile in conflict with the law.

1.4 Juvenile justice shall be conceived as an integral part of the national development process of each country, within a comprehensive framework of social justice for all juveniles, thus, at the same time, contributing to the protection of the young and the maintenance of a peaceful order in society.

1.5 These Rules shall be implemented in the context of economic, social and cultural conditions prevailing in each Member State.

1.6 Juvenile justice services shall be systematically developed and co-ordinated with a view to improving and sustaining the competence of personnel involved in the services, including their methods, approaches and attitudes.

Commentary

These broad fundamental perspectives refer to comprehensive social policy in general and aim at promoting juvenile welfare to the greatest possible extent, which will minimize the necessity of intervention by the juvenile justice system, and in turn, will reduce the harm that may be caused by any intervention. Such care measures for the young, before the onset of delinquency, are basic policy requisites designed to obviate the need for the application of the Rules.

Rules 1.1 to 1.3 point to the important role that a constructive social policy for juveniles will play, inter alia, in the prevention of juvenile crime and delinquency. Rule 1.4 defines juvenile justice as an integral part of social justice for juveniles, while rule 1.6 refers to the necessity of constantly improving juvenile justice, without falling behind the development of progressive social policy for juveniles in general and bearing in mind the need for consistent improvement of staff services.

Rule 1.5 seeks to take account of existing conditions in Member States which would cause the manner of implementation of particular rules necessarily to be different from the manner adopted in other States.

2. Scope of the Rules and definitions used

2.1 The following Standard Minimum Rules shall be applied to juvenile offenders impartially, without distinction of any kind, for example as to race, colour, sex, language, religion, political or other opinions, national or social origin, property, birth or other status.

2.2 For the purposes of these Rules, the following definitions shall be applied by Member States in a manner which is compatible with their respective legal systems and concepts:

(a) A juvenile is a child or young person who, under the respective legal systems, may be dealt with for an offence in a manner which is different from an adult;

(b) An offence is any behaviour (act or omission) that is punishable by law under the respective legal systems;

(c) A juvenile offender is a child or young person who is alleged to have committed or who has been found to have committed an offence.

2.3 Efforts shall be made to establish, in each national jurisdiction, a set of laws, rules and provisions specifically applicable to juvenile offenders and institutions and bodies entrusted with the functions of the administration of juvenile justice and designed:

(a) To meet the varying needs of juvenile offenders, while protecting their basic rights;

(b)   To meet the needs of society;

(c)   To implement the following rules thoroughly and fairly.

Commentary

The Standard Minimum Rules are deliberately formulated so as to be applicable within different legal systems and, at the same time, to set some minimum standards for the handling of juvenile offenders under any definition of a juvenile and under any system of dealing with juvenile offenders. The Rules are always to be applied impartially and without distinction of any kind.

. . . It should be noted that age limits will depend on, and are explicitly made dependent on, each respective legal system, thus fully respecting the economic, social, political, cultural and legal systems of Member States. This makes for a wide variety of ages coming under the definition of 'juvenile', ranging from 7 years to 18 years or above. Such a variety seems inevitable in view of the different national legal systems and does not diminish the impact of these Standard Minimum Rules.

. . .

4. Age of criminal responsibility

4.1   In those legal systems recognizing the concept of the age of criminal responsibility for juveniles, the beginning of that age shall not be fixed at too low an age level, bearing in mind the facts of emotional, mental and intellectual maturity.

Commentary

The minimum age of criminal responsibility differs widely owing to history and culture. The modern approach would be to consider whether a child can live up to the moral and psychological components of criminal responsibility; that is, whether a child, by virtue of her or his individual discernment and understanding, can be held responsible for essentially antisocial behaviour. If the age of criminal responsibility is fixed too low or if there is no lower age limit at all, the notion of responsibility would become meaningless. In general, there is a close relationship between the notion of responsibility for delinquent or criminal behaviour and other social rights and responsibilities (such as marital status, civil majority, etc.).

Efforts should therefore be made to agree on a reasonable lowest age limit that is applicable internationally.

5. Aims of juvenile justice

5.1   The juvenile justice system shall emphasize the well-being of the juvenile and shall ensure that any reaction to juvenile offenders shall always be in proportion to the circumstances of both the offenders and the offence.

Commentary

Rule 5 refers to two of the most important objectives of juvenile justice. The first objective is the promotion of the well-being of the juvenile. This is the main focus of those legal systems in which juvenile offenders are dealt with by family courts or administrative authorities, but the well-being of the juvenile should also be emphasized in legal systems that follow the criminal court model, thus contributing to the avoidance of merely punitive sanctions.

The second objective is 'the principle of proportionality'. This principle is well-known as an instrument for curbing punitive sanctions, mostly expressed in terms of just deserts in relation to the gravity of the offence. The response to young offenders should be based on the consideration not only of the gravity of the offence but also of personal circumstances. The individual circumstances of the offender (for example social status, family situation, the harm caused by the offence or other factors affecting personal circumstances) should influence the proportionality of the reactions (for example by having regard to the offender's endeavour to indemnify the victim or to her or his willingness to turn to wholesome and useful life).

By the same token, reactions aiming to ensure the welfare of the young offender may go beyond necessity and therefore infringe upon the fundamental rights of the young individual, as has been observed in some juvenile justice systems. Here, too, the proportionality of the reaction to the circumstances of both the offender and the offence, including the victim, should be safeguarded.

In essence, rule 5 calls for no less and no more than a fair reaction in any given cases of juvenile delinquency and crime. The issues combined in the rule may help to stimulate development in both regards: new and innovative types of reactions are as desirable as precautions against any undue widening of the net of formal social control over juveniles.

. . .

7. Rights of juveniles

7.1 Basic procedural safeguards such as the presumption of innocence, the right to be notified of the charges, the right to remain silent, the right to counsel, the right to the presence of a parent or guardian, the right to confront and cross-examine witnesses and the right to appeal to a higher authority shall be guaranteed at all stages of proceedings.

Commentary
Rule 7.1 emphasizes some important points that represent essential elements for a fair and just trial and that are internationally recognized in existing human rights instruments

. . .

8. Protection of privacy

8.1 The juvenile's right to privacy shall be respected at all stages in order to avoid harm being caused to her or him by undue publicity or by the process of labelling.

8.2 In principle, no information that may lead to the identification of a juvenile offender shall be published.

Commentary
Rule 8 stresses the importance of the protection of the juvenile's right to privacy. Young persons are particularly susceptible to stigmatization. Criminological research into labelling processes has provided evidence of the detrimental effects (of different kinds) resulting from the permanent identification of young persons as 'delinquent' or 'criminal'.

Rule 8 stresses the importance of protecting the juvenile from the adverse effects that may result from the publication in the mass media of information about the case (for example the names of young offenders, alleged or convicted). The interest of the individual should be protected and upheld, at least in principle.

. . .

PART TWO
INVESTIGATION AND PROSECUTION
10. Initial contact

10.1 Upon the apprehension of a juvenile, her or his parents or guardian shall be immediately notified of such apprehension, and, where such immediate notification is not possible, the parents or guardian shall be notified within the shortest possible time thereafter.

10.2 A judge or other competent official or body shall, without delay, consider the issue of release.

10.3 Contacts between the law enforcement agencies and a juvenile offender shall be managed in such a way as to respect the legal status of the juvenile, promote the well-being of the juvenile and avoid harm to her or him, with due regard to the circumstances of the case.

Commentary

. . .

The question of release (rule 10.2) shall be considered without delay by a judge or other competent official. The latter refers to any person or institution in the broadest sense of the term, including community boards or police authorities having power to release an arrested person.

Rule 10.3 deals with some fundamental aspects of the procedures and behaviour on the part of the police and other law enforcement officials in cases of juvenile crime. To 'avoid harm' admittedly is flexible wording and covers many features of possible interaction (for example the use of harsh language, physical violence or exposure to the environment). Involvement in juvenile justice processes in itself can be 'harmful' to juveniles; the term 'avoid harm' should be broadly interpreted, therefore, as doing the least harm possible to the juvenile in the first instance, as well as any additional or undue harm. This is especially important in the initial contact with law enforcement agencies, which might profoundly influence the juvenile's attitude towards the State and society. Moreover, the success of any further intervention is largely dependent on such initial contacts. Compassion and kind firmness are important in these situations.

11. Diversion

11.1 Consideration shall be given, wherever appropriate, to dealing with juvenile offenders without resorting to formal trial by the competent authority, referred to in rule 14.1 below.

11.2 The police, the prosecution or other agencies dealing with juvenile cases shall be empowered to dispose of such cases, at their discretion, without recourse to formal hearings, in accordance with the criteria laid down for that purpose in the respective legal system and also in accordance with the principles contained in these Rules.

11.3 Any diversion involving referral to appropriate community or other services shall require the consent of the juvenile, or her or his parents or guardian, provided that such decision to refer a case shall be subject to review by a competent authority, upon application.

11.4 In order to facilitate the discretionary disposition of juvenile cases, efforts shall be made to provide for community programmes, such as temporary supervision and guidance, restitution, and compensation of victims.

Commentary

Diversion, involving removal from criminal justice processing and, frequently, redirection to community support services, is commonly practised on a formal and informal basis in many legal systems. This practice serves to hinder the negative effects of subsequent proceedings in juvenile justice administration (for example the stigma of conviction and sentence). In many cases, non-intervention would be the best response. Thus, diversion at the outset and without referral to alternative (social) services may be the optimal response. This is especially the case where the offence is of a non-serious nature and where the family, the school or other informal social control institutions have already reacted, or are likely to react, in an appropriate and constructive manner.

As stated in rule 11.2, diversion may be used at any point of decision-making by the police, the prosecution or other agencies such as the courts, tribunals, boards or councils. It may be exercised by one authority or several or all authorities, according to the rules and policies of the respective systems and in line with the present Rules. It need not necessarily be limited to petty cases, thus rendering diversion an important instrument.

Rule 11.3 stresses the important requirement of securing the consent of the young offender (or the parent or guardian) to the recommended diversionary measure(s). (Diversion to community service without such consent would contradict the Abolition of Forced Labour Convention.) However, this consent should not be left unchallengeable, since it might sometimes be given out of sheer desperation on the part of the juvenile. The rule underlines that care should be taken to minimize the potential for coercion and intimidation at all levels in the diversion process. Juveniles should not feel pressured (for example in order to avoid court appearance) or be pressured into consenting to diversion programmes. Thus, it is advocated that provision should be made for an objective appraisal of the appropriateness of dispositions involving young offenders by a 'competent authority upon application'. (The 'competent authority' may be different from that referred to in rule 14.)

Rule 11.4 recommends the provision of viable alternatives to juvenile justice processing in the form of community-based diversion. Programmes that involve settlement by victim restitution and those that seek to avoid future conflict with the law through temporary supervision and guidance are especially commended. The merits of individual cases would make diversion appropriate, even when more serious offences have been committed (for example first offence, the act having been committed under peer pressure, etc.).

. . .

13. Detention pending trial

13.1 Detention pending trial shall be used only as a measure of last resort and for the shortest possible period of time.

13.2 Whenever possible, detention pending trial shall be replaced by alternative measures, such as close supervision, intensive care or placement with a family or in an educational setting or home.

13.3 Juveniles under detention pending trial shall be entitled to all rights and guarantees of the Standard Minimum Rules for the Treatment of Prisoners adopted by the United Nations.

13.4 Juveniles under detention pending trial shall be kept separate from adults and shall be detained in a separate institution or in a separate part of an institution also holding adults.

13.5 While in custody, juveniles shall receive care, protection and all necessary individual assistance – social, educational, vocational, psychological, medical and physical – that they may require in view of their age, sex and personality.

Commentary

The danger to juveniles of 'criminal contamination' while in detention pending trial must not be underestimated. It is therefore important to stress the need for alternative measures. By doing so, rule 13.1 encourages the devising of new and innovative measures to avoid such detention in the interest of the well-being of the juvenile.

. . .

Rule 13.4 does not prevent States from taking other measures against the negative influences of adult offenders which are at least as effective as the measures mentioned in the rule.

Different forms of assistance that may become necessary have been enumerated to draw attention to the broad range of particular needs of young detainees to be addressed (for example females or males, drug addicts, alcoholics, mentally ill juveniles, young persons suffering from the trauma, for example, of arrest, etc.).

Varying physical and psychological characteristics of young detainees may warrant classification measures by which some are kept separate while in detention pending trial, thus contributing to the avoidance of victimization and rendering more appropriate assistance.

. . . [P]re-trial detention should be used only as a last resort, that no minors should be held in a facility where they are vulnerable to the negative influences of adult detainees and that account should always be taken of the needs particular to their stage of development.

PART THREE
ADJUDICATION AND DISPOSITION
14. Competent authority to adjudicate

14.1 Where the case of a juvenile offender has not been diverted (under rule 11), she or he shall be dealt with by the competent authority (court, tribunal, board, council, etc.) according to the principles of a fair and just trial.

14.2 The proceedings shall be conducive to the best interests of the juvenile and shall be conducted in an atmosphere of understanding, which shall allow the juvenile to participate therein and to express herself or himself freely.

Commentary

It is difficult to formulate a definition of the competent body or person that would universally describe an adjudicating authority. 'Competent authority' is meant to include those who preside over courts or tribunals (composed of a single judge or of several members), including professional and lay magistrates as well as administrative boards (for example the Scottish and Scandinavian systems) or other more informal community and conflict resolution agencies of an adjudicatory nature.

The procedure for dealing with juvenile offenders shall in any case follow the minimum standards that are applied almost universally for any criminal defendant under the procedure known as 'due process of law'. In accordance with due process, a 'fair and just trial' includes such basic safeguards as the presumption of innocence, the presentation and examination of witnesses, the common legal defences, the right to remain silent, the right to have the last word in a hearing, the right to appeal, etc.

15. Legal counsel, parents and guardians

15.1 Throughout the proceedings the juvenile shall have the right to be represented by a legal adviser or to apply for free legal aid where there is provision for such aid in the country.

15.2 The parents or the guardian shall be entitled to participate in the proceedings and may be required by the competent authority to attend them in the interest of the juvenile. They may, however, be denied participation by the competent authority if there are reasons to assume that such exclusion is necessary in the interest of the juvenile.

Commentary

. . . Whereas legal counsel and free legal aid are needed to assure the juvenile legal assistance, the right of the parents or guardian to participate as stated in rule 15.2 should be viewed as general psychological and emotional assistance to the juvenile – a function extending throughout the procedure.

The competent authority's search for an adequate disposition of the case may profit, in particular, from the co-operation of the legal representatives of the juvenile (or, for that matter, some other personal assistant who the juvenile can and does really trust). Such concern can be thwarted if the presence of parents or guardians at the hearings plays a negative role, for instance, if they display a hostile attitude towards the juvenile, hence, the possibility of their exclusion must be provided for.

16. Social inquiry reports

16.1 In all cases except those involving minor offences, before the competent authority renders a final disposition prior to sentencing, the background and circumstances in which the juvenile is living or the conditions under which the offence has been committed shall be properly investigated so as to facilitate judicious adjudication of the case by the competent authority.

Commentary

Social inquiry reports (social reports or pre-sentence reports) are an indispensable aid in most legal proceedings involving juveniles. The competent authority should be informed of relevant facts about the juvenile, such as social and family background, school career, educational experiences, etc. For this purpose, some jurisdictions use special social services or personnel attached to the court or board. Other personnel, including probation officers, may serve the same function. The rule therefore requires that adequate social services should be available to deliver social inquiry reports of a qualified nature.

17. Guiding principles in adjudication and disposition

17.1 The disposition of the competent authority shall be guided by the following principles:

(a) The reaction taken shall always be in proportion not only to the circumstances and the gravity of the offence but also to the circumstances and the needs of the juvenile as well as to the needs of the society;

(b) Restrictions on the personal liberty of the juvenile shall be imposed only after careful consideration and shall be limited to the possible minimum;

(c) Deprivation of personal liberty shall not be imposed unless the juvenile is adjudicated of a serious act involving violence against another person or of persistence in committing other serious offences and unless there is no other appropriate response;

(d) The well-being of the juvenile shall be the guiding factor in the consideration of her or his case.

17.2 Capital punishment shall not be imposed for any crime committed by juveniles.

17.3 Juveniles shall not be subject to corporal punishment.

17.4 The competent authority shall have the power to discontinue the proceedings at any time.

Commentary

The main difficulty in formulating guidelines for the adjudication of young persons stems from the fact that there are unresolved conflicts of a philosophical nature, such as the following:

(a) Rehabilitation versus just desert;
(b) Assistance versus repression and punishment;
(c) Reaction according to the singular merits of an individual case versus reaction according to the protection of society in general;
(d) General deterrence versus individual incapacitation.

The conflict between these approaches is more pronounced in juvenile cases than in adult cases. With the variety of causes and reactions characterizing juvenile cases, these alternatives become intricately interwoven.

It is not the function of the Standard Minimum Rules for the Administration of Juvenile Justice to prescribe which approach is to be followed but rather to identify one that is most closely in consonance with internationally accepted principles. Therefore the essential elements as laid down in rule 17.1, in particular in sub-paragraphs (a) and (c), are mainly to be understood as practical guidelines that should ensure a common starting point; if heeded by the concerned authorities, they could contribute considerably to ensuring that the fundamental rights of juvenile offenders are protected, especially the fundamental rights of personal development and education.

Rule 17.1 (b) implies that strictly punitive approaches are not appropriate. Whereas in adult cases, and possibly also in cases of severe offences by juveniles, just desert and retributive sanctions might be considered to have some merit, in juvenile cases such considerations should always be outweighed by the interest of safeguarding the well-being and the future of the young person.

. . . rule 17.1 (b) encourages the use of alternatives to institutionalization to the maximum extent possible, bearing in mind the need to respond to the specific requirements of the young. Thus, full use should be made of the range of existing alternative sanctions and new alternative sanctions should be developed, bearing the public safety in mind. Probation should be granted to the greatest possible extent via suspended sentences, conditional sentences, board orders and other dispositions.

Rule 17.1 (c) ... aims at avoiding incarceration in the case of juveniles unless there is no other appropriate response that will protect the public safety.

. . .

The power to discontinue the proceedings at any time (rule 17.4) is a characteristic inherent in the handling of juvenile offenders as opposed to adults. At any time, circumstances may become known to the competent authority which would make a complete cessation of the intervention appear to be the best disposition of the case.

18. Various disposition measures

18.1 A large variety of disposition measures shall be made available to the competent authority, allowing for flexibility so as to avoid institutionalization to the greatest extent possible. Such measures, some of which may be combined, include:

(a) Care, guidance and supervision orders;
(b) Probation;
(c) Community service orders;
(d) Financial penalties, compensation and restitution;
(e) Intermediate treatment and other treatment orders;
(f) Orders to participate in group counselling and similar activities;
(g) Orders concerning foster care, living communities or other educational settings;
(h) Other relevant orders.

18.2 No juvenile shall be removed from parental supervision, whether partly or entirely, unless the circumstances of her or his case make this necessary.

Commentary
Rule 18.1 attempts to enumerate some of the important reactions and sanctions that have been practised and proved successful thus far, in different legal systems ...

The examples given in rule 18.1 have in common, above all, a reliance on and an appeal to the community for the effective implementation of alternative dispositions. Community-based correction is a traditional measure that has taken on many aspects. On that basis, relevant authorities should be encouraged to offer community-based services.

Rule 18.2 points to the importance of the family which, according to article 10, paragraph 1, of the International Covenant on Economic, Social and Cultural Rights, is 'the natural and fundamental group unit of society'. Within the family, the parents have not only the right but also the responsibility to care for and supervise their children. Rule 18.2, therefore, requires that the separation of children from their parents is a measure of last resort. It may be resorted to only when the facts of the case clearly warrant this grave step (for example child abuse).

19. Least possible use of institutionalization

19.1 The placement of a juvenile in an institution shall always be a disposition of last resort and for the minimum necessary period.

Commentary

Progressive criminology advocates the use of non-institutional over institutional treatment. Little or no difference has been found in terms of the success of institutionalization as compared to non-institutionalization. The many adverse influences on an individual that seem unavoidable within any institutional setting evidently cannot be outbalanced by treatment efforts. This is especially the case for juveniles, who are vulnerable to negative influences. Moreover, the negative effects, not only of loss of liberty but also of separation from the usual social environment, are certainly more acute for juveniles than for adults because of their early stage of development.

Rule 19 aims at restricting institutionalization in two regards: in quantity ('last resort') and in time ('minimum necessary period'). Rule 19 reflects one of the basic guiding principles . . .: a juvenile offender should not be incarcerated unless there is no other appropriate response. The rule, therefore, makes the appeal that if a juvenile must be institutionalized, the loss of liberty should be restricted to the least possible degree, with special institutional arrangements for confinement and bearing in mind the differences in kinds of offenders, offences and institutions. In fact, priority should be given to 'open' over 'closed' institutions. Furthermore, any facility should be of a correctional or educational rather than of a prison type.

20. Avoidance of unnecessary delay

20.1 Each case shall from the outset be handled expeditiously, without any unnecessary delay.

Commentary

The speedy conduct of formal procedures in juvenile cases is a paramount concern. Otherwise whatever good may be achieved by the procedure and the disposition is at risk. As time passes, the juvenile will find it increasingly difficult, if not impossible, to relate the procedure and disposition to the offence, both intellectually and psychologically.

. . .

PART FOUR
NON-INSTITUTIONAL TREATMENT

. . .

24. Provision of needed assistance

24.1 Efforts shall be made to provide juveniles, at all stages of the proceedings, with necessary assistance such as lodging, education or vocational training, employment or any other assistance, helpful and practical, in order to facilitate the rehabilitative process.

Commentary

The promotion of the well-being of the juvenile is of paramount consideration. Thus, rule 24 emphasizes the importance of providing requisite facilities, services and other necessary assistance as may further the best interests of the juvenile throughout the rehabilitative process.

. . .

PART FIVE
INSTITUTIONAL TREATMENT
26. Objectives of institutional treatment

26.1 The objective of training and treatment of juveniles placed in institutions is to provide care, protection, education and vocational skills, with a view to assisting them to assume socially constructive and productive roles in society.

26.2 Juveniles in institutions shall receive care, protection and all necessary assistance – social, educational, vocational, psychological, medical and physical – that they may require because of their age, sex, and personality and in the interest of their wholesome development.

26.3 Juveniles in institutions shall be kept separate from adults and shall be detained in a separate institution or in a separate part of an institution also holding adults.

26.4 Young female offenders placed in an institution deserve special attention as to their personal needs and problems. They shall by no means receive less care, protection, assistance, treatment and training than young male offenders. Their fair treatment shall be ensured.

26.5 In the interest and well-being of the institutionalized juvenile, the parents or guardians shall have a right of access.

26.6 Inter-ministerial and inter-departmental co-operation shall be fostered for the purpose of providing adequate academic or, as appropriate, vocational training to institutionalized juveniles, with a view to ensuring that they do not leave the institution at an educational disadvantage.

Commentary

. . .

Medical and psychological assistance, in particular, are extremely important for institutionalized drug addicts, violent and mentally ill young persons.

. . . The rule does not prevent States from taking other measures against the negative influences of adult offenders, which are at least as effective as the measures mentioned in the rule.

Rule 26.4 addresses the fact that female offenders normally receive less attention than their male counterparts . . .

. . .

28. Frequent and early recourse to conditional release

28.1 Conditional release from an institution shall be used by the appropriate authority to the greatest possible extent, and shall be granted at the earliest possible time.

28.2 Juveniles released conditionally from an institution shall be assisted and supervised by an appropriate authority and shall receive full support by the community.

Commentary

. . .

Circumstances permitting, conditional release shall be preferred to serving a full sentence. Upon evidence of satisfactory progress towards rehabilitation, even offenders who had been deemed dangerous at the time of their institutionalization can be conditionally released whenever feasible. Like probation, such release may be conditional on the satisfactory fulfilment of the requirements specified by the relevant authorities for a period of time established in the decision, for example relating to 'good behaviour' of the offender, attendance in community programmes, residence in half-way houses, etc.

In the case of offenders conditionally released from an institution, assistance and supervision by a probation or other officer (particularly where probation has not yet been adopted) should be provided and community support should be encouraged.

29. Semi-institutional arrangements

29.1 Efforts shall be made to provide semi-institutional arrangements, such as half-way houses, educational homes, day-time training centres and other such appropriate arrangements that may assist juveniles in their proper reintegration into society.

Commentary

The importance of care following a period of institutionalization should not be underestimated. This rule emphasizes the necessity of forming a net of semi-institutional arrangements.

This rule also emphasizes the need for a diverse range of facilities and services designed to meet the different needs of young offenders re-entering the community and to provide guidance and structural support as an important step towards successful reintegration into society.

6.15.1.2 *The Convention on the Rights of the Child (1990):*

<http://www.un.org/children/conflict/keydocuments/english/theconventionont6.html>

Article 37

States Parties shall ensure that:

(a) No child shall be subjected to torture or other cruel, inhuman or degrading treatment or punishment. Neither capital punishment nor life imprisonment without possibility of release shall be imposed for offences committed by persons below eighteen years of age;

(b) No child shall be deprived of his or her liberty unlawfully or arbitrarily. The arrest, detention or imprisonment of a child shall be in conformity with the law and shall be used only as a measure of last resort and for the shortest appropriate period of time;

(c) Every child deprived of liberty shall be treated with humanity and respect for the inherent dignity of the human person, and in a manner which takes into account the needs of persons of his or her age. In particular, every child deprived of liberty shall be separated from adults unless it is considered in the child's best interest not to do so and shall have the right to maintain contact with his or her family through correspondence and visits, save in exceptional circumstances;

(d) Every child deprived of his or her liberty shall have the right to prompt access to legal and other appropriate assistance, as well as the right to challenge the legality of the deprivation of his or her liberty before a court or other competent, independent and impartial authority, and to a prompt decision on any such action.

. . .

Article 40

1. States Parties recognize the right of every child alleged as, accused of, or recognized as having infringed the penal law to be treated in a manner consistent with the promotion of the child's sense of dignity and worth, which reinforces the child's respect for the human rights and fundamental freedoms of others and which takes into account the child's age and the desirability of promoting the child's reintegration and the child's assuming a constructive role in society.

2. To this end, and having regard to the relevant provisions of international instruments, States Parties shall, in particular, ensure that:

   (a) No child shall be alleged as, be accused of, or recognized as having infringed the penal law by reason of acts or omissions that were not prohibited by national or international law at the time they were committed;

   (b) Every child alleged as or accused of having infringed the penal law has at least the following guarantees:

      (i) To be presumed innocent until proven guilty according to law;

      (ii) To be informed promptly and directly of the charges against him or her, and, if appropriate, through his or her parents or legal guardians, and to have legal or other appropriate assistance in the preparation and presentation of his or her defence;

      (iii) To have the matter determined without delay by a competent, independent and impartial authority or judicial body in a fair hearing according to law, in the presence of legal or other appropriate assistance and, unless it is considered not to be in the best interest of the child, in particular, taking into account his or her age or situation, his or her parents or legal guardians;

      (iv) Not to be compelled to give testimony or to confess guilt; to examine or have examined adverse witnesses and to obtain the participation and examination of witnesses on his or her behalf under conditions of equality;

      (v) If considered to have infringed the penal law, to have this decision and any measures imposed in consequence thereof reviewed by a higher competent, independent and impartial authority or judicial body according to law;

      (vi) To have the free assistance of an interpreter if the child cannot understand or speak the language used;

      (vii) To have his or her privacy fully respected at all stages of the proceedings.

3. States Parties shall seek to promote the establishment of laws, procedures, authorities and institutions specifically applicable to children alleged as, accused of, or recognized as having infringed the penal law, and, in particular:

   (a) The establishment of a minimum age below which children shall be presumed not to have the capacity to infringe the penal law;

   (b) Whenever appropriate and desirable, measures for dealing with such children without resorting to judicial proceedings, providing that human rights and legal safeguards are fully respected.

4. A variety of dispositions, such as care, guidance and supervision orders; counselling; probation; foster care; education and vocational training programmes and other alter-

natives to institutional care shall be available to ensure that children are dealt with in a manner appropriate to their well-being and proportionate both to their circumstances and the offence.

. . .

6.15.1.3 Recommendation No. R(87)20 of the Committee of Ministers to Member States on Social Reactions to Juvenile Delinquency

See <https://wcm.coe.int/ViewDoc.jsp?id=704821&Lang=en>.
   This recommends:

I. Prevention

1. to undertaking or continuing particular efforts for the prevention of juvenile mal-adjustment and delinquency, in particular:

    a. by implementing a comprehensive policy promoting the social integration of young people;
    b. by providing special assistance and the introduction of specialised programmes, on an experimental basis, in schools or in young peoples' or sports' organisations for the better integration of young people who are experiencing serious difficulties in this field;
    c. by taking technical and situational measures to reduce the opportunities offered to young people to commit offences;

II. Diversion – mediation

2. to encouraging the development of diversion and mediation procedures at public prosecutor level (discontinuation of proceedings) or at police level, in countries where the police has prosecuting functions, in order to prevent minors from entering into the criminal justice system and suffering the ensuing consequences; to associating Child Protection Boards or services to the application of these procedures;
3. to taking the necessary measures to ensure that in such procedures:

    – the consent of the minor to the measures on which the diversion is conditional and, if necessary, the co-operation of his family are secured;
    – appropriate attention is paid to the rights and interests of the minor as well as to those of the victim;

III. Proceedings against minors

4. to ensuring that minors are tried more rapidly, avoiding undue delay, so as to ensure effective educational action;
5. to avoiding committing minors to adult courts, where juvenile courts exist;
6. to avoiding, as far as possible, minors being kept in police custody and, in any case, encouraging the prosecuting authorities to supervise the conditions of such custody;
7. to excluding the remand in custody of minors, apart from exceptional cases of very serious offences committed by older minors; in these cases, restricting the length of

remand in custody and keeping minors apart from adults; arranging for decisions of this type to be, in principle, ordered after consultation with a welfare department on alternative proposals;

8. to reinforcing the legal position of minors throughout the proceedings, including the police investigation, by recognising, inter alia:

   – the presumption of innocence;
   – the right to the assistance of a counsel who may, if necessary, be officially appointed and paid by the State ;
   – the right to the presence of parents or of another legal representative who should be informed from the beginning of the proceedings;
   – the right of minors to call, interrogate and confront witnesses;
   – the possibility for minors to ask for a second expert opinion or any other equivalent investigative measure;
   – the right of minors to speak and, if necessary, to give an opinion on the measures envisaged for them;
   – the right to appeal;
   – the right to apply for a review of the measures ordered;
   – the right of juveniles to respect for their private lives;

9. to encouraging arrangements for all the persons concerned at various stages of the proceedings (police, counsel, prosecutors, judges, social workers) to receive specialised training on the law relating to minors and juvenile delinquency;

10. to ensuring that the entries of decisions relating to minors in the police records are treated as confidential and only communicated to the judicial authorities or equivalent authorities and that these entries are not used after the persons concerned come of age, except on compelling grounds provided for in national law;

IV. Interventions

11. to ensuring that interventions in respect of juvenile delinquents are sought preferably in the minors' natural environment, respect their right to education and their personality and foster their personal development;

12. to providing that intervention is of a determined length and that only the judicial authorities or equivalent administrative authorities may fix it, and that the same authorities may terminate the intervention earlier than originally provided;

13. when residential care is essential:

   – to diversifying the forms of residential care in order to provide the one most suited to the minor's age, difficulties and background (host families, homes);
   – to establishing small-scale educational institutions integrated into their social, economic and cultural environment;
   – to providing that the minor's personal freedom shall be restricted as little as possible and that the way in which this is done is decided under judicial control;
   – in all forms of custodial education, to fostering, where possible, the minor's relations with his family:
   – avoiding custody in places which are too distant or inaccessible;
   – maintaining contact between the place of custody and the family;

14. with the aim of gradually abandoning recourse to detention and increasing the number of alternative measures, to giving preference to those which allow greater opportunities for social integration through education, vocational training as well as through the use of leisure or other activities;

15. among such measures, to paying particular attention to those which:

    – involve probationary supervision and assistance;
    – are intended to cope with the persistence of delinquent behaviour in the minor by improving his capacities for social adjustment by means of intensive educational action (including 'intensive intermediary treatment');
    – entail reparation for the damage caused by the criminal activity of the minor;
    – entail community work suited to the minor's age and educational needs;

16. in cases where, under national legislation, a custodial sentence cannot be avoided:

    – to establishing a scale of sentences suited to the condition of minors, and to introducing more favourable conditions for the serving of sentences than those which the law lays down for adults, in particular as regards the obtaining of semi-liberty and early release, as well as granting and revocation of suspended sentence;
    – to requiring the courts to give reasons for their prison sentences;
    – to separating minors from adults or, where in exceptional cases integration is preferred for treatment reasons, to protecting minors from harmful influence from adults;
    – to providing both education and vocational training for young prisoners, preferably in conjunction with the community, or any other measure which may assist reinsertion in society;
    – to providing educational support after release and possible assistance for the social rehabilitation of the minors;

17. to reviewing, if necessary, their legislation on young adult delinquents, so that the relevant courts also have the opportunity of passing sentences which are educational in nature and foster social integration, regard being had for the personalities of the offenders

. . .

6.15.1.4 Recommendation Rec(2003)20 of the Committee of Ministers to Member States concerning new ways of dealing with Juvenile Delinquency and the role of Juvenile Justice

See <https://wcm.coe.int/ViewDoc.jsp?id=70063&Lang=en>.

This Recommendation was adopted by the Committee of Ministers on 24 September 2003:

II. A more strategic approach

1. The principal aims of juvenile justice and associated measures for tackling juvenile delinquency should be:

    i.   to prevent offending and reoffending;
    ii. to (re)socialise and (re)integrate offenders; and
    iii. to address the needs and interests of victims.

2. The juvenile justice system should be seen as one component in a broader, community-based strategy for preventing juvenile delinquency, that takes account of the wider family, school, neighbourhood and peer group context within which offending occurs.

3. Resources should in particular be targeted towards addressing serious, violent, persistent and drug- and alcohol-related offending.

4. More appropriate and effective measures to prevent offending and reoffending by young members of ethnic minorities, groups of juveniles, young women and those under the age of criminal responsibility also need to be developed.

5. Interventions with juvenile offenders should, as much as possible, be based on scientific evidence on what works, with whom and under what circumstances.

6. In order to prevent discrimination public authorities should produce 'impact' statements on the potential consequences of new policies and practices on young members of ethnic minorities.

III. New responses

7. Expansion of the range of suitable alternatives to formal prosecution should continue. They should form part of a regular procedure, must respect the principle of proportionality, reflect the best interests of the juvenile and, in principle, apply only in cases where responsibility is freely accepted.

8. To address serious, violent and persistent juvenile offending, Member States should develop a broader spectrum of innovative and more effective (but still proportional) community sanctions and measures. They should directly address offending behaviour as well as the needs of the offender. They should also involve the offender's parents or other legal guardian (unless this is considered counter-productive) and, where possible and appropriate, deliver mediation, restoration and reparation to the victim.

9. Culpability should better reflect the age and maturity of the offender, and be more in step with the offender's stage of development, with criminal measures being progressively applied as individual responsibility increases.

10. Parents (or legal guardians) should be encouraged to become aware of and accept their responsibilities in relation to the offending behaviour of young children. They should attend court proceedings (unless this is considered counter-productive) and, where possible, they should be offered help, support and guidance. They should be required, where appropriate, to attend counselling or parent training courses, to ensure their child attends school and to assist official agencies in carrying out community sanctions and measures.

11. Reflecting the extended transition to adulthood, it should be possible for young adults under the age of 21 to be treated in a way comparable to juveniles and to be subject to the same interventions, when the judge is of the opinion that they are not as mature and responsible for their actions as full adults.

12. To facilitate their entry into the labour market, every effort should be made to ensure that young adult offenders under the age of 21 should not be required to disclose their criminal record to prospective employers, except where the nature of the employment dictates otherwise.

13. Instruments for assessing the risk of future reoffending should be developed in order that the nature, intensity and duration of interventions can be closely matched to the

risk of reoffending, as well as to the needs of the offender, always bearing in mind the principle of proportionality. Where appropriate, relevant agencies should be encouraged to share information, but always in accordance with the requirements of data protection legislation.

14. Short time periods for each stage of criminal proceedings should be set to reduce delays and ensure the swiftest possible response to juvenile offending. In all cases, measures to speed up justice and improve effectiveness should be balanced with the requirements of due process.

15. Where juveniles are detained in police custody, account should be taken of their status as a minor, their age and their vulnerability and level of maturity. They should be promptly informed of their rights and safeguards in a manner that ensures their full understanding. While being questioned by the police they should, in principle, be accompanied by their parent/legal guardian or other appropriate adult. They should also have the right of access to a lawyer and a doctor. They should not be detained in police custody for longer than forty-eight hours in total and for younger offenders every effort should be made to reduce this time further. The detention of juveniles in police custody should be supervised by the competent authorities.

16. When, as a last resort, juvenile suspects are remanded in custody, this should not be for longer than six months before the commencement of the trial. This period can only be extended where a judge not involved in the investigation of the case is satisfied that any delays in proceedings are fully justified by exceptional circumstances.

17. Where possible, alternatives to remand in custody should be used for juvenile suspects, such as placements with relatives, foster families or other forms of supported accommodation. Custodial remand should never be used as a punishment or form of intimidation or as a substitute for child protection or mental health measures.

18. In considering whether to prevent further offending by remanding a juvenile suspect in custody, courts should undertake a full risk assessment based on comprehensive and reliable information on the young person's personality and social circumstances.

19. Preparation for the release of juveniles deprived of their liberty should begin on the first day of their sentence. A full needs and risk assessment should be the first step towards a reintegration plan which fully prepares offenders for release by addressing, in a co-ordinated manner, their needs relating to education, employment, income, health, housing, supervision, family and social environment.

20. A phased approach to reintegration should be adopted, using periods of leave, open institutions, early release on licence and resettlement units. Resources should be invested in rehabilitation measures after release and this should, in all cases, be planned and carried out with the close co-operation of outside agencies.

. . .

6.16 YOUTH JUSTICE: WHAT HAPPENS NEXT?

In its consultation paper, *Every Child Matters – Next Steps* (<http://www.home-office.gov.uk/documents/259029/cons-youth-jus-next-steps-summ?view=Binary>), the Government sets out its plans for the system of youth justice in England and Wales, making the point that some of the action to put its decisions into effect will depend on resources or parliamentary time. It says that: 'our youth justice approach . . . focuses on preventing offending but also on tackling the factors which underlie it.' The conclusions are set out under a series of headings:

Pre-court interventions

We have decided not to change the existing statutory framework on reprimands and final warnings because it provides speed, simplicity and effective sanctions for failure to comply. We do propose to take administrative action to ensure that the scheme is used to its full capacity and we shall issue guidance so that reasons are stated in open court whenever the scheme is bypassed. We also intend to put forward legislation at a suitable opportunity to amend the Rehabilitation of Offenders Act to ensure that reprimands and final warnings are not citable to prospective employers.

General sentencing principles and structure

We unreservedly accept that welfare is an important consideration when a court has to make a decision on the appropriate sentence for a young offender. But we believe that the main purpose of a sentence imposed by a court on conviction of a criminal offence by a juvenile should be to prevent their further offending and we shall legislate to clarify this in law. Courts will also be required to have regard to other factors including public protection, welfare, punishment and reparation. The interventions which are used to help the young person deal with their offending behaviour would include activities and support which have been assessed as appropriate for the individual. The sentencing guidelines council will also provide guidance to courts on juveniles. In addition, we will include preventing antisocial behaviour in the duties of the Youth Justice Board and Youth Offending Teams.

Families and communities

We shall promote the fuller use of parenting measures, including family group conferencing and family therapy, by youth justice agencies and shall issue guidance. We shall also provide parenting programmes for young offenders who are themselves parents. We recognise that some of these offenders are 'hard to reach' and their needs are not being met by current programmes. We plan to establish family group conferencing in 15 Youth Offending Team areas to promote this technique as a form of restorative justice.

Policing, public order and courts

We propose to develop a young defendant's pack to help young people and their parents or carers understand and prepare for their court experience – to promote understanding and acceptance of responsibility. We shall also examine the scope for involving voluntary agencies in supporting them at and before court, and further promote simpler language in court. We propose to discuss with the Judicial Studies Board ways in which the particular needs of young defendants can be met through training for crown court judges and with the relevant professional bodies in respect of training for lawyers.

Remands

We shall issue guidance to ensure pre-sentence reports are consistently well targeted and provide the information courts need. We propose to provide a wider range of supported accommodation for young people on bail or community sentence. We also propose to encourage the use of remand fostering and consider how to increase the provision of places.

We also propose to legislate to treat 17 year olds as juveniles for the purposes of remand

and bail. There will be separate consultation on the question of the status of 17 year olds being interviewed by the police under PACE legislation.

Sentencing in the community

We believe that it is important for the sentencing options to be simpler and more flexible. The reparation order and referral order will maintain their distinct roles but otherwise we shall legislate to introduce a new generic juvenile community sentence with a wide menu of interventions. This new juvenile rehabilitation order will replace the eight current community sentences.

. . . Youth Justice Centres [will] provide a wider range of activities in support of the sentence – including counselling, sport, education (basic and life skills), training, employment and community service.

. . . [w]e shall build on the success of acceptable behaviour contracts and encourage their use with positive requirements as part of the early intervention work by youth inclusion and support panels.

We propose to improve the leverage of Youth Offending Teams in accessing local accommodation for young defendants on bail and for convicted young offenders through buying retainers on emergency beds, bonds and specialist advice or placement services. They need to be able to make full use of existing accommodation in the community – whether provided by local authorities, housing associations or private landlords. We also propose to pilot intensive fostering as an alternative to custody for convicted young offenders.

We shall establish outreach services for young offenders serving sentences in the community, including those leaving custody. These services will provide practical advice and help to the young person to re-engage with the statutory and other services in the community. We shall also negotiate with local authorities to identify more reparation projects suitable for juvenile offenders which help local communities.

We propose a limited extension to referral orders to allow them on a later court appearance, for example where the young person has not previously received one or did so at least two years ago.

More intensive sentences, including custody

. . . [w]e shall legislate to establish a new intensive supervision and surveillance order as a robust alternative to custody for the more serious or persistent offenders. We shall retain the detention and training order (DTO) and also provide that 12–14 year olds would no longer need to be both serious and persistent to receive a DTO, but that the maximum term for them would drop from 24 to 12 months.

During the community part of a DTO we shall bring a particular focus on activities to help young offenders re-engage with education, training and employment. In addition supervising officers will be able to choose from the same range of interventions as are available to offenders serving a community sentence. We shall explore further how to improve the continuity between education in custody and in the community.

For a critique of these proposals in the context of the history of juvenile justice, see Caroline Ball, 'Youth Justice? Half a Century of Responses to Youth Offending' [2004] Crim LR 167.

For a discussion of the youth rehabilitation order created by the Criminal Justice and Immigration Act 2008, see Chapter 21.

Chapter 7

Appeals from magistrates' courts and youth courts

7.1 INTRODUCTION

In this chapter, we look at the mechanisms which exist for appealing against the decisions of a magistrates' court or a youth court. We examine the appellate jurisdiction of the Crown Court (which is completely different to its jurisdiction as a court of first instance when defendants are tried by a judge and jury) and we also consider the supervisory jurisdiction which the High Court exercises over magistrates' courts and youth courts by means of appeal by way of case stated and by means of judicial review.

Thus, there are three forms to appeal against the decisions of a magistrates' court or a youth court:

- appeal to the Crown Court;
- appeal to the High Court by way of case stated; and
- judicial review.

7.2 APPEAL TO THE CROWN COURT

The most common form of appeal from the magistrates' court and youth court is to the Crown Court. This is governed by s 108 of the Magistrates' Courts Act 1980. Under s 108(1):

A person convicted by a magistrates' court may appeal to the Crown Court—

(a) if he pleaded guilty, against his sentence;
(b) if he did not, against the conviction or sentence.

Thus, a defendant who pleaded guilty cannot appeal against his conviction (unless the plea was equivocal, considered later in this chapter) but can appeal against the sentence imposed. If he pleaded not guilty but was convicted by the magistrates, he can appeal against conviction and/or sentence.

Where an offender is dealt with by means of an absolute or conditional discharge (dealt with in Chapter 19), he is (by virtue of s 14 of the Powers of Criminal Courts (Sentencing) Act 2000) deemed not to have been convicted of the offence except for certain purposes. However, s 108(1A) of the 1980 Act specifically stipulates that this provision does not prevent an appeal (whether against conviction or sentence) pursuant to s 108. Moreover, s 108(2) specifically allows for an appeal against sentence where a conditional discharge was ordered.

Section 108(3)(b) specifically excludes costs orders from the definition of 'sentence' for these purposes, and so a costs order cannot be the subject of an appeal under s 108.

7.2.1 Procedure for appeal to the Crown Court

The procedure for appeal to the Crown Court is set out in Pt 63 of the Criminal Procedure Rules. It is as follows:

- notice of appeal must be given to the magistrates' court and to the prosecutor (r 63.2(2));
- this notice must be given within 21 days of the passing of the sentence (r 63.2(3));
- the notice of appeal must state the grounds of appeal (r 63.2(4));
- leave to appeal is not required;
- the time for giving notice of appeal may be extended, either before or after it expires, by the Crown Court (r 63.2(5)).

It should be emphasised that the 21-day period for giving notice of appeal runs from the date when sentence is passed even if the appeal is against conviction only.

An application to extend that 21-day period has to be made to the Crown Court in writing, specifying the grounds on which it is made (r 63.2(6)). The court will take account of the merits of the case as well as the reason for the delay when deciding whether to extend the time limit (*R v Stafford Crown Court ex p Reid* (1995) *The Independent*, March 13).

7.2.2 Bail pending appeal

Where the defendant is given a custodial sentence, bail pending appeal may be granted by the magistrates who passed sentence (s 113 of the Magistrates' Courts Act 1980). However, there is no presumption in favour of bail, as s 4 of the Bail Act 1976 (see Chapter 3) does not apply.

If the magistrates do not grant bail, the Crown Court may do so (under s 81(1)(b) of the Supreme Court Act 1981). The strongest argument that can usually be advanced in support of bail pending the hearing of the appeal is that a short sentence may have been served before the appeal is heard.

The right to apply for bail to a High Court judge in chambers under s 22(1) of the Criminal Justice Act 1967 was removed by the Criminal Justice Act 2003.

7.2.3 The hearing of the appeal in the Crown Court

The appeal is heard by a judge (a Circuit Judge or a Recorder) and at least two (but not more than four) lay justices (s 74(1) of the Supreme Court Act 1981).

Under r 63.7 of the Criminal Procedure Rules, where the Crown Court is hearing an appeal from a youth court, the Crown Court must consist of a judge sitting with two justices (one male, one female) each of whom is authorised to hear youth court cases.

Rule 63.8(1) provides that the Crown Court may hear an appeal even if not properly constituted as required by s 74(1) of the 1981 Act or r 63.7, if it appears to the judge that the court could not be so constituted without 'unreasonable delay' and the court includes one lay justice (where the appeal is from a youth court, he or she must be authorised to hear youth court cases). Moreover, under r 63.8(2), the Crown Court may continue hearing an appeal even if one or more of the justices who was sitting has withdrawn, or is absent for any reason.

Section 73(3) of the Supreme Court Act 1981 stipulates that where a Crown Court judge sits with justices of the peace:

- he shall preside;
- the decision of the Crown Court may be a majority decision; and
- if the members of the court are equally divided, the Crown Court judge has a second and casting vote.

7.2.3.1 Appeals against conviction

An appeal against conviction takes the form of a complete re-hearing, and so the procedure is the same as the trial in the magistrates' court or youth court (s 79(3) of the Supreme Court Act 1981).

Because an appeal against conviction is a re-hearing, the parties are not limited to evidence which was called at the original trial. This has the important consequence that either party can call witnesses who were not called in the magistrates' court trial, or refrain from calling witnesses who did give evidence in the magistrates' court.

However, the Crown Court cannot amend the charge on which the appellant was convicted (*Garfield v Maddocks* [1974] QB 7; *R v Swansea Crown Court ex p Stacey* [1990] RTR 183).

7.2.3.2 Appeals against sentence

An appeal against sentence similarly mirrors the sentencing procedure in the magistrates' court or youth court, with the prosecution summarising the facts and the defence making a plea in mitigation.

The Crown Court carries out a complete re-hearing of the issues and forms an independent view as to the correct sentence. In *R v Swindon Crown Court ex p Murray* (1998) 162 JP 36, the Divisional Court held that, when dealing with an appeal against sentence, the Crown Court should not ask itself whether the sentence was within the discretion of the magistrates (the test which would be appropriate in judicial review) but should consider whether, in the light of all the matters which the Crown Court had heard, the sentence passed by the magistrates was the correct one. If it was not the correct sentence, the Crown Court should replace it with the sentence which that court holds to be the right one.

It is not the function of the Crown Court when considering an appeal against sentence to address perceived procedural errors made by the magistrates. In *R (Lees-Sandey) v Chichester Crown Court* [2004] EWHC 2280; (2004), *The Times*, 15 October, it was held that where the Crown Court is hearing an appeal against a sentence imposed by a magistrates' court, the Crown Court is not entitled to increase the sentence on the basis that the magistrates ought to have committed the offender to the Crown Court for sentence in the first place.

In Chapter 16 we consider the situation where a defendant pleads guilty but does so on a different factual basis to that put forward by the prosecution. In such a case the court must either accept the defendant's version of events and sentence accordingly, or else hear evidence and make findings of fact on the disputed issues (a so-called 'Newton' hearing, as the procedure was laid down in *R v Newton* (1983) 77 Cr App R 13). In *Bussey v DPP* [1999] 1 Cr App R(S) 125, the defendant pleaded guilty to the offence of driving whilst disqualified. He maintained that he only drove because his wife had been taken ill and he had to take her to hospital. The prosecution disputed this version of events, but the magistrates decided (without hearing evidence) to accept the defendant's version. The defendant felt that the sentence imposed was nonetheless excessive and he appealed to the Crown Court. It was held that the Crown Court is not bound by findings of fact made by a magistrates' court in a way that could limit the Crown Court's sentencing powers. It follows that, where a defendant appeals against sentence to the Crown Court, the court is entitled to decide the appeal on a different factual basis from that accepted by the magistrates' court. However, where the Crown Court is minded to reject the view taken by the magistrates' court, the court should make the position clear to the appellant and give him an opportunity, under the *Newton* principle, to challenge the Crown Court's view of the facts.

7.2.4 Decision

The decision of the Crown Court is a majority decision. This means that the lay justices can out-vote the Crown Court judge. The lay justices must, however, accept any decisions on questions of law made by the judge.

In *R v Orpin* [1975] QB 283 at p 287, Lord Widgery CJ said that:

> in matters of law the lay justices must take a ruling from the presiding judge in precisely the same way as the jury is required to take his ruling when the jury considers its verdict . . . [it should be] clearly understood: first, that decisions are the product of all members of the court but, secondly, that any question of law is a question upon which the lay members of the court must defer to the views of the qualified presiding judge.

Thus, the justices are just as much judges of the Crown Court as the judge who presides, although on questions of law they should defer to the professional judge. The role of the justices was further considered in *R v Newby* (1984) 6 Cr App R (S) 148, an appeal against sentence passed by a court consisting of a recorder and two justices. Criticising the recorder for announcing sentence immediately after defence counsel's plea in mitigation and without any apparent consultation with the justices (although there had in fact been consultation before coming into court and the passing of notes during counsel's speech), Caulfield J said (at p 150):

> One would hardly need *Orpin* to recognise that where a recorder or any other judge is sitting with justices, the court consists of the presiding judge and the justices who sit with the judge, and of course on matters of fact the majority decision decides. So obviously there has to be consultation between the presiding judge and the justices who sit with him . . . This

Court would like to emphasise that where a learned judge is sitting with magistrates, not only should he consult his fellow-magistrates by law but he should make sure that the court appreciates that he has consulted. It is not necessary for the court to retire after each particular case. There is nothing wrong in notes being passed between members of the court. But when it comes to the point of sentence having to be given, it is far wiser for the court to show the public that the court is a composite court and that each member has a view which is expressed eventually through the president or chairman of the court.

It is submitted that his Lordship's remarks are applicable to all decisions (whether interlocutory or final) taken by a court which includes justices.

There is discussion of the role of the lay justices in the Crown Court in Bohlander, M, *'Take it from me . . .' – The Roles of the Judge and Lay Assessors in Deciding Questions of Law in Appeals to the Crown Court* (2005) 69 J Crim L 442. He makes the point that it is clear that in the magistrates' court, the justices are judges both of law and of fact. The justices have the benefit from advice on points of law from the court clerk/legal adviser, but (although they are strongly encouraged to follow that advice, as in *Jones v Nicks* [1977] RTR 72), decisions on questions of law are ultimately a matter for them. He argues that it is therefore anomalous that they are stripped of their power to decide points of law when sitting in the Crown Court. He takes the view, therefore, that the justices ought to be able to outvote the judge on points of law, as well as questions of fact.

Taking an even broader view it is perhaps questionable whether the presence of lay justices on the Crown Court bench when the court is hearing an appeal from a magistrates' court serves much purpose or is even appropriate. One useful by-product of the presence of justices in the Crown Court, however, is that it helps to foster good relationships between the magistracy and the Crown Court judges. So far as appropriateness is concerned, it may seem anomalous that an appeal is heard, at least in part, by a court which comprises judges of the same 'rank' as the original decision-makers; however, this can also occur in the Court of Appeal, where designated Circuit Judges are allowed to sit.

7.2.4.1 Reasons for the decision

Where the Crown Court dismisses an appeal against conviction, the judge must give reasons (and judicial review can be sought to compel the judge to do so if necessary). The reasons need not be elaborate, but the judge must say enough to demonstrate that the court has identified the main contentious issues in the case and how it has resolved each of them. The appellant is entitled to know the basis upon which the prosecution case had been accepted by the court (*R v Harrow Crown Court ex p Dave* [1994] 1 WLR 98 per Pill J at 107). In *R v Snaresbrook Crown Court ex p Input Management Ltd* (1999) 163 JP 533, the Divisional Court said that the reasons given by the court should enable the defendant to see the nature of the criminality found to exist by the court and to consider properly whether there are grounds for a further appeal to the Divisional Court by way of case stated.

In *R v Kingston Crown Court ex p Bell* (2000) 164 JP 633, the Divisional Court re-affirmed that, in the ordinary way, when the Crown Court hears an appeal from the magistrates' court, the Crown Court is under a duty to give reasons for its decision. Jackson J, giving the judgment of the court, said (at para 34):

> a failure to give reasons will vitiate the Crown Court's decision. However, this is not a universal rule: for example, the reasons may be obvious, or the case may be simple or the subject matter of the appeal may be unimportant. In cases of that nature, a failure to give reasons would not be fatal.

7.2.5 Equivocal pleas

Section 108(1)(a) of the Magistrates Courts Act 1980 limits the right of appeal in the case of a defendant who pleaded guilty to appeal against sentence. It follows that a defendant who pleads guilty in the magistrates' court cannot usually challenge that conviction by appealing to the Crown Court. However, if the plea of guilty was 'equivocal', the defendant can appeal against conviction despite having pleaded guilty. There are two types of equivocal plea:

1   The plea which is equivocal in court (that is, becomes equivocal because of something said prior to the passing of sentence). This will be the case if either:

    i   when the charge is put, the defendant says 'Guilty but . . .'. In other words, at the time of entering the guilty plea, the defendant says something which raises a defence (for example, 'guilty of theft but I thought the property was mine'); or

    ii   when the charge is put, the defendant says only 'Guilty', but this straight-forward plea is followed by a plea in mitigation which raises a defence and so is inconsistent with the guilty plea (for example, *R v Durham Quarter Sessions ex p Virgo* [1952] 2 QB 1, where an unrepresented defendant pleaded guilty to stealing a motorbike. Before sentence was passed, he made a statement to the effect that his taking of the motorbike was a mistake as he thought it belonged to a friend of his who had told him to take it home. It was held that the justices should have entered a plea of not guilty in view of the defendant's statement, and the case was remitted to the magistrates' court with a direction to hear the case on the basis of a plea of not guilty).

2   The plea which is made equivocal not because of anything the defendant says in court but because the defendant pleaded guilty as a direct result of threats from a third party. Then, at some time after the passing of sentence, the defendant alleges that he only pleaded guilty as a result of duress and now maintains that he is innocent (for example, *R v Huntingdon Crown Court ex p Jordan* [1981] QB 857, where the defendant, in the course of an appeal to the Crown Court, said that she had been threatened by her husband that he would physically ill-treat her if she did not plead guilty. It was held that the Crown Court should investigate the matter where it is alleged that there has been an equivocal plea in that sense and, if satisfied that there was an equivocal plea, send the matter back to the justices to enable them to re-hear the case on the basis of a not guilty plea).

In the case of the first type of equivocal plea, the problem should, of course, be dealt with at the original hearing. The charge should be put again by the magistrates' court once the relevant law has been explained to the defendant. If the plea remains equivocal, a 'not guilty' plea should be entered by the court on the defendant's behalf.

If this does not occur, or if the plea is equivocal because of duress, the defendant should apply to the Crown Court to declare the plea equivocal. In this type of appeal, the only inquiry undertaken by the Crown Court is whether or not the plea was equivocal. If the Crown Court decides that the plea was indeed equivocal, it will remit the case to the magistrates' court for trial. If not, the conviction based on the guilty plea will be upheld.

Provided the Crown Court conducts a proper inquiry into what happened in the magistrates' court (the court clerk or the chairman of the bench which convicted the defendant may have to supply a statement to assist the Crown Court in that inquiry), a direction from the Crown Court regarding remission for trial is binding on the magistrates' court (*R v Plymouth Justices ex p Hart* [1986] QB 950).

There are no other grounds for going behind a plea of guilty and so no other cases where a defendant can appeal to the Crown Court after pleading guilty (*R v Marylebone Justices ex p Westminster London Borough Council* [1971] 1 WLR 567). It is therefore not sufficient for the defendant merely to show that he regrets pleading guilty and that he has an arguable defence.

7.2.6 Powers of the Crown Court

The powers of the Crown Court when disposing of an appeal under s 108 of the Magistrates' Courts Act 1980 are set out in s 48(2) of the Supreme Court Act 1981. This provides that, following an appeal from the magistrates' court, the Crown Court:

(a) may confirm, reverse or vary any part of the decision appealed against, including a determination not to impose a separate penalty in respect of an offence; or

(b) may remit the matter with its opinion thereon to the authority whose decision is appealed against; or

(c) may make such other order in the matter as the court thinks just, and by such order exercise any power which the said authority might have exercised.

This means that, on an appeal against conviction, the Crown Court may:

- dismiss the appeal (and so uphold the conviction), or
- allow the appeal (and quash the conviction, placing the defendant in the position he would have been in had the magistrates acquitted him), or
- remit the case to the magistrates' court (as would be the case where the Crown Court holds a plea of guilty to be equivocal).

The Crown Court can also vary the sentence imposed by the magistrates' court. Section 48(4) of the 1981 Act says that:

if the appeal is against a conviction or a sentence, the preceding provisions of this section shall be construed as including power to award any punishment, whether more or less severe than that awarded by the magistrates' court whose decision is appealed against, if that is a punishment which that magistrates' court might have awarded.

The Crown Court may thus vary the sentence imposed by the magistrates, and this includes the power to increase the sentence, but not beyond the maximum sentence which the magistrates' court could have passed.

Section 48(5) provides that s 48 'applies whether or not the appeal is against the whole of the decision' and, as we have seen, s 48(2) refers to varying 'any part' of the decision under appeal. The effect of these provisions is that, if the defendant appeals against only part of the decision of the magistrates' court, every aspect of the magistrates' decision can be reconsidered by the Crown Court. For example:

- even if the defendant appeals only against conviction, the Crown Court can still vary the sentence;
- if the defendant was convicted of two offences and appeals against only one conviction, the Crown Court could allow the appeal (and quash the conviction that is being appealed) but also vary the sentence for the other offence;
- if the defendant was convicted by the magistrates of one offence but acquitted of another and he now appeals against the conviction, the Crown Court could convict the defendant of the offence of which the magistrates' court acquitted him.

It should be emphasised that, if the Crown Court does vary the sentence, it cannot impose a sentence greater than the sentence that the magistrates could have imposed.

7.2.7 Abandonment of appeal

Under r 63.5 of the Criminal Procedure Rules, an appellant may abandon an appeal by giving notice in writing (to the magistrates' court, the Crown Court, and the prosecution) not later than the third day before the day fixed for hearing the appeal.

It is, however, open to the Crown Court to allow an appeal to be abandoned even if these requirements are not satisfied.

In *R v Gloucester Crown Court ex p Betteridge* (1997) 161 JP 721, the Divisional Court held that, once the Crown Court gives leave to an appellant to abandon his appeal from the decision of the magistrates' court, the Crown Court no longer has the power to increase the sentence imposed by the magistrates.

In *R (Hayes) v Chelmsford Crown Court* [2003] EWHC 73 (Admin); (2003) 167 JP 65, the defendant was sentenced to six months' imprisonment by a magistrates' court. He was released on bail pending appeal. The terms of his bail required him to be present at the appeal. The defendant failed to attend court on the date fixed for the hearing of the appeal. He also failed to appear on subsequent dates, although he was represented by counsel. The judge dismissed the appeal, holding that the defendant had effectively abandoned his appeal. The Divisional Court held that it is not open to the Crown Court to treat the absence of the appellant as *de facto* abandonment of the appeal. Henriques J, at para 18, said that whenever it appears to a Crown Court in its appellate capacity that an appellant obliged to attend has deliberately absented himself, the appropriate course is to hear the appeal in the absence of the appellant.

7.2.8 Further appeal from the Crown Court

The decision of the Crown Court on an appeal from a magistrates' court or youth court can only be challenged by means of an appeal to the Divisional Court by way of case stated or judicial review. There is no further appeal to the Court of Appeal.

Recommendation 306 of the Lord Justice Auld's *Review of the Criminal Courts of England and Wales* (the *Auld Review*) was that there should no longer be an appeal to the High Court (either by way of case stated or judicial review) from the Crown Court sitting in its appellate capacity, but that there should be an appeal to the Court of Appeal; however, this appeal should be subject to the permission of the Court of Appeal, which it should only give in a case involving an important point of principle or practice or where there is some other compelling reason for the court to hear it. This suggestion was not taken up by the Government. However, appeals from the Crown Court to the High Court have been the subject of a Law Commission consultation exercise (<http://www.lawcom.gov.uk/docs/cp184_tso.pdf>).

7.3 APPEAL TO THE DIVISIONAL COURT BY WAY OF CASE STATED

Appeal to the Divisional Court (part of the High Court of Justice) is made possible by s 111(1) of the Magistrates' Courts Act 1980, which provides as follows:

> Any person who was a party to any proceeding before a magistrates' court or is aggrieved by the conviction, order, determination or other proceeding of the court may question the proceeding on the ground that it is wrong in law or is in excess of jurisdiction by applying to the justices composing the court to state a case for the opinion of the High Court on the question of law or jurisdiction involved . . .

The right to appeal by way of case stated is only available where there has been a 'final determination' of the case in the magistrates' court (*Streames v Copping* [1985] QB 920 and *Loade v DPP* [1990] 1 QB 1052). It follows that s 111 does not apply to interlocutory decisions, such as a decision to commit the defendant to the Crown Court to be sentenced. The case law is fairly clear that that there must have been a final determination before an appeal by way of case stated may be brought, but in *Essen v DPP* [2005] EWHC 1077 (Admin), Sedley LJ said (at para 34):

> It may be . . . this . . . could usefully be revisited. If neither judicial review nor appeal by a case stated is available against an interlocutory decision which would arguably have been dispositive of a case at an early and much less costly stage, a fixed rule that any challenge must abide a final outcome is capable of working injustice.

In *Essen*, the challenge was in respect of an adjournment. By the time the trial had concluded, the defendant was out of time to seek judicial review of the decision on the adjournment. It is submitted, however, that it will be in only rare cases that the defendant will be left without a remedy because judicial review is not available.

Unlike the appeal to the Crown Court, appeal to the High Court by way of case stated is available to the prosecution as well as the defence. However, under s 111 of the Magistrates' Courts Act 1980, it is available only where the decision of the magistrates' court or youth court is:

- wrong in law; or
- in excess of jurisdiction.

This procedure is perhaps best suited to cases where it is suggested that the magistrates got the law wrong when coming to their decision – for example, that they misconstrued a statutory provision.

Where the challenge that is being made to the conviction is essentially about the correctness of the findings of fact by the magistrates, the correct course is to appeal to the Crown Court, where the matter can be quickly resolved, and not to the High Court by way of case stated (*Spillman v DPP* [2006] EWHC 1197 (Admin)). Indeed, in *Braintree District Council v Thompson* [2005] EWCA Civ 178 (a case involving appeals to a social security commissioner), Ward LJ said (at para 19):

> Findings of fact which are challenged as erroneous for being against the weight of the evidence do not involve any error of law. It only becomes an error of law if the finding of fact is perverse in the sense that no reasonable Tribunal could have reached that conclusion. An example of such perversity would be where the fact-finding body proceeded upon a blatant misunderstanding or in total ignorance of an established and relevant fact. It must be established that the Tribunal acted upon a wholly incorrect basis of fact but that only arises where the fact is plain and incontrovertible and where there is no room for difference of view about it.

The Divisional Court will not readily 'second guess' the magistrates. In *H v DPP* [2007] EWHC 2192 (Admin), Auld LJ (at para 19) noted the well-established approach of the Court of Appeal to cases under s 78 of the Police and Criminal Evidence Act 1984 (exclusion of prosecution evidence on the ground of unfairness), when invited to consider the trial judge's exercise of judgment as to fairness. The court will only interfere with the judge's ruling if it is *Wednesbury* irrational or perverse (i.e. a decision so unreasonable that no judge properly directing himself could have reached it). His Lordship said that the Divisional Court should adopt the same approach on appeals to it by way of case stated on such matters (concerning as they do an exercise of judgment): anything falling short of *Wednesbury* irrationality will not suffice.

7.3.1 Procedure for appealing by way of case stated

Section 111(2) requires that an application under s 111 must be made 'within 21 days after the day on which the decision of the magistrates' court was given'. Sub-section (3) defines the date of decision where the defendant has been convicted by the magistrates as 'the day on which the court sentences or otherwise deals with the offender'.

The appellant begins the appeal by making an application to the magistrates to state a case. In accordance with s 111, this application must be made within 21 days of conviction (or sentence, if later) and must identify the question of law or jurisdiction at issue. This 21-day period cannot be extended (see *Michael v Gowland* [1977] 1 WLR 296, decided under earlier legislation).

Where the final termination of proceedings is a decision on an application for costs, the 21-day time limit for asking the magistrates to state a case begins to run from the date of the decision on costs (*Liverpool City Council v Worthington* (1998), *The Times*, 16 June).

7.3.2 Refusal to state a case

By virtue of s 111(5), the justices may refuse to state a case if they are of opinion that the application is 'frivolous'. If the magistrates refuse to state a case on this basis, the applicant may seek a certificate confirming their refusal to state a case. Under sub-s (6), where justices refuse to state a case, the applicant may seek judicial review of the refusal and the High Court may make an order requiring the justices to state a case.

The test of whether a request to state a case is 'frivolous' is whether the application raises an 'arguable point of law' (*R v City of London Justices ex p Ocansey* (1995, QBD, 17 February, unreported), and *R v East Cambridgeshire Justices ex p Stephenson* (1995), QBD, 24 February, unreported). In *R v Mildenhall Magistrates' Court ex p Forest Heath District Council* (1997) 161 JP 401, it was held that the word 'frivolous' in this context means that the justices consider the application to be 'futile, misconceived, hopeless, or academic'. Lord Bingham CJ went on to say that such a conclusion will be reached only rarely: it is not enough that the justices consider that their original decision was correct. Furthermore, where justices do refuse to state a case, they should give brief reasons explaining why they have done so. Lord Bingham added that a finding of fact may be challenged if it is perverse. This would be the case if, for example, the finding had no evidential foundation whatsoever (as Lord Goddard CJ put it in *Bracegirdle v Oxley* [1947] 1 KB 349, at 353, findings of fact may be challenged if the justices 'come to a decision of fact without evidence to support it'). However, a decision (even if mistaken) is not perverse if the justices prefer A's evidence to that of B and resolve the question of fact on the basis of A's evidence.

Where the magistrates refuse to state a case and the appellant seeks judicial review of that refusal, the usual remedy (if the Divisional Court holds that the refusal to state a case was wrong) is for the Divisional Court to quash the refusal to state a case, so the magistrates have to state a case. However, it is open to the Divisional Court, when considering the application for judicial review of the refusal to state a case, to regard the written evidence used in the judicial review proceedings as the case stated and to treat the application for judicial review as if it were an appeal by way of case stated. In this way, the Divisional Court can, for example, quash a conviction without waiting for the case to go back to the magistrates to state a case (see, for example, *R v Ealing Justices ex p Woodman* (1994) 158 JP 997).

This approach was followed in *R v Crown Court at Blackfriars ex p Sunworld Ltd* [2000] 1 WLR 2102, where Simon Brown LJ (at p 2106–7), giving the judgment of the Divisional Court, handed down guidance on the approach to be adopted by that court in a case where the magistrates' court (or indeed the Crown Court, on appeal from the magistrates' court) has refused to state a case:

(1) Where a court, be it a magistrate's court or the Crown Court, refuses to state a case, then the party aggrieved should without delay apply for permission to bring judicial review, either (a) to mandamus it to state a case and/or (b) to quash the order sought to be appealed.

(2) If the court below has already (a) given a reasoned judgment containing all the necessary findings of fact and/or (b) explained its refusal to state a case in terms which clearly raise the true point of law in issue, then the correct course would be for the single judge, assuming he thinks the point properly arguable, to grant permission for judicial review which directly challenges the order complained of, thereby avoiding the need for a case to be stated at all.

(3) If the court below has stated a case but in respect of some questions only, as here, the better course may be to apply for the case stated to be amended unless again, as here, there already exists sufficient material to enable the Divisional Court to deal with all the properly arguable issues in the case.

(4) This court for its part will adopt whatever course involves the fewest additional steps and the least expense, delay and duplication of proceedings. Whether ... it will be possible to proceed at once to a substantive determination of the issues must inevitably depend in part upon whether all interested parties are represented and prepared, and in part upon the availability of court time.

Another reason for refusing to state a case is contained in s 114 of the Magistrates' Courts Act 1980, which empowers the magistrates to require the appellant to enter into a recognisance (that is, promise to pay a specified sum of money if the condition is not complied with) to pursue the appeal without delay and to pay any costs awarded against him by the High Court. If this power is invoked, a case will not be stated until the appellant has entered into a recognisance.

The fact that the applicant's defence is publicly funded does not, of itself, mean that the justices cannot require him to enter into a recognisance; the defendant must satisfy the court that he has no means of raising sufficient capital to comply with the condition (*R v Croydon Magistrates' Court ex p Morgan* (1997) 161 JP 169).

7.3.3 The statement of case

The procedure for an appeal by way of case stated is governed by Pt 64 of the Criminal Procedure Rules. It provides as follows:

64.1 Application to a magistrates' court to state a case

(1) An application under section 111(1) of the Magistrates' Courts Act 1980(1) shall be made in writing and signed by or on behalf of the applicant and shall identify the question or questions of law or jurisdiction on which the opinion of the High Court is sought.

(2) Where one of the questions on which the opinion of the High Court is sought is whether there was evidence on which the magistrates' court could come to its decision, the particular finding of fact made by the magistrates' court which it is claimed cannot be supported by the evidence before the magistrates' court shall be specified in such application.

(3) Any such application shall be sent to a court officer for the magistrates' court whose decision is questioned.

. . .

64.6 Content of case stated by a magistrates' courts

(1) A case stated by the magistrates' court shall state the facts found by the court and the question or questions of law or jurisdiction on which the opinion of the High Court is sought.

(2) Where one of the questions on which the opinion of the High Court is sought is whether there was evidence on which the magistrates' court could come to its decision, the particular finding of fact which it is claimed cannot be supported by the evidence before the magistrates' court shall be specified in the case.

(3) Unless one of the questions on which the opinion of the High Court is sought is whether there was evidence on which the magistrates' court could come to its decision, the case shall not contain a statement of evidence.

Thus, the statement of the case should set out:

- the charge(s) being tried by the magistrates;
- the facts as found by the magistrates (but not the evidence upon which those findings of fact were based, unless the basis of the appeal is that the decision of the justices was entirely unsupported by the evidence which they had heard);
- any submissions (including names of any authorities cited in argument) made to the magistrates by the prosecution and defence, and the magistrates' decision on those submissions;
- the question(s) for determination by the High Court.

In *Oladimeji v DPP* [2006] EWHC 1199 (Admin), the Divisional Court emphasised that, when appealing to the High Court by way of case stated, r 64.6 must be followed. Keene LJ, giving the judgment of the court, said (at para 4):

> What this court does need in all cases are clear findings of fact, and a clear identification of the questions of law which are said to arise. The justices should decline to pose questions for this court unless those questions are ones of law. If there is no evidence for a finding of fact, that will give rise to an error of law. But the weight to be attached to particular pieces of evidence is a matter for the justices. Only if no reasonable Bench could have reached the finding in question will that finding produce an error of law or amount to an *ultra vires* act. If a defendant believes that the justices have arrived at a finding for which there was evidence but at which he contends they should not have arrived (for example, because it was against the weight of the evidence), his remedy lies in an appeal to the Crown Court, not in an appeal by case stated to this court.

In *Vehicle Inspectorate v George Jenkins Transport Ltd* [2003] EWHC 2879 (Admin); (2003) *The Times*, 5 December, it was said that a stated case should set out the facts as found or accepted for the purposes of the magistrates' ruling (with reference to any relevant documents); it should set out in summary form the submissions made on each side; it should set out the conclusions of the magistrates' court on the matters in issue and the question(s) for the consideration of the Divisional Court. Kennedy LJ added (at para 39): 'Where advocates appear in the magistrates' court, there is no reason why the court, if minded to state a case, should not invite the advocates for the parties to submit a first draft, indicating any areas of disagreement.'

Following receipt of the application to state a case, the magistrates' clerk prepares a draft case and sends it to the prosecution and defence for comment. This should be done within 21 days of receipt of the application (r 64.2(1) of the Criminal Procedure Rules). The parties have 21 days from receipt of the draft case in which to comment (r 64.2(2)).

The final version (amended in the light of any comments made by prosecution or defence and signed by the clerk or by two of the magistrates whose decision is under appeal) is sent to the appellant; this must be done within 21 days of the last day on which representations may be made (r 64.3). A properly drafted question should not be altered without the party who framed the original question being given the opportunity to comment on the changes (*Waldie v DPP* (1995) 159 JP 514).

The appellant should lodge the stated case at the Administrative Court Office (in the Royal Courts of Justice) within 10 days of receiving it from the magistrates' court (Civil Procedure Rules Practice Direction 52, para 18.4) and must serve the appellant's notice and accompanying documents on all respondents within four days after they are filed or lodged at the appeal court (ibid para 18.6).

It should be borne in mind that when magistrates are asked to state a case, it is not open to them to put forward reasons their decision should not be challenged where those reasons were not part of their original decision (*Kent County Council v Curtis* (1998) EGCS 100). Furthermore, the justices should not change, or put a gloss on, the reasons which they gave in court for convicting or acquitting the defendant (*Evans v DPP* [2001] EWHC 369 (Admin); (2001) *The Times*, 9 July).

7.3.4 Bail pending appeal

If the defendant was given a custodial sentence, the magistrates may grant bail pending appeal under s 113 of the Magistrates' Courts Act 1980. If the magistrates refuse, the defendant can apply to a High Court judge in chambers under s 37(1)(b) of the Criminal Justice Act 1948. This jurisdiction to grant bail is preserved by the Criminal Justice Act 2003 (which otherwise removed the bail jurisdiction of the High Court).

7.3.5 The hearing

The appeal is heard by a Divisional Court (that is, two or more High Court judges in open court). If a two-judge court hears the appeal but cannot agree on the outcome, the appeal fails (*Flannagan v Shaw* [1920] 3 KB 96 at 107, per Scrutton LJ, obiter).

The hearing of the appeal takes the form of legal argument based on the facts stated in the case; no evidence is called, and so there are no witnesses.

In *Skipaway Ltd v Environment Agency* [2006] EWHC 983 (Admin), Stanley Burnton J noted that there is a 'surprisingly common misconception that once an appeal by way of case stated is before the court, the parties may refer to evidence, or at least undisputed evidence, that was before the lower court in addition to that set out in the case'. To correct that misconception, his Lordship said (at para 15):

On an appeal by way of case stated, the Court is confined to the facts set out in the case. It is therefore important that the parties ensure that the case includes all those matters that should be before the Court when deciding the issues raised on the appeal. If a party to an appeal considers that the case produced by the lower court omits relevant matters, he should seek to have the case supplemented either by agreement with the other party and the lower court or by application to this Court under s 28A(2) of the Supreme Court Act 1981 for an order for the amendment of the case stated.

A corollary of this is that a party is not entitled to take a new point, the decision of which might be affected by evidence which could have been, but was not, adduced before the magistrates. Similarly, where a defendant has been convicted by the magistrates and appeals to the Divisional Court, it is not possible to raise the issue that certain prosecution evidence should have been excluded under s 78 of the Police and Criminal Evidence Act 1984 if the defence had not asked the magistrates to exclude the evidence under s 78. Such matters cannot be raised for the first time in the Divisional Court (see *Braham v DPP* (1995) 159 JP 527).

7.3.6 Powers of the Divisional Court

The powers of the Divisional Court on an appeal by way of case stated are contained in s 28A(3) of the Supreme Court Act 1981, which provides that the High Court may:

(a) reverse, affirm or amend the determination in respect of which the case has been stated; or

(b) remit the matter to the magistrates' court, or the Crown Court, with the opinion of the High Court,

and may make such other order in relation to the matter (including as to costs) as it thinks fit.

It follows that:

- where the defendant was convicted by the magistrates' court the Divisional Court may replace the conviction with an acquittal;
- where the defendant was acquitted after a full trial (that is, not after a successful submission of no case to answer at the close of the prosecution case), the Divisional Court may remit the case back to the magistrates' court with a direction to convict and proceed to sentence (or, if it is plain what sentence should be passed, the Divisional Court may itself convict the appellant and then proceed to sentence him);
- where the defendant was acquitted otherwise than after a full trial (for example, following a successful submission of no case to answer), the Divisional Court may remit the case to the magistrates' court with a direction to continue with the trial or to start the trial afresh in front of a fresh bench.

The Divisional Court cannot quash only part of an order and leave the rest intact. So, in *R v Old Street Magistrates ex p Spencer* (1994) *The Times*, 8 November, a costs order for £930 had been made. The Divisional Court felt that £150–250 was the appropriate bracket. However, the Divisional Court lacked the power to substitute a different amount. All it could do was to quash the original order and remit the case to the magistrates.

In *Griffith v Jenkins* [1992] 2 AC 76, the House of Lords confirmed that the Divisional Court has the power to remit a case for a rehearing before the same or a different bench of magistrates. Thus, it does not matter if the original court cannot be reconstituted for some reason (for example, one of the justices has retired or died). A rehearing of the case will only be ordered if a fair trial is still possible given the lapse of time since the alleged offence. Lord Bridge of Harwich (at p 84) said:

> . . . there is always power in the court on hearing an appeal by case stated . . . to order a rehearing before either the same or a different bench when that appears to be an appropriate course and the court, in its discretion, decides to take it. It is axiomatic, of course, that a rehearing will only be ordered in circumstances where a fair trial is still possible. But where errors of law by justices have led to an acquittal which is successfully challenged and where the circumstances of the case are such that a rehearing is the only way in which the matter can be put right, . . . the court will normally, though not necessarily, exercise its discretion in favour of that course. I recognise that very different considerations may apply to the exercise of discretion to order a rehearing following a successful appeal against conviction by the defendant in circumstances where the error in the proceedings which vitiated the conviction has left the issue of the defendant's guilt or innocence unresolved. In some such cases to order a rehearing may appear inappropriate or oppressive. But this must depend on how the proceedings have been conducted, the nature of the error vitiating the conviction, the gravity of the offence and any other relevant consideration . . .

7.3.7 Abandonment of appeal

An appellant who has made an appeal by way of case stated is entitled to withdraw that appeal without the leave of the High Court (*Collett v Bromsgrove District Council* (1996) 160 JP 593).

7.3.8 Effect on the right of appeal to the Crown Court

The making of an application to the magistrates to state a case removes the defendant's right to appeal to the Crown Court (s 111(4) of the Magistrates' Courts Act 1980). Tactically, therefore, it is wise to appeal to the Crown Court first and, if that appeal is unsuccessful, to appeal against the decision of the Crown Court to the Divisional Court if there is a point of law on which to base that appeal.

7.4 JUDICIAL REVIEW

Like appeal by way of case stated, judicial review is available to the prosecution as well as the defence. However, an acquittal will not be quashed unless the trial was a nullity and so the defendant was not in danger of a valid conviction (for example, the purported summary trial of an indictable-only offence, or where the magistrates acquit without hearing any prosecution evidence, as in *R v Dorking Justices ex p Harrington* [1984] AC 743).

Unlike appeal by way of case stated, for judicial review to be available, there does not have to have been a final determination of the case. Nonetheless, any application for judicial review should usually be made at the conclusion of the proceedings in the magistrates' court. In *R v Rochford Justices ex p Buck* (1978) 68 Cr App R 114, the prosecution had sought to introduce certain evidence which the justices ruled inadmissible; the matter was then adjourned to enable the prosecution to test the ruling in the Divisional Court. Lord Widgery CJ said (at p 118) that it was 'very unsatisfactory' for the Divisional Court to review proceedings in a lower court which have not run their course and which are still pending, so that the application is in respect of an interlocutory matter; the obligation of the Divisional Court is to 'keep out of the way' until the magistrates' court has finished its determination. Similarly, in *R (Hoar-Stevens) v Richmond-upon-Thames Magistrates* [2003] EWHC 2660 (Admin), the Divisional Court held that, normally, it will not entertain an application for a quashing order in relation to a decision made in a magistrate's court where the proceedings in that court are not complete. Kennedy LJ (at para 18) said:

> It is of the utmost importance that the course of a criminal trial in the Magistrates' Court should not be punctuated by applications for an adjournment to test a ruling in this court, especially when in reality if the case proceeds the ruling may turn out to be of little or no importance ... I am satisfied that even when ... there is an important substantive point which arises during a trial this court should not and indeed cannot intervene. The proper course is to proceed to the end of the trial in the lower court and then to test the matter, almost certainly by way of case stated.

However, in *R (Watson) v Dartford Magistrates' Court* [2005] EWHC 905 (Admin), the court entertained a challenge to an interlocutory decision on an application for an adjournment. Mitting J said (at para 7):

> ... in some ... cases, the prosecution would no doubt say at the conclusion of a trial resulting in a conviction that it was too late for the claimant to complain about an adjournment that should not have been granted before. In a case such as this, where the issue is straightforward and the principle clear, I do not see that there is any fetter on this court intervening.

It seems that the rule that the Divisional Court should not interfere until the proceedings have been concluded is far from absolute. Where the issue before the magistrates is whether the trial should go ahead or not, as where the defence ask for the case to be dismissed as an abuse of process (see Chapter 1) and the magistrates reject that application, it would be appropriate for any challenge of that decision by way of judicial review to be heard before the trial commences.

Where the defendant pleaded guilty and wishes to challenge his conviction on the basis of a complaint about the conduct of the prosecution, the court will only entertain an application for judicial review of the conviction where the conduct of the prosecution can be 'fairly categorised as being analogous to fraud'; however, it is possible for conduct to be so categorised where there is no actual fraud or dishonesty. Thus the question is whether the prosecutor has acted in a way which has misled the defendant, whether deliberately or not (*R v Burton-on-Trent Justices ex p Woolley* (1995) 159 JP 165, followed in *R v Dolgellau Justices ex p Cartledge* [1996] RTR 207).

7.4.1 Grounds for seeking judicial review

Detailed consideration of the scope of judicial review is beyond the scope of the present work. However, the traditional statement of the ambit of judicial review comes from the speech of Lord Diplock in *Council of Civil Service Unions v Minister for the Civil Service* [1985] AC 374 at 410:

> ... one can conveniently classify under three heads the grounds upon which administrative action is subject to control by judicial review. The first ground I would call 'illegality', the second 'irrationality' and the third 'procedural impropriety'.

Another analysis of the ambit of judicial review suggests that the following are the main grounds:

* error of law on the face of the record (that is, an error disclosed in the court records). This would include passing a sentence in excess of the relevant statutory maximum for that offence;
* excess of jurisdiction (that is, the decision was *ultra vires*). This would include, for example, a magistrates' court trying an either-way offence without the defendant having first consented to summary trial;
* breach of the rules of natural justice (for example, bias or failing to allow both sides to put their case).

7.4.1.1 Bias

So far as bias is concerned, in *R v Gough* [1993] AC 646, the House of Lords held that the court should ask itself whether there was a 'real danger' of bias. In *Porter v Magill* [2002] 2 AC 357, the House of Lords considered the question of bias in relation to the courts generally. Lord Hope (at para 103) approved the test derived from *Re Medicaments and Related Classes of Goods (No 2)* [2000] 1 WLR 700 (per Lord Phillips of Worth Matravers MR at para 85), namely:

> whether those circumstances would lead a fair-minded and informed observer to conclude that there was a real possibility, or a real danger, the two being the same, that the tribunal was biased.

This test is in accordance with that adopted by the European Court of Human Rights in *Sander v UK* (2001) 31 EHRR 44 (where the Court considered the allegation being made in that case were capable of causing both 'the applicant and any objective observer legitimate doubts as to the impartiality of the court') and is effectively the same as the test propounded in *R v Liverpool Justices ex p Topping* [1983] 1 WLR 119 (per Ackner LJ at p 123): 'Would a reasonable and fair-minded person sitting in court and knowing all the relevant facts have a reasonable suspicion that a fair trial for the defendant was not possible?'

7.4.1.2 Breach of natural justice

Breach of natural justice has been widely construed. It includes, for example:

a the unreasonable refusal of an adjournment to enable a defendant to prepare his case (*R v Thames Magistrates' Court ex p Polemis* [1974] 1 WLR 1371);

b refusing an adjournment where a defence witness could not attend on the day of the trial without first considering the effect on the defence of having to go ahead without that witness (*R v Bracknell Justices ex p Hughes* (1990) 154 JP 98);

c failure by the prosecution to notify the defence of the existence of witnesses who could support the defence case (*R v Leyland Justices ex p Hawthorn* [1979] QB 283);

d failure by the prosecution to inform the defence that a key prosecution witness had a previous conviction for wasting police time, arising out of a false allegation of theft (*R v Knightsbridge Crown Court ex p Goonatilleke* [1986] QB 1, where the accused was charged with shoplifting);

e ordering a defendant to pay costs without considering his means to pay them (*R v Newham Justices ex p Samuels* [1991] COD 412).

7.4.1.3 Availability of appeal to the Crown Court

In *R v Peterborough Justices ex p Dowler* [1997] QB 911, where the appellant claimed that his conviction for careless driving should be set aside because the prosecution had failed to disclose a witness statement which might have helped his case, it was held that it is unnecessary to grant judicial review of a conviction by magistrates where the procedural unfairness complained of could be rectified by a fair hearing (by way of appeal) before the Crown Court, appealing to that court being 'clearly more effective and more convenient as well as being more expeditious' (per Henry LJ at 923).

In *R v Hereford Magistrates' Court ex p Rowlands* [1998] QB 110, Lord Bingham CJ noted (at p 118) that appeal to the Crown Court 'is the ordinary avenue of appeal for a defendant who complains that the magistrates' court reached a wrong decision of fact, or a wrong decision of mixed law and fact'. On the other hand, appeal by way of case stated:

> is the ordinary avenue of appeal for a convicted defendant who contends that the justices erred in law: the usual question posed for the opinion of the High Court is whether on the facts which they found the justices were entitled to convict the defendant; but sometimes the question is whether there was any evidence upon which the justices could properly convict the defendant, which has traditionally been regarded as an issue of law ... [I]f a magistrates' court convicts a defendant after radically departing from well known principles of justice and procedure, the defendant may challenge his conviction as wrong in law by way of case stated.

Judicial review, said Lord Bingham (at p 120) 'has provided the usual if not invariable means of pursuing challenges based on unfairness, bias or procedural irregularity in magistrates' courts'.

His Lordship went on to hold that the decision in *Dowler*, although correct on its facts, should not be treated as authority that a party complaining of procedural unfairness in a magistrates' court should invariably exercise his right of appeal to the Crown Court rather than seek judicial review. However, his Lordship said (at p 125):

> Two notes of caution should however be sounded. First, leave to [seek judicial review] should not be granted unless the applicant advances an apparently plausible complaint which, if made good, might arguably be held to vitiate the proceedings in the magistrates' court. Immaterial and minor deviations from best practice would not have that effect, and the court should be respectful of discretionary decisions of magistrates' courts as of all other courts. This court should be generally slow to intervene, and should do so only where good (or arguably good) grounds for doing so are shown. Secondly, the decision whether or not to grant relief by way of judicial review is always, in the end, a discretionary one. Many factors may properly influence the exercise of discretion, and it would be both foolish and impossible to seek to anticipate them all. The need for an applicant to make full disclosure of all matters relevant to the exercise of discretion should require no emphasis. We do not, however, consider that the existence of a right of appeal to the Crown Court, particularly if unexercised, should ordinarily weigh against the grant of leave to move for judicial review, or the grant of substantive relief, in a proper case.

7.4.2 Procedure

Judicial review is governed by Pt 54 of the Civil Procedure Rules (CPR). There is a strict time limit of three months from the date of the decision complained of (and the applicant must act promptly even within the three months). The first stage is to seek permission to pursue a claim for judicial review (s 31(3) of the Supreme Court Act 1981). The procedure to be followed is this:

a   The first step in a claim for judicial review is to file a claim form. As well as the matters that normally have to appear in a claim form (see CPR 8.2), CPR 54.6 provides that the claimant has to identify interested parties and must state the remedy sought. The claim form has to be accompanied by the documents required by the Practice Direction which supplements CPR Pt 54. Paragraph 5.6 of the Practice Direction says that the claim form must include or be accompanied by a detailed statement of the claimant's grounds for bringing the claim for judicial review and a statement of the facts relied upon. Paragraph 5.7 of the Practice Direction says that the claim form must also be accompanied by any written evidence in support of the claim (or in support of any application to extend time), a copy of any order that the claimant seeks to have quashed, an approved copy of the lower court's reasons for reaching the decision under challenge, copies of any documents on which the claimant proposes to rely, copies of any relevant statutory material, and a list of essential documents for reading in advance by the court (with page references to the passages relied on). Where the claim is for judicial review of a decision of a magistrates' court or the Crown Court, the prosecution must always be named as an interested party (para 5.2 of the Practice Direction).

b   The defendant must file an acknowledgment of service not more than 21 days after the service of the claim form (r 54.8). The acknowledgment of service must be served on the claimant, and on any other person named in the claim form, not later than seven days after it is filed (ibid). The acknowledgment of service must (if the person filing it intends to contest the claim) set out a summary of the grounds for contesting the claim (r 54.8(4)).

c   Paragraph 8.4 of the Practice Direction says that the court will generally consider the question of permission without a hearing. Where there is a hearing, neither the defendant nor any other interested party need attend the hearing unless the court directs otherwise (para 8.5 of the Practice Direction). Where the defendant or any interested party does attend a hearing, the court will not generally make an order for costs against the claimant (para 8.6 of the Practice Direction). If there has not been undue delay, the judge will go on to consider the merits of the application. The test applied by the single judge is whether the claimant's application for judicial review discloses an arguable case. Rule 54.12 provides that if the court, without a hearing, refuses permission to proceed or gives permission that is subject to conditions or on certain grounds only, the court will serve its reasons for making the order along with the order itself. Under r 54.12(3), the claimant may not appeal but may request the decision to be reconsidered at a hearing. Neither the defendant nor anyone else serviced with the claim form may apply to set aside an order giving the claimant permission to proceed (r 54.13).

d   Under r 54.14, once the claimant has been given permission to proceed, the defendant (and anyone else served with the claim form who wishes to contest the claim or support it on additional grounds) must, within 35 days after service of the order giving permission, serve detailed grounds for contesting the claim, and any written evidence.

e   Where all the parties agree, the court may decide the claim for judicial review without a hearing (r 54.18).

f   Otherwise, the claimant must file and serve a skeleton argument not less than 21 working days before the date of the hearing of the judicial review claim (para 15.1 of the Practice Direction). The defendant (and any other party wishing to make representations at the hearing) must file and serve a skeleton argument not less than 14 working days before the date of the hearing (para 15.2 of the Practice Direction). The skeleton arguments must contain a list of issues, a list of the legal points to be taken (together with any relevant authorities), a chronology of events, a list of essential documents for advance reading by the court, and a list of persons referred to (para 15.3).

g   Where the claimant seeks to rely on grounds other than those for which the court gave permission to proceed, he must first obtain the court's permission (r 54.15).

In a criminal case, a judicial review hearing takes place before a Divisional Court (that is, two or more High Court judges sitting in an open court). It usually takes the form of legal argument based on the written evidence, though it is possible for oral evidence to be called if necessary. The court then reaches its decision and, if it decides in favour of the claimant, can make any of the orders set out below.

7.4.3 Bail

Where the defendant was given a custodial sentence by the magistrates and is applying to the Divisional Court to quash the conviction, the magistrates do not have the power to grant bail pending the hearing of the application for judicial review. An application for bail may, however, be made to a single High Court judge in chambers under s 37(1)(d) of the Criminal Justice Act 1948.

7.4.4 Remedies

The main judicial review remedies (listed in s 31(1)(a) of the Supreme Court Act 1981) are:

- quashing order (formerly called 'certiorari'), which has the effect of quashing the original decision (where a conviction is quashed, the defendant stands acquitted of the offence);
- mandatory order (formerly called 'mandamus'), which requires the lower court to do something, for example, to go through the mode of trial procedure again or to rehear an application for public funding of the case;
- prohibiting order (formerly called 'prohibition'), which prevents the lower court from doing something that it should not do, for example, trying the defendant in circumstances that amount to an abuse of process.

Sometimes more than one order is made: for example, there might be a quashing order to quash the decision of the court below, and a mandatory order compelling the lower court to reconsider the matter.

Section 31(5) of the Supreme Court Act 1981 (as amended by s 141 of the Tribunals, Courts and Enforcement Act 2007) provides that if, on an application for judicial review, the High Court quashes the decision to which the application relates, it may also (a) remit the matter to the original decision-maker, with a direction to reconsider the matter and reach a decision in accordance with the findings of the High Court, or (b) substitute its own decision for the decision in question. Under sub-s (5A), it may substitute its own decision only if the decision in question was made by a court or tribunal, the decision is quashed on the ground that there has been an error of law, and without the error, there would have been only one decision which the court or tribunal could have reached.

It must be underlined that the granting of a judicial review remedy is always discretionary. Even if the applicant is able to succeed on the merits, the High Court may decide that it is inappropriate to grant a remedy (see, for example, *R v Oxford City Justices ex p Berry* [1988] QB 507). Delay in making the application for permission to seek judicial review is a fairly common ground for withholding relief. In *R v Neath and Port Talbot Justices ex p DPP* [2000] 1 WLR 1376, Simon Brown LJ (at p 1381) said that the circumstances to be taken into account when the court is exercising its discretion in criminal proceedings whether to grant relief in a judicial review application (or indeed an appeal by way of case stated) where there has been delay include:

(a) the seriousness of the criminal charges,
(b) the nature of the evidence in the case and in particular the extent to which its quality may be affected by the delay,
(c) the extent, if any, to which the defendant has brought about or contributed to the justice's error,

(d) the extent, if any, to which the defendant has brought about or contributed to the delay in the hearing of the challenge, and

(e) how far the complainant would feel justifiably aggrieved by the proceedings being halted and the defendant would feel justifiably aggrieved by their being continued.

7.5 APPEALS AGAINST SENTENCE

Although it would theoretically be possible to appeal by way of case stated (or to seek judicial review) if the magistrates impose a sentence which is beyond their powers, it is quicker and easier simply to appeal to the Crown Court against sentence.

Even where the appeal is on the basis that the sentence is wrong in law (or outside jurisdiction) because it is so severe that no reasonable bench could impose such a sentence, the proper appeal is to the Crown Court rather than to the Divisional Court. In *Tucker v DPP* (1992) 13 Cr App R(S) 495, Woolf LJ said (at p 498):

> If a person who is convicted by the magistrates wishes to challenge the sentence which is imposed, in all but the most exceptional case, the appropriate course for them to adopt is to go before the Crown Court where there will be a rehearing.

In *R v Gloucester Crown Court ex p McGeary* [1999] 2 Cr App R(S) 263, Lord Bingham CJ said (at p 268) that, 'before any challenge can succeed, the departure of the sentencing court from normal standards or levels or practice of sentencing must be so great as to constitute an excess of jurisdiction or an error of law'.

In *Allen v West Yorkshire Probation Service* [2001] EWHC 2 (Admin); (2001) 165 JP 313, the Divisional Court repeated that appeals by way of case stated or applications for judicial review are not usually appropriate procedures for appeals against sentence. If a sentence imposed by magistrates is wrong, the defendant should appeal to the Crown Court unless there are clear and substantial reasons for believing that an appeal by way of case stated or judicial review would be appropriate.

7.6 CASE STATED OR JUDICIAL REVIEW?

The grounds on which judicial review can be sought and an appeal by way of case stated made are virtually the same: an error of law or jurisdiction.

In *R v Oldbury Justices ex p Smith* (1994) 159 JP 316, it was said that where appeal by way of case stated is available, it is preferable to challenge a decision of a magistrates' court by means of appeal by way of case stated rather than judicial review. This is because judicial review is to be regarded as a remedy of last resort and because on an appeal by way of case stated the Divisional Court is presented with all the findings of fact made by the magistrates.

It has to be borne in mind that appeal by way of case stated is available only when there has been a final determination of the proceedings in the lower court (see above). However, where a magistrate is deciding a preliminary issue as to jurisdiction, his ruling upon that is final and so can properly be challenged by way of case stated or judicial review (*R (Donnachie) v Cardiff Magistrates' Court* [2007] EWHC 1846 (Admin); [2007] 1 WLR 3085, per Nelson J at para 6).

It should also be added that judicial review is particularly appropriate where the *procedure* adopted by the lower court is being questioned. In *R v North Essex Justices ex p Lloyd* [2001] 2 Cr App R(S) 15, the Divisional Court said that the most appropriate procedure for challenging a decision of a magistrates' court where the issue is the extent of their jurisdiction, and the procedure which should ordinarily be used, is judicial review. Lord Woolf CJ (at para 11) said:

> A case stated for appeal is very useful and valuable when the magistrates have determined facts. It is a useful vehicle for them to record their findings of fact. But in a case where the issue is of the sort that exists here as to the extent of their jurisdiction to commit for sentence, an application for judicial review is the most convenient procedure and it is the procedure which should ordinarily be used. It has the advantage, first of all, that it saves the cumbersome procedure of appealing by way of case stated; and secondly, it has the advantage that the matter comes before a judge of the High Court who decides whether or not to give permission to apply for judicial review. That avoids this Court being troubled with cases which lack merit. It also provides assistance to the applicant because at relatively modest cost he knows whether or not he has an arguable case.

In *R (P) v Liverpool City Magistrates* [2006] EWHC 887 (Admin), Collins J (at paras 6–8) said:

> . . . I recognise that there are some conflicting authorities, which do not make it necessarily easy to decide whether judicial review or case stated is appropriate in the circumstances of a given case. Judicial review is obviously more appropriate where, for example, there is an issue of fact which may have to be raised and decided and which the Justices cannot have decided for themselves.
>
> Those rather cryptic observations are intended to relate to a situation where it is alleged that there has been unfairness in the way that the Justices conducted the case, obviously where for example it is suggested that there was bias in the manner in which they conducted themselves, or the defendant in question was prevented from properly putting his or her case, or the Clerk to the Justices interfered in a way in which he should not have interfered.
>
> . . . Generally speaking, where it is alleged that Justices have misdirected themselves or got the law wrong in their approach to a decision, case stated is the appropriate way of dealing with it. Generally speaking a failure to go by way of case stated in such a situation is likely to result in a refusal of permission for judicial review on the basis that it is the wrong way of dealing with it . . .

It follows that, provided there has been a final determination, if it is alleged that the magistrates have (for example) misconstrued a statutory provision, appeal by way of case stated is preferable as it enables the question(s) at issue to be set out more clearly.

In *R (White) v Crown Court at Blackfriars* [2008] EWHC 510 (Admin), a claim for judicial review was made because an appeal by way of case stated would have been out of time. Richards LJ said (at para 25) that the court should 'be slow to entertain an application for judicial review as an alternative to an appeal by way of case stated just because the time limit for an appeal has been missed, even if the fault lies with the claimant's solicitors rather than with the claimant personally' However, His Lordship added that there 'may be cases where judicial review is nonetheless appropriate, in particular to avoid a serious injustice'.

7.7 FURTHER APPEALS

If the initial appeal is unsuccessful, a further appeal may be possible.

7.7.1 From the Crown Court

Where the Crown Court is sitting in an appellate capacity from the magistrates' court, the appellant may appeal against the decision of the Crown Court to the Divisional Court by way of case stated, or seek judicial review, but only where the Crown Court has made an error of law or jurisdiction (ss 28(1) and 29(3) of the Supreme Court Act 1981).

In *R v Gloucester Crown Court ex p Chester* [1998] COD 365, it was held by the Divisional Court that, where a person is convicted by a magistrates' court and appeals to the Crown Court, further appeal against conviction to the High Court on a point of law should be by way of case stated, not judicial review.

An application to the Crown Court to state a case for the opinion of the Divisional Court (following the Crown Court's determination of an appeal from a magistrates' court) must be made within 21 days of the decision complained of (r 64.7(1) of the CPR). Unlike the time limit applicable to challenging the decision of a magistrates' court, r 64.7(14) allows any time limit (including the initial 21-day period) under r 64.7 to be extended by the Crown Court. In *DPP v Coleman* [1998] 1 WLR 1708 (a case where the prosecution sought the quashing of an acquittal), it was held that the decision to extend time can be taken by a judge alone (that is, without lay justices), that the respondent (at least where he is an acquitted defendant) must be given the chance to make representations, and that extensions of time should only be granted for cogent reasons. The court added that the application for an extension of time can normally be considered on the basis of written representations and the need for an oral hearing will rarely arise.

In *R (Gillan) v DPP* [2007] EWHC 380; [2007] 1 WLR 2214, the court confirmed that appeal from the Crown Court by way of case stated under s 28(1) of the Supreme Court Act 1981 is not available in respect of interlocutory decisions (as there has to have been a final determination of the case) and that judicial review should only be granted in exceptional cases where there has not been a final decision in the case. Forbes J, giving the judgment of the court, said at (para 13):

> . . . the word 'decision' in s 28(1) of the 1981 Act means 'final decision'. It therefore does not include an interlocutory decision in criminal proceedings, such as the one under challenge in this case. However, the Crown Court is amenable to judicial review except in matters relating to trial on indictment (see s 29(3) of the 1981 Act) which this is not. Accordingly, in my view, the correct procedure for challenging the lawfulness of an interlocutory decision in criminal proceedings such as the present one is by way of an appropriate claim for judicial review, although the circumstances in which that is likely to be necessary will, as it seems to me, be relatively rare and exceptional.

7.7.2 Appeal from the Divisional Court

Appeal from the Divisional Court lies direct to the House of Lords (to be replaced by the Supreme Court in due course), bypassing the Court of Appeal (s 1(1)(a) of the Administration of Justice Act 1960). The Divisional Court must certify that there is a point of law of general public importance involved and either the Divisional Court or the House of Lords must give leave to appeal (s 1(2)).

7.8 REFLECTING ON THE SYSTEM OF APPEALS FROM MAGISTRATES' COURTS

Lord Justice Auld, in Chapter 12 of his *Review of the Criminal Courts in England and Wales*, noted (in para 16) that the incidence of appeals from decisions of magistrates is comparatively low. He noted that in 2000, there were nearly 14,000 appeals against conviction and/or sentence to the Crown Court, 125 appeals by way of case stated to the Divisional Court and 336 claims of judicial review in criminal cases to the Divisional Court. This meant that less than one per cent of magistrates' courts' decisions are appealed.

Kate Malleson in 'Streamlining and clarifying the appellate process' [2002] Crim LR 272, points out that this figure of one per cent includes both conviction and sentence appeals; for conviction appeals alone, the rate was a mere 0.4 per cent in 2000 (compared with four per cent of defendants convicted in the Crown Court appealing against conviction during the same period). The fact that so few defendants appeal against the decisions of magistrates (even though there is no requirement to obtain leave to appeal) might appear to suggest an extremely high satisfaction rating for summary trial. However, it should be borne in mind that the power of the Crown Court to review sentence (with the risk that the sentence might be increased) may be a significant deterrent to would-be appellants. As we have seen, the Crown Court has the power to increase the sentence to the maximum the magistrates could have imposed (and it has this power whether the appeal is against conviction, or sentence, or both); given that very few defendants in the magistrates' court receive the maximum sentence the magistrates could impose, most would-be appellants are at risk of an increase in sentence if the Crown Court takes the view that the original sentence was overly lenient. Another reason for the low rate of appeals might be that, because the sentences imposed by magistrates are generally lenient compared to the Crown Court, dissatisfied defendants simply do not bother to appeal.

According to the official Judicial Statistics for 2006, of defendants appealing to the Crown Court in 2006, 42 per cent had their appeals allowed or their sentence varied. Of the remainder, 30 per cent were dismissed and 28 per cent were abandoned or otherwise disposed.

Chapter 12 of the *Auld Review* identifies a number of unsatisfactory features in the system of appeals from magistrates' courts:

> 24 . . . First, there are the three partially overlapping routes of appeal. Depending on the matter challenged, a defendant can take his point of law to the Crown Court by way of rehearing or by one of two different procedures to the same tribunal in the High Court.

Depending on the selection made, a convicted defendant may make his way on a point of law to the High Court via a rehearing in the Crown Court or lose his right to such a rehearing if he proceeds straight to the High Court. Choosing the most appropriate route and form of relief in the High Court is not always straightforward.

25   Second, it is anomalous that there should be an appeal as of right capable of turning on points of law from a magistrates' court to the Crown Court when the two other forms of challenges on points of law going to the High Court require some form of judicial filter.

26   Third, it is equally anomalous that there should be a right of appeal on issues of fact, by way of rehearing from a magistrates' court to the Crown Court . . . District Judges and increasingly well trained magistrates now give reasons for their decision which require them to justify why and on what evidence they decided the matter and, where there was a conflict of evidence, why they preferred one version to the other. Where magistrates have taken the decision, the appeal is heard by a similarly constituted tribunal, save only that one of its fact finders is a judge. Where the appeal is from a District Judge, it is equally anomalous that a defendant should then be able to repeat the process before a mixed tribunal of professional and lay judges. It is also an unsatisfactory feature of a normal appeal process, particularly one exercisable by a defendant as of right, that witnesses should have to attend court twice to give evidence.

27   Fourth, there seems little point in retaining two distinct and partially overlapping procedures for challenging magistrates' courts' jurisdictional and other legal errors in the same tribunal in the High Court.

28   Fifth, depending on the form of challenge chosen, different time limits apply either to the start of the process or the stages by which it reaches hearing.

One particular feature of the system of appeals from magistrates' courts that has attracted criticism is the fact that appeals to the Crown Court (a) do not require leave (unlike appeal to the Court of Appeal following conviction following trial on indictment), and (b) take the form of a rehearing (again, unlike appeals to the Court of Appeal following conviction on indictment, where the appeal takes the form of legal argument based on specific grounds of appeal). A complete rehearing of the case is a much lengthier process than a review of the decision of the lower court. It is perhaps strange that this 'resource-hungry' method of hearing appeals applies to appeals from magistrates' court (dealing with generally less serious offences) but not to appeals from Crown Court trial (where the offences are generally more serious). The *Auld Review* (para 17) suggests that the right of appeal from magistrates' courts by way of rehearing has its origins in a general and historical lack of confidence in the impartiality and competence of magistrates' courts, a fact perhaps connected with the fact that they used to be known as 'police courts' and so were perceived as working hand-in-hand with the police, together with a perception that magistrates are drawn from a narrow social spectrum and receive little training. The Review notes that this perception, to the extent it still exists today, bears very little relation to reality: magistrates now receive much more training (under the auspices of the Judicial Studies Board); they have the benefit of advice and support from the court legal adviser; and significant effort is being made to recruit magistrates from a much wider social and ethnic background. Moreover, confidence in the fairness of the decisions of magistrates is boosted by the fact that they now give reasons for their decisions.

The *Auld Review* goes on to make a number of recommendations. Recommendation 300 is that there should be the same tests for appeal against conviction and sentence for appeals from both magistrates' courts and the Crown Court, and that those tests should be the ones currently used by the Court of Appeal (see Chapter 13). This would involve the abolition of the defendant's right of appeal against conviction and/or sentence in the magistrates' court to the Crown Court by way of rehearing (Recommendation 302). The current entitlement to appeal without leave and to have the case reheard would be replaced by a requirement for leave to appeal to the Crown Court, on the same grounds as are applicable in the Court of Appeal (Recommendation 303), with the appeal being heard in the Crown Court by a judge sitting alone, not sitting with justices (Recommendation 304), and hearing submissions about the safety of the conviction or the severity of the sentence in the same way that the Court of Appeal hears appeals.

The *Auld Review* was also critical of the fact that there are currently three separate forms of appeal from the magistrates' court. Lord Justice Auld took the view that it was unnecessary to have three different avenues of appeal, and accordingly recommended that there should be no right of appeal from the magistrates' courts to the High Court through appeal by way of case stated or by a claim for judicial review (Recommendation 305). There are comparatively few appeals to the High Court; this may well be due to the fact that such appeals can only be on points of law or jurisdiction. The small number of appeals to the High Court suggests that the existence of the two routes of appeal to that court (in addition to appeal to the Crown Court) does not have significant resource implications. Moreover, decisions of the High Court on significant points of law are reported in Law Reports in a way that decisions of the Crown Court are not. This means that the appeals to the High Court enable a body of case law to be developed and reported in a way that is accessible to courts throughout the country. Appeals to the High Court thus have a valuable role to play in providing guidance on such matters as the interpretation of statutory provisions and on the way in which magistrates' court procedures should operate.

For a wide-ranging critique of the present system of appeals, see JR Spencer, 'Does our present criminal appeal system make sense?' [2006] Crim LR 677.

Chapter 8

Disclosure under the Criminal Procedure and Investigations Act 1996

8.1 DISCLOSURE OF UNUSED MATERIAL UNDER THE CRIMINAL PROCEDURE AND INVESTIGATIONS ACT 1996

We have already seen that the prosecution have to disclose the evidence that they will be adducing against the defendant, under the 'advance information' rules contained in Pt 21 of the Criminal Procedure Rules in cases tried in the magistrates' court or through the process by which cases are sent to Crown Court for trial. It is noteworthy that, in his *Review of the Criminal Courts of England and Wales*, Lord Justice Auld notes (paras 117–20 of Chapter 10) that the rules on disclosure of evidence that the prosecution intend to adduce are rather piecemeal. He recommends that there should be a single set of statutory rules imposing on the prosecution in all cases a duty to provide its proposed evidence in sufficient time to enable the defence adequately to prepare for trial, the precise timescale to be prescribed by rules (Recommendation 194). The Government chose not to take up this recommendation.

In this chapter we focus on the disclosure by the prosecution of 'unused material' (that is, material that has been gathered during the investigation of the offence but which the prosecution do not propose to put forward at the trial), together with the obligation on the defence to provide a 'defence statement' setting out the basis of the defence case.

The rules relating to the disclosure of 'unused material' are contained principally in the Criminal Procedure and Investigations Act (CPIA) 1996 (as amended by the Criminal Justice Act 2003). However, reference also has to be made to a number of other sources, including:

- the Code of Practice issued under s 23 of the CPIA 1996: <http://police.home-office.gov.uk/news-and-publications/publication/operational-policing/Disclosure_code_of_practice.pdf?view=Binary>;
- the Attorney General's Guidelines on Disclosure of Information in Criminal Proceedings: <http://www.cps.gov.uk/legal/section20/chapter_c.html>;
- guidance to the police and to the Crown Prosecution Service (CPS) on the operation of the CPIA 1996 can be found in the Joint Operational Instructions (JOPI): <http://www.cps.gov.uk/publications/docs/jopimay2004.pdf>;
- the Protocol of Disclosure (Disclosure: A Protocol for the Control and Management of Unused Material in The Crown Court), dated 20 February 2006 and

available in the website of HM Courts Service: <http://www.hmcourts-service. gov.uk/cms/files/disclosure_protocol.pdf>. (In *R v K* [2006] EWCA Crim 724; [2006] 2 All ER 552 (Note), the Court of Appeal said that this protocol should be applied by trial judges and those who act for the prosecution, and that the defence should ensure that they familiarise themselves with it).

Under s 1 of the CPIA 1996, the statutory disclosure provisions apply to all trials in the magistrates' court or youth court where the defendant pleads not guilty and to all cases being tried in the Crown Court.

8.1.1 The duty of the investigator

A system of disclosure of unused material held by the prosecution will only be as good as the investigation which was conducted by the police, since the prosecution cannot disclose material that has not been found during the investigation. Furthermore, the system depends on relevant information that is discovered during the investigation being retained and its existence accurately recorded. It is essential that the police draw up accurate schedules of the material in their possession, and that those schedules contain sufficient detail when describing that material to enable the prosecutor to make an informed judgment as to whether the material should be disclosed (and for the defence to challenge non-disclosure). The investigating officer is therefore under a duty to retain material obtained in a criminal investigation which may be relevant to that investigation. Paragraph 5.4 of the Code of Practice issued under s 23 of the CPIA 1996 provides a non-exhaustive list of the material that should be retained, which includes:

- crime reports (including crime report forms, relevant parts of incident report books or police officers' notebooks);
- custody records;
- records derived from tapes of telephone messages (for example, 999 calls) containing descriptions of the alleged offence or offender;
- final versions of witness statements (and draft versions where their content differs from the final version), including any exhibits mentioned (unless these have been returned to their owner on the understanding that they will be produced in court if required);
- interview records (written records, or audio or video tapes, of interviews with actual or potential witnesses or suspects);
- communications between police and experts such as forensic scientists, reports of work carried out by experts, and schedules of scientific material prepared by the expert for the investigator, for the purposes of criminal proceedings;
- records of the first description of a suspect by each potential witness who purports to identify or describe the suspect, whether or not the description differs from that of subsequent descriptions by that or other witnesses;
- any material casting doubt on the reliability of a witness.

Paragraph 5.5 says that there is also a duty to retain material which may satisfy the test for prosecution disclosure in the Act, such as:

- information provided by an accused person which indicates an explanation for the offence with which he has been charged;
- any material casting doubt on the reliability of a confession;
- any material casting doubt on the reliability of a prosecution witness.

Because of concerns about this important stage of the process, the *Auld Review* recommended that:

199 The police should retain responsibility for retaining, collating and recording any material gathered or inspected in the course of the investigation; police officers should be better trained for what, in many cases, may be an extensive and difficult exercise regardless of issues of disclosability, and subject, in their exercise of it to statutory guidelines and a rigorous system of 'spot' audits by HM Inspectorates of Constabulary and/or of the Crown Prosecution Service.

200 Such responsibility as the police have for identifying and considering all potentially disclosable material should be removed to the prosecutor.

201 The prosecutor should retain ultimate responsibility for the completeness of the material recorded by the police and assume sole responsibility for primary and all subsequent disclosure.

The suggestion that the responsibility that the police currently have for identifying all potentially disclosable material should be transferred to the prosecutor might raise some practical difficulties, not least because of the massive increase in workload for prosecutors that this would entail. The Criminal Justice Act 2003 did not enact this suggestion.

8.1.2 Disclosure of unused material by the prosecution

Section 3(1) of the CPIA 1996 requires the prosecutor to:

(a) disclose to the accused any prosecution material which has not previously been disclosed to the accused and which might reasonably be considered capable of undermining the case for the prosecution against the accused or of assisting the case for the accused, or

(b) give to the accused a written statement that there is no material of a description mentioned in paragraph (a).

'Prosecution material' is defined by s 3(2) as material which 'is in the prosecutor's possession, and came into his possession in connection with the case for the prosecution against the accused' or which 'he has inspected in connection with the case for the prosecution against the accused'. This would seem to represent a narrowing of the common law duty of disclosure, which extended to material of which the prosecuting lawyers were unaware (for example, forensic evidence which had not been passed on to the lawyers).

Before this version of s 3 was enacted, there were two stages for prosecution disclosure:

1   primary disclosure, when the prosecution had to disclose material which might, in the opinion of the prosecutor (that is, a subjective test) undermine the prosecution case against the accused;

2   after the defence had provided a defence statement (see below), the prosecution had to disclose material which might reasonably be expected (an objective test) to assist the accused's defence as disclosed in the defence statement.

There had been some criticism of the subjective nature of the original version of the test contained in s 3, and of the potential difficulty of deciding whether a particular item of unused material undermines the prosecution case or supports the defence case. The *Auld Review* concluded that:

195 The Criminal Procedure and Investigations Act 1996 scheme of material disclosure should be retained, in particular, two stages of prosecution disclosure under which the second stage is informed by and conditional on a defence statement indicating the issues that the defendant proposes to take at trial.

196 The present mix of primary and subsidiary legislation, Code, Guidelines and Instructions should be replaced by a single and simply expressed instrument setting out clearly the duties and rights of all parties involved.

197 There should be the same test of disclosability for both stages of prosecution disclosure providing in substance and, for example, for the disclosure of 'material which, in the prosecutor's opinion, might reasonably affect the determination of any issue in the case of which he knows or should reasonably expect' or, more simply but tautologically, 'material which in the prosecutor's opinion might weaken the prosecution case or assist that of the defence'.

The current version of s 3 brings these two stages into a single test, makes the test an objective one throughout, and does not confine the requirement to disclose material which might assist the defence to material disclosed in the defence statement. However, the reforms brought about by the Criminal Justice Act 2003 do not address the need to ensure that the police pass on all the necessary information to the prosecution. In 'Criminal Justice Act 2003: disclosure and its discontents' [2004] Crim LR 441, Mike Redmayne comments that:

These changes . . . make the prosecution's obligations clearer and simpler. But their significance should not be overstated. The problems that afflict prosecution disclosure are too deep-rooted to be cured by legislative tweaking. They stem from the fact that the police are naturally reluctant to reveal information which may damage the prosecution case, and that they know that undisclosed material will often not be discovered. Because the police are the ones with the key obligations here – to draw up accurate schedules which contain sufficient detail for judgments to be made by prosecutors, and for challenges to be made by the defence – failings on their part are difficult to remedy later in the process. The Criminal Justice Act does nothing to address these problems.

The CPIA 1996 came into being largely because of concerns that under the pre-existing common law rules, the defence were able to go on fishing expeditions, trawling through everything the prosecution had in their possession. The Government wanted to place a limit on the material that the defence could demand to see by defining what the prosecution were under a duty to disclose (as well as ensuring that if material fell within that definition, it could only be withheld from the defence on the authority of a judge). It seems inevitable that there should be some limit on what the defence should be allowed to see. As Redmayne (ibid) puts it:

> Even giving the defence access to all unused material will not ensure that it gets to see everything that is important: if the police really want to hide information, it is not too difficult for them to do so. And in terms of resources, open access for the defence is no magic solution . . . [S]o long as someone has to comb though the material deciding what is relevant and what is not, there will be a large bill to pay.

8.1.3 The scope of the prosecution disclosure obligations under s 3

The disclosure requirements enacted in s 3 cover a wide range of material. Paragraph 10 of the *Attorney General's Guidelines: Disclosure of Information in Criminal Proceedings* says that:

> Generally, material which can reasonably be considered capable of undermining the prosecution case against the accused or assisting the defence case will include anything that tends to show a fact inconsistent with the elements of the case that must be proved by the prosecution. Material can fulfil the disclosure test:
>
> (a) by the use to be made of it in cross-examination; or
> (b) by its capacity to support submissions that could lead to:
>
> > (i)   the exclusion of evidence; or
> > (ii) a stay of proceedings; or
> > (iii) a court or tribunal finding that any public authority had acted incompatibly with the accused's rights under the ECHR, or
>
> (c) by its capacity to suggest an explanation or partial explanation of the accused's actions.

Paragraph 12 goes on to say that:

> Examples of material that might reasonably be considered capable of undermining the prosecution case or of assisting the case for the accused are:
>
> (i)   Any material casting doubt upon the accuracy of any prosecution evidence.
> (ii)   Any material which may point to another person, whether charged or not (including a co-accused) having involvement in the commission of the offence.
> (iii) Any material which may cast doubt upon the reliability of a confession.
> (iv)   Any material that might go to the credibility of a prosecution witness.
> (v)   Any material that might support a defence that is either raised by the defence or apparent from the prosecution papers.
> (vi)   Any material which may have a bearing on the admissibility of any prosecution evidence.

On the basis of this guidance, a useful rule-of-thumb test is that material ought to be disclosed if it would give the defence a useful basis for cross-examination or if it would support defence arguments that prosecution evidence is inadmissible or that the proceedings should be stayed.

In *R v Makin* [2004] EWCA Crim 1607, Hooper LJ (construing the original version of s 3) summarised (at para 30) the prosecution disclosure obligations as including:

> ... an obligation to disclose material if it assists the defence by allowing the defendant to put forward a tenable case in the best possible light or if the material could assist the defence to make further inquiries and those inquiries might assist in showing the defendant's innocence or avoid a miscarriage of justice.

Plainly, information which must be disclosed under s 3 includes anything that casts doubt on the reliability of a prosecution witness by undermining their credibility. So, for example, the prosecution should disclose any previous convictions of their witnesses (see *R v Vasiliou* [2000] Crim LR 845), or the fact that a prosecution witness has sought a reward payable on the defendant's conviction (as in *R v Rasheed* (1994) 158 JP 914). Likewise, in *R v Guney* [1998] 2 Cr App R 242, the Court of Appeal held that the defence are entitled to be informed of any convictions or disciplinary findings recorded against a police officer involved in the present case, and of any decisions by trial judges where a trial was stopped, or Court of Appeal judgments where a conviction was quashed, because of misconduct or lack of veracity of identified police officers who are also involved in the present case.

Section 3(6) enables the prosecutor to withhold material if 'the court, on an application by the prosecutor, concludes it is not in the public interest to disclose it and orders accordingly'. The question of 'public interest immunity' is considered in detail later in this chapter. However, the key point to emphasise at this stage is that if material should be disclosed under s 3, the prosecution may withhold that material from the defence only if permitted to do so by the court.

8.1.3.1 Common law rules on disclosure

Although s 21(1) of the CPIA 1996 dis-applies the common law rules on disclosure, some case law pre-dating the CPIA is likely to remain valid, in that the outcome would be the same under the CPIA.

In *R v Brown* [1998] AC 367, the prosecution had failed to disclose to the defence information which reflected on the credibility of two defence witnesses. It was held by the House of Lords that the Crown is not under a duty to disclose to the defence material which is relevant only to the credibility of defence witnesses. Although this case was not one to which the CPIA 1996 applied (since the relevant provisions of the Act were not in force at the relevant time), the House of Lords held that such material is not material which might assist the defence case; it follows that it would not be disclosable under the CPIA 1996.

In *R v Mills* [1998] AC 382, the House of Lords held that the prosecution should provide the defence with a copy of the statement containing relevant material made by a witness whom the prosecution does not propose to call at the trial (not just supply the defence with the name and address of that witness) even if the prosecution take the view that the witness is not a credible witness. Failure to do so may render a conviction unsafe. Such statements would now have to be disclosed under the CPIA 1996 if they might assist the defence case.

In *R v DPP ex p Lee* [1999] 1 WLR 1950, the Divisional Court noted that the CPIA 1996 does not specifically address disclosure during the period between arrest and the case being sent to the Crown Court. The court said that, in most cases, prosecution disclosure can wait until after the case has been sent to the Crown Court without jeopardising the defendant's right to a fair trial. However, the court said that the prosecutor must always be alive to the need to make advance disclosure of material that should be disclosed at an earlier stage. Examples given by Kennedy LJ at p 1962 include:

a previous convictions of a complainant or deceased if that information could reasonably be expected to assist the defence when applying for bail;

b material which might enable a defendant to make an early application to stay the proceedings as an abuse of process;

c material which might enable a defendant to submit that he should only be sent for trial on a lesser charge, or perhaps that he should not be sent for trial at all;

d material which will enable the defendant and his legal advisers to make preparations for trial which may be significantly less effective if disclosure is delayed (e.g. names of eye-witnesses who the prosecution do not intend to use).

Similarly, in *DPP v Ara* [2002] 1 WLR 815, it was held that, where the police are willing to caution a suspect in relation to an offence, rather than prosecute him, the suspect is entitled to disclosure of such material as is necessary to enable his legal adviser to assess the prosecution case and to give informed advice as to whether or not the suspect should consent to the caution. The court added that this does not mean that there is a general obligation on the police to disclose material prior to charge.

8.1.4 Disclosure by the defence

Where the case is to be tried in the Crown Court, the defence are required, by s 5 of the CPIA 1996, to serve a 'defence statement'. Where the case is to be tried in a magistrates' court or youth court, service of a defence statement is voluntary (see s 6 of the Act).

The requirement in s 5 of the CPIA 1996 for compulsory disclosure by the defendant where the case is to be tried in the Crown Court applies once the prosecution have made disclosure of their material under s 3. The defence statement must be served within 14 days of the date on which the prosecution comply (or purport to comply) with the duty of primary disclosure under s 3 of the CPIA 1996 (see para 2 of the Criminal Procedure and Investigations Act 1996 (Defence Disclosure Time Limits) Regulations 1997 (SI 1997/684)).

Section 5(5) requires the defendant to give a defence statement to both the court and the prosecution. This 'defence statement' is defined by s 6A(1) as 'a written statement':

(a) setting out the nature of the accused's defence, including any particular defences on which he intends to rely,

(b) indicating the matters of fact on which he takes issue with the prosecution,

(c)   setting out, in the case of each such matter, why he takes issue with the prosecution, and

(d)   indicating any point of law (including any point as to the admissibility of evidence or an abuse of process) which he wishes to take, and any authority on which he intends to rely for that purpose.

Section 60(1) of the Criminal Justice and Immigration Act 2008 adds a new subsection, (ca), to s 6A(1) of the 1996 Act, requiring the defence statement to '[set] out particulars of the matters of fact on which he intends to rely for the purposes of his defence'.

Section 6A(2) makes specific provision for cases where the defendant relies on an alibi (see below).

Prior to the amendment of the CPIA 1996 by the Criminal Justice Act 2003, defence statements tended to be fairly brief, somewhat anodyne, documents. Lord Justice Auld, in his *Review of the Criminal Courts of England and Wales*, had said:

202   The requirements of a defence statement should remain as at present, as should the requirements for particulars where the defence is alibi and/or the defence propose to adduce expert evidence.

203   More effective use of defence statements should be facilitated by the general improvements to the system for preparation for trial that I have recommended, and encouraged through professional conduct rules, training and, in the rare cases where it might be appropriate, discipline, to inculcate in criminal defence practitioners the propriety of and need for compliance with the requirements.

Thus, the Review recommends no more than greater encouragement, through professional conduct rules and otherwise, for the provision of adequate defence statements. The Criminal Justice Act 2003 went further by making the statutory duty of the defence more onerous than it had been.

Defence statements are normally drafted by the accused's solicitor, since counsel may not be involved during the early stages of the life of the case. However, counsel will sometimes be instructed to draft a defence statement. The Bar Standards Board has approved guidance on the involvement of counsel in the drafting of defence statements (see Guidance on Preparation of Defence Case Statements: <http://www.barstandardsboard.org.uk/standardsandguidance/codeguidance/thepreparationofdefencecasestatements/>). In particular, counsel must ensure that the defendant:

a   understands the importance of the accuracy and adequacy of the defence statement; and

b   has had the opportunity of carefully considering the statement drafted by counsel and has approved it.

What can go wrong is illustrated by *R v Wheeler* (2000) 164 JP 565. The defendant was convicted of importing controlled drugs following his arrest at Gatwick airport, when he was found to be concealing drugs internally. At trial, an inconsistency had become apparent between the defence statement which had been served by his solicitors (in which he said that he knew he was carrying the drugs when he arrived in the UK) and his evidence during cross-examination (in which he maintained that he believed he had vomited up all of the packets before travelling to the UK). The defence statement had not been signed by the defendant, who alleged that his solicitor had made a mistake in serving an incorrect statement of his case. Whilst referring to the alleged mistake in his summing up, the trial judge had provided the jury with no specific guidance. The Court of Appeal held that the judge had erred in failing to give specific directions as to the inconsistency, given that the jury would be affected by it. The court added that it is advisable that defence statements be signed by a defendant in preference to them being permitted to be served by solicitors on a defendant's behalf without procedures being followed to verify accuracy.

Even though it is desirable that the defendant should sign the defence statement, it should be noted that the court has no power to impose a requirement that a defence statement be signed personally by the defendant (*R (Sullivan) v Maidstone Crown Court* [2002] EWHC 967; [2002] 1 WLR 2747).

In some cases, the issue arose as to whether a defence statement drafted by a solicitor could be regarded as putting forward assertions made by the accused himself. To remove doubt as to whether a defence statement served by the defendant's solicitor is to be regarded as being given on behalf of the defendant, s 6E(1) of the 1996 Act (inserted by the Criminal Justice Act 2003) provides that:

> Where an accused's solicitor purports to give on behalf of the accused—
>
> (a) a defence statement under section 5, 6 or 6B, or
> (b) a statement of the kind mentioned in section 6B(4),
>
> the statement shall, unless the contrary is proved, be deemed to be given with the authority of the accused.

Section 6E(4) of the CPIA increases the importance of the defence statement by empowering the judge to direct that a copy of the defence statement (edited, if necessary, to remove any inadmissible evidence) be shown to the jury. Under sub-s (5), such a direction may be given of the judge's own motion or on the application of any party; however, the direction may be made only if the judge is of the opinion that seeing a copy of the defence statement would help the jury to understand the case or to resolve any issue in the case.

In *Murphy v DPP* [2006] EWHC 1753 (Admin), however, the court said that a defendant does not lose his entitlement to disclosure under the CPIA 1996 merely because he serves his defence case statement out of time.

Redmayne (ibid) considers in detail the philosophical arguments for and against any disclosure being required of the defence. One key argument in favour of requiring at least some disclosure is that it tends to make it more likely that the final verdict will be factually correct, since the issues will have been defined before the start of the trial. On the other hand, requiring the defence to reveal information to the prosecution seems to go against the privilege against self-incrimination and the widely held view that an accused should not be required to assist the prosecution to build up their case against him.

8.1.4.1 Disclosure of expert evidence

The defence also have a duty to disclose expert evidence to the prosecution (see Pt 24 of the Criminal Procedure Rules). In *R v Davies* [2002] EWCA Crim 85; (2002) 166 JP 243, the defendant was charged with murder. The main defence to the murder charge was diminished responsibility. Prior to the trial, a consultant psychiatrist had been instructed by the defendant's solicitors to examine him and to write a report on him. After she had provided her report, the defence decided that she would not be called to give evidence and that the report would not be disclosed. The prosecution applied for an order that the report be disclosed. The judge ordered disclosure. It was held by the Court of Appeal (applying the case of *R v R (Blood Sample: Privilege)* [1994] 1 WLR 758) that the judge had erred in ordering disclosure of the report. Where, in criminal proceedings, the opinion of an expert has been obtained at the request of the solicitors to a party to the proceedings, and that opinion is derived from privileged information from which it cannot be separated, it is itself privileged.

8.1.4.2 Alibi evidence

Special provisions apply where the defendant relies on an alibi. Evidence in support of an alibi is defined in the following terms by s 6A(3):

> . . . evidence in support of an alibi is evidence tending to show that by reason of the presence of the accused at a particular place or in a particular area at a particular time he was not, or was unlikely to have been, at the place where the offence is alleged to have been committed at the time of its alleged commission.

The defence of alibi applies only to offences which are linked to a particular time and place. In *R v Hassan* [1970] 1 QB 423, for example, the defendant was charged with living off immoral earnings and claimed in his defence that he was out of the country at the time he was alleged to have been so doing. This defence was held not to amount to an alibi because the allegation was not specific to a particular place. The court said that the statutory definition of an alibi contemplated the commission of an offence at a particular place; the present offence was anchored to no particular location.

An alibi is concerned with the defendant's whereabouts at the time when the offence is alleged to have been committed. Evidence as to his whereabouts on another occasion does not amount to alibi evidence, however significant that circumstantial evidence might be. In *R v Lewis* [1969] 2 QB 1, the defendant was charged with dishonestly receiving two stolen postal orders on 14 February. The prosecution adduced evidence that he cashed the two postal orders on 16 February, as part of the evidence showing that he had dishonestly received them on 14 February. It was held that his whereabouts on 16 February were so removed from the offence itself as not to amount to an alibi. This case should be contrasted with *R v Fields and Adams* [1991] Crim LR 38, where the defendant was allegedly seen twice by a prosecution witness, once during the robbery with which he was charged and once three hours before the robbery. The defendant had no alibi for the time of the robbery itself but said that three hours before the robbery he was 25 miles away and so could not have been the person seen by the witness. This was held to amount to an alibi even though it did not relate to the time of the offence itself.

This decision of the Court of Appeal is a rather surprising one; however, it may be justified on the basis that the two sightings were very close together in time and that they were inextricably linked given the evidence of the witness; also, that the person seen three hours before the robbery was at the scene in order to prepare for the robbery and so his presence there could (loosely) be said to be part of the robbery itself. Nonetheless, this decision should probably be confined to its facts.

In *R v Johnson* [1995] 2 Cr App R 1, it was held that evidence only amounts to alibi evidence if it is evidence that the defendant was somewhere other than the place where the offence was allegedly committed at the relevant time; evidence which simply shows that the defendant was not present at the commission of the offence is not alibi evidence.

Where the defence statement discloses an alibi, s 6A(2) requires the defence statement to give particulars of the alibi. Those particulars must include:

(a) the name, address and date of birth of any witness the accused believes is able to give evidence in support of the alibi, or as many of those details as are known to the accused when the statement is given;

(b) any information in the accused's possession which might be of material assistance in identifying or finding any such witness in whose case any of the details mentioned in paragraph (a) are not known to the accused when the statement is given.

Presumably the particulars of an alibi should set out where the defendant claims to have been at the relevant time even if the only evidence in support of that alibi is to come from the defendant himself (cf *R v Jackson* [1973] Crim LR 356, a case decided under the legislation which dealt with alibi evidence prior to the enactment of the CPIA 1996, which prevented alibi evidence being adduced without leave of the court if the prosecution had not been supplied with details of the alibi prior to the trial).

8.1.4.3 *Updating the defence statement*

Section 5 as originally enacted had envisaged a single defence statement. However, s 6B requires defence statements to be updated. It provides that where the accused has already served a defence statement under ss 5 or 6, he must (before the trial) serve an updated defence statement or else give a written statement stating that he has no changes to make to the defence statement that was served under ss 5 or 6, as the case may be.

8.1.4.4 *Notification of intention to call defence witnesses*

Section 6C of the CPIA 1996 (another section added by the Criminal Justice Act 2003) provides as follows:

(1) The accused must give to the court and the prosecutor a notice indicating whether he intends to call any persons (other than himself) as witnesses at his trial and, if so—

(a) giving the name, address and date of birth of each such proposed witness, or as many of those details as are known to the accused when the notice is given;

(b) providing any information in the accused's possession which might be of material assistance in identifying or finding any such proposed witness in whose case any of the details mentioned in paragraph (a) are not known to the accused when the notice is given.

. . .

(4) If, following the giving of a notice under this section, the accused—

(a) decides to call a person (other than himself) who is not included in the notice as a proposed witness, or decides not to call a person who is so included, or

(b) discovers any information which, under sub-section (1), he would have had to include in the notice if he had been aware of it when giving the notice,

he must give an appropriately amended notice to the court and the prosecutor.

The proposal that the defence should have to reveal details of their witnesses to the prosecution was a cause of some concern. It is highly likely that the police will want to interview some or all of the witnesses who are named, and there is a risk that the witnesses may be put off from testifying. In an attempt to allay these fears, s 21A(1) of the 1996 Act requires the Secretary of State to publish a Code of Practice which gives guidance to police officers (and other people who are responsible for investigating offences) in respect of arranging and conducting of interviews of defence witnesses. Section 21A(2) requires that the Code should, in particular, give guidance in relation to:

(a) information that should be provided to the interviewee and the accused in relation to such an interview;

(b) the notification of the accused's solicitor of such an interview;

(c) the attendance of the interviewee's solicitor at such an interview;

(d) the attendance of the accused's solicitor at such an interview;

(e) the attendance of any other appropriate person at such an interview taking into account the interviewee's age or any disability of the interviewee.

In 2004, the Home Office published a draft Code of Practice under s 21A governing police interviews of defence witnesses notified under s 6C: see Annex C of the Home Office Consultation Document on Disclosure Codes of Practice (Code of Practice for Police Interviews of Witnesses Notified by Accused), <http://www.homeoffice.gov.uk/documents/2004-cons-cja-implementation/2004-cons-cja-implementation-doc?view=Binary>. The draft provides as follows:

1. Where a police officer or other investigator wishes to interview a witness identified by the accused in a statement given in accordance with section 6A(2), or a notice served under section 6C of the Criminal Procedure and Investigations Act 1996, he must:

(a) notify the accused's solicitor of the proposed interview;

(b) unless the witness indicates before the interview that he does not wish the accused's solicitor to be present, invite the accused's solicitor to be present at the proposed interview;

(c) notify the witness that he may, if he wishes, invite his own solicitor to be present at the proposed interview;

(d) make an accurate record of the interview, whether it takes place at a police station or elsewhere. A record may be made in writing or by audio-recording where this is appropriate and practicable;

(e) at the beginning of the interview, advise the witness that a record will be made of the interview that will be copied to both the witness and the accused, unless the witness has indicated that he does not wish the accused's solicitor to be present, in which case the witness should be asked if he would consent to a copy being supplied to the accused; and if such consent is not given, the witness should be advised that the record will be copied to him alone but may be disclosed later to the accused and any co-accused.

(f) at the conclusion of, or following the interview provide a copy of the record taken to the witness or, as the case may be, the witness and the accused.

2. Where an accused is not legally represented, the police officer or other investigator must:

(a) inform the accused that he intends to interview a witness identified in a statement given in accordance with section 6A(2), or a notice served under section 6C of the Criminal Procedure and Investigations Act 1996; and

(b) invite the accused to appoint a solicitor to be present at the interview, unless the witness indicates before the interview that he does not wish the accused's solicitor to be present.

3. In the case of a witness who is a juvenile or a person who is mentally disordered or otherwise mentally vulnerable, it is recommended that arrangements should be made for an appropriate adult to be present during the interview.

...

However, at the time of writing, s 6C had not been brought into force (and no final version of the Code of Practice had been published). In *R (Kelly) v Warley Magistrates' Court* [2007] EWHC 1836 (Admin); (2007) 171 JP 585, the defence were ordered (under Pt 3.10 of the Criminal Procedure Rules) to supply the full names, dates of birth and addresses of all defence witnesses to be called at trial. The defendant applied to have the direction quashed. The court held that the subject-matter of the direction was covered by both litigation privilege and legal professional privilege, and the court did not have power to override them. Such a requirement would require statutory authority, and the relevant provisions of the Criminal Justice Act 2003 had not yet been brought into force. Since this case was decided, r 3.5(6) of the Criminal Procedure Rules came into being, giving the courts sanctions for non-compliance with orders under the Rules.

8.1.4.5 Notification of names of experts instructed by accused

As we have already noted, there is a duty to disclose the evidence that will be adduced by an expert witness to be called by the defence. Section 6D of the CPIA 1996 (inserted by the Criminal Justice Act 2003) creates an additional obligation to reveal the identity of experts who have been instructed on behalf of the defence, whether or not they are called as defence witnesses. Section 6D provides as follows:

(1) If the accused instructs a person with a view to his providing any expert opinion for possible use as evidence at the trial of the accused, he must give to the court and the prosecutor a notice specifying the person's name and address.

(2) A notice does not have to be given under this section specifying the name and address of a person whose name and address have already been given under section 6C.

...

This provision had not been brought into force at the time of writing. Redmayne, in 'Criminal Justice Act 2003: disclosure and its discontents' [2004] Crim LR 441 suggests that this provision will usually be of little practical value to the prosecution:

> There is no property in an expert witness: by instructing an expert a litigant does not prevent that expert being used by the other side. However, the expert may still not be of very much use to the prosecution, because the most useful information she can give will often be subject to privilege ... In some cases, however, litigation privilege will not be an obstacle. If the defence supply the expert with material which was not created for the purposes of litigation, then, while any instructions given to the expert and the expert's report to the solicitor are privileged, the pre-existing material and the expert's opinion based on it are not. And there may be cases where disclosure will alert the prosecution to the existence of an expert whose opinion will be useful to it even though it has access to exactly the same material as the defence. The expert instructed by the defence may be relying on a theory or piece of technology which the prosecution and its experts did not know about. In that situation, the defence's disclosure of the expert's name and address might give the prosecution an important lead in the case.

8.1.4.6 Cases where there is more than one defendant

Section 5(5A) applies where there is more than one defendant. It empowers the court to order a defendant to give a copy of the defence statement to each other defendant specified by the court (the implication being that the court may order disclosure of the defence statement of one defendant to some but not all of the co-defendants). Under s 5(5B), the court may make such an order either of its own motion or on the application of any party.

This provision essentially gives statutory effect to the decision of the Court of Appeal in *R v Cairns* [2002] EWCA Crim 2838; [2003] 1 WLR 796, where the Court of Appeal held that, in cases in which there are a number of co-defendants, the prosecution are not automatically required to disclose to any defendant the defence statement of another. However, if the prosecution, having received the defence statements of the co-defendants, form the view that the statement of one might reasonably be expected to assist the defence of another, that statement should be disclosed to the defence. Disclosure in these circumstances is necessary in order to give effect to the defendant's right to a fair trial under Art 6 of the European Convention on Human Rights.

8.1.4.7 Summary trial: voluntary disclosure by defence

Where the defendant is to be tried in the magistrates' court (or, if a juvenile, the youth court), s 6 of the CPIA 1996 makes provision for voluntary disclosure by the defence.

Section 6(2) provides that in those cases the defendant may give a defence statement to the prosecutor and, if he does so, must also give such a statement to the court.

The incentive for the defence to make disclosure even though it is not compulsory is that, if they do so, this will assist the prosecution to identify any material which has not been disclosed thus far and which might assist the defence.

8.1.5 Continuing disclosure duty of the prosecution

Section 7A of the 1996 Act (inserted by the Criminal Justice Act 2003) imposes a continuing duty on prosecutors to disclose unused material. Section 7A(2) provides that, in the period between the prosecution complying with s 3 and the disposal of the case (i.e. when the accused is acquitted or convicted, or when the prosecutor decides not to proceed with the case), the prosecutor must:

> ... keep under review the question whether at any given time (and, in particular, following the giving of a defence statement) there is prosecution material which—
>
> (a) might reasonably be considered capable of undermining the case for the prosecution against the accused or of assisting the case for the accused, and
> (b) has not been disclosed to the accused.

Under sub-s (3), any such material must be disclosed to the accused as soon as is reasonably practicable. However, sub-s (8) permits material to be withheld from the defence if the court, on an application by the prosecution, concludes it is not in the public interest to disclose it.

8.1.6 Sanctions for failure to comply with defence disclosure obligations

The sanction for non-compliance with the defence disclosure obligations is set out in s 11 of the CPIA 1996. Section 11 applies in three situations:

The first is where the accused is to be tried in the Crown Court (and so is required by s 5 to provide a defence statement) and he:

a   fails to give an initial defence statement under s 5; or
b   provides an initial defence statement but does so late; or
c   fails to provide an updated defence statement (or a statement that there are no changes); or
d   provides an updated statement (or a statement that there are no changes) but does so late; or
e   sets out inconsistent defences in the defence statement; or
f   at the trial, puts forward a defence which was not mentioned in his defence statement or is different from any defence set out in that statement; or
g   at the trial, relies on a matter which was not mentioned in his defence statement but which should have been so mentioned; or
h   at the trial, adduces evidence in support of an alibi without having given particulars of the alibi in the defence statement; or

i   at the trial, calls an alibi witness without having given appropriate notice of the alibi, or details of that particular witness, in the defence statement.

The second is where the accused is to be tried in a magistrates' court and gives an initial defence statement voluntarily but does so late or does any of the things set out in paragraphs (c) to (i) in the preceding paragraph.

The third is where the accused gives a witness notice (under s 6C) but does so late or, at the trial, calls a witness who was not included, or not adequately identified, in a witness notice.

Under s 11(5), where s 11 applies:

(a)   the court or any other party may make such comment as appears appropriate;

(b)   the court or jury may draw such inferences as appear proper in deciding whether the accused is guilty of the offence concerned.

Section 11(6) provides that where adverse inferences could be drawn as a result of failure to mention a point of law (including any point as to the admissibility of evidence or an abuse of process) or an authority, any comment by another party may be made only with the leave of the court. Subsection (7) provides that where the failure in question is a failure to comply with the witness notice requirements (s 6C), comment by another party may be made only with the leave of the court.

Under s 11(8), where the accused puts forward a defence which is different from any defence set out in his defence statement, the court must have regard (a) to the extent of the differences in the defences, and (b) to whether there is any justification for it.

Section 11(9) stipulates that where the accused calls a witness whom he has failed to include, or to identify adequately, in a witness notice, the court must have regard to whether there is any justification for the failure.

Crucially, s 11(10) confirms that 'a person shall not be convicted of an offence solely on an inference drawn under sub-section (5)'. This mirrors the other 'adverse inference' provisions (under the Criminal Justice and Public Order Act 1994).

The matters that must be revealed in a defence statement are construed broadly. In *R v Terry* [2003] EWCA Crim 1800, for example, the defendant served a defence state-ment in which he alleged that police officers had entrapped him to commit the offence. At trial, however, he ran a defence of duress. The prosecution cross-examined the defendant on his apparent change of defence from entrapment to duress. The judge subsequently directed the jury that it was a matter for them if they chose to draw an inference from the defendant's change of defence. The defendant appealed against conviction on the ground that the judge had erred in his ruling because entrapment was not capable of constituting a defence but would only have been potential grounds for an abuse of process argument. The Court of Appeal held that the defence statement contained material which the defendant sought to put forward to prevent his convic-tion. It might or might not amount to a defence in law or on the facts; nevertheless, it was within s 5 of the Act and therefore was capable of being used under s 11. Accord-ingly, the judge had been entitled to allow the jury to draw appropriate inferences.

8.1.7 Defence application for disclosure

Section 8(2) of the CPIA 1996 provides that, where the accused has given a defence statement under ss 5, 6 or 6B and has, at any time, reasonable cause to believe that there is prosecution material which should have been disclosed to him but which has not been disclosed, he may apply to the court for an order requiring the prosecution to disclose it to him. Again, it is open to the prosecutor to argue that disclosure is not in the public interest, in which case the court may authorise the withholding of the material from the defence (s 8(5)). Defence applications are dealt with in more detail later in this Chapter.

8.1.8 Third party disclosure

Sometimes material that may support the defence case is in the hands of a third party. For example, the accused might be charged with a sexual offence involving a child, and the child's school, or the relevant social services department, might have records of false allegations made by the child who is the alleged victim of the offence (as in *R v Brushett* [2001] Crim LR 471). If the material comes into the hands of the police, it should be retained and would fall within the ordinary disclosure regime under the CPIA 1996.

Otherwise, the Attorney General's Guidelines on Disclosure distinguish between two situations. First, there is material held by Government departments or other Crown bodies. Paragraph 47 says that:

> Where it appears to an investigator, disclosure officer or prosecutor that a Government department or other Crown body has material that may be relevant to an issue in the case, reasonable steps should be taken to identify and consider such material. Although what is reasonable will vary from case to case, the prosecution should inform the department or other body of the nature of its case and of relevant issues in the case in respect of which the department or body might possess material, and ask whether it has any such material.

Paragraph 50 adds that:

> Where, after reasonable steps have been taken to secure access to such material, access is denied the investigator, disclosure officer or prosecutor should consider what if any further steps might be taken to obtain the material or inform the defence.

Secondly, there is material held by other agencies. Paragraphs 51–54 state that:

> 51. There may be cases where the investigator, disclosure officer or prosecutor believes that a third party (for example, a local authority, a social services department, a hospital, a doctor, a school, a provider of forensic services) has material or information which might be relevant to the prosecution case. In such cases, if the material or information might reasonably be considered capable of undermining the prosecution case or of assisting the case for the accused prosecutors should take what steps they regard as appropriate in the particular case to obtain it.
>
> 52. If the investigator, disclosure officer or prosecutor seeks access to the material or information but the third party declines or refuses to allow access to it, the matter should not be left. If despite any reasons offered by the third party it is still believed that

it is reasonable to seek production of the material or information, and the requirements of section 2 of the Criminal Procedure (Attendance of Witnesses) Act 1965 or as appropriate section 97 of the Magistrates' Courts Act 1980 are satisfied, then the prosecutor or investigator should apply for a witness summons causing a representative of the third party to produce the material to the Court.

53. Relevant information which comes to the knowledge of investigators or prosecutors as a result of liaison with third parties should be recorded by the investigator or prosecutor in a durable or retrievable form (for example potentially relevant information revealed in discussions at a child protection conference attended by police officers).

54. Where information comes into the possession of the prosecution in the circumstances set out in paragraphs 51–53 above, consultation with the other agency should take place before disclosure is made: there may be public interest reasons which justify withholding disclosure and which would require the issue of disclosure of the information to be placed before the court.

If material remains in the hands of the third party, then the accused is obviously entitled to request it. If the third party is not prepared to hand it over, then the accused can seek a witness summons (using the procedure laid down by s 2 of the Criminal Procedure (Attendance of Witnesses) Act 1965 in Crown Court cases, or s 97 of the Magistrates' Courts Act 1980 in magistrates' court cases). The accused would have to be able to show that the third party is likely to be able to give or produce material evidence in the case, and that it is in the interests of justice to issue a summons.

Rule 28.5(3) of the Criminal Procedure Rules requires the applicant to serve notice of the application on the proposed witness (unless the court otherwise directs) and, if the court so directs, on any person to whom the proposed evidence relates. Under r 28.6(1), a person served with an application for a witness summons requiring production of a document or other evidence may object to its production on the ground that either it is not likely to be material evidence, or the duties or rights (including rights of confidentiality) of the proposed witness or of any person to whom the document or thing relates outweigh the reasons for issuing a summons. Under r 28.6(2), the court may require the proposed witness to make the document or thing available for the objection to be assessed by the court. In the context of disclosure, a third party would be to able to argue, for example, that the evidence should not be disclosed on grounds of public interest immunity (see below).

The *Auld Review* also considered the question of third party disclosure, and recommends (Recommendation 206) that:

There should be consideration of a new statutory scheme for third party disclosure, including its cost implications to all concerned, to operate alongside and more consistently with the general provisions for disclosure of unused material.

So far, this suggestion has not been taken up by the Government.

8.2 PUBLIC INTEREST IMMUNITY

Sections 3(6) (initial duty of disclosure) and 7A(8) (continuing duty of disclosure) enable the prosecutor to withhold material that would normally have to be disclosed if the court, on an application by the prosecutor, concludes that it is not in the public interest to disclose it and orders accordingly. For these purposes, the relevant court is the court in which the defendant is to be tried (so the magistrates' court has no jurisdiction in respect of disclosure once the defendant has been sent to the Crown Court for trial: *R v CPS ex p Warby* (1994) 158 JP 190). Public interest immunity (PII) is similarly relevant under s 8(5) (defence applications for disclosure).

A common example of a case where PII is raised is where the prosecution wish to protect the identity of an informant whom the prosecutor does not intend to call as a witness at the trial (as in *R v Turner* [1995] 1 WLR 264, discussed below). A similar example is where the police wish to keep secret the location of an observation post from which they were watching the movements of the accused (as in *R v Johnson* [1988] 1 WLR 1377, where the court observed that, at the heart of the problem is the desirability, as far as possible, of reassuring people who are asked to help the police that their identities will never be disclosed lest they become the victims of reprisals by wrongdoers for performing a public service. On the other hand, the court has to ensure that the accused has a fair trial, and his ability to challenge the accuracy of observation evidence may be prejudiced if he does not know from where the observation was being carried out).

The essence of the PII provisions in the CPIA 1996 is that if material should otherwise be disclosed because it undermines the prosecution case or assists the defence case, that material must be disclosed to the defence unless the court gives permission for it to be withheld from the defence.

The Attorney General's Guidelines on Disclosure, dealing with applications for non-disclosure in the public interest, state (paras 20–22) that:

20. Before making an application to the court to withhold material which would otherwise fall to be disclosed, on the basis that to disclose would give rise to a real risk of serious prejudice to an important public interest, prosecutors should aim to disclose as much of the material as they properly can (for example, by giving the defence redacted or edited copies or summaries). Neutral material or material damaging to the defendant need not be disclosed and must not be brought to the attention of the court. It is only in truly borderline cases that the prosecution should seek a judicial ruling on the disclosability of material in its possession.

21. Prior to or at the hearing, the court must be provided with full and accurate information. Prior to the hearing the prosecutor and the prosecution advocate must examine all material, which is the subject matter of the application and make any necessary inquiries of the investigator. The prosecutor (or representative) and/or investigator should attend such applications.

22. The principles set out at paragraph 36 of *R v H & C* should be rigorously applied firstly by the prosecutor and then by the court considering the material. It is essential that these principles are scrupulously attended to to ensure that the procedure for examination of material in the absence of the accused is compliant with Article 6 of ECHR.

Where a magistrates' court has ruled that it is not in the public interest to disclose prosecution material, the defendant may apply to the magistrates for a review of the question whether it is still not in the public interest to disclose that material (s 14(2)).

Where a Crown Court has ruled that it is not in the public interest to disclose prosecution material, the court itself must keep under review the question whether it is still not in the public interest to disclose that material (s 15(3)). Although the Crown Court has to keep the matter under review without the need for any application by the defence, it is nonetheless open to the defendant to apply to the court for a review of the question (s 15(4)).

Where magistrates rule on disclosure, it may be that they hear matters which are prejudicial to the defendant. In these circumstances, it is a matter for their discretion whether they disqualify themselves from conducting the trial itself so that the trial is heard by a different bench (*R v South Worcestershire Justices ex p Lilley* [1995] 1 WLR 1595).

8.2.1 Public interest immunity ('PII') and the European Convention on Human Rights

In *Jasper v UK* (2000) 30 EHRR 441, the European Court of Human Rights said (at para 51):

> It is a fundamental aspect of the right to a fair trial that criminal proceedings . . . should be adversarial and that there should be equality of arms between the prosecution and defence. The right to an adversarial trial means, in a criminal case, that both prosecution and defence must be given the opportunity to have knowledge of and comment on the observations filed and the evidence adduced by the other party. In addition Article 6(1) requires . . . that the prosecution authorities should disclose to the defence all material evidence in their possession for or against the accused.

In para 52, however, the Court noted that it is not only the interests of the accused that have to be taken into account. It follows that:

> . . . the entitlement to disclosure of relevant evidence is not an absolute right. In any criminal proceedings there may be competing interests, such as national security or the need to protect witnesses at risk of reprisals or keep secret police methods of investigation of crime, which must be weighed against the rights of the accused. In some cases it may be necessary to withhold certain evidence from the defence so as to preserve the fundamental rights of another individual or to safeguard an important public interest. However, only such measures restricting the rights of the defence which are strictly necessary are permissible under Article 6(1). Moreover, in order to ensure that the accused receives a fair trial, any difficulties caused to the defence by a limitation on its rights must be sufficiently counterbalanced by the procedures followed by the judicial authorities.

The Court emphasised that its role was to 'scrutinise the decision-making procedure to ensure that, as far as possible, it complied with the requirements to provide adversarial proceedings and equality of arms and incorporated adequate safeguards to protect the interests of the accused' (para 53).

In the present case, the defence had been notified that a PII application to withhold material was to be made, but were not told of the category of material which the prosecution sought to withhold. The defence were given the opportunity to outline the defence case to the trial judge and to ask the judge to order disclosure of any evidence relevant to that case. On this basis, the Court (at para 55) said that it was:

> ... satisfied that the defence were kept informed and permitted to make submissions and participate in the above decision-making process as far as was possible without revealing to them the material which the prosecution sought to keep secret on public interest grounds.

Jasper was decided in favour of the UK Government by the slenderest of majorities. It is worthwhile examining briefly the views of some of the judges who were in the minority:

> We note that, although the defence in this case were notified that an ex parte application was to be made by the prosecution for material to be withheld on grounds of public interest immunity, they were not informed of the category of material which the prosecution sought to withhold, they were not – by definition – involved in the ex parte proceedings, and they were not informed of the reasons for the judge's subsequent decision that the material should not be disclosed. This procedure cannot, in our view, be said to respect the principles of adversarial proceedings and equality of arms, given that the prosecuting authorities were provided with access to the judge and were able to participate in the decision-making process in the absence of any representative of the defence. We do not accept that the opportunity given to the defence to outline their case before the trial judge took his decision on disclosure can affect the position, as the defence were unaware of the nature of the matters they needed to address. It was purely a matter of chance whether they made any relevant points.
>
> The fact that the judge monitored the need for disclosure throughout the trial cannot remedy the unfairness created by the defence's absence from the ex parte proceedings. In our view, the requirements ... that any difficulties caused to the defence by a limitation on defence rights must be sufficiently counterbalanced by the procedures followed by the judicial authorities, are not met by the mere fact that it was a judge who decided that the evidence be withheld ... Our concern is that, in order to be able to fulfil his functions as the judge in a fair trial, the judge should be informed by the opinions of both parties, not solely the prosecution.

The minority went on to suggest that the use of special counsel (see below) might go some way to redress the balance.

In *R v Davis, Rowe and Johnson* (2000) *The Times*, 24 April, the Court of Appeal noted that the judgment of the European Court of Human Rights in the case of *Rowe and Davis v UK* (2000) 30 EHRR 1 had been highly critical of the procedure adopted prior to the coming into force of the CPIA 1996 but did not criticise the procedure used under that Act to deal with public interest immunity applications.

In *Edwards and Lewis v UK* (2003) 15 BHRC 189, the European Court of Human Rights quoted extensively from its judgment in *Jasper*. However, the Court distinguished *Jasper* on the basis that, in the present case, it appeared that 'the undisclosed evidence related, or may have related, to an issue of fact decided by the trial judge' (namely whether or not there had been entrapment). At para 57, the Court noted that:

> Had the defence been able to persuade the judge that the police had acted improperly, the prosecution would, in effect, have had to be discontinued. The applications in question were, therefore, of determinative importance to the applicants' trials, and the public interest immunity evidence may have related to facts connected with those applications.

The Court (at para 58) said that:

> Despite this, the applicants were denied access to the evidence. It was not, therefore, possible for the defence representatives to argue the case on entrapment in full before the judge.

The Court went on (at para 59) to hold that it did:

> ... not consider that the procedure employed to determine the issues of disclosure of evidence and entrapment complied with the requirements to provide adversarial proceedings and equality of arms and incorporated adequate safeguards to protect the interests of the accused. It follows that there has been a violation of Article 6 § 1 in this case.

It has to be noted that this decision has a fairly limited application. It appears to be relevant only where the defendant's ability to make an application to the judge for the case to be dismissed or stayed is diminished through the withholding of potentially relevant evidence. It does not apply where the guilt or innocence of the accused is a matter for the jury.

8.2.2 Domestic case law on public interest immunity

Prior to the enactment of the CPIA 1996, disclosure was governed almost exclusively by case law. Section 21 of the CPIA 1996 provides that the Act replaces the common law regarding the circumstances in which disclosure has to be made (s 21(1)). However, the Act does not 'affect the rules of common law as to whether disclosure is in the public interest' (s 21(2)).

Many of the public interest cases are ones where the prosecution did not want to reveal to the defence the identity of a person because the prosecution feared that the person would be intimidated or otherwise put at risk (for example, a regular police informant). However, as was said in *R v Keane* [1994] 1 WLR 746, if the evidence proves the defendant's innocence, or would assist in avoiding a miscarriage of justice, the balance must come down resoundingly in favour of disclosing that evidence (per Lord Taylor CJ at p 752).

In *R v Reilly* [1994] Crim LR 279, the prosecution refused to disclose the identity of an informant who was not going to be called as a prosecution witness. It was held by the Court of Appeal that the need to protect an informant had to give way to the need to allow the defence to present a tenable case in its best light (which may involve impugning the informant). The Crown had to choose between disclosing the identity of the informant or discontinuing the case against the defendant (and in fact chose the latter course). This invidious choice meant that a large number of prosecutions had to be dropped rather than placing informants at risk. In *R v Turner* [1995] 1 WLR 264, the Court of Appeal took a slightly tougher line, making the point that a distinction has to be drawn between cases where there is no reasonable possibility that information about the informant will bear upon the issues and cases where it will; even where the informant may have participated in the events constituting, surrounding, or following the crime, the judge will need to consider whether his role so impinges on an issue of interest to the defence as to make disclosure necessary (per Lord Taylor CJ at p 267). It follows that the court should only accede to an application by the defence for disclosure of the identity of an informant if it is satisfied that the information is essential to the running of the defence. In the instant case, it appeared that the informant had participated in the events surrounding the crime and the defence case was that the defendant had been set up. Accordingly, the judge should have decided that the balance came down firmly in favour of disclosure.

The prosecution generally cannot claim immunity from disclosure in respect of documents which the trial judge has not viewed personally (*R v K* (1993) 97 Cr App R 342). However, in *R v Whittle* [1997] 1 Cr App R 166, it was said to be sufficient for the judge to rely on the judgment of an independent barrister appointed to read the documents where the volume of papers is such that the judge does not have time to read them personally.

In *R v Templar* [2003] EWCA Crim 3186, the Court of Appeal accepted the assertion by prosecuting counsel that if the material in respect of which immunity is sought 'was properly the subject of public interest immunity, the judge was entitled to order that it be withheld from the [defendant] unless it provided any support for the [defendant]'s case or could be said to harm or undermine that of the prosecution'. This raises a key problem in the law of disclosure: if the material is not relevant (in the sense that it undermines the prosecution case or supports the defence case) it does not have to be disclosed in the first place. On the other hand, if it does in fact undermine the prosecution case or support the defence case to any significant extent, it seems inconsistent with the defendant's right to a fair trial for that material to be withheld, however sensitive it might be. In 'Fairness and public interest immunity: inconsistent concepts?' (2004) 154 NLJ 46, Stephen Parkinson suggests that:

- Where the public interest in withholding material is weak and it has a central relevance to the defence case, then clearly he must order disclosure.
- Equally, where the public interest against disclosure is strong and the material is of peripheral relevance to the defence case, though falling within CPIA 1996 tests, he will rule against disclosure.
- If both competing interests are equally strong, or equally weak, then he will apply the test used by the Court of Appeal: would a conviction that follows when disclosure is withheld be unsafe? If not, then he will not order disclosure.

Thus Parkinson suggests that where the matter cannot be resolved by comparing the damage that would be done by disclosing the information with the prejudice the defendant will suffer in the conduct of his defence if the material is withheld, disclosure should be withheld only if doing so will not render the conviction unsafe.

8.2.3 Procedure for determining public interest immunity claims

Some applications for permission to withhold material held by the prosecution take place without the defence even knowing that such an application is being made. This raises obvious concerns about the fairness of the procedure that is adopted for the determination of PII applications.

The procedure for determining claims of public interest immunity was originally set out in *R v Ward* [1993] 1 WLR 619 and *R v Davis* [1993] 1 WLR 613 at 617–18. The Court of Appeal identified three classes of case, which Lord Bingham, in *R v H; R v C* [2004] UKHL 3; [2004] 2 AC 134, summarised in the following terms (see para 20):

> In the first, comprising most of the cases in which a PII issue arises, the prosecution must give notice to the defence that they are applying for a ruling of the court, and must indicate to the defence at least the category of the material they hold (that is, the broad ground upon which PII is claimed), and the defence must have the opportunity to make representations to the court. There is thus an *inter partes* hearing conducted in open court with reference to at least the category of the material in question. The second class comprises cases in which the prosecution contend that the public interest would be injured if disclosure were made even of the category of the material. In such cases the prosecution must still notify the defence that an application to the court is to be made, but the category of the material need not be specified: the defence will still have an opportunity to address the court on the procedure to be adopted but the application will be made to the court in the absence of the defendant or anyone representing him. If the court considers that the application falls within the first class, it will order that procedure to be followed. Otherwise it will rule. The third class, described as 'highly exceptional', comprises cases where the public interest would be injured even by disclosure that an *ex parte* application is to be made. In such cases application to the court would be made without notice to the defence. But if the court considers that the case should be treated as falling within the second or the first class, it will so order.

Thus, the prosecution should, whenever possible, notify the defence that it is applying for a ruling by the court, and indicate to the defence at least the category of the material to which the application relates. The defence should then be given the opportunity of making representations to the court. Where disclosure even of the category of material would be tantamount to revealing whatever it is that the prosecution are seeking not to disclose, the prosecution should still notify the defence of the application, but need not specify the category of material; in such a case, the application will be *ex parte* (though it would be open to the defence to submit written representations to the judge). If the court, on hearing the application, considers that the normal procedure should have been followed, it will order that the application should be renewed *inter partes*, otherwise it will rule on the *ex parte* application. If the prosecution believe that to reveal even the fact that an *ex parte* application is to be made could 'let the cat out of the bag' (thereby defeating the purpose of the application), they may apply to the court *ex parte* without notice to the defence. If the court, on hearing the application considers that notice should have been given to the defence, or even that the normal *inter partes* procedure should have been adopted, it will so order.

The Court of Appeal in *Ward* and *Davis* also made the point that, even if the judge rules in favour of non-disclosure, the position may change during the course of the trial, and so the court will have to monitor the question of disclosure. If the public interest in non-disclosure is then outweighed by the need to order disclosure in the interests of securing fairness to the defendant, the prosecution will have to decide whether to disclose the material in question or to offer no further evidence in the case.

The procedural regime established by *R v Davis* and *R v Ward* is mirrored by Pt 25 of the Criminal Procedure Rules, which sets out the procedure to be adopted where the prosecution wish to seek the court's permission to withhold from the defence material that would otherwise have to be disclosed. Rule 25.1 provides as follows:

(3) Subject to paragraphs (4) and (5) below, a copy of the notice of application shall be served on the accused by the prosecutor.

(4) Where the prosecutor has reason to believe that to reveal to the accused the nature of the material to which the application relates would have the effect of disclosing that which the prosecutor contends should not in the public interest be disclosed, paragraph (3) above shall not apply but the prosecutor shall notify the accused that an application to which this rule applies has been made.

(5) Where the prosecutor has reason to believe that to reveal to the accused the fact that an application is being made would have the effect of disclosing that which the prosecutor contends should not in the public interest be disclosed, paragraph (3) above shall not apply.

The procedure for the hearing itself is contained in r 25.2, which provides as follows:

(3) . . . subject to paragraphs (4) and (5) below . . .

   (b) the hearing shall be inter partes; and
   (c) the prosecutor and the accused shall be entitled to make representations to the court.

(4) Where the prosecutor applies to the court for leave to make representations in the absence of the accused, the court may for that purpose sit in the absence of the accused and any legal representative of his.

(5) . . . where a copy of the notice of application has not been served on the accused in accordance with rule 25.1(3).

   (a) the hearing shall be ex parte;
   (b) only the prosecutor shall be entitled to make representations to the court;
   (c) the accused shall not be given notice [of the hearing].

. . .

Under r 25.8(2), the hearing of the prosecution application may be held in private.

8.2.3.1 Guidance on how to approach PII hearings

In *R v H; R v C* [2004] UKHL 3; [2004] 2 AC 134, the Court of Appeal had certified two points of law of general public importance:

(1) Are the procedures for dealing with claims for public interest immunity made on behalf of the prosecution in criminal proceedings compliant with Article 6 of the European Convention for the Protection of Human Rights and Fundamental Freedoms?

(2) If not, in what way are the procedures deficient and how might the deficiency be remedied?

The opinion of the House of Lords was delivered by Lord Bingham on behalf of all the Law Lords who heard this appeal. Lord Bingham took as his starting point the principle established in *R v Horseferry Road Magistrates' Court ex p Bennett* [1994] 1 AC 42 at 68, and *Attorney General's Reference (No 2 of 2001)* [2003] UKHL 68; [2004] 2 AC 72, para 13, that it is 'axiomatic' that a person charged with a criminal offence should receive a fair trial and that, if he cannot be tried fairly for that offence, he should not be tried for it at all.

Lord Bingham noted that Art 6 of the European Convention requires that the trial process, viewed as a whole, must be fair; it followed that the answers to the questions posed by the Court of Appeal (and the other issues considered by the House of Lords) had to be governed by that 'cardinal and overriding requirement' (para 10).

At para 12, Lord Bingham quotes from Lord Steyn in *Attorney General's Reference (No 3 of 1999)* [2001] 2 AC 91, 118:

> The purpose of the criminal law is to permit everyone to go about their daily lives without fear of harm to person or property. And it is in the interests of everyone that serious crime should be effectively investigated and prosecuted. There must be fairness to all sides. In a criminal case this requires the court to consider a triangulation of interests. It involves taking into account the position of the accused, the victim and his or her family, and the public.

Lord Bingham makes the point that, while the focus of Art 6 is on the right of a criminal defendant to a fair trial, it is a right that has to be exercised within the framework of the administration of the criminal law. It follows from this that rights of people other than the defendant have to be taken into account. His Lordship also repeats (in para 13) that the duty of prosecuting counsel is not to obtain a conviction at all costs but to act as a minister of justice (*Randall v The Queen* [2002] UKPC 19; [2002] 1 WLR 2237, para 10).

In para 14, Lord Bingham refers to what he calls 'the golden rule': that fairness ordinarily requires disclosure to the defence of any material held by the prosecution which weakens its case or strengthens that of the defendant (assuming this material is not part of the formal prosecution case against the defendant, in which it will have been disclosed anyway). This duty has been enshrined in statute, in the CPIA 1996.

Turning to public interest immunity justifying the withholding of material that tends to undermine prosecution or assist the defence, Lord Bingham notes that the public interest most regularly engaged in this context is the need for the effective investigation and prosecution of serious crime; this may involve the following (para 18):

> ... resort to informers and under-cover agents, or the use of scientific or operational techniques (such as surveillance) which cannot be disclosed without exposing individuals to the risk of personal injury or jeopardising the success of future operations. In such circumstances some derogation from the golden rule of full disclosure may be justified but such

derogation must always be the minimum derogation necessary to protect the public interest in question and must never imperil the overall fairness of the trial.

Lord Bingham emphasised that material only has to be disclosed to the defence if it is relevant. After considering the background of both English law and the jurisprudence of the Strasbourg Court, his Lordship concluded that (para 35):

> If material does not weaken the prosecution case or strengthen that of the defendant, there is no requirement to disclose it . . . Neutral material or material damaging to the defendant need not be disclosed and should not be brought to the attention of the court. Only in truly borderline cases should the prosecution seek a judicial ruling on the disclosability of material in its hands . . .

In other words, in most cases the prosecution will not need to make an application: if it is clear that a judge would order disclosure, then the prosecution should either disclose the material to the defence or drop the case.

Lord Bingham went on to give detailed guidance on how the courts should approach public interest immunity hearings (at paras 36 and 37):

36. When any issue of derogation from the golden rule of full disclosure comes before it, the court must address a series of questions:

    (1) What is the material which the prosecution seek to withhold? This must be considered by the court in detail.

    (2) Is the material such as may weaken the prosecution case or strengthen that of the defence? If No, disclosure should not be ordered. If Yes, full disclosure should (subject to (3), (4) and (5) below) be ordered.

    (3) Is there a real risk of serious prejudice to an important public interest (and, if so, what) if full disclosure of the material is ordered? If No, full disclosure should be ordered.

    (4) If the answer to (2) and (3) is Yes, can the defendant's interest be protected without disclosure or can disclosure be ordered to an extent or in a way which will give adequate protection to the public interest in question and also afford adequate protection to the interests of the defence?
    This question requires the court to consider, with specific reference to the material which the prosecution seek to withhold and the facts of the case and the defence as disclosed, whether the prosecution should formally admit what the defence seek to establish or whether disclosure short of full disclosure may be ordered. This may be done in appropriate cases by the preparation of summaries or extracts of evidence, or the provision of documents in an edited or anonymised form, provided the documents supplied are in each instance approved by the judge. In appropriate cases the appointment of special counsel may be a necessary step to ensure that the contentions of the prosecution are tested and the interests of the defendant protected (see paragraph 22 above). In cases of exceptional difficulty the court may require the appointment of special counsel to ensure a correct answer to questions (2) and (3) as well as (4).

    (5) Do the measures proposed in answer to (4) represent the minimum derogation

necessary to protect the public interest in question? If No, the court should order such greater disclosure as will represent the minimum derogation from the golden rule of full disclosure.

(6) If limited disclosure is ordered pursuant to (4) or (5), may the effect be to render the trial process, viewed as a whole, unfair to the defendant? If Yes, then fuller disclosure should be ordered even if this leads or may lead the prosecution to discontinue the proceedings so as to avoid having to make disclosure.

(7) If the answer to (6) when first given is No, does that remain the correct answer as the trial unfolds, evidence is adduced and the defence advanced?

It is important that the answer to (6) should not be treated as a final, once-and-for-all, answer but as a provisional answer which the court must keep under review.

37. Throughout his or her consideration of any disclosure issue the trial judge must bear constantly in mind the overriding principles referred to in this opinion. In applying them, the judge should involve the defence to the maximum extent possible without disclosing that which the general interest requires to be protected but taking full account of the specific defence which is relied on. There will be very few cases indeed in which some measure of disclosure to the defence will not be possible, even if this is confined to the fact that an ex parte application is to be made. If even that information is withheld and if the material to be withheld is of significant help to the defendant, there must be a very serious question whether the prosecution should proceed, since special counsel, even if appointed, cannot then receive any instructions from the defence at all.

Importantly, Lord Bingham concludes (at para 39) that:

Provided the existing procedures for dealing with claims for public interest immunity made on behalf of the prosecution in criminal proceedings are operated with scrupulous attention to the governing principles referred to and continuing regard to the proper interests of the defendant, there should be no violation of Article 6 of the Convention.

In *R v G* [2004] EWCA Crim 1368; [2004] 1 WLR 2932, the Court of Appeal had to consider a case where sensitive information had been disclosed to the defence inadvertently. In a PII hearing, held *ex parte*, the judge had ordered non-disclosure of certain material to the defence. Subsequently, the prosecution had inadvertently disclosed some highly confidential and sensitive material in a document sent to the defendants' counsel. The judge ordered a ban on dissemination by the lawyers 'in the know' to anyone, including their clients. The judge made an express finding that the legal representatives could continue to represent their clients properly and effectively. The Court of Appeal said that there is no reason in principle why a Crown Court judge should not restrain the use of material inadvertently disclosed, although the particular circumstances of the case will dictate whether justice requires such an order. On the facts of the present case, it would have wholly undermined the lawyers' relationship with their client if they were privy to issues in court but could not reveal those issues to the client. Moreover, the court said that it is not for the judge to determine whether counsel or solicitors are capable of continuing to represent their client: the question of whether a lawyer can properly continue to represent his client is one for the lawyer, not the court.

8.2.3.2 Use of 'special counsel' in public interest immunity applications

The role of the judge in PII hearings is clearly a crucial one so far as the European Court is concerned. Indeed, in *PG and JH v UK* [2002] Crim LR 308, the court said that:

> ... The fact that the need for disclosure was at all times under assessment by the trial judge provided a further, important safeguard in that it was his duty to monitor throughout the trial the fairness or otherwise of the evidence being withheld. It has not been suggested that the judge was not independent and impartial within the meaning of Article 6(1). He was fully versed in all the evidence and issues in the case and in a position to monitor the relevance to the defence of the withheld information both before and during the trial.

Two points arise from this. First, in a case such as *Jasper* (where the defendant knew that an application to withhold material was being made and had a chance to make representations to the judge), the judge can only safeguard the interests of the accused if he or she has received sufficient information from the defence as to its case. Inevitably, the judge will not be as well-briefed on the details of the defence case as defence counsel would be. Nonetheless, it is probably true that (in most cases at least) knowledge of the broad thrust of the defence case will be sufficient to evaluate the potential relevance of the material that the prosecution are seeking to withhold. However, the second point is that, in a case where the defence do not know that an application to withhold material is being made, the only information that the judge is likely to have about the defence case will be based on (a) what the accused said when interviewed by the police, and (b) the content of the 'defence statement' served under the CPIA 1996. This information may well be inadequate to brief the judge sufficiently to appreciate the relevance of the withheld material. Also, if the defendant remains silent in interview and/or serves a defence statement that lacks detail, he not only faces the possibility of adverse inferences being drawn by the jury but also is depriving the judge of information that might help in assessing the relevance of withheld material. This in turn makes it more difficult, if not impossible, for the judge to ensure that the accused has a fair trial.

The *Auld Review* recommended the use of 'special counsel' in cases where the prosecution wished to seek non-disclosure on grounds of public interest immunity on an *ex parte* basis. Paragraph 194 of Chapter 10 of the Review refers to a paper prepared for the Review by Tim Owen QC, who argued that the use of special counsel would:

> ... restore some adversarial testing of the issues presently absent in the determination of these often critical and finely balanced applications. It should not be generally necessary for special counsel to be present throughout the trial. Mostly the matter should be capable of resolution by the court before trial and, if any question about it arises during trial, he could be asked to return ...

However, at para 197 of the Review, Lord Justice Auld notes that the efficacy of the disclosure regime does not depend wholly on court procedures. He says that:

> ... even the introduction of special counsel ... would not solve the root problem ... of police failure, whether out of incompetence or dishonesty, to indicate to the prosecutor the

existence of critical information. Unless . . . the police significantly improve their performance in that basic exercise, there will be no solid foundation for whatever following safeguards are introduced into the system.

Recommendation 206 of the *Auld Review* is as follows:

A scheme should be introduced for instruction by the court of special independent counsel
to represent the interests of the defendant in those cases at first instance and on appeal
where the court now considers prosecution applications in the absence of the defence in
respect of the non-disclosure of sensitive material.

This recommendation was apparently not accepted by the Government. The Criminal
Justice Act 2003 makes a number of changes to the law relating to the disclosure of
unused material, but does not make provision for use of special counsel.

It therefore fell to the courts to decide whether to sanction the use of special counsel.
In *R v H* (see above), the House of Lords considered the potential role for 'special
independent counsel' in PII hearings. It is interesting that the role of special independent counsel was not mentioned specifically in the questions certified by the Court of
Appeal, even though the role of such counsel was central to the appeal. It seems likely
that the Court of Appeal did not want to limit the scope of the inquiry by the House
of Lords into general issues surrounding the fairness or otherwise of PII hearings.

At para 21, Lord Bingham turns to what he describes as the 'novel procedure' of
appointing special independent counsel or a 'special advocate' to protect the interests
of the defendant but who may not disclose to the defendant the secret material that is
disclosed to him in order to make representations on behalf of the defendant and who
is not, in the ordinary sense, professionally responsible to the defendant. Despite
describing the procedure as 'novel', his Lordship goes on to identify a number of cases
where the use of special advocates has been sanctioned by statute or by the courts. It is
interesting to note in this context that the Government did not include any reference to
the use of special counsel when it amended the CPIA 1996 in the Criminal Justice Act
2003.

Turning to the jurisprudence of the European Court of Human Rights, Lord Bingham
referred to *Chahal v UK* (1996) 23 EHRR 413 (an immigration case which raised issues
of national security and where security-cleared counsel, instructed by the court, was
appointed to cross-examine the witnesses and generally assist the court to test the
strength of the State's case). The European Court accepted (at para 131) 'that there are
techniques which can be employed which both accommodate legitimate security concerns about the nature and sources of intelligence information and yet accord the
individual a substantial measure of procedural justice'. A similar point was made in
Tinnelly & Sons Ltd and McElduff v UK (1998) 27 EHRR 249, where special counsel
was appointed in a discrimination case that raised national security issues.

Of relevance to the appeal in *R v H*, the European Court in *Jasper* had held that the
use of special counsel was not necessary in that case. At para 56, the Court said that:

The fact that the need for disclosure was at all times under assessment by the trial judge
provided a further, important, safeguard in that it was his duty to monitor throughout the
trial the fairness or otherwise of the evidence being withheld . . . He was fully versed in all

the evidence and issues in the case and in a position to monitor the relevance to the defence of the withheld information both before and during the trial.

Lord Bingham, in *R v H*, expresses concern (at para 22) that the appointment of special counsel raises:

> ... ethical problems, since a lawyer who cannot take full instructions from his client, nor report to his client, who is not responsible to his client and whose relationship with the client lacks the quality of confidence inherent in any ordinary lawyer-client relationship, is acting in a way hitherto unknown to the legal profession. While not insuperable, these problems should not be ignored, since neither the defendant nor the public will be fully aware of what is being done. The appointment is also likely to cause practical problems: of delay, while the special counsel familiarises himself with the detail of what is likely to be a complex case; of expense, since the introduction of an additional, high-quality advocate must add significantly to the cost of the case; and of continuing review, since it will not be easy for a special counsel to assist the court in its continuing duty to review disclosure, unless the special counsel is present throughout or is instructed from time to time when need arises.

However, his Lordship concludes that:

> None of these problems should deter the court from appointing special counsel where the interests of justice are shown to require it. But the need must be shown. Such an appointment will always be exceptional, never automatic; a course of last and never first resort. It should not be ordered unless and until the trial judge is satisfied that no other course will adequately meet the overriding requirement of fairness to the defendant.

The House of Lords also considered whether it was right to question the suitability of the Attorney General (who effectively oversees the work of the Director of Public Prosecutions) to be the officer responsible for the appointment of special counsel in cases where the necessity for such appointment arises. Lord Bingham says (at para 46):

> In our opinion such doubt is misplaced. It is very well-established that when exercising a range of functions the Attorney General acts not as a minister of the Crown ... and not as the public officer with overall responsibility for the conduct of prosecutions, but as an independent, unpartisan guardian of the public interest in the administration of justice ... It is in that capacity alone that he approves the list of counsel judged suitable to act as ... special counsel ... It would perhaps allay any conceivable ground of doubt, however ill-founded, if the Attorney General were to seek external approval of his list of eligible advocates by an appropriate professional body or bodies, but such approval is not in current circumstances essential to the acceptability of the procedure.

His Lordship (at para 44) also gives general guidance on PII hearings in magistrates' courts, affirming the approach taken in *R (DPP) v Acton Youth Court* [2001] EWHC 402 (Admin); [2001] 1 WLR 1828:

> If PII applications are confined, as they should be, to material which undermines the prosecution case or strengthens that of the defence, the bench will not be alerted to material

damaging to the defendant. If it is, the principles which should govern the court's decision whether to recuse itself are the same as in the case of any other tribunal of fact, but the court's duty of continuing review ordinarily militates in favour of continuing the proceedings before the court which determines the PII application. If a case raises complex and contentious PII issues, and the court has discretion to send the case to the crown court for trial, the magistrates' court should carefully consider whether those issues are best resolved in the crown court. The occasions on which it will be appropriate to appoint special counsel in the magistrates' court will be even rarer than in the Crown Court.

8.3 DEFENCE APPLICATIONS TO THE COURT UNDER THE CRIMINAL PROCEDURE AND INVESTIGATIONS ACT 1996

The defence can seek a review of an earlier finding upholding a prosecution claim for public interest immunity. The defence can also make a free-standing application for disclosure if they think that the prosecution have wrongly withheld material.

8.3.1 Applications for review

It is open to the defence to seek a review by the court of an order permitting non-disclosure of material, under ss 14(2) (summary trials) or 15(4) (Crown Court trials). Rule 25.4 of the Criminal Procedure Rules governs applications by the defence for the review of non-disclosure orders, and provides as follows:

(6) Where such an application is made in the Crown Court, the judge shall consider whether the application may be determined without a hearing . . .

(7) No application to which this rule applies shall be determined by the Crown Court without a hearing if it appears to the judge that there are grounds on which the court might conclude that it is in the public interest to disclose material to any extent.

(8) Where a magistrates' court considers that there are no grounds on which it might conclude that it is in the public interest to disclose material to any extent it may determine an application to which this rule applies without hearing representations from the accused, the prosecutor or any person claiming to have an interest in the material to which the application relates.

(9) Subject to paragraphs (10) and (11) of this rule . . . the hearing of an application to which this rule applies shall be inter partes and the accused and the prosecutor shall be entitled to make representations to the court.

(10) Where after hearing the accused's representations the prosecutor applies to the court for leave to make representations in the absence of the accused, the court may for that purpose sit in the absence of the accused and any legal representative of his.

(11) . . . where the order to which the application relates was made following an application of which the accused was not notified . . . the hearing shall be ex parte and only the prosecutor shall be entitled to make representations to the court.

8.3.2 Defence application for disclosure

If the defence believe that the prosecution have failed to disclose material that should have been disclosed, they may make an application to the court under s 8(2) of the CPIA 1996, which provides that, so long as the accused has supplied a defence statement under ss 5, 6 or 6B, he may, if he has 'reasonable cause to believe that there is prosecution material which is required by s 7A to be disclosed to him and has not been', apply to the court for an order requiring the prosecutor to disclose it to him.

The procedure for defence applications for orders for disclosure of specific material is governed by Pt 25.6 of the Criminal Procedure Rules. Under r 25.6(5), when the prosecution receive notice of the accused's application, they have to inform the court whether they wish to make representation to the court about the material being sought by the defence or whether they are willing to disclose that material without further ado. The rule goes on to set out what happens where the prosecution oppose the defence application:

(6) A court may determine an application to which this rule applies without hearing representations from the applicant or the prosecutor unless—

  (a) the prosecutor has given notice [that he wishes to make representations] and the court considers that the representations should be made at a hearing; or
  (b) the court considers it necessary to hear representations from the applicant or the prosecutor in the interests of justice for the purposes of determining the application.

(7) Subject to paragraph (8), where a hearing is held in pursuance of this rule—
  . . .

  (b) the hearing shall be inter partes; and
  (c) the prosecutor and the applicant shall be entitled to make representations to the court.

(8) Where the prosecutor applies to the court for leave to make representations in the absence of the accused, the court may for that purpose sit in the absence of the accused and any legal representative of his.

Under r 25.8(2), hearings of defence applications for review of non-disclosure orders and applications for specific disclosure orders may be held in private.

8.4 CONFIDENTIALITY

Where prosecution material has been disclosed to the defendant, the defendant may only use that material in connection with the forthcoming trial or an appeal following that trial, unless the material is in the public domain because it has been displayed or communicated to the public in open court (s 17). Contravention of s 17 is a contempt of court (s 18(1)). Where the prosecution disclosure was in the context of a summary trial, the contempt will be dealt with by the magistrates' court and the penalty is a custodial sentence of up to six months and/or a fine of up to £5,000; where the prosecution disclosure was in the context of trial on indictment, the contempt will be dealt with by the Crown Court and the penalty is up to two years' custody and/or a fine.

8.5 ASSESSING THE EFFECTIVENESS OF THE DISCLOSURE REGIME

In May 2008, HM Crown Prosecution Service Inspectorate published a report, 'A thematic review of the duties of disclosure of unused material undertaken by the CPS' (<http://www.hmcpsi.gov.uk/reports/DCL_thm_report.pdf>). The finding are summarised in para 2.16:

> Our overall key finding was that the current disclosure regime is not being adhered to fully. On the one hand less than full compliance by police disclosure officers and crown prosecutors manifests itself in inadequately described material and a lack of either informed decision-making or recording reasons for decisions. On the other there is too often a decision not to apply the statutory test, so that blanket disclosure is allowed by the prosecution (or influenced or ordered by some courts) so that responsibility and added resource costs are passed to the defence (and Legal Aid budget). We recognise that for the disclosure regime to work properly there is a need for sufficient time, effort and attention to be devoted to the task by investigators and lawyers who fully understand the nature of it. At present this is too often the exception rather than the rule.

The next paragraph goes on to note that:

> The resource demands are without question considerable. The Association of Chief Police Officers (ACPO) considers the effort disproportionate, particularly in relation to cases dealt with in the magistrates' courts, and not fully workable within existing resources. Many CPS prosecutors consider that they do not have sufficient time to undertake the duties fully. Defence lawyers vary between an acceptance of proportionality and a desire in principle to see all unused material when they think it appropriate. The costs to the public through the funding of both public and private participants in the criminal process are considerable . . .

The researchers inspected a total of 152 files. The results are set out in para 2.19:

> The CPS complied with its duties of disclosure in the majority of cases. However, this was not universal and throughout this review we found frequent non compliance within the linked processes which support the disclosure regime. In the 152 cases in our file sample the initial duty of disclosure was properly complied with in 56.6 per cent (86). In the 72 magistrates' courts' cases the initial duty of disclosure was complied with in 55.0 per cent (40) and in the 80 Crown Court cases in 57.5 per cent (46). The duty of continuing disclosure was properly complied with in 71.3 per cent (62 of 87) of all relevant cases. This was made of up 81.8 per cent (nine of 11) of cases in the magistrates' courts and 69.7 per cent (53 of 76) in the Crown Court. The handling of sensitive material was properly complied with in 47.5 per cent (28 of 59) of cases, which was made up of 26.6 per cent (four of 15) of magistrates' courts' cases and 54.5 per cent (24 of 44) of those from the Crown Court.

In para 2.20, the Report notes that very few cases were seen where there was total compliance with all the procedures and guidance within the disclosure regime. However, in the cases examined 'this did not result in any findings of abuse of process or cases being dismissed prematurely'. The failures were either rectified on the morning of, or during the course of, the trial. At para 22, the Report says that in 8 cases (5.3 per cent), some aspects of the non-compliance resulted in adjournments and ineffective trials. The researchers also observed significant delays on the morning of trials whilst the trial advocates sorted out disclosure issues; they were told that these delays, often lasting for two to four hours or more, were not uncommon. This clearly has an adverse effect on the administration of justice.

An important issue is highlighted in para 2.34:

> It is arguable that the present arrangements require police officers to make decisions which they are not equipped to take. The police find it too onerous within their priorities and resources. The arrangements for describing material in schedules as the basis for prosecutorial consideration means that many decisions by crown prosecutors are taken on the basis of inadequate information; and they do not always examine sufficient material themselves or record the reasons for their decisions in appropriate detail.

The same paragraph goes on to argue that a single regime for all cases calls into question its proportionality within the field of summary justice in the magistrates' courts.

Paragraphs 2.38 and 2.39 of the Report make some detailed recommendations 'to secure improvement not only in actual compliance with CPIA, but also in *demonstrating* compliance with the Act'.

Chapter 9

Transferring cases to the Crown Court for trial

9.1 INTRODUCTION

We have already seen that all criminal cases begin in the magistrates' court (the requisition or summons requires the defendant to attend the magistrates' court, or else the defendant is arrested, charged and either bailed to appear at the magistrates' court or kept in custody and brought before the magistrates' court). If the offence is triable only in the Crown Court, it must be transferred to that court. If it is triable either way, it will be transferred to the Crown Court for trial only if the accused indicates a not guilty plea at the 'plea before venue' hearing (or gives no indication of plea and so is deemed to be indicating a not guilty plea) and the mode of trial hearing that follows results in a decision in favour of Crown Court trial (either because the magistrates decline jurisdiction or because the accused elects Crown Court trial).

9.1.1 Background

The original version of the Magistrates' Courts Act 1980 provided two alternative methods for transferring a case from the magistrates' court so that it could be tried in the Crown Court. The first, committal 'without consideration of the evidence' under s 6(2) of the Magistrates' Courts Act 1980, currently remains in force for either-way offences (but not indictable-only offences) and is described below. However, it is due to be abolished when the relevant provisions of the Criminal Justice Act 2003 come into force.

The second was a version of committal 'with consideration of the evidence', which was significantly different from the version of committal under s 6(1) of the 1980 Act which is described below (and which will also be abolished when the relevant provisions of the 2003 Act are implemented). Under the original version of s 6(1), the procedure for a committal with consideration of the evidence was very similar to that of an ordinary trial, with witnesses being subject to examination-in-chief, cross-examination and re-examination. A contemporaneous note of the evidence was taken down and, when each witness had finished testifying, the notes were read back to the witness, who was then given an opportunity to make any amendments. The witness then signed the notes (which became a 'deposition'). After the prosecution witnesses had given evidence, the defence had a chance to make a submission that there was no case to answer. If that submission was unsuccessful, the defence had the opportunity to call evidence and make a second submission of no case to answer (though it was very rare for the defence to call any evidence at this stage). If a submission of no case to answer was successful, the defendant was 'discharged'.

Under the Criminal Justice and Public Order Act 1994, a new system called 'transfer for trial' was set up to replace both forms of committal. The essence of the system was that the prosecution would serve a notice on the defendant and on the magistrates' court and then, following receipt of the notice, the magistrates would transfer the case to the Crown Court for trial. This procedure did not involve a hearing in court. It was, however, open to a defendant to make representations to the effect that the prosecution witness statements did not disclose a case to answer and in that case there could be a hearing. However, these provisions never came into force and were, under s 47 of the Criminal Procedure and Investigations Act (CPIA) 1996, replaced by a new system of committal proceedings set out in Sched 1 to the CPIA 1996.

Under this new system, committal without consideration of the evidence remained in its original version, but committal with consideration of the evidence was amended so that witness statements are read out but the witnesses do not attend the hearing.

A further change was made by the enactment of s 51 of the Crime and Disorder Act 1998, which abolished committal proceedings in the case of indictable-only offences, replacing them with a system under which the case was transferred to the Crown Court at a very early stage (often after only one appearance in the magistrates' court).

Finally, the Criminal Justice Act 2003 makes provision for the abolition of committal proceedings for either-way offences as well, applying the system of transfer in s 51 of the Crime and Disorder Act 1998 to either-way offences as well as indictable-only offences.

9.2 INDICTABLE-ONLY OFFENCES: TRANSFER UNDER S 51 OF THE CRIME AND DISORDER ACT 1998

Section 51 of the Crime and Disorder Act 1998 abolishes the requirement of committal proceedings in the case of offences which are triable only on indictment. The detailed provisions for the transfer of indictable-only offences to the Crown Court are set out in Sched 3 to the 1998 Act.

The version of s 51(1) in force at the time of writing provides that where an adult appears before a magistrates' court charged with an offence that is triable only on indictment, the court shall send him 'forthwith' to the Crown Court for trial for that offence, and (under s 51(1)(b)) for any either-way or summary offence with which he is charged and which appears to the court to be related to the indictable-only offence (in the case of a summary offence, it must also be punishable with imprisonment or involve obligatory or discretionary disqualification from driving: s 51(11)). In selecting which location of the Crown Court to send the defendant to for trial, the magistrates' court must have regard to the convenience of the defence, the prosecution and the witnesses; the desirability of expediting the trial; and any directions given by the Lord Chief Justice on the allocation of Crown Court business (s 51(10)).

In *R (Salubi) v Bow Street Magistrates' Court* [2002] EWHC 919 (Admin); [2002] 1 WLR 3073, it was held that the fact that a magistrate's court has a duty under s 51(1) to send an indictable-only case to the Crown Court 'forthwith' does not necessarily preclude it from exercising its jurisdiction to stay the proceedings as an abuse of process in an appropriate case, i.e. where the application for a stay is based on matters directly affecting the fairness of a trial before it, such as delay or unfair manipulation of court procedures (per Auld LJ at para 20). However, his Lordship added that it should be remembered that the onus is on the defence to establish bad faith or serious misconduct and that incorrect procedure based on lack of judgment does not suffice; in most cases the Crown Court is likely to be better equipped to make such value judgments (para 21).

Within 70 days (50 if the defendant is in custody) of the transfer, the prosecution must serve on the defence copies of the documents containing the evidence on which the charge(s) are based: reg 2 of the Crime and Disorder Act (Service of Prosecution Evidence) Regulations 2005 (SI 2005/902). In *Fehily v Governor of Wandsworth Prison* [2002] EWHC 1295; [2003] 1 Cr App R 10, it was held that the Crown Court has jurisdiction to extend time for service of the documents on an application by the prosecution even if the application is made after the expiry of the time limit.

9.2.1 Submissions of no case to answer

Paragraph 2(1) of Sched 3 says that at any time after the service of the documents containing the evidence on which the charge(s) are based but before he has been arraigned (i.e. before he is asked to plead guilty or not guilty), the defendant may apply, orally or in writing, to the Crown Court to which he has been sent for trial for the charge(s) to be dismissed. The application is heard by a judge, who is required (under para 2(2)) to dismiss a charge (and where the indictment has been preferred, to quash any count on the indictment relating to that charge) if it appears to him 'that the evidence against the applicant would not be sufficient for him to be properly convicted'.

Paragraph 2(3) says that an oral application may be made only if the applicant has given written notice of his intention to make the application. Paragraph 2(4) says that oral evidence may be given on such an application only with the leave of the judge, and that leave is only to be given where it is in the interests of justice to do so. When the amending provisions in the Criminal Justice Act 2003 come into force, the possibility of oral evidence being heard will be removed.

In *R (Snelgrove) v Crown Court at Woolwich* [2004] EWHC 2172 (Admin); [2005] 1 WLR 3223 (followed in *R (O) v Central Criminal Court* [2006] EWHC 256 (Admin)), it was held that a judge's decision to refuse to dismiss a case under para 2(1) is a matter relating to trial on indictment (an integral part of the trial process and an issue between the Crown and the defendant arising out of issues formulated by the charge), and therefore not susceptible to judicial review (as a result of s 29(3) of the Supreme Court Act 1981).

In *R (IRC) v Kingston Crown Court* [2001] EWHC 581 (Admin); [2001] 4 All ER 721, Stanley Burnton described the approach that a judge ought to take when dealing with such a submission of no case to answer in such a case. His Lordship said (at para 16) that the judge is required 'to take into account the whole of the evidence against a defendant'. Therefore, 'it is not appropriate for the judge to view any evidence in isolation from its context and other evidence'. His Lordship went on to reject the argument that the judge is bound to assume that a jury might make every possible inference capable of being drawn against the defendant. The key question for the judge is the sufficiency of the evidence:

That exercise requires the judge to assess the weight of the evidence. This is not to say that the judge is entitled to substitute himself for the jury. The question for him is not whether the defendant should be convicted on the evidence put forward by the prosecution, but the sufficiency of that evidence. Where the evidence is largely documentary, and the case depends on the inferences or conclusions to be drawn from it, the judge must assess the inferences or conclusions that the prosecution propose to ask the jury to draw from the documents, and decide whether it appears to him that the jury could properly draw those inferences and come to those conclusions.

The decision in *Snelgrove* means that the court in *R (IRC) v Crown Court at Kingston* should not have entertained the application for judicial review of the decision of the Crown Court judge, but the Court's ruling about the test to be applied in such cases remains valid nonetheless.

Paragraph 2(6) provides that where a charge has been dismissed under para 2(2), further proceedings on that charge can only be brought by means of an application to a High Court judge for a voluntary bill of indictment (see below). This provision excludes any application for judicial review by the prosecution.

9.2.2 Reporting restrictions

Paragraph 3 of Sched 3 imposes reporting restrictions. Under para 3(8), the only detail that may be reported about the case includes:

- the identity of the court and the name of the judge;
- the names, ages, home addresses and occupations of the accused and witnesses;
- the offence(s) with which the accused is charged;
- the names of counsel and solicitors engaged in the proceedings;
- where the proceedings are adjourned, the date and place to which they are adjourned;
- the arrangements as to bail;
- whether legal aid was granted.

Under para 3(2), the judge may lift the reporting restrictions. Where there are two or more accused and one of them objects to the lifting of the restrictions, the judge can make the order if, and only if, he is satisfied (after hearing the representations of the accused) that it is in the interests of justice to do so (para 3(3)).

Breach of the reporting restrictions is an offence punishable on summary conviction with a fine not exceeding level 5 on the standard scale, namely £5,000. Proceedings may only be instituted by, or with the consent, of the Attorney General (para 3(11)).

9.2.3 Linked offences

Paragraph 6 of Sched 3 deals with the power of the Crown Court to deal with cases where summary offences are sent to the Crown Court under s 51. All the related indictable-only and either-way offences appear on the indictment. If the defendant is convicted on that indictment, the Crown Court must first consider whether the summary offence is related to the indictable offence(s) that were sent for trial (para

6(2)). Paragraph 6(12) provides that an offence is related to another offence for these purposes 'if it arises out of circumstances which are the same as or connected with those giving rise to the other offence'. If the summary offence is related to the indictable offence for which the defendant was sent for trial, the court asks the defendant whether he pleads guilty or not guilty to the summary offence (para 6(3)). If he pleads guilty, the Crown Court will proceed to sentence him for that offence, but may not impose a greater sentence than a magistrates' court could have imposed (para 6(4))). If he pleads not guilty, the Crown Court has no further part to play in respect of that offence (para 6(5)), unless the prosecution indicate that they do not wish to proceed with the offence, in which case the Crown Court can formally dismiss it, with the effect that the defendant is acquitted of it (para 6(6)). Paragraph 6(8) makes it clear that the provisions of para 6 do not apply where the summary offence is tried on indictment under s 40 of the Criminal Justice Act 1988 (see Chapter 4).

In *R v Nembhard* [2002] EWCA Crim 134; (2002) 166 JP 363, the defendant was charged with attempted robbery (an indictable-only offence) and was sent to the Crown Court under s 51; he was also sent to the Crown Court (under s 51(1)(b)) for the summary offence of assaulting a police officer. The attempted robbery charge was subsequently replaced with a charge of attempted theft (an either-way offence). The defendant indicated a guilty plea to that charge, and so was deemed to have pleaded guilty to it (para 7(6) of Sched 3). The defendant also pleaded guilty to the summary offence (para 6(2) of Sched 3). The question to be resolved was whether the Crown Court had jurisdiction to sentence the defendant for the summary offence, given the fact that the indictable-only offence was no longer before the court. It was held that the court did have jurisdiction to deal with the summary offence in these circumstances (its sentencing powers being limited to those of the magistrates' court).

The procedure under para 6 is of course very similar to that set out in s 41 of the Criminal Justice Act 1988 (see Chapter 4) and achieves the same objectives. It is for this reason that s 41 of the 1988 Act will be repealed when the relevant provisions of the 2003 Act come into force, making s 51 applicable to either-way as well as indictable-only offences.

Paragraph 6(9) provides that where the Court of Appeal quashes a conviction for an indictable offence, it must also set aside any conviction for a summary offence where the accused was dealt with for that offence by the Crown Court following conviction for the indictable offence.

Section 51(2) currently provides that, where an adult has already been sent for trial under s 51(1) and then appears before a magistrates' court charged with a related either-way offence (or a related summary offence, provided that it carries imprisonment or disqualification from driving), the magistrates may send him to the Crown Court for trial for that either-way or summary offence.

Paragraph 7 of Sched 3 deals with the situation where the defendant is sent for trial for an indictable-only offence but is not arraigned for such an offence. If the indictment still contains any either-way offences, the Crown Court must go through the indication as to plea ('plea before venue') procedure. If the defendant indicates a guilty plea, he is deemed to have pleaded guilty, and the court proceeds to the sentencing stage (para 7(6)); if the defendant indicates a not guilty plea (or gives no indication), the court must go on to decide whether the offence is more suitable for summary trial or for trial on indictment (para 7(7)). Under para 9, the Crown Court has to deal with question of mode of trial in the same way as a magistrates' court has to deal with that issue (see Chapter 4); in particular, the key question is whether the sentence which a magistrates' court would have power to impose for the offence would be adequate. If the Crown Court decides that the case is suitable for summary trial, the defendant is asked whether or not he consents to summary trial; if he does, the case will be remitted to the magistrates' court for trial, and if he does not, the trial of the offence will take place in the Crown Court (para 10(3)). If the Crown Court decides that the offence is not suitable for summary trial, the trial will take place in the Crown Court (para 11).

In *R v Haye* [2002] EWCA Crim 2476, the defendant was charged with robbery. He was sent for trial at the Crown Court. The prosecution then dropped the charge of robbery and replaced it with a charge of theft. The defendant pleaded not guilty to theft. When the matter came on for trial, the defendant was re-arraigned on the theft charge and entered a guilty plea. However, he subsequently appealed against conviction on the ground that the procedure set out in para 7 of Sched 3 had not been followed prior to the arraignment on the theft charge; in particular, he complained that proper consideration had not been given to the question of whether he should be tried summarily or whether the Crown Court should continue to deal with the case. He argued that the proceedings which followed the plea of guilty were, therefore, a nullity. The Court of Appeal agreed, holding that any failure to comply with the statutory procedure in relation to the right of a defendant to make representations and/or to exercise choice as to mode of trial would render any subsequent hearing in respect of that offence *ultra vires*. In the present case, the defendant had been deprived of an opportunity of seeking to persuade the judge that summary trial would be more suitable and so the proceedings in relation to the theft charge were a nullity. It seems, however, that *Haye* is no longer good law. In *R v Thwaites* [2006] EWCA Crim 3235, the defendant was sent for trial to the Crown Court charged with conspiracy to handle stolen goods. However, he was arraigned and tried on an indictment containing counts of burglary, but no indictable-only offence. During the course of the trial, it was discovered that the judge had failed to conduct the mode of trial procedure required by para 7 in respect of the either-way charges on the indictment. The trial judge ruled that, had the correct procedure been followed, the case would have been found as suitable only for trial on indictment, and so the defendant had suffered no prejudice from the failure to conduct the mode of trial procedure. The Court of Appeal held, following *R v Ashton* [2006] EWCA Crim 794, that where a court is confronted by a procedural failure, it should first consider whether the intention of Parliament was that any act done following that procedural failure should be invalid. If not, the court should go on to consider the interests of justice and, in particular, whether there is a real possibility that either the prosecution or defence might suffer prejudice on account of the procedural failure. It follows that earlier authorities, such as *R v Haye*, are no longer good law. In the present case, there was no unfairness or prejudice to the defendant, who had received a fair trial.

9.2.4 Other defendants

Section 51(3) currently provides that where an adult is sent to the Crown Court for trial under s 51(1), and another adult, either then or on a subsequent occasion, appears at the magistrates' court charged jointly with him with an either-way offence which is related to the indictable-only offence, the court must (if it is the same occasion) or may (if it is a subsequent occasion) send the other adult to the Crown Court for trial for the either-way offence. Under s 51(4), the magistrates must also send him to the Crown Court for trial for any either-way or summary offence (in the case of the latter, provided that it is imprisonable or carries disqualification from driving) which is related to the indictable offence.

Under s 51(5), where an adult is sent for trial under s 51(1) or (3) and a juvenile is charged jointly with the adult with the indictable offence for which the adult has been sent for trial, the magistrates' court should only send the juvenile to the Crown Court for trial for the indictable offence 'if it considers it necessary in the interests of justice'. Under s 51(6), where a juvenile is sent for trial for an indictable offence under s 51(5), the court may also send him for trial for any related either-way or summary offence (in the case of the latter, provided that it is imprisonable or carries disqualification from driving).

9.3 EITHER-WAY OFFENCES: COMMITTAL PROCEEDINGS

Until they are abolished when the relevant provisions of the Criminal Justice Act 2003 come into force, committal proceedings have to be held in order for an either-way offence to be transferred from the magistrates' court to the Crown Court for trial. When magistrates are conducting committal proceedings, they are known as 'examining justices'. They have jurisdiction to hold committal proceedings no matter where in England and Wales the offence was allegedly committed.

Section 6 of the Magistrates' Courts Act 1980 currently provides for two methods of committing a defendant from the magistrates' court to the Crown Court. One method (under s 6(1) of the Magistrates' Courts Act 1980) involves a consideration of the evidence by the magistrates; the other (under s 6(2) of the 1980 Act) does not.

If there is more than one defendant, and the defendants are jointly charged, there will be joint committal proceedings. If the defendants are not jointly charged, joint committal proceedings only take place if the charges against the defendants are sufficiently linked that it is likely that they will be tried together in the Crown Court (*R v Camberwell Green Magistrates ex p Christie* [1978] QB 602).

Section 4(3) of the Magistrates' Courts Act 1980 provides that the defendant must be present at committal proceedings unless (under s 4(4)):

a   his disorderly conduct makes it impracticable for him to remain in court; or
b   he is unwell but is legally represented and consents to the proceedings taking place in his absence.

If the defendant fails without good cause to attend the committal proceedings, he will be in breach of his bail and a warrant for his arrest will be issued.

9.3.1 Committal without consideration of the evidence under s 6(2)

The vast majority of committals are without consideration of the evidence, under s 6(2). This form of committal is possible only if all of the following requirements are satisfied.

1   Under s 5A of the Magistrates' Courts Act 1980, the prosecution evidence must comprise written statements which comply with s 5B of the Act (which requires that the statement must be signed by its maker; the statement must contain a declaration by the maker that 'it is true to the best of my knowledge and belief and I make it knowing that, if it is tendered in evidence, I shall be liable to prosecution if I have wilfully stated in it anything which I know to be false or do not believe to be true'; and that a copy of the statement must be served on the (or each) defendant).

2   Under s 6(2)(a), the (or each) defendant must have a legal representative acting for him in the case.

3   Under s 6(2)(b), the defendant must not have requested the magistrates' court to consider a submission that there is insufficient evidence to put him on trial for the offence. If there is more than one defendant, committal under s 6(2) is not possible if any of them wishes to submit that there is no case to answer.

9.3.1.1 Procedure

Prior to the hearing, the prosecution will have served on the defendant(s) the bundle of prosecution witness statements (assuming these statements have not already been served on the defence pursuant to the 'advance information' rules in Pt 21 of the Criminal Procedure Rules – see Chapter 4).

At the hearing, the bundle of witness statements will be handed to the magistrates. The magistrates will not read the witness statements but will check that there is no submission on behalf of the defendant(s) that there is no case to answer. Assuming there is no such submission, the defendant will be committed to stand trial at the Crown Court and will be told the date of his first appearance at the Crown Court (for the Plea and Case Management Hearing). The magistrates will also consider ancillary matters such as bail.

Under para 12 of the Schedule to the Justices' Clerks Rules 2005 (SI 2005/545), a clerk may commit a defendant for trial provided that he is already on bail and is committed to the Crown Court on bail with the same conditions (if any) as before.

The presumption in favour of bail continues to apply where the defendant has been committed for trial to the Crown Court. Where the defendant was on bail prior to committal, bail will be continued unless the prosecution can satisfy the magistrates that any of the statutory reasons for withholding bail now apply. Where the defendant is in custody at the time of the committal proceedings, the committal hearing may present an opportunity to make a bail application, not least because the strength of the prosecution case (something which the magistrates have to consider under the Bail Act 1976) may well be much clearer. See Chapter 3 for a fuller discussion of bail.

9.3.1.2 Reporting restrictions

Section 8(1) of the Magistrates' Courts Act 1980 makes it unlawful to publish a report (written or broadcast) of any information other than that specified by s 8(4) of the Magistrates' Courts Act 1980. This allows the publication of only basic details about the case such as:

*   the identity of the court and the names of the examining justices;

- the names, addresses and occupations of the parties and witnesses and the ages of the accused and witnesses;
- the offence or offences, or a summary of them, with which the accused is or are charged;
- the names of the legal representatives engaged in the proceedings;
- any decision of the court to commit the accused or any of the accused for trial, and any decision of the court on the disposal of the case of any accused not committed;
- where the court commits the accused or any of the accused for trial, the charge or charges, or a summary of them, on which he is committed and the court to which he is committed;
- any arrangements as to bail;
- whether legal aid was granted.

These restrictions mean that any evidence read out, and any arguments put forward, at committal proceedings cannot be reported by the media. This is so that the people who eventually sit on the jury that tries the defendant will not be biased against the defendant because of unfavourable pre-trial publicity.

Breach of the restrictions is a summary offence carrying a maximum fine of £5,000 (s 8(5)).

Under s 8(3) of the Magistrates' Courts Act 1980, these restrictions apply to all stages of the case against the defendant prior to and including the committal and, unless lifted, also apply until the Crown Court trial is over.

Under s 8(2), these statutory reporting restrictions may be lifted by the magistrates. An application for the restrictions to be lifted may be made at the committal proceedings or at any remand hearing before those proceedings take place. If there is only one defendant and he asks for the reporting restrictions to be lifted, the magistrates must comply with this request and lift the restrictions (s 8(2)). If there is more than one defendant and one defendant asks for the reporting restrictions to be lifted, but another defendant opposes this application, the court may make the order if, and only if, it is satisfied, after hearing the representations of the accused, that it is in the interests of justice to do so (s 8(2A)). This means that the defendant who wants the restrictions lifted must show that it is in the interests of justice for this to be done (*R v Leeds Justices ex p Sykes* [1983] 1 WLR 132). A powerful argument in favour of lifting the restrictions is that publicity is necessary in order to encourage potential witnesses to come forward.

In *Sykes*, Griffiths LJ (at p 136) said that: 'If the reporting restrictions are to be lifted, then they are to be lifted in respect of the committal proceedings in their entirety. They cannot be lifted piecemeal.' Thus, if the restrictions are lifted, then all of the restrictions have to be lifted: the justices cannot pick and choose which of the restrictions are lifted and which remain. However, if the justices wish to lift the reporting restrictions which apply under s 8 of the Magistrates' Courts Act 1980 but nonetheless wish to prevent the full reporting of all the details of the case, they can lift the s 8 restrictions but then make an order under s 4(2) of the Contempt of Court Act 1981. This allows the court to order postponement of the contemporaneous reporting of some or all of any legal proceedings where such action is necessary to prevent a 'substantial risk of prejudice to the administration of justice'. Thus, if the s 8 restrictions have been lifted, the court can effectively define what may be reported by making an order under the Contempt of Court Act 1981.

In *R v Sherwood ex p Telegraph Group plc* [2001] EWCA Crim 1075; [2001] 1 WLR 1983, the Court of Appeal issued guidance on applications to postpone media coverage of court proceedings under s 4(2). The court should adopt a three-stage test, set out by Longmore J at para 22:

(1) The first question is whether reporting would give rise to a 'not insubstantial' risk of prejudice to the administration of justice in the relevant proceedings. If not, that will be the end of the matter.

(2) If such a risk is perceived to exist, then the second question arises: would a section 4(2) order eliminate it? If not, obviously there could be no necessity to impose such a ban. Again, that would be the end of the matter. On the other hand, even if the judge is satisfied that an order would achieve the objective, he or she would still have to consider whether the risk could satisfactorily be overcome by some less restrictive means. If so, it could not be said to be 'necessary' to take the more drastic approach . . .

(3) Suppose that the judge concludes that there is indeed no other way of eliminating the perceived risk of prejudice; it still does not follow necessarily that an order has to be made. The judge may still have to ask whether the degree of risk contemplated should be regarded as tolerable in the sense of being 'the lesser of two evils'. It is at this stage that value judgments may have to be made as to the priority between 'competing public interests' . . .

These guidelines are equally applicable to magistrates' courts.

Where the court is minded to make an order under the Contempt of Court Act 1981, it should listen to any representations made on behalf of the press (*R v Clerkenwell Magistrates ex p The Telegraph plc* [1993] QB 462 and para I.3.2 of the *Consolidated Practice Direction*).

9.3.2 Committal with consideration of the evidence

As we have seen, committal without consideration of the evidence under s 6(2) of the Magistrates' Courts Act 1980 is possible only if the defendant concedes that the prosecution witness statements disclose a case to answer against him. In those comparatively rare cases where the defendant does not concede that this is so, the magistrates have to consider the evidence against the defendant under s 6(1). Under s 6(1), the magistrates must commit the accused for trial if they are of the opinion that there is 'sufficient evidence to put him on trial by jury for any indictable offence'; otherwise, they must 'discharge' him.

Under s 5B(4), unless the committal is without consideration of the evidence under s 6(2), each prosecution witness statement must be 'read aloud at the hearing'. This is subject to the proviso that, 'where the court so directs an account shall be given orally of so much of any statement as is not read aloud'.

The hearing at which the magistrates consider whether the witness statements disclose a case to answer against the defendant begins with a short opening speech by the prosecutor. The prosecutor then reads out the written statements made by the witnesses upon whose evidence the prosecution case is based (or, with the permission of the court, the prosecutor summarises the effect of any part of a statement which is not read out loud). No witnesses will be called to give oral evidence. When the prosecution statements have been read to the court, the defence have the opportunity to submit that there is no case to answer on the basis of those witness statements; the prosecutor is entitled to reply to that submission in order to try to persuade the magistrates that there is a case to answer. Having heard the submission of no case to answer from the defence and a reply from the prosecution, the examining justices consider whether there is sufficient evidence to justify committing the defendant to stand trial at the Crown Court. The test they have to apply is whether there is a prima facie case against the accused. In other words, they have to ask themselves whether there is sufficient evidence on which a reasonable jury *could* convict him (not whether they *would* convict him).

Thus, the only evidence tendered at a s 6(1) committal is prosecution evidence, and all that evidence must be in writing. There is no defence evidence at all. This procedure for committal with consideration of the evidence is of comparatively little use to defendants. It will be very rare that the witness statements do not disclose a case to answer. Because the s 6(1) procedure does not allow oral evidence to be heard, there is no possibility of cross-examining a prosecution witness to probe potential weaknesses in their evidence. Furthermore (under paras 25 and 26 of Sched 1 to the CPIA 1996), ss 76 and 78 of the Police and Criminal Evidence Act 1984 (which enable a court to exclude prosecution evidence as being inadmissible) do not apply to committal proceedings.

In *Wilkinson v CPS* (1998) 162 JP 591, the Crown Prosecution Service (CPS) served a bundle of witness statements on the defendant. The defendant opted for committal proceedings with consideration of the evidence under s 6(1) of the Magistrates' Courts Act 1980. At the committal proceedings, the CPS relied solely on the statement of the alleged victim of the offence. The defence argued that the decision not to read any of the other witness statements created a false picture. The Divisional Court held that the prosecution may choose which witnesses to rely on for the purposes of committal proceedings. Lord Bingham of Cornhill CJ said that:

> the prosecutor need not tender before examining justices more than a small part of the evidence which may be called at the trial. It is enough for the prosecutor to show the examining justices that there is sufficient evidence to put a defendant on trial for an indictable offence provided always that, in deciding what evidence to tender, the prosecutor does not mislead the court or take unfair advantage of the defendant.

Under s 6(1), it is open to the magistrates to decide that there is insufficient evidence to justify the defendant being committed for trial in respect of the offence for which the prosecution seek committal but that there is sufficient evidence to justify committal for trial for another offence. Provided that the offence in respect of which the magistrates find a case to answer is an indictable offence (whether triable only in the Crown Court or triable either-way), they may commit him for trial for that offence. An example would be where the prosecution seek committal for murder but the magistrates decide that there is only sufficient evidence to support a charge of manslaughter. Where the justices are minded to hold that there is a case to answer on a charge other than the original one, the parties should be given the opportunity to address the bench before the magistrates reach a final decision (*R v Gloucester Magistrates Court ex p Chung* (1989) 153 JP 75).

Where the magistrates decide that there is insufficient evidence to justify a Crown Court trial in respect of any indictable offence, they must discharge the defendant. A 'discharge' at committal proceedings does not have the same effect as an acquittal, since the prosecution can re-prosecute the defendant for the same offence (something that cannot be done where the defendant has been acquitted following a trial).

If the prosecution wish to challenge a discharge, there are two ways of doing so:

1   The prosecution can bring fresh committal proceedings alleging the same offence (*R v Manchester City Stipendiary Magistrate ex p Snelson* [1977] 1 WLR 911). Normally, the prosecution will only bring fresh proceedings if, for example, the decision to discharge the defendant was clearly unreasonable, or new evidence against the accused comes to light. If the prosecution behave oppressively by bringing fresh committal proceedings where the defendant has already been discharged, the Divisional Court may (on an application for judicial review) grant an order of prohibition to prevent further committal proceedings which amount to an 'abuse of process' (*R v Horsham Justices ex p Reeves* (1980) 75 Cr App R 236 – see Chapter 1 for discussion of abuse of process).
2   Instead of bringing fresh committal proceedings, the prosecution may decide instead to seek a 'voluntary bill of indictment' (see below).

9.3.2.1 Challenging the decision to commit for trial under s 6(1)

In most cases, there will be no remedy for a defendant who thinks that he should not have been committed for trial; all he can do is wait for the Crown Court trial and make a submission that there is no case to answer at the close of the prosecution case.

If the defendant is committed for trial, there is no possibility of an appeal to the Divisional Court by way of case stated as there has been no final determination of the case (*Cragg v Lewes District Council* [1986] Crim LR 800).

In *R v Bedwellty Justices ex p Williams* [1997] AC 225, the House of Lords held that the decision of a magistrates' court to commit a defendant for trial is susceptible to judicial review. However, a committal will only be quashed in rare cases. Lord Cooke of Thorndon said (at p 236) that 'a committal by examining justices can and normally should be quashed in judicial review proceedings if there was before them no admissible evidence of the defendant's guilt'. His Lordship continued (at p 237):

> If justices have been of the opinion on admissible evidence that there is sufficient to put the accused on trial, I suggest that normally on a judicial review application a court will rightly be slow to interfere at that stage. The question will more appropriately be dealt with on a no case submission at the close of the prosecution evidence, when the worth of that evidence can be better assessed by a judge who has heard it, or even on a pre-trial application grounded on abuse of process.

However, his Lordship also left open the possibility of a committal being quashed where it was 'much influenced by inadmissible evidence, yet some admissible evidence remaining on which the justices might properly have committed, although it cannot be assumed that they would have done so' (as in *Neill v North Antrim Magistrates' Court* [1992] 1 WLR 1221 (HL).

It is submitted that, for the sake of consistency with the usual approach to judicial review, a decision based on admissible evidence that there is a prima facie case against the accused should be quashed only if no reasonable bench of magistrates could have come to the view that there was sufficient evidence (that is, the decision to commit the accused for trial was perverse).

9.4 NOTICES OF TRANSFER

A separate transfer procedure exists for two specific types of offence:

a   serious or complex fraud cases, and
b   cases where a child will be called as a witness at the trial.

The transfer of serious or complex cases is dealt with by s 4 of the Criminal Justice Act 1987, which will be replaced by s 51B of the Crime and Disorder Act 1998 (added by the Criminal Justice Act 2003), when that provision is implemented. Section 4 of the 1987 Act and s 51B of the 1998 Act are in virtually identical terms (set out below).

The provisions relating to child witnesses are dealt with by s 53 of the Criminal Justice Act 1991, which will be replaced by s 51C of the Crime and Disorder Act 1998 (added by the Criminal Justice Act 2003) when that provision is brought into force. The two provisions are in slightly different terms, and so both are set out below.

9.4.1 Serious or complex fraud cases

Section 51B(1) of the 1998 Act applies where the prosecution is brought by the Director of Public Prosecutions (DPP), the Director of the Serious Fraud Office, the Director of Revenue and Customs Prosecutions, or a Secretary of State (s 51B(9)), and the prosecutor:

> is of the opinion that the evidence of the offence charged—
>
> (a) is sufficient for the person charged to be put on trial for the offence; and
> (b) reveals a case of fraud of such seriousness or complexity that it is appropriate that the management of the case should without delay be taken over by the Crown Court.

The prosecuting authority serves a notice on the magistrates' court specifying the proposed place of trial (sub-s 3). The effect of such a notice is that the functions of the magistrates' court cease in respect of the case (sub-s (6)) and the Crown Court has jurisdiction to try the case on the basis of the notice.

9.4.2 Child witness cases

Section 53 of the Criminal Justice Act 1991 applies where the DPP (this includes any Crown Prosecutor):

> is of the opinion—

(a) that the evidence of the offence would be sufficient for the person charged to be committed for trial;

(b) that a child who is alleged—

(i) to be a person against whom the offence was committed; or

(ii) to have witnessed the commission of the offence,

will be called as a witness at the trial; and

(c) that, for the purpose of avoiding any prejudice to the welfare of the child, the case should be taken over and proceeded with without delay by the Crown Court.

In such a case, the DPP (or a Crown Prosecutor) can issue a notice of transfer which has the effect of sending the case to the Crown Court for trial.

Section 53 applies only to offences specified in s 32(2) of the Criminal Justice Act 1988 (see s 53(1)). In fact s 32 has been repealed but it is legitimate to assume (given the lack of any consequential amendment to s 53) that Parliament's intention is that the offences originally listed in s 32 continue to define the ambit of s 53 (sexual offences and offences involving an assault on, or injury or a threat of injury to, any person).

Section 51C of the Crime and Disorder Act 1998 applies where the DPP (again, this means any Crown Prosecutor):

. . . is of the opinion—

(a) that the evidence of the offence would be sufficient for the person charged to be put on trial for the offence;

(b) that a child would be called as a witness at the trial; and

(c) that, for the purpose of avoiding any prejudice to the welfare of the child, the case should be taken over and proceeded with without delay by the Crown Court.

Under sub-s (3), s 51C applies only to certain offences, including those which involve 'an assault on, or injury or a threat of injury to, a person' and offences under the Protection of Children Act 1978 and the Sexual Offences Act 2003.

As with s 51B, the effect of such a notice is that the functions of the magistrates' court cease in respect of the case and the Crown Court has jurisdiction to try the case on the basis of the notice.

Where the defendant is under 18 and the offence is one that falls within the ambit of s 91 of the Powers of Criminal Courts (Sentencing) Act 2000 (see Chapter 6), there should be no transfer to the Crown Court for trial unless the prosecution could conclude that a magistrates' court would be likely to find that the case falls within the requirements of seriousness that would enable them to commit the case to the Crown Court for trial (*R v T and K* [2001] 1 Cr App R 32 at para 37).

9.4.3 Submissions of no case

Where a notice of transfer has been served, the defendant may apply to a Crown Court judge to dismiss the charge(s) on the basis that there is no case to answer (s 6 of the Criminal Justice Act 1987; Sched 6, para 5, of the Criminal Justice Act 1991). There is no specific provision for such submissions in respect of transfers under ss 51B and 51C of the Crime and Disorder Act 1998, but it is submitted that it would be open to a court to construe para 2 of Sched 3 to that Act as applying to ss 51B and 51C, thus enabling a submission of no case to answer to be made.

9.4.4 Linked offences

In *R v Wrench* [1996] 1 Cr App R 340, it was held that, if one of the offences of which the defendant is accused is one to which the transfer provisions apply, then the procedure can also be used in respect of any other offences provided that they can validly be joined on the same indictment (see Chapter 10 for discussion of joinder of offences in an indictment). This aspect of *Wrench* is not affected by the disapproval of that case in *R v T and K* [2001] 1 Cr App R 32.

9.5 EXTENDING S 51 TO EITHER-WAY OFFENCES (THE CRIMINAL JUSTICE ACT 2003)

Lord Justice Auld, in his *Review of the Criminal Courts of England and Wales* (the *Auld Review*), concluded that committal proceedings should be abolished for either-way offences in the same way that they had been abolished for indictable-only offences, on the basis that they serve little useful purpose. Accordingly, Recommendation 35 was that either-way cases should be sent to the Crown Court in the same way as indictable-only cases. The Criminal Justice Act 2003 made provision for the amendment of s 51 (and Sched 3) of the Crime and Disorder Act. At the time of writing, however, these amendments had not been brought into force.

First of all, s 50A of the Crime and Disorder Act 1998 sets out the order in which the magistrates must take the various steps where the defendant is charged with an either-way offence (s 50A(1)). Under sub-s (3), the magistrates should take the following steps:

- a 'plea before venue' hearing;
- in the event of an indication of a 'not guilty' plea, the mode of trial procedure;
- if the magistrates decline jurisdiction or the defendant elects trial on indictment, transfer the case to the Crown Court under s 51.

When the amended version of s 51 of the Crime and Disorder Act 1998 is brought into force, it will cover all indictable offences (both indictable-only and either-way offences), so that the same transfer process will apply to all indictable offences.

The amended s 51(1) will provide that, where an adult (i.e. someone who has attained the age of 18) appears before a magistrates' court and any of the conditions set out in sub-s (2) is satisfied, the court shall send him 'forthwith' to the Crown Court for trial for the offence. The conditions in sub-s (2) are that:

- the offence is an offence triable only on indictment; or
- the offence is an triable either way, the defendant has indicated that he intends to plead not guilty (or has given no indication as to plea) and either the magistrates have declined jurisdiction or the defendant has chosen Crown Court trial; or

- a notice is given to the court under ss 51B or 51C (see above) in respect of the offence.

Under sub-s (3), where the court sends an adult for trial under s 51(1), it must also send him to the Crown Court for trial for any either-way or summary offence with which he is charged and which:

a   (if it is an either-way offence) appears to the court to be related to the offence that has been sent for trial; or
b   (if it is a summary offence) appears to the court to be related to the offence that has been sent for trial or to the either-way offence referred to in (a), and is punishable with imprisonment or involves obligatory or discretionary disqualification from driving.

Section 51E provides that:

. . .

(c)   an either-way offence is related to an indictable offence if the charge for the either-way offence could be joined in the same indictment as the charge for the indictable offence;
(d)   a summary offence is related to an indictable offence if it arises out of circumstances which are the same as or connected with those giving rise to the indictable offence.

Section 51E(c) thus applies the usual test for joinder of offences in an indictment (set out in r 14.2(3) of the Criminal Procedure Rules); this is discussed in Chapter 10. The test for summary offences (s 51E(d)) requires a weaker link between the offences.

Under s 51(4), the magistrates may send a defendant for trial in the Crown Court in respect of such a related either-way or summary offence if he subsequently appears in the magistrates' court charged with that offence after he has been sent for trial for the 'main' offence. Where an either-way offence is sent to the Crown Court under sub-s (3) or (4), this is done without first going through 'plea before venue' or mode of trial procedure. Any summary offence must be punishable with imprisonment or involve obligatory or discretionary disqualification from driving to fall within the ambit of sub-s (4).

Under s 51(5), where the magistrates send an adult defendant for trial under s 51 and another adult appears before the court on the same or a subsequent occasion charged jointly with the first adult with an either-way offence that appears to the court to be related to an offence for which the first adult was sent for trial, the court must (where it is the same occasion) and may (where it is a subsequent occasion) send the second adult forthwith to the Crown Court for trial for the either-way offence. Under s 51(6), where the court sends an adult for trial under sub-s (5), it must also send him to the Crown Court for trial for any either-way offence with which he is charged if that offence is related to the offence for which he is sent for trial (and for any summary offence, so long as it is punishable with imprisonment or disqualification from driving, that is related to any of the indictable offences that have been sent for trial).

Under s 51(7), if an adult is sent for trial under s 51, and a child or young person appears before the court on the same or a subsequent occasion charged jointly with the adult with an indictable offence for which the adult is sent for trial or with an indictable offence which appears to the court to be related to that offence, the court 'shall, if it considers it necessary in the interests of justice to do so, send the child or young person forthwith to the Crown Court for trial for the indictable offence'. Under sub-s (8), if a juvenile has been sent for trial under sub-s (7), it may at the same time send him to the Crown Court for trial for any indictable offence (or summary offence punishable with imprisonment or disqualification from driving) with which he is charged and which is related to the offence(s) for which he is sent for trial.

Where a summary offence is sent for trial under these provisions, the proceedings in respect of that offence are deemed to have been adjourned 'sine die', that is without fixing the time and place for their resumption. Any summary offences sent for trial under these provisions (unless they fall within the scope of s 40 of the Criminal Justice Act 1988 – see Chapter 4) will not appear on the indictment when the defendant is tried in the Crown Court, and so will not be tried by a jury.

Under para 6(2) of Sched 3, if the defendant is convicted on the indictment, the Crown Court then considers whether the summary offence is related to the indictable offence (or any of the indictable offences) for which he was sent for trial. In this context, an offence is related to another offence if it arises out of circumstances which are the same as or connected with those giving rise to the other offence (para 6(12)). If the court considers that the summary offence is so related, the defendant is asked whether he pleads guilty or not guilty (para 6(3)). If he pleads guilty, the Crown Court passes sentence in respect of the summary offence but its sentencing powers are limited to those of a magistrates' court (para 6(4)). Under para 6(5), if he pleads not guilty, the powers of the Crown Court cease in respect of the summary offence, save that (under para 6(6)) if the prosecution inform the court that they would not desire to submit evidence in respect of the summary offence, the court will dismiss that charge. It is submitted, however, that there would be nothing to prevent the Crown Court judge from trying the summary offence himself, exercising the power (conferred by s 66 of the Courts Act 2003) to sit as a District Judge.

Under s 51(13), the functions of a magistrates' court under s 51 may be discharged by a single justice.

Section 51D requires the provision of a notice which specifies the offence(s) for which the defendant has been sent for trial and specifying the location of the Crown Court at which he is to be tried. Under sub-s (4), when selecting the place of trial, the magistrates' court must have regard to:

a   the convenience of the defence, the prosecution and the witnesses;
b   the desirability of expediting the trial; and
c   any directions about allocation of Crown Court business given by the Lord Chief Justice under s 75(1) of the Supreme Court Act 1981.

9.6 REPORTING RESTRICTIONS

Section 52A of the Crime and Disorder Act 1998 (not in force at the time of writing) sets out reporting restrictions to prevent prejudicial pre-trial reportage of cases. Under s 52A(1), the restrictions apply to any allocation or sending proceedings, and cover both written reports and broadcast programmes. Section 52A(6) provides that it is unlawful to publish, or include in a broadcast programme, any matters except those specified in sub-s (7). In other words, s 52A(7) sets out the matters that can be reported, namely:

- the identity of the court and the name of the justice or justices;
- the name, age, home address and occupation of the accused;
- in the case of an accused charged with an offence in respect of which notice has been given to the court under s 51B (serious or complex fraud cases), any relevant business information (defined in sub-s (9) to include the name(s) and address(es) of the business(es) in question;
- the offence or offences, or a summary of them, with which the accused is or are charged;
- the names of counsel and solicitors engaged in the proceedings;
- details of any adjournments;
- the arrangements as to bail;
- whether legal aid was granted.

Under s 52A(2), the magistrates have the power to lift these reporting restrictions. Where the accused (or any of the accused) objects to the lifting of the restrictions, the court may lift the restrictions only if it is satisfied, after hearing representations from (each of) the accused, that it is in the interests of justice to do so (s 52A(3) and (4)). It is submitted that if there is only one defendant, and he asks for the restrictions to be lifted, the court should make an order lifting the restrictions.

Under s 52B, breach of the reporting restrictions set out in s 52A is a summary offence, punishable (under s 52B(2)) with a level 5 fine (currently up to £5,000). Proceedings under s 52B can only be brought by, or with the consent of, the Attorney General (s 52B(3)).

9.7 VOLUNTARY BILLS OF INDICTMENT

Another way of securing the Crown Court trial of a defendant is for the prosecution to seek a 'voluntary bill of indictment'. Essentially, this is an order by a High Court judge requiring the defendant to stand trial for the offence(s) specified in the order.

The obtaining of a voluntary bill of indictment is made possible by s 2(2)(b) of the Administration of Justice (Miscellaneous Provisions) Act 1933 and the procedure for doing so is set out in para IV.35 of the *Consolidated Practice Direction*.

To obtain a voluntary bill of indictment, the prosecution have to make a written application to a High Court judge. Paragraph IV.35.2 requires the prosecution to provide the judge with:

(a) a copy of any charges on which the defendant has been committed for trial;

(b) a copy of any charges on which his committal for trial was refused by the magistrates' court;

(c) a copy of any existing indictment which has been preferred in consequence of his committal;

(d) a summary of the evidence or other document which (i) identifies the counts in the proposed indictment on which he has been committed for trial (or which are substantially the same as charges on which he has been so committed), and (ii) in relation to each other count in the proposed indictment, identifies the pages in the accompanying statements and exhibits where the essential evidence said to support that count is to be found . . .

The Practice Direction also provides as follows:

IV.35.5 [Prosecutors are required]:

(a) on the making of application for consent to preferment of a voluntary bill, forthwith to give notice to the prospective defendant that such application has been made;

(b) at about the same time, to serve on the prospective defendant a copy of all the documents delivered to the judge (save to the extent that these have already been served on him);

(c) to inform the prospective defendant that he may make submissions in writing to the judge, provided that he does so within nine working days of the giving of notice under (a) above. . . . [T]hese procedures should be followed unless there are good grounds for not doing so, in which case prosecutors will inform the judge that the procedures have not been followed and seek his leave to dispense with all or any of them. Judges should not give leave to dispense unless good grounds are shown.

IV.35.6 A judge to whom application for consent to the preferment of a voluntary bill is made will, of course, wish to consider carefully the documents submitted by the prosecutor and any written submissions timeously made by the prospective defendant, and may properly seek any necessary amplification. The judge may invite oral submissions from either party, or accede to a request for an opportunity to make such oral submissions, if the judge considers it necessary or desirable to receive such oral submissions in order to make a sound and fair decision on the application. Any such oral submissions should be made on notice to the other party, who should be allowed to attend.

Paragraph IV.35.3 makes it clear that the voluntary bill procedure should not be used routinely and that consent should be given 'only where the interests of justice, rather than considerations of administrative convenience, require it'.

In *R v Raymond* [1981] QB 910, it was said that the proposed defendant had no right to attend the hearing of the application, although the judge did have a discretion to receive written representations. Watkins LJ, at p 921, said that there was no discretion to permit the making of oral representations. It is submitted that this no long represents the law, given that para 35.6 of the *Practice Direction* says that (as well as considering any written submissions), the judge may invite oral submissions from either party, or accede to a request for permission to make such oral submissions.

The main uses of this procedure are as follows:

a   Where committal proceedings have taken place and the defendant has been discharged, the voluntary bill procedure is an alternative to bringing fresh committal proceedings. However, in *Brooks v DPP of Jamaica* [1994] 1 AC 568, the Privy Council said that in a case where magistrates have discharged a defendant a judge should only direct the preferment of a voluntary bill of indictment in exceptional circumstances.

b   Where the defendant disrupts the committal proceedings but for some reason the justices decide not to use their power (under s 4 of the Magistrates' Courts Act 1980) to proceed in his absence, the voluntary bill procedure can be used.

c   Where one defendant has already been sent for trial and another suspect is arrested shortly before the trial of the first defendant, it is desirable that there be a joint trial. If it is undesirable to seek an adjournment of the first defendant's trial, the voluntary bill procedure is a speedy way of getting the second suspect to the Crown Court so that there can be a joint trial.

In *R v Muse* [2007] EWHC 2924 (QB), on an application for a voluntary bill of indictment, the CPS had decided not to rely on certain evidence. The judge found that there was insufficient evidence to put the defendants on trial. The CPS subsequently reconsidered the matter, and sought a voluntary bill of indictment in respect of the same incident on the basis of the evidence that it had chosen not to use at the previous hearing. It was held that it would be wrong in principle for the prosecution to be able to get round a decision that it did not like by inviting another judge to take a different view of the same material that had been before the judge who had dismissed the charges. However, a voluntary bill may be granted to correct a mistaken decision by the CPS or to reflect a change of mind within the CPS. The power to do so should be used sparingly, in truly exceptional cases. Relevant factors include the public interest in putting defendants on trial where there is sufficient evidence to justify doing so and the offence is a serious one. On the other hand, given the desirability of finality in criminal matters, it would not usually be in the interests of justice that persons should have to face a second prosecution in relation to the same offence if the evidence relied on was in fact available at the earlier hearing, particularly when a deliberate decision had been taken not to rely on that evidence. Each case has to be decided on its own facts.

If the judge directs that a voluntary bill of indictment be preferred (that is, orders the defendant to stand trial in the Crown Court), that decision cannot be challenged by way of judicial review (*R v Manchester Crown Court ex p Williams* (1990) 154 JP 589). Similarly, the judge who presides over the trial in the Crown Court cannot quash the indictment if he disagrees with the decision of the High Court judge (*R v Rothfield* (1937) 26 Cr App R 103 at 105, per Humphreys J). Moreover, the Court of Appeal will not inquire into the exercise of the discretion of a judge to direct the preferment of a voluntary bill, so long as it is clear that he had jurisdiction to entertain the application (*Rothfield*, at p 106).

Even though the decision of a High Court judge to issue a voluntary bill of indictment is not subject to judicial review, the decision of a prosecutor to *seek* a voluntary bill is susceptible to review, but only on very limited grounds, such as bad faith or alleged personal malice on the part of the prosecutor (*R v Inland Revenue Commissioners ex p Dhesi* (1995) *The Independent*, 14 August).

Simon Farrell and Daniel Friedman, in 'Voluntary bills of indictment: the administration of justice or a rubber stamp?' [1998] Crim LR 616, are highly critical of this procedure, contending that the defendant loses the right to make representations that (for example) he has been the victim of administrative inefficiency or that criminal proceedings have been initiated by way of misleading information, and they argue that in such cases the defendant should have the right to object to the initiation of criminal proceedings from the outset. They contend that the system of voluntary bills is defective because it does not readily allow for such objections. Indeed, recommendation 167 of the *Auld Review* was that the voluntary bill of indictment should be abolished, on the basis that it no longer serves a useful purpose (especially bearing in mind that its main use is to bypass committal proceedings, which have been abolished in the case of indictable-only offences and will be abolished in the case of either-way offences when the relevant provisions of the Criminal Justice Act 2003 come into force).

9.8 MOVING THE TRIAL

The justices will usually send the defendant to the nearest location of the Crown Court which is competent to deal with the case (see Pt III.21 of the *Consolidated Practice Direction*). It may be, however, that there are reasons why this may not be appropriate. For example, the offence with which the defendant is charged may have aroused such ill feeling locally that a fair trial at the nearest location of the Crown Court may not be possible. In such a case, the magistrates may be asked to send the defendant to a different Crown Court. If the magistrates do not accede to this application, or if no such application is made, there are two other ways of moving the trial:

- s 76(2) of the Supreme Court Act 1981 empowers an officer of the Crown Court to alter the place of trial;
- if the transfer is not effected administratively, either party may make an application to the Crown Court, under s 76(3) of the Supreme Court Act 1981, for the venue of the trial to be altered. Such applications are heard by a Crown Court judge, sitting in chambers.

9.9 CASE MANAGEMENT STANDARD DIRECTIONS WHEN CASE SENT TO CROWN COURT

The following directions apply unless the court specifies a different timetable:

- Within 70 days of the case being sent for trial (50 days if the defendant is in custody): prosecution to serve draft indictment, case papers and initial disclosure under the CIPA 1996 (see Chapter 8).
- 14 days after service of draft indictment etc: defence to notify prosecution of witness requirements, prosecution to serve any application for hearsay or defendant's bad character, defence to serve defence statement (including any alibi details) or notification of guilty plea, any application for hearsay/bad character, and any notice of application to dismiss charges.
- 28 days after service of draft indictment etc: prosecution to serve final draft indictment and any 'special measures' applications.
- 14 days after defence notification of prosecution witness requirements etc:

prosecution to serve responses to hearsay/bad character/dismissal of charges applications; defence to serve response to hearsay/bad character application by prosecution.

- 14 days after service of final draft indictment etc: defence to serve response to any prosecution application for special measures; prosecution and defence to notify Crown Court of names of trial advocate and time estimate; defence to notify Crown Court of non-availability of expert witnesses, with reasons; Witness Care Unit to notify Crown Court and prosecution of dates when witnesses required by defence are unavailable, with reasons.

Chapter 10

Indictments

10.1 INTRODUCTION

In this chapter, we examine the rules which govern the form and content of the indictment upon which a Crown Court trial is based. The key legislative provisions governing the form and content of indictments are to be found in ss 3 and 5 of the Indictments Act 1915, s 2 of the Administration of Justice (Miscellaneous Provisions) Act 1933. The rules setting out the practice relating to indictments may be found in Pt 14 of the Criminal Procedure Rules and para IV.34 of the *Consolidated Practice Direction*.

10.2 TERMINOLOGY

The indictment is simply the formal document setting out the charges which the defendant faces at the Crown Court. Each offence charged is known as a 'count'. An indictment is only valid when it is signed by an appropriate officer of the Crown Court. Until signed, it is a draft indictment.

10.3 DRAFTING THE INDICTMENT

It used to be the case that an officer of the Crown Court would draft the indictment. Nowadays, however, the Crown Prosecution Service (CPS) will usually send a draft indictment to the Crown Court and an officer of the court simply signs it. In most cases, the drafting is done by a Crown Prosecutor, although in difficult cases the Crown Prosecution Service may instruct a barrister to do the drafting.

Although the drafting of the indictment is the responsibility of the prosecution, under s 2(1) of the Administration of Justice (Miscellaneous Provisions) Act 1933, a proper officer of the Crown Court must sign the draft indictment before it can become an indictment.

In *R v Morais* [1988] 3 All ER 161, it was held by the Court of Appeal that this requirement is a mandatory requirement. It followed that a draft indictment which had been initialled by a High Court judge after giving leave to the prosecution to prefer a voluntary bill of indictment, but which had not been signed by the proper office of the court, was not a valid indictment. In *R v Clarke* [2006] EWCA Crim 1196 the Court of

Appeal held that *Morais* could not stand in light of the line of authority to the effect that procedural irregularities do not necessarily invalidate the proceedings that follow. However, when *Clarke* went to the House of Lords ([2008] UKHL 8; [2008] 1 WLR 338), it was held that the decision in *Morais* was correct. Lord Rodger of Earlsferry said (at para 26) that the only step which changes a bill of indictment (i.e. a draft indictment) into an indictment is the signing of the bill (draft) by the proper officer of the court. That step is accordingly 'indispensable'. In *Clarke* the indictment had been signed during the course of the trial but, as Lord Bingham put it (at para 21) this could not 'throw a blanket of legality over the invalid proceedings already conducted'. Accordingly, it is essential that the indictment is signed before the trial commences.

10.4 TIME LIMIT

Part 14.1 of the Criminal Procedure Rules provides that:

(1) The prosecutor must serve a draft indictment on the Crown Court officer not more than 28 days after—

  (a) service on the defendant and on the Crown Court officer of copies of the documents containing the evidence on which the charge or charges are based, in a case where the defendant is sent for trial;
  (b) a High Court judge gives permission to serve a draft indictment;
  (c) the Court of Appeal orders a retrial; or
  (d) the committal or transfer of the defendant for trial.

(2) The Crown Court may extend the time limit, even after it has expired.
(3) Unless the Crown Court otherwise directs, the court officer must—

  (a) sign and date the draft, which then becomes an indictment; and
  (b) serve a copy of the indictment on all parties.

Thus, the draft indictment has to be served on the Crown Court within 28 days of the case being sent from the magistrates' court to the Crown Court. This 28-day period may be extended by the court (and an application for an extension of time can be made even after the time limit has expired).

In any event, even if the indictment is not signed within the 28-day period, this does not give rise to a ground of appeal against conviction (*R v Sheerin* (1976) 64 Cr App R 68; *R v Soffe* (1982) 75 Cr App R 133). It must, however, be signed before the start of the trial.

10.5 FORM OF INDICTMENT

Section 3 of the Indictments Act 1915 provides that:

(1) Every indictment shall contain, and shall be sufficient if it contains, a statement of the specific offence or offences with which the accused person is charged, together with

such particulars as may be necessary for giving reasonable information as to the nature of the charge.

(2) Notwithstanding any rule or law or practice, an indictment shall, subject to the provisions of this Act, not be open to objection in respect of its form or contents if it is framed in accordance with the rules under this Act.

More detailed rules on the form and content of an indictment are to be found in r 14.2 of the Criminal Procedure Rules. This provides as follows:

(1) An indictment must be in one of the forms set out in the Practice Direction and must contain, in a paragraph called a 'count'—

   (a) a statement of the offence charged that—
      (i) describes the offence in ordinary language, and
      (ii) identifies any legislation that creates it; and
   (b) such particulars of the conduct constituting the commission of the offence as to make clear what the prosecutor alleges against the defendant.

(2) More than one incident of the commission of the offence may be included in a count if those incidents taken together amount to a course of conduct having regard to the time, place or purpose of commission.

(3) An indictment may contain more than one count if all the offences charged—

   (a) are founded on the same facts; or
   (b) form or are a part of a series of offences of the same or a similar character.

(4) The counts must be numbered consecutively.

(5) An indictment may contain—

   (a) any count charging substantially the same offence as one—
      (i) specified in the notice of the offence or offences for which the defendant was sent for trial,
      (ii) on which the defendant was committed for trial, or
      (iii) specified in the notice of transfer given by the prosecutor; and
   (b) any other count based on the prosecution evidence already served which the Crown Court may try.

The 'statement of offence' is a brief description of the offence; if the offence is a statutory one, the relevant section of the statute will be given. The 'particulars of offence' summarise what is alleged against the defendant. The particulars should set out who is charged, the date of the alleged offence, the act allegedly done, an allegation of *mens rea* (that is, the mental element of the crime), and the identity of the alleged victim.

Where more than one offence is charged in an indictment, the statement and particulars of each offence have to be set out in a separate paragraph, known as a 'count'.

Precedents to assist in the drafting of indictments can be found in *Blackstone's Criminal Practice* and in *Archbold*.

An indictment therefore looks like this:

No 08/01321

INDICTMENT
THE CROWN COURT AT CROYDON
THE QUEEN v VICTOR JAMES WARD

VICTOR JAMES WARD is charged as follows:

COUNT 1
Statement of Offence

Burglary, contrary to s 9(1)(b) of the Theft Act 1968. Particulars of Offence VICTOR
JAMES WARD, on 2 September 2008, having entered as a trespasser a building known as 17
Maidwell Avenue, Croydon, stole therein a television set and a video recorder, the
property of John Green.

COUNT 2
Statement of Offence

Unlawful wounding, contrary to section 20 of the Offences Against the Person Act 1861.

Particulars of Offence

VICTOR JAMES WARD, on 2 September 2008, unlawfully and maliciously wounded John
Green.

BR SMITH
Officer of the Crown Court
Date: 1 December 2008

Where the date of the commission of the offence is not known for certain, it is
usual to say either 'on or about [date]' or 'on a date unknown between [day before
the earliest date when the offence could have been committed] and [day after the
latest date when the offence could have been committed]'. If the date is incorrectly
stated, that is not fatal to the prosecution case since the indictment can be amended,
though the defendant may well be entitled to an adjournment if necessary to
prepare his defence on the basis of the new date (cf *Wright v Nicholson* [1970]
1 WLR 142).

In *R v Ike* [1996] STC 391, the defendant was charged with tax offences relating
to VAT. On appeal against conviction, she argued that the indictment was defective
because it failed to spell out the *mens rea* which the prosecution had to prove in relation
to acts which she was alleged to have done. The Court of Appeal held that the indictment should indeed have spelled out the necessary *mens rea* and that those words
should have appeared before any reference to the conduct which was alleged (so each
count should have alleged that, with the necessary *mens rea*, the defendant carried out
the *actus reus*). However, the jury had been correctly directed on the mental element of
the offences and so the conviction was not unsafe; the appeal was therefore dismissed.
In *R v Hodgson* [2008] EWCA Crim 895, the accused were charged with wounding with

intent contrary to s 18 of the Offences Against the Person Act 1861. The form of the indictment was defective in that it did not spell out the mental element of the offence in the usual manner. However, the Court of Appeal held that it did not follow that the indictment failed to give reasonable information as to the nature of the charge as required by r 14.2(1) of the Criminal Procedure Rules.

Where there is more than one defendant, the order in which the names of defendants are placed on an indictment is the responsibility of the prosecutor, who has a discretion as to that order. The mere fact that a co-defendant named later on the indictment might give evidence adverse to a defendant after that defendant has given evidence provides no basis for regarding the prosecution's exercise of its discretion in drafting the indictment as improper (*R v Cairns* [2002] EWCA Crim 2838; [2003] 1 WLR 796).

Each count in an indictment is a separate entity. In *R v O'Neill* [2003] EWCA Crim 411, the defendant was charged in an indictment which included a count that was defective, in that it was based on a statutory provision which had not been in force at the relevant time. The Court of Appeal confirmed that even if one count charges an offence not known to the law, any other counts in the same indictment can stand and need not be quashed.

10.6 THE RULE AGAINST DUPLICITY

Subject to r 14.2(2) (quoted above), each count in an indictment should allege only one offence.

The specimen indictment shown above has as its first count an allegation of burglary involving the theft of two items. This is proper, as the activity of burglary can and usually will involve more than one act. Where the acts form part of 'the same transaction', they may properly be said to amount to a single offence (*DPP v Merriman* [1973] AC 584). Indeed r 14.2(2) makes specific provision for cases where 'those incidents taken together amount to a course of conduct'. This means, for example, that if a defendant steals a number of items from the same person at more or less the same time, it will be regarded as a single act of theft (*R v Wilson* (1979) 69 Cr App R 83). In that case, the defendant was charged with stealing three jumpers, a pair of shorts, two pairs of trousers, four dimmer switches and a cassette tape from Debenhams (count 1) and stealing eight records and a bottle of aftershave from Boots (count 2). It was argued on behalf of the defendant that both counts were bad for duplicity as the stolen items came from different departments of the stores in question. The argument was rejected on the basis that each count alleged acts forming a single activity, and so neither count was duplicitous. Thus, where a series of acts in effect amounts to a single course of conduct, those acts can validly be regarded as amounting to a single offence. For example, in *DPP v McCabe* (1993) 157 JP 443, it was held by the Divisional Court that an allegation that the defendant stole 76 library books between two specified dates was a single offence and so a count alleging this theft was not bad for duplicity.

Paragraph IV.34.10 of the *Consolidated Practice Direction* deals with indictments where a single count charges more than one incident. It provides as follows:

> Rule 14.2(2) of the Criminal Procedure Rules allows a single count to allege more than one incident of the commission of an offence in certain circumstances. Each incident must be of

the same offence. The circumstances in which such a count may be appropriate include, but are not limited to, the following:

(a) the victim on each occasion was the same, or there was no identifiable individual victim as, for example, in a case of the unlawful importation of controlled drugs or of money laundering;

(b) the alleged incidents involved a marked degree of repetition in the method employed or in their location, or both;

(c) the alleged incidents took place over a clearly defined period, typically (but not necessarily) no more than about a year;

(d) in any event, the defence is such as to apply to every alleged incident without differentiation. Where what is in issue differs between different incidents, a single 'multiple incidents' count will not be appropriate, though it may be appropriate to use two or more such counts according to the circumstances and to the issues raised by the defence.

Where there are several victims, it is usual to have a separate count for each victim, as in *R v Mansfield* [1977] 1 WLR 1102, where the defendant was charged with seven different counts of murder arising from a single act of arson. This is so even though a single count would have been valid in that particular case, since only one act was involved.

However, a count which alleged that the defendant stole £200 from A one day and £200 from B the next would certainly be duplicitous because there are two separate acts of theft.

If a section of a statute creates one offence which may be committed in a number of ways, the alternatives may be charged in a single count (although it might sometimes be better to charge them in separate counts if this would make the task of the jury easier). If, however, the section creates more than one offence, each offence that the prosecution wish the jury to consider must be put in a separate count.

An example of where this might arise is to be found in respect of handling stolen goods contrary to s 22 of the Theft Act 1968. Handling effectively comprises two different offences. The first is that of dishonestly receiving stolen goods; the second comprises all the other ways of handling (these ways are all different ways of committing a single offence). The various ways of committing the second form of handling can, and usually will, be charged in a single count. However, a count which charged receiving and the other forms of handling together would be regarded as defective. Thus, there are two basic handling counts; either:

* AB on [date] dishonestly received stolen goods, namely [description of goods], knowing or believing the same to be stolen goods; or
* AB on [date] dishonestly undertook or assisted in the retention, removal, disposal or realisation of stolen goods, namely [description of goods], by or for the benefit of another, or dishonestly arranged to do so, knowing or believing the same to be stolen goods.

If a count alleges more than one offence and the defence raise an objection to this, the prosecution will usually seek leave to amend the indictment under s 5(1) of the Indictments Act 1915 to split the 'duplicitous' count into two separate counts.

Even if a count includes allegations which do not amount to a single course of conduct (as permitted by r 14.2(2)), this does not necessarily mean that a conviction would be quashed. In *R v Levantiz* [1999] 1 Cr App R 465, several discrete acts of supplying a controlled drug were alleged in a single count in the indictment. The Court of Appeal held (following *R v Thompson* [1914] 2 KB 99) that, where a count in an indictment is duplicitous (that is, charges more than one offence), that count is not void and the conviction is not necessarily unsafe. It follows that an appeal against conviction on that count can be dismissed if the Court of Appeal decides that the conviction is safe despite the irregularity in the indictment. In deciding whether a conviction based on a duplicitous count is safe, it is submitted that the court should ask itself whether the accused was prejudiced by the duplicitous nature of the count. If it is the case that the defendant must have been guilty of everything alleged in the count – or nothing alleged in the count – it is unlikely that he would have been prejudiced by the duplicity.

In *R v Marchese* [2008] EWCA Crim 389, the Court of Appeal reiterated that an indictment is not rendered a nullity because a count in that indictment is duplicitous, and so the fact that a count is held to be duplicitous does not necessarily require the quashing of the conviction.

10.7 CO-DEFENDANTS

Where there is alleged to have been more than one participant in the offence, all the parties to an offence may be joined in a single count (*DPP v Merriman* [1973] AC 584). The jury will be directed that they must consider each defendant separately, so where there are two defendants, they may acquit both defendants, convict both defendants or convict one and acquit the other.

10.7.1 Secondary parties

Secondary parties (that is, those who aid, abet, counsel or procure the commission of the offence) are usually charged as principal offenders (s 8 of the Accessories and Abettors Act 1861). Thus, in a burglary case where one person enters the premises and another person stays outside as a look-out, both will usually be charged with burglary contrary to s 9(1)(b) of the Theft Act 1968 and the particulars will allege that both entered the premises and stole. Similarly, the getaway driver in a robbery will usually be charged in the same count as the defendants who actually carry out the robbery.

The fact that a defendant is really alleged to have been a secondary party is thus not apparent from the indictment itself, but is made clear to the jury in the course of the prosecution opening speech.

Nonetheless, there will be cases where the prosecution choose to draft a count which specifically alleges aiding and abetting.

10.8 JOINDER OF COUNTS

A single indictment may (and often will) allege several different offences (each set out in a different 'count'). An indictment which contains two or more counts must comply with r 14.2(3). The effect of this rule is that all the counts on the indictment must be either:

- founded on the same facts; or
- form, or be part of, a series of offences of the same or a similar character.

Joinder is permissible if either or these two 'limbs' is satisfied.

10.8.1 Same facts

Two offences may be said to be founded on the same facts if either:

- they arise from a single incident or are part of the same 'transaction'. For example, in the specimen indictment shown above, the defendant wounds the householder in the course of committing the burglary. The same principles would apply where someone steals a car in order to use it as a getaway vehicle in a robbery: the taking of the car and the robbery would be charged in a single indictment. Similarly, someone who causes criminal damage in order to commit a burglary may be charged with both offences in a single indictment (the criminal damage being charged pursuant to s 40 of the Criminal Justice Act 1988 if the value of the damage is less than £5,000); or
- a later offence would not have been committed but for the commission of an earlier offence. For example, see *R v Barrell and Wilson* (1979) 69 Cr App R 250, where a defendant was charged with affray and assault (both arising out of a single incident) and with attempting to pervert the course of justice, as the defendant had tried to bribe witnesses to the affray and assault not to give evidence against him. The defence objected to the joinder of the latter charge. However, the Court of Appeal held that, because the attempt at bribery would not have taken place but for the charges arising out of the affray, the charges all had a 'common factual origin' (per Shaw LJ at p 253). It was held, therefore, that all these charges could appear in a single indictment.

10.8.1.1 Contradictory counts

In *R v Bellman* [1989] AC 836, the House of Lords held that counts can be joined in an indictment even if they are mutually contradictory. The defendant in that case was charged with conspiracy to evade the prohibition on the importation of controlled drugs and with obtaining property by deception. If the defendant had intended to import the drugs, he was guilty of the first offence; if he took the money from the buyers but did not intend to import the drugs to give to them, he was guilty of the second offence. The House of Lords ruled that these inconsistent allegations could properly appear in a single indictment.

Another example is *R v Shelton* (1986) 83 Cr App R 379, where the defendant was charged with two counts, one alleging theft and the other alleging the second form of handling. The Court of Appeal said that it did not matter that these allegations were contradictory.

It will generally be unusual for the prosecution to include inconsistent counts in an indictment. The jury will be directed to consider each count separately. A conviction in respect of a given count is only possible if the jury are satisfied beyond reasonable doubt that the defendant is guilty under that particular count. If the prosecution are making contradictory allegations, the jury may well think that the defendant is guilty of something but may not be satisfied so that they are sure that he is guilty of a particular offence.

10.8.2 Same or similar character

In *Ludlow v Metropolitan Police Commissioner* [1971] AC 29, the House of Lords had to consider whether two offences formed, or were part of, a series of offences of the same or a similar character. The defendant faced two allegations, one of attempted theft on 20 August 1968 (the theft allegedly taking place at a public house in Acton) and one of robbery on 5 September 1968 (the allegation arising out of an altercation with a barman in a public house in Acton). The House of Lords held that these two allegations could be made in the same indictment. In coming to this conclusion, the following points were made:

- two offences are capable of amounting to a 'series';
- for counts to be joined in an indictment, there must be a 'nexus' between them both in law and in fact. In other words, the offences must be both legally and factually similar;
- the evidence in respect of one count need not be admissible by way of similar fact evidence in respect of the other count(s).

In *R v Harward* (1981) 73 Cr App R 168, the defendant was charged with conspiracy to defraud and with handling stolen goods. Despite the legal similarity (dishonesty), there was no factual link between the offences (apart from the fact that the stolen goods were found when his home was being searched during the fraud investigation). Two offences do not form (part of) a series of offences merely because evidence relating to one offence is uncovered during the investigation into the other. The indictment was therefore defective.

In *R v Marsh* (1985) 83 Cr App R 165, the defendant was charged with criminal damage and reckless driving (the same victim) and assault (a different victim). It was held that criminal damage and reckless driving were validly joined as they arose out of a single act (causing damage by using the car). However, there was an insufficient legal link between either of these offences and the assault, and the only factual link between those offences was the use of violence. The addition of the assault charge thus rendered the indictment defective. Mustill LJ (at p 171) said that:

> those faced with the question of joinder should approach the matter by seeking to ascertain whether or not the counts have similar or dissimilar legal characteristics, whether or not they have similar or dissimilar factual characteristics, and whether or not in all the circumstances such features of similarity as are found enable the offences to be properly described as a series.

In *R v McGlinchey* (1983) 78 Cr App R 282, it was held that two counts alleging handling stolen goods were correctly joined. The first alleged receiving photographic equipment on 19 July 1982 and the second receiving a stolen credit card on 2 September 1982. There was clearly a legal nexus, in that the same offence was alleged in both counts. The only factual nexus was that they were committed two months apart, but that was held to be sufficient. French J (at p 285) considered the rules on joinder of counts and said:

> All that is necessary to satisfy the rule is that the offences should exhibit such similar features that they can conveniently be tried together in the general interests of justice, including those of the defendants, the Crown, the witnesses and the public.

In *R v Mariou* [1992] Crim LR 511, the defendant was charged with burglary, robbery, aggravated burglary and possession of a firearm with intent to endanger life. The Court of Appeal upheld the joinder of these counts as the burglary and robbery charges were legally similar and were all linked by violent entry into a dwelling-house and the subsequent use or threat of violence. The firearms offence was validly joined as it arose on the same facts as the others – the gun was carried when the offences were being committed.

In *R v Baird* (1993) 97 Cr App R 308, the defendant was charged with sexual assault on two different boys. The alleged offences were separated by a period of nine years. The Court of Appeal held that the offences nevertheless formed a series and so could validly be joined in a single indictment. The court said that coincidence in point of time, like a coincidence in point of location, may be an important factor in determining whether or not particular offences can be regarded as being or forming part of a series, but every case must depend upon its own facts, the correct approach being to discover whether the alleged offences claimed by the prosecution to form part of a series are linked by a sufficiently close nexus to bring them within the Rule (per Nolan LJ at 313–4).

In *R v Williams* [1993] Crim LR 533, the defendant was charged with sexual assault on a 13-year-old girl on 8 June 1991 and with false imprisonment of the same girl on 13 June 1991. It was held that, had these two offences been committed on the same occasion, they could have been joined in a single indictment; however, they were different incidents (it was the same victim but different offences, thus lacking a legal nexus) and so they could not be validly joined on the same indictment.

10.8.3 Joinder of defendants

The provisions of r 14.2(3) apply whether the counts are against the same defendant or different defendants; all that matters is that the offences themselves are sufficiently linked to satisfy the provisions of that rule. Thus, a number of defendants may be joined in the same indictment even if no count applies to all of them, provided that the counts are sufficiently linked for the rule to be satisfied. For example, the person who is alleged to have handled the proceeds of a burglary could be charged in the same indictment as the alleged burglar.

For example, in *R v Assim* [1966] 2 QB 249, there were two defendants, a receptionist and a doorman at a night club. The receptionist was charged with wounding one person (s 20 of the Offences Against the Person Act 1861) and the doorman with assault occasioning actual bodily harm (s 47 of the same Act) against a different person. Even though there was no joint count in the indictment, the indictment was held to be valid as there was sufficient link in time and place: both victims had tried to leave without paying; D1 allegedly attacked one victim with a knife; the other victim intervened and was attacked by D2. Thus, there was sufficient legal and factual nexus for the two counts to be joined in the same indictment. Sachs J (at p 260) said:

> Where . . . the matters which constitute the individual offences of the several offenders are upon the available evidence so related, whether in time or by other factors, that the interests of justice are best served by their being tried together, then they can properly be the subject of counts in one indictment and can, subject always to the discretion of the court, be tried together. Such a rule, of course, includes cases where there is evidence that several offenders acted in concert but is not limited to such cases.

10.8.4 Joinder of summary offences under s 40 of the Criminal Justice Act 1988

Section 40 of the Criminal Justice Act 1988 enables a specified summary offence (including common assault, taking a motor vehicle or other conveyance without authority, driving a motor vehicle while disqualified, and criminal damages where the value of the damage is less than £5,000) to be added to an indictment if it:

(a) is founded on the same facts or evidence as a count charging an indictable offence; or
(b) is part of a series of offences of the same or similar character as an indictable offence which is also charged.

This requirement mirrors the wording of r 14.2(3).

In *R v Callaghan* (1992) 94 Cr App R 226, the appellant was charged with six offences: one count of arson (an indictable offence), two counts of theft (an indictable offence), two counts of taking a conveyance without the consent of the owner (a summary offence to which s 40 of the Criminal Justice Act 1988 applies) and one count of driving while disqualified (a summary offence to which s 40 applies). The two counts of taking a conveyance without the owner's consent were held to be properly joined since they were of the same or a similar character to the two theft charges (which both involved motor vehicles). However, the charge of driving while disqualified related to his driving of a vehicle which he had taken without consent (the subject of one of the other counts on the indictment). The Court of Appeal held that the charge of driving while disqualified should not have been included in the indictment, since that charge was not linked with an *indictable* offence. The only link was with a summary offence validly added under s 40, and that was held not to be enough.

10.9 DISCRETION TO ORDER SEPARATE TRIALS

Where an indictment validly alleges that a defendant committed more than one offence or alleges that more than one defendant was involved in the offence(s), the judge may nevertheless order that separate trials take place.

10.9.1 Separate counts

Section 5(3) of the Indictments Act 1915 provides:

> Where, before trial, or at any stage of a trial, the court is of the opinion that a person accused may be prejudiced or embarrassed in his defence by reason of being charged with more than one offence in the same indictment, or that for any other reason it is desirable to direct that the person should be tried separately for any one or more offences charged in an indictment, the court may order a separate trial of any count or counts of such indictment.

This provision thus empowers a Crown Court judge to order separate trials of offences on an indictment. This power is sometimes known as 'severing the indictment'. It applies both to a defendant who seeks separate trials for a number of offences and to co-defendants who seek separate trials. This power applies only to an indictment that complies with r 14.2(3), and so this power to 'sever' cannot be used to cure misjoinder of counts (*R v Newland* [1988] QB 402).

The power to 'sever' applies if the defendant can show that he would be 'prejudiced or embarrassed in his defence' or there is some other good reason. In other words, the defendant has to show that he will not receive a fair trial if all the counts are dealt with together.

In *Ludlow v Metropolitan Police Commissioner* [1971] AC 29, the House of Lords said that if the counts are validly joined, those counts should usually be tried together and the defendant must show a 'special feature' (per Lord Pearson at p 41) in the case if there are to be separate trials. In other words, the burden rests on the defendant to show that exceptional circumstances merit separate trials.

In *R v Christou* [1997] AC 117, where the defendant was charged with sexual offences against more than one person, Lord Taylor of Gosforth CJ said (at p 129) that:

> the essential criterion is the achievement of a fair resolution of the issues. That requires fairness to the accused but also to the prosecution and those involved in it. Some, but by no means an exhaustive list, of the factors which may need to be considered are:- how discrete or inter-related are the facts giving rise to the counts; the impact of ordering two or more trials on the defendant and his family, on the victims and their families, on press publicity; and importantly, whether directions the judge can give to the jury will suffice to secure a fair trial if the counts are tried together. In regard to that last factor, jury trials are conducted on the basis that the judge's directions of law are to be applied faithfully.

In *R v Trew* [1996] 2 Cr App R 138, the defendant was charged with attacks on four different women. Only one of the women (B) picked him out at an identification parade. The trial judge refused to sever the counts relating to the attack on B from the counts relating to the other attacks. The Court of Appeal said that the judge should have taken account of the fact that evidence relating to the attack on B was inadmissible as regards the other alleged attacks. It followed that the presence of all the counts in the same indictment would have the sole effect of making it more likely that the appellant would be convicted. Accordingly, the appeal was allowed and a retrial ordered.

Another example may be found in *R v D* [2003] EWCA Crim 2424; [2004] 1 Cr App

R 19; Nelson J (at para 26) said that where charges involving different victims are not severed:

> it is essential that the jury is directed in clear terms that the evidence on each set of allegations is to be treated separately and that the evidence in relation to an allegation in respect of one victim cannot be treated as proof of an allegation against the other victim.

Arguments in favour of severance which may succeed in appropriate cases include the following:

- the jury may find it difficult to disentangle the evidence, with the risk that they will rely on evidence which does not relate to a particular count when considering that count;
- one count is of a nature likely to arouse hostility in the minds of the jurors, and so they may not approach the other counts with open minds;
- the evidence on one count is strong but on the other is weak, and there is a risk that the jury will assume the defendant is guilty of the second count merely because they find him guilty of the first;
- the evidence in respect of each count is weak, but the jury may convict on the basis that there is 'no smoke without fire', taking an overview of the allegations rather than (as they should) considering each count individually;
- the number of counts and/or defendants is such that the jury will be overwhelmed by the sheer weight of evidence, and the interests of justice are therefore better served by having a number of shorter trials (see, for example, *R v Novac* (1976) 65 Cr App R 107, where the Court of Appeal said that if multiplicity of defendants and charges threatens undue length and complexity of trial then a heavy responsibility must rest on the prosecution to consider whether joinder is essential in the interests of justice or whether the case can reasonably be subdivided).

It has to be borne in mind that the effect of all these risks, except the last, can be minimised, if not removed altogether, by appropriately worded directions from the judge on how the jury should approach the task of analysing the evidence. A defendant seeking separate trials would therefore have to show why such a direction would not provide sufficient protection in his case.

An example of where severance would have been appropriate is *R v Laycock* [2003] EWCA Crim 1477; [2003] Crim LR 803, where the defendant was charged with a number of offences, including possession of a firearm when a prohibited person (namely having been sentenced to imprisonment for more than three years). The very nature of this offence revealed the fact that he had previously been convicted of a serious offence. The court criticised the number of counts, saying that in formulating an indictment an excessive number of counts should not be included, since this overloads the indictment. Furthermore, the court went on to say that prosecutors should be careful not to charge counts that would prejudice a defendant unless there is a real purpose to be served. In the present case, the possession offence should not have been joined in the indictment since it did not give the judge any additional sentencing powers. If the prosecution wanted to seek a conviction for the offence in question, a separate trial of that count would have been fairer.

10.9.2 Co-defendants

Where two or more defendants are charged in a single count, the judge has a discretion to order separate trials. Again, it has to be shown that a fair trial cannot be achieved without severance. Judges are reluctant to order separate trials of defendants charged with the same offence: if there are two separate trials, the cost of the proceedings will be doubled, the witnesses will have to testify twice, and there is a risk of inconsistent verdicts. It is for this reason that separate trials will only be ordered if there are exceptional circumstances which require this course of action.

In *R v Grondkowski and Malinowski* [1946] KB 369, separate trials were not ordered even though the defendants were blaming each other (the so called 'cut throat defence'), a defence which often results in both defendants being convicted.

In *R v Lake* (1976) 64 Cr App R 172, the trial judge's refusal to order separate trials was upheld by the Court of Appeal even though there was some evidence in the case which was admissible against one defendant but inadmissible against (and highly prejudicial to) the other. This will be the case if D1 confesses to the police and in that confession implicates D2 (the out-of-court statement by D1 is inadmissible against D2, but the jury will hear about that statement as they hear about the case against D1). The Court of Appeal agreed with the trial judge that the danger of prejudice could be removed by an appropriate direction to the jury. Similarly, in *R v Crawford* [1997] 1 WLR 1329, the Court of Appeal upheld the decision of the trial judge not to order separate trials in a case where D1 was going to give evidence (in the course of her defence) against D2 and so D2 would be able to cross-examine D1 on her previous convictions (and it should be borne in mind that if D1 gives evidence in the witness box that implicates D2, that is admissible evidence against D2). Lord Bingham of Cornhill CJ (at p 1335–36) said:

> The trial of both defendants together, with each cross-examining the other on the other's previous convictions, may indeed have increased the chances of both defendants being convicted as compared with their chances of conviction had they been tried separately. To that extent it must be accepted that a joint trial was prejudicial to them. It is, however, to be remembered that the whole trial process is prejudicial to a defendant in the sense that it is intended to convict that defendant. What the court must be concerned to ensure is that there is no unfair prejudice to a defendant.
>
> In our judgment there was no trace of unfair prejudice to this appellant in the course adopted here. This was pre-eminently a discretionary decision for the [trial judge]. He had to weigh the risk of unfair prejudice to the defendants against the disadvantages of repeated trials with repeated appearances to testify by the victim and the obvious risk of an unjust result. The [judge] was plainly alive to the risk that the jury would stray from considering the credibility of the appellant into considering her propensity to commit offences of this kind and gave a direction on this matter which [was] clear . . . We have no reason whatever to suppose that the jury would not have paid full attention to that direction.

Similarly, in *R v Eriemo* [1995] 2 Cr App R 206, it was held that a judge was justified in refusing an application to sever an indictment where one defendant intends to argue that he was acting under the duress of another defendant.

The usual response to the argument that the jury will hear evidence that is inadmissible against one defendant, or that they might give undue weight to the evidence of one defendant if he gives evidence that implicates his co-accused, is that the jury will be directed by the judge to consider the case of each defendant separately and to ignore any evidence that has been ruled inadmissible against a particular defendant when they consider the case against that defendant (and that they should bear in mind that one defendant might be serving his own interests by giving evidence against a co-accused). Critics of the efficacy of such directions suggest that jurors are being asked to perform 'mental gymnastics'. In 'The prejudiced defendant: unfairness suffered by a defendant in a joint trial' [2003] Crim LR 432, Peter Thornton QC suggests that:

> There is certainly an argument that severance should take place more frequently than at present, with the object of achieving fairness for all defendants. The decision whether to order severance is now made much easier for judges in the light of modern rules of disclosure, both by prosecution and defence. It is not right that a defendant should be put at risk of a conviction based partly on inadmissible evidence. There is no way of knowing, in the absence of jury research, how juries cope with this problem and what notice they take of the judge's warnings. After all, the necessity for consistency, the principle that drives the concept of the joint trial, is frequently not achieved in a joint trial. The evidence against one defendant may be weaker than against another, producing different verdicts, even where it is alleged that both defendants were present and jointly participating in the crime. That applies whether they are tried together or separately. Similarly unequal 'treatment' can easily be avoided by one judge trying both cases and passing sentence in the event of convictions. At the very least the judge's direction to ignore inadmissible evidence should be given to the jury in writing for them to take with them when they retire.

He concludes that:

> While it must be recognised that the interest of the prejudiced defendant in the context of a joint trial will always be only one of several competing interests, the time may have come for greater flexibility in favour of that defendant and a less restrictive approach.

Where the defence would prefer separate trials of the defendants (for example, where the confession of one defendant implicates the other), it is worth making an application for separate trials to the trial judge but, if the judge refuses, the Court of Appeal is unlikely to interfere with his decision unless it is manifestly unreasonable (*R v Josephs* (1977) 65 Cr App R 253 and *R v Myers* [1996] 2 Cr App R 335).

10.10 MISJOINDER

If an indictment contains counts which should not be joined together in the same indictment, two questions arise. First, how can the defect be cured before the trial proceeds? Secondly, what happens if no remedial steps are taken and the defendant is convicted on the basis of the defective indictment?

10.10.1 Curing the defect

What should the Crown Court do if faced with an indictment which breaches r 14.2(3)?

In *R v Newland* [1988] QB 402, the defendant was charged with a drugs offence and three counts alleging assault which were wholly unconnected with the drugs charge. The trial judge simply ordered separate trials (purporting to 'sever' the indictment under s 5(3) of the Indictments Act 1915), so that the drugs offence and the assault charges were tried separately. The Court of Appeal held that the judge had no power to 'sever' the indictment under s 5(3), since this power applies only to a valid indictment, and the indictment in the present case was invalid because it failed to comply with what is now r 14.2(3) of the Criminal Procedure Rules. The court went on to say that the trial judge should have deleted from the indictment either the drugs charge or the assault charges, and proceeded with the trial on that indictment. The allegations deleted from the indictment could only be proceeded with if the prosecution brought fresh proceedings in the magistrates' court in respect of them or else sought a voluntary bill of indictment.

On the other hand, in *R v Follett* [1989] QB 338, a differently constituted Court of Appeal accepted a rather simpler solution. In this case, the indictment was invalid because it contained counts which were not sufficiently linked. The Court of Appeal upheld the decision of the trial judge to stay proceedings on the indictment as drafted and to give the prosecution leave to prefer fresh indictments (each complying with r 14.2(3)) out of time. The effect of this is that the original (defective) indictment remains in existence but becomes irrelevant. Two or more trials then follow, based on the new indictments, without the need for fresh proceedings in the magistrates' court or a voluntary bill of indictment.

In the light of the case law set out below, it seems that it is not strictly correct to label an indictment 'invalid' because of misjoinder. However, there is no reason to suppose that the methods for curing the defect of misjoinder which these two cases suggest should not be followed where the misjoinder becomes apparent at the Crown Court trial. Thus, the 'cure' is either (a) to delete sufficient counts to leave an indictment which complies with r 14.2(3) or (b) with the leave of the court, to prefer fresh indictments, each of which must comply with that rule.

10.10.2 Validity of the indictment

There has been a plethora of case law on the exact status of proceedings on an indictment which contains counts that are improperly joined. The question which the Court of Appeal has had to consider on several occasions is this: if a person is convicted on the basis of an indictment which does not comply with r 14.2(3), should all the convictions on that indictment be quashed, or just the convictions on counts which were improperly joined?

In *R v Bell* (1984) 78 Cr App R 305, Lord Lane CJ said that it cannot be the law that an indictment could be made a complete nullity by the addition of a count or counts contrary to r 14.2(3). In *Newland*, however, Watkins LJ said that although the indictment itself could not, in the light of *Bell*, properly be described as a nullity, 'the proceedings flowing from the arraignment of the appellant upon that indictment must surely be a nullity'. This was followed in *R v O'Reilly* (1990) 90 Cr App R 40.

In *R v Callaghan* (1992) 94 Cr App R 226, the Court of Appeal had to consider a case where a summary offence was added to an indictment pursuant to s 40 of the Criminal Justice Act 1988 but where the required link (which is in the same terms as r 14.2(3)) between the summary offence and the indictable offence was missing. The Court of Appeal held cases such as *Newland* and *Follett* do not decide that an indictment becomes a nullity by the addition of a count which involves a breach of r 14.2(3). The result of this was that the misjoinder did not nullify all the proceedings on the indictment. It followed that only the conviction for the improperly joined count should be quashed.

R v Lewis (1992) 95 Cr App R 131 was another case involving the addition of a summary offence under s 40 of the Criminal Justice Act 1988. The defendant was arrested for a number of offences. While he was at the police station he spat at one of the police officers; this resulted in a charge of common assault (a summary offence to which s 40 of the Criminal Justice Act 1988 applies). The Court of Appeal held that the common assault could not be regarded as being founded on the same facts as the other offences: what occurred at the police station took place too long after the other offences to be founded on the same facts as those offences. The Court of Appeal, reaching the opposite conclusion to *R v Callaghan*, went on to hold that the indictment was invalid and so technically there had been no convictions. Thus, all the convictions on the defective indictment had to be quashed.

In *R v Simon* [1992] Crim LR 444, the appellant took one car without authority. That car ran out of petrol. He then took another car without authority and used it to get to a place where he and another defendant committed a robbery. The Court of Appeal held that the taking of the first car was properly joined, since the whole evening's criminality needed to be looked at as a continuous series of events; thus, there was no misjoinder. However, the court went on to say (*obiter*) that *Callaghan*, having been decided earlier than *Lewis*, was to be preferred.

In *R v Smith* [1997] QB 836, three summary offences were added to an indictment under s 40 of the Criminal Justice Act 1988; joinder of two of those summary offences was improper because there was no sufficient link with the indictable offence which was also on the indictment. The Court of Appeal followed *Callaghan* and the *obiter dictum* in *Simon* and held that convictions for offences which are correctly joined are valid convictions. Accordingly, the convictions on the indictable offence and the correctly joined summary offence stood; only the convictions for the two improperly joined summary offences were quashed.

In *R v Lockley and Sainsbury* [1997] Crim LR 455, the appellants were charged with conspiracy to commit burglary and dangerous driving (on the basis that the car they used in connection with the burglary was dangerously defective). Both offences are indictable offences and so only r 14.2(3) of the Criminal Procedure Rules had to be considered. The Court of Appeal held that the dangerous driving charge was improperly joined. The court confirmed that s 40 of the Criminal Justice Act 1988 and r 14.2(3) are in all material respects in the same terms, and so the same principles regarding misjoinder and the consequences thereof must apply to both. The court went on to hold that misjoinder does not nullify the whole indictment. It followed that only the conviction on the wrongly joined count(s) should be quashed.

It is thus clear that misjoinder of counts does not render the entire indictment invalid.

10.11 DECIDING THE CONTENTS OF THE INDICTMENT

In most cases, the counts on the indictment are the same as the charges in respect of which the defendant was sent for trial. However, s 2(2) of the Administration of Justice (Miscellaneous Provisions) Act 1933 states that where a defendant has been sent for trial at the Crown Court, the draft indictment against the person charged may include, either in substitution for or in addition to counts charging the offence(s) for which the defendant was sent for trial, any counts founded on the evidence contained in the witness statements relied on by the prosecution, provided that the various counts may 'lawfully be joined in the same indictment'.

Section 2(2) effectively confers two powers:

- the power to indict an offender for offences in addition to those for which he has been sent for trial by the magistrates; and
- the power to replace the offences for which he has been sent for trial with different offences.

In *R v Biddis* [1993] Crim LR 392, it was held that there need not be conclusive evidence in the prosecution papers supporting the new count(s); it is enough if there is some evidence in respect of them.

10.11.1 Substituting offences

An example of the power in s 2 of the Administration of Justice (Miscellaneous Provisions) Act 1933 to substitute a different offence would be a case where the magistrates send the defendant for trial on a charge of burglary (entering premises as a trespasser and then stealing). The prosecution, after the case has been sent to the Crown Court, decide that the evidence on the issue of trespass is very weak, but that they can prove that the defendant stole what he is alleged to have stolen during the course of the 'burglary'. The prosecution could indict the defendant for theft instead of burglary.

Similarly, if the magistrates send the defendant for trial on a charge of theft but the prosecution subsequently decide that there is sufficient evidence to prove that the theft was committed in the course of a burglary, the prosecution could indict the defendant for burglary instead of theft.

The power to indict for offences which differ from those in respect of which the justices sent the defendant for trial applies even if the justices expressly refused to send him for trial in respect of a particular offence but sent him to the Crown Court in respect of another offence (*R v Moloney* [1985] AC 905). The abolition of committal proceedings means that this principle will only be relevant in very rare cases (since the magistrates do not consider the evidence when sending a case to the Crown Court under s 51 of the Crime and Disorder Act 1998). However, there may be exceptional cases where abuse of process arguments are used in the magistrates' court in an attempt to prevent the court from sending a case to the Crown Court for trial. In *R v C* (1995) 159 JP 205, the magistrates had stayed certain charges on the ground of abuse of process but the defendant was sent for trial on other charges. Evidence of the charges which had been stayed was contained in the witness statements which formed the bundle of evidence relied on by the prosecution. The prosecution sought leave from the Crown Court to add to the indictment the charges which had been stayed by the magistrate. Leave was given and the Court of Appeal upheld this decision, holding that the trial judge had power to include in an indictment counts for any offences disclosed in the prosecution witness statements, even where those charges had been stayed by the magistrates' court on the grounds of abuse of process.

10.11.2 Adding offences

Section 2(2) of the Administration of Justice (Miscellaneous Provisions) Act 1933 also enables the prosecution to indict the defendant for charges which are additional to those in respect of which he was sent for trial. The essential restriction on this power is that the resulting indictment must satisfy the requirements of r 14.2(3) of the Indictment Rules (*R v Lombardi* [1989] 1 WLR 73).

An example of the operation of the power to add offences would be where the defendant is sent for trial on a single charge of robbery. The prosecution witness statements relied upon by the prosecution also disclose the fact that the defendant was in possession of a firearm when carrying out the robbery. The prosecution could add a firearms offence to the indictment. Even though the defendant has not been sent for trial in respect of the firearms charge, it is a charge which is sufficiently closely related to the charge in respect of which the defendant has been sent for trial to permit joinder of the two charges under r 14.2(3).

An example of where it would not be open to the prosecution to add a count to the indictment would be where the defendant is sent for trial on a charge on burglary. The prosecution witness statements also reveal evidence which would support a completely unrelated drugs charge. However, the defendant has not been sent for trial in respect of that charge. The prosecution cannot add the drugs charge to the indictment which contains the burglary charge. The two charges are wholly unrelated and so to put them on the same indictment would infringe r 14.2(3).

10.11.3 More than one indictment

In *Lombardi*, Lord Lane CJ said (at p 77) that where the magistrates have sent a defendant to the Crown Court on more than one charge, the prosecution are at liberty to prefer a number of separate indictments if they feel that it is appropriate to do so. Take, for example, the defendant who is sent for trial on a charge of burglary and a completely unrelated drugs charge. Although the two charges (being unrelated) cannot appear on the same indictment (because of r 14.2(3)), the prosecution can nonetheless prefer two separate indictments (one for the burglary and the other for the drugs offence), since the defendant has been sent for trial in respect of both offences.

However, what the prosecution cannot do is to prefer one indictment containing the charge(s) in respect of which the defendant was sent for trial, and a second indictment containing only charges in respect of which the defendant has not been sent for trial. Take, for example, a case where the defendant is sent to the Crown Court for trial on a charge of burglary, but the prosecution witness statements also reveal evidence of a drugs offence. The prosecution can prefer an indictment for burglary because the defendant has been sent for trial in respect of that charge. They cannot add the unrelated drugs offence to that indictment, because that would contravene r 14.2(3), and they cannot prefer a separate indictment in respect of the drugs offence, because the defendant has not been sent for trial in respect of that offence and that offence is not being substituted for an offence in respect of which the defendant was sent for trial.

10.11.4 More than one defendant

If the magistrates send two or more defendants for trial at the same time, it is open to the prosecution to draft separate indictments against them if the prosecution feel that it would be appropriate to do so or if the defendants are charged with different offences and joinder of the offences in one indictment would breach r 14.2(3).

If defendants are not sent for trial at the same time, it is nevertheless open to the prosecution to join those defendants in the same indictment, assuming r 14.2(3) is satisfied (see *R v Groom* [1977] QB 6). This is so even if an indictment in respect of a defendant who has been sent for trial has already been signed: see para IV.34.2 of the *Consolidated Practice Direction*, which provides as follows:

> There is no rule of law or practice which prohibits two indictments being in existence at the same time for the same offence against the same person and on the same facts. But the court will not allow the prosecution to proceed on both indictments. They cannot be tried together and the court will require the prosecution to elect the one on which the trial will proceed. Where different defendants have been separately sent or committed for trial for offences which can lawfully be charged in the same indictment then it is permissible to join in one indictment counts based on the separate sendings or committals for trial even if an indictment based on one of them already has been signed. Where necessary the court should be invited to exercise its powers of amendment under s 5 of the Indictments Act 1915.

10.11.5 Alternative counts

In many cases, the prosecution will include alternative counts on the indictment. For instance, an allegation of wounding with intent (s 18 of the Offences Against the Person Act 1861) may be accompanied by a separate count alleging unlawful wounding (s 20 of the same Act). This would be appropriate where the prosecution are not sure that they can prove that the accused had the requisite intent to commit the s 18 offence. There is nothing on the indictment to show that these are alternatives (the word 'or' does not appear) but counsel for the prosecution, during the opening speech, will inform the jury that the prosecution seek a conviction on one or other of the two counts but not both.

10.11.6 Overloading the indictment

In *R v Novac* (1976) 65 Cr App R 107 and *R v Thorne* (1977) 66 Cr App R 6, the Court of Appeal warned against the danger of having too many counts or too many defendants in a single trial. Splitting the case into a series of shorter trials may, in the long run, be easier. It is for this reason that detailed guidance is given in para IV.34.3 of the *Consolidated Practice Direction*:

Save in the special circumstances described in the following paragraphs of this Practice Direction, it is undesirable that a large number of counts should be contained in one indictment. Where defendants on trial have a variety of offences alleged against them then in the interests of effective case management it is the court's responsibility to exercise its powers in accordance with the overriding objective set out in Part 1 of the Criminal Procedure Rules. The prosecution may be required to identify a selection of counts on which the trial should proceed, leaving a decision to be taken later whether to try any of the remainder. Where an indictment contains substantive counts and one or more related conspiracy counts the court will expect the prosecution to justify the joinder. Failing justification the prosecution should be required to choose whether to proceed on the substantive counts or on the conspiracy counts. In any event, if there is a conviction on any counts that are tried then those that have been postponed can remain on the file marked 'not to be proceeded with without the leave of the court'. In the event that a conviction is later quashed on appeal, the remaining counts can be tried. Where necessary the court has power to order that an indictment be divided and some counts removed to a separate indictment.

10.12 AMENDING THE INDICTMENT

Section 5(1) of the Indictments Act 1915 provides:

Where, before trial, or at any stage of a trial, it appears to the court that the indictment is defective, the court shall make such order for the amendment of the indictment as the court thinks necessary to meet the circumstances of the case, unless, having regard to the merits of the case, the required amendments cannot be made without injustice.

This provision thus allows the amendment of a defective indictment at any stage, provided the amendment can be made without causing injustice. Amendment may be necessary, for example, where the evidence at trial shows that the prosecution have charged the wrong offence.

The amendment may take the form of inserting a new count in the indictment, whether in addition to or instead of the original count (*R v Johal* [1973] QB 475). Where there is no injustice to the defendant, an indictment can even be amended under s 5(1) so as to add a new defendant (*R v Palmer* [2002] EWCA Crim 892; (2002) *The Times*, 18 April).

In *R v Osieh* [1996] 1 WLR 1260, prior to the start of the trial, the judge gave leave for the indictment to be amended to include a count of attempted theft. The appellant argued that the judge should not have allowed this to be done, since there was no evidence relating to the attempted theft in the papers on the basis of which the case was sent to the Crown Court (as is required by s 2(2) of the Administration of Justice (Miscellaneous Provisions) Act 1933). The Court of Appeal held that the 1933 Act and the Indictments Act 1915 are two entirely different statutory regimes. The Administration of Justice (Miscellaneous Provisions) Act 1933 governs the signing of the draft indictment; the Indictments Act 1915 governs the indictment itself. Accordingly, the requirement in the Administration of Justice (Miscellaneous Provisions) Act 1933 that there must be evidence in the prosecution papers to support a count on the indictment does not apply to the power conferred by the Indictments Act 1915. The court went on to say that where the amendment relates to matters which are not foreshadowed in the prosecution papers, it may be appropriate for the judge to exercise his discretion against giving leave for the amendment (or else allowing the amendment but adjourning the case to enable the defence to review their case). The court went on to make the point that the 1915 Act confers a wide discretion; the Court of Appeal will not interfere lightly with the exercise of such a discretion.

Applications to amend the indictment may be made at the Plea and Case Management Hearing (PCMH). If an amendment is made just before the start of the trial, and the amendment changes the nature of the prosecution case, the defence must be allowed an adjournment to enable them to review their case in the light of the new allegations (see s 5(4) of the Indictments Act 1915). If a jury has already been empanelled, it may be necessary for the judge to discharge that jury and order a retrial (see s 5(5)(a) of the Indictments Act 1915).

It is permissible (subject to the possible need for an adjournment) for the indictment to be amended in the course of the trial (although if the amendment is a fundamental one, so that defence would need a long adjournment, it may be appropriate for the judge to discharge the jury and order a retrial).

In *R v Pople* [1951] 1 KB 53, it was held that it is not necessary that an indictment, in order to be 'defective' within the meaning of s 5(1) of the Indictments Act 1915, should be one which is bad on its face (for example, one which charges an offence unknown to the law). On the contrary, said the court, any alteration in matters of description may be made in order to meet the evidence in the case so long as the amendment causes no injustice to the accused. In that case, the appellants were charged in an indictment alleging that they had obtained sums of money by false pretences; the trial judge allowed the indictment to be amended by replacing the sums in question with the words 'a valuable security, to wit, a cheque'. The Court of Appeal upheld this amendment. They held that the defendant was not prejudiced, since the substance of the allegation was unaltered.

In *R v Foster* [2007] EWCA Crim 2869, Sir Igor Judge P said (at para 65):

> . . . it is now common practice to permit amendments to the indictment at any stage of the trial, whether by amending or adding or substituting new counts, provided that these steps may be taken without unfairness to the accused. Whether unfairness results will usually depend on the purpose of the amendment, the stage of the trial at which the amendment is sought, the degree, if any, to which the defendant is required by the amendment to meet a new prosecution case and whether he would be disadvantaged in the presentation of his defence.

Such an amendment may even be permitted after the jury had retired to consider their verdict. In *R v Collison* (1980) 71 Cr App R 249, the defendant was charged with one count of wounding with intent (s 18 of the Offences Against the Person Act 1861). The jury was unable to reach either a unanimous or a majority verdict on this count, but wanted to convict the defendant of the lesser offence of unlawful wounding (s 20 of the 1861 Act). Since they could not agree on an acquittal of the offence on the indictment, they could not simply return a verdict of guilty to the lesser offence under s 6(3) of the Criminal Law Act 1967, since that provision only applies where the jury first acquits of the offence on the indictment (see Chapter 12). The judge therefore allowed the prosecution to add a further count (alleging the s 20 offence) to the indictment. The Court of Appeal upheld this course of action, as no injustice was caused to the defendant by the addition of the new count. Given their power to acquit of s 18 but convict instead of s 20, the lesser offence was, effectively, already before the jury.

The important question in deciding whether or not to allow an amendment once the trial has started is whether the defence case would have been conducted differently had the amendment taken place at the outset. In *R v Harris* (1993) *The Times*, 22 March, the defendant was charged with rape but, at the close of the defence case, the prosecution applied to add an alternative count alleging attempted rape to the indictment. The judge allowed this amendment, but the Court of Appeal held that this decision was wrong, since the defence case would have been put differently (different cross-examination of prosecution witnesses and different defence evidence). Similarly, in *R v Thomas* [1983] Crim LR 619, the Court of Appeal quashed a conviction where a count of receiving stolen property was added to an indictment which hitherto alleged only theft. This amendment took place after the close of the prosecution case and the defence would have cross-examined the prosecution witnesses differently if both allegations had been made at the outset.

In *R v Piggott and Litwin* [1999] 2 Cr App R 320, the Court of Appeal reaffirmed that the test to determine whether an amendment after the close of the prosecution case should be permitted is whether the trial itself can be continued without injustice. The power to amend does not affect the principle that the defendant is entitled to know the case he has to meet and the right to a fair trial. Accordingly, the prosecution are not entitled to present the case to the jury in one way and hope that leave to amend will be given if there is a successful submission of no case to answer.

Once an indictment has been signed and preferred following the granting of a voluntary bill of indictment (see Chapter 9), the indictment is like any other indictment. It follows that the trial judge can give leave for that indictment to be amended if it is defective (for example, it does not include offences disclosed in the witness statements which were considered by the High Court judge (*R v Wells* [1995] 2 Cr App R 417)).

Where the Court of Appeal quashes a conviction but orders a retrial under s 7 of the Criminal Appeal Act 1968, the trial judge has power under s 5(1) of the Indictments Act 1915 to allow the indictment to be amended, even if the amendment results in the defendant being tried for offences for which the Court of Appeal had no power to order a retrial. However, this is only permissible so long as the amendment does not put the defendant in a worse position than he was in after the original trial (*R v Hemmings* [2000] 1 WLR 661).

10.13 QUASHING THE INDICTMENT

It is open to the defence to make an application to 'quash' the indictment. Such an application would normally be made at the PCMH which precedes the trial itself.

There are three grounds for quashing an indictment. Those grounds are:

a the indictment (or a count on the indictment) is bad on its face, as it alleges an offence which is not known to the law or a single count alleges more than one offence;

b   the indictment (or one of its counts) has been preferred without authority, in that there has been no valid transfer of the case from the magistrates' court to the Crown Court, and no voluntary bill of indictment;

c   the indictment contains a count in respect of which the defendant was not sent for trial (and there was no voluntary bill of indictment in respect of that count) *and* the prosecution witness statements do not disclose a case to answer on that count.

The distinction between (b) and (c) is that in the case of (b), there was no valid transfer of the case to the Crown Court; in the case of (c), there was a valid transfer of the case to the Crown Court, but the person drafting the indictment added a new offence in addition to the offence(s) in respect of which the defendant was originally sent for trial.

The only instance in which the trial judge is entitled to look at the prosecution witness statements to see if they disclose a case to answer is in case (c), in respect of the 'new' count (*R v Jones* (1974) 59 Cr App R 120). It follows that if the offence is one in respect of which the defendant was sent for trial, the judge cannot be asked to quash the indictment on the basis that there is insufficient evidence in respect of that offence (*R v London Quarter Sessions ex p Downes* [1954] 1 QB 1).

Motions to quash are of little practical importance since these grounds are very limited and, in any event, most errors can be cured by the prosecution seeking to amend the defective indictment under s 5(1) of the Indictments Act 1915.

Furthermore, if the indictment is quashed, the defendant is not regarded as having been acquitted and so can be prosecuted again. However, if the whole indictment is quashed, the defendant can only be indicted for the same offence again if he is sent for trial a second time for that offence by the magistrates or a voluntary bill of indictment obtained (*R v Thompson* [1975] 1 WLR 1425).

10.14 SHOULD INDICTMENTS BE MORE DETAILED?

In 1994, the Law Commission published a paper (which is no longer available) entitled 'Counts in an Indictment'. It proposed that counts in an indictment should be drafted in a way that sets out the prosecution case in greater detail. The main objectives of this would be to:

*   assist with ensuring that the prosecution has evidence to support each of the elements of the offence charged (by setting out each element that has to be proved);
*   assist the prosecutor when opening the case to the jury, by setting out (from the prosecution's perspective) the agenda for the trial;
*   assist the jury's comprehension of the issues in the trial (so that they can follow more easily the evidence that they hear during the trial);
*   assist in 'stock-taking' at the end of the trial (and to assist the jury when considering their verdict).

The proposal was not intended to require the prosecution to plead law or evidence, but simply to set out the factual nature of their case in greater detail. Two examples given by the Law Commission illustrated what was being proposed.

One example is theft of a handbag. The 'particulars of offence' for theft would currently read:

> [Defendant] on [date] stole a handbag belonging to [victim].

A more detailed indictment in that case might allege:

> [Defendant] on [date] in the White Horse Public House, Croydon, removed a handbag belonging to [victim] from the chair on which [victim] had placed it, thereby dishonestly assuming [victim's] rights as owner of the handbag and its contents. [Defendant] intended permanently to deprive [victim] of the handbag and its contents.

A second example is assault occasioning actual bodily harm. The particulars for this offence would currently read:

> [Defendant] on [date] assaulted [victim], thereby occasioning him actual bodily harm.

A more detailed indictment might allege:

> [Defendant] on [date], in the Prince of Wales Public House, Croydon, at about 10.45 pm intentionally punched [victim], causing him bruising around the mouth.

One potential drawback of setting out such factual detail is that the evidence may not come out exactly as the prosecution anticipated (for example, in the theft case illustrated above, it might turn out that the handbag was under the chair, not on the chair). There would therefore probably be more cases where the indictment would have to be amended during the course of the trial.

It was also suggested by the Law Commission that the defence should also be required to set out the basis of their case. This is now done through the defence statements required by the Criminal Procedure and Investigations Act 1996, especially given the greater level of detail required as a result of the amendments to the 1996 Act contained in Pt 5 of the Criminal Justice Act 2003 (see Chapter 8).

Chapter 11

Crown Court trial: preliminaries

11.1 INTRODUCTION

In this chapter, we examine some of the preliminary matters which are dealt with before a Crown Court trial takes place. In the next chapter, we follow the course of the trial itself.

11.2 DISCLOSURE OF EVIDENCE TO THE DEFENCE

It is a vital principle that the defence are entitled to know in advance what case they have to meet.

11.2.1 Witness to be called by the prosecution

The prosecution may only call as witnesses at the Crown Court people whose written statements have previously been served on the defence. Most of these witness statements will have been served on the defence as part of the process whereby the case is transferred from the magistrates' court to the Crown Court (see Chapter 9).

If the prosecution wish to adduce the evidence of a witness whose statement was not served on the defence when the case was sent to the Crown Court, a 'notice of additional evidence' (including a copy of the written statement by the witness) must first be served on the defence. There is no specified time by which the notice must have been served on the defence; however, if the notice is served just before (or even during) the trial, so that there is insufficient time for the defence to consider the effect which the extra evidence has on the defence case, the judge should grant an adjournment.

11.2.2 Editing prosecution evidence

It will sometimes be necessary for the witness statements of some prosecution witnesses to be edited. This might be a witness who has made more than one statement and it would be better to reduce these statements into a single comprehensive statement of their evidence, or it might be that a statement contains inadmissible, prejudicial or irrelevant material. Paragraph III.24.1 of *Consolidated Practice Direction* requires that any such editing be done by a Crown Prosecutor (not by the police).

Paragraph III.24.3(a) says that a statement should normally be edited by:

marking copies of the statement in a way which indicates the passages on which the prosecution will not rely. This merely indicates that the prosecution will not seek to adduce the
evidence so marked. The original signed statement to be tendered to the court is not
marked in any way. The marking on the copy statement is done by lightly striking out the
passages to be edited so that what appears beneath can still be read, or by bracketing, or by a
combination of both . . . Whenever the striking out/bracketing method is used, it will assist if
the following words appear at the foot of the frontispiece or index to any bundle of copy
statements to be tendered: 'The prosecution does not propose to adduce evidence of those
passages of the attached copy statements which have been struck out and/or bracketed (nor
will it seek to do so at the trial unless a notice of further evidence is served).'

Alternatively, a fresh statement may be obtained, signed by the witness, which omits the
offending material. According to paragraph III.24.4, this is preferable:

(a)   When a police (or other investigating) officer's statement contains details of interviews
      with more suspects than are eventually charged, a fresh statement should be prepared
      and signed omitting all details of interview with those not charged except, insofar as it is
      relevant, for the bald fact that a certain named person was interviewed at a particular
      time, date and place.
(b)   When a suspect is interviewed about more offences than are eventually made the
      subject of . . . charges, a fresh statement should be prepared and signed omitting all
      questions and answers about the uncharged offences unless either they might appropri-
      ately be taken into consideration or evidence about those offences is admissible on the
      charges preferred, such as evidence of system. It may, however, be desirable to replace
      the omitted questions and answers with a phrase such as: 'After referring to some
      other matters, I then said . . .', so as to make it clear that part of the interview has been
      omitted.
(c)   A fresh statement should normally be prepared and signed if the only part of the
      original on which the prosecution is relying is only a small proportion of the whole,
      although it remains desirable to use the alternative method if there is reason to believe
      that the defence might itself wish to rely, in mitigation or for any other purpose, on at
      least some of those parts which the prosecution does not propose to adduce.
(d)   When the passages contain material which the prosecution is entitled to withhold from
      disclosure to the defence.

Paragraph III.24.7 stipulates that whenever a fresh statement is taken from a witness, a
copy of the earlier, unedited statement(s) of that witness must be given to the defence in
accordance with the rules governing disclosure of unused material unless there are
grounds for withholding such disclosure.

Editing may also be necessary in the case of evidence which the jury will see. For
example, the accused might make a statement to the police from which it becomes
apparent that he has previous convictions (unless those previous convictions are ruled
admissible) or is accused of other offences. The transcript of this interview may well
become an exhibit in the case which the jury will see. Such a document has to be edited
so that the inadmissible material which is deleted is no longer visible.

11.2.3 Witnesses whom the prosecution do not intend to call: unused material

The prosecution have a duty (under the Criminal Procedure and Investigations Act (CPIA) 1996) to disclose to the defence any material which has not already been disclosed but which might undermine the prosecution case against the defendant or assist the defence case. This is considered in detail in Chapter 8.

11.3 DISCLOSURE BY THE DEFENCE

The defence also have a duty of disclosure.

11.3.1 Disclosure of the defence case

Under the CPIA 1996, the defence have a duty to give the prosecution a written statement of the nature of the defence case and to set out the matters upon which the defence take issue with the prosecution. In particular, the defence must give full particulars of any alibi which is going to be raised at trial. Failure to comply with these requirements enables adverse inferences to be drawn by the jury. Full details of these provisions are contained in Chapter 8.

11.3.2 Expert evidence

The other specific duty of pre-trial disclosure with which the defence have to comply is Pt 24.1 of the Criminal Procedure Rules, which requires disclosure of a statement in writing of any finding or opinion which an expert witness proposes to adduce as evidence. Part 24 applies to the prosecution as well as the defence, but the prosecution have to disclose all the evidence they wish to rely on anyway. Under r 24.3, a party who seeks to adduce expert evidence but fails to comply with r 24.1, cannot adduce that evidence without the leave of the court.

11.4 SECURING THE ATTENDANCE OF WITNESSES

Section 2 of the Criminal Procedure (Attendance of Witnesses) Act 1965 enables the Crown Court to grant a witness summons requiring the attendance at the Crown Court of a person who is likely to be able to give material evidence but who will not attend voluntarily.

Section 2 provides that:

(1)   This section applies where the Crown Court is satisfied that –

    (a)   a person is likely to be able to give evidence likely to be material evidence, or produce any document or thing likely to be material evidence, for the purpose of any criminal proceedings before the Crown Court, and

    (b)   it is in the interests of justice to issue a summons under this section to secure the attendance of that person to give evidence or to produce the document or thing.

(2) In such a case the Crown Court shall, subject to the following provisions of this section, issue a summons (a witness summons) directed to the person concerned and requiring him to –

(a) attend before the Crown Court at the time and place stated in the summons, and
(b) give the evidence or produce the document or thing.

(3) A witness summons may only be issued under this section on an application; and the Crown Court may refuse to issue the summons if any requirement relating to the application is not fulfilled.

Under sub-ss (4)–(6), an application for a witness summons must be made as soon as reasonably practicable after the defendant has been sent to the Crown Court for trial.

Under s 2C(1) of the Criminal Procedure (Attendance of Witnesses) Act 1965, a person against whom a witness summons was made and who was not present or represented when the order was made may apply to the Crown Court for the order to be discharged provided that he:

(b) satisfies the court that he was not served with notice of the application to issue the summons and that he was neither present nor represented at the hearing of the application, and
(c) satisfies the court that he cannot give any evidence likely to be material evidence or, as the case may be, produce any document or thing likely to be material evidence . . .

Section 4(1) of the Act enables pre-emptive action if a witness summons has been obtained and there are grounds to believe that the person will not attend court. It provides that:

(1) If a judge of the Crown Court is satisfied by evidence on oath that a witness in respect of whom a witness summons is in force is unlikely to comply with the summons, the judge may issue a warrant to arrest the witness and bring him before the court before which he is required to attend:

Provided that a warrant shall not be issued under this sub-section unless the judge is satisfied by such evidence as aforesaid that the witness is likely to be able to give evidence likely to be material evidence or produce any document or thing likely to be material evidence in the proceedings.

Section 4(2) and (3) deals with the situation where the witness fails to attend court:

(2) Where a witness who is required to attend before the Crown Court by virtue of a witness summons fails to attend in compliance with the summons, that court may—

(a) in any case, cause to be served on him a notice requiring him to attend the court forthwith or at such time as may be specified in the notice;
(b) if the court is satisfied that there are reasonable grounds for believing that he has failed to attend without just excuse, or if he has failed to comply with a notice under paragraph (a) above, issue a warrant to arrest him and bring him before the court.

(3) A witness brought before the court in pursuance of a warrant under this section may be remanded by that court in custody or on bail (with or without sureties) until such time as the court may appoint for receiving his evidence or dealing with him under section 3 of this Act . . .

Thus, if the person who is the subject of a witness summons fails to attend court, and there are reasonable grounds for believing that there is no just excuse for this non-attendance, a warrant for the arrest of the witness may be issued by the judge. Otherwise, a notice is served on the witness requiring him to attend court on a specified date (and if he fails to do so, a warrant for his arrest may be issued). Someone arrested under such a warrant will be taken before the Crown Court and may be remanded in custody or on bail until the time his evidence is required.

Failure to comply with a witness summons amounts to contempt of court under s 3(1) of the 1965 Act, which provides that:

Any person who without just excuse disobeys a witness summons requiring him to attend before any court shall be guilty of contempt of that court and may be punished summarily by that court as if his contempt had been committed in the face of the court.

Under s 3(2), the maximum sentence under s 3(1) is 3 months' imprisonment.

The power to remand a witness in custody, pursuant to s 4(3) of the Criminal Procedure (Attendance of Witnesses) Act 1965, does not expire merely upon the commencement of a witness giving evidence on the first day; rather it continues for as long as it is anticipated that the witness might be required to give evidence on subsequent days. The correct test is whether there is a real possibility that either side might recall the witness: *R (TH) v Crown Court at Wood Green* [2006] EWHC 2683 (Admin); [2007] 1 WLR 1670.

11.5 PREPARATORY AND PRE-TRIAL HEARINGS; PLEA AND CASE MANAGEMENT HEARINGS

The CPIA 1996 makes provision for preliminary hearings to take place prior to Crown Court trials. Para IV.41 of the *Consolidated Practice Direction* also requires the convening of a 'plea and case management hearing' (PCMH) where a case is sent for trial.

11.5.1 Preparatory hearings

Section 29(1) of the CPIA 1996 empowers a Crown Court judge to order that a 'preparatory hearing' be held; such power may be exercised where 'an indictment reveals a case of such complexity, a case of such seriousness or a case whose trial is likely to be of such length, that substantial benefits are likely to accrue from [such] a hearing'. Thus, a preparatory hearing can be held on the basis that the case appears to be:

• complex; or
• serious; or
• lengthy.

Section 29(2) sets out the purposes of the preparatory hearing:

(a) identifying issues which are likely to be material to the determinations and findings which are likely to be required during the trial,

(b) if there is to be a jury, assisting their comprehension of those issues and expediting the proceedings before them,

(c) determining an application to which s 45 of the Criminal Justice Act 2003 [an application for trial without a jury] applies,

(d) assisting the judge's management of the trial,

(e) considering questions as to the severance or joinder of charges.

Section 30 says that the arraignment (i.e. the defendant being asked to plead guilty or not guilty) will take place at the start of the preparatory hearing, unless it has taken place before then.

Section 31(3) sets out the powers which the judge may exercise at the preparatory hearing. He may make a ruling as to:

(a) any question as to the admissibility of evidence;

(b) any other question of law relating to the case;

(c) any question as to the severance or joinder of charges.

Under s 31(4)(a), the judge may also require the prosecution to supply the defence with a written statement (a 'case statement') setting out the matters listed in s 31(5), namely:

(a) the principal facts of the case for the prosecution;

(b) the witnesses who will speak to those facts;

(c) any exhibits relevant to those facts;

(d) any proposition of law on which the prosecutor proposes to rely;

(e) the consequences in relation to any of the counts in the indictment that appear to the prosecutor to flow from the matters falling within paragraphs (a) to (d).

Section 31(4)(b) and (c) enable the judge to order the prosecution:

(b) to prepare the prosecution evidence and any explanatory material in such a form as appears to the judge to be likely to aid comprehension by a jury and to give it in that form to the court and to the accused or, if there is more than one, to each of them;

(c) to give the court and the accused or, if there is more than one, each of them written notice of documents the truth of the contents of which ought in the prosecutor's view to be admitted and of any other matters which in his view ought to be agreed;

Under s 31(7), where the judge has ordered the prosecution to give a notice under sub-s (4)(c) and the prosecutor has complied with the order, the judge may order the defence to supply a written notice stating the extent to which the defence agree with the prosecutor as to documents and other matters to which the notice under sub-s (4)(c) relates, and also the reason for any disagreement.

Section 34(1) provides that a party may depart from the case disclosed under s 31. However, s 34(2) provides that if a party departs from the case disclosed under s 31, or fails to comply with a requirement imposed under s 31, the judge or (with the leave of the judge) any other party may make such comment as appears to be appropriate and the jury may draw such inference as appears proper. Under s 34(3), the judge must have regard to the extent of the departure or failure, and to whether there is any justification for it.

A Crown Court judge is entitled to hold separate preparatory hearings under s 29 in respect of defendants who are charged jointly in the same indictment (*Kanaris v Governor of Pentonville Prison* [2003] UKHL 2; [2003] 1 WLR 443).

Under s 31(11), any order or ruling made at a preparatory hearing has effect throughout the trial, unless it appears to the judge (following an application by the prosecution or the defence) that the interests of justice require him to vary or discharge it. In *R v M (No 2)* [2007] EWCA Crim 970; [2007] 3 All ER 53, it was held that, although rulings made in the course of preparatory hearings should normally continue throughout the trial, they are not immutable. If the interests of justice as a whole so require, a ruling at a preparatory hearing might be changed. Moreover, any rulings of law at preparatory hearings must correctly reflect the law which will govern the trial (and so may need to be reviewed in light of any changes in the law).

In *R v K* [2006] EWCA Crim 724; [2006] 2 All ER 552, the Court of Appeal said that the new case management powers of judges in the Criminal Procedure Rules mean that a judge dealing with matters preliminary to a trial may, if he thinks it right to do so, deal with the issues exclusively by reference to written submissions, or to place a time limit on oral submissions. He is not bound to allow oral submissions and, if he does hear oral submissions, is entitled to place a time limit on them. The necessary public element of any hearing is sufficiently achieved if the defendants, and any representatives of the media, are supplied with copies of written submissions, if they wish to see them (per Sir Igor Judge P, at para 6).

11.5.2 Appeals from preparatory hearings

Section 35(1) of the CPIA provides that an appeal may be made to the Court of Appeal against any ruling s 31(3), but only with the leave of the judge or of the Court of Appeal.

Under s 35(2), the judge may continue a preparatory hearing notwithstanding that leave to appeal has been granted, but the trial itself cannot start until after the appeal has been determined or abandoned. The procedure for such an appeal is set out in Pt 66 of the Criminal Procedure Rules.

The scope of preparatory hearings, and appeals therefrom, was considered in *R v Claydon* [2001] EWCA Crim 1359; [2004] 1 WLR 1575. In the preparatory hearing in that case, a number of issues were raised which were formulated as abuse of process issues and issues under s 78 of the PACE 1984. The judge rejected submissions based on abuse of process but held that some evidence should be excluded because it would be unfair to admit it on the ground of entrapment. The defendants sought leave to appeal the judge's ruling. The first issue that arose was whether the Court of Appeal had jurisdiction under the 1996 Act to hear the appeal. The Court of Appeal held that for there to be an interlocutory appeal, there has not only to be a ruling as to admissibility or law made at a hearing held pursuant to the judge's order that there be a preparatory hearing, but the ruling has also to be for a purpose covered by s 29(2). In the present case, it could be said that the object of the hearing was for the limited purpose of securing a fair trial by excluding or admitting evidence (usually within the context of s 78) and so was not a purpose listed in s 29(2). However, the court took the view that Parliament clearly intended, by s 31(3)(a) of the 1996 Act, to empower rulings concerning questions of admissibility of evidence to be made at a preparatory hearing and for such rulings to be subject to appeal (if leave is given). Such questions preeminently arise under s 78, and it would largely emasculate s 31 if rulings given under s 78 were held to be outside its scope. Accordingly, the court held that the making of such rulings should be treated as being for the purpose of 'expediting the proceedings before the jury' (s 29(2)(b)). The trial judge therefore has power to determine s 78 issues within the context of the preparatory hearing (and so his rulings are, to that extent, subject to appeal); however, rulings as to abuse of process are not subject to appeal.

In *R v Ward* [2003] EWCA Crim 814; [2003] 2 Cr App R 20, the issue as to whether the case was likely to be long or complex had never been addressed by the trial judge. It followed that the judge had erred in concluding that the case fell within s 29. The judge was entitled to make a pre-trial ruling on a point of law, but that power came from s 40 of the 1996 Act (see below), not s 31(3). It followed that the Court of Appeal did not have jurisdiction to hold an interlocutory appeal, since there was no right of pre-trial appeal against a ruling under s 40.

Similarly, in *R v van Hoogstraten* [2003] EWCA Crim 3642; (2003) The Times, 24 December, the defendant was to be retried for manslaughter (his original conviction having been quashed by the Court of Appeal). The defence made an application to the trial judge that the case should not proceed to trial because, even if the prosecution proved their factual allegations, the jury would not in law be able to convict the defendant of manslaughter. The judge acceded to the application. The prosecution sought to appeal to the Court of Appeal, arguing that the judge's ruling had been made in a preparatory hearing under s 29 of the CPIA 1996. The Court of Appeal held that where the object of the defence application before the start of the trial is to prevent the trial occurring, that application falls outside the scope of the preparatory hearing under s 29(2) of the CPIA 1996, and so there can be no appeal to the Court of Appeal. It should be noted that the facts of this case would now be covered by the provisions of Pt 9 of the Criminal Justice Act 2003 (prosecution appeal against terminating rulings: see Chapter 13).

In *Attorney General's Reference (No 1 of 2004); R v Crowley* [2004] EWCA Crim 1025; [2004] 1 WLR 2111, it was held that, before ordering a preparatory hearing under the CPIA 1996, the judge must identify factors relevant to the criteria set out in s 29(2) of the Act. The judgment cannot be made solely on the basis of a study of the terms or length of the specific indictment. The judge is entitled to consider the evidence which is likely to be called and to make his own judgment as to whether he should order a preparatory hearing. If the judge has addressed the statutory criteria for such hearings, the Court of Appeal will be reluctant to set aside what is a matter for judicial assessment and decision by the trial judge. However, if there was no relevant material on which the judge could properly conclude that the case falls within s 29(1), there is no jurisdiction to make an order for a preparatory hearing and the Court of Appeal similarly lacks jurisdiction.

In *R v H (Interlocutory application: Disclosure)* [2007] UKHL 7; [2007] 2 AC 270 (decided under equivalent provisions contained in the Criminal Justice Act 1987), Lord Nicholls of Birkenhead (at para 7) said that:

in deciding whether to order a preparatory hearing, judges will always have in mind that the underlying object of a preparatory hearing is to conduct part of the trial before the jury is sworn because of the benefits this course is likely to have. The preparatory hearing procedure is not intended to be the means for deciding questions which can and should be decided in advance of the trial.

Lord Scott of Foscote observed (at para 32) that:

> The common thread that runs through all these purposes is, surely, that of producing an efficient and expeditious disposal of the criminal proceedings in question and thereby of avoiding, or reducing to a minimum, any waste of the judge's time, the jury's time or the time of the lawyers engaged in the case.

The House of Lords confirmed that a judge may determine other interlocutory applications at the same time as the preparatory hearing, but that there is no appeal to the Court of Appeal unless the ruling in question is for one of the purposes for which a preparatory hearing may be held. In the present case, the ruling was made in response to a defence application for disclosure under s 8 of the CPIA 1996 Act; this would qualify for an appeal only if it involves the determination of a question of law (in the instant case, it did not, since the issues raised were entirely factual).

There is detailed discussion of *R v H* in the Law Commission Consultation Paper, *The High Court's Jurisdiction in Relation to Criminal Proceedings* (Consultation Paper No 184), <http://www.lawcom.gov.uk/docs/cp184_tso.pdf>, para 2.70–2.89.

11.5.3 Pre-trial hearings

The procedure that we have just looked at is concerned only with complex, lengthy or serious trials. Section 39 of the CPIA 1996 provides for pre-trial hearings in other cases to be tried in the Crown Court. These hearings take place before the jury is empanelled.

Under s 40(1), a judge may make at a pre-trial hearing a ruling as to:

(a) any question as to the admissibility of evidence;
(b) any other question of law relating to the case concerned.

Under s 40(2), a ruling may be made either following an application by a party to the case, or of the judge's own motion.

Section 40(3) states that a ruling made under s 40 is binding from the time it is made until the case against the accused is disposed of (that is when the accused is acquitted or convicted, or the prosecutor decides not to proceed with the case).

Section 40(4) empowers the judge to discharge or vary a ruling made under s 40 (following an application by a party to the case, or of the judge's own motion) if it appears to him that it is in the interests of justice to do so. Under sub-s (5), an application for a ruling to be discharged or varied cannot be made unless there has been a material change of circumstances since the ruling was made.

Section 40(6) makes it clear that these provisions apply whether or not the pre-trial hearing and the trial itself are presided over by the same judge.

11.5.4 Plea and case management hearings

Paragraph IV.41 of *Consolidated Practice Direction* (which needs to be read in the light of the general case management powers contained in Pt 3 of the Criminal Procedure Rules) makes detailed provision for preliminary hearings in Crown Court cases.

Paragraph IV.41.3 provides that where a case is sent for trial under s 51 of the Crime and Disorder Act 1998, a preliminary hearing should normally only be ordered by the magistrates' court or by the Crown Court where:

(i)   there are case management issues which call for such a hearing;

(ii) the case is likely to last for more than 4 weeks;

(iii) it would be desirable to set an early trial date;

(iv) the defendant is a child or young person;

(v)   there is likely to be a guilty plea and the defendant could be sentenced at the preliminary hearing; or

(vi) it seems to the court that it is a case suitable for a preparatory hearing in the Crown Court.

Under para IV.41.5 and 6, where the magistrates' court does not order a preliminary hearing, it should order a plea and case management hearing (PCMH) to be held within about 14 weeks after sending for trial where a defendant is in custody and within about 17 weeks after sending for trial where a defendant is on bail. Where the case is committed for trial under s 6 of the Magistrates' Courts Act 1980 (until committal proceedings for either-way offences are abolished), a PCMH should be ordered by the magistrates' court in every case; it should be held within about 7 weeks after committal. Where the parties realistically expect to have completed their preparation for the PCMH in less time than that, the magistrates' court should order it to be held earlier. The paragraph goes on to point out that to order that a PCMH be held before the parties have had a reasonable opportunity to complete their preparation in accordance with the Criminal Procedure Rules 'risks compromising the effectiveness of this most important pre-trial hearing and risks wasting their time and that of the court'.

It follows that, whether or not there is a 'preliminary hearing', there will always be a PCMH. Indeed, r 3.8(3) of the Criminal Procedure Rules requires the Crown Court to conduct a plea and case management hearing 'unless the circumstances make that unnecessary'.

Paragraph IV.41.8 of the Practice Direction emphasises the importance of the PCMH:

> Active case management at the PCMH is essential to reduce the number of ineffective and cracked trials and delays during the trial to resolve legal issues. The effectiveness of a PCMH hearing in a contested case depends in large measure upon preparation by all concerned and upon the presence of the trial advocate or an advocate who is able to make decisions and give the court the assistance which the trial advocate could be expected to give. Resident Judges in setting the listing policy should ensure that list officers fix cases as far as possible to enable the trial advocate to conduct the PCMH and the trial.

Paragraph IV.41.11 says that, 'Additional pre-trial hearings should be held only if needed for some compelling reason. Such hearings – often described informally as "mentions" – are expensive and should actively be discouraged'.

At the PCMH, the defendant is asked to enter a plea to the offence(s) on the indictment (this is sometimes known as 'arraigning' the defendant). The indictment is read out by the clerk of the court and after each count the defendant says 'guilty' or 'not guilty'. Each count must be 'put' to the defendant separately and a separate plea must be entered on each count. The plea must be entered by the defendant personally (not through his advocate), at least if the plea is one of guilty (*R v Ellis* (1973) 57 Cr App R 571; *R v Williams* [1978] QB 373).

If the defendant pleads guilty, the judge should proceed to sentencing whenever possible, although it may be necessary to adjourn in order for a pre-sentence report to be prepared.

The *Auld Review* recommended that, in the preparation for trial in all criminal courts, there should be a move away from pre-trial hearings to co-operation between the parties according to standard timetables (wherever necessary, seeking written directions from the court). Lord Justice Auld recommended a written 'pre-trial assessment' by the court of the parties' readiness for trial, with a pre-trial hearing only if the court or the parties are unable to resolve all matters in this way (see Recommendations 210–221). However, this proposal was not adopted, perhaps because of the desire to ensure that the court should actively supervise the progress of the case.

Indeed, active judicial management of cases is becoming increasingly important. In *R v Jisl* [2004] EWCA Crim 696, for example, the Court of Appeal observed that whilst the defendant is entitled to a fair trial, the prosecution are equally entitled to a reasonable opportunity to present the evidence against the defendant. The court said that it is not a concomitant of the entitlement to a fair trial that either or both sides are entitled to take as much time as they like or, for that matter, as long as counsel and solicitors or defendants themselves think appropriate. Resources are limited. Time itself is a resource. Active, hands-on case management, both pre-trial and throughout the trial itself, is now regarded as an essential part of a judge's duty. The profession must understand that this has become and will remain part of the normal trial process, and that cases must be prepared and conducted accordingly (see paras 114–16 of the judgment of Judge LJ).

See also the PCHM Advocates Questionnaire: <http://www.justice.gov.uk/criminal/procrules_fin//contents/practice_direction/forms_anx_e%20pdf/anx_e1page1-19.pdf>.

11.6 THE TRIAL

Now, we start to examine in detail the early stages of a trial on indictment.

11.6.1 Presence of the defendant

In the Crown Court, the defendant must be present in order to enter a plea to the counts on the indictment. In the magistrates' court, the position is slightly different, as it is possible (where a defendant fails to attend court) for a not guilty plea to be entered on his behalf (although if the offence is triable either way, this is only possible if the accused had consented to summary trial at an earlier hearing).

If, after entering a plea, the defendant absconds (or misbehaves and disrupts the proceedings), the trial judge has a discretion to continue the trial in the defendant's absence. It will almost invariably be the case that the trial will continue where there is another defendant being tried at the same time and it would be unfair on that defendant to postpone the trial (see *R v Jones (No 2)* [1972] 1 WLR 887, where it was held that the defendant, by his conduct in absconding, had waived his right to be present at the trial and, in such circumstances, the judge had a discretion to allow the trial to proceed in the applicant's absence).

Further guidance was given by the House of Lords in *R v Jones* [2002] UKHL 5; [2003] 1 AC 1, where the defendants had pleaded not guilty on arraignment but absconded before the date fixed for the trial. The judge (after a number of adjournments) decided to try them in their absence. It was held by the House of Lords that the discretion to commence a trial in the absence of the defendant should be exercised (per Lord Bingham at para 6)

> with great caution and with close regard to the overall fairness of the proceedings; a defendant afflicted by involuntary illness or incapacity will have much stronger grounds for resisting the continuance of the trial than one who has voluntarily chosen to abscond.

At para 13, Lord Bingham reiterated that:

> the discretion to commence a trial in the absence of a defendant should be exercised with the utmost care and caution. If the absence of the defendant is attributable to involuntary illness or incapacity it would very rarely, if ever, be right to exercise the discretion in favour of commencing the trial, at any rate unless the defendant is represented and asks that the trial should begin.

In the same case, the Court of Appeal ([2001] EWCA Crim 168; [2001] QB 862 at 872–3, per Rose LJ) had set out, in detail, the principles which should guide the English courts in relation to the trial of a defendant in his absence. They are as follows:

(1) A defendant has, in general, a right to be present at his trial and a right to be legally represented.

(2) Those rights can be waived, separately or together, wholly or in part, by the defendant himself. They may be wholly waived if, knowing, or having the means of knowledge as to, when and where his trial is to take place, he deliberately and voluntarily absents himself and/or withdraws instructions from those representing him. They may be waived in part if, being present and represented at the outset, the defendant, during the course of the trial, behaves in such a way as to obstruct the proper course of the proceedings and/or withdraws his instructions from those representing him.

(3) The trial judge has a discretion as to whether a trial should take place or continue in the absence of a defendant and/or his legal representatives.

(4) That discretion must be exercised with great care and it is only in rare and exceptional cases that it should be exercised in favour of a trial taking place or continuing, particularly if the defendant is unrepresented.

(5) In exercising that discretion, fairness to the defence is of prime importance but fairness to the prosecution must also be taken into account. The judge must have regard to all

the circumstances of the case including, in particular: (i) the nature and circumstances of the defendant's behaviour in absenting himself from the trial or disrupting it, as the case may be and, in particular, whether his behaviour was deliberate, voluntary and such as plainly waived his right to appear; (ii) whether an adjournment might result in the defendant being caught or attending voluntarily and/or not disrupting the proceedings; (iii) the likely length of such an adjournment; (iv) whether the defendant, though absent, is, or wishes to be, legally represented at the trial or has, by his conduct, waived his right to representation; (v) whether an absent defendant's legal representatives are able to receive instructions from him during the trial and the extent to which they are able to present his defence; (vi) the extent of the disadvantage to the defendant in not being able to give his account of events, having regard to the nature of the evidence against him; (vii) the risk of the jury reaching an improper conclusion about the absence of the defendant; (viii) the seriousness of the offence, which affects defendant, victim and public; (ix) the general public interest and the particular interest of victims and witnesses that a trial should take place within a reasonable time of the events to which it relates; (x) the effect of delay on the memories of witnesses; (xi) where there is more than one defendant and not all have absconded, the undesirability of separate trials, and the prospects of a fair trial for the defendants who are present.

(6) If the judge decides that a trial should take place or continue in the absence of an unrepresented defendant, he must ensure that the trial is as fair as the circumstances permit. He must, in particular, take reasonable steps, both during the giving of evidence and in the summing up, to expose weaknesses in the prosecution case and to make such points on behalf of the defendant as the evidence permits. In summing up he must warn the jury that absence is not an admission of guilt and adds nothing to the prosecution case.

When the case went to the House of Lords, Lord Bingham made two observations about these principles. The first (as regards (5)(viii)), at para 14 of his speech, was that the seriousness of the offence should not be taken into account, since the trial judge's

> overriding concern will be to ensure that the trial, if conducted in the absence of the defendant, will be as fair as circumstances permit and lead to a just outcome. These objects are equally important, whether the offence charged be serious or relatively minor.

Paragraph I.13.19 of the *Consolidated Practice Direction* makes it clear that 'due regard' should be had to the judgment of Lord Bingham in *Jones* but adds that other relevant considerations include 'the seriousness of the offence and likely outcome if the defendant is found guilty'. This provision, however, is explained by the words which follow it, which make the point that the seriousness of the offence may be relevant in magistrates' court cases, since if the defendant is only likely to be fined for a summary offence this can be relevant, since the costs that a defendant might otherwise be ordered to pay as a result of an adjournment could be disproportionate; moreover, in the case of summary proceedings the fact that there can be an appeal in the form of a complete rehearing is also relevant, as is the power to reopen the case under s 142 of the Magistrates' Court Act 1980.

Lord Bingham also added (at para 15) that:

it is generally desirable that a defendant be represented even if he has voluntarily absconded. The task of representing at trial a defendant who is not present, and who may well be out of touch, is of course rendered much more difficult and unsatisfactory, and there is no possible ground for criticising the legal representatives who withdrew from representing the appellant at trial in this case. But the presence throughout the trial of legal representatives, in receipt of instructions from the client at some earlier stage, and with no object other than to protect the interests of that client, does provide a valuable safeguard against the possibility of error and oversight. For this reason trial judges routinely ask counsel to continue to represent a defendant who has absconded during the trial, and counsel in practice accede to such an invitation and defend their absent client as best they properly can in the circumstances.

Where a defendant is taken ill during the course of the trial and cannot attend court, the usual practice is for the trial to continue in his absence if he consents; if he does not consent to the trial continuing in his absence, and the illness is likely to last more than a few days, the jury will be discharged and a new trial will begin when the defendant is well enough to attend court.

In *R v Kepple* [2007] EWCA Crim 1339, the Court of Appeal said that where the defendant is being tried in his absence but counsel continues to act, he should conduct the case as though his client were still present in court but had decided not to give evidence, on the basis of any instruction he had received. He is free to use any material contained in his brief and may cross-examine prosecution witnesses and call defence witnesses. Counsel is entitled to ask questions of prosecution witnesses in as much detail as he wishes based on his instructions, but without indicating what the defendant's evidence might have been and in the knowledge that he will not be able to call evidence to contradict the answers given. He is entitled to conduct cross examination on this basis in the hope of either showing that his absent client's instructions are accepted by the witnesses or casting doubt upon the coherence or accuracy of their accounts.

In *R v O'Hare* [2006] EWCA Crim 471, Thomas LJ (at para 35) said that, contrary to observations by the Court of Appeal in *R v Jones* (above), it should be

> made clear to each defendant that if he fails to attend a trial, the consequences may well be that the trial will proceed in his absence and without legal representation. An analysis of the speeches in the House of Lords [in *R v Jones*] points to the conclusion that, if waiver is to be established, then knowledge of, or indifference to, the consequences of being tried in his absence and without legal representation would have to be proved. A direction to the defendant (of the nature suggested) upon the grant of bail as the provision to the defendant of a written statement (to the same effect) would, we think, generally provide an incontrovertible means of proof.

11.6.2 Bail

If the defendant is remanded in custody prior to his trial, he will remain in custody during the trial itself (unless the trial judge grants bail, which is very unlikely).

In *R v Central Criminal Court ex p Guney* [1996] AC 616, the House of Lords held that when a defendant who has not previously surrendered to the custody of the court is arraigned (i.e. called upon to plead guilty or not guilty), he thereby surrenders to the custody of the court at that moment. The result is that the Crown Court judge then has to decide whether or not to grant him bail; unless the judge grants bail, the defendant will remain in custody pending and during the trial.

In *R v Maidstone Crown Court ex p Jodka* (1997) 161 JP 638, the court held that bail granted by magistrates ceases when the defendant surrenders to the custody of the Crown Court, whether or not the defendant is arraigned at the hearing at which he surrenders. Where the magistrates grant bail subject to a surety, the responsibility of that surety under the magistrates' court order ceases once the defendant surrenders to the custody of the Crown Court. If the Crown Court wishes to grant bail subject to the same surety, the court must consider the position of that surety before imposing such a condition. However, in *Choudhry v Birmingham Crown Court* [2007] EWHC 2764 (Admin); (2008) 172 JP 33, Gibbs J (at para 35) said that it is both possible and lawful for a recognizance in Crown Court proceedings to be expressed as continuous until the conclusion of proceedings in the Crown Court. Any order varying the conditions of bail, unconnected with the sureties in question, does not give rise to the need for sureties to be taken afresh. His Lordship added (at para 36) that, assuming that a defendant who is on bail at the commencement of trial is then allowed to continue on bail, whether on the same or varied terms, that amounts to a fresh grant of bail (rather than a continuation of previous bail). However, provided that the recognizances were in terms which made it clear that they continued to bind the surety until the end of the trial, they will remain in force so long as bail was granted in terms which required that they did so, and so the sureties do not have to be taken again (para 37).

It follows from this that the question of bail will have to be considered at the pre-trial hearing. In any event, if the defendant is on bail before the trial, his bail effectively expires at the start of the trial. It is therefore a matter for the trial judge whether or not bail is granted to the defendant for lunch-time and/or overnight adjournments. Some judges usually withhold bail at lunch-time; some grant bail on the condition that the defendant remains in the company of his solicitor; others are happy to grant unconditional bail unless there seems to be a risk of the defendant absconding. Bail might be withdrawn if, for example, the likelihood of the defendant absconding increases because the case starts to go badly for him. If a custodial sentence is likely in the event of conviction, bail is normally withheld once the judge has begun the summing up. These issues are dealt with in para III.25 of the *Consolidated Practice Direction*, which provides as follows:

> III.25.2 Once a trial has begun the further grant of bail, whether during the short adjournment or overnight, is in the discretion of the trial judge. It may be a proper exercise of this discretion to refuse bail during the short adjournment if the accused cannot otherwise be segregated from witnesses and jurors.

> III.25.3 An accused who was on bail while on remand should not be refused overnight bail during the trial unless in the opinion of the judge there are positive reasons to justify this refusal. Such reasons are likely to be:

> (a) that a point has been reached where there is a real danger that the accused will abscond, either because the case is going badly for him, or for any other reason;
> (b) that there is a real danger that he may interfere with witnesses or jurors.

III.25.4 There is no universal rule of practice that bail shall not be renewed when the summing-up has begun. Each case must be decided in the light of its own circumstances and having regard to the judge's assessment from time to time of the risks involved.

III.25.5 Once the jury has returned a verdict a further renewal of bail should be decided in the light of the gravity of the offence and the likely sentence to be passed in all the circumstances of the case.

11.6.3 Unrepresented defendants

Where the defendant is unrepresented:

(a) the trial judge should ask such questions as he sees fit, to test the reliability of the prosecution witnesses and may ask the defendant whether there are certain matters he wishes to be put to the witnesses;
(b) the jury should be instructed (at the start of the trial and in the summing up) that the defendant is entitled to represent himself and they should also be warned of the difficulty of his doing so properly;
(c) the judge should prevent repetitious questioning of prosecution witnesses by the defendant.

It should be noted that s 34 of the Youth Justice and Criminal Evidence Act (YJCEA) 1999 provides that no person charged with a sexual offence may cross-examine the complainant, either in connection with that offence or in connection with any other offence (of whatever nature) with which that person is charged in the proceedings. Under s 35 of the Act, unrepresented defendants are not allowed to cross-examine in person a child who is either the complainant of, or a witness to the commission of, an offence of kidnapping or any offence which involves an assault on, or injury or a threat of injury to, any person. Section 36 gives courts the power to prohibit unrepresented defendants from cross-examining witnesses in cases where a mandatory ban does not apply under ss 34 and 35, but where the court is satisfied:

(a) that the quality of evidence given by the witness on cross-examination—

   (i)   is likely to be diminished if the cross-examination (or further cross-examination) is conducted by the accused in person, and
   (ii) would be likely to be improved if a direction were given under this section, and

(b) that it would not be contrary to the interests of justice to give such a direction.

Article 6(3)(c) of the European Convention on Human Rights guarantees the right to legal representation and legal aid. However, the European Court of Human Rights has held that a court may place restrictions on the right of a defendant to appear without a lawyer, so long as there are relevant and sufficient grounds for holding that this is necessary in the interests of justice (*Croissant v Germany* (1993) 16 EHRR 135). The provisions of the 1999 Act would therefore seem to be within Art 6.

11.6.4 Adjournments

In *R v Chaaban* [2003] EWCA Crim 1012; (2003) *The Times*, 8 May, the Court of Appeal said that adjournments must be justified and, if at all possible, should be avoided. When asked to consider an adjournment, the judge must closely scrutinise the application and, unless satisfied that it is indeed necessary and justified, should refuse it. However, the Court noted that the decision whether or not to adjourn is pre-eminently a matter for the trial judge, and so the Court of Appeal will not interfere with that decision unless it can be demonstrated that the decision to refuse an adjournment was wholly unreasonable and caused real as opposed to fanciful prejudice to the defendant, undermining the safety of the conviction (per Judge LJ at para 36).

11.7 THE JURY

In this section, we examine the composition of the jury, and how the jury to try a defendant is chosen.

11.7.1 Who can serve on a jury?

Jurors are drawn from the electoral register. Anyone on the register and aged between 18 and 70 can be summoned for jury service (s 1 of the Juries Act 1974). The principle underpinning the operation of the Juries Act 1974 is that the jury should be a cross-section of society, drawn at random.

Prior to the amendment of the Juries Act 1974 by the Criminal Justice Act 2003, some people were ineligible to serve on a jury. This category included the judiciary (including lay magistrates), lawyers, those concerned in the administration of justice (for example, police officers, prison officers, and probation officers), the clergy and the mentally disordered. Other people had the right to be excused from jury service if they so wished. This category included those aged 65 or over, those who had served on a jury within the last two years, Members of Parliament, full time serving members of the armed forces, and medical personnel (such as doctors, dentists, nurses and vets).

A major change recommended by the *Auld Review* was that those with criminal convictions and mental disorder should continue to be excluded from jury service, but that no one else should be ineligible for, or excusable as of right from, it (Recommendation 20). This proposal was enacted by the Criminal Justice Act 2003.

By virtue of the amendments made by the 2003 Act, s 1 of the Juries Act 1974 (qualification for jury service) now reads as follows:

(1) Subject to the provisions of this Act, every person shall be qualified to serve as a juror in the Crown Court ... and be liable accordingly to attend for jury service when summoned under this Act if—

    (a) he is for the time being registered as a parliamentary or local government elector and is not less than eighteen nor more than seventy years of age;

    (b) he has been ordinarily resident in the United Kingdom, the Channel Islands or the Isle of Man for any period of at least five years since attaining the age of thirteen;

    (c) he is not a mentally disordered person; and

(d) he is not disqualified for jury service.

(2) In sub-section (1) above 'mentally disordered person' means any person listed in Part 1 of Schedule 1 to this Act.

(3) The persons who are disqualified for jury service are those listed in Part 2 of that Schedule.

Under Pt 1 of Sched 1 to the 1974 Act (as substituted by the 2003 Act), only mentally disordered people are ineligible for jury service (and there is a comprehensive definition of mental disorder in that Schedule).

The Criminal Justice Act 2003 also amended the categories of those who are disqualified from jury service (set out in Pt 2 of Sched 1 to the Juries Act 1974). The following people are disqualified from jury service:

- a person who is on bail in criminal proceedings at the relevant time;
- a person who has at any time been sentenced in the UK to imprisonment or detention for life, to detention during Her Majesty's pleasure, to imprisonment or detention for public protection, to an extended sentence under ss 227 or 228 of the Criminal Justice Act 2003, or to a term of imprisonment or detention of five years or more;
- a person who at any time in the last 10 years has, in the UK, served any part of a sentence of imprisonment or detention, or has had passed on him a suspended sentence of imprisonment or detention;
- a person who at any time in the last 10 years has, in England and Wales, had made in respect of him a community order under s 177 of the Criminal Justice Act 2003, a community rehabilitation order, a community punishment order, a community punishment and rehabilitation order, a drug treatment and testing order or a drug abstinence order.

Under the revised rules on eligibility for jury service, even lawyers and judges, and police officers, are now eligible for jury service. Such jurors will (according to guidance issued by the Central Summoning Bureau) be asked to sit in a court other than one in which they regularly appear or sit as the case may be. The *Auld Review* specifically rejected the argument that such a person might (albeit unintentionally) unduly influence their fellow jurors (citing the fact that in some American states, where lawyers and judges are eligible for jury service, such problems do not seem to have arisen (see paras 27–32 of Chapter 5)).

In *R v Abdroikov* [2007] UKHL 37, [2007] 1 WLR 2679, three defendants had been tried on indictment in different courts on unrelated charges and were convicted. In the first two cases the trial jury included among its members a serving police officer, and in the third case it included a solicitor employed by the Crown Prosecution Service (CPS). The House held (by a 3:2 majority) that the question to be asked was whether, on the particular facts of each of the cases, a fair-minded and informed observer would conclude that there was a real possibility that the jurors in question were biased, having regard to the fact that Parliament had declared that in England and Wales such persons were eligible to sit on juries, envisaging that any objection to their sitting would be the subject of judicial decision. They went on to hold that the convictions should be quashed in the case where one of the jurors was an employee of CPS (that fact was enough to create a suspicion of bias in a case where the prosecution was brought by CPS) and the case where one of the jurors was a serving police officer who worked in the same area as police witnesses in the case; however, the conviction should not be quashed in the other case, where the police officer who was on the jury did not work in the same area as the police witnesses. Lord Bingham quotes from the Morris Committee in 1965 (Cmnd 2627) and cites para 103 of their report:

> If juries are to continue to command public confidence it is essential that they should manifestly represent an impartial and lay element in the workings of the courts. It follows that all those whose work is connected with the detection of crime and the enforcement of law and order must be excluded, as must those who professionally practise the law, or whose work is concerned with the functioning of the courts.

Paragraph 104 of the report went on:

> ... it seems to us necessary to secure the exclusion from juries of any person who, in the words of one memorandum submitted to us, 'because of occupation or position, has knowledge or experience of a legal or quasi-legal nature which is likely to enable him to exercise undue influence over his fellow jurors'. If justice is not only to be done but to be seen to be done, such persons must not be allowed to serve on juries lest the specialist knowledge and prestige attaching to their occupations might cause them to be what has been described to us as 'built-in leaders'.

His Lordship then pointed out that when Lord Justice Auld considered this issue in his *Review of the Criminal Courts of England and Wales*, he came to a different view, recognising concerns about the risk of prejudice or partiality, but suggesting that any question about the suspicion or apprehension of bias on the part of any particular juror could be resolved by the trial judge on the facts of the particular case. In para 30 of Chapter 5, he wrote:

> There is also the anxiety voiced by some that those closely connected with the criminal justice system, for example, a policeman or a prosecutor, would not approach the case with the same openness of mind as someone unconnected with the legal system. I do not know why the undoubted risk of prejudice of that sort should be any greater than in the case of many others who are not excluded from juries and who are trusted to put aside any prejudices they may have. Take, for example shopkeepers or house-owners who may have been burgled, or car owners whose cars may have been vandalised, many government and other employees concerned in one way or another with public welfare and people with strong views on various controversial issues, such as legalisation of drugs or euthanasia. I acknowledge that there may be Article 6 considerations in this. But it would be for the judge in each case to satisfy himself that the potential juror in question was not likely to engender any reasonable suspicion or apprehension of bias so as to distinguish him from other members of the public who would normally be expected to have an interest in upholding the law. Provided that the judge was so satisfied, the over-all fairness of the tribunal and of the trial should not be at risk.

Baroness Hale noted that the essential question is whether, on the particular facts of each of these cases, a fair-minded and informed observer would conclude that there was a real possibility that the jury was biased. At para 51, she considers the appeal where a member of the staff of the CPS was one of the jurors. She says:

> It is inconceivable that the Director of Public Prosecutions could sit as a juror in a case prosecuted by the CPS, irrespective of whether or not he had been personally involved in the decision to prosecute. There would be no objection to his sitting in a case prosecuted by some other person or authority. The same must apply to a CPS lawyer, who is employed to decide upon whether or not to prosecute and to conduct the prosecutions decided upon. Whether the same would apply to other CPS employees, whose role in the prosecution process or whose connection with the organisation is rather more peripheral, is a separate question which does not arise here. One could imagine that it might not apply to temporary or short term employees in junior positions unless the prosecution were brought by the office in which they served. There would, of course, be no objection to CPS lawyers or other employees serving on juries in prosecutions brought by other persons or authorities. This view is consistent with Parliament's lifting the ban upon members of the DPP's staff serving on juries, while leaving intact the common law and Convention rules against bias.

In the next paragraph, Baroness Hale goes on to consider the position of police officers as members of a jury. She says:

> Police officers are in a rather different position. Their professional role is the prevention of crime and the apprehension of criminals and persons suspected of crime. They arrest, question and charge people but they do not prosecute. These may seem like technical distinctions when the police are so closely associated in the public mind with the fight against crime. If one asked a member of the public whether he would rather be tried by a jury containing one or more police officers or a jury containing one or more CPS employees, his preference might well be for the CPS over the police. But we are here talking of identification with the prosecution process and the police are further removed from that than are the CPS. Furthermore, while it is consistent with the legislation to distinguish between CPS and other prosecutions the objection to the police is their identification with the fight against crime generally rather than with the prosecution process in particular. Parliament obviously intended that police officers should be eligible to serve on juries in some cases (although they may well have contemplated a rather closer inquiry into the circumstances of each individual police juror than in fact takes place). The difficulty therefore is to identify a criterion by which to judge when they can and when they cannot do so.

It was this distinction between the roles of employees of CPS and police officers which enabled the House of Lords to rule that there should be an absolute bar on CPS employees sitting on juries in cases where CPS is the prosecutor, but that a police officer could sit on a jury unless connected in some way (for example, by place of work) to the police witnesses in the particular case.

Lord Rodger of Earlsferry dissented in the outcome. He observed at para 33 that the law takes steps to minimise the risk of prejudice or bias

> by making jurors take an oath or affirm that they will 'faithfully try the defendant and give a

true verdict according to the evidence'. It makes them sit and listen to the evidence in a solemn setting. It requires the judge to give them a direction that they must assess the evidence impartially. Of course, it would be naïve to suppose that these safeguards will always work with every juror. The law is not naïve: it stipulates that there should be 12 men and women on a jury. The assumption is that, among them, the twelve will be able to neutralise any bias on the part of one or more members and so reach an impartial verdict – by a majority, if necessary. If any of the jurors consider that the jury will be unable to do so, then they must tell the judge, who can then deal with the matter – by discharging the jury, if necessary. So the mere fact that there is a real possibility that a juror may be biased does not mean that there is a real possibility that the jury will be incapable of returning an impartial verdict.

In the next para, he goes on:

> The reality therefore is that the jury system operates, not because those who serve are free from prejudice, but despite the fact that many of them will harbour prejudices of various kinds when they enter the jury box. In the United States a voir dire is held to try to select jurors who are free from relevant prejudices. In Britain, with its very different history, such a procedure has not been adopted – indeed it has been specifically rejected. If experience had shown that British juries, made up of people drawn at random from all kinds of backgrounds, could not act impartially, the system would long since have lost all credibility. But Parliament must consider that it works, since it has not abolished it or introduced a new procedure for selecting jurors, even though it has had opportunities to do so. Juries also seem to enjoy the confidence of the general public. The fair-minded and informed observer will be well aware of this.

At para 38 he says that there is:

> no reason why the fair-minded and informed observer should single out juries with police officers and CPS lawyers as being constitutionally incapable of following the judge's directions and reaching an impartial verdict.

He concludes, at para 44 that:

> although the fair-minded and informed observer would see that it was possible that a police officer or CPS lawyer would be biased, he would also see that the possibility of the jury's verdict being biased as a result was no greater than in many other cases. In other words, the mere presence of these individuals, without more, would not give rise to a real possibility that the jury had been unable to assess the evidence impartially and reach an unbiased verdict.

Lord Carswell, who also dissented in the outcome, said (at para 68) that he had concluded that

> . . . the fair-minded and informed observer would not necessarily conclude that the mere presence on a jury of a police officer or CPS staff member would create such a possibility of bias as to deny the defendant a fair trial. Such an observer would in my view wish to know more about the circumstances of the case, the issues to be decided, the background of the

juror in question and the closeness of any connection which he or she might have to the case to be tried.

A review of the statutory rules governing eligibility to sit on a jury may well follow this decision. In the meantime, the effect of this case was considered in *R v Alan I* [2007] EWCA Crim 2999. Nelson J, at para 29, said:

> In all cases the test is one of apparent bias. This will depend on the facts. If, for example, a potential juror knows a witness personally, it is common for such a juror to stand down. Where, however, the witness he knows is not contentious and not to be called, but is taken simply as read as an agreed statement, there may well be no possibility of bias. It is therefore necessary for the judge to make all appropriate factual enquiries. Usually, this is by posing questions, either in court or in writing to the potential juror. The manner in which the questions are asked will depend on the circumstances. Sometimes a few questions in open court will suffice. In other cases, where the information might be sensitive, or more detail is required, the matter may have to be dealt with in writing.

His Lordship went on to hold (at para 35) that any potential juror who knows witnesses who are to be called to give oral evidence should be stood down at the outset, 'unless it can be said with certainty that the evidence of the witnesses who are known will play no contested part in the determination of the matter'. His Lordship concluded (at para 36):

> ... if it cannot be so determined with certainty, the potential juror who knows witnesses personally should be asked to stand down, whether he be a policeman or not a policeman ... unless it can be said with certainty that the known witnesses to be called will play no contested as opposed to an agreed part in the determination of the issues, a juror who personally knows a witness or witnesses should normally be asked to stand down.

In *R v Khan* [2008] EWCA Crim 531, the Court of Appeal gave detailed consideration to the effect of the decision of the House of Lords in *R v Abdroikov*. In *Khan*, the appeals were each based on the ground that a member of the jury had, by reason of their occupation, an appearance of bias. The relevant jurors were a serving police officer, an employee of the CPS (in a case being prosecuted by the Department of Trade and Industry), and two prison officers. Giving the judgement of the Court of Appeal, Lord Phillips of Worth Matravers CJ said (at para 10):

> Where an impartial juror is shown to have had reason to favour a particular witness, this will not necessarily result in the quashing of a conviction. It will only do so if this has rendered the trial unfair, or given it an appearance of unfairness. To decide this it is necessary to consider two questions:
>
> (i)   Would the fair minded observer consider that partiality of the juror to the witness may have caused the jury to accept the evidence of that witness? If so
>
> (ii)   Would the fair minded observer consider that this may have affected the outcome of the trial?
>
> If the answer to both questions is in the affirmative, then the trial will not have the appearance of fairness. If the answer to the first or the second question is in the negative, then the

partiality of the juror to the witness will not have affected the safety of the verdict and there will be no reason to consider the trial unfair.

His Lordship confesses to finding it difficult to deduce from *Abdroikov* clear principles that apply where a juror is a police officer. However, at para 29, his Lordship said that the Court had concluded that

> ... the fact that a police juror may seem likely to favour the evidence of a fellow police officer will not, automatically, lead to the appearance that he favours the prosecution. If the police evidence is not challenged or does not form an important part of the prosecution case, we do not consider that it will normally do so. None the less it will be appropriate to quash the conviction if, but only if, the effect of the juror's partiality towards a brother officer puts in doubt the safety of the conviction and thus renders the trial unfair.

At para 48, Lord Phillips adds:

> If one starts, as one must, from the premise that police officers are not, by reason simply of their occupations, considered to be biased in favour of the prosecution, we do not consider that the fact that a police officer has taken part in operations involving the type of offence with which a defendant is charged, gives rise, of itself, to an appearance of bias on the part of the police officer. Most police officers are likely to have had experience of most of the common types of criminal offence, not least drug dealing. We do not consider that familiarity with the particular offence charged against an offender would lead the objective observer to suspect a police juror of bias.

Lord Phillips also points out (at para 97), that it is clear from *Abdroikov* that 'there could be no objection to a member of the Crown Prosecution Service sitting in a case prosecuted by some other authority.'

Dealing with the prison officer jurors, Lord Phillips noted (at para 117) that, as a result of the enactment of the Criminal Justice Act 2003, 'evidence of bad character is now routinely placed before the jury in specified situations where it has particular relevance'. His Lordship concluded (at para 120) that:

> ... knowledge of a defendant's bad character will not automatically result in the juror ceasing to qualify as 'independent and impartial'. The mere suspicion that a juror might, by reason of having been employed as a prison officer in a prison where the defendant was held, have acquired knowledge of that defendant's bad character could not, of itself, lead an objective observer to conclude that the juror had an appearance of bias.

At the end of the judgement in *Khan*, Lord Phillips said (at para 131) that it was 'undesirable that the apprehension of the jury bias should lead to appeals' and that it is 'particularly undesirable if such appeals lead to the quashing of convictions so that re-trials have to take place'. His Lordship said it was therefore 'desirable that any risk of jury bias, or of unfairness as a result of partiality to witnesses should be identified before the trial begins. If such a risk may arise, the juror should be stood down' (ibid). His Lordship concludes (at para 132) that it is 'essential that the trial judge should be aware at the stage of jury selection if any juror in waiting is or has been, a police officer or a member of the prosecuting authority, or is a serving prison officer'.

The virtue of having representative juries is discussed by Gwynedd Parry in 'Jury Service for All? Analysing Lawyers as Jurors' (2006) 70 J Crim L 163. She says:

> It is because almost all members of the community are summonable for jury service that the jury becomes a representative body, and it is this feature that gives it its democratic quality. Representativeness is in one sense an intrinsic value that legitimises the process. On the other hand, it may equally be seen as a means to an end, which is the facilitation of an independent and unbiased tribunal that commands public confidence.

One of the other concerns about jury trial has been that a substantial number of people are not summoned for jury service because they are not on the electoral role. In his *Review of the Criminal Courts of England and Wales,* Lord Justice Auld quotes (Chapter 5, para 22) some Home Office research showing that in 1999 some eight per cent of people who were eligible to register on the electoral roll had not done so. Those aged 20–24, ethnic minorities and those living in rented accommodation were most under-represented on the electoral roll. Indeed, people who move house frequently, for whatever reason, are less likely to be on the electoral roll. Lord Justice Auld said that jurors should be more representative than they currently are of the national and local communities from which they are drawn. To this end, Recommendation 18 in the Review is that:

> The law should be amended to substitute for the condition of registration on an electoral roll, inclusion in such a roll and/or on any one or more of a number of other specified publicly maintained lists or directories, but excluding anyone listed who, on investigation at the summons stage, is found not to be entitled to registration as an elector.

Thus, entitlement to, rather than actual, entry on an electoral role would be the basis for eligibility; this would make it possible to use other sources of information (public registers and lists) to track down people who are eligible to be on the electoral roll but are not in fact on it. The Government has not so far acted upon this suggestion.

11.7.2 Excusal

Under the original version of the Juries Act 1974, as well as a list of those ineligible to serve, there was also a list of people who were entitled to be 'excused as of right' from jury service (for example medical practitioners). This provision was repealed by the Criminal Justice Act 2003. The effect of this repeal is that no one is entitled to automatic excusal from jury service.

The Auld Review had noted the number of people who sought – and obtained – excusal from jury service (during a sample period in 1999, 38 per cent of those summoned), and quotes the axiom that the scope for excusal created the impression that jury service is only for those not important or clever enough to get out of it (para 13 in Chapter 5). The effect of this (especially in the case of longer trials) was that the jury did not represent a true cross-section of the community at large. To deal with this problem, the Review made three recommendations:

> **22** Save for those who have recently undertaken, or have been excused by a court from, jury service, no-one should be excusable from jury service as of right, only on showing good reason for excusal.
>
> **23** The Central Summoning Bureau or the court, in examining a claim for discretionary excusal, should consider its power of deferral first.
>
> **24** The Bureau should treat all subsequent applications for deferral and all applications for excusal against clear criteria identified in the jury summons.

The effect of the reforms made by the 2003 Act is that anyone who is not ineligible through mental illness, or disqualified because of a previous conviction, is required to attend for jury service if summoned. However:

- s 9(2) of the Juries Act 1974 provides that a person who has been summoned for jury service may seek excusal if they can show a 'good reason' for this;
- s 9A(1) enables a person summoned for jury service to seek deferral of that service if there is good reason (and so if, for example, the dates specified in the summons clash with the person's holiday arrangements or business commitments, attendance can be deferred to a later date);
- s 9B enables a person to be excused from jury service because he or she is not capable of acting effectively as a juror because of a physical disability.

The discretion to excuse or defer is exercised by the Jury Central Summoning Bureau which administers the jury summoning system on behalf of the Crown Court in England and Wales.

Under s 9AA of the 1974 Act, guidance has to be given on the exercise of the discretion to excuse or defer. The guidance (<http://www.hmcourts-service.gov.uk/courtfinder/forms/js_guidance_0404.pdf>) that has been issued states that excusal should be reserved for cases where it would be 'unreasonable to require the person to serve at any time within the following 12 months' (see para 2), and that a person should be excused from jury service only in 'extreme circumstances' (para 4).

In *R v Guildford Crown Court ex p Siderfin* [1990] 2 QB 683, the Divisional Court said that it would be appropriate to excuse from jury service a practising member of a religious society or order the tenets or beliefs of which are incompatible with jury service.

Another concern that is considered in the *Auld Review* is the number of people who evaded jury service. In para 25 of Chapter 5, Lord Justice Auld refers to Home Office research showing that some 15 per cent of summoned jurors failed to attend court. To endeavour to counter this, the Review suggests (Recommendation 18) that:

> There should be rigorous and well publicised enforcement of the obligation to undertake jury service when required, and consideration should be given to doing so by way of a system of fixed penalties subject to a right of appeal to the magistrates.

This suggestion was not taken up in the Criminal Justice Act 2003, and so it remains incumbent on the Crown Court to deal with those who fail to answer their summons for jury service. A person who is summoned for jury service and who fails to attend without reasonable cause is guilty of an offence punishable with a fine of up to £1,000 (s 20 of the Juries Act 1974).

Paragraph IV.42 of the *Consolidated Practice Direction* states:

> IV.42.1 . . . Jury service is an important public duty which individual members of the public are chosen at random to undertake. The normal presumption is that everyone, unless mentally disordered or disqualified, will be required to serve when summoned to do so . . . [T]rial judges must continue to be alert to the need to exercise their discretion to adjourn a trial, excuse or discharge a juror should the need arise. Whether or not an application has already been made to the jury summoning officer for deferral or excusal it is also open to the person summoned to apply to the court to be excused. Such applications must be considered with common sense and according to the interests of justice. An explanation should be required for an application being much later than necessary.

> IV.42.2 Where a juror appears on a jury panel, it may be appropriate for a judge to excuse the juror from that particular case where the potential juror is personally concerned with the facts of the particular case or is closely connected with a prospective witness. Where the length of the trial is estimated to be significantly longer than the normal period of jury service, it is good practice for the trial judge to enquire whether the potential jurors on the jury panel foresee any difficulties with the length and if the judge is satisfied that the jurors' concerns are justified he may say that they are not required for that particular jury. This does not mean that the judge must excuse the juror from sitting at that court altogether as it may well be possible for the juror to sit on a shorter trial at the same court.

> IV.42.3 Where a juror unexpectedly finds him or herself in difficult professional or personal circumstances during the course of the trial, jurors should be encouraged to raise such problems with the trial judge. This might apply, for example, to a parent whose childcare arrangements unexpectedly fail or a worker who is engaged in the provision of services the need for which can be critical or Member of Parliament who has deferred their jury service to an apparently more convenient time, but is unexpectedly called back to work for a very important reason. Such difficulties would normally be raised through a jury note in the normal manner. In such circumstances, the judge must exercise his or her discretion according to the interests of justice and the requirements of each individual case. The judge must decide for himself whether the juror has presented a sufficient reason to interfere with the course of the trial. If the juror has presented a sufficient reason, in longer trials it may well be possible to adjourn for a short period in order to allow the juror to overcome the difficulty. In shorter cases it may be more appropriate to discharge the juror and to continue the trial with a reduced number of jurors. The power to do this is implicit in section 16 (1) Juries Act 1974. In unusual cases (such as an unexpected emergency arising overnight) a juror need not be discharged in open court. The good administration of justice depends on the co-operation of jurors who perform an essential public service. All such applications should be dealt with sensitively and sympathetically and the trial judge should always seek to meet the interests of justice without unduly inconveniencing any juror.

11.7.3 Empanelling a jury

The term 'jury panel' is used to describe the body of people who have been summoned for jury service at a particular Crown Court.

Where a defendant has pleaded not guilty to an indictment, at least 12 members of the jury panel are brought into the court room; they are then known as the 'jury in waiting'. The clerk of the court calls out the names of 12 of them, chosen at random.

Once 12 people are in the jury box, the clerk says to the defendant, 'the names that you are about to hear are the names of the jurors who are to try you. If you wish to object to them or to any of them, you must do so as they come to the book to be sworn, and before they are sworn, and your objection shall be heard'. The nature of the objection referred to is considered below when we examine challenges to jurors.

Each of the jurors (one after the other) takes the juror's oath, reading the words from a card and holding in his right hand the appropriate Holy Book (New Testament for Christians, Old Testament for Jews, Koran for Muslims). Jurors who do not wish to swear an oath are permitted to make an affirmation instead. The terms of the oath/affirmation are set out in para IV.42.4 of the *Consolidated Practice Direction*, which stipulates that:

> The wording of the oath to be taken by jurors is: 'I swear by Almighty God that I will faithfully try the defendant and give a true verdict according to the evidence.' Any person who objects to being sworn shall be permitted to make his solemn affirmation instead. The wording of the affirmation is 'I do solemnly, sincerely and truly declare and affirm that I will faithfully try the defendant and give a true verdict according to the evidence.'

Note that Recommendation 295 of the *Auld Review* was for a simpler form:

> The juror's oath and affirmation should be replaced with a promise in the following or similar form: 'I promise to try the defendant and to decide on the evidence whether he is guilty or not.'

Once all 12 have taken the oath (or affirmed), the clerk reads out the indictment and then says, 'To this indictment the defendant has pleaded not guilty. It is your charge, having heard the evidence, to say whether he be guilty or not'. Note that if the defendant has pleaded guilty to some of the counts on the indictment, but not guilty to the others, the jury will not be told about the guilty pleas.

In some cases, there have been attempts to 'nobble' the jury. If the police fear that such an attempt is likely, an application may be made for the jurors to receive special protection. In *R v Comerford* [1998] 1 WLR 191, it was held that an application for jury protection should normally be made in the presence of the defendant, and should be supported by evidence of the need for such protection (which the defendant can cross-examine). Any departure from this approach is only possible if the trial judge is satisfied that it is necessary and would not render the trial process unfair. Furthermore, the jury must be directed not to hold it against the defendant that protective measures have been taken. In that case, the clerk in the Crown Court did not reveal the names of the jurors. The Court of Appeal held that, although the defendant is entitled under s 5(2) of the Juries Act 1974, if he wishes, to know the names of all the people on the jury panel (that is, all those summoned for jury service at that court), it is permissible, in an appropriate case, for the clerk not to follow the usual practice of calling out the names of the individual jurors as they enter the jury box.

11.8 CHALLENGES TO JURORS

The clerk tells the defendant that he can challenge the jury, or individual jurors. In this section, we consider the challenges which can be made to the jury as a whole and to individual jurors.

11.8.1 Challenging the whole jury

Theoretically, it is open to the defendant to challenge the way in which the jury panel was selected; this is known as 'challenging the array'. In practice, this never occurs. The only basis for objecting to the entire jury panel would be that the population of the area served by that particular Crown Court would be hostile to the defendant because of the notoriety of the case. In such a case, the appropriate course of action would be to seek a change in the location of the trial.

11.8.2 Challenging individual jurors

Both the prosecution and the defence can challenge a would-be juror on the ground that he or she may be biased for or against the accused. The prosecution and the judge also have the right to stand a potential juror by, so that he or she does not sit on that jury.

11.8.2.1 Challenging for cause

The party who alleges that a juror is biased bears the burden of proving bias.

To challenge for cause, counsel says 'challenge' just before the would-be juror takes his oath. The reason for the challenge is then explained to the judge. In a straightforward case, the judge will ask the would-be juror to leave the jury box, having heard submissions from counsel. Otherwise, jurors who have already been sworn in and the rest of the 'jury in waiting' will be asked to leave the court room and evidence will be called to substantiate the challenge.

Unlike the position in the United States (where jurors are questioned at length on their suitability to try the case in question), the challenger must provide prima facie evidence in support of the challenge before being allowed to question the juror (*R v Chandler (No 2)* [1964] 2 QB 322). An example of this taking place is *R v Kray* (1969) 53 Cr App R 412. The activities of the accused had been the subject of sensational reporting in a newspaper; counsel for the accused persuaded the trial judge that anyone who had read the graphic and inaccurate material would be predisposed to convict the accused. Once the judge was satisfied of this, he allowed the defence to ask each potential juror if they had read the offending press reports.

Questioning of potential jurors can only take place in exceptional cases. In *R v Andrews* [1999] Crim LR 156, the appellant claimed that her conviction for murder was unsafe because of adverse pre-trial publicity. It was argued on her behalf that potential jurors should have been asked whether they had read or heard the reports in question. It was held that such questioning of jurors (whether done orally or by means of a questionnaire) is of doubtful efficacy and may even be counter-productive (by reminding the jurors of the adverse publicity); it should therefore only be done in the most exceptional circumstances. In *Montgomery v HM Advocate; Coulter v HM Advocate* [2003] 1 AC 641, the Privy Council (hearing a Scottish appeal) held that, where there has been prejudicial pre-trial publicity, the court is entitled to expect the jury to follow the directions which they receive from the trial judge and to return a true verdict based only on the evidence they have heard in court. Lord Hope of Craighead said (at p 674) that:

> the entire system of trial by jury is based upon the assumption that the jury will follow the instructions which they receive from the trial judge and that they will return a true verdict in accordance with the evidence.

On that basis, a defendant may be regarded as having received a fair trial even if there has been adverse pre-trial publicity. The Court of Appeal took the same view in *R v Stone* [2001] EWCA Crim 297; (2001) *The Times*, 22 February, where it was held that in deciding whether to order a retrial in a case that had attracted widespread publicity, the court has to consider whether it could be satisfied, on the balance of probabilities, that if the jury empanelled at the retrial returned a verdict of guilty, the effect of the pre-trial publicity would be such as to render that conviction unsafe. In the present case, any retrial would not start until nearly three years after the relevant publicity, and the public would have largely forgotten about that publicity. Even if they did not forget it entirely, the passage of time made it easier for them to set aside that which they would be told to disregard. It was, said the court, in the interests of justice to both the victims and the wider community that there should be a retrial.

If the challenge for cause is successful the would-be juror cannot try the present case but, depending on the nature of the challenge (is he or she unsuitable to be a juror or just biased in this particular case?), may be called upon to try another case.

The question to be asked where it is suspected that the would-be juror might be biased is whether the fair-minded and informed observer, having considered the facts, would conclude that there was a real possibility that the he or she was biased: see *Porter v Magill* [2002] 2 AC 357. In that case, Lord Hope of Craighead notes (at para 88) that there is a close relationship between the concept of independence and that of impartiality. He quotes from the case of *Findlay v UK* (1997) 24 EHRR 221 at 244–45 (para 73), where the European Court said:

> . . . in order to establish whether a tribunal can be considered as 'independent', regard must be had inter alia to the manner of appointment of its members and their term of office, the existence of guarantees against outside pressures and the question whether the body presents an appearance of independence. As to the question of 'impartiality', there are two aspects to this requirement. First, the tribunal must be subjectively free from personal prejudice or bias. Secondly, it must also be impartial from an objective viewpoint, that is, it must offer sufficient guarantees to exclude any legitimate doubt in this respect. The concepts of independence and objective impartiality are closely linked . . .

Lord Hope comments that, in both cases, the concept requires not only that the tribunal must be truly independent and free from actual bias (proof of which is likely to be very difficult), but also that it must not appear, in the objective sense, to lack these essential qualities.

The test for apparent bias had been set out by Lord Goff of Chieveley in *R v Gough* [1993] AC 646 at 670 in these terms:

> I think it unnecessary, in formulating the appropriate test, to require that the court should look at the matter through the eyes of a reasonable man, because the court in cases such as these personifies the reasonable man; and in any event the court has first to ascertain the relevant circumstances from the available evidence, knowledge of which would not necessarily be available to an observer in court at the relevant time . . . I prefer to state the test in terms of real danger rather than real likelihood, to ensure that the court is thinking of possibility rather than probability of bias. Accordingly, having ascertained the relevant circumstances, the court should ask itself whether, having regard to those circumstances, there was a real danger of bias on the part of the relevant member of the tribunal in question, in the sense that he might unfairly regard (or have unfairly regarded) with favour, or disfavour, the case of a party to the issue under consideration by him . . .

In *Porter v Magill*, Lord Hope notes that the 'reasonable likelihood' and 'real danger' tests propounded by Lord Goff in *R v Gough* had been criticised on the ground that they tend to emphasise the court's view of the facts and to place inadequate emphasis on the public perception of the irregular incident. The Scottish courts (see, for example, *Bradford v McLeod* 1986 SLT 244) had adopted a test which looked at the question of whether there was suspicion of bias through the eyes of the reasonable man who was aware of the circumstances. Lord Hope observed that this approach (sometimes described as 'the reasonable apprehension of bias' test) is in line with that adopted in most common law jurisdictions and by the European Court of Human Rights (which looks at the question of whether there was a risk of bias objectively in the light of the circumstances which the court has identified: *Piersack v Belgium* (1982) 5 EHRR 169 at 179–80 (paras 30–31); *Pullar v UK* (1996) 22 EHRR 391 at 402–03 (para 30); and *Hauschildt v Denmark* (1989) 12 EHRR 266 at 279 (para 48)).

In *R v Bow Street Metropolitan Stipendiary Magistrate ex p Pinochet Ugarte (No 2)* [2000] 1 AC 119, the House of Lords declined to review the *Gough* test. In that case, Lord Hope had expressed the view that the English and Scottish tests were described differently but their application was likely, in practice, to lead to results that were so similar as to be indistinguishable (p 142). Moreover, the Court of Appeal, having examined the question whether the 'real danger' test might lead to a different result from that which the informed observer would reach on the same facts, concluded in *Locabail (UK) Ltd v Bayfield Properties Ltd* [2000] QB 451 at 477 (para 17) that, in the overwhelming majority of cases, the application of the two tests would lead to the same outcome. However, in *Re Medicaments and Related Classes of Goods (No 2)* [2001] 1 WLR 700, the Court of Appeal reconsidered the question of bias. Lord Phillips of Worth Matravers MR, giving the judgment of the court, concluded as follows (at para 35):

> When the Strasbourg jurisprudence is taken into account, we believe that a modest adjustment of the test in *R v Gough* is called for, which makes it plain that it is, in effect, no different

from the test applied in most of the Commonwealth and in Scotland. The court must first ascertain all the circumstances which have a bearing on the suggestion that the judge was biased. It must then ask whether those circumstances would lead a fair-minded and informed observer to conclude that there was a real possibility, or a real danger, the two being the same, that the tribunal was biased.

In *Porter v Magill*, Lord Hope (with whom the other Law Lords agreed) approved this 'modest adjustment' of the test in *R v Gough* subject to one modification. Lord Hope (at para 103) said the test formulated by Lord Phillips:

> . . . expresses in clear and simple language a test which is in harmony with the objective test which the Strasbourg court applies when it is considering whether the circumstances give rise to a reasonable apprehension of bias. It removes any possible conflict with the test which is now applied in most Commonwealth countries and in Scotland. I would however delete from it the reference to 'a real danger'. Those words no longer serve a useful purpose here, and they are not used in the jurisprudence of the Strasbourg court. The question is whether the fair-minded and informed observer, having considered the facts, would conclude that there was a real possibility that the tribunal was biased.

In *R v Abu Hamza* [2006] EWCA Crim 2918; [2007] 3 All ER 451, the Court of Appeal observed that the risk that members of a jury may be affected by prejudice is one that cannot wholly be eliminated. Prejudicial publicity renders more difficult the task of the court in trying the case fairly. However, the fact that adverse publicity may have risked prejudicing a fair trial is no reason for not proceeding with the trial if the judge concludes that, with his assistance, it will be possible to have a fair trial. In considering this question it is right for the judge to have regard to his own experience and that of his fellow judges as to the manner in which juries normally perform their duties.

11.8.2.2 The prosecution stand by

It used to be the case that each defendant could challenge potential jurors 'peremptorily' (that is, without giving a reason). This right came to be restricted so that each defendant could challenge up to three potential jurors peremptorily, and it was finally abolished in 1988. The only challenge the defence can now make is the challenge for cause described above. The prosecution, however, have retained their right to challenge a juror without giving reasons; this is known as the prosecution right to stand a juror by. To exercise this right, prosecuting counsel says 'stand by' just before the juror takes his oath. It is then explained to the juror that he cannot sit on this jury, but will go back to the jury panel and may be called on to try another case.

As it may be seen as unfair that the prosecution should be able to challenge a juror without giving any reason but the defence do not have such a right, guidance on jury vetting is given to Crown Prosecutors (<http://www.cps.gov.uk/legal/section17/chapter_k.html#_Toc3179589>):

> The circumstances in which it would be proper for the Crown to exercise its right to stand by a member of the jury panel are:

- • to remove a manifestly unsuitable juror, but only if the defence agree; and
- • to remove a juror in a terrorist or security case in which the Attorney General has authorised a check of the jury list, but only on the authority of the Attorney General.

The Attorney General also issued guidelines (*Attorney General's Guidelines (Juries: Right to Stand By)* [1988] 3 All ER 1086) which make it clear that the right of stand by should only be used in exceptional cases. In cases involving national security or terrorism, the jury panel will be 'vetted' extensively to ensure that they are suitable to try such a sensitive case. In other cases, the only check that will be carried out is to see which members of the jury panel have previous convictions. Some may have convictions which disqualify them from jury service (and this would be the subject of a challenge for cause); others may not be disqualified from service but may be unsuitable to try a particular case (for example, someone who has just been fined for theft may not be the best person to try a theft case). Apart from any previous convictions, a would-be juror may be manifestly unsuitable to try the case (for example, someone who clearly has difficulty in reading the words on the card when trying to take the oath is unsuited to try a case where a number of documents have to be read).

11.8.2.3 The judge's right of stand by

The judge has an inherent power to stand a juror by. This power is hardly ever exercised and would only be appropriate where a juror is manifestly unsuitable to try a particular case.

In *R v Ford* [1989] QB 868, the Court of Appeal held that a judge must not use his power to stand jurors by in order to try to ensure a racially balanced jury. Lord Lane CJ said (at page 872) that the judge's right of stand by:

> is to be exercised to prevent individual jurors who are not competent from serving. It has never been held to include a discretion to discharge a competent juror or jurors in an attempt to secure a jury drawn from particular sections of the community, or otherwise to influence the overall composition of the jury. For this latter purpose the law provides that 'fairness' is achieved by the principle of random selection.

The essence of the decision is that statutory procedure for selecting jurors is intended to ensure random selection and the judge should not interfere with this randomness.

Ford was followed in *R v Tarrant* [1998] Crim LR 342, where the Court of Appeal repeated that a judge cannot use his discretion to discharge individual jurors in order to interfere with the composition of the jury panel (in the present case, to select jurors from outside the court's catchment area in order to minimise the risk of intimidation). In *R v Smith* [2003] EWCA Crim 283; [2003] 1 WLR 2229, a black defendant was tried by an all-white jury with causing serious injury to a white victim. It was held that the jury summoning procedure in the Juries Act 1974 is not inconsistent with Art 6 of the European Convention on Human Rights. Pill LJ, at para 40, said:

> We do not accept that it was unfair for the defendant to be tried by a randomly selected all-white jury or that the fair-minded and informed observer would regard it as unfair. We do not accept that, on the facts of this case, the trial could only be fair if members of the

defendant's race were present on the jury. It was not a case where a consideration of the evidence required knowledge of the traditions or social circumstances of a particular racial group. The situation was an all too common one, violence late at night outside a club, and a randomly selected jury was entirely capable of trying the issues fairly and impartially. Public confidence is not impaired by the composition of this jury.

The observation that the evidence in the present case did not require knowledge of the traditions or social circumstances of a particular racial group (even though there was a racial element to the offence) appears to leave open the possibility that the judge might be allowed take steps to include ethnic minority representation on the jury if the case were one that required such knowledge.

Davies and Edwards, in *'A Jury of Peers': A Comparative Analysis* (2004) 68 J Crim L 150, are highly critical of the approach taken in *Ford*. They conclude that:

> ensuring at least some representation on the jury of defendant's peers would produce a fairer result. Indeed from the point of view of the defendant, it may be argued that even a more substantive approach would be fairer, i.e. if it is accepted that having members of one's own social group is beneficial to the jury's understanding of the facts of the case, the jury should comprise persons with a common understanding of the defendant's background . . . Further, if it is accepted that having a member of the defendant's own ethnic group represented on the jury is beneficial to understanding the facts of the case more fully, and consequentially goes further in upholding principles of justice and fairness, then random selection is clearly not the best way of ensuring an impartial jury.

In light of the rule that a judge cannot use the power of stand by to try to achieve a racially balanced jury, it has been a source of concern that juries do not necessarily represent the ethnic diversity of our society. It is not uncommon, for example, for a defendant to be tried by 12 people none of whom shares his ethnicity. The *Auld Review* said that provision should be made to enable ethnic minority representation on juries where race is likely to be relevant to an important issue in the case (not on the basis that people have a right to have on the jury someone from their background but on the basis of studies suggesting that white juries are, or are perceived to be, less fair to black than to white people). Recommendation 25 of the Review suggests that:

> A scheme should be devised . . . for cases in which the court considers that race is likely to be relevant to an issue of importance in the case, for the selection of a jury consisting of, say, up to three people from any ethnic minority group.

The detail of this proposal, which was not acted upon in the Criminal Justice Act 2003, is set out in paras 60 and 61 of Chapter 5 of the Review:

> The parties could be required to indicate early in their preparation for the pre-trial assessment whether race is likely to be a relevant issue and, if so, whether steps should be taken to attempt to secure some ethnic minority representation on the jury. This could be done by the empanelment of a larger number of jurors than normal from which the jury for the case is to be selected, some of whom would be identified by their juror cards as from ethnic minorities . . . The first nine selected would be called to serve and, if they did not include a

minimum of – say three – ethnic minority jurors, the remainder would be stood down until the minimum was reached . . .

61 . . . the judge's ruling would be for a racially diverse jury in the form that I have suggested, not that it should contain representatives of the particular ethnic background on either side.

11.8.3 Discharge of individual jurors during the trial

A jury always starts off with 12 jurors. However, under s 16 of the Juries Act 1974, up to three jurors may be discharged during the course of the trial in case of illness or other reason (for example, bereavement). What constitutes a valid reason is a matter for the trial judge. In *R v Hambery* [1977] 1 QB 924, a juror was discharged because the trial went on longer than expected and she would otherwise have had to cancel a holiday. If more than three jurors can no longer serve, the trial has to be abandoned; a fresh trial will take place later.

Paragraphs 17–20 of Chapter 5 of the *Auld Review* discuss the (comparatively) rare cases where a trial has to be aborted because the number of jurors falls below the crucial figure of nine. This does not happen often but is a cause for concern in cases that last a very long time. Recommendation 16 of the Review is that:

A system should be introduced for enabling judges in long cases, where they consider it appropriate, to swear alternate or reserve jurors to meet the contingency of a jury other-wise being reduced in number by discharge for illness or any other reason of necessity.

This suggestion was not adopted by the Government.

11.8.4 Discharge of the entire jury

The entire jury may be discharged if, for example,

- the jury hears evidence which is inadmissible and prejudicial to the defendant and the judge decides that a direction to ignore this evidence would not be sufficient. Where something prejudicial to the defendant has inadvertently been admitted in evidence, it is not necessarily the case that the jury should be discharged; whether or not the jury should be discharged is a matter for the discretion of the trial judge (*R v Weaver and Weaver* [1968] 1 QB 353); the test to be applied is the usual test for bias, namely whether there is real possibility or real danger of injustice occurring because the jury, having heard the prejudicial matter, might be biased against the accused (*R v Docherty* [1999] 1 Cr App R 274);
- the jury cannot agree on a verdict (see below);
- an individual juror has to be discharged and there is a risk that he may have contaminated the rest of the jury – for example, he happens to know that the defendant has previous convictions which have not been ruled admissible or is facing further trials for other offences (*R v Hutton* [1990] Crim LR 875).

Where the jury is discharged from giving a verdict, the defendant can be retried, as he is not regarded as having been acquitted.

If members of the jury misbehave during the course of the trial, the jury should be discharged if there is a 'real danger of prejudice' to the accused (*R v Spencer* [1987] AC 128). In *R v Sawyer* (1980) 71 Cr App R 283, for example, some jurors were seen in conversation with prosecution witnesses during an adjournment. The trial judge questioned them and it transpired that the conversation had been on subjects unconnected with the trial. The decision of the judge not to discharge the jury was upheld by the Court of Appeal.

Where a juror has specialised knowledge of something relevant to the case against the defendant, and has communicated that knowledge to the rest of the jury, the judge is obliged to discharge the jury if this comes to light at a stage of the trial such that the defendant has had no opportunity to challenge what amounts to new evidence or to put forward his own explanation (*R v Fricker* (1999) *The Times*, 13 July).

In *R v Blackwell* [1995] 2 Cr App R 625, the Court of Appeal gave guidance on the approach to be taken by a judge where there is a suspicion that a member of the public has tried to influence members of the jury. The member of the public should be questioned by the judge (or by court officials or police at the direction of the judge) and, if it appears that there has been an attempt to influence the jurors, the jurors should be questioned to establish if their independence has been compromised. Only after a full investigation has been completed does the judge have sufficient information to decide whether any or all of the jurors should be discharged.

In *R v Azam* [2006] EWCA Crim 161, the Court of Appeal confirmed that the judge has, and where necessary should exercise, a discretionary power to discharge the jury. It is open to the judge to exercise this power whichever side invites him to do so, and also when neither side does, and even when both sides submit that he should not. The judge must make his own judgment whether the interests of justice require the discharge of the jury. If the judge concludes that there were 'real grounds for doubting the ability of the jury to bring an objective judgment to bear' on the issues, the jury should be discharged. The decision requires a balanced judgment of the things said to create the risk of bias in the jury, while also taking account of the directions available to be given by the trial judge to address and extinguish the risk (per Sir Igor Judge P at para 50). The Court of Appeal added that it will not interfere with decisions made by the trial judge about the proper conduct of the case unless satisfied that they are wrong, and that in consequence the conviction is unsafe (ibid, para 57).

Paragraphs IV.42.6–9 of the *Consolidated Practice Direction* give guidance on what should be said to the jury about misconduct by its members (particularly in light of the fact that, where matters come to light after the verdict has been delivered, it is too late to do anything because of the rule that the deliberations of the jury must remain secret – see Chapter 13). It says:

> Trial judges should ensure that the jury is alerted to the need to bring any concerns about fellow jurors to the attention of the judge at the time, and not to wait until the case is concluded. At the same time, it is undesirable to encourage inappropriate criticism of fellow jurors, or to threaten jurors with contempt of court.
>
> Judges should therefore take the opportunity, when warning the jury of the importance of not discussing the case with anyone outside the jury, to add a further warning. It is for the trial judge to tailor the further warning to the case, and to the phraseology used in the usual warning. The effect of the further warning should be that it is the duty of jurors to bring to

the judge's attention, promptly, any behaviour among the jurors or by others affecting the jurors, that causes concern. The point should be made that, unless that is done while the case is continuing, it may be impossible to put matters right.

The Judge should consider, particularly in a longer trial, whether a reminder on the lines of the further warning is appropriate prior to the retirement of the jury.

11.8.5 Composition of the jury as a ground of appeal

Composition of the jury as a ground of appeal is dealt with in Chapter 13.

11.9 SPECIAL MEASURES DIRECTIONS AND LIVE LINKS

In this section, we look at the measures which can be adopted to help witnesses who might otherwise find it difficult to testify and the use of live links to enable a witness to testify from outside the courtroom.

11.9.1 Special measures directions

Sections 16–33 of the Youth Justice and Criminal Evidence Act 1999 contain provision for various 'special measures' which the court can direct in respect of certain witnesses. An application can be made under s 19 of the Youth Justice and Criminal Evidence Act 1999 for special measures:

a   screening the witness from the accused (under s 23);
b   giving evidence by live link (under s 24), although this provision will become less relevant as s 51 of the Criminal Justice Act 2003 (at the time of writing, in force only with regard to the offences specified in the *Criminal Justice Act 2003 (Commencement No 18 and Transitional Provisions) Order 2007*), will enable a court to authorise witnesses, other than the accused, to give evidence through a live link in criminal proceedings;
c   giving evidence in private, in a sexual offence case, or where there is a fear that the witness may be intimidated (under s 25);
d   video recording of evidence-in-chief (under s 27) – again, this provision will be made less relevant once s 137 of the CJA 2003 extends the circumstances in which evidence-in-chief can take the form of a video-recorded statement;
e   video recording of cross-examination and re-examination where the evidence-in-chief of the witness has been video recorded (under s 28);
f   in the case of a young or incapacitated witness, examination through an intermediary (under s 29) to communicate questions to the witness and their answers to the questioner;
g   provision of aids to communication for a young or incapacitated witness (under s 30).

The procedure for making (and opposing) applications for special measures directions is set out in Pt 29 of the Criminal Procedure Rules.

Rule 29.4 makes provision for applications to vary or discharge a special measures direction. Under s 20 of the 1999 Act, such applications must be based on a 'material change of circumstances' since the direction was made. Also, under r 29.5, where an application for a special measures direction has been refused by the court, the application may be renewed, but only where there has been a 'material change of circumstances' since the court refused the application.

In *R (S) v Waltham Forest Youth Court* [2004] EWHC 715 (Admin); [2004] 2 Cr App R 335, the accused (who was aged 13) wanted to testify in her own defence but said that she was too scared to do so because of the physical presence in court of her co-accused. The question arose whether the court could make a 'special measures' direction in respect of the accused. The Divisional Court held that there is no power to make a direction under the 1999 Act in relation to the evidence of the accused. It should, however, be borne in mind that one special measure (namely, testifying via a 'live link') is available for the accused under s 33A of the 1999 Act (inserted by the s 47 of the Police and Justice Act 2006, with effect from January 2007 – see below).

In *R v Brown* [2004] EWCA Crim 1620, the appeal concerned a special measures direction whereby two witnesses were permitted to give evidence from behind screens but a third witness did not wish to do so; also, the applications for special measures were not made within the 28 day time limit envisaged in r 29.1 of the Criminal Procedure Rules. The Court of Appeal held that, provided that the jury are correctly instructed as to the implications of the use of screens, the fact that one witness gives evidence without screens does not require the rest to do so as well; it is a matter for the judge to determine whether the justice of the case, fairness to the defendants and fairness to the witnesses require or permit him to allow them to give evidence in different ways. It was also held that the time limits provided for by the Rules are not mandatory, but are directory; any significant handicap to the defence by a late application is for the judge to take very carefully into account. The court added that where a special measures direction has been given to the jury before a witness gave evidence, the judge is not required to repeat the direction in the summing up. The question is whether the judge had got across to the jury effectively the essential matter of the use of screens and the conclusions that should and should not be drawn therefrom. Doing so is much more likely to impress itself on the jury if it is given at the time of the witness' evidence than if it is repeated on a later date in the summing up. Further, any reversion to the matter might, in some cases, give it more emphasis (derogatory to the defendant) than it deserves.

In *Krasniki v The Czech Republic* (Application No 51277/99), in February 2006, the ECtHR accepted that the Convention rights of witnesses include, where necessary, the preservation of their anonymity. The Court of Appeal, in *R v Davis; R v Ellis* [2006] EWCA Crim 1155; [2006] 1 WLR 3130, said that it follows that the concealment of the identity of witnesses is not inconsistent with the right to a fair trial, provided that the need for anonymity is clearly established. The ultimate test, said the Court, is that the trial must be fair. The Court pointed out that the House of Lords, in *R (Al-Fawwaz) v Governor of Brixton Prison* [2002] 1 AC 556 and *R (D) v Camberwell Green Youth Court* [2005] 1 WLR 393, had made it plain that the discretion to permit evidence to be given by witnesses whose identity might not be known to the defendant is now beyond question. Provided that appropriate safeguards are applied, and the judge is satisfied that a fair trial can take place, the trial can proceed and any conviction is not to be regarded as unsafe simply because the evidence of anonymous witnesses might have been decisive.

11.9.1.1 *Video testimony*

Rule 29.7 of the Criminal Procedure Rules deals with video recording of testimony from witnesses. Where an application is made for a special measures direction enabling a video recording of an interview of a witness to be admitted as evidence-in-chief of the witness, the application must be accompanied by the video recording which it is proposed to tender in evidence and must include the information specified by r 29.7(2), which includes a statement of the circumstances in which the recording was made. This statement must comply with the requirements of r 29.7(4), which sets out a series of detailed questions about the making of the recording. Where a party opposes the use of the video recording, he must lodge a notice giving reasons why it would not be in the interests of justice for the recording (or part of it) to be admitted (r 29.7(7)(a) and (8)).

Rule 29.7(10) stipulates that any video recording which the defendant proposes to tender in evidence need not be sent to the prosecution until the close of the prosecution case at the trial.

In *R v Mullen* [2004] EWCA Crim 602; [2004] 2 Cr App R 18, at the defendant's trial for indecent assault, video-recorded interviews were admitted under ss 19 and 27 of the Youth Justice and Criminal Evidence Act 1999 of the evidence-in-chief of both the complainant and her young brother. The jury, while considering their verdict, sent a note indicating that they wished to see the video evidence again. The judge acceded to this request and the video was replayed in open court. The Court of Appeal held that there is no reason why, as an exercise of discretion, the judge should not permit the video of the complainant's evidence to be replayed. However, the replaying of video evidence is a departure from the normal method of conducting a criminal trial, and should only take place where there are exceptional reasons. Nonetheless, this is a proper course of action where the jury request to see the evidence again for the purpose of seeing *how* the complainant gave his or her evidence (as opposed simply to being reminded of the content of that evidence), provided that a 'balancing' direction is given to the jury in order to avoid any potential advantage for the prosecution which might render the trial unfair and any resulting conviction unsafe. The same applies to the evidence of a supporting child witness, but if the evidence goes no further than evidence as to recent complaint and opportunity, it is (said the court) difficult to envisage circumstances in which it would not be sufficient for the judge merely to remind the jury of the content of the evidence without replaying it. The Court went on to say that it would be inappropriate to propound any rule for the exclusion of members of the public during the giving of the evidence-in-chief of a vulnerable witness. The playing or replaying of an interview tape relied upon as the evidence-in-chief of a vulnerable witness is as much a part of the proceedings as the evidence of other witnesses.

Section 137(1) of the Criminal Justice Act 2003, when it comes into force, will also extend the cases where evidence can be given by means of a video recording. It empowers the court to allow a video recording of an interview with a witness (other than the defendant), or a part of such a recording, to be admitted as evidence-in-chief of the witness (that is, to replace live evidence-in-chief of that witness) provided that the person is called as a witness in proceedings for an offence which is triable only on indictment, or for a prescribed either-way offence, and:

i   the person claims to have witnessed the offence or events closely connected with it;
ii   he has previously given an account of those events in question;

iii the account was given at a time when those events were fresh in the person's memory;

iv a video recording was made of the account.

Under s 137(3)(b), an order may only be made under s 137 if it appears to the court that:

i   the witness's recollection of the events in question is likely to have been significantly better when he gave the recorded account than it will be when he gives oral evidence in the proceedings, and

ii it is in the interests of justice for the recording to be admitted into evidence.

In considering the interests of justice under s 137(3)(b), the court must have regard to the matters set out in sub-s (4):

(a) the interval between the time of the events in question and the time when the recorded account was made;

(b) any other factors that might affect the reliability of what the witness said in that account;

(c) the quality of the recording;

(d) any views of the witness as to whether his evidence-in-chief should be given orally or by means of the recording.

Section 138 stipulates that where a video recording has been admitted into evidence under s 137, the witness cannot give examination-in-chief in any other way.

11.9.1.2 'Live links'

Part 8 of the Criminal Justice Act, when it is brought into force, will extend the circumstances where live links can be used. A 'live link' (defined in s 56(2)) will usually mean a closed circuit television link, but could apply to any technology with the same effect, such as video-conferencing facilities or the internet. Under s 51(3), a direction may be given on an application by a party to the proceedings or of the court's own motion. However, s 51(4) provides that a direction may not be given unless the court is satisfied that it is 'in the interests of the efficient or effective administration of justice for the person concerned to give evidence in the proceedings through a live link'. Under s 51(6), the court must consider all the circumstances of the case, and in particular (s 51(7)):

(a) the availability of the witness;

(b) the need for the witness to attend in person;

(c) the importance of the witness's evidence to the proceedings;

(d) the views of the witness;

(e) the suitability of the facilities at the place where the witness would give evidence through a live link;

(f) whether a direction might tend to inhibit any party to the proceedings from effectively testing the witness's evidence.

Under s 51(8), the court must state in open court its reasons for refusing an application for a direction where one is sought.

Under s 52(2), where the court has given a direction under s 51 for a person to give evidence through a live link in particular proceedings, the person concerned may not give evidence in those proceedings after the direction is given otherwise than through a live link unless the court rescinds the direction, which it can do under s 52(3) (on the application of a party or of its own motion), if it appears to the court to be in the interests of justice to do so.

Section 47 of the Police and Justice Act 2006 inserts some new sections (in force from January 2007) into the Youth Justice and Criminal Evidence Act 1999. Section 33A allows the court (whether the Crown Court or a magistrates' court), on application by the accused, to direct that any evidence given by him should be given via a 'live link'. Section 33B defines 'live link' very broadly: it encompasses any technology that enables the accused to see and hear a person in the courtroom, and to be seen and heard by the persons listed in s 33B(2), namely the judge and the jury (if there is one), any co-accused, the legal representatives acting in the proceedings and any interpreter or other person appointed by the court to assist the accused.

Before giving a live link direction, the court must be satisfied that it would be in the interests of justice to do so, and:

a   if the accused is under the age of 18, that his ability to participate effectively as a witness giving oral evidence is compromised by his 'level of intellectual ability or social functioning', and that use of a live link would enable him to participate more effectively as a witness, whether by improving the quality of his evidence or otherwise (s 33A(4)); or

b   if the accused is aged 18 or over, that he is unable to participate effectively in the proceedings effectively as a witness giving oral evidence because he has a mental disorder (within the meaning of the Mental Health Act 1983) or a 'significant impairment of intelligence and social function', and that use of a live link would enable him to participate more effectively as a witness, whether by improving the quality of his evidence or otherwise (s 33A(5)).

The Explanatory Notes that accompany the 2006 Act make it clear that the presumption in the case of adult defendants is that they should give evidence in court. The criteria set out in s 33A(5) are intended to ensure that the use of live links is reserved for exceptional cases where the accused has a condition that prevents effective participation as a witness and so may prevent a fair trial from taking place. In the case of a juvenile accused, however, the test is less strict (in that there is no reference to a mental disorder or impairment); it is sufficient that the accused's ability to participate is compromised. The Notes make the point that this 'lower threshold recognises that it may be more common for juveniles to experience difficulties during the trial through limited intelligence and social development, than it would be for adults' but goes on the emphasise that s 33A(4) 'is aimed at juvenile defendants with a low level of intelligence or a particular problem in dealing with social situations, and is not intended to operate merely because an accused is a juvenile and is nervous, for example'.

Section 33A(6) provides that, where a live link direction has been given, the accused must give all his evidence in that way. It follows that any cross-examination of the accused also has to take place via a live link. However, the court may, in the exercise of its discretion, discharge a live link direction if it appears to the court to be in the interests of justice to do so (s 33A(7)). This may be appropriate where, for example, the accused finds that giving evidence over a live link is more difficult than expected and believes that giving evidence in open court would allow him to give better quality evidence.

11.9.1.3 Reporting directions

Part 16 of the Criminal Procedure Rules makes provision for the making of 'reporting directions' under s 46 of the YJCEA 1999. The effect is that no matter relating to the witness may be included in any publication during the lifetime of the witness, if that matter is likely to lead members of the public to identify that person as a witness in the proceedings. The application may be made in writing or orally (r 16.1). Under r 16.2, any party may oppose the application for a 'reporting direction' and must state whether they dispute that the witness is eligible for protection under s 46 or that the granting of protection would be likely to improve the quality of the evidence given by the witness or the level of co-operation given by the witness to any party to the proceedings in connection with that party's preparation of its case. Under r 16.7(4), the court may hear and take into account representations made to it by any person who in the court's view has a legitimate interest in the application before it.

Crown Court trial: the course of the trial

12.1 THE START OF THE TRIAL

Once the jury has been empanelled, the prosecution present their case. Counsel for the prosecution begins by making an opening speech.

12.1.1 Content of the prosecution opening speech

In the opening speech, the prosecutor reminds the jury of the offences to which the defendant has pleaded not guilty. If those offences are complicated, the prosecutor will summarise the relevant legal principles (making it clear, however, that the judge is the final arbiter of the law). It should also be made clear at this stage that the prosecution bear the burden of proof and that the jury must be satisfied so that they are sure of the defendant's guilt in order to convict. Prosecutors normally indicate who they will be calling as witnesses and how these witnesses fit into the overall story. The purpose of the opening speech is to enable the jury to make sense of the evidence that they will now be hearing.

In most cases, any questions of admissibility of evidence should be dealt with at the plea and case management hearing (PCMH). However, if this has not happened for any reason, and counsel for the defence has indicated to the prosecution before the start of the trial that the defence will be challenging the admissibility of some of the prosecution evidence, the opening speech by the prosecution should make no mention of that evidence. If, however, the evidence in dispute is so crucial to the prosecution case that an opening speech cannot be made without referring to it, the jury will be sent out of the court room and the admissibility of this evidence will be determined before the trial begins. Usually, where such crucial evidence is ruled inadmissible at the outset, the prosecution would have little choice but to abandon the case.

In *R v Lashley* [2005] EWCA Crim 2016; (2005), *The Times*, 28 September, the Court of Appeal said that the presumption should be that an opening address by counsel for the Crown should not address the law, save in cases of real complication and difficulty where counsel believes (and the trial judge agrees) that the jury may be assisted by a brief and well-focussed submission (per Judge LJ at para 13).

12.2 THE PROSECUTION CASE

If the defendant pleads not guilty, the prosecution are put to proof of their entire case, and so must adduce evidence on all the elements of the alleged offence(s). The only exception to this rule is where the defence make a 'formal admission' so that something which would otherwise be in issue is no longer an issue.

12.2.1 Formal admissions

Under s 10 of the Criminal Justice Act 1967, the prosecution or the defence (in practice, usually the defence) may admit any fact which would otherwise be in issue; this admission is conclusive evidence of the fact admitted. If, for example, the defendant is charged with causing death by dangerous driving, he might admit that he was driving the car at the time of the accident.

In the Crown Court, the admission may be made in writing (in which case, it will be signed by the person making it) or orally in court by counsel. In the magistrates' court, a formal admission must be made in writing (under r 37.4 of the Criminal Procedure Rules).

Formal admissions are not made very frequently. It is usually apparent from questions asked in cross-examination if some of what the witness says is accepted by the defence. If all of the evidence of a particular witness is accepted by the defence, the defence will consent to that witness's statement being read to the court (see below).

12.2.2 Prosecution witnesses

The prosecution witnesses whose written statements the defence do not allow to be read to the court each give evidence. Evidence is usually given under oath, the witness saying 'I swear by almighty God that the evidence I shall give shall be the truth, the whole truth, and nothing but the truth'. A witness who does not wish to take the oath may affirm instead, promising to tell the truth.

Each witness is examined-in-chief by the prosecution (who are not allowed to ask leading questions, that is, questions which contain or suggest their own answer), then cross-examined by the defence, and (if necessary) re-examined by the prosecution (the rule against leading questions applying to re-examination as well).

In *R v Butt* [2005] EWCA Crim 805; (2005), *The Times*, 2 May, the Court of Appeal said that, although defence counsel has a duty to present the defence fearlessly, there is an obligation to avoid repetition and a duty to discriminate between relevant and irrelevant features (per Dyson LJ at para 10). The judge is therefore entitled to impose a time limit on cross-examination.

Where a witness made a contemporaneous note of the matters on which he is about to give evidence, it is open to the party calling that witness to apply to the judge for the witness to be given permission to refresh his memory by referring to those notes (*R v Da Silva* [1990] 1 WLR 31). This is invariably done to enable police officers to refer to their notebooks while giving evidence.

In *Da Silva*, Stuart-Smith LJ at p 36, added that the judge has a discretion, where it is in the interests of justice, to permit a witness who has begun to give evidence to refresh his memory from a statement made near to the time of events in question, even though it does not come within the definition of contemporaneous, provided he is satisfied that the witness indicates that he cannot now recall the details of events because of the lapse of time since they took place, that he made a statement much nearer the time of the events and that the contents of the statement represented his recollection at the time he made it; that he had not read the statement before coming into the witness box; and that he wished to have an opportunity to read the statement before he continued to give evidence. The statement must be removed from him when he comes to give his evidence and he should not be permitted to refer to it again (unlike a contemporaneous statement which may be used to refresh memory while giving evidence). In *R v South Ribble Stipendiary Magistrate ex p Cochrane* [1996] 2 Cr App R 544, the Divisional Court held all of the requirements set out in *Da Silva* do not necessarily have to be satisfied; the court must consider the requirements of fairness and justice in exercising that discretion. Section 139 of the Criminal Justice Act 2003 puts the matter on a statutory footing. Section 139(1) provides that:

> A person giving oral evidence in criminal proceedings about any matter may, at any stage in the course of doing so, refresh his memory of it from a document made or verified by him at an earlier time if—
>
> (a) he states in his oral evidence that the document records his recollection of the matter at that earlier time, and
>
> (b) his recollection of the matter is likely to have been significantly better at that time than it is as the time of his oral evidence.

Section 139(2) allows a witness to refresh his memory from the transcript of a sound recording in the same circumstances.

12.2.3 Reading witness statements with the consent of the defence

Section 9(1) of the Criminal Justice Act 1967 provides that a written statement is admissible in evidence as if it were oral testimony provided that the requirements set out in sub-s (2) are satisfied, namely:

> (a) the statement purports to be signed by the person who made it;
>
> (b) the statement contains a declaration by that person to the effect that it is true to the best of his knowledge and belief and that he made the statement knowing that, if it were tendered in evidence, he would be liable to prosecution if he wilfully stated in it anything which he knew to be false or did not believe to be true;
>
> (c) before the hearing at which the statement is tendered in evidence, a copy of the statement is served, by or on behalf of the party proposing to tender it, on each of the other parties to the proceedings; and
>
> (d) none of the other parties or their solicitors, within seven days from the service of the copy of the statement, serves a notice on the party so proposing objecting to the statement being tendered in evidence under this section:
>
> Provided that the conditions mentioned in paragraphs (c) and (d) of this sub-section shall not apply if the parties agree before or during the hearing that the statement shall be so tendered.

This very useful provision will be invoked, for example, where the defence in a theft case is not that the property was not stolen but that the defendant was not the thief: the evidence of the loser of the property, saying that the property is his and that he gave no-one permission to take it, will not therefore be disputed by the defence and so the written statement of the loser will be read out to the court. The judge should direct the jury that a statement read out under this provision has the same evidential value as 'live' testimony.

12.2.4 Reading witness statements without the consent of the defence

Section 116 of the Criminal Justice Act 2003 makes provision for the reading of witnesses' statements, without the consent of the defence, in cases where the witness is unavailable. It provides as follows:

(1) In criminal proceedings a statement not made in oral evidence in the proceedings is admissible as evidence of any matter stated if—

    (a) oral evidence given in the proceedings by the person who made the statement would be admissible as evidence of that matter,

    (b) the person who made the statement (the relevant person) is identified to the court's satisfaction, and

    (c) any of the five conditions mentioned in sub-section (2) is satisfied.

(2) The conditions are—

    (a) that the relevant person is dead;

    (b) that the relevant person is unfit to be a witness because of his bodily or mental condition;

    (c) that the relevant person is outside the United Kingdom and it is not reasonably practicable to secure his attendance;

    (d) that the relevant person cannot be found although such steps as it is reasonably practicable to take to find him have been taken;

    (e) that through fear the relevant person does not give (or does not continue to give) oral evidence in the proceedings, either at all or in connection with the subject matter of the statement, and the court gives leave for the statement to be given in evidence.

(3) For the purposes of sub-section (2)(e) 'fear' is to be widely construed and (for example) includes fear of the death or injury of another person or of financial loss.

(4) Leave may be given under sub-section (2)(e) only if the court considers that the statement ought to be admitted in the interests of justice, having regard—

    (a) to the statement's contents,

    (b) to any risk that its admission or exclusion will result in unfairness to any party to the proceedings (and in particular to how difficult it will be to challenge the statement if the relevant person does not give oral evidence),

    (c) in appropriate cases, to the fact that a direction under section 19 of the Youth Justice and Criminal Evidence Act 1999 (special measures for the giving of evidence by fearful witnesses etc) could be made in relation to the relevant person, and

(d) to any other relevant circumstances.

(5) A condition set out in any paragraph of sub-section (2) which is in fact satisfied is to be treated as not satisfied if it is shown that the circumstances described in that paragraph are caused—

(a) by the person in support of whose case it is sought to give the statement in evidence, or

(b) by a person acting on his behalf,

in order to prevent the relevant person giving oral evidence in the proceedings (whether at all or in connection with the subject matter of the statement).

This provision is based on earlier legislation – s 23 of the Criminal Justice Act 1988 – and it is submitted that case law decided under that provision is relevant to s 116 of the 2003 Act. In particular, where the ground relied upon that the witness is not testifying because of fear, that fear must be proved by admissible evidence (*Neill v North Antrim Magistrates' Court* [1992] 1 WLR 1221). In *R v Belmarsh Magistrates' Court ex p Gilligan* [1998] 1 Cr App R 14, the Divisional Court held that the court must hear oral evidence (for example, from a police officer) as to the fear of the witness: the fear cannot be proved by a written statement made by the witness who claims to be in fear.

In *R v Ricketts* [1991] Crim LR 915, it was said that the jury must not be told that a statement is being read to them on the ground that the maker of the statement is absent because of fear for his personal safety resulting from threats by the accused. Obviously this would be extremely prejudicial to the defendant.

In *R v Waters* (1997) 161 JP 249, the victim of an assault made a statement to the police in which he identified the appellant as one of his assailants. At the appellant's trial, the witness started to give evidence but then ceased to give evidence through fear, saying that he could not now remember what had happened and could not identify his assailants. The Court of Appeal (following *R v Ashford Justices ex p Hilden* [1993] QB 555) upheld the decision of the trial judge to allow the witness's earlier statement to be read to the jury. The court said that what mattered was whether or not there was, at the time when the statutory provision for reading witness statements was invoked, any relevant oral evidence which the witness was still expected to give. If there is such evidence, and it was proved beyond reasonable doubt that he did not give that evidence through fear, the statement is admissible.

In *R v Sellick* [2005] EWCA Crim 651 [2005] 1 WLR 3257, the Court of Appeal held that where the statement of a witness is read because the court is satisfied that he has been kept away by the defendant through fear, or that he cannot be found and that it is highly probable that he is in fear, the defendant cannot complain that his right under Art 6(3)(d) of the European Convention on Human Rights (ECHR) (to examine witnesses against him) is thereby infringed. The fact that the statement is decisive or the sole evidence against the defendant does not automatically mean that its admission infringes the right to a fair trial under Art 6 of the Convention. The Court went on to say that care should be taken to ensure that the legislative provisions concerning evidence not given through fear are not abused. The more decisive the evidence in the statements, the greater the care needed to be sure of why the witness could not give evidence. The court should be astute to examine the quality and reliability of the evidence in the statement, and should consider the interests of justice (including justice to the defendant and the victim(s)). The judge should give warnings to the jury stressing the disadvantage to the defendant in not being able to examine the witness (per Waller LJ at para 57).

Section 116(4)(c), quoted above, makes it clear that where the fear of the witness could be addressed through special measures, that it is what should be done (rather than allowing the statement of the witness to be read to the court).

The prosecution will not be allowed to rely on a witness statement, rather than oral evidence, where there would be another way of getting the evidence before the court. In *R v Radak* [1999] 1 Cr App R 187, the trial judge allowed a witness statement to be read to the jury on the basis that the maker of the statement was in the United States and would not come to court to give evidence through fear. The Court of Appeal held that this decision was wrong. The witness's evidence was an essential link in the prosecution case and the defence had little or no evidence to controvert the contents of the statement; it would therefore be unfair to admit that evidence without the defence being able to cross-examine the witness. Furthermore, the prosecution had known from the outset that the witness might not attend voluntarily, and so should have taken steps to have his evidence taken in the United States. The witness statement should therefore not have been admitted.

Where the prosecution seek to adduce the written statement of a witness on the ground that the witness is unfit through illness to attend, the defence should ordinarily be given the opportunity to cross-examine the doctor who provides support for the application. If the defence dispute the unfitness of the witness, the prosecution cannot rely on a written statement setting out the doctor's view that the witness is unfit (*R v Elliott* [2003] EWCA Crim 1695; (2003) *The Times*, 15 May).

Where a statement is read to the jury without the consent of the defence, the jury should be warned that the evidence needs to be viewed in light of the fact that the defence have not had the opportunity to cross-examine the witness. It is not sufficient simply to draw the jury's attention to the fact that evidence has been given by way of a witness statement. The jury should be warned to use particular care when considering the witness statement, since the maker of the statement was not in court to be cross-examined as to its contents. Where the witness statement is vital to the prosecution case, failure to give such a direction will render any subsequent conviction unsafe (*R v Curry* (1998) *The Times*, 23 March).

Article 6(3)(d) of the ECHR guarantees the right to examine and call witnesses. The admission of hearsay evidence without an opportunity for the defence to cross-examine may render the trial unfair if the conviction is based wholly or mainly on such evidence (*Unterpertinger v Austria* (1991) 13 EHRR 175). In *R v Arnold* [2004] EWCA Crim 1293, Leveson J pointed out the importance of compliance with the European Convention on Human Rights, saying (at para 30):

> Very great care must be taken in each and every case to ensure that attention is paid to the letter and spirit of the Convention and judges should not easily be persuaded that it is in the interests of justice to permit evidence to be read. Where that witness provides the sole or determinative evidence against the accused, permitting it to be read may well, depending on

the circumstances, jeopardise infringing the defendant's Article 6(3)(d) rights; even if it is not the only evidence, care must be taken to ensure that the ultimate aim of each and every trial, namely, a fair hearing, is achieved.

12.2.5 Real evidence

Real evidence means tangible evidence such as the murder weapon or the stolen goods. An item of real evidence has to be 'produced' (that is, formally identified and its relevance established) by a witness. Once this has been done, counsel says to the judge 'may this be exhibit [number]?' and (assuming the judge agrees) the item then becomes an exhibit in the case. Exhibits are numbered sequentially.

12.3 CHALLENGING THE ADMISSIBILITY OF PROSECUTION EVIDENCE

If the defence object to some of the prosecution evidence, arguing that it is inadmissible, this matter may be dealt with at the PCMH (at which the judge is empowered to give binding rulings on the admissibility of evidence). Otherwise, the objection is made (in the absence of the jury) during the course of the trial. If the objection is made during the course of the trial, the prosecution evidence is called in the usual way until the part of the evidence to which there is objection is reached. At that point the jury is invited to retire to the jury room.

Although s 82 of the Police and Criminal Evidence Act 1984 (PACE) expressly preserved the common law rules on the admissibility of evidence, objections to prosecution evidence are usually made under ss 76 or 78 of PACE.

12.3.1 Section 76 of the Police and Criminal Evidence Act 1984

Section 76 of PACE provides as follows:

(1) In any proceedings a confession made by an accused person may be given in evidence against him in so far as it is relevant to any matter in issue in the proceedings and is not excluded by the court in pursuance of this section.

(2) If, in any proceedings where the prosecution proposes to give in evidence a confession made by an accused person, it is represented to the court that the confession was or may have been obtained—

(a) by oppression of the person who made it; or
(b) in consequence of anything said or done which was likely, in the circumstances existing at the time, to render unreliable any confession which might be made by him in consequence thereof,

the court shall not allow the confession to be given in evidence against him except in so far as the prosecution proves to the court beyond reasonable doubt that the confession (notwithstanding that it may be true) was not obtained as aforesaid.

. . .

(8)   In this section 'oppression' includes torture, inhuman or degrading treatment, and the use or threat of violence (whether or not amounting to torture).

It must be underlined that s 76 applies only to confessions. Where the defence allege that a confession has been obtained by oppression or in circumstances likely to render it unreliable, the prosecution must prove beyond reasonable doubt that the confession was not so obtained. The requirement for the prosecution to prove this fact means that they must call evidence on the point and so a voir dire ('trial within a trial') takes place.

Unless the witness is in the middle of giving (or has already given) evidence in the course of the trial, a witness giving evidence on a voir dire takes a special form of oath: 'I swear by almighty God that I will answer truthfully all such questions as the court may ask.'

Each prosecution witness called in the voir dire may be cross-examined by the defence. When the relevant prosecution witnesses have given evidence, the defence may call evidence (including the evidence of the defendant himself); each defence witness may be cross-examined by the prosecution.

After the evidence has been called, both advocates may address the judge and the judge then rules on the admissibility of the confession. The only question to be determined under s 76 is how the confession was obtained. It is wholly irrelevant whether the confession was true or not.

If the defence case is simply that the police have fabricated the confession, that is a matter for the jury to decide and not a question of admissibility. However, there are cases where the defence allege that the confession has been fabricated but also argue that, even if that was not so, the confession is inadmissible anyway. In *Thongjai v The Queen* [1998] AC 54, the Privy Council (following *Ajodha v The State* [1982] AC 204) said that if the defendant denies confessing and also alleges that he was ill treated by the police before or at the time of the alleged confession, the two issues are not mutually exclusive. The judge has to assume that the admission was made and decide whether it is admissible; if (and only if) the judge decides that the evidence is admissible, it is for the jury to decide whether the admission was in fact made.

Where a judge conducts a voir dire and holds that a confession is admissible, the judge should not tell the jury of the ruling (the trial should simply continue with the prosecution leading evidence of the confession); if the judge indicates that he has ruled against the accused, this might lead the jury to think that the judge does not believe the accused (*Mitchell v The Queen* [1998] AC 695).

12.3.2 Section 78 of the Police and Criminal Evidence Act 1984

Section 78(1) of PACE provides as follows:

In any proceedings the court may refuse to allow evidence on which the prosecution proposes to rely to be given if it appears to the court that, having regard to all the circumstances, including the circumstances in which the evidence was obtained, the admission of the evidence would have such an adverse effect on the fairness of the proceedings that the court ought not to admit it.

Section 78 (unlike s 76) applies to any prosecution evidence. Where the defence object to prosecution evidence on the ground that its admission would be unfairly prejudicial, this objection is made in the absence of the jury but need not involve the judge hearing evidence. In other words, a voir dire need not take place if the judge is able to decide the question of admissibility under s 78 just by hearing legal argument from counsel and without hearing evidence. This will be the case, for example, where the breach of provisions of the Codes of Practice made under PACE are apparent from the custody record and/or the witness statements of the prosecution witnesses and the judge merely has to decide the effect of those breaches (as in *R v Keenan* [1990] 2 QB 54).

12.3.3 The European Convention on Human Rights

Under the European Convention on Human Rights, there is no absolute requirement that illegally obtained evidence should be excluded, but use of such evidence may give rise to unfairness in a particular case (*Schenk v Switzerland* (1991) 13 EHRR 242). The broad discretion conferred by s 78 of PACE appears to accord with this principle. Admission of a confession which was obtained through maltreatment of the suspect will inevitably violate Art 6. Section 76 of the 1984 Act accords with this principle.

12.4 WITNESSES WHOM THE PROSECUTION MUST CALL

The prosecution must call all the witnesses whose statements were served on the defence when the case was transferred to the Crown Court (*R v Balmforth* [1992] Crim LR 825). In *R v Russell-Jones* [1995] 1 Cr App R 538 at 544, Kennedy LJ summarised the relevant principles as follows:

- Generally speaking the prosecution must have at court all the witnesses whose statements have been served on the defence as witnesses on whom the prosecution intend to rely, if the defence want those witnesses to attend (i.e. the defence have not consented to the statements of those witnesses being read to the court under s 9 of the Criminal Justice Act 1967).
- The prosecution enjoy a discretion whether to call any witness it requires to attend, but the discretion is not unfettered. This discretion must be exercised in the interests of justice, so as to promote a fair trial.
- The next principle is that the prosecution ought normally to call or offer to call all the witnesses who give direct evidence of the primary facts of the case, unless for good reason, in any instance, the prosecutor regards the witness's evidence as unworthy of belief. In most cases the jury should have available all of the evidence as to what actually happened, which the prosecution, when serving statements, considered to be material, even if there are inconsistencies between one witness and another. If what a witness has to say is properly regarded by the prosecution as being 'incapable of belief', then his evidence cannot help the jury assess the overall picture of the crucial events; hence, it is not unfair that he should not be called.
- The prosecutor cannot properly condemn a witness as incredible merely because, for example, he gives an account at variance with that of a larger number of witnesses, and one which is less favourable to the prosecution case than that of the others.

- A prosecutor properly exercising his discretion will not therefore be obliged to proffer a witness merely in order to give the defence material with which to attack the credit of other witnesses on whom the Crown relies.
- In every case, the judgment to be made is primarily that of the prosecutor, and, in general, the court will only interfere with it if he has gone wrong in principle.

Thus, the main exceptions to the rule are as follows:

- the defence consent to the written statement of the witness being read to the court (under s 9 of the Criminal Justice Act 1967); or
- the prosecution take the view that the witness is no longer credible (as in *R v Oliva* [1965] 1 WLR 1028); or
- the witness would so fundamentally contradict the prosecution case that it would be better for that witness to be called by the defence (as in *R v Nugent* [1977] 1 WLR 789).

In *R v Cairns* [2002] EWCA Crim 2838; [2003] 1 WLR 796, the appeal was based partly on the fact that the prosecution had called a witness, part of whose evidence the prosecutor conceded to be unreliable. The Court of Appeal rejected this ground of appeal, holding that the overriding consideration in the exercise of the prosecution's discretion as to whether to call a witness is the interests of justice. As there is no reason why a jury should not accept the evidence of a witness in part only, there is no principle of law which requires the prosecution to regard the whole of a witness's evidence as reliable before calling that person to testify. If the prosecution consider that part of the evidence of a witness is capable of belief, then, even though they might not rely upon other parts of his evidence, it is a proper exercise of their discretion to call the witness. The court said that, since part of the evidence of the witness might be of assistance to the jury in performing its task, it would be contrary to the interests of justice to deprive them of that assistance.

12.4.1 'Tendering' witnesses for cross-examination

If a witness simply duplicates the evidence of another witness, the prosecution may simply 'tender' that witness, that is, call him, establish his identity and relevance to the case, and then invite the defence to cross-examine. This is often done with police witnesses, where the evidence of one officer largely repeats that of another.

12.5 SUBMISSION OF NO CASE TO ANSWER

After the close of the prosecution case, the defence may make a submission that there is no case to answer. This submission is made in the absence of the jury, who might otherwise be prejudiced against the defendant if the submission fails (*R v Smith* (1987) 85 Cr App R 197; *Crosdale v R* [1995] 1 WLR 864).

In the next sections we examine the two key cases on submissions of no case to answer: *R v Galbraith* [1981] 1 WLR 1039 (which sets out the general principles) and *R v Turnbull* [1977] QB 224 (which deals with the special status of identification evidence).

12.5.1 Principles applicable to a submission of no case to answer

The principles governing this submission are to be found in *R v Galbraith* [1981] 1 WLR 1039 (per Lord Lane CJ) at p 1042:

> How . . . should the judge approach a submission of 'no case'? (1) If there is no evidence that the crime alleged has been committed by the defendant, there is no difficulty. The judge will of course stop the case. (2) The difficulty arises where there is some evidence but it is of a tenuous character, for example because of inherent weakness or vagueness or because it is inconsistent with other evidence. (a) Where the judge comes to the conclusion that the prosecution evidence, taken at its highest, is such that a jury properly directed could not properly convict upon it, it is his duty, upon a submission being made, to stop the case. (b) Where however the prosecution evidence is such that its strength or weakness depends on the view to be taken of a witness's reliability, or other matters which are generally speaking within the province of the jury and where on one possible view of the facts there is evidence upon which a jury could properly come to the conclusion that the defendant is guilty, then the judge should allow the matter to be tried by the jury . . .
>
> There will of course, as always in this branch of the law, be borderline cases. They can safely be left to the discretion of the judge.

Two key principles flow from **Galbraith**:

a   if the judge comes to the conclusion that the prosecution evidence, taken at its highest, is such that a jury properly directed could not properly convict upon it, it is his duty to hold that there is no case to answer; and

b   if the strength or weakness of the prosecution evidence depends on the view to be taken of a witness's reliability, and on one possible view there is evidence on which a jury could properly convict, the judge should allow the matter to be tried by the jury.

Thus, a judge should only accept a submission of no case to answer in a clear case; otherwise he is trespassing on the function of the jury.

The phrase 'taken at its highest' is generally taken to require the judge to assume that the prosecution witnesses are telling the truth. However, in *R v Shippey* [1988] Crim LR 767, for example, Turner J found no case to answer in a rape trial because of 'really significant inherent inconsistencies' in the complainant's uncorroborated evidence, which his Lordship found 'frankly incredible'. It had been conceded by the defence that there was undoubtedly some evidence which went to support the prosecution case. However, the judge agreed that taking the prosecution case at its highest did not mean 'picking out the plums and leaving the duff behind'. Rather, the judge ruled that he must assess the evidence as a whole. It would, he said, not be right to interpret *Galbraith* as saying that if there are parts of the evidence which support the charge then, no matter what the state of the rest of the evidence, that is enough to leave the matter to the jury.

It is clear from this that the case must not be withdrawn from the jury simply because the judge doubts whether the principal prosecution witnesses are telling the truth, since that would be to usurp the function of the jury. However, the judge is entitled to rule that there is no case to answer if he takes the view that no reasonable jury could find that the prosecution witnesses are telling the truth. If that is so, there would of course be no point in leaving the case to them, since they would inevitably acquit.

It follows that the judge can have regard to:

- the sheer improbability of what a witness says;
- internal inconsistencies in the testimony of a particular witness; and
- inconsistencies between one prosecution witness and another.

In *R v Silcock* [2007] EWCA Crim 2176, Hooper LJ (at para 32) said that *Shippey* [1988] Crim LR 767 establishes no principle of law. The Court of Appeal had made the same point in *R v Pryer* [2004] EWCA Crim 1163 (where Hooper LJ said (at para 27) that *Shippey* is a decision on the facts, not a decision on the law). However, as Keene LJ said in *R v Broadhead* [2006] EWCA Crim 1705 (at para 17), Turner J's ruling in *Shippey* embodied a 'valid and important point'; his Lordship went on to say that

> The judge's task in considering such a submission at the end of the prosecution's case is to assess the prosecution's evidence as a whole. He has to take into account the weaknesses of the evidence as well as such strengths as there are. He needs to look at the evidence at that stage in the trial in the round therefore.

The essential point is that the testimony of a 'good' witness will not usually be nullified merely because other witnesses are poor or incredible; similarly, a jury might sometimes have reason to believe one part of a witness's testimony without necessarily believing another part of it. In *Silcock*, for example, the evidence of one witness was clear and the judge was entitled to hold that the jury could properly decide that this evidence was not invalidated by the confused or uncertain testimony of other witnesses.

It should be noted that where identification is in issue, special rules apply. In *R v Turnbull* [1977] QB 224, the Court of Appeal said that a judge should withdraw an identification case from the jury if the quality of the identification is poor (taking into account the circumstances of the identification – length of view, distance, lighting, etc) and there is no other evidence supporting the correctness of the identification. This case is so widely used in the courts that it is worth quoting at length from the judgment of Lord Widgery CJ (at pp 228–31):

> In our judgment the danger of miscarriages of justice occurring can be much reduced if trial judges sum up to juries in the way indicated in this judgment.
>
> First, whenever the case against an accused depends wholly or substantially on the correctness of one or more identifications of the accused which the defence alleges to be mistaken, the judge should warn the jury of the special need for caution before convicting the accused in reliance on the correctness of the identification or identifications. In addition he should instruct them as to the reason for the need for such a warning and should make some reference to the possibility that a mistaken witness can be a convincing one and that a number of such witnesses can all be mistaken. Provided this is done in clear terms the judge need not use any particular form of words.

Secondly, the judge should direct the jury to examine closely the circumstances in which the identification by each witness came to be made. How long did the witness have the accused under observation? At what distance? In what light? Was the observation impeded in any way, as for example by passing traffic or a press of people? Had the witness ever seen the accused before? How often? If only occasionally, had he any special reason for remembering the accused? How long elapsed between the original observation and the subsequent identification to the police? Was there any material discrepancy between the description of the accused given to the police by the witness when first seen by them and his actual appearance? If in any case, whether it is being dealt with summarily or on indictment, the prosecution have reason to believe that there is such a material discrepancy they should supply the accused or his legal advisers with particulars of the description the police were first given. In all cases if the accused asks to be given particulars of such descriptions, the prosecution should supply them. Finally, he should remind the jury of any specific weaknesses which had appeared in the identification evidence.

Recognition may be more reliable than identification of a stranger; but even when the witness is purporting to recognise someone whom he knows, the jury should be reminded that mistakes in recognition of close relatives and friends are sometimes made.

All these matters go to the quality of the identification evidence. If the quality is good and remains good at the close of the accused's case, the danger of a mistaken identification is lessened, but the poorer the quality, the greater the danger.

In our judgment when the quality is good, as for example when the identification is made after a long period of observation, or in satisfactory conditions by a relative, a neighbour, a close friend, a workmate and the like, the jury can safely be left to assess the value of the identifying evidence even though there is no other evidence to support it: provided always, however, that an adequate warning has been given about the special need for caution . . .

When, in the judgment of the trial judge, the quality of the identifying evidence is poor, as for example when it depends solely on a fleeting glance or on a longer observation made in difficult conditions, the situation is very different. The judge should then withdraw the case from the jury and direct an acquittal unless there is other evidence which goes to support the correctness of the identification. This may be corroboration in the sense lawyers use that word; but it need not be so if its effect is to make the jury sure that there has been no mistaken identification . . .

The trial judge should identify to the jury the evidence which he adjudges is capable of supporting the evidence of identification. If there is any evidence or circumstances which the jury might think was supporting when it did not have this quality, the judge should say so . . .

Care should be taken by the judge when directing the jury about the support for an identification which may be derived from the fact that they have rejected an alibi. False alibis may be put forward for many reasons: an accused, for example, who has only his own truthful evidence to rely on may stupidly fabricate an alibi and get lying witnesses to support it out of fear that his own evidence will not be enough. Further, alibi witnesses can make genuine mistakes about dates and occasions like any other witnesses can. It is only when the jury is satisfied that the sole reason for the fabrication was to deceive them and there is no other explanation for its being put forward can fabrication provide any support for identification evidence. The jury should be reminded that proving the accused has told lies about where he was at the material time does not by itself prove that he was where the identifying witness says he was . . .

> A failure to follow these guidelines is likely to result in a conviction being quashed and will do so if in the judgment of this court on all the evidence the verdict is either unsatisfactory or unsafe.

Section 34(2)(c) of the Criminal Justice and Public Order Act 1994 provides that adverse inferences can be drawn from failure to answer police questions when the court is considering a submission of no case to answer. However, s 34(2)(c) can only be relied upon to take the case past half time if a fact has been relied on by the defence which brings s 34 into play. In *R v Webber* [2004] UKHL 1; [2004] 1 WLR 404, the question of law certified by the Court of Appeal was: 'Can a suggestion put to a witness by or on behalf of a defendant amount to a fact relied upon in his defence for the purpose of s 34 of the Criminal Justice and Public Order Act 1994, if that suggestion is not adopted by the witness?' The House of Lords ruled that s 34 might apply if a defendant fails to mention when questioned by the police a significant matter on which he seeks to rely in his defence at trial (a) by giving evidence of it, (b) by adducing evidence of it from another witness, or (c) by putting it to a prosecution witness. A defendant relies on a fact or matter in his defence not only when he gives or adduces evidence of it but also when counsel, acting on his instructions, puts a specific and positive case to prosecution witnesses, as opposed to asking questions intended to probe or test the prosecution case; this is so whether or not the witness accepts the suggestion put (per Lord Bingham at para 34).

If the submission of no case to answer succeeds in respect of all the counts being tried, the judge directs the jury to acquit the defendant on all those counts. If the submission fails on all counts, the trial proceeds and the jury know nothing about the making of submission. If the submission succeeds on some, but not all, of the counts in the indictment, the trial of those counts in respect of which the judge has found there to be a case to answer continues; the jury are told that they are to consider only the counts that are left, and a formal acquittal on those counts where the submission succeeded will be directed when the jury give their verdict on the remaining counts.

The Court of Appeal has cautioned against the tactical use of submissions of no case to answer. If defence counsel notices a procedural error on the part of the prosecution, he should take the point at the outset, and not wait until the close of the prosecution case. For example, in *R v Gleeson* [2003] EWCA Crim 3357; [2004] 1 Cr App R 29, the defendant was charged with conspiracy. The charge was inappropriate and the trial judge accepted a submission of no case to answer. However, the judge also gave the prosecution leave to amend the indictment to allege a different offence. Giving the judgment of the court, Auld LJ (at paras 35–36) said:

> . . . just as a defendant should not be penalised for errors of his legal representatives in the conduct of his defence if he is unfairly prejudiced by them, so also should a prosecution not be frustrated by errors of the prosecutor, unless such errors have irremediably rendered a fair trial for the defendant impossible. For defence advocates to seek to take advantage of such errors by deliberately delaying identification of an issue of fact or law in the case until the last possible moment is, in our view, no longer acceptable, given the legislative and procedural changes to our criminal justice process in recent years. . .
>
> In this context we take the opportunity to repeat and adopt the extra-judicial sentiments

of one of us in the Report of the Criminal Courts Review (October 2001), in para 154 of Ch 10:

> 'To the extent that the prosecution may legitimately wish to fill possible holes in its case once issues have been identified by the defence statement, it is understandable why as a matter of tactics a defendant might prefer to keep his case close to his chest. But that is not a valid reason for preventing a full and fair hearing on the issues canvassed at the trial. A criminal trial is not a game under which a guilty defendant should be provided with a sporting chance. It is a search for truth in accordance with the twin principles that the prosecution must prove its case and that a defendant is not obliged to inculpate himself, the object being to convict the guilty and acquit the innocent. Requiring a defendant to indicate in advance what he disputes about the prosecution case offends neither of those principles.'

If the judge wrongly holds that there is a case to answer, evidence called after the submission will not be considered by the Court of Appeal, as no further evidence would have been called had the submission been upheld. Thus, an appeal against conviction would succeed even if the defendant was clearly incriminated by evidence given on behalf of the defence. In *R v Smith* [2000] 1 All ER 263, Mantell LJ said:

> What if a submission is wrongly rejected but the defendant is cross-examined into admitting his guilt? Should the conviction be said to be unsafe? We think it should. The defendant was entitled to be acquitted after the evidence against him had been heard. To allow the trial to continue beyond the end of the prosecution case would be an abuse of process and fundamentally unfair. So even in the extreme case, the conviction should be regarded as unsafe . . .

Similarly, in *R v Abbott* [1955] 2 QB 497, it had been held that the appellant was entitled to have his appeal allowed as the judge had come to a wrong decision in rejecting the submission of no case and thereby leaving the case to the jury when there was no evidence against him at the close of the case for the prosecution. In those circumstances, the Court of Appeal ruled that it was not obliged to take into account the adverse evidence given against him when the case had been wrongly left to the jury.

The same had been held to apply in *R v Juett* [1981] Crim LR 113 where, at the close of the prosecution case there was no evidence against D1 but no submission was made on his behalf. D2 then incriminated D1 in the course of his (D2's) defence. D1 did not testify. D1's conviction was quashed because a submission of no case to answer should have been made (and upheld).

In *R v Powell* [2006] EWCA Crim 685, Moore-Bick LJ (at para 19) said that where a submission of no case to answer is made but rejected, the judge should give brief reasons for deciding that there is sufficient evidence to go before a jury:

> both to enable the defendant and those representing him to understand clearly the grounds upon which the application has failed and to demonstrate that the decision rests on a rational basis rather than on any personal whim.

12.5.2 Acquittal by judge of his own motion

The judge can order an acquittal of his own motion (in other words, without the need for a submission of no case to answer). However, in *Attorney General's Reference (No 2 of 2000)* [2001] 1 Cr App R 36, the Court of Appeal held that where a prosecution has been properly brought (that is, it is not an 'abuse of process' – a concept considered in Chapter 1), a trial judge has no power to prevent the prosecution from calling evidence, or to direct the jury to acquit, simply on the basis that he thinks a conviction unlikely. In the case which gave rise to the Reference, when the defendant was brought before the court, the judge encouraged the prosecution to offer no evidence because he considered that it was unlikely that the defendant would be convicted. The prosecution declined to do so. A jury was empanelled and the judge informed them that he had formed a view about the quality of the evidence and that once the prosecution had begun he intended to order a verdict of not guilty. Prosecuting counsel opened the case to the jury and the judge then directed the jury to return a verdict of not guilty before the prosecution had called any of its witnesses. The Court of Appeal noted that the judge had not decided that the case was oppressive, vexatious or an abuse of process, but rather that the accused had a defence and that to proceed with the case would be a waste of time. The decision of the judge to stop the case, which had otherwise been properly brought, trespassed upon the right of the Crown Prosecution Service (CPS) to present its case in court, and the right of the jury to form their own view of the evidence and to express it by their verdict. Accordingly, the decision of the trial judge to direct an acquittal after the prosecution had opened its case had been wrong in law.

In *R v Brown* [2001] EWCA Crim 961; [2002] 1 Cr App R 5, the Court of Appeal held that a Crown Court judge is entitled, even at the end of the defence case, to rule that there is no case to go before the jury if there is no evidence on a count or if no reasonable jury could convict on the evidence available. A judge is under a duty to keep under review the question of whether a properly directed jury could convict at the close of evidence before leaving the matter to the jury. However, the judge's power to rule that there is no case to go before the jury should be exercised very sparingly and only if the judge is satisfied that no properly directed reasonable jury could safely convict on the evidence (per Longmore J at para 12).

12.5.3 Power of the jury to acquit at any time after the close of the prosecution case

Not to be confused with the right of the defence to seek a ruling from the judge that there is no case to answer, the jury themselves have the power to stop the case and acquit the defendant at any time after the close of the prosecution case. Jurors are, of course, generally unaware that they have this power and it is only in exceptional cases that they will be told of this power. In *R v Kemp* [1995] 1 Cr App R 151, the Court of Appeal said that where the judge does remind the jury that they may acquit the defendant without hearing further evidence, he should be cautious not to do anything other than merely inform them of their right to stop the case. Thus, the judge should not in effect invite the jury to acquit the defendant. If the judge considers that the case against the defendant is too weak to be left to the jury, then he should stop the case himself.

In *R v Speechley* [2004] EWCA Crim 3067; [2005] 2 Cr App R (S) 15, the Court of

Appeal held that the common law right of the jury to acquit a defendant after the conclusion of the prosecution case is exercisable only where they have been invited to do so by the trial judge. The court reasoned that it is the duty of the judge to ensure that the trial is fair, both to the defence and to the prosecution, and he has therefore to be in a position to decide when the time has come for the jury to be permitted to reach a decision. In almost every case, in order to do justice, the jury need to listen to all of the evidence, the submissions of counsel and the directions in law of the judge. Otherwise, for example, where an alternative verdict is available (e.g. under s 6 of the Criminal Law Act 1967), the jury might acquit without realising that an alternative verdict is possible. Accordingly, if a jury is invited by counsel, or seeks of its own motion, to return a verdict before being asked by the judge to do so, the judge should direct the jury that it is his duty to ensure that justice is done and that it is not open to them to return a verdict until he has invited them to do so (per Kennedy LJ at para 51). Kennedy LJ went on (at para 53) to observe that, bearing in mind that in an exceptional case a judge can consider a submission of no case to answer, or decide of his own motion that there is no case to answer, as late as the close of the defence case, it is difficult to envisage any circumstance where in reality it will be appropriate in the interests of justice for a judge to invite the jury to acquit.

More recently, in *R v Collins* [2007] EWCA Crim 854, the court said that it thought it 'strongly arguable' that the common law right of a jury to stop a case after the close of the prosecution case cannot survive Art 6 of the ECHR but that it is possible to envisage circumstances in which the jury could be reminded of this right in such a way as not to breach Art 6. However, the practice of inviting a jury to exercise such a right has been comprehensively disapproved by the Court of Appeal and should be exercised only in the most exceptional circumstances, and certainly not in a multi-handed case of some complexity (per Gage LJ at para 48).

12.5.4 'Judge-ordered' and 'judge-directed' acquittals – a critical evaluation

'Ordered' acquittals are those in which the judge orders an acquittal before the trial starts (usually because the prosecution has decided to offer no evidence); 'directed' acquittals occur where the judge directs the jury to acquit after the trial has started.

The Table which follows contains figures based on data from the Annual Reports produced by the CPS.

According to the official Judicial Statistics for 2006 (which cover all prosecutions, not just those brought by the CPS), during 2006, 59 per cent of the defendants who pleaded not guilty to all counts were acquitted. Of these, 10 per cent were acquitted on the direction of the judge. In both 2003 and 2004, 11 per cent of acquittals were on the direction of the judge; in 2005, the figure was 12 per cent.

Whichever set of figures is used, the rate of non-jury acquittals is very high. John Baldwin conducted a study of judge-ordered and judge-directed acquittals (see 'Understanding judge ordered and directed acquittals in the Crown Court' [1997] Crim LR 536). He was concerned to find out the principal reasons why cases ended as such acquittals and whether those acquittals were foreseeable and (if so) preventable. In his detailed study of 173 prosecution files, he found that early warning signs about the likelihood of the prosecution ending in acquittal were noted in no fewer than

Year	%age of acquittals that were judge-directed	%age of contested cases resulting in judge-directed acquittal
2006–07	18	7
2005–06	21	8
2004–05	24	9
2003–04	18	7
2002–03	18.5	7
2001–02	18.5	8
2000–01	20	9
1999–2000	20.5	9
1998–99	21	9

87.3 per cent of judge-ordered acquittals, 73.1 per cent of judge-directed acquittals and 58.8 per cent of jury acquittals. It is tempting to use figures such as these to suggest that the CPS is simply allowing too many weak cases to proceed. There may be some substance to this, in that some of the CPS lawyers interviewed by Baldwin suggested that case reviews had to be carried out too quickly for the evidential sufficiency test to be applied rigorously; that some reviewing lawyers may lack the necessary experience to help them spot evidential weaknesses; and that some reviewing lawyers:

> . . . far from conducting a dispassionate examination of a case, uncritically accepted the initial police view. . . . It was sometimes clear that reviewing lawyers had been blinkered in the approach they had adopted, merely following the line that the police had already taken and not subjecting the evidence supplied by the police to a rigorous or critical examination . . . Put bluntly, weak cases continue to be committed to the Crown Court because of a reluctance, even a disinclination, on the part of certain reviewing lawyers to make the tough decisions in serious cases required of them under the Code for Crown Prosecutors.

It also transpired that several CPS lawyers were considering the strength of the case as it stood, rather than considering whether the prosecution case could be improved. Baldwin also noticed a tendency to adopt 'in effect a weaker test of evidential sufficiency where allegations or injuries are serious'. Baldwin said that:

> . . . the interviews also showed that some CPS lawyers share a common value system with the police, a core element of which is that serious cases ought to be prosecuted, almost irrespective of considerations as to evidential strength. Cases have developed a considerable momentum by the time of committal, and expectations build up that cases will proceed to the Crown Court. In such circumstances, it is easy to understand why some prosecutors, particularly when lacking experience or self-confidence, hesitate in making hard decisions in complex or serious cases.

He also noted that:

> ... requests to the police, in so far as they were made at all, were overwhelmingly for clarification of the detail or for the taking of statements which had for some reason been overlooked by police. There were only isolated instances in the files where suggestions had been made by reviewing lawyers about the need to pursue further or fresh lines of inquiry. In practice, it seems, case review is much more concerned with tinkering with points of detail in what has already been done by police than with tackling the fundamentals in the approach adopted.

(Indeed some prosecutors complain, though Baldwin does not note this as an issue, that requests for further evidence rarely result in action by the police.) It also became apparent during Baldwin's research that some prosecuting counsel were not carrying out a review of the evidence at all (or at least not until very close to the trial date, making it too late to take remedial action). Some barristers felt that it was not appropriate for them to advise on evidence unless specifically instructed to do so; some barristers felt reluctant to point out weaknesses in the case, lest doing so jeopardised their relationship with the CPS.

A major reason for the failure of the prosecution to obtain convictions was the fact that witnesses either failed to attend court or else did not 'come up to proof' (in other words, gave evidence that was inconsistent with their original statements to the police). In some cases, there were clear warning signs that there were, or might be, problems with particular witnesses, but little or no action was taken to address the problem.

It is clear from Baldwin's research that there are many reasons why so many cases fail to get past 'half time' but many of those reasons are capable of remedy.

One way of reducing the number of cases that collapse might be pre-trial interviewing of prosecution witnesses by Crown Prosecutors. This suggestion is controversial because of the obvious risk of 'coaching'. However, pre-trial witness interviewing by Crown Prosecutors has been tested in a limited pilot exercise undertaken in four CPS Areas between January 2006 and February 2007. An evaluation of the pilot was carried out by Paul Roberts and Candida Saunders (<http://www.cps.gov.uk/victims_witnesses/interviews_report.html>). Their main conclusion was such interviews are 'capable of delivering a range of benefits, to prosecutors, to victims, to other criminal justice professionals and agencies, and to the higher ideals of criminal justice policy, across a range of cases – including crimes of serious violence and sexual assault'. The writers concluded that such interviewing 'improves the quality of prosecutorial decision-making both by strengthening cases that proceed to trial and by timely rejection of evidentially weak cases'. In several cases, the result of the interview was a decision not to charge the suspect, or to discontinue proceedings or offer no evidence at trial; in a similar number of cases, however, the interviews confirmed the prosecutor's inclination to proceed, 'by resolving any residual doubts or contributing important evidential clarifications'. It was noted that there were several notable instances in which interviews 'rescued' prosecutions which would otherwise have been abandoned. It should be noted, however, that in some cases the interview 'failed to clarify the situation, and the prosecutor essentially remained none the wiser about how to proceed'. The writers also note that several concerns about interviewing witnesses emerged. These included the risk of, or allegations of, witness 'coaching', witness non-cooperation or hostility, and the possibility that the interview may generate material that is damaging to the witness's credibility. Moreover, it is conceivable that such interviews could create an additional procedural hurdle for complainants and other prosecution witnesses to surmount, potentially 'setting up the prosecutor as judge and jury' and 'contributing to the deterioration of conviction rates in already-hard-to-prosecute cases'.

12.6 THE DEFENCE CASE

If there is no submission of no case to answer, or a submission is made and the judge finds a case to answer in respect of some or all of the counts, evidence may then be adduced on behalf of the defendant.

Counsel for the defence may begin the defence case by making an opening speech if he proposes to call one or more witnesses (other than the defendant) as to the facts. If the only witness as to the facts is the defendant (that is, only the defendant gives evidence or there is evidence only from the defendant and character witnesses) there will be no defence opening speech. This is based on s 2 of the Criminal Evidence Act 1898, which provides that:

> Where the only witness to the facts of the case called by the defence is the person charged, he shall be called as a witness immediately after the close of the evidence for the prosecution.

12.6.1 Defence evidence

Where there is more than one defence witness including the defendant, the defendant must give evidence first unless the court otherwise directs, under s 79 of PACE, which states:

> If at the trial of any person for an offence—
>
> (a)   the defence intends to call two or more witnesses to the facts of the case; and
> (b)   those witnesses include the accused,
>
> the accused shall be called before the other witness or witnesses unless the court in its discretion otherwise directs.

Each defence witness (including the defendant himself, if he chooses to give evidence) is liable to be cross-examined by the prosecution and may then be re-examined by defence counsel, if necessary.

12.6.2 Adverse inferences

There is no obligation on the defence to call any evidence: counsel for the defence could simply address the jury and ask them to find that the prosecution have failed to prove the guilt of the accused beyond reasonable doubt. However, s 35 of the Criminal Justice and Public Order Act 1994, whilst not rendering the accused compellable to give evidence on his own behalf, does enable the court to draw such inferences as appear proper from the failure of the accused to give evidence or from his refusal, without good cause, to answer any question.

Where the accused has taken the oath but then refuses to answer a question, he will only be regarded as having good cause not to answer the question if either he is entitled to refuse to answer by virtue of an Act of Parliament or on the ground of privilege, or the court, in the exercise of its general discretion, excuses him from answering it.

Section 35 requires the defendant to be warned that adverse inferences may be drawn from his silence unless he (or his barrister) has informed the court that he will give evidence. The details of what the judge should say are set out in para IV.44 of the *Consolidated Practice Direction*:

IV.44 Defendant's right to give or not to give evidence

IV.44.1 At the conclusion of the evidence for the prosecution, section 35(2) of the Criminal Justice and Public Order Act 1994 requires the court to satisfy itself that the accused is aware that the stage has been reached at which evidence can be given for the defence and that he can, if he wishes, give evidence and that, if he chooses not to give evidence, or having been sworn, without good cause refuses to answer any question, it will be permissible for the jury to draw such inferences as appear proper from his failure to give evidence or his refusal, without good cause, to answer any question.

If the accused is legally represented

IV.44.2 Section 35(1) provides that section 35(2) does not apply if at the conclusion of the evidence for the prosecution the accused's legal representative informs the court that the accused will give evidence. This should be done in the presence of the jury. If the representative indicates that the accused will give evidence the case should proceed in the usual way.

IV.44.3 If the court is not so informed, or if the court is informed that the accused does not intend to give evidence, the judge should in the presence of the jury inquire of the representative in these terms:

'Have you advised your client that the stage has now been reached at which he may give evidence and, if he chooses not to do so or, having been sworn, without good cause refuses to answer any question, the jury may draw such inferences as appear proper from his failure to do so?'

IV.44.4 If the representative replies to the judge that the accused has been so advised, then the case shall proceed. If counsel replies that the accused has not been so advised, then the judge shall direct the representative to advise his client of the consequences set out in paragraph 44.3 and should adjourn briefly for this purpose before proceeding further.

If the accused is not legally represented

IV.44.5 If the accused is not represented, the judge shall at the conclusion of the evidence for the prosecution and in the presence of the jury say to the accused:

'You have heard the evidence against you. Now is the time for you to make your defence. You may give evidence on oath, and be cross-examined like any other witness. If you do not give evidence or, having been sworn, without good cause refuse to answer any question the jury may draw such inferences as appear proper. That means they may hold it against you. You may also call any witness or witnesses whom you have arranged to attend court. Afterwards you may also, if you wish, address the jury by arguing your case from the dock. But you cannot at that stage give evidence. Do you now intend to give evidence?'

In *R v Bevan* (1994) 98 Cr App R 354, the Court of Appeal said that if the defendant chooses not to give evidence in his own defence, counsel should make sure that this decision is recorded (usually, this will be done by an endorsement on the brief). Watkins LJ said (at p 358) that:

it should be the invariable practice of counsel to have that decision recorded and to cause the defendant to sign the record, giving a clear indication that (1) he has by his own will decided not to give evidence and (2) that he has so decided bearing in mind the advice, if any, given to him by his counsel.

12.6.3 Defendant's previous convictions

A detailed discussion of the rules relating to the admissibility of any previous convictions recorded against the defendant is outside the scope of this textbook (there is a useful discussion of the relevant law in Adrian Keane's *Modern Law of Evidence* (OUP, 2008)).

The statutory provisions are contained in Chapter 1 of Pt 11 of the Criminal Justice Act 2003. Section 101(1) provides that:

(1) In criminal proceedings evidence of the defendant's bad character is admissible if, but only if—

(a) all parties to the proceedings agree to the evidence being admissible,

(b) the evidence is adduced by the defendant himself or is given in answer to a question asked by him in cross-examination and intended to elicit it,

(c) it is important explanatory evidence,

(d) it is relevant to an important matter in issue between the defendant and the prosecution,

(e) it has substantial probative value in relation to an important matter in issue between the defendant and a co-defendant,

(f) it is evidence to correct a false impression given by the defendant, or

(g) the defendant has made an attack on another person's character.

Under s 101(3), the court must not admit evidence under sub-s (1)(d) or (g) if, on an application by the defendant to exclude it, it appears to the court that the admission of the evidence 'would have such an adverse effect on the fairness of the proceedings that the court ought not to admit it'. Section 101(4) goes on to provide that the court, when considering an application to exclude evidence under sub-s (3), must 'have regard, in particular, to the length of time between the matters to which that evidence relates and the matters which form the subject of the offence charged'.

One of the leading authorities is *R v Hanson* [2005] EWCA Crim 824; [2005] 1 WLR 3169, where the Court of Appeal held that, on an application by the prosecution under s 101(1), to show his propensity to commit offences of the kind with which he was charged, the trial judge has to consider three questions:

i   did the history of his convictions establish a propensity to commit offences of the kind charged;

ii   did that propensity make it more likely that the defendant had committed the offence charged; and

iii was it unjust to rely on convictions of the same description or category; and, in any event, would the proceedings be unfair if they were admitted?

The court added that where the application is made in order to show that the defendant had a propensity to untruthfulness, this is not the same as a propensity to dishonesty. Accordingly, previous convictions, whether for offences of dishonesty or otherwise, are only likely to be capable of showing a propensity to untruthfulness where, in the case being tried, truthfulness is an issue and, in the earlier cases, either there was a plea of not guilty and the defendant gave an account which the jury must have disbelieved, or the way in which the offence was committed showed a propensity for untruthfulness, for example by the making of false representations.

12.6.4 Judicial control of the trial

To what extent can the judge intervene during the questioning of witnesses? This point was addressed by Stuart-Smith LJ in *R v Sharp* [1994] QB 261 (at p. 273), where his Lordship said:

> When a judge intervenes in the course of examination, or particularly cross-examination, a number of problems can arise depending on the frequency and manner of the interruptions. First the judge may be in danger of seeming to enter the arena in the sense that he may appear partial to one side or the other. This may arise from the hostile tone of questioning or implied criticism of counsel who is conducting the examination or cross-examination, or if the judge is impressed by a witness, perhaps suggesting excuses or explanations for a witness's conduct which is open to attack by counsel for the opposite party. Quite apart from this, frequent interruptions may so disrupt the thread of cross-examination that counsel's task may be seriously hampered. In a case of any complexity cross-examination of the principal witnesses is something that calls for careful preparation and planning. It is the most important part of the advocate's art, because a competent cross-examination is designed to weaken or destroy the opponent's case and to gain support for the client's case. But it is easier said than done. If the judge intervenes at a crucial point where the witness is being constrained to make an important admission, it can have an adverse effect on the trial.
>
> In general, when a cross-examination is being conducted by competent counsel a judge should not intervene, save to clarify matters he does not understand or thinks the jury may not understand. If he wishes to ask questions about matters that have not been touched upon it is generally better to wait until the end of the examination or cross-examination.

This is no doubt a counsel of perfection and a judge should not be criticised for occasional transgressions; still less can it be said in such cases that there is any irregularity in the conduct of the trial or that the verdict is unsafe or unsatisfactory. But there may come a time, depending on the nature and frequency of the interruptions that a reviewing court is of the opinion that defence counsel was so hampered in the way he properly wished to conduct the cross-examination that the judge's conduct amounts to a material irregularity.

In *R v Denton* [2007] EWCA Crim 1111, the Court of Appeal considered judicial interventions during the trial on indictment in the light of this guidance, holding that judges must be free to clarify the true state of the evidence. There can be no fixed rules as to when it is appropriate for a judge to intervene. All must depend on the facts of the individual case. Sustained questioning by the judge should be embarked on only with caution, having regard to the need for judicial restraint and the preservation both of impartiality and the appearance of impartiality. It does not, however, follow that even judicial interventions which of themselves might raise an eyebrow necessarily result in an unfair trial or an unsafe conviction. Such interventions or questions must be considered in the context of the evidence as a whole, of the conduct of the trial as a whole and also with regard to the summing-up (per Gross J at para 18).

12.7 CLOSING SPEECHES

Once all the defence evidence has been called, both counsel may generally make a closing speech. The prosecution make the first speech (although prosecuting counsel may decide not to make a speech if the trial has been a very short one).

If the accused is unrepresented and either calls no evidence at all or else was himself the only witness as to the facts, then the prosecution have no right to make a closing speech (*R v Mondon* (1968) 52 Cr App R 695). In *R v Stovell* [2006] EWCA Crim 27, the Court of Appeal doubted whether this was an invariable rule. Rose LJ said that the court was by no means satisfied that in all cases, particularly when a defendant has been represented substantially throughout the trial and there are issues arising during the defence upon which the jury would be assisted by comment from prosecuting counsel, it is necessarily inappropriate for prosecuting counsel to make a closing speech (para 36).

R v Bryant [1979] QB 108 confirms that the prosecution has the right to make a closing speech to the jury even when a defendant represented by counsel has called no evidence and has not given evidence himself.

Where the prosecutor does make a closing speech, s 1(b) of the Criminal Procedure (Right of Reply) Act 1964 requires that such a speech must 'be after the close of the evidence for the defence and before the closing speech (if any) by or on behalf of the accused'. Thus the prosecutor has the first closing speech and the defence advocate has the last word before the judge's summing up.

12.8 VARIATION IN PROCEDURE WHERE THERE IS MORE THAN ONE DEFENDANT

The procedure for putting the defence case before the jury varies slightly if there is more than one defendant.

12.8.1 Defendants separately represented

Where two or more defendants are charged in the same indictment and are separately represented, their cases are presented in the order in which their names appear on the indictment. So:

Regina   v   D1
                       D2

Prosecution witnesses are cross-examined first on behalf of D1, then on behalf of D2.
  The defence case is then presented as follows:

* opening speech on behalf of D1;
* D1 called as a witness (if he chooses to give evidence):

  a   examination-in-chief by his own counsel;
  b   cross-examination on behalf of D2;
  c   cross-examination by prosecution;
  d   re-examination by his own counsel (if necessary);

* any witnesses called on behalf of D1 give evidence; the order of questioning is the same as above;
* opening speech on behalf of D2;
* D2 called as a witness (if he chooses to give evidence):

  a   examination-in-chief by his own counsel;
  b   cross-examination on behalf of D1;
  c   cross-examination by prosecution;
  d   re-examination by his own counsel (if necessary);

* any witnesses called on behalf of D2 give evidence; the order of questioning is the same as the point above;
* prosecution closing speech;
* closing speech on behalf of D1;
* closing speech on behalf of D2.

12.8.2 Defendants jointly represented

If the defendants are jointly represented, they are regarded as presenting a joint defence. Consequently, the defence case will be presented as follows:

* a single opening speech on behalf of all the defendants;
* D1 gives evidence if he wishes to do so;

- D2 gives evidence if he wishes to do so;
- any other defence witnesses give evidence;
- prosecution closing speech;
- closing speech on behalf of all defendants.

12.9 REOPENING THE PROSECUTION CASE

In exceptional cases, the judge has a discretion to allow the prosecution to call add-itional evidence after the close of the prosecution case. In *R v Munnery* (1992) 94 Cr App R 164, for example, after the close of the prosecution case, the defence indicated that they wished to submit that there was no case to answer. The next morning, when the judge was to consider this submission, the prosecution stated that they wished to call a new witness. The Court of Appeal upheld the decision of the judge to allow this witness to be called. No injustice was done to the defendant as the defence case had not yet started. The court emphasises that the discretion to admit fresh evidence after the close of the prosecution case might be exercised with great caution.

In *R v Patel* [1992] Crim LR 739, further evidence against the defendant unexpect-edly came to light in the context of an unrelated investigation. The prosecution were allowed to adduce this additional evidence even though closing speeches had already been made. The Court of Appeal said that judges should generally be reluctant to grant such late applications. However, the judge had invited the defence to seek an adjourn-ment and to call fresh evidence if they wished and so no harm had been done. Any prejudice to the defendant was, said the court, far outweighed by the strong probative quality of the evidence in question.

If the judge takes the view that it would be unduly prejudicial to the defence to allow the prosecution to reopen their case, it is open to him to discharge the jury (with the effect that a new trial will take place later).

12.10 THE JUDGE'S SUMMING UP

After the prosecution and defence counsel have made their closing speeches, the judge sums the case up to the jury. The judge must do this in all cases, however simple the case may seem. Although traditionally the judge produces the summing up without refer-ence to counsel, in *R v Taylor* [2003] EWCA Crim 2447; (2003) *The Times*, 8 October, the Court of Appeal said that where complex directions are to be given to the jury, counsel in the case should be permitted to consider and comment upon the draft directions before the judge addresses the jury.

A very useful resource is the Criminal Bench Book published by the Judicial Studies Board. It contains a set of specimen directions which cover all the major matters which have to be covered in a summing up. These specimen directions are freely available on the web: <http://www.jsboard.co.uk/criminal_law/cbb/index.htm>. For discussion of the advantages and disadvantages of the use of specimen directions, see Roderick Munday, 'Exemplum Habemus: Reflections on the Judicial Studies Board's Specimen Directions' (2006) 70 J Crim L 27.

In October 2007, Lord Phillips CJ announced that, because of concern at the number of directions that are given to juries on matters that could be regarded as no more than common sense, Latham LJ had been asked to lead a working party to see whether some of those directions could be dispensed with, or at least simplified. In this connection, it is worth noting that, in *R v C* [2007] EWCA Crim 2859, the Court of Appeal observed that every summing up, particularly one delivered extempore, could, with hindsight, be rewritten or have incorporated into it other features. However, that is nowhere near sufficient to demonstrate that a conviction is unsafe. A summing up is an individual creation, in which virtually everyone who hears it who is a party to a case on either side will find something that he would prefer to be expressed differently. However, it is important to bear in mind that a summing up is not written for the Court of Appeal, which has not heard the evidence, but rather it is written for the jury who have been listening to the evidence. It is written for those who know, in particular, what is not disputed.

12.10.1 The respective functions of the judge and the jury

Matters of law are for the judge whereas matters of fact are for the jury. This means that the jury must accept what the judge says about the law, whether they agree or not. The judge should be careful not to express an opinion on the facts and should make it clear to the jury that if he does express an opinion on the facts, the jury are free to come to a different conclusion. The direction approved in *R v Jackson* [1992] Crim LR 214 was:

> It is my job to tell you what the law is and how to apply it to the issues of fact that you have to decide and to remind you of the important evidence on these issues. As to the law, you must accept what I tell you. As to the facts, you alone are the judges. It is for you to decide what evidence you accept and what evidence you reject or of which you are unsure. If I appear to have a view of the evidence or of the facts with which you do not agree, reject my view. If I mention or emphasise evidence that you regard as unimportant, disregard that evidence. If I do not mention what you regard as important, follow your own view and take that evidence into account.

In the most recent edition of the Judicial Studies Board standard directions, the suggested wording is:

> Our functions in this trial have been and remain quite different. Throughout this trial the law has been my area of responsibility, and I must now give you directions as to the law which applies in this case. When I do so, you must accept those directions and follow them.
>
> I must also remind you of the prominent features of the evidence. However, it has always been your responsibility to judge the evidence and decide all the relevant facts of this case, and when you come to consider your verdict you, and you alone, must do that.
>
> You do not have to decide every point which has been raised; only such matters as will enable you to say whether the charge laid against the defendant has been proved. You will do that by having regard to the whole of the evidence [including the agreed/admitted evidence] and forming your own judgment about the witnesses, and which evidence is reliable and which is not. [The defendant has chosen to give evidence (and call witnesses). You must

judge that evidence by precisely the same fair standards as you apply to any other evidence in the case].

[Add something along the following lines, if you believe it may be of assistance in the particular case: You must decide this case only on the evidence which has been placed before you. There will be no more. You are entitled to draw inferences, that is come to common sense conclusions based on the evidence which you accept, but you may not speculate about what evidence there might have been or allow yourselves to be drawn into speculation.]

The facts of this case are your responsibility. You will wish to take account of the arguments in the speeches you have heard, but you are not bound to accept them. Equally, if in the course of my review of the evidence, I appear to express any views concerning the facts, or emphasise a particular aspect of the evidence, do not adopt those views unless you agree with them; and if I do not mention something which you think is important, you should have regard to it, and give it such weight as you think fit. When it comes to the facts of this case, it is your judgment alone that counts.

12.10.2 Burden and standard of proof

Every summing up must contain at least a direction to the jury as to the burden and standard of proof (*R v McVey* [1988] Crim LR 127).

12.10.2.1 Burden of proof

The recommended wording is as follows:

> In this case the prosecution must prove that the defendant is guilty. He does not have to prove his innocence. In a criminal trial the burden of proving the defendant's guilt is on the prosecution.

12.10.2.2 Standard of proof

The recommended wording is as follows:

> How does the prosecution succeed in proving the defendant's guilt? The answer is – by making you sure of it. Nothing less than that will do. If after considering all the evidence you are sure that the defendant is guilty, you must return a verdict of 'Guilty'. If you are not sure, your verdict must be 'Not Guilty'.

It will be noted that the Judicial Studies Board recommends that, when describing the standard of proof, the judge should tell the jury that they have to be satisfied so that they are 'sure' of the defendant's guilt. This is in preference to the well-known phrase 'beyond reasonable doubt'. However, in *Ferguson v The Queen* [1979] 1 WLR 94, it was put thus:

> It is generally sufficient and safe to direct a jury that they must be satisfied beyond reasonable doubt so that they feel sure of the defendant's guilt.

In *R v Stephens* [2002] EWCA Crim 1529; (2002) *The Times*, 27 June, the jury retired and sent a note asking the judge (a) what constituted reasonable doubt and (b) how certain was it necessary for them to be. The appeal concerned the answer which should be given in such a case. The court said that the Judicial Studies Board guideline to direct a jury to be satisfied so that they were sure of guilt is a well-established direction. It is not helpful for a judge to direct a jury to distinguish between being sure and being certain and a judge should avoid doing so. If necessary, a judge should direct a jury that they have to be sure of guilt before they can convict, and that is the limit of the help that he can give them (per Keene LJ at para 15).

Exceptionally, the defendant may bear a burden of proof. For example, if the defendant is charged with possession of an offensive weapon, it is open to him to show that he had lawful authority or reasonable excuse. In such a case, it must be made clear to the jury that the defendant can satisfy this burden of proof on the balance of probabilities (that is, showing that it is more likely than not that he had lawful authority or reasonable excuse). There is only a burden of proof on the defendant if statute clearly so provides; otherwise it is for the prosecution to disprove any defence. Thus, for example, if the defendant raises the defence of self-defence, it is for the prosecution to prove beyond reasonable doubt that he was not so acting. If an issue does arise on which the defence bears the burden of proof, the appropriate direction is:

> If the prosecution has not made you sure that the defendant has (set out what the prosecution must prove), that is an end of the matter and you must find the defendant 'Not Guilty'. However, if and only if, you are sure of those matters, you must consider whether the defendant [e.g. had a reasonable excuse etc. for doing what he did]. The law is that that is a matter for him to prove on all the evidence; but whenever the law requires a defendant to prove something, he does not have to make you sure of it. He has to show that it is probable, which means it is more likely than not, that [e.g. he had reasonable excuse etc. for doing it]. If you decide that probably he did [e.g. have a reasonable excuse etc. for doing it], you must find him 'Not Guilty'. If you decide that he did not, then providing that the prosecution has made you sure of what it has to prove, you must find him 'Guilty'.

12.10.3 Explanation of the law involved and how it relates to the facts

Even in a straightforward case, directions on the ingredients of the offence are an essential part of the summing up (*R v McVey* [1988] Crim LR 127). Thus, the judge must explain what the prosecution have to prove and must remind the jury of the evidence they have heard. The judge should remind the jury of the main features of the prosecution and defence evidence, even if the case is a straightforward one (*R v Gregory* [1993] Crim LR 623). In *R v Lawrence* [1982] AC 510, Lord Hailsham of St Marylebone LC (at p 519) said that the summing up must:

> include a succinct but accurate summary of the issues of fact as to which a decision is required, a correct but concise summary of the evidence and arguments on both sides, and a correct statement of the inferences which the jury are entitled to draw from their particular conclusions about the primary facts.

With the help of the summing up, the jury should thus be able to relate the evidence which they have heard to the legal principles which they have to apply.

In *R v Bowerman* [2000] 2 Cr App R 189, the grounds of appeal concerned the judge's decision not to sum up the facts of the case to the jury. After giving legal directions the judge told the jury that they had the advantage of two speeches, from the defence and prosecution counsel, who were very experienced and had covered every salient point in the case. He told them that any repetition by him of the evidence would be otiose. On appeal, it was submitted in particular that the jury were not reminded of the evidence which supported the defence case. Henry LJ (at pp 191–3) said that counsels' closing speeches are no substitute for an impartial review of the facts from the trial judge, who is responsible for ensuring that an accused has a fair trial. The first step to a fair trial is for the trial judge to focus the jury's attention on the issues he identifies; that responsibility should not be delegated to counsel. The fact that members of the jury were taking notes did not relieve a judge of his responsibility; evidence needs to be marshalled and arranged issue by issue by the judge and that task could not be passed to the jurors. Whilst it might be unnecessary for the judge to review the evidence if the trial was a very short one (as in *R v Wilson* [1991] Crim LR 838),

> in a trial lasting several days or more, it is generally of assistance to the jury if the judge summarises those factual issues which are not disputed, and, where there is a significant dispute as to material facts, identifies succinctly those pieces of evidence which are in conflict. By so doing, the judge can focus the jury's attention on those factual issues which they must resolve. It is never appropriate, however, for a summing-up to be a mere rehearsal of the evidence.

12.10.4 Such warnings as are appropriate

12.10.4.1 Co-defendants or more than one count

Where there is more than one count and/or more than one defendant, the judge must direct the jury to consider each count and each defendant separately.

In *R v Jones and Jenkins* [2003] EWCA Crim 1966; [2004] 1 Cr App R 5 (at para 47, per Auld LJ), it was held that, where there are co-defendants and each defendant says that he is not responsible for the alleged crime, the jury should be directed as follows:

> First, the jury should consider the case for and against each defendant separately. Second, the jury should decide the case on all the evidence, including the evidence of each defendant's co-defendant. Third, when considering the evidence of co-defendants, the jury should bear in mind that he or she may have an interest to serve or, as it is often put, an axe to grind. Fourth, the jury should assess the evidence of co-defendants in the same way as that of the evidence of any other witness in the case.

If one defendant implicated another in a police interview, the judge should instruct the jury to disregard the out-of-court statement of that defendant in so far as it implicates the other defendant (*R v Rhodes* (1960) 44 Cr App R 23). Note that if a defendant implicated a co-defendant in the witness box when giving evidence on his own behalf, that evidence is admissible against the co-defendant (*R v Rudd* (1948) 32 Cr App R 138).

12.10.4.2 Identification evidence

If the case rests on identification evidence, the judge must warn the jury that such evidence is notoriously unreliable and that they should examine very closely the circumstances in which the identification took place when assessing the weight of that evidence (*R v Turnbull* [1977] QB 224). The judge should give a detailed direction on the factors which strengthen or weaken the identification evidence (see above, in the section discussing the submission of no case to answer, for further detail).

12.10.4.3 Adverse inferences for silence

Given the fact that a jury may draw adverse inferences from the failure of a defendant to answer police questions (under s 34 of the Criminal Justice and Public Order Act 1994) or to testify in court (s 35), they have to be given some guidance on how to approach this aspect of the case.

In *R v Cowan* [1996] QB 373, the Court of Appeal considered what should be said in the summing up if the case is one where adverse inferences might be drawn under s 35 from the defendant's failure to testify. Lord Taylor CJ (at p 381) said that the essential elements of the direction are as follows:

(1) The judge will have told the jury that the burden of proof remains upon the prosecution throughout and what the required standard is.

(2) It is necessary for the judge to make clear to the jury that the defendant is entitled to remain silent. That is his right and his choice. The right of silence remains.

(3) An inference from failure to give evidence cannot on its own prove guilt. That is expressly stated in section 38(3) of the Act.

(4) Therefore, the jury must be satisfied that the prosecution have established a case to answer before drawing any inferences from silence. Of course, the judge must have thought so or the question whether the defendant was to give evidence would not have arisen. But the jury may not believe the witnesses whose evidence the judge considered sufficient to raise a prima facie case. It must therefore be made clear to them that they must find there to be a case to answer on the prosecution evidence before drawing an adverse inference from the defendant's silence.

(5) If, despite any evidence relied upon to explain his silence or in the absence of any such evidence, the jury conclude the silence can only sensibly be attributed to the defendant's having no answer or none that would stand up to cross-examination, they may draw an adverse inference.

In other words, the defendant's failure to answer police questions or testify cannot be the sole basis for his conviction and so the jury must be directed not to convict just because the defendant has not testified. Nevertheless, if the evidence adduced by the prosecution calls for an explanation which the defendant should be in a position to give, the jury may be rightly suspicious of a defendant who declines to give an explanation unless they accept any explanation for the silence.

The same approach was followed in *R v Birchall* [1999] Crim LR 311. In that case, the Court of Appeal held that where the defendant fails to testify, the judge must tell the jury that they should not start to consider whether to draw adverse inferences from the defendant's failure to testify until they have concluded that there is a case to answer (that is, that the prosecution case against him is sufficiently compelling to call for an answer by him). This is so even if there is plainly sufficient evidence to amount to a prima facie case against the defendant. Thus, there are two key steps before adverse inferences can be drawn under s 35:

a   is the jury satisfied that the prosecution have established a case to answer against the defendant?; and
b   has the jury rejected any explanation put forward by the defendant for his refusal to give evidence?

If the answer to these questions is 'yes', the jury may draw adverse inferences from the defendant's silence.

In *R v Argent* [1997] 2 Cr App R 27, Lord Bingham identified the conditions which have to be satisfied before adverse inferences can be drawn, under s 34 of the 1994 Act. The final condition his Lordship identified (at p 33) was that:

> the appellant failed to mention a fact which in the circumstances existing at the time the accused could reasonably have been expected to mention when so questioned. The time referred to is the time of questioning, and account must be taken of all the relevant circumstances existing at that time. The courts should not construe the expression 'in the circumstances' restrictively: matters such as time of day, the defendant's age, experience, mental capacity, state of health, sobriety, tiredness, knowledge, personality and legal advice are all part of the relevant circumstances; and those are only examples of things which may be relevant. When reference is made to 'the accused' attention is directed not to some hypothetical, reasonable accused of ordinary phlegm and fortitude but to the actual accused with such qualities, apprehensions, knowledge and advice as he is shown to have had at the time. It is for the jury to decide whether the fact (or facts) which the defendant has relied on in his defence in the criminal trial, but which he had not mentioned when questioned under caution before charge by the constable investigating the alleged offence for which the defendant is being tried, is (or are) a fact (or facts) which in the circumstances as they actually existed the actual defendant could reasonably have been expected to mention.
>
> Like so many other questions in criminal trials this is a question to be resolved by the jury in the exercise of their collective common-sense, experience and understanding of human nature . . .

Where the silence was failure to answer police questions, it may be that the defendant will explain this silence when he gives evidence. If the silence is a failure to testify, any explanation could come from the questions asked during the cross-examination of the prosecution witnesses. In *R v Chenia* [2002] EWCA Crim 2345; [2003] 2 Cr App R 6, the Court of Appeal gave further detailed guidance on the drawing of adverse inferences under s 34 of the Criminal Justice and Public Order Act 1994. In that case, evidence was adduced of interviews under caution in which the appellant made no comment. He did not give evidence, but his case was put through counsel in cross-examination. The Court of Appeal ruled as follows:

a   whilst merely putting the prosecution to proof of its case would not amount to reliance upon a fact for the purposes of s 34, an adverse inference might be drawn even though the defendant did not give evidence or call witnesses. A fact might be relied upon whether it was adduced in evidence in the course of either the prosecution or defence case. The mere putting of a fact to a witness in cross-examination might, in certain circumstances, be sufficient to amount to reliance upon it for the purposes of s 34 (see also *R v Bowers* (1999) 163 JP 33 and *R v Webber* [2004] UKHL 1; [2004] 1 WLR 404);

b   discussion between the advocates and the judge before the commencement of speeches, aimed at determining whether a s 34 direction is appropriate and, if so, how that direction should be tailored to meet the facts of the particular case, is a sensible and necessary precaution;

c   under s 34, the jury should, in respect of any fact relied on by a defendant in his defence but not mentioned in interview, first resolve whether he could, in the circumstances existing at the time, have been expected to mention it and, if so, go on to draw such inferences as might appear proper. The facts relied upon by way of defence, but not mentioned in interview, should be identified by the trial judge to the jury. The direction must not give the impression that the jury might draw an adverse inference because the appellant was sheltering behind his solicitor's advice not to answer questions: such an inference can only be drawn if the jury are sure that the defendant had, at that stage, no explanation to offer or none that would have withstood questioning or investigation;

d   the fact that the s 34 direction given by the trial judge was inadequate does not necessarily render either the trial unfair or the conviction unsafe. Whether there was a breach of Art 6 as the result of a failure to direct a jury in a particular way depends upon all the circumstances of the individual case.

In *R v Petkar* [2003] EWCA Crim 2668; [2004] 1 Cr App R 22, Rix LJ (at para 51) said that a well crafted and careful jury direction on s 34 should include: identification of the facts the accused failed to mention but which were relied on in his defence and of the inferences which it is suggested might be drawn from the failure, to the extent that they might go beyond the standard inference of late fabrication; that if an inference is drawn, the jury should not convict wholly or mainly on the strength of it; that an inference should only be drawn if the jury think it a fair and proper conclusion and that the only sensible explanation for the failure was that the defendant had no answer to the accusation or none that would have stood up to scrutiny; that no inference should be drawn unless the prosecution case was so strong that it clearly called for an answer.

In *R v Bresa* [2005] EWCA Crim 1414, the Court of Appeal said that, among the key features of a direction under s 34 are the following (per Waller LJ at para 16):

First there needs to be the striking of a fair balance between telling the jury of a defendant's rights [to remain silent or not to disclose advice], and telling the jury that the defendant has a choice not to rely on those rights. Second there needs to be an accurate identification of the facts which it is alleged a defendant might reasonably have mentioned. Third there needs to be a warning that there must be a case to answer and the jury cannot convict on inference alone. Fourth there must be a direction to the effect that the key question is whether the jury can be sure that the accused remains silent not because of any advice but because he had no satisfactory explanation to give.

Where the case is one where the jury might be inclined to draw adverse inferences but it is not open to them to do so, the judge should make this clear. In *R v McGarry* [1999] 1 WLR 1500, the prosecution had accepted that the defendant had not relied on anything in his defence that he had not mentioned when interviewed, and so no inferences could be drawn from his failure to answer questions in those interviews. It was held that the trial judge should have given the jury a specific direction that no adverse inference should be drawn from the defendant's silence; otherwise, the jury might have been left in doubt as to whether or not it was proper to hold the defendant's silence against him. However, according to *R v Francom* [2001] 1 Cr App R 237, failure to give such a direction will render a conviction unsafe only if it resulted in unfairness to the accused.

The right to a fair trial guaranteed by Art 6 of the European Convention on Human Rights includes 'the right of anyone charged with a criminal offence to remain silent and not to contribute to incriminating himself' (*Funke v France* (1993) 16 EHRR 297). The case of *Condron* (see above) went to the European Court of Human Rights (*Condron v UK* (2001) 31 EHRR 1). On the basis that the defendant had testified at trial and had offered an explanation for remaining silent during the police interview, the Court held that the jury should have been directed that if they were satisfied that the defendant's silence at the police interview could not sensibly be attributed to his having no answer, or none that would stand up to cross-examination, it should not draw an adverse inference.

In *R v Betts & Hall* [2001] EWCA Crim 224; [2001] 2 Cr App R 257, the court said that if it was a plausible explanation that the reason for not mentioning facts when interviewed was that the particular defendant had acted on the advice of his solicitor and not because he had had no answer, or no satisfactory answer, to give, then no inference could be drawn. In the present case, the jury might have failed to appreciate that they could only draw inferences against a particular defendant if they were sure that he had no explanation to offer, or none that he believed would stand up to questioning or investigating. The approach taken by the Court of Appeal in this case was approved by the European Court of Human Rights in *Beckles v UK* (2003) 36 EHRR 13.

In *R v Beckles* [2004] EWCA Crim 2766; [2005] 1 WLR 2829, the Court of Appeal re-visited the effect of legal advice, holding that in a case where a solicitor's advice is relied upon by the defendant, the ultimate question for the jury under s 34 remains whether the facts relied on at the trial were facts which the defendant could reasonably have been expected to mention at interview. If they were not, that is the end of the matter. If the jury consider that the defendant genuinely relied on the advice, that is not necessarily the end of the matter. It may still not have been reasonable for him to rely on the advice, or the advice may not have been the true explanation for his silence. If it is possible to say that the defendant genuinely acted upon the advice, the fact that he did so because it suited his purpose may mean he was not acting reasonably in not mentioning the facts. His reasonableness in not mentioning the facts remains to be determined by the jury. If they conclude he was acting unreasonably, they can draw an adverse inference from the failure to mention the facts (per Lord Woolf CJ at para 46).

If the defendant explains his failure to reveal a fact that he later relies on in court on the basis of legal advice he had received, the issue of waiver of legal privilege (i.e. the confidentiality of that advice) might arise. In *R v Condron* [1997] 1 WLR 827 at 837, the Court of Appeal said that:

> If an accused person gives as a reason for not answering questions that he has been advised by his solicitor not to do so, that advice, in our judgment, does not amount to a waiver of privilege. But, equally, for reasons which we have already given, that bare assertion is unlikely by itself to be regarded as a sufficient reason for not mentioning matters relevant to the defence. So it will be necessary, if the defendant wishes to invite the court not to draw an adverse inference, to go further and state the basis or reason for the advice. Although the matter was not fully argued, it seems to us that once this is done it may well amount to a waiver of privilege so that the defendant or, if his solicitor is also called, the solicitor can be asked whether there were any other reasons for the advice, and the nature of the advice given, so as to explore whether the advice may also have been given for tactical reasons.

Further guidance on this point was given by the Court of Appeal in *R v Bowden* [1999] 1 WLR 823, where it was held if a defendant says (either at his interview in the police station or at trial) that he refused to answer police questions because he was advised to remain silent by his solicitor, he does not thereby waive legal professional privilege. However, if the defendant or his solicitor (at the time of the interview or at trial) explains the basis for that advice, the defendant has waived privilege and it is open to the prosecution to cross-examine the defendant about the information he gave to his solicitor (that is, he can be cross-examined on the nature of that advice and the factual premises on which it had been based).

In *R v Hoare; R v Pierce* [2004] EWCA Crim 784; [2005] 1 WLR 1804, the court commented on the rationale behind s 34, saying (at paras 53–55, per Auld LJ):

> The whole basis of s 34 of the 1994 Act, in its qualification of the otherwise general right of an accused to remain silent and to require the prosecution to prove its case, is an assumption that an innocent defendant – as distinct from one who is entitled to require the prosecution to prove its case – would give an early explanation to demonstrate his innocence. If such a defendant is advised by a solicitor to remain silent, why on earth should he do so, unless . . . he might wrongly inculpate himself?
>
> It is not the purpose of s 34 of the 1994 Act to exclude a jury from drawing an adverse inference against a defendant because he genuinely or reasonably believes that, regardless of his guilt or innocence, he is entitled to take advantage of that advice to impede the prosecution case against him. In such a case the advice is not truly the reason for not mentioning the facts. The s 34 inference is concerned with flushing out innocence at an early stage or supporting other evidence of guilt at a later stage, not simply with whether a guilty defendant is entitled, or genuinely or reasonably believes that he is entitled, to rely on legal rights of which his solicitor has advised him. Legal entitlement is one thing. An accused's reason for exercising it is another. His belief in his entitlement may be genuine, but it does not follow that his reason for exercising it is . . .

The question in the end, which is for the jury, is whether regardless of advice, genuinely given and genuinely accepted, an accused has remained silent not because of that advice but because he had no or no satisfactory explanation to give . . .

Given that the purpose of s 34 is to prevent the accused from 'ambushing' the prosecution by revealing important facts for the first time at trial, one stratagem that is often employed is the provision to the police of a statement, followed by a refusal to answer questions. Thus, the accused is able to reveal the facts that will be relied on in court but still give a 'no-comment' interview.

This stratagem was considered in *R v Knight* [2003] EWCA Crim 1977; [2004] 1 WLR 340, at the beginning of the accused's interview with police, his solicitor read out a prepared statement giving an account which was wholly consistent with the testimony that he gave later at trial. On his solicitor's advice, he declined to answer any questions in interview, stating at trial that he did so because he was worried about getting confused and answering police questions incorrectly. The judge directed the jury that they might draw the adverse inference from the defendant's silence that he wished to prevent his account being scrutinised by police questioning because he believed that it would not stand up to it. The Court of Appeal said that the purpose of s 34 is to procure the early disclosure of a suspect's account, not the scrutiny and testing of it by the police in interview. That, said the court, would be a significantly greater intrusion into a suspect's general right to silence than the requirement to disclose his factual defence. There can be no adverse inference where the defendant gives his full account in the statement given to the police, mentioning all the facts he later relies on and from which he does not depart in the witness box. The fact that he does not mention the facts specifically in response to police questions is immaterial. The judge's direction therefore rendered the conviction unsafe. The court noted that a prepared statement does not of itself give automatic immunity against adverse inferences under s 34. It might be incomplete in comparison with the account given at trial or in some respects inconsistent with it.

In *R v Turner* [2003] EWCA Crim 3108; [2004] 1 All ER 1025, the defendant again relied on a pre-prepared statement in his interview with the police. The Court of Appeal ruled that where a defendant produces a pre-prepared statement in a police interview, directions to the jury in relation to potential adverse inferences should include a comparison of the defendant's evidence at trial with the pre-prepared statement to see whether there was any fact relied on at trial which the defendant did not mention in the pre-prepared statement. It is only on the basis of such unmentioned facts that the jury is entitled to draw an adverse inference and the judge should give a specific direction in that regard. The court pointed out that the growing practice of submitting a pre-prepared statement and declining to answer any questions in interview may prove a dangerous course for an innocent person who subsequently discovers at the trial that something significant was omitted; no such problems would arise following an interview where the suspect gave appropriate answers to all the questions asked. The court added that where the prosecution propose to invite the jury to draw an adverse inference under s 34, the alleged discrepancy should ordinarily be ventilated in cross-examination so that the defendant has an opportunity to deal with it, and that where there are discrepancies between the prepared statement and the defendant's evidence at trial, it may be more appropriate to deal with this through a direction on previous lies rather than a direction under s 34.

Given the importance of ss 34 and 35 of the 1994 Act, it is appropriate to set out those provisions in more detail:

34. Effect of accused's failure to mention facts when questioned or charged.

(1) Where, in any proceedings against a person for an offence, evidence is given that the accused—

    (a) at any time before he was charged with the offence, on being questioned under caution by a constable trying to discover whether or by whom the offence had been committed, failed to mention any fact relied on in his defence in those proceedings; or

    (b) on being charged with the offence or officially informed that he might be prosecuted for it, failed to mention any such fact,

being a fact which in the circumstances existing at the time the accused could reasonably have been expected to mention when so questioned, charged or informed, as the case may be, sub-section (2) below applies.

(2) Where this sub-section applies—

. . .

    (c) the court, in determining whether there is a case to answer; and

    (d) the court or jury, in determining whether the accused is guilty of the offence charged,

may draw such inferences from the failure as appear proper.

(2A) Where the accused was at an authorised place of detention at the time of the failure, sub-sections (1) and (2) above do not apply if he had not been allowed an opportunity to consult a solicitor prior to being questioned, charged or informed as mentioned in sub-section (1) above.

(3) Subject to any directions by the court, evidence tending to establish the failure may be given before or after evidence tending to establish the fact which the accused is alleged to have failed to mention.

. . .

35. Effect of accused's silence at trial.

(1) At the trial of any person for an offence, sub-sections (2) and (3) below apply unless—

    (a) the accused's guilt is not in issue; or

    (b) it appears to the court that the physical or mental condition of the accused makes it undesirable for him to give evidence;

but sub-section (2) below does not apply if, at the conclusion of the evidence for the prosecution, his legal representative informs the court that the accused will give evidence or, where he is unrepresented, the court ascertains from him that he will give evidence.

(2) Where this sub-section applies, the court shall, at the conclusion of the evidence for the prosecution, satisfy itself (in the case of proceedings on indictment with a jury, in the presence of the jury) that the accused is aware that the stage has been reached at

which evidence can be given for the defence and that he can, if he wishes, give evidence and that, if he chooses not to give evidence, or having been sworn, without good cause refuses to answer any question, it will be permissible for the court or jury to draw such inferences as appear proper from his failure to give evidence or his refusal, without good cause, to answer any question.

(3)   Where this sub-section applies, the court or jury, in determining whether the accused is guilty of the offence charged, may draw such inferences as appear proper from the failure of the accused to give evidence or his refusal, without good cause, to answer any question.

(4)   This section does not render the accused compellable to give evidence on his own behalf, and he shall accordingly not be guilty of contempt of court by reason of a failure to do so.

(5)   For the purposes of this section a person who, having been sworn, refuses to answer any question shall be taken to do so without good cause unless—

(a)   he is entitled to refuse to answer the question by virtue of any enactment, when-ever passed or made, or on the ground of privilege; or

(b)   the court in the exercise of its general discretion excuses him from answering it.

. . .

Note also s 38(3) which provides that a person shall not have a case to answer or be convicted of an offence solely on an inference drawn under ss 34 or 35.

12.10.4.4 Alibi evidence

Where the defendant puts forward an alibi, the judge must direct the jury that the burden of proof rests on the prosecution to disprove it (not on the defendant to prove it) beyond reasonable doubt. Where the defendant relies on an alibi at trial but either failed to give particulars of that alibi to the prosecution or gave particulars which are inconsistent with the story told in court, the judge may direct the jury that they are entitled to draw adverse inferences against the defendant (see s 11(2)(f) and (5) of the Criminal Procedure and Investigations Act (CPIA) 1996). A conviction cannot, how-ever, be based solely on such an adverse inference (s 11(10)). Where the evidence in court is different from the particulars of alibi given to the prosecution, regard must be had to the degree of divergence in the stories and to any justification which the defence put forward for the divergence (s 11(8)).

The specimen direction recommended by the Judicial Studies Board is:

> The defence is one of alibi. The defendant says that he was not at the scene of the crime when it was committed. As the prosecution has to prove his guilt so that you are sure of it, he does not have to prove he was elsewhere at the time. On the contrary, the prosecution must disprove the alibi.
>
> Even if you conclude that the alibi was false, that does not by itself entitle you to convict the defendant. It is a matter which you may take into account, but you should bear in mind that an alibi is sometimes invented to bolster a genuine defence.

A failure to give such a direction does not automatically render a conviction unsafe; the Court of Appeal will consider whether the jury might have come to a different conclusion had the direction been given (*R v Harron* [1996] 2 Cr App R 457; *R v Lesley* [1996] 1 Cr App R 39).

12.10.4.5 Lies by the defendant

Where there is evidence before the jury that the defendant has lied about something, and there is a risk of the jury thinking that, because the defendant has lied, he must therefore be guilty of the offence with which he is charged, they should be directed that proof of lying is not proof of guilt (in that an innocent defendant might lie). See *R v Lucas* [1981] QB 720, where Lord Lane CJ said (at p 724):

> To be capable of amounting to corroboration the lie told out of court must first of all be deliberate. Secondly it must relate to a material issue. Thirdly the motive for the lie must be a realisation of guilt and a fear of the truth. The jury should in appropriate cases be reminded that people sometimes lie, for example, in an attempt to bolster up a just cause, or out of shame or out of a wish to conceal disgraceful behaviour from their family. Fourthly the statement must be clearly shown to be a lie ... by admission or by evidence from an independent witness.

The specimen direction recommended by the Judicial Studies Board puts it thus:

> [If the issue arises] You must decide whether the defendant did in fact deliberately tell [these] lies. If you are not sure he did, ignore this matter. If you are sure, consider:
>
> Why did the defendant lie? The mere fact that a defendant tells a lie is not in itself evidence of guilt. A defendant may lie for many reasons, and they may possibly be 'innocent' ones in the sense that they do not denote guilt, for example, (add as appropriate) lies to bolster a true defence, to protect somebody else, to conceal some disgraceful conduct [other than] [short of] the commission of the offence, or out of panic, distress or confusion. In this case the explanation for his lies is [. . . .].
>
> If you think that there is, or may be, an innocent explanation for his lies then you should take no notice of them. It is only if you are sure that he did not lie for an innocent reason that his lies can be regarded by you as evidence [going to prove guilt] [supporting the prosecution case].

12.10.4.6 The defendant's previous convictions

The judge's summing up must reflect the principles governing the admissibility of previous convictions under ss 98 to 112 of the Criminal Justice Act 2003, detailed consideration of which is beyond the scope of the present work.

The leading case is *R v Hanson* [2005] EWCA Crim 824; [2005] 1 WLR 3169, where (at para 18), Rose LJ said that:

> in any case in which evidence of bad character is admitted to show propensity, whether to commit offences or to be untruthful, the judge in summing up should warn the jury clearly against placing undue reliance on previous convictions. Evidence of bad character cannot be used simply to bolster a weak case, or to prejudice the minds of a jury against a defendant. In particular, the jury should be directed; that they should not conclude that the defendant is

guilty or untruthful merely because he has these convictions; that, although the convictions may show a propensity, this does not mean that he has committed this offence or been untruthful in this case; that whether they in fact show a propensity is for them to decide; that they must take into account what the defendant has said about his previous convictions; and that, although they are entitled, if they find propensity as shown, to take this into account when determining guilt, propensity is only one relevant factor and they must assess its significance in the light of all the other evidence in the case.

12.10.4.7 The defendant's good character

Where the defendant has no previous convictions, the jury should be directed that this is relevant both to his credibility as a witness and to the likelihood of his having commit- ted the offence. If the defendant does not testify, then his previous good character goes to the credibility of any denial that he made to the police when interviewed as well as being relevant to the likelihood of his having committed the offence alleged (*R v Vye* [1993] 1 WLR 471; *R v Teasdale* [1993] 4 All ER 290). In *R v Aziz* [1996] 1 AC 41, the House of Lords confirmed that a defendant who does not have any relevant previous convictions and who has testified or made pre-trial answers or statements containing admissions as well as self-exculpatory explanations is prima facie entitled to a good character direction going both to credibility and propensity.

In *R v Gray* [2004] EWCA Crim 1074; [2004] 2 Cr App R 30, the Court considered the law on good character directions. Rix LJ (at para 57) summarises the law as follows:

(1) The primary rule is that a person of previous good character must be given a full direction covering both credibility and propensity. Where there are no further facts to complicate the position, such a direction is mandatory and should be unqualified.

(2) If a defendant has a previous conviction which, either because of its age or its nature, may entitle him to be treated as of effective good character, the trial judge has a discretion so to treat him, and if he does so the defendant is entitled to a direction; but

(3) Where the previous conviction can only be regarded as irrelevant or of no significance in relation to the offence charged, that discretion ought to be exercised in favour of treating the defendant as of good character. In such a case the defendant is again entitled to a *Vye* direction ... where there is room for uncertainty as to how a defendant of effective good character should be treated, a judge would be entitled to give an appropriately modified *Vye* direction.

(4) Where a defendant of previous good character, whether absolute or, we would suggest, effective, has been shown at trial, whether by admission or otherwise, to be guilty of criminal conduct, the prima facie rule of practice is to deal with this by qualifying a *Vye* direction rather than by withholding it; but

(5) In such a case, there remains a narrowly circumscribed residual discretion to withhold a good character direction in whole, or presumably in part, where it would make no sense, or would be meaningless or absurd or an insult to common sense, to do otherwise.

(6) Approved examples of the exercise of such a residual discretion are not common ...

(7) A direction should never be misleading. Where therefore a defendant has withheld something of his record so that otherwise a trial judge is not in a position to refer to it,

the defendant may forfeit the more ample, if qualified, direction which the judge might have been able to give.

In *Teeluck v State of Trinidad and Tobago* [2005] UKPC 14; [2005] 1 WLR 2421, the PC (following earlier cases such as *Barrow v The Queen* [1998] AC 846 and *Thompson v The Queen* [1998] AC 811) held as follows (at para 33):

(i)   When a defendant is of good character, i.e. has no convictions of any relevance or significance, he is entitled to the benefit of a good character direction from the judge when summing up to the jury, tailored to fit the circumstances of the case.

(ii) The direction should be given as a matter of course, not of discretion. It will have some value and will therefore be capable of having some effect in every case in which it is appropriate for such a direction to be given. If it is omitted in such a case it will rarely be possible for an appellate court to say that the giving of a good character direction could not have affected the outcome of the trial.

(iii) The standard direction should contain two limbs, the credibility direction, that a person of good character is more likely to be truthful than one of bad character, and the propensity direction, that he is less likely to commit a crime, especially one of the nature with which he is charged.

(iv) Where credibility is in issue, a good character direction is always relevant.

(v)   The defendant's good character must be distinctly raised, by direct evidence from him or given on his behalf or by eliciting it in cross-examination of prosecution witnesses. It is a necessary part of counsel's duty to his client to ensure that a good character direction is obtained where the defendant is entitled to it and likely to benefit from it. The duty of raising the issue is to be discharged by the defence, not by the judge, and if it is not raised by the defence the judge is under no duty to raise it himself.

12.10.4.8 Corroboration

Where an accomplice testifies as a prosecution witness against a defendant, there is no duty to warn the jury about the dangers of convicting on the basis of that evidence (s 32 of the Criminal Justice and Public Order Act 1994 removed the mandatory corroboration warning). However, the trial judge nevertheless has residual discretion to warn the jury in regard to a particular witness. In *R v Makanjuola* [1995] 1 WLR 1348 (at pp 1351-2), Lord Taylor CJ summarised the law as follows:

. . . (2) It is a matter for the judge's discretion what, if any warning, he considers appropriate in respect of such a witness as indeed in respect of any other witness in whatever type of case. Whether he chooses to give a warning and in what terms will depend on the circumstances of the case, the issues raised and the content and quality of the witness's evidence. (3) In some cases, it may be appropriate for the judge to warn the jury to exercise caution before acting upon the unsupported evidence of a witness. This will not be so . . . because a witness is alleged to be an accomplice. There will need to be an evidential basis for suggesting that the evidence of the witness may be unreliable. An evidential basis does not include mere suggestion by cross-examining counsel. (4) If any question arises as to whether the judge should give a special warning in respect of a witness, it is desirable that the question be resolved by discussion with counsel in the absence of the jury before final speeches. (5)

Where the judge does decide to give some warning in respect of a witness, it will be appropriate to do so as part of the judge's review of the evidence and his comments as to how the jury should evaluate it rather than as a set-piece legal direction. (6) Where some warning is required, it will be for the judge to decide the strength and terms of the warning. It does not have to be invested with the whole florid regime of the old corroboration rules . . . (8) Finally, this court will be disinclined to interfere with a trial judge's exercise of his discretion save in a case where that exercise is unreasonable in the *Wednesbury* sense . . .

12.10.4.9 *Expert evidence*

In a case involving expert evidence, it is important for the judge to direct the jury that they are not bound by the opinion of an expert witness: *R v Stockwell* (1993) 97 Cr App R 260 and *R v Fitzpatrick* [1999] Crim LR 832. In the former case, Lord Taylor CJ said (at p 266):

> It is . . . important that the judge should make clear to the jury that they are not bound by the expert's opinion, and that the issue is for them to decide.

12.10.5 Alternative counts

If the indictment contains alternative counts where one is more serious than the other (for example, ss 18 and 20 of the Offences Against the Person Act 1861), the judge will tell the jury to consider the more serious count first. If they convict on that count, they should not go on consider the other count; if they acquit on the more serious count, they should proceed to consider the less serious charge.

If the alternative counts are of more or less equal gravity (for example, theft and handling), the jury will simply be told to consider both but either to acquit on both or convict on only one.

12.10.6 Unanimous verdict

The jury must be directed to return a unanimous verdict; a majority verdict is only possible after an appropriate direction given later. The form of words suggested by the Judicial Studies Board is:

> You must reach, if you can, a unanimous verdict. As you may know, the law allows me in certain circumstances to accept a verdict which is not the verdict of you all. Those circumstances have not arisen, so when you retire I ask you to reach a verdict on which each one of you is agreed. Should, however, the time come when I can accept a majority verdict, I shall call you back into court and give you a further direction.

Finally, the jury will also be advised to elect a foreman to chair their discussions and announce their verdict.

12.10.7 Summing up fairly

The judge must take care to sum up fairly. He must, for example, ensure that the defence case is put fully and fairly. The judge should deal with the case impartially. Sarcastic and extravagant language disparaging the defence must be avoided. In the event of an appeal against conviction, the Court of Appeal will look at 'the impact of the summing up as a whole' when considering its fairness (*R v Berrada* (1990) 91 Cr App R 131).

In *R v Spencer* [1995] Crim LR 235, the defendant's conviction was held to be unsafe as a result of excessive and largely one-sided comment made by the judge when directing the jury. It was said by Henry LJ that some comment is permissible, but not to the extent that the rehearsal of the evidence is interrupted and the jury's task made more difficult.

In *R v Reid* (1999) *The Times*, 17 August, Beldam LJ said:

> The case against this appellant was strong. His defence correspondingly weak. But it is just in these circumstances that a judge has to be scrupulous to ensure that the accused's defence is presented to the jury in an even handed and impartial manner. Justice is not served by a one-sided account given to the jury shortly before they retire to consider their verdict. It is best served by a constant striving to give the accused what is his absolute right, that is a fair trial by an impartial tribunal, guided and directed by an impartial judge.

The judge has to make sure that the defence case is left to the jury properly. In *R v Curtin* [1996] Crim LR 831, Rose LJ said:

> . . . it is a judge's duty, in summing up to a jury, to give directions about the relevant law, to refer to the salient pieces of evidence, to identify and focus attention upon the issues, and in each of those respects to do so as succinctly as the case permits. It follows that as part of this duty a judge must identify the defence. The way in which he does so will necessarily depend on all the circumstances of the particular case. When the defendant has given evidence it will usually be desirable, though it may not always be necessary, to summarise his evidence. When the defendant has answered questions in police interviews, as well as giving evidence, it may be appropriate for the judge to draw attention to consistencies or inconsistencies between the interviews and the evidence. When the defendant has neither answered questions in interview nor given evidence, it will often be very difficult for the judge to say much in relation to the defence, though it will usually be appropriate in such a case for him to remind the jury of significant points made in defence counsel's speech.

It should be noted that it is generally inappropriate for the judge to comment on the failure of the defence to call a particular witness, as such comment can easily detract from what is said about the burden of proof (see *R v Wheeler* [1967] 1 WLR 1531, 1536; *R v Wright* [2000] Crim LR 510).

It should be borne in mind that where the judge fails to direct the jury adequately on a particular point, and that failure appears to provide a ground of appeal, defence counsel should not remain silent but should draw the matter to the attention of the judge; indeed, the duty to assist the judge rests upon both the prosecution and the defence (*R v Langford* (2001) *The Times*, 12 January).

In *R v Wang* [2005] UKHL 9; [2005] 1 WLR 661, the House of Lords held that there are no circumstances in which a judge is entitled to direct a jury to return a verdict of guilty. However, *Wang* does not support the proposition that in every case where a judge had given a direction to convict, the conviction has automatically to be considered unsafe, although the conviction will be unsafe if the judge effectively takes the decision away from the jury because they are given no opportunity to retire and consider the matter for themselves (*R v Caley-Knowles; R v Jones* [2006] EWCA Crim 1611; [2006] 1 WLR 3181).

12.11 RETIREMENT OF THE JURY

After the summing up, the jury are delivered into the custody of the jury bailiff, who takes an oath to take them to a private place to consider their verdict and to prevent anyone from communicating with them. The jury then go to the jury room to consider their verdict.

In a serious case (especially where there are several counts and/or several defendants), the judge should not send the jury out after 3 pm save in exceptional cases. It would be better for them to start their deliberations the following day (*R v Birch* (1992) *The Times*, 27 March).

The *Consolidated Practice Direction* provides as follows:

Guidance to jurors

IV.42.6 Trial judges should ensure that the jury is alerted to the need to bring any concerns about fellow jurors to the attention of the judge at the time, and not to wait until the case is concluded. At the same time, it is undesirable to encourage inappropriate criticism of fellow jurors, or to threaten jurors with contempt of court.

IV.42.7 Judges should therefore take the opportunity, when warning the jury of the importance of not discussing the case with anyone outside the jury, to add a further warning. It is for the trial judge to tailor the further warning to the case, and to the phraseology used in the usual warning. The effect of the further warning should be that it is the duty of jurors to bring to the judge's attention, promptly, any behaviour among the jurors or by others affecting the jurors, that causes concern. The point should be made that, unless that is done while the case is continuing, it may be impossible to put matters right.

IV.42.8 The judge should consider, particularly in a longer trial, whether a reminder on the lines of the further warning is appropriate prior to the retirement of the jury.

IV.42.9 In the event that such an incident does occur, trial judges should have regard to the remarks of Lord Hope of Craighead in R v Mirza [2004] 2 WLR 201, 241–42, paras 127–28 and consider the desirability of preparing a statement that could be used in connection with any appeal arising from the incident to the Court of Appeal (Criminal Division) . . .

12.11.1 Separation of the jury

During lunchtime and overnight adjournments during the trial, the jury are allowed to go their separate ways. Formerly, the jury were not allowed to separate after the judge had finished the summing up. However, s 13 of the Juries Act 1974, as amended, now enables the court to allow the jury to separate after (as well as before) they have been sent out to consider their verdict.

Before being allowed to separate, the jurors should be warned not to discuss the case with anyone who is not on the jury (*R v Prime* (1973) 57 Cr App R 632). The jury should also be told not to continue their deliberations except when they are together in the jury room, otherwise there is a risk that discussions might take place without all jurors being present (*R v Tharakan* [1995] 2 Cr App R 368). In *R v Oliver* [1995] 2 Cr App R 514 at 520, the Court of Appeal gave guidance on the directions which should be given to a jury which was allowed to separate before delivering its verdict. The following elements should be contained in such a direction:

1. That the jury must decide the case on the evidence and the arguments that they have seen and heard in court, and not on anything they may have seen or heard or may see or hear outside the court.

2. That the evidence has been completed and that it would be wrong for any juror to seek for or to receive further evidence or information of any sort about the case.

3. That the jury must not talk to anyone about the case, save to the other members of the jury and then only when they are deliberating in the jury room. They must not allow anyone to talk to them about the case unless that person is a juror and he or she is in the jury room deliberating about the case.

4. When they leave court they should try to set the case they are trying on one side until they return to court and retire to their jury room to continue the process of deliberating about their verdict or verdicts.

It is not necessary for the judge to use any precise form of words provided that the matters set out above are properly covered in whatever words he chooses to use. We consider it would be desirable for this direction to be given in full on the first dispersal of the jury and a brief reminder to be given at each subsequent dispersal.

In *R v Hastings* [2003] EWCA Crim 3730; (2003) *The Times*, 12 December, the Court of Appeal reiterated that it is extremely important that the judge warns the jury not to deliberate on their verdict until all jury members are present (per Lord Woolf CJ at para 19).

12.11.2 No further evidence

Once the jury has retired, no further evidence can be called (*R v Owen* [1952] 2 QB 362). In that case, the jury came out of retirement to ask whether the premises where a sexual assault was alleged to have taken place would have been occupied or not at the relevant time. The Court of Appeal held that no further evidence (whether from a witness who has already been called or from a fresh witness) can be called after the jury has retired to consider its verdict. However, in *R v Hallam* [2007] EWCA Crim 1495, Toulson LJ said (at para 22) that there is no longer an absolute rule to the effect that evidence cannot be admitted after the retirement of the jury; rather, 'the question is what justice requires'. The same view was expressed by Gage

LJ in *R v Khan* [2008] EWCA Crim 1112 (at para 39), where his Lordship said that although, historically, the authorities state that there is an absolute principle that no further evidence should be given after the judge's summing-up has been concluded and the jury has retired, this principle has, in recent years, been subject to some relaxation.

The judge does have a discretion to permit an exhibit to be taken into the jury room for further examination (*R v Wright* [1993] Crim LR 607). In *R v Tonge* (1993) 157 JP 1137, the Court of Appeal considered what should be done if the jury (after they have retired) ask to hear a tape-recording. It was said that if the tape-recording had not been played in open court during the trial and the jury ask to hear the tape, it should usually be played in open court. However, if the tape has already been played in court, the jury may be allowed to hear it again in the jury room. This followed the approach suggested in *R v Emmerson* (1991) 92 Cr App R 284 at 287, where Lloyd LJ said that if the whole of the tape was played in open court, there is no reason why the jury should not have the tape (and any transcript) if either side or the jury want. If only part of the tape was played in open court but the jury have a transcript of the whole tape, there is no reason why the jury should not have the whole tape. If only part of the tape has been played in open court and the jury have no transcript, the tape should be edited so as to ensure that the jury do not have anything that has not been given in evidence.

In *R v Karakaya* [2005] EWCA Crim 346; [2005] 2 Cr App R 5, it was held that documents downloaded from the internet by a juror and taken into the jury room during the deliberations of the jury contravene the principle which prohibits the jury from relying upon anything seen or heard outside the courtroom.

12.11.3 Questions from the jury after retirement

If the jury wish to communicate with the judge (for example, they need further directions on the law or to be reminded of some of the evidence), they do so by means of a note sent to the judge via the jury bailiff. If the judge receives such a note, he should show it to both counsel in open court and should invite submissions from them before sending for the jury. In *R v Gorman* [1987] 1 WLR 545 (at 550–1), Lord Lane CJ said that

> ... certain propositions can now be set out as to what should be done by a judge who receives a communication from a jury which has retired to consider its verdict.
>
> First of all, if the communication raises something unconnected with the trial, for example a request that some message be sent to a relative of one of the jurors, it can simply be dealt with without any reference to counsel and without bringing the jury back to court ...
>
> Secondly, in almost every other case a judge should state in open court the nature and content of the communication which he has received from the jury and, if he considers it helpful so to do, seek the assistance of counsel. This assistance will normally be sought before the jury is asked to return to court, and then, when the jury returns, the judge will deal with their communication.
>
> Exceptionally if, as in the present case, the communication from the jury contains

information which the jury need not, and indeed should not, have imparted, such as details of voting figures, as we have called them, then, so far as possible the communication should be dealt with in the normal way, save that the judge should not disclose the detailed information which the jury ought not to have revealed.

... the object of these procedures ... is this: first of all, to ensure that there is no suspicion of any private or secret communication between the court and jury, and secondly, to enable the judge to give proper and accurate assistance to the jury upon any matter of law or fact which is troubling them ...

In *Ramstead v The Queen* [1999] 2 AC 92, the Privy Council emphasised that any communication between the judge and jury has to take place in open court in the presence of the entire jury, both counsel and the defendant. The Privy Council reiterated that where the judge receives a note from the jury, he should follow the procedure laid down in *R v Gorman*.

In *R v McQuiston* [1998] 1 Cr App R 139, it was held that where the judge reads substantial parts of the complainant's evidence to the jury after they have retired to consider their verdict (as may be the case if the jury ask for their memory of certain evidence to be refreshed), the judge must warn the jury not to give disproportionate weight to that evidence simply because it was repeated well after the other evidence had been heard; the judge must also remind the jury of the cross-examination of the complainant and of any part of the defendant's evidence that may be relevant.

12.12 RETURNING A VERDICT

When the jury come back into court, the clerk asks them: 'Have you reached a verdict upon which you are all agreed?' If the answer is 'yes', the foreman will be asked to announce the verdict on each count of the indictment. If the answer is 'yes', and the defendant is acquitted on all counts, he is told that he is free to go.

Where the defendant is charged with a number of offences and the jury indicate that they have agreed verdicts on some, but not all, of the offences, it is good practice to take the verdicts on those counts upon which the jury are agreed before they carry on considering the other counts. That course should be adopted save in the most exceptional circumstances (*R v F* [1994] Crim LR 377).

Lord Justice Auld's *Review of the Criminal Courts of England and Wales* (paras 99–108) considers the ability of the jury to announce a verdict that does not accord with the evidence they have heard or the law as expounded to them by the judge. Where the decision is to convict, the accused can of course appeal against that conviction. However, there is no remedy for the prosecution against a perverse acquittal. Some see this as one of the great strengths of the system of jury trial: if the jury feel that the law is wrong or is being applied oppressively, they can acquit the defendant. Others argue that a defendant has no right to be acquitted just because 12 people think that they know better than the Government. Lord Justice Auld recommends (Recommendation 30) that:

> The law should be declared, by statute, if need be, that juries have no right to acquit defendants in defiance of the law or in disregard of the evidence, and that judges and advocates should conduct criminal cases accordingly.

This comparatively limited recommendation needs to be seen in the context of Recommendation 310 of the Review, which states that:

> 310 Where any special verdict [i.e. a verdict where the judge has required the jury to answer publicly a series of questions fashioned by the judge to the issues in the case] of a jury reveals on its terms that it is perverse:
>
> 310.1 if the verdict is guilty, the defence should have a right of appeal to the Court of Appeal, subject to the usual leave procedure, on the ground that the perversity renders the conviction unsafe; and
>
> 310.2 if the verdict is not guilty, the prosecution should have a right of appeal to the Court of Appeal, also subject to leave, on the ground that the perversity indicates that the verdict is probably untrue or unfair and such as to merit a retrial.

This proposal is a very controversial one, since it would enable an appeal against an acquittal by the jury. However, as Lord Justice Auld points out in para 67 of Chapter 12, perverse decisions of magistrates have always been open to scrutiny on appeal, by the defence or the prosecution, through appeal by way of case stated to the Divisional Court. In the event, this suggestion was not taken up in the Criminal Justice Act 2003.

12.12.1 Guilty verdict

If the defendant is convicted on some or all of the counts, the prosecution will tell the judge whether the defendant has any previous convictions and will say what else is known about him (education, family situation, employment, etc). The judge may hear a plea in mitigation or may adjourn the case for a pre-sentence report to be produced. If there is an adjournment, the plea in mitigation will be delivered when the report has been prepared. The usual period of an adjournment for a report is three weeks if the defendant is remanded in custody, four weeks if he is on bail.

12.12.2 Alternative counts

If the indictment contains counts which are in the alternative, the usual practice is for the clerk to ask for a verdict on the more serious allegation first. If the verdict on that count is 'not guilty', the clerk will go on to ask for the verdict on the other count. If, on the other hand, the verdict on the more serious count is 'guilty', the jury should be discharged from giving a verdict on the less serious charge.

This should not be confused with the power of the jury to return an alternative verdict, acquitting the defendant of the count on the indictment but convicting him of an offence which is not on the indictment, a power that is discussed below.

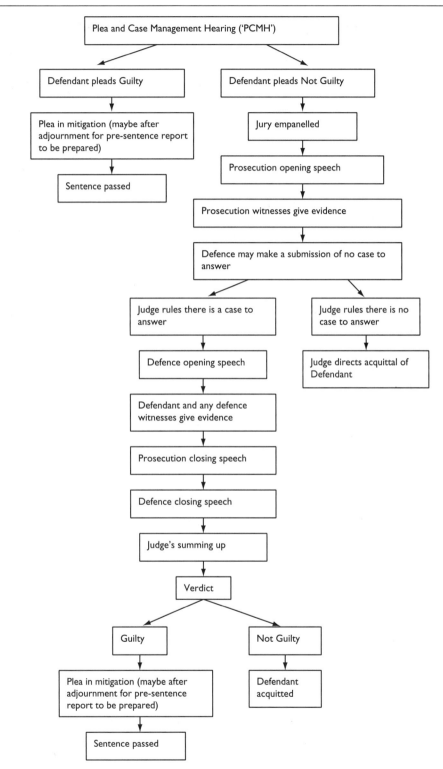

Figure 12.1 Outline of a Crown Court trial.

12.13 WHAT HAPPENS IF THE JURY IS UNABLE TO REACH A VERDICT

The answer to the question 'Have you reached a verdict upon which you are all agreed?' will be 'no' if the jury have returned to court to ask the judge for further assistance or if they have been considering the case for some time and cannot reach a verdict. In the latter case, a majority verdict direction may be appropriate.

12.14 MAJORITY VERDICTS

According to the official Judicial Statistics for 2006, 18 per cent of convictions that year were by way of majority verdict (21 per cent in 2005, 23 per cent in 2004, and 22 per cent in 2003). The law relating to majority verdicts is to be found in s 17 of the Juries Act 1974 and para IV.46 of *Consolidated Practice Direction*.

Section 17 of the 1974 Act provides as follows:

(1) Subject to sub-sections (3) and (4) below, the verdict of a jury . . . need not be unanimous if—

   (a) in a case where there are not less than eleven jurors, ten of them agree on the verdict; and
   (b) in a case where there are ten jurors, nine of them agree on the verdict.

. . .

(3) The Crown Court shall not accept a verdict of guilty by virtue of sub-section (1) above unless the foreman of the jury has stated in open court the number of jurors who respectively agreed to and dissented from the verdict.

(4) No court shall accept a verdict by virtue of sub-section (1) or (2) above unless it appears to the court that the jury have had such period of time for deliberation as the court thinks reasonable having regard to the nature and complexity of the case; and the Crown Court shall in any event not accept such a verdict unless it appears to the court that the jury have had at least two hours for deliberation.

Paragraph IV.46 of the *Practice Direction* states:

IV.46.1 It is important that all those trying indictable offences should so far as possible adopt a uniform practice when complying with section 17 of the Juries Act 1974, both in directing the jury in summing-up and also in receiving the verdict or giving further directions after retirement. So far as the summing-up is concerned, it is inadvisable for the judge, and indeed for advocates, to attempt an explanation of the section for fear that the jury will be confused. Before the jury retire, however, the judge should direct the jury in some such words as the following:

'As you may know, the law permits me, in certain circumstances, to accept a verdict which is not the verdict of you all. Those circumstances have not as yet arisen, so that when you retire I must ask you to reach a verdict upon which each one of you is agreed.

Should, however, the time come when it is possible for me to accept a majority verdict, I will give you a further direction.'

IV.46.2 Thereafter the practice should be as follows: Should the jury return before two hours and ten minutes since the last member of the jury left the jury box to go to the jury room (or such longer time as the judge thinks reasonable) has elapsed (see section 17(4)), they should be asked:

(a)   'Have you reached a verdict upon which you are all agreed? Please answer Yes or No';
(b)   (i)   If unanimous, 'What is your verdict?';
       (ii)   If not unanimous, the jury should be sent out again for further deliberation with a further direction to arrive if possible at an unanimous verdict.

IV.46.3 Should the jury return (whether for the first time or subsequently) or be sent for after the two hours and ten minutes (or the longer period) has elapsed, questions (a) and (b)(i) in paragraph IV.46.2 should be put to them and, if it appears that they are not unanimous, they should be asked to retire once more and told that they should continue to endeavour to reach an unanimous verdict but that, if they cannot, the judge will accept a majority verdict as in section 17(1).

IV.46.4 When the jury finally return they should be asked:

(a)   'Have at least ten (or nine as the case may be) of you agreed on your verdict?';
(b)   If 'Yes', 'What is your verdict? Please only answer Guilty or Not Guilty';
(c)   (i)   If 'Not Guilty', accept the verdict without more ado;
       (ii)   If 'Guilty', 'Is that the verdict of you all or by a majority?';

(d)   If 'Guilty' by a majority, 'How many of you agreed to the verdict and how many dissented?'

IV.46.5   At whatever stage the jury return, before question (a) is asked, the senior officer of the court present shall state in open court, for each period when the jury was out of court for the purpose of considering their verdict(s), the time at which the last member of the jury left the jury box to go to the jury room and the time of their return to the jury box and will additionally state in open court the total of such periods.

IV.46.6   The reason why section 17(3) is confined to a majority verdict of guilty and for the somewhat complicated procedure set out in paragraph IV.46.3 and paragraph IV.46.4 is to prevent it being known that a verdict of 'Not Guilty' is a majority verdict. If the final direction in paragraph IV.46.3 continues to require the jury to arrive, if possible, at a unanimous verdict and the verdict is received as in paragraph IV.46.4, it will not be known for certain that the acquittal is not unanimous.

IV.46.7   Where there are several counts (or alternative verdicts) left to the jury the above practice will, of course, need to be adapted to the circumstances. The procedure will have to be repeated in respect of each count (or alternative verdict), the verdict being accepted in those cases where the jury are unanimous and the further direction in paragraph IV.46.3 being given in cases in which they are not unanimous. Should the jury in the end be unable to agree on a verdict by the required majority (i.e. if the answer to the question in paragraph

IV.46.4(a) be in the negative) the judge in his discretion will either ask them to deliberate further or discharge them.

...

There is no minimum length of deliberation required before a *unanimous* verdict can be delivered. However, under s 17 of the Juries Act 1974, a *majority* verdict cannot be accepted until at least two hours, or such longer period as the judge considers necessary having regard to the nature and complexity of the case, have elapsed since the jury first retired to consider their verdict. The *Practice Direction* adds a further 10 minutes, to allow the jury to settle down in the jury room and elect a foreman.

If a majority verdict were to be accepted before two hours have elapsed from the time the jury left the courtroom to begin its deliberations, that verdict would be a nullity.

The only permissible majorities are:

- for 12 jurors: 11–1 or 10–2;
- where one juror has been discharged, leaving 11 jurors: 10–1;
- where two jurors have been discharged, leaving 10: 9–1.

A nine person jury (where three jurors have been discharged) can only deliver a unanimous verdict. If more than three jurors have to be discharged, the trial has to be aborted and a retrial takes place later.

If the judge considers that the jury have had long enough to come to a verdict (subject to the two hour minimum set out in s 17), the judge can send for the jury and give a majority verdict direction. Sometimes, however, the jury will take the initiative and send a note to the judge saying that they are deadlocked; if at least two hours have elapsed, the judge may, if he thinks it appropriate, give a majority verdict direction.

12.14.1 Content of majority verdict direction

The Judicial Studies Board recommends this form of words:

> I ask you once more to retire and to continue to try to reach a unanimous verdict; but if you cannot, I will accept a majority verdict. This is a verdict with which at least ten of you agree.

Some judges give a slightly longer version, along these lines:

> Members of the jury, it is desirable for you to reach a verdict upon which you are all agreed if that is possible. However, the time has now come when I can accept a verdict which is the verdict of at least 10 of you. Please go back into the jury room and try once again to reach a unanimous verdict or, if you are unable to do that, a verdict upon which at least 10 of you are agreed.

12.14.2 Errors in procedure for accepting a majority verdict

The Practice Direction, quoted above, sets out in detail how a majority verdict is to be taken. If the majority verdict is 'guilty' but the size of the majority in favour of conviction is not stated as required by s 17(3) of the 1974 Act, the verdict is a nullity (*R v Barry* [1975] 1 WLR 1190; *R v Austin* [2002] EWCA Crim 1796; [2003] Crim LR 426). In *R v Pigg* [1983] 1 WLR 6 at 13, the House of Lords held that:

> ... compliance with the requirement of s 17(3) of the Act of 1974 is mandatory before a judge can accept a majority verdict of guilty; but the precise form of words used by the clerk of the court when asking questions of the foreman of the jury, and the precise form of words used by the latter in answer to such questions, as long as they make it clear to an ordinary person how the jury was divided, do not constitute any essential part of that requirement.

If, however, the error in failing to ascertain how many jurors agreed with, and how many dissented from, the majority verdict is realised after the jury has been discharged, and it is possible to reconvene the jury, the error may be rectified (*R v Maloney* [1996] 2 Cr App R 303).

As is clear from the *Practice Direction*, the key points are that (a) it must not be known whether an acquittal is unanimous or by majority; and (b) in the case of a conviction, it is essential to know whether it was unanimous or by majority and, if the latter, the size of the majority (not least to ensure that the majority was a lawful one).

12.14.3 Discharge of jury

If the jury, having been given a majority verdict direction, cannot reach a majority verdict, the foreman will be asked by the judge if there is any prospect of the jury reaching a verdict. If there is a possibility, the judge will almost certainly give the jury more time. If there is no possibility of the jury reaching a verdict within what the judge regards as a reasonable time, the jury will be discharged. This does not count as an acquittal and so the accused can be retried (and there is no need for the case to go back to the magistrates' court to be re-sent to the Crown Court). If the second jury is 'hung' (i.e. unable to reach a verdict) too, the prosecution are unlikely to insist on a third trial.

12.15 THE *WATSON* DIRECTION

The judge must not exert undue pressure on the jury to reach a verdict (*R v McKenna* [1960] 1 QB 411; *R v Duggan* [1992] Crim LR 513). However, the judge can inquire if there is a reasonable prospect of a verdict being reached; the judge may tell the jury that if there is no reasonable prospect of them reaching a verdict they will be discharged and if there is then they can have as much time as they need (*R v Modeste* [1983] Crim LR 746).

In *R v Watson* [1988] QB 690, the Court of Appeal said that a judge must not point out to the jury that if they do not reach a verdict there will have to be a retrial which will cause inconvenience and expense. However, Lord Lane CJ said (at p 700) that:

... there is no reason why a jury should not be directed as follows:

'Each of you has taken an oath to return a true verdict according to the evidence. No one must be false to that oath, but you have a duty not only as individuals but collectively. That is the strength of the jury system. Each of you takes into the jury box with you your individual experience and wisdom. Your task is to pool that experience and wisdom. You do that by giving your views and listening to the views of the others. There must necessarily be discussion, argument and give and take within the scope of your oath. That is the way in which agreement is reached. If, unhappily, [10 of] you cannot reach agreement you must say so.'

In *R v Buono* (1992) 95 Cr App R 338, the Court of Appeal said that a *Watson* direction should not be given at the same time as a majority verdict direction. Watkins LJ said (at p 344):

there is rarely any need for the *Watson* direction to be given and that when given it should be given either during the summing-up or after the jury have had a reasonable time to consider the majority direction. It should never be combined with the majority direction. Moreover, judges should confine themselves to the precise wording of the *Watson* direction and not add anything to it . . .

Thus, the judge should give the majority verdict direction and then wait to see if the jury can reach a majority verdict; if the jury is still unable to reach a verdict, a *Watson* direction may then be given.

In *R v Morgan* [1997] Crim LR 593, the Court of Appeal reiterated that judges should follow precisely the terms of the direction as laid down in *Watson*. If they do not do so, there is a risk that the verdict would be rendered unsafe, particularly if what was said could be construed as imposing on the jury improper pressure to reach a verdict.

In *R v Atlan* [2004] EWCA Crim 1798; [2005] Crim LR 63, the jury sent a note to the judge saying that they were unanimous on all counts except for one, and that they wanted assistance. The judge gave a modified *Watson* direction, telling the jury that they had to try harder as it was not yet time to allow a majority verdict, but that 'there might have to be a bit of give and take in your deliberations and your thoughts'. Shortly afterwards, the jury convicted the defendant under the count in question. The Court of Appeal said that a *Watson* direction has to make it clear that any 'give and take' should be within the scope of the juror's oath. It is, said the court, just as dangerous to omit words from the *Watson* direction as to add them. Moreover, such a direction should not be given after the jury have retired unless a majority verdict is to be permitted. In the present case, the direction might have put undue pressure on the jury to compromise, and so the subsequent conviction was unsafe.

12.16 THE VERDICT OF GUILTY TO AN ALTERNATIVE OFFENCE

Under s 6(3) of the Criminal Law Act 1967, where 'the allegations in the indictment amount to or include (expressly or by implication) an allegation of another offence' which may be tried on indictment, the jury may acquit on the offence charged and convict on the included offence.

12.16.1 Express inclusion

An offence is *expressly* included in the indictment if words can be deleted from the existing count so as to leave words alleging another offence. This is sometimes called the 'red pencil' test (*R v Lillis* [1972] 2 QB 236).

Suppose, for example, that it is alleged that the defendant 'entered 4 Gray's Inn Place as a trespasser and stole therein a computer'. If the words 'entered 4 Gray's Inn Place as a trespasser and' and 'therein' are deleted, that leaves an allegation that the defendant 'stole a computer'. Therefore, theft (s 1 of the Theft Act 1968) is expressly included in an allegation of burglary (s 9(1)(b) of the Theft Act 1968).

Thus, if a jury decides that they are not satisfied so that they are sure that the defendant entered as a trespasser but are sure that he stole the goods alleged in the indictment, they can acquit of burglary but convict of theft.

12.16.2 Implied inclusion

The meaning of *implied* inclusion was considered by the House of Lords in *Metropolitan Police Commissioner v Wilson* [1984] AC 242. Where the commission of the offence alleged in the indictment will, in the normal course of events (that is, in the great majority of cases) involve the commission of another offence, that other offence is impliedly included in the offence charged in the indictment.

In *Wilson*, for example, it was held that inflicting grievous bodily harm (s 20 of the Offences Against the Person Act 1861) usually involves assault occasioning actual bodily harm (s 47 of the Offences Against the Person Act 1861), and so the jury can acquit of grievous bodily harm but convict of actual bodily harm. It may well be possible to inflict grievous bodily harm without assaulting the victim (for example, by deliberately creating a panic in a crowded building intending that people are seriously hurt in the rush to escape), but, in the normal course of events, grievous bodily harm will involve assault occasioning actual bodily harm.

The same would apply to an allegation of wounding under s 20 of the Offences Against the Person Act 1861, so s 47 is an alternative offence to that charge too (*R v Savage* [1992] 1 AC 699).

A charge of causing grievous bodily harm with intent (s 18 of the Offences Against the Person Act 1861) includes a charge of inflicting grievous bodily harm (s 20 of the Offences Against the Person Act 1861) (*R v Mandair* [1995] 1 AC 208). Likewise, indecent assault is an alternative to rape (*R v Hodgson* [1973] QB 565) and theft is an alternative to robbery.

Where a defendant is charged with attempted murder, an alternative verdict of attempting to cause grievous bodily harm with intent can be left to the jury, since a defendant who intends to murder someone clearly intends to cause them grievous bodily harm as well (*R v Morrison* [2003] EWCA Crim 1722; [2003] 1 WLR 1859).

12.16.3 Other statutory provisions

There are also a number of statutory provisions which set out possible alternative offences:

- s 6(2) of the Criminal Law Act 1967: the jury may acquit of murder but convict of (inter alia) manslaughter or causing grievous bodily harm with intent;
- s 6(4) of the Criminal Law Act 1967: the jury may acquit of the offence charged but convict of attempt to commit that offence or of attempt to commit an offence which is expressly or implied included in the offence charged. Thus, if the indictment alleges robbery, the jury could acquit of robbery but convict of attempted robbery or attempted theft;
- s 12(4) of the Theft Act 1968: on a count of theft, the jury may acquit of theft but convict the defendant of taking a vehicle without the owner's consent (even though the latter is a summary offence);
- s 24 of the Road Traffic Offenders Act 1988: for example, on a count alleging dangerous driving or causing death by dangerous driving or causing death by careless driving when under influence of drink or drugs, the jury may convict the defendant instead of careless driving (again, even though the latter is a summary offence).

12.16.4 Summary offences

Section 6(3) of the Criminal Law Act 1967 makes it clear that the included offence must be one which can be tried in the Crown Court – hence the need for provisions such as s 12(4) of the Theft Act 1968 and s 24 of the Road Traffic Offenders Act 1988. The included offences they permit are summary offences and, but for statutory provision to the contrary, the jury would not be able to convict of those summary offences.

Section s 6(3) is also qualified by s 6(3A), which provides that summary offences to which s 40 of the Criminal Justice Act 1988 applies (common assault etc.) come within the ambit of sub-s (3), and that this is so even if a count charging that summary offence is not included in the indictment. For example, if the accused is charged with assault occasioning actual bodily harm (s 47 of the Offences Against the Person Act 1861) but the jury find that no actual bodily harm was caused, they may acquit of that charge but convict of common assault (to which s 40 of the 1988 Act applies) even though that charge does not appear on the indictment.

Under sub-s (3B), a person convicted of an offence by virtue of sub-s (3A) may only be dealt with for it in a manner in which a magistrates' court could have dealt with him. Section 6(3A) was enacted to reverse the effect of *R v Mearns* [1991] 1 QB 82 and other cases where it had been held that s 6(3) did not apply to summary offences falling with s 40 of the 1988 Act.

Where a summary offence is tried with an indictable offence (pursuant to s 40 of the Criminal Justice Act 1988), but the judge rules that there is no case to answer on the indictable offence, the summary offence does not have to be withdrawn from the jury and retried before a magistrates' court (*R v Plant* [2008] EWCA Crim 960).

12.16.5 Scope of s 6(3) of the Criminal Law Act 1967

Convicting of an alternative offence is only possible if the jury first agree to acquit on the offence on the indictment. If the jury cannot agree on an acquittal of the offence charged, the only way they can convict of another offence is if that offence is added to the indictment as a new count. See, for example, *R v Collison* (1980) 71 Cr App R 249, where a count was added to the indictment after the jury had been considering their verdict for some while for this very reason.

A finding of no case to answer results in an acquittal and so s 6(3) may come into play. In *R v Livesey* [2006] EWCA Crim 3344; [2007] 1 Cr App R 35, the judge informed the jury that there was no case to answer on the offence on the indictment but, rather than taking a verdict at that stage, he was allowing the count to remain on the indictment so that jury could consider the alternative offence. The Court of Appeal held that, where the judge upholds a submission of no case to answer in respect of a count to which there is a statutory alternative verdict, he is entitled to leave the count on the indictment in order to allow the jury to return a verdict on the statutory alternative offence.

In *R v Khela* [2005] EWCA Crim 3446; [2006] 1 Cr App R 23, the Court of Appeal said that where a jury has been discharged from returning a verdict (e.g. after a successful application to stay the proceedings for abuse of process, or because the jury were unable to reach a verdict) the jury cannot then proceed to return verdicts of guilty to lesser offences where the relevant statute provides that they can convict of the lesser offence only if the defendant has been found not guilty of the more serious offence.

12.16.6 Directing the jury on alternative offences

The jury will only know about the possibility of convicting of an offence other than the offence on the indictment if they are told that they have this power. So, when should the judge direct the jury about the possibility of convicting on an alternative offence? In *Metropolitan Police Commissioner v Wilson* [1984] AC 242, Lord Roskill said (p 261) that the trial judge:

> must always ensure, before deciding to leave the possibility of conviction of another offence to the jury under s 6(3), that that course will involve no risk of injustice to the defendant and that he has had the opportunity of fully meeting that alternative in the course of his defence.

If the possibility of an alternative offence is only canvassed at the end of the trial, the key question is whether the defence would have cross-examined prosecution witnesses differently or would have adduced different defence evidence had the alternative offence been mentioned at the start of the trial. In *R v Hammett* [1993] RTR 275, for example, the possibility of convicting of an alternative offence was first mentioned in the judge's summing up. Even though the judge then gave counsel the opportunity of addressing the jury further, it was held by the Court of Appeal to be unfair to raise the issue of an alternative offence so late in the proceedings.

In *R v Fairbanks* [1986] 1 WLR 1202 at 1205–6, it was said that the judge should direct the jury that it is possible for them to acquit of the offence charged but convict of an alternative offence only if this is necessary in the interests of justice. In applying that test it should be borne in mind that:

- the possibility that the defendant is guilty only of a lesser offence must have fairly arisen on the basis of the way in which the case had been presented to the court (e.g. it would be inappropriate for the judge to leave a lesser offence to the jury if it is inappropriate given the way the defence has been conducted, as where the defence is one of alibi); and

• directing the jury about the possibility of convicting the defendant of an alternative offence should not unnecessarily complicate the case (e.g. where the principal offence is very serious and the alternative may fairly be described as trifling by comparison).

The arguments in favour of letting the jury consider an alternative offence were considered in *Fairbanks*. From the prosecution point of view, where the evidence is such that it is clear that the defendant ought to be convicted (at least) of the lesser offence, it would be wrong for the jury to have to acquit him altogether merely because they cannot be sure that he is guilty of the more serious offence. From the defence point of view, if the judge does not allow the jury to consider the lesser offence, it is possible that the jury will convict the defendant of the more serious offence, not because they are sure that he is guilty of it, but so as to convict him of something rather than allowing him to escape without any penalty at all.

The question was revisited by the House of Lords in *R v Maxwell* [1990] 1 WLR 401. The defendant was charged with robbery. He indicated that he would have been willing to plead guilty to burglary. However, the prosecution did not wish to add a count alleging burglary to the indictment. Burglary is not an alternative to robbery, but theft (a constituent of one type of burglary) is an alternative to robbery (which comprises theft together with the use or threat of violence). The judge refused to allow the jury to consider convicting of theft instead of robbery. This refusal was upheld by the House of Lords. The essential issue, as defined by the prosecution, was whether the defendant had used violence; theft was trivial by comparison and would merely have distracted the jury from the main issue of the case. The implication of *Maxwell* is that it is for the prosecution to define the main issue(s) in the case and the judge should not subvert their decision by directing the jury to consider an alternative offence. It should be noted that even if defence counsel takes the initiative and tells the jury that they can convict of an alternative offence, the judge could direct the jury that they are not to consider this possibility.

In *R v Bergman and Collins* [1996] 2 Cr App R 399, the Court of Appeal decided that the trial judge should have directed the jury about the possibility of convicting the defendants of a lesser offence but the convictions for the offence charged on the indictment were nonetheless upheld since there was no evidence which tended to show that the jury's verdict would have been different if they had been directed on the possibility of convicting of a lesser offence.

Similarly, in *R v Hussain* [2004] EWCA Crim 325, where the defendant was charged with causing death by dangerous driving, the trial judge rejected an application to leave the alternative offence of careless driving to the jury. Kay LJ (at paras 17–19) said this:

> When a judge comes to consider whether or not to leave an alternative lesser charge to the jury he has a number of different considerations that he has to take into account. The first is whether there is any sensible basis upon which the jury could reach a conclusion that the more serious offence was not made out but that a lesser offence was made out. . . .
>
> The next consideration for the judge is whether in fact leaving a lesser charge even though

it might be open on the facts may unnecessarily complicate the jury's consideration and lead to the element of confusion to which we have already referred. Where that is the situation the authorities make clear that it is perfectly proper for the judge not to leave such a charge.

There is, however, a third category of case, and that is one in which a judge concludes that the charge that is being tried is of so much greater gravity than the alternative that it really is unnecessary and undesirable to leave the jury to have to trouble over the much lesser matter. In such circumstances, even if that means that the position is slightly over-favourable to the defendant it may be proper for the judge to conclude that the lesser charge is not what this case is all about and to leave the jury properly with the stark choice between guilt of the full offence or acquitting altogether. What the decision in *Maxwell* makes clear is that the judge contemplating that sort of course must be mindful to the possibility that if the jury find the conduct of the appellant reprehensible it may induce in them a willingness to convict of the full offence even though that is not properly made out simply because of the undesirability of the defendant getting away altogether with the reprehensible conduct.

Where an alternative offence is not left to the jury, a conviction might be rendered unsafe if the jury convicted the defendant out of reluctance to see an acquittal where they had found some misconduct. In those circumstances, the court said that it is incumbent on the judge to direct the jury exactly as to what they have to find in order to convict. On the facts of the present case, it was open to the judge not to leave the alternative to the jury, and the direction to the jury was clearly designed to ensure that the jury only convicted the defendant if the offence on the indictment was made out. The conviction was therefore safe.

It was held in *Maxwell* that, where a judge refuses to leave an alternative offence to the jury, the Court of Appeal will only quash a conviction for the offence charged on the indictment if satisfied that 'the jury may have convicted out of a reluctance to see the defendant get clean away with what, on any view, was disgraceful conduct' (per Lord Ackner at p 408). Similarly it was held in *R v O'hAdhmaill* [1996] Crim LR 509 that the conviction should only be quashed if the Court of Appeal is satisfied that the jury convicted the defendant only because it was reluctant to allow him to get away completely with his misconduct.

However, in *R v Coutts* [2006] UKHL 39; [2006] 1 WLR 2154 this approach to appeals was disapproved. Lord Hutton, at paras 60 and 61, said that he considered that the approach taken in *Maxwell* is:

> an unsatisfactory one and should no longer be taken. It requires the appellate court, without having material before it to enable a proper assessment to be made, to attempt to make an assessment whether a jury has returned a verdict of guilty, not on a proper and fair weighing of the evidence in the light of the judge's directions as to the law, but from reluctance to see a defendant, who has behaved disgracefully, get clean away. In reality, it appears to oblige the appellate court to engage in speculation as to the factors which may have influenced the jury's decision . . . Therefore I consider that the House should . . . hold that, save in exceptional circumstances, an appellate court should quash a conviction, whether for murder or for a lesser offence, as constituting a serious miscarriage of justice where the judge has erred in failing to leave a lesser alternative verdict obviously raised by the evidence.

Lord Mance, at paras 99 and 100, expressed a similar view:

> I am persuaded that this is an unworkable test to apply to a jury trial. There is no reliable means by which an appellate court can, on so particular a basis, measure whether or how a jury may react to an unnatural limitation of the choices put before it. One is entitled to assume that juries go about their task in the utmost good faith, but the concern is with subconscious as well as conscious reactions . . . Accordingly, in my view, where . . . an obvious alternative verdict presents itself in respect of some more than trifling offence and can without injustice be left for the jury to consider, the judge should in fairness ensure that this is done, even if the alternative only arises on the defence case in circumstances where as a matter of law there should apart from that alternative be a complete acquittal.

Lord Bingham of Cornhill said (at para 12):

> The interests of justice are not served if a defendant who has committed a lesser offence is either convicted of a greater offence, exposing him to greater punishment than his crime deserves, or acquitted altogether, enabling him to escape the measure of punishment which his crime deserves. The objective must be that defendants are neither over-convicted nor under-convicted, nor acquitted when they have committed a lesser offence of the type charged.

His Lordship carried on, at paras 23 and 24:

> The public interest in the administration of justice is . . . best served if in any trial on indictment the trial judge leaves to the jury, subject to any appropriate caution or warning, but irrespective of the wishes of trial counsel, any obvious alternative offence which there is evidence to support . . . I would also confine the rule to alternative verdicts obviously raised by the evidence . . . Application of this rule may in some cases benefit the defendant, protecting him against an excessive conviction. In other cases it may benefit the public, by providing for the conviction of a lawbreaker who deserves punishment . . .
>
>   It is of course fundamental that the duty to leave lesser verdicts to the jury should not be exercised so as to infringe a defendant's right to a fair trial. This might be so if it were shown that decisions were made at trial which would not have been made had the possibility of such a verdict been envisaged . . . nor will it ordinarily be unfair to leave an alternative where a defendant who, resisting conviction of a more serious offence, succeeds in throwing doubt on an ingredient of that offence and is as a result convicted of a lesser offence lacking that ingredient. There may be unfairness if the jury first learn of the alternative from the judge's summing-up, when counsel have not had the opportunity to address it in their closing speeches. But that risk is met if the proposed direction is indicated to counsel at some stage before they make their closing speeches. They can continue to discount the alternative in their closing speeches, but they can address the jury with knowledge of what the judge will direct . . . It is not unfair to deprive a defendant, timeously alerted to the possibility, of what may be an adventitious acquittal.

In *R v Foster* [2007] EWCA Crim 2869, the Court of Appeal had to consider the effect of *Coutts*. Sir Igor Judge P said (at para 51):

Coutts . . . provides unequivocal authority that whenever alternative verdicts should be left to the jury, whether in the narrow or broad context, then the judge should so direct them, notwithstanding united submissions on behalf of both the prosecution and the defence to the contrary. In making this judgment, of course, the judge must be alert to and have in mind the possibility of any consequent unfairness, usually to the defendant, but not excluding the possibility of unfairness to the prosecution. In recent years, with increasing emphasis, the entire structure of the trial process has been revisited to ensure that the real issues should be identified before, or certainly not later than the start of the trial, and that the evidence on both sides should be presented accordingly. That said, experience shows that the evidence by the end of the trial may not always mirror the anticipation of either side, and any 'fairness' question should be addressed at the close of the evidence, before speeches, but always in the context of the issues to which the evidence has given rise.

His Lordship went on to say (paras 59–61):

. . . it does not necessarily follow from the defendant's admission of a lesser or different crime to the crime charged in the indictment that the jury must be given an opportunity to return a verdict on the basis of the admitted criminal conduct . . . when cases like these arise, the alternative verdict may very well be remote from the more serious allegation made by the prosecution and the real issues in the case.

The danger highlighted by some of the speeches in *Coutts*, underlining the duty of the trial judge to leave alternative verdicts to the jury, is the risk that faced with the stark choice between convicting a defendant whose behaviour was on any view utterly deplorable, and acquitting him altogether, the jury may unconsciously but wrongly allow its decision to be influenced by considerations extraneous to the evidence and convict of the more serious charges rather than acquit altogether. In such circumstances to omit directions about a possible lesser alternative verdict may therefore work to the defendant's disadvantage . . . *Coutts* does not suggest that such a risk is always present. Indeed our entire system for the administration of criminal justice in the Crown Court depends on the conscientious and impartial determination of the issues by the jury, following and applying the directions of law which they receive from the judge . . .

Accordingly, not every alternative verdict must be left to the jury. In addition to any specific issues of fairness, there is . . . a proportionality consideration. The judge is not in error if he decides that a lesser alternative verdict should not be left to the jury if that verdict can properly be described in its legal and factual context as trivial, or insubstantial, or where any possible compromise verdict would not reflect the real issues in the case. He must, of course, reconsider any decision he may have reached about alternative verdicts in the light of any question which the jury may see fit to ask . . . However when the defence to a specific charge amounts to the admission or assertion of a lesser offence, the primary obligation of the judge is to ensure that the defence is left to the jury . . . the judge must examine whether the absence of a direction about a lesser alternative verdict or verdicts would oblige the jury to make an unrealistic choice between the serious charge and complete acquittal which would unfairly disadvantage the defendant . . .

The nature of the defence being put forward remains a very important consideration. In *R v Banton* [2007] EWCA Crim 1847, the defendant was charged with wounding with intent (s 18 of the Offences Against the Person Act). The basis of the prosecution case against the defendant was that she smashed a bottle in the victim's face. The defendant denied it, presenting the jury with a stark question of fact. It would have been unfair to leave the offence of unlawful wounding to the jury on the alternative basis because the case had been about whether the defendant had deliberately smashed a bottle in the victim's face, and the possible alternative issue as to whether she had recklessly wounded the victim by throwing the bottle had not been explored. At para 25, Toulson J said:

> The existence of some possible evidential basis for such an alternative verdict would be by no means necessarily a sufficient basis for putting it to the jury. The judge would be justified in not leaving it to the jury if he reasonably considered it to be remote from the real point of the case. A fortiori, it would be wrong for the judge to leave it to the jury if it would cause a real possibility of unfairness to the defendant.

In *R v Mandair* [1995] 1 AC 208, Lord Mackay LC said that the simpler (and better) course of action is to add a count to the indictment alleging the lesser offence, rather than relying on s 6(3) of the Criminal Law Act 1967. Similarly, in *R v Lahaye* [2005] EWCA Crim 2847; [2006] 1 Cr App R 11, Sir Igor Judge P said (at para 21):

> In circumstances where as a matter of law s 20 [of the Offences Against the Person Act 1861] is available as an alternative to s 18, and where the application of s 6(3) of the 1967 Act means that that alternative would be available even if s 20 were not alleged, we consider that it would be better practice for the s 20 count to be included on the face of the indictment.

It is submitted that these remarks are of general application, and should not be confined to offences under the 1861 Act.

12.16.7 Summary: alternative verdicts

For the judge to leave the alternative offence to the jury:

- it must be appropriate (for example, it would not be appropriate where the defence is one of alibi, since it would distract the jury from the main issue in the case, namely the whereabouts of the defendant at the time of the alleged offence);
- it must have been at least implicit in the defence questioning of prosecution witnesses and the defence evidence (otherwise, it will be unfair to the defence);
- if the alternative is trivial in comparison with the offence charged, it may be an unnecessary and undesirable complication.

12.17 GUILTY PLEAS

If the defendant pleads guilty to all the counts on the indictment (or pleads guilty to some of the counts and the prosecution do not proceed with the others), no trial takes place.

If the defendant pleads guilty to all the counts, the prosecution summarise the facts of the case. Details of the defendant's previous convictions (if any) are handed to the judge and he will indicate which (if any) he wishes prosecuting counsel to read aloud. Usually, it is only the most recent previous convictions that are read out. The prosecution will also tell the judge what is known about the defendant's personal circumstances (employment, housing, etc); this is based on what the defendant has told the police and will be very brief.

The defence then make a plea in mitigation. If a pre-sentence report is not available, the judge may adjourn the case until one is prepared. In that case, there is a presumption in favour of bail as s 4 of the Bail Act 1976 still applies. When the case is resumed, the prosecution will again summarise the facts and the defence will make a plea in mitigation. The usual period for the adjournment is three weeks if the defendant is in custody, four weeks if he is on bail.

If the defendant pleads guilty but challenges the version of events put forward by the prosecution, and the difference is one which will affect the sentence that is passed, the court can only reject the defence version of events after hearing evidence as to what happened. Such a hearing is known as a *Newton* hearing (from *R v Newton* (1983) 77 Cr App R 13) – see Chapter 16.

If the defendant pleads guilty to some counts but not guilty to others, sentence will be postponed until the trial on the counts to which the defendant has pleaded not guilty has been completed, assuming that the prosecution wish to proceed with the trial of the offences to which the defendant pleaded not guilty. This raises the question of plea bargaining between the prosecution and the defence.

12.18 'PLEA BARGAINING'

The usual basis of a plea bargain is either:

- that if the defendant will plead guilty to some counts on the indictment, the prosecution will not proceed with the remainder; or
- that if the defendant will plead guilty to a lesser offence, the prosecution will not proceed with the more serious offence.

This form of plea bargaining is widely accepted as a way of saving time and money. From the prosecution point of view, it may well be better to have a conviction for something rather than risk a jury acquitting on all counts.

Pleading guilty to a lesser offence is possible in the following two circumstances.

12.18.1 Pleading guilty to an offence which is not on the indictment

Under s 6(1)(b) of the Criminal Law Act 1967, the defendant 'may plead not guilty of the offence specifically charged in the indictment but guilty of another offence of which he might be found guilty on that indictment'. In other words, the defendant may enter a plea of not guilty to the count on the indictment but also offer a plea of guilty to a lesser offence of which the jury would be able to convict him under s 6(3) of the Criminal Law Act 1967. If this plea is accepted, the defendant stands acquitted of the offence charged but convicted of the lesser offence, for which he will then be sentenced.

If the plea of guilty to the lesser offence is not accepted by the prosecution (or the judge refuses to accept it), the trial will proceed on the basis of a not guilty plea to the offence on the indictment. The defendant's plea of guilty to the lesser offence is impliedly withdrawn (so, if the jury acquit the defendant of the offence on the indict-ment, and do not convict of the lesser offence under s 6(3), the defendant cannot then be sentenced for the lesser offence (*R v Hazeltine* [1967] 2 QB 857)). *Hazeltine* was followed in *R v Yeardley* [2000] 1 QB 374, where the defendant was arraigned on an indictment charging possession of a Class A drug with intent to supply contrary to the Misuse of Drugs Act 1971. He pleaded not guilty to that charge but guilty to simple possession of the drug. However, his guilty plea was not accepted by the prosecution, and the trial proceeded on the charge of possession with intent to supply. The prosecu-tion did not seek a conviction for, nor were the jury directed that they could find the defendant guilty of, simple possession. The jury returned a verdict of not guilty of possession with intent to supply. The judge then sentenced the defendant for simple possession. The Court of Appeal held that the defendant's plea of guilty, having been rejected by the prosecution, was a nullity; there was therefore no conviction and no basis on which he could lawfully have been sentenced.

Note that if a guilty plea to a lesser offence is rejected and there is a trial on the original offence, the prosecution could adduce evidence of the defendant's earlier plea of guilty to the lesser offence if they so wish. So (using the facts of *Yeardley*) if the accused had, during his trial for possession with intent to supply, denied being in possession of the drugs, the prosecution could have adduced evidence of his plea of guilty to the possession charge.

The acceptance of a plea of guilty to a lesser offence is subject to the agreement of the judge, but it would be very rare for the judge to insist on a trial of the more serious offence if the prosecution do not wish that to happen. However, there may be cases where the judge expresses misgivings about the decision of the prosecutor to accept a plea to a lesser charge. In *R v Mulla* [2003] EWCA Crim 1881; [2004] 1 Cr App R 6, the defendant was charged with causing death by dangerous driving; he offered to plead guilty to the lesser offence of causing death by careless driving. The prosecutor initially agreed to that course of action, but the trial judge invited the prosecutor to reconsider this decision. The prosecutor subsequently decided to proceed on the original charge. The defendant argued that this amounted to an abuse of process. The Court of Appeal rejected this argument, holding (at para 22):

> This was not a case in which the defendant's hopes were raised, later to be dashed. He knew from the beginning of the proceedings in court . . . that the judge did not approve of the course which the prosecution were proposing to take. He had not had his hopes raised by anything which counsel had privately said to him . . . Other factors include what view is expressed by the judge when the prosecution gives its indication, the period of time over

which the prosecution reconsiders the matter, before they change their mind, whether or not the defendant's hopes have been inappropriately raised, and whether there has been, by reason of the change of course by the prosecution, any prejudice to the defence.

12.18.2 Pleading guilty to an alternative count on the indictment

The indictment may contain alternative counts. The word 'or' does not appear, and so there is nothing on the face of the indictment to indicate that the counts are in the alternative. For example, there might be one count alleging a s 18 offence under the Offences Against the Person Act 1861 and another alleging s 20. If the defendant pleads not guilty to both counts, the trial will proceed on both counts and the jury will be told that the prosecution are not seeking a conviction on both counts.

If the defendant pleads not guilty to the more serious offence but guilty to the lesser offence, it is up to the prosecution to decide whether to proceed with a trial of the count to which the defendant pleads not guilty. If a trial does follow and the defendant is acquitted of the more serious offence, he will then be sentenced for the lesser offence to which he pleaded guilty. If he is convicted of the more serious offence, the lesser offence will be ignored for sentencing purposes.

Normally, the prosecution will indicate to the defence beforehand whether a plea of guilty to the lesser offence will be acceptable. Where the plea to the lesser offence is acceptable, the lesser offence is put to the defendant first and (assuming he pleads guilty to it as anticipated) the second offence will either not be put to the defendant or it will be put and the prosecution will either offer no evidence or ask it to be left on the file.

12.18.3 Plea-bargaining in fraud cases

In 2008, the Attorney General's office published a consultation paper on *The Introduction of a Plea Negotiation Framework for Fraud Cases in England and Wales*. It contained the following:

(1) *General Principles*

  (1) Before charge, Prosecutors and a person suspected of involvement in a criminal offence may discuss and reach an agreement in respect of a basis of plea.

  (2) The court must not participate or be involved in these discussions.

  (3) It will be presumed that nothing said by the suspect in the course of such discussions will subsequently be used against him. However, Prosecutors may agree with the suspect the circumstances in which anything said by him in furtherance of the discussions can be used by the Prosecution in evidence against him. This should be reduced to writing in advance.

  (4) Consonant with the general common law duty of the Prosecution to act fairly and assist in the administration of justice, the Prosecutor must provide to the defence any material which he does not intend to use but which he, as a responsible prosecutor, recognises should be disclosed at an early stage.

  (5) Where the suspect indicates a willingness to plead guilty, Prosecutors should only agree to accept the suspect's plea (such agreement being subject where necessary

to the approval of the Court) if the charge or charges to which the suspect is willing to plead guilty:

    (5.1) reflect the seriousness and extent of the offending;

    (5.2) gives the court adequate powers to sentence and impose any appropriate post-conviction order; and therefore

    (5.3) enable the public, and any victim(s), to have confidence in the outcome.

(6) The decision whether a person should be charged and if so, with what offence, rests with the Prosecutor.

(7) Where the suspect indicates a willingness to plead guilty to charges acceptable to the Prosecution, the basis of the guilty plea must be agreed with the Prosecution and reduced to writing (the 'plea agreement').

(8) The plea agreement may, inter alia, specify that the Prosecution will:

    (8.1) not bring other charges (additional to those to which the suspect has indicated a willingness to plead guilty);

    (8.2) agree (but without in any way binding the exercise by the Court of its own powers in the matter) that a specific sentence or sentencing range is appropriate (whether as to any term of imprisonment or otherwise).

(2) *Judicial Consideration of a Plea Agreement*

(9) A plea agreement will usually be submitted to the Court at the Defendant's first appearance before the Crown Court. The Court may then consider the plea agreement or adjourn consideration of the matter to a separate hearing.

(10) The hearing at which the plea agreement is considered will normally take place in open court and in the Defendant's presence.

(11) The Court may be invited to impose reporting restrictions, but they should be lifted once a guilty plea has been entered or a Defendant has been found guilty.

(12) The Judge may:

    (12.1) Deal with the plea agreement as he sees fit, whether by accepting it (including any provision as to sentence), rejecting it, or deferring a decision until the court has obtained further information, and/or;

    (12.2) Of his own motion, or if invited by the Prosecution or the Defendant to do so, indicate his view of the maximum sentence (whether as to any term of imprisonment or otherwise) which would be imposed on the basis of the plea agreement.

(13) Where the court accepts the plea agreement and the Defendant pleads guilty, the plea agreement will form the basis upon which the Defendant is sentenced.

(14) Where an indication of sentence is given, the court is bound by it, but the indication ceases to have effect if, after having a reasonable opportunity to consider it, the Defendant declines to plead guilty.

(15) Where the court rejects the plea agreement, or the Defendant declines to plead guilty in accordance with it, the Prosecution may (if so entitled) discontinue the proceedings so as to be able to make further enquiries and, if so advised, to prefer more extensive charges; alternatively an adjournment or stay of proceedings will normally be granted at the request of the Prosecution to enable the Prosecution to make such enquiries and, if so advised, to bring further charges.

Fraud trials are very costly and the complexity of the issues can mean that is hard to secure a conviction. However, there may be little incentive for the accused to co-operate.

12.19 ADVISING THE DEFENDANT ON PLEA

Care must be taken that a plea of guilty is entered voluntarily. If it is not entered voluntarily, the Court of Appeal will quash the conviction and will usually order a retrial.

In the next section, we look at safeguards to prevent pressure from the judge. However, pressure can also be exerted by the defendant's own lawyers. It would be wholly improper to advise a client to plead guilty if the defendant reveals facts amounting to a defence. If, however, the facts revealed by the defendant show that he is effectively admitting the offence, then this should be made clear to him.

The decision as to plea must be that of the accused. The defendant's legal adviser may express advice in strong terms but must make it clear that the defendant has complete freedom of choice.

It should be added that if the defendant confesses to the crime to his advocate, he can only continue to represent the defendant if he pleads guilty (otherwise the advocate would effectively be misleading the court).

If the defendant insists on pleading guilty but maintains to the advocate that he is in fact innocent, the advocate may continue to represent the defendant but cannot say anything in mitigation which is inconsistent with the plea of guilty. This should be made clear to the defendant. Where the client is represented by counsel, the client should be asked to write a signed note on counsel's brief saying that he wishes to plead guilty against the advice of counsel.

12.19.1 Seeing the judge in his chambers: indications as to sentence

When a solicitor or barrister is advising a defendant as to plea, the client will inevitably want to know the likely sentence in the event of a conviction. Experienced lawyers are usually able to predict sentences with a reasonable degree of accuracy. Sometimes, however, the question arises whether the judge can give a preliminary indication of the sentence he is minded to impose (based on a view of the offence founded on the witness statements sent from the magistrates' court and a pre-sentence report if one is already available).

The leading case on this topic used to be *R v Turner* [1970] 2 QB 321, where the trial judge told defence counsel that if the defendant pleaded guilty, he would not be sent to prison but if he was convicted by the jury, a prison sentence was a very real possibility. The Court of Appeal said that a judge must not say (or imply) that the sentence is likely to take one form if the defendant pleads guilty and a different form if the defendant is convicted following a not guilty plea, since this could be construed as putting pressure on the defendant to plead guilty. The judge was only allowed to say that, whether the defendant pleads guilty or is found guilty, the sentence will (or will not) take a particular form.

However, this strict approach was modified by the Court of Appeal in *R v Goodyear* [2005] EWCA Crim 888; [2005] 1 WLR 2532 (decided by a five-judge court). Lord Woolf CJ gave the judgment of the court. At para 50 he said:

> We . . . do not seek to water down the essential principle that the defendant's plea must always be made voluntarily and free from any improper pressure. On closer analysis, how-

ever, we cannot discern any clash between this principle, and a process by which the defendant personally may instruct his counsel to seek an indication from the judge of his current view of the maximum sentence which would be imposed on the defendant. In effect, this simply substitutes the defendant's legitimate reliance on counsel's assessment of the likely sentence with the more accurate indication provided by the judge himself. In such circumstances, the prohibition against the judge giving an unsolicited sentence indication would not be contravened, and any subsequent plea, whether guilty or not guilty, would be voluntary. Accordingly it would not constitute inappropriate judicial pressure on the defendant for the judge to respond to such a request if one were made.

Paras 53 to 77 of Lord Woolf's judgment then give detailed guidelines on advance indications of sentence. The key points made include the following:

- Any advance indication of sentence given by the judge should normally be confined to the maximum sentence if a plea of guilty were tendered at the stage at which the indication is sought.
- The judge should not give an advance indication of sentence unless one has been sought by the defendant.
- The judge remains entitled, if he sees fit, to exercise the power recognised in *Turner* (see above) to indicate that the sentence, or type of sentence, on the defendant would be the same, whether the case proceeded as a plea of guilty or went to trial, with a resulting conviction.
- The judge is also entitled in an appropriate case to remind the defence advocate that the defendant is entitled to seek an advance indication of sentence.
- In whatever circumstances an advance indication of sentence is sought, the judge retains an unfettered discretion to refuse to give one.
- The judge may alternatively reserve his position until such time as he feels able to give an indication, for example, when a pre-sentence report is available.
- In many cases involving an outright refusal, the judge would probably conclude that it would be inappropriate to give his reasons. If he has in mind to defer an indication, the probability is that he would explain his reasons, and further indicate the circumstances in which, and when, he would be prepared to respond to a request for a sentence indication.
- If at any stage the judge refuses to give an indication (as opposed to deferring it) it remains open to the defendant to seek a further indication at a later stage.
- Once an indication has been given, it is binding on the judge who has given it, and it also binds any other judge who becomes responsible for the case.
- If, after a reasonable opportunity to consider his position in the light of the indication, the defendant does not plead guilty, the indication will cease to have effect.
- An indication should not be sought on a basis of hypothetical facts. Where appropriate, there must be an agreed, written basis of plea (and unless there is, the judge should refuse to give an indication).
- The defendant's advocate should not seek an indication without written authority, signed by his client, that he (the client) wishes to seek an indication.
- The advocate is personally responsible for ensuring that his client fully appreciates that:

a   he should not plead guilty unless he is guilty;

b   any sentence indication given by the judge remains subject to the entitlement of the Attorney General (where it arises) to refer an unduly lenient sentence to the Court of Appeal;

c   any indication given by the judge reflects the situation at the time when it is given, and that if a guilty plea is not tendered in the light of that indication the indication ceases to have effect;

d   any indication which may be given relates only to the matters about which an indication is sought (and so does not include, for example confiscation proceedings).

- The judge should never be invited to give an indication on the basis of what would be, or what would appear to be a 'plea bargain' and so should not become involved in discussions linking the acceptability to the prosecution of a plea or basis of plea, and the sentence which may be imposed.
- If an indication is sought, the prosecution should normally inquire whether the judge is in possession of, or has had access to, all the evidence relied on by the prosecution, including any personal impact statement from the victim of the crime, as well as any information of relevant previous convictions recorded against the defendant.
- Any sentence indication should normally be sought at the plea and case management hearing.
- At least seven days' notice in writing of an intention to seek an indication should normally be given in writing to the prosecution, and the court.
- The hearing should normally take place in open court, with a full recording of the entire proceedings, and both sides represented, in the defendant's presence.
- The fact that the accused has sought an indication of sentence would be inadmissible in any subsequent trial should he maintain his 'not guilty' plea.
- Reporting restrictions should normally be imposed, to be lifted if and when the defendant pleads or is found guilty.

It is a well-established principle that if the judge does give an indication of the likely sentence, he cannot then change his mind. For example, in *R v Johnson and Lorraine* (1990) 12 Cr App R(S) 219, the judge indicated that he would impose either a community order or a suspended sentence but, when he came to pass sentence, imposed immediate custody. The Court of Appeal said that even though the sentences were proper in themselves, a sense of injustice would result from the earlier comments of the judge if the promises made were not honoured, and so the custodial sentences had to be quashed. Similarly, in *R v Ryan* (1999) 163 JP 849, Gray J said that:

> where the defendant has changed his or her plea, in the light of such an indication from the judge, but has subsequently been subjected to a more severe sentence than that indicated, this Court will often but not invariably feel constrained to reduce the sentence to that indicated, even if the indicated sentence was lower than that which the offence, in all the circumstances, merited. Otherwise, the defendant would or might have reason to feel aggrieved.

In *R v Smith* [1990] 1 WLR 1311, the Court of Appeal emphasised the importance of a shorthand writer being present (or the use of a recording device) if counsel see the judge in his chambers. This will prevent an 'unseemly dispute' arising later as to exactly what was said.

Some of these principles have been summarised in para IV.45 of the *Consolidated Practice Direction*:

> IV.45.1 An advocate must be free to do what is his duty, namely to give the accused the best advice he can and, if need be, in strong terms. It will often include advice that a guilty plea, showing an element of remorse, is a mitigating factor which may well enable the court to give a lesser sentence than would otherwise be the case. The advocate will, of course, emphasise that the accused must not plead guilty unless he has committed the acts constituting the offence(s) charged.
>
> IV.45.2 The accused, having considered the advocate's advice, must have complete freedom of choice whether to plead guilty or not guilty.
>
> IV.45.3 There must be freedom of access between advocate and judge. Any discussion must, however, be between the judge and the advocates on both sides. If counsel is instructed by a solicitor who is in court, he too should be allowed to attend the discussion. This freedom of access is important because there may be matters calling for communication or discussion of such a nature that the advocate cannot, in his client's interest, mention them in open court, e.g. the advocate, by way of mitigation, may wish to tell the judge that the accused has not long to live because he is suffering maybe from cancer of which he is and should remain ignorant. Again, the advocates on both sides may wish to discuss with the judge whether it would be proper, in a particular case, for the prosecution to accept a plea to a lesser offence. It is imperative that, so far as possible, justice must be administered in open court. Advocates should, therefore, only ask to see the judge when it is felt to be really necessary. The judge must be careful only to treat such communications as private where, in fairness to the accused, this is necessary.
>
> . . .
>
> IV.45.5 Where any such discussion takes place it should be recorded either by a tape recorder or a shorthand writer.

Paragraph IV.45.4 of the *Consolidated Practice Direction* says that:

> The judge should, subject to one exception, never indicate the sentence he is minded to impose. The exception is that it should be permissible for a judge to say, if it be the case, that, whatever happens, whether the accused pleads guilty or not guilty, the sentence will or will not take a particular form. Where any such discussion on sentence has taken place, the advocate for the defence should disclose it to the accused and, subject to the exception of those matters of which he should remain ignorant, such as cancer, of which he is unaware, inform him of what took place.

The first sentence is inconsistent with *Goodyear*, and so should be regarded as having been superseded by the principles laid down by the Court of Appeal in that case.

Lord Justice Auld, in Chapter 10 of his *Review* (paras 91–114), considers whether there should be greater freedom for courts to give advance indications of likely sentence. He considers the rule set out in *Turner* (see above) restricting what the judge can say about likely sentence, and notes that:

98 The Bar Council and many others have urged a relaxation of the Turner rules. They propose a system of advance indication of sentence in the event of a possible plea of guilty, but without commitment as to the likely sentence in the event of a trial. They suggest that that such a system should have the following features:

(a) a publicly well defined and consistently applied scale of minimum discounts according to the stage in the proceedings that the plea is offered;

(b) the discounts should be such as to secure for the defendant a significant reduction in sentence;

(c) the level of discount above the appropriate minimum would remain a matter for the judge's discretion, but in exercising it, he should disregard the strength of the prosecution case since otherwise that could undermine the incentive to a defendant to enter an early plea;

(d) the judge should indicate the sentence he would give in the event of a plea of guilty and what his sentence might be if the matter went to trial;

(e) the present disincentive to early pleas of guilty of loss of bail or change of status for remand prisoners should be removed; and

(f) the procedure should be subject to review by the Court of Appeal on a reference by the Attorney General, but without power to the Court of Appeal to increase individual sentences.

99 The Bar Council suggests the following procedure. It would be for the defendant, through his advocate, to initiate it by requesting an advance indication of sentence from the judge. Before doing so, his advocate should advise him firmly that he should not plead guilty unless he is guilty. The application would be made formally in court, though sitting in private, in the presence of the defendant and his legal advisers and of the prosecution advocate. The proceedings would be recorded. The judge should satisfy himself through canvassing the matter with both advocates as to the mental competence and emotional state of the defendant and as to whether he might be under any pressure falsely to admit guilt. He should firmly warn the defendant that he should not plead guilty unless he is guilty. If satisfied as to those matters and as to the sufficiency of the information before him of the circumstances of the offence, the judge should indicate the maximum sentence he would give in the event of a plea of guilty.

However, Lord Justice Auld goes on to note that these proposals are far from uncontroversial. He says:

100 Arrayed against that seemingly just and pragmatic solution to the long-standing problems of 'cracked' and unnecessary trials and the advantage to defendants in knowing where they stand, there are powerful arguments of principle voiced in the main by leading academics. They are directed, not so much against a clearer articulation of the system of sentence discounting for a plea of guilty or the relaxation of the Turner rule, but at the very existence of pleas of guilty as part of our criminal justice process and, in any event, against the practice of discounting sentence for a plea of guilty.

101 As to the former, Professor Ashworth and others have referred to the general absence in European jurisdictions of a procedure for pleading guilty and have urged consideration of abolition of the guilty plea itself, say, in indictable cases. They suggest replacing it with some form of judicial scrutiny of the acknowledgement of guilt. However, Professor Ashworth rightly acknowledges that 'there would be tremendous difficulties in such a great cultural change'. I have to confess to timidity about such a radical approach given the state of development of our sentencing law and practice. There would be obvious problems in devising a new criminal justice system equipped to subject every serious criminal case to judicial scrutiny of some sort to test an acknowledgement of guilt against all the other evidence, in order to evaluate the fact of guilt and the extent of it. I cannot see in what practical way it would improve the quality or administration of justice or what significant, if any, advantage the public or defendants would gain from it. The comparison, often made in this context, with bench trials in Philadelphia, is unhelpful. There, they have earned the description of 'slow pleas of guilty' to meet those cases in which, under that State's plea bargaining system, the prosecutor and defendant have been unable to make a bargain as to the disposal of the case, and the defendant opts instead for trial by judge alone in the hope of persuading him of the level of culpability for which he contends.

Having considered each of these arguments, Lord Justice Auld concludes as follows:

186 There should be introduced, by way of a judicial sentencing guideline for later incorporation in a Sentencing Code, a system of sentencing discounts graduated so that the earlier the tender of plea of guilty the higher the discount for it, coupled with a system of advance indication of sentence for a defendant considering pleading guilty.

187 On the request of a defendant, through his advocate, the judge should be entitled formally to indicate the maximum sentence in the event of a plea of guilty at that stage and the possible sentence on conviction following a trial.

188 The request to the judge and all related subsequent proceedings should be in court, in the presence of the prosecution, the defendant and his advisers and a court reporter, but otherwise in private, and should be fully recorded.

189 The judge should enquire, by canvassing the matter with both advocates, as to the mental competence and emotional state of the defendant and as to whether he might be under any pressure falsely to admit guilt.

190 The prosecution and defence should be equipped to put before the judge all relevant information about the offence(s) and the defendant, including any pre-sentence or other reports and any victim impact statement, to enable the judge to give an indication.

191 The judge should only give an indication if and when he is satisfied that he has sufficient information and if he considers it appropriate to do so.

192 Where, as a result of such an indication, a defendant's advocate indicates to the judge that he wishes to plead guilty, the judge should, by questioning the defendant direct, satisfy himself that the defendant understands the effect of his proposed plea, that it would be true and that it would be voluntary.

193 The judge should be bound by his indication, as should any other judge before whom
the defendant may appear for sentence, on the consequent plea of guilty.

The Sentencing Guidelines Council has produced definitive Guidelines on sentencing
where the defendant pleads guilty. These make provision for the discount for pleading
guilty to be reduced depending on how late in the process the guilty plea is entered (see
Chapter 12).

It should also be noted that procedures outlined in *Goodyear* for seeking advance
indications of sentence in the Crown Court brings that court into line with magistrates'
courts where, under changes brought about by the Criminal Justice Act 2003, a defendant may seek a broad indication of sentence at the allocation (mode of trial) stage. He is
entitled to request an indication of sentence, whether 'a custodial sentence or non-
custodial sentence would be more likely to be imposed if he were to be tried summarily
. . . and to plead guilty'. The court is entitled, but not obliged, to respond to such a
request (see Chapter 4).

12.20 CHANGE OF PLEA

The defendant may change his plea from not guilty to guilty at any stage before the
verdict is given. Counsel for the defendant simply asks for the indictment to be put again,
and the defendant pleads guilty. According to *R v Heyes* [1951] 1 KB 29, the jury should
then be asked by the judge to return a formal verdict of guilty. However, in *R v Poole*
[2001] EWCA Crim 2664; [2002] 1 WLR 1528 (followed in *R v McPeake* [2005] EWCA
Crim 3162; [2006] Crim LR 376), the Court of Appeal held that, where a defendant
pleads not guilty but then changes the plea to guilty during the course of the trial, there
is no requirement that the judge should ask the jury for a formal verdict of guilty; it is
permissible for the judge simply to discharge the jury and proceed to sentencing.

The judge has a discretion to allow the defendant to change his plea of guilty to one
of not guilty at any stage before sentence has been passed (*R v Dodd* (1982) 74 Cr App
R 50, following *S v Recorder of Manchester* [1971] AC 481, which concerned change of
plea in the magistrates' court). The defendant will obviously have to give a reason for
his change of mind. Permission to withdraw the guilty plea is unlikely to be given unless
the defendant did not realise that he had a defence when he pleaded guilty (*R v McNally*
[1954] 1 WLR 933). In *R v Drew* [1985] 1 WLR 914 at 923, Lord Lane CJ said that only
rarely would it be appropriate for the trial judge to exercise his discretion in favour of
an accused person wishing to change an unequivocal plea of guilty to one of not guilty.
In *R v B* [2002] EWCA Crim 3020, Laws LJ (at para 19) said that the discretion must be
exercised judicially and there must be some objective basis for allowing the plea to be
changed.

So far as appeals against the refusal to allow a change of plea from guilty to not
guilty are concerned, in *R v Mason* [2004] EWCA Crim 2848, Potter LJ said (at para 53)
that if the trial judge investigates the question why the defendant wishes to change his
plea fully and fairly, taking into account the various factors brought to his notice, and
concludes that there are no good grounds for allowing a change of plea because the plea
represents a 'free and genuine acknowledgement of guilt', then it is inappropriate for
the Court of Appeal to interfere.

In *R v Sheikh* [2004] EWCA Crim 492; [2004] 2 Cr App R 13, the defendants applied to withdraw their pleas of guilty. The basis of their application was that they had not been informed that they could be made the subject of confiscation proceedings in the event of conviction. The trial judge refused to allow a change of plea, and the Court of Appeal upheld the refusal. At para 16, Mantell LJ said:

> It is well accepted that quite apart from cases where the plea of guilty is equivocal or ambiguous, the court retains a residual discretion to allow the withdrawal of a guilty plea where not to do so might work an injustice. Examples might be where a defendant might be misinformed about the nature of the charge or the availability of the defence or where he has been put under pressure to plead guilty in circumstances where he is not truly admitting guilt. It is not possible to attempt a comprehensive catalogue of the circumstances in which the discretion might be exercised. Commonly, however, it is reserved for cases where there is doubt that the plea represents a genuine acknowledgement of guilt.

However, in the present case, the possibility of confiscation proceedings taking place could not, of itself, have any bearing upon the defendant's acceptance of guilt.

So far as appeals are concerned, his Lordship went on to say (at para 18):

> . . . it must be shown that the judge misdirected himself or took account of matters which he should not have taken account of or failed to take account of matters to which he should have had regard or that he exercised his discretion in a wholly unreasonable manner.

The procedure for seeking to change a plea from guilty to not guilty is set out in r 39.3 of the Criminal Procedure Rules, which provides as follows:

(1) The defendant must apply as soon as practicable after becoming aware of the grounds for making an application to change a plea of guilty, and may only do so before the final disposal of the case, by sentence or otherwise.

(2) Unless the court otherwise directs, the application must be in writing and it must—

   (a) set out the reasons why it would be unjust for the guilty plea to remain unchanged;
   (b) indicate what, if any, evidence the defendant wishes to call;
   (c) identify any proposed witness; and
   (d) indicate whether legal professional privilege is waived, specifying any material name and date.

(3) The defendant must serve the written application on—

   (a) the court officer; and
   (b) the prosecutor.

12.21 ALTERNATIVES TO TRIAL: OFFERING NO EVIDENCE; LEAVING COUNTS ON FILE

We have already seen that there may be circumstances where the prosecution do not wish to proceed with the trial. Once the indictment has been signed, it is too late to serve a notice of discontinuance under s 23 or 23A of the Prosecution of Offences Act 1985 (since that power only applies during the preliminary stages of the case) but there are two other ways of achieving the same objective.

12.21.1 Offering no evidence

Section 17 of the Criminal Justice Act 1967 provides that:

> Where a defendant arraigned on an indictment or inquisition pleads not guilty and the prosecutor proposes to offer no evidence against him, the court before which the defendant is arraigned may, if it thinks fit, order that a verdict of not guilty shall be recorded without any further steps being taken in the proceedings, and the verdict shall have the same effect as if the defendant had been tried and acquitted on the verdict of a jury or a court.

This section thus allows the prosecution to 'offer no evidence' in respect of one or more counts on an indictment. This may be appropriate, for example, where a key prosecution witness refuses to testify, or where evidence exonerating the defendant comes to light, or where the defendant pleads guilty to one offence and the prosecution do not wish to proceed with another.

Section 17 says that the court 'may' enter a finding of not guilty where the prosecution offer no evidence. The use of the word 'may' suggests that the court can refuse and can empanel a jury. In practice, however, the judge would not force the prosecution to present its case. Indeed, in *R v Grafton* [1993] QB 101, the Court of Appeal said that before the completion of the prosecution case, the decision whether or not to continue had to be that of the prosecution and that a trial judge therefore has no power to refuse to permit discontinuance of the prosecution. Taylor LJ (at p 107) said:

> It is well established that the judge in a criminal trial has power to call a witness. It is, however, a power which should be used most sparingly and rarely exercised . . . It cannot in our judgment be right that a judge can refuse to allow the prosecution to discontinue before their case is concluded if he believes the evidence already called raises a prima facie case. The effect would be that after a complainant gave evidence which the judge thought credible, if the prosecution at that point decided on due reflection to discontinue, the judge could go on to call all the remaining prosecution witnesses himself. In doing so, he would inevitably have descended into the arena in a totally unacceptable way.

It is submitted that the same principles must necessarily apply where the prosecution do not even wish to open their case. It would seem to be wrong in principle to require a prosecutor to continue with a case that he does not wish to proceed with, and it would be wholly wrong for the judge to call and question prosecution witnesses himself. It is suggested that if a judge is unhappy with a decision to offer no evidence, he should contact the Chief Crown Prosecutor for the area and ask for the case to be reviewed.

12.21.2 Leaving counts on file

The prosecution may alternatively ask for one or more counts to be 'left on the file marked not to be proceeded with without leave of the Crown Court or the Court of Appeal'. This may be appropriate where the defendant pleads guilty to some counts but not guilty to others, since leaving a count on the file does not amount to an acquittal. Thus, if the conviction is for some reason overturned on appeal, the prosecution can proceed with the other counts if the Crown Court or Court of Appeal gives permission. This could happen if the trial judge gives a preliminary ruling on the law adverse to the accused, so the accused then pleads guilty but then challenges the judge's ruling by means of an appeal against conviction; the prosecution could then seek leave to proceed with the other counts.

Thus, the main difference between offering no evidence and leaving counts on the file is that in the former case an acquittal is entered (so the defendant cannot – subject to the reforms made by Pt 10 of the Criminal Justice Act 2003 – be prosecuted again for the same offence) whereas, in the latter case, it is possible (with the leave of the court) for the case against the defendant to be revived.

12.22 DIFFERENT PLEAS FROM DIFFERENT DEFENDANTS

If more than one defendant is charged in the same indictment, it may well be that one defendant will plead guilty and another will plead not guilty.

12.22.1 What to tell the jury

Where one defendant pleads guilty but another not guilty, counsel for the prosecution should only tell the jury which tries the defendant who pleads not guilty that '[name of defendant who pleads guilty], of whom you may hear mention in the course of this case, is not before you and is none of your concern'.

Reference to the guilty plea of a co-defendant is only possible with leave of the judge, which can only be given where the evidence of the plea of the former co-defendant is admissible in evidence (in the circumstances set out in s 74 of PACE 1984) (*R v Kempster* [1989] 1 WLR 1125). For example, in *R v Manzur and Mahmood* [1997] 1 Cr App R 414, three people had been charged with rape. One defendant pleaded guilty; the other two pleaded not guilty, saying that the victim had consented to sexual intercourse. The judge allowed the jury to be told of the third defendant's plea of guilty. The Court of Appeal accepted the argument that the jury might have taken the view, on the basis of the third defendant's guilty plea, that the two appellants must have known that the victim was not consenting and so may not have given sufficient consideration to the evidence of the two appellants that they believed the woman to be consenting to intercourse. The admission of the evidence of the plea of the third defendant was therefore unduly prejudicial to the appellants and so a retrial was ordered.

12.22.2 When should sentence be passed on the defendant who pleads guilty?

Where one defendant pleads guilty and the other not guilty, the usual procedure is to adjourn sentence of the defendant who pleads guilty until after the trial of the defendant who pleads not guilty. There is less risk of disparity between the sentences if the judge sentences the defendants together, and the judge is in a better position to sentence as he will have heard the evidence about the gravity of the offence and the respective roles played by the defendants during the course of the trial (*R v Payne* [1950] 1 All ER 102).

However, where it is accepted by the prosecution that the defendant who pleads guilty played a very minor role in the offence, or where the other defendant absconds, the defendant who pleads guilty will generally be sentenced as soon as the plea is entered.

12.22.3 'Turning Queen's evidence'

If the defendant who pleads guilty also indicates that he is willing to give evidence for the prosecution, the arguments are slightly different. This is because 'turning Queen's evidence' attracts a discount in sentence well beyond the one-third discount that a plea of guilty normally receives. Such a person becomes a 'competent' witness (i.e. is legally able to testify) for the prosecution once he has pleaded guilty.

In *Payne* (see above), it was said that where the defendant who pleads guilty is going to be called as a witness, the general practice is that he should be sentenced there and then, so that there should be no suspicion of his evidence being affected by the fact that he hopes to get a lighter sentence because of the evidence which he gives. It should also be borne in mind that, if a defendant is sentenced before he gives his evidence, he will receive a substantial discount for his promise to give evidence for the Crown and if (having achieved a more lenient sentence) he then refuses to testify, he cannot be re-sentenced (see *R v Stone* [1970] 1 WLR 1112). On the other hand, however, another argument is that if a defendant who pleads guilty is sentenced after he has given evidence against the other accused, it could be thought that the sentence is determined by the quality of his evidence for the Crown rather than by the level of criminality revealed in his involvement in the offence. In *R v Weekes* (1982) 74 Cr App R 161, the Court of Appeal ruled that in such a case sentence should normally be postponed until after the trial of the defendant who pleads not guilty so the defendants are sentenced together (assuming that the defendant who pleaded not guilty is convicted).

Ultimately, however, it is a matter for the trial judge whether he sentences the defendant who is expected to testify for the Crown immediately after his plea of guilty or after the trial of the other defendant. In *R v Clement* (1991) *The Times*, 12 December, it was held that the decision whether or not to postpone sentence on a defendant who pleads guilty and indicates that he is willing to give evidence against a co-defendant until the end of the trial is a matter for the discretion of the trial judge, and would not in itself give rise to a ground of appeal.

Sections 70–75A of the Serious Organised Crime and Police Act 2005 make provision for immunity from prosecution and for sentence reductions for offenders who assist investigations into, and prosecutions of, serious offences. See Chapter 16 for discussion of these provisions.

12.23 VARIATION OF SENTENCE

Section 155 of the Powers of Criminal Courts (Sentencing) Act 2000 states:

(1) Subject to the following provisions of this section, a sentence imposed, or other order made, by the Crown Court when dealing with an offender may be varied or rescinded by the Crown Court within the period of 28 days beginning with the day on which the sentence or other order was imposed or made or, where sub-section (2) below applies, within the time allowed by that sub-section.

(2) Where two or more persons are jointly tried on an indictment, then, subject to the following provisions of this section, a sentence imposed, or other order made, by the Crown Court on conviction of any of those persons on the indictment may be varied or rescinded by the Crown Court not later than the expiry of whichever is the shorter of the following periods, that is—

   (a) the period of 28 days beginning with the date of conclusion of the joint trial;
   (b) the period of 56 days beginning with the day on which the sentence or other order was imposed or made.

(3) For the purposes of sub-section (2) above, the joint trial is concluded on the latest of the following dates, that is any date on which any of the persons jointly tried is sentenced or is acquitted or on which a special verdict is brought in.

(4) A sentence or other order shall not be varied or rescinded under this section except by the court constituted as it was when the sentence or other order was imposed or made, or, where that court comprised one or more justices of the peace, a court so constituted except for the omission of any one or more of those justices.

Section 155 thus enables the judge who imposed a sentence to vary or rescind that sentence within 28 days of the sentence being passed. This power is rarely invoked. It would be appropriate where, for example, an unlawful sentence has inadvertently been passed. However, it can also be used to increase sentence in exceptional cases where the original sentence was imposed on an erroneous factual basis. In *R v Hart* (1983) 5 Cr App R(S) 25, for example, a defendant boasted to the press that he had invented a false story to trick the judge into passing a lenient sentence. The judge re-listed the case and replaced a suspended sentence of imprisonment with immediate custody. The Court of Appeal upheld this use of s 155 (although on the facts quashed the decision as the judge had varied the sentence outside the time-limit permitted by the Act).

The power to vary a sentence (which can only be exercised by the judge who imposed the original sentence (s 155(4)) can be used to substitute one form of sentence for another. In *R v Sodhi* (1978) 66 Cr App R 260, for example, a prison sentence was replaced with a hospital order under the Mental Health Act 1983. In *R v Hadley* (1995) 16 Cr App R(S) 358, the judge thought that the maximum sentence for the offence of which the defendant had been convicted was lower than in fact it was. When the judge discovered his error, he increased the defendant's sentence. The Court of Appeal upheld this use of the power to vary the sentence, saying that where a judge decides that the original sentence is too low, in the sense that it is outside the bracket of sentences which could reasonably be imposed for a particular offence, the judge will be justified in increasing the sentence.

Where the Crown Court intends to exercise its power to vary a sentence which has been imposed, it should do so in the presence of the defendant and after affording him an opportunity to make representations, particularly when it is intended to increase the sentence which was imposed (*R v May* (1981) Cr App R(S) 165). The defendant or his counsel must be given the opportunity to address the court. If the court purports to alter a sentence without giving the offender this opportunity, the variation in the sentence will be null and void (*R v Cleere* (1983) 5 Cr App R (S) 465). Sentence should only be varied in open court (*R v Dowling* (1989) 88 Cr App R 88).

Subject to the provision about joint trials, the power to vary a sentence under s 155 can only be exercised within the period of 28 days from the passing of the sentence (*R v Menocal* [1980] AC 598). This means that not only must the original sentence be rescinded but a new sentence must be imposed within the 28 day period (*R v Stillwell* (1991) 94 Cr App R 65).

12.24 OTHER PLEAS

In this section, we consider the case where the plea of the defendant is unclear and we look at the special situations where the accused may not be fit to plead or where he claims the benefit of the doctrine of *autrefois convict* or *autrefois acquit* (otherwise known as 'double jeopardy').

12.24.1 The ambiguous plea

If the defendant pleads guilty but, either then or when addressing the court in mitigation, says something which shows that he may have a defence, the judge will explain to the defendant that he is putting forward a defence and the defendant will be asked to plead again. If the defendant confirms his plea of guilty but still tries to put forward a defence, a not guilty plea will be entered by the court.

12.24.2 If the defendant refuses to plead

If the defendant refuses to enter a plea of guilty or not guilty when the indictment is put to him, a not guilty plea will be entered on his behalf.

12.24.3 Fitness to plead

Either the prosecution or the defence may raise the issue of whether the accused is fit to plead.

A defendant is unfit to plead if he suffers from a disability which prevents him from being able to understand the course of the proceedings and the evidence which is given. Such a defendant would not be able to give proper instructions to his lawyer. It is not enough for the accused to be mentally disturbed or to be suffering from amnesia so that he cannot remember the events in question (see *R v Podola* [1960] 1 QB 325).

The procedure to be followed in such a case is contained in the Criminal Procedure (Insanity) Act 1964. Section 4 provides as follows:

> (1) This section applies where on the trial of a person the question arises (at the instance of the defence or otherwise) whether the accused is under a disability, that is to say, under any disability such that apart from this Act it would constitute a bar to his being tried.
>
> (2) If, having regard to the nature of the supposed disability, the court are of opinion that it is expedient to do so and in the interests of the accused, they may postpone consideration of the question of fitness to be tried until any time up to the opening of the case for the defence.
>
> (3) If, before the question of fitness to be tried falls to be determined, the jury return a verdict of acquittal on the count or each of the counts on which the accused is being tried, that question shall not be determined.
>
> (4) Subject to sub-sections (2) and (3) above, the question of fitness to be tried shall be determined as soon as it arises.
>
> (5) The question of fitness to be tried shall be determined by the court without a jury.
>
> (6) The court shall not make a determination under sub-section (5) above except on the written or oral evidence of two or more registered medical practitioners at least one of whom is duly approved.

It will be noted that, under s 4(2), the court may postpone consideration of the question of the defendant's fitness to be tried until any time up to the opening of the defence case if this is in the defendant's interests. This means that there is an opportunity for a submission of no case to answer to be made before the question of fitness is considered. If the submission of no case to answer is successful, an acquittal is entered and the issue of fitness is not determined.

The issue of fitness to plead is determined by the judge. The evidence of at least two doctors (at least one of whom must specialise in mental disorder) is required.

Until the 1964 Act was amended by the Domestic Violence, Crime and Victims Act 2004, the issue of fitness to plead had to be determined by a jury. Paragraphs 212–13 of the *Auld Review* considered how the question of fitness to plead should be determined. Lord Justice Auld notes that in the majority of cases the question of unfitness is little more than a formality, since there is no dispute between the prosecution and the defence that the defendant is unfit to plead. However, the procedure remained cumbersome because of the need to empanel a jury. Lord Justice Auld took the view that it is difficult to see what a jury can bring to the determination of the issue that a judge cannot. Accordingly, Recommendation 51 was that: 'Legislation should be introduced to require a judge, not a jury, to determine the issue of fitness to plead.'

If the issue of fitness is determined at the start of the trial and the defendant is found fit to plead, a jury is empanelled to try the case in the usual way and the trial will take its usual course.

Where the defendant is found unfit to plead, a jury has to consider whether the defendant committed the act or omission charged against him (i.e. where he committed the *actus reus* of the offence). The procedure for this is governed by s 4A of the 1964 Act, which provides as follows:

(1)   This section applies where in accordance with section 4(5) above it is determined by a court that the accused is under a disability.

(2)   The trial shall not proceed or further proceed but it shall be determined by a jury—

  (a)   on the evidence (if any) already given in the trial; and

  (b)   on such evidence as may be adduced or further adduced by the prosecution, or adduced by a person appointed by the court under this section to put the case for the defence,

  whether they are satisfied, as respects the count or each of the counts on which the accused was to be or was being tried, that he did the act or made the omission charged against him as the offence.

(3)   If as respects that count or any of those counts the jury are satisfied as mentioned in sub-section (2) above, they shall make a finding that the accused did the act or made the omission charged against him.

(4)   If as respects that count or any of those counts the jury are not so satisfied, they shall return a verdict of acquittal as if on the count in question the trial had proceeded to a conclusion.

(5)   Where the question of disability was determined after arraignment of the accused, the determination under sub-section (2) is to be made by the jury by whom he was being tried.

If determination of the question of fitness to plead was postponed, the issue of fitness has to be considered by the jury trying the case. If the jury finds that he did not do the act alleged, then he must be acquitted (s 4A(4)).

The procedure laid down by s 4A for determining whether the accused has done the act charged against him does not involve the determination of a criminal charge but is, in any event, compatible with the rights of the accused under Art 6 of the European Convention on Human Rights (*R v H* [2003] UKHL 1; [2003] 1 WLR 411).

Section 5(2) and (3) of the Criminal Procedure (Insanity) Act 1964 sets out the powers of the court where the defendant is found unfit to plead and it is also found that he committed the *actus reus* of the offence. The court is empowered to make a hospital order, a supervision order, or to grant an absolute discharge.

12.24.4 *Autrefois convict* and *autrefois acquit* (double jeopardy)

The basic principle of *autrefois convict* and *autrefois acquit* is that a person should not be tried twice for the same offence. In other words, a person should not be tried for a crime in respect of which he has already been acquitted or convicted (*Connelly v DPP* [1964] AC 1254). From the speeches in *Connelly*, it is possible to identify three other principles:

- the defendant cannot be tried for a crime in respect of which he could have been convicted on an earlier occasion (that is, he cannot be convicted of an offence which was an alternative offence of which the jury could have convicted him under s 6(3) of the Criminal Law Act 1967). Thus, if the defendant was earlier tried for robbery, he cannot now be tried for the theft which comprised that robbery;

- the defendant cannot be tried for a crime, proof of which would necessarily entail proof of another crime of which he has already been acquitted (that is, the offence of which he has been acquitted is a necessary step towards establishing the second offence). Thus, if the defendant is acquitted of theft, he cannot later be charged with robbery alleging that same theft; and
- the defendant cannot be tried for a crime which is, in effect, the same (or substantially the same) as one of which he has previously been acquitted or convicted, or of which he could have been convicted by way of a verdict of guilty to an alternative offence.

In *R v Beedie* [1998] QB 356, a tenant died from carbon monoxide poisoning due to a defective gas fire. Her landlord was convicted of offences under health and safety legislation. He was subsequently charged with manslaughter, arising from the same facts. The Court of Appeal pointed out that in *Connelly*, the majority of the House of Lords had confined the strict operation of the *autrefois convict* doctrine to cases where the second indictment charged the same offence as the first; in such a case, the later prosecution must be struck out as an abuse of process. In the other three situations identified in *Connelly*, the court has a discretion whether or not to strike out the later prosecution. In the present case, the court decided that a stay should have been ordered, because the manslaughter charge was based on substantially the same facts as the earlier prosecution and gave rise to a prosecution for an offence of greater gravity, no new facts having occurred.

In *R v Dabhade* [1993] QB 329, the Court of Appeal confirmed the general principle that where a charge is dismissed without a hearing, the prosecution may not thereafter institute fresh proceedings on the same or an essentially similar charge or count. However, the court held that if the summary dismissal of the charge is because it is defective or because the prosecution wished to reorganise their case (because the charge was inappropriate given the evidence they had), it cannot properly be said that the defendant was ever in jeopardy of conviction. Wright J, giving the judgment of the court, said (at p 341):

1. For the principle of *autrefois* to apply, the defendant must have been put in jeopardy. Quite apart from all other requirements, he must demonstrate that the earlier proceedings that he relies upon must have been commenced . . .

2. If, thereafter, a charge or count is dismissed, albeit without a hearing on the merits (e.g. on the basis that the prosecution are unable to proceed), there is a well-established principle that the prosecution may not thereafter institute fresh proceedings on the same or an essentially similar charge or count. [His Lordship added that this may be explicable on the basis of the jurisdiction of the court to prevent an abuse of process, rather than the *autrefois* doctrine.]

3. If, however, the summary dismissal of the charge or count is because it is apparent that it is defective, either as a matter of law (e.g. for duplicity) or because the evidence available to the prosecution on any view, given the application of proper legal principles, is insufficient to sustain a conviction on the charge as laid, then, in our view, it cannot be properly said that the defendant has ever been in jeopardy of conviction . . . As a matter of general principle, it does not seem to us to make any difference whether the evidence that the prosecution might

otherwise have wished to rely upon is excluded because of some rule of law or statute . . . or simply because the evidence on its face is incapable of proving the particulars of the offence alleged.

4. If, moreover, the context in which a charge is summarily dismissed is a rationalisation or reorganisation of the prosecution's case, so that, no doubt in recognition of the difficulties that may lie ahead in the successful prosecution of the original charge, it is decided to substitute therefor a new charge which is regarded as more appropriate to the facts, then the consensual dismissal of the original charge, upon the substitution of the new one, will not give rise to the application of the doctrine of *autrefois acquit* . . .

In *Dabhade*, the defendant was originally charged with obtaining property by deception, but the prosecution offered no evidence on that charge (which was then dismissed). The prosecution then brought proceedings on a charge of theft arising out of the same incident, as this was felt to be more appropriate given the facts. The Court of Appeal rejected the argument that the defendant could plead *autrefois acquit*, holding that the original charge was so fundamentally incorrectly framed that the prosecution had decided before a trial could take place that a different charge would have to be brought; the defendant was therefore never, in any real sense, in jeopardy of being convicted on that original charge.

Dabhade applies only where the original charge is fundamentally flawed. In *R v G* [2001] EWCA Crim 1215; [2001] 1 WLR 1727, the appellant was charged with common assault and pleaded not guilty. Counsel for the prosecution then applied to amend the indictment by adding a count of assault occasioning actual bodily harm. The prosecution offered no evidence on the common assault charge and a verdict of not guilty was entered under s 17 of the Criminal Justice Act 1967. The question to be decided was whether the defendant was entitled to rely on *autrefois acquit* to avoid prosecution on the actual bodily harm charge. It was held that where the prosecution offer no evidence against a defendant and a verdict of not guilty is entered, the prosecution cannot then proceed against the defendant on a charge alleging a more serious offence based on the same facts, as the defendant is entitled to rely on the defence of *autrefois acquit*.

Section 122 of the Criminal Justice Act 1988 provides that where the issue of *autrefois* is raised, it must be determined by a judge alone (that is, sitting without a jury).

12.24.5 Summary: the scope of the *autrefois* doctrine

The following situations do not amount to acquittal and so the defendant can be re-prosecuted:

- the quashing of an indictment (for example, because it is defective) (*R v Newland* [1988] QB 402);
- the withdrawal of a summons in the magistrates' court at any time prior to the defendant entering a plea (*R v Grays Justices ex p Low* [1990] 1 QB 54);
- the dismissal of an information by the magistrates where the prosecution failed to attend court or where the information is defective in a way that cannot be cured by amendment (*R v Dabhade* [1993] QB 329);

- the prosecution serve a notice of discontinuance under s 23 or s 23A of the Prosecution of Offences Act 1985 (sub-s (9) and (5) respectively providing that the discontinuance of any proceedings does not prevent the institution of fresh proceedings in respect of the same offence);
- the jury is discharged from giving a verdict.

In all of these cases, the defendant cannot be said to have been in jeopardy of a conviction.

12.25 TRIALS ON INDICTMENT WITHOUT A JURY

The *Auld Review* made the controversial suggestion that some trials on indictment should take place without a jury:

a defendants in the Crown Court should be entitled, with the court's consent, to opt for trial by judge alone (Recommendation 31);
b in serious and complex frauds, the trial judge should have the power to direct trial by himself and two lay members or, if the defendant so requests, by himself alone (Recommendation 37).

In paras 110–18 of Chapter 5 of the *Review*, Lord Justice Auld considers the arguments for and against the defendant having the option to choose trial by judge alone ('bench trial' or 'jury waiver'). This mode of trial (which is available in some other jurisdictions) might be attractive to defendants in a number of circumstances, for instance in cases where the defendant is concerned about whether a jury would understand the defence case (perhaps where the defence is a technical one), or where the defendant is charged with an offence which might evoke strong emotional reactions or where there has been adverse pre-trial publicity, or where the evidence against the accused rests on evidence, such as identification evidence, which needs very careful and thorough scrutiny. Lord Justice Auld concluded that there may be cases where this form of trial would not be appropriate (and so the court needs to be able to insist that the ordinary trial process should take place) but that little harm can be done by giving the accused the option to choose trial by judge alone. Accordingly, Recommendation 31 of the Review was to the effect that defendants, with the consent of the court (given after hearing representations from both sides), should be able to opt for trial by judge alone in all cases tried on indictment. This recommendation was accepted by the Government and appeared in the Criminal Justice Bill 2003; however, it was removed at the last minute as part of a deal with the Opposition to enable the Bill to receive Royal Assent.

It is perhaps odd that judge-only trial without the agreement of the defence – surely the more controversial measure – remained in the Bill. In paras 173–206 of Chapter 5, the *Auld Review* considers whether there should continue to be trial by jury in fraud and other complex cases. This topic has been considered on several previous occasions; for example, by the Fraud Trials Committee chaired by Lord Roskill, which reported in 1986 (the 'Roskill Committee'). Lord Justice Auld helpfully sets out the arguments for and against in para 181:

The arguments for and against the present form of jury trial in cases of serious and complex fraud have been canvassed many times. Arguments for include:

- jury trial is a hallowed democratic institution and a citizen's right in all serious cases which necessarily include serious and complex frauds;
- the random nature of selection of juries ensures their fairness and independence;
- mostly the question is one of dishonesty, which is essentially a matter for a jury who, by reason of their number and mix, are as well as, or better equipped than, a smaller tribunal, however professional, to assess the reliability and credibility of witnesses;
- there is no evidence, for example in the form of jury research, that juries cannot cope with long and complex cases or that their decisions in them are contrary to the evidence; on the contrary, most judges and legal practitioners' assessment, based on their trial experience, is that their verdicts are in the main 'correct'; and
- there is an openness and public intelligibility in the parties having to accommodate the jury's newness to the subject matter by presenting their respective cases in a simple and easily digestible form, and that there is scope for improvements in such presentation.

Arguments against include:

- if jurors are truly to be regarded as the defendant's peers, they should be experienced in the professional or commercial discipline in which the alleged offence occurred;
- although the issue of dishonesty is essentially a matter for a jury, the volume and complexities of the issues and the evidence, especially in specialist market frauds, may be too difficult for them to understand or analyse so as to enable them to determine whether there has been dishonesty;
- the length of such trials, sometimes of several months, is an unreasonable intrusion on jurors' personal and, where they are in employment, working lives, going way beyond the conventional requirement for such duty of about two weeks' service;
- that has the effect of making juries even less representative of the community than they are already, since the court excuses many who would otherwise be able and willing to make short-term arrangements to do their civic duty;
- such long trials are also a great personal strain and burden on everyone else involved, not least the defendant, the victim and witnesses;
- judges, with their legal and forensic experience, and/or specialist assessors would be better equipped to deal justly and more expeditiously with such cases;
- that would also have the benefit of greater openness, since there would then be a publicly reasoned and appealable decision instead of the present inscrutable and largely unappealable verdict of the jury; and
- the length of jury trials in fraud cases is very costly to the public and also, because of limited judicial and court resources, unduly delays the efficient disposal of other cases waiting for trial.

In para 182, Lord Justice Auld writes:

I have considered these conflicting arguments with care. Like the Roskill Committee, I have concluded that those for replacing trial by judge and jury with some other form of tribunal in serious and complex fraud cases are the more persuasive.

On this basis, the *Auld Review* makes the following Recommendations:

37 As an alternative to trial by judge and jury in serious and complex fraud cases, the nominated trial judge should be empowered to direct trial by himself sitting with lay members or, where the defendant has opted for trial by judge alone, by himself alone.

38 The category of cases to which such a direction might apply should, in the first instance, be frauds of seriousness or complexity within sections 4 and 7 of the Criminal Justice Act 1987.

39 The overriding criterion for directing trial without jury should be the interests of justice.

40 Either party should have a right of appeal against such decision to the Court of Appeal (Criminal Division).

41 Judges trying such cases, by whatever form of procedure, should be specially nominated for the purpose as now, and provided with a thorough, structured and continuing training for it.

42 There should be a panel of experts, established and maintained by the Lord Chancellor in consultation with professional and other bodies, from which lay members may be selected for trials.

43 The nominated trial judge should select the lay members after affording the parties an opportunity to make written representations as to their suitability.

44 Lay members should be paid appropriately for their service.

45 In a court consisting of a judge and lay members, the judge should be the sole judge of law, procedure, admissibility of evidence and as to sentence; as to conviction, all three should be the judges of fact.

46 The decision of a court so constituted should wherever possible be unanimous, but a majority of any two could suffice for a conviction.

47 The judge should give the court's decision by a public and fully reasoned judgment.

Part 7 of the Criminal Justice Act 2003 makes provision for trial by judge alone in complex fraud cases, but makes no provision for the judge to sit with lay members. Part 7 also enables trial by judge alone to take place in cases where there is a danger of jury tampering. We will now examine the detail of those provisions (which were not in force at the time of writing).

12.25.1 Complex or lengthy fraud trials

Section 43 of the Criminal Justice Act 2003 enables an application to be made by the prosecution for certain fraud trials to be conducted without a jury. Such an order can only be made with the approval of the Lord Chief Justice or a judge nominated for this purpose by the Lord Chief Justice (s 43(4)). It only applies where notice has been given under s 51B of the Crime and Disorder Act 1998 (notices in serious or complex fraud cases) in respect of the offence(s) (s 43(1)(b)). The judge can accede to the request only if (s 43(5)):

... the complexity of the trial or the length of the trial (or both) is likely to make the trial so burdensome to the members of a jury hearing the trial that the interests of justice require that serious consideration should be given to the question of whether the trial should be conducted without a jury.

In deciding whether or not he is satisfied that this condition is fulfilled, the judge must have regard to any steps which might reasonably be taken to reduce the complexity or length of the trial (s 43(6)); in other words, a trial without a jury is very much a last resort. However, under s 43(7), 'a step is not to be regarded as reasonable if it would significantly disadvantage the prosecution'.

12.25.2 Jury tampering

Section 44 of the 2003 Act enables an application to be made by the prosecution for a trial to be conducted without a jury where there is a danger of jury tampering. The judge may make such an order only if two conditions are satisfied: the first condition is that 'there is evidence of a real and present danger that jury tampering would take place' (s 44(4)) and the second condition is that 'notwithstanding any steps (including the provision of police protection) which might reasonably be taken to prevent jury tampering, the likelihood that it would take place would be so substantial as to make it necessary in the interests of justice for the trial to be conducted without a jury' (s 44(5)). Section 44(6) gives some examples of cases where there may be evidence of a real and present danger that jury tampering would take place:

(a) a case where the trial is a retrial and the jury in the previous trial was discharged because jury tampering had taken place,

(b) a case where jury tampering has taken place in previous criminal proceedings involving the defendant or any of the defendants,

(c) a case where there has been intimidation, or attempted intimidation, of any person who is likely to be a witness in the trial.

The use of the word 'examples' indicates that this is not intended to be an exhaustive list of the circumstances where s 44 might apply.

12.25.3 Procedure for applications for judge-only trials

Under s 45(2) of the Criminal Justice Act 2003, an application for an order under s 43 or s 44 must be made at a 'preparatory hearing' held pursuant to s 29 of the Criminal Procedure and Investigations Act 1996 (see Chapter 11); all parties must be given an opportunity to make representations about the application (s 45(3)). Section 45(9) enables an appeal to the Court of Appeal against the decision of the judge on an application under ss 43 or s 44.

12.25.4 Discharge of jury because of jury tampering

Section 46 of the Criminal Justice Act 2003 makes provision for the discharge of a jury because of jury tampering:

(1) This section applies where—

  (a) a judge is minded during a trial on indictment to discharge the jury, and
  (b) he is so minded because jury tampering appears to have taken place.

(2) Before taking any steps to discharge the jury, the judge must—

  (a) inform the parties that he is minded to discharge the jury,
  (b) inform the parties of the grounds on which he is so minded, and
  (c) allow the parties an opportunity to make representations.

(3) Where the judge, after considering any such representations, discharges the jury, he may make an order that the trial is to continue without a jury if, but only if, he is satisfied—

  (a) that jury tampering has taken place, and
  (b) that to continue the trial without a jury would be fair to the defendant or defendants;

  but this is subject to sub-section (4).

(4) If the judge considers that it is necessary in the interests of justice for the trial to be terminated, he must terminate the trial.

(5) Where the judge terminates the trial under sub-section (4), he may make an order that any new trial which is to take place must be conducted without a jury if he is satisfied in respect of the new trial that both of the conditions set out in section 44 are likely to be fulfilled.

  . . .

Section 47 of the 2003 Act makes provision for an appeal to the Court of Appeal against an order under s 46(3) or (5). However, under s 47(2), such an appeal may be brought only with the leave of the trial judge or the Court of Appeal.

12.25.5 Giving of reasons for convicting a defendant following a judge-only trial

In an attempt to allay fears about potential unfairness in a trial by judge alone, s 48(5)(a) requires the judge to give reasons for convicting the defendant. It provides that where a trial is conducted or continued without a jury and the court convicts a defendant, 'the court must give a judgment which states the reasons for the conviction at, or as soon as reasonably practicable after, the time of the conviction'. Under sub-s (b), the time limit for lodging an appeal against conviction does not start to run until that judgment has been given.

12.25.6 Are jurors competent to try fraud cases?

The basis of the recommendation by Lord Justice Auld, in the *Review of the Criminal Courts of England and Wales* (and that of the Fraud Trials Committee Report (1986)), was essentially that jurors are ill-equipped to understand the evidence in such cases, and it is very difficult to find jurors who cannot validly seek excusal from sitting on a trial lasting several months (in para 183 of Chapter 5, Lord Justice Auld quotes the Director of the Serious Fraud Office as saying that in fraud trials lasting upwards of six months, the jury consists largely of 'the unemployed and the unemployable').

Some would argue that rather than removing the right to trial by jury in complex cases, efforts should be made to find ways of presenting complex cases to jurors in a way that they will be able to comprehend. This may be something of a counsel of perfection. However, jury comprehension is not the only issue: given the length of the trial that is necessary to deal with a very complex case, many of those who are summoned for jury service will have valid reasons to seek excusal from trying such a case (because of family and/or work commitments). This means that juries in such cases tend to be drawn exclusively from those people with time on their hands, thus subverting the randomness which is supposed to be a feature of the system of trial by jury.

In 'Trying fraud cases without juries' [2002] Crim LR 282, David Corker argues that the safeguards suggested by Auld were inadequate. He argues that the 'interests of justice' and 'complexity' tests are too vague (leaving what he calls 'undue and excessive scope for subjective and relativist judicial decision-making'); and that the right of appeal to the Court of Appeal will be 'emasculated' by the fact that the Court of Appeal will probably be reluctant to interfere with the exercise of the trial judge's discretion. He goes on to argue that:

> The absence of the jury combined with the new role of trier of fact will inevitably cause the judge to play a far greater role. His/her position of judge both of law and fact, likely long experience of trials and ability to explore issues of fact with witnesses must place the judge in a position of near-dominance in the courtroom . . . The enhanced role of the judge is . . . likely to have implications upon adversarial protections for the defence. If for example the judge will be free to open up new lines of inquiry not known in advance to the defence, to cross-examine witnesses and generally act more like a coroner than a judge this must surely entail that there must be far greater interaction, if not challenge, between judge and counsel than at present . . . It is submitted that whatever the consequences of a non-jury trial, the character of the trial will be significantly changed. The vacuum left behind by the jury will be filled somehow by an active and dominant judge.

He also considers the requirement that the judge must produce a judgment explaining why the defendant has been convicted. He writes:

> This requirement . . . has perhaps been commonly regarded as the most important safeguard ensuring a fair conviction. The assumption is that whatever prejudicial evidence the tribunal has heard, the eventual judgment will be untainted because of the need to justify it on the basis of the admissible evidence with detailed reasoning. Thus if error or prejudice has crept in, this will be exposed upon scrutiny of the judgment leading to a successful appeal . . . Two

issues arise in consequence. First the workload of the Crown Court judiciary ... will be substantially increased. The intellectual feat of writing an inevitably lengthy and detailed judgment should not be underestimated and trial judges may need a considerable period of time away from the courtroom to accomplish this. Secondly it is also inevitable that there will be an increased number of appeals by those convicted. In a complex case it would be rare for them not to find some inaccuracy or infelicity in the written judgment about which to appeal. The Court of Appeal, already overworked, will be awarded a burdensome new source of business.

S Wooler, in *Review of the Investigation and Criminal Proceedings Relating to the Jubilee Line Case (HM Crown Prosecution Service Inspectorate)* (June 2006: <http://www. attorneygeneral.gov.uk/attachments/JubileeLineRep_pt_1.pdf>) reviews the experience of the jurors in a lengthy and complex case that involved charges of corruption and conspiracy to defraud in relation to contracts for major construction work extending London Underground's Jubilee Line in the 1990s. The trial collapsed in March 2005 after the case had been running for some 21 months. Wooler interviewed 11 of the jurors after the collapse of the trial. He notes (at para 11.7) that:

Taken as a whole they did not appear to have had difficulty understanding the evidence or the essentials of the case presented to them. Most of them insisted they had a good or very good grasp of what the case was about from the prosecution opening onwards; that they understood very well the charges and the different combinations of defendants and counts; and that when the case collapsed they had a clear understanding of the evidence. During a group interview in early August 2005 they showed quite impressive familiarity with the charges, issues and evidence, despite the length of time that had elapsed, and the fact that they did not have their notes or access to documents nor an opportunity to think back and refresh their memories. They recalled particular parts of the evidence, particular witnesses and the substance of their evidence. They recalled the different counts ... Occasionally, there were individual failures of recollection, but one advantage of the jury system is that not all jurors are likely to have forgotten the same piece of evidence, if it is of any importance.

Wooler's report is discussed by Sally Lloyd-Bostock, 'The Jubilee Line Jurors: does their experience strengthen the argument for judge-only trial in long and complex fraud cases?' [2007] Crim LR 255. She points out that juror comprehension did not appear to be a problem and concludes that the problem with that particular case was not the jury's ability to cope, but the unnecessarily excessive length of the case.

Robert F Julian (a Justice of the New York State Supreme Court) in 'Judicial perspectives on the conduct of serious fraud trials' [2007] Crim LR 751 describes the results of interviews with nine judges who had extensive experience of presiding over serious fraud trials. None of the judges expressed support for judge-only trials in serious fraud cases:

Permeating every interview was the strong belief expressed by each of the judges that trial by jury was entirely appropriate in serious fraud cases and that trial by judge should not replace trial by jury. The judges unanimously voiced their faith in, and commitment to, the jury system. The common rationale of the judges interviewed was that juries were usually able to understand a complex fraud case upon the completion of the trial, explaining that usually the complexity of a serious fraud case gradually evaporates as the trial progresses when the proof is competently and carefully presented. They further suggest that a longer trial can sometimes give jurors a greater understanding of the facts. Finally each judge expressed a very high rate of agreement with jury verdicts in the cases they have presided over.

12.25.7 Trial by judge following trial by jury on sample counts

Section 17 of the Domestic Violence, Crime and Victims Act 2004 (in force from January 2007) makes further provision for Crown Court trial without a jury, building on the provisions contained in the Criminal Justice Act 2003. Section 17(1) enables the prosecution to apply to a Crown Court judge for an order that some, but not all, of the counts included in the indictment should be tried without a jury. Under s 17(2), the judge may make such an order if the conditions set out in sub-ss (3)–(5) are satisfied, namely:

(3)   The first condition is that the number of counts included in the indictment is likely to mean that a trial by jury involving all of those counts would be impracticable.

(4)   The second condition is that, if an order under sub-section (2) were made, each count or group of counts which would accordingly be tried with a jury can be regarded as a sample of counts which could accordingly be tried without a jury.

(5)   The third condition is that it is in the interests of justice for an order under sub-section (2) to be made.

Section 17(6) stipulates that the judge 'must have regard to any steps which might reasonably be taken to facilitate a trial by jury' but, under sub-s (7), 'a step is not to be regarded as reasonable if it could lead to the possibility of a defendant in the trial receiving a lesser sentence than would be the case if that step were not taken'.

Section 19(1) sets out the effect of an order under s 17(2). Where an order is made under s 17(2) and the defendant is found guilty by a jury on a count which may be regarded as a sample of other counts to be tried in those proceedings, those other counts may then be tried without a jury (i.e. by a judge alone). Under s 19(4), where the trial of a count is conducted without a jury by virtue of s 17(2) and the court convicts the defendant, the court must give a judgment stating the reasons for the conviction at, or as soon as reasonably practicable after, the time of the conviction, and the time limit for lodging an appeal against conviction does not start to run until that judgment has been given.

Section 18 requires that applications under s 17 must be determined at a preparatory hearing (under s 29 of the Criminal Procedure and Investigations Act 1996). Section 18(4) requires that the parties to the preparatory hearing must be given an opportunity to make representations with respect to the application. Section 18(5) makes provision for appeal to the Court of Appeal from the decision of the judge in respect of an application under s 17.

12.25.8 Research in how juries reach their verdicts

In 'Summing up to juries in criminal cases: what jury research says about current rules and practice' [2003] Crim LR 665, William Young notes some of the research that has been done about how juries reach their verdicts. He suggests that reluctance to countenance research into real juries (as opposed to research using mock juries or shadow juries) might be explicable on the basis of concern about what such research might reveal. However, his verdict on the system suggests that these fears are unfounded. He says that:

> Overall, the research . . . suggests that the strength of the jury system lies in the collective understanding, recall and diligence of the jury as a whole and that in most (but not all) cases, inadequacy, misunderstanding, predisposition, or prejudice on the part of individual jurors do not adversely impact on the ultimate determination.

However, he does not suggest that the system is perfect. He says:

> Plainly there are imperfections in the system. A significant proportion of acquittals and a much smaller proportion of convictions are highly suspect. A perverse verdict may result from a jury consciously setting out to decide the case outside the legal framework identified by the judge. Sometimes the random nature of jury selection produces a jury without sufficient unprejudiced and competent jurors to ensure that a rational approach is taken. Occasionally, the complexity of a case is beyond the collective competence of the jury. These risks are inherent in the jury system. But a wayward verdict is perhaps more likely to result from the jury misunderstanding either the law or the evidence. It follows that if such misunderstandings can be avoided, the likelihood of perverse verdicts is much reduced.

In 'What can we learn from published jury research? Findings for the criminal courts review' [2001] Crim LR 969, Penny Darbyshire considers the question whether s 8 of the Contempt of Court Act 1981 should be repealed, so as to enable research to be carried out amongst jurors. She begins by considering the composition of juries. She found that:

> The new central summoning system for jurors has not solved the problem of a high avoidance and excusal rate. In London in 2000, the [Jury Summoning Central] Bureau found they had to summon six times as many jurors as needed and four times as many elsewhere in England and Wales. We found if jurors ignore their summons and reminder letter, many Crown Court centres will take no steps to pursue a non-respondent.

She notes that:

> Research in England and Wales, California and New Zealand found that the causes for high excusal and avoidance rates are problems with childcare, family commitments, employment problems and potential lost income.

She also notes that some people escape from the pool of potential jurors. She comments that:

... selection from the electoral roll is a flawed system. Research as long ago as the 1960s, in the USA, showed electoral lists are not representative of communities and this has since been confirmed in Australia and New Zealand. This is caused by factors such as population mobility and residential status, which are linked to class and income levels. Census data in England and Wales show non-registration to be high among ethnic minorities, the 20–24 age group and renters. Also, it is well known that non-registration may be an attempt to evade council tax. As long ago as 1968, Federal US legislation required supplementary source lists, such as drivers' licence and public utility lists to be used to correct this unrepresentativeness. Most research shows that merging electoral rolls with other lists increases the proportion of young people and non-whites in jury pools.

On the decision-making process, Darbyshire notes that:

... there is much sophisticated research on jury instruction in the United States. Virtually every involved researcher agrees that juries have a great deal of difficulty in understanding instructions, even though research shows that most juries conscientiously try to follow them ... Improvements in comprehension have been achieved experimentally in the United States, by reorganising instructions, reducing sentence length and complexity, avoiding jargon and uncommon words and using concrete rather than abstract concepts ... It is well known that audible information is lost soon after receipt. Written instructions do not reduce deliberation time but they result in better comprehension, retention and application. They make jurors more satisfied and efficient and they participate in higher quality deliberations. American researchers have suggested a juror notebook with witness photos, key documentation and a written instruction. Similar conclusions have been reached in recent New Zealand research on real jurors, who found a written summary of the law useful. We encountered English circuit judges who have given word-processed instructions to juries for some years. The pros and cons of pre-instruction have been analysed. Most writers appear to conclude in favour of pre-instruction, which confirms accounts of real jurors in England and Wales that it is illogical and confusing to receive a mass of verbal information (the trial evidence) and then be verbally instructed on the decisions the group has to reach on that information. Judges were less surprised by and more satisfied with the verdicts of pre-instructed juries (in American experiments with real juries) and tend to favour their use, finding no difficulty and no extra burden in preparing them.

Accordingly, she recommends that:

Juries should be given written as well as verbal instructions on the law after the trial. These should be drafted by the judge and agreed by counsel and explained verbally by the judge. Where possible, juries should be given a pre-trial summary of the issues. Certain basic instructions, such as on burden and quantum of proof could be written into the juror's introductory pamphlet and pinned, as reminders, onto the walls of the jury room.

In a similar vein, Young (in the article mentioned at the beginning of this section) concludes that:

If some of the rules which have developed around the way judges sum up are underpinned by unnecessarily gloomy views of juror competence, many practical aspects of the criminal trial process rest on unrealistically high assessments of juries' powers of analysis, comprehension and recall. Jurors are unlikely to have had experience in breaking down complex factual controversies into issues of manageable size. If there are a number of such issues, they will struggle to match these issues to the relevant evidence. Limits to their collective powers of comprehension and recall will be most apparent in lengthy or complex cases. All of this requires inputs from the judge. This should be in language that is appropriate to the occasion – simple concrete language firmly tied to the facts of the case at hand. At the start of the trial, jurors should be told what is truly in issue. In the summing up, if not before, the judge should marshal the evidence around those questions. In cases of any length, the oral process of the criminal trial process requires some written supplementation if jurors are to recall enough of the evidence and the summing up to be able to deliberate efficiently and to reach verdicts on the evidence and in accordance with the law.

The point is reiterated by Nic Madge, in 'Summing up – a judge's perspective' [2006] Crim LR 817. He notes that his own practice of handing out written directions to the jury seems to have almost eliminated requests from juries for reminders or further guidance on the law. Moreover, juries also seem to be reaching verdicts more quickly. He also notes that there has also been an increase in the proportion of convictions. The latter effect might be explicable on the basis that uncertainty and confusion about the legal directions that the judge gave in the summing up may lead to doubt and so to acquittals.

An important issue is whether the jurors understand the direction that they receive from the judge on the standard of proof. Darbyshire (in the article mentioned above) noted that:

> Recent English research found that subjects thought the quantum of proof varied with the gravity of the offence. Most subjects instructed with the English instruction, including the word 'sure' equated BRD ['beyond reasonable doubt'] with an impossible 100 per cent proof and this was confirmed by very recent English research. A survey of American studies showed that the percentage proof at which jurors were prepared to convict varied from 51 to 92 per cent, very close to their interpretation of the balance of probabilities.

She concludes that:

> Juries have immense difficulty in understanding 'beyond reasonable doubt'. Depending on how it is interpreted by the judge, they may equate it with 51–100 per cent proof. Modern lay persons are used to evaluating probability in terms of percentages. English research findings confirm real jurors' accounts that when judges use the word 'sure', some or even the majority of jurors will equate BRD with absolute proof. On the other hand, with different instructions, jurors may equate BRD with the balance of probabilities. It may be thought desirable to describe BRD in percentage proof terms. In any event, the word 'sure' should be eliminated from the BRD direction.

Young raises the same issue. He notes that:

In Professor JW Montgomery's study (The Criminal Standard of Proof (1998) 148 NLJ 582), 73.5 per cent of those surveyed took the 'satisfied so that you are sure' formula to require 100 per cent confidence of guilt.

Professor Michael Zander carried out a broadly similar study ('The criminal standard of proof' (2000) 150 NLJ 1517). In that study, the formula used was 'Only convict if the prosecution have made you sure of the defendant's guilt [which is the same as proving the case beyond reasonable doubt]'. Half of those surveyed received the words included in square brackets and the other half did not. Just over half the respondents regarded the direction (in both forms) as requiring 100 per cent certainty. Young suggests that:

> The difference between that figure and the corresponding figure of 73.5 per cent in Professor Montgomery's survey may suggest that the formula that Professor Zander used (in both its iterations) is less stringent than the 'satisfied so that you are sure' formula used by Professor Montgomery.

This is a rather worrying conclusion, since a number of judges seem to use 'sure' and 'satisfied so you are sure' interchangeably.

A Research Study carried out in 2001 for the Home Office by Matthews, Hancock and Briggs, *Jurors' perceptions, understanding, confidence and satisfaction in the jury system: a study in six courts*, discovered that the main impediment to understanding proceedings was the use of legal terminology. There was also confusion about whether or not they should take notes during a trial or whether it was appropriate to ask questions. Jurors also felt that evidence was not always presented in the clearest ways and that maps, diagrams, photographs and other visual aids were under-used in courts. So far as jurors being encouraged to take notes is concerned, Darbyshire (above) suggests that, in fact, this would be disadvantageous, as it is more difficult to concentrate on observing witnesses if one is taking notes.

Nic Madge (in the article mentioned above) also suggests that judges should be discouraged from commenting on the evidence, given that when it comes to the facts, it is the jurors' judgment alone that counts. He points out that in the majority of American state jurisdictions it is the duty of the trial judge to abstain from any expression of opinion or comment on the facts or evidence. He argues that this 'no-judge-comment' rule is designed to safeguard the role of the jury as the sole judge of the facts on the issue of guilt or innocence.

In his *Review of the Criminal Courts in England and Wales*, Lord Justice Auld made several recommendations aimed at making the task of the juror more manageable. He recommends that jurors should receive more assistance to help them understand what is going on. Recommendation 235 is as follows:

> In all cases tried by judge and jury:
>
> 1   each juror should be provided at the start of the trial with a copy of the charge or charges;
> 2   the judge at the start of the trial should address the jury, introducing them generally to their task as jurors and giving them an objective outline of the case and the questions they are there to decide;

3   the judge should supplement his opening address with, and provide a copy to each juror of, a written case and issues summary prepared by the parties' advocates and approved by him;

4   the judge, in the course of his introductory address, and the case and issues summary, should identify:

(a)   the nature of the charges;

(b)   as part of a brief narrative, the evidence agreed, reflecting the admissions of either side at the appropriate point in the story;

(c)   also as part of the narrative, the matters of fact in issue; and

(d)   with no, or minimal, reference to the law, a list of likely questions for their decision.

Thus, the judge, by reference to a case and issues summary produced by the parties, would give the jury a fuller introduction to the case than is now conventional. Given the fact that the issues can change during the course of a trial, Recommendation 236 is that:

> If and to the extent that the issues narrow or widen in the course of the trial, the case and issues summary should be amended and fresh copies provided to the judge and jury.

Recommendation 238 concerns the role of defence counsel in setting the scene for the jury. It states that:

> I endorse the Runciman Royal Commission's recommendation that a defence advocate should be entitled to make a short opening speech to the jury immediately after that of the prosecution advocate, but normally of no more than a few minutes.

Recommendation 240 makes it clear that:

> . . . a defence advocate who makes a short opening speech after the prosecution opening should not, thereby, forfeit his right to make an opening speech at the beginning of the defence case.

In his *Review*, Lord Justice Auld took the view (Recommendation 241) that defence counsel should always have the right to make an opening speech:

> A defence advocate's entitlement to make an opening speech at the start of the defence case should no longer depend on whether he intends to call a witness as to fact other than the defendant.

To give further assistance to the jury, the *Auld Review* recommends as follows:

> 242   At the close of evidence and before speeches, the judge and advocates, in the absence of the jury, should finally review the case and issues summary and, if necessary, amend it for the jury.

> . . .

244 If, and to the extent that, the law and professional codes of conduct do not require a defending, as well as a prosecuting, advocate to seek to correct a judge's error of law or of material fact of which he becomes aware, both the law and the codes should be changed to require it.

The *Auld Review* also looks at the role of the summing up in helping the jury with their task. The Recommendations are:

245 Consideration should be given to . . . a requirement that a judge should use a case and issues summary and any other written or visual aid provided to a jury, as an integral part of his summing-up, referring to the points in them, one by one, as he deals with them orally.

246 Courts should equip judges with, and in cases meriting it they should consider using, other visual aids to their summings-up, such as PowerPoint and evolving forms of presentational soft-ware.

247 So far as possible, the judge should not direct the jury on the law, save by implication in the questions of fact that he puts to them for decision.

248 The judge should continue to remind the jury of the issues and, save in the most simple cases, the evidence relevant to them, and should always give the jury an adequate account of the defence; but he should do it in more summary form than is now common.

249 The judge should devise and put to the jury a series of written factual questions, the answers to which could logically lead only to a verdict of guilty or not guilty; the questions should correspond with those in the updated case and issues summary, supplemented as necessary in a separate written list prepared for the purpose; and each question should be tailored to the law as the judge knows it to be and to the issues and evidence in the case.

250 The judge, where he considers it appropriate, should be permitted to require a jury to answer publicly each of his questions and to declare a verdict in accordance with those answers.

Thus, Lord Justice Auld suggests that in the summing up the judge should make use of the written case and issues summary, and should try, so far as possible, to 'filter out' the law and devise factual questions (tailored by the legal, evidential and factual issues in the case). Where he considers it appropriate, the judge should require the jury publicly to answer each of the questions and to declare a verdict in accordance with those answers. These proposals would perhaps have made the task of the jury a little easier (and the requirement to answer a series of questions, as well as delivering a verdict on guilt or innocence, might answer the point made by some that the right to a fair trial should require juries to give reasons for their verdict). However, the Criminal Justice Act 2003 did not enact these suggestions.

12.25.9 The Jury Diversity Project

A major piece of research was conducted by Cheryl Thomas and Nigel Balmer: *Diversity and Fairness in the Jury System* (Ministry of Justice Research Series 2/07,

June 2007): <http://www.justice.gov.uk/publications/research130607.htm>. A key aspect was the Jury Diversity Project, which was based on continuing concerns about the under-representation of ethnic minorities on juries in this country. It addressed two key questions: how representative of the local community are those summoned for jury service and those serving as jurors in England and Wales; and does ethnicity affect jury decision-making? The research used case simulation with real jurors, along with a study of jury verdicts in real cases.

A key finding of the Jury Diversity Project is that most current thinking about jury service in this country is based on myth, not reality. The report found that there was no significant under-representation of black and minority ethnic (BME) groups among those summoned for jury service; that ethnic minorities are summoned in proportion to their representation in the local population (in almost all courts – 81 of the 84 surveyed – there was no significant difference between the proportion of BME jurors serving and the BME population levels in the local juror catchment area for each court); that the main factor affecting non-responses to summonses is high residential mobility, not ethnicity (a survey conducted for the project found no significant differences between BME and White respondents in their willingness to do jury service or support for the jury system, which was high for both groups).

The study found that the most significant factors predicting whether a summoned juror will actually serve on a jury are income and employment status, not ethnicity: summoned jurors in lower income brackets and those who are economically inactive are far less likely to serve than those in medium to high income brackets and those who are employed. The study found no indication that the middle classes or the important and clever in society avoid jury service. Instead, it established that the highest rates of jury service are among middle to high-income earners and that those in higher status professions are fully represented among serving jurors. The employed are over-represented among serving jurors, and the retired and unemployed are in fact under-represented.

The study also established that jury pools at individual courts closely reflect the local population in terms of gender and age, and the self-employed are represented among serving jurors in direct proportion to their representation in the population.

In 2005, 85 per cent of those summoned replied to their summonses. Of all those who replied their summonses, 64 per cent of jurors served, nine per cent were disqualified or ineligible, 27 per cent were excused. Of those excused, most were for medical reasons that prevented serving (34 per cent), or child care (15 per cent) and work reasons (12 per cent). Fifteen per cent of all the summonses in the survey were either returned to the JCSB as undeliverable (five per cent) or not responded to (ten per cent), which occurred most often in areas of high residential mobility. Where ethnic minorities did not serve, this was primarily due to ineligibility or disqualification (residency or language).

Surveys conducted both before and after the changes to juror eligibility in the Criminal Justice Act 2003 came into effect in 2004 showed that the new rules increased the proportion of those summoned that served from 54 per cent to 64 per cent. Those serving on the date summoned increased by a third, disqualifications fell by a third and excusals fell by a quarter. These changes did not affect any single socio-economic group, with one exception (the proportion of serving jurors aged 65 to 69 doubled from three per cent in 2003 to six per cent in 2005, after their right of excusal was removed).

The report noted that the final stage of jury selection (empanelling) is the only stage that does not involve computerised random selection of jurors. It noted that there was some evidence that BME jurors on jury panels appeared to be selected to serve on juries less often than White jurors on jury panels, which may be the result of court clerks inadvertently avoiding reading out juror names that are difficult to pronounce.

The study determined that racially mixed juries are only likely to exist in courts where BME groups make up at least ten per cent of the entire juror catchment area. The report concluded that this does not reflect any failure in summoning. It is simply the consequence of BME population levels in these catchment areas and the process of random selection.

The report also noted that whilst the proportion of BME people summoned for jury service and serving on juries was more or less in accordance with the ethnic mix of the court's catchment area as a whole, within that catchment area there may be areas with a high BME population concentrated in particular places. In these courts, there is likely to be a public expectation that juries will be racially mixed, even though summoning will not usually produce this. This may be particularly problematic because a high proportion of BME defendants and racially-aggravated crimes are prosecuted at some of these courts.

Concern about the possible under-representation of ethnic minorities on juries assumes that the ethnic composition of juries can affect jury outcomes. The research included case simulation that was done in as authentic a way as possible (based on a real case, using a real courtroom, with a real judge, barristers, court staff, police and witnesses; real jurors were the study participants, with jury panels being selected by the Court Service random selection programme and jurors deliberating in a real deliberating room). The main finding of the case simulation study was that the verdicts of racially mixed juries did not discriminate against defendants based on the defendant's race. The outcomes for the White, Black and Asian defendants were remarkably similar.

The writers concluded that this study provided the first evidence to support the widely held belief that racially mixed juries do not discriminate against defendants based on the defendant's ethnic background (the assumption had been that racially mixed juries will not discriminate against ethnic minority defendants, but this study showed that racially mixed juries also did not discriminate against White defendants).

Even though the defendant's ethnicity did not have an impact on jury verdicts, the research did find that in certain cases ethnicity did have a significant impact on the individual votes of some jurors who sat on these juries. Statistical analysis of the individual votes of the jurors who took part in the case simulation showed that, in certain cases, BME jurors were significantly less likely to vote to convict a BME defendant than a White defendant. The study also found that 'same race leniency' among BME jurors was only present when race was not an explicit element of the case; when the offence was prosecuted on the basis that it had been racially-aggravated, BME jurors and White jurors had similar conviction rates for both the White and BME defendants. The report suggests that 'same race leniency' among BME jurors appeared to reflect their belief that the courts treat ethnic minority defendants more harshly than White defendants.

The study found that same race leniency did not occur among all BME jurors for all BME defendants: both Black and Asian jurors showed leniency for the Black defendant, but there was no evidence of leniency for the Asian defendant by either Asian or Black jurors. There was evidence that White jurors showed some same race leniency towards White defendants, but only in cases where race was not an explicit element of the case.

The report noted the benefits of permitting majority verdicts and of having 12-member juries. The fact that 12 jurors must try to reach a joint decision and that majority verdicts are possible meant that more verdicts are achieved and individual biases do not dictate the decision-making of racially mixed juries. The report argued that, if juries were smaller or if unanimous verdicts were required, then individual juror bias might potentially have a greater impact on jury verdicts.

The report also noted that the main effect of deliberating on the verdict was to increase the proportion of jurors who felt completely confident in their votes. The analysis also showed that the probability of a BME juror voting to convict a White defendant fell following deliberation, suggesting that the process of deliberating on racially mixed juries may influence the decision-making of ethnic minority jurors. Analysis of individual juror votes also indicated that White jurors on these racially mixed juries were sensitive to the plight of a Black victim. White jurors were most likely to convict a defendant when the victim was Black and defendant was White or Asian (but not when the defendant was Black).

The analysis of jury verdicts in actual trials at different courts showed that there are likely to be court-based differences in jury verdicts: some courts had comparatively low conviction rates and others comparatively high conviction rates, regardless of the jury's racial composition.

The study was based on ethnically mixed juries and the conclusion points out that what remains to be answered is whether all-White juries, which decide cases in most Crown Courts, also do not discriminate against defendants based on race.

This Report is summarised by Cheryl Thomas in 'Exposing the myths of jury service' [2008] Crim LR 415. She concludes that article by saying:

> For too many years myths about jury service have clouded perceptions and policy debates about the jury system. It can serve no purpose for jurors, court users or the legal profession to mistakenly believe that jurors are unrepresentative and are not important or clever enough to avoid serving. It is now clear that serving jurors closely reflect the diversity of their local communities and that there is no widespread avoidance of jury service by the public in England and Wales. This was true even before the recent introduction of new juror eligibility rules, which have nonetheless increased participation in the jury system. The research also provides evidence to support the Lord Chief Justice's call to trust in the common sense of the jury. Despite the fact that some jurors did show bias towards defendants based on race, the verdicts of the juries on which these jurors sat did not discriminate against defendants based on race. By laying to rest a number of long-standing myths about juries and exploring how juries make decisions, this research has also highlighted how valuable empirical research on juries can be and just how much jury research can be conducted in this country within existing legal restrictions.

Chapter 13

Appeals to the Court of Appeal

13.1 INTRODUCTION

Appeal against conviction and/or sentence lies from the Crown Court to the Court of Appeal (Criminal Division). In this chapter, we look at the procedure for appealing against conviction and/or sentence following trial on indictment and at the criteria applied by the Court of Appeal when disposing of such appeals.

Criminal appeals are governed by:

- the Criminal Appeal Act 1968;
- Parts 65–70 of the Criminal Procedure Rules; and
- Part II of the Consolidated Practice Direction.

There is also very helpful information in 'A guide to the proceedings of the Court of Appeal Criminal Division' (1997), available online at <http://www.hmcourts-service.gov.uk/docs/proc_guide.pdf>.

13.2 THE COURT OF APPEAL

The constitution of the Court of Appeal (Criminal Division) is governed by the Supreme Court Act 1981. The court is presided over by the Lord Chief Justice of England (although, of course, he will not hear every appeal). It comprises Lords Justices of Appeal, together with High Court judges whom the Lord Chief Justice has asked to assist with the work of the Court of Appeal (ss 2, 3 and 9 of the Supreme Court Act 1981).

The number of judges required for a sitting of the Court of Appeal is governed by s 55 of the Supreme Court Act 1981:

- when determining an appeal against conviction, the Court of Appeal must comprise at least three judges; one or more of the judges must be a Lord Justice of Appeal. The decision is by majority (the presiding judge does not have a casting vote). Usually, only one judgment will be delivered;
- when determining an appeal against sentence, the Court of Appeal may consist of only two judges, but again one of them should be a Lord Justice of Appeal. Should an appeal be heard by a two-judge court (again, one would have to be a Lord

Justice of Appeal) and the two judges disagree, the appeal will be re-heard by a three-judge court.

We shall see later that some of the powers of the Court of Appeal may be exercised by a single judge (for example, the granting of leave to appeal). The single judge may be a Lord Justice of Appeal or else a High Court judge whom the Lord Chief Justice has asked to assist with the work of the Court of Appeal.

Certain Circuit judges may be approved by the Lord Chancellor to sit in the Court of Appeal (Criminal Division). A sitting of the court must not include more than one Circuit judge (s 55(6)), and a Circuit judge is not permitted to exercise the powers of the single judge. Following the repeal of s 56A of the 1981 Act by s 67 of the Courts Act 2003, the selected Circuit judges who sit in the Court of Appeal are permitted to hear any appeal against conviction and/or sentence, even if the judge who presided at the trial, or passed the sentence, was a High Court judge.

The administrative work of the court is carried out by the Registrar of Criminal Appeals.

Recommendation 314 of Lord Justice Auld's *Review of the Criminal Courts of England and Wales* considers the composition of the Court of Appeal and would require amendment of s 55 of the 1981 Act. It includes the following:

> 314.2 In straightforward appeals against conviction, or in respect of short sentences where the law and procedures are clear and the only issue is whether the trial judge has correctly followed them, or where the issue turns on his treatment of the facts, the Court should consist of two High Court Judges or one High Court Judge and one Circuit Judge; and
>
> 314.3 Consideration should be given to introducing a system under which, in cases of exceptional legal importance and complexity, a distinguished academic could either be appointed ad hoc to act as a judge of the Court or be invited to submit a written brief to the Court on the point(s) in issue.

J R Spencer, in 'Does our present criminal appeal system make sense?' [2006] Crim LR 677 (a wide-ranging critique of the current system of appeals both from magistrates' courts and the Crown Court) comments on this proposal as follows:

> A better way to reform the system of criminal appeals would be to set up regional Courts of Appeal for criminal cases, which would handle all appeals against sentences imposed in the Crown Court, except for the small minority that involve points of legal principle, and which would also deal with the simpler appeals against conviction. They could be staffed, I believe, by senior circuit judges – possibly presided over by a High Court judge. Such a court, I believe, would be well able to cope with the type of work that would be sent to it. The Court of Appeal (Criminal Division) in London would then sit to deal with the most difficult and important cases only: so relieving the senior and experienced judges who sit in it of a mass of relatively routine work, so enabling them to devote their time to work that is worthy of their talents.

13.3 APPEAL AGAINST CONVICTION: PROCEDURE

13.3.1 The need for leave to appeal

Under s 1(2) of the Criminal Appeal Act 1968 (as amended by the Criminal Appeal Act 1995), an appeal against conviction may only be made if either:

a   the Court of Appeal gives leave to appeal (s 1(2)(a)); or
b   the trial judge certifies that the case is 'fit for appeal' (s 1(2)(b)).

Certificates from the trial judge are very rare and are only granted if the case has raised a point of law where there is no authority giving an answer or where there are conflicting decisions of the Court of Appeal. In *R v Inskip* [2005] EWCA Crim 3372 (following *R v Bansal* [1999] Crim LR 484), it was emphasised such certificates should be granted only in exceptional cases. The normal rule is that it should be left to the Court of Appeal to decide whether a case is suitable for the grant of leave to appeal (per Richards LJ at para 28). It follows that it is not enough that the trial judge simply disagrees with the verdict, and so leave to appeal is required in almost every case.

Again, in *R v Harries* [2007] EWCA Crim 820, Scott Baker LJ (at para 4) said:

> It is only in exceptional circumstances that appeals come before this court by way of certificate from the trial judge rather than through the ordinary process of leave being granted by members of this court. A certificate would ordinarily be granted if there was a very clear reason for doing so, such as an unresolved issue of law or where there were clear reasons for supposing that the appeal was likely to succeed.

It should be noted that although Art 6 of the European Convention on Human Rights does not necessarily require there to be a possibility of appeal against conviction or sentence, where there is a mechanism for appeal, any appellate proceedings will be treated as an extension of the trial process and so will be subject to the requirements of Art 6 of the Convention, which guarantees the right to a fair trial. It should also be borne in mind that, for the purposes of the European Convention on Human Rights, unfairness at first instance can be remedied by an effective appellate process (*Adolf v Austria* (1982) 4 EHRR 313).

13.3.2 Appeal against conviction where the defendant has pleaded guilty

A defendant who pleads guilty in the magistrates' court cannot appeal against conviction to the Crown Court if he pleaded guilty (see s 108 of the Magistrates' Courts Act 1980). There is no such rule in the Criminal Appeal Act 1968. However, the Court of Appeal is very unwilling to give leave to appeal against conviction to a defendant who pleaded guilty in the Crown Court. In *R v Forde* [1923] 2 KB 400, Avory J said (at p 403):

> A plea of Guilty having been recorded, this Court can only entertain an appeal against conviction if it appears (1) that the appellant did not appreciate the nature of the charge or

did not intend to admit he was guilty of it, or (2) that upon the admitted facts he could not in law have been convicted of the offence charged.

Nonetheless, there have been several cases where a defendant who has pleaded guilty has been allowed to appeal against conviction. For example, if a defendant is pressurised (for example, by comments from the judge) into pleading guilty, he will be allowed to appeal (*R v Turner* [1970] 2 QB 321). Similarly, in *R v Bane* [1994] Crim LR 134, the judge told counsel that he was not willing to leave the defence of self-defence to the jury. The defendant changed his plea to guilty. The conviction was quashed because of the pressure to plead guilty which was caused by the judge's refusal to allow the jury to consider Bane's defence. Similarly, in *R v Boal* [1992] QB 591, the defendant pleaded guilty because of erroneous legal advice by his counsel and so the Court of Appeal entertained his appeal against conviction. Another situation where the defendant might be able to appeal against conviction even though he pleaded guilty is where the plea of guilty was entered after the judge made an incorrect ruling on the law. In *R v Kenny* [1994] Crim LR 284, for example, the defendant (who was mentally handicapped) changed his plea to guilty following a decision by the trial judge that a confession (the only evidence against him) was admissible.

In *R v Eriemo* [1995] 2 Cr App R 206, the Court of Appeal reaffirmed its reluctance to entertain appeals where the defendant pleaded guilty. In that case, the applicant (who had changed his plea to guilty following the trial judge's refusal to sever the indictment on the basis that the applicant was going to allege that he committed the offence under the duress of the co-defendant) was refused leave to appeal. It was said by Glidewell LJ (at p 210) that where a defendant pleads guilty, he is making an admission of the facts which form the basis of the offence with which he is charged and therefore loses his right to appeal against conviction.

Similarly, in *R v Greene* [1997] Crim LR 659, the Court of Appeal took a tough line. The defendant had changed his plea to guilty following the rejection by the trial judge of a submission that the confession should be excluded under s 78 of the Police and Criminal Evidence Act 1984. The Court of Appeal said that his plea of guilty was an acknowledgment of the truth of the confession and the commission of the offence. The court said that had the defendant maintained his plea of not guilty and been convicted, he could then have complained on appeal about the judge's ruling under s 78.

In *R v Chalkley* [1998] QB 848, the Court of Appeal returned to the question of whether a defendant who pleads guilty in the Crown Court can appeal against conviction to the Court of Appeal. The defendants had originally pleaded not guilty, but the judge ruled that certain evidence against them (covertly obtained tape-recordings of conversations) was admissible; the defendants then changed their pleas to guilty. It was held that the Court of Appeal may quash a conviction based on a guilty plea 'where the plea was mistaken or without intention to admit the truth of the offence charged'. Furthermore, Auld LJ said (at p 864) that:

> a conviction would be unsafe where the effect of an incorrect ruling of law on admitted facts was to leave an accused with no legal escape from a verdict of guilty on those facts. But a conviction would not normally be unsafe where an accused is influenced to change his plea to guilty because he recognises that, as a result of a ruling to admit strong evidence against him, his case on the facts is hopeless. A change of plea to guilty in such circumstances would

normally be regarded as an acknowledgement of the truth of the facts constituting the offence charged.

In other words, a conviction would be unsafe where, on the basis of the erroneous ruling, an acquittal would be legally impossible (for example, where the judge rejects the defendant's submission that admitted facts do not in law amount to the offence charged, and so there is no issue of fact for the jury to try). In such a case, an appeal will be entertained despite the guilty plea. Otherwise (for example, where the defendant pleads guilty following an erroneous ruling to admit strong evidence against the defendant), the guilty plea amounts to an admission of the truth of the allegations made against the defendant, and so no appeal will be entertained.

In *R v Sales* [2000] 2 Cr App R 431, the Court of Appeal reiterated that because a plea of guilty is normally to be regarded as an acknowledgment of the truth of the facts constituting the offence charged, it can only be in a very rare case that a defendant who, either by his plea or in his evidence before the jury, has acknowledged that he did the criminal act on which the prosecution relies, can subsequently be heard to say in the Court of Appeal that his conviction was unsafe because he did not do the act relied on (per Rose LJ at p 436). However, such rare cases do occur. In *R v Early* [2002] EWCA Crim 1904; [2003] 1 Cr App R 288, it was held that where the prosecution have failed to make proper pre-trial disclosure and prosecution witnesses have lied to the court on a voir dire, and the defendant enters a plea of guilty on the assumption that full disclosure has been made, the Court of Appeal will set aside that guilty plea however strong the prosecution case might appear to be. Rose LJ (at p 295) said that freely entered pleas of guilty will not be interfered with by the Court of Appeal unless the prosecution's misconduct is of a category which justifies this. A plea of guilty is binding unless the defendant was ignorant of evidence going to innocence or guilt; ignorance of material which goes merely to credibility of a prosecution witness does not justify reopening a plea of guilty.

Furthermore, in *R v Togher* [2001] 1 Cr App R 33, it was held that the strict approach taken in *Chalkley* could not be applied to a situation where the appeal is based on alleged abuse of process and the defendants were unaware, when they pleaded guilty, of the matters relied upon in the appeal as amounting to the abuse of process. Lord Woolf CJ said (at para 33) that if the appellants can establish an abuse, the Court of Appeal will give very serious consideration to whether justice requires the conviction to be set aside; however, it has to be a situation where it would be inconsistent with the due administration of justice to allow the pleas of guilty to stand.

An example of an exceptional case, where an appeal was permitted despite a guilty plea, may be found in *R v Montague-Darlington* [2003] EWCA Crim 1542. The defendant had pleaded guilty to illegal importation of a Class A drug. Almost a year after the conviction, it came to light that the prosecution were in possession of certain information that would have been disclosable under the Criminal Procedure and Investigations Act 1996 (see Chapter 8) but which was highly sensitive and therefore likely to attract public interest immunity. The court held that the prosecution would have been obliged to disclose the material (in other words, the right of the defendant to a fair trial would have overridden the public interest immunity in withholding the material from the defence). The result would have been that the prosecution would have been dropped. The Court of Appeal reaffirmed that it will only consider an appeal against conviction following a guilty plea in rare cases. The court's task was to determine whether the appellant had had a fair trial. It was said to be difficult to see how she could have had a fair trial when she should not have been tried at all had the sensitive material been available at that stage. The conviction was therefore set aside.

In *R v Saik* [2004] EWCA Crim 2936; (2004) *The Times*, 29 November, Scott Baker LJ said (at para 57) that for an appeal against conviction to succeed on the basis that a guilty plea was tendered following erroneous advice, the facts must be so strong as to show that the plea of guilty was not a true acknowledgement of guilt. The advice, he said, must go to the heart of the plea, so that the plea would not be a free plea and what followed would be a nullity. His Lordship went on say that it is very difficult to see how erroneous advice as to the length of sentence could ever go to the heart of a plea – except perhaps where the maximum penalty for the offence is understated, since the decision on length of sentence lies with the judge or the Court of Appeal. This aspect of the decision is not affected by the successful appeal to the House of Lords [2006] UKHL 18; [2007] 1 AC 18.

13.3.3 Procedure for obtaining leave to appeal

A barrister (usually, but not necessarily, the one who conducted the case in the Crown Court) will be asked to write an advice on the merits of an appeal. If the barrister advises that an appeal is appropriate, draft grounds of appeal will be attached to the advice.

As a matter of professional conduct, counsel should only advise in favour of an appeal if there are proper grounds for doing so (*R v Morson* (1976) 62 Cr App R 236). Paragraph 2.4 of the Guide to the Proceedings of the Court of Appeal (Criminal Division) states that:

> Counsel should not settle or sign grounds unless they are reasonable, have some real prospect of success and are such that he is prepared to argue them before the Court.

In a similar vein, para II.15.1 of *Consolidated Practice Direction* states:

> Advocates should not settle grounds or support them with written advice unless they consider that they are properly arguable. Grounds should be carefully drafted and properly particularised. Advocates should not assume that the Court will entertain any ground of appeal not set out and properly particularised. Should leave to amend the grounds be granted it is most unlikely that further grounds will be entertained.

A notice of application for leave to appeal is then lodged at the Crown Court where the defendant was convicted (see r 68.2(1) of the Criminal Procedure Rules and para II.14.1 of the *Practice Direction*). The notice must identify each ground of appeal on which the appellant relies, concisely outlining each argument in support (r 68.3(2)(b) of the Criminal Procedure Rules). The Crown Court then passes the papers to the Criminal Appeal Office.

13.3.4 Time limit

The notice of application for leave to appeal against conviction (or, in those rare cases where the trial judge certified the case fit for appeal, the notice of appeal) must be lodged within 28 days of conviction (s 18(2) of the Criminal Appeal Act 1968). The text of s 18(2) is as follows:

> Notice of appeal, or of application for leave to appeal, shall be given within twenty-eight days from the date of the conviction, verdict or finding appealed against, or in the case of appeal against sentence, from the date on which sentence was passed or, in the case of an order made or treated as made on conviction, from the date of the making of the order.

In *R v Long* [1998] 2 Cr App R 326, the Court of Appeal pointed out that, under s 18(2), a notice of application for leave to appeal against conviction must be lodged within 28 days of conviction even if there is lapse of time between conviction and sentence. In other words, for an appeal against conviction, time begins to run from the date of conviction (and not from the date of sentence).

The time for giving notice under s 18 may be extended, either before or after it expires, by the Court of Appeal (s 18(3)). In *R v Hawkins* [1997] 1 Cr App R 234 at 239, it was noted that the Court of Appeal has 'traditionally been reluctant to do so save where the extension sought is relatively short and good reason is shown for the failure to apply in time'. It follows that the time limit will normally not be extended unless there is a 'very good' and 'exceptional reason' for doing so (*R v Burley* (1994) *The Times*, 9 November).

13.3.5 Transcript of evidence and summing up

The Registrar (when he receives the grounds of appeal) decides whether a transcript is necessary and, if so, how extensive it should be. Normally, the transcript is limited to the summing up and to any judgment given by the judge during the course of the trial. If counsel for the would-be appellant wants a more extensive transcript, reasons for this request must be given. A transcript of the evidence should only be sought if genuinely essential, as it is an expensive and time consuming procedure (*R v Flemming* (1987) 86 Cr App R 32). Similarly, para 3.3 of the *Guide* says that it is important that a transcript should only be requested if it is essential for the proper conduct of the appeal. The Registrar will normally decline to obtain a transcript he considers to have been requested without justification. Counsel who seek excessive quantities of transcript are likely to face criticism from the court.

13.3.6 'Perfecting' the grounds of appeal

The original advice and grounds of appeal will be based on counsel's notes taken at the time of the trial. It may be that these notes are not entirely accurate (for example, some of the judge's comments may have been omitted or noted down incorrectly). The transcript of the summing up is sent to counsel for the would-be appellant (free of charge if the appellant is publicly funded), who then has the chance to 'perfect' the grounds of appeal. Paragraph 4.2 of the *Guide* says that:

> The purpose of perfection is (a) to give counsel the opportunity to reconsider his original grounds in the light of the transcript and (b) to save valuable judicial time by enabling the judge or Court to identify at once the relevant parts of the transcript.

Paragraph 4.4. of the *Guide* goes on to say:

> Perfected grounds should consist of a fresh document which supersedes the original grounds of appeal and contains inter alia references by page number and letter to all relevant passages in the transcript. Authorities on which counsel relies should be cited, where possible in the Criminal Appeal Reports . . .

Thus, counsel should amend the original grounds of appeal so that they refer to specific passages of the transcript – for example, 'the learned trial judge erred in that at [specific page number] he . . .'. The grounds of appeal, or the advice on appeal written by counsel which accompanies the grounds, should also cite any authorities upon which counsel for the appellant proposes to rely.

Once the grounds of appeal have perfected, the papers are referred to a single judge to decide the question of leave to appeal.

13.3.7 Granting of leave to appeal: the single judge

The single judge considers the papers (without a hearing) and decides whether the appeal has a sufficient prospect of success to justify the granting of leave of appeal (s 31(2)(a) of the Criminal Appeal Act 1968).

In most cases, a single judge granting leave to appeal will give leave to appeal generally. However, the single judge may grant leave on some grounds and expressly refuse leave on others. Where leave to appeal has been refused on particular grounds, those grounds can only be argued before the court with its leave (*R v Cox* [1999] 2 Cr App R 6; *R v Jackson* [1999] 1 All ER 572).

In *Monnell and Morris v UK* (1988) 10 EHRR 205, the European Court of Human Rights held that the consideration of an application for leave to appeal constitutes part of the determination of a criminal charge and so Art 6 of the Convention is applicable. However, the Court went on to hold that the manner in which Art 6 applies depends on the nature of the proceedings. The determination of the application for leave to appeal without the applicant being present or represented is not incompatible with Art 6.

13.3.8 Challenging the decision of the single judge

If the single judge refuses leave to appeal, the appellant has 14 days (which can only be extended if there is very good reason (*R v Doherty* [1971] 1 WLR 1454)) in which to renew the application for leave (r 65.5(2)). If the appellant does renew the application, it will be heard by two or three Court of Appeal judges sitting in open court (s 31(3) of the Criminal Appeal Act 1968).

If the applicant is serving a custodial sentence, there is a risk in renewing the application for leave – namely that a 'direction for loss of time' (see below) could be made if the Court of Appeal confirms the refusal of leave to appeal.

13.3.9 Procedure where leave is not required

In the very few cases where leave to appeal is not required because the trial judge certified that the case was fit for appeal, grounds of appeal still have to be drafted. The only difference in procedure is that the Registrar will not refer the papers to a single judge; instead, the case will be listed for a full hearing by the Court of Appeal.

13.3.10 Frivolous appeals

Section 20 of the Criminal Appeal Act 1968 provides as follows:

> If it appears to the registrar that a notice of appeal or application for leave to appeal does not show any substantial ground of appeal, he may refer the appeal or application for leave to the Court for summary determination; and where the case is so referred the Court may, if they consider that the appeal or application for leave is frivolous or vexatious, and can be determined without adjourning it for a full hearing, dismiss the appeal or application for leave summarily, without calling on anyone to attend the hearing or to appear for the Crown thereon.

Thus, if the Registrar of Criminal Appeals takes the view that a notice of appeal or an application for leave to appeal is frivolous or vexatious, he can refer it to a sitting of the Court of Appeal for summary determination without a full hearing. If the Court of Appeal dismisses the application summarily, this decision cannot be challenged. The Court of Appeal may thus dispose summarily of appeals which are unarguable and bound to fail (*R v Taylor* [1979] Crim LR 649).

13.3.11 Other powers of the Registrar of Criminal Appeals

Under s 31A(2) of the Criminal Appeal Act 1968, the Registrar of Criminal Appeals is empowered to:

a   extend the time within which notice of appeal or of application for leave to appeal may be given;
b   order a witness to attend for examination;
c   vary the conditions of bail granted to an appellant by the Court of Appeal or the Crown Court but only if the respondent does not object (s 31A(3));
d   make orders under s 23(1)(a) of the Act (order for the production of any document or exhibit connected with the proceedings, the production of which appears necessary for the determination of the case).

If the Registrar refuses an application on behalf of an appellant to exercise any of these powers, the appellant is 'entitled to have the application determined by a single judge' (s 31A(4)).

13.4 OTHER POWERS OF THE SINGLE JUDGE

As well as granting leave to appeal, the single judge also has jurisdiction (under s 31 of the Criminal Appeal Act 1968) to deal with various other matters.

13.4.1 Presence of the appellant

Where the appellant is not in custody, he may be present on any occasion when his appeal is being heard or where interlocutory applications in respect of his appeal are being made in open court. However, an appellant who is in custody has no right to attend interlocutory applications in respect of his appeal or, if the appeal is on a ground of law alone, the hearing of the appeal itself. Section 22 of the Criminal Appeal Act 1968 provides as follows:

(1)   Except as provided by this section, an appellant shall be entitled to be present, if he wishes it, on the hearing of his appeal, although he may be in custody.

(2)   A person in custody shall not be entitled to be present—

    (a)   where his appeal is on some ground involving a question of law alone; or

    (b)   on an application by him for leave to appeal; or

    (c)   on any proceedings preliminary or incidental to an appeal; or

    (d)   where he is in custody in consequence of a verdict of not guilty by reason of insanity or of a finding of disability,

unless the Court of Appeal give him leave to be present.

(3)   The power of the Court of Appeal to pass sentence on a person may be exercised although he is for any reason not present.

Where the appellant is in custody, the single judge may make an order permitting him to be present at the hearing of the appeal if he does not have a right to attend (s 31(2)(c)). No order is needed, as the appellant has the right to attend, if the appeal involves questions of fact.

Under s 22(4), the Court of Appeal may give a 'live link direction' in relation to a hearing at which the appellant is expected to be in custody but is entitled to be present. This is a direction that the appellant, if he is being held in custody at the time of the hearing, is to attend the hearing through a live link from the place where he is held; the live link must enable him to see and hear, and to be seen and heard by, the Court of Appeal.

Where an appellant absconds before his appeal has been heard, the normal practice is to adjourn the appeal or, if the justice of the case permits, to dismiss the appeal. However, in exceptional cases, the court might allow the appeal to be heard in the absence of the appellant (*R v Gooch* [1998] 1 WLR 1100). In *R v Charles* [2001] EWCA Crim 129; [2001] 2 Cr App R 15, the defendant had absconded during his trial. After his capture, he sought leave to appeal against his conviction. The Court of Appeal held that, notwithstanding policy issues regarding absconders, the defendant should not be denied the right to apply for leave to appeal simply because of the delay caused by his being at large (since that might be a breach of his right to a fair trial under Art 6(1) of the Convention). The court went on to hold that it is open to the Court of Appeal to consider such applications by assuming that the legal representatives of an absconder had instructions to act.

13.4.2 Bail

Bail may be granted to the appellant under s 19 of the Criminal Appeal Act 1968, which empowers the Court of Appeal to:

a grant an appellant bail pending the determination of his appeal; or
b revoke bail granted to an appellant by the Crown Court under s 81(1)(f) of the Supreme Court Act 1981 or by the Court of Appeal under para (a); or
c vary the conditions of bail granted to the appellant.

An application for bail is considered by the single judge (under s 31(2)(e)) without a hearing. If the single judge refuses bail, the appellant can renew his bail application in open court if he gives notice that he wishes to do so within 14 days of the single judge's decision.

Bail pending appeal will be granted only 'where it appears prima facie that the appeal is likely to be successful or where there is a risk that the sentence will have been served by the time the appeal is heard'; the question to be addressed is whether there are 'exceptional circumstances, which would drive the Court to the conclusion that justice can only be done by the granting of bail'? (*R v Watton* (1979) 68 Cr App R 293 at 296–7 per Lord Lane CJ).

13.4.2.1 Restrictions on Crown Court granting bail pending appeal

It should be noted that the Crown Court only has jurisdiction to grant bail to someone who is appealing against conviction and/or sentence if the trial judge has certified that the case is fit for appeal (s 81(1)(f) of the Supreme Court Act 1981). Such certificates are, as we have seen, very rare, and so in most cases it will only be the single judge of the Court of Appeal who can grant bail to an appellant.

In *R v Harries* [2007] EWCA Crim 820, the trial judge granted bail, having certified that the case was fit for appeal. The Court of Appeal described this as an 'unsatisfactory course' for the judge to take, particularly without making any prior inquiry of the Criminal Appeal Office as to the speed with which an appeal could be heard. The Court reasoned that it is undesirable that somebody who has been convicted should be granted bail and then find that his appeal fails and so he has to begin to serve his sentence at a later point. It is therefore only in rare cases that bail should be granted. The ordinary course is to take steps for the hearing of the appeal to be expedited (per Scott Baker LJ at para 5).

13.4.2.2 Potential injustice of the approach to bail

If the defendant was wrongly convicted, or received an excessive prison sentence, and is not granted bail pending appeal, this of course means that he will have to serve a period of imprisonment whilst waiting for his conviction or his sentence to be quashed. If the conviction of an appellant who is serving a custodial sentence is quashed, the successful appellant has no right to compensation for the period of wrongful incarceration (compensation for miscarriages of justices is limited to cases where convictions are quashed after the normal appeal process has been exhausted). It is interesting to note that in many continental jurisdictions, the general rule is that where the defendant enters an appeal, the execution of his sentence is automatically suspended. J R Spencer in 'Does our present criminal appeal system make sense?' [2006] Crim LR 677 argues that:

> once we have accepted that the defendant must be allowed to appeal against the initial decision on its merits, we have officially accepted the possibility that the initial decision might be wrong. And if that is so, it is unacceptable for the legal system to make him undergo his punishment while this question is resolved – let alone, as we do, to make him do so without the right to compensation.

The only mitigation of the potential injustice comes from the possibility of the hearing of the appeal being expedited.

13.4.3 Public funding

Under s 26 of the Access to Justice Act 1999, representation under the trial representation order includes advice on the question of whether there appear to be reasonable grounds of appeal and, if such grounds appear to exist, assistance in the preparation of an application for leave to appeal or in the giving of a notice of appeal.

Publicly funded representation is also available for the appeal itself. Regulation 10 of the Criminal Defence Service (General) (No 2) Regulations 2001 (SI 2001/1437) governs the making of applications for representation orders. Such applications are considered in the first place by the Registrar. Under reg 10(4), he may either grant the application, or refer it to the full court or to a single judge (in other words, the Registrar cannot simply refuse an order).

13.4.4 Procedural directions

Under s 31B(1) of the Criminal Appeal Act 1968, both the single judge and registrar are empowered to give procedural directions, defined in sub-s (2) as directions for the efficient and effective preparation of an application for leave to appeal or of an appeal.

Section 31C deals with appeals against procedural directions: appeal from the single judge lies to the full court, and appeal from the registrar lies to a single judge.

13.5 THE HEARING OF THE APPEAL

Paragraph II.2.4 of the *Consolidated Practice Direction* sets out targets for hearing dates in the Court of Appeal: for sentencing appeals, 28 days from receipt by the listing officer; for conviction appeals, 63 days from receipt by the listing officer; for conviction appeals where witnesses are to attend, 80 days from receipt by the listing officer.

Prior to the hearing, the judges and all counsel will have received a summary of the case from the Registrar. These case summaries are prepared by the Registrar's staff.

Paragraph II.17 of the *Practice Direction* requires the production of skeleton arguments. The advocate for the appellant must lodge a skeleton argument with the Registrar, and serve it on the prosecuting authority, within 14 days of receipt by the advocate of notification of the grant of leave to appeal against conviction (unless a longer period is directed). The prosecutor should lodge a skeleton argument within 14 days of receipt of the appellant's skeleton argument (unless directed otherwise).

At the hearing, counsel for the appellant presents his case first and counsel for the respondent (the prosecution) then replies. The appeal takes the form of argument based on the grounds of appeal, the transcript of the summing up and any other documentary evidence. Unless it is a case where the conviction is said to be unsafe because of fresh evidence, no oral evidence will be heard by the court.

13.6 GROUNDS OF APPEAL AGAINST CONVICTION

Section 2(1) of the Criminal Appeal Act 1968, in its original form, was in the following terms:

> Except as provided by this Act, the Court of Appeal shall allow an appeal against conviction if they think—
>
> (a) that the conviction should be set aside on the ground that under all the circumstances of the case it is unsafe or unsatisfactory,
> (b) that the judgment of the court of trial should be set aside on the ground of a wrong decision of any question of law:
> (c) that there was a material irregularity in the course of the trial, and in any other case shall dismiss the appeal:
>
> Provided that the court may, notwithstanding that they are of opinion that the point raised in the appeal might be decided in favour of the appellant, dismiss the appeal if they consider that no miscarriage of justice has actually occurred.

However s 2 of the 1968 Act was subsequently amended by the Criminal Appeal Act 1995, to provide as follows:

> (1) Subject to the provisions of this Act, the Court of Appeal—
>
>> (a) shall allow an appeal against conviction if they think that the conviction is unsafe; and
>> (b) shall dismiss such an appeal in any other case.
>
> (2) In the case of an appeal against conviction the Court shall, if they allow the appeal, quash the conviction.
> (3) An order of the Court of Appeal quashing a conviction shall, except when under section 7 below the appellant is ordered to be retried, operate as a direction to the court of trial to enter, instead of the record of conviction, a judgment and verdict of acquittal.

Thus, the Court of Appeal must allow an appeal against conviction if they think that the conviction is unsafe; otherwise, they must dismiss the appeal. The proviso that featured in the original version of s 2(1) does not appear in the amended version as it is unnecessary: a conviction could not be 'safe' if a miscarriage of justice has occurred.

According to the Home Secretary, who had consulted with the Lord Chief Justice, the revised version of s 2(1), 'in substance . . . restates the existing practice of the Court of Appeal' (Hansard, HC (6 March 1995) cols 53–55 and Hansard, HL (15 May 1995) cols 310–12).

There is no statutory definition of the word 'unsafe'. However, under the original version of s 2(1), a conviction would be held to be 'unsafe' if the members of the Court of Appeal feel that there is 'some lurking doubt in our minds which makes us wonder whether an injustice has been done' (*R v Cooper* [1969] 1 QB 267 at p 271, per Lord Widgery CJ). In *Stafford v DPP* [1974] AC 878 at p 912, Lord Kilbrandon expressed the question a judge of the Court of Appeal should pose: 'Have I a reasonable doubt, or perhaps even a lurking doubt, that this conviction may be unsafe or unsatisfactory? If I have I must quash. If I have not, I have no power to do so.'

In *R v Graham* [1997] 1 Cr App R 302 at p 308, Lord Bingham CJ said of the amended s 2(1):

> This new provision . . . is plainly intended to concentrate attention on one question: whether in the light of any arguments raised or evidence adduced on appeal the Court of Appeal considers a conviction unsafe. If the Court is satisfied despite any misdirection of law or any irregularity in the conduct of the trial or any fresh evidence, that the conviction is safe, the Court will dismiss the appeal. But if, for whatever reason, the Court concludes that the appellant was wrongly convicted of the offence charged or is left in doubt whether the appellant was rightly convicted of that offence or not, then it must of necessity consider the conviction unsafe. The Court is then subject to a binding duty to allow the appeal . . . Where the condition in s 2(1)(a) . . . is satisfied, the Court has no discretion to exercise.

It follows from this that the Court of Appeal is not concerned with the guilt or innocence of appellants, but only with the safety of their convictions.

In *R v Farrow* [1999] Crim LR 306, the Court of Appeal deprecated the use of the 'lurking doubt' test for appeals against conviction and said that the court should focus on the wording of the statutory test of whether the conviction is unsafe, rather than applying a gloss to that test. In *R v Heron* [2005] EWCA Crim 3245, Scott Baker LJ said (at para 38) that:

> if we are not persuaded for some specific reason that the conviction is unsafe, the appellant does not succeed on lurking doubt or any general feeling of unease about the conviction.

However, in *R v Melville* [2005] EWCA Crim 1668, Hughes J said (at para 15) that:

> This Court does, of course, have the power to [regard a conviction as unsafe, that is to say that there is a lurking doubt about the appellant's guilt] in an appropriate case, though it must be careful not to substitute its own assessment of witnesses whom it has not seen for the judgment of the jury which has seen them.

In *R v Criminal Cases Review Commission ex p Pearson* [2000] 1 Cr App R 141, Lord Bingham CJ (at pp 146–47) said:

> The expression 'unsafe' in s 2(1)(a) of the 1968 Act does not lend itself to precise definition. In some cases unsafety will be obvious, as (for example) where it appears that someone other than the appellant committed the crime and the appellant did not, or where the appellant has been convicted of an act that was not in law a crime, or where a conviction is shown to be vitiated by serious unfairness in the conduct of the trial or significant legal misdirection, or where the jury verdict, in the context of other verdicts, defies any rational explanation. Cases however arise in which unsafety is much less obvious: cases in which the Court, although by no means persuaded of an appellant's innocence, is subject to some lurking doubt or uneasiness whether an injustice has been done . . . If, on consideration of all the facts and circumstances of the case before it, the Court entertains real doubts whether the appellant was guilty of the offence of which he has been convicted, the Court will consider the conviction unsafe. In these less obvious cases the ultimate decision of the Court of Appeal will very much depend on its assessment of all the facts and circumstances.

L H Leigh in 'Lurking doubt and the safety of convictions' [2006] Crim LR 809 discusses the concept of lurking doubt and analyses the case law on the use of this phrase to justify upholding appeals against conviction. He concludes that the cases show that the Court of Appeal has not in fact sought to substitute its view of the facts for that of a fully and properly-instructed jury in determining whether a verdict is unsafe, and he points out that, were it to do so, the court would fall foul of *R v Pendleton* [2001] UKHL 66; [2002] 1 WLR 72, where Lord Bingham pointed out (at para 19) that the Court of Appeal is not, and should never become, the primary decision-maker (and so it follows that the Court of Appeal should be slow to second-guess the verdict of the jury).

13.6.1 Errors in the course of the trial

Matters which are capable of rendering a conviction unsafe include the following:

(a) *A decision by the judge that certain evidence against the defendant was admissible.* If the Court of Appeal decides that the evidence in question ought to have been excluded, the judges will go on to consider what impact this mistake had on the trial: for example, how strong was the other (admissible) evidence against the accused.

(b) *The wrongful rejection by the judge of a submission that there is no case to answer.* Where a defendant appeals against conviction on the ground that the trial judge wrongly rejected a submission of no case to answer at the end of the prosecution case, the Court of Appeal should ignore any evidence admitted after the submission of no case. Therefore, if the defendant admits his guilt during cross-examination, the conviction should still be set aside if the submission of no case was rejected wrongly. The defendant was entitled to be acquitted after the evidence against him had been heard, and so to allow the trial to continue beyond the end of the prosecution case would be an abuse of process and fundamentally unfair (*R v Smith* [1999] 2 Cr App R 238 per Mantell LJ at p 242). The Criminal Justice and Immigration Bill in 2007–08 proposed the reversal of the effect of cases such as *Smith*, by providing that:

> In determining an appeal . . ., the Court of Appeal shall not disregard any evidence solely on the ground that it was given after the judge at the appellant's trial wrongly permitted the trial to continue after the close of the evidence for the prosecution.

However, this clause was dropped from the Bill during its Parliamentary journey, and so *Smith* remains good law.

(c) *Irregularities occurring during the course of the trial.* This includes, for example, misconduct on the part of a juror (as where a juror is seen in conversation with a prosecution witness during an adjournment). A further example of something going wrong in the course of the trial is provided by *R v Maguire* [1997] 1 Cr App R 61. A witness called by the defendant repeatedly refused to answer certain questions regarding his own whereabouts at the time of the alleged offence. The judge, in the presence of the jury, ordered the witness to be arrested and taken down to the cells. The Court of Appeal accepted the argument that the jury might have been affected by seeing an important defence witness being arrested. The judge should have invited the jury to retire before ordering the arrest of the witness. The appeal was therefore allowed and a retrial was ordered.

(d) *Errors in the summing up*: details of what the summing up must contain and how the various components should be dealt with are set out Chapter 12. In *R v Lambert* [2006] EWCA Crim 827, Lord Phillips CJ said (at para 57) that:

> The Judicial Studies Board publishes specimen directions which judges are advised to use, many of which are no more than propositions of common sense, albeit propositions that may be more self-evident to those accustomed to the evaluation of evidence than to juries approaching such a task for the first time. Sometimes in the conduct of a trial, particularly one as lengthy as that with which we are concerned, as a result of an oversight on the part of counsel and the judge, or the judge alone, a direction is omitted or material is placed before the jury which should not have been. It is wrong to start with the premise that such an oversight vitiates the trial. The question must always be whether, when viewed in the context of the trial as a whole, the safety of any verdict which has been given or is to be given, has been put in jeopardy or the fairness of the trial has otherwise been prejudiced to an extent that calls for the discharge of the jury or the quashing of a verdict.

(e) *The judge's conduct of the trial*: in *R v Whybrow* (1994) 144 NLJ 124, the Court of Appeal expressed support for the recommendation of the 1993 Royal Commission on Criminal Justice that judges should be more interventionist in order to prevent trials becoming protracted. However, such intervention must not go beyond legitimate bounds. If, for example, a witness gives an ambiguous answer, the judge should have it clarified. If a witness gives a long answer, the judge may ask the witness to confirm the gist of that answer so that there is no misunderstanding. What the judge must not do is to become an advocate. The court approved a dictum of Cumming-Bruce LJ in *R v Gunning* (1994) 98 Cr App R 303 at 306, comparing the function of the judge with that of an umpire in a cricket match:

> The judge is not an advocate. Under the English and Welsh system of criminal trials he is much more like the umpire at a cricket match. He is certainly not the bowler, whose business

it is to get the batsman out. If a judge, without any conscious intention to be unfair, descends into the forum and asks great numbers of pointed questions of the accused when he is giving his evidence in-chief, the jury may very well get the impression that the judge does not believe a word that the witness is saying and by putting these pointed questions, to which there is sometimes only a lame answer, blows the evidence out of the water during the stage that counsel ought to be having the opportunity to bring the evidence of the accused to the attention of the jury in its most impressive pattern and shape. The importance of counsel having that opportunity is not diminished – indeed it is enhanced – if the evidence emerging in-chief is a story that takes a bit of swallowing. If the judge, when the witness is skating over thin ice, asks pointed questions so that the ice seems to crack, the jury may well get the impression, however perfectly the judge may later sum up the case, that the judge has seen through the evidence in-chief so that the jury do not take it very seriously either.

In *R v Wiggan* (1999) *The Times*, 22 March, after the defendant had been re-examined by her counsel, the judge asked some 64 questions of a testing nature, suggesting scepticism of the defendant's evidence. The Court of Appeal held that after a witness has been re-examined, it is open to the judge to ask questions to clear up uncertainties, to fill gaps, or to answer queries which might be lurking in the jury's mind. However, it is not appropriate for the judge to cross-examine the witness. Similarly, in *R v Tuegel* [2000] 2 All ER 872, the Court of Appeal held that although a judge should avoid asking a witness questions which appear to suggest that the judge is taking sides, he has a duty to ask questions which clarify ambiguities in answers previously given or which identify the nature of the defence, if that is unclear. Such questions should usually be asked at, or close to, the time when the ambiguity first becomes apparent. The court went on to say that although it might exceptionally be necessary for a judge, in the presence of the jury, to interrupt a speech by counsel, it is generally preferable for him not to do so. Ideally, interventions for the purpose of clarifying or correcting something said, either by judge or counsel, should be made in the first instance in the absence of the jury and at a break in the proceedings, so that, if necessary, the point can be dealt with before the jury in an appropriate fashion.

In *R v Cordingley* [2007] EWCA Crim 2174, there were heated exchanges between the judge and defence counsel, as the judge was highly critical of the time estimate for the trial. It was held that the safety of a conviction does not depend merely on the strength of the evidence that has been heard, but also on the observance of due process. Every defendant is entitled to be treated fairly, courteously, and with due regard to the presumption of innocence. In the present case there had been a failure of due process on account of the judge's conduct (per Laws LJ at para 15).

(f) *Errors by defence counsel*: in *R v Ullah* [2000] 1 Cr App R 351, defence counsel was aware of the existence of evidence that cast doubt on the veracity of the complainant's evidence; this evidence was not put before the court (possibly because its admissibility was rather doubtful). Had the jury known about this evidence, it would have seriously damaged the prosecution case. The Court of Appeal held that a conviction will not be unsafe merely because defence counsel took a decision that another advocate might not have taken; the Court of Appeal will only have regard to 'significant' fault by trial counsel or solicitor. The court said that it may well be appropriate to apply the *Wednesbury Corporation* ([1948] 1 KB 223) test of unreasonableness: was the decision one that no reasonable advocate could have reached? In *Boodram v State of Trinidad & Tobago*

[2001] UK PC 20; [2002] 1 Cr App R 12, the Privy Council said that when the conduct of a case forms the ground of appeal against conviction, the court ought normally to focus on the impact which the faulty conduct of the case had on the trial and the verdict. However, where counsel's conduct was so extreme as to result in a denial of due process to his client, the question of the impact of counsel's conduct on the result of the case is no longer of any relevance: whenever a person is convicted without having enjoyed the benefit of due process, there is a miscarriage of justice, regardless of his guilt or innocence. In such circumstances, the conviction has to be quashed, since a conviction following a fundamental flaw in the conduct of a trial cannot be allowed to stand.

In *R v Thakrar* [2001] EWCA Crim 1096, the appeal was brought on the grounds that the appellant had not had a fair trial because his solicitors did not properly prepare or advise on his case prior to trial. It was held that the appellant's solicitors had fallen below the level of reasonably competent solicitors in the way in which they had prepared the trial on behalf of the appellant. However, the mere fact that an appellant's solicitors may have failed to carry out their duties to an appellant in a proper manner does not of itself mean that a conviction is automatically unsafe. Nor could a conviction be quashed as a means of expressing the court's disapproval of a solicitor's failure. The issue, said the court, was whether the failures had prevented the appellant from having a fair trial within the meaning of Art 6 of the European Convention on Human Rights (per Keene LJ at para 34).

(g) *Events before the trial*: a conviction may be rendered unsafe by events which occurred before the trial started. In *R v Mullen* [2000] QB 520, for example, the appellant's deportation to this country had been procured by unlawful means. There was no complaint about the conduct of the trial, but it was argued that the trial should never have taken place, since there had been abuse of process by the prosecution prior to the trial. The Court of Appeal confirmed that a conviction can be 'unsafe' under s 2 of the Criminal Appeal Act 1968 as a result of matters occurring prior to the trial itself.

13.6.2 Safety of conviction and fairness of trial

A key question is the relationship between the 'safety' of the conviction (the test applicable under the Criminal Appeal Act) and the 'fairness' of the trial (the test applicable under Art 6 of the European Convention on Human Rights). Put simply, the question is whether a conviction can be regarded as 'safe' if the trial process was 'unfair'.

In *R v Chalkley* [1998] QB 848 (where the defendants pleaded guilty following an erroneous ruling by the trial judge on a question of admissibility), Auld LJ said (at p 868), 'The Court has no power under [s 2(1) of the Criminal Appeal Act 1968] to allow an appeal if it does not think the conviction unsafe but is dissatisfied in some way with what went on at trial'. However, his Lordship went on to say that this is subject to the jurisprudence of the European Court of Human Rights.

The view of the European Court was given in *Condron v UK* (2001) 31 EHRR 1, where the Court said (at para 65) that 'the question whether or not the rights of the defence guaranteed to an accused under Article 6 were secured in any given case cannot be assimilated to a finding that his conviction was safe in the absence of any enquiry into the issue of fairness'. This is significant, as it suggests that the European Court was concerned that the two tests – the safety of the conviction and the fairness of the trial – might not necessarily lead to the same result.

In *R v Francom* [2001] 1 Cr App R 237, the Court of Appeal agreed that the two tests are different but said that this does not mean that the results of applying the two tests should be different. Lord Woolf CJ said (at para 43) that the test of whether a conviction is unsafe applied by the Court of Appeal is not identical to the issue of unfairness before the European Court of Human Rights. In particular, the term 'unfair' is not limited to the safety of the conviction itself, but encompasses the entire prosecution process. However, his Lordship said (at para 47) that in a case involving misdirection of the jury, the Court of Appeal should approach the issue of lack of safety in the same way that the European Court of Human Rights approaches lack of fairness. The appeal is this case arose (as in *Condron v UK*) from the failure of the trial judge to direct the jury correctly on adverse inferences under s 34 of the Criminal Justice and Public Order Act 1994. Lord Woolf CJ said that the issue was whether the omission of the required direction had in fact resulted in unfairness or had impaired the safety of the conviction. No distinction should be drawn between the two tests (para 48). In the present case, no reasonable jury, properly directed, could have reached a different conclusion, and so the conviction was not unsafe and there had been no unfairness to the defendants.

Similarly, in *R v Togher* [2001] 1 Cr App R 33, the Court of Appeal said that since the coming into force of the Human Rights Act 1998, it would be extremely rare for there to be room for a different result before the Court of Appeal and before the European Court of Human Rights. Lord Woolf CJ said that 'if a defendant has been denied a fair trial it will almost be inevitable that the conviction will be regarded as unsafe' (para 30). It followed that, if it would have been right to stop a prosecution on the basis that it was an abuse of process, the Court of Appeal would be most unlikely to conclude that the conviction should not be set aside.

In *R v Davies, Rowe and Johnson* [2001] 1 Cr App R 115, the Court of Appeal had to decide how to deal with the fact that the European Court of Human Rights had held that there had been a breach of Art 6(1) of the Convention during the trial of these defendants, and that this had not been cured by the appeal process. In other words, the court had to consider the effect of this ruling on the application of s 2 of the Criminal Appeal Act 1968 to the defendants' convictions. It held that the Court of Appeal is concerned only with the safety of a conviction, whereas the jurisdiction of the European Court of Human Rights is to examine the fairness of the trial, not to express an opinion on the safety of the conviction under domestic law. Even if there has been a finding by the European Court that Art 6(1) of the Convention has been violated, that would not necessarily lead to the quashing of a conviction, since it is for the domestic court to examine the safety of the conviction in accordance with s 2 of the 1968 Act. Mantell LJ said (at para 56) that a conviction can never be safe if there is doubt about the appellant's guilt. However, his Lordship said that the converse is not true: a conviction might be unsafe even where there is no doubt about guilt, but the trial process was vitiated by serious unfairness or significant legal misdirection. It follows that if a trial is found to be unfair, that could have an impact on the safety of the conviction even in the face of overwhelming evidence against the defendant (see, for example, *R v Smith* [1999] 2 Cr App R 238). His Lordship went on (at para 56) to hold that, usually, the court should apply the test in *Stirland v DPP* [1944] AC 315 and ask itself: 'Assuming the wrong decision on law or the misdirection had not occurred and the trial had been free

from legal error, would the only reasonable and proper verdict have been one of guilty?'
At para 65, his Lordship notes that the European Court is charged with inquiring into
whether there has been a breach of a Convention right; the Court of Appeal is concerned with the safety of the conviction. Obviously, the first question might intrude
upon the second, but the extent to which it does so would depend upon the circumstances of the particular case. A finding of a breach of Art 6(1) of the Convention
would not lead 'inexorably' to the quashing of a conviction. The effect of any unfairness upon the safety of a conviction would vary according to its nature and degree. The
court went on to hold that, in the present case, the unfairness did cast doubt on the
safety of the convictions, which were accordingly quashed.

In *R v Williams* [2001] EWCA Crim 932; (2001) *The Times*, 30 March, the Court of
Appeal reiterated the point made in *R v Davis, Rowe and Johnson* that a conviction
following a trial which involved a breach of Art 6 of the European Convention is not
necessarily unsafe. In the case of a misdirection or failure to give a direction, the court
should ask itself whether, if an appropriate direction had been given, the jury might
have acquitted the defendant. If the answer is no, then the conviction should
be regarded as safe. Similarly, in *R v Dundon* [2004] EWCA Crim 621, Rose LJ said (at
para 15):

> In many cases, breach of an Article 6 right will result in the quashing of a conviction as unsafe.
> But that is not necessarily the result in all cases . . . In every case the outcome depends on
> the kind of breach and the nature and quality of the evidence in the case. Just and pro-
> portionate satisfaction may, in an appropriate case, be provided, for example, by a declar-
> ation of breach or a reduction in sentence, rather than the quashing of a conviction. Breach
> arising from delay may have such a consequence . . . And there may be other exceptional
> cases in which a conviction may not be unsafe, for example if there has been unfairness
> because of a legal misdirection but the evidence is overwhelming . . . or, possibly, if the trial is
> unfair because of inadequate prosecution disclosure on a peripheral issue but compelling
> evidence of guilt makes the conviction safe.

However, his Lordship went on to say (at para 16): 'We are unable to envisage any
circumstance in which, an Article 6 breach having arisen from want of independence
and impartiality in the tribunal, it would be possible to conclude that the conviction is
safe.' It is clear that this would encompass cases where the defendant was clearly guilty.

The position was expressed succinctly by Mitting J giving the judgment of the Divisional Court in *Dowsett v Criminal Cases Review Commission* [2007] EWHC 1923
(Admin), at para 16: 'not every breach of Article 6 will make a conviction unsafe. The
nature of the breach and the facts of the case must in every case be analysed.'

In *R v A (No 2)* [2002] 1 AC 45, Lord Steyn said (at para 38):

> It is well established that the guarantee of a fair trial under Article 6 is absolute: a conviction
> obtained in breach of it cannot stand . . . The only balancing permitted is in respect of what
> the concept of a fair trial entails: here account may be taken of the familiar triangulation of
> interests of the accused, the victim and society.

It is submitted that this approach may offer one way of resolving the uncertainty in the
case law: a breach of the right to a fair trial should result in the conviction being held

unsafe, but not every error in the course of a trial is of sufficient gravity to result in unfairness. In *R v Lambert* [2002] 2 AC 545, Lord Clyde (at para 159) said that:

> ... an unfairness is not always fatal to a conviction ... If there is doubt about guilt then the conviction must be held to be unsafe. But if there is no doubt about guilt it is not every case where an unfairness can be identified that will necessarily and inevitably lead to a quashing of the conviction.

In *R v Hanratty* [2002] EWCA Crim 1141; [2002] 2 Cr App R 30, Lord Woolf (at para 95) reiterated the point that a conviction can be unsafe even if the defendant is in fact guilty of the offence:

> Here it is important to have in mind that a conviction may be unsafe for two distinct reasons that may, but do not necessarily, overlap. The first reason being that there is a doubt as to the safety of the conviction and the second being that the trial was materially flawed. The second reason can be independent of guilt because of the fundamental constitutional requirement that even a guilty defendant is entitled, before being found guilty, to have a trial which conforms with at least the minimum standards of what is regarded in this jurisdiction as being an acceptable criminal trial.

The jurisdiction of the Court of Appeal is limited to assessing whether the convictions are safe, and not every departure from good practice will render a trial unfair. However, as Lord Bingham put it in *R v Randall* [2002] UKPC 19; [2002] 1 WLR 2237, at para 28:

> ... it is not every departure from good practice which renders a trial unfair ... But the right of a criminal defendant to a fair trial is absolute. There will come a point when the departure from good practice is so gross, or so persistent, or so prejudicial, or so irremediable that an appellate court will have no choice but to condemn a trial as unfair and quash a conviction as unsafe, however strong the grounds for believing the defendant to be guilty. The right to a fair trial is one to be enjoyed by the guilty as well as the innocent, for a defendant is presumed to be innocent until proved to be otherwise in a fairly conducted trial.

In a similar vein, in *Sinclair v Her Majesty's Advocate* [2005] UKPC D2; [2005] HRLR 26, the Privy Council held that the right to a fair trial is an absolute right which cannot be compromised. If the accused has not had a fair trial, the verdict cannot stand and the conviction should be quashed. In the present case, the failure by the prosecution to provide copies of statements made to the police by one of its witnesses breached the appellant's right to a fair trial, as he had been denied the opportunity to cross-examine the witness (whose evidence at trial was inconsistent with the statements made to the police) so as to undermine the witness's reliability and credibility. This Scottish case underlines the importance of compliance in England and Wales with the provisions of the Criminal Procedure and Investigations Act 1996 (see Chapter 8).

In a similar vein, *R v Cordingley* [2007] EWCA Crim 2174 concerned a case where the judge failed to behave with appropriate courtesy towards the accused and his counsel. Laws LJ said, at para 15:

> The safety of a conviction does not merely depend upon the strength of the evidence that the jury hears. It depends also on the observance of due process. In this case it seems to us inescapable that the effect of the judge's conduct must have been to inhibit the defendant in the course of his defence. He clearly felt that the judge was prejudiced against him . . . [I]t is to be remembered that every defendant . . . is entitled to be tried fairly – that is courteously and with due regard for the presumption of innocence . . . There was a failure of due process by reason of the judge's conduct.

Nick Taylor and David Ormerod, in 'Mind the gaps: safety, fairness and moral legitimacy' [2004] Crim LR 266, suggest that:

> the appropriate benchmark for the degree of unfairness sufficient to constitute unsafety is not a question of 'grossness' but a matter of when the procedure is flawed to the extent that it jeopardises the moral integrity of the process. In such cases, the conviction cannot be upheld even if the defendant is factually guilty, and conversely can be upheld in the face of minor infractions of 'fairness' . . . Explicit adoption of this benchmark would provide a principled dividing line between tolerable unfairness and unfairness leading to unsafety . . . We would . . . submit that failings in fairness that would not fall within the scope of unsafety should be restricted to technical breaches that do not prejudice the accused. There ought to be only a small gap between unsafety and unfairness. Viewed from a different angle, it is easier to identify what should be treated as being so unfair as to constitute unsafety. Breaches of Convention rights should presumptively be viewed as generating such unfairness as to render a conviction unsafe.

Given the uncertainty created by conflicting dicta in the case law, it is perhaps unsurprising that in the *Auld Review*, Lord Justice Auld notes the potential tension between safety of conviction and fairness of trial. Recommendation 301 is that:

> Consideration should be given to amendment of the statutory test of unsafety as the ground for quashing a conviction so as to clarify whether and to what extent it is to apply to convictions that would be regarded as safe in the ordinary sense, but that follow want of due process before or during trial.

13.6.3 What if the appellant was guilty of the offence?

The Criminal Justice and Immigration Bill 2007–08 proposed the addition of two new sub-s to s 2 of the Criminal Appeal Act 1968:

> (1A) For the purposes of sub-section (1)(a), the conviction is not unsafe if the Court think that there is no reasonable doubt about the appellant's guilt.
> (1B) Sub-section (1A) does not require the Court to dismiss the appeal if they think that it would seriously undermine the proper administration of justice to allow the conviction to stand.

In a later version of the Bill the wording was slightly different:

(1A)   For the purposes of sub-section (1)(a), a conviction is not unsafe if the Court of Appeal are satisfied that the appellant is guilty of the offence.

(1B)   Sub-section (1A) does not prevent the Court of Appeal from allowing an appeal against conviction where they think that it would be incompatible with the appellant's Convention rights to dismiss the appeal.

The change to the drafting of sub-s (1A) clarified the need for the Court of Appeal to be sure of the appellant's guilt before dismissing an appeal on the basis that he committed the offence in question. The original version of sub-s (1B) provided a safeguard based purely on the appellant's rights under the European Convention on Human Rights. We saw in Chapter 1 that the rights of the accused, whilst very important, are not the only rights that need to be safeguarded by the criminal justice system. The broader wording in the re-drafted sub-section – referring to the 'proper administration of justice' – encompasses considerations that include, but are not limited to, the rights of the defendant.

Because of concerns that the ability of the Court of Appeal to quash a conviction, irrespective of the strength of the case against the defendant, where there had been an abuse of process on the part of the prosecution was a powerful deterrent to such misconduct, the Bill provided that:

> If it appears to the Court of Appeal, in determining an appeal under this Part, that there has been serious misconduct by any person involved in the investigation or prosecution of the offence the Court may refer the matter to the Attorney-General.

The Government decided to remove these clauses from the Bill (and so they do not appear in the final Act), as the extent of the opposition to them meant that the Parliamentary progress of the Bill would otherwise have been impeded. It is possible that similar clauses will appear in a subsequent Bill, and so it worth considering the thinking which underpinned the Government's proposals for reform.

A copy of the author's response to the consultation paper that preceded the Bill is available on the companion website for this work.

J R Spencer in 'Quashing convictions for procedural irregularities' [2007] Crim LR 835 discusses the Government's wish to change the law so that the Court of Appeal would no longer be able to quash convictions on 'purely procedural grounds' if it was sure that the defendant was factually guilty. It is perhaps telling that the consultation paper issued by the Home Office made it clear that 'whilst the Government is open to suggestions about how we achieve the aims, we are not consulting on the aims themselves or therefore whether the law should be changed'. The responses to the consultation paper were overwhelmingly negative. However, the Criminal Justice and Immigration Bill originally contained a clause aimed at altering the powers of the Court of Appeal in the way the Government wanted. Spencer sets out the objections to this reform in these terms:

> The first is that it fails to recognise that the criminal appeal process exists not only to ensure that the factually innocent are not punished, but also to uphold the rule of law. Thus the function of criminal appeals is not just to see that in a given case the 'right result' is reached, but also to ensure that the law of the land in general, and the rules of criminal procedure and

evidence in particular, are respected and properly applied. Because of this, it is inevitable that the Court of Appeal must sometimes quash convictions that are tainted by grave breaches of the law, or serious failures to apply the rules – irrespective of the factual guilt or innocence of the accused. This is so for two good reasons, one theoretical, and one practical. The theoretical reason is that a criminal conviction is only acceptable if it carries moral authority, and a decision reached in defiance of the basic rules that society prescribes for criminal investigations and criminal trials does not. And the practical reason is that, if convictions can be upheld where the authorities have flouted the basic rules, this will undermine the self-restraint we expect the authorities to show in keeping to them. If the police know that if they break the rules, the resulting conviction will be appeal-proof as long as nobody finds out until afterwards, this 'sends a signal' – to borrow the phrase so popular with the Home Office – that breaking rules can pay.

The second objection is that the proposal is unnecessary, because it fails to understand the way in which the rules of criminal appeal currently operate.

Behind the proposal is the notion that, as the law now stands, defendants who are clearly guilty regularly escape punishment because the Court of Appeal quashes their convictions on account of footling procedural irregularities. But in fact this is not so. In the first place, for most procedural irregularities the Court of Appeal will uphold the conviction if it is convinced that the defendant is really guilty, and would still have been convicted even if the irregularity had not taken place. An abundant case law makes it clear that it is only for the most serious procedural irregularities that the Court of Appeal will quash the conviction of a defendant who is plainly guilty. And secondly, in those comparatively rare cases where the Court of Appeal considers the procedural flaw too grave for the conviction of a visibly guilty person to be allowed to stand, it will usually order a retrial where – as is usually the case – a new trial can 'cure' the problem.

It is only in the rarest cases that a retrial is not possible, and these will usually be where some misconduct by the investigating authorities has been so grave that anything that follows must of necessity be tainted . . . In such a case, as the law stands it is indeed true that a guilty person may escape the punishment he would have suffered had the authorities pursued him using lawful means. This is regrettable, of course: but it is, surely, the price that society must pay to ensure that the executive, and the police, remember that the law of the land applies to them, and not just to the rest of us.

Spencer concludes that, on principle, it is right that: (i) some 'purely procedural errors' should cause the conviction to be quashed, irrespective of the defendant's factual guilt or innocence, and (ii) that in some of these cases, it should not be possible for the defendant to be retried.

Spencer goes on to list the broad categories of cases where convictions should be quashed irrespective of the factual guilt of the accused:

a   where the court had no jurisdiction to try the offence;
b   where the court below fundamentally misapplied the substantive criminal law (in this type of case, the Court of Appeal can, and often does, order a retrial, or in an appropriate case may substitute a conviction for a different offence);
c   where the rules of natural justice were broken;
d   where there has been a disregard of other procedural rules of major importance that exist for the particular protection of the defendant;

e   where some formal bar to prosecution exists;

f   where there is gross misconduct in the course of investigating the offence, or preparing for the trial.

He adds that he can see no reason in principle for refusing to order a retrial in any of
the cases (a) to (d) inclusive (unless, for example, the Court of Appeal takes the view
that a retrial is not worth the trouble and expense or is for some reason impracticable).
However, he says that a retrial should not be possible in cases (e) and (f), since in both
cases the prosecution should not have taken place at all and the court below, if it had
done its job properly, would have stopped it.

13.6.4 Appeals relating to the jury

There are special rules which deal with appeals which are based on complaints about
the jury. Those rules are contained in s 18 of the Juries Act 1974. This provides that a
conviction may not be quashed on any of the following grounds:

a   that the provisions of the Act regarding the selection of the jury have not been
complied with;

b   that a juror was not qualified to serve;

c   that a juror was unfit to serve. In *R v Chapman and Lauday* (1976) 63 Cr App R 75,
this was held to include an allegation that one of the jurors was partially deaf and
so missed much of the evidence. The Court of Appeal did say in that case that
although such unfitness could not amount to a material irregularity, it could be
used as one factor amongst others rendering the conviction unsafe. In *R v Richard-
son* [2004] EWCA Crim 2997, one of the jurors was disqualified from jury service as
a result of a previous conviction. It was argued that this rendered the defendant's
conviction unsafe. The Court of Appeal disagreed, holding that the conviction was
not rendered unsafe. The court cited with approval the judgment of Garland J in *R
v Bliss* (1986) 84 Cr App R 1, where it was held (at p 6) that the Court of Appeal
'will not interfere with the verdict of a jury unless there is either evidence pointing
directly to the fact, or evidence from which a proper inference may be drawn, that
the defendant may have been prejudiced or may not in fact have received a fair
trial', and also referred to the decision in *R v Spencer* (1985) 80 Cr App R 264 (at
p 279) that, in this type of case, the court 'must ask itself whether it thinks there is
anything in the events which *ex hypothesi* should not have occurred which leads it
to the conclusion that an injustice may have been done, or that there is a real danger
that the appellant may have been prejudiced by what has gone on'.

13.6.4.1 The secrecy of the jury room

In addition to the statutory restriction contained in s 18, it is a strict rule that the Court
of Appeal will not investigate what went on in the jury room while the jury were
considering their verdict: see, for example, *R v Bean* [1991] Crim LR 843, where the
defence wanted to adduce evidence from the jury bailiff that he had overheard an
exchange which could be regarded as one juror being pressurised into voting in favour
of conviction, but the Court of Appeal refused to entertain this evidence. This is a long-

standing rule. In *R v Thompson* [1962] 1 All ER 65, the Court of Appeal refused to hear evidence that most of the jury had been in favour of an acquittal until the foreman of the jury had read out a list of the defendant's previous convictions (which had not been referred to in court). Likewise, in *R v Roads* [1967] 2 QB 108, the Court of Appeal would not hear evidence that one of the jurors had in fact disagreed with the verdict announced by the foreman. In *R v Less* (1993) *The Times*, 30 March, the Court of Appeal disregarded letters from jurors saying that they disagreed with the verdict. Similarly, in *R v Schofield* [1993] Crim LR 217, the Court of Appeal refused to entertain evidence of a conversation between a juror and the jury bailiff in which it became apparent that the jury did not understand the legal definition of the charge. In *R v Miah; R v Akhbar* [1997] 2 Cr App R 12, the Court of Appeal reaffirmed once again the rule that 'an appellate court will not receive evidence from jurors about discussions or other matters that took place in the jury box or jury room concerning the cases in which they were acting' (per Kennedy LJ at p 18).

In any event, it was pointed out in *R v Mickleburgh* [1995] 1 Cr App R 297 that taking a statement from a juror about the deliberations which took place in the jury room could well amount to contempt under s 8 of the Contempt of Court Act 1981; following *R v McCluskey* (1994) 98 Cr App R 216, it was held that such inquiries should only take place with the consent of the Court of Appeal. This point is considered in more detail below.

In *R v Millward* [1999] 1 Cr App R 61, after a majority verdict direction had been given, the jury later returned to court. They were asked if they had reached a verdict on which at least 10 of them were agreed. The foreman said that they had. The verdict was guilty. The clerk asked whether it was a verdict of all the jury or by a majority. The foreman replied 'all'. The foreman subsequently wrote to the court saying that she had made a mistake and in fact it was a 10:2 majority verdict in favour of conviction. The Court of Appeal said that there had been a clear statement from the foreman that the verdict was unanimous, and so the court did not have to make the further inquiries required by s 17(3) of the Juries Act 1974. In any event, the Court of Appeal is not entitled to inquire into what went on in the jury room.

Allegations of dissent amongst a jury remain immune from investigation notwithstanding the coming into force of the Human Rights Act 1998: *R v Lewis* [2001] EWCA Crim 749; (2001) *The Times*, 26 April; *R v Qureshi* [2001] EWCA Crim 1807; [2002] 1 WLR 518. In *R v Austin* [2002] EWCA Crim 1796; [2003] Crim LR 426, the jury verdict was announced as unanimous but the following day one of the jurors stated that he and possibly other jurors had in fact disagreed with the verdict. The judge refused to make any inquiries of jurors in relation to the verdict. The Court of Appeal held that where a verdict is given in the sight and hearing of the entire jury without any dissent by any member of it, there is a presumption that they all assent to it. There was nothing in the present case to rebut that presumption.

In *Gregory v UK* (1998) 25 EHRR 577, nearly two hours after retiring to consider its verdict, a note was passed from the jury to the judge. It read: 'Jury showing racial overtones. One member to be excused.' The trial judge showed the note to the prosecution and defence. He subsequently warned the jury to try the case according to the evidence and to put aside any prejudice. The jury eventually, by a majority of 10 to 2, returned a verdict of guilty. The European Court of Human Rights observed (at para 44):

... the rule governing the secrecy of jury deliberations is a crucial and legitimate feature of English trial law which serves to reinforce the jury's role as the ultimate arbiter of fact and to guarantee open and frank deliberations among jurors on the evidence which they have heard.

The rationale of the secrecy rule was explained by Arbour J, in giving the judgment of the Canadian Supreme Court in *Sawyer* [2001] 2 SCC 344 at pp 373–75:

The first reason supporting the need for secrecy is that confidentiality promotes candour and the kind of full and frank debate that is essential to this type of collegial decision making. While searching for unanimity, jurors should be free to explore out loud all avenues of reasoning without fear of exposure to public ridicule, contempt or hatred. This rationale is of vital importance to the potential acquittal of an unpopular accused, or one charged with a particularly repulsive crime. In my view, this rationale is sound, and does not require empirical confirmation.

The Court of Appeal also placed considerable weight on the second rationale for the secrecy rule: the need to ensure finality of the verdict. Describing the verdict as the product of a dynamic process, the court emphasized the need to protect the solemnity of the verdict, as the product of the unanimous consensus which, when formally announced, carries the finality and authority of a legal pronouncement. That rationale is more abstract, and inevitably invites the question of why the finality of the verdict should prevail over its integrity in cases where that integrity is seriously put in issue. In a legal environment such as ours, which provides for generous review of judicial decisions on appeal, and which does not perceive the voicing of dissenting opinions on appeal as a threat to the authority of the law, I do not consider that finality, standing alone, is a convincing rationale for requiring secrecy.

[T]he third main rationale for the jury secrecy rule [is] the need to protect jurors from harassment, censure and reprisals. Our system of jury selection is sensitive to the privacy interests of prospective jurors ... and the proper functioning of the jury system, a constitutionally protected right in serious criminal charges, depends upon the willingness of jurors to discharge their functions honestly and honourably. This in turn is dependent, at the very minimum, on a system that ensures the safety of jurors, their sense of security, as well as their privacy.

I am fully satisfied that a considerable measure of secrecy surrounding the deliberations of the jury is essential to the proper functioning of that important institution and that the preceding rationales serve as a useful guide to the boundaries between the competing demands of secrecy and reviewability.

The competing demands of 'secrecy and reviewability' mirror the tension that permeates the criminal process between the need for finality (an important goal for adherents of Herbert Packer's 'crime control' perspective) and fairness (an essential element of 'due process').

In *R v Connor; R v Mirza* [2004] UKHL 2; [2004] 1 AC 1118, the House of Lords was called upon to review the rule that the court will not investigate, or receive evidence about, anything said in the course of the jury's deliberations while they are considering their verdict in their retiring room. The questions certified by the Court of Appeal were:

1. Should the common law prohibition on the admission of evidence of the jury's deliber-ations prevail even if the Court of Appeal is presented with a statement from the juror, which, if admitted, would provide prima facie evidence of jury partiality in breach of Article 6?

2. Does section 8 of the Contempt of Court Act 1981, when interpreted in the light of section 3 of the Human Rights Act 1998 and Article 6 of the European Convention, prohibit the admission into evidence of a statement from a juror which if admitted, would provide prima facie evidence of partiality in breach of Article 6? If so, is section 8 incompatible with Article 6 to the extent that it prohibits the admission into evidence of such a statement?

Section 8 of the Contempt of Court Act 1981 provides:

(1) Subject to sub-section (2) below, it is a contempt of court to obtain, disclose or solicit any particulars of statements made, opinions expressed, arguments advanced or votes cast by members of a jury in the course of their deliberations in any legal proceedings.

(2) This section does not apply to any disclosure of any particulars—

(a) in the proceedings in question for the purpose of enabling the jury to arrive at their verdict, or in connection with the delivery of that verdict; or

(b) in evidence in any subsequent proceedings for an offence alleged to have been committed in relation to the jury in the first mentioned proceedings,

or to the publication of any particulars so disclosed.

There have been many calls for s 8 of the Contempt of Court Act 1981 to be amended to enable research to take place into how juries reach their verdicts. The *Auld Review* concluded that the law should not be amended to permit more intrusive research than is already possible into the workings of juries. However, Lord Justice Auld did add that, in appropriate cases, trial judges and/or the Court of Appeal should be entitled to exam-ine alleged improprieties in the jury room. On the issue of research into jury verdicts, the Recommendations steer a very cautious path. They are:

26 There should be no amendment of section 8 of the Contempt of Court Act 1981 to enable research into individual juries' deliberations.

27 Careful consideration should be given to existing research material throughout the common law world on jury trial in criminal cases, with a view to identifying and responding appropriately to all available information about how juries arrive at their verdicts.

28 If and to the extent that such research material is insufficient, consideration should be given to jury research of a general nature that does not violate the 1981 Act.

29 Section 8 of the Contempt of Court Act 1981 should be amended to permit, where appropriate, enquiry by the trial judge and/or the Court of Appeal (Criminal Division) into alleged impropriety by a jury, whether in the course of its deliberations or otherwise.

It is submitted that this final recommendation is unnecessary in so far as the trial judge is concerned, in that the trial judge is already fully entitled to inquire into irregularities that occur during the course of the trial (that is, prior to the verdict).

In January 2005, the Department for Constitutional Affairs published a consultation paper about research into jury deliberations (<http://www.dca.gov.uk/consult/jury-research/juryresearch_cp0405.pdf>). It suggests a number of options:

- to leave s 8 of the Contempt of Court Act 1981 and the common law principle that evidence of a jury's deliberations is generally inadmissable as it is. This would not only prohibit investigation of a jury's deliberations beyond the court, but debar any research into jury deliberations;
- to amend the law to permit research into a jury's deliberations subject to safeguards;
- to amend the law so as to clarify the circumstances in which allegations of jury impropriety can be investigated, but not to allow research into a jury's deliberations;
- to amend the law both to permit research into the process by which a jury reaches its verdict and to clarify the circumstances in which investigations into allegations of juror impropriety can be conducted.

The paper states that the Government does not propose a repeal of s 8 of the 1981 Act, since this provision was implemented to ensure that there could be no publication of a jury's deliberations such as to identify a particular case, and to repeal s 8 in its entirety would, in the view of the Government, 'unacceptably undermine the confidentiality of the jury'. The paper goes on to note that, apart from that, the Government has an 'open mind on whether or not research into a jury's deliberations should be permitted'. The paper confirms the Government's view that allegations of juror impropriety should continue to be handled by the courts on a case-by-case basis, given the diverse nature of behaviour that may be legitimately complained of.

In *Mirza*, it becomes clear that the rules preventing the Court of Appeal from inquiring into what takes place in the jury room result from the common law, not from the effect of s 8. *Mirza* involved two separate appeals. In one of them, it was suggested that some of the jurors may have been motivated by racism; in the other, it was contended that the jury had decided to convict both of them because it would have taken too long to consider the case against each of them separately and, in any event, this would 'teach them a lesson'. In both appeals the allegations were based on a letter sent by a member of the jury after the trial was over. The House of Lords had to consider both the common law rules relating to the secrecy of the jury room and the effect of s 8 of the Contempt of Court Act 1981.

Lord Slynn of Hadley says (at para 55) that:

> The admission of evidence as to what happened in the jury room cannot be allowed without seriously detracting from the advantages which flow from the present system and which in my view need to be protected. If a case arose when all the jurors agreed that something occurred which in effect meant that the jury abrogated its functions and e.g. decided on the toss of a coin the case might be, and in my opinion would be, different.

His Lordship then refers to *R v Young* [1995] QB 324 (where it was alleged that four jurors, during their accommodation overnight in an hotel, had conducted a session with an Ouija board and that a discussion had taken place about this with the other jurors afterwards). In that case, Lord Taylor of Gosforth CJ had said at p 330F–H:

... As a matter of principle, the object of [s 8] is clearly to maintain the secrecy of the jury's deliberations in their retiring room. To give the court power, after verdict, to inquire into those deliberations, would force the door of the jury room wide open. If one dissentient juror or sharp-eared bailiff alleged irregularities in the jury room, the court would be pressed to inquire into the jury's deliberations. We are in no doubt that s 8(1) applies to the court as to everyone else.

Lord Slynn, holding that *Young* was wrongly decided on this point, says (at para 57):

... in enacting s 8 of the Contempt of Court Act 1981 ... Parliament did not intend to fetter the power of a court to make investigation as to the conduct of a trial. Properly construed, s 8(1) does not apply to the court of trial or to the Court of Appeal hearing an appeal in that case. It cannot properly be read as categorising what the court does in the course of its investigation as a contempt of the court itself. What was said in *R v Young* [1995] QB 324, at p 330 should not be followed. The court is restricted in its inquiry into what happened in the jury's deliberations, not by s 8 of the Act but by the longstanding rule of the common law.

Lord Hope said (at para 90):

... a court cannot be in contempt of itself. In my opinion s 8(1) is addressed to third parties who can be punished for contempt, and not to the court which has the responsibility of ensuring that the defendant receives a fair trial. The observations to the contrary in *R v Young* at p 330 F–H should now be disapproved.

It follows, said his Lordship (para 92), that:

Where allegations are made which suggest that a defendant is not receiving, or did not receive, the fair trial to which he was entitled under Article 6(1) of the Convention, they must be considered and investigated. Any investigation must, of course, be within the limits that are set by the common law. Evidence which is struck at by the common law rule will be inadmissible, and the court should not ask for or receive such evidence.

But there is nothing in the statute that expressly inhibits or restricts the court in its performance of this task ...

Lord Hope went on (para 93) to say:

... it is going too far to suggest, as the Court of Appeal appears to have done in *Young*'s case, that the trial court will be in contempt of itself if during the trial, having received allegations such as those made by the jurors in these cases, it investigates them and discloses the result of these investigations to counsel so that they may have an opportunity of making submissions about them to the court; or that the Court of Appeal in its turn, or persons acting under its direction, will be in contempt if the Court of Appeal decides that in the interests of justice the allegations must be investigated. The court must look to the common law for guidance as to the extent to which any such investigation is permissible.

Having established that the only restriction on the court is to be found in the common law, his Lordship went on to consider the common law rules (and whether those rules are compatible with Art 6(1) of the European Convention on Human Rights). He takes as his starting point three propositions (para 61): that confidentiality is essential to the proper functioning of the jury process; that there is merit in finality; and that jurors must be protected from harassment. At para 107, Lord Hope summarises the exceptions to the common law rules as disclosed by case law:

- matters which were extrinsic to the deliberations in the jury room;
- events that took place outside the jury room;
- irregularities which may have led to the jury being provided with information which they should not have had;
- the possession by a juror of knowledge or characteristics which made it inappropriate for that person to serve on the jury.

The present appeals concerned allegations that were directed to what took place during the jury's deliberations in the jury room and so fell squarely within the common law rule.

Lord Hope refers to the dictum of the Canadian judge, Arbour J (cited above) and comments (at para 115) that:

> These observations take us to the heart of the matter. The appeals raise questions about a rule which makes it impossible, after a guilty verdict has been returned, to investigate allegations that the jurors were biased or that they ignored directions by the trial judge. But the rigour of the secrecy rule operates, and is designed to operate, in exactly the same way if the verdict is one of not guilty. A defendant does not need to invoke his article 6(1) right where he has been acquitted. But the rule protects jurors who acquit the unpopular, such as members of minority groups, or who acquit those accused of crimes that the public regards as repulsive, such as the abuse of children who were in their care. It protects them too against pressure that might otherwise be brought to bear, in less enlightened times, by the executive.

He goes on (para 116):

> This is an important safeguard against biased verdicts. One cannot have a rule that operates in one way where the jury acquits but operates differently where they convict. Full and frank discussion, in the course of which prejudices may indeed be aired but then rejected when it comes to the moment of decision-taking, would be inhibited if everything that might give rise to allegations of prejudice after the verdict is delivered were to be opened up to scrutiny. Attempts to soften the rule to serve the interests of those who claim that they were unfairly convicted should be resisted in the general public interest, if jurors are to continue to perform their vital function of safeguarding the liberty of every individual.

Lord Hope concludes (at para 123) that he would be:

> . . . inclined to make only one modification to the rule that distinguishes, after the verdict has been delivered, between things which are intrinsic to the deliberation process and those which are extrinsic to it . . . it is arguable that an allegation that the jury as a whole declined to deliberate at all, but decided the case by other means such as drawing lots or by the toss

of a coin, can be placed into a different category. Conduct of that kind, were it ever to occur, would amount to a complete repudiation by the jury of their only function which, as the juror's oath puts it, is to give a true verdict according to the evidence. A trial which results in a verdict by lot or the toss of a coin, or was reached by consulting an Ouija board in the jury room, is not a trial at all. If that is what happened, the jurors have no need to be protected as the verdict was not reached by deliberation – that is, by discussing and debating the issues in the case and arriving at a decision collectively in the light of that discussion. The law would be unduly hampered if the court were to be unable to intervene in such a case and order a new trial.

Having held that the common law should continue to require that the deliberations of the jury must remain confidential, Lord Hope suggested two 'refinements to current practice with a view to strengthening the system of jury trial and retaining public confidence': first, that jurors should be informed that they are under a duty to inform the court at once of any irregularity which occurs during their deliberations (if that step is taken before the verdict is delivered, the trial judge can – indeed must – investigate and deal with the matter); second, that where an irregularity involving the jury is a ground of appeal, the Court of Appeal should call for a report from the trial judge, so that the Court of Appeal has a complete and accurate account of the events of the trial.

Lord Hobhouse of Woodborough, at para 131, makes the point that 'it is fundamentally wrong to use the phrase "miscarriage of justice" selectively as if it only related to perverse convictions . . . a perverse verdict of not guilty, whatever the reason for it, is also a miscarriage of justice'. His Lordship points out (at para 135) that approximately 20 per cent of all convictions after a trial on indictment result from majority verdicts and suggests that:

> This is inevitably a fertile scenario for a dissident juror, maybe honestly, maybe not, to claim that the majority disregarded or misunderstood the judge's direction, did not understand the facts, were not prepared to listen to argument or were prejudiced in some way.

At para 142, Lord Hobhouse reiterates the arguments in favour of the confidentiality of jury deliberations:

> It underpins the independence and impartiality of the jury as a whole. It enables them to be true to their oath to return a true verdict according to the evidence without fearing the consequences of the reporting of things individual jurors have said or the arguments they have advanced. They can play their part in the collective deliberations of the jury without fear of quotation, embarrassment or victimisation.

Lord Rodger of Earlsferry recalls (at para 156) that:

> Allegations of misconduct by jurors may surface at any stage of a trial before the jury has returned a verdict. In such cases there is no reason why the allegations should not be investigated. Judges must accordingly take appropriate steps to investigate and deal with any such matter that arises then . . . If it turns out on investigation of an allegation that the jury as a whole is fatally compromised, the judge will discharge them. Where only one particular juror is fatally compromised, the judge will discharge that juror and the trial will proceed

with the remaining jurors. In less serious cases the judge will deal with the matter by giving the jury appropriate directions.

His Lordship quotes from the judgment of the European Court of Human Rights in *Gregory v UK* (1997) 25 EHRR 577, and comments (at para 160):

> In other words, faced with a situation where the rule that jurors' deliberations had to be kept secret made it impossible for the trial judge to find out what had given rise to the note, the European Court acknowledged that that rule was not only a legitimate, but a 'crucial', feature of English trial law which served worthwhile objectives. Thus the incorporation of Article 6 of the Convention into our domestic law can be regarded as reinforcing, rather than as calling into question, the rule that jury deliberations should be kept secret.

At para 165, his Lordship says that:

> Once returned . . . the verdict becomes the verdict of the jury as a whole and, as such, it cannot be impugned by any of the individual jurors who have publicly assented to it. To hold otherwise would not only call into question the entire status and authority of the jury's verdict but would also expose jurors to pressure, especially from convicted defendants and their associates, to make such allegations.

At para 173, Lord Rodgers points out that the *Auld Review* (Chapter 5, para 98) recommended that the Court of Appeal should be able to inquire into alleged impropriety by a jury, whether in the course of their deliberations or otherwise. His Lordship continues:

> This would involve a substantial, if not complete, departure from the present law and from its underlying policies. There is, as yet, no sign that the Government intend to bring forward legislation to implement the recommendation. Any such far-reaching reform of the law on this topic must, however, be a matter for Parliament rather than for this House in its judicial capacity. Only Parliament is in a position to weigh the competing policy arguments and, if so advised, to produce a new and suitably sophisticated solution. Unless and until that happens, the existing law must be applied.

It seems likely that this factor will have weighed heavily on the other three Law Lords who agreed that the House of Lords should affirm the common law rules on the secrecy of the jury room. It could be argued that if Parliament is examining an area of law, the courts should not pre-empt that examination by making their own modifications to that area of law.

Nonetheless, in a powerful dissenting speech, Lord Steyn disagreed vehemently with the view expressed by the other four Law Lords:

> If the law requires individual cases to be subordinated to systemic considerations affecting the jury system, one may question whether the law has not lost its moral underpinning (para 5).

Lord Steyn emphasises the importance of the jury to public confidence in our criminal justice system. At para 7, his Lordship says:

Lord Devlin observed 'that trial by jury is more than an instrument of justice and more than one wheel of the constitution: it is the lamp that shows that freedom lives': Trial by Jury, (1956), p 164 . . . The jury is an integral and indispensable part of the criminal justice system. The system of trial by judge and jury is of constitutional significance. The jury is also, through its collective decision-making, an excellent fact finder. Not surprisingly, the public trust juries. What public opinion would not tolerate are jury verdicts arrived at by perverse processes.

To ensure the integrity of the jury system, Lord Steyn said (para 8) that:

> . . . it is necessary to accept that the Court of Appeal has the power in exceptional cases to examine material regarding jury deliberations tending to show that the jury or some of them were false to their oath.

His Lordship accepted that 'there must be a general rule that the deliberations of the jury must remain secret' (para 9). However, he took the view that there should be exceptions to this rule where the justice of the case so requires. At para 12, he quotes from the commentary to the Court of Appeal decision in *R v Qureshi* [2002] Crim LR 62 by the late Professor Sir John Smith QC:

> If the allegations in the present case were true and if the court had been able to inquire into them, it seems likely that the conviction would have been held to be unsafe. As it is, we shall never know. Not a happy situation . . .

Lord Steyn goes on to quote from Professor J R Spencer [2002] 61 CLJ 291 at p 293:

> The nub of the decision in *Qureshi*, one suspects, is the remark that if the appeal were allowed it might lead 'to many such complaints, some perhaps owing their origin to friends or relatives of the defendant'. But this simply will not do. The fact that many allegations of this sort are false cannot justify ignoring all of them because, as *Young* [the ouija board case] so painfully reminds us, some of them regrettably are true.

Turning to the interpretation of the decided cases, Lord Steyn said (at para 14):

> In none of the judgments is there any clear indication that the courts would have been prepared to uphold an absolute rule excluding evidence about jury deliberations in cases where there is credible evidence, disclosed after verdict, showing that the jury was not impartial. In none of the decided cases has it been held that the court may in the interests of the efficient functioning of the jury system tolerate real identifiable risks of miscarriages of justice.

At para 16, Lord Steyn says:

> In cases where there is cogent evidence demonstrating a real risk that the jury was not impartial and that the general confidence in jury verdicts was in the particular case ill reposed, what possible public interest can there be in maintaining a dubious conviction?

At para 19, Lord Steyn says:

In my view it would be an astonishing thing for the ECHR to hold, when the point directly arises before it, that a miscarriage of justice may be ignored in the interests of the general efficiency of the jury system . . . such a view would be utterly indefensible.

At para 22, Lord Steyn says that the consequence of the ruling of the majority is that the jury is immune from scrutiny:

... on the basis that such immunity is a price worth paying. This restrictive view will gnaw at public confidence in juries. It is likely in the long run to increase pressure for reducing the scope of trial by jury. A system which forfeits its moral authority is not likely to survive intact. The question will be whether such a system provides a better quality of justice than trial by professionals.

There is discussion of the issues raised by the rule relating to the secrecy of the deliberation of the jury by Katie Quinn in 'Jury Bias and the European Convention on Human Rights: a Well-Kept Secret' [2004] Crim LR 998 and by Laura McGowan in 'Trial by Jury: Still a Lamp in the Dark?' (2005) 69 J Crim L 518. McGowan lists the main reasons given for continuing the secrecy of the jury room and responds to each of those reasons:

i   it would undermine public confidence in the jury system, to which she responds if verdicts are being reached on an improper basis (for example on the basis of racism) then this should be exposed, since it is only when this emerges that such improper behaviour can be rooted out and the system reformed;
ii it would compromise frank discussion among the jury in reaching their verdict, to which she responds that it would be wholly unacceptable to tolerate prejudicial discussion when deciding on a verdict;
iii it would undermine finality of verdicts to the extent that justice cannot be effectively administered, to which she responds that the finality of verdicts has already been compromised by the provisions of Pts 9 and 10 of the Criminal Justice Act 2003 (allowing retrial for serious offences where compelling new evidence comes to light and casts doubt on an acquittal, and prosecution appeals against terminating rulings) and that if a verdict is based on bias or impropriety it should not have the legal or moral character of being final but should be questioned; and
iv it would prejudice the privacy or safety of the jury or expose them to intimidation, to which she responds that measures can be put in place to prevent intimidation of jurors.

McGowan concludes that an investigation into jury deliberations should be permitted 'where there is a real risk that the jury has not tried the defendant according to the evidence' (in other words, has not acted in accordance with the jury oath). This echoes the response of JUSTICE to the Government's Consultation Paper on Jury Research (<http://www.justice.org.uk/images/pdfs/jurydca.pdf>), which recommended that 'the Court of Appeal should be able to order an investigation if there is prima facie evidence that if proved would give rise to a reasonable apprehension of unfairness or the appearance of unfairness'. JUSTICE came to this view on the basis that such a reform would enhance the credibility of jury trial.

Nicola Haralambous, in 'Investigating Impropriety in Jury Deliberations: A Recipe for Disaster' (2204) 68 J Crim L 411, made a similar point, arguing that there should be an exception to the rule upholding the secrecy of jury deliberations where there is a real risk that those deliberations were vitiated by bias. She argues that where it comes to light that a jury has behaved improperly, there must be some recourse for the defendant, and she adds that individual jurors could be protected, for example through reporting restrictions preventing the publication of information which might lead to a particular juror being identified.

The decision in *Connor* was considered by the House of Lords in R *v Smith; R v Mercieca* [2005] UKHL 12; [2005] 1 WLR 704. After the jury had been deliberating for some time, the judge received a letter from one of the jurors, stating that a certain group of jurors had been badgering, coercing and intimidating other jurors into changing their verdicts. The judge, after consulting with counsel, gave a further direction to the jury, telling them that there had to be discussion and give and take, and exhorting them not to be bullied or cajoled into giving a verdict with which they did not agree. The jury returned majority verdicts of guilty against both defendants. It was held that the judge was not obliged to question the jurors about the contents of the letter, nor would it have been appropriate for him to do so. If he had gone into the allegations, he would inevitably have had to question them about the subject of their deliberations (namely, whether the defendants were guilty of any of the offences charged). The common law prohibition against inquiring into events in the jury room extends to matters connected with the subject matter of the jury's deliberations. Moreover, where the juror's communication alleges wilful misconduct on the part of certain jurors and deliberate disregard of the judge's directions on the law, the prospects of obtaining satisfactory answers to questioning would be rather limited. The judge in such a case is left with the choice of discharging the jury or giving them a further direction. If the jury have been behaving as alleged in the juror's letter, they require a strong, even stern, warning that they have to follow the judge's directions on the law, adhere to the evidence without speculation, and decide on the verdicts without pressure or bargaining. Without strong and detailed guidance and instruction it would be difficult for the Court of Appeal to be satisfied that the discussion in the jury room was conducted in the proper manner.

In *Attorney General v Scotcher* [2005] UKHL 36; [2005] 1 WLR 1867, the House of Lords held that a juror who discloses to the court, whether directly or indirectly, what was said or done during the jury's deliberations, with the intention of prompting an investigation, is not (without more) in contempt of court under s 8(1) of the Contempt of Court Act 1981. Thus, a juror who writes to the Crown Court or to the Court of Appeal, or who speaks or writes to the jury bailiff or to the clerk of the court, is not in contempt. Similarly, a juror who sends a sealed letter containing his complaint to the defendant's solicitors or counsel (or even to a Citizens' Advice Bureau or similar organisation, asking them to forward it unopened to the appropriate court authorities) does not fall within s 8(1). However, writing to a third party (in the case, the defendants' mother) with the intention that the matter should be raised by lawyers presenting an appeal to the Court of Appeal is not sufficient to exclude the juror from the scope of s 8(1).

In *R v Adams* [2007] EWCA Crim 1; [2007] 1 Cr App R 34, the Court of Appeal said that it is highly undesirable for any person to seek to interview a juror without first obtaining the leave of the court. Circumstances in which the Court of Appeal will need to hear evidence from a juror or jurors are likely to be rare and exceptional. In light of paras IV.42.5–9 of the *Consolidated Practice Direction*, which advises judges to tell jurors that they should report any irregularities occurring during the course of the trial to the court, silence as to any such irregularity will almost certainly mean that the Court of Appeal will assume that none occurred (per Gage LJ at para 180).

In *R v Pintori* [2007] EWCA Crim 1700, Dyson LJ (at para 19) reiterated that the

> general rule is that evidence of the jury's deliberations is inadmissible and it seems to us that this must extend to evidence not only of the jury's discussions but also to evidence of how and why a particular juror reached his or her verdict.

However, in the present case, evidence that the juror in question was a civilian police employee and of the extent of her knowledge of the officers in the case was admissible. The fact that the juror knew the officers in the case reasonably well and had worked with them was enough to satisfy the bias test as regards her. There was a real possibility that she would have been influenced by those factors in reaching her verdict, and there was no doubt that the fair-minded informed observer would have concluded that there was a real possibility that the biased juror had influenced her fellow jurors. The risk of contamination could not safely be excluded.

13.7 FRESH EVIDENCE IN THE COURT OF APPEAL

One reason for a conviction being unsafe may be that new evidence has come to light which casts doubt on the safety of the conviction. Another reason is that the trial judge wrongly declared certain evidence to be inadmissible. In either case, the Court of Appeal has a discretion to receive evidence which was not adduced at the trial. Section 23(1) of the Criminal Appeal Act 1968 empowers the Court of Appeal to receive fresh evidence.

The Court of Appeal decides whether or not to receive fresh evidence on the basis of written witness statements. If the Court of Appeal decides to receive the evidence, the witnesses have to attend court to give their evidence unless the court regards the written statement it has already seen as sufficient. Each witness is usually examined-in-chief on behalf of the appellant and cross-examined on behalf of the Crown.

Under s 23(2) of the 1968 Act:

> The Court of Appeal shall, in considering whether to receive any evidence, have regard in particular to—
>
> (a) whether the evidence appears to the Court to be capable of belief;
> (b) whether it appears to the Court that the evidence may afford any ground for allowing the appeal;
> (c) whether the evidence would have been admissible in the proceedings from which the appeal lies on an issue which is the subject of the appeal; and
> (d) whether there is a reasonable explanation for the failure to adduce the evidence in those proceedings.

Thus, the criteria to which the court must have regard when deciding whether or not to receive fresh evidence are:

- the credibility of the new evidence (s 23(2)(a));
- the relevance of the new evidence – would it have made a difference had it been adduced at trial? (s 23(2)(b));
- the admissibility of the evidence, applying the usual rules of evidence (s 23(2)(c)); and
- the reason for that evidence not being adduced at trial (s 23(2)(d)).

In assessing credibility, the court will consider whether the evidence is intrinsically credible and whether it fits in with at least some of the evidence adduced at trial (*R v Parks* [1961] 1 WLR 1484). To assess the credibility of the witness for the purpose of s 23(2)(a), the court should either be provided with an affidavit or a written witness statement or else the Registrar must have been asked to arrange for an out-of-court deposition to be taken by an examiner appointed by the court. In *R v Gogana* (1999) *The Times*, 12 July, the Court of Appeal emphasised the importance of this require-ment, particularly where it is suggested that a witness who has previously made a statement is now prepared to give different evidence. In such a case, the court must be supplied with affidavit evidence from all those involved in the taking of the new state-ment (since the circumstances in which that new statement came into existence are highly relevant to its potential credibility).

As far as s 23(2)(b) is concerned, in *R v Gilfoyle* [1996] 3 All ER 883, Beldam LJ said (at p 898):

> In our judgment the court has not only the power to receive admissible evidence which would afford a ground for allowing the appeal but has a wider discretion, if it thinks it necessary or expedient in the interests of justice, to order any witness to attend for examin-ation and to be examined before the court whether or not he testified at the trial. We are satisfied that the interests of justice are not simply confined to receiving evidence which would result in an appeal being allowed, particularly when the court is being asked to review as unsafe and unsatisfactory the verdict of a jury after an impeccable summing-up on the ground that it has a lurking doubt.

The court is therefore empowered to receive admissible evidence which reinforces or dispels a lurking doubt.

Section 23(2)(c) simply requires that the evidence be admissible. Where the trial judge ruled that certain evidence was inadmissible, it is of course open to the Court of Appeal, if it rules that the evidence was in fact admissible, to receive that evidence itself.

The fact that counsel for the defence took a tactical decision not to call a particular witness is not generally regarded as a reasonable explanation for the failure to adduce the evidence at trial for the purpose of s 23(2)(d), and so the Court of Appeal is unlikely to hear the evidence of that witness. In *R v Sharp* [2003] EWCA Crim 3870, the Court of Appeal was asked to entertain evidence relating to diminishing responsibility even though that defence had not been raised at the trial. The court noted that there are two conflicting principles. The first principle is that facts 'establishing innocence should not be excluded because of a previous mistaken decision by the appellant or by his advisers'. The second (and conflicting) principle is that it is not open to appellants to choose not to run a defence at trial and then to go back on that decision at the appeal. The Court of Appeal cited with approval the words of Lord Bingham CJ in *R v Campbell* [1997] 1 Cr App R 199 (at p 204):

> This Court has repeatedly underlined the need for defendants in criminal trials to advance their full defence before the jury and call any necessary evidence at that stage. It is not permissible to advance one defence before the jury and, when that has failed, to devise a new defence, perhaps many years later, and then seek to raise that defence on appeal.

This dictum was itself based closely on earlier guidance given by Lord Taylor CJ in *R v Ahluwalia* (1992) 96 Cr App R 133 (at p 142):

> Ordinarily, of course, any available defences should be advanced at trial. Accordingly, if medical evidence is available to support a plea of diminished responsibility, it should be adduced at the trial. It cannot be too strongly emphasised that this court would require much persuasion to allow such a defence to be raised for the first time here if the option had been exercised at the trial not to pursue it. Otherwise, as must be clear, defendants might be encouraged to run one defence at trial in the belief that if it fails, this court would allow a different defence to be raised and give the defendant, in effect, two opportunities to run different defences. Nothing could be further from the truth.

In *Sharp*, the Court of Appeal concluded that the inhibition on running a different defence on appeal is not limited to cases where the original decision was in some way dishonest or manipulative, or one purely of tactics. It will only be in very exceptional cases that a different defence can be adduced (per Buxton LJ at para 32).

In *R v Hampton* [2004] EWCA Crim 2139; (2004), *The Times*, 13 October, it was held that, if a defendant, who was in a position to call a witness at trial, deliberately took an informed decision not to call the witness, he could not expect an appeal based on fresh evidence to succeed. At para 101, Hooper LJ summarises the relevant principles thus:

(1) The cases demonstrate that all applications to adduce evidence on appeal under s 23 turn on their own particular facts . . .

(2) The fundamental question in each case is whether the Court of Appeal thinks it is either necessary or expedient in the interests of justice to receive the evidence sought to be adduced.

(3) In answering that question the Court of Appeal must have regard to the four factors that are set out in section 23(2). They are not prerequisites that must be fulfilled before the Court of Appeal will receive the evidence that is sought to be adduced on appeal. But . . . the cases do identify certain features which are likely to weigh more or less heavily against the reception of evidence on appeal . . .

(4) In relation to the fourth factor, which is set out at s 23(2)(d), viz. whether there is a reasonable explanation of the failure to adduce the evidence at the trial, even if it is held that there is no reasonable explanation, that is not necessarily fatal to the application to adduce evidence on appeal. The Court of Appeal still has a duty to consider whether it is necessary or expedient in the interests of justice to receive the evidence . . .

(5)   In general a defendant is only entitled to one trial, so that it is his duty (as it is that of the prosecution) to put forward all his case and all the evidence that he wishes to be considered at that trial . . .

(6)   If the reason for a case not being argued or evidence not being adduced at the trial is that the defendant's legal advisers acted in such a way as to deprive the defendant of a fair trial, then that could amount to a reasonable explanation for the failure to adduce the evidence at the trial. However, if there was a deliberate, informed decision by a defendant and his advisers not to advance a defence or evidence known to be available and that decision is made for tactical reasons, then that will not amount to a reasonable explanation for the failure to adduce that evidence at trial . . .

The court went on to note that a decision on whether to call a witness to support an alibi can only be said to have been made in a deliberate and informed way if the defendant and his advisers had all relevant and accurate information available at the time that the decision is made. However, an informed decision not to call an alibi witness for sound tactical reasons is (for the purposes of s 23(2)(d)) regarded as not being a 'reasonable explanation' for a failure to call a witness. At para 103, his Lordship concluded:

> In any case, the Court of Appeal has always to ask the ultimate question: is it necessary or expedient in the interests of justice to receive the evidence that the appellant wishes to adduce at the appeal? If an informed decision was made by the appellant and his advisers, for sound tactical reasons, not to call a witness at the trial, then even if the factors in s 23(2)(a) (b) and (c) are in the appellant's favour, the Court of Appeal is most likely to conclude that it is not expedient in the interests of justice to permit the evidence of that witness to be adduced on appeal.

It follows that, even if there is no reasonable explanation for the failure to adduce particular evidence at trial, it might nevertheless be expedient in the interests of justice to receive that fresh evidence (provided that it would have been admissible at the trial, is capable of belief, and might afford a ground for allowing the appeal): see *R v Cairns* [2000] Crim LR 473, where the Court of Appeal noted that it is possible for the court to receive fresh evidence under s 23 of the 1968 Act even if all of the four criteria in sub-s (2)(a)–(d) are not satisfied.

In *R v Sales* [2000] 2 Cr App R 431, the Court of Appeal said that it is only in rare cases that the Court of Appeal will receive fresh evidence in respect of a defence that was not only not advanced at trial but was completely different to the defence given at trial, and that it is also rare for the Court of Appeal to receive evidence from an appellant who chose not to give evidence before the jury. However, the court confirmed that it is possible for the Court of Appeal to receive fresh evidence even if all four of the considerations under s 23(2) of the 1968 Act are not satisfied, providing that the Court of Appeal has had regard to those matters (per Rose LJ at p 437).

In *R v Gautier* (Court of Appeal, 9 May 2007, unreported), it was held that where an appellant seeks to rely on fresh evidence by calling a witness who was not called at trial as a result of the advice or decision of the defendant's counsel and it is alleged that the advice or decision was mistaken, the Court of Appeal will not admit the evidence unless there is a lurking doubt that injustice was caused by flagrantly incompetent advocacy. It would seldom, if ever, be a reasonable explanation for not calling a witness that the risk of calling him was considered to be too great and counsel had advised that he should not be called.

Where evidence could not have been obtained with 'reasonable diligence' in time for the trial (for example, a relevant witness has only just come forward), there is of course a reasonable explanation for not adducing that evidence at the trial. However, the defendant has to co-operate in the preparation of the defence case. In *R v Beresford* (1972) 56 Cr App R 143, where the appellant wished to rely on the evidence of alibi witnesses who had not been called at the trial, the defence solicitors had not been given the names and addresses of the potential witnesses. However, as the appellant could have supplied this information to his solicitors before the trial, the Court of Appeal held that there was no reasonable explanation for the failure to adduce the evidence at trial.

In *R v Jamil* [2001] EWCA Crim 1687; (2001) *The Times*, 25 October, the appeal was based on the existence of a police report which had not been disclosed to the defence. It was held that in cases in which fresh evidence is uncovered following a trial, this evidence should be considered within the actual context of the case, bearing in mind the material available to the defence at the time, the instructions given by the defendant and the manner in which the defence conducted the trial. The test as to whether or not the fresh evidence is such as to render the conviction unsafe is whether, having regard to all these matters, the fresh evidence is likely to have been used by the defence. If the answer to this question is in the negative, then it is very unlikely that the discovery of the fresh evidence will render the conviction unsafe (per Hooper J at para 44).

In *R v Jones* [1997] 1 Cr App R 86, the Court of Appeal considered the position of expert witnesses. The court noted that s 23(2)(d) applies more aptly to factual evidence of which a party was unaware or could not adduce at the trial. Expert witnesses, unlike factual witnesses, even though they may vary in standing, are interchangeable. A defendant who is unable to call a particular expert at the trial should either apply for a postponement of the trial or else should try to find a different expert witness. Having said that, the Court of Appeal decided that it was in the interests of justice in the present case to receive the evidence of the three expert witnesses upon whom the appellant wished to rely.

In *R v Garner* (Court of Appeal, 20 December 1996, unreported), Potter LJ drew a distinction between (on one hand) cases involving the late discovery of some earlier suppression or mistake, or evidence dealing with some feature of the case which had hitherto been unknown, unappreciated or misunderstood, or some advancement in scientific techniques, or changes in scientific and technical perception, or indeed confession of error or change of opinion on the part of expert witnesses who were called at the original trial, and (on the other hand) cases where expert evidence related to matters of professional duty and practice in fields largely governed by codes of conduct, rulings of professional bodies, or matters of generally accepted practice within the profession concerned. If, in such a case, the position appears to be that, on the basis of the facts known and available for comment at the trial, opinion within the profession (as represented by the expert for the prosecution and the experts consulted by the defence) is broadly agreed, but that the defence have since discovered an expert who is in significant disagreement with such opinion, the Court of Appeal should hesitate long before permitting his evidence to be adduced on appeal.

Most applications to receive fresh evidence are made by the appellant. However, there is no reason why the prosecution cannot invite the court to receive fresh evidence. In *R v Hanratty* [2002] EWCA Crim 1141; [2002] 3 All ER 534, the Court of Appeal said that the overriding consideration, when deciding whether to admit fresh evidence at the request of the prosecution, is whether that evidence could assist the court to achieve justice, bearing in mind that the conviction could be unsafe either because there was a doubt as to the guilt of the defendant or because the trial was materially flawed. The court rejected the submission that the prosecution could only place evidence before the court if it was used to evaluate or rebut fresh evidence adduced by the appellant.

In *R v Pendleton* [2001] UKHL 66; [2002] 1 WLR 72, the House of Lords considered the test to be applied in deciding whether or not to allow an appeal against conviction where fresh evidence has been received under s 23 of the Criminal Appeal Act 1968. It was held (following *Stafford v DPP* [1974] AC 878) that the Court of Appeal should consider the effect of the fresh evidence on the minds of the members of the court, and not the effect that it would have had on the minds of the jury, so long as the court bears very clearly in mind that the question for its consideration is whether the conviction is safe and not whether the accused was guilty. Such a test reminds the Court of Appeal that it is not and should never become the primary decision-maker, and that it has an imperfect and incomplete understanding of the full processes which had led the jury to convict. The court can make its assessment of the fresh evidence it has heard but, save in a clear case, it is at a disadvantage in seeking to relate that evidence to the rest of the evidence which the jury heard. It would therefore usually be wise for the Court of Appeal, in a case of any difficulty, to test their own provisional view by asking whether the evidence, if given at the trial, might reasonably have affected the decision of the trial jury to convict. If it might, the conviction must be thought to be unsafe (per Lord Bingham at para 19).

In *Dosoruth v State of Mauritius* [2004] UKPC 51; [2005] Crim LR 474, the Privy Council, considering fresh evidence as a ground of appeal, held that the mere fact that additional evidence might have made a difference to the result had it been available at trial is an insufficient reason for ordering a retrial. Not only does it have to be shown that the additional evidence is relevant to the issue before the trial court and that, if steps had been taken to lead the evidence at that stage, it would have been admissible, but the court also has to be satisfied that it is in the interests of justice, having regard to the right of the defendant to a fair hearing, for the additional evidence to be taken into account at the stage of the appeal (per Lord Hope at para 22).

13.8 RESULT OF APPEAL AGAINST CONVICTION

The Court of Appeal has a number of options open to it when disposing of an appeal against conviction.

13.8.1 Appeal dismissed

If the Court of Appeal decides that the appellant's conviction was safe, it will dismiss the appeal and the appellant's conviction will stand.

13.8.2 Successful appeal

If the Court of Appeal decides that the conviction was unsafe, it has up to four options.

13.8.2.1 Quashing the conviction

If the conviction is quashed, the appellant is regarded for all purposes as if he had been acquitted by the jury. The doctrine of *autrefois acquit* applies, so the appellant cannot be re-prosecuted for the same offence (save in the limited circumstances set out in the Criminal Justice Act 2003). If the Court of Appeal allows the appellant's appeal on some counts of an indictment but not others, the Court of Appeal may also review the sentence. However, if the sentence is altered, it must not be more severe than that imposed by the Crown Court.

13.8.2.2 Ordering a retrial

Section 7(1) of the Criminal Appeal Act 1968 provides that the Court of Appeal may order a retrial where the court allows an appeal against conviction and it appears to the court that the interests of justice so require.

Under s 7(2), a retrial may be ordered only in respect of:

a the offence of which the appellant was convicted at the original trial and in respect of which his appeal has been allowed;
b an offence of which he could have been convicted at the original trial (i.e. by way of alternative verdict under s 6(3) of the Criminal Law Act 1967); or
c an offence which was charged in an alternative count at the original trial.

In *R v Graham* [1997] 1 Cr App R 302 (at p 318), Lord Bingham CJ said that the interests of justice:

> ... requires an exercise of judgment, and will involve consideration of the public interest and the legitimate interests of the defendant. The public interest is generally served by the prosecution of those reasonably suspected on available evidence of serious crime, if such prosecution can be conducted without unfairness to or oppression of the defendant. The legitimate interests of the defendant will often call for consideration of the time which has passed since the alleged offence, and any penalty the defendant may already have paid before the quashing of the conviction.

If the appeal is allowed after the Court of Appeal has heard fresh evidence, a retrial will usually be ordered so that a jury can hear all the evidence. If, however, the fresh evidence clearly establishes that the appellant is innocent of the charge, the Court of Appeal will simply quash the conviction. No retrial will be ordered if the original trial took place so long ago that the memories of the witnesses would have faded, making a fair trial impossible (*R v Saunders* (1974) 58 Cr App R 248). Furthermore, if the appellant has already spent time in custody so that he has, in effect, already served whatever sentence would be appropriate were he to be found guilty on a retrial, no retrial will be ordered (*R v Newland* [1988] QB 402, at 408).

In *Nicholls v The State* (2001) *The Times*, 30 January, it was held by the Privy Council that where an appeal against conviction is allowed because the trial judge failed to mention to the jury that there were inadequacies in the prosecution case, and those inadequacies could have been remedied by the prosecution calling further evidence (in the present case, expert evidence), the proper course is simply to quash the conviction, and not to order a retrial. It would be wrong in principle to allow the prosecution another chance to make good the deficiencies in its case by calling further evidence.

Section 8 of the Criminal Appeal Act 1968 says that where a retrial has been ordered, a fresh indictment must be preferred (i.e. delivered to the Crown Court) within two months of the order; if it is not preferred within that time, the defendant may apply to the Court of Appeal for the order to be set aside. Such an application will succeed unless the prosecution can show that they have acted with all due expedition (that is, all reasonable promptness) and there is good and sufficient cause for a retrial despite the delay.

It is permissible to introduce a new count to the indictment where there is a retrial, provided that this can be done without injustice to the defendant (*R v Swaine* (2000) *The Times*, 1 November).

13.8.2.3 Venire de novo

There will be some (very rare) cases where the statutory power to order a retrial is not available. This will be the case where the proceedings at the trial were a nullity. Examples of this are where some irregularity of procedure has occurred so that no trial was validly commenced (an extreme instance of this would be if a defendant were to be tried in the Crown Court without having been sent for trial by a valid method) or where the trial comes to an end without a properly constituted jury ever having returned a valid verdict (an instance of this would be where the number of jurors remaining falls below the statutory minimum of nine but the judge nevertheless allows the trial to continue and accepts a 'verdict' from the remaining jurors). In such a case, if the Court of Appeal wishes to order a retrial, it does so by means of a writ of *venire de novo* (see *R v Rose* [1982] AC 822). In *R v O'Donnell* [1996] 1 Cr App R 286, for example, the defendant was tried despite having been found unfit to plead (see Chapter 12). Because the trial should not have continued after the finding that the defendant was unfit to plead, the conviction was a nullity; thus, there was no conviction for the defendant to appeal against for the purposes of s 2 of the Criminal Appeal Act 1968. Nonetheless, the Court of Appeal used its inherent jurisdiction to set aside and annul the 'conviction' and then exercised its discretion to order a *venire de novo*.

Where the Court of Appeal allows an appeal on the ground that there has been an irregularity which vitiates the whole trial but decides not to grant an order for retrial (*venire de novo*), the proper form of order is that the conviction 'be set aside and annulled and that there be no new trial'. There is no conviction to quash (since the purported conviction is a nullity) and so there is no power to grant a statutory acquittal under the Criminal Appeal Act 1968 (*R v Booth* [1999] 1 Cr App R 457).

13.8.2.4 Substituting a conviction for an alternative offence

Section 3 of the Criminal Appeal Act 1968 provides that where the appellant has been convicted of an offence to which he did not plead guilty, and the jury could on the indictment have found him guilty of another offence, and on the finding of the jury it appears to the Court of Appeal that the jury must have been satisfied of facts which proved him guilty of the other offence, the court may, instead of allowing or dismissing the appeal, substitute for the verdict of the jury a verdict of guilty of the other offence. Therefore, if:

a   the jury could, on the indictment, have found the appellant guilty of some other offence; and
b   the jury must have been satisfied of facts which proved him guilty of the other offence,

the Court of Appeal may quash the conviction appealed against but replace it with a conviction for that other offence. For example, in *R v Spratt* [1980] 1 WLR 554, a conviction for manslaughter was substituted for the conviction of murder and, in *R v Blackford* (1989) 89 Cr App R 239, a conviction for possession of cannabis with intent to supply was replaced by a conviction for simple possession of cannabis.

The first requirement in s 3 means that the Court of Appeal must consider whether the jury could, on the indictment they were trying, have found the appellant guilty of some other offence (under s 6 of the Criminal Law Act 1967 or other statutory provisions dealing with specific offences). The second requirement in s 3 means that the Court of Appeal has to consider the evidence which was put before the jury. In *R v Graham* [1997] 1 Cr App R 302 (at 312–13), Lord Bingham CJ said that:

> Before this Court could substitute a conviction of an alternative offence the prosecution would have to establish two requirements: (1) that the jury could on the indictment have found the appellant guilty of some other offence (offence B) and (2) that the jury must have been satisfied of facts which proved the appellant guilty of offence B. As to (1) it would be sufficient if looking at the indictment (not the evidence) the allegation in the particular count in the indictment expressly or impliedly included an allegation of offence B. A count charging offence A impliedly contains an allegation of offence B if the allegation in the particular count would ordinarily involve an allegation of offence B and on the facts of the particular case did so. As to (2) this Court has only the verdict of the jury to go on. The fact that the jury did not have a proper direction as to offence B is a highly relevant consideration, as is the question whether there are reasonable grounds for concluding that the conduct of the defence would have been materially affected if the appellant had been charged with offence B . . .

If the Court of Appeal does quash the conviction appealed against but substitutes a conviction for a different offence, it must then go on to review the sentence imposed by the Crown Court. If the Court of Appeal alters the sentence, it must not impose a sentence which is more severe than the original sentence (see s 3(2)).

In *R v Horsman* [1998] QB 531, the Court of Appeal held that where the defendant pleads guilty in the Crown Court to an offence and then appeals against that conviction, and the Court of Appeal quashes the conviction, the Court of Appeal has no power under s 3 of the Criminal Appeal Act 1968 to substitute a conviction for an alternative offence. The effect of this case is reversed by s 3A of the Criminal Appeal Act 1968. This applies where

a   the appellant has been convicted of an offence to which he pleaded guilty;
b   if he had not so pleaded, he could have pleaded guilty to, or been found guilty of, another offence; and
c   it appears to the Court of Appeal that the plea of guilty indicates an admission by the appellant of facts which prove him guilty of the other offence.

In that case, the Court of Appeal may, instead of allowing or dismissing the appeal, substitute for the appellant's plea of guilty a plea of guilty of the other offence.

13.8.2.5 Unmeritorious appeals: directions for loss of time

Directions for loss of time are governed by s 29 of the Criminal Appeal Act 1968 and para II.16 of *Consolidated Practice Direction*. Section 29 of the 1968 Act says:

(1) The time during which an appellant is in custody pending the determination of his appeal shall, subject to any direction which the Court of Appeal may give to the contrary, be reckoned as part of the term of any sentence to which he is for the time being subject.
(2) Where the Court of Appeal give a contrary direction under sub-section (1) above, they shall state their reasons for doing so; and they shall not give any such direction where—

(a) leave to appeal has been granted; or
(b) a certificate has been given by the judge of the court of trial [that the case is fit for appeal]; or
(c) the case has been referred to them [by the Criminal Cases Review Commission].

Paragraph II.16.1 of the *Consolidated Practice Direction* says:

Both the court and the single judge have power in their discretion to direct that part of the time during which an applicant is in custody after putting in his notice of application for leave to appeal should not count towards sentence. Those who contemplate putting in such a notice and their legal advisers should bear this in mind. It is important that those contemplating an appeal should seek advice and should remember that it is useless to appeal without grounds and that grounds should be substantial and particularised and not a mere formula. Where an application devoid of merit has been refused by the single judge and a direction for loss of time has been made, the full court, on renewal of the application, may direct that additional time shall be lost if it, once again, thinks it right so to exercise its discretion in all the circumstances of the case.

A 'direction for loss of time' is relevant only if the appellant is serving a custodial sentence. The direction is that some or all of the sentence served by the appellant between the date of the commencement of the appeal proceedings and the date when the application for leave or (as the case may be) the renewed application for leave to appeal is dismissed does not count towards the service of the appellant's sentence.

Where the single judge gives leave to appeal (or the application is successfully renewed) but the Court of Appeal ultimately dismisses the appeal, a direction for loss of time cannot be made even though the appeal is ultimately unsuccessful (s 29(2)(a) of the Criminal Appeal Act 1968).

A direction for loss of time under s 29 does not amount to arbitrary detention and pursues a legitimate aim under Art 5(1)(a) and so is compatible with the right to liberty under Art 5 of the European Convention on Human Rights (*Monnell and Morris v UK* (1988) 10 EHRR 205 at para 46).

The Court reasoned that:

> the power of the Court of Appeal to order loss of time . . . is a component of the machinery existing under English law to ensure that criminal appeals are considered within a reasonable time and, in particular, to reduce the time spent in custody by those with meritorious grounds waiting for their appeal to be heard . . . In sum, it is a power exercised to discourage abuse of the court's own procedures. As such, it is an inherent part of the criminal appeal process following conviction of an offender and pursues a legitimate aim under sub-paragraph (a) of Art 5(1).

This reasoning was echoed in *R v Greaves* [2008] EWCA Crim 647, where Sir Igor Judge P said that, if the applicant had still been serving his sentence the court would unhesitatingly have ordered that the maximum permissible period should not count towards his sentence. His Lordship said (at para 57), that 'justice for cases with merit has been delayed by this wholly unmeritorious, renewed application. That is unfair to those appellants'. Similarly, in *R v Brind* [2008] EWCA Crim 934, Latham LJ said (at para 1) that 'if the application is without merit then this court will consider ordering that time served should not count for the good reason that the renewal of such an application has a significant effect on the work of this court and adds to the potential backlog of cases to the detriment of those who have legitimate arguments to put before this court'. His Lordship added (at para 2) that if the single judge expressed the view that the application is 'without merit . . . the would-be applicant must expect that this court will order that time served should not count'.

In *R v Kuimba* [2005] EWCA Crim 955; (2005), *The Times*, 17 May, the Court of Appeal said that, having regard to delays caused to the hearing of meritorious appeals by unmeritorious applications, the fact that warnings are given before an applicant signs his notice and grounds of appeal, and the fact the European Court of Human Rights has considered the compatibility of the court's powers with the European Convention on Human Rights, there should be greater use of the court's powers to make directions for loss of time.

In *R v Hart* [2006] EWCA Crim 3239; [2007] 1 Cr App R 31, the court considered its power to direct that some or all of the period served by the applicant since he was sentenced should not count towards his sentence on the grounds that his application lacks merit. Latham LJ expressed concern that a significant number of applications for leave to appeal against conviction or sentence are wholly without merit and are taking up the time of single judges and being renewed to the full court. He concluded at para 43:

We hope that both applicants and counsel will heed the fact that this court is prepared to exercise its power and will do so more frequently in the future than it has done so in the past. The mere fact that counsel has advised that there are grounds of appeal will not always be a sufficient answer to the question as to whether or not an application has indeed been brought which was totally without merit. It should not be thought that this court will not exercise its power on other occasions even if there is an advice from counsel supporting grounds of appeal.

13.9 APPEAL AGAINST SENTENCE

Section 9(1) of the Criminal Appeal Act 1968 provides that a person who has been convicted of an offence on indictment may appeal to the Court of Appeal against any sentence (not being a sentence fixed by law) passed on him for that offence. 'Sentence' includes an order to pay prosecution costs (*R v Hayden* [1975] 1 WLR 852) and a compensation order (*R v Vivian* [1979] 1 WLR 291).

Under s 10 of the Criminal Appeal Act 1968, where an offender has been committed to the Crown Court for sentence, he may appeal to the Court of Appeal against any sentence passed on him for the offence by the Crown Court.

13.9.1 Leave to appeal

Section 11(1) and (1A) of the Criminal Appeal Act 1968 provide that leave is required in order to appeal against sentence unless the trial judge certifies the sentence fit for appeal. Certificates are hardly ever given and are strongly discouraged by the Court of Appeal. In *R v Grant* (1990) 12 Cr App R(S) 441 at 443, for example, it was said that if the judge has second thoughts about a sentence he has imposed, he should use his power under what is now s 155 of the Powers of Criminal Courts (Sentencing) Act 2000 to vary the sentence (provided that no more than 28 days have elapsed since the sentence was imposed) or else allow the case to proceed through the ordinary process of appeal; he should not grant a certificate that the sentence is fit for appeal.

It should be emphasised that leave to appeal is needed even if the sentence is wrong in law.

13.9.2 Procedure

The procedure for obtaining leave to appeal is virtually identical to that for obtaining leave to appeal against conviction. Within 28 days of the date on which sentence was passed (see s 18(2) of the 1968 Act), the appellant has to lodge a notice of application for leave to appeal against sentence at the Crown Court which passed the sentence. Grounds of appeal (usually drafted by counsel), based on the remarks made by the judge when passing sentence, are drafted (see rr 68.2 and 68.3 of the Criminal Procedure Rules). The papers are sent to the Registrar of Criminal Appeals, who refers them to a single judge to decide whether leave to appeal should be given. The test is whether the appeal has a reasonable prospect of success. The appellant has 14 days to renew the application for leave to appeal if the single judge refuses leave (r 65.5(2))

13.9.3 The hearing

At the hearing of the appeal (assuming leave is granted), the appellant will usually be represented by counsel (and the single judge will grant public funding for this purpose if the appellant's means are insufficient).

The Crown will not usually be represented, however, as it is not part of the role of the prosecution to advocate for a higher sentence. It should be noted, however, that Recommendation 321 of the *Auld Review* says that:

> The Crown Prosecution Service should consider on a case by case basis whether to appear on the hearing of an appeal against sentence so as to be able to assist the Court, if required, on matters of fact, including the effect on any victim, or of law.

Paragraph II.1.1 of the *Consolidated Practice Direction* provides that the prosecution should be notified if a defendant has been granted leave to appeal against sentence so that they may be represented at the hearing if they so wish. The ever-increasing complexity of sentencing legislation means that it is more often desirable for the Court of Appeal to hear adversarial argument rather than simply hearing argument from the appellant.

A cautionary note on the use of authorities in sentencing appeals was sounded in *Attorney General's Reference (No 17 of 2002)* [2002] EWCA Crim 1292 (at para 21), where Judge LJ said:

> Before leaving this case, we would like to highlight the authorities cited in the reference. Some of the authorities appear in well-known, respected reports. But two of the authorities include sentencing decisions of this Court, which appear in the neutral citation system only. Ignoring guideline decisions, sentencing decisions by this Court almost always reflect the specific and individual facts of the offence and the circumstances of the offender. Accordingly, generally speaking, citation of sentencing decisions should, to put it no higher, be circumspect. If a sentencing decision is not regarded as worthy of the attention of the Criminal Appeal (Sentencing) Reports, or the Criminal Law Review, or The Times or any other recognised authoritative series of reports, we believe that it can only be in the most exceptional circumstances that unreported decisions will be of any value to the Court. The wonder of modern technology means that all the decisions of this Court are preserved and published and available through the neutral citation system. That, however, does not normally justify citation of them on sentencing appeals, whether those appeals are brought by an appellant or take form of a reference by the Attorney General.

This was echoed in *R v Lyon* [2005] EWCA Crim 1365; (2005), *The Times*, 19 May, where Rose LJ (at paras 16 and 17) said:

> . . . one or two decisions of this Court, which are neither guideline cases nor expressed to be of general application, are unlikely to be a reliable guide to the appropriate sentencing bracket for a particular type of offence, because the facts and circumstances of cases vary infinitely. That is why, generally, this Court is, and will continue to be, reluctant in sentence appeals to look at cases which are merely illustrative of the sentence appropriate on particular facts.

> ... particular caution is necessary in relation to judgments given on Attorney General References, which, unless they expressly contain statements of general application, are unlikely to identify a general sentencing level.

In any event, care should also be taken in citing older authorities. Laws LJ, in *R v Royal* [2003] EWCA Crim 1152; [2004] 1 Cr App R(S) 2, said (at para 13):

> It is often said that when the Court declares a principle of the common law, it is as if the principle had always been the law. But this does not generally apply to matters of practice or tariff sentencing. As the Vice President said in *Graham* [1999] 2 Cr App R(S) 312 at p 315:
>
> > ... sentencing decisions of this court, whether by way of guidelines or otherwise, are not intended to and do not have retrospective effect. They reflect no more than the current tariff which, as we have sought to explain, can and does change over the years.

13.10 GROUNDS OF APPEAL AGAINST SENTENCE

Unlike appeals against conviction, the Criminal Appeal Act 1968 does not specify grounds for appeal against sentence. However, case law suggests that a sentence may be appealed on the basis that it is wrong in law, passed on an incorrect factual basis, manifestly excessive or wrong in principle.

13.10.1 Sentence is wrong in law

If the judge imposes a sentence which he has no jurisdiction to impose, that sentence can be set aside by the Court of Appeal. This would apply, for example, if the judge imposed a sentence of three years' imprisonment for an offence which carries a maximum of two years' imprisonment. In *R v Corcoran* (1986) 8 Cr App R(S) 118, a Crown Court judge imposed a sentence of long-term detention on a juvenile, purportedly under what is now s 91 of the Powers of Criminal Courts (Sentencing) Act 2000, even though that power was not available in the circumstances of the case being dealt with; that sentence was therefore unlawful.

Such cases are, of course, very rare as most judges know the extent of their sentencing power. Furthermore, it is the duty of both prosecuting and defence counsel to make themselves aware of the sentencing options that are available and to draw the judge's attention to any mistake he makes (*R v Clarke* (1974) 59 Cr App R 298; *R v Komsta* (1990) 12 Cr App R(S) 63; *R v Hartrey* (1993) 14 Cr App R(S) 507; *R v Brown* [1996] 2 Cr App R(S) 2). In *Hartrey*, Wright J said (at p 510):

> without in any way wishing to derogate from the responsibility of the judge himself to be alert to the limitations imposed upon him by statute, we stress that it is the duty of both prosecuting and defence counsel to inform themselves of the extent of the court's powers in any case in which they are instructed, to know what options are open to the trial judge and to correct him if, as it is unfortunately only too easy to do in the morass of legislation which governs the subject, he should make a mistake.

In *R v Pepper* [2005] EWCA Crim 1181; [2006] 1 Cr App R (S) 20, the court made the point that, if an error is made by the judge in sentencing, particularly regarding his sentencing powers, counsel, whether for the prosecution or the defence, should be alive to the possibility of rectifying the sentence under s 155 of the Powers of Criminal Courts (Sentencing) Act 2000.

13.10.2 Sentence is wrong in principle

A sentence which is wrong in principle occurs where the Crown Court judge imposes the wrong form of sentence. For example, an appellant who receives a custodial sentence argues that the offence was not so serious that only a custodial sentence was appropriate and so the custody threshold had not been crossed. To succeed on this basis, the appellant must show that he was dealt with in a way which was outside the broad range of penalties appropriate to the case.

13.10.3 Sentence is manifestly excessive

A sentence is manifestly excessive where the judge imposed the correct form of sentence but nevertheless imposed too severe a sentence. For example, the judge imposes a sentence of three years' imprisonment in a case where 18 months would be more appropriate. In *R v Gumbs* (1927) 19 Cr App R 74, Lord Hewart CJ said that the Court of Appeal

> . . . never interferes with the discretion of the Court below merely on the ground that this Court might have passed a somewhat different sentence; for this Court to revise a sentence there must be some error in principle.

For example, in *R v Gleeson* [2001] EWCA Crim 2023; [2002] 1 Cr App R(S) 112, the Court of Appeal found that the case was one where some judges might have passed a slightly shorter sentence. However, the court repeated that, save in wholly exceptional cases, it does not interfere with sentences passed in the Crown Court unless the sentence passed was wrong in principle or manifestly excessive (per Rose LJ at para 16).

13.10.4 Wrong approach to sentencing

The Court of Appeal will interfere with a sentence if the judge adopted the wrong approach to the sentencing process. This occurs where the judge ignores relevant factors or takes account of irrelevant factors. In *R v Skone* (1967) 51 Cr App R 165 and *R v Evans* (1986) 8 Cr App R (S) 197, for example, the judge incorrectly penalised the defendant for casting imputations on the veracity of the prosecution witnesses. Similarly, in *R v Doab* [1983] Crim LR 569, the judge wrongly increased the sentence because the defendant had chosen Crown Court trial for an offence which could have been tried in the magistrates' court.

13.10.5 Procedural errors

The Court of Appeal will also interfere if there has been a procedural error. An example of a procedural error is where the judge failed to hold a *Newton* hearing (see Chapter 16) where defence and prosecution versions of events differ significantly where the defendant has pleaded guilty.

13.10.6 Legitimate sense of grievance

If a judge gives an indication that a custodial sentence will not be imposed, the Court of Appeal will interfere if a custodial sentence is subsequently imposed for that offence (*R v Gillam* (1980) 2 Cr App R(S) 267; *R v Moss* (1983) 5 Cr App R(S) 209). If a court adjourns for pre-sentence reports, it should therefore be made clear to the defendant that the court is nevertheless keeping all its sentencing options open (*R v Horton* (1985) 7 Cr App R(S) 299).

13.10.7 Disparity

Where two offenders are sentenced for an offence which they have committed jointly, any difference in sentence should only result from differing degrees of involvement in the offence or from personal mitigating circumstances. Even if a difference cannot be so justified, an appeal on the basis of disparity will only succeed in rare cases.

If the heavier of the two sentences is the correct one, the Court of Appeal will not generally reduce it to bring it into line with the more lenient sentence: this would convert one right sentence and one wrong sentence into two wrong sentences. The main question is whether the appellant's sentence is excessive in itself (*R v Stroud* (1977) 65 Cr App R 150). In *R v Tate* [2006] EWCA Crim 2373, it was said that, where a lenient sentence is passed on one co-defendant, it does not follow that the other defendant's sentence must be reduced on appeal. It would be wrong to replace one injustice with another by reducing the defendant's sentence to an unjustifiable level, and imposing one which would be less than the facts of the case merited. Thus, a co-defendant's good fortune in receiving a lesser sentence is not a reason to impose a lesser sentence than the facts of the case merited.

An appeal will only succeed on the ground of disparity if the appellant would otherwise be left with a justifiable and burning sense of grievance (*R v Potter* [1977] Crim LR 112 and *R v Dickinson* [1977] Crim LR 303). As Lawton LJ put it in *R v Fawcett* (1983) 5 Cr App R(S) 158 (at p 161):

> would right thinking members of the public, with full knowledge of the facts and circumstances, hearing of this sentence consider that something has gone wrong with the administration of justice?

13.11 EFFECT OF APPEAL AGAINST A SENTENCE

If the appeal is dismissed, the original sentence stands. If the Court of Appeal allows the appeal, it may quash the sentence and replace it with the appropriate sentence. Section 11(3) of the Criminal Appeal Act 1968 provides that:

On an appeal against sentence the Court of Appeal, if they consider that the appellant should be sentenced differently for an offence for which he was dealt with by the court below may—

(a) quash any sentence or order which is the subject of the appeal; and

(b) in place of it pass such sentence or make such order as they think appropriate for the case and as the court below had power to pass or make when dealing with him for the offence;

but the Court shall so exercise their powers under this sub-section that, taking the case as a whole, the appellant is not more severely dealt with on appeal than he was dealt with by the court below.

Thus, taking the case as a whole, the appellant should not be dealt with more severely by the Court of Appeal than he was dealt with by the Crown Court. Two examples may assist in interpreting the restrictions imposed by s 11(3):

- An appellant is sentenced to two years' imprisonment on count 1 and 12 months' imprisonment on count 2 and the judge ordered the terms to run consecutively, making a total of three years. The Court of Appeal could (for example) substitute sentences of 12 months on count 1 (a reduction) and two years on count 2 (an increase), to run consecutively: the original total of three years is not exceeded.
- An appellant is sentenced to two years on count 1 and three years on count 2, these terms to run consecutively (making a total of five years). The Court of Appeal could theoretically substitute sentences of five years on each count to run concurrently, as the total of five years is not exceeded.

Note that the Court of Appeal cannot replace a suspended sentence of imprisonment with a sentence of immediate custody, even if the term is the same as or less than the original term that was suspended (*R v Peppard* (1990) 12 Cr App R(S) 88).

13.12 APPEALS BY THE PROSECUTION

In contrast to acquittals in the magistrates' court, the prosecution cannot appeal against an acquittal if the acquittal was based on a mistaken understanding of the law. However, the prosecution can (through an Attorney General's Reference) ask the Court of Appeal to clarify the law. The prosecution can also, in certain cases, challenge an excessively lenient sentence imposed by the Crown Court. Moreover, Pt 9 of the Criminal Justice Act 2003 confers a right to appeal against terminating and evidentiary rulings, and Pt 10 enables someone who has been acquitted of a serious offence to be re-tried if compelling new evidence comes to light.

13.12.1 Attorney General's reference following acquittal

Where a defendant has been acquitted following trial on indictment and the Attorney General thinks that the trial judge misdirected the jury on a point of law, he may refer the case to the Court of Appeal under s 36 of the Criminal Justice Act 1972. The acquittal is not in jeopardy as the Court of Appeal cannot reverse that acquittal, but the reference does enable the Court of Appeal to clarify the law. Thus, judges in subsequent trials will not make the same mistake. The acquitted defendant cannot be named unless he gives his permission (see r 70.3(2) of the Criminal Procedure Rules).

This power is only relevant to acquittal following trial on indictment. Where the defendant was acquitted following summary trial and there was an error of law, the prosecution can challenge the acquittal by asking the magistrates to state a case for the opinion of the High Court (under s 111 of the Magistrates' Courts Act 1980) and the High Court has power to quash the acquittal.

13.12.2 Attorney General's reference: unduly lenient sentences

Sections 35 and 36 of the Criminal Justice Act 1988 enable the Attorney General to appeal against excessively lenient sentences imposed by the Crown Court. Three restrictions apply:

- this power only applies in respect of offences which are triable only on indictment or which are triable either way and have been prescribed by statutory instrument (currently the latter category comprises a comparatively small number of either-way offences);
- the Attorney General requires leave from a single judge of the Court of Appeal in order to bring such an appeal;
- the Court of Appeal may increase the sentence (but not beyond the maximum which the Crown Court could have imposed) only if it holds that the original sentence was 'unduly lenient'.

In *Attorney General's Reference (No 4 of 1989)* [1990] 1 WLR 41 (at 46, per Lord Lane CJ), the Court of Appeal gave guidance on the use of s 36 references:

- a sentence is unduly lenient if it 'falls outside the range of sentences which the judge, applying his mind to all the relevant factors, could reasonably consider appropriate';
- even if the Court of Appeal does consider the original sentence to be unduly lenient, it does not have to increase that sentence. It may be that the sentence can be justified in the light of events since the trial or that increasing the sentence would be unfair to the offender or detrimental to others for whose well-being the court should be concerned;
- if the Attorney General is given leave to refer a sentence to the Court of Appeal on the ground that it is unduly lenient, the court's powers are not confined to increasing the sentence. In theory, the sentence could be reduced.

In *Attorney General's Reference (No 31 of 2004); R v McInerney* [2004] EWCA Crim 1934; [2005] 1 Cr App R (S) 76, the Court of Appeal reiterated that it will only interfere with a sentence under s 36 if it is shown that there was some error of principle in the sentence, so that public confidence would be damaged if the sentence were not altered.

The court will not interfere with a sentence on an Attorney General's reference unless it is manifestly not sufficiently severe. Where the sentence under appeal is a community order, the court should be provided with up-to-date information on the progress made by the offender since the sentence was passed: even if such a sentence were not appropriate at the time it was passed, the fact that the offender is responding to the community order could affect the outcome of the reference.

Where a sentence is referred to the Court of Appeal by the Attorney General under s 36, the Court of Appeal will not inquire into the facts of the offence but will base its decision on the findings made by the Crown Court (*Attorney General's Reference (No 95 of 1998); R v Highfield* (1999) *The Times*, 21 April). Likewise, in *Attorney General's Reference (No 19 of 2005)* [2006] EWCA Crim 785, the court noted that where the Attorney General seeks to refer a sentence to the Court of Appeal as unduly lenient, it is not open to the court to take into account new material which had not been available to the sentencing judge. The task of the Court of Appeal is to decide whether the judge's sentence, in the light of the material then before him, could properly be characterised as unduly lenient (per Rose LJ at para 10).

In *Attorney General's Reference (No 17 of 1998); R v Stokes* [1999] 1 Cr App R(S) 407, a judge gave an indication that he was not minded to impose a sentence of immediate custody. The defendant pleaded guilty (and received a suspended sentence). The prosecution sought to appeal against the sentence as unduly lenient. The Court of Appeal rejected the argument that it should not increase the sentence because the defendant had pleaded guilty on the basis of the judge's indication as to likely sentence. In *Attorney General's References (Nos 87 & 86 of 1999); R v Webb & Simpson* [2001] 1 Cr App R(S) 141, the Court of Appeal said that the fact that a trial judge gives an indication that he feels a custodial sentence to be inappropriate does not fetter the discretion of the Court of Appeal on an appeal by the Attorney General under s 36, although it is a relevant factor (especially where the defendant acted to his detriment, for example, by pleading guilty in light of that indication).

Where a reference is heard and an unduly lenient sentence is quashed, under s 36 of the Criminal Justice Act 1988, the Court of Appeal has the same powers as a sentencing court to remand a defendant in custody pending reports before deciding the appropriate sentence (*Attorney General's Reference (No 129 of 2004)* [2005] EWCA Crim 363).

An order deferring sentence (s 1 of the Powers of Criminal Courts (Sentencing) Act 2000) is a sentence within the meaning of s 36 of the Criminal Justice Act 1988 and so the Attorney General can seek leave to refer that order to the Court of Appeal as unduly lenient (*R v L; R v Jones* [1999] 1 WLR 479). In *R v Barrett; Attorney General's Reference (No 118 of 2004)* [2004] EWCA Crim 3220; [2005] 2 Cr App R (S) 18, it was held that the proper time for the Attorney General to seek leave to refer a deferred sentence is within 28 days from the date on which the sentence was deferred.

In *R v Lea; R v Shatwell* [2002] EWCA Crim 215; [2002] 2 Cr App R 24, the Court of Appeal said that where the defendant is convicted following a retrial ordered by the Court of Appeal, the Attorney General has no power to appeal against the sentence imposed following the retrial if he feels it is unduly lenient, as the judge is precluded (by para 2(1) of Sched 2 to the Criminal Appeal Act 1968) from passing a greater sentence than that passed at the original trial. In appropriate cases, the Attorney

General would therefore have to appeal against the sentence passed at the original trial.

Where the Court of Appeal increases a sentence following a reference by the Attorney General, it invariably adopts the practice of allowing a 'double jeopardy discount' by not increasing the sentence as much as it would otherwise do, on the grounds that the defendant is suffering distress and anxiety from going through the sentencing process a second time. Section 46(2) of the Criminal Justice and Immigration Act 2008 amends s 36 to make it clear that, in the case of life sentences and imprisonment under the 'dangerous offender' provisions of the Criminal Justice Act 2003, the 'Court of Appeal shall not, in deciding what sentence is appropriate for the case, make any allowance for the fact that the person to whom it relates is being sentenced for a second time'.

13.12.3 Prosecution appeals under the Criminal Justice Act 2003

Prior to the enactment of Pt 9 of the Criminal Justice Act 2003, there was statutory provision only for appeals to the Court of Appeal by the defendant. Whereas the defendant has a right of appeal at the end of the trial against conviction and/or sentence, there was no corresponding right for the prosecution to appeal against an acquittal. In some ways this was anomalous, since the prosecution enjoy a right of appeal to the High Court (through an appeal by way of case stated or through judicial review) if an acquittal in the magistrates' court is based on an error of law.

13.12.3.1 The advantages and disadvantages of a prosecution right of appeal

The possibility of a right of appeal against certain acquittals was considered in the Law Commission's Paper *Double Jeopardy and Prosecution Appeals* (Law Com 267). In that Paper, the Commission endeavoured to identify 'the main principles and aims which have a bearing on the question whether it would be fair to extend the prosecution's existing rights of appeal'. They identified two such aims:

a   'accuracy of outcome' – to ensure, as far as possible, that those who are guilty are convicted and that those who are not guilty are acquitted; and
b   a 'process aim' – ensuring that the system shows respect for the fundamental rights and freedoms of the individual.

They noted that accuracy of outcome may benefit either the prosecution or the defendant, depending on whether the defendant is guilty or innocent. Process aims, however, by their nature work only in favour of the defendant (see para 7.12). When this approach was first mooted in a Law Commission Consultation Paper (Law Com 158), it was criticised by some on the basis that the prosecution and defendant are not the only interested parties in a criminal trial. The victim of the alleged offence, for example, clearly has an interest in the case.

The Law Commission argued that, in general, the existence of prosecution rights of appeal may be expected to militate in favour of accurate outcomes, because an accurate outcome is more likely to be achieved if the law is correctly applied than if it is not; on the other hand, they noted that the existence of such rights might detract from the process aims of the system. They decided that the correct approach to the question whether to grant the prosecution a particular right of appeal was (para 7.13):

(1) to identify the extent (if any) to which that right of appeal would enhance or detract from the aim of ensuring accuracy of outcome;

(2) to identify the extent (if any) to which it would detract from process aims; and,

(3) by balancing these factors, to come to a conclusion whether the trial process would thus be rendered unfair.

On this basis, the Commission recommended (in para 7.49) that:

. . . the prosecution should have a right of appeal against an acquittal arising from a terminating ruling made during the trial up to the conclusion of the prosecution evidence.

The Law Commission gave separate consideration to rulings that there is no case to answer. In its Consultation Paper (Law Com 158), the Commission had argued that the existence of a prosecution right of appeal against a successful submission of no case would put the defence in an invidious position: if a submission of no case is made, and is successful, there is a danger that the prosecution will appeal and there will be a re-trial (and so it might be better for the defence not to make a submission of no case, simply hoping that the jury will acquit at the end of the trial). In that Consultation Paper, the Law Commission concluded that it would be wrong for the defence to face this disincentive to the making of a submission of no case, and they concluded that there should be no right of appeal by the prosecution against a ruling of no case to answer made at the conclusion of the prosecution case. On the other hand, the possibility of a prosecution appeal in such a case already exists in the context of magistrates' courts. If the magistrates uphold a submission of no case to answer, it is open to the prosecution to ask the magistrates to state a case for the opinion of the High Court if it appears that the ruling may be based on an error of law; the High Court may then quash the acquittal. This possibility does not seem to have dissuaded defendants in the magistrates' court from making submissions of no case to answer.

At para 7.56 of the Report (Law Com 267), the Commission summarises some of the arguments in favour of allowing a challenge to erroneous acquittals following submissions of no case in this way:

A successful submission of no case, erroneously acceded to, deprives the jury of a proper opportunity to judge the case, diminishes the legitimacy of the resulting acquittal, may appear to interested persons and the public to be the product of bizarre technicality, and damages public confidence in the system.

In the next paragraph, they put forward a further argument:

The possibility of an appeal against an acquittal arising from an erroneous ruling of no case would help to 'keep the judges honest'. A senior trial judge with Court of Appeal experience argued that 'It is a temptation for a weak judge with a difficult case to rule against there being a case to answer . . .'

The Law Commission's conclusions were as follows:

7.61 . . . we agree that there is no logical distinction between a terminating ruling of law made during the prosecution case and one made at its conclusion.

7.62 We also accept that there may be a temptation for trial judges too readily to accept defence submissions where they know that their reasoning will not be susceptible to scrutiny by the Court of Appeal. In any event the discipline of possible appeal to the Court of Appeal would serve to concentrate minds and improve both the quality of decision taken and its expression.

7.63 If a case is to fail on a legal argument it is better for public confidence in the system of criminal justice that it be susceptible to the second opinion of a higher court than that it be unappealable.

7.64 We also agree that the case stated procedure in the magistrates' court is a template, at least for a prosecution appeal on a point of law, and that there is no evidence that defendants labour under a disadvantage in pursuing a submission of no case at that level because of it.

7.65 On the other hand we do not accept the arguments which seek to diminish the dilemma for the defence which we described . . . Arguments were presented which suggested that there is no particular disadvantage to a defendant in being required either (i) to make a submission and to face a retrial after an appeal; or (ii) to forgo a submission and give evidence for fear that an appealed ruling of no case would deprive the defendant of the chance of an acquittal by a jury in a trial which is going well . . . It is a truism, recognised by most experienced practitioners, that the high point of the defence case is invariably at the close of the prosecution case. This is quite apart from the obvious fact that at a retrial witnesses will have had a dry run, tactics will have been revealed and weaknesses in the prosecution case will have been spotted and possibly plugged.

7.66 In our view, it is possible to reconcile these different arguments in a principled way.

7.67 There is no doubt that the two limbs identified in *Galbraith* are distinct. The first limb [that there is no evidence that the alleged offence was committed by the defendant] concerns a question of law, and there is no logical reason why the prosecution should not have a right of appeal against an acquittal arising from such a terminating decision if it is to have a right of appeal against acquittals arising from other terminating rulings made in the course of its case.

7.68 On the other hand, the second limb of *Galbraith* [that the prosecution evidence, taken at its highest, is such that a jury properly directed could not properly convict on it] does not involve a point of law at all. Rather, the judge is required to perform a quasi-jury role. Without usurping the role of the jury, the judge has to assess the strength of the prosecution case. If the judge is of the view that, taking that case at its highest, no jury properly directed could properly convict, the judge's duty is to protect the defendant from any further risk by removing the case from the jury.

7.69 There is no more reason to give the prosecution a right of appeal against such a decision than there is to give it a right of appeal against an acquittal by a jury . . .

7.70 In CP 158 we expressed the opinion that it would be difficult in practice to distinguish the two limbs of *Galbraith* . . . on reflection we believe that we were over-pessimistic on this score. The limbs are distinct. Whilst submissions are often made under both limbs and the arguments may merge, the tests are sufficiently distinct so that we are confident that trial judges will be able sufficiently to separate them in their own minds, and in their reasons for their decisions, to enable the parties and the court of appeal to see whether the ruling is one of law under limb one, susceptible to appeal, or one of no case on the basis of limb two, not susceptible to appeal. Where the ruling is on both bases, in practice there would, of course, be no appeal.

...

7.72 . . . if the defence has decided to try to persuade the judge to dismiss the case on a legal basis which turns out to be wrong, it can have no cause to complain if on appeal it is denied the benefit of an error of law which it by its own arguments has induced.

7.73 It follows from the above analysis that we do not recommend any prosecution right of appeal where the case is one of identification and it is withdrawn from the jury because the quality of the identifying evidence is poor, such as where it depends solely on a 'fleeting glance'. The judge in such a case is as much exercising a quasi-jury function as in applying *Galbraith* limb two . . .

7.74 We recommend that the prosecution should have a right of appeal against an acquittal arising from a ruling of no case to answer made at the conclusion of the prosecution evidence, but only where that ruling is made on a point of law under the first limb of *Galbraith* . . .

The Law Commission's proposals (as contained in the original consultation paper no 158) were considered by Rosemary Pattenden in 'Prosecution appeals against judges' rulings' [2000] Crim LR 971. She says that, 'the question is whether an innovation that promotes accuracy, and is therefore presumptively desirable, detracts so seriously from process values that lend the criminal justice system moral authority that it must be rejected', and concludes that 'judges are at present unaccountable to the Court of Appeal as to a crucial aspect of their responsibilities: directed acquittals and other rulings that abort the proceedings' and that this should be remedied in order to 'protect public confidence in the criminal process'.

In Recommendation 309 of the *Review of the Criminal Courts of England and Wales*, Lord Justice Auld says:

I . . . support the general thrust of the Law Commission's recommendations for:

309.1 extending the present preparatory hearing regime to include appealable rulings on potentially terminating matters such as severance, joinder, quashing the indictment or staying the prosecution as an abuse of process;

309.2 giving the prosecution a right of appeal against an acquittal in certain cases arising from a terminating ruling during the trial up to the close of the prosecution case; and

309.3 giving the prosecution a right of appeal against an acquittal arising from a ruling of no case to answer under the first limb of the rule in R v *Galbraith*.

13.12.3.2 Part 9 of the Criminal Justice Act 2003: appeals against terminating and evidentiary rulings

Part 9 of the 2003 Act introduces an interlocutory prosecution right of appeal against two categories of ruling by Crown Court judges: (a) rulings, made either at a pre-trial hearing or at any time during the trial before the start of the summing up, that have the effect of terminating the trial (this includes both rulings that are terminating in themselves and also those that are so fatal to the prosecution case that the prosecution proposes to treat them as terminating and, in the absence of the right of appeal, would offer no, or no further, evidence); and (b) evidentiary rulings made in certain trials for qualifying offences where the ruling significantly weakens the prosecution case. Thus, the 2003 Act does not entirely accord with the recommendations of the Law Commission and the *Auld Review*, in that it does not exclude any submissions of no case to answer from the prosecution right of appeal against terminating rulings (in s 58), and it goes further than the Law Commission recommendation by including rulings that are, in effect, terminating rulings where key prosecution evidence is excluded (s 62).

By virtue of s 74(5), where a ruling affects several defendants, the prosecution may (if they so wish) appeal against that ruling in so far as it relates to just one of the defendants.

Under s 57(4) of the Act, an appeal under Pt 9 may be brought only with the leave of the trial judge or the Court of Appeal.

13.12.3.3 The right of appeal against 'terminating' rulings

Section 58 of the 2003 Act sets out the procedure to be followed when the prosecution wish to appeal against a terminating ruling. Under s 58(4), following the ruling, the prosecution must either inform the court that they intend to appeal or request an adjournment to consider whether to appeal (s 58(4)(a)). If such an adjournment is requested, the judge has a discretion to grant it (s 58(5)). Following such an adjournment, the prosecution must inform the court whether or not they in fact intend to appeal (s 58(4)(b)). By virtue of s 58(3), (10) and (11), the judge's ruling has no effect while the prosecution are considering whether to appeal or are pursuing an appeal. However, if the prosecution inform the court under s 58(4) that they intend to appeal, proceedings may be continued in respect of any offence which is not the subject of the appeal (s 60). Under s 58(8) and (9), where the prosecution either fail to obtain leave to appeal or abandon the appeal, the prosecution must agree that the defendant should be acquitted.

In *R v A* [2008] EWCA Crim 1034, the Court of Appeal noted that where notice of appeal is given, the Crown Court proceedings stand adjourned pending the hearing of the appeal, and the ruling in question has no effect pending the outcome of the appeal. It follows that where a defendant has been acquitted following a ruling by the judge, the prosecution cannot *then* seek to appeal against that ruling. The prosecutor must give notice that he intends to appeal the ruling before an acquittal is entered (and if he does so, the ruling has no effect pending appeal).

Section 59 provides two different appeal routes (an 'expedited' appeal and a 'non-expedited' appeal). The judge must decide whether or not the appeal should be expedited (s 59(1)). If the judge decides that the appeal should be expedited, the trial may be adjourned pending the outcome of the appeal (s 59(2)). If the judge decides that the appeal should not be expedited, he may either adjourn the trial or discharge the jury, if one has been sworn in (s 59(3)).

Under s 61, the Court of Appeal may confirm, reverse or vary the ruling that is under appeal. Under s 61(3) and (7), where the Court of Appeal confirms the ruling, it must order the acquittal of the defendant(s) for the offence(s) which are the subject of the appeal. If the Court of Appeal reverses or varies a ruling, it must (under s 61(4)) also order that:

- the proceedings be resumed in the Crown Court; or
- a fresh trial should take place; or
- the defendant(s) should be acquitted of the offence(s) that are subject to the appeal.

The Court of Appeal will only order the resumption of the Crown Court proceedings or the start of a fresh trial where it considers it 'necessary in the interests of justice to do so' (s 61(5)). However, s 44 of the Criminal Justice and Immigration Act 2008 amends s 61(5) to alter the test for ordering a re-trial (or that the trial should resume) where the Court of Appeal allows a prosecution appeal against a terminating ruling. The substituted sub-s (5) has the effect that the trial *must* continue, or a fresh trial must take place, unless the court considers that the defendant 'could not receive a fair trial'. This makes it clear that there is a strong presumption that the proceedings against the accused should continue.

In *R v Thompson* [2006] EWCA Crim 2849; [2007] 1 WLR 1123, it was held that the Crown's right of appeal under s 58 does not extend to a judge's ruling pursuant to para 2 of Sched 3 to the Crime and Disorder Act 1998 (application to dismiss the charge prior to arraignment – see Chapter 9), since that procedure can only lead to the dismissal of a charge or the quashing of an indictment, rather than the acquittal of the defendant. The only remedy for the prosecution in the face of a dismissal of a charge or the quashing of an indictment is to seek the preferment of a voluntary bill of indictment under para 2(6) of Sched 3 to the 1998 Act.

In *R v Clarke* [2007] EWCA Crim 2532; [2008] 1 Cr App R 33, the Court of Appeal held that the right to appeal granted by s 58 of the Criminal Justice Act 2003 extends to case management decisions and so a case management decision refusing to order an adjournment may constitute a terminating ruling against which a prosecutor can appeal, where that ruling effectively terminates the trial.

Under s 57(2)(a), however, there is no right of appeal under Pt 9 in respect of a ruling that a jury be discharged.

13.12.3.4 'Evidentiary' rulings

Section 62 of the 2003 Act (which was not in force at the time of writing) confers on the prosecution a right of appeal in respect of 'qualifying evidentiary' rulings. Section 62(9) defines an evidentiary ruling as 'a ruling which relates to the admissibility or exclusion of any prosecution evidence'. Under s 62(2), a 'qualifying evidentiary ruling' is one made by a judge in relation to a trial on indictment at any time before the opening of the case of the defence (as defined in s 62(8)). Under s 62(3) and (4), the prosecution may only appeal against evidentiary rulings that relate to 'qualifying' offences (whether

or not the ruling also relates to other, non-qualifying, offences); s 62(9) defines a qualifying offence as an offence listed in Pt 1 of Sched 4.

To appeal under s 62, the prosecution must (before the opening of the defence case)
inform the court that they intend to appeal and identify the ruling(s) and the qualifying
offence(s) to which the appeal relates (s 62(5)).

Section 63 places a further limitation on the right of the prosecution to appeal under
s 62. It provides that leave to appeal should not be given (whether by the trial judge or
by the Court of Appeal itself) unless the effect of the ruling(s) is to 'significantly
weaken' the prosecution case in relation to the offence(s) subject to appeal.

As is the case with the general right of appeal against terminating rulings, appeals
under s 62 can be either expedited or non-expedited, and it is a matter for the trial judge
to decide which (s 64). Section 65 provides that where the trial involves one or more
offences which are not subject to appeal, the proceedings in respect of those offences
may be continued.

Section 66 empowers the Court of Appeal to confirm, reverse or vary any ruling to
which the appeal relates. Under s 66(2), the Court of Appeal must also order that:

- the proceedings be resumed in the Crown Court; or
- a fresh trial should take place; or
- the defendant(s) should be acquitted of the offence(s) that are subject to the
  appeal.

In *R v Y* [2008] EWCA Crim 10; [2008] 1 Cr App R 34, the Court of Appeal had to
consider whether an interlocutory appeal under s 58 could be brought where the ruling
was as to admissibility of evidence. The Court said that there is no reason why a single
ruling should not qualify both as a s 58 ruling in relation to a count on the indictment
(assuming the Crown agree to an acquittal if the appeal fails) and also as an evidentiary
ruling under s 62 (when it is brought into force). Many rulings made by trial judges can
properly be described both as relating to counts on the indictment and as being evidentiary; the difference between the two types of interlocutory appeal lies in the s 58(8)
condition. Where the Judge first excludes evidence which the Crown wants admitted
and then, because of its absence, finds that there is no case to answer, the Crown can
(provided it complies with s 58(8)), challenge not only the no case decision, but also the
evidentiary ruling which preceded it.

13.12.3.5 Reversal of rulings

Section 67 applies to both appeals against terminating rulings and appeals against
evidentiary rulings. It states that the Court of Appeal may not reverse such a ruling
unless satisfied:

(a) that the ruling was wrong in law,
(b) that the ruling involved an error of law or principle, or
(c) that the ruling was a ruling that it was not reasonable for the judge to have made.

Section 67(c) seems to suggest that the Court of Appeal should interfere with a
ruling only if the trial judge reached a decision that no reasonable judge, properly

directing himself on the law, could have reached (in other words, the *Wednesbury* standard of unreasonableness familiar within the field of judicial review). This would seem appropriate, since the Court of Appeal is carrying out a task very similar to the judicial review task carried out by the High Court in relation to errors of law in the magistrates' court. Furthermore, it seems likely to be Parliament's intention that the prosecution right to appeal should be exercised sparingly, and certainly not routinely.

In *R v B* [2008] EWCA Crim 1144, Sir Igor Judge P (at para 19), said that leave to appeal under s 67 will not be given by the Court of Appeal unless it is seriously arguable, not that the judge's discretion might have been exercised differently, but that it was unreasonable for it to have been exercised in the way that it was. His Lordship said that the mere fact that the judge could have reached an opposite conclusion to the one he did does not begin to provide a basis for a successful appeal.

In *State of Trinidad and Tobago v Boyce* [2006] UKPC 1; [2006] 2 AC 76, the Privy Council held that a statutory provision enabling the prosecution to appeal against the acquittal of a defendant on the direction of the trial judge does not infringe the defendant's constitutional rights to 'due process'.

13.12.3.6 Custody time limits

Under s 22(6B) of the Prosecution of Offences Act 1985, any period during which proceedings for an offence are adjourned pending the determination of an appeal under Pt 9 of the Criminal Justice Act 2003 is to be disregarded for the purpose of calculating the custody time limit (see Chapter 3) applicable to that offence.

13.12.3.7 Reporting restrictions

Section 71 of the Criminal Justice Act 2003 prevents reporting of appeal proceedings under Pt 9, except the reporting of basic factual details (set out in s 71(8)), for example, details of the court, the defendants, witnesses, legal representatives and the offences charged. Section 71(2), (3) and (4) enable the reporting restrictions to be lifted either completely or to a specified extent. Where a defendant objects to the lifting of the restrictions, the restrictions may only be lifted if the court is satisfied, after hearing the representations of the defendant, or (if more than one) each of the defendants, that it is in the interests of justice to do so (s 71(5) and (6)).

Under s 72, breach of the reporting restrictions is a summary offence punishable with a fine up to level 5 (£5,000) (s 72(9)); proceedings for such an offence can only be instituted by or with the consent of the Attorney General (s 72(10)).

13.12.3.8 Retrials following 'tainted' acquittals

An exception to the *autrefois acquit* doctrine (which generally prevents someone from being tried twice for the same offence) was introduced by ss 54–57 of the Criminal Procedure and Investigations Act 1996. Section 54 provides that where a defendant has been acquitted of an offence and:

a person has been convicted of an administration of justice offence involving interference with or intimidation of a juror or a witness (or potential witness) in any proceedings which led to the acquittal

then the court before which the latter person was convicted may certify that:

i   there is a real possibility that, but for the interference or intimidation, the acquitted person would not have been acquitted; and
ii   it is not contrary to the interests of justice (because of lapse of time or for any other reason) for the acquitted person to be re-prosecuted.

An application may then be made to the High Court for an order quashing the acquittal. The acquitted person may then be re-prosecuted for the offence of which he was acquitted. Section 55 requires that four conditions must be satisfied before the High Court will quash the acquittal:

(a)   it must appear to the High Court likely that, but for the interference or intimidation, the acquitted person would not have been acquitted;
(b)   it must not appear to the Court that, because of lapse of time or for any other reason, it would be contrary to the interests of justice to take proceedings against the acquitted person for the offence of which he was acquitted;
(c)   it must appear to the Court that the acquitted person has been given a reasonable opportunity to make written representations to the Court;
(d)   it must appear to the Court that the conviction for the administration of justice offence will stand.

Under r 40.1 of the Criminal Procedure Rules, certification by the court under s 54 must take place no later than immediately after the court has sentenced or otherwise dealt with the person convicted of the administration of justice offence.

13.12.3.9 Retrials under Pt 10 of the Criminal Justice Act 2003

Part 10 of the Criminal Justice Act 2003 sets out another exception to the 'double jeopardy' rule). This was one of the most controversial provisions in that Act, since it enables a retrial to take place if new evidence comes to light.

Section 75 sets out the types of case which may be retried. The main restriction is that these provisions apply only to 'qualifying offences' (defined in s 75(8) as offences listed in Pt 1 of Sched 5); the offences in the list are all very serious ones (most of them carry a maximum sentence of life imprisonment). As the Explanatory Notes issued along with the Act suggest, these offences were chosen because they are 'considered to have a particularly serious impact either on the victim or on society more generally'.

For s 75 to apply, the defendant must have been:

•   acquitted of the qualifying offence at the Crown Court; or ,
•   acquitted of the qualifying offence through the quashing of his conviction on appeal (but note that in the latter case the Court of Appeal would have the power to order a retrial under s 7 of the Criminal Appeal Act 1968, which empowers the Court of Appeal to order a retrial when it considers that it is in the interests of

justice to do so, if the fresh evidence had come to light before the appeal was disposed of); or

- (under s 75(2)) impliedly acquitted of a lesser qualifying offence of which he could have been convicted at the time (this would apply where the jury could have convicted of an alternative offence under s 6 of the Criminal Law Act 1967 but did not do so – for example, an acquittal for murder may also imply an acquittal for the lesser offence of manslaughter, but new evidence may then come to light which would support a charge of manslaughter).

Where s 75 applies, s 76 allows a prosecutor (defined in s 95) to apply to the Court of Appeal for an order quashing the defendant's acquittal and ordering him to be retried for the qualifying offence. Under s 76(3), a prosecutor may make an application under s 76 only with the written consent of the Director of Public Prosecutions (DPP). Under s 76(4), the DPP may give his consent only if satisfied that:

- there is evidence which meets the requirements of s 78 (see below);
- it is in the public interest for the application to proceed; and
- any retrial under these provisions would not breach the UK's international obligations.

Furthermore, to protect against possible abuse of process, s 76(5) provides that only one application for an acquittal to be quashed may be made in respect of any acquittal, giving the prosecution only one further 'bite at the cherry'.

The powers of the Court of Appeal are set out in s 77(1): if satisfied that the requirements of ss 78 and 79 are met, it must make the order applied for; otherwise, it must dismiss the application.

The key criteria, which are relevant both to the decision of the DPP to permit an appeal and to the Court of Appeal in deciding whether to order a retrial, are set out in ss 78 and 79 of the 2003 Act. Section 78 set out the requirement for 'new and compelling evidence':

(1) The requirements of this section are met if there is new and compelling evidence against the acquitted person in relation to the qualifying offence.

(2) Evidence is new if it was not adduced in the proceedings in which the person was acquitted (nor, if those were appeal proceedings, in earlier proceedings to which the appeal related).

(3) Evidence is compelling if—

   (a) it is reliable,
   (b) it is substantial, and
   (c) in the context of the outstanding issues, it appears highly probative of the case against the acquitted person.

(4) The outstanding issues are the issues in dispute in the proceedings in which the person was acquitted and, if those were appeal proceedings, any other issues remaining in dispute from earlier proceedings to which the appeal related.

(5) For the purposes of this section, it is irrelevant whether any evidence would have been admissible in earlier proceedings against the acquitted person.

The retrial must also be in the 'interests of justice', as defined in s 79:

(1) The requirements of this section are met if in all the circumstances it is in the interests of justice for the court to make the order under section 77.

(2) That question is to be determined having regard in particular to—

(a) whether existing circumstances make a fair trial unlikely;

(b) for the purposes of that question and otherwise, the length of time since the qualifying offence was allegedly committed;

(c) whether it is likely that the new evidence would have been adduced in the earlier proceedings against the acquitted person but for a failure by an officer or by a prosecutor to act with due diligence or expedition;

(d) whether, since those proceedings or, if later, since the commencement of this Part, any officer or prosecutor has failed to act with due diligence or expedition.

. . .

Thus, s 78 requires the court to make a decision on the strength of the new evidence and the impact it would have had if it had been adduced at the original trial. In considering the interests of justice under s 79, the court will have regard to factors such as whether a fair trial would be made more difficult because of, for example, adverse publicity about the case or the length of time that has elapsed since the original trial. The court is specifically required to consider whether the police and prosecution acted with due diligence and expedition in relation to both the original trial and the new evidence that has come to light.

In *R v Dunlop* [2006] EWCA Crim 1354; [2007] 1 WLR 1657, it was held that it is in the interests of justice to order a retrial where the application for a retrial is based on confessions made by the accused after his acquittal even if he would not have made those confessions had he appreciated that they might lead to his retrial. However, in *R v Miell* [2007] EWCA Crim 3130; [2008] 1 WLR 627, the defendant was acquitted of murder. He later confessed to the murder. He subsequently pleaded guilty to perjury arising out of untruthful evidence he gave at the murder trial. The Crown Prosecution Service (CPS) sought to have the acquittal for murder quashed, and a retrial ordered, under s 76 of the 2003 Act. It was held that s 78 requires the court to form its own view of whether the defendant's conviction for perjury was, in fact, compelling, reliable and highly probative evidence that he was guilty of the original murder. On the facts, the court concluded that it was not. Lord Phillips CJ added (at para 52) that it would have been contrary to the interests of justice to order the defendant to stand trial again given that s 74 of the Police and Criminal Evidence Act 1984 (conviction as evidence of commission of offence) would, on the facts of the case, effectively shift the burden of proof onto the defendant at any retrial.

Under s 80(5), the acquitted person is entitled to be present at the hearing of the s 76 application, and to be represented. Under s 81(2), there is a right to appeal on a point of law to the House of Lords from decisions made by the Court of Appeal under s 77.

Under s 84, the acquitted person must be arraigned for the retrial within two months (or such longer time as the Court of Appeal may allow); if this does not occur, he can apply to the Court of Appeal to set aside the order for retrial and restore the previous acquittal.

Section 82(1) empowers the Court of Appeal to impose reporting restrictions to ensure that any potential jury is not influenced by these developments:

> Where it appears to the Court of Appeal that the inclusion of any matter in a publication would give rise to a substantial risk of prejudice to the administration of justice in a retrial, the court may order that the matter is not to be included in any publication while the order has effect.

In *Re D (Acquitted person: Retrial)* [2006] EWCA Crim 828; [2006] 1 WLR 1998, the Court of Appeal observed that, where an application is made to quash an acquittal and a new trial is ordered, publicity of the fact that the Court of Appeal has concluded that there is compelling evidence for making such an order might reasonably be regarded as prejudicial to the subsequent trial. The court should only make the order if satisfied that it was necessary, in the interests of justice, to require the imposition of reporting restrictions. Sir Igor Judge P (at para 18) said that:

> In making its decision, the court will also address the principle, not simply of open justice in the sense that the proceedings themselves will take place in a public court, but also the responsibility of the media for reporting legal proceedings. It will no doubt remind itself without any necessity to cite authority, of the common judicial experience that juries are, and should be treated as if they are, robust and independent-minded, capable of evaluating the evidence called before them, and distinguishing it from pre-trial gossip and irrelevant comment.

There is a further safeguard for acquitted defendants in s 85, which requires the police to obtain the consent of the DPP before re-investigating cases where new evidence has come to light (or where there are reasonable grounds to believe that new evidence is likely to be obtained as a result of reinvestigation) if the previous acquittal would ordinarily constitute a bar to prosecution (on the basis of the *autrefois* doctrine). Under s 85(3), the DPP's consent is required before the police can arrest or question the defendant; search him, or premises owned or occupied by him; search a vehicle owned by him, or anything in or on such a vehicle; seize anything in his possession; or take his fingerprints or a sample from him. Under s 85(6), the DPP is only allowed to give his consent if:

(a) there is, or there is likely as a result of the investigation to be, sufficient new evidence to warrant the conduct of the investigation, and
(b) it is in the public interest for the investigation to proceed.

These restrictions are intended to provide a safeguard against any potential harassment of acquitted persons. As is pointed out in the Explanatory Notes that accompany the Act, there must be some 'trigger' for the application to the DPP, since it is not intended that the reinvestigation of an acquitted person can take place without any element of new evidence. It should be noted, however, that the DPP's consent is not required in order to enable the police to make inquiries that do not directly affect the acquitted person (for example, interviewing new or previous witnesses, or comparing fingerprint or DNA samples with records which they already hold).

Section 86 provides for the situation where investigative steps have to be taken urgently and there is insufficient time to seek consent from the DPP. In such a case, a police officer of at least the rank of Superintendent can authorise the action. In such a case, s 87 empowers a magistrate to issue an arrest warrant in respect of the acquitted person. After his arrest under the warrant, he can be charged with the offence for which he has been arrested if there is sufficient evidence to do so but only with the agreement of an officer of the rank of Superintendent or above.

13.12.3.10 Critical analysis of the prosecution appeals introduced by the Criminal Justice Act 2003

The prosecution appeals introduced by the Criminal Justice Act 2003 are discussed by Ian Dennis in 'Prosecution appeals and retrial for serious offences' [2004] Crim LR 619. He argues that, although these reforms were controversial, they are sound in principle:

> They are justified by their tendency to promote accuracy of outcome of criminal proceedings, on the basis that accuracy is the major component of the legitimacy of verdicts. Arguments that these reforms are unfair to defendants or unconstitutional are not convincing.
>
> The main concern in relation to Pt 9 is the prospect of a significantly increased workload for the Court of Appeal as many prosecutors take the opportunity to try and rescue their cases from the damage done by adverse rulings. A flood of cases is not a realistic worry in relation to Pt 10. The battery of restrictive conditions on mounting a successful challenge to a jury acquittal means that the importance of this new exception to double jeopardy will almost certainly be more symbolic than real. But the new exception is without doubt symbolically important. It shows that a constitutional rule of finality of jury acquittals has now become a constitutional presumption of finality. The presumption can be rebutted in a limited class of cases, although the number and difficulty of the obstacles to rebuttal shows that the presumption is a powerful one.
>
> Taken together, the exceptions to the rule against double jeopardy for new evidence of guilt and for tainted acquittals have a theoretical coherence. By focusing on the factual accuracy of the acquittal and its moral authority respectively they acknowledge the key features of the legitimacy of jury acquittals, and recognise how legitimacy may be put in doubt in certain cases.

13.13 APPEALS TO THE HOUSE OF LORDS

Under ss 33 and 34 of the Criminal Appeal Act 1968, either the prosecution or the defence can appeal to the House of Lords against a decision of the Court of Appeal. This is subject to two conditions:

- the Court of Appeal must certify that a point of law of general public importance is involved; and
- leave to appeal is given by the Court of Appeal or by the House of Lords.

Given the ability of the prosecution to appeal, it should be noted that even if a conviction is quashed by the Court of Appeal, that conviction could be reinstated by the House of Lords.

When it comes into being, the role of the House of Lords will be taken over by the new Supreme Court.

13.14 THE ROLE OF THE DIVISIONAL COURT

Under s 28(1) of the Supreme Court Act 1981, an order, judgment or other decision of the Crown Court may be questioned by any party to the proceedings, on the ground that it is wrong in law or is in excess of jurisdiction, by applying to the Crown Court to state a case for the opinion of the High Court. However, sub-s (2) excludes any 'judgment or other decision of the Crown Court *relating to trial on indictment*'. It follows that appeal by way of case stated is not available in respect of matters relating to trial on indictment.

Similarly, s 29(3) of the Supreme Court Act 1981 provides that, in relation to the jurisdiction of the Crown Court, other than its jurisdiction in matters *relating to trial on indictment*, the High Court has the power to make mandatory, prohibiting or quashing orders. Thus, the High Court may judicially review a decision of the Crown Court provided that the decision was not in respect of a matter relating to trial on indictment. In *DPP v Manchester Crown Court and Huckfield* [1993] 1 WLR 1524, Lord Browne-Wilkinson suggested (at p 1530) that one 'pointer' to the true construction of s 29 would be:

> . . . to ask the question, 'Is the decision sought to be reviewed one arising in the issue between the Crown and the defendant formulated by the indictment (including the costs of such issue)?' If the answer is 'Yes', then to permit the decision to be challenged by judicial review may lead to delay in the trial: the matter is therefore probably excluded from review by the section. If the answer is 'No', the decision of the Crown Court is truly collateral to the indictment of the defendant and judicial review of that decision will not delay his trial: therefore it may well not be excluded by the section.

In that case, the decision of a Crown Court judge to quash an indictment was held to be incapable of judicial review. This followed the earlier decision of the House of Lords in *DPP v Manchester Crown Court and Ashton* [1994] 1 AC 9, where it was held by the House of Lords that an order made on an application to stay proceedings for abuse of process (see Chapter 1) could not be the subject of judicial review, whether the order is that the proceedings shall or shall not be stayed, since it is an order affecting the conduct of the trial.

In *R v Leeds Crown Court ex p Hussain* [1995] 1 WLR 1329, the Divisional Court held that the decision when to arraign a defendant (and indeed the conduct of the plea and case management hearing generally) is sufficiently closely related to the trial on indictment that s 29 operates to exclude judicial review of the decision.

However, the Divisional Court does have jurisdiction to entertain an application for judicial review of an order made by the Crown Court lifting reporting restrictions imposed under s 39 of the Children and Young Persons Act 1933: *R v Manchester Crown Court ex p H* [2000] 1 WLR 760 (*R v Winchester Crown Court ex p B* [1999] 1 WLR 788 followed). In that case Rose LJ called for urgent legislation to clarify the ambit of s 29.

In *R (Snelgrove) v Woolwich Crown Court* [2004] EWHC 2172 (Admin); [2005] 1 WLR 3223, the accused was charged with an indictable-only offence. He made an application for the charge to be dismissed (under para 2 of Sched 3 to the Crime and Disorder Act 1998). The judge refused to dismiss the charge against the accused, who then applied for judicial review. The question at issue was whether the decision under challenge was a matter relating to trial under indictment for the purposes of s 29 of the Supreme Court Act 1981. The court held that a decision under Sched 3 not to dismiss the charge is an order in a matter relating to trial on indictment for the purposes of s 29, and so judicial review is not available. Following the sending of a case to the Crown Court, that court is seized of the matter and of all decisions concerning the issue between the accused and the Crown which necessarily relate to the trial on indictment. The availability of judicial review would inject delay and uncertainty into proceedings in the Crown Court, which was contrary to parliamentary intention. Auld LJ (at para 43) said that *R v Central Criminal Court, ex p Director of Serious Fraud Office* [1993] 1 WLR 949 (where the contrary conclusion had been reached) should no longer be regarded as good law. This would also seem to mean that the court in *R (Inland Revenue Commissioners) v Crown Court at Kingston* [2001] 4 All ER 721, should not have entertained the application for judicial review of a decision to dismiss a case under s 6 of the Criminal Justice Act 1987 (although the court's ruling about the test to be applied under s 6 remains valid). The decision in *Snelgrove* will be of even greater significance when the s 51 transfer procedure is extended to either-way offences (when Sched 3 to the Criminal Justice Act 2003 comes into force).

In *R (CPS) v Crown Court at Guildford* [2007] EWHC 1798 (Admin); [2007] 1 WLR 2886, the Divisional Court reiterated that it has no power to quash an unlawful sentence imposed on a defendant by a Crown Court judge following trial on indictment. Similarly, in *R (Faithfull) v Crown Court at Ipswich* [2007] EWHC 2763 (Admin), it was held that the Divisional Court does not have jurisdiction to hear an application for judicial review of a decision of a judge in the Crown Court to make, or not to make, a compensation order (the court pointed out that such orders form part of the defendant's sentence, which can be appealed to the Court of Appeal, and that if a compensation order is not made, the victim can take action against the defendant in the civil courts).

For a comprehensive discussion of cases which do – and do not – fall within the ambit of the definition of the phrase 'relating to trial on indictment', see paras 2.100–2.103 of the Law Commission Consultation Paper, *The High Court's Jurisdiction in Relation to Criminal Proceedings* (Consultation Paper No 184), at <http://www.lawcom.gov.uk/docs/cp184_tso.pdf>.

The Law Commission had been asked to consider the limitations upon the High Court's criminal jurisdiction (by way of case stated and judicial review) over the Crown Court, and how those jurisdictions could best be transferred to the Court of Appeal, together with the implications of any such reform for the High Court's criminal jurisdiction over the magistrates' court. The Paper makes a number of provisional proposals, which are summarised in Chapter 8 of the paper. Those provisional proposals include the following:

- All appeals against convictions and/or sentences of the Crown Court (whether exercising its first instance jurisdiction, its appellate jurisdiction or its committal for sentence jurisdiction) should lie to the Court of Appeal. This would be achieved by amending the Criminal Appeal Act 1968 so that it is extended to cover convictions and sentences of the Crown Court exercising its appellate jurisdiction.

- All appeals against convictions and/or sentences of the Crown Court when exercising its appellate jurisdiction should require the leave of the Court of Appeal.
- Section 58 of the Criminal Justice Act 2003 should be extended so as to apply to all 'terminating' rulings made by the Crown Court irrespective of whether the ruling was made in relation to an offence being tried on indictment.
- Section 36 of the Criminal Law Act 1972 should be extended so as to permit the Attorney General, following an acquittal by the Crown Court when exercising its appellate jurisdiction, to refer to the Court of Appeal a point of law which has arisen in the case.
- Sections 28 and 29 of the Supreme Court Act 1981 should be amended so as to remove the possibility of decisions of the Crown Court made in criminal proceedings being challenged by way of appeal by case stated or judicial review.
- There should be a new statutory appeal to the Court of Appeal to enable the Court of Appeal to entertain challenges to decisions and rulings of the Crown Court on the grounds that the decision or ruling:

1   is wrong in law;
2   involves a serious procedural or other irregularity; or
3   is one that no competent and reasonable tribunal could properly have made.

- This new statutory appeal should be subject to leave being granted by the Crown Court.
- The Court of Appeal, when determining a statutory appeal, should be able to confirm, reverse or vary a decision, or to remit the case to the Crown Court with its opinion for a further decision to be made.

13.15 THE CRIMINAL CASES REVIEW COMMISSION

Section 8(1) of the Criminal Appeal Act 1995 created the Criminal Cases Review Commission. Its function is to investigate possible miscarriages of justice. The Commission must consist of at least 11 members (s 8(3)), appointed by the Queen on the recommendation of the Prime Minister (s 8(4)). At least one-third of the members have to be legally qualified and at least two-thirds must have 'knowledge or experience of any aspect of the criminal justice system' (s 8(5), (6)).

13.15.1 References

Section 9(1) of the Criminal Appeal Act 1995 says that where a person has been convicted on indictment by the Crown Court, the Commission may, at any time, refer the conviction and/or the sentence to the Court of Appeal.

Section 11(1) of the Act says that where a person has been convicted by a magistrates' court, the Commission may, at any time, refer the conviction and/or the sentence to the Crown Court. The power to refer a conviction to the Crown Court applies whether or not the defendant pleaded guilty (s 11(2)). Section 11(6) says that on a reference under s 11, the Crown Court may not impose a more severe punishment than that inflicted by the magistrates' court. Section 11(7) empowers the Crown Court to grant bail to someone whose conviction or sentence has been referred to the Crown Court under s 11.

Section 13(1)(a)–(c) sets out the three conditions which have to be satisfied before a reference can be made:

(a) the Commission consider that there is a real possibility that the conviction, verdict, finding or sentence would not be upheld were the reference to be made,

(b) the Commission so consider—

(i) in the case of a conviction, verdict or finding, because of an argument, or evidence, not raised in the proceedings which led to it or on any appeal or application for leave to appeal against it, or

(ii) in the case of a sentence, because of an argument on a point of law, or information, not so raised, and

(c) an appeal against the conviction, verdict, finding or sentence has been determined or leave to appeal against it has been refused.

Section 13(2) says that:

nothing in sub-s 1(b)(i) or (c) shall prevent the making of a reference if it appears to the Commission that there are exceptional circumstances which justify making it.

Thus, the commission may only refer a conviction to the Court of Appeal if it considers that there is a real possibility that the court would not uphold the conviction because of new argument or evidence, or because there are exceptional circumstances for making it.

Under s 14(4A), where the reference is made under s 9 (cases dealt with on indictment), the appeal may not be on any ground which is not related to any reason given by the Commission for making the reference. This is subject, however, to s 14(4B), which provides that the Court of Appeal may give leave for such an appeal to be on a ground which is not related to any reason given by the Commission for making the reference. Under s 15(5), where the reference is made under s 11 (cases dealt with summarily), the appeal may be on any ground (whether or not related to any reason given by the Commission for making the reference).

The grounds of appeal may consist of, or include, a ground that has already been aired in a previous appellate hearing in the matter; however, the proper exercise of the court's discretion in cases which would involve departure from its previous reasoning should be confined to exceptional circumstances (*R v Thomas* [2002] EWCA Crim 941; [2003] 1 Cr App R 168). In *R v Mills and Poole* [2003] EWCA Crim 1753; [2003] 1 WLR 2931, the Court of Appeal noted that such exceptional circumstances may exist where, for example, there was some cogent argument advanced but not properly developed at the previous appellate hearing, but which, as now developed, could persuade the court that the conviction was unsafe; or where there has been a development of the law requiring the adoption of a different approach by the court to the issue before it. The exceptional circumstances must be such as would convince the court that if the matter had been arguable and argued in that way before the previous court, it would (not might) have quashed the conviction. The court should in any such cases be very slow to differ from its previous judgment. The court must also keep in mind that it needs to be sure of the safety of the conviction, as distinct from sureness of the appellant's guilt (per Auld LJ at paras 57 and 58). However, this requirement of exceptional circumstances does not govern the court's consideration of grounds rejected by the Commission. Whilst the court will treat the Commission's reasoning on making a reference with considerable respect, its discretion to consider a ground not included in the Commission's reasons for the reference, or to reject the Commission's reasoning on any matter considered by it, is unfettered (at para 60). The court added that the *Pendleton* 'jury impact' test ([2001] UKHL 66; [2002] 1 WLR 72), looked at as a range of permissible intrusion into the jury's thought processes for confirmatory purposes, is equally applicable where the new matter is one of argument, either of law or of interpretation of (or of inference from) the evidence at trial. The court may also have to ask itself similar questions as to the effect on the jury of evidence improperly given or of other irregularities at trial (at para 64).

In *R v Cottrell; R v Fletcher* [2007] EWCA Crim 2016; [2008] 1 Cr App R 7, the Court of Appeal said that the Commission should not normally refer a conviction to the Court of Appeal on the basis of a change of law. A defendant seeking leave to appeal out of time is generally expected to point to something more than the fact that the criminal law has changed. If the appeal is effectively based on a change of law, and nothing else, but the conviction was properly returned at the time, after a fair trial, the court reasoned that it is unlikely that a substantial injustice has occurred (per Sir Igor Judge P, at para 46). Indeed, s 42 of the Criminal Justice and Immigration Act 2008 reinforces this position by inserting a new section, s 16C, into the Criminal Appeal Act 1968. This provides that, where an appeal follows a reference by the Criminal Cases Review Commission, the Court of Appeal may dismiss the appeal if (a) the only ground for allowing it would be that there has been a development in the law since the date of the conviction, and (b) if the reference had not been made, but the appellant had made (and had been entitled to make) an application for an extension of time within which to seek leave to appeal on the ground of the development in the law, the Court would not think it appropriate to grant the application by exercising its power to extend time under s 18(3) of the 1968 Act.

13.15.2 Power to order investigations

Under s 23A (1) of the Criminal Appeal Act 1968, on an appeal against conviction (or an application for leave to appeal against conviction), the Court of Appeal may direct the Commission to investigate and report to the court on any matter if it appears to the court that:

(a) in the case of an appeal, the matter is relevant to the determination of the appeal and ought, if possible, to be resolved before the appeal is determined;

(aa) in the case of an application for leave to appeal, the matter is relevant to the determination of the application and ought, if possible, to be resolved before the application is determined;

(b)   an investigation of the matter by the Commission is likely to result in the Court being able to resolve it; and

(c)   the matter cannot be resolved by the Court without an investigation by the Commission.

The court may make the Commission's report available to the appellant and the respondent (s 23A(4)).

Under s 23A(1A), a direction to the Commission to investigate may not be given by a single judge of the Court of Appeal when considering an application for leave to appeal. The purpose of this stipulation is to require the full court to consider such directions before they are made, and thus ensure that they are used sparingly.

Section 15(2) of the Criminal Appeal Act 1995 provides that where, in investigating a matter pursuant to a direction from the Court of Appeal, it appears to the Commission that another matter which is relevant to the determination of the case by the Court of Appeal ought, if possible, to be resolved before the case is determined by that court, and an investigation of that other matter 'is likely to result in the Court's being able to resolve it', the Commission may investigate the related matter.

13.16 COMPENSATION FOR MISCARRIAGES OF JUSTICE

If a defendant successfully appeals against conviction, so that his conviction is quashed, and this occurs within the ordinary time limits for appeals, there is no right to compensation. However, where a conviction is quashed after the defendant has been allowed to appeal out of time, there may be a right to compensation. Section 133 of the Criminal Justice Act 1988 provides as follows:

(1)   Subject to sub-section (2) below, when a person has been convicted of a criminal offence and when subsequently his conviction has been reversed or he has been pardoned on the ground that a new or newly discovered fact shows beyond reasonable doubt that there has been a miscarriage of justice, the Secretary of State shall pay compensation for the miscarriage of justice to the person who has suffered punishment as a result of such conviction or, if he is dead, to his personal representatives, unless the non-disclosure of the unknown fact was wholly or partly attributable to the person convicted.

(2)   No payment of compensation under this section shall be made unless an application for such compensation has been made to the Secretary of State.

(3)   The question whether there is a right to compensation under this section shall be determined by the Secretary of State.

(4)   If the Secretary of State determines that there is a right to such compensation, the amount of the compensation shall be assessed by an assessor appointed by the Secretary of State.

(4A) In assessing so much of any compensation payable under this section to or in respect of a person as is attributable to suffering, harm to reputation or similar damage, the assessor shall have regard in particular to—

(a)   the seriousness of the offence of which the person was convicted and the severity of the punishment resulting from the conviction;

(b)   the conduct of the investigation and prosecution of the offence; and

(c)   any other convictions of the person and any punishment resulting from them.

(5) In this section 'reversed' shall be construed as referring to a conviction having been quashed—

  (a) on an appeal out of time; or
  (b) on a reference—
       (i)   under the Criminal Appeal Act 1995; . . .

In *R v Secretary of State for the Home Department ex p Mullen* [2004] UKHL 18; [2005] 1 AC 1, the House of Lords had to grapple with the meaning of the phrase 'miscarriage of justice'. Counsel for the Secretary of State argued that, in its context, 'miscarriage of justice' in s 133 refers to the 'wrongful conviction' of an innocent accused. Lord Bingham of Cornhill said (at para 4):

> The expression 'wrongful conviction' is not a legal term of art and it has no settled meaning. Plainly the expression includes the conviction of those who are innocent of the crime of which they have been convicted. But in ordinary parlance the expression would, I think, be extended to those who, whether guilty or not, should clearly not have been convicted at their trials. It is impossible and unnecessary to identify the manifold reasons why a defendant may be convicted when he should not have been. It may be because the evidence against him was fabricated or perjured. It may be because flawed expert evidence was relied on to secure conviction. It may be because evidence helpful to the defence was concealed or withheld. It may be because the jury was the subject of malicious interference. It may be because of judicial unfairness or misdirection. In cases of this kind, it may, or more often may not, be possible to say that a defendant is innocent, but it is possible to say that he has been wrongly convicted. The common factor in such cases is that something has gone seriously wrong in the investigation of the offence or the conduct of the trial, resulting in the conviction of someone who should not have been convicted.

His Lordship went to say (at para 9):

> '[M]iscarriage of justice' is an expression which, although very familiar, is not a legal term of art and has no settled meaning. Like 'wrongful conviction' it can be used to describe the conviction of the demonstrably innocent . . . but, again like 'wrongful conviction', it can be and has been used to describe cases in which defendants, guilty or not, certainly should not have been convicted . . . courts of appeal, although well used to deciding whether convictions are safe, or whether reasonable doubts exist about the safety of a conviction, are not called upon to decide whether a defendant is innocent and in practice very rarely do so.

Lord Steyn, however, concluded that the term 'a miscarriage of justice' extends only to 'clear cases of miscarriage of justice, in the sense that there would be acknowledgment that the person concerned was clearly innocent' (para 56). Lords Rodgers and Walker adopted the narrower interpretation put forward by Lord Steyn. Lord Scott declined to express a preference as between the views put forward by Lords Bingham and Steyn. The view of the majority – the narrow interpretation of 'miscarriage of justice' – may be thought preferable on the basis that it would seem to be an inappropriate use of public funds to pay compensation to someone who is not 'clearly innocent' of the offence of which he was wrongly convicted. Nonetheless, it is possible to conceive of cases where it cannot be said with certainty that the defendant was innocent but where the trial process (or events which preceded that trial) was vitiated by such unfairness that there ought to be financial recompense.

In *R (Murphy) v Secretary of State for the Home Department* [2005] EWHC 140 (Admin); [2005] 1 WLR 3516, the Divisional Court held that, for the purposes of s 133, where new evidence results in a finding of fact and the fact so found could properly be described as a new or newly discovered fact, s 133(1) is satisfied even if the evidence and the resulting finding of fact relate to a matter that was in issue at trial. However, the disclosure of a fact between trial and the determination of an appeal brought within the normal time limit cannot engage the operation of s 133 (since s 133 is concerned only with facts that emerge after the ordinary appellate process has been exhausted). Further, the words 'on the ground that' in s 133(1) mean that the new or newly discovered fact has to be the principal, if not the only, reason for the quashing of the conviction. Only then can it be said that the new or newly discovered fact showed beyond reasonable doubt that there had been a miscarriage of justice.

Section 61 of the Criminal Justice and Immigration Act 2008 makes a number of amendments to the compensation scheme in s 133. Section 61(3) amends s 133(2) of the 1988 Act to require an application for compensation to be made within two years of the date on which the conviction of the applicant was reversed or the date on which he was granted a pardon. However, under s 133(2A) (inserted by s 61(3)), an application may be accepted even though it was made outside the new time limit if the Secretary of State considers that there are 'exceptional circumstances which justify doing so'.

As we have seen, compensation can only be paid to those who have been pardoned or whose convictions have been 'reversed'. Section 61(5) inserts two new sub-sections, (5A) and (5B), into s 133. Sub-section (5A) amends the definition of 'reversed' where the conviction has been quashed on an appeal out of time but a retrial has been ordered. In such a case the conviction will now only be regarded as having been reversed if the person is acquitted of all offences at the re-trial (or if the prosecution decide not to proceed with a retrial). The new sub-s (5B) provides that references to a re-trial in sub-s (5A) include proceedings in a magistrates' court following remission of a case from the Crown Court.

If the Secretary of State decides that there is a right to compensation under s 133, the amount of compensation is assessed by an assessor. Section 61(7) of the Criminal Justice and Immigration Act 2008 inserts a new s 133A into the 1988 Act. Under s 133A(2), in assessing the amount of any compensation for suffering, harm to reputation or similar damage, the assessor must have regard, in particular, to (a) the seriousness of the offence of which the person was convicted and the severity of the punishment suffered as a result of the conviction, and (b) the conduct of the investigation and prosecution of the offence. Under s 133A(3), the assessor may make any deductions he considers appropriate by reason of any conduct on the part of the applicant which appears to the assessor to have caused or contributed to the conviction in question, and/ or any other convictions recorded against the applicant, and any punishment suffered as a result of them. If the assessor considers that there are exceptional circumstances which justify doing so, these deductions may result in the award of only a nominal amount of compensation (sub-s (4)). The award of only a nominal amount might be appropriate if, for example, the applicant's own conduct was a major contributory factor in the miscarriage of justice, or he has either a lengthy criminal record or has been convicted of particularly serious offences (whether before or after the miscarriage of justice in respect of which the claim is being made).

In so far as the compensation includes loss of earnings, s 133A(6) limits the compensation payable in respect of any one year to an amount 'equal to 1.5 times the median annual gross earnings according to the latest figures published by the Office of National Statistics at the time of the assessment'. Moreover, s 133A(5) limits the total amount of compensation payable in respect of a particular miscarriage of justice under s 133 to £500,000, unless the applicant has been detained for 10 years or more before the conviction is overturned, in which case the maximum is £1,000,000. These limits are intended to bring the compensation scheme under s 133 into line with the Criminal Injuries Compensation Scheme.

As well as the statutory scheme, there used to be an *ex gratia* scheme under which the Home Secretary could award compensation to claimants who fell outside s 133 but whose claim was nonetheless meritorious. However, this scheme was withdrawn in April 2006. In *R (Niazi) v Secretary of State for the Home Department* [2007] EWHC 1495 (Admin), it was held that the withdrawal (which took place without notice or consultation) of the *ex gratia* scheme was not unlawful.

13.17 FREE PARDONS

It is open to the Home Secretary to advise the Queen to pardon someone who has been convicted of an offence. This may be the only remedy if appeal to the Court of Appeal has failed to secure the quashing of the conviction.

This exercise of the royal prerogative of mercy does not, however, have the effect of quashing the conviction (*R v Foster* [1985] QB 115); only a successful appeal to the Court of Appeal (or House of Lords, on further appeal) can achieve that.

Chapter 14

Public funding of criminal litigation

In this chapter, we look at the mechanism for the State to fund the costs incurred by the defence in a criminal case. Legal aid is a very complex topic, and so this chapter will only be able to provide an overview of some of the key points.

14.1 THE ROLE OF LEGAL AID IN THE CRIMINAL JUSTICE SYSTEM

The provision of legal aid is a vital aspect of the right to a fair trial guaranteed by Art 6 of the European Convention on Human Rights. Article 6(3) includes the following rights:

(b) to have adequate time and facilities for the preparation of his defence;

(c) to defend himself in person or through legal assistance of his own choosing or, if he has not sufficient means to pay for legal assistance, to be given it free when the interests of justice so require.

A Fairer Deal for Legal Aid (2005, Department for Constitutional Affairs, <http://www.dca.gov.uk/laid/laidfullpaper.pdf>) had this to say about the role of legal aid in 'protecting people's rights and supporting the delivery of justice':

4.4 Legal aid ensures a fair trial for defendants by providing public funds for legal advice and representation in those criminal cases where defendants cannot afford to pay for it themselves. Legal aid therefore makes a vital contribution to the effective operation of our fair and effective CJS.

4.5 Providing this essential component of a fair and decent society means that criminal legal aid represents more than half of the entire legal aid budget. Because this is one element of a single budget for all publicly funded legal services it is vital that:

• the demands made on legal aid by the CJS are appropriate and proportionate;
• it makes the most effective contribution to the overall aims of the CJS;
• it is procured in ways which incentivise these objectives and provide the best value for money.

4.6 Legal aid can make an effective contribution to achieving our goals for the CJS. Where defendants plead not guilty, the way in which legal help is provided can help to ensure that the trial is focused on the key issues. Effective legal advice can also help those who intend to plead guilty to do so at the earliest opportunity. Not only is this the most efficient outcome for the CJS and legal aid, but more importantly, it provides the best deal for victims and witnesses, who are spared the ordeal of an unnecessarily protracted trial process. A system that delivers justice quickly and that is focused on the needs of victims and witnesses whilst safeguarding fairness and the rule of law, will attract higher levels of public confidence.

The premium placed on early guilty pleas is redolent of the 'crime control' model put forward by Herbert Packer (see Chapter 1).

In *Delivering Value for Money in the Criminal Defence Service – A Consultation on Proposed Changes to the Criminal Defence Service* (<http://www.dca.gov.uk/consult/leg-aid/cdserv.htm>), published in June 2003, the Government expressed concern at the escalating cost of providing representation for defendants in criminal cases, making the point that:

Legal aid has to compete with other calls on taxpayers' money, such as schools and hospitals. Any efficient publicly funded system of legal aid must be clearly focused on eliminating duplication and waste where they exist and delivering efficient, effective and sustainable services within budget.

The Paper expressed the desire to ensure that the legal aid scheme is focused firmly on what it describes as the 'core functions' of a Criminal Defence Service:

which are to ensure that people have the right to a fair trial and that people accused of a crime have their rights protected and are treated fairly.

This in turn requires, according to the Paper, that resources should be focused primarily in two areas:

- advice in the police station where such advice is necessary to protect and advance the client's interests;
- representation in court where the interests of justice require such representation.

It is perhaps important to remember the words of Lord Justice Auld in his *Review of the Criminal Courts of England and Wales* (the *Auld Review*). He was critical of the funding arrangements for defence lawyers (see paras 13–27 of Chapter 10). Recommendation 153 is that:

Urgent consideration should be given to changing the structure of public funding of defence fees in the criminal courts so as properly to reward and encourage adequate and timely preparation of cases for disposal on pleas of guilty or by trial, rather than discourage such preparation as it perversely does at present.

A thorough review of the whole legal aid system was carried out by Lord Carter, whose dedicated website is <http://www.legalaidprocurementreview.gov.uk/publications.htm>.

One of his key recommendations as regards criminal legal aid was that the basis of payment should change, with a move to a 'graduated fee system'. Such a scheme would 'provide suppliers with a fee for a case that is not connected to the number of hours they work but to the complexity of the case. This would allow those suppliers who are most efficient to benefit financially from their efficiencies' (see Chapter 2, para 36 of the Review). He concluded that the 'graduated fee scheme better rewards efficiency and encourages advocates to bring cases to a timely disposal' (para 42). The conclusions of the Carter Review are very much resource-driven, looking to reduce the amount of public money spent on legal aid. Many criminal practitioners are worried about the effect of such proposals on the viability of publicly-funded criminal work. The response of the Legal Action Group (published in October 2006, <http://www.lag.org.uk/ Shared_ASP_Files/UploadedFiles/AB0B7478-B50C-4439-9349-2E5F1BEBFCF6_ CACInquiryOct06. pdf>), for example, suggests that these proposals would have the effect of restricting choice and reducing access to justice and expresses concern that increasing pressure to drive down costs will mean that quality of service suffers.

14.2 THE CRIMINAL DEFENCE SERVICE

The Access to Justice Act 1999 (which replaced the Legal Aid Act 1988) created the Criminal Defence Service (CDS), the civil counterpart of the Community Legal Service). The CDS (<http://www.legalservices.gov.uk/criminal.asp>) is run by the Legal Services Commission (LSC) (the successor to the Legal Aid Board). Its purpose is set out in s 12(1) of the 1999 Act:

> . . . securing that individuals involved in criminal investigations or criminal proceedings have access to such advice, assistance and representation as the interests of justice require.

The legislation generally refers to representation 'funded by the Commission as part of the Criminal Defence Service'. In this chapter, such publicly funded representation will be described as 'legal aid'.

14.2.1 How the system works

Since 2001, solicitors' firms wishing to carry out publicly funded criminal defence services have been required to obtain a 'General Criminal Contract' from the Legal Services Commission. Solicitors in private practice are authorised to carry out publicly funded criminal defence work only if they have such a contract. Once it has been awarded, the firm is subject to a periodic audit to ensure that it meets the standards set out in the contract.

For the vast majority of criminal defence work, firms obtain cases when suspects arrested by the police either choose their own solicitor or request a duty solicitor. Suspects choose their own solicitor in approximately half of all cases. If a suspect asks for a solicitor, but does not know a particular solicitor who can attend the police station, they will be offered a solicitor from the duty solicitor scheme. Under the duty solicitor scheme, solicitors are placed on a duty rota for a particular police station or a group of stations, and when someone in police custody requests a duty solicitor, a solicitor from the rota is called. In most cases the solicitor will attend the police station (and sit in on any interview of the suspect) but in some cases (probably around one-fifth) the assistance is limited to advice given over the telephone. All requests for publicly-funded police station work, including 'own solicitor' requests, must be made through the Defence Solicitor Call Centre (DSCC).

The CDS is currently piloting 'CDS Direct' aimed at formalising the use of telephone advice by providing telephone advice to clients detained at a police station for a limited number of minor offences (and replacing telephone advice via the DSCC). The main benefit of telephone advice is that the suspect does not have to wait for the duty solicitor to arrive. It is hoped by the Government that this innovation will lead to a reduction in the overall time that suspects are held in the police station and a reduction in expenditure on criminal legal aid.

The DSCC or CDS Direct will determine whether legal advice should be limited to telephone advice or whether a solicitor should attend. Legal advice will be by telephone if a detainee is detained for a non-imprisonable offence, arrested on a bench warrant for failing to appear (and so is being held for production before the court, arrested on suspicion of drink-driving, or detained in relation to breach of police or court bail conditions. However, personal attendance by a solicitor for an offence suitable for telephone advice may be appropriate where, for example, the police are going to carry out an interview or an identification procedure.

14.2.1.1 Public defenders

Traditionally, defendants in criminal cases have been represented by lawyers who are in private practice and whose fee is paid either by the client or by the State. However, in 2001, the Government established a Public Defender Service (PDS), initially available in certain areas only, to provide salaried criminal defence service lawyers (along the lines of the public defender system that is a feature of American criminal justice). The basis of the Government's decision to establish a PDS is set out in *Criminal Defence Service: Establishing a Salaried Defence Service – The Government's Conclusions*, <http://www.dca.gov.uk/consult/saldef/saldefresp.htm>. This Paper announces the intention to employ as public defenders lawyers with higher rights of audience (whether barristers or solicitors who have completed the Rights of Audience in the Higher Courts training), as well as those who would be limited to appearing in the magistrates' court. The salaried defenders are also entitled to instruct specialist advocates (whether solicitors or barristers). The public service is governed by the same quality standards and system of auditing that applies to contracted firms.

Despite some negative responses from practitioners and interest groups during the consultation exercise which preceded the establishment of the scheme, the Government maintained its view that the independence of the Public Defenders could be assured 'by the appointment of a professional head of service and the effective implementation of the Code of Conduct'. Nonetheless, the Government accepted that 'public perception of independence will remain a concern until experience proves otherwise'. It is note-worthy that the Paper points out a particular clause (cl 2.2) in the Code of Conduct for Salaried Defenders, designed to ensure that public defenders are not 'too ready to plea bargain':

A professional employee shall not put a client under pressure to plead guilty, and in particular, shall not advise a client that it is in his or her interests to plead guilty unless satisfied that the prosecution is able to discharge the burden of proof.

The ultimate objective is to achieve a CDS which uses both lawyers in private practice and salaried defenders. Suspects and defendants seeking publicly funded representation would therefore be able to choose between a solicitor in private practice who has a contract with the LSC, or a salaried defender employed by the LSC.

There is discussion of public defenders in Cyrus Tata et al, 'Does mode of delivery make a difference to criminal case outcomes and client' satisfaction? The public defence solicitor experiment' [2004] Crim LR 120 (focusing on the Public Defence Solicitors' Office in Scotland).

14.2.1.2 'Advice and assistance'

Under reg 4 of the Criminal Defence Service (General) (No 2) Regulations 2001 (SI 2001/1437), the LSC is required to 'fund such advice and assistance, including advocacy assistance, as it considers appropriate in relation to any individual' who:

(a) is the subject of an investigation which may lead to criminal proceedings;
(b) is the subject of criminal proceedings;
(c) requires advice and assistance regarding his appeal or potential appeal against the outcome of any criminal proceedings or an application to vary a sentence;
(d) requires advice and assistance regarding his sentence;
(e) requires advice and assistance regarding his application or potential application to the Criminal Cases Review Commission;
. . .
(j) is a volunteer [this means a person attending a police station voluntarily, 'helping the police with their inquiries']
. . .

Regulation 5 covers 'advice and assistance'. Under para 5(1):

The following advice and assistance may be granted without reference to the financial resources of the individual:

(a) all advice and assistance provided to an individual who is arrested and held in custody at a police station or other premises;
(b) all advocacy assistance before a magistrates' court or the Crown Court;
(c) all advice and assistance provided by a court duty solicitor in accordance with his contract with the Commission;
(d) all advice and assistance provided to a volunteer during his period of voluntary attendance;
. . .

Under reg 5(4), except where reg 5(1) applies, the financial eligibility of the individual has to be determined. For these purposes, an individual is eligible for advice and assistance if his weekly disposable income does not exceed £95 and his disposable capital does not exceed £1,000 (these figures are amended periodically for inflation) (reg 5(5)). A person is deemed to be financially eligible if in receipt of means-tested State benefits such as income support and income-based jobseeker's allowance (reg 5(8)).

14.2.1.3 Representation orders

Under the original scheme established by the Access to Justice Act 1999 (mirroring the scheme under the Legal Aid Act 1988), responsibility for the grant of legal aid rested with the court. The Government felt that the magistrates' courts were not applying the merits ('interests of justice') test with sufficient rigour, and so it was decided that responsibility for the grant of legal aid should pass to the LSC. In practice, this has made little difference, as legal aid decisions are taken by court staff acting on behalf of the LSC.

Nonetheless, reg 3 of the Criminal Defence Service (Representation Orders and Consequential Amendments) Regulations 2006 (SI 2006/2493) makes it clear that the granting of legal aid in criminal proceedings in the magistrates' court is the responsibility of the LSC. Under reg 4, a representation order extends to the Crown Court, if the proceedings continue there, and to any incidental proceedings. However, it does not extend to any appeal. Under reg 5(1), where any charge against the individual is varied, the representation authority must consider whether the interests of justice require that he be represented in respect of the varied charge (and must withdraw the representation order if the interests of justice do not so require).

Regulation 6 of the Criminal Defence Service (General) (No 2) Regulations 2001 (SI 2001/1437) provides that the date of any representation order is the date on which the application for the grant of such an order is received in accordance with the Regulations.

Under reg 7 of the 2001 Regulations, the court, a judge of the court, or the registrar of criminal appeals may grant a representation order at any stage of criminal proceedings, other than proceedings in a magistrates' court. Under reg 9(1) of those Regulations, an application for a representation order in respect of proceedings in the Crown Court may be made, where an application for such an order in respect of the proceedings in a magistrates' court has not been made or has been refused, orally or in writing to the Crown Court; in writing to the magistrates' court at the conclusion of the proceedings in that magistrates' court; or (where the accused has been sent for trial to the Crown Court), in writing to the magistrates' court which sent the case to the Crown Court. Under reg 9(1A), where a representation order has been granted in respect of proceedings in a magistrates' court, an application for a representation order in respect of an appeal to the Crown Court in those proceedings may be made orally or in writing to the magistrates' court, or orally or in writing to the Crown Court. Under reg 17(1), where the charge(s) against the assisted person are varied, the court before which the proceedings are heard must consider whether the interests of justice continue to require that he be represented (and must withdraw the representation order if the interests of justice do not so require).

14.2.2 Grant of right to representation: the merits test

The decision whether or not to grant representation by the CDS is determined 'according to the interests of justice' set out in para 5 of Sched 3 to the Access to Justice Act 1999. Paragraph 5 provides as follows:

(1) Any question as to whether power to grant a right to representation should be exercised shall be determined according to the interests of justice.

(2) In deciding what the interests of justice consist of in relation to any individual, the following factors must be taken into account—

(a) whether the individual would, if any matter arising in the proceedings is decided against him, be likely to lose his liberty or livelihood or suffer serious damage to his reputation,

(b) whether the determination of any matter arising in the proceedings may involve consideration of a substantial question of law,

(c) whether the individual may be unable to understand the proceedings or to state his own case,

(d) whether the proceedings may involve the tracing, interviewing or expert cross-examination of witnesses on behalf of the individual, and

(e) whether it is in the interests of another person that the individual be represented.

The factors set out in para 5(2) mirror those that were relevant under s 22 of the Legal Aid Act 1988, and so case law decided under s 22 is relevant to the criteria contained in para 5(2).

In assessing whether the accused is likely to lose his liberty, regard must be had to the facts alleged by the prosecution, rather than the maximum penalty that could theoretically be imposed in respect of the offence with which the defendant is charged.

There must be a real and practical (as opposed to a theoretical) risk of a custodial sentence being imposed. Thus, it is not enough that the offence carries a custodial sentence: the court must consider whether a custodial sentence might actually be imposed in this particular case *R (Sonn Macmillan Solicitors) v Gray's Magistrates' Court* [2006] EWHC 1103 (Admin).

In *R v Liverpool City Magistrates ex p McGhee* (1994) 158 JP 275, the Divisional Court rejected the contention that what would now be a community order with an unpaid work requirement (see Chapter 18) could be regarded as a sentence which deprives the accused of liberty. However, Rose LJ emphasised that the list of criteria in s 22 (now para 5) is not exhaustive, and so the possibility that such an order may be made may be a factor in deciding whether or not to make a representation order.

The factor which includes 'expert cross-examination of witnesses' refers to the need to have an advocate cross-examination of witnesses, not cross-examination of expert witnesses (*R v Liverpool City Magistrates ex p McGhee*). In *R v Scunthorpe Justices ex p S* (1998) *The Times*, 5 March, the Divisional Court considered that refusal of legal aid to a defendant aged 16, in a case where the prosecution witnesses were all police officers, was irrational. The expertise needed to cross-examine police witnesses, and to trace and interview potential defence witnesses, would be beyond an accused aged 16.

In *R (Matara) v Brent Magistrates' Court* [2005] EWHC Admin 1829 (Admin); (2005) 169 JP 576, the defendant was charged with failure to provide a specimen of breath. He made an application for legal aid. It was argued that he would be unable to understand the court proceedings because his understanding of English was inadequate; the court's response was that an interpreter would be provided. It was held that at least one of the 'interests of justice' criteria in para 5 was met. The availability of an interpreter did not meet the point that it was the defendant's case that he was unable to understand what was being said at the time of his arrest, a point which lay at the heart of his defence. It went to his ability to state his own case and the overall fairness of the trial. The decision to refuse legal aid was therefore quashed.

In *R v Oates* [2002] EWCA Crim 1071; [2002] 1 WLR 2833, the applicant sought permission to appeal to the Court of Appeal against her conviction (see Chapter 13 for discussion of appeals to the Court of Appeal). The application had been refused by the single judge and she now wished to renew the application orally. She sought public funding for representations to be made on her behalf. It was held that, whilst legal aid is available to cover the drafting of the grounds of appeal and (if leave to appeal is granted) the appeal hearing itself, legal aid will not be granted on a renewed application for permission to appeal against conviction following refusal by the single judge. The court added that this restriction is not contrary to Art 6(3)(c) of the European Convention on Human Rights (quoted above). Rose LJ pointed out (at para 10) that counsel often appear before the Court of Appeal on a pro bono (i.e. without fee) basis to renew an application for leave to appeal, following refusal by the single judge. If such an application is successful, and leave to appeal is granted, legal aid will then invariably be granted (subject to any questions of means) for the hearing of the appeal. It is submitted, however, that it is questionable whether representation should depend on the goodwill of the legal profession. Perhaps a better justification for the decision was the fact that the applicant's legal aid had covered the provision of advice by counsel, and the drafting of grounds of appeal, that the particular appeal was based on issues of law, and that such grounds could fairly be considered by the court on the basis of written submissions by defence counsel, without an oral hearing, and so without the defendant being present and without prosecution or defence being represented by counsel (at para 11).

For a discussion of the application of the merits test, see Richard Young and Aidan Wilcox, 'The merits of legal aid in the magistrates' courts revisited' [2007] Crim LR 109.

14.2.2.1 Appeals against refusal of legal aid on the merits test

The Criminal Defence Service (Representation Orders: Appeals etc.) Regulations 2006 (SI 2006/2494) provide for appeals or renewed applications where an applicant has been refused publicly funded representation on the ground that the interests of justice do not require him to be granted legal aid.

Under reg 3(3), an appeal or a renewed application is determined without a hearing unless the person determining the appeal or application directs otherwise. Written reasons must be given for any decision on an appeal or a renewed application (reg 3(5)).

Regulation 4 deals with appeals in magistrates' court cases. Under reg 4(2) an individual may appeal to the magistrates' court (which for these purposes includes a single justice) against a decision to refuse to grant a representation order on the grounds that the interests of justice do not require such an order to be granted. The court must either uphold the refusal of legal aid or else decide that it would be in the interests of justice for a representation order to be granted (reg 4(3)). In the latter case, the individual may then apply for a representation order. If the individual states in writing, verified by a statement of truth, that his financial resources have not changed since the date of his original application so as to make him financially ineligible for a representation order, the representation authority must grant the order; if his financial resources may have so changed, the representation authority must determine whether he is financially eligible for legal aid and, if so, must grant the order (reg 4(4)).

Regulation 5 makes it clear that there is no appeal against a decision to refuse legal aid on the ground that the individual is not financially eligible to be granted legal aid.

Regulation 6 deals with cases which are to be heard in the Crown Court where a representation order has been refused on the grounds that the interests of justice do not require such an order to be granted. In such a case, under reg 6(1), the individual may make a renewed application to the appropriate officer who, or court which, refused the application. Under reg 6(2), where the renewed application is made to the appropriate officer, he may either grant the order or refer the application to a Crown Court judge or, if the case is still in the magistrates' court, to the court or a District Judge, who may either grant the order or refuse the application.

Regulation 8 covers cases where an application for the grant of legal aid in respect of proceedings other than proceedings in a magistrates' court has been refused on the ground that the interests of justice do not require such an order to be granted. The applicant may make a renewed application to the Commission, which may grant the order or refuse the application.

14.2.3 The means test

As well as having to satisfy the merits test (set out above) applicants for legal aid in the magistrates' court also have to satisfy the means test, namely that they are financially eligible for legal aid, taking account of their income and expenses (capital is not included).

There had been a means test under the Legal Aid Act 1988 but it had been scrapped when that Act was replaced by the Access to Justice Act 1999. However, the means test was reintroduced for magistrates' court cases in October 2006 (and the intention is to extend the means test to Crown Court cases as well).

The Criminal Defence Service (Financial Eligibility) Regulations 2006 (SI 2006/2492) set out the criteria relating to financial eligibility which must be satisfied before individuals involved in criminal proceedings in a magistrates' court may be granted legal aid. Regulation 5(1) provides that the representation authority (magistrates' court staff working on behalf of the Legal Services Commission) must assess whether the financial resources of the individual are such that he is eligible to be granted a representation order.

Under reg 5(2), applicants under the age of 18 are deemed to be financially eligible. Under reg 5(3), applicants who are in receipt of a qualifying benefit are also deemed to be financially eligible for legal aid. The qualifying benefits are income support; income-based jobseeker's allowance; guarantee credit under s 1(3)(a) of the State Pension Credit Act 2002.

Regulation 7(1) stipulates that, in calculating the applicant's income, the resources of his partner must be treated as those of the applicant, unless the partner has a 'contrary interest in the proceedings'. A contrary interest would exist, for example, where the partner is the alleged victim in the case, or is a prosecution witness in the case, or is a co-defendant with a contrary interest (e.g. running a 'cut-throat' defence).

Regulation 8 contains an anti-avoidance provision to the effect that, if it appears to the representation authority that the applicant (or his partner) has, with intent to reduce the amount of his resources, directly or indirectly deprived himself of any resources, or transferred any resources to another person, such resources are to be treated as part of the individual's resources. This is so whether or not the intention of the applicant was to reduce his resources to the level at which he would become financially eligible for legal aid or for some other purpose.

Under reg 9(1), where an individual applies for a representation order, the representation authority must calculate his gross annual income and, where he has a partner or has children living in his household, must divide the total according to the scale set out in the Schedule, which provides for adding the 'relevant figure' to 1.00 and dividing the individual's gross annual income (including that of any partner) by the total.

The 'relevant figure' for reg 9 is as follows:

A partner	0.64
Each child of the applicant in his household, aged 0–1	0.15
Each child aged 2–4	0.30
Each child aged 5–7	0.34
Each child aged 8–10	0.38
Each child aged 11–12	0.41
Each child aged 13–15	0.44
Each child aged 16–18	0.59

Under reg 9(2), an individual is eligible for a representation order if his gross annual income, as adjusted under reg 9(1), is £12,475 or less. Regulation 9(3) provides that an individual is not eligible for legal aid if his gross annual income (as adjusted under reg 9(1)) is £22,325 or more (these figures are adjusted periodically to take account of inflation).

Regulation 10(1) requires that, where an individual's gross annual income (as adjusted under reg 9(1)) is more than £12,475 and less than £22,325, the representation authority must calculate the individual's annual disposable income in accordance with reg 10(2). This is a more complex calculation, requires various items of expenditure to be deducted from the applicant's gross annual income. Deductions include:

- income tax;
- national insurance contributions;
- council tax;
- rent or mortgage payments on his only or main dwelling (less any housing benefit);
- child care costs;
- bona fide payments for the maintenance of a former partner or of a child or a relative who is not a member of his household;
- living expenses, fixed at £5,676 per annum (this figure is adjusted periodically for inflation) or, if applicant has a partner or has children living in his household, an amount calculated in accordance with the scale set out above: the 'relevant figure' is added to 1.00 and multiplied by £5,676.

Under reg 10(3), an applicant is eligible for legal aid if his annual disposable income, as calculated according to the formula in reg 10(2), does not exceed £3,398 (this figure is also adjusted periodically for inflation).

A couple of examples (based on ones that appear on the CDS website) will help to demonstrate how the initial means test operates:

Example 1
The applicant has a partner and three children (aged 2, 5 and 9). He earns £20,800 and his partner earns £11,000. The calculation is as follows:

Applicant = 1
Partner = 0.64
Child 1 = 0.38
Child 2 = 0.34
Child 3 = 0.30
The weighting factor totals 2.66.

The total income received in the family is £31,800. Dividing this figure by 2.66 gives £11,955. This applicant therefore passes the financial eligibility test (he will of course have to satisfy the merits test as well in order to qualify for legal aid).

Example 2
The applicant has a partner and one child aged 6. She earns £20,800 and her partner earns £11,000. The calculation is as follows:

Applicant = 1
Partner = 0.64
Child = 0.34
The weighting factor totals 1.98.

The total income received by the family is £31,800. Dividing this figure by 1.98 gives £16,061. This applicant therefore has to undergo a full means test.

To assist practitioners, the CDS has produced an online eligibility calculator: see <http://www.legalservices.gov.uk/criminal/getting_legal_aid/eligibility_calculator. asp>. Where an individual has been granted a representation order, reg 11(1) requires him to inform the representation authority of any change in his financial circumstances. Where the effect of such a change is that the individual is no longer financially eligible for legal aid, the representation authority must withdraw the grant of representation (reg 11(2)).

Regulation 12 provides for recalculation of the applicant's income: if it appears to the representation authority that there has been an error in the calculation of the individual's income, or new information comes to light, the representation authority must recalculate the applicant's income and, if he is no longer financially eligible for a representation order, must withdraw the order.

Regulation 13 provides for renewal of the application for legal aid: if an applicant is refused legal aid on the ground that he is not financially eligible, he may renew his application if, but only if, there is a change in his financial circumstances.

Under reg 14(1), an applicant who has been refused legal aid on the ground that he is not financially eligible may apply for a review of the decision:

a   to the representation authority, on the ground that there has been a miscalculation of his income or an administrative error; or
b   to the Commission, on the ground that he does not have sufficient means to pay for the cost of legal assistance, notwithstanding that his financial resources are such that he is not financially eligible for a representation order (in which case, the applicant must provide full particulars of his income and expenditure and a certificate by a solicitor as to the likely costs of the proceedings). Cases falling within this provision might include, for example, cases where the costs are likely to be particularly high, or where the applicant has unusually high outgoings (e.g. having to pay care costs for a disabled relative).

Under reg 14(6), the Commission may, if it thinks that the application raises a question of such importance that it should be decided by the High Court, refer that question to the High Court for its decision.

14.2.4 Nature of representation

Section 15(1) of the Access to Justice Act 1999 provides that where an individual has been granted a right to representation, he may select any representative willing to act for him, and the Commission has to fund representation by that representative. This is subject to the proviso in reg 11 of the Criminal Defence Service (General) (No 2) Regulations 2001 (S.I. 2001/1437), that this right is exercisable only in relation to representatives who are either employed by the LSC (i.e. as public defenders) to provide such representation, or authorised to provide such representation under the General Criminal Contract with the LSC.

Under reg 12(1), a representation order in respect of proceedings before a magistrates' court may only include representation by an advocate if the offence is indictable (this includes either-way offences) and the court is of the opinion that, because of circumstances which make the proceedings unusually grave or difficult, representation by both a litigator (normally a solicitor) and an advocate would be desirable. Regulation 12(3) provides that a representation order for magistrates' court proceedings may provide for the services of a Queen's Counsel or of more than one advocate only where the court is of the opinion that the assisted person could not be adequately represented except by a Queen's Counsel or by more than one advocate.

Regulation 14 deals with cases in the Crown Court, High Court, Court of Appeal, and House of Lords. Under reg 14(1), a representation order for proceedings in these courts will always include representation by one junior advocate (a barrister or a solicitor with a right of audience in the higher courts), and may (if the complexity of the case so requires) include representation by a Queen's Counsel or by more than one advocate.

Regulation 16(2) empowers the court to allow a change of legal representative if the original litigator (usually a solicitor) considers himself to be under a duty to withdraw from the case in accordance with his professional rules of conduct, or there has been a breakdown in the relationship between the assisted person and the litigator such that effective representation can no longer be provided, or (through circumstances beyond his control) the litigator is no longer able to represent the assisted person, or some other substantial compelling reason exists.

In the interests of keeping costs to a minimum, reg 16A provides that where the person who has been granted a right to representation is one of two or more co-defendants whose cases are to be heard together, he must select the same litigator as the co-defendant(s) unless there is, or is likely to be, a conflict of interest.

Paragraph 19 covers the need for authorisation of expenditure. Where it appears to the litigator that it is necessary to obtain a written report or opinion of one or more experts or to perform an act which is unusual in its nature or involves large expenditure, he should apply to the Costs Committee of the LSC for prior authority to do so. Where the Costs Committee authorises such action, it will also fix the maximum to be paid in respect of it.

Regulation 24 places a duty on legal representatives to report abuse of the system. It provides that:

> Notwithstanding the relationship between or rights of a representative and client or any privilege arising out of such relationship, where the representative for an applicant or assisted person knows or suspects that that person:
>
> (a) has intentionally failed to comply with any provision of regulations made under the Act concerning the information to be furnished by him; or
>
> (b) in furnishing such information has knowingly made a false statement or false representation,
>
> the representative shall immediately report the circumstances to the Commission.

14.2.5 Provisional grant of representation

Section 56 of the Criminal Justice and Immigration Act 2008 amends Sched 3 to the 1999 Act to allow for the *provisional* grant of a right to representation in certain circumstances. Section 56(6) inserts a new paragraph 1A into Sched 3 to the 1999 Act. This provides for regulations to set out circumstances in which a right to representation may be granted provisionally to individuals involved in an investigation which may result in criminal proceedings, for the purpose of those proceedings. The regulations will also make provision about the stage of an investigation at which the right may be granted provisionally, and the circumstances in which any provisional grant ceases to be provisional (thereby becoming a full grant), or where it is to be withdrawn. Any provisional grant of a right to representation will be made by the LSC (para 2A of Sched 3 to the 1999 Act).

14.3 RECOVERY OF COSTS

Regulation 3(1) of the Criminal Defence Service (Recovery of Defence Costs Orders) Regulations 2001 (SI 2001/856) provides that the court before which the proceedings are heard, unless it is a magistrates' court, shall make an order requiring a publicly funded defendant to pay some or all of the cost of any representation so funded if the case falls within the circumstances set out in the regulations. This is known as a Recovery of Defence Costs Order (RDCO) (reg 3(2)). It follows from the exclusion of magistrates' courts from para 3 that a person convicted by a magistrates' court cannot be required to contribute to the costs incurred on their behalf by the CDS.

Under reg 4, the judge must make an RDCO unless the case falls within reg 4(2), which provides:

> (2) An RDCO shall not be made against a [publicly] funded defendant who:
>
> > (a) has appeared in the magistrates' court only;
> > (b) is committed for sentence to the Crown Court;
> > (c) is appealing against sentence to the Crown Court; or
> > (d) has been acquitted, other than in exceptional circumstances.

The effect of this is that a Crown Court judge will only make an RDCO if the defendant was tried in the Crown Court and was convicted, or if the defendant appealed unsuccessfully to the Crown Court against conviction in the magistrates' court (note that reg 4(2)(c) excludes only appeals against sentence). It is clear from reg 4(2)(d) that an RDCO may be made where the defendant was acquitted, but only in exceptional circumstances. Paragraph XI.1.5 of the *Practice Direction (Costs: Criminal Proceedings)* [2004] 2 All ER 1070 says that where a funded defendant has been acquitted, the judge 'must consider whether it is reasonable in all the circumstances to make such an order'. Paragraph XI.1.6 of the *Practice Direction* goes on to say that 'where a person of modest means properly brings an appeal against conviction, it should be borne in mind that it will not usually be desirable or appropriate for the court to make an RDCO for a significant amount, if to do so would inhibit an appellant from bringing an appeal'.

The Court of Appeal may make an RDCO where the defendant appeals unsuccessfully to that Court against conviction and/or sentence in the Crown Court.

Under reg 5(1), an RDCO may be made for the 'full cost of the representation incurred in any court under the representation order' (or such lesser amount as the judge determines). This includes costs incurred in the magistrates' court before the case was sent to the Crown Court for trial. The order may require payment to be made forthwith, or in specified instalments (reg 5(2)).

The means of the defendant have to be taken into account. Under reg 9(1) the amount or value of every source of income and every resource of capital available to the defendant may be taken into account, along with the financial resources of any partner. However, under reg 9(2), the court will disregard the first £3,000 of capital available to him, the first £100,000 of equity in his principal residence, and his income if it does not exceed £25,250 (this figure is adjusted periodically for inflation).

Chapter 15

Costs in criminal cases

In this chapter we consider various costs orders that can be made by the criminal courts.

15.1 POWER TO AWARD COSTS

The powers of the criminal courts to award costs are contained in ss 16–21 of the Prosecution of Offences Act 1985 and the Costs in Criminal Cases (General) Regulations 1986 (SI 1986/1335). Reference should also be made to *Practice Direction (Costs: Criminal Proceedings)* [2004] 2 All ER 1070, which gives detailed guidance on costs in criminal cases.

Three main types of costs order have to be considered:

- an order that the defendant's costs be paid out of central funds (s 16 of the 1985 Act);
- an order that the prosecution costs be paid out of central funds (s 17); and
- an order that the defendant pay the prosecution costs (s 18).

15.2 DEFENDANT'S COSTS ORDER

Section 16 makes provision for the award of defence costs out of central funds (that is, Government funds pay some or all of the defendant's legal bill). Such an order may be made in any of the following circumstances:

- the prosecution decide not to proceed with a charge;
- the defendant is discharged when the magistrates find no case to answer in committal proceedings (this will cease to be relevant when committal proceedings are abolished for either-way offences in the same way they have been for indictable-only offences, save for the exceptional cases where the magistrates refuse to send a case for trial to the Crown Court on the basis that it would be an abuse of process);
- the defendant is acquitted following summary trial;
- the prosecution at the Crown Court offer no evidence or ask that all counts remain on the file marked not to be proceeded with without leave;
- the defendant is acquitted following trial on indictment;
- the defendant successfully appeals against conviction and/or sentence.

Paragraphs II.1.1 (magistrates' courts) and II.2.1 (Crown Court) of the *Practice Direction* stipulate that where s 16 of the Act applies, 'an order should normally be made unless there are positive reasons for not doing so. For example, where the defendant's own conduct has brought suspicion on himself and has misled the prosecution into thinking that the case against him was stronger than it was, the defendant can be left to pay his own costs'. However, para II.1.2 (dealing with magistrates' courts) makes it clear that the decision 'whether to make such an award is a matter in the discretion of the court in the light of the circumstances of each particular case', effectively reducing the scope for challenging a refusal to make an order under s 16. This paragraph makes it clear that magistrates' courts should adopt the same approach as the Crown Court to the making of orders under s 16. Paragraph II.2.1, dealing with the Crown Court, says that if the court declines to make an order under s 16, it should be explained, in open court, 'that the reason for not making an order does not involve any suggestion that the defendant is guilty of any criminal conduct but the order is refused because of the positive reason that should be identified'.

Paragraph II.2.2 goes on to provide that where a person is convicted of one count but acquitted on another, the court may exercise its discretion to make a defendant's costs order but may order that only part of the costs incurred be paid. The court should make whatever order seems just having regard to the relative importance of the two charges and the conduct of the parties generally. Where the court considers that it would be inappropriate that the defendant should recover all of the costs properly incurred, the amount must be specified in the order. The same approach applies in the magistrates' court (para II.1.1).

Paragraph II.4.3 provides that where the Court of Appeal has jurisdiction to make an order under s 16 in favour of a successful appellant, the court will bear in mind the principles applied by the Crown Court in relation to acquitted defendants.

It is clear from the *Practice Direction* that (unless the defence is publicly funded) there is a strong presumption that a costs order should be made in favour of a defendant who has been acquitted. Where the prosecution resist an application for costs on the basis that the defendant brought suspicion on himself, the court is entitled to rely on a statement of facts from the prosecution (provided that statement contains sufficient facts for the justices to be justified in reaching the conclusion that the defendant has brought the proceedings on himself) – the court does not have to hear oral evidence on this matter (*Mooney v Cardiff Justices* (2000) 164 JP 220).

A defendant's costs order under s 16 does not have to be made by the bench which acquits the defendant, and so a differently constituted court (for example, the bench which sentences the defendant for other offences) can make such an order regarding an earlier acquittal (*R v Clerk to Liverpool Justices ex p Abiaka* (1999) 163 JP 497).

R (McCormick) v Liverpool City Magistrates' Court [2001] 2 All ER 705 concerned costs incurred by a defendant before he was granted publicly funded representation. The defendant did not have the means to pay those costs. It was held that costs are incurred by a defendant for the purpose of s 16(6) of the Act if he is contractually obliged to pay for them. There is no requirement for the defendant to prove that he has in fact paid, or is likely to pay, those costs.

In *R (Cunningham) v Exeter Crown Court* [2003] EWHC 184 (Admin); (2003) 167 JP 93, it was held that, where the court takes the view that there are positive reasons for not awarding costs, it should set out (albeit briefly) its reasons for coming to that view. In *R*

(Barrington) v Preston Crown Court [2001] EWHC 599 (Admin), the defendant was convicted in the magistrates' court and appealed to the Crown Court. At the Crown Court, the prosecution offered no evidence after a crucial witness failed to attend and so the defendant's conviction was quashed. However, the judge refused an application for a defendant's costs order under s 16. Having regard to the fact that the case against the defendant collapsed not because of anything she had said or done, or any misleading behaviour on her part, but simply because a prosecution witness had failed to attend court, it was held that an application for a defendant's costs order should have been successful.

In *R (Stoddard) v Oxford Magistrates' Court* [2005] EWHC 2733 (Admin); (2005) 169 JP 683, the prosecution indicated that they were willing to conclude the proceedings by way of a formal caution, and the defendants accepted that offer. The case was subsequently dismissed, with the prosecution offering no evidence. The defendants sought a defendant's costs order but the application was refused, the court holding that a defendant who had accepted a formal caution should be in no better position in terms of costs than a defendant who had pleaded guilty to a charge. The Divisional Court overturned the refusal, holding that a caution is not to be equated with a conviction. Though in accepting the caution the defendant had accepted that there had been wrongdoing, he had been acquitted of the offence, did not have a criminal record, and had not been subjected to any penalty. Where a prosecution is withdrawn following the acceptance by the accused of a caution, the defendant stands acquitted for the purposes of the making of a defendant's costs under s 16 of the 1985 Act.

Some care must be taken by the court when explaining a refusal to award costs. In *Hussain v United Kingdom* (2006) 43 EHRR 22, counsel for the Crown informed the court that a key witness did not want to give evidence and that the prosecution did not feel that she ought to be compelled to give evidence; they accordingly offered no evidence. The defendant was duly acquitted. He made an application for a defendant's costs order under s 16 of the 1985 Act. The judge stated that there was compelling evidence against the defendant on the court papers and that he was not going to exercise his discretion to make an order for costs. The European Court of Human Rights held that the presumption of innocence enshrined in Art 6(2) is violated if a statement of a public official reflects an opinion that a person charged with an offence is guilty unless he has been proved guilty. The Convention does not guarantee a defendant who had been acquitted the right to reimbursement of his costs. However, the only interpretation which could be put on the judge's words was that he was refusing the order because he was of the view that, although the defendant had been acquitted, he was in fact guilty of the offence. That was incompatible with the presumption of innocence and a breach of the Convention (see paras 19–24).

The amount of the costs order is governed by s 16(6) which provides that amount is to be what the court considers 'reasonably sufficient' to compensate the defendant for 'any expenses properly incurred by him in the proceedings'. The order cannot include expenses that do not relate directly to the proceedings themselves, such as loss of earnings. See also para I.3.1 of the *Practice Direction*.

In *R v Dudley Magistrates' Court ex p Power City Stores Ltd* (1990) 154 JP 654, where the defendant wanted to recover the cost of employing leading counsel (that is, a QC), the Divisional Court held that in calculating the amount of costs to be paid under s 16, the officer doing the assessment has to carry out a two-stage test. First, he has to consider whether the expenses claimed were properly incurred by the defendant. If so, the second step is to ask what amount would be reasonably sufficient to compensate the defendant for those costs. The test is whether the defendant acted reasonably in instructing the counsel he did. There are cases in which junior counsel or a solicitor could conduct the case, but in which it is nonetheless reasonable to instruct leading counsel. In *R (Hale) v North Sefton Justices* [2002] EWHC 257 (Admin); (2002) *The Times*, 29 January, it was held that the question to be decided under s 16(6) is whether the defendant had acted reasonably in the circumstances by instructing a solicitor at a particular hourly rate, not whether he could have instructed a more junior solicitor. In the instant case, the justices' clerk had applied the statutory criterion of reasonable sufficiency in s 16(6) to the wrong issue, namely the quality of representation, rather than the costs incurred.

In *Henry A Coff Ltd v Environment Agency* [2003] EWHC 1305 (Admin), a District judge declined to make a defendant's costs order under s 16 on the ground that the amount sought was unreasonable on its face and the court should not allow costs that reflect extravagance. The Divisional Court said that the District judge was wrong to refuse to make a defendant's costs order on this basis. What had been asked for was an order for costs to be assessed. It would therefore be for the person subsequently assessing the costs to determine whether the costs claimed were excessive.

Under s 16(7), where a court makes a defendant's costs order but is of the opinion that there are circumstances which make it inappropriate that the person in whose favour the order is made should recover the full amount they would otherwise receive, the court may assess what amount would, in its opinion, be just and reasonable and specify that amount in the order. This allows the court to make a defendant's costs order in respect of only part of the costs incurred. If, for example, the defendant is convicted of some offences but acquitted of others, it may be appropriate to award him some costs, or none at all.

15.3 PROSECUTION COSTS FROM CENTRAL FUNDS

An order that the prosecutor's costs be paid out of central funds may be made under s 17 of the Prosecution of Offences Act 1985. Section 17 applies only to private prosecutors, and so excludes the Crown Prosecution Service and any other public authority (for example, HM Revenue and Customs, local authorities, etc.). Furthermore, this section applies only to the prosecution of indictable offences (whether triable only on indictment or triable either way). According to para III.1.1 of the *Practice Direction*, an order should be made, save where there is good reason for not doing so, for example, where 'proceedings have been instituted or continued without good cause'. Such an order can be made even though the defendant was acquitted.

The order under s 17(1) is an order for the payment out of central funds of such amount as the court considers 'reasonably sufficient' to compensate the prosecutor for any 'expenses properly incurred' in the proceedings. Section 17(3) enables the court to award a lesser amount.

15.4 DEFENDANT TO PAY PROSECUTION COSTS

Section 18(1) of the Prosecution of Offences Act 1985 provides that where:

- a defendant is convicted of an offence by a magistrates' court;
- the Crown Court dismisses an appeal against such a conviction or against the sentence imposed by a magistrates' court; or
- a defendant is convicted of an offence by the Crown Court,

the court may make 'such order as to the costs to be paid by the accused to the prosecutor as it considers just and reasonable'.

Section 18(2) allows the Court of Appeal to make a similar order where it dismisses an appeal or an application for leave to appeal.

Under s 18(5), where a defendant under the age of 18 is convicted of an offence by a magistrates' court (this term includes a youth court), the amount of any costs ordered to be paid by the accused under s 18 must not exceed the amount of any fine imposed on him.

Paragraph VI.1.4 of the *Practice Direction* says that an order for costs under s 18 against a person convicted of an offence or an unsuccessful appellant 'should be made where the court is satisfied that the offender or appellant has the means and the ability to pay', thus establishing a clear presumption (subject to means) that an order will be made. Such an order will, however, only be made if the defendant has sufficient means to enable him to pay some or all of the prosecution costs. In *R v Newham Justices ex p Samuels* [1991] COD 412, for example, the Divisional Court quashed a costs order which had been made without proper account being taken of the defendant's means.

In *R v Northallerton Magistrates' Court ex p Dove* [2000] 1 Cr App R(S) 136, Lord Bingham CJ (at p 142) set out the following principles:

(1) An order to pay costs to the prosecutor should never exceed the sum which, having regard to the defendant's means and any other financial order imposed upon him, the defendant is able to pay and which it is reasonable to order the defendant to pay.

(2) Such an order should never exceed the sum which the prosecutor has actually and reasonably incurred.

(3) The purpose of such an order is to compensate the prosecutor and not to punish the defendant. Where the defendant has by his conduct put the prosecutor to avoidable expense he may, subject to his means, be ordered to pay some or all of that sum to the prosecutor. But he is not to be punished for exercising a constitutional right to defend himself . . .

(4) While there is no requirement that any sum ordered by justices to be paid to a prosecutor by way of costs should stand in any arithmetical relationship to any fine imposed, the costs ordered to be paid should not in the ordinary way be grossly disproportionate to the fine. Justices should ordinarily begin by deciding on the appropriate fine to reflect the criminality of the defendant's offence, always bearing in mind his means and his ability to pay, and then consider what, if any, costs he should be ordered to pay to the prosecutor. If, when the costs sought by the prosecutor are added to the proposed fine, the total exceeds the sum which in the light of the defendant's means and all other relevant circumstances the defendant can reasonably be ordered to

pay, it is preferable to achieve an acceptable total by reducing the sum of costs which the defendant is ordered to pay rather than by reducing the fine.

(5) It is for the defendant facing a financial penalty by way of fine or an order to pay costs to a prosecutor to disclose to magistrates such data relevant to his financial position as will enable justices to assess what he can reasonably afford to pay. In the absence of such disclosure justices may draw reasonable inferences as to the defendant's means from evidence they have heard and from all the circumstances of the case . . .

(6) It is incumbent on any court which proposes to make any financial order against a defendant, whether by way of fine or costs, to give the defendant a fair opportunity to adduce any relevant financial information and make any appropriate submissions. If the court has it in mind to make any unusual or unconventional order potentially adverse to a defendant, it should alert the defendant and his advisers to that possibility.

Where the court wishes to impose costs in addition to a fine, compensation and/or the victim surcharge (see Chapters 19 and 22) but the offender has insufficient resources to pay the total amount, the order of priority is:

i   compensation;
ii   victim surcharge;
iii   fine;
iv   costs.

Where costs are awarded against several defendants and one of them lacks the means to pay costs, the court should divide the total amount payable between the number of defendants (not just those who are able to pay) so that each defendant pays only his own share of the costs and does not subsidise the defendant who cannot pay (*R v Ronson* (1992) 13 Cr App R(S) 153). In *Ronson*, there were four defendants of whom one could not afford to pay costs. It was held by the Court of Appeal that the defendants who could afford to pay costs should each pay one-quarter of the total, not one-third. In *R v Harrison* (1993) 14 Cr App R(S) 419, however, the Court of Appeal upheld an order made against only one of the defendants: he was the principal offender (the other defendants had played relatively minor roles in the offences) and he had the means to pay the amount ordered.

In *R v Associated Octel Co Ltd* [1997] 1 Cr App R (S) 435, the Court of Appeal held that where a defendant is ordered to pay costs under s 18, the amount can include the cost of investigating the offence (as well as the costs of preparing and presenting the prosecution). In *R v Bow Street Stipendiary Magistrate ex p Multimedia Screen Ltd* (1998) *The Times*, 28 January, the defendant sought judicial review of a costs order requiring him to pay £15,000 although he had made only a tiny profit from the offence of which he was convicted. The Divisional Court held that the prosecution had had to do a lot of research and so the order was appropriate.

A judge in the Crown Court should not use a costs order as a means of penalising a defendant for electing Crown Court trial of an offence which could have been dealt with in the magistrates' court (*R v Hayden* [1975] 1 WLR 852). Nevertheless, it has been recognised by the Court of Appeal that trial on indictment is necessarily more expensive than summary trial and this will inevitably be reflected in the costs order (*R v Bushell* (1980) 2 Cr App R(S) 77; *R v Boyle* (1995) 16 Cr App R(S) 927).

A costs order is more likely to be made against a defendant where the prosecution case is manifestly strong and the defendant must have known all along that he was guilty (*R v Singh* (1982) 4 Cr App R(S) 38; *R v Mountain* (1979) 68 Cr App R 41).

If the prosecution in the Crown Court accept a plea of guilty to an offence to which the defendant would have pleaded guilty in the magistrates' court if the prosecution had not at that stage wanted to proceed with a more serious offence, the defendant will only be ordered to pay the costs appropriate to a guilty plea in the magistrates' court (*R v Hall* (1988) 10 Cr App R(S) 456; *R v Sentonco* [1996] 1 Cr App R(S) 174).

A costs order may (and, subject to means, usually will) be made where the defendant pleads guilty. However, the order will be for less than would be the case upon conviction following a not guilty plea, not least because less expense will probably have been incurred, especially if a plea of guilty is intimated at the earliest opportunity (see *R v Maher* [1983] QB 784).

15.5 PUBLICLY FUNDED DEFENDANTS

Section 21(4A)(a) of the Prosecution of Offences Act 1985 provides that where the defendant is a legally aided then, for the purposes of ss 16 and 17 of the Act, his costs shall be taken not to include the cost of representation funded for him by the Legal Services Commission (LSC). Thus, a defendant's costs order will not be made in respect of costs covered by a representation order, as these costs are being paid out of the public purse anyway.

15.6 WASTED COSTS ORDERS

There are two types of 'wasted costs' orders, one against a party to the proceedings and the other against the legal representative.

15.6.1 Costs in respect of 'unnecessary or improper acts or omissions'

Regulation 3 of the Costs in Criminal Cases (General) Regulations 1986 (SI 1986/1335) provides that where a magistrates' court, the Crown Court, or the Court of Appeal

> is satisfied that costs have been incurred in respect of the proceedings by one of the parties as a result of an unnecessary or improper act or omission by, or on behalf of, another party to the proceedings, the court may, after hearing the parties, order that all or part of the costs so incurred by that party shall be paid to him by the other party.

In *R (Commissioners of Customs & Excise) v Crown Court at Leicester* [2001] EWHC 33 (Admin); (2001) *The Times*, 23 February, Lord Woolf CJ ruled (at para 16) that:

> ... the proper exercise of the jurisdiction under reg 3 requires, first, the judge to consider whether there has been an unnecessary or improper act or omission. Secondly, the judge has to consider whether costs have been incurred as a result of that unnecessary or

improper act or omission by one of the parties. Thirdly, the court has to consider whether it will as a matter of discretion order all or part of the costs so incurred to be paid to the other party by the party in default. It is implicit in the last stage that, before an order is made, the judge is required to identify the costs so incurred (that is the costs incurred as a result of the unnecessary or improper act or omission). Having performed those exercises, finally, the judge will have to specify the amount of costs to be paid. There is therefore a formal structure to be followed before an order is made.

In *Crowch v DPP* [2008] EWHC 948 (Admin), it was held that a wasted costs order cannot be made to compensate an unrepresented defendant for his own loss of time in preparing his case and attending court (the reasoning in *R v Bedlington Magistrates' Court ex p Wilkinson* (1999) 164 JP 156, construing s 16 of the Act, was held to apply equally to s 19).

15.6.2 Wasted costs orders against representatives

Section 19A of the Prosecution of Offences Act 1985 empowers a magistrates' court, the Crown Court, or the Court of Appeal, to make a 'wasted costs order' against the representative acting for a party to criminal proceedings. Paragraph VIII.1.1 of the *Practice Direction* makes it clear that the power under s 19A of the Act to 'disallow or order the legal or other representative to meet the whole or any part of the wasted costs' is applicable against 'any person exercising a right of audience or a right to conduct litigation (in the sense of acting for a party to the proceedings)'. The paragraph says that 'wasted costs' are:

> costs incurred by a party (which includes an LSC-funded party) as a result of any improper, unreasonable or negligent act or omission on the part of any representative or his employee, or which, in the light of any such act or omission occurring after they were incurred, the court considers it unreasonable to expect that party to pay . . .

Paragraph VIII.1.2 stipulates that:

> the Judge . . . should keep the question of costs in the forefront of his mind at every stage of the case and ought to be prepared to take the initiative himself without any prompting from the parties.

Paragraph VIII.1.4 makes reference to the guidance given by the Court of Appeal in *Re a Barrister (Wasted Costs Order) (No 1 of 1991)* [1993] QB 293:

> (i)   There is a clear need for any judge or court intending to exercise the wasted costs jurisdiction to formulate carefully and concisely the complaint and grounds upon which such an order may be sought. These measures are draconian and . . . the grounds must be clear and particular . . .
>
> (iv) A three-stage test or approach is recommended when a wasted costs order is contemplated: (a) Has there been an improper, unreasonable or negligent act or omission? (b) As a result have any costs been incurred by a party? (c) If the answers to (a) and (b) are 'yes', should the court exercise its discretion to disallow or order the representative to

meet the whole or any part of the relevant costs, and if so what specific sum is involved? . . .

Paragraph VIII.1.5 goes on to refer to the further guidance in *Re P (a barrister)* [2001] EWCA Crim 1728, [2002] 1 Cr App R 207:

(i)   The primary object is not to punish but to compensate, albeit as the order is sought against a non-party, it can from that perspective be regarded as penal.

(ii) The jurisdiction is a summary jurisdiction to be exercised by the court which has 'tried the case in the course of which the misconduct was committed'.

(iii) Fairness is assured if the lawyer alleged to be at fault has sufficient notice of the complaint made against him and a proper opportunity to respond to it.

(iv) Because of the penal element a mere mistake is not sufficient to justify an order there must be a more serious error.

(v)   Although the trial judge can decline to consider an application in respect of costs, for example on the ground that he or she is personally embarrassed by an appearance of bias, it will only be in exceptional circumstances that it will be appropriate to pass the matter to another judge, and the fact that, in the proper exercise of his judicial function, a judge has expressed views in relation to the conduct of a lawyer against whom an order is sought, does not of itself normally constitute bias or the appearance of bias so as to necessitate a transfer.

(vi) If the allegation is one of serious misconduct or crime the standard of proof will be higher but otherwise it will be the normal civil standard of proof.

It was held in *Re a Barrister (Wasted Costs Order) (No 9 of 1999)* (2000) *The Times*, 18 April (following the civil case of *Ridehalgh v Horsefield* [1994] Ch 205) that such an order is only appropriate where the lawyer has made an error that no reasonably well-informed and competent lawyer could have made. A wasted costs order against a solicitor is not appropriate where the solicitor relied on the advice of experienced counsel; such a solicitor cannot be said to have acted in a way that no reasonably competent solicitor could have acted (*Re Hickman and Rose (Wasted Costs Order) (No 10 of 1999)* (2000) *The Times*, 3 May).

Paragraph VIII.1.7 of the *Practice Direction* notes that the court may postpone the making of a wasted costs order to the end of the case if it appears more appropriate to do so. This might be the case if, for example, there is a possibility of conflict between the legal representatives as to the apportionment of blame, or the legal representative concerned is unable to make full representations because of a possible conflict with their duty to the client.

15.7 APPEALS ON COSTS

Neither party has a right of appeal to the Crown Court in respect of a costs order made by a magistrates' court: the prosecution have no right of appeal to the Crown Court, and s 108(3)(b) of the Magistrates' Courts Act 1980 specifically precludes a defence appeal to the Crown Court against a costs order.

However, in *Hamilton-Johnson v RSPCA* (2000) 164 JP 345, it was held that, when the Crown Court dismisses an appeal against conviction or sentence, it has power to vary an order made by the magistrates' court requiring the defendant to pay the costs of the prosecutor in relation to the proceedings in the magistrates' court (either under s 18(1) of the Prosecution of Offences Act 1985 or s 48(2) of the Supreme Court Act 1981). The court added that, in the usual case where the issue is whether the magistrates' order in respect of costs should be modified after an unsuccessful appeal, the Crown Court should hesitate to do so. Usually, the magistrates will be far better placed than the Crown Court judge to decide how much of the costs of legal proceedings before them the prosecution should recover. Also, if the prosecutor wishes to seek an increase in the costs the defendant has to pay, he should give written notice to this effect to the defendant, so that the defendant is aware of the possible consequences of pursuing an appeal against conviction.

So far as costs orders made by the Crown Court are concerned, s 50 of the Criminal Appeal Act 1968 provides that, for the purpose of appealing against sentence, the word 'sentence' includes 'any order made by a court when dealing with an offender'. In *R v Heyden* [1975] 1 WLR 852, the Court of Appeal held that an order that the defendant pay part of the prosecution costs came within the definition of a 'sentence' under s 50, and so the defendant may appeal against the costs order under s 9 of the 1968 Act.

15.8 AWARD OF COSTS AGAINST THIRD PARTIES

Section 19B(3) of the Prosecution of Offences Act 1985 enables costs to be awarded against a third party where there has been 'serious misconduct' by the third party. Part IIB of the Costs in Criminal Cases (General) Regulations 1986 (SI 1986/1335) provides more detail on the power to make a third party costs order (which is available to magistrates' courts, the Crown Court and the Court of Appeal).

Regulation 3F(1) provides that if:

(a) there has been serious misconduct (whether or not constituting a contempt of court) by a third party; and
(b) the court considers it appropriate, having regard to that misconduct, to make a third party costs order against him

the court may order the third party to pay all or part of the costs incurred or wasted by any party as a result of the misconduct.

Under reg 3F(3),

The court shall make a third party costs order during the proceedings only if it decides that there are good reasons to do so, rather than making the order after the proceedings, and it shall notify the parties and the third party of those reasons and allow any of them to make representations.

Regulation 3F(4) provides that:

Before making a third party costs order the court shall allow the third party and any party to make representations and may hear evidence.

Under Regulation 3G, where a party applies to the court for a third party costs order or the court decides that it might make a third party costs order of its own initiative, the third party must receive written notice of the application; this written notice must include details of the alleged misconduct of the third party.

Regulation 3H makes provision for appeals against third party costs orders. In the case of an order made by a magistrates' court, appeal lies to the Crown Court; in the case of an order made at first instance by the Crown Court, appeal lies to the Court of Appeal. The appeal has to be instituted (by written notice to the court which made the order, stating the grounds of appeal) within 21 days of the order being made. This time limit may be extended where there is good reason (reg 3H(4)). Under reg 3H(6), the appeal court may affirm, vary or revoke the order as it thinks fit.

Chapter 16

Sentencing procedure and principles

In this chapter, we examine the procedure which takes place between conviction and the passing of sentence and at some of the factors which affect the sentence passed by the court.

16.1 THE PURPOSES OF SENTENCING

For the first time, the objectives of sentencing have been enshrined in statute: s 142(1) of the Criminal Justice Act 2003 describes the purposes of sentencing, to which 'any court dealing with an offender in respect of his offence must have regard' as:

(a) the punishment of offenders,
(b) the reduction of crime (including its reduction by deterrence),
(c) the reform and rehabilitation of offenders,
(d) the protection of the public, and
(e) the making of reparation by offenders to persons affected by their offences.

Section 142(2) states that sub-s (1) does not apply in a number of cases:

- offenders who are aged under 18 at the time of conviction (see below);
- where the sentence is fixed by law (that is, murder);
- where the sentence is a mandatory one (ss 110 or 111 of the Powers of Criminal Courts (Sentencing) Act 2000 (repeat offending – Class A drug trafficking or domestic burglary)), s 51A of the Firearms Act 1968 (possession of illegal weapons), s 29(4) or (6) of the Violent Crime Reduction Act 2006 (minimum sentences in certain cases of using someone to mind a weapon), or ss 225 to 228 of the 2003 Act (dangerous offenders); or
- in relation to the making of hospital orders under the Mental Health Act 1983.

Section 9 of the Criminal Justice and Immigration Act 2008 inserts a new section, s 142A, into the 2003 Act to set out the purposes of sentencing in the case of offenders under the age of 18 (subject to the same exceptions that apply to adult offenders, set out in s 142(2)). Section 142A (when it comes into force) will provide as follows:

(2) The court must have regard to—

  (a) the principal aim of the youth justice system (which is to prevent offending (or re-offending) by persons aged under 18: see section 37(1) of the Crime and Disorder Act 1998),

  (b) in accordance with section 44 of the Children and Young Persons Act 1933, the welfare of the offender, and

  (c) the purposes of sentencing mentioned in sub-s (3) (so far as it is not required to do so by paragraph (a)).

(3) Those purposes of sentencing are—

  (a) the punishment of offenders,
  (b) the reform and rehabilitation of offenders,
  (c) the protection of the public, and
  (d) the making of reparation by offenders to persons affected by their offences.

The statutory purposes for sentencing are very similar in the case of adults and young offenders. The key difference is that, in the case of offenders who are under the age of 18, the court is required to have regard to the 'welfare' of the offender, a feature that does not feature in the sentencing of adults.

The enumeration of a variety of sentencing aims is perhaps of comparatively little assistance to judges and magistrates when passing sentence, not least because the legislation makes no attempt to identify the relative importance of the goals that it sets out: which of the aims should be prioritised? If there is conflict between the effect of the aims in a particular case, which should prevail?

Moreover, some of the aims may themselves be regarded as questionable. Andrew von Hirsch and Julian V Roberts, in 'Legislating sentencing principles: the provisions of the Criminal Justice Act 2003 relating to sentencing purposes and the role of previous convictions' [2004] Crim LR 639 point out the lack of evidence to support the effectiveness of deterrence. They refer to three major analyses of statistical studies of general deterrence (A von Hirsch et al, *Criminal Deterrence and Sentence Severity* (1999); A Doob and C Webster, 'Sentence Severity and Crime: Accepting the Null Hypothesis' in M Tonry (ed), (2003) *Crime and Justice* Vol 30; D Nagin, 'Criminal Deterrence Research at the Beginning of the Twenty-first century' in M Tonry (ed), (1998) *Crime and Justice*), all of which conclude that variations in sentence severity have only marginally discernible impacts, if any, on the incidence of crime. Discernible effects on crime rates were significantly associated only with changes in the likelihood of being caught and convicted. Thus 'there is scant empirical basis for assigning deterrence an enhanced role in the determination of sentence'. The conclusion that the real deterrent is the risk of being caught (rather than the sentence that is likely to be imposed) is, of course, a very significant one. The likely sentence is not an effective deterrent if the would-be perpetrator does not think they are likely to get caught in the first place.

16.2 THE HALLIDAY REPORT AND THE PRINCIPLES OF SENTENCING

In July 2001, John Halliday's *Report of the Review of the Sentencing Framework for England and Wales: Making Punishments Work* (the Halliday report) was published. Halliday's brief was to examine whether the sentencing framework for England and Wales could be changed to improve results, especially by reducing crime, at justifiable expense. To this end, the Review looked at a broad range of matters, including:

- the types of sentence that should be available to the courts (with the aim of designing more flexible sentences that work effectively whether the offender is in prison or in the community);
- the ways in which sentences are enforced;
- the systems that govern release from prison;
- the role of the courts in decision-making while the sentence is in force;
- judicial discretion in sentencing and the guidelines governing its use.

The Halliday Report begins by identifying the perceived deficiencies in the sentencing framework in existence at the time. The shortcomings identified included the following:

- the system was too narrowly focused on 'just deserts' and did not encourage sentencers to consider crime reduction and reparation (paras 1.8–1.10);
- the system adopted a 'muddled approach' towards persistent offenders (paras 1.11–1.15) and failed to deal satisfactorily with the relevance of previous convictions (para 1.34);
- short-term prison sentences (that is, those under 12 months) were felt to be inadequate because they 'literally mean half what they say' and 'to all intents and purposes [the second half] is meaningless and ineffective' (paras 1.16–1.19 and 3.13);
- although longer prison terms were 'closer to meaning what they say', the last quartile of the sentence lacked 'any obvious purpose' and had a questionable impact on offenders' behaviour (paras 1.20–1.23);
- community sentences did not inspire confidence because their purpose and 'punitive weight' lack clarity and transparency (paras 1.24–1.27);
- the arrangements for sentence enforcement were 'inconsistent and unclear' and lack continuity (paras 1.28–1.30);
- the statutory sentencing framework was unnecessarily rigid; in particular, the division that the 'community sentence threshold' created between financial and non-financial community penalties was said to be irrational (paras 1.31–1.33);
- the 'just deserts' approach had 'failed to take root because deterrence was soon reinstated [by the courts] as an aim of sentencing' (paras 1.34–1.36);
- the sentencing framework was said to be inaccessible and lacking in transparency (paras 1.37–1.41) (put another way, the system was felt to be overly complicated); and
- significant disparities existed in sentencing patterns, particularly as between magistrates' courts (paras 1.42–1.44).

In considering the case for change, the Report highlighted two particular shortcomings in the existing system of sentencing:

- the unclear and unpredictable approach to persistent offenders; and
- the fact that prison sentences of less than 12 months had little meaningful impact on criminal behaviour.

The Report points out that the purpose of sentencing is not confined to punishment; rather, the aims of sentencing should include both crime reduction and reparation. The Report therefore concluded that the sentencing framework should do more to reduce re-offending through working with offenders under sentence, and that more should be done to build on the contributions that reparation and 'restorative justice' schemes can make.

The Report also concluded that the principles that severity of sentence should be 'proportionate' to the seriousness of criminal conduct, and that imprisonment should be reserved for cases in which no other sentence will do, both remain valid. Thus, the Report says that the principle of 'just deserts' should be retained (so that the sentence ought to be commensurate with the seriousness of the offence) but that in assessing the seriousness of the offence, greater account should be taken of any previous convictions recorded against the offender. Thus, persistent criminality would result in more severe sentencing than would otherwise have been the case (para 2.7). The reasoning goes along the lines that the existence of previous convictions is a strong indicator of the risk that the offender will re-offend and therefore, if a key aim of sentencing is crime reduction, previous convictions must be an essential part of the information that is taken into account in deciding how to deal with the offender.

The Report therefore called for a reform of the law relating to the relevance of previous convictions in the sentencing process. It argued in favour of a new presumption that the severity of the sentence should be increased by the existence of recent and relevant convictions showing a continuing course of criminal conduct. To prevent sentencing practice becoming unpredictable and to prevent disproportionately severe sentences being passed, the Report also recommended that guidelines be created to help sentencers match the severity of sentence with the seriousness of the offence and to show the ranges within which previous convictions might impact on sentence severity.

The Report also suggests that sentencing decisions should be structured so that sentencers would consider whether a non-custodial sentence would meet the needs of crime reduction, punishment and reparation rather than imposing a short custodial sentence.

The Report called for the general principles of sentencing to be set out in statute. It identified the key principles as being that:

- the severity of the sentence should reflect the seriousness of the offence(s), and the offender's criminal history;
- the seriousness of the offence should reflect the harm caused, threatened or risked, and the offender's degree of blame in committing the offence;
- the severity of the sentence should increase as a consequence of sufficiently recent and relevant previous convictions;

- a custodial sentence should be imposed only when no other sentence would be adequate to reflect the need for punishment;
- non-custodial sentences (including financial penalties) should be used, when they are adequately punitive, in ways designed to reduce the risk of reoffending and to protect the public.

A critique of the Halliday Report can be found in E Baker and C Clarkson, 'Making punishments work? An evaluation of the Halliday Report on sentencing in England and Wales' [2002] Crim LR 81. Their first criticism is that the Report's approach seems to give undue weight to previous convictions:

> . . . the Report proposes that, in future, sentencing should be based on 'limited retributivism'. This means that the limits of punishment (the punitive envelope) would be shaped by desert while the content of the envelope would be determined according to utilitarian objectives. In principle, the pursuit of such a strategy is intellectually defensible. However, there are good reasons for questioning the manner in which the Report's proposals would put it into effect.
>
> The first difficulty lies with the way in which, in seeking to ensure that persistence is punished more effectively, the Report's modified just deserts philosophy has the potential to attach a disproportionate weight to an offender's criminal history in defining the punitive envelope. Although it is asserted that 'sentence severity should be commensurate with the seriousness of criminal conduct', later in the same paragraph [para 2.7] the Report proceeds to propose 'a clear presumption that sentence severity should increase as a consequence of sufficiently recent and relevant previous convictions'. Allowing previous convictions to lead to an increase in sentence severity can be reconciled with desert-based sentencing through the principle of 'progressive loss of mitigation' [see M Wasik and A von Hirsch, 'Section 29 revisited: previous convictions in sentencing' [1994] Crim LR 409]. At the outset of a criminal career an offender can argue that a first offence was 'out of character' and that this should be reflected in mitigated punishment. However, with each successive conviction the argument loses plausibility as the offender's failure to respond to the State's censure and to learn lessons from previous convictions and punishments becomes increasingly patent. Consequently, the degree of mitigation of subsequent sentences progressively diminishes. Importantly, though, the reasoning that supports this principle suggests that there ought to be a ceiling on the extent to which previous convictions can justifiably increase sentencing severity.

This leads onto another key criticism made by Baker and Clarkson, that the Halliday approach, as well as being based on predictive sentencing (itself controversial), will lead to an unacceptable level of disparity in the sentencing process:

> Having established the parameters of the [punitive] envelope according to the Report's modified desert principles, the next stage in the proposed sentencing process is all-important. The actual sentence to be imposed will be determined by utilitarian considerations. Within the range the sentencer will select the punishment that would most closely serve the purpose of crime reduction (and reparation) in the individual case [see para 2.30]. This will involve an assessment of the likelihood of reoffending and the measures most likely to reduce that risk [see para 2.31]. It is, of course, appropriate that crime reduction should be a consideration in sentencing, particularly with regard to the type of sentence imposed, as

opposed to the severity of sentence. However, the difficulty with the Report's proposals is that they invite inconsistent results. Because the 'desert'-based sentencing range is defined according to previous convictions and aggravating and mitigating circumstances, two offenders who commit substantially similar crimes with similar records could end up receiving very different sentences on the grounds that their predicted risk and assessed suitability for programmes aimed at reducing reoffending were significantly divergent . . . The important point to note is this. While predictive sentencing is already practised in relation to 'dangerous' offenders (and would continue in the guise of the new 'special' and discretionary life sentences), the effect of the Report's proposals would be to extend a risk assessment approach to all cases. The only possible outcome is sentencing disparity, the avoidance of which is one of the Report's stated goals [in paras 1.42–1.44].

16.3 PROCEDURE FOLLOWING A PLEA OF GUILTY

Where the defendant pleads guilty, the first step is for the court to ascertain the facts of the case. The prosecution therefore summarise the facts of the offence so that the court is able to form a view of how serious the offence was. The prosecutor will also draw the court's attention to the defendant's antecedents (i.e. his personal circumstances), including any previous convictions. The prosecution adopt a neutral stance when it comes to sentencing. It is considered wrong for a prosecutor to try to persuade the court to impose a heavy sentence or to argue for a particular sentence. The prosecutor should therefore summarise the facts fairly.

All the allegations which are made by the prosecution should be based on admissible evidence and should be apparent from the written witness statements which have been disclosed to the defence. In *R v Hobstaff* (1993) 14 Cr App R(S) 605, for example, the Court of Appeal criticised prosecuting counsel for making allegations about the effect of the offence on the victim because he used emotive language and made allegations which were not contained in the witness statements which had been supplied to the defence.

16.3.1 The *Newton* hearing

In cases where the defendant pleads guilty but does so on a factual basis which is different from the prosecution version of what took place, the conflict must be resolved in accordance with the rules laid down by the Court of Appeal in *R v Newton* (1983) 77 Cr App R 13.

In *Newton*, the defendant was charged with buggery of his wife. He claimed that she consented to this (at that time not a defence, but relevant to sentence) but the prosecution alleged that she had not consented. The judge wrongly accepted the prosecution version without hearing evidence on the issue of consent. The Court of Appeal held that if, on a plea of guilty, there is a substantial conflict between the prosecution and the defence (that is, there is sharp divergence between the prosecution version of the facts and the defence version of the facts), the judge or magistrates must either:

- accept the defence version and sentence accordingly; or

- hear evidence on what happened and then make a finding of fact as to what happened, and sentence accordingly.

In other words, where there is a substantial divergence between the two stories (that is, a divergence which will have a material effect on the sentence imposed), the judge or magistrates can only reject the defence version after hearing evidence on what happened.

In the Crown Court, if the judge hears evidence, then he sits alone (that is, a jury is not empanelled for the *Newton* hearing). The parties are given the opportunity to call such evidence as they wish and to cross-examine witnesses called by the other side.

An example of a situation where the principles set out in *Newton* apply may be found in the facts of *R v McFarlane* (1995) 16 Cr App R(S) 315. The defendant was charged with assault occasioning actual bodily harm. The prosecution case was that he had jabbed his wife in the face with a fork and repeatedly punched her about the face. The defendant pleaded guilty but claimed that he had not jabbed her in the face with a fork and that he had slapped her (and had not punched her).

The judge cannot compel the prosecution or the defence to call evidence or cross-examine witnesses. However, if a party refuses to co-operate, the judge is entitled to draw the appropriate adverse inferences. In *R v Mirza* (1993) 14 Cr App R(S) 64, for example, the trial judge directed that a *Newton* hearing should take place. The defendant refused to give evidence, however. The judge accepted the prosecution version of events, and the defendant appealed on the ground that a *Newton* hearing had not taken place. Not surprisingly, the Court of Appeal dismissed the appeal.

If the defendant wants to plead guilty on the basis that he committed the offence but not in the way alleged by the prosecution (for example, he might admit the offence but deny the presence of aggravating features alleged by prosecution witnesses), the defence should warn the prosecution that this is so, so that the prosecution can ensure that the relevant witnesses attend court on the relevant date (see *R v Mohun* (1993) 14 Cr App R(S) 5). That way, a *Newton* hearing can take place without the need for an adjournment.

As we have seen, a *Newton* hearing in the Crown Court takes the form of the judge himself hearing evidence and deciding issues of the fact. However, in *R v Newton*, it was suggested that there may be cases where the difference between the versions put forward by the prosecution and the defence ought to be resolved by use of a jury. This can only be done where the difference in stories amounts to an allegation that the defendant committed an additional offence. For example, in a robbery case, if the offender admits threatening the use of violence but denies brandishing a weapon, this dispute should be resolved by adding a count alleging possession of an offensive weapon (s 1 of the Prevention of Crime Act 1953). Indeed, the *Newton* hearing should not be used in a way that effectively defeats the defendant's right to be tried by a jury for an allegation which amounts to an additional offence. For example, in *R v Eubank* [2001] EWCA Crim 891; [2002] 1 Cr App R(S) 4, the defendant was charged with robbery. The prosecution alleged that he was carrying a firearm in the course of the robbery. The defendant pleaded guilty to robbery but denied carrying a firearm. The judge held a *Newton* hearing and decided that the defendant was carrying a firearm. The Court of Appeal said that the judge had been wrong to resolve the question through a *Newton* hearing. The allegation that the defendant had a firearm amounted to a separate and additional offence, on which the defendant was entitled to the verdict of a jury, and so that allegation should have been reflected by a separate count on the indictment (per Lord Woolf CJ at para 9).

Another example of where it would have been appropriate to empanel a jury comes from the case of *R v Gandy* (1989) 11 Cr App R(S) 564. The defendant pleaded guilty to a charge of violent disorder. The prosecution alleged that, during the course of the incident, the defendant threw a glass, causing serious injury to the victim. The defendant denied that this was the case. The judge held a *Newton* hearing, but the Court of Appeal said (obiter) that it would have been more appropriate to add a count alleging wounding with intent (s 18 of the Offences Against the Person Act 1861) or a count alleging unlawful wounding (s 20 of the Offences Against the Person Act 1861); this would have enabled a jury to determine whether the defendant threw the glass.

In fact, cases where this method of resolving the difference between the two versions of events will be quite rare. A jury should not be empanelled needlessly. In *R v Dowdall* (1992) 13 Cr App R(S) 441, for example, the defendant was charged with stealing a pension book from a bag carried by a woman in a supermarket. He offered to plead guilty to theft on the basis that he had found the book and subsequently dishonestly appropriated it, but he denied that he had taken the book from the victim's bag (which would have been a more serious offence, given the closer proximity to the victim). The judge allowed the prosecution to amend the indictment so that it contained a count alleging theft by finding and an alternative count alleging theft from the woman's bag. The Court of Appeal said that the judge erred in allowing the prosecution to amend the indictment in this way. He should have accepted the defendant's plea of guilty and should then have held a *Newton* hearing (without empanelling a jury) to determine the circumstances in which the defendant stole the pension book. It is only appropriate to empanel a jury where the prosecution allege one offence and the defendant admits a different offence; in the present case, the only offence alleged was theft.

In the magistrates' court, where the dispute amounts to an allegation that the defendant committed an additional offence, the proper procedure is for this additional offence to be the subject of a new charge, which is then tried by the magistrates in the usual way.

It should be borne in mind that if there is a *Newton* hearing and the judge rules against the accused (in other words, having heard evidence, the judge accepts the prosecution version), the accused will lose some (though not all) of the credit that he would otherwise have received for pleading guilty (see, for example, *R v Webster* [2004] EWCA Crim 417; [2004] 2 Cr App R (S) 77). Indeed, para 4.3(iv) of the Sentencing Guidelines Council guidance on *Reduction in Sentence for a Guilty Plea* (see below) makes the point that:

> if after pleading guilty there is a *Newton* hearing and the offender's version of the circumstances of the offence is rejected, this should be taken into account in determining the level of reduction.

Sentencing procedure and principles

16.3.2 Exceptional cases where *Newton* does not have to be applied

A *Newton* hearing need not be held where the defendant's story is manifestly false or implausible. See, for example, *R v Hawkins* (1985) 7 Cr App R(S) 351, where the Court of Appeal said that the story told by the defendant was 'so manifestly false that the judge was entitled to reject it' without further ado (per Lord Lane at p 353). Likewise, in *R v Walton* (1987) 9 Cr App R(S) 107 at 109, Kennedy J, giving the judgment of the court said that 'the words used by this Court in the case of *Newton* do not mean that in every case a judge must hear evidence before he rejects a version of the facts put forward in mitigation, but which for good reason he regards as untenable'. In such cases, the court can accept the prosecution versions of events without having first heard evidence to support that version.

16.3.3 Standard of proof in a *Newton* hearing

In a *Newton* hearing, the judge must approach the questions of fact which he has to decide in accordance with the criminal burden and standard of proof. Therefore, the judge, in making findings of fact on a *Newton* hearing, must be satisfied so that he is sure that the prosecution version is correct before sentencing on that basis (*R v Kerrigan* (1993) 14 Cr App R(S) 179).

In *R v Gandy* (1989) 11 Cr App R(S) 564 (mentioned above), it was stressed by the Court of Appeal that where the judge holds a *Newton* hearing, the rules of evidence must be followed strictly and the judge must direct himself in the same terms as he would direct a jury. In that case, for example, the Court of Appeal rejected the finding of fact made by the judge that it was the defendant that had caused injury to the victim because the judge had not taken proper account of the weaknesses in the identification evidence against the accused (cf *R v Turnbull* [1977] QB 224).

16.3.4 Appeals

In *R v Ahmed* (1985) 80 Cr App R 295 (followed in *R v Wood* (1992) 13 Cr App R (S) 207), the Court of Appeal said that it would not interfere with the judge's findings of fact in a *Newton* hearing unless no reasonable jury could have reached the conclusion reached by the judge (per Parker LJ at p 297).

In appropriate cases, the Court of Appeal may conduct a *Newton* hearing itself (see *R v Guppy* [1995] 16 Cr App R(S) 25). However, if the judge wrongly fails to conduct a *Newton* hearing, the Court of Appeal will usually allow an appeal against sentence and will impose the sentence which would be appropriate on the basis that the defendant's version of events is the correct one (*R v Mohun* (1993) 14 Cr App R(S) 5), effectively giving the benefit of the doubt to the defendant.

16.3.5 Responsibility of the sentencer and of counsel

In *Attorney General's Reference (Nos 3 and 4 of 1996)* [1997] 1 Cr App R(S) 29, the defendants pleaded guilty to robbery but, when speaking to the probation officer, denied some of the allegations made by the victim. These denials were set out in the pre-sentence report. Counsel for the defendants, when addressing the court in mitigation, referred to the pre-sentence report but did not make specific reference to the fact that the defendants denied some of the allegations made by the prosecution. The Court of Appeal (following *R v Gardener* (1994) 15 Cr App R(S) 667) said that it was the duty of defence counsel to make the dispute known to the prosecution, and that the court should be informed of the dispute at the outset of the sentencing hearing (so that the judge can decide whether a *Newton* hearing is necessary). The Court of Appeal went on to consider the dispute (since it had not been considered in the Crown Court) but upheld the sentence on the basis that a *Newton* hearing need not be held if the defendant's story is manifestly false or implausible. In *R v Oakley* [1998] 1 Cr App R(S) 100, it was said that the court itself must also be alert to differences between the prosecution case and the defence case. In that case, sentence was passed on a factual basis which was inconsistent with the defence version of what had happened as set out in the pre-sentence report. Defence counsel did not invite the judge to hold a *Newton* hearing. The Court of Appeal held that the judge should have been alert to the conflict and should have resolved the conflict with the *Newton* hearing whether or not the defence or prosecution asked for such a hearing.

In *R v Tolera* [1999] 1 Cr App R 29, the Court of Appeal re-emphasised that it is not enough for the defence version of events to be set out in the pre-sentence report. It was said that while the judge will normally read that part of the report, he will not ordinarily pay attention, for the purposes of sentence, to any account of the crime given by the offender to the probation officer where it conflicts with the prosecution case. If the defendant wants to rely on such an account, the defence must expressly draw those paragraphs to the court's attention and ask that sentence be passed on that basis, thus triggering the need for a *Newton* hearing in an appropriate case (per Lord Bingham at p 32).

Tolera also gives guidance on what should be done where the defendant puts forward a version of events which is inconsistent with the prosecution case but which the prosecutor is unable to challenge by adducing evidence to contradict what the defendant is saying. This might be the case if, for example, the defendant alleges the existence of mitigating circumstances relating to the commission of the offence. If the court is unwilling to accept the defence version, the court should make its views known so that a *Newton* hearing can take place before sentence is passed. That will normally involve the defendant giving evidence; the prosecutor should ask appropriate questions to test the defendant's evidence rather than simply leaving it to the court to question the defendant.

16.3.6 Summary

In *R v Underwood* [2004] EWCA Crim 2256; [2005] 1 Cr App R 13, Judge LJ provided a helpful and comprehensive summary of the principles laid down in *Newton* and in subsequent case law. It is worth setting out in full.

> 1. In these appeals ... we are concerned with what can compendiously be described as *Newton* hearings. Although the principles are clear, they are not always fully understood or applied. These appeals have therefore been listed together to enable this Court to repeat and emphasise general guidance about the procedure to be adopted where the defendant pleads guilty on a factual basis different to that which appears from the Crown's case, or,

indeed, a study of the papers. In short, we are concerned with the process which will achieve the sentence appropriate to reflect the justice of the case where there is a plea of guilty, but some important fact or facts relating to the offence which the defendant is admitting, of potential significance to the sentencing decision, are in dispute.

2. The essential principle is that the sentencing judge must do justice. So far as possible the offender should be sentenced on the basis which accurately reflects the facts of the individual case. In *R v Newton* (1983) 77 Cr App R 13 itself, Newton was charged with and pleaded guilty to very serious sexual offences involving his wife. As the law then stood, her consent provided no defence. It hardly needs saying that for sentencing purposes the differ-ence between forced and consensual sexual activity was huge. It was therefore a classic example of an imperative need to establish the facts. To proceed to sentence without doing so, would have been productive of injustice. Lord Lane CJ identified one method of approach where there was a sharp divergence between the differing accounts of the offence:

> 'the second method which could be adopted by the judge in these circumstances is himself to hear the evidence on one side and another, and come to his own conclusion, acting so to speak as his own jury on the issue which is the root of the problem.'

This is the *Newton* hearing . . .

3. The starting point has to be the defendant's instructions. His advocate will appreciate whether any significant facts about the prosecution evidence are disputed and the factual basis on which the defendant intends to plead guilty. If the resolution of the facts in dispute may matter to the sentencing decision, the responsibility for taking any initiative and alerting the prosecutor to the areas of dispute rest with the defence. The Crown should not be taken by surprise, and if it is suddenly faced with a proposed basis of plea of guilty where important facts are disputed, it should, if necessary, take time for proper reflection and consultation to consider its position and the interests of justice. In any event, whatever view may be formed by the Crown on any proposed basis of plea, it is deemed to be conditional on the judge's acceptance of it.

4. The Crown may accept and agree the defendant's account of the disputed facts. If so, the agreement should be reduced into writing and signed by both advocates. It should then be made available to the judge before the start of the Crown's opening, and, if possible, before he is invited to approve the acceptance of any plea or pleas. If, however, pleas have already been accepted and approved, then it should be available before the sentencing hearing begins. If the agreed basis of plea is not signed by the advocates for both sides, the judge is entitled to ignore it; similarly, if the document is not legible. The Crown may reject the defendant's version. If so, the areas of dispute should be identified in writing and the document should focus the court's attention on the precise fact or facts which are in dispute.

5. The third, and most difficult, situation arises when the Crown may lack the evidence positively to dispute the defendant's account. In many cases an issue raised by the defence is outside the knowledge of the prosecution. The prosecution's position may well be that they had no evidence to contradict the defence assertions. That does not mean that the truth of matters outside their own knowledge should be agreed. In these circumstances, particularly if the facts relied on by defendant arise from his personal knowledge and depend on his own account of the facts, the Crown should not normally agree the defendant's account unless

it is supported by other material. There is, therefore, an important distinction between assertions about the facts which the Crown is prepared to agree, and its possible agreement to facts about which, in truth, the prosecution is ignorant. Neither the prosecution nor the judge is bound to agree facts merely because, in the word currently in vogue, the prosecution cannot 'gainsay' the defendant's account. Again, the court should be notified at the outset in writing of the points in issue and the Crown's responses. We need not address those cases where the Crown occupies a position which straddles two, or even all three, of these alternatives.

6. After submissions from the advocates the judge should decide how to proceed. If not already decided, he will address the question whether he should approve the Crown's acceptance of pleas. Then he will address the proposed basis of plea. We emphasise that whether or not the basis of plea is 'agreed', the judge is not bound by any such agreement and is entitled of his own motion to insist that any evidence relevant to the facts in dispute should be called before him. No doubt, before doing so, he will examine any agreement reached by the advocates, paying appropriate regard to it, and any reasons which the Crown, in particular, may advance to justify him proceeding immediately to sentence. At the risk of stating the obvious, the judge is responsible for the sentencing decision and he may therefore order a *Newton* hearing and to ascertain the truth about disputed facts.

7. The prosecuting advocate should assist him by calling any appropriate evidence and testing the evidence advanced by the defence. The defence advocate should similarly call any relevant evidence and, in particular, where the issue arises from facts which are within the exclusive knowledge of the defendant and the defendant is willing to give evidence in support of his case, be prepared to call him. If he is not, and subject to any explanation which may be proffered, the judge may draw such inferences he thinks fit from that fact. An adjournment for these purposes is often unnecessary. If the plea is tendered late when the case is due to be tried the relevant witnesses for the Crown are likely to be available. The *Newton* hearing should proceed immediately. In every case, or virtually so, the defendant will be present. It may be sufficient for the judge's purpose to hear the defendant. If so, again, unless it is impracticable for some exceptional reason, the hearing should proceed immediately.

8. The judge must then make up his mind about the facts in dispute. He may, of course, reject evidence called by the prosecution. It is sometimes overlooked that he may equally reject assertions advanced by the defendant, or his witnesses, even if the Crown does not offer positive contradictory evidence.

9. The judge must, of course, direct himself in accordance with ordinary principles, such as, for example, the burden and standard of proof. In short, his self-directions should reflect the relevant directions he would have given to the jury. Having reached his conclusions, he should explain them in a judgment.

10. Again, by way of reminder, we must explain some of the limitations on the *Newton* hearing procedure.

(a)   There will be occasions when the *Newton* hearing will be inappropriate. Some issues require a verdict from the jury. To take an obvious example, a dispute whether the necessary intent under section 18 of the Offences against the Person Act 1861 has been proved should be decided by the jury. Where the factual issue is not encapsulated in a distinct count in the indictment when it should be, then, again, the indictment should be amended and the issue resolved by the jury. We have in mind, again for example, cases where there is a dispute whether the defendant was carrying a firearm to commit a robbery. In essence, if the defendant is denying that a specific criminal offence has been committed, the tribunal for deciding whether the offence has been proved is the jury.

(b) At the end of the *Newton* hearing the judge cannot make findings of fact and sentence on a basis which is inconsistent with the pleas to counts which have already been accepted by the Crown and approved by the court. Particular care is needed in relation to a multi-count indictment involving one defendant, or an indictment involving a number of defendants, and to circumstances in which the Crown accepts, and the court approves, a guilty plea to a reduced charge.

(c) Where there are a number of defendants to a joint enterprise, the judge, while reflecting on the individual basis of pleas, should bear in mind the relative seriousness of the joint enterprise on which the defendants were involved. In short, the context is always relevant. He should also take care not to regard a written basis of plea offered by one defendant, without more, as evidence justifying an adverse conclusion against another defendant.

(d) Generally speaking, matters of mitigation are not normally dealt with by way of a *Newton* hearing. It is, of course, always open to the court to allow a defendant to give evidence of matters of mitigation which are within his own knowledge. From time to time, for example, defendants involved in drug cases will assert that they were acting under some form of duress, not amounting in law to a defence. If there is nothing to support such a contention, the judge is entitled to invite the advocate for the defendant to call his client rather than depend on the unsupported assertions of the advocate.

(e) Where the impact of the dispute on the eventual sentencing decision is minimal, the *Newton* hearing is unnecessary. The judge is rarely likely to be concerned with minute differences about events on the periphery.

(f) The judge is entitled to decline to hear evidence about disputed facts if the case advanced on the defendant's behalf is, for good reason, to be regarded as absurd or obviously untenable. If so, however, he should explain why he has reached this conclusion.

11. The final matter for guidance is whether the defendant should lose the mitigation available to him for his guilty plea if, having contested facts alleged by the prosecution, the issues are resolved against him. The principles are clear. If the issues at the *Newton* hearing are wholly resolved in the defendant's favour, the credit due to him should not be reduced. If for example, however, the defendant is disbelieved, or obliges the prosecution to call evidence from the victim, who is then subjected to a cross-examination, which, because it is entirely unfounded, causes unnecessary and inappropriate distress, or if the defendant conveys to the judge that he has no insight into the consequences of his offence and no genuine remorse for it, these are all matters which may lead the judge to reduce the discount which the defendant would otherwise have received for his guilty plea, particularly if that plea is tendered at a very late stage. Accordingly, there may even be exceptional cases in which the normal entitlement to a credit for a plea of guilty is wholly dissipated by the *Newton* hearing. In such cases, again, the judge should explain his reasons.

16.4 PROCEDURE FOLLOWING CONVICTION AFTER A NOT GUILTY PLEA

Where the defendant was convicted following a plea of not guilty, the facts of the offence will have emerged during the evidence. However, the prosecution may still have to summarise the facts of the case where there has been an adjournment after conviction, as will usually be the case where a pre-sentence report has to be prepared. In the Crown Court, it is usually the judge who presided over the trial who passes sentence and it is likely that he will use his note of the evidence to refresh his memory, and so will not need the prosecution to remind him of the facts. In magistrates' courts, however, it is very common for a bench other than the bench which convicted the defendant to pass sentence, and so the bench which passes sentence will need a summary of the facts from the prosecution.

16.5 PROCEDURE AFTER THE PROSECUTION SUMMARY OF FACTS (IF GIVEN)

After the prosecution have summarised the facts of the case (if the defendant pleaded guilty), or after the defendant has been found guilty, the prosecution supply the court with details of the defendant's character and antecedents. In *R v Egan* [2004] EWCA Crim 630; (2004) *The Times*, 9 March, the Court of Appeal pointed out that sentencers should have available to them, as part of a defendant's antecedent history, details of any previous sentences imposed, the dates of release from such sentences and the relevant sentence expiry dates. The way in which the court is made aware of the defendant's previous convictions is dealt with in detail in para III.27 of the *Consolidated Practice Direction*.

Under para III.27.3, the antecedents form should contain:

a   personal details (domestic circumstances, financial commitments, employment, etc; this is based on information provided by the defendant to the police following arrest and no action will be taken by the police to verify this information);

b   a list of previous convictions (showing, for each conviction, the date of the conviction, the court, the offence, and the sentence imposed);

c   details of any cautions recorded against the offender.

In cases being dealt with by the Crown Court, the antecedents form should also:

a   show the circumstances of the last three similar convictions and/or of convictions likely to be of interest to the court; and

b   set out the circumstances of the offence leading to any community order which is still in force (in case the Crown Court decides to revoke the community order and re-sentence for the earlier offence).

The information is conveyed to the court by the prosecutor, who simply reads details from the standard forms.

Where the defendant disputes the accuracy of the information provided by the police, this matter should (where possible) be raised at least seven days before the date of the hearing.

If the offender disputes the accuracy of the list of previous convictions, the convictions which he disputes have to be proved. Section 73 of the Police and Criminal Evidence Act 1984 enables proof of previous convictions to be by way of a certificate of conviction from the convicting court. Alternatively, someone (for example, a police officer) may give evidence that he was present in court when the defendant was convicted of the offence on the earlier occasion and that that person is the defendant in the present proceedings.

If the present conviction means that the offender is in breach of a previous order (for example, a suspended sentence or conditional discharge), it is necessary to ask the defendant whether he admits that he is in breach of the earlier order. If the defendant denies the breach, the breach has to be proved by means of admissible evidence that the earlier order was made.

16.6 PRE-SENTENCE REPORTS ON THE OFFENDER

As well as considering the prosecution summary of the facts (if given) and the defendant's antecedents, the court will often consider a pre-sentence report. In the case of offenders who have attained the age of 18, pre-sentence reports are compiled by probation officers. For offenders who are under 13, reports are prepared by local authority social workers. In the case of young offenders who have attained the age of 13, reports are usually prepared by a social worker, but the report would be prepared by a probation officer if, for example, the probation service was already having dealings with a member of the offender's family.

The court is not bound to accept the conclusions in a pre-sentence report. So, for example, if the report says that the offender is suitable for a community order, the court does not have to accept that view.

16.6.1 Circumstances where a pre-sentence report is required

Section 156 of the Criminal Justice Act 2003 sets out when a pre-sentence report has to be obtained. It provides that before forming an opinion about the appropriateness of a community sentence or the appropriateness of a custodial sentence, the court 'must take into account all such information as is available to it about the circumstances of the offence . . . [and any] offences associated with it, including any aggravating or mitigating factors'; also, in forming an opinion about the suitability of imposition of specific requirements as part of a community sentence, the court may take into account any information about the offender which is before it.

In particular, s 156(3) provides that a court must obtain and consider a pre-sentence report before:

a   in the case of a custodial sentence, deciding that:

- the case is so serious that neither a fine nor a community sentence could be justified (s 152(2)),
- the term imposed is commensurate with the seriousness of the offence (s 153(2)),
- life imprisonment is necessary for the protection of the public because of the risk of serious harm posed by the offender (s 225(1)(b); s 226(1)(b) for young offenders),
- an extended sentence is necessary to protect the public where the offender is convicted of certain violent or sexual offences and poses a significant risk to the public (s 227(1)(b); s 228(1)(b)(i) for young offenders);

b   in the case of a community sentence, deciding that:

- the offence is sufficiently serious to warrant a community sentence (s 148(1)),
- the restrictions on the offender's liberty are commensurate with the seriousness of the offence (s 148(2)(b); s 148(3)(b) for young offenders), or
- forming any opinion as to the suitability for the offender of the particular requirement(s) to be imposed by the community order.

Under s 156(4), the court need not obtain and consider a pre-sentence report if, in the circumstances of the case, the court is of the opinion that it is unnecessary to obtain one. However, where the offender is under the age of 18, the court cannot dispense with a pre-sentence report unless (a) there exists a previous pre-sentence report obtained in respect of the offender, and (b) the court has had regard to the information contained in that report or, if there is more than one such report, the most recent report (s 156(5)).

Section 156(6) provides that no custodial sentence or community sentence is invalidated by the failure of a court to obtain and consider a pre-sentence report as required by s 156. However, if the sentencing court did not obtain a pre-sentencing report in a case where one was required under s 156, the court hearing the appeal should obtain a pre-sentence report unless that court is of the opinion (a) that the sentencing court was justified in forming an opinion that it was unnecessary to obtain a pre-sentence report, or (b) that although the court below was not justified in forming that opinion, in the circumstances of the case at the time it is before the appeal court, it is unnecessary to obtain a pre-sentence report (s 156(7)). If the offender is under 18, the appeal court can only dispense with a pre-sentence report if (a) there exists a previous pre-sentence report obtained in respect of the offender, and (b) the court has had regard to the information contained in that report, or, if there is more than one such report, the most recent report (s 156(8)).

In summary, then, in relation to an offender aged 18 or over, unless the court considers a report to be unnecessary, it is required to request a pre-sentence report before deciding:

- that the community or custody threshold has been crossed;
- what is the shortest term of a custodial sentence that is commensurate with the seriousness of the offence;

- whether the restrictions on liberty in a community order are commensurate with the seriousness of the offence; and
- whether the requirements of a community order are suitable for the offender.

It follows that a pre-sentence report should not normally be requested where the court considers that it is appropriate to impose a fine.

A report may be oral or written. Written reports may be either:

a fast delivery reports (FDR), which are completed without a full Offender Assessment System (OASys) assessment. Where community orders are being considered, this form of report is generally appropriate for low or medium seriousness cases. The report should normally be available within 24 hours;

b standard delivery reports (SDR), which are based on a full OASys assessment. Such reports are generally appropriate where a custodial sentence is being considered, although in some straightforward cases a fast delivery PSR may be sufficient. Where community orders are being considered, this form of report is generally appropriate for high seriousness cases. Such reports should normally be available within 15 working days (10 working days if the offender has been remanded in custody).

All pre-sentence reports should contain:

- basic facts about the offender and the sources used to prepare the report;
- an offence analysis;
- an assessment of the offender;
- an assessment of the risk of harm to the public and the likelihood of reoffending;
- a sentencing proposal.

Section 12 of the Criminal Justice and Immigration Act 2008 inserts new sub-sections into s 158 of the Criminal Justice Act 2003 to provide that the court may accept a pre-sentence report given orally in open court (s 158(1A)) unless the report relates to an offender aged under 18 and has to be considered (under s 156(3)(a)) before the passing of a custodial sentence, in which case the report must be in writing (s 158(1B)).

16.6.2 Disclosure of the pre-sentence report

Disclosure of the pre-sentence report is governed by s 159 of the Criminal Justice Act 2003.

The defence advocate invariably has sight of a copy of the pre-sentence report if one has been prepared. It is good practice to ask the defendant if he has seen a copy of the report. If he has not, then he should be asked to read through it and check its accuracy (or the advocate should summarise its contents). The report is normally based on a single interview between the defendant and a probation officer and there is the potential for errors to creep in. In any event, s 159(2) requires the pre-sentence report to be disclosed to the offender and to his legal representative.

Section 159(2)(c) also requires the report to be disclosed to the prosecutor. This may seem unnecessary, since the prosecutor generally has little further part to play once a conviction has been recorded (apart from ensuring that the court does not exceed its sentencing powers and drawing the courts attention to any relevant sentencing guidelines). Section 159(5) stipulates that the prosecutor can only use information gleaned from the report for the purpose of deciding whether to make representations to the court about the content of the report and for making any such representations. The disclosure of the report to the prosecutor under this provision means that prosecutors have a chance to check that any factual information contained in the report agrees with information contained in the prosecution file. Any representations made by the prosecutor are likely to be confined to drawing the attention of the court to any factual inaccuracies in the report.

16.6.3 Juveniles

Under s 159(2)(b) of the 2003 Act, if the offender is under 18, a copy of the report must also be given to a parent or guardian (if present in court); this is subject to the proviso in s 159(3) that:

> If the offender is aged under 18 and it appears to the court that the disclosure to the offender or to any parent or guardian of his of any information contained in the report would be likely to create a risk of significant harm to the offender, a complete copy of the report need not be given to the offender or, as the case may be, to that parent or guardian.

Where the offender is under 18 and is in local authority care, a copy of the report goes to the local authority (s 159(6)).

Before passing sentence on a juvenile, a youth court must give the juvenile and a parent or guardian a chance to make representations about the appropriate sentence. The court must also consider all available information about the offender's general conduct, home environment, school record and medical history. In addition to the report from a local authority social worker (or a probation officer), there will also be a report from the juvenile's school (and, if appropriate, their GP) (see Pt 44 of the Criminal Procedure Rules, s 9 of the Children and Young Persons Act 1969, and s 160 of the Criminal Justice Act 2003).

16.6.4 Adjournments prior to sentence

Section 10(3) of the Magistrates' Courts Act 1980 empowers a magistrates' court to adjourn before passing sentence in order to enable inquiries to be made as to the most suitable method of dealing with the offender. Under s 10(3), adjournments between conviction and sentence should be for no more than four weeks at a time if the offender is on bail (note that the presumption in favour of bail created by s 4 of the Bail Act 1976 applies to such an offender) and for no more than three weeks at a time if the offender is in custody. The Crown Court has inherent jurisdiction to adjourn and there is no statutory limit on the length of the adjournment; however, the Crown Court will usually adopt the same periods as magistrates' courts.

16.6.5 Other reports

Under s 157 of the 2003 Act, where the offender is (or appears to be) mentally disordered, the court must obtain and consider a medical report before passing a custodial sentence unless (under sub-s (2)) the court is of the opinion that it is unnecessary to obtain a medical report.

Section 161 of the 2003 Act provides for pre-sentence drug testing where the offender is aged 14 or over and the court is considering passing a community sentence or a suspended sentence. Failure, without reasonable excuse, to comply with the order is punishable with a fine of up to £2,500.

16.6.6 Keeping sentencing options open

When the court adjourns the case so that a report can be prepared, great care must be exercised when the court explains to the defendant what is happening. In *R v Gillam* (1980) 2 Cr App R(S) 267, the judge adjourned the case so that a report could be prepared to assess whether the defendant was suitable for what was then known as community service (unpaid work under a community order). The circumstances were such that the defendant was led to believe that if the report was favourable, he would receive community service rather than a custodial sentence. In the event, the report was favourable but a custodial sentence was passed nonetheless. The Court of Appeal said that the judge should have imposed a non-custodial sentence. Watkins LJ (at p 269) said that when a judge in such circumstances purposely postpones sentence so that an alternative to prison can be examined and that alternative is found to be a satisfactory one in all respects, the court ought to adopt the alternative; otherwise, a feeling of injustice is aroused. Similarly, in *R v Howard* (1989) 11 Cr App R(S) 583, the court adjourned for a pre-sentence report and the defendant was told that the court was minded to deal with the case by means of a community order. A custodial sentence was subsequently imposed and this sentence was quashed by the Court of Appeal.

Lord Bingham CJ in *R v Nottingham Magistrates' Court* [2001] Cr App R (S) 167 (at p 169) expressed the position thus:

> If a court at a preliminary stage of the sentencing process gives to a defendant any indication as to the sentence which will or will not be thereafter passed upon him, in terms sufficiently unqualified to found a legitimate expectation in the mind of the defendant that any court which later passes sentence upon him will act in accordance with the indication given, and if on a later occasion a court, without reasons which justify departure from the earlier indication, and whether or not it is aware of that indication, passes a sentence inconsistent with, and more severe than, the sentence indicated, the court will ordinarily feel obliged, however reluctantly, to adjust the sentence passed so as to bring it into line with that indicated.

This principle applies only if there was something 'in the nature of a promise, express or implied, that, if a particular proposal is recommended, it will be adopted' (*R v Moss* (1983) 5 Cr App R(S) 209, per Croom-Johnson LJ at p 213). Thus, if the court makes it clear that it is not committing itself to a non-custodial sentence even if the pre-sentence report recommends a non-custodial sentence, no legitimate sense of injustice is created if a custodial sentence is passed, even if the court rejects a recommendation for a non-custodial sentence contained in the report (*R v Horton* (1985) 7 Cr App R(S) 299). Thus, in *R v Renan* (1994) 15 Cr App R(S) 722, the judge granted the defendant bail pending the preparation of a pre-sentence report, but said nothing about sentencing options. It was held that this did not, in the circumstances of the particular case, create an expectation that a custodial sentence would not be passed. A custodial sentence was, accordingly, upheld.

In *R v Jones* [2003] EWCA Crim 1631; [2004] Cr App R(S) 23, the judge adjourned sentence with a view to hearing an application for a confiscation order, but made no mention of the possibility of making a compensation order; at the adjourned hearing, the judge imposed a compensation order. It was held (quashing the compensation order) that the sentencer must spell out clearly and precisely the purpose(s) of any postponement of the sentence (or part of it) at the time of postponement. It is not permissible to adjourn for a specified purpose but subsequently to pass a sentence which was not expressed to be in contemplation at the time when the hearing was adjourned.

16.7 THE PLEA IN MITIGATION

A plea in mitigation usually comprises a speech by the advocate appearing for the defence. If the defendant is unrepresented, he will be asked if there is anything he wishes to say before sentence is passed.

Occasionally, witnesses will be called to show the previous good character of the offender or to explain why he acted out of character by committing an offence.

The plea in mitigation by the defence will usually address the seriousness of the offence, together with mitigating factors relating to the offender.

The decision on the sentence to be passed will take account of guidance from case law and from the Sentencing Guidelines Council, and the defence advocate will have to make use of those resources when preparing the plea in mitigation.

16.8 SENTENCING GUIDELINES

There are currently three sources of guidelines: Magistrates' Court Sentencing Guidelines, formerly issued by the Magistrates' Association but now issued by the Sentencing Guidelines Council (for offences triable in the magistrates' court), guideline judgments of the Court of Appeal (for some offences triable in the Crown Court), and 'definitive' guidelines (both on general principles relating to sentencing and for specific offences) issued by the Sentencing Guidelines Council. These sources are very useful for identifying aggravating and mitigating factors associated with particular offences.

Prior to the passing of the Criminal Justice Act 2003, the Court of Appeal was assisted in its task of handing down sentencing guidelines for particular offences by the Sentencing Advisory Panel. The Panel would identify those offences where it felt that guidelines (or revised guidelines) were required, and would suggest specific guidelines to the Court of Appeal. It was a matter for the Court of Appeal whether it acceded to the suggestion that it lay down guidelines for a particular offence, and it was open to the Court of Appeal to accept or reject (wholly or in part) the suggestions made by the Panel.

Dealing with the Sentencing Advisory Panel, the *Review of the Criminal Courts of England and Wales* by Lord Justice Auld recommended as follows:

> 324 The law should be amended to widen the remit of the Sentencing Advisory Panel to include general principles of sentencing, in particular as to the courts' use of the various sentencing options available to them regardless of the category of offence.
>
> 325 The law should be amended, to enable the Court of Appeal to work more closely with and respond more speedily to the Panel's advice, by empowering it to issue guidelines without having to tie them to a specific appeal before it.

To ensure consistency in applying these principles, the Halliday Report called for new guidelines to be provided for sentencers. The Report said that these guidelines should apply to all criminal courts (rather than having separate guidelines for magistrates' courts and the Crown Court). The guidelines should:

- specify graded levels of seriousness of offence;
- provide 'entry points' of sentence severity in relation to each level of seriousness;
- set out how severity of sentence should increase in relation to numbers and types of previous convictions;
- explain other possible grounds for mitigation and aggravation.

The Report argued that responsibility for producing, monitoring, revising and accounting for the guidelines should be placed on an independent judicial body. The Report sets out various options for the composition of this body:

- the Court of Appeal (Criminal Division) sitting in a new capacity, with the Sentencing Advisory Panel in an expanded remit providing a resource to the court;
- a new judicial body set up for the purpose, which would be independent of the Court of Appeal, but under strong judicial leadership complemented by professionals and academics. The Sentencing Advisory Panel could be subsumed within this body; or
- an independent body with a more mixed membership, not necessarily judicially dominated, and into which the Sentencing Advisory Panel would be subsumed.

16.8.1 The Sentencing Guidelines Council

Rather than widening the remit of the Sentencing Advisory Panel, the Criminal Justice Act 2003 created a new body, the 'Sentencing Guidelines Council', which (working alongside the Panel) took over responsibility for issuing guidelines on sentencing matters. The Council is chaired by the Lord Chief Justice and comprises seven other 'judicial members' and four 'non-judicial members'. To be eligible to act as one of the judicial members, a person must be a Lord Justice of Appeal, a High Court judge, a Circuit judge, a District judge (magistrates' courts) or a lay justice; the judicial members must include a Circuit judge, a District judge (magistrates' courts) and a lay justice. To be eligible for appointment as a non-judicial member, a person must have experience in policing, criminal prosecution, criminal defence, or the promotion of the welfare of victims of crime; the non-judicial members must include at least one person with experience in each of these areas. Section 167(9) empowers the Lord Chancellor to appoint a person with experience of sentencing policy and the administration of sentences to attend and speak at any meeting of the Council.

The function of the Sentencing Guidelines Council is to promulgate guidelines to enable all courts dealing with criminal cases to approach the sentencing of offenders from a common starting point. The Council works alongside the Sentencing Advisory Panel, whose continued existence is confirmed by s 169(1).

The functions of the Council are set out in s 170 of the 2003 Act. Under s 170(1), two type of guidelines are identified:

> (a) 'sentencing guidelines' means guidelines relating to the sentencing of offenders, which may be general in nature or limited to a particular category of offence or offender, and
> (b) 'allocation guidelines' means guidelines relating to decisions by a magistrates' court under section 19 of the Magistrates' Courts Act 1980 as to whether an offence is more suitable for summary trial or trial on indictment.

Under s 170(3), the Council may consider whether to frame sentencing guidelines or allocation guidelines and it must do so if it receives a proposal from the Panel under s 171(2), or a proposal under sub-s (2) from the Secretary of State under s 170(2).

Section 170(4) requires the Council to consider, from time to time, whether existing guidelines ought to be revised.

Importantly, s 170(5) set out the matters to which the Council must have regard when it is framing or revising sentencing guidelines:

> (a) the need to promote consistency in sentencing,
> (b) the sentences imposed by courts in England and Wales for offences to which the guidelines relate,
> (c) the cost of different sentences and their relative effectiveness in preventing re-offending,
> (d) the need to promote public confidence in the criminal justice system, and
> (e) the views communicated to the Council, in accordance with s 171(3)(b), by the Panel.

Section 170(6) makes similar provisions for the framing or revision of allocation guidelines, requiring the Council to have regard to:

> (a) the need to promote consistency in decisions under s 19 of the Magistrates' Courts Act 1980, and
> (b) the views communicated to the Council, in accordance with s 171(3)(b), by the Panel.

Section 170(7) says that:

> Sentencing guidelines in respect of an offence or category of offences must include criteria for determining the seriousness of the offence or offences, including (where appropriate) criteria for determining the weight to be given to any previous convictions of offenders.

The role of the Sentencing Advisory Panel is set out in s 171 of the Act. Under s 171(1), if the Council decides to frame or revise any sentencing or allocation guidelines, otherwise than in response to a proposal from the Panel, the Council must notify the Panel. Under s 171(2), the Panel may propose to the Council the framing or revising of sentencing or allocation guidelines (so the Panel make proposals for guidelines to the Council, not direct to the Court of Appeal as was previously the case).

The force of the sentencing guidelines issued by the Council is spelled out by s 172(1) of the 2003 Act, which states that:

> Every court must—
>
> (a) in sentencing an offender, have regard to any guidelines which are relevant to the offender's case, and
> (b) in exercising any other function relating to the sentencing of offenders, have regard to any guidelines which are relevant to the exercise of the function.

In *R v Doidge* [2005] EWCA Crim 273; (2005), *The Times*, 19 March, the Court of Appeal said that, when sentencing, the court should have regard to the definitive guidelines produced by the Sentencing Guidelines Council, not the advice given by the Sentencing Advisory Panel. Moreover, sentencing judges should be extremely cautious about looking at and having regard to consultation guidelines issued by the Sentencing Guidelines Council: it is only after it becomes a definitive guideline that there is a statutory requirement to have regard to it under s 172 of the Criminal Justice Act 2003 (*R v Lloyd* [2007] EWCA Crim 590).

The Sentencing Guidelines Council has issued a number of Guidelines, some dealing with general principles, others with specific offences. In particular, there is general guidance on assessing the 'seriousness' of an offence, and guidance on the approach to be taken where the accused pleads guilty. The latter guidance was revised in 2007.

It must be borne in mind that guidelines, whether laid down by the Court of Appeal or the Sentencing Guidelines Council, are only guidelines. There will be cases where there is good reason to depart significantly from the guidelines. In particular, this might be appropriate where the facts of the offence diminish its seriousness in comparison to the norm, or where there is particularly powerful personal mitigation (*R v Krivec (Attorney General's Reference No 8 of 2007)* [2007] EWCA Crim 922; [2008] 1 Cr App R (S) 1 per Lord Phillips CJ at para 16). Moreover, the Court of Appeal pointed out, in *R v Martin* [2006] EWCA Crim 1035; [2007] 1 Cr App R (S) 3, that sentencing is not a mathematical exercise. It involves the weighing up of sometimes conflicting mitigating and aggravating factors. Although the court has a duty to consider 'definitive' guidelines under s 172 of the Criminal Justice Act 2003, the guidelines of Sentencing Guidelines Council remain guidelines. For those purposes, the term 'definitive guidelines' meant simply guidelines that have been through the process outlined in s 170 of the Act (Sir Igor Judge P at para 15).

16.8.1.1 *Moves towards a structured sentencing framework*

In December 2007 Lord Carter, who had been asked the Lord Chancellor to consider options for improving the balance between the supply of and demand for prison places, produced a Report entitled 'Securing the Future' (<http://www.justice.gov.uk/docs/securing-the-future.pdf>). Amongst his proposals was a recommendation that 'a structured sentencing framework and permanent Sentencing Commission should be developed, with judicial leadership, to improve the transparency, predictability and consistency of sentencing and the criminal justice system'. In 2008, a working party, chaired by Lord Justice Gage, was set up. The working party issued a consultation paper (<http://www.judiciary.gov.uk/docs/consultation_ssfsc_310308.pdf>). The consultation paper notes (at para 1.5) that, in assessing the possible improvements that could be made to the sentencing process, 'as a matter of principle and practice, individual sentencers would not under any of the measures discussed here be required to have regard to resources at the time they sentence in individual cases' and that 'it is important to understand that sentencing encompasses custodial and non custodial sentences. A structured sentencing framework will need to cover both aspects of sentencing and the appropriate balance between them'. The consultation paper acknowledges the work already being done by the Sentencing Guidelines Council but points out (at para 3.6) that the SGC 'has not created a table that ranks all offences by seriousness – this means that it does not employ an overarching guide as to the relative severity of different offences when selecting guideline starting points and sentencing ranges. The SGC has instead adopted an offence by offence approach to the development of its guidelines'. The paper goes on to assert that this 'offence by offence approach may ultimately result in a framework of guidelines that is not relative and proportionate in its construction' and to suggest that 'an offence severity scale may contribute to more informed choices about the correct starting points and sentencing ranges for different offences'. The paper gives particular consideration to the effect of previous convictions. Paragraph 3.10 points out that s 143(2) of the 2003 Act, together with the guidance issued by the SGC, has the effect that 'sentencers are free to judge the specific weight to be applied to each previous conviction'. Paragraph 3.12 says that

> The Working Group wishes to explore whether specific guidance on the treatment of previous criminal convictions would be of use to sentencers in England and Wales. It is argued the provision of such guidance may:
>
> - Aid consistency of approach in relation to the judicial interpretation of the terms 'relevant' and 'recent'.
> - Allow the body charged with producing sentencing guidelines the option of influencing more precisely how its guidelines ought to apply to offenders with previous convictions.
> - Properly determine the weight that sentencers ought to give to the seriousness of the current offence, relative to the criminal record.

Paragraph 3.13 explains that, 'Consistency of approach in sentencing practice plays a role in bringing certainty to future predictable sentencing behaviour'.

To achieve this 'structured sentencing' framework, the consultation paper effectively adopts Lord Carter's recommendation, that a Sentencing Commission should oversee the establishment of a set of indicative sentence ranges and have a continuing role to monitor the impact of those ranges on the sentencing framework.

Martin Wasik, who was chairman of the Sentencing Advisory Panel from 1999 to 2007, notes in his article 'Sentencing guidelines in England and Wales - state of the art?' [2008] Crim LR 253, that

> it is hard to conceive of a sentencing commission working alongside the existing SGC/SAP arrangements. The likely scenarios seem to be: (1) requiring the SGC to take on the additional responsibility of having regard to resources when devising guidelines; or (2) abolishing the SGC/SAP and replacing it with an American-style sentencing commission.

In 'Aggravating and mitigating factors at sentencing: towards greater consistency of application' [2008] Crim LR 264, Julian Roberts calls for a more comprehensive sentencing guidance system for the exercise of discretion with respect to sentencing factors. He notes that such a system would:

- provide a general list of the principal mitigating and aggravating factors, and also for specific offence categories or offences;
- clarify the different standard of proof for contested claims for mitigation and aggravation;
- distinguish between factors of low and high importance;
- provide specific principles of application to ensure uniform consideration of the factors;
- identify specific factors that should not be considered in mitigation or aggravation;
- provide judicial discretion to apply factors not identified in the guidelines or Court of Appeal judgments, provided they are relevant;
- encourage sentencers to consider the justification for invoking specific factors;
- encourage sentencers to identify the most important sentencing factors taken into account as well as the specific way in which these factors influenced the sentencing outcome.

His conclusion is that, so long as it does not unduly impair a court's ability to impose an appropriate disposition, any attempt to structure judicial discretion is welcome and that 'there is reason to believe that courts in England and Wales would benefit from more detailed and structured guidance regarding the use of mitigating and aggravating factors at sentencing. Such guidance would result in more consistency in the use of these factors, and ultimately more equitable and proportionate sentencing outcomes'.

Cooper, J, 'The Sentencing Guidelines Council - a practical perspective' [2008] Crim LR 277, concludes that

> From a practitioner's point of view there remains a fundamental conflict between the need for conformity and certainty in sentencing and the reality that each case will inevitably depend upon its own facts . . . The overall impact of the guidelines has been perceived to have increased the likelihood of a custodial sentence, with stress being placed upon prescriptive lists of aggravating features to the detriment of personal mitigation. Inherent within this problem is the erosion of judicial discretion to deal with each case before the court individually and, ultimately, fairly. In undoubtedly achieving a desired level of consistency and coherency in areas of criminal law requiring these elements, the SGC must regularly remind itself that its other stated purpose, that of increasing public confidence that justice is being

done, and ensure that this objective should not be interpreted in such a way as to emaciate a flexible and dynamic sentencing regime.

16.8.2 Guidance on overarching principles: seriousness

In December 2004, the Sentencing Guidelines Council issued guidance on the concept of seriousness (see <http://www.sentencing-guidelines.gov.uk/docs/Seriousness_guideline.pdf>).

> This guideline applies only to sentences passed under the sentencing framework applicable to those aged 18 or over although there are some aspects that will assist courts assessing the seriousness of offences committed by those under 18. The Council has commissioned separate advice from the Sentencing Advisory Panel on the sentencing of young offenders.
>
> . . .
>
> 1.2 The Act does not indicate that any one purpose should be more important than any other and in practice they may all be relevant to a greater or lesser degree in any individual case – the sentencer has the task of determining the manner in which they apply.
>
> 1.3 The sentencer must start by considering the seriousness of the offence, the assessment of which will:
>
> * determine which of the sentencing thresholds has been crossed;
> * indicate whether a custodial, community or other sentence is the most appropriate;
> * be the key factor in deciding the length of a custodial sentence, the onerousness of requirements to be incorporated in a community sentence and the amount of any fine imposed.
>
> 1.4 A court is required to pass a sentence that is commensurate with the seriousness of the offence. The seriousness of an offence is determined by two main parameters; the **culpability** of the offender and the **harm** caused or risked being caused by the offence.
>
> . . .
>
> **B. Culpability**
>
> 1.6 Four levels of criminal culpability can be identified for sentencing purposes:
>
> 1.7 Where the offender:
>
> (i) has the **intention** to cause harm, with the highest culpability when an offence is planned. The worse the harm intended, the greater the seriousness.
> (ii) is **reckless** as to whether harm is caused, that is, where the offender appreciates at least some harm would be caused but proceeds giving no thought to the consequences even though the extent of the risk would be obvious to most people.
> (iii) has **knowledge** of the specific risks entailed by his actions even though he does not intend to cause the harm that results.
> (iv) is guilty of **negligence.**
>
> **Note:** There are offences where liability is strict and no culpability need be proved for the purposes of obtaining a conviction, but the degree of culpability is still important when

deciding sentence. The extent to which recklessness, knowledge or negligence are involved in a particular offence will vary.

C. Harm

1.8 The relevant provision is widely drafted so that it encompasses those offences where harm is caused but also those where neither individuals nor the community suffer harm but a risk of harm is present.

To Individual Victims

1.9 The types of harm caused or risked by different types of criminal activity are diverse and victims may suffer physical injury, sexual violation, financial loss, damage to health or psychological distress. There are gradations of harm within all of these categories.

1.10 The nature of harm will depend on personal characteristics and circumstances of the victim and the court's assessment of harm will be an effective and important way of taking into consideration the impact of a particular crime on the victim.

1.11 In some cases no actual harm may have resulted and the court will be concerned with assessing the relative dangerousness of the offender's conduct; it will consider the likelihood of harm occurring and the gravity of the harm that could have resulted.

To the Community

1.12 Some offences cause harm to the community at large (instead of or as well as to an individual victim) and may include economic loss, harm to public health, or interference with the administration of justice.

Other Types of harm

1.13 There are other types of harm that are more difficult to define or categorise. For example, cruelty to animals certainly causes significant harm to the animal but there may also be a human victim who also suffers psychological distress and/or financial loss.

1.14 Some conduct is criminalised purely by reference to public feeling or social mores. In addition, public concern about the damage caused by some behaviour, both to individuals and to society as a whole, can influence public perception of the harm caused, for example, by the supply of prohibited drugs.

D. The Assessment of Culpability and Harm

1.15 Section 143(1) makes clear that the assessment of the seriousness of any individual offence must take account not only of any harm actually caused by the offence, but also of any harm that was intended to be caused or might foreseeably be caused by the offence.

1.16 Assessing seriousness is a difficult task, particularly where there is an imbalance between culpability and harm:

- sometimes the harm that actually results is greater than the harm intended by the offender;
- in other circumstances, the offender's culpability may be at a higher level than the harm resulting from the offence.

1.17 Harm must always be judged in the light of culpability. The precise level of culpability will be determined by such factors as motivation, whether the offence was planned or spontaneous or whether the offender was in a position of trust.

Culpability will be greater if:

- an offender deliberately causes more harm than is necessary for the commission of the offence, or
- where an offender targets a vulnerable victim (because of their old age or youth, disability or by virtue of the job they do).

1.18 Where unusually serious harm results and was unintended and beyond the control of the offender, culpability will be significantly influenced by the extent to which the harm could have been foreseen.

1.19 If much **more** harm, or much **less** harm has been caused by the offence than the offender intended or foresaw, the culpability of the offender, depending on the circumstances, may be regarded as carrying greater or lesser weight as appropriate.

The culpability of the offender in the particular circumstances of an individual case should be the initial factor in determining the seriousness of an offence.

(i) Aggravating Factors

1.20 Sentencing guidelines for a particular offence will normally include a list of aggravating features which, if present in an individual instance of the offence, would indicate either a higher than usual level of culpability on the part of the offender, or a greater than usual degree of harm caused by the offence (or sometimes both).

1.21 The lists below bring together the most important aggravating features with potential application to more than one offence or class of offences. They include some factors (such as the vulnerability of victims or abuse of trust) which are integral features of certain offences; in such cases, the presence of the aggravating factor is already reflected in the penalty for the offence and cannot be used as justification for increasing the sentence further. The lists are not intended to be comprehensive and the aggravating factors are not listed in any particular order of priority. On occasions, two or more of the factors listed will describe the same feature of the offence and care needs to be taken to avoid 'doublecounting' . . .

1.22 **Factors indicating higher culpability:**

- Offence committed whilst on bail for other offences
- Failure to respond to previous sentences
- Offence was racially or religiously aggravated
- Offence motivated by, or demonstrating, hostility to the victim based on his or her sexual orientation (or presumed sexual orientation)
- Offence motivated by, or demonstrating, hostility based on the victim's disability (or presumed disability)
- Previous conviction(s), particularly where a pattern of repeat offending is disclosed
- Planning of an offence
- An intention to commit more serious harm than actually resulted from the offence
- Offenders operating in groups or gangs
- 'Professional' offending
- Commission of the offence for financial gain (where this is not inherent in the offence itself)

- High level of profit from the offence
- An attempt to conceal or dispose of evidence
- Failure to respond to warnings or concerns expressed by others about the offender's behaviour
- Offence committed whilst on licence
- Offence motivated by hostility towards a minority group, or a member or members of it
- Deliberate targeting of vulnerable victim(s)
- Commission of an offence while under the influence of alcohol or drugs
- Use of a weapon to frighten or injure victim
- Deliberate and gratuitous violence or damage to property, over and above what is needed to carry out the offence
- Abuse of power
- Abuse of a position of trust

1.23 **Factors indicating a more than usually serious degree of harm:**

- Multiple victims
- An especially serious physical or psychological effect on the victim, even if unintended
- A sustained assault or repeated assaults on the same victim
- Victim is particularly vulnerable
- Location of the offence (for example, in an isolated place)
- Offence is committed against those working in the public sector or providing a service to the public
- Presence of others e.g. relatives, especially children or partner of the victim
- Additional degradation of the victim (e.g. taking photographs of a victim as part of a sexual offence)
- In property offences, high value (including sentimental value) of property to the victim, or substantial consequential loss (e.g. where the theft of equipment causes serious disruption to a victim's life or business)

(ii) Mitigating factors

1.24 Some factors may indicate that an offender's culpability is unusually low, or that the harm caused by an offence is less than usually serious.

1.25 **Factors indicating significantly lower culpability:**

- A greater degree of provocation than normally expected
- Mental illness or disability
- Youth or age, where it affects the responsibility of the individual defendant
- The fact that the offender played only a minor role in the offence

(iii) Personal mitigation

. . .

1.27 When the court has formed an initial assessment of the seriousness of the offence, then it should consider any offender mitigation. The issue of remorse should be taken into account at this point along with other mitigating features such as admissions to the police in interview.

(iv) Reduction for a guilty plea

1.28 Sentencers will normally reduce the severity of a sentence to reflect an early guilty plea. This subject is covered by a separate guideline and provides a sliding scale reduction with a normal maximum one-third reduction being given to offenders who enter a guilty plea at the first reasonable opportunity.

1.29 Credit may also be given for ready co-operation with the authorities. This will depend on the particular circumstances of the individual case.

E. The Sentencing Thresholds

1.30 Assessing the seriousness of an offence is only the first step in the process of determining the appropriate sentence in an individual case. Matching the offence to a type and level of sentence is a separate and complex exercise assisted by the application of the respective threshold tests for custodial and community sentences.

The Custody Threshold

. . .

1.32 In applying the threshold test, sentencers should note:

- the clear intention of the threshold test is to reserve prison as a punishment for the most serious offences;
- it is impossible to determine definitively which features of a particular offence make it serious enough to merit a custodial sentence;
- passing the custody threshold does not mean that a custodial sentence should be deemed inevitable, and custody can still be avoided in the light of personal mitigation or where there is a suitable intervention in the community which provides sufficient restriction (by way of punishment) while addressing the rehabilitation of the offender to prevent future crime. For example, a prolific offender who currently could expect a short custodial sentence (which, in advance of custody plus, would have no provision for supervision on release) might more appropriately receive a suitable community sentence.

1.33 The approach to the imposition of a custodial sentence under the new framework should be as follows:

(a) has the custody threshold been passed?
(b) if so, is it unavoidable that a custodial sentence be imposed?
(c) if so, can that sentence be suspended? (sentencers should be clear that they would have imposed a custodial sentence if the power to suspend had not been available)
(d) if not, can the sentence be served intermittently?
(e) if not, impose a sentence which takes immediate effect for the term commensurate with the seriousness of the offence.

The Threshold for Community Sentences

. . .

1.35 In addition, the threshold for a community sentence can be crossed even though the seriousness criterion is not met. Section 151 of the Criminal Justice Act 2003 provides that, in relation to an offender aged 16 or over on whom, on 3 or more previous occasions, sentences had been passed consisting only of a fine, a community sentence may be imposed (if it is in the interests of justice) despite the fact that the seriousness of the current offence (and others associated with it) might not warrant such a sentence.

1.36 Sentencers should consider all of the disposals available (within or below the threshold passed) at the time of sentence before reaching the provisional decision to make a community sentence, so that, even where the threshold for a community sentence has been passed, a financial penalty or discharge may still be an appropriate penalty.

Summary
1.37 It would not be feasible to provide a form of words or to devise any formula that would provide a general solution to the problem of where the custody threshold lies. Factors vary too widely between offences for this to be done. It is the task of guidelines for individual offences to provide more detailed guidance on what features within that offence point to a custodial sentence, and also to deal with issues such as sentence length, the appropriate requirements for a community sentence or the use of appropriate ancillary orders.

Having assessed the seriousness of an individual offence, sentencers must consult the sentencing guidelines for an offence of that type for guidance on the factors that are likely to indicate whether a custodial sentence or other disposal is most likely to be appropriate.

F. Prevalence
1.38 The seriousness of an individual case should be judged on its own dimensions of harm and culpability rather than as part of a collective social harm. It is legitimate for the overall approach to sentencing levels for particular offences to be guided by their cumulative effect. However, it would be wrong to further penalise individual offenders by increasing sentence length for committing an individual offence of that type.

1.39 There may be exceptional local circumstances that arise which may lead a court to decide that prevalence should influence sentencing levels. The pivotal issue in such cases will be the harm being caused to the community. It is essential that sentencers both have supporting evidence from an external source (for example the local Criminal Justice Board) to justify claims that a particular crime is prevalent in their area and are satisfied that there is a compelling need to treat the offence more seriously than elsewhere.

The key factor in determining whether sentencing levels should be enhanced in response to prevalence will be the level of harm being caused in the locality. Enhanced sentences should be exceptional and in response to exceptional circumstances. Sentencers must sentence within the sentencing guidelines once the prevalence has been addressed.

In summary, the decision as to what sentence to pass involves a two-stage process:

- the court first has to decide what sentence is appropriate given the seriousness of the offence committed by the defendant;
- the court then goes on to consider whether that sentence should be reduced in the light of any mitigating circumstances which relate to the defendant.

Thus, the court looks first at the offence and then at the offender. Section 143(1) of the Criminal Justice Act 2003 states that:

> In considering the seriousness of any offence, the court must consider the offender's culpability in committing the offence and any harm which the offence caused, was intended to cause or might foreseeably have caused.

In other words, the starting point is to consider the harm that was actually caused and the harm that the offender intended to cause.

In assessing seriousness where there is more than one offence, the court looks at the seriousness of the combination of associated offences. Section 161(1) of the Powers of Criminal Courts (Sentencing) Act 2000 provides that an offence is associated with another offence (which we may call the main offence) if:

- it is an offence of which the defendant has been convicted, or for which he is to be sentenced, in the same proceedings as the main offence; or
- it is an offence which the offender has asked the court to take into consideration when passing sentence for the main offence (see below for discussion of offences that are taken into consideration).

The factors identified in paras 1.22–25 of the Guidelines were already established as relevant to the sentencing practice of the courts. For example, it has long been established that:

- in a case involving money, the amount involved is an important factor in determining the seriousness of the offence: the greater the sum stolen or the greater the value of the property damaged, the more serious the offence;
- using, or threatening the use of violence, makes the offence more serious, and the use or threatened use of a weapon makes it more serious still;
- the offence is more serious if the victim is vulnerable. The term vulnerable includes not only the aged and infirm, but also those whose work brings them into contact with the public, and so places them at greater risk (for example, police officers, civil enforcement officers, taxi drivers, bus drivers, publicans).
- where an offence is committed in breach of trust, the offence is made more serious by that breach (see *R v Barrick* (1985) 81 Cr App R 78 and *R v Clark* [1998] 2 Cr App R 137). This includes the employee who steals from his employer and the postman who steals or destroys the mail. In a case involving breach of trust, a custodial sentence may be appropriate even if the sum involved is small (as in *R v McCormick* (1995) 16 Cr App R(S) 134);
- if the offence was committed on impulse, that is a mitigating factor. On the other hand, an offence is made more serious if it is premeditated. The greater the degree of planning and sophistication, the more serious the offence;
- where more than one person is involved in the commission of an offence, this fact may make the offence more serious. A 'mugging' by a gang, for example, is even worse than a mugging carried out by one person;
- where more than one person is involved, the level of a particular person's involvement affects the seriousness of the offence as regards that offender. For example, the lookout and the getaway driver will be dealt with more leniently than those who actually carry out the burglary or the robbery, as the case may be;
- if the offender is able to show that the offence was committed out of something

approaching necessity (but the necessity falls short of being a defence), that offence may be regarded as less serious than one committed for purely personal gain;

- provocation is only a defence to murder but may be used as a mitigating circumstance for any offence. Usually, of course, the question of provocation arises only in offences of violence. See, for example, *R v Brookin* (1995) 16 Cr App R(S) 78.

Another very important factor is the impact of the offence on the victim. The use of statements from victims of crime about the impact of the offence is governed by para III.28 of *Consolidated Practice Direction*. Paragraph III.28.2 says that:

> When a police officer takes a statement from a victim the victim will be told about the scheme and given the chance to make a victim personal statement. A victim personal statement may be made or updated at any time prior to the disposal of the case. The decision about whether or not to make a victim personal statement is entirely for the victim. If the court is presented with a victim personal statement the following approach should be adopted:
>
> (a) The victim personal statement and any evidence in support should be considered and taken into account by the court prior to passing sentence.
> (b) Evidence of the effects of an offence on the victim contained in the victim personal statement or other statement must be in proper form, that is a witness statement made under section 9 of the Criminal Justice Act 1967 or an expert's report, and served upon the defendant's solicitor or the defendant, if he is not represented, prior to sentence. Except where inferences can properly be drawn from the nature of or circumstances surrounding the offence, a sentencer must not make assumptions unsupported by evidence about the effects of an offence on the victim.
> (c) The court must pass what it judges to be the appropriate sentence having regard to the circumstances of the offence and of the offender, taking into account, so far as the court considers it appropriate, the consequences to the victim. The opinions of the victim or the victim's close relatives as to what the sentence should be are therefore not relevant, unlike the consequence of the offence on them. Victims should be advised of this. If, despite the advice, opinions as to sentence are included in the statement, the court should pay no attention to them.
> (d) The court should consider whether it is desirable in its sentencing remarks to refer to the evidence provided on behalf of the victim.

The point to emphasise is that the court is only concerned with the impact of the offence on the victim, not with the victim's views on how severe – or lenient – the sentence should be.

In *R v Oosthuizen* [2005] EWCA Crim 1978; [2006] 1 Cr App R (S) 73, the court referred to para 1.39 (local prevalence) of the SGC's Guidelines on Seriousness (see above). Rose LJ said, at paras 15 and 16:

> If, in any particular town or city, there are statistics available to the Crown Prosecution Service, the Local Criminal Justice Board or otherwise, which demonstrate a prevalence greater than that nationally of a particular type of offence, those statistics can and should be made available to the Court.

In the absence of such statistics or other evidence identifying particular prevalence in a particular area, a judge, however experienced in a particular area, should not make the assumption that prevalence of that offence is more marked in the area with which he is familiar than it is nationally.

16.8.3 Guidance on reduction in sentence for guilty pleas

Section 144(1) of the Criminal Justice Act 2003 gives statutory effect to the already well-established principle that credit should be given for pleading guilty. It provides that:

In determining what sentence to pass on an offender who has pleaded guilty to an offence in proceedings before that or another court, a court must take into account—

(a) the stage in the proceedings for the offence at which the offender indicated his intention to plead guilty, and

(b) the circumstances in which this indication was given.

There is, however, no statutory guidance on the amount of the discount: guidance on that issue comes from the Sentencing Guidelines Council (see below).

The main reasons for giving credit to someone for pleading guilty are:

- it shows contrition on the part of the defendant;
- it saves court time, in that no trial takes place;
- if the defendant admitted the offence when first questioned by the police (or, better still, surrendered himself to police custody), police time is saved, in that unnecessary enquiries do not have to be made;
- in cases where the experience of giving evidence would be traumatic to a witness (for example, a victim of a sexual assault), the plea of guilty spares the witness this trauma.

Guidance on guilty pleas was originally issued by the Sentencing Guidelines Council in December 2004, along with the guidance on the concept of seriousness. This guidance confirmed that an offender who pleads guilty should receive a reduction in sentence to reflect the guilty plea. The guidance confirmed that the usual starting-point for giving credit for pleading guilty is a one-third reduction in that sentence (which was the position according to earlier case law, for example *R v Buffery* (1993) 14 Cr App R(S) 511).

Under s 144(1)(a), the court is specifically required to have regard to when the defendant pleads guilty. In *R v Barber* [2001] EWCA Crim 2267; [2002] 1 Cr App R(S) 130, and in *R v Wilson* [2004] EWCA Crim 281; (2004) *The Times*, 12 February, the Court of Appeal emphasised the importance of giving credit to those who enter pleas of guilty at the earliest reasonable opportunity. The Guidelines from the Sentencing Guidelines Council confirm the effect of such case law and show how the phrase 'earliest reasonable opportunity' should be interpreted. In the case of an offence which is triable either way, the earliest stage at which the defendant can effectively enter a plea of guilty is at the 'plea before venue' hearing. If the defendant indicates an intention to plead not guilty (or gives no indication of likely plea) at the 'plea before venue' hearing, but then (at the trial) enters a plea of guilty, he will forfeit some of the credit which he would otherwise have earned for pleading guilty. In the case of an offence which is triable only on indictment, the earliest point at which the defendant can plead guilty is when he is arraigned in the Crown Court (at the plea and case management hearing); however, the defendant can nevertheless give an informal indication that he intends to plead guilty at an earlier stage.

Section 174(2)(d) of the Criminal Justice Act 2003 provides that where, because of a guilty plea, the court imposes a punishment on the offender which is less severe than the punishment it would otherwise have imposed, the judge must say so. However, it was held in *R v Wharton* [2001] EWCA Crim 622; (2001) *The Times*, 27 March, construing earlier legislation, that this requirement is purely procedural and so the court, on an appeal, is not required to interfere with what is otherwise an appropriate sentence merely on the ground that the sentencer failed to state expressly that the guilty plea had been taken into account.

Earlier case law made it clear that the discount for pleading guilty could be withheld if it was clear that the offender is only pleading guilty because the prosecution case against him is overwhelming (sometimes referred to as cases where the defendant was caught 'red-handed'). However, the first edition of the Sentencing Guidelines Council Guidelines said that the full discount for pleading guilty should be given even if the prosecution case was overwhelming. That guidance proved to be very controversial, and it was revised in July 2007 to reduce (from one-third to one-fifth) the discount to be given in such cases.

The revised guidance on guilty pleas is as follows (<http://www.sentencing-guidelines.gov.uk/docs/Reduction%20in%20Sentence-final.pdf>):

B Statement of Purpose

. . .

2.2 A reduction in sentence is appropriate because a guilty plea avoids the need for a trial (thus enabling other cases to be disposed of more expeditiously), shortens the gap between charge and sentence, saves considerable cost, and, in the case of an early plea, saves victims and witnesses from the concern about having to give evidence. The reduction principle derives from the need for the effective administration of justice and not as an aspect of mitigation.

2.3 Where a sentencer is in doubt as to whether a custodial sentence is appropriate, the reduction attributable to a guilty plea will be a relevant consideration. Where this is amongst the factors leading to the imposition of a non-custodial sentence, there will be no need to apply a further reduction on account of the guilty plea. A similar approach is appropriate where the reduction for a guilty plea is amongst the factors leading to the imposition of a financial penalty or discharge instead of a community order.

2.4 When deciding the most appropriate length of sentence, the sentencer should address separately the issue of remorse, together with any other mitigating features, before calculating the reduction for the guilty plea. Similarly, assistance to the prosecuting or enforcement authorities is a separate issue which may attract a reduction in sentence under other procedures; care will need to be taken to ensure that there is no 'double counting'.

2.5 The implications of other offences that an offender has asked to be taken into consideration should be reflected in the sentence before the reduction for the guilty plea has been applied.

2.6 A reduction in sentence should only be applied to the punitive elements of a penalty. The guilty plea reduction has no impact on sentencing decisions in relation to ancillary orders, including orders of disqualification from driving.

3.1 Recommended Approach

The court decides sentence for the offence(s) taking into account aggravating and mitigating factors and any other offences that have been formally admitted (TICs)

↓

The court selects the amount of the reduction by reference to the sliding scale

↓

The court applies the reduction

↓

When pronouncing sentence the court should usually state what the sentence would have been if there had been no reduction as a result of the guilty plea

D. Determining the Level of Reduction

4.1 The level of reduction should be a proportion of the total sentence imposed, with the proportion calculated by reference to the circumstances in which the guilty plea was indicated, in particular the stage in the proceedings. The greatest reduction will be given where the plea was indicated at the 'first reasonable opportunity'.

4.2 Save where section 144(2) of the 2003 Act applies, the level of the reduction will be gauged on a sliding scale ranging from a recommended one third (where the guilty plea was entered at the first reasonable opportunity in relation to the offence for which sentence is being imposed), reducing to a recommended one quarter (where a trial date has been set) and to a recommended one tenth (for a guilty plea entered at the 'door of the court' or after the trial has begun).

4.3 The level of reduction should reflect the stage at which the offender indicated a willingness to admit guilt to the offence for which he is eventually sentenced:

(i)   the largest recommended reduction will not normally be given unless the offender indicated willingness to admit guilt at the first reasonable opportunity; when this occurs will vary from case to case (see Annex 1 for illustrative examples);

(ii) where the admission of guilt comes later than the first reasonable opportunity, the reduction for guilty plea will normally be less than one third;

(iii) where the plea of guilty comes very late, it is still appropriate to give some reduction;

(iv) if after pleading guilty there is a *Newton* hearing and the offender's version of the circumstances of the offence is rejected, this should be taken into account in determining the level of reduction;

(v)   if the not guilty plea was entered and maintained for tactical reasons (such as to retain privileges whilst on remand), a late guilty plea should attract very little, if any, discount.

In each category, there is a presumption that the recommended reduction will be given unless there are good reasons for a lower amount.

First reasonable opportunity: recommended $\frac{1}{3}$

After a trial date is set: recommended $\frac{1}{4}$

Door of the court/after trial has begun: recommended $\frac{1}{10}$

E. Withholding a Reduction
On the basis of dangerousness

5.1 Where a sentence for a 'dangerous offender' is imposed under the provisions in the Criminal Justice Act 2003, whether the sentence requires the calculation of a minimum term or is an extended sentence, the approach will be the same as for any other determinate sentence (see also section G below).

Where the prosecution case is overwhelming

5.2 The purpose of giving credit is to encourage those who are guilty to plead at the earliest opportunity. Any defendant is entitled to put the prosecution to proof and so every defendant who is guilty should be encouraged to indicate that guilt at the first reasonable opportunity.

5.3 Where the prosecution case is overwhelming, it may not be appropriate to give the full reduction that would otherwise be given. Whilst there is a presumption in favour of the full reduction being given where a plea has been indicated at the first reasonable opportunity, the fact that the prosecution case is overwhelming without relying on admissions from the defendant may be a reason justifying departure from the guideline.

5.4 Where a court is satisfied that a lower reduction should be given for this reason, a recommended reduction of 20% is likely to be appropriate where the guilty plea was indicated at the first reasonable opportunity.

5.5 A Court departing from a guideline must state the reasons for doing so.

Where the maximum penalty for the offence is thought to be too low

5.6 The sentencer is bound to sentence for the offence with which the offender has been charged, and to which he has pleaded guilty. The sentencer cannot remedy perceived defects (for example an inadequate charge or maximum penalty) by refusal of the appropriate discount.

Where jurisdictional issues arise

(i) *Where sentencing powers are limited to 6 months imprisonment despite multiple offences*

5.7 When the total sentence for both or all of the offences is 6 months imprisonment, a court may determine to impose consecutive sentences which, even allowing for a reduction for a guilty plea where appropriate on each offence, would still result in the imposition of the maximum sentence available. In such circumstances, in order to achieve the purpose for which the reduction principle has been established, some modest allowance should normally be given against the total sentence for the entry of a guilty plea.

(ii) *Where a maximum sentence might still be imposed*

5.8 Despite a guilty plea being entered which would normally attract a reduction in sentence, a magistrates' court may impose a sentence of imprisonment of 6 months for a single either-way offence where, but for the plea, that offence would have been committed to the Crown Court for sentence.

5.9 Similarly, a detention and training order of 24 months may be imposed on an offender aged under 18 if the offence is one which would but for the plea have attracted a sentence of long-term detention in excess of 24 months under the Powers of Criminal Courts (Sentencing) Act 2000, section 91.

[F. Application to Sentencing for Murder]
Omitted
ANNEX I
FIRST REASONABLE OPPORTUNITY
1. The critical time for determining the reduction for a guilty plea is the first reasonable opportunity for the defendant to have indicated a willingness to plead guilty. This opportunity will vary with a wide range of factors and the Court will need to make a judgment on the particular facts of the case before it.

2. The key principle is that the purpose of giving a reduction is to recognise the benefits that come from a guilty plea not only for those directly involved in the case in question but also in enabling Courts more quickly to deal with other outstanding cases.

3. This Annex seeks to help Courts to adopt a consistent approach by giving examples of circumstances where a determination will have to be made:

(a)   the first reasonable opportunity may be the first time that a defendant appears before the court and has the opportunity to plead guilty;
(b)   but the court may consider that it would be reasonable to have expected an indication of willingness even earlier, perhaps whilst under interview;
      Note: For (a) and (b) to apply, the Court will need to be satisfied that the defendant (and any legal adviser) would have had sufficient information about the allegations.
(c)   where an offence triable either way is committed to the Crown Court for trial and the defendant pleads guilty at the first hearing in that Court, the reduction will be less than if there had been an indication of a guilty plea given to the magistrates' court (recommended reduction of one third) but more than if the plea had been entered after a trial date had been set (recommended reduction of one quarter), and is likely to be in the region of 30%;
(d)   where an offence is triable only on indictment, it may well be that the first reasonable opportunity would have been during the police station stage; where that is not the case, the first reasonable opportunity is likely to be at the first hearing in the Crown Court;
(e)   where a defendant is convicted after pleading guilty to an alternative (lesser) charge to that to which he/she had originally pleaded not guilty, the extent of any reduction will be determined by the stage at which the defendant first formally indicated to the court willingness to plead guilty to the lesser charge, and the reason why that lesser charge was proceeded with in preference to the original charge.

Discount for pleading guilty should be withheld only in the circumstances where that is permitted by the Guidelines set out above. In *R v March* [2002] EWCA Crim 551; [2002] 2 Cr App R(S) 98, the judge had refused to give any discount for the defendant's guilty plea on the basis that he felt that the Crown had wrongly decided to accept pleas to lesser offences. It was held that he had erred in not giving some discount for the guilty plea. A judge cannot pass a sentence which reflects charges which the Crown has chosen not to pursue.

16.8.3.1 Mitigation associated with guilty pleas

Paragraph 2.4 of the Guidelines draws a clear distinction between remorse and credit for pleading guilty. In *R v Barney* [2007] EWCA Crim 3181, the court said that, in the context of dealing with the issue of remorse on the one hand and pleas of guilty on the other, sentencing is not simply a matter of arithmetical precision. The question of remorse cannot be entirely divorced from the question of a defendant's guilty plea. Where an entirely fictitious story was told to the police, that is a matter which the court is entitled to take into account when deciding upon the credit to be given for a subsequent guilty plea. A remorseful plea of guilty will not necessarily result in a discount of greater than a third, although there are some circumstances in which clear remorse might be taken into account as an additional factor. A reduction in the credit due for a guilty plea on the basis of lack of remorse might not in itself be appropriate. However, where a defendant went out of his way to seek to avoid responsibility (e.g. denying responsibility in the defence case statement), that can be taken into account in the context of remorse and the plea of guilty (per Cooke J at paras 19 and 21).

Coupled with a guilty plea, it is of course very good mitigation that the offender has tried to compensate the victim of the crime, since it is evidence of remorse.

Also likely to be linked to a guilty plea, credit should also be given if the offender has assisted the police, perhaps by helping them to trace stolen property or to arrest other offenders. Where an accomplice pleads guilty and gives evidence for the prosecution against his erstwhile co-defendants, substantial credit should be given. In *R v Wood* [1997] 1 Cr App R(S) 347, the Court of Appeal said that the discount for someone who 'turns Queen's evidence' (that is, gives evidence against an accomplice) should reflect the seriousness of the offence, the importance of the evidence, and the effect which giving the evidence will have on the future circumstances of the witness (for example, placing him in danger of retribution).

In *R v A (Informer: Reduction of Sentence)* [1999] 1 Cr App R(S) 52, the Court of Appeal reiterated that where defendants co-operate with the prosecuting authorities, not only by pleading guilty but by testifying or expressing willingness to testify against a co-defendant, they will ordinarily earn an enhanced discount in their sentences, particularly where such conduct leads to the conviction of a co-defendant or induces a co-defendant to plead guilty. Moreover, it is the long-standing practice of the courts to recognise by a further discount help given to the authorities in the investigation, detection, suppression and prosecution of serious crime. The extent of the discount will ordinarily depend on the value of the help given. If the information given is unreliable, vague, lacking in practical utility or already known to the authorities, no identifiable discount may be given or, if given, any discount will be minimal. If, however, the information given is accurate, particularised, useful in practice, and hitherto unknown to the authorities, enabling serious criminal activity to be stopped and serious criminals brought to book, the discount may be substantial. Furthermore, where, by supplying valuable information to the authorities, a defendant exposes himself or his family to personal jeopardy, it will ordinarily be recognised in the sentence passed (per Lord

Bingham CJ at p 56). In *R v R (Informer: Reduction in Sentence)* (2002) *The Times*, 18 February, the Court of Appeal said that where the defendant pleads guilty and, within a reasonable time of sentence being passed, gives information to the authorities (albeit in relation to a different case), he is entitled to rely on that subsequent information. Information given in those circumstances, however, will not carry the same discount potential as would have been the case had the same information been provided prior to sentence.

Sections 70-75A of the Serious Organised Crime and Police Act 2005 make provision for immunity from prosecution or sentence reductions for offenders who assist investigations into, and prosecutions of, serious offences. Section 71 provides for a designated prosecutor from the Crown Prosecution Service, the Revenue and Customs Prosecutions Office, or the Serious Fraud Office to grant a person conditional immunity from prosecution. The immunity notice must be in writing and must specify the offences for which the person will be immune from prosecution. The notice will normally include conditions, breach of which would lead to the immunity being revoked. Under s 73, the Crown Court, when sentencing a defendant who has pleaded guilty and has entered into a written agreement to provide assistance in any investigation or prosecution, may take account of the nature and extent of that assistance. Section 73(3) requires the court, if it passes a lower sentence than it would otherwise have done, to set out what the sentence would otherwise have been. Under s 74, where a person is still serving a sentence imposed by the Crown Court and one of the conditions in sub-s (2) applies, a specified prosecutor may refer the sentence back to the court for review if he considers it to be in the interests of justice to do so. The conditions in sub-s (2) are that the defendant received a reduced sentence on the basis of an agreement to assist, but then knowingly failed to give that assistance; or the defendant gives or agrees to give assistance after he has been sentenced. Section 74(5) gives the court the power to substitute a greater sentence (not exceeding that which it would have passed but for the agreement to give assistance) where it considers the person has knowingly failed to assist. Where a person has provided assistance or offered to assist, sub-s (6) gives the court the power to take that into account and to reduce the individual's sentence accordingly. Subsections (8) and (9) provide that normal avenues of appeal against sentence apply.

In *R v P* [2007] EWCA Crim 2290, the Court of Appeal gave detailed guidance on the effect of these provisions. At para 27, Sir Igor Judge P noted that, 'the essential feature of [this] statutory framework is that the offender must publicly admit the full extent of his own criminality and agree to participate in a formalised process'. His Lordship added (at para 28) that 'the process is not confined to offenders who provide assistance in relation to crimes in which they were participants, or accessories, or with which they were otherwise linked'. Moreover, the common law principles have not been abolished: 'there will be occasions when a defendant has provided assistance to the police which does not fall within [these] arrangements, and in particular the written agreement. He is not thereby deprived of whatever consequent benefit he should receive' (para 34). Concerning the sentence to be imposed on an offender who has entered into an agreement under the Act, his Lordship said (at paras 39 and 40):

> The first factor in any sentencing decision is the criminality of the defendant, weight being given to such mitigating and aggravating features as there may be. Thereafter, the quality and quantity of the material provided by the defendant in the investigation and subsequent

prosecution of crime falls to be considered. Addressing this issue, particular value should be attached to those cases where the defendant provides evidence in the form of a witness statement or is prepared to give evidence at any subsequent trial, and does so, with added force where the information either produces convictions for the most serious offences, including terrorism and murder, or prevents them, or which leads to disruption to or indeed the break up of major criminal gangs. Considerations like these then have to be put in the context of the nature and extent of the personal risks to and potential consequences faced by the defendant and the members of his family. In most cases the greater the nature of the criminality revealed by the defendant, the greater the consequent risks . . .

The SOCPA procedure requires the defendant to reveal the whole of his previous criminal activities. This will almost inevitably mean that he will admit, and plead guilty to offences which would never otherwise have been attributed to him, and may indeed have been unknown to the police. In order for the process to work as intended, sentencing for offences which fall into this category should usually be approached with these realities in mind and . . . should normally lead to the imposition of concurrent sentences . . .

His Lordship emphasised (at para 41) that the process does not provide immunity from punishment and, subject to appropriate discounts, 'an effective sentence remains a basic characteristic of the process'. Therefore, it is only in the most exceptional case that the appropriate level of reduction would exceed ¾ of the total sentence which would otherwise be passed, and the normal reduction should be between ½ and ⅔ of that sentence.

16.8.3.2 Criticism of the system of discounts for guilty pleas

The system of giving a discount for a guilty plea has been heavily criticised. One major concern is that defendants who are innocent might plead guilty rather than face the ordeal of a trial. For a wide-ranging critique of the system, see R Henham, 'Bargain justice and justice on demand? Sentence discounts and the criminal process' (1999) 62 MLR 515 and P Darbyshire, 'The mischief of plea bargaining and sentencing rewards' [2000] Crim LR 895.

In para 102 of Chapter 10 his *Review of the Criminal Courts of England and Wales*, Lord Justice Auld considers the arguments that have been put forward against having a system of discounting sentence for pleas of guilty (for example, by Andrew Ashworth in *The Criminal Process: An Evaluative Study* (OUP, 1998, pp 276–97; now OUP, 2005, pp 275–78) and Penny Darbyshire in 'The mischief of plea bargaining and sentencing rewards' [2000] Crim LR 895). He summarises the arguments against discounts for guilty pleas as follows:

- defendants who plead guilty, and by that means secure a lower sentence than would have been imposed on conviction, receive a benefit that they do not deserve, since a plea of guilty does not reduce their culpability or need for punishment and/or containment;
- it is contrary to the presumption of innocence and, by implication, the defendant's entitlement to require the prosecution to prove his guilt that, as a result of requiring it to do so, he should receive a more severe sentence than if he had admitted guilt;

- although a defendant can waive that entitlement, a system of discounting sentences is an incentive and is therefore capable of amounting to an improper pressure on him to do so;
- in other jurisdictions, for example, Scotland, no discount is given for a plea and to do so would be regarded as an improper inducement; and in many European countries, at least formally, admission of guilt is not a mitigating factor for the purpose of determining sentence;
- victims, though relieved of the ordeal of having to give evidence, may be unhappy about the lower sentence secured by the plea and untested mitigation; and
- discounting sentence for pleas of guilty indirectly discriminates against defendants from ethnic minorities who, regardless of their guilt or innocence, tend to maintain a plea of not guilty and, in consequence on conviction, face a greater risk of custody and longer sentences than white offenders.

Having considered and rejected each of these arguments, Lord Justice Auld concludes (Recommendation 186) that there should be a 'system of sentencing discounts graduated so that the earlier the tender of plea of guilty the higher the discount for it'.

The other side of the coin is that the defendant should not be penalised for pleading not guilty. In *R v Blaize* (1997) *The Times*, 12 June, for example, the Court of Appeal said that a defendant ought to be sentenced for the offence of which he has been convicted, not for the manner in which the defence was conducted. By contesting the charge, the defendant loses the benefit of the discount which a plea of guilty usually earns but, by pleading not guilty, the defendant should not run the risk of the sentence being increased. It followed, said the Court of Appeal, that false accusations of racial prejudice made in the course of the defence case should not serve to increase the sentence imposed on conviction.

16.9 STATUTORY AGGRAVATING FACTORS

A number of specific aggravating features are identified by statute. We will consider these factors in turn.

16.9.1 Previous convictions

Section 143(2) of the Criminal Justice Act 2003, appears to place greater emphasis on previous convictions than was the case under earlier legislation (following recommendations of the Halliday Report, discussed earlier in this chapter). It says that:

> In considering the seriousness of an offence ('the current offence') committed by an offender who has one or more previous convictions, the court must treat each previous conviction as an aggravating factor if (in the case of that conviction) the court considers that it can reasonably be so treated having regard, in particular, to—
>
> (a) the nature of the offence to which the conviction relates and its relevance to the current offence, and
>
> (b) the time that has elapsed since the conviction.

Sub-section (2)(a) requires the court to assess the relevance of any previous convictions, particularly taking into account whether they relate to similar offences to the offence(s) now being dealt with. It follows that if someone is being sentenced for an offence of violence, the existence of previous convictions for offences of dishonesty will have a lesser adverse effect on the offender than previous convictions for offences of violence. Sub-section (2)(b) makes it clear that, if the offender has previous convictions, but those convictions were some time ago, this conviction-free period should be taken into account when sentence is passed.

Prior to the implementation of the Criminal Justice Act 2003, the general view of the effect of previous convictions was one of 'progressive loss of mitigation' (see, for example *R v Carlton* (1994) 15 Cr App R(S) 335, where it was said that the only relevance of previous convictions to the sentence to be passed is that the offender cannot pray in aid his good character). The effect of good character mitigation is that, if the defendant is of previous good character, a more lenient sentence may be imposed than that justified by the seriousness of the offence. The more previous convictions recorded against an offender, the greater the loss of this 'good character' mitigation. So the effect of previous convictions was to deprive the offender of what would otherwise have been the very strong mitigation that he has no previous convictions: a defendant who had previous convictions would not receive the discount in sentence which a person without previous convictions would receive. It was generally accepted, however, that it would be wrong in principle to impose a sentence greater than that appropriate to the seriousness of the offence merely because the offender has previous convictions. In *R v Queen* (1981) 3 Cr App R (S) 245, for example, it was said that it would be wrong in principle to sentence the offender not merely for the offences of which he has been convicted, but also for his record: no-one is to be sentenced for the offences which he has committed in the past and for which he has already been punished. Adopting this approach, the court must not impose a sentence greater than that justified by the seriousness of the offence merely because the offender has previous convictions. To do so would, in effect, be to sentence the defendant again for his previous misdemeanours. So, to take a case where the custody threshold has been met, if the appropriate sentence is between six and nine months, an offender with previous convictions might receive a sentence closer to nine months than six. However, it would be wrong in such a case to impose 12 months.

Section 143 of the 2003 Act, however, seems to give effect to the views set out in the Halliday Report, that an offence is more serious if committed by someone with relevant previous convictions than if committed by someone of good character or with fewer previous convictions.

The fact that the defendant has a bad record does not necessarily mean that a custodial sentence is inevitable. It has often been recognised (for example, in *R v Bowles* [1996] 2 Cr App R(S) 248) that there are occasions when, in the case of persistent offenders, it is appropriate to impose a community order, rather than a custodial sentence, provided that there is sufficient reason to think that it might be possible to break the defendant's cycle of offending once and for all. To take such a course of action, the court should be satisfied that the offender is highly motivated to change his ways.

The phrase 'previous good character' is often taken to connote merely the absence of previous convictions. However, it can be very strong mitigation to have good character that goes beyond merely a lack previous convictions. For example, in *R v Clark (Joan)*

(1999) *The Times*, 27 January, the defendant had defrauded the public of a total of £18,000 over a period of six years (a very serious offence, almost certain to carry a lengthy prison sentence). However, there was a moving tribute from the nephews and nieces whom she had brought up following the death of their mother, and her parish priest gave evidence of a number of local community and charitable activities with which she had been involved. The Court of Appeal held (maybe a little surprisingly) that the judge should have placed greater weight on her positive good character (that is, good character going beyond the legal sense of an absence of convictions); the sentence of six months' imprisonment was reduced to seven days, enabling her immediate release.

Under earlier legislation, the court was specifically entitled to take account of 'failure to respond' to earlier sentences: if the sentence appropriate to the seriousness of the offence was a custodial sentence but it was argued on behalf of the defendant that a non-custodial sentence should be imposed instead, that argument could be rejected if the offender had previously been given a community sentence but had nonetheless re-offended. Reoffending could thus be taken as showing that non-custodial sentences do not prevent this offender from reoffending (see, for example, *R v Oliver and Little* [1993] 1 WLR 177 at 182, where the defendants reoffended during the currency of a community order). This argument is strongest where the offender has committed offences whilst being subject to a community order.

The provision about failures to respond does not feature in the Criminal Justice Act 2003. However, the fact that the offender has previously received non-custodial sentences, and yet has reoffended, may well be relevant under s 143(2).

Andrew von Hirsch and Julian V Roberts, in 'Legislating sentencing principles: the provisions of the Criminal Justice Act 2003 relating to sentencing purposes and the role of previous convictions' [2004] Crim LR 639, discuss the effect of s 143(2). They say:

> A sentencing scheme that resorts to cumulative sentence increases for repeat offenders will make the criminal law's public valuation of criminal conduct much more diffuse. The focus would no longer be on the degree of harmfulness of the offence and the offender's culpability, but rather on the extent of the offender's previous convictions. An offender who commits a lesser offence, having repeatedly been convicted of such conduct before, could receive nearly as much condemnation through his increased sentence as someone who has committed a much more harmful and reprehensible act. As a result, the severity of the criminal sanction will no longer reflect recognition of the degree of wrongfulness of criminal acts.

They go on to note that the Halliday Report called for a ceiling on the extent to which sentence severity could be increased on account of prior convictions. The 2003 Act, however, makes no such provision for upper limits. Indeed, it could be interpreted as doing the opposite, since s 143(2) requires *each* previous conviction to be treated as aggravating, if the convictions are considered to be sufficiently recent and related to the current offence.

16.9.2 Offences committed whilst on bail

Section 143(3) of the Criminal Justice Act 2003 provides that if an offence is committed whilst the offender is on bail in respect of another offence, that is an aggravating factor as far as the later offence is concerned. This is so even if the two offences are different in nature or relative seriousness, and even if the accused is in fact acquitted of the first offence. In *R v Thackwray* [2003] EWCA Crim 3362; (2003) *The Times*, 25 November, the defendant was sentenced for an offence committed while he was on bail for another offence; the judge treated that fact as an aggravating feature even though the defendant had been acquitted of the original offence. The Court of Appeal confirmed that this was the correct approach, saying that the fact that he was subsequently acquitted of the offence for which he was on bail made no difference. The fact that he was on bail at the time of the present offence is to be regarded as an aggravating feature, whether or not the defendant was subsequently convicted of that other offence (per Lord Woolf CJ at para 7).

16.9.3 Racial or religious aggravation

The fact that an offence was 'racially or religiously aggravated' must be treated as an aggravating factor which increases the seriousness of the offence (s 145 of the Criminal Justice Act 2003). In *R v Saunders* [2000] 1 Cr App R 458, the Court of Appeal said that where an offence involves racial aggravation, a term of up to two years' custody may be added to the sentence. Also, the presence of racial aggravation may make a custodial sentence appropriate for an offence which would otherwise have merited a non-custodial sentence (per Rose LJ at p 462).

16.9.4 Aggravation related to disability or sexual orientation

Section 146(3) of the Criminal Justice Act 2003 requires the court to treat as an aggravating factors the fact that:

    (a) that, at the time of committing the offence, or immediately before or after doing so, the offender demonstrated towards the victim of the offence hostility based on—

        (i)   the sexual orientation (or presumed sexual orientation) of the victim, or
        (ii) a disability (or presumed disability) of the victim, or

    (b) that the offence is motivated (wholly or partly)—

        (i)   by hostility towards persons who are of a particular sexual orientation, or
        (ii) by hostility towards persons who have a disability or a particular disability.

Under sub-s (4), it is immaterial whether or not the offender's hostility was also based, to any extent, on any other factors apart from disability or sexual orientation.

16.10 MITIGATION RELATING TO THE OFFENDER

Paragraph 1.27 of the Guidelines on Seriousness (see above) makes reference to 'offender mitigation'. Mitigation may be derived from the personal circumstances of the offender. The courts tend to look more favourably on people who have stable homes and secure jobs, partly by giving credit for a past contribution to society and partly because such people have more to lose as a result of acquiring a criminal record (effect-ively a punishment in addition to the sentence imposed by the court).

In appropriate cases, a plea in mitigation should try to explain why the offender has turned to crime. For example, it may well be that a person with no previous convictions suddenly starts committing offences at a time when suffering stress at work or as a result of a family break-up. A related argument is that, if the source of the stress has been removed, the risk of reoffending is negligible. See, for example, *R v Edney* (1994) 15 Cr App R(S) 889.

The age of the offender may be relevant. Account is taken particularly of the youth of an offender, perhaps because the young are more easily led astray. However, in *R v Dodds* (1997) *The Times*, 28 January, the Court of Appeal said that, in a serious case, such as aggravated burglary involving the use of violence, a substantial reduction in sentence should no longer be given because of the offender's youth. It should also be added that where an offence is committed predominantly by young offenders (such as taking cars without the owner's consent), the fact that the offender is young will not amount to mitigation.

The fact that the offender was acting under the influence of drink or drugs is regarded by some as a mitigating factor on the basis that the offender did not know what he was doing. Others, however, regard it as an aggravating factor that the offender deprived himself of self-control.

In some cases, it will be appropriate to consider the likely effect of a particular sentence on people other than the offender. For example, if a single parent is sent to prison, the children may well have to go into the care of the local authority. In *Attorney General's Ref (Nos 132 and 133 of 2004)* [2005] EWCA Crim 354; (2005), *The Times*, 21 March, the Court of Appeal took account of the interests of the children who were being cared for by the offender.

16.10.1 The effectiveness of pleas in mitigation

In *Mitigation: the role of personal factors in sentencing* (Prison Reform Trust, 2007), Jessica Jacobson and Mike Hough (<http://www.prisonreformtrust.org.uk>), con-ducted empirical research into sentencing decisions in a number of Crown Courts (a total of 132 cases involving 162 defendants and 52 sentencers) and concluded that:

- personal mitigation takes many forms. It can, for example, relate to: the offender's past; the offender's circumstances at the time of the offence; the offender's response to the offence and prosecution; and the offender's present and future;
- personal mitigation plays an important part in the sentencing decision; it can be the decisive factor in choosing a community penalty in preference to imprisonment;
- judges cited at least some factor of personal mitigation as relevant to sentencing in almost half of the cases observed in the study;
- in just under a third of the cases where the judge made the role of mitigation explicit, personal mitigation was a major – usually the major – factor which pulled the sentence back from immediate custody;
- in a just over a quarter of the cases observed, mitigation including personal factors resulted in a shorter custodial sentence.

The researchers asked judges to rate the importance of different mitigating factors; they were in agreement about the importance of some forms of personal mitigation, but expressed very mixed views on others. Jacobson and Hough take the view that:

> There is a clear case for structuring judicial discretion as it relates to personal mitigation.
>
> The argument is persuasive that judicial discretion enables sentencers to retain the humanity in sentencing. By implication, the extensive scope for personal mitigation is something to be valued rather than discarded. However, the study has shown that there is plenty of room for idiosyncratic decisions on mitigation, and it seems wrong that judges should apply conflicting principles in their decisions about mitigation.
>
> Our analysis has shown that there are at least four types of factor that sentencers take into account in personal mitigation:
>
> - those that indicate reduced culpability, such as youth or mental health problems, pressing need, previous good character and exceptional disadvantage
> - those that indicate limited risk of further offending – relating to remorse and attempts to make reparation, the offender's circumstances, or steps taken towards rehabilitation
> - those that indicate particular sensibility to punishment, such as the strain of prosecution, the loss of reputation and standing or the fact that the offender is unusually poorly equipped to handle a prison sentence
> - factors that call for clemency, such as the victim's support for the offender, family responsibilities and the 'collateral damage' that imprisonment would inflict on relatives, or the social contribution made by the offender.

They identify a number of matters where there is disagreement and suggest that guidance from the Sentencing Guidelines Council would be helpful. These matters include:

> - whether and why securing or retaining employment should be regarded as a mitigating factor
> - whether disadvantage and social exclusion should be regarded as mitigating factors, and whether advantage should be regarded as an aggravating factor
> - whether and why family and childcare responsibilities should be treated as mitigating factors, and whether fathers should be treated differently from mothers
> - whether offender 'sensibility' to particular punishments should be taken into account, by analogy to the means test applied in unit fine systems
> - to what extent and in what circumstances the prospect of rehabilitation, e.g. through drug treatment, can override the principle of proportionate punishment
> - the scope for personal mitigation a) where there is a plea of not guilty, and b) where the offence is so serious as to make custody inevitable.

Following interviews with the judges, Jacobson and Hough were able to produce a checklist setting out the attributes of a good plea in mitigation (at p 46). The plea should be:

> *Realistic and informed*
>
> - Realism is about acknowledging and dealing with the bad features of the case straight away, before moving on to the other aspects.

- A good plea should be understated, should acknowledge the downsides of a case, and then 'marshal in a logical and coherent way' the positive issues.
- Realism is also about providing 'the hooks on which to hang a sentence' that is considerably more lenient than one would have thought, by providing a 'realistic, intellectual framework to justify the sentence'.
- The good advocates are those who 'give you pause for thought, lead you by the hand and persuade you that you don't have to send him to prison, and that it would be wrong to do so: not for emotional but for intellectual reasons'.

Creative

- A good plea 'draws your attention to matters you have not previously considered, or lays appropriate emphasis on matters that you have not thought important'.
- Good pleas are those that 'really go for it': there is a 'real art' in persuading someone to do something that is more lenient than he would otherwise do.
- Under the pressure of a long court list, 'skilful mitigation makes the task of identifying those unusual features or novel features [of a case] that much easier'. This is a matter of 'giving some life to the sort of formulaic mitigation that most practitioners can do in their sleep'.
- If mitigation is to have an impact, it needs to contain something 'slightly out of the ordinary [that] sounds genuine', and to engage the interest of the judge.

Structured

- A good advocate will 'enumerate in a logical order' the main points of the case, without adopting a 'hectoring manner'.
- A good plea is 'relevant, concise, well-informed and realistic'.
- A good plea has 'tersity (sic), lack of repetition, clarity and relevance to the nature of the offence'.
- A good plea is organised, succinct, in bullet points. Attractive presentation counts, and there is no need for 'hours of oratory'.

16.11 RULE THAT THE DEFENDANT SHOULD BE SENTENCED ONLY FOR OFFENCES OF WHICH HE HAS BEEN CONVICTED

It is an important principle of sentencing that the offender should only be sentenced for offences to which he has pleaded guilty or been found guilty. For example, if the offender is charged with an indictment containing a count alleging wounding with intent (s 18 of the Offences Against the Person Act 1861) and an alternative count alleging unlawful wounding (s 20), and the jury acquits the offender of the s 18 offence but convicts him of the s 20 offence, the judge must ensure that the sentence reflects the fact that the offender is guilty only of the lesser offence. This is so even if the judge disagrees with the verdict of the jury. The same applies where the prosecution agree to accept a plea of guilty to a lesser offence and the more serious offence is left on the file or the prosecution offer no evidence in respect of it (see *R v Stubbs* (1989) 88 Cr App R 53).

Moreover, the judge must not sentence the offender on the basis that he has committed similar offences on other occasions, even if the circumstances of the offence of which the defendant has been convicted (or even admissions made by the defendant to the police) suggest that the offence of which the defendant has been convicted is just part of a course of criminal conduct (*R v Ayensu* (1982) 4 Cr App R(S) 248; *R v Reeves* (1983) 5 Cr App R(S) 292).

In *R v Perkins* (1994) 15 Cr App R(S) 402, the defendant was accused of breaching a notice under planning legislation preventing him from tipping waste onto certain land. The charge alleged a breach of the notice on one particular day. However, the judge imposed a fine on the basis not of one incident, but on the basis that breaches of the notice had been taking place over an extensive period of several months. The Court of Appeal said that since the basis of the appellant's conviction was a single breach of the notice, that should be the basis of the sentence. The appellant had not admitted other breaches of the notice and so should only have been sentenced for the offence of which he had actually been convicted.

The same principle applies to compensation orders. In *R v Crutchley and Tonks* (1994) 15 Cr App R(S) 627, the offenders pleaded guilty to specimen offences arising out of a social security fraud; the appellants accepted that the charges to which they had pleaded guilty were sample counts representing a substantial number of other offences. However, no other offences were formally taken into consideration. The compensation order made by the Crown Court reflected the whole amount lost as a result of the fraud, not just the offences to which the appellants had pleaded guilty. The Court of Appeal held that there was no power to make such an order since it was not open to the court to make a compensation order in respect of loss or damage arising from offences which, even though admitted by the defendant, have not been subject to a conviction and have not been taken into consideration.

16.11.1 Offences taken into consideration (TICs)

It is very common for an offender to ask for offences with which he is not charged to be taken into consideration when he is sentenced for the offences with which he is charged and to which he pleads guilty. These other offences are colloquially known as 'TICs'.

Suppose that a person is arrested for an offence and when he is interviewed by the police admits that he has committed a large number of similar offences. In such a case, the defendant is usually charged with a number of the offences which he has admitted. The prosecution also draw up a list of the other offences which the offender has admitted to the police. The offender is asked to sign the list to confirm that he wishes those offences to be taken into consideration. Any offences which he subsequently denies should be deleted from the list. When the prosecution summarise the facts of the case, they will refer to the list of TICs and the court will ask the offender to confirm that he wishes the offences to be taken into consideration.

The offender does not stand convicted of offences which are taken into consideration. This means that the maximum sentence which the court may impose is fixed by the offences to which the offender has pleaded guilty or of which he has been found guilty.

It follows from this that no separate penalty can be imposed in respect of an offence which has been taken into consideration. However, TICs are regarded as associated offences under s 161 of the Powers of Criminal Courts (Sentencing) Act 2000 and so the presence of TICs may result in an increase in the sentence imposed for the offences of which the defendant actually stands convicted.

Because the offender does not stand convicted of offences which have been taken into consideration, the doctrine of *autrefois convict* does not apply to those offences (*R v Nicholson* [1947] 2 All ER 535). Thus, in theory, the offender could subsequently be prosecuted for offences which have been taken into consideration. However, such action would only be taken in exceptional circumstances.

There is no statutory basis for the practice of taking offences into consideration. However, it enables the police to close their files on the offences which have been dealt with in this way (which has a good effect on their 'clear up rate'). As far as the offender is concerned, although the existence of TICs may result in a slightly increased sentence, the defendant is able to 'wipe the slate clean' (which is a good indicator of remorse) at a minimal cost in terms of increased sentence. The amount of the increase will almost certainly be considerably less than the sentence would have been had the offences been prosecuted separately.

The court has a discretion whether or not to comply with the defendant's request to take offences into consideration. It is generally regarded as inappropriate for offences to be taken into consideration if they are of a different type to the offence(s) of which the defendant actually stands convicted. In *R v Simons* [1953] 1 WLR 1014, it was held that if a court has no jurisdiction to try a particular offence, it ought not to take that offence into account; it follows from this that magistrates should not take into consideration offences which are triable only on indictment. In *R v Collins* [1947] KB 560, it was held that a court should not take into consideration offences which carry endorsement or disqualification from driving unless the offences of which the offender stands convicted also carry such penalty.

In *R v Miles* [2006] EWCA Crim 256; (2006), *The Times*, 10 April, the Court of Appeal made some observations about offences taken into consideration. Sir Igor Judge P, at paras 10 and 11, said:

> In relation to offences taken into consideration, we have these observations: the sentence is intended to reflect a defendant's overall criminality. Offences cannot be taken into consideration without the express agreement of the offender. That is an essential prerequisite. The offender is pleading guilty to the offences. If they are to be taken into account (and the court is not obliged to take them into account) they have relevance to the overall criminality. When assessing the significance of TICs, as they are called, of course the court is likely to attach weight to the demonstrable fact that the offender has assisted the police, particularly if they are enabled to clear up offences which might not otherwise be brought to justice. It is also true that co-operative behaviour of that kind will often provide its own very early indication of guilt, and usually means that no further proceedings at all need be started. They may also serve to demonstrate a genuine determination by the offender . . . to wipe the slate clean, so that when he emerges from whatever sentence is imposed on him, he can put his past completely behind him, without having worry or concern that offences may be revealed as that he is then returned to court.
>
> As in so many aspects of sentencing, of course, the way in which the court deals with offences to be taken into consideration depends on context. In some cases the offences taken into consideration will end up by adding nothing or nothing very much to the sentence which the court would otherwise impose. On the other hand, offences taken into consider-

ation may aggravate the sentence and lead to a substantial increase in it. For example, the offences may show a pattern of criminal activity which suggests careful planning or deliberate rather than casual involvement in a crime. They may show an offence or offences committed on bail, after an earlier arrest. They may show a return to crime immediately after the offender has been before the court and given a chance that, by committing the crime, he has immediately rejected. There are many situations where similar issues may arise. One advantage to the defendant, of course, is that once an offence is taken into consideration, there is no likely risk of any further prosecution for it. If, on the other hand, it is not, that risk remains. In short, offences taken into consideration are indeed taken into consideration. They are not ignored or expunged or disregarded.

16.11.2 'Specimen' or 'sample' counts

A 'specimen' (or 'sample') count is where the defendant is charged with one or more offences occurring on specific occasions, but the prosecution allege that such conduct was representative of other criminal conduct of the same kind on other occasions which are not the subject of specific charges. Take, for example, the case of a defendant who uses a stolen credit card on 20 occasions: if the indictment contains three counts relating to the use of the card, those three counts would be sample counts.

In a number of cases, such as *R v Huchison* [1972] 1 WLR 398, *R v McKenzie* (1984) 6 Cr App R(S) 99 and *R v Burfoot* (1990) 12 Cr App R(S) 252, the Court of Appeal made it clear that the offender could only be sentenced on the basis that the counts of which he stood convicted were sample counts, illustrative of an overall course of conduct (rather than being sentenced on the basis that he had only committed the offences of which he stood convicted), if the offender accepted that the convictions represented an overall course of conduct.

In *R v Clark* [1996] 2 Cr App R(S) 351, the appellant was convicted of a single count of indecent assault. This single count was said by the prosecution to reflect a series of offences committed over a two-year period. However, the appellant did not admit committing any offence. The judge passed sentence on the basis that the defendant had committed a series of offences. The Court of Appeal said that, having been convicted on a single count particularising a single act and not having admitted any offence beyond that, the appellant could only be sentenced on the basis of that single act.

In *R v Kidd; R v Canavan* [1998] 1 WLR 604, the Court of Appeal went further and effectively put a stop to the practice of using counts as 'specimen counts'. The court held that the defendant can only be sentenced for an offence which has been proved against him (that is, where he pleads guilty to it or is found guilty of it) or which he has asked the court to take into consideration when passing sentence (per Lord Bingham CJ at p 607). His Lordship thought it 'inconsistent with principle that a defendant should be sentenced for offences neither admitted nor proved by verdict' (p 608). Therefore, when passing sentence, the court must not take account of the fact that the charges are said by the prosecution to be 'specimen' or 'sample' charges. If the prosecution want other incidents to be taken account of, those other incidents must be the subject of individual charges (or offences 'taken into consideration' under the procedure set out in the previous section). In *R v Rosenburg* [1999] 1 Cr App R(S) 365 and *R v T (Michael Patrick)* [1999] 1 Cr App R(S) 419, the Court of Appeal repeated that a defendant should not be sentenced for offences of which he has not been convicted (whether by pleading guilty or being found guilty) and which he has not asked the court to take into consideration under the TIC procedure. If the prosecution wish to rely on a continuous course of conduct, they must give a sufficient number of instances of that conduct in distinct counts in the indictment.

In *R v Smith; R v Tovey* [2005] EWCA Crim 530; [2005] 2 Cr App R (S) 100, the Court of Appeal noted that the proper approach is that identified in *R v Canavan* [1998] 1 Cr App R 70, namely that an offender should be sentenced only for an offence which has been proved against him or admitted by him. That approach is not to be qualified based on reasonable inferences drawn by the judge from the evidence he or she has heard (per Lord Woolf CJ at para 16). Where an offender pleads guilty and admits that his plea embraces a wider course of conduct than that specifically charged, that is the equivalent of an informal invitation to the court to take into consideration the other offences and a sentencing judge can properly proceed to pass sentence on the wider basis admitted (para 22). The court added that, where the evidence of the prosecution and defence does not raise different issues in respect of all the acts said to be part of the same activity, it is perfectly acceptable to charge the defendant with the single activity representing more than one act, provided that there is no unfairness caused to the defendant. The court approved *Barton v DPP* [2001] EWHC Admin 223; (2001) 165 JP 779, where there were 94 takings from a cash register over a period of a year; the Divisional Court concluded that it was permissible to charge the whole course of conduct as a continuous offence because the defendant had no specific explanation for the individual takings and put forward the same defence for all the takings (and so there was no discernible prejudice or unfairness to the defendant). The court in *Smith* added that, in preparing the indictment, the prosecution should always have in mind, in a situation of multiple offending, the need to provide the sentencing judge with sufficient examples (and no more) of the offending to enable the judge to impose a sentence which properly reflects the offender's criminal behaviour (para 33). It is also important to draft the counts that are included in the indictment so as to establish the period during which the offending occurred (e.g. whether the offences occurred regularly over a significant period). With offences involving money, the period over which offences occurred can be as significant as the total sum involved (para 34).

If the prosecution do use specimen counts, but the offender pleads guilty to an indictment on an agreed factual basis that it charges a course of conduct involving multiple offences, he is admitting to having committed those multiple offences and may therefore be sentenced accordingly (*Attorney General's Reference (No 82 of 2002)* [2003] EWCA Crim 1078; [2003] 2 Cr App R(S) 115).

16.12 REASONS FOR SENTENCING DECISIONS

Section 174 of the Criminal Justice Act 2003 imposes a general statutory duty on courts to give reasons for, and to explain the effect of, the sentence passed. Section 174(1) provides that:

> . . . any court passing sentence on an offender—

(a) must state in open court, in ordinary language and in general terms, its reasons for deciding on the sentence passed, and

(b) must explain to the offender in ordinary language—

    (i) the effect of the sentence,

    (ii) where the offender is required to comply with any order of the court forming part of the sentence, the effects of non-compliance with the order,

    (iii) any power of the court, on the application of the offender or any other person, to vary or review any order of the court forming part of the sentence, and

    (iv) where the sentence consists of or includes a fine, the effects of failure to pay the fine.

This requires the court to explain its reasons for passing a particular sentence in non-technical terms. The aim of this is to ensure that the offender and other interested parties (such as the victim of the offence, and the family and friends of the victim) understand why the particular sentence was chosen by the court. The court is also required to explain to the offender what the sentence requires him to do, what will happen if he fails to comply, and any power that exists to vary or review the sentence. Section 174(2) requires the court to deal with certain additional specific matters. Under sub-s (2)(a), where the Sentencing Guidelines Council has issued definitive guidelines relevant to the sentence, and the court departs from those guidelines, it must give reasons for doing so.

In the case of a custodial sentence or a community sentence, the court must explain why it regards the offence as being sufficiently serious to warrant such a sentence (s 174(2)(b) and (c)).

By virtue of s 174(2)(d), where, as a result of taking account of a plea of guilty, the court imposes a less severe sentence than it would otherwise have done, it must state that fact.

Under s 174(2)(e), the court must mention any aggravating or mitigating factors which the court has regarded as being of particular importance.

In *Attorney General's References (Nos 115 and 116 of 2007)* [2008] EWCA Crim 795, the Court of Appeal observed that the requirements of s 174(2)(a) are not an idle formality. The public, the victim, and the defendant are entitled to know why there has been a departure from sentencing guidelines. If the judge is going to pass a non-custodial sentence, where it is obvious that the guidelines require a custodial sentence, and the judge knows that the victim might not understand it, it is essential that the reasons for the departure are set out, so the victim and public can understand why the court is departing from the norm. The giving of reasons strengthens the confidence of the public in the administration of justice. Moreover, the thought process of producing reasons can point to a potential error in adopting the course of action contemplated.

16.13 SENTENCING THE DEFENDANT IN HIS ABSENCE

Section 11 of the Magistrates' Courts Act 1980 empowers a magistrates' court to try a defendant in his absence in certain circumstances (see Chapter 5). This power extends to sentencing a defendant who has been convicted in his absence. The power to sentence a defendant in his absence is subject to two restrictions:

- a person may not be sentenced to a custodial sentence in his absence (s 11(3)); and
- a person may not have any disqualification imposed on him in his absence (s 11(4)).

Section 11(4) applies to any disqualification and so would include, for example, the most common disqualification, namely, disqualification from driving under the Road Traffic Offenders Act 1988, but would also include, for example, disqualification from keeping an animal under the Animal Welfare Act 2006. However, under s 11(5) – added by s 54(6) of the Criminal Justice and Immigration Act 2008 – this restriction will only apply where the proceedings were commenced by the laying of an information or by the issue of a written charge and requisition (and so do not apply to cases where the accused was arrested and charged).

If a custodial sentence or a disqualification is imposed in the absence of the defendant, the order is a nullity and would be quashed by the Divisional Court on an application for judicial review (*R v Llandrindod Wells Justices ex p Gibson* [1968] 1 WLR 598).

Where the defendant has pleaded guilty by post under s 12 of the Magistrates' Courts Act 1980, the court will have to adjourn the case if it is minded to impose a custodial sentence or to make an order involving disqualification. There is no power to issue an arrest warrant against the defendant unless the court has adjourned once and the defendant fails to appear on the occasion of the adjourned hearing.

Where the defendant was tried in his absence under s 11, the court has the power to issue a warrant for the defendant's arrest under s 13(1) if the offence is an imprisonable one (s 13(3)(a)) or if the defendant has been convicted of a non-imprisonable offence and the court is minded to impose a disqualification on him (s 13(3)(b)).

16.14 DUTIES OF THE ADVOCATES

In cases such as *R v Hartrey* (1993) 14 Cr App R(S) 507 and in *R v Street* (1997) 161 JP 281, the Court of Appeal reiterated that it is the duty of both prosecution and defence counsel to acquaint themselves with the sentencing powers of the court in the particular case, and to correct the judge if he purports to pass a sentence which is unlawful. In *Hartrey*, Wright J said (at p 510):

> without in any way wishing to derogate from the responsibility of the judge himself to be alert to the limitations imposed upon him by statute, we stress that it is the duty of both prosecuting and defence counsel to inform themselves of the extent of the court's powers in any case in which they are instructed, to know what options are open to the trial judge and to correct him if, as it is unfortunately only too easy to do in the morass of legislation which governs the subject, he should make a mistake. Prosecuting counsel, in particular, is not there merely to recite a brief resume of the facts, to produce the antecedent history of the defendant, and thereafter to take no further interest in the proceedings.

In *Attorney General's Reference (No 52 of 2003)* [2003] EWCA Crim 3731; (2003) *The Times*, 12 December, Lord Woolf CJ (at para 5) emphasised that it is the duty of prosecuting counsel to draw relevant guideline cases (or, it should be added, guidelines issued by the Sentencing Guidelines Council) to the judge's attention:

> It is part of the duty of prosecuting counsel to draw to the judge's attention before sentence is passed any relevant guideline cases and to have copies available for him (or her) to look at if he (or she) wishes to do so. The judge, if he (or she) is unaware of the authorities or needs reminding of them, should take advantage of that offer so that he (or she) can have the guidelines well in mind when he (or she) comes to pass sentence . . .

In *R v Cain* [2006] EWCA Crim 3233; [2007] 2 Cr App R (S) 25, Lord Phillips CJ again had cause to admonish counsel. At paras 1–3, his Lordship said:

> It is of course the duty of a judge to impose a lawful sentence, but sentencing has become a complex matter and a judge will often not see the papers very long before the hearing and does not have the time for preparation that advocates should enjoy. In these circumstances a judge relies on the advocates to assist him with sentencing. It is unacceptable for advocates not to ascertain and be prepared to assist the judge with the legal restrictions on the sentence that he can impose on their clients.
>
> This duty is not restricted to defence advocates. We emphasise the fact that advocates for the prosecution also owe a duty to assist the judge at the stage of sentencing. It is not satisfactory for a prosecuting advocate, having secured a conviction, to sit back and leave sentencing to the defence. Nor can an advocate, when appearing for the prosecution for the purpose of sentence on a plea of guilty, limit the assistance that he provides to the court to the outlining of the facts and details of the defendant's previous convictions.
>
> The advocate for the prosecution should always be ready to assist the court by drawing attention to any statutory provisions that govern the court's sentencing powers. It is the duty of the prosecuting advocate to ensure that the judge does not, through inadvertence, impose a sentence that is outside his powers. The advocate for the prosecution should also be in a position to offer to draw the judge's attention to any relevant sentencing guidelines or guideline decisions of this court.

At para 5, his Lordship confirmed that these principles are equally applicable to those appearing for prosecution and defence in the magistrates' court.

In a similar vein, para B4 of the *Attorney General's Guidelines on the Acceptance of Pleas and the Prosecutor's Role in the Sentencing Exercise* (<www.attorneygeneral. gov.uk>) says:

> The appropriate disposal of a criminal case after conviction is as much a part of the criminal justice process as the trial of guilt or innocence. The prosecution advocate represents the public interest, and should be ready to assist the court to reach its decision as to the appropriate sentence. This will include drawing the court's attention to:
>
> - any victim personal statement or other information available to the prosecution advocate as to the impact of the offence on the victim;
> - where appropriate, to any evidence of the impact of the offending on a community;
> - any statutory provisions relevant to the offender and the offences under consideration;
> - any relevant sentencing guidelines and guideline cases; and

- the aggravating and mitigating factors of the offence under consideration.

The prosecution advocate may also offer assistance to the court by making submissions, in the light of all these factors, as to the appropriate sentencing range.

In all cases, it is the prosecution advocate's duty to apply for appropriate ancillary orders, such as anti-social behaviour orders and confiscation orders. When considering which ancillary orders to apply for, prosecution advocates must always have regard to the victim's needs, including the question of his or her future protection.

16.15 DEFERRING SENTENCE

Section 1 of the Powers of Criminal Courts (Sentencing) Act 2000 empowers the Crown Court and magistrates' courts to defer passing sentence on an offender. Under s 1(4), the maximum period of deferment is six months. The purpose of the deferment (under s 1(1)) must be to enable the court, when passing sentence, to have regard to:

(a) his conduct after conviction (including, where appropriate, the making by him of reparation for his offence); or
(b) any change in his circumstances.

Under s 1(3), sentence may be deferred only if:

(a) the offender consents;
(b) the offender undertakes to comply with any requirements as to his conduct during the period of the deferment that the court considers it appropriate to impose; and
(c) the court is satisfied, having regard to the nature of the offence and the character and circumstances of the offender, that it would be in the interests of justice to exercise the power.

A court which defers passing sentence on an offender must not then remand him, and so when released he is not on bail (s 1(6)). If the offender does not return to court on the specified date, the court may issue a summons or an arrest warrant to secure his attendance (s 1(7)).

The court may deal with the offender before the end of the period of deferment if satisfied that he has failed to comply with one or more requirements imposed under s 1(3)(b) (s 1B(1)(b)), or if, during that period, he is convicted in Great Britain of any offence (s 1C(1)). Where the offender has reoffended during the period of deferment, the court which sentences him for the later offence may also deal with him for the offence(s) for which sentence has been deferred (s 1C(3)); however, this power cannot be exercised by a magistrates' court if the court which deferred sentence was the Crown Court (s 1C(3)(a)), and if the Crown Court passed sentence in respect of an offence where sentence was deferred by a magistrates' court, it cannot pass a sentence which could not have been passed by the magistrates' court had they not deferred sentence (s 1C(3)(b)).

Under s 1D(2), when the court deals with the offender at the end of the period of deferment (or earlier if he does not comply with the requirements or commits another offence), it can deal with him in any way in which it could have done had sentence not been deferred (including, where the offence is triable either way and the court which deferred sentence was a magistrates' court, committing him to the Crown Court for sentence).

Given the comparatively short period of deferment, it may well be that the offender is charged with a further offence allegedly committed during the period of the deferment but the offender has not been convicted of that offence before the date when the court passes sentence in respect of the original offence. In such a case, the allegation of a later offence should be ignored by the court dealing with the offence for which sentence was deferred. It is only where the offender has been *convicted* of an offence committed during the period of deferment that account can be taken of the later offence when sentence is passed for the offence in respect for which sentence was deferred. An unproved allegation of a further offence should be disregarded (*R v Aquilina* (1989) 11 Cr App R(S) 431).

R v George [1984] 1 WLR 1082 was decided at a time when the statutory provisions relating to deferral of sentence were slightly different, but most of the comments made by the Court of Appeal about deferring sentence remain valid:

- the power to defer is not to be used as an easy way out for a court which is unable to make up its mind about the correct sentence;
- it is essential that the deferring court should make a careful note of the purposes for which the sentence is being deferred and what steps, if any, it expects the defendant to take during the period of deferment. Ideally the defendant himself should be given notice in writing of what he is expected to do or refrain from doing, so that there can be no doubt in his mind what is expected of him;
- when the court comes to deal with the offender at the end of the period of deferment, it must determine if the defendant has substantially conformed or attempted to conform with the proper expectations of the deferring court. If he has, then the defendant may legitimately expect that an immediate custodial sentence will not be imposed. If he has not, then the court should be careful to state with precision in what respects he has failed.

It will always be a requirement that the offender does not commit any further offences, but merely refraining from committing further offences will not be enough. Requirements that may imposed when sentence is deferred are at the discretion of the court, but may include (for example) making a real effort to find work (*R v George*).

In *Attorney General's Reference (No 22 of 1992)* [1994] 1 All ER 105, it was held that a deferred sentence is a sentence (as defined by s 50(1) of the Criminal Appeal Act 1968) for the purposes of appeal, and so the Attorney General may use his powers under s 36 of the Criminal Justice Act 1988 to appeal to the Court of Appeal on the ground that it is too lenient.

The Sentencing Guidelines Council, in its guidance on the sentencing regime established by the Criminal Justice act 2003 (<http://www.sentencing-guidelines.gov.uk/docs/New_sentences_guideline1.pdf>), gave the following guidance on deferred sentences:

B. Use of Deferred Sentences

1.2.6 Under the new framework, there is a wider range of sentencing options open to the courts, including the increased availability of suspended sentences, and deferred sentences are likely to be used in very limited circumstances. A deferred sentence enables the court to review the conduct of the defendant before passing sentence, having first prescribed certain requirements. It also provides several opportunities for an offender to have some influence as to the sentence passed—

(a)   it tests the commitment of the offender not to reoffend;

(b)   it gives the offender an opportunity to do something where progress can be shown within a short period;

(c)   it provides the offender with an opportunity to behave or refrain from behaving in a particular way that will be relevant to sentence.

1.2.7 Given the new power to require undertakings and the ability to enforce those undertakings before the end of the period of deferral, the decision to defer sentence should be predominantly for a small group of cases at either the custody threshold or the community sentence threshold where the sentencer feels that there would be particular value in giving the offender the opportunities listed because, if the offender complies with the requirements, a different sentence will be justified at the end of the deferment period. This could be a community sentence instead of a custodial sentence or a fine or discharge instead of a community sentence. It may, rarely, enable a custodial sentence to be suspended rather than imposed immediately.

The use of deferred sentences should be predominantly for a small group of cases close to a significant threshold where, should the defendant be prepared to adapt his behaviour in a way clearly specified by the sentencer, the court may be prepared to impose a lesser sentence.

1.2.8 A court may impose any conditions during the period of deferment that it considers appropriate. These could be specific requirements as set out in the provisions for community sentences, or requirements that are drawn more widely. These should be specific, measurable conditions so that the offender knows exactly what is required and the court can assess compliance; the restriction on liberty should be limited to ensure that the offender has a reasonable expectation of being able to comply whilst maintaining his or her social responsibilities.

1.2.9 Given the need for clarity in the mind of the offender and the possibility of sentence by another court, the court should give a clear indication (and make a written record) of the type of sentence it would be minded to impose if it had not decided to defer and ensure that the offender understands the consequences of failure to comply with the court's wishes during the deferral period.

When deferring sentence, the sentencer must make clear the consequence of not complying with any requirements and should indicate the type of sentence it would be minded to impose. Sentencers should impose specific, measurable conditions that do not involve a serious restriction on liberty.

16.16 REHABILITATION OF OFFENDERS: SPENT CONVICTIONS

The Rehabilitation of Offenders Act 1974 allows a person who has been convicted of an offence to regard himself as 'rehabilitated' after a period of time has elapsed and the conviction is deemed to be 'spent' (s 4(1)). However, s 7(2)(a) of the Rehabilitation of Offenders Act 1974 says that the provisions of the Act do not apply to criminal proceedings. Nonetheless, para I.6 of the *Consolidated Practice Direction* sets out the following principles:

> I.6.4 ... both court and advocates should never [refer] to a spent conviction when such reference can reasonably be avoided.

> I.6.5 After a verdict of guilty the court must be provided with a statement of the defendant's record for the purposes of sentence. The record supplied should contain all previous convictions, but those which are spent should, so far as practicable, be marked as such.

> I.6.6 No one should refer in open court to a spent conviction without the authority of the judge, which authority should not be given unless the interests of justice so require.

> I.6.7 When passing sentence the judge should make no reference to a spent conviction unless it is necessary to do so for the purpose of explaining the sentence to be passed.

The rehabilitation period (that is, the time which must elapse before the conviction is regarded as spent) depends on the sentence imposed for the original offence. In some cases, the rehabilitation period is shortened if the offender was under 18 at the date of conviction. Some of the main rehabilitation periods (set out in s 5) are as follows:

- A custodial sentence of 6 months – 2½ years (30 months): 10 years
- A custodial sentence of 6 months or less: 7 years
- Community Order; fine: 5 years
- Conditional discharge: 1 year
- Absolute discharge: 6 months

The rehabilitation period for a sentence of imprisonment is the same whether the imprisonment is immediate or suspended. A conviction which resulted in a sentence of more than 2½ years can never be spent (s 5(1)(a) and (b)).

If the offender is convicted of a further offence during the rehabilitation period, the rehabilitation period for the first offence continues to run until the expiry of the rehabilitation period for the subsequent offence (s 6(4)).

Chapter 17

Adult offenders: custodial sentences

In this chapter, we examine the sentences of imprisonment (immediate and suspended) which may be imposed on an offender who has attained the age of 21.

17.1 STATUTORY CRITERIA FOR IMPOSING CUSTODIAL SENTENCES

The Criminal Justice Act (CJA) 2003 replaces earlier legislation on the imposition of custodial sentences. However, it maintains the position (established by earlier legislation) that a custodial sentence may only be passed where no other sentence would be appropriate; in other words, the 'custody threshold' must have been crossed.

17.1.1 The custody threshold under the Criminal Justice Act 2003

The threshold test is set out in s 152(2), which provides:

> The court must not pass a custodial sentence unless it is of the opinion that the offence, or the combination of the offence and one or more offences associated with it, was so serious that neither a fine alone nor a community sentence can be justified for the offence.

This is subject to the rider contained in s 152(3), that:

> Nothing in sub-section (2) prevents the court from passing a custodial sentence on the offender if—
>
> (a) he fails to express his willingness to comply with a requirement which is proposed by the court to be included in a community order and which requires an expression of such willingness, or
> (b) he fails to comply with an order under section 161(2) (pre-sentence drug testing).

The similarity between s 152 of the 2003 Act and the earlier legislation on custodial sentences means that the case law decided under the former provisions remains valid when the courts consider how to apply the new provision.

A very important case (decided under earlier legislation) on the 'custody threshold' was *R v Howells* [1999] 1 WLR 307. In it, Lord Bingham CJ gave detailed guidance on the application of the test of whether an offence is so serious that only a custodial sentence can be justified. Lord Bingham described the problem of dealing with cases which are on the borderline of the custody threshold as 'one of the most elusive problems of criminal sentencing'.

The earlier legislation had been interpreted by Lawton LJ in *R v Bradbourn* (1985) 7 Cr App R(S) 180, at 183 thus:

> . . . the phrase, 'so serious that a non-custodial sentence cannot be justified' comes to this: the kind of offence which . . . would make right-thinking members of the public, knowing all the facts, feel that justice had not been done by the passing of any sentence other than a custodial one.

This approach was approved in *R v Cox* [1993] 1 WLR 188. However, in *Howells*, Lord Bingham said that this test is unhelpful, since the sentencing court has no means of ascertaining the views of right-thinking members of the public and inevitably attributes to such right-thinking members its own views. So, when applying this test, the sentencing court is doing little more than reflect its own opinion whether justice would or would not be done and be seen to be done by the passing of a non-custodial sentence. Thus, the test is saying little more than 'a custodial sentence is justified if the court thinks it is justified'. His Lordship then went on to offer some general guidance on the process for determining which side of the line a particular case may fall. His comments (at pages 311–12) are worth quoting at length:

> . . . in approaching cases which are on or near the custody threshold courts will usually find it helpful to begin by considering the nature and extent of the defendant's criminal intention and the nature and extent of any injury or damage caused to the victim. Other things being equal, an offence which is deliberate and premeditated will usually be more serious than one which is spontaneous and unpremeditated or which involves an excessive response to provocation; an offence which inflicts personal injury or mental trauma, particularly if permanent, will usually be more serious than one which inflicts financial loss only . . .
>
> In deciding whether to impose a custodial sentence in borderline cases the sentencing court will ordinarily take account of matters relating to the offender. (a) The court will have regard to an offender's admission of responsibility for the offence, particularly if reflected in a plea of guilty tendered at the earliest opportunity and accompanied by hard evidence of genuine remorse, as shown (for example) by an expression of regret to the victim and an offer of compensation . . . (b) Where offending has been fuelled by addiction to drink or drugs, the court will be inclined to look more favourably on an offender who has already demonstrated (by taking practical steps to that end) a genuine, self-motivated determination to address his addiction. (c) Youth and immaturity, while affording no defence, will often justify a less rigorous penalty than would be appropriate for an adult. (d) Some measure of leniency will ordinarily be extended to offenders of previous good character, the more so if there is evidence of positive good character (such as a solid employment record or faithful discharge of family duties) as opposed to a mere absence of previous convictions. It will sometimes be appropriate to take account of family responsibilities, or physical or mental disability. (e) While the court will never impose a custodial sentence unless satisfied that it is

necessary to do so, there will be even greater reluctance to impose a custodial sentence on an offender who has never before served such a sentence.

Courts should always bear in mind that criminal sentences are in almost every case intended to protect the public, whether by punishing the offender or reforming him, or deterring him and others, or all of these things. Courts cannot and should not be unmindful of the important public dimension of criminal sentencing and the importance of maintaining public confidence in the sentencing system.

As regards the first of the factors listed by Lord Bingham, it should be borne in mind that s 144 of the Criminal Justice Act 2003 requires the court to take account of the fact that the defendant pleaded guilty, and to have regard to the stage in the proceedings at which he indicated his intention to plead guilty (see Chapter 16).

So far as deterrence is concerned, in *Attorney General's References (Nos 62 and 63 of 1997); R v McMaster* [1998] 2 Cr App R(S) 300, the Court of Appeal referred to the need for sentences to have a proper deterrent effect on those who embark on brutal attacks. In a similar vein, in *R v Cunningham* [1993] 1 WLR 183, it was held that the sentencing judge is entitled to take the need for deterrence into account (per Lord Taylor CJ at p 186). His Lordship went on to say (at p 187) that prevalence of the particular kind of offence is a legitimate factor in determining the length of the custodial sentence to be passed, since the 'seriousness of an offence is clearly affected by how many people it harms and to what extent'.

It should be emphasised that, in assessing the seriousness of the offence, the court should consider the facts of the case and not just the label which is attached to the offence. For example, although most cases involving the burglary of a dwelling house will result in a custodial sentence, domestic burglary should not be regarded as automatically so serious that a custodial sentence is justified.

Where the offender is convicted of two or more offences, the court should consider the offences together and should decide whether the combination of offences is such that a custodial sentence is justified. In *R v Oliver and Little* [1993] 1 WLR 177 (at 182), the Court of Appeal considered what should be done where an offender is convicted of a number of offences, some of which merit a custodial sentence and some of which do not. It was held that, once an offender has qualified for a custodial sentence, the court is not precluded from passing, on the same occasion, custodial sentences for offences which did not themselves satisfy the statutory requirements. However, it would usually be inappropriate for consecutive sentences to be passed for offences which did not themselves satisfy the requirements relating to custody (and so those sentences should be concurrent with the sentences for the offences which do merit custody, not adding to the total period of custody to be served).

In *R v Oliver and Little*, the Court of Appeal also noted that there may well be cases where, notwithstanding that the offence itself passes the custody threshold, there is sufficient mitigation to lead the court to impose a community sentence instead. This mirrors the approach taken in *R v Cox* [1993] 1 WLR 188, where the Court of Appeal pointed out that even if the court decides that an offence is sufficiently serious to justify the imposition of a custodial sentence, the court is not prevented from imposing a non-custodial sentence in the light of mitigating circumstances. In this connection, it should be noted that s 166(1) provides that nothing in ss 152, 153 or 157 (imposing custodial sentences) prevents a court from mitigating an offender's sentence by taking into account any such matters as, in the opinion of the court, are relevant in mitigation of sentence. Moreover, s 166(2) provides that s 152(2):

> does not prevent a court, after taking into account such matters, from passing a community sentence even though it is of the opinion that the offence, or the combination of the offence and one or more offences associated with it, was so serious that a community sentence could not normally be justified for the offence.

In *R v Oliver and Little*, the court also considered the approach to be taken where a court is re-sentencing the offender for an earlier offence (for example, where the offender commits an offence during the currency of a community order and is re-sentenced for the original offence). The Court of Appeal said that if a further offence is committed while the community order was in force, and the defendant was brought to court for sentence, he would have deprived himself of much of the mitigation, such as good character, genuine remorse, isolated lapse and similar considerations, which had led the original court to pass a community rather than a custodial sentence (per Lord Taylor CJ at p 182).

Severe prison over-crowding has led the courts to emphasise the importance of alternatives to custody in appropriate cases. In *R v Kefford* [2002] EWCA Crim 519; [2002] 2 Cr App R(S) 106, Lord Woolf (at paras 7 and 10) said:

> Nothing that we say in this judgment is intended to deter courts from sending to prison for the appropriate period those who commit offences involving violence or intimidation or other grave crimes. Offences of this nature, particularly if they are committed against vulnerable members of the community undermine the public's sense of safety and the courts must play their part in protecting the public from these categories of offences. There are, however, other categories of offences where a community punishment or a fine can be sometimes a more appropriate form of sentence than imprisonment . . . In the case of economic crimes, for example obtaining undue credit by fraud, prison is not necessarily the only appropriate form of punishment. Particularly in the case of those who have no record of previous offending, the very fact of having to appear before a court can be a significant punishment. Certainly, having to perform a form of community punishment can be a very salutary way of making it clear that crime does not pay, particularly if a community punishment order is combined with a curfew order. In the appropriate cases, it can be better that an offender repays his debt to society by performing some useful task for the public than spending a short time in prison . . .

Similarly, in *R v Baldwin* [2002] EWCA Crim 2647; (2002) *The Times*, 22 November, Lord Woolf CJ (at para 9) said:

> It is not today the practice to use the penalty of a fine as frequently as it has been used in the past. Bearing in mind the stress in our prisons today from overcrowding, if there are good prospects that an offender is not going to prey upon the public again, there are advantages in using the penalty of a fine rather than sentencing someone to a further period of imprisonment. This is especially true in the case of an offender . . . who is able to gain steady employment and is able to earn a substantial salary . . .

This has to be handled quite carefully in a plea in mitigation, as it would be wrong to give the impression that the offender is trying to 'buy his way out of prison' by offering to pay a substantial fine. The essential point is that a fine can have a substantial punitive effect.

In *Attorney General's Reference (No 11 of 2006)* [2006] EWCA Crim 856; [2006] 2 Cr App R (S) 108, Lord Phillips CJ (at para 20) observed that:

> When prisons are overcrowded the result is to hinder or prevent the valuable work of rehabilitation that a prison should normally provide. The fact that prisons are overcrowded may, for this reason, be a relevant factor where the sentencer's decision is on the cusp, so that there is a real issue as to whether a community sentence can be justified rather than a custodial sentence.

Similarly, in *R v Seed* [2007] EWCA Crim 254; [2007] 2 Cr App R (S) 69 (Lord Phillips CJ, at paras 1–7) said:

> Once again judges who have to sentence offenders are confronted with the fact that the prisons are full. When they impose sentences of imprisonment – and very often the nature of the offence will mean that there is no alternative to this course – the prison regime that the offender will experience will be likely to be more punitive because of the consequence of overcrowding and the opportunities for rehabilitative intervention in prison will be restricted. Those already serving sentences are subject to the same adverse consequences . . .
>
> Section 152(2) of the 2003 Act . . . requires the court, when looking at the particulars of the offence, to decide whether the 'custodial threshold' has been passed. If it has not, then no custodial sentence can be imposed. If it has, it does not follow that a custodial sentence must be imposed. The effect of a guilty plea or of personal mitigation may make it appropriate for the sentencer to impose a non-custodial sentence . . .
>
> [W]hen considering the length of a custodial sentence, the court should properly bear in mind that the prison regime is likely to be more punitive as a result of prison overcrowding . . .
>
> Unless imprisonment is necessary for the protection of the public the court should always give consideration to the question of whether the aims of rehabilitation and thus the reduction of crime cannot better be achieved by a fine or community sentence rather than by imprisonment and whether punishment cannot adequately be achieved by such a sentence. We believe that there may have been a reluctance to impose fines because fines were often not enforced. Enforcement of fines is now rigorous and effective and, where the offender has the means, a heavy fine can often be an adequate and appropriate punishment. If so, the 2003 Act requires a fine to be imposed rather than a community sentence.
>
> Particular care should be exercised before imposing a custodial sentence on a first offender. Association with seasoned criminals may make reoffending more likely rather than deter it, particularly where the offender is young. A clean record can be important personal mitigation and may make a custodial sentence inappropriate, notwithstanding that the custodial threshold is crossed.

17.1.2 Length of sentence under the Criminal Justice Act 2003

If the case is sufficiently serious to justify the imposition of a custodial sentence, the next question is how long that sentence should be. Section 153 of the Criminal Justice Act 2003 provides as follows:

(1) This section applies where a court passes a custodial sentence other than one fixed by law or falling to be imposed under section 225 or 226 [imprisonment for protection of public].

(2) Subject to section 51A(2) of the Firearms Act 1968, sections 110(2) and 111(2) of the Sentencing Act, section 29(4) or (6) of the Violent Crime Reduction Act 2006 [mandatory minimum sentences] and sections 227(2) and 228(2) of this Act [extended sentences for certain violent or sexual offences], the custodial sentence must be for the shortest term (not exceeding the permitted maximum) that in the opinion of the court is commensurate with the seriousness of the offence, or the combination of the offence and one or more offences associated with it.

The principle underpinning the restriction is that of 'just deserts', in other words that there should be a direct correlation between the sentence imposed and the seriousness of the offence that is being dealt with.

In *R v Cunningham* [1993] 1 WLR 183, the Court of Appeal considered the question of deterrence. Lord Taylor of Gosforth CJ said (at p 186) that the phrase 'commensurate with the seriousness of the offence' must mean 'commensurate with the punishment and deterrence which the seriousness of the offence requires'. His Lordship went on to say (at p 187) that the court should not add 'any extra length to the sentence which by those criteria is commensurate with the seriousness of the offence, simply to make a special example of the defendant'. However, his Lordship then said that prevalence of the particular kind of offence is a legitimate factor in determining the length of the custodial sentence to be passed (presumably with the implication that a stiff sentence on the present occasion might make it less prevalent in the future!).

In *R v Howells* [1999] 1 WLR 307, Lord Bingham CJ said (at p 312):

Where the court is of the opinion that an offence, or the combination of an offence and one or more offences associated with it, is so serious that only a custodial sentence can be justified and that such a sentence should be passed, the sentence imposed should be no longer than is necessary to meet the penal purpose which the court has in mind.

His Lordship went on to endorse the observations of Rose LJ in *R v Ollerenshaw* [1999] 1 Cr App R(S) 65 (at p 67):

When a court is considering imposing a comparatively short period of custody, that is of about 12 months or less, it should generally ask itself, particularly where the defendant has not previously been sentenced to custody, whether an even shorter period might be equally effective in protecting the interests of the public, and punishing and deterring the criminal. For example, there will be cases where, for these purposes, six months may be just as effective as nine, or two months may be just as effective as four.

This echoes observations made by Lord Lane CJ in *R v Bibi* [1980] 1 WLR 1193 at p 1195, where he said that a custodial sentence should be 'as short as possible, consistent only with the duty to protect the interests of the public and to punish and deter the criminal'. This point will be of particular relevance where the offender has been remanded in custody prior to conviction and/or sentence: it may well be possible to mitigate on the basis that the period already spent behind bars on remand is sufficient punishment.

Guidance on length of sentence for specific offences can be found in definitive guidelines issued by the Sentencing Guidelines Council and in guideline judgments of the Court of Appeal.

In *R v Johnson* (1994) 15 Cr App R(S) 827, Roch LJ said (at p 830):

> The decisions of this Court are no more than guidelines to judges who have the task of sentencing in the Crown Court. Within the guidelines there is a great deal of flexibility . . . [S]entences should be broadly in line with guideline cases, unless there are factors applicable to the particular case which require or enable the judge to depart from the normal level of sentence . . .

The same approach applies to the guidelines issued by the Sentencing Guidelines Council, which are gradually replacing the Court of Appeal guideline judgments.

To a large extent, the provisions of the Criminal Justice Act 2003 mirror earlier legislation (such as the Criminal Justice Act 1991) in requiring the sentence to be proportionate to the offence. However, the 2003 Act moves away from the concept of proportionality to the extent that it requires the sentencer to have regard to a number of aims (set out in s 142 and discussed in the previous chapter) which are not necessarily related to the seriousness of the offence, and it requires the court to regard previous convictions as an aggravating factor, resulting in a higher sentence. Laurence Koffman, in 'The rise and fall of proportionality: the failure of the Criminal Justice Act 1991' [2006] Crim LR 281 compares the approaches taken by the 1991 and 2003 Act and concludes as follows:

> Advocates of the proportionality model rightly stress its importance in restricting potentially unjust utilitarian sentencing aims, and in safeguarding fairness and fundamental rights. It represents an honest approach to sentencing in making just deserts the primary rationale, rather than unsupported claims about rehabilitation, deterrence and public protection. It provides sentencers with a consistent starting point, eschewing the 'menu-of-aims' approach which the recent legislation has restored to the sentencing process. In view of these important qualities, and its support amongst many experts on sentencing, it is surprising that the proportionality principle has failed to become more firmly entrenched in sentencing law and practice. In concluding, it is instructive to consider why, although proportionality has not been 'jettisoned' by the 2003 legislation, it has declined in importance since the 1991 Act.
>
> One possibility is that proportionality has a rather negative quality. Supporters advocate its pre-eminence by reference to the fact that other sentencing objectives are not effective or, at least, that there is little evidence to suggest that they are. Academics and others whose training encourages an evidence-based approach have no difficulty adopting a 'rationalist' position. However, amongst the general public (and the media) there is an enduring expectation and belief that sentencing policy can achieve utilitarian goals. This 'aspirational' (or intuitive) approach persists despite the lack of empirical evidence to support it, and the two

major political parties have encouraged this belief increasingly since 1993. The general public is not well informed about current levels of sentencing, and survey research has repeatedly suggested that the public overestimates the leniency of the courts. There is, inevitably perhaps, considerable popular support for harsher sentences for persistent offenders and those regarded (accurately or not) as dangerous. The public believes implicitly that persistent offenders can be deterred by longer sentences, and also that they are safer as a result of special provisions for dealing with 'dangerous' offenders. Although public attitudes to sentencing are undoubtedly complex, with the public not necessarily as punitive as is sometimes assumed, research also suggests that 'the public is interested in the reduction of crime by whatever means'.

. . . Governments need to convince the public that their legislation and policies can make a difference; accordingly, the more limited, justice-based, claims of proportionality are not sufficiently attractive to today's politicians. The government seeks to persuade the public that with clearer goals, and better integration and management of the criminal justice system, crime reduction can be achieved through sentencing and punishment.

17.1.3 Procedural requirements before imposing a custodial sentence

Section 156 of the Criminal Justice Act 2003 requires the court to obtain and consider a pre-sentence report before deciding that a case is sufficiently serious to justify the imposition of a custodial sentence and, if so, the length of sentence that would be commensurate with the seriousness of the offence (s 156(3)). Where the offender has attained the age of 18, the court may refrain from seeking a pre-sentence report if it considers that it is unnecessary to obtain one (s 156(4)).

In *R v Gillette* (1999) *The Times*, 3 December, the Court of Appeal said that in all cases where a court is contemplating sentencing a defendant to prison for the first time, other than for a very short period, it should be the invariable practice that a pre-sentence report should be obtained before such a sentence is passed. However, the Court of Appeal subsequently reconsidered this point in *R v Armsaramah* [2001] 1 Cr App R(S) 133, holding that there may be cases where it is permissible for the court to pass a first custodial sentence without first obtaining a pre-sentence report. In the instant case, it was held that the judge had been entitled to decide that a pre-sentence report would have added nothing.

Under s 174(2)(b) of the 2003 Act, the court has to explain why it is of the view that the offence is so serious that neither a fine alone nor a community sentence can be justified for it.

17.1.4 Dangerous offenders under the Criminal Justice Act 2003

Chapter 5 of Pt 12 of the Criminal Justice Act 2003 (ss 224–36) deals with 'dangerous offenders'. These provisions apply only to certain offences. Section 224 defines the key terms used in Chapter 5 of the Act. A 'specified offence' means a violent offence specified in Pt 1 of Sched 15 to the Act or a sexual offence specified in Pt 2 of that Schedule. A 'serious offence' means a violent or sexual offence specified in Sched 15 and punishable (ignoring the effect of s 225, below) with life imprisonment or a determinate sentence of at least 10 years' imprisonment. The phrase 'serious harm' means death or serious personal injury, whether physical or psychological (s 224(3)).

17.1.4.1 *Life sentence or imprisonment for public protection*

Section 225 enables the court to impose imprisonment for public protection where an offender aged 18 or over is convicted of a 'serious offence' and the court is of the opinion that there is a 'significant risk to members of the public of serious harm occasioned by the commission by him of further specified offences' (that is, offences specified in Sched 15).

Under s 225(2), if the offence is punishable with life imprisonment and the court considers that the seriousness of the offence (or of the offence and one or more offences associated with it) is such as to justify the imposition of a sentence of imprisonment for life, then the court must impose a life sentence. In all other cases which fall within s 225 but not within s 225(2), the court must impose a sentence of imprisonment for public protection (s 225(3)); this sentence is for an indeterminate period (s 225(4)). Section 13 of the Criminal Justice and Immigration Act 2008 amends s 225(3), so that where the case does not fall within s 225(2), the court may impose a sentence of imprisonment for public protection if, at the time the offence was committed, the offender had been convicted of an offence specified in a new Sched 15A added to the 2003 Act (s 225(3A)), or the notional minimum term is at least two years (s 225(3B)).

Section 226 (which is amended by s 14 of the 2008 Act) deals with cases where the offender is under 18. It provides that where an offender under the age of 18 is convicted of an offence that falls within s 225, the same consequences result, save that the sentence is detention for life (or for an indeterminate period, as the case may be) under s 91 of the Powers of Criminal Courts (Sentencing) Act 2000.

17.1.4.2 *Extended sentences for violent or sexual offences*

We have already seen that the usual principle of sentencing is based on the principle of 'just deserts', so that the length of any custodial sentence should be commensurate with the seriousness of the offence. Section 227, however, empowers the court to impose an 'extended sentence' where the offender has attained the age of 18 and is convicted of a specified violent or sexual offence and the court considers that there is 'a significant risk to members of the public of serious harm occasioned by the commission by the offender of further specified offences' (that is, offences specified in Sched 15), but the court is not required by s 225(2) to impose a sentence of imprisonment for life. Section 15 of the Criminal Justice and Immigration Act 2008 amends s 227(2), so that in such a case the court may impose an extended sentence of imprisonment if, at the time the offence was committed, the offender had been convicted of an offence specified in new Sched 15A added to the 2003 (s 227(2A)) or, if the court were to impose an extended sentence of imprisonment, the term that it would specify as the appropriate custodial term would be at least 4 years (s 227(2B)). Section 229 defines the phrase 'extended sentence of imprisonment' as meaning:

> . . . the term of which is equal to the aggregate of—
>
> (a) the appropriate custodial term, and

(b) a further period ('the extension period') for which the offender is to be subject to a licence and which is of such length as the court considers necessary for the purpose of protecting members of the public from serious harm occasioned by the commission by him of further specified offences.

Sub-section (3) defines 'the appropriate custodial term' as a term of imprisonment:

... (not exceeding the maximum term permitted for the offence) which—

(a) is the term that would (apart from this section) be imposed in compliance with section 153(2) [commensurate with seriousness of offence], or

(b) where the term that would be so imposed is a term of less than 12 months, is a term of 12 months.

Under sub-s (4), the extension period must not exceed:

(a) five years in the case of a specified violent offence, and

(b) eight years in the case of a specified sexual offence. In any event, the term of an extended sentence of imprisonment must not exceed the maximum term permitted for the offence.

Section 228 (which is amended by s 16 of the 2008 Act) applies similar provisions to offenders under the age of 18.

In *R v S* [2005] EWCA 3616 Crim; (2006) 170 JP 145, the Court of Appeal said that, under ss 227 and 228 of the CJA 2003, the extension period is intended to follow the custodial term, not the custodial period as reduced by release on licence. Accordingly, an extension period under ss 227 or 228 begins to run at the end of the custodial period determined by the court whether or not part of the custodial period has been 'served' on licence.

17.1.4.3 Assessing dangerousness

Section 229 sets out the criteria for assessing dangerousness in cases to which any of ss 225–28 apply.

Section 229(2), as amended by s 17 of the Criminal Justice and Immigration Act 2008, provides that, in making the assessment of dangerousness, the court

(a)   must take into account all such information as is available to it about the nature and circumstances of the offence,

(aa) may take into account all such information as is available to it about the nature and circumstances of any other offences of which the offender has been convicted by a court anywhere in the world,

(b)   may take into account any information which is before it about any pattern of behaviour of which the offence forms part, and

(c)   may take into account any information about the offender which is before it.

Under s 229(3), where the offender had previous convictions for specified offences, the court was required to presume that there was a significant risk to members of the public of serious harm through him committing further specified offences. This seemed to create a strong presumption that such a defendant should be found to be dangerous, and it was questionable whether it was compatible with the Human Rights Act. This sub-section will, however, be repealed when s 17(4) of the 2008 Act comes into effect.

In *R v Lang* [2005] EWCA Crim 2864; [2006] 1 WLR 2509, the Court of Appeal held that significant risk to members of the public from serious harm by the commission of further specified offences requires significant risk to be shown in relation to two matters: the commission of further specified, but not necessarily serious, offences; and the causing thereby of serious harm to members of the public. Rose LJ (at para 17) then gave the following detailed guidance:

... the following factors should be borne in mind when a sentencer is assessing significant risk.

(i)   The risk identified must be significant. This is a higher threshold than mere possibility of occurrence and in our view can be taken to mean (as in the Concise Oxford Dictionary) 'noteworthy, of considerable amount ... or importance'.

(ii) In assessing the risk of further offences being committed, the sentencer should take into account the nature and circumstances of the current offence; the offender's history of offending including not just the kind of offence but its circumstances and the sentence passed, details of which the prosecution must have available and whether the offending demonstrates any pattern; social and economic factors in relation to the offender including accommodation, employability, education, associates, relationships and drug or alcohol abuse and the offender's thinking, attitude towards offending and supervision and emotional state. Information in relation to these matters will most readily, though not exclusively, come from antecedents and pre-sentence probation and medical reports ... The sentencer will be guided, but not bound by, the assessment of risk in such reports. A sentencer who contemplates differing from the assessment in such a report should give both counsel the opportunity of addressing the point.

(iii) If the foreseen specified offence is serious, there will clearly be some cases, though not by any means all, in which there may be a significant risk of serious harm. For example, robbery is a serious offence. But it can be committed in a wide variety of ways many of which do not give rise to a significant risk of serious harm. Sentencers must therefore guard against assuming there is a significant risk of serious harm merely because the foreseen specified offence is serious. A pre-sentence report should usually be obtained before any sentence is passed which is based on significant risk of serious harm. In a small number of cases, where the circumstances of the current offence or the history of the offender suggest mental abnormality on his part, a medical report may be necessary before risk can properly be assessed.

(iv) If the foreseen specified offence is not serious, there will be comparatively few cases in which a risk of serious harm will properly be regarded as significant. The huge variety of offences in Sched 15 to the Act of 2003, includes many which, in themselves, are not suggestive of serious harm. Repetitive violent or sexual offending at a relatively low level without serious harm does not of itself give rise to a significant risk of serious harm in the future. There may, in such cases, be some risk of future victims being more adversely affected than past victims but this, of itself, does not give rise to significant risk of serious harm.

(v)   In relation to the rebuttable assumption to which section 229(3) of the 2003 Act gives rise, the court is accorded a discretion if, in the light of information about the current offence, the offender and his previous offences, it would be unreasonable to conclude that there is a significant risk. The exercise of such a discretion is, historically, at the very heart of judicial sentencing and the language of the statute indicates that judges are expected, albeit starting from the assumption, to exercise their ability to reach a reasonable conclusion in the light of the information before them. It is to be noted that the assumption will be rebutted, if at all, as an exercise of judgment, the statute includes no reference to the burden or standard of proof . . . it will usually be unreasonable to conclude that the assumption applies unless information about the offences, pattern of behaviour and offender show a significant risk of serious harm from further offences.

(vi) In relation to offenders under 18 and adults with no relevant previous convictions at the time the specified offence was committed, the court's discretion under section 229(2) of the 2003 Act is not constrained by any initial assumption such as, under section 229(3) of the Act, applies to adults with previous convictions. It is still necessary, when sentencing young offenders, to bear in mind that, within a shorter time than adults, they may change and develop. This and their level of maturity may be highly pertinent when assessing what their future conduct may be and whether it may give rise to significant risk of serious harm.

(vii) In relation to a particularly young offender, an indeterminate sentence may be inappropriate even where a serious offence has been committed and there is a significant risk of serious harm from further offences . . .

(viii) It cannot have been Parliament's intention, in a statute dealing with the liberty of the subject, to require the imposition of indeterminate sentences for the commission of relatively minor offences . . .

(ix) Sentencers should usually, and in accordance with section 174(1)(a) of the Criminal Justice Act 2003 give reasons for all their conclusions: in particular, that there is or is not a significant risk of further offences or serious harm; where the assumption under section 229(3) of the 2003 Act arises for making or not making the assumption which the statute requires unless this would be unreasonable; and for not imposing an extended sentence under sections 227 and 228 of the Act. Sentencers should, in giving reasons, briefly identify the information which they have taken into account.

In *R v Johnson* [2006] EWCA Crim 2486; [2007] 1 WLR 585, the Court of Appeal handed down further guidance about the 'dangerous offender' provisions. Sir Igor Judge P, at paras 10 and 11, says this:

(i) Just as the absence of previous convictions does not preclude a finding of dangerousness, the existence of previous convictions for specified offences does not compel such a finding. There is a presumption that it does so, which may be rebutted.

(ii) If a finding of dangerousness can be made against an offender without previous specified convictions, it also follows that previous offences, not in fact specified for the purposes of section 229, are not disqualified from consideration. Thus, for example, as indeed the statute recognises, a pattern of minor previous offences of gradually escalating seriousness may be significant. In other words, it is not right . . . that unless the previous offences were specified offences they were irrelevant.

(iii) Where the facts of the instant offence, or indeed any specified offences for the purposes of section 229(3) are examined, it may emerge that no harm actually occurred.

That may be advantageous to the offender . . . On the other hand the absence of harm may be entirely fortuitous . . . It does not automatically follow from the absence of actual harm caused by the offender to date, that the risk that he will cause serious harm in the future is negligible . . . *R v Shaffi* [2006] EWCA Crim 418 . . . is not authority for the proposition that as a matter of law offences which did not result in harm to the victim should be treated as irrelevant.

(iv) . . . the inadequacy, suggestibility, or vulnerability of the offender . . . may bear on dangerousness. Such characteristics may serve to mitigate the offender's culpability. In the final analysis however they may also serve to produce or reinforce the conclusion that the offender is dangerous . . .

. . . this court will not normally interfere with the conclusions reached by a sentencer who has accurately identified the relevant principles, and applied his mind to the relevant facts.

In *R v Reynolds* [2007] EWCA Crim 538; [2007] 2 Cr App R (S) 87, the Court of Appeal observed that the 'dangerous offender' regime requires the court to carry out a careful step by step evaluation of the sentencing consequences of the type of offence, the age of the offender and the assessment of his dangerousness. Latham LJ, at para 5, provided a helpful synopsis of the way in which that exercise should be carried out:

(a) As far as the type of offence is concerned, the first question to ask is whether or not the offence is a 'specified' offence, and the second is whether it is a 'serious' offence.

(b) If it is a 'specified' offence, whether 'serious' or not, the court must determine whether the defendant meets the criteria of dangerousness . . .

(c) If the criteria of dangerousness are met and the defendant is aged 18 or over,

   (i) where the offence is a 'serious' offence, he must be sentenced to an indeterminate sentence under section 225 of the 2003 Act,

   (ii) otherwise he must be sentenced to an extended sentence under section 227 of the 2003 Act.

(d) If the criteria of dangerousness are met, and the offender is under 18:

   (i) If the offence is a 'serious' offence and an offence to which he would be liable to a sentence of detention for life under s 91 of the 2000 Act, and it justifies (together with any associated offence) detention for life; he must be sentenced to detention for life;

   (ii) if the court considers in such a case that such a sentence is not justified, and, pursuant to section 226(3) of the 2003 Act, it considers that an extended sentence under section 228 of the 2003 Act would be inadequate to protect the public, it must impose detention for public protection;

   (iii) in any other case the defendant must be sentenced to an extended sentence under section 227 of the 2003 Act.

(e) By virtue of sections 227 and 228 of the 2003 Act a court must impose an extended sentence on a defendant who meets the criteria of dangerousness if he has been convicted of a 'specified' but not 'serious' offence, even if he has been convicted at the same time of an offence carrying an indeterminate sentence, and has been sentenced accordingly.

In *R v Considine* [2007] EWCA Crim 1166; [2007] 3 All ER 621, Sir Igor Judge P ruled (at para 27) that the information to be taken into account when making the assessment of 'dangerousness':

> ... is not limited to the offender's previous convictions or a pattern of behaviour established by them, or indeed information about the offender which is limited to them ... relevant information bearing on the assessment of dangerousness may take the form of material adverse to the offender which is not substantiated or proved by criminal convictions.

At para 37, his Lordship continued:

> ... there will be very few cases in which a fair analysis of all the information in the papers prepared by the prosecution, events at the trial, if there has been one, the judicial assessment of the defendant's character and personality (always a critical feature in the assessment), the material in mitigation drawn to the attention of the court by the defendant's advocate, the contents of the pre-sentence report, and any psychiatric or psychological assessment prepared on behalf of the defendant, or at the behest of the court itself, should not provide the judge with sufficient appropriate information on which to form the necessary judgment in relation to dangerousness.

The importance of having a sound basis for the assessment of dangerousness was re-emphasised in *R v Xhelollari* [2007] EWCA Crim 2052, where the imposition of a sentence of imprisonment for public protection was held to be wrong in principle, as the pre-sentence report did not identify factors which led to a conclusion that there was a significant risk of serious harm posed by the defendant. The risk assessment of the report was based entirely upon the perceived vulnerability of the victim and the unwillingness of the appellant to acknowledge guilt. The court stressed that the conclusion that there is a significant risk of serious harm from future offending 'must be founded upon evidence rather than speculation or mere apprehension of some risk of future harm' (per McCombe J at para 24).

The *Sentencing Guidelines Council* has issued guidance entitled *Dangerous Offenders: Guide for Sentencers and Practitioners* (available on their website at <http://www.sentencing-guidelines.gov.uk/docs/SGC%20Dangerous%20Offenders.pdf>). It contains detailed guidance (including a summary of relevant case law) on the 'dangerous offender' provisions in the Criminal Justice Act 2003. Annex A contains useful flow charts for both adult offenders and young offenders.

17.1.5 Concurrent and consecutive sentences

Where an offender is convicted of more than one offence, a separate sentence will usually be imposed for each offence. In the case of custodial sentences, the terms may be concurrent or consecutive. Sentences are concurrent if they are to be served simultaneously (e.g. a sentence of nine months on count 1 and three months concurrent on count 2 means that the offender receives a total sentence of nine months); sentences are consecutive if they have to be served one after the other (e.g. a sentence of nine months on count 1 and three months consecutive on count 2 means that the offender receives a total sentence of 12 months). If the court fails to specify whether sentences are concurrent or consecutive, they are deemed to be concurrent.

It is possible to have a mixture of consecutive and concurrent sentences. For example, an offender could be sentenced to six months on count 1, nine months consecutive on count 2 and three months concurrent on count 3. The total sentence would be 15 months.

It would be wrong in principle to impose consecutive sentences if the two offences in question essentially amount to a single crime. For example, in *R v Coker* [1984] Crim LR 184, the defendant was convicted of sexual assault and assault occasioning actual bodily harm. He had struck a young woman repeatedly about the face, removed most of her clothes and then indecently assaulted her. The judge imposed consecutive terms of imprisonment but the Court of Appeal held that the two offences were so inextricably linked that the sentences should have been concurrent.

Generally, concurrent sentences will be imposed where the offences arise out of the same transaction; for example, dangerous driving and driving while disqualified on the same occasion (*R v Skinner* (1986) 8 Cr App R(S) 166), driving with excess alcohol and driving while disqualified on the same occasion (*R v Jones* (1980) 2 Cr App R(S) 152). However, this is not an invariable rule. In *R v Wheatley* (1983) 5 Cr App R(S) 417, consecutive sentences were imposed for driving while disqualified and driving with excess alcohol on the same occasion on the ground that, given his 'bad record', it would be wrong to lead the offender to believe that he could drive with excess alcohol and incur no extra penalty for driving while disqualified: though the offences were committed on the same occasion, they were in fact completely separate offences.

In *R v Ling* (1993) 157 JP 931, the defendant was convicted of burglary, affray, dangerous driving, driving while disqualified, refusing to provide a specimen, and making off without payment. It was said that his offending, which took place over a single (and rather eventful!) evening, was due to the effects of diabetes. The Court of Appeal held that these events should therefore have been regarded as a single ongoing offence. Likewise, in *R v Tutu Sikwabi* (1993) 157 JP 1182, the defendant was convicted of making off without payment, taking without consent, reckless driving and driving while disqualified. The offences took place over three days, beginning with the taking of the car, and ending only after a police car chase. It was held that the offences arose out of a single series of events and that the sentences for the various parts of the series should therefore be concurrent.

Consecutive sentences are usually imposed where the offences are committed on different occasions, even if there is a link between the offences. In *Attorney General's Reference (No 1 of 1990)* (1990) 12 Cr App R(S) 245, for example, it was held that where an offender is convicted of an offence, and of an attempt to pervert the course of justice in relation to his trial for that offence, the sentence for the offence of attempting to pervert the course of justice should normally be consecutive to the sentence for the principal offence. See also *Attorney General's Reference (No 4 of 1994)* (1995) 16 Cr App R(S) 81, where consecutive sentences were imposed for robbery and wounding with intent committed on separate occasions.

Consecutive sentences are also appropriate where, though the offences were committed on the same occasion, they are not part of the same transaction. Thus, a sentence for using violence to resist arrest or in an attempt to escape from the scene of the crime will normally lead to a consecutive sentence being imposed (*R v Fitter* (1983) 5 Cr App

R(S) 168). Similarly, a sentence for a firearms offence will usually be consecutive to the sentence for the main offence where that offence involves the use or possession of a firearm (*R v French* (1982) 4 Cr App R(S) 57). For example, in *R v Greaves* [2003] EWCA Crim 3229; [2004] 2 Cr App R(S) 10, it was held that if a defendant uses a weapon in the course of committing a robbery, the proper course as regards sentencing is to impose a separate and consecutive sentence in respect of possession of the weapon (giving a clear message to those who commit crimes of this nature that if they carry a weapon when committing a robbery they will receive an additional sentence). Likewise, in *R v McNaughten* [2003] EWCA Crim 3479; (2004) *The Times*, 15 January, which concerned a woman who had been the subject of systematic and very brutal domestic violence, the court observed that if there had been a separate victim for each count, consecutive sentences would have been justified. The court could see no reason why consecutive sentences would be inappropriate simply because the victim of each assault was the same person.

Terms of imprisonment may be ordered to run consecutively even if the total sentence is greater than the maximum which could have been imposed for one of the offences. For example, in *R v Backwell* [2003] EWCA Crim 3213; (2003) *The Times*, 15 December, the defendant pleaded guilty to seven offences of sexual assault, for which the statutory maximum (for a single offence) was 10 years' imprisonment. The judge passed six sentences of six years to run concurrently for six of the offences, and a further six years to run consecutively for the seventh offence (making a total of 12 years). The Court of Appeal upheld this sentence, holding that it was not wrong in principle even though it exceeded the statutory maximum for a single offence. There is, said the court, no legal principle that consecutive sentences for a series of offences cannot be passed which exceed the statutory maximum for a single offence.

17.1.6 The principle of 'totality'

Sentencers must, however, have regard to the total length of sentence passed, particularly where consecutive sentences have been imposed, to ensure that the sentence properly reflects the overall seriousness of the behaviour (*R v Jones* [1996] 1 Cr App R(S) 153). Thus, where an offender is being sentenced for a number of offences, and terms of imprisonment are ordered to run consecutively rather than concurrently, the court should ensure that the total sentence is commensurate with the overall seriousness of the offender's crimes. This is known as the principle of 'totality', a principle expressly preserved by s 166(3)(b) of the Criminal Justice Act 2003.

17.1.7 Effect of time spent on remand

Section 240(3) of the Criminal Justice Act 2003 provides that, if an offender has spent time in custody awaiting trial and/or sentence, 'the court must direct that the number of days for which the offender was remanded in custody in connection with the offence or a related offence is to count as time served by him as part of the sentence'. This means that, where an offender has been remanded in custody before conviction and/or sentence, the period for which he has already been detained is deducted from the sentence he has to serve. Under sub-s (4), however, the court may refrain from making such a direction if it is in the opinion of the court 'just in all the circumstances' not to do so. Where the court does not give a direction under sub-s (3), or makes a limited direction (i.e. a direction that fewer than the total number of days spent on remand should count as part of the sentence), the court must give reasons for its decision (sub-s (6)).

Section 240 applies to sentences of imprisonment, detention in a young offender institution, and long-term detention under s 91 of the 2000 Act (but it does not apply to detention and training orders).

In *R v Barber* [2006] EWCA Crim 162; [2006] 2 Cr App R (S) 81, the Court of Appeal said that it is plainly good practice for a judge to inform defence counsel if he is considering making no direction under s 240(3), thus giving counsel the opportunity of addressing him on that issue and of seeking to persuade him that the circumstances are not such that it would be just for the period spent in custody on remand not to count as part of the sentence to be served.

The Guidelines from the Sentencing Guidelines Council on the sentences created by the Criminal Justice Act 2003 (at <http://www.sentencing-guidelines.gov.uk/docs/New_sentences_guideline1.pdf>) included an annex setting out advice from the Sentencing Advisory Panel on the effect of time spent on remand:

ANNEX A
Time Spent on Remand – Sentencing Advisory Panel's Advice
The Act makes provision for a sentencer to give credit for time spent on remand in custody where a custodial sentence is passed. It also empowers the court to have regard to time spent on remand in custody when determining the restrictions on liberty to be imposed by a community order or youth community order. Where an offender has spent several weeks in custody, this may affect the nature of the offence that is passed. For example, where the court decides that a custodial sentence is justified some sentencers may decide to pass a community sentence instead, on the basis that the offender has already completed the equivalent of a punitive element in a sentence. The Panel takes the view that, given the changes in the content of the second part of a custodial sentence, in such cases it will be more appropriate to pass a custodial sentence knowing that licence requirements will be imposed on release from custody (which may be immediate). Recommendations made by the court at the point of sentence will then be of particular importance in influencing the content of the licence. This will help to ensure that the record clearly shows the assessment of seriousness of the offending behaviour.

Whereas the Act clearly states that time spent on remand is to be regarded as part of a custodial sentence unless the Court considers it unjust, it states that sentencers passing a community sentence may have regard to time spent on remand, but no further information is given on how this discretion should be exercised. The Panel recognises that giving credit for time spent on remand is likely to be easier to apply in relation to punitive requirements rather than the rehabilitative elements of a community sentence. For example, reducing the number of unpaid work hours could be fairly easy, whereas reducing the length of a rehabilitation programme might not be appropriate as it could undermine its effectiveness. Where an offender has been kept on remand, one could take the view that this action was justified by the bail provisions and that the sentencer should not, therefore, feel obliged to adjust the terms of the community sentence. However, in principle, the Panel recommends that the court should seek to give credit for time spent on remand in all cases and should explain its reasons for not doing so when it considers either that this is not justified, would not be practical, or would not be in the best interests of the offender.

The court should seek to give credit for time spent on remand in all cases. It should make clear, when announcing sentence, whether or not credit for time on remand has been given and should explain its reasons for not giving credit when it considers either that this is not justified, would not be practical, or would not be in the best interests of the offender.

Where, following a period of time spent in custody on remand, the court decides that a custodial sentence is justified then, given the changes in the content of the second part of a custodial sentence, the court should pass a custodial sentence in the knowledge that licence requirements will be imposed on release from custody.

Recommendations made by the court at the point of sentence will be of particular importance in influencing the content of the licence.

Section 21 of the Criminal Justice and Immigration Act 2008 inserts a new section, s 240A, into the Criminal Justice Act 2003. The effect of this new section, when it comes into force, will be that if the offender was remanded on bail, and was subject to a curfew condition (requiring him to remain at one or more specified places for a total of not less than 9 hours in any given day) and an electronic monitoring condition, then the court must (unless it is of the opinion that it is just in all the circumstances not to do so) direct that the 'credit period' (i.e. half of the number of days on which the offender was subject to those bail conditions) is to count as time served by the offender as part of the sentence.

17.1.8 Criminal Justice Act 2003: Prison sentences of less than 12 months

Section 181 of the CJA 2003 (not in force at the time of writing) provides that, in general, all prison sentences of less than 12 months should consist of a short period of custody (the 'custodial period') followed by a longer period on licence (the 'licence period'), during which the offender has to comply with requirements fixed by the court as part of the 'custody plus order'. Section 181(2) stipulates that the term of the sentence:

(a) must be expressed in weeks,
(b) must be at least 28 weeks,
(c) must not be more than 51 weeks in respect of any one offence, and
(d) must not exceed the maximum term permitted for the offence.

Under s 181(5), the custodial period must be between two and 13 weeks for each offence; under s 181(6), the licence period must be at least 26 weeks.

Section 181(7) provides for consecutive sentences and limits the total term of imprisonment for two or more offences to 65 weeks (15 months), with a maximum of 26 weeks (six months) in custody.

Section 182 of the 2003 Act lists the requirements which the court may attach to the licence period under the 'custody plus order' provided for by s 181. Under s 182(1), the following conditions may be attached:

(a) an unpaid work requirement (as defined by s 199);

(b) an activity requirement (as defined by s 201);

(c) a programme requirement (as defined by s 202);

(d) a prohibited activity requirement (as defined by s 203);

(e) a curfew requirement (as defined by s 204);

(f) an exclusion requirement (as defined by s 205);

(g) a supervision requirement (as defined by s 213); and

(h) where the offender is aged under 25, an attendance centre requirement (as defined by s 214).

Sections 182(3) and (4) provide for electronic monitoring requirements to be added; and s 182(5) adds the stipulation that where the licence contains two or more different requirements, the court must consider whether, in the circumstances of the case, the requirements are compatible with each other.

17.1.9 Prison sentences of 12 months or more: guidance from the Sentencing Guidelines Council

In December 2004, the Sentencing Guidelines Council issued guidance on the sentencing regime established by the Criminal Justice Act 2003 entitled *New Sentences: Criminal Justice Act 2003* (see <http://www.sentencing-guidelines.gov.uk/docs/New_sentences_guideline1.pdf>).

SECTION 2 – CUSTODIAL SENTENCES
PART 1 – CUSTODIAL SENTENCES OF 12 MONTHS OR MORE

. . .

B. Imposition of Custodial Sentences of 12 Months or more
(i) Length of Sentence

. . .

Transitional arrangements

2.1.7 In general, a fixed term custodial sentence of 12 months or more under the new framework will increase the sentence actually served (whether in custody or in the community) since it continues to the end of the term imposed. Existing guidelines issued since 1991 have been based on a different framework and so, in order to maintain consistency between the lengths of sentence under the current and the new framework, there will need to be some adjustment to the starting points for custodial sentences contained in those guidelines (subject to the special sentences under the 2003 Act where the offender is a 'dangerous' offender).

. . .

2.1.9 . . . As a guide, the Council suggests the sentence length should be reduced by in the region of 15%.

2.1.10 The changes in the nature of a custodial sentence will require changes in the way the sentence is announced. Sentencers will need to continue to spell out the practical implications of the sentence being imposed so that offenders, victims and the public alike all understand that the sentence does not end when the offender is released from custody. The fact that a breach of the requirements imposed in the second half of the sentence is likely to result in a return to custody should also be made very clear at the point of sentence.

- When imposing a fixed term custodial sentence of 12 months or more under the new provisions, courts should consider reducing the overall length of the sentence that would have been imposed under the current provisions by in the region of 15%.
- When announcing sentence, sentencers should explain the way in which the sentence has been calculated, how it will be served and the implications of non-compliance with licence requirements. In particular, it needs to be stated clearly that the sentence is in two parts, one in custody and one under supervision in the community.
- This proposal does not apply to sentences for dangerous offenders, for which separate provision has been made in the Act.

(ii) Licence conditions

. . .

2.1.12 When passing such a sentence, the court will not know with any certainty to what extent the offender's behaviour may have been addressed in custody or what the offender's health and other personal circumstances might be on release and so it will be extremely difficult, especially in the case of longer custodial sentences, for sentencers to make an informed judgment about the most appropriate licence conditions to be imposed on release. However, in most cases, it would be extremely helpful for sentencers to indicate areas of an offender's behaviour about which they have the most concern and to make suggestions about the types of intervention whether this, in practice, takes place in prison or in the community.

2.1.13 The involvement of the Probation Service at the pre-sentence stage will clearly be pivotal. A recommendation on the likely post-release requirements included in a pre-sentence report will assist the court with the decision on overall sentence length, although any recommendation would still have to be open to review when release is being considered. A curfew, exclusion requirement or prohibited activity requirement might be suitable conditions to recommend for the licence period. A court might also wish to suggest that the offender should complete a rehabilitation programme, for example for drug abuse, anger management, or improving skills such as literacy and could recommend that this should be considered as a licence requirement if the programme has not been undertaken or completed in custody.

2.1.14 The Governor responsible for authorising the prisoner's release, in consultation with the Probation Service, is best placed to make recommendations at the point of release; this is the case at present and continues to be provided for in the Act. Specific court recommendations will only generally be appropriate in the context of relatively short sentences, where it would not be unreasonable for the sentencer to anticipate the relevance of particular requirements at the point of release. Making recommendations in relation to longer sentences (other than suggestions about the types of intervention that might be appropriate at some point during the sentence) would be unrealistic. The Governor and Probation Service should have due regard to any recommendations made by the sentencing court and the final recommendation to the Secretary of State on licence conditions will need to build upon any interventions during the custodial period and any other changes in the offender's circumstances.

- A court may sensibly suggest interventions that could be useful when passing sentence, but should only make specific recommendations about the requirements to be imposed on licence when announcing short sentences and where it is reasonable to anticipate their relevance at the point of release. The Governor and Probation Service should have due regard to any recommendations made by the sentencing court but its decision should be contingent upon any changed circumstances during the custodial period.
- The court should make it clear, at the point of sentence, that the requirements to be imposed on licence will ultimately be the responsibility of the Governor and Probation Service and that they are entitled to review any recommendations made by the court in the light of any changed circumstances.

17.1.10 Intermittent custody

Following a recommendation in the Halliday Report (see Chapter 16), s 183 of the CJA 2003 makes provision for 'intermittent custody'. Under s 183(1), a court passing a sentence of imprisonment of under 12 months may specify the number of days the offender must serve in prison, and at the same time provide for his release on licence, subject to specified conditions, at set intervals throughout his sentence. Such a sentence cannot be passed without the consent of the offender (s 183(6)). Under s 183(4), the sentence must be at least 28 weeks (14 where the sentence was passed by a magistrates' court) but no more than 51 weeks (26 where the sentence was passed by a magistrates' court) in respect of any one offence. Section 183(5) specifies that the number of custodial days must be at least 14 and (in respect of any one offence) must not be more than 90 (45 where the sentence was passed by a magistrates' court). Section 183(7) makes provision for consecutive sentences, but limits the total term to 65 weeks (52 where the sentence was passed by a magistrates' court), with a maximum of 180 days (90 where the sentence was passed by a magistrates' court) in custody (see also s 264A of the Act).

Section 185(1) limits requirements which can be added to the licence conditions for intermittent custody to: unpaid work requirement, activity requirement, programme requirement, prohibited activity requirement. Section 185(2) provides for electronic monitoring of licence conditions.

Paragraph 6 of Sched 10 to the Act enables the court to amend the order, for example to provide that the offender is to remain in prison until the number of days served by him in prison is equal to the number of custodial days. This provision could be used if (for example) the offender loses his job, which had provided the reason for intermittence. In such a case, the offender might wish to serve his sentence in the normal manner in order to get the custodial days over with as soon as possible.

Guidance by the Sentencing Guidelines Council on intermittent sentences, in Pt 3 of the Guidance of the CJA 2003 Sentencing regime (see <http://www. sentencing-guidelines.gov.uk/docs/New_sentences_guideline1.pdf>) includes the following:

B. Imposing an Intermittent Custody Order

2.3.6 Intermittent custody must be used only for offences that have crossed the custodial threshold. It is an alternative to immediate full-time custody and so must meet all the criteria that apply to such a sentence, in particular the need to pass the custody threshold and the need to ensure that the sentence is for the shortest term commensurate with the seriousness of the offence.

. . .

(i) Circumstances when intermittent custody may be appropriate

2.3.9 . . . intermittent custody is not intended to be used for sex offenders or those convicted of serious offences of either violence or burglary. There may be other offences which by their nature would make intermittent custody inappropriate and public safety should always be the paramount consideration.

2.3.10 The circumstances of the offender are likely to be the determining factor in deciding whether an intermittent custody order is appropriate. It is only appropriate where the custody threshold has been crossed and where suspending the custodial sentence or imposing a non-custodial sentence have been ruled out. Suitable candidates for weekend custody might include offenders who are: full-time carers; employed; or in education.

2.3.11 . . . For the purposes of intermittent custody the relevant steps are:

(a)   has the custody threshold been passed?
(b)   if so, is it unavoidable that a custodial sentence be imposed?
(c)   if so, can that sentence be suspended? (sentencers should be clear that they would have imposed a custodial sentence if the power to suspend had not been available)
(d)   if not, can it be served intermittently?
(e)   if not, impose a sentence which takes immediate effect for the term commensurate with the seriousness of the offence.

- Courts must be satisfied that a custodial sentence of less than 12 months is justified and that neither a community sentence nor a suspended sentence is appropriate before considering whether to make an intermittent custody order.
- When imposing a custodial sentence of less than 12 months, the court should always consider whether it would be appropriate to sentence an offender to intermittent custody; primary considerations will be public safety, offender suitability and sentence availability.
- Courts should strive to ensure that the intermittent custody provisions are applied in a way that limits discrimination and they should, in principle, be considered for all offenders.

(ii) Licence requirements

2.3.12 As a primary objective of being able to serve a custodial sentence intermittently is to enable offenders to continue to fulfil existing obligations in the community, and since the time spent in custody is utilised extensively for activities, experience has so far shown that additional, similar, requirements to be completed whilst on licence are not practical. However, requirements such as curfews, prohibited activity and exclusion requirements might be appropriate in a particular case.

The practical workings of an intermittent custody sentence will effectively rule out the use of some of the longer or more intensive community requirements. Requirements such as curfews, prohibited activity and exclusion requirements might be appropriate in a particular case.

(iii) Sentence length

2.3.13 The demands made on the offender by this sentence will generally be considerably greater than for a custodial sentence to be served immediately in full. The disruptive effect on family life, the psychological impact of going in and out of custody and the responsibility on the offender to travel to and from the custodial establishment on many occasions all make the sentence more onerous.

Once a court has decided that an offender should be sent to prison and has determined the length of the sentence, it should reduce the overall length of the sentence because it is to be served intermittently.

The provisions in the 2003 Act relating to intermittent custody remain in force, but the Home Office announced that Intermittent Custody Orders were to be withdrawn with effect from 20 November 2006.

17.2 RELEASE ON LICENCE

Section 244 of the Criminal Justice Act 2003 sets out when prisoners (other than those subject to life sentences or to sentences under the 'dangerous offender' provisions) must be released. Prisoners must spend the 'requisite custodial period' in custody before the Secretary of State is required to release them on licence. This period varies according to the length of the sentence:

- prisoners serving a sentence of 12 months or more (apart from dangerous offenders and life sentence prisoners) must be released on licence after serving one-half of their sentence;
- prisoners serving a sentence of less than 12 months must be released at the end of the 'custodial period' defined by s 181 (see above);

Where a fixed term prisoner is released on licence, the licence remains in force (unless he is recalled to prison) for the remainder of his sentence: s 249(1).

Section 247 deals with the release on licence of prisoners who are serving extended sentences under ss 227 or 228 (see above). Under s 247(2), once the offender has served one-half of the 'appropriate custodial term', he must be released on licence.

17.2.1 Conditions of release on licence

The Halliday Report called for greater supervision of prisoners following their release. It proposed that the supervisory period should run until the end of the total sentence, making (as the Report suggests) these sentences more 'real' and increasing opportunities for crime reduction through work with offenders after release. In essence the sentence is being served in full, the first part in custody and the second part under supervision in the community (with that second part being subject to conditions whose breach could result in recall to prison). It is perhaps noteworthy that this was the model already adopted for juvenile offenders (the detention and training order, which is a period of custody, followed by the same period being supervised in the community: see Chapter 20).

Section 250 of the Criminal Justice Act 2003 sets out the licence conditions that may be imposed. Under s 250(2), where the prisoner is serving a sentence of less than 12 months, the conditions must include:

a   the conditions required by the relevant court order; and
b   the 'standard conditions' in so far as they are not inconsistent with (a).

The conditions may also include conditions authorised by ss 62 or 64 of the Criminal Justice and Court Services Act 2000 (electronic monitoring or drug testing requirements) or other conditions of a kind prescribed by the Secretary of State.

Under s 250(4), where the prisoner is serving a sentence of 12 months or more, the conditions must include the standard conditions and may include conditions authorised by ss 62 or 64 of the Criminal Justice and Court Services Act 2000 (electronic monitoring or drug testing requirements), s 28 of the Offender Management Act 2007 (polygraph conditions, available in the case of certain sex offenders), or other conditions of a kind prescribed by the Secretary of State.

The Criminal Justice (Sentencing) (Licence Conditions) Order 2005 (SI 2005/648) sets out conditions of licences upon release from prison under s 250 of the CJA 2003: there are 'standard' conditions and 'additional' conditions that may be imposed. The 'standard' conditions of licence (under para 2) are that the prisoner must:

(a)   keep in touch with the responsible officer as instructed by him;
(b)   receive visits from the responsible officer as instructed by him;
(c)   permanently reside at an address approved by the responsible officer and obtain the prior permission of the responsible officer for any stay of one or more nights at a different address;
(d)   undertake work (including voluntary work) only with the approval of the responsible officer and obtain his prior approval in relation to any change in the nature of that work;
(e)   not travel outside the United Kingdom, the Channel Islands or the Isle of Man without the prior permission of the responsible officer, except where he is deported or removed from the United Kingdom . . .
(f)   be of good behaviour, and not behave in a way which undermines the purposes of the release on licence, which are to protect the public, prevent reoffending and promote successful reintegration into the community;
(g)   not commit any offence.

Other conditions of licence that may be imposed on a prisoner (under para 3) are:

(a)   a requirement that he reside at a certain place;
(b)   a requirement relating to his making or maintaining contact with a person;
(c)   a restriction relating to his making or maintaining contact with a person;
(d)   a restriction on his participation in, or undertaking of, an activity;
(e)   a requirement that he participate in, or co-operate with, a programme or set of activities designed to further one or more of the purposes referred to in section 250(8) of the Act;
(f)   a requirement that he comply with a curfew arrangement;

(g) a restriction on his freedom of movement (which is not a requirement referred to in sub-paragraph (f));

(h) a requirement relating to his supervision in the community by a responsible officer.

Section 238 (which does not apply to sentences of detention under s 91 of the Powers of Criminal Courts (Sentencing) Act 2000) empowers the court to recommend licence conditions when sentencing an offender to imprisonment for 12 months or more (such recommendations are not binding on the Secretary of State).

17.2.2 Early release under s 246

Section 246 of the CJA 2003 makes provision for release prisoners on licence before they are required to be released. Under s 246(1), the Secretary of State may release a prisoner on licence at any time during the period of 135 days ending with the day on which the prisoner will have served the custodial period under the sentence. Under s 246(4), prisoners serving one of the sentences applicable to dangerous offenders are not eligible for this scheme. Under s 246(2), where the length of the custodial period is at least six weeks, the offender must have served at least four weeks, and at least one-half, of the custodial period. Under s 250(5), a licence under s 246 must also include a curfew condition.

The curfew element is governed by s 253. The curfew condition specifies periods during which the offender must remain in a specified place, and includes a requirement that the curfew is electronically monitored. Under sub-s (2) the curfew condition can specify more than one place and/or more than one period but cannot last for less than 9 hours in any one day. Under sub-s (3), the curfew condition lasts until the date the offender would have been released on licence under s 244.

17.2.3 Revocation of licence

Section 254(1) of the CJA 2003 empowers the Secretary of State to revoke a prisoner's licence and thereby to recall the prisoner to prison. Section 254(2) provides that a person recalled to prison:

(a) may make representations in writing with respect to his recall, and

(b) on his return to prison, must be informed of the reasons for his recall and of his right to make representations.

Section 255 governs the recall of prisoners who have been released under s 246 (see above). Such recall may be ordered where the offender fails to comply with any licence condition or if his whereabouts can no longer be electronically monitored.

Finally, s 257 of the Criminal Justice Act 2003 enables additional days to be added to a prisoner's sentence if he is found guilty of disciplinary offences whilst in custody.

17.3 SUSPENDED SENTENCES OF IMPRISONMENT

The Halliday Report recommended the replacement of the existing form of suspended sentence with a new version, which would combine a community sentence with a suspended sentence of imprisonment (which could be activated if the offender fails to comply with the conditions of the non-custodial part of the sentence). The basis of this recommendation was that under the original form of suspended sentence, there was no engagement with the offender following the passing of the sentence, unless he reoffended during the currency of the sentence. The effect of the suspended sentence was based entirely on the so-called 'sword of Damocles' effect (that the custodial term would have to be served in the event of reoffending). Halliday took the view that greater engagement with the offender would make it less likely that he would reoffend.

The CJA 2003 made radical changes to the law relating to suspended sentences. The key changes were:

a   the removal of the requirement that there must be 'exceptional circumstances' before the court can impose a suspended sentence; and

b   the inclusion of a supervisory element into the suspended sentence to increase the rehabilitative effect of the sentence.

The law on suspended sentences is contained in s 189 of the 2003 Act. Section 189(1) enables a court which passes a prison sentence of between 28 and 51 weeks (prior to the implementation of changes to the sentencing powers of magistrates' courts, at least 14 days but not more than 12 months, or in the case of a magistrates' court, at least 14 days but not more than six months) to suspend that sentence for a period of between six months and two years and to order the offender to undertake certain requirements in the community. Under s 189(2), where consecutive sentences are imposed for two or more offences, the custodial term must be between 28 and 65 weeks (prior to the implementation of changes to the sentencing powers of magistrates' courts, up to 12 months, or in the case of a magistrates' court, six months).

The custodial part of the sentence only takes effect if the offender either fails to comply with the community requirements or commits another offence during the period of suspension.

The period during which the offender undertakes the community requirements is called 'the supervision period' and the entire length of period of suspension is called 'the operational period'.

Under s 189(3), the supervision period and the operational period must each be between six months and two years. Section 189(4) provides that the supervision period must not end later than the operational period. However, the supervision period may be less than the operational period.

Section 189(5) prohibits the court from imposing a community sentence at the same time as a suspended sentence (although it is open to the court to impose a fine or compensation order at the same time). Indeed, it would be unnecessary to impose a community sentence as well, given the range of requirements that can be added to a suspended sentence.

Section 189(6) provides that a suspended sentence is to be treated as a sentence of imprisonment.

17.3.1 Requirements that may be added to a suspended sentence

Section 190(1) of the 2003 Act sets out the requirements that may be imposed under a suspended sentence order:

(a) an unpaid work requirement (as defined by s 199),

(b) an activity requirement (as defined by s 201),

(c) a programme requirement (as defined by s 202),

(d) a prohibited activity requirement (as defined by s 203),

(e) a curfew requirement (as defined by s 204),

(f) an exclusion requirement (as defined by s 205),

(g) a residence requirement (as defined by s 206),

(h) a mental health treatment requirement (as defined by s 207),

(i) a drug rehabilitation requirement (as defined by s 209),

(j) an alcohol treatment requirement (as defined by s 212),

(k) a supervision requirement (as defined by s 213), and

(l) in a case where the offender is aged under 25, an attendance centre requirement (as defined by s 214).

Section 190(3) requires that where the court makes a suspended sentence order imposing a curfew requirement or an exclusion requirement, it must also impose an electronic monitoring requirement (as defined by s 215) unless, in the particular circumstances of the case, it would be inappropriate to do so. Under s 190(4), where the court makes a suspended sentence order imposing any of the other requirements listed above, it may also impose an electronic monitoring requirement. Where two or more different requirements are imposed, the court must consider whether, in the circumstances of the case, the requirements are compatible with each other (sub-s (5)).

Section 191(1) confers a discretion on the court to provide that a suspended sentence order passed under s 189(1) should be subject to periodic review at review hearings (which the offender is required to attend). Sub-section (2) excludes cases where the offender is subject to an order that imposes a drug rehabilitation requirement that is subject to court review, since reviews will be taking place anyway (under s 210).

Section 192 sets out what is to take place at a review hearing. Section 192(1) provides that the court may amend the community requirements of the suspended sentence order, following consideration of a report from the officer responsible for supervising the offender. However, under s 192(2)(a), the court cannot impose a requirement of a different kind unless the offender consents, although (under s 192(3)) a community requirement falling within any paragraph of s 190(1) is regarded as being of the same kind as any other community requirement falling within that paragraph. The offender's consent is required before a mental health treatment, drug rehabilitation or alcohol treatment requirement can be amended (s 192(2)(b)). The court may extend the supervision period, but not so that it lasts longer than two years or ends later than the operational period (s 192(2)(c)); however, the court has no power to amend the operational period (s 192(2)(d)).

Where (based on a report from the responsible officer who is supervising the offender) the court is of the opinion that 'the offender's progress in complying with the community requirements of the order is satisfactory', it can dispense with a review hearing, or may amend the order to provide that subsequent reviews can be held without a hearing (s 192(4)). Under s 192(5), if a review is held without a hearing and the court takes the view that the offender's progress is no longer satisfactory, the offender may be required to attend a review hearing.

17.3.2 Breach of suspended sentence orders

Schedule 12 to the Act provides for the revocation or amendment of suspended sentence orders, and sets out the effect of further convictions.

Paragraph 4 of Sched 12 provides that if the responsible officer is of the opinion that the offender has failed without reasonable excuse to comply with any of the community requirements of a suspended sentence order, the officer must give him a warning unless either the offender has received a similar warning within the previous 12 months or the officer refers the matter back to the court. A warning under para 4 must inform the offender that if, within the next 12 months, he again fails to comply with any requirement of the order, he will be liable to be brought before a court.

Paragraph 5(1) sets out the consequences of a breach of the order after a warning has been administered. If, within the next 12 months, the responsible officer is again of the opinion that the offender has failed without reasonable excuse to comply with any of the community requirements of the order, the officer must refer the matter back to the court.

Under para 6, where a suspended sentence order was made by a magistrates' court, or by the Crown Court but including a direction that any failure to comply with the community requirements of the order is to be dealt with by a magistrates' court, and it appears to a justice of the peace that the offender has failed to comply with any of the community requirements of the order, the justice may issue a summons requiring the offender to appear at the court or (if the allegation of non-compliance is in writing and substantiated on oath) issue a warrant for his arrest.

Paragraph 7 confers the same power on the Crown Court where the suspended sentence order was made by the Crown Court and does not include a direction that any failure to comply with the community requirements of the order is to be dealt with by a magistrates' court.

Under para 8(6) of Sched 12, where the suspended sentence order was made by the Crown Court and the offender is appearing before a magistrates' court, the magistrates may commit him (in custody or on bail) to the Crown Court to be dealt with.

Under para 8(8), if the Crown Court has to decide whether the offender has failed to comply with the community requirements of a suspended sentence order, this question is dealt with by a judge sitting alone.

Paragraph 10(1) makes it clear that an offender who is subject to a suspended sentence order that contains a mental health treatment, drug rehabilitation or alcohol treatment requirement, and who refuses to undergo any surgical, electrical or other treatment, is not to be regarded as being in breach of the order if the court takes the view that his refusal was, in all the circumstances, reasonable having regard to all the circumstances. Under para 10(2), the court cannot amend a mental health treatment, drug rehabilitation or alcohol treatment requirement unless the offender agrees to comply with the requirement as amended.

Paragraph 11 sets out which court may deal with a breach of a suspended sentence order. Paragraph 11(1) provides that the Crown Court may deal with breach of any suspended sentence (whether imposed by the Crown Court or a magistrates' court), and that any magistrates' court dealing with the offender can deal with breach of a suspended sentence order made by that or any other magistrates' court. Under para 11(2), where an offender is convicted by a magistrates' court of an offence committed during the operational period of a suspended sentence passed by the Crown Court, the magistrates may commit him (in custody or on bail) to the Crown Court, otherwise they must give written notice of the conviction to the appropriate officer of the Crown Court. In the latter case, para 12 enables the Crown Court to issue a summons requiring the offender to appear before the court, or to issue a warrant for his arrest.

Detailed guidance on the effect of some of the committal powers under Sched 12 of the CJA 2003 was given by the Court of Appeal in *R v Majury* [2007] EWCA Crim 2968. Paragraph 8(6) applies only to a breach of a suspended sentence order with which the magistrates themselves can deal. Magistrates can deal with breach of a suspended sentence passed by a magistrates' court, or where the breach comprises a failure to comply with a community requirement in a suspended sentence order and the Crown Court directed when the sentence was passed that failures to comply should be dealt with by the magistrates' court (see para 6(2) and para 11(1)). Paragraph 8(6) does not, however, apply to breach of a suspended sentence when the sentence was passed by the Crown Court and the breach is comprised in the commission of a further offence. Furthermore, para 11(2) does not apply to new offences committed in breach of the suspended sentence. If the offender is committed to the Crown Court, then the Crown Court can deal with the breach under Schedule 12, para 8(1)(b) (see para 11(1)). If the offender is not committed to the Crown Court, but the Crown Court receives notice of the breach, it can take its own enforcement proceedings by issuing a summons or a warrant for his arrest under para 12(1). Paragraph 11(2) does not of itself give the Crown Court power to deal with the offences committed during the operational period of the suspended sentence; rather, it is the means by which the breach of the suspended sentence is brought before the Crown Court to be dealt with under para 8(1)(b). If the justices want the Crown Court to deal with the original offence and the 'new' offences, and the latter are triable either way, the justices should decide whether the powers of the Crown Court to sentence for the new offences should be those of the Crown Court or of the magistrates' court. If the former, then the committal of those offences would take place under s 3 of the Powers of Criminal Courts (Sentencing) Act 2000, and if the latter, committal would be under s 6 of the 2000 Act (per Hooper LJ at paras 8-11).

17.3.2.1 Consequences of breaching suspended sentence order

Paragraph 8 sets out the powers of the court following the breach of a community requirement or where the offender is convicted of a further offence. Under this paragraph, where:

a   it is proved to the satisfaction of the court that the offender has failed, without reasonable excuse, to comply with any of the community requirements of the suspended sentence order; or b   the offender is convicted of an offence committed during the operational period of a suspended sentence,

the court must deal with him in one of the following ways (set out in para 8(2)):

a   make an order that the suspended sentence is to take effect with its original term unaltered (this is sometimes known as 'activating' the suspended sentence); or
b   make an order that the sentence is to take effect but with the substitution of a lesser term (i.e. activating the suspended sentence only in part); or
c   amend the order by:

  i   imposing more onerous community requirements;
  ii   extending the supervision period (i.e. extending the period during which the offender is subject to community requirements); or
  iii extending the operational period (so that the offender is at risk for a longer period than was originally the case of the activation of the suspended sentence).

Paragraph 8(3) stipulates that the court must activate the whole or part of the suspended term of imprisonment unless it is of the opinion that it would be unjust to do so in view of all the circumstances, including the matters mentioned in sub-para (4). The factors set out in para 8(4) are:

a   the extent to which the offender has complied with the community requirements of the suspended sentence order; and
b   where the offender has been convicted of a subsequent offence, the facts of that subsequent offence.

Where the court does not order that the suspended sentence is to take effect, it must state its reasons (para 8(3)).

These provisions thus include a presumption that a suspended sentence will be activated following a breach, unless the court finds that it would be unjust to do so. If it does activate the suspended sentence, the court can set a shorter custodial term for the offender to serve if it wishes. If the court finds that it would be unjust to activate the suspended sentence, it can maintain the sentence suspended but amend the order to make the community requirements more onerous or to extend either the supervision or operational periods.

In *R v Sheppard* [2008] EWCA Crim 799, the Court of Appeal gave further guidance on the activation of suspended sentences under Sched 12 of the Criminal Justice Act 2003, holding that the statutory provisions envisage a two stage test. First, where there has been a breach, the court must order that the suspended sentence take effect either in whole or in part unless it would be unjust to do so. The extent of compliance with the original order is relevant to that decision. So, for example, if 95 per cent of the order had been complied with, a court might conclude that it was unjust to order that any part of the custodial term take effect. Secondly, if it is not unjust to activate the suspended sentence, then the court must decide whether or not to impose the original sentence or modify the term. Either option is available where there has been part compliance. If there has been substantial and prompt compliance with the order then, even if a suspended sentence is to be activated, the court may be minded to impose a lesser term than that originally specified (per Coulson J at para 14).

Many of the cases decided under the earlier system of suspended sentences are still relevant to the question of what action should be taken in the event of the offender committing a further offence. Where the court activates all or part of a suspended sentence, it should be ordered to run consecutively to a prison sentence for the later offence unless there are exceptional circumstances (*R v Ithell* [1969] 1 WLR 272). This is because the offender is being sentenced for two separate offences. However, in *R v Bocskei* (1970) 54 Cr App R 519, it was pointed out that the 'totality' principle applies to the activation of suspended sentences. Therefore, if the activation of a suspended sentence to run consecutively with a custodial sentence for the present offence would result in a total sentence which is too harsh, the court may activate part of the suspended sentence and/or order that the two sentences be served concurrently.

It must be emphasised that a defendant is only in breach of a suspended sentence if he commits an imprisonable offence during the operational period of the suspended sentence. It follows from this that the defendant will be in breach of the suspended sentence even if he is convicted of the later offence after the expiry of the operational period, provided that the offence was committed during the operational period. It is the date of the commission of the later offence, not the date when the defendant is convicted of that offence, which determines whether there is a breach of a suspended sentence.

In *R v Craine* (1981) 3 Cr App R(S) 198, it was emphasised that it is only in exceptional circumstances that a suspended sentence will not be activated if a further imprisonable offence is committed. The mere fact that the later offence is of a different type to the offence for which the suspended sentence was imposed does not justify refraining from activating the suspended sentence (see also *R v Saunders* (1970) 54 Cr App R 247; *R v Clitheroe* (1987) 9 Cr App R(S) 159).

However, in most cases (though not all), it will be inappropriate to activate a suspended sentence where the later offence is dealt with by means of a non-custodial sentence (*R v McElhorne* (1983) 5 Cr App R(S) 53; *R v Dobson* (1989) 11 Cr App R(S) 332). In *R v Stewart* (1984) 6 Cr App R (S) 166, it was said that the appropriate method of dealing with such cases is to look first at the 'breach offence', to determine whether it is sufficiently serious to warrant a custodial sentence; if it does not, that is a strong circumstance for not bringing the suspended sentence into operation (per Beldam J at p 169). This is so even if the later offence is of the same nature as the offence for which the suspended sentence was imposed. In *R v Brooks* (1990) 12 Cr App R(S) 756, the defendant was convicted of possessing a small quantity of cannabis for his own use. This conviction placed him in breach of a suspended sentence for possession of cannabis with intent to supply. It was held by the Court of Appeal that the later offence was not sufficiently serious to justify a custodial sentence. The comparative triviality of the second offence, making a custodial sentence for that offence inappropriate, meant that it would be wrong to activate the suspended sentence for the earlier offence.

Another argument in favour of leniency is that the later offence was committed when the operational period of the suspended sentence had almost expired (*R v Carr* (1979) 1 Cr App R(S) 53; *R v Fitton* (1989) 11 Cr App R(S) 350). In *Carr*, the later offence was committed when the offender had completed 22 months of a two-year suspended sentence. He was sentenced to two years' imprisonment for the later offence, but the Court of Appeal ordered that the suspended sentence run concurrently with the sentence for the later offence. An alternative in such a case may well be to activate only part of the suspended sentence.

17.3.3 Amendment of suspended sentence orders

Paragraph 13(1) of Sched 12 to the CJA 2003 empowers the court to cancel the community requirements that form part of a suspended sentence order if it appears to the court (on the application of the offender or the responsible officer) that, having regard to the circumstances which have arisen since the order was made, it would be in the interests of justice to do so. Paragraph 13(2) states that the circumstances to be taken into account include 'the offender's making good progress or his responding satisfactorily to supervision'. Another reason might be illness or disability making it impossible for the offender to comply with the original requirements.

Paragraph 15(1) empowers the court (upon application by the offender or the responsible officer) to amend any community requirement of a suspended sentence order either by cancelling the requirement, or by replacing it with a requirement of the same kind. Under para 15(3), the court cannot amend a mental health treatment, drug rehabilitation or alcohol treatment requirement without the consent of the offender; however, where the offender withholds consent, the court may (under para 15(4)) revoke the suspended sentence order, and deal with the offender for the offence in respect of which the suspended sentence was imposed in any way in which it could deal with him if he had just been convicted by the court of it. If the court does re-sentence the offender, it must take into account the extent to which the offender has complied with the requirements of the order (para 15(5)).

Paragraph 16 provides that where a community order includes a drug rehabilitation, alcohol treatment or mental health treatment requirement and the medical practitioner responsible for the treatment is of the opinion that:

- the treatment should be extended beyond the period specified in the order;
- the offender should receive different treatment;
- the offender is not susceptible to treatment; or
- the offender does not require further treatment,

he must make a report to the responsible officer. Similarly, if for any reason the medical practitioner is unwilling to continue to treat the offender, he must report this fact to the responsible officer. Where this has occurred, the responsible officer will apply to the court to have the requirement amended or cancelled.

Under para 18, where the suspended sentence order includes an unpaid work requirement, the offender or the responsible officer may apply to the court to extend the 12 months limit for the completion of the unpaid work if it is in the interests of justice to do so. This might be necessary if, for example, the offender became ill during the 12 months and was unable to complete all the hours of unpaid work during the first 12 months.

17.3.4 Sentencing Guidelines Council guidance on suspended sentences

The Guidelines on the sentencing regime created by the CJA 2003 contain the following:

B. Imposing a Suspended Sentence

2.2.6 A suspended sentence is a sentence of imprisonment. It is subject to the same criteria as a sentence of imprisonment which is to commence immediately. In particular, this requires a court to be satisfied that the custody threshold has been passed and that the length of the term is the shortest term commensurate with the seriousness of the offence.

. . .

(i) The decision to suspend

2.2.10 There are many similarities between the suspended sentence and the community sentence. In both cases, requirements can be imposed during the supervision period and the court can respond to breach by sending the offender to custody. The crucial difference is that the suspended sentence is a prison sentence and is appropriate only for an offence that passes the custody threshold and for which imprisonment is the only option. A community sentence may also be imposed for an offence that passes the custody threshold where the court considers that to be appropriate.

2.2.11 . . . For the purposes of suspended sentences the relevant steps are:

(a)   has the custody threshold been passed?
(b)   if so, is it unavoidable that a custodial sentence be imposed?
(c)   if so, can that sentence be suspended? (sentencers should be clear that they would have imposed a custodial sentence if the power to suspend had not been available);
(d)   if not, can the sentence be served intermittently?
(e)   if not, impose a sentence which takes immediate effect for the term commensurate with the seriousness of the offence.

(ii) Length of sentence

2.2.12 Before making the decision to suspend sentence, the court must already have decided that a prison sentence is justified and should also have decided the length of sentence that would be the shortest term commensurate with the seriousness of the offence if it were to be imposed immediately. The decision to suspend the sentence should not lead to a longer term being imposed than if the sentence were to take effect immediately.

A prison sentence that is suspended should be for the same term that would have applied if the offender were being sentenced to immediate custody.

2.2.13 When assessing the length of the operational period of a suspended sentence, the court should have in mind the relatively short length of the sentence being suspended and the advantages to be gained by retaining the opportunity to extend the operational period at a later stage (see below).

The operational period of a suspended sentence should reflect the length of the sentence being suspended. As an approximate guide, an operational period of up to 12 months might normally be appropriate for a suspended sentence of up to 6 months and an operational period of up to 18 months might normally be appropriate for a suspended sentence of up to 12 months.

(iii) Requirements

2.2.14 The court will set the requirements to be complied with during the supervision period. Whilst the offence for which a suspended sentence is imposed is generally likely to be more serious than one for which a community sentence is imposed, the imposition of the custodial sentence is a clear punishment and deterrent. In order to ensure that the overall terms of the sentence are commensurate with the seriousness of the offence, it is likely that the requirements to be undertaken during the supervision period would be less onerous than if a community sentence had been imposed. These requirements will need to ensure that they properly address those factors that are most likely to reduce the risk of reoffending.

Because of the very clear deterrent threat involved in a suspended sentence, requirements imposed as part of that sentence should generally be less onerous than those imposed as part of a community sentence. A court wishing to impose onerous or intensive requirements on an offender should reconsider its decision to suspend the sentence and consider whether a community sentence might be more appropriate.

C. Breaches

2.2.15 The essence of a suspended sentence is to make it abundantly clear to an offender that failure to comply with the requirements of the order or commission of another offence will almost certainly result in a custodial sentence . . .

. . .

2.2.19 If an offender near the end of an operational period (having complied with the requirements imposed) commits another offence, it may be more appropriate to amend the order rather than activate it.

2.2.20 If a new offence committed is of a less serious nature than the offence for which the suspended sentence was passed, it may justify activating the sentence with a reduced term or amending the terms of the order.

2.2.21 It is expected that any activated suspended sentence will be consecutive to the sentence imposed for the new offence.

2.2.22 If the new offence is non-imprisonable, the sentencer should consider whether it is appropriate to activate the suspended sentence at all.

Where the court decides to amend a suspended sentence order rather than activate the custodial sentence, it should give serious consideration to extending the supervision or operational periods (within statutory limits) rather than making the requirements more onerous.

17.4 LIFE SENTENCES

Murder is punishable with imprisonment for life: such a sentence is mandatory. There are several offences (such as manslaughter, rape, inflicting grievous bodily harm with intent, and robbery) which *may* result in a life sentence.

17.4.1 Mandatory life sentences

Section 269 of the Criminal Justice Act 2003 governs the determination of the minimum term in relation to mandatory life sentences. Under s 269(2), a court passing a mandatory life sentence must make an order specifying a period of time the prisoner must serve before the Parole Board can consider release on licence under the provisions of s 28 of the Crime (Sentences) Act 1997 (often called the 'minimum term'). Under subs (3), the minimum term is to be such as the court considers appropriate taking into account the seriousness of the offence(s).

However, under s 269(4), where the offender was aged 21 or over at the time of the offence, and the court takes the view that the offence is so serious that the offender ought to spend the rest of his life in prison, the court must order that the early release provisions are not to apply. Under s 269(5)(a), the court must have regard to the principles set out in Sched 21 to the Act.

Schedule 21 provides that where the offender was aged 21 or over when he committed the offence, the appropriate starting point is a 'whole life order' if the court considers the seriousness of the offences is 'exceptionally high'. Under para 4(2), cases that would normally fall within this category include:

(a) in the case of the murder of two or more persons, each murder involves any of the following—

  (i) a substantial degree of premeditation or planning,
  (ii) the abduction of the victim, or
  (iii) sexual or sadistic conduct,

(b) the murder of a child, if involving the abduction of the child or sexual or sadistic motivation,
(c) a murder done for the purpose of advancing a political, religious or ideological cause, or
(d) a murder by an offender previously convicted of murder.

Where the offender was aged 18 or over when he committed the offence, the appropriate starting point is a minimum term of 30 years if the court considers that the seriousness of the offence is 'particularly high'. Under para 5(2), cases that would normally fall within this category include:

(a) the murder of a police officer or prison officer in the course of his duty,
(b) a murder involving the use of a firearm or explosive,
(c) a murder done for gain (such as a murder done in the course or furtherance of robbery or burglary, done for payment or done in the expectation of gain as a result of the death),
(d) a murder intended to obstruct or interfere with the course of justice,
(e) a murder involving sexual or sadistic conduct,
(f) the murder of two or more persons,
(g) a murder that is racially or religiously aggravated or aggravated by sexual orientation, or
(h) a murder falling within paragraph 4(2) [quoted above] committed by an offender who was aged under 21 when he committed the offence.

In other cases where the offender was aged 18 or over when he committed the offence, the appropriate starting point, in determining the minimum term, is 15 years (para 6). If the offender was aged under 18 when he committed the offence, the appropriate starting point, in determining the minimum term, is 12 years (para 7).

Paragraph 8 goes on to provide that:

> Having chosen a starting point, the court should take into account any aggravating or mitigating factors, to the extent that it has not allowed for them in its choice of starting point.

These aggravating or mitigating factors may result in a minimum term of any length (whatever the starting point), or in the making of a whole life order (para 9).

Paragraph 10 lists some aggravating factors (additional to those mentioned in paras 4(2) and 5(2)):

(a) a significant degree of planning or premeditation,
(b) the fact that the victim was particularly vulnerable because of age or disability,
(c) mental or physical suffering inflicted on the victim before death,
(d) the abuse of a position of trust,
(e) the use of duress or threats against another person to facilitate the commission of the offence,
(f) the fact that the victim was providing a public service or performing a public duty, and
(g) concealment, destruction or dismemberment of the body.

Paragraph 11 lists some mitigating factors that may be relevant to the offence of murder:

(a) an intention to cause serious bodily harm rather than to kill,
(b) lack of premeditation,
(c) the fact that the offender suffered from any mental disorder or mental disability which (although not falling within section 2(1) of the Homicide Act 1957), lowered his degree of culpability,
(d) the fact that the offender was provoked (for example, by prolonged stress) in a way not amounting to a defence of provocation,
(e) the fact that the offender acted to any extent in self-defence,
(f) a belief by the offender that the murder was an act of mercy, and
(g) the age of the offender.

In *R v Last* [2005] EWCA Crim 106; [2005] 2 Cr App R (S) 64, the Court of Appeal said that judges are free to depart from the guidelines contained in Sched 21 (and in guidance issued by the Sentencing Guidelines Council), provided that valid reasons are given for doing so.

17.4.2 Discretionary life sentences

When imposing a discretionary life sentence, the trial judge is empowered to specify a minimum length of time which the offender should serve before release on licence (s 82A of the Powers of Criminal Courts (Sentencing) Act 2000). A minimum recommendation should be made unless the case is an exceptional one, where the judge considers the offence to be so serious that detention for life is justified by the seriousness of the offence alone, irrespective of the risk to the public. Guidance is given in para IV.47 of the *Consolidated Practice Direction*.

In *R v Whittaker* [1997] 1 Cr App R(S) 261, Lord Bingham CJ said (at p 264) that before a discretionary life sentence can be imposed, there must be:

> good grounds for believing that the offender may remain a serious danger to the public for a period which cannot be reliably estimated at the date of sentence. By 'serious danger' the Court has in mind particularly serious offences of violence and serious offences of a sexual nature. The grounds which may found such a belief will often relate to the mental condition of the offender.

Further guidance on discretionary life sentences was given in *R v Chapman* [2000] 1 Cr App R 77, where the offender was given a discretionary life sentence after pleading guilty to arson. The offender, aged 19, had started a fire in the room he shared in an adult residential unit where it could be, and was, quickly discovered and extinguished. The property had not been extensively damaged; no personal injuries had been sustained, nor were they likely or intended to have been. The Court of Appeal held that an indeterminate life sentence may be imposed if the offender has committed an offence grave enough to merit an extremely long sentence, and there are good grounds for believing that the offender might remain a serious danger to the public for a period which could not be reliably estimated at the date of sentence. The court added that the 'more likely it is that an offender will offend again, and the more grave such offending is likely to be if it does occur, the less emphasis the court may lay on the gravity of the original offence'. However, a life sentence should never be imposed 'unless the circumstances are such as to call for a severe sentence based on the offence which the offender has committed' (per Lord Bingham CJ at p 85). In the present case, the offence was not sufficiently grave to justify imposition of a life sentence.

In *R v Kehoe* [2008] EWCA Crim 819, however, the Court of Appeal ruled that where an offender meets the criteria of dangerousness (under the CJA 2003), there is no longer any need to protect the public by passing a sentence of life imprisonment, since the public are now protected by the imposition of the sentence of imprisonment for public protection under the 2003 Act. The cases decided before the 2003 Act came into effect therefore 'no longer offer guidance on when a life sentence should be imposed'. Now, 'when the court finds that the defendant satisfies the criteria for dangerousness, a life sentence [under s 225 of the 2003 Act] should be reserved for those cases where the culpability of the offender is particularly high or the offence itself particularly grave' (per Openshaw J at para 17).

17.4.3 Release of life prisoners

Section 28 of the Crime Sentences Act 1997 deals with the release of mandatory life prisoners. Prior to the amendment of this provision, the trial judge made a recommendation as to the minimum period which should elapse before the offender was released on licence; this recommendation was communicated to the Home Secretary, along with the view of the Lord Chief Justice. The recommendation was not binding on the Home Secretary, who could shorten or lengthen the period. The prisoner's case would, in due course, be reviewed by the Parole Board, which could recommend that the prisoner be released on licence. However, the Home Secretary was not bound by that recommendation. The law relating to the release of prisoners serving mandatory life sentences was amended by the CJA 2003 in order to give effect to the ruling of the European Court of Human Rights in *Stafford v UK* (2002) 35 EHRR 32 (where it was held that the fixing of a tariff (i.e. the minimum time to be served) is to be regarded as a sentencing exercise rather than the administrative implementation of a life sentence that has already been passed) and *R (Anderson) v Secretary of State for the Home Department* [2002] UKHL 46; [2003] 1 AC 837 (where the House of Lords held that the Home Secretary's power to fix sentencing tariffs was incompatible with the right to a fair trial guaranteed by Art 6 of the European Convention, since this function should be performed by an independent and impartial tribunal). Now, the minimum term to be served is specified by the court (guidance on the fixing of the minimum term is contained in para IV.49 of the *Consolidated Practice Direction*).

Release on licence of life prisoners is considered by the Parole Board. Under s 28(5) of the Crime (Sentences) Act 1997, once the prisoner has served the minimum period specified by the court, he must be released if the Parole Board so directs. Under sub-s (6), the Parole Board can only give a direction under sub-s (5) if the Secretary of State has referred the prisoner's case to the Board, and the Board is 'satisfied that it is no longer necessary for the protection of the public that the prisoner should be confined'. Sub-section (7) enables the prisoner to require the Secretary of State to refer his case to the Parole Board once he has served the minimum term specified by the court. If the Board does not decide to release the prisoner, he can require his case to be considered every two years (s 28(7)(b)).

17.5 MANDATORY SENTENCES

For some offences, a minimum sentence has been prescribed by Parliament.

17.5.1 Minimum sentences for a third Class A drug trafficking offence

Section 110 of the Powers of Criminal Courts (Sentencing) Act 2000 provides for the imposition of a minimum sentence of seven years for conviction of a third Class A drug trafficking offence. The section states that where:

a   a person is convicted of a Class A drug trafficking offence (as defined by the Proceeds of Crime Act 2002); and

b   at the time when that offence was committed the offender was 18 or over and had been convicted in any part of the United Kingdom of two other Class A drug trafficking offences; and

c   one of those other offences was committed after he had been convicted of the other (so where the offender is convicted of more than one offence on a single occasion that only counts as one conviction for these purposes),

then the court must impose a custodial sentence of at least seven years unless the court takes the view that there are particular circumstances which relate to any of the offences or to the offender and which would make it unjust in all the circumstances to impose the minimum sentence.

In *R v Stenhouse* [2000] 2 Cr App R(S) 386, the Court of Appeal decided that there were 'particular circumstances' making it unjust to impose the seven-year minimum: the last of the offender's previous convictions had led to a community order; that fact, together with other mitigating features, made the minimum sentence unjust in all the circumstances.

17.5.2 Minimum sentence for a third domestic burglary

Section 111 of the Powers of Criminal Courts (Sentencing) Act 2000 prescribes a minimum sentence of three years for conviction of a third domestic burglary. It states that where:

a a person is convicted of a domestic burglary (that is, a burglary committed in respect of a building or part of a building which is a dwelling); and

b at the time when that offence was committed the offender had attained the age of 18 and had been convicted in England or Wales of two other domestic burglaries; and

c one of those other burglaries was committed after he had been convicted of the other, and both were committed after 30 November 1999,

then the court must impose a custodial sentence of at least three years unless the court takes the view that there are particular circumstances which relate to any of the offences or to the offender and which would make it unjust in all the circumstances to impose the minimum sentence.

17.5.3 Minimum sentence for certain firearms offences

Section 51A of the Firearms Act 1968 (inserted by the Criminal Justice Act 2003 in response to the rapid growth of gun-crime) prescribes minimum sentences for certain firearms offences under the Firearms Act 1968. Under s 51A(5), the minimum sentence for a person aged 18 or over at the time of the offence is five years (three years where the offender was under 18 at the time of the offence). Section 51A(2) provides that the court must impose a custodial sentence for a term of at least the required minimum unless it is of the opinion that there are exceptional circumstances relating to the offence or to the offender which justify its not doing so.

In *R v Rehman; R v Wood* [2005] EWCA Crim 2056; [2006] 1 Cr App R (S) 77, the court held that the mandatory minimum sentence under s 51A should not be imposed if it would result in an 'arbitrary and disproportionate sentence'.

17.5.4 Violent Crime Reduction Act 2006

Section 29 of the Violent Crime Reduction Act 2006 sets minimum sentences for offences under s 28 of that Act (using someone to mind dangerous weapons). Where the offender is aged 18 or over at the date of conviction, the minimum sentence is five years;

where he is aged under 18, the minimum sentence is three years (s 29(4) and (6) respectively). In both instances, the court may refrain from imposing the minimum sentence if it is of the opinion that there are 'exceptional circumstances relating to the offence or to the offender' which justify it doing so.

17.5.5 Discount for guilty plea

Where ss 110 or 111 of the 2000 Act are applicable, the court can still give credit for a guilty plea under s 144 of the CJA 2003. However, the amount of discount is limited by s 144(2) of the 2003 Act, which provides that in a case under ss 110 or 111, the court can take account of a guilty plea by passing a sentence which is not less than 80 per cent of what would otherwise be the minimum sentence prescribed by the 2000 Act.

Similar provision is not made for the other mandatory minimum sentences discussed above. In *R v Jordan* [2004] EWCA Crim 3291; [2005] 2 Cr App R (S) 44, the court considered whether there should be a discount for pleading guilty where s 51A of the Firearms Act 1968 applies. It was held that the absence from s 51A of any reference to s 144 of the CJA 2003 (credit for guilty pleas) is to be regarded as deliberate. However, the court added that the rigour of s 51A is mitigated by the possibility of there being exceptional circumstances. The court concluded that, once a judge has properly identified exceptional circumstances, the sentence is at large. The minimum sentence provided in s 51A is a factor which the judge can take into account, and he will also take into account the relevant sentencing guidelines and any available mitigation. This will only arise, said the court, where there are real exceptional circumstances; such cases will be rare (per Douglas Brown J at para 30).

17.6 SENTENCING POWERS OF MAGISTRATES' COURTS

The sentence which may be imposed by a magistrates' court often depends on whether the offence is summary or triable either way.

17.6.1 Summary offences

The statute creating a summary offence will indicate whether or not the offence is punishable with imprisonment. Prior to the implementation of the changes made by the CJA 2003, if the summary offence is an imprisonable offence, the maximum sentence is six months or that prescribed by the statute which creates the offence, whichever is less (s 78(1) of the Powers of Criminal Courts (Sentencing) Act 2000). If the statute creating the offence expressly overrides the limit of six months, then the statute creating the offence prevails (s 78(2)).

These powers are altered by the CJA 2003. Schedule 26 lists a number of summary offences where the maximum term of imprisonment is increased to 51 weeks (to fit in with the new framework of custodial sentences created by the Act). Section 281(4) and (5) provides for all summary offences contained in Acts passed before or in the same Parliamentary Session as the 2003 Act with a maximum penalty of six months' imprisonment to have this maximum penalty raised to 51 weeks.

17.6.2 Offences which are triable either way

The maximum sentence for an offence which is triable either way because it is listed in Sched 1 to the Magistrates' Courts Act 1980 is currently six months' imprisonment (s 32(1)).

Where the offence is triable either way because the statute creating it gives alternative penalties for summary conviction and conviction on indictment, the maximum penalty is six months' imprisonment or the term specified in the statute creating the offence, whichever is the less (s 78(1) of the Powers of Criminal Courts (Sentencing) Act 2000). If the statute creating the offence expressly overrides the six-month limit, the statute creating the offence prevails (s 78(2)).

Section 282(1) of the CJA 2003 (not in force at the time of writing) increases the maximum custodial term that may be imposed following summary conviction of an either way offence from six months to 12 months. Furthermore, under s 154(1) of the CJA 2003 (also not in force at the time of writing), the powers of magistrates are extended, so that they can pass a sentence of up to 12 months' custody for a single either-way offence.

17.6.3 Consecutive terms of imprisonment

Section 133(1) of the Magistrates' Courts Act 1980 empowers a magistrates' court to order custodial sentences to run consecutively. However, the maximum aggregate sentence which may be imposed is six months (s 133(1)) unless the court is dealing with the offender for two or more offences which are triable either way, in which case the maximum aggregate sentence is 12 months (s 133(2)).

Thus, if an offender is convicted of three summary offences each of which is punishable with three months' imprisonment, the maximum aggregate term is six months. The magistrates could, for example, impose a sentence of three months on each offence but one of the terms would have to be concurrent, so that the maximum does not exceed six months; alternatively, they could impose a sentence of two months on each to run consecutively. If the offender is being dealt with for one either-way offence and a number of summary offences, the maximum aggregate sentence remains six months. It is only where the court is dealing with an offender for at least two either-way offences that a total of up to 12 months' custody may be imposed.

It should be noted that where a magistrates' court activates a suspended sentence (which it can only do if that sentence was imposed by a magistrates' court), the provisions of s 133 do not apply; the effect of this is that whilst the sentence(s) for the present offence(s) must not exceed the limit set by s 133, the suspended sentence may be activated even if doing so has the effect of imposing a total term in excess of the limit set by s 133 (*R v Chamberlain* (1992) 13 Cr App R(S) 525).

Section 155(1) of the CJA 2003 amends s 133 of the Magistrates' Court Act 1980 to empower magistrates to impose consecutive sentences such that the aggregate term is up to 65 weeks (which equates roughly to 15 months) when passing sentence in respect of two or more offences.

Chapter 18

Adult offenders:
community sentences

In this chapter, we look at the community sentences which may be imposed on adult offenders under the Criminal Justice Act 2003.

18.1 COMMUNITY SENTENCES UNDER THE CRIMINAL JUSTICE ACT 2003

Prior to the implementation of the community sentence provisions of the Criminal Justice Act (CJA) 2003, a range of separate community orders was available for adult offenders. These orders included 'community service orders', which were re-named 'community punishment orders' (requiring unpaid community work); probation orders, which were re-named 'community rehabilitation orders' (placing the offender under the supervision of a probation officer), and 'community punishment and rehabilitation orders' (which effectively combined probation and community service).

The Halliday Report (see Chapter 16) said that in order to ensure that non-custodial sentences reduce the likelihood of reoffending, courts should have the power to impose a single, non-custodial penalty made up of specific elements. This new sentence would replace all existing community sentences. The Report said that supervision in all cases would be geared towards managing and enforcing the sentence, and supporting resettlement. In deciding which particular elements to include in the sentence passed on an offender, the court should, said the Report, consider the aims of punishment, including reparation and prevention of reoffending. The 'punitive weight' of the sentence should reflect the seriousness of offence(s), subject to any increase in the severity of the offence resulting from the existence of previous convictions.

The Report also expressed the view that 'visible involvement' of the court for the duration of the sentence would exert additional leverage over the offender during periods in the community (whether after release from prison, or under a community sentence) and would make community sentences more transparent to the public (and, it might be added, increase the level of public confidence in community sentences as an effective form of punishment rather than some sort of 'let-off' or 'soft option').

The broad thrust of these proposals was accepted by the Government. The CJA 2003 therefore aimed to simplify the regime of community sentences. Essentially it gives the court a 'pick and mix' menu to enable it to construct a community order that is appropriate to the particular offender.

18.1.1 Definition of community order

The starting point is the definition of 'community order' in s 177(1) of the Act. This provides that where a person aged 16 or over is convicted of an offence, the court may make a 'community order' imposing on him any one or more of the following requirements:

(a)   an unpaid work requirement (as defined by s 199),
(b)   an activity requirement (as defined by s 201),
(c)   a programme requirement (as defined by s 202),
(d)   a prohibited activity requirement (as defined by s 203),
(e)   a curfew requirement (as defined by s 204),
(f)   an exclusion requirement (as defined by s 205),
(g)   a residence requirement (as defined by s 206),
(h)   a mental health treatment requirement (as defined by s 207),
(i)   a drug rehabilitation requirement (as defined by s 209),
(j)   an alcohol treatment requirement (as defined by s 212),
(k)   a supervision requirement (as defined by s 213), and
(l)   where the offender is aged under 25, an attendance centre requirement (as defined by s 214).

Under s 177(5), the community order must specify a date, not more than three years after the date of the order, by which all the requirements in it must have been complied with. Where two or more different requirements are imposed, the order may specify different completion dates for them. An order may only impose two or more different requirements if those requirements are compatible with each other (sub-s (6)).

The two key points, therefore, are that:

- a community order can last for up to three years; and
- the components of the order must be compatible with each other.

As was the case prior to the passing of the CJA 2003, a community sentence can be imposed only if the seriousness of the case merits such a sentence; in other words, the community sentence 'threshold' has to be met. Section 148 of the 2003 Act provides that:

(1)   A court must not pass a community sentence on an offender unless it is of the opinion that the offence, or the combination of the offence and one or more offences associated with it, was serious enough to warrant such a sentence.

(2)   Where a court passes a community sentence which consists of or includes a community order—

(a)   the particular requirement or requirements forming part of the community order must be such as, in the opinion of the court, is, or taken together are, the most suitable for the offender, and

(b)   the restrictions on liberty imposed by the order must be such as in the opinion of the court are commensurate with the seriousness of the offence, or the combination of the offence and one or more offences associated with it.

Section 10 of the Criminal Justice and Immigration Act 2008 amends the restrictions on imposing community sentences set out in s 148 of the 2003 Act. A new sub-section (sub-s (5)) is inserted to make it clear that nothing in s 148 requires the court to impose a community sentence even though the offence is serious enough to justify such a sentence (and so the court may, for example, impose a fine instead). This amendment reflects the existing practice of the courts, which is that an offence may cross a particular threshold but a more lenient sentence may nevertheless be imposed if there is (for example) compelling mitigation.

It may well be that an offender who ultimately receives a community sentence was remanded in custody prior to conviction and/or sentence. Section 149(1) of the 2003 Act provides that in such a case:

In determining the restrictions on liberty to be imposed by a community order or youth community order in respect of an offence, the court may have regard to any period for which the offender has been remanded in custody in connection with the offence or any other offence the charge for which was founded on the same facts or evidence.

In other words, the offender may receive a more lenient community sentence to reflect the fact that he has already spent some time in custody in connection with the offence for which sentence is now being passed. This enshrines in statute the effect of previous case law.

The next stage in understanding the community sentencing regime introduced by the CJA 2003 is to examine each of the requirements that may be imposed as part of a community order (listed in s 177(1), quoted above).

18.1.2 Unpaid work requirement (s 199)

Section 199 empowers the court to include an 'unpaid work requirement' as part of a community order. The number of hours work to be carried out must be specified in the order and must be between 40 and 300 (s 199(2)).

Under an unpaid work requirement, the offender works for the specified number of hours on local community projects under close supervision. The order may be seen as a way of getting the offender to 'repay their debt to society': charities, community organisations and local authorities provide work places and benefit from the offender's contribution. Moreover, these orders are also intended to help the offender to develop new skills, hopefully increasing their employability and so reducing the risk of reoffending. The work that can be required under the order is extremely varied. It might, for example, involve conservation work (such as tidying up local beauty spots), removing graffiti, or helping with anti-crime measures such as installing security locks, working with the elderly or vulnerable (perhaps doing decorating). It could include working in a charity shop.

Where the offender has attained the age of 18, the work is carried out under the supervision of a probation officer. Where the offender is 16 or 17 (16 being the minimum age for a community order under the 2003 Act), supervision may be provided by a probation office, local authority social worker, or a member of a youth offending team (s 199(4)).

Under s 199(3), the court may not impose an unpaid work requirement unless satisfied (e.g. through the pre-sentence report) that the offender is a 'suitable person to perform work under such a requirement'.

Where the court imposes an unpaid work requirement in respect of two or more offences, it may direct that the hours of work imposed for one offence are to be concurrent with, or additional to, the hours specified for another offence. However, the total number of hours must not exceed 300 (s 199(5)).

Section 200(2) stipulates that the unpaid work should normally be performed within 12 months. However, under sub-s (3), unless it is revoked, a community order imposing an unpaid work requirement remains in force until the offender has completed the number of hours specified in the order.

Under s 200(4), where an unpaid work requirement is imposed as part of a suspended sentence order (see Chapter 17), the supervision period of the suspended sentence continues until the offender has completed the number of hours specified in the order, subject to the proviso that the supervision period cannot continue beyond the end of the operational period of the suspended sentence.

18.1.3 Activity requirements (s 201)

Section 201(1) of the Act makes provision for the imposition of an 'activity requirement'. This enables the court to include a requirement that the offender participate in a specified activity for the number of days specified in the order. Under sub-s (5), the maximum number of days that may be specified is 60.

Section 201(2) says that the specified activities may consist of, or include, activities whose purpose is that of reparation, such as activities involving contact between offenders and persons affected by their offences (and so could include a meeting with the victim of the offence and the making of reparation to the victim or to the community at large). The activity may also require such things as participation in day centre activities, education, or basic skills training.

An activity requirement will normally be combined with a supervision requirement to support and reinforce the offender's rehabilitation and to provide him with additional support.

Before including an activity requirement on an offender who has attained the age of 18, the court must consult a probation officer (in the case of an offender who is 16 or 17, a probation officer or a member of a youth offending team), and must be satisfied that it is feasible to secure compliance with the requirement (sub-s (3)).

18.1.4 Programme requirements (s 202)

Under s 202, the court may impose a 'programme requirement' which requires the offender to attend a group or individual programme (defined in sub-s (3) as a 'systematic set of activities'). The programmes are designed to address the activities and patterns of behaviour that contribute to committing crime.

The programmes currently fall into five broad categories:

- general offending
- violence
- sex offending
- substance misuse
- domestic violence

Under sub-s (4), a court may only include a programme requirement if satisfied that it is suitable for the offender and that a place is available.

18.1.5 Prohibited activity requirements (s 203)

Section 203 of the Act enables the court to include a 'prohibited activity requirement', defined in sub-s (1) as a requirement that the offender must refrain from participating in the activities specified in the order either on specified days or for a specified period. This requirement is designed to prevent the offender from becoming involved in an activity that might lead to them committing more crime.

Before imposing such a requirement, the court must consult a probation officer or, if the offender is aged 16 or 17, a probation officer or a member of a youth offending team (sub-s (2)).

18.1.6 Curfew requirements (s 204)

Section 204 of the 2003 Act covers 'curfew requirements'. Sub-section (1) defines a 'curfew requirement' as a requirement that the offender must remain, for periods specified in the order, at a place so specified.

Under s 204(2), the court may specify different places or different periods for different days. However, the period of curfew must be between two and 12 hours in any day to which the order applies. A curfew requirement can be imposed for a maximum period of six months (s 204(3)).

Section 204(6) stipulates that, before imposing a curfew requirement, the court must obtain and consider information about the place proposed to be specified in the order (including information as to the attitude of persons likely to be affected by the enforced presence there of the offender).

A curfew order is similar in effect to house arrest. The offender has to stay at the specified address (usually at their home) for the curfew period. A tag, worn on the ankle or wrist, notifies monitoring services if the offender is absent during the curfew hours.

The main purpose of the requirement is to reduce the offender's opportunities to take part in criminal activity. It may also help to provide some structure to the life of the offender, and of course also operates as a punishment (by curtailing the offender's liberty). It is most appropriate for offenders who do not need rehabilitative supervision.

Curfew hours are often set in order to take account of the times when the offending has taken place (often during the hours of darkness).

18.1.7 Exclusion requirements (s 205)

Section 205 of the Act provides for the imposition of an 'exclusion requirement', defined in sub-s (1) as meaning a provision prohibiting the offender from entering a place or area specified in the order for a period so specified.

The maximum duration of such a requirement is two years (sub-s (2)). Under sub-s (3), the exclusion can be limited to particular periods and may specify different places for different periods or days.

The offender will be electronically monitored unless the facility is not available or the court considers it unnecessary.

18.1.8 Residence requirements (s 206)

Section 206(1) empowers the court to impose a 'residence requirement', namely a requirement that, during the period specified in the order, the offender must reside at the place specified in the order. Under sub-s (2), the court may make provision for the offender to reside at a different address with the prior approval of his probation officer.

Under sub-s (3), before imposing a residence requirement, the court must consider the home surroundings of the offender.

Sub-section (4) stipulates that the court may not specify a hostel or similar institution as the place where an offender must reside unless a probation officer so recommends. Residence at an approved hostel automatically includes a supervised curfew.

18.1.9 Mental health treatment requirements (s 207)

Section 207 of the Act provides for the making of a 'mental health treatment requirement', defined in sub-s (1) as a requirement that the offender must submit, during the period(s) specified in the order, to treatment by or under the direction of a registered medical practitioner or a chartered psychologist (or both, for different periods) with a view to the improvement of the offender's mental condition. Under sub-s (2), the treatment required may be:

- treatment as a resident patient;
- treatment as a non-resident patient;
- treatment by or under the direction of such registered medical practitioner or chartered psychologist (or both).

Sub-section (3) sets out the restrictions that apply such requirements:

- the court must be satisfied, on the evidence of a registered medical practitioner, approved for the purposes of s 12 of the Mental Health Act 1983, that the mental condition of the offender requires and may be susceptible to treatment (but is not such as to warrant the making of a hospital order or guardianship order under the 1983 Act);
- arrangements can be made for the treatment needed; and
- the offender has expressed his willingness to comply with such a requirement.

18.1.10 Drug rehabilitation requirements (s 209)

Section 209 covers the imposition of a 'drug rehabilitation requirement'. This is defined in sub-s (1) as a requirement that for the period specified in the order (known as 'the treatment and testing period') the offender:

a   must submit to treatment with a view to the reduction or elimination of his dependency on, or propensity to misuse, drugs; and

b   for the purpose of ascertaining whether he has any drug in his body during that period, must provide urine or blood samples.

Under sub-s (2), the court may only impose a drug rehabilitation requirement if satisfied that the offender is dependent on (or has a propensity to misuse) drugs, and that his dependency or propensity is such as requires and may be susceptible to treatment. Such a requirement may only be imposed on the recommendation of a probation officer (or, if the offender is aged 16 or 17, a probation officer or member of a youth offending team). Moreover, the offender must express willingness to comply with the requirement before it can be imposed.

The treatment and testing period must be at least six months (sub-s (3)). The treatment can be in-patient or out-patient treatment (sub-s (4)).

The purpose of a drug rehabilitation requirement is to provide fast access to a drug treatment programme, with the goal of reducing drug-related offending. Offenders agree their treatment plan with the probation and treatment services. The plan sets out the level of treatment and testing and what is required at each stage of the order. This type of sentence is appropriate for problem drug users who commit crime in order to fund their drug habit and who have shown a willingness to co-operate with treatment. The treatment programme requires motivation and determination on the part of the offender, but support is provided by probation and treatment staff to complete the programme successfully. The treatment is intended to:

- help offenders produce a personal action plan so that they can identify what they must do to reduce offending and stop their use of drugs;
- explain the links between drug use and offending and how drugs affect health;
- help offenders identify realistic ways of changing their lives for the better.

The offender may also receive clinical treatment; a day care programme; health education; activities to improve social skills, education and career prospects; and the chance to participate in an offending behaviour programme.

Section 210 provides for periodic review by the court where a drug rehabilitation requirement has been imposed. Failure to comply with the treatment plan will result in the offender having to return to court for breach of the order. Under s 211, this could mean that the order is revoked and the offender is re-sentenced for the original offence.

The power to impose a drug rehabilitation requirement replaces the power under earlier legislation to make a 'drug treatment and testing order' (DTTO). Some of the points made in case law about those orders may be regarded as equally applicable to the drug rehabilitation requirement. For example, in *Attorney General's Reference No 64 of 2003* [2003] EWCA Crim 3514; [2004] 2 Cr App R (S) 22, Rose LJ said (at para 14):

(i)   judges should be alert to pass sentences which have a realistic prospect of reducing drug addiction whenever it is possible sensibly to do so;

(ii)   many offences are committed by an offender under the influence of drugs. The fact that a defendant was so acting is not in itself a reason for making a DTTO;

(iii)   a necessary prerequisite to the making of such an order is clear evidence that a defendant is determined to free himself or herself from drugs;

(iv)   a DTTO is likely to have a better prospect of success early rather than late in a criminal career, though there will be exceptional cases in which an order may be justified for an older defendant;

(v)   it will be very rare for a DTTO to be appropriate for an offence involving serious violence or threat of violence with a lethal weapon;

(vi)   the type of offence for which a DTTO will generally be appropriate is an acquisitive offence carried out to obtain money for drugs, though the fact that the motive was to feed drug addiction does not compel the conclusion that a DTTO should be made;

(vii)   a DTTO may be appropriate even when a substantial number of offences have been committed;

(viii) a DTTO is unlikely to be appropriate for a substantial number of serious offences which either involve minor violence, or have a particularly damaging effect on the victim or victims. There must be a degree of proportionality between offence and sentence, so that excessive weight is not given to the prospect of rehabilitation at the expense of proper regard for the criminality of the offender;

. . .

In *R (Inner London Probation Service) v Tower Bridge Magistrates' Court* [2001] EWHC 401 (Admin); [2002] 1 Cr App R(S) 43, it was held by the Divisional Court that where a court is considering the imposition of a DTTO and the pre-sentence report says that the defendant is not suitable for such an order, the court should be slow to act against the conclusions of that assessment unless it has cogent reasons for doing so. In such a case, the court should ask the person who made the assessment to attend court, so that the court can discuss the matter. Where the court disagrees with the assessment of the probation service, it should set out the reasons for its decision.

18.1.11 Alcohol treatment requirements (s 212)

Section 212 deals with the imposition of an 'alcohol treatment requirement', defined in sub-s (1) as a requirement that the offender must submit, during the period specified in the order, to treatment with a view to the reduction or elimination of his dependency on alcohol.

Under sub-s (2), the court may only impose an alcohol treatment requirement if satisfied that the offender is dependent on alcohol and that dependency is such as requires, and may be susceptible to, treatment. Such a requirement may only be imposed if the offender expresses his willingness to comply with it (sub-s (3)). The order must last for at least six months (sub-s (4)). The treatment can be in-patient or out-patient treatment (sub-s (5)).

The alcohol treatment requirement provides access to a tailored treatment programme with the aim of reducing drink dependency.

18.1.12 Supervision requirements (s 213)

Section 213 enables the court to impose a 'supervision requirement'. This is defined in sub-s (1) as a requirement that, for the period specified by the court, the offender must attend appointments with his probation officer. Sub-section (2) states that a supervision requirement may be imposed in order to promote the offender's rehabilitation. The length of a supervision requirement must be the overall period for which the community order is in force (sub-s (3)).

Under this requirement the offender is required to attend regular appointments with an Offender Manager from the Probation Service. The frequency of contact will be specified in the sentence plan. During supervision sessions offenders may:

- undertake work aimed at promoting personal and behaviour change;
- monitor and review patterns of behaviour and personal activity;
- undertake work to increase motivation and provide practical support to increase compliance with other requirements;
- support and re-enforce learning undertaken as part of a programme or activity requirement;
- undergo individual counselling;
- get support from their probation officer on fulfilling other aspects of their community order.

18.1.13 Attendance centre requirements (s 214)

Section 221(2) defines an 'attendance centre' as 'a place at which offenders aged under 25 may be required to attend and be given under supervision appropriate occupation or instruction . . .'.

Attendance centre requirements are governed by s 214, which provides that the court may impose a requirement that the offender must attend an attendance centre for the number of hours specified in the order (sub-s (1)). Sub-section (2) states that the aggregate number of hours for which the offender may be required to attend an attendance centre must not be less than 12 or more than 36. Under sub-s (6), an offender may not be required to attend an attendance centre on more than one occasion on any one day, or for more than three hours on any occasion.

The attendance centre requirement offers a structured opportunity for offenders to address their offending behaviour in a group environment while imposing a restriction on leisure time at the weekend.

18.1.14 Electronic monitoring requirements

Section 215 enables the court to impose an 'electronic monitoring requirement', defined in sub-s (1) as a requirement for securing the electronic monitoring of the offender's compliance with other requirements imposed by the community order. Thus an electronic monitoring requirement is ancillary to other requirements under the community order. Where there is someone other than the offender without whose co-operation it will not be practicable to secure the monitoring, the requirement may only be included in the order with that person's consent (sub-s (2)).

18.1.15 Restrictions on community orders

Section 217 requires that:

(1)   The court must ensure, as far as practicable, that any requirement imposed by a relevant order is such as to avoid—

(a)   any conflict with the offender's religious beliefs or with the requirements of any other relevant order to which he may be subject; and

(b)   any interference with the times, if any, at which he normally works or attends school or any other educational establishment.

(2)   The responsible officer in relation to an offender to whom a relevant order relates must ensure, as far as practicable, that any instruction given or requirement imposed by him in pursuance of the order is such as to avoid the conflict or interference mentioned in sub-section (1).

18.1.16 Other duties of offenders subject to community orders

Section 220(1) imposes a duty on the offender to keep in touch with the responsible officer and to notify him of any change of address. This is a requirement of all community orders and, under s 220(2), these obligations are enforceable as if they were requirements imposed by the order itself. In *Richards v National Probation Service* [2007] EWHC 3108 (Admin); (2008) 172 JP 100, it was held that, in the context of community punishments, a responsible officer is entitled to set conditions that require the offender to inform the officer in advance if he knows he cannot keep an appointment to do unpaid work. This falls within the words 'keep in touch' in s 220(1)(a). The officer may require that information to be in writing and to be supported by evidence from a third party. It is permissible for the conditions to provide that the officer may relax that requirement in the circumstances of a given case, so that the information is to be provided within a short period thereafter. However, s 220 cannot be read as enabling the responsible officer to request the information *ex post facto* unless the request is to provide the information in advance and a concession is then made to allow it to be provided later.

18.2 REVOCATION AND AMENDMENT OF COMMUNITY ORDERS UNDER THE CRIMINAL JUSTICE ACT 2003

Schedule 8 to the Criminal Justice Act 2003 deals with breach, revocation and amendment of community orders. Part 2 of Sched 8 deals with breach of community orders.

18.2.1 Breach of community orders

Under para 5(1), if the responsible officer is of the opinion that the offender has failed without reasonable excuse to comply with any of the requirements of a community order, the officer must give him a warning unless either he has been given a warning in the previous 12 months or the officer refers the case back to the court. Under para 5(2), the warning must inform the offender that, if he fails again to comply with any requirement of the order during the next 12 months, he will be liable to be brought before a court.

Prior to the implementation of these provisions, there had been some concern that the Probation Service has been insufficiently robust in bringing offenders before the court when they fail to comply with community orders. It should be noted that para 6(1), which deals with further non-compliance after a warning, is cast in mandatory terms. It provides that, if the responsible officer has given a warning under para 5 and, within the next 12 months, the responsible officer is of the opinion that the offender has again failed without reasonable excuse to comply with any of the requirements of the order, the officer must refer the offender back to the court.

Under para 7, a justice of the peace may issue a summons requiring the attendance of the offender, or (if the allegation of breach is in writing and substantiated on oath) a warrant for his arrest, if it appears that he has failed to comply with any of the requirements of:

a   a community order made by a magistrates' court; or
b   a community order made by the Crown Court which includes a direction that any failure to comply with the requirements of the order is to be dealt with by a magistrates' court.

However, para 7(2) makes it clear that this power only applies if the community order is still in force (thus preventing enforcement proceedings being commenced after the order has expired). Under para 7(4), if the offender fails to appear in answer to the summons, the magistrates' court may issue a warrant for his arrest.

Paragraph 8 confers the same powers on the Crown Court where it has made a community order which does not include a direction that a failure to comply with the requirements be dealt with by the magistrates' court.

Paragraph 9(1) provides that if it is proved to the satisfaction of the magistrates' court that the offender has failed without reasonable excuse to comply with any of the requirements of the community order, the court must deal with him in one of the following ways:

a   by amending the terms of the community order so as to impose more onerous requirements;
b   where the community order was made by a magistrates' court, by dealing with him, for the offence in respect of which the order was made, in any way in which the court could deal with him if he had just been convicted by it of the offence;
c   where—

   i   the community order was made by a magistrates' court,
   ii   the offence in respect of which the order was made was not an offence punishable by imprisonment,
   iii   the offender is aged 18 or over, and
   iv   the offender has wilfully and persistently failed to comply with the requirements of the order,

   by dealing with him, in respect of that offence, by imposing a sentence of imprisonment for a term not exceeding six months [51 weeks when the changes to magistrates' sentencing powers are implemented].

Option (a) would, for example, empower the court to extend the duration of a particular requirement, but not beyond the maximum duration applicable to that requirement and not beyond the three-year limit applicable to the duration of a community order (para 9(3)).

Option (b) involves revocation of the order (if it is still in force at the date of the hearing) and then re-sentencing (subject to the limitation on the court's sentencing powers when it was first dealing with the offender). Paragraph 9(4) empowers the court to impose a custodial sentence, even if the original offence did not cross the custody threshold, where the offender has 'wilfully and persistently' failed to comply with the requirements of the community order.

Option (c) enables the court to punish wilful and persistent non-compliance by means of a custodial sentence even though the offence for which the order was made was non-imprisonable. As with (b), the community order is revoked if this option is chosen.

When dealing with the non-compliance, the court must take into account the extent to which the offender has complied with the order (para 9(2)).

If the offender is re-sentenced, he can appeal to the Crown Court against the new sentence (para 9(8)).

Where the order was made by the Crown Court (and that court directed that failures to comply should be dealt with by the magistrates' court), the magistrates' court dealing with the breach can (instead of dealing with the offender themselves) commit him, in custody or on bail, to be dealt with by the Crown Court (para 9(6)).

Paragraph 10 sets out how the Crown Court must deal with failure to comply with a community order (whether the Crown Court is dealing with the case under para 8 or para 9). The options open to the Crown Court are the same as those available to the magistrates' court (making the order more onerous; revoking the order and re-sentencing the offender; imposing a custodial sentence for up to 6 months (to be increased to 51 weeks) even though the offence for which the order was made is non-imprisonable). The determination of whether or not the defendant is in breach of the order (if the breach is not admitted by the defendant) is made by a Crown Court judge sitting alone.

Section 38 of the Criminal Justice and Immigration Act 2008 amends paras 9 and 10 of Sched 8 to the CJA 2003 so that where the court amends the terms of the community order so as to impose more onerous requirements under paras 9(1)(a) or 10(1)(a), the minimum period of unpaid work that may be imposed for breach of a community order is reduced from 40 to 20 hours where the community order does not already contain an unpaid work requirement.

Paragraph 11(1) provides that:

(a) if an offender has refused to comply with a mental health treatment requirement, a drug rehabilitation requirement or an alcohol treatment requirement; and
(b) the refusal was a refusal to undergo 'any surgical, electrical or other treatment'; and
(c) the court decides that the refusal was reasonable in all the circumstances,

then the refusal is not to be treated as a breach of the order.

Under para 11(2), the court may not amend a mental health treatment requirement, a drug rehabilitation requirement or an alcohol treatment requirement 'unless the offender expresses his willingness to comply with the requirement as amended'.

Paragraph 12 deals with cases where a community order was made by a magistrates' court in respect of an offender who was being dealt with for an indictable-only offence and who was under 18 years of age when the order was made but has attained the age of 18 by the time of the enforcement proceedings. Where the court revokes the community order and re-sentences the offender, its powers are limited to:

(a) imposing a fine not exceeding £5,000 for the offence in respect of which the order was made; or
(b) dealing with the offender for that offence in any way in which a magistrates' court could deal with him if it had just convicted him of an offence punishable with imprisonment for a term not exceeding six months [to be increased to 51 weeks].

In *West Yorkshire Probation Board v Boulter* [2005] EWHC 2342; [2006] 1 WLR 232, it was held that a breach of a community order is within the criminal process and so has to be proved to the criminal standard (namely, beyond reasonable doubt).

In *Greater Manchester Probation Committee v Bent* (1996) 160 JP 297, it was held that the fact that an appeal had been lodged did not mean that the probation service could not institute proceedings for breach of an order which was under appeal. The same approach was adopted in *West Midlands Probation Board v Sutton Coldfield Magistrates' Court* [2008] EWHC 15 (Admin); (2008) 172 JP 169. Dyson LJ said (at para 13):

> [L]ike any other sentence, a community order takes effect when it is imposed and it remains in full force and effect until and unless it is quashed on appeal or revoked or amended by order of the court. The lodging of an appeal does not of itself have any effect on the enforceability of the order.

His Lordship continued (at para 15):

> Although the concept of "reasonable excuse" is broad, I do not consider that it can have been intended by Parliament to be stretched to include the mere fact that the defendant has lodged an appeal against the community order or the conviction on which it is based. To do that would be to undermine the general principle that community orders take effect from the date on which they are made and remain in force until and unless they are quashed on appeal or revoked or amended by order of the court. To accept non-compliance with a community order as a reasonable excuse merely because the defendant is appealing would amount to an acknowledgement that defendants may pick and choose whether and in what circumstances they will comply. That is wrong in principle.

18.2.2 Revocation of community orders other than for breach

Part 3 of Sched 8 deals with the revocation of community orders other than in the case of a breach of the requirement of the order.

Paragraph 13(1) states that (provided the order is still in force) either the offender or the responsible officer may apply to the magistrates' court for the revocation of the order, or for the offender to be dealt with in some other way for the offence in respect of which the order was made, if – having regard to circumstances which have arisen since the order was made – it would be in the interests of justice to do so. Under para 13(2), a magistrates' court may simply revoke the order, or it may revoke the order and re-sentence the offender (although a magistrates' court cannot re-sentence the offender if the original sentence was passed by the Crown Court).

Under para 13(3), the circumstances in which a community order may be revoked include the fact that the offender is 'making good progress' or is 'responding satisfactorily' to supervision or treatment under the order. The revocation of the order may also be appropriate if, for example, the offender is taken ill or becomes disabled, and so becomes unable to complete the requirements of the order.

If the court re-sentences the offender, it must take into account the extent to which the offender has complied with the original order (para 13(4)). If a new sentence is passed, the offender can appeal to the Crown Court against that sentence (para 13(5)).

Unless it is the offender who is applying for the revocation of the order, the court must summon him to appear in order to revoke, or to revoke and re-sentence; if he does not appear in answer to the summons, the court may issue a warrant for his arrest (para 13(6)).

Paragraph 14 confers the same powers to the Crown Court in the case of orders it has made which do not contain a direction that failure to comply with the requirements is to be dealt with by the magistrates' court.

Under para 15, if the offender was convicted of an indictable-only offence and was under the age of 18 when the community order was made, but attained the age of 18 by the time the court is considering revocation, the court can impose a fine of up to £5,000 or else re-sentence him as if he had just been convicted of an offence punishable with imprisonment for up to 6 months (to be increased to 51 weeks).

18.2.3 Amendment of community orders

Part 4 of Sched 8 deals with the amendment of community orders.

Paragraph 16 deals with amendments made necessary because the offender has changed residence and is now living in a different local justice area.

Under para 17(1), the court may, on the application of the offender or the responsible officer, amend a community order by cancelling any of the requirements of the order, or by replacing any of those requirements with a requirement of the same kind and which the court could include if it were then making the order. The court cannot add a wholly new requirement or substitute a different requirement for one that was originally specified in the order. However, the court can cancel a requirement or adjust it (for example, changing the hours of a curfew or substituting one specified activity for another). The court is also empowered to add electronic monitoring to any of the original requirements under the order.

Under para 17(2), the court may not amend a mental health treatment, drug rehabilitation, or alcohol treatment requirement unless the offender expresses his willingness to comply with the requirement as amended. However, if the offender fails to express his willingness to comply, the court may revoke the community order and deal with him, for the offence in respect of which the order was made, in any way in which he could have been dealt with for that offence by the court which made the order (para 17(3)). If the court re-sentences the offender, it must take account of the extent to which the offender has complied with the requirements of the order, and may impose a custodial sentence if the original offence was punishable with imprisonment (para 17(4)).

Paragraph 18 provides that, where a community order includes a drug rehabilitation, alcohol treatment or mental health treatment requirement, and the medical practitioner responsible for the treatment is:

a   of the opinion that:

   i   the treatment of the offender should be continued beyond the period specified in the order;

   ii   the offender needs different treatment;

   iii the offender is not susceptible to treatment; or

   iv   the offender does not require further treatment; or

b   is for any reason unwilling to continue to treat or direct the treatment of the offender,

he must make a written report to that effect to the responsible officer; the responsible officer must then apply (under para 17) to the court for the variation or cancellation of the requirement.

Paragraph 19 provides that where a community order includes a drug rehabilitation requirement with provision for review, the responsible officer may apply to the court (under para 17) to amend the order to provide for each subsequent periodic review (see s 211) to be made without a hearing instead of at a review hearing, or vice versa.

Paragraph 20 provides that, on the application of the offender or the responsible officer, the court may extend an unpaid work requirement beyond the 12-month limit (specified in s 200(2)) for completion of the work if it believes it to be in the interests of justice to do so, having regard to circumstances which have arisen since the order was made.

18.2.4 Commission of further offences

Part 5 of Sched 8 deals with the powers of the court in relation to a community order where the offender is convicted of another offence during the currency of the community order.

Paragraph 21 provides that where an offender, in respect of whom a community order made by a magistrates' court is in force, is convicted of an offence by a magistrates' court, and it appears to the court that it would be in the interests of justice to do so (having regard to circumstances which have arisen since the community order was made), the magistrates' court may either (a) revoke the order, or (b) revoke the order and deal with the offender, for the offence in respect of which the order was made, in any way which he could have been dealt with for that offence by the court which made the order.

If it re-sentences him, the court must take into account the extent to which he complied with the order (para 21(3)), and the offender has a right of appeal to the Crown Court (para 21(4)).

If the magistrates' court is dealing with the later offence but the community order was made in the Crown Court, the magistrates may commit the offender (in custody or on bail) to appear at the Crown Court (para 22(1)).

Paragraph 23 confers the same power to revoke, or to revoke and re-sentence, on the Crown Court where the offender is convicted by the Crown Court of an offence committed during the currency of a community order (or where the offender is committed to the Crown Court under para 22). If the Crown Court re-sentences the offender for an offence where the original sentence was passed by a magistrates' court, the Crown Courts sentencing powers are limited to those of a magistrates' court.

18.3 GUIDANCE FROM THE SENTENCING GUIDELINES COUNCIL ON COMMUNITY SENTENCES

In December 2004, the Sentencing Guidelines Council issued guidance on the sentencing regime established by the Criminal Justice Act 2003. It is entitled *New Sentences: Criminal Justice Act 2003* (see <http://www.sentencing-guidelines.gov.uk/docs/New_sentences_guideline1.pdf>).

> This guideline applies only to sentences passed under the sentencing framework applicable to those aged 18 or over.

SECTION I PART I – COMMUNITY SENTENCES

. . .

B. Imposing a Community Sentence – The Approach

1.1.9 . . . Sentencers must consider all of the disposals available (within or below the threshold passed) at the time of sentence, and reject them before reaching the provisional decision to make a community sentence, so that even where the threshold for a community sentence has been passed a financial penalty or discharge may still be an appropriate penalty. Where an offender has a low risk of reoffending, particular care needs to be taken in the light of evidence that indicates that there are circumstances where inappropriate intervention can increase the risk of re-offending rather than decrease it. In addition, recent improvements in enforcement of financial penalties make them a more viable sentence in a wider range of cases.

1.1.10 Where an offender is being sentenced for a non-imprisonable offence or offences, great care will be needed in assessing whether a community sentence is appropriate since failure to comply could result in a custodial sentence.

1.1.11 Having decided (in consultation with the Probation Service where appropriate) that a community sentence is justified, the court must decide which requirements should be included in the community order. The requirements or orders imposed will have the effect of restricting the offender's liberty, whilst providing punishment in the community, rehabilitation for the offender, and/or ensuring that the offender engages in reparative activities.

The key issues arising are:

(i)   which requirements to impose;

(ii)   how to make allowance for time spent on remand; and

(iii) how to deal with breaches.

(i) Requirements

1.1.12 When deciding which requirements to include, the court must be satisfied on three matters—

i.   that the **restriction on liberty is commensurate with the seriousness** of the offence(s);

ii.   that the **requirements are the most suitable** for the offender; and

iii. that, where there are two or more requirements included, they are **compatible with each other**.

1.1.13 Sentencers should have the possibility of breach firmly in mind when passing sentence for the original offence. If a court is to reflect the seriousness of an offence, there is little value in setting requirements as part of a community sentence that are not demanding enough for an offender. On the other hand, there is equally little value in imposing requirements that would 'set an offender up to fail' and almost inevitably lead to sanctions for a breach.

In community sentences, the guiding principles are proportionality and suitability. Once a court has decided that the offence has crossed the community sentence threshold and that a community sentence is justified, the initial factor in defining which requirements to include in a community sentence should be the seriousness of the offence committed.

1.1.14 This means that 'seriousness' is an important factor in deciding whether the Court chooses the low, medium or high range (see below) but, having taken that decision, selection of the content of the order within the range will be determined by a much wider range of factors.

• Sentencing ranges must remain flexible enough to take account of the suitability of the offender, his or her ability to comply with particular requirements and their availability in the local area.

• The justification for imposing a community sentence in response to persistent petty offending is the persistence of the offending behaviour rather than the seriousness of the offences being committed. The requirements imposed should ensure that the restriction on liberty is proportionate to the seriousness of the offending, to reflect the fact that the offences, of themselves, are not sufficiently serious to merit a community sentence.

(a) Information for Sentencers

1.1.15 In many cases, a pre-sentence report will be pivotal in helping a sentencer decide whether to impose a custodial sentence or whether to impose a community sentence and, if so, whether particular requirements, or combinations of requirements, are suitable for an individual offender. The court must always ensure (especially where there are multiple requirements) that the restriction on liberty placed on the offender is proportionate to the seriousness of the offence committed. The court must also consider the likely effect of one requirement on another, and that they do not place conflicting demands upon the offender.

1.1.16 The Council supports the approach proposed by the Panel at paragraph 78 of its Advice that, having reached the provisional view that a community sentence is the most appropriate disposal, the sentencer should request a pre-sentence report, indicating which of the three sentencing ranges is relevant and the purpose(s) of sentencing that the package of requirements is required to fulfil. Usually the most helpful way for the court to do this would be to produce a written note for the report writer, copied on the court file. If it is known that the same tribunal and defence advocate will be present at the sentencing hearing and a probation officer is present in court when the request for a report is made, it may not be necessary to commit details of the request to writing. However, events may change during the period of an adjournment and it is good practice to ensure that there is a clear record of the request for the court. These two factors will guide the Probation Service in determining the nature and combination of requirements that may be appropriate and the onerousness and intensity of those requirements. A similar procedure should apply when ordering a pre-sentence report when a custodial sentence is being considered.

1.1.17 There will be occasions when any type of report may be unnecessary despite the intention to pass a community sentence though this is likely to be infrequent. A court could consider dispensing with the need to obtain a pre-sentence report for adult offenders—

- where the offence falls within the LOW range of seriousness . . . *and*
- where the sentencer was minded to impose a single requirement, such as an exclusion requirement (where the circumstances of the case mean that this would be an appropriate disposal without electronic monitoring) *and*
- where the sentence will not require the involvement of the Probation Service, for example an electronically monitored curfew (subject to the court being satisfied that there is an appropriate address at which the curfew can operate).

(b) Ranges of Sentence Within the Community Sentence Band

1.1.18 To enable the court to benefit from the flexibility that community sentences provide and also to meet its statutory obligations, any structure governing the use of community requirements must allow the courts to choose the most appropriate sentence for each individual offender.

1.1.19 Sentencers have a statutory obligation to pass sentences that are commensurate with the seriousness of an offence. However, within the range of sentence justified by the seriousness of the offence(s), courts will quite properly consider those factors that heighten the risk of the offender committing further offences or causing further harm with a view to lessening that risk. The extent to which requirements are imposed must be capable of being varied to ensure that the restriction on liberty is commensurate with the seriousness of the offence.

1.1.20 The Council recognises that it would be helpful for sentencers to have a framework to help them decide on the most appropriate use of the new community sentence. While there is no single guiding principle, the seriousness of the offence that has been committed is an important factor. Three sentencing ranges (low, medium and high) within the community sentence band can be identified. It is not possible to position particular types of offence at firm points within the three ranges because the seriousness level of an offence is largely dependent upon the culpability of the offender and this is uniquely variable. The difficulty is particularly acute in relation to the medium range where it is clear that requirements will need to be tailored across a relatively wide range of offending behaviour.

1.1.21 In general terms, the lowest range of community sentence would be for those offenders whose offence was relatively minor within the community sentence band and would include persistent petty offenders whose offences only merit a community sentence by virtue of failing to respond to the previous imposition of fines. Such offenders would merit a 'light touch' approach, for example, normally a single requirement such as a short period of unpaid work, or a curfew, or a prohibited activity requirement or an exclusion requirement (where the circumstances of the case mean that this would be an appropriate disposal without electronic monitoring).

1.1.22 The top range would be for those offenders who have only just fallen short of a custodial sentence and for those who have passed the threshold but for whom a community sentence is deemed appropriate.

1.1.23 In all three ranges there must be sufficient flexibility to allow the sentence to be varied to take account of the suitability of particular requirements for the individual offender and whether a particular requirement or package of requirements might be more effective at reducing any identified risk of reoffending. It will fall to the sentencer to ensure that the sentence strikes the right balance between proportionality and suitability.

There should be three sentencing ranges (low, medium and high) within the community sentence band based upon seriousness.

It is not intended that an offender necessarily progress from one range to the next on each sentencing occasion. The decision as to the appropriate range each time is based upon the seriousness of the new offence(s).

The decision on the nature and severity of the requirements to be included in a community sentence should be guided by:

(i)   the assessment of offence seriousness (LOW, MEDIUM OR HIGH);
(ii)   the purpose(s) of sentencing the court wishes to achieve;
(iii) the risk of reoffending;
(iv) the ability of the offender to comply, and
(v)   the availability of requirements in the local area.

The resulting restriction on liberty must be a proportionate response to the offence that was committed.

1.1.24 Below we set out a non-exhaustive description of examples of requirements that might be appropriate in the three sentencing ranges. These examples focus on punishment in the community, although it is recognised that not all packages will necessarily need to include a punitive requirement. There will clearly be other requirements of a rehabilitative nature, such as a treatment requirement or an accredited programme, which may be appropriate depending on the specific needs of the offender and assessment of suitability. Given the intensity of such interventions, it is expected that these would normally only be appropriate at medium and high levels of seriousness, and where assessed as having a medium or high risk of reoffending. In addition, when passing sentence in any one of the three ranges, the court should consider whether a rehabilitative intervention such as a programme requirement, or a restorative justice intervention might be suitable as an additional or alternative part of the sentence.

LOW

1.1.25 For offences only just crossing the community sentence threshold (such as persistent petty offending, some public order offences, some thefts from shops, or interference with a motor vehicle, where the seriousness of the offence or the nature of the offender's record means that a discharge or fine is inappropriate).

1.1.26 Suitable requirements might include:

- 40 to 80 hours of unpaid work or
- a curfew requirement within the lowest range (e.g. up to 12 hours per day for a few weeks) or
- an exclusion requirement (where the circumstances of the case mean that this would be an appropriate disposal without electronic monitoring) lasting a few months or
- a prohibited activity requirement or
- an attendance centre requirement (where available).

1.1.27 Since the restriction on liberty must be commensurate with the seriousness of the offence, particular care needs to be taken with this band to ensure that this obligation is complied with. In most cases, only one requirement will be appropriate and the length may be curtailed if additional requirements are necessary.

MEDIUM

1.1.28 For offences that obviously fall within the community sentence band such as handling stolen goods worth less than £1000 acquired for resale or somewhat more valuable goods acquired for the handler's own use, some cases of burglary in commercial premises, some cases of taking a motor vehicle without consent, or some cases of obtaining property by deception.

1.1.29 Suitable requirements might include:

- a greater number (e.g. 80 to 150) of hours of unpaid work or
- an activity requirement in the middle range (20 to 30 days) or
- a curfew requirement within the middle range (e.g. up to 12 hours for 2–3 months) or
- an exclusion requirement lasting in the region of 6 months or
- a prohibited activity requirement.

1.1.30 Since the restriction on liberty must be commensurate with the seriousness of the offence, particular care needs to be taken with this band to ensure that this obligation is complied with.

HIGH

1.1.31 For offences that only just fall below the custody threshold or where the custody threshold is crossed but a community sentence is more appropriate in all the circumstances, for example some cases displaying the features of a standard domestic burglary committed by a first-time offender.

1.1.32 More intensive sentences which combine two or more requirements may be appropriate at this level. Suitable requirements might include an unpaid work order of between 150 and 300 hours; an activity requirement up to the maximum 60 days; an exclusion order lasting in the region of 12 months; a curfew requirement of up to 12 hours a day for 4–6 months.

(c) Electronic Monitoring

1.1.33 The court must also consider whether an electronic monitoring requirement should be imposed which is mandatory in some circumstances.

Electronic monitoring should be used with the primary purpose of promoting and monitoring compliance with other requirements, in circumstances where the punishment of the offender and/or the need to safeguard the public and prevent reoffending are the most important concerns.

(d) Recording the Sentence Imposed

1.1.34 Under the new framework there is only one (generic) community sentence provided by statute. This does not mean that offenders who have completed a community sentence and have then reoffended should be regarded as ineligible for a second community sentence on the basis that this has been tried and failed. Further community sentences, perhaps with different requirements, may well be justified.

1.1.35 Those imposing sentence will wish to be clear about the 'purposes' that the community sentence is designed to achieve when setting the requirements. Sharing those purposes with the offender and Probation Service will enable them to be clear about the goals that are to be achieved.

1.1.36 Any future sentencer must have full information about the requirements that were inserted by the court into the previous community sentence imposed on the offender (including whether it was a low/medium/high level order) and also about the offender's response. This will enable the court to consider the merits of imposing the same or different requirements as part of another community sentence. The requirements should be recorded in such a way as to ensure that they can be made available to another court if another offence is committed.

When an offender is required to serve a community sentence, the court records should be clearly annotated to show which particular requirements have been imposed.

(ii) Time Spent on Remand

1.1.37 The court will need to consider whether to give any credit for time spent in custody on remand . . .

The court should seek to give credit for time spent on remand (in custody or equivalent status) in all cases. It should make clear, when announcing sentence, whether or not credit for time on remand has been given (bearing in mind that there will be no automatic reduction in sentence once section 67 of the Criminal Justice Act 1967 is repealed) and should explain its reasons for not giving credit when it considers either that this is not justified, would not be practical, or would not be in the best interests of the offender.

1.1.38 Where an offender has spent a period of time in custody on remand, there will be occasions where a custodial sentence is warranted but the length of the sentence justified by the seriousness of the offence would mean that the offender would be released immediately. Under the present framework, it may be more appropriate to pass a community sentence since that will ensure supervision on release.

1.1.39 However, given the changes in the content of the second part of a custodial sentence of 12 months or longer, a court in this situation where the custodial sentence would be 12 months or more should, under the new framework, pass a custodial sentence in the knowledge that licence requirements will be imposed on release from custody. This will ensure that the sentence imposed properly reflects the seriousness of the offence.

1.1.40 Recommendations made by the court at the point of sentence will be of particular importance in influencing the content of the licence. This will properly reflect the gravity of the offence(s) committed.

(iii) Breaches
1.1.41 Where an offender fails, without reasonable excuse, to comply with one or more requirements, the 'responsible officer' can either give a warning or initiate breach proceedings. Where the offender fails to comply without reasonable excuse for the second time within a 12-month period, the 'responsible officer' must initiate proceedings.

1.1.42 In such proceedings the court must either **increase the severity of the existing sentence** (i.e. impose more onerous conditions including requirements aimed at enforcement, such as a curfew or supervision requirement) or **revoke the existing sentence and proceed as though sentencing for the original offence**. The court is required to take account of the circumstances of the breach, which will inevitably have an impact on its response.

1.1.43 In certain circumstances (where an offender has wilfully and persistently failed to comply with an order made in respect of an offence that is not itself punishable by imprisonment), the court can **impose a maximum of 51 weeks custody**.

1.1.44 When increasing the onerousness of requirements, the court must consider the impact on the offender's ability to comply and the possibility of precipitating a custodial sentence for further breach. For that reason, and particularly where the breach occurs towards the end of the sentence, the court should take account of compliance to date and may consider that extending the supervision or operational periods will be more sensible; in other cases it might choose to add punitive or rehabilitative requirements instead. In making these changes the court must be mindful of the legislative restrictions on the overall length of community sentences and on the supervision and operational periods allowed for each type of requirement.

1.1.45 The court dealing with breach of a community sentence should have as its primary objective ensuring that the requirements of the sentence are finished, and this is important if the court is to have regard to the statutory purposes of sentencing. A court that imposes a custodial sentence for breach without giving adequate consideration to alternatives is in danger of imposing a sentence that is not commensurate with the seriousness of the original offence and is solely a punishment for breach. This risks undermining the purposes it has identified as being important. Nonetheless, courts will need to be vigilant to ensure that there is a realistic prospect of the purposes of the order being achieved.

Having decided that a community sentence is commensurate with the seriousness of the offence, the primary objective when sentencing for breach of requirements is to ensure that those requirements are completed.

1.1.46 A court sentencing for breach must take account of the extent to which the offender has complied with the requirements of the community order, the reasons for breach and the point at which the breach has occurred. Where a breach takes place towards the end of the operational period and the court is satisfied that the offender's appearance before the court is likely to be sufficient in itself to ensure future compliance, then given that it is not open to the court to make no order, an approach that the court might wish to adopt could be to re-sentence in a way that enables the original order to be completed properly – for example, a differently constructed community sentence that aims to secure compliance with the purposes of the original sentence.

1.1.47 If the court decides to increase the onerousness of an order, it must give careful consideration, with advice from the Probation Service, to the offender's ability to comply. A custodial sentence should be the last resort, where all reasonable efforts to ensure that an offender completes a community sentence have failed.

- The Act allows for a custodial sentence to be imposed in response to breach of a community sentence. Custody should be the last resort, reserved for those cases of deliberate and repeated breach where all reasonable efforts to ensure that the offender complies have failed.
- Before increasing the onerousness of requirements, sentencers should take account of the offender's ability to comply and should avoid precipitating further breach by over-loading the offender with too many or conflicting requirements.
- There may be cases where the court will need to consider re-sentencing to a differently constructed community sentence in order to secure compliance with the purposes of the original sentence, perhaps where there has already been partial compliance or where events since the sentence was imposed have shown that a different course of action is likely to be effective.

18.4 COMMUNITY ORDERS FOR PERSISTENT PETTY OFFENDERS

Section 151 of the Criminal Justice Act 2003 enables the court to impose community orders on persistent offenders even if the offence in question does not cross the community sentence threshold. This is intended to be a limited exception to the rule that a community order may be imposed only if the community sentence threshold is crossed. Section 11 of the Criminal Justice and Immigration Act 2008 inserts a new section, s 150A, into the 2003 Act to make it clear (in s 150A(1)) that the power to make a community order is only exercisable in respect of an offence if either the offence is punishable with imprisonment or, in any other case, s 151(2) confers power to make such an order. Section 11 of the 2008 Act also amends s 151. When the amended version of s 151 comes into effect, its provisions will apply in two categories of case. The first (s 151(1)) is where the current offence is punishable with imprisonment, the offender was aged 16 or over when he was convicted, on three or more previous occasions the offender has (since attaining the age of 16) been fined, and the court would not regard the current offence as being serious enough to warrant a community sentence. The second (s 151(1A)) is where the current offence is not punishable with imprisonment, the offender was aged 16 or over when he was convicted, and on three or more previous occasions the offender has (since attaining the age of 16), had passed on him a sentence consisting only of a fine. In either situation, s 151(2) provides that the court may make a community order in respect of the current offence, instead of imposing a fine, if it considers that it would be in the interests of justice to make such an order. In coming to that decision, the court has to take into account (under s 151(3)) the nature of the previous offences and their relevance to the current offence(s), and the time that has elapsed since the offender's conviction of each of those offences.

Chapter 19

Fines, discharges and binding over to keep the peace

In this chapter, we consider fines, conditional and absolute discharges, and the power to bind a person over. These powers apply irrespective of the age of the offender, although special limits exist on the amount of a fine that may be imposed on a juvenile.

19.1 FINES

A fine may be imposed for any offence except one which carries mandatory life imprisonment. There has been some encouragement for the courts to make greater use of the fine as a penalty. In *R v Baldwin* [2002] EWCA Crim 2647; (2002) *The Times*, 22 November, for example, Lord Woolf CJ, at para 9, said that, particularly in light of prison overcrowding, 'if there are good prospects that an offender is not going to prey upon the public again, there are advantages in using the penalty of a fine rather than sentencing someone to a further period of imprisonment'.

19.1.1 Crown Court fines

Section 163 of the Criminal Justice Act (CJA) 2003 empowers the Crown Court, when sentencing an offender who has been convicted following trial on indictment, to impose a fine on the offender instead of, or in addition to, dealing with him in any other way. This power also applies when the offender was convicted by a magistrates' court but committed for sentence under s 3 of the Powers of Criminal Courts (Sentencing) Act 2000, since the powers of the Crown Court following such a committal are the same as if the offender had been convicted on indictment. Section 163 of the 2003 Act excludes only offences for which the sentence is fixed by law or falls to be imposed under ss 110(2) or 111(2) of the 2000 Act (mandatory minimum sentences for drug trafficking and domestic burglary), or under ss 225 to 228 of the 2003 Act (dangerous offenders).

There is no statutory limit on the amount of a fine imposed by the Crown Court following conviction on indictment (or following committal for sentence under s 3 of the 2000 Act). Note, however, that where a Crown Court is dealing with an offence following committal under s 6 of the 2000 Act, the Crown Court cannot exceed the amount of the fine which the magistrates could have imposed (since the object of that committal is not to increase the sentencing powers available to the court).

19.1.2 Magistrates' courts fines

The amount of fine which may be imposed by a magistrates' court depends on whether the offence is summary or triable either way.

19.1.2.1 Magistrates' courts fines for summary offences

The maximum fine for a summary offence is that prescribed by the statute which creates the offence. Most enactments refer to a level on 'the standard scale' of fines, rather than to a specific sum of money. Under s 37(2) of the Criminal Justice Act 1982, the standard scale has five levels:

Level	Current maximum fine (£)
1	200
2	500
3	1,000
4	2,500
5	5,000

If the statute creating the offence refers only to imprisonment as a punishment, a fine on level 3 (£1,000) is deemed to be included (s 34(3) of the Magistrates' Courts Act 1980).

19.1.2.2 Magistrates' courts fines for either-way offences

Where a magistrates' court convicts a person of an offence which is triable either way because it is listed in Sched 1 to the Magistrates' Courts Act 1980, the court may impose a fine not exceeding the 'prescribed sum' (s 32(1) of the Magistrates' Courts Act 1980. The prescribed sum is currently £5,000 (sub-s (9)).

Where a magistrates' court convicts a person of an offence which is triable either way because the statute creating the offence specifies penalties both for summary conviction and conviction on indictment, the court may impose a fine not exceeding the amount fixed in the statute creating the offence or the prescribed sum (that is, £5,000), whichever is greater (s 32(2)). Where the statute creating the offence states that the fine may not exceed 'the statutory maximum', the maximum referred to is the prescribed sum (that is, £5,000).

Although there is a limit to the amount of a fine for an individual offence, there is no limit on the aggregate fine which may be imposed. Thus, if the court is dealing with an offender for 10 offences which are triable either way, it could impose a fine of £5,000 on each, making a total of £50,000.

19.1.3 Fixing the amount of the fine

Section 164 of the CJA 2003 sets out the procedure for fixing the amount of a fine:

(1) Before fixing the amount of any fine to be imposed on an offender who is an individual, a court must inquire into his financial circumstances.

(2) The amount of any fine fixed by a court must be such as, in the opinion of the court, reflects the seriousness of the offence.

(3) In fixing the amount of any fine to be imposed on an offender (whether an individual or other person), a court must take into account the circumstances of the case including, among other things, the financial circumstances of the offender so far as they are known, or appear, to the court.

(4) Sub-section (3) applies whether taking into account the financial circumstances of the offender has the effect of increasing or reducing the amount of the fine.

It should be noted that sub-s (1) applies only where the offender is an individual (that is, not a company), whereas sub-s (3) applies both to individuals and to companies.

Sub-section (4) requires the means of the offender to be taken into account whether this has the effect of increasing or reducing the amount of the fine. The purpose of sub-s (4) is to ensure that no-one is ordered to pay a fine that is beyond their financial means (and to try to ensure that the effect of the fine on this particular offender would be the same as the effect of an equivalent fine on someone who is noticeably richer or poorer than this offender).

Thus, under s 164, the court first fixes an amount related to the seriousness of the offence (taking account of any aggravating features, and any relevant mitigating circumstances) and then considers whether that amount should be increased or reduced as a result of the offender's means. See, for example, *R v Cowley* (1995) *The Times*, 2 February, where a fine was reduced because proper account had not been taken of the offender's means.

In *R v Warden* (1996) 160 JP 363, it was held that in determining the amount of a fine in a case where the offender has been remanded in custody in connection with the offence, some credit should be given for the time spent on remand. In that case, a fine of £2,000 was reduced to £1,000 on that basis.

In *R v Chelmsford Crown Court ex p Birchall* (1989) 11 Cr App R(S) 510, the Divisional Court emphasised that where the offender is fined for a number of offences, the court must ensure that the total amount to be paid is proportionate to the totality of the offending.

19.1.3.1 The means of the offender

If the offender does not have the means to pay a fine which adequately reflects the seriousness of the offence but the offence is not sufficiently serious to justify a custodial sentence, it is wrong in principle to impose a custodial sentence (*R v Reeves* (1972) 56 Cr App R 366). The same applies even if the sentence of imprisonment is to be suspended. On the other hand, if the seriousness of the offence does justify a custodial sentence, the offender should not escape custody merely because he has the means to pay a large fine (*R v Markwick* (1953) 37 Cr App R 125).

A fine may be imposed at the same time as a compensation order. However, s 130(12) of the Powers of Criminal Courts (Sentencing) Act 2000 provides that if an offender has insufficient means to pay both a fine and a compensation order, the compensation order takes priority; thus, in such a case, the fine will be reduced or a different sentence altogether imposed. A fine may be imposed in addition to an order to pay the costs incurred by the prosecution (see Chapter 15), but the court should ensure that the total sum is within the offender's means.

In *R v F Howe & Son Ltd* [1999] 2 All ER 249, the Court of Appeal gave some guidance on fines where the defendant is a company. The starting point should be the company's annual accounts; these need to be scrutinised with some care to avoid reaching a superficial or erroneous conclusion. Where accounts or other financial information are deliberately not supplied, the court is entitled to conclude that the company can afford to pay any fine the court is minded to impose. The fine needs to be large enough to bring home the seriousness of the offending to the managers and to the shareholders (per Scott Baker J at p 44). Where the defendant is a small company, with limited resources, it must be borne in mind that the fine (and costs) are not tax deductible and so the full burden will fall on the company (at p 45).

In *R v Rollco Screw and Rivet Co Ltd* [1999] 2 Cr App R(S) 436, the Court of Appeal pointed out that, in a small company, the directors might also be the shareholders and so the court must be alert to this if a fine is imposed on both the directors and on the company; however, the penalties imposed should make it clear that there is personal responsibility on the part of the directors which cannot be 'shuffled off' to the company.

The guidance on corporate fines laid down in *R v Howe & Co (Engineers) Ltd* [1999] 2 Cr App R (S) 37 was affirmed in *R v Balfour Beatty Rail Infrastructure Services Ltd* [2006] EWCA Crim 1586; [2007] 1 Cr App R(S) 65. In that case, the court accepted (at paras 22 and 23) that a fine does not have to stand in any specific relationship with a turnover or net profit of the defendant; each case must be dealt with according to its own circumstances. The defendant's resources and the effect of a fine on its business are important; any fine should reflect the means of the offender, and the court should consider the whole sum it is minded to order the defendant to pay including any order for costs. Where a defendant is a public body, it is not immune from criminal penalties because it has no shareholder or well-paid directors; however, if a very substantial financial penalty will inhibit the cost of performance by a statutory body of a public function which it is set up to perform, that is not something to be disregarded.

19.1.3.2 *Obtaining information about the offenders' means*

Section 162 of the CJA 2003 empowers a court to make a 'financial circumstances order' against any person convicted by that court. The order requires the offender to provide a statement of his financial circumstances within the period specified in the order.

Under sub-s (4), failure to comply without reasonable excuse is a summary offence punishable with a fine not exceeding level 3 (£1,000). Where a financial circumstances order has been made, it is an offence (punishable with a fine not exceeding level 4 (£2,500)) under sub-s (5) to make a statement which is known to be false, or recklessly to furnish a statement which is false, or knowingly to fail to disclose a material fact.

Moreover, under s 164(5) where the offender has failed to comply with an order under s 162(1), or has otherwise failed to co-operate with the court in its inquiry into his financial circumstances, and 'the court considers that it has insufficient information to make a proper determination of the financial circumstances of the offender, it may make such determination as it thinks fit'. The effect of this provision is mitigated by s 165, which applies where a court has, in fixing the amount of a fine, determined the offender's financial circumstances under s 164(5). Under s 165(2), if, on subsequently inquiring into the offender's financial circumstances, the court is satisfied that had it had the results of that inquiry when sentencing the offender it would either have fixed a smaller amount or would not have fined him, then it may remit the whole or part of the fine.

19.1.3.3 Guidelines on fixing fines in the magistrates' court

The Guidelines issued by the Sentencing Guidelines Council for use in magistrates' courts give detailed guidance about the imposition of fines. The Guidelines provide three 'bands' (A, B and C) representing levels of seriousness where the court is to impose a fine. The starting points for those bands are 50 per cent, 100 per cent and 150 per cent (respectively) of the offender's weekly income. There is also provision for a range of fines within each band, recognising that there will be variations in the seriousness of offences within each of those bands.

	Starting point	Range
Fine band A	50% of relevant weekly income	25–75% of relevant weekly income
Fine band B	100% of relevant weekly income	75–125% of relevant weekly income
Fine band C	150% of relevant weekly income	125–175% of relevant weekly income

In most cases where an offender is in receipt of earned income, his weekly income will be his actual income less deductions for tax and national insurance. In general, no adjustments are made for the normal range of expenditure on housing and living costs, or for dependants, as these elements have been taken into account in deciding the proportions of weekly income that are the starting points and ranges for each fine band.

The definition of weekly income is adapted for those in receipt of low income (including those whose primary source of income is State benefit). The aim is to ensure that the resulting fine is realistic and fair but also, so far as possible, that a fine has an equal impact on offenders with different circumstances. For those offenders for whom State benefit is their primary source of income, the deemed weekly income is £100 (this applies regardless of whether the actual amount received by the offender is in fact more or less); where the offender is in receipt of earned income, the deemed weekly income of £100 applies where his earned income is £100 or less per week after deduction of tax and national insurance. It follows that where the offender is not in receipt of State benefits and has an earned weekly income in excess of £100, the starting point for a fine will be based on a proportion of his actual income.

Where the offender has an unusually high income, it is necessary to limit the risk that, solely because of his financial circumstances, the fine will be disproportionately high in comparison with the seriousness of the offence. It is for this reason that the Guidelines suggest an upper limit: a fine for a first time offender convicted after pleading not guilty should generally not exceed 75 per cent of the maximum fine for the offence.

Where an offender has savings these will not normally be relevant to the assessment of the amount of a fine, although they may influence the decision on time to pay.

In all cases, a fine should be reduced by one-third where there has been a guilty plea at the first reasonable opportunity.

The Guidelines contain two additional fine 'bands' to assist the court in calculating a fine where the offence would otherwise justify a community order (band D) or a custodial sentence (band E) but the court has decided that it need not impose such a sentence (usually because of compelling mitigation) and that a financial penalty is appropriate.

	Starting point	*Range*
Fine band D	250% of relevant weekly income	200–300% of relevant weekly income
Fine band E	400% of relevant weekly income	300–500% of relevant weekly income

---

19.1.4 Summary: fixing the amount of a fine

The fixing of a fine is essentially a three-stage process:

- deciding what amount would appropriately reflect the seriousness of the offence;
- considering whether that amount should be reduced in light of personal mitigation relating to the offender; and
- considering whether the amount reached after the second stage should be increased or decreased in light of the offender's means.

19.1.5 Enforcement of fines

Whether the fine was imposed by the Crown Court or a magistrates' court, enforcement is the responsibility of a magistrates' court. If the fine was imposed by a magistrates' court, enforcement is the responsibility of that court. If the fine was imposed by the Crown Court, responsibility for enforcement rests with the magistrates' court which sent the offender for trial or committed him for sentence (as the case may be). If the offender resides outside the area served by the enforcing magistrates' court, the order will usually be transferred to the offender's local magistrates' court.

Under s 75 of the Magistrates' Courts Act 1980, the court may allow time (or extend the time already allowed) for payment or may order payment by instalments. Where a fine is to be paid by instalments, the instalments should usually be calculated so that the fine is paid off within 12 months. However, there is no rule of law to this effect and there may be cases where a period longer than a year may be appropriate (*R v Olliver* (1989) 11 Cr App R(S) 10). Where the court allows time (or further time), it may also set a date when the offender must attend court for an inquiry into his means if any part of the fine remains unpaid (s 86).

Under s 85(1) of the Magistrates' Courts Act 1980, where a fine has been imposed by a magistrates' court, the court may at any time remit the whole or any part of the fine, but only 'if it thinks it just to do so having regard to a change of circumstances'. Under sub-s (2), where the court remits the whole or part of the fine after a term of imprisonment has been fixed (as will always be the case with Crown Court fines – see below), it must also reduce the term by a proportionate amount (or remit the whole term if the whole fine is cancelled). It should be noted that the power to remit is restricted to fines; there is no equivalent power in respect of compensation orders (s 85(4)).

Under s 85A of the 1980 Act, where the court has ordered (under s 75) that the fine be paid by instalments, the court may, on application by the offender, vary the number of instalments payable, the amount of any instalment payable, and the date on which any instalment becomes payable.

Assuming the fine is not remitted, the court has at its disposal a wide array of enforcement mechanisms to ensure that fines are paid.

19.1.5.1 Sanctions for non-payment of fines

Sanctions for non-payment of a fine include the following:

- Issuing a 'warrant of distress' authorising the seizure and sale of goods belonging to the offender, with the proceeds of sale going to meet the outstanding fine (s 76 of the Magistrates' Courts Act 1980). These warrants are re-named 'warrants of control' by s 62 of the Tribunals, Courts and Enforcement Act 2007.
- Where the offender is in employment, making an 'attachment of earnings order', which requires the offender's employer to deduct a regular sum from the offender's wages and to pay that sum direct to the court (the Attachment of Earnings Act 1971).
- Where the offender is in receipt of income support or income-based jobseeker's allowance, to make an order for the deduction of regular sums from the offender's income support (under the Fines (Deduction from Income Support) Regulations 1992 (SI 1992/2182)).
- Committing the offender to prison (s 82(4) of the 1980 Act). This is possible if either:
  - the offence for which the fine was imposed was imprisonable and it appears to the court that the offender has the means to pay the outstanding amount forthwith; or
  - the court is satisfied that the offender's failure to pay the fine is due to 'wilful refusal or culpable neglect', and the court 'has considered or tried all other methods of enforcing payment of the sum and it appears to the court that they are inappropriate or unsuccessful'.

  Where a term of imprisonment is ordered, it must be for the term originally specified as the term in default (see below); if no term in default was specified when the fine was imposed, the court dealing with the default fixes a term, which must not exceed the term which could have been fixed in the first place (under Sched 4 to the Magistrates' Courts Act 1980).
- Under s 300(2) of the CJA 2003 (not in force at the time of writing), where a court has the power to commit an offender to prison in default of payment of a fine, the court may instead order the offender to comply with an unpaid work or curfew requirement (this provision is based on s 35 of the Crime (Sentences) Act 1997).

Section 40 of the Criminal Justice and Immigration Act 2008 amends s 300(2), to enable an attendance centre requirement to be imposed on a defaulter under the age of 25 (as an alternative to an unpaid work requirement or a curfew requirement).

- Under s 301 of the CJA 2003 (not in force at the time of writing), instead of committing an offender to custody in default of payment, the court may disqualify the offender from driving for a period of up to 12 months (this provision is based on s 40 of the Crime (Sentences) Act 1997).

19.1.5.2 Imprisonment in default

Section 139(2) of the Powers of Criminal Courts (Sentencing) Act 2000 provides that where the Crown Court imposes a fine, it must fix a term of imprisonment (if the offender is 21 or over) or detention in a young offender institution (if the offender is aged between 18 and 20) in default. Sub-section (4) sets out the maximum term of imprisonment or detention which may be imposed under s 139. This depends on the amount of the fine:

Fine (£)	Term
1–200	7 days
201–500	14 days
501–1,000	28 days
1,001–2,500	45 days
2,501–5,000	3 months
5,001–10,000	6 months
10,001–20,000	12 months
20,001–50,000	18 months
50,001–100,000	2 years
100,001–250,000	3 years
250,001–1,000,000	5 years
over 1,000,000	10 years

Section 82(1) of the Magistrates' Courts Act 1980 provides that a magistrates' court which imposes a fine may fix a term of imprisonment (or detention in a young offender institution) in default only if:

- the offence is punishable with imprisonment and it appears to the court that the offender has sufficient means to pay the fine immediately; or
- it appears to the court that the offender is unlikely to remain long enough at an address where he can be found so that enforcement of the fine by other methods is possible; or
- the court also imposes a custodial sentence on the offender, or the offender is already serving a custodial sentence.

Where a magistrates' court does fix a term of imprisonment in default of payment of a fine, the same periods apply as in the Crown Court (see table above), save that a magistrates' court cannot fix more than 12 months' imprisonment in default (Sched 4 to the Magistrates' Courts Act 1980).

19.1.5.3 Enforcement of fines under the Courts Act 2003

Schedule 5 to the Courts Act 2003 puts in place an additional set of powers to aid the enforcement of fines, complementing (rather than replacing) the other mechanisms for enforcement. It applies to the collection of any sum imposed on conviction (such as fines, costs or sums required to be paid under a compensation order or a confiscation order), regardless of whether those sums are imposed together with a fine, or on their own without a fine (see para 1).

Part 3 of the schedule covers attachment of earnings orders and applications for deduction from benefits (income support or jobseeker's allowance). Under para 7A (where the sum due consists of or includes a sum due under a compensation order) and under para 8 (in the case of other sums due, such as fines, where the offender is an existing defaulter), the court must make an attachment of earnings order if the offender is in employment and it is not impracticable or inappropriate to make the order; if the offender is on benefit, the court must make an application for benefit deductions if it is not impracticable or inappropriate to make the application.

Part 4 governs the making of 'collection orders'. The court must, in every case in which a fine or compensation order is imposed, make a collection order relating to the payment of the sum due, unless it appears to the court that it is impracticable or inappropriate to do so (para 12(1)). Under para 14, if the court has not made an attachment of earnings order or an application for benefit deductions, the collection order must state the payment terms (requiring the offender to pay the sum due within a specified period or by instalments of specified amounts on or before specified dates).

Part 6 enables the 'fines officer' (the person responsible for collecting the fine) to vary the payment terms in the collection order. Under para 22, the offender can apply for such a variation (provided that he is not in default) if there has been a material change in his circumstances since the collection order was made (or since the fines officer last varied the collection order), or if the offender has since provided more information about his circumstances. The offender might seek, for example, to be allowed to pay the sum due by instalments rather than within a fixed period, or (if the order requires payment by instalments) to vary the number or amount of the instalments.

Part 7 of the schedule sets out the effect of the first default on a collection order containing payment terms. Under para 26, if an offender defaults on a collection order and he is not already subject to an attachment of earning order or application for benefit deductions, the fines officer must (provided it is not 'impracticable or inappropriate' to do so) either make an attachment of earnings order (if the offender is employed) or apply for deductions to be made from benefit. Part 9, para 37, provides if the offender is in default on a collection order, and an attachment of earnings order or application for deductions from benefit was not made under para 26, the fines officer must either refer the case to the magistrates' court, or deliver a 'further steps notice' to the offender stating that he intends to take one or more of the steps listed in para 38. These steps include:

- issuing a warrant of distress (to be renamed 'warrant of control') for seizure and sale of goods;
- registering the sum in the register of judgments set up under the Act (which may adversely affect the offender's credit rating);
- make an attachment of earnings order or apply for deduction from benefits;
- make a clamping order (that a vehicle registered in the offender's name be immobilised; the magistrates can then order the sale of the vehicle under para 41);
- take enforcement proceedings in the High Court or County Court (under s 87(1) of the Magistrates' Courts Act 1980).

The offender may appeal to the magistrates' court against the further steps notice (para 37(9)). Under para 39(4), the court may (inter alia) vary the notice so as to specify any step listed in para 38 or vary the payment terms.

Paragraph 42 enables the fines officer to refer a case to the magistrates' court (and, if necessary, issue a summons requiring the offender to attend court) at any time before the fine is paid in full. This would be appropriate if circumstances arise which require action but the fines officer lacks the necessary powers. This would be the case if, for example, the offender fails to co-operate with the fines officer, or circumstances arise under which the offender ceases to have the means to pay any fine.

Paragraph 42A enables the court to increase the fine. Where the offender is in default on a collection order, the sum due consists of or includes a fine, the fines officer has referred the case to the court, and the court is satisfied that the default is due to the offender's 'wilful refusal or culpable neglect', the court may increase the fine. The amount of the increase must not be greater than 50 per cent of the fine.

Schedule 6 to the Courts Act 2003 is even more innovative. It enables the court to allow an offender to discharge a fine by means of unpaid work (under a 'work order'). This power only applies to offenders who are over the age of 18. Under para 2, a 'work order' may be made if it appears to the court that, in view of the offender's financial circumstances, the normal methods of fine collection are likely to be 'impracticable or inappropriate'. The court must be satisfied that the offender appears suitable to carry out the work; also, the order can only be made with the consent of the offender.

Under para 3(3), the number of hours to be worked is calculated by dividing the sum owed by the prescribed hourly sum, which is fixed by regulations (the *Discharge of Fines by Unpaid Work (Prescribed Hourly Sum) Regulations 2004* (SI 2004/2196) fixed the hourly sum at £6). The order must specify a date by which the number of hours is to be performed (para 3(4)). Under para 6(3), if the work is completed before the specified date, the liability to pay the amount due is discharged. Paragraph 7 allows the offender to discharge his liability by paying the sum in respect of which the work was set; he can also reduce the number of hours he has to work by paying part of the sum.

Under para 8, the work order may be revoked or varied by the court (on application of the fines officer) if the offender fails without reasonable excuse to comply with the work order. If the offender fails to carry out the work but has a reasonable excuse (or if a change in circumstances means that he is unlikely to be able to comply), the court may revoke the order or allow more time to do the work. Where a work order is revoked and the offender has carried out some work under it, the sum due is reduced pro rata (para 9).

19.1.6 The use of fines

In 'The use of financial penalties and the amounts imposed: the need for a new approach' [2003] Crim LR 13, Robin Moore notes that use of the fine had declined, and that there were growing concerns regarding its credibility as a means of punishment. Those concerns arose from the fact that a large proportion of those ordered to pay fines were in arrears, and significant amounts of money were simply being written-off. He says that:

> . . . it is important to clarify the underlying principles behind any proposals for change. One such principle is that the fine should have a detrimental impact upon offenders' means, short of actual financial hardship. It should also be capable of payment within 12 months, enabling offenders to make a fresh start once a year has passed.

He advocates a return to a version of the short-lived 'unit fines' system, which was related much more closely to ability to pay. Under that system, the fine was essentially based on weekly disposable income: s 18(2) of the Criminal Justice Act 1991 provided that the amount of the fine should be the product of a number of units, 'commensurate with the seriousness of the offence', and the value given to each unit, representing 'the offender's disposable [weekly] income'. However, after being in force for only a very short time, the unit fine system was abolished by s 65 of the Criminal Justice Act 1993. The system had attracted criticism from magistrates and from the media, with magistrates saying that the scheme was too rigid and the press protesting at the fact that people who had committed similar offences were receiving very different fines (which was, of course, the whole point of the scheme!). The unit fines scheme was replaced with the more general requirement that the court should take account of the offender's means when fixing a fine (whether doing so served to decrease or increase the amount of the fine). Moore suggests a modification of the short-lived 'unit fines' scheme:

> First, a financial penalty could be imposed for a specified number of weeks according to the gravity of the offence. The offence would rightly remain paramount, and fines, like other sentencing disposals, would be imposed for a period of time. Second, the amount to be paid in each week throughout the specified period could be set according to the offender's spare income, subject to a fixed minimum and maximum so as to maintain a level of proportionality with the offence. To maintain correspondence with both offence and offender, subsequent financial penalties would need to be set consecutively, unless the offender was judged able to afford concurrent maximum rates of payment. The time periods appropriate for the various offences, along with the maximum and minimum rates of payment, would have to be calculated carefully and set out in the magistrates' guidelines.

We have seen (above) that the provision of 'bands' for fines in the magistrates' court represents an attempt to relate the fine to the income of the offender (without engaging in complex calculations that would cause undue delay). Concerted efforts to ensure that fines are actually paid by the offender (for example 'Operation Payback' in 2004–05) have increased the credibility of the fine as an effective disposal.

Moore also comments on the dilemma faced by courts where a fine is the appropriate sentence but the offender lacks the means to pay. Often the only alternative is a conditional discharge (which is regarded by many as a complete 'let-off'). Moore concludes that 'the full range of community sentences should be available as options so that the sentence can be tailored to both offence and offender'. This would, however, mean doing away with the community sentence threshold (the requirement that a community sentence may be imposed only if the seriousness of the offence so warrants), since many of the offences that are dealt with by way of a fine would currently not be regarded as serious enough to justify a community sentence. An extension of community sentences would have significant resource implications, given the need to supervise the offender's performance of the requirements of the sentence.

In 'The methods for enforcing financial penalties: the need for a multi-dimensional approach' [2004] Crim LR 728, Robin Moore advocates use of a variety of enforcement methods, and greater attention being paid to the reasons for default. He concludes that, if defaulters' circumstances have changed, the total amount payable and/or the instalment rate should be altered accordingly (this is generally done). For those unable to pay at a sufficient minimum rate and/or complete payment within 12 months, other options should be explored (in this regard, the unpaid work option is valuable addition to the court's armoury for fine defaulters). Moore says that 'for those defaulters who can pay, the initial efforts should be upon ensuring payment. Direct deductions are particularly effective and should be employed against those who forgot to pay and those who decided not to do so'. For those who have decided not to pay, he says that 'firmer "enforcing" responses are then justifiable, with imprisonment being retained as a last resort'.

19.2 ABSOLUTE AND CONDITIONAL DISCHARGES

Section 12(1) of the Powers of Criminal Courts (Sentencing) Act 2000 provides that where a court has convicted a person of an offence but is of the opinion, having regard to the nature of the offence and the character of the offender, that it is 'inexpedient to inflict punishment', the court may either:

- discharge the offender absolutely; or
- discharge the offender subject to a condition that he does not commit a further offence during the period (of up to three years) specified in the order.

19.2.1 Absolute discharge

The effect of an absolute discharge is that, apart from the fact that a conviction is recorded against the offender, no penalty is imposed.

An absolute discharge is appropriate where the court decides that it would be wrong to take any action against the accused. For example, an absolute discharge may be ordered if the defendant is convicted of a very trivial offence or if the circumstances of the commission of the offence show little or no blame on the part of the defendant. In *R v O'Toole* (1971) 55 Cr App R 206, for example, an ambulance driver who collided with another vehicle while answering a 999 call received an absolute discharge.

19.2.2 Conditional discharge

The only condition of a conditional discharge is that the offender does not commit another offence during the period of the conditional discharge. No other condition may be imposed. If the offender commits another offence during the period of the conditional discharge, he is liable to be sentenced for the original offence as well as for the subsequent offence.

A conditional discharge may be appropriate instead of a fine where the offence is not sufficiently serious to justify a community sentence or there is sufficient personal mitigation to render a community sentence too harsh.

Since a discharge is only to be imposed where it is inexpedient to inflict punishment (s 12(1) of the 2000 Act), it would be wrong in principle to combine a discharge with any other sentence for the same offence (see, for example, *R v Sanck* (1990) 12 Cr App R(S) 155, where it was held that a conditional discharge cannot be combined with a fine for the same offence).

Section 12(7) of the 2000 Act, however, enables the court to make an order for costs and/or compensation even if it discharges the offender. Moreover, an offender may also be disqualified (for example, from driving) even though he has been discharged.

19.2.2.1 Breach of conditional discharge

If the offender commits an offence during the period of a conditional discharge, the court dealing with the breach may deal with the offender in any way in which the offender could have been dealt with when the conditional discharge was ordered (s 13(6) of the Powers of Criminal Courts (Sentencing) Act 2000).

If a person who is subject to a conditional discharge imposed by a magistrates' court is convicted by a magistrates' court of any offence committed during the period of that conditional discharge, the convicting court may deal with him for the original offence (as well as for the later offence); if the convicting court is not the same court that imposed the conditional discharge, the convicting court must obtain the consent of the court which made the order before re-sentencing for the original offence (s 13(8)). Where a person who is subject to a conditional discharge is convicted by the Crown Court of an offence committed during the period of that conditional discharge, the Crown Court may re-sentence for the original offence whether the conditional discharge was imposed by the Crown Court or by a magistrates' court. If the order was made by a magistrates' court, the powers of the Crown Court are limited to those of a magistrates' court if it re-sentences the offender for the original offence (s 13(7)). A magistrates' court which convicts someone of an offence committed during the currency of a conditional discharge imposed by the Crown Court cannot re-sentence the offender for the original offence but the magistrates may commit the offender (in custody or on bail) to the Crown Court to be dealt with for the breach (s 13(5)).

In practice, little is usually done in respect of a breach of a conditional discharge. A custodial sentence can only be imposed in respect of the original offence if that offence was sufficiently serious to justify a custodial sentence; this will rarely be the case. Similarly, a community sentence can only be imposed if the original offence merited such a sentence but there was sufficient personal mitigation in respect of the offender for a conditional discharge to be imposed instead.

Thus, the breach of a conditional discharge is often ignored, or else a fine is imposed for the original offence.

19.2.3 Effect of conditional or absolute discharge

Section 14(1) of the Powers of Criminal Courts (Sentencing) Act 2000 provides that a conditional or absolute discharge only counts as a conviction for certain purposes.

It follows that where an offence is dealt with by way of a discharge, conviction for that offence cannot amount to a breach of an earlier order. So, for example, if the offender commits an offence during the currency of a conditional discharge or during the operational period of a suspended sentence, but the later offence is dealt with by way of a discharge, the court cannot re-sentence the offender for the earlier offence or activate the suspended sentence.

However, an offence which is dealt with by way of conditional discharge does amount to a conviction where a further offence is committed during the currency of that conditional discharge and the offender is re-sentenced for the offence for which the conditional discharge was imposed (s 14(2) of the Powers of Criminal Courts (Sentencing) Act 2000).

Furthermore, an offence dealt with by way of discharge appears on the offender's criminal record.

19.3 BINDING OVER TO KEEP THE PEACE

Section 1(7) of the Justices of the Peace Act 1968 declares that any 'court of record' with criminal jurisdiction (that is, a magistrates' court, the Crown Court or the Court of Appeal) has the power to bind a person over to be of good behaviour. This may be done by requiring the person to enter into his own recognisance or to find sureties, or both, and he may be committed to prison if he does not comply. The Justices of the Peace Act 1361 is interpreted as conferring a similar power to bind people over to be of good behaviour and to keep the peace. Section 115 of the Magistrates' Courts Act 1980 also contains a power to make a bind over order requiring a person to keep the peace or to be of good behaviour, but this is in the context of 'complaints' (and so is of more relevance to the civil jurisdiction of the magistrates' court).

The effect of the order is that the offender promises to pay a specified sum of money (or sureties promise to pay money on his behalf) if he misbehaves during a period specified by the court.

When exercising its power to bind over, the court must fix the period during which the bind over is to last (that is, the period during which misbehaviour will result in forfeiture of the recognisance) and must also fix the amount to be forfeited if the person breaches the order.

There is no statutory maximum for the amount of the recognisance. A person could, therefore, be convicted of an offence and bound over in a sum which exceeds the maximum fine that could be imposed for that offence (*R v Sandbach Justices ex p Williams* [1935] 2 KB 192). Similarly, there is no statutory maximum for the length of time for which the order is to run.

A person may be bound over at any stage of criminal proceedings. It may be done, for example, where the prosecution discontinue the case, or offer no evidence. The power to bind over arises 'not by reason of any offence having been committed, but as a measure of preventive justice, that is to say, where the person's conduct is such as to lead the justice to suspect that there may be a breach of the peace, or that he may misbehave' (*Veater v Glennon* [1981] 1 WLR 567 at 574 (per Lord Lane CJ)). It follows that:

- the power to bind over does not apply only to defendants. It also applies to a witness appearing before the court (see *Sheldon v Bromfield Justices* [1964] 2 QB 573) and to the alleged victim of the defendant's wrongdoing (see *R v Wilkins* [1907] 2 KB 380);
- it does not depend on a conviction being recorded against the person to be bound over. So, a defendant who has been acquitted can be bound over (*R v Inner London Crown Court ex p Benjamin* (1987) 85 Cr App R 267). However, in *R v Middlesex Crown Court ex p Khan* (1997) 161 JP 240, the Divisional Court held that where a defendant is acquitted, he may only be bound over if the judge is satisfied beyond reasonable doubt that he is a person of violence and potential threat to other people.

The jurisdiction to make binding over orders was considered by the European Court of Human Rights in *Steel v UK* (1999) 28 EHRR 603 (followed in *Hashman and Harrup v UK* (2000) 30 EHRR 241). The Court said that the expression 'to be of good behaviour' was 'particularly imprecise and offered little guidance to the person bound over as to the type of conduct which would amount to a breach of the order' (para 76). However, in the present case, the binding over order had been imposed after a finding that the defendants had committed a breach of the peace, and the Court was satisfied that it was sufficiently clear that they were being asked to agree to refrain from causing further, similar, breaches of the peace during the next 12 months.

Section III.31 of the *Consolidation Practice Direction* gives guidance on the power to bind over, including the following:

> III.31.2 Before imposing a binding over order, the court must be satisfied that a breach of the peace involving violence or an imminent threat of violence has occurred or that there is a real risk of violence in the future. Such violence may be perpetrated by the individual who will be subject to the order or by a third party as a natural consequence of the individual's conduct.

> III.31.3 In light of the judgment in *Hashman and Harrup*, courts should no longer bind an individual over 'to be of good behaviour'. Rather than binding an individual over to 'keep the peace' in general terms, the court should identify the specific conduct or activity from which the individual must refrain.

19.3.1 Procedure

Where the court is minded to bind over a person who has not been charged with an offence, or a defendant who has been acquitted, that person should be given the opportunity to make representations (*R v Hendon Justices ex p Gorchein* [1973] 1 WLR 1502; *R v Woking Justices ex p Gossage* [1973] QB 448). Where the court proposes to bind over a defendant who has been convicted (in other words, using the power to bind over as a form of sentence), the defendant must be given the opportunity to make representations and the amount of the recognisance must take account of the defendant's means (*R v Central Criminal Court ex p Boulding* [1984] QB 813).

The *Consolidated Practice Direction* provides that:

III.31.4 . . . The court should state its reasons for the making of the order, its length and the amount of the recognisance. The length of the order should be proportionate to the harm sought to be avoided and should not generally exceed 12 months.

. . .

III.31.11 When fixing the amount of the recognisance, courts should have regard to the individual's financial resources and should hear representations from the individual or his legal representatives regarding finances.

19.3.2 Refusal to enter into recognisance

In *R v Lincoln Crown Court ex p Jude* [1998] 1 WLR 1403, the Divisional Court held that where a court intends to bind a person over, there is no requirement that the person must consent to the order. However, if the person refuses to be bound over, the court can impose a custodial sentence. There is no statutory limit to the custodial sentence where the defendant refuses to be bound over under s 1 of the Justices of the Peace Act 1968, although it would seem to be wrong in principle for a magistrates' court to exceed the usual limit on its sentencing powers.

Although the penalty for failing to enter into the recognisance is expressed to be committal to prison, this is deemed to include detention in a young offender institution where the defendant is aged 18 to 20 (*Howley v Oxford* (1985) 81 Cr App R 246).

There is no power in these circumstances to order the detention of a person who is under the age of 18.

Section III.31 of the *Consolidated Practice Direction* states that:

III.31.13 Before the court exercises a power to commit the individual to custody, the individual should be given the opportunity to see a duty solicitor or another legal representative and be represented in proceedings if the individual so wishes. Public funding should generally be granted to cover representation.

III.31.14 In the event that the individual does not take the opportunity to seek legal advice, the court shall give the individual a final opportunity to comply with the request and shall explain the consequences of a failure to do so.

19.3.3 Failure to comply with conditions of bind over

If the person who has been bound over fails to comply with the terms of the bind over, the court may order the payment of some or all of the amount of the recognisance.

The Crown Court, when forfeiting a recognisance, must fix a term of imprisonment or detention to be served in default (s 139(2) of the Powers of Criminal Courts (Sentencing) Act 2000).

Forfeiture proceedings in respect of a bind over ordered by a magistrates' court are commenced by means of a complaint to the court which made the original order (under s 120(2) of the Magistrates' Courts Act 1980). In *R v Marlow Justices ex p O'Sullivan* [1984] QB 381, it was held that such forfeiture proceedings are to be regarded as civil, not criminal, and so the civil standard of proof (the balance of probabilities) applies. However, para III.31.9 of the *Consolidated Practice Direction* states that:

> Where there is an allegation of breach of a binding over order, the court should be satisfied beyond reasonable doubt that a breach has occurred before making any order for forfeiture of a recognisance. The burden of proof shall rest on the prosecution.

In any event, the person should be given an opportunity to present evidence (including calling witnesses) and to make representations as to why the recognisance should not be forfeited (*R v McGregor* (1945) 30 Cr App R 155).

Chapter 20

Young offenders: custodial sentences

There are currently three types of custodial sentence which apply to offenders who have not attained the age of 21:

- 'detention in a young offender institution', under s 96 of the Powers of Criminal Courts (Sentencing) Act 2000 (18–20 year olds);
- a 'detention and training order', under s 100 of the Act (offenders under 18); and
- long-term detention under s 91 of the Act (offenders under 18).

The two main differences between custodial sentences for those under 21 as against those over 21 are:

- young offenders and adults do not serve their sentences together: young offenders are detained separately from adult offenders;
- unlike a sentence of imprisonment, a detention and training order cannot be suspended.

20.1 DETENTION AND TRAINING ORDERS

Section 100 of the Powers of Criminal Courts (Sentencing) Act 2000 provides for the making of a 'detention and training order' (DTO) where an offender between the ages of 12 and 17 is convicted of an offence which (in the case of an adult offender) is punishable with imprisonment.

A DTO is a custodial sentence and so may be imposed only if the offence is so serious that neither a fine alone, nor a community sentence, can be justified (s 152(2) of the Criminal Justice Act (CJA) 2003, which applies to all custodial sentences).

Where the offender has not attained the age of 15 at the date of conviction, a DTO may be imposed only if he is a 'persistent offender' (s 100(2)(a)). The term 'persistent offender' is (rather surprisingly) not defined in the legislation. In *R v Charlton* [2001] 1 Cr App R(S) 120, the court noted Home Office guidance which suggested that the phrase meant that the offender had been convicted on three or more separate occasions in the past. In the present case, however, the offender had been held by the Crown Court to be a persistent offender solely on the basis of the offences currently before the court (of which there were several!). The Divisional Court held that it would not be appropriate to adopt the Home Office guidance as the definition of the term 'persistent offender'; the court went on to say that the sentencing court in the present case was entitled to regard the offender as a persistent offender on the basis of the offences currently before the court. Similarly, in *R v B (A Juvenile)* [2001] 1 Cr App R(S) 113, Turner J (at para 13) said:

> We conclude that it was the intention of Parliament to leave the question whether or not any given offender had achieved that degree of persistence in his offending to qualify with the sub-section to the good sense of the court which was called upon to sentence, in any given case.

The court declined to provide a more precise definition of the term 'persistent offender'. At para 14, Turner J said:

> It is not necessary . . . that before a person should be categorised as a persistent offender he should have been committing a string of offences either of the same or a similar character, or that his failure to address his offending behaviour arose by his failure to comply with previous orders of a relevant court. The Act . . . leaves the matter wide open. It is for the good sense of judges who are called upon to operate that Act to come to a conclusion on all the evidence before them whether or not the offender satisfies the court as to its opinion that the offender is indeed a persistent offender.

It is clear from the case law that a juvenile may be regarded as a 'persistent offender' for these purposes on the basis of previous findings of guilt and/or the number of offences being dealt with by the court. It is, however, unfortunate that there is no clear definition of the term 'persistent offender', given that the definition affects the liberty of young (and potentially vulnerable) offenders.

Where the offender is aged 10 or 11 at the date of conviction, a DTO cannot be imposed unless the Secretary of State extends such orders to offenders of this age group (this had not happened at the time of writing) and if the court is of the opinion that only a custodial sentence would be adequate to protect the public from further offending by the offender (s 100(2)(b)).

20.1.1 Duration of a detention and training order

Section 100(3) defines a DTO as a sentence comprising 'a period of detention and training followed by a period of supervision'. The total length of a DTO 'shall be 4, 6, 8, 10, 12, 18 or 24 months' (s 101(1)). However, the term of a DTO must not exceed the maximum term of imprisonment that the Crown Court could impose on an adult offender for that offence (s 101(2)). In the case of summary offences, the maximum DTO is six months (s 101(2A)), and so the maximum DTO for a summary offence will remain six months even when, for adults, the maximum sentence for some summary-only offences is increased from six months to 51 weeks. Where the offender is convicted of more than one offence, the court may impose consecutive DTOs (s 101(3)), but the total term imposed must not exceed 24 months (s 101(4)). Under s 101(8), in determining the length of a DTO, the court must take account of any period for which the offender has been remanded in custody in connection with the offence.

In *R (A) v The Governor of Huntercombe Young Offenders' Institute* [2006] EWHC

2544 (Admin); (2007) 171 JP 65, the court noted that it is not open to a criminal court to impose a detention and training order of a duration other than one of those specified in s 101(1).

Section 102(2) provides that the period of detention under a DTO is to be one-half of the total term of the order.

Section 101 empowers both the Crown Court and a youth court to impose a detention and training order for up to 24 months. As half of the period of the detention and training order is spent in custody, this means that the youth court is empowered to impose 12 months' custody (plus 12 months' supervision) for a single offence. The youth court's powers in this regard are therefore greater than those currently enjoyed by the adult magistrates' court (although the powers of that court are due to be increased when the relevant provisions of the Criminal Justice Act 2003 are implemented). In *R v Medway Youth Court ex p A* [2000] 1 Cr App R(S) 191, the Divisional Court declined to imply into the statutory provisions a restriction that the youth court could not impose on a juvenile a longer period of custody than a magistrates' court could in the case of an adult. So, for example, in *C (A Child) v DPP* [2001] EWHC 453 (Admin); [2002] 1 Cr App R(S) 45, an aggregate sentence of 10 months' detention and training was held to be permissible even though a magistrates' court dealing with an adult offender would have been limited to a total of six months' imprisonment.

However, the length of a DTO cannot exceed the maximum sentence that may be passed in respect of the particular offence. In *Pye v Leeds Youth Court* [2006] EWHC 2527, for example, the offence carried a maximum sentence of three months, and so the court quashed a four-month DTO, holding that where the maximum sentence for the offence is less than four months, it is not possible to impose a DTO (which cannot be less than four months).

20.1.2 Supervision under a detention and training order

Section 103(1) provides that the period of supervision under a DTO begins with the offender's release from custody (whether that is at the half-way point or not) and lasts until the expiry of the total term of the order. During the period of supervision, the offender is under the supervision of a probation officer, a social worker or a member of a youth offending team (s 103(3)).

The offender receives a notice setting out any requirements with which he must comply during the period of supervision (s 103(6)(b)). Section 104 provides that failure to comply with such requirements will lead to the issue of a summons requiring the offender to appear before the youth court which made the order or the youth court for the area where the offender now lives (if the allegation of breach is in writing and substantiated on oath, an arrest warrant may be issued instead). If breach of the requirement(s) is proven, the court may order the detention of the offender for a period of up to three months, or the remainder of the term of the detention and training order (whichever is shorter) or it may impose a fine of up to £1,000 (s 104(3)).

20.1.3 Commission of further offences during the supervision period of a detention and training order

Section 105 applies where a person is convicted of an imprisonable offence committed after release from detention but before the expiry of the term of a DTO (that is, during the period of supervision). The court which convicts him of the later offence may (as well as dealing with him for the later offence) order his detention for a period equal in length to the period between the date of the commission of the later offence and the date when the original DTO would have expired.

20.1.4 Early release from a detention and training order

Section 102(4) provides for discretionary early release:

(a) in the case of an order for a term of eight months or more but less than 18 months, at any time during the period of one month ending with the half-way point of the term of the order; and

(b) in the case of an order for a term of 18 months or more, at any time during the period of two months ending with that point.

Time spent in custody on remand prior to the imposition of a detention and training order is not automatically deducted, so s 101(8) requires the court, when determining the duration of a detention and training order, to take account of any period for which the offender was remanded in custody in connection with that or a closely related offence. In *R v Ganley* [2001] 2 Cr App R(S) 17, the Court of Appeal highlighted the fact that time spent in custody on remand is not automatically deducted from the period to be served under a DTO but has to be taken into account by the court when passing sentence.

20.2 DETENTION IN A YOUNG OFFENDER INSTITUTION

Section 96 of the Powers of Criminal Courts (Sentencing) Act 2000 provides that where an offender who has attained the age of 18 but is under 21 is convicted of an offence which is punishable with imprisonment in the case of an offender who has attained the age of 21, the court may impose a sentence of 'detention in a young offender institution'. Because this is a custodial sentence, it can only be imposed if the offence crosses the custody threshold in s 152(2) of the CJA 2003.

The Criminal Justice and Court Services Act 2000 abolishes the sentence of the detention in a young offender institution. However, this repealing provision had not been brought into force at the time of writing. When this sentence is abolished, a court imposing a custodial sentence on a defendant aged 18 or over at the time of sentence will impose a sentence of imprisonment (as it would in the case of an offender who has attained the age of 21).

Under s 189(1) of the Criminal Justice Act 2003, a sentence of detention in a young offender institution may be suspended in the same way that a sentence of imprisonment can. The discussion of suspended sentences in Chapter 17 is therefore equally applicable to detention in a young offender institution.

20.2.1 Length of detention

The minimum period of detention in a young offender institution is 21 days (s 97(2) of the Powers of Criminal Courts (Sentencing) Act 2000). The maximum period of detention is the same as the maximum sentence of imprisonment in the case of an offender who has attained the age of 21 (s 97(1)). It follows that where a young offender aged between 18 and 21 is convicted of a single offence which is triable either way, the magistrates may impose up to six months' detention; where such an offender is convicted of two or more offences which are triable either way, the magistrates may impose up to 12 months' detention. The Crown Court may impose detention of any length up to the maximum sentence applicable to the offence in question (that is, the maximum prison sentence for an adult offender). When the provisions of CJA 2003 which increase the powers of the magistrates when dealing with adult offenders (generally speaking, 51 weeks' custody for a single offence and 65 weeks for two or more offences) are implemented, they will apply equally to detention in a young offender institution.

Section 97(4) of the 2000 Act allows the court to impose consecutive sentences of detention in the same way that consecutive sentences of imprisonment can be imposed on an offender who has attained the age of 21.

20.3 DETENTION UNDER S 91 OF THE POWERS OF CRIMINAL COURTS (SENTENCING) ACT 2000

As we have seen, once an offender has attained the age of 18, the courts can impose the same length of custody (by way of detention in a young offender institution) that they could in the case of an adult (by way of imprisonment). However, in the case of an offender who is under 18 at the date of conviction, the usual custodial sentence (the detention and training order) is limited to a total of 24 months (of which only half is served in custody). Plainly, this would not be adequate punishment where an offender under the age of 18 has committed a really serious offence. Section 91 of the Powers of Criminal Courts (Sentencing) Act 2000 provides for long-term detention in the following cases:

- an offence punishable (in the case of an adult offender) with 14 years' imprisonment or more; or
- an offence under s 3 of the Sexual Offences Act 2003 (sexual assault); or
- an offence under s 13 of the 2003 Act (child sex offences committed by children or young persons); or
- an offence under s 25 of the 2003 Act (sexual activity with a child family member); or
- an offence under s 26 of the 2003 Act (inciting a child family member to engage in sexual activity).

Under s 91(3), a sentence of detention under s 91 may be imposed only if the court is of the opinion that neither a community sentence nor a detention and training order is suitable.

Section 91 can also be used to enable the passing of the minimum sentences required under s 51A of the Firearms Act 1968 and s 29 of the Violent Crime Reduction Act 2006 (see s 91(1A)–(1C)).

Section 91 currently only applies to an offender who has been convicted in the Crown Court following trial on indictment. Thus, a youth court cannot impose a sentence under this section. When the 'plea before venue' procedure (see Chapter 4) is extended to the youth court in cases where the juvenile is charged with an offence that falls within the ambit of s 91, the youth court will be then empowered to commit the juvenile to the Crown Court for sentence if the juvenile indicates a guilty plea and the magistrates take the view that a sentence of detention under s 91 may well be appropriate given the seriousness of the offence (see s 24A of the Magistrates' Courts Act 1980).

20.3.1 Length of detention

The maximum sentence which can be imposed under s 91 is the same as the maximum sentence of imprisonment which can be imposed on an adult offender for that offence (s 91(3)). If the offence carries life imprisonment in the case of an adult, detention for life can be ordered under s 91.

Usually, a sentence under s 91 will be for more than two years (since a sentence of up to 24 months can be achieved through a detention and training order, described above). However, unless the Secretary of State exercises his power under s 100(2) of the Act to extend the scope of detention and training orders to 10–11 year olds, there is no custodial sentence for offenders in that age group apart from detention for life for murder (under s 90 – see below) or detention under s 91. In the case of offenders in that age group, a relatively short sentence under s 91 may be appropriate in some cases. In *R v LH* [1997] 2 Cr App R(S) 319, for example, the Court of Appeal upheld a sentence of 12 months' detention under what is now s 91 for indecent assault where the offender was too young for any other custodial sentence; see also *R v Nicholls and Warden* [1998] 1 Cr App R(S) 66, where the Court of Appeal reduced a sentence on two such youngsters to 12 months' detention.

20.3.2 Effect of time spent on remand

Where a young offender has spent time in custody (or in local authority secure accommodation) because bail was withheld before conviction and/or sentence, the time spent in custody (or secure accommodation) counts towards the service of any custodial sentence (whether detention in a young offender institution or long-term detention under s 91 of the 2000 Act) subsequently imposed for the offence for which bail was withheld, and so that period will be deducted from the sentence which is imposed by the court in order to calculate how long the offender will actually have to serve in custody (s 240(10) of the CJA 2003).

20.4 DANGEROUS OFFENDERS

Section 226 of the CJA 2003 applies where a person aged under 18 is convicted of a 'serious' offence (as defined in s 224) and the court 'is of the opinion that there is a significant risk to members of the public of serious harm occasioned by the commission by him of further specified offences' (sub-s (1)). Where the offence is one in respect of which the offender would otherwise be liable to a sentence of detention for life under s 91 of the Powers of Criminal Courts (Sentencing) Act 2000, and the court considers that the seriousness of the offence(s) is such as to justify the imposition of a sentence of detention for life, the court must impose a sentence of detention for life under s 91 (s 226(2)). Under sub-s (3), if the case does not fall within sub-s (2), and the court considers that an extended sentence under s 228 (see below) 'would not be adequate for the purpose of protecting the public from serious harm occasioned by the commission by the offender of further specified offences', then the court must impose a sentence of detention for public protection (i.e. a sentence of detention for an indeterminate period (sub-s (4)).

Section 228 of the 2003 Act applies where a person aged under 18 is convicted of a specified offence (as defined in s 224) and the court considers that 'there is a significant risk to members of the public of serious harm occasioned by the commission by the offender of further specified offences' and, where the specified offence is also a 'serious' offence (again as defined in s 224), that the case is not one in which the court is required by s 226(2) to impose a sentence of detention for life or by s 226(3) to impose a sentence of detention for public protection (s 228(1)). Under s 228(2), the court must impose an extended sentence of detention. This is defined in sub-s (2) as a sentence of detention the term of which is equal to the aggregate of (a) the 'appropriate custodial term', and (b) a further period ('the extension period') for which the offender is to be on licence and which 'is of such length as the court considers necessary for the purpose of protecting members of the public from serious harm occasioned by the commission by him of further specified offences'. Sub-section (3) defines 'appropriate custodial term' as such term as the court considers appropriate, and which is at least 12 months but must not exceed the maximum term of imprisonment permitted for the offence in the case of an adult offender. Under sub-s (4), the 'extension period' must not exceed five years in the case of a specified violent offence or eight years in the case of a specified sexual offence. Sub-section (5) makes it clear that the term of an extended sentence of detention must not exceed the maximum term of imprisonment permitted for the offence.

These provisions mirror the provisions applicable to adult offenders, which are discussed in detail in Chapter 17.

20.5 CUSTODY FOR LIFE/DURING HER MAJESTY'S PLEASURE

Section 90 of the Powers of Criminal Courts (Sentencing) Act 2000 requires the court to detain the offender 'during Her Majesty's pleasure' (effectively a life sentence) where he is convicted of murder (or any other offence the sentence for which is fixed by law as life imprisonment) and he was under 18 at the time the offence was committed.

Where a person aged between 18 and 21 is convicted of murder, s 93 of the 2000 Act requires the court to pass a sentence of custody for life. This provision will be repealed (by the Criminal Justice and Court Services Act 2000 – the repealing provision was not in force at the time of writing) when imprisonment becomes available in the case of offenders who have attained the age of 18 (and so a sentence of life imprisonment will be possible).

Section 94 of the 2000 Act provides that where an offender aged 18–20 is convicted of an offence which carries discretionary life imprisonment in the case of an adult offender, the Crown Court may impose custody for life. This section is also due to be repealed (by the Criminal Justice and Court Services Act 2000); when the repealing provision is implemented, offenders aged 18–20 who would have been sentenced to custody for life will be sentenced to life imprisonment instead.

20.6 RELEVANT DATE FOR DETERMINING THE AGE OF THE OFFENDER

In *R v Danga* [1992] QB 476, the Court of Appeal ruled that the sentence to be imposed is determined according to the offender's age at the date of conviction, not at the date when sentence is passed. Thus, an offender who is 20 when convicted, but 21 at the date of sentence, would be sentenced to detention in a young offender institution, not to imprisonment. Thus, in *R v Cassidy* (2000) *The Times*, 13 October, the offender was aged 17 when convicted but was 18 at the date of sentence. The question at issue was whether the appropriate sentence was one of detention in a young offender institution or a detention and training order (see above). The Court of Appeal held that the appellant fell to be sentenced as a 17-year-old because the determining factor is the date of conviction.

In *Aldis v DPP* [2002] EWHC 403 (Admin); [2002] 2 Cr App R(S) 88, the defendant, who was aged 17 at the time of the offence, was charged with wounding with intent. The youth court decided that it would not be appropriate to commit him to the Crown Court for trial (to enable a sentence of detention under s 91 of the Powers of Criminal Courts (Sentencing) Act 2000 to be imposed in the event of conviction). The defendant pleaded not guilty. Before the trial started, the defendant had had his 18th birthday. The Divisional Court was asked whether the court could impose a detention and training order on a youth who had attained the age of 18 prior to conviction and sentence. The court held that s 100 of the 2000 Act plainly contemplates the possibility of a detention and training order being made in respect of someone over 18, since the crucial date is the date of conviction. The justices were therefore entitled to sentence a defendant to a DTO even though the defendant had attained the age of 18 prior to the sentencing hearing.

In *R v Ghafoor* [2002] EWCA Crim 1857; [2003] 1 Cr App R(S) 84, the offender was 17 at the date of the offence but, by the time he pleaded guilty, he had reached the age of 18. The court confirmed that the relevant date for determining a defendant's age when the court is about to exercise its powers of sentence is the date of conviction, since the form of sentence is dictated by the defendant's age at that date. In the present case, since the offender had passed his 18th birthday before he pleaded guilty, the sentencing powers available to the court permitted the judge to pass a sentence of up to a maximum of 10 years' detention in a young offender institution. If he had pleaded guilty when he was still only 17, the maximum available custodial sentence would have been a term of 24 months' detention and training order. Dyson LJ at para 31 said that:

The approach to be adopted where a defendant crosses a relevant age threshold between the date of the commission of the offence and the date of conviction should now be clear. The starting point is the sentence that the defendant would have been likely to receive if he had been sentenced at the date of the commission of the offence . . . It should be noted that the 'starting point' is not the maximum sentence that could lawfully have been imposed, but the sentence that the offender would have been likely to receive.

His Lordship went on, at paras 32–34, to say:

So the sentence that would have been passed at the date of the commission of the offence is a 'powerful factor'. It is the starting point, and other factors may have to be considered. But in our judgment, there have to be good reasons for departing from the starting point . . . That is because justice requires there to be good reason to pass a sentence higher than would have been passed at the date of the commission of the offence.

That is not to say that the starting point may not be tempered somewhat in certain cases. We have in mind in particular cases where there is a long interval between the date of commission of the offence and the date of conviction. By the date of conviction, circumstances may have changed significantly. The offender may now have been revealed as a dangerous criminal, whereas at the date of the offence that was not so. By the date of conviction, the tariff for the offence in question may have increased. These are factors that can be taken into account, and can, in an appropriate case, properly lead to the passing of a sentence somewhat higher than the sentence that would have been passed at the date of the commission of the offence. It will rarely be necessary for a court even to consider passing a sentence that is more severe than the maximum that it would have had jurisdiction to pass at the date of commission of the offence.

But in a case such as the present where the date of conviction is only a few months after the date of the offence, we think that it would rarely be appropriate to pass a longer sentence than that which would have been passed at the date of the offence.

In *R v Bowker* [2007] EWCA Crim 1608; [2008] 1 Cr App R(S) 72, the Court of Appeal emphasised that the principle that culpability should be judged by reference to the offender's age at the time of the offence is only a starting point. The sentence that would have been imposed at the time of the commission of the offence is a 'powerful', not sole or determining, factor. The sentencer also has to take account of the matters set out in s 142 of the CJA 2003, including deterrence.

Chapter 21

Young offenders: non-custodial sentences

In this chapter we look at the various non-custodial sentences that are applicable to young offenders.

21.1 POWERS OF AN ADULT MAGISTRATES' COURT

As we saw in Chapter 6, there are some circumstances in which a juvenile may be tried and sentenced by an adult magistrates' court. However, the range of sentences available to the adult court is very limited. Pursuant to s 8(8) of the Powers of Criminal Courts (Sentencing) Act 2000, an adult magistrates' court may:

- order an absolute or conditional discharge;
- impose a fine (see below);
- order the parents of the juvenile to enter into a recognisance to take proper care of, and to exercise proper control over, him (see below).

The court may also make ancillary orders, such as compensation and disqualification from driving or from holding a driving licence.

21.2 POWERS OF THE YOUTH COURT AND CROWN COURT

As regards non-custodial sentences, the powers of the youth court and the Crown Court are identical.

21.2.1 Fines

A fine may be imposed on a juvenile (that is, someone under the age of 18) by a youth court, an adult magistrates' court and by the Crown Court.

21.2.1.1 Maximum fine

Under s 135(1) of the Powers of Criminal Courts (Sentencing) Act 2000, the maximum fine which may be imposed by a youth court or an adult magistrates' court on an offender who has not attained the age of 18 is £1,000. Where the offender has not attained the age of 14, the fine is limited to a maximum of £250 (sub-s (2)). There is, however, no limit on the fine which may be imposed by the Crown Court.

21.2.1.2 Payment of fine

Under s 137(1) of the Powers of Criminal Courts (Sentencing) Act 2000, where the offender is under 16, the court must order that any fine (or compensation order) be paid by the parent or guardian of the offender unless either:

- the parent or guardian cannot be found; or
- it would be unreasonable to order the parent or guardian to pay the fine.

Section 137(1A) makes identical provision for surcharges under s 161A of the Criminal Justice Act (CJA) 2003.

Under s 137(3) of the 2000 Act, where the offender has attained the age of 16, the court has a power (not a duty) to order the parent or guardian to pay the fine.

Where a parent or guardian is ordered to pay the fine, it is the means of the parent or guardian (not those of the young offender) which are taken into account in fixing the amount of the fine (s 138). Accordingly, s 136 empowers the court to make a 'financial circumstances order' requiring the parent or guardian to provide a statement of means.

Enforcement of fines is considered in detail in Chapter 19. However, some particular provisions apply to young offenders. For example, under s 81 of the Magistrates' Courts Act 1980, where a magistrates' court would have power to commit an adult to prison for non-payment (but cannot do so in the case of a juvenile because of s 89 of the Powers of Criminal Courts (Sentencing) Act 2000, which prevents imprisonment of young offenders), the court may either (a) make an order requiring the defaulter's parent or guardian to enter into a recognisance to ensure that the defaulter pays so much of the fine as remains unpaid (but only if the parent or guardian consents), or (b) make an order directing that the outstanding amount be paid by the defaulter's parent or guardian instead of by the defaulter (but only if the court is satisfied in all the circumstances that it is reasonable to make the order).

When it comes into force, s 39 of the Criminal Justice and Immigration Act 2008 will enable a magistrates' court to impose a 'youth default order' instead. The order may contain an unpaid work requirement (if the offender is aged 16 or 17), an attendance centre requirement, or a curfew requirement (s 39(2)). Section 39(4) enables the imposition of electronic monitoring of the curfew requirement. Section 39(7) provides for the youth default order to cease to have effect if the sum owed is paid in full, or for the total number of hours or days specified in the default order to be reduced by the appropriate proportion if part payment is made. Paragraph 2 of Sched 7 to the Act sets out the maximum number of hours of unpaid work which may be required (this differs according to the amount which the offender has failed to pay). Paragraph 3 does the same as regards the number of hours which the offender may be required to attend an attendance centre, and para 4 sets out the maximum number of days of curfew which may be imposed.

21.2.2 Parental recognisance

Section 150(1) of the Powers of Criminal Courts (Sentencing) Act 2000 empowers the Crown Court, a youth court or a magistrates' court to order the parent or guardian of an offender who has not attained the age of 18 to enter into a recognisance to take proper care of the offender and to exercise proper control over him. The effect of such an order is that the parent or guardian promises to pay a sum specified by the court, which must not exceed £1,000 (sub-s (3)), if they fail to comply with the terms of the order. Such an order can only be made if the court is satisfied that it is desirable to do so in the interests of preventing the offender from committing further offences.

Where the offender has not attained the age of 16 (that is, he is under school-leaving age), the court must state in open court why it has not exercised the power under s 150 if it decides not to bind the parents over.

Paragraph III.31.17 of the Consolidated Practice Direction states that:

> Where a court is considering binding over a parent or guardian under section 150 of the Powers of Criminal Courts (Sentencing) Act 2000 to enter into a recognisance to take proper care of and exercise proper control over a child or young person, the court should specify the actions which the parent or guardian is to take.

A parent or guardian can only be ordered to enter into a recognisance with their consent. However, a parent or guardian who unreasonably refuses to consent may be fined up to £1,000 (s 150(2)).

The duration of the bind over is limited to three years, or the period until the offender's 18th birthday, whichever is shorter (s 150(4)).

In fixing the amount of the recognisance, the court must take account of the means of the parent or guardian, whether this has the effect of increasing or reducing the amount of the recognisance (subject always to the maximum of £1,000): s 150(7).

Under s 150(2), when a court imposes a community sentence on a young offender, the order may include a requirement that the offender's parent or guardian enter into a recognisance to ensure that the young offender complies with the terms of the order.

21.2.3 Community orders

Where the juvenile has attained the age of 16, the court may impose a community order under s 177 of the CJA 2003. It should be noted that s 148(3) of the 2003 Act provides that:

> Where a court passes a community sentence which consists of or includes one or more youth community orders—
>
> (a) the particular order or orders forming part of the sentence must be such as, in the opinion of the court, is, or taken together are, the most suitable for the offender, and
>
> (b) the restrictions on liberty imposed by the order or orders must be such as in the opinion of the court are commensurate with the seriousness of the offence, or the combination of the offence and one or more offences associated with it.

In the case of all offenders under the age of 18, the court may impose a variety of

892 Criminal Procedure and Sentencing

community-based sentences which are described in the sections which follow. Where the offender is aged 16 or 17, the court therefore has a choice of imposing an adult community order (under the 2003 Act) or one of the sentences described below.

The Criminal Justice and Immigration Act 2008 makes provision for the replacement of the current range of youth sentences with a single generic community order (see below).

21.3 SUPERVISION ORDERS

Section 63 of the Powers of Criminal Courts (Sentencing) Act 2000 enables a youth court or the Crown Court (but not an adult magistrates' court) to make a supervision order against an offender who has attained the age of 10 but who is under 18.

The effect of a supervision order is to place the juvenile under the supervision of a social worker, a member of a youth offending team or a probation officer. The supervisor will usually be a social worker unless the probation service is already in contact with other members of the offender's family. The role of the supervisor, according to s 64(4) of the Act, is to 'advise, assist and befriend' the offender.

A young person who is subject to a supervision order is also required to take part in activities set by the youth offending team (YOT), which could include repairing the harm done by their offence either to the victim or the community, or participating in programmes to address their offending behaviour, such as anger management.

A supervision order may last for up to three years (s 63(7) of the 2000 Act).

21.3.1 Additional requirements

A range of conditions can be attached to a supervision order when the sentence is used for more serious offences. The additional requirements that may be added to a supervision order are set out in Sched 6 to the 2000 Act.

21.3.1.1 Residence

Paragraph 1 of Sched 6 allows the court to require the offender to reside with an individual named in the order. Before such a requirement may be imposed, the person named in the order must agree to the offender residing with him.

21.3.1.2 Complying with directions of supervisor

Paragraph 2(1) of Sched 6 enables the court to require a person who is subject to a supervision order to comply with any directions given by the supervisor to:

- live at a specified place for a specified period;
- present himself to a specified person at a specified place on a specified day;
- participate in activities specified by the supervisor.

Paragraph 2(5) stipulates that the maximum number of days in respect of which the supervisor may give directions is 180. These days need not be consecutive.

The directions are at the discretion of the supervisor, in that it is for the supervisor to decide whether to exercise any of the powers conferred by the order. These directions are intended to help the offender to develop his abilities and to become involved in worthwhile activities. The object is essentially to show the offender that spare time can be used constructively.

Examples of 'specified activities' include participation in an Intensive Supervision and Surveillance Programme ('ISSP' – see below), drug treatment (for offenders who have attained the age of 16), curfews or a residence requirement (which might require a young person to live in local authority accommodation for the period of the sentence). Other directions may involve, for example, learning a new skill or going on an outward-bound adventure holiday.

The ISSP has been described as the most rigorous non-custodial intervention available for young offenders. It combines community-based supervision with a comprehensive and sustained focus on tackling the factors that contribute to the young person's offending behaviour. ISSPs are aimed at the most 'active' repeat young offenders, and those who commit the most serious crimes. The programme aims to:

- reduce the frequency and seriousness of offending in the target groups;
- tackle the underlying needs of offenders which give rise to offending, with a particular emphasis on education and training;
- provide reassurance to communities through close surveillance backed up by rigorous enforcement.

Information on the Youth Justice Board website (see <http://www.yjb.gov.uk/en-gb/yjs/SentencesOrdersandAgreements/IntensiveSupervisionAndSurveillanceProgramme/>) notes that, since the programme started in July 2001, up to the end of March 2006, 19,037 persistent young offenders have been referred to an ISSP. During 2005/06 alone, there were 5,564 young people starting the ISSP. Most young people will spend six months on ISSP. The most intensive supervision (25 hours a week) lasts for the first three months of the programme. Following this, the supervision continues at a reduced intensity (a minimum of five hours a week, and weekend support) for a further three months. On completion of ISSP the young person will continue to be supervised for the remaining period of their supervision order.

21.3.1.3 Court-nominated activities

Under para 3(2)(a)–(c) of Sched 6, the court may itself specify requirements that the offender live at a specified place for a specified period or participate in specified activities on specified days. In other words, the court removes the discretionary element from the directions under para 2(1) of Sched 6 by deciding itself what the offender is to do.

The maximum number of days in respect of which the court may impose such requirements is 180 (para 3(3)).

21.3.1.4 Reparation

Paragraph 3(2)(d) of Sched 6 enables the court to add a requirement to a supervision order that the offender make reparation (otherwise than by payment of compensation) to the victim(s) of the offence or to the community at large.

21.3.1.5 Negative requirements

Under para 3(2)(f) of Sched 6, the court may order the supervised person to refrain from participating in specified activities on specified days or for a specified period. The restrictions may apply for the entire duration of the supervision order.

21.3.1.6 Procedural requirements for an order under para 3(2)

Before making an order under any of the provisions of para 3(2), the court must be satisfied:

a   that compliance with the requirement(s) is feasible (para 3(4)(a));
b   that the requirements are necessary for securing the good conduct of the supervised person or for preventing him from committing further offences (para 3(4)(b)).

Where the offender is under 16, the court also has to consider the likely effect of the requirements it wishes to impose upon the offender's family circumstances (para 3(4)(c)).

Where compliance with the requirement requires the co-operation of a third party, the requirement can only be imposed with that person's consent (para 3(5)).

21.3.1.7 Requirement of residence in local authority accommodation

Under para 5 of Sched 6, the court may add a requirement that the supervised person live in local authority accommodation for a specified period. The maximum period which may be specified in a residence requirement is six months (para 5(6)).

The residence requirement may also stipulate that the supervised person must not live with a person named in the order (para 5(5)).

A residence requirement may only be added to a supervision order if all of the conditions laid down in para 5(2) are met. Those conditions are as follows:

- a supervision order has previously been made in respect of the offender;
- the supervision order contained a requirement of residence, or compliance with supervisor's directions, or court-nominated directions, an education requirement, or a local authority residence requirement;
- the offender has failed to comply with the requirement, or has been found guilty of an offence which was committed while the original supervision order was in force;
- the court is satisfied that the failure to comply with the requirement, or the behaviour which constituted the offence was due, to a significant extent, to the circumstances in which the offender was living and that the imposition of a local authority residence requirement will assist in his rehabilitation.

The other requirements which may be added to a supervision order may be imposed in addition to a residence requirement (para 5(9)).

21.3.1.8 Requirement to live for specified period with local authority foster parent

Under para 5A of Sched 6, the court may add a requirement that the offender must live for a specified period with a local authority foster parent. Under para 5A(2), such a requirement may be added on if:

- the offence is punishable with imprisonment in the case of an adult offender;
- the offence is so serious that a custodial sentence would normally be appropriate; and
- the court is satisfied that the behaviour which constituted the offence was due to a significant extent to the circumstances in which the offender was living, and that the imposition of a foster parent residence requirement will assist in his rehabilitation.

The maximum duration of such a requirement is 12 months (para 5A(5)), although this period may be extended up to a total of 18 months under para 5(2A) of Sched 7.

The other requirements which may be added to a supervision order may be imposed in addition to a residence requirement (para 5A(8)).

21.3.1.9 Treatment for a mental condition

Paragraph 6 of Sched 6 enables the court to include a requirement that the offender receive treatment for a mental condition. The court must have evidence from a duly qualified medical practitioner that the mental condition of the offender is such as requires, and may be susceptible to, treatment but is not sufficiently serious to require a hospital order or guardianship order under the Mental Health Act 1983. Such a requirement may specify treatment by a qualified medical practitioner, treatment (as an in-patient or out-patient) at a place specified in the order, or treatment in a mental hospital.

The consent of the offender is required if he has attained the age of 14. A condition requiring mental treatment lapses when the offender attains the age of 18 (para 6(3)).

21.3.1.10 Drug treatment and testing requirements

Paragraph 6A of Sched 6 provides for the imposition of a drug treatment and testing requirement.

Such a requirement may be added where the court is satisfied that the offender is dependent on, or has a propensity to misuse, drugs and that his dependency or propensity is such as requires, and may be susceptible to, treatment. The object of the treatment (which may be in-patient or out-patient treatment) is to reduce or eliminate the offender's dependency on, or propensity to misuse, drugs (para 6A(2)). The purpose of adding such a requirement is to enable the offender's drug misuse and offending behaviour to be addressed at the same time.

The testing element may only be included if the offender has attained the age of 14 and consents to the inclusion of that requirement (para 6A(6)).

21.3.1.11 Educational requirements

Paragraph 7 of Sched 6 enables the court to add a requirement to a supervision order that the offender, so long as he is of compulsory school age (that is, under 16), must comply with arrangements made by his parents and approved by the local education authority for his education.

Under para 7(5), such a requirement may only be imposed if it is necessary to secure the good conduct of the offender or to prevent the commission of further offences by him.

21.3.1.12 Breach of a supervision order

Schedule 7 to the Powers of Criminal Courts (Sentencing) Act 2000 deals with the enforcement of supervision orders. A person who fails to comply with a supervision order and who is under the age of 18 will be summoned to appear before the youth court; if the offender has attained the age of 18, he will be summoned to attend before the adult magistrates' court (para 1).

Paragraph 2 of Sched 7 enables the supervisor to take action in respect of a breach of a supervision order. Where it is proved to the satisfaction of the court that the offender has failed to comply with any of the requirements of the supervision order, the court may impose a fine of up to £1,000, or may make a curfew order or an attendance centre order (para 2(2)(a) of Sched 7). The fine or curfew order or attendance centre order may be imposed in addition to, or instead of, the discharge of the order.

Under para 2(2)(b), where the supervision order was made by a magistrates' court or youth court, the magistrates' court dealing with the breach can revoke the order and re-sentence the offender for the original offence. The court can impose any sentence which could have been passed for that offence by the court which made the order.

If the supervision order was made by the Crown Court, the magistrates' court dealing with the breach may simply commit the offender (in custody or on bail) to the Crown Court (para 2(2)(c)). The Crown Court may then revoke the supervision order and re-sentence the offender for the original offence (para 2(4)).

When an offender is re-sentenced following breach of a supervision order, the court must take into account the extent to which the offender has complied with the requirements of the order (and make any necessary reduction) (para 2(7)).

21.3.1.13 Revocation or amendment of an order

We have already seen that a supervision order can be discharged under para 2 of Sched 7 if the offender fails to comply with any of its requirements. Paragraph 5 of Sched 7 enables the supervisor, or the supervised person, to make an application for the order to be discharged or varied. The application is made to the youth court if the offender is under 18 and to the adult magistrates' court if he has attained the age of 18.

If the court decides to vary the order, it may do so by cancelling any of the additional requirements imposed in the original order or by adding any requirement which could have been imposed originally.

Paragraph 8(1) stipulates that a youth court cannot exercise its powers under para 5(1) by revoking a supervision order, or inserting in it an additional requirement or varying or cancelling such a requirement, unless it is 'satisfied that the offender either is unlikely to receive the care or control he needs unless the court makes the order or is likely to receive it notwithstanding the order'.

21.4 ATTENDANCE CENTRE ORDERS

The object of an attendance centre order is partly punitive, in that the offender is deprived of free time on a Saturday morning or afternoon, and partly preventative (a Home Office Circular from 1990 pointed out that such an order can be effective in keeping football hooligans away from matches). There is also a substantial element of rehabilitation. The 1990 Home Office Circular said that such an order should benefit the offender by 'bringing him under the influence of representatives of the authority of the State' and by 'teaching him something of the constructive use of leisure'. Thus, there should be firm discipline at an attendance centre, but the emphasis will be on physical exercise and skills. The programmes run at attendance centres concentrate on group work to give attendees basic skills (such as literacy and numeracy, life skills, cookery, first aid and money management), as well as encouraging attendees to make better use of leisure time. The programme may also include victim awareness sessions (which consider the impact of offending on individuals and the community and how the young person might make amends), and sessions on drug and alcohol awareness and sexual health matters. Attendance centres are generally run by off-duty police officers or teachers on Saturday mornings or afternoons. Premises such as schools, youth clubs and church/community halls are often used.

The power to make an attendance centre order is conferred by s 60 of the Powers of Criminal Courts (Sentencing) Act 2000. The offender must be under the age of 16 (if over 16, an attendance centre requirement can be added to the adult community order under s 214 of the CJA 2003) and must have been convicted of an imprisonable offence.

An attendance centre order may only be made if an appropriate centre is reasonably accessible to the offender (s 60(6)).

An attendance centre order may be made as an alternative to the imposition of a custodial term for non-payment of a fine (s 60(1)(b)) and (as we saw above) it can be used as a method of punishing a failure to comply with the requirements of a supervision order.

21.4.1 Number of hours

The aggregate number of hours must be specified in the order and must be not be less than 12, unless the offender is under 14 and the court takes the view that 12 hours would be excessive (s 60(3)). The aggregate number of hours must not exceed 12 unless the court takes the view that, in all the circumstances, 12 hours would be inadequate. In that case, the total number of hours must not exceed 24 in the case of an offender who is under 16 and must not exceed 36 hours if the offender is aged between 16 and 20.

This maximum aggregate number of hours applies only to attendance centre orders made on the same occasion. If an attendance centre order is made against someone who has not yet completed the number of hours under an earlier attendance centre order, the earlier order is disregarded in fixing the number of hours under the later order (s 60(5)).

Under s 60(10), an offender may not be required to attend a centre on more than one occasion on any day and cannot be ordered to attend for more than three hours on any one occasion.

21.4.2 Breach of an attendance centre order

Paragraph 1 of Sched 5 to the Powers of Criminal Courts (Sentencing) Act 2000 empowers a magistrates' court to require the offender to attend before it where the person in charge of the attendance centre alleges that he has failed to attend or has broken the rules of the centre.

Where the original order was made by a magistrates' court, the magistrates' court dealing with the breach may either impose a fine of up to £1,000 (para 2(1)(a)) or revoke the order and re-sentence the offender for the original offence. Any sentence which could have been imposed by the original court may be imposed by the court dealing with the breach (para 2(1)(b)).

If the original order was made by the Crown Court, the magistrates' court may impose a fine of up to £1,000 for the breach but it cannot re-sentence the offender for the original offence. It can, however, commit the offender (in custody or on bail) to the Crown Court to be dealt with for the breach (para 2(1)(c)). The Crown Court can then re-sentence the offender for the original offence (para 3(1)).

Where the offender is re-sentenced for the original offence, account must be taken of the extent to which he has complied with the original order (paras 2(5)(a) and 3(3)(a)).

It should also be noted that if the offender has 'wilfully and persistently failed to comply' with an attendance centre order, the court may impose a custodial sentence notwithstanding anything in s 152(2) of the CJA 2003 (paras 2(5)(b) and 3(3)(b)).

21.4.3 Discharge or variation of an attendance centre order

As well as the power to deal with a breach of an attendance centre order under paras 2 and 3 of Sched 5, the court may discharge or vary an order, on the application of the person in charge of the attendance centre or of the offender, under para 4 of Sched 5. If the order is revoked, the court has the power to re-sentence for the original offence under para 4(3) of Sched 5.

21.5 CURFEW ORDERS

Where the offender is under the age of 16, s 37(1) of the Powers of Criminal Courts (Sentencing) Act 2000, empowers the court to make a curfew order, defined as an order requiring him to remain, for periods specified in the order, at a place so specified. Where the offender has attained the age of 16 a curfew requirement may be added to an adult community order under s 204 of the CJA 2003.

The time period for the curfew must be between two and 12 hours a day and the order can last no more than six months (s 37(3)).

Under s 37(5), the requirements in a curfew order must, as far as practicable, avoid any conflict with the offender's religious beliefs or with the requirements of any other youth community order to which he may be subject, and any interference with the times, if any, at which he normally works or attends school or any other educational establishment.

Curfew orders are enforced by means of electronic monitoring ('tagging') under s 36B of the 2000 Act.

21.6 EXCLUSION ORDERS

Section 40A(1) of the Powers of Criminal Courts (Sentencing) Act 2000 provides that where a person aged under 16 is convicted of an offence, the court may make an order prohibiting him from entering a specified place for a specified period of up to three months. Such an order is known as an 'exclusion order' (s 40A(2)).

Under sub-s (3), the order may provide for the prohibition to operate only during the periods specified in the order (during its three-month currency) and may specify different places for different periods or days. The order should contain provision for monitoring the offender's whereabouts during the periods when the prohibition is operative (sub-s (6)).

Under sub-s (9), before making an exclusion order, the court shall obtain and consider information about the offender's family circumstances and the likely effect of such an order on those circumstances.

Breach of an exclusion order is dealt with under the procedure set out in Sched 3 to the Powers of Criminal Courts (Sentencing) Act 2000.

21.7 ACTION PLAN ORDERS

An Action Plan order is an intensive, community-based programme lasting three months. The order is supervised by the youth offending team (YOT). The programme developed by the YOT is specifically tailored to the risks and needs of the young person in question. It can include repairing the harm done to the victim of the offence or the community, education and training, attending an attendance centre or a variety of other programmes to address the young person's offending behaviour.

Under s 69(1) of the Powers of Criminal Courts (Sentencing) Act 2000, where a person aged under 18 is convicted of an offence, the court may, if it considers it desirable in the interests of securing his rehabilitation or preventing him from reoffending (s 69(3)), make an action plan order. This is an order which (under s 69(1)):

a   requires the offender, for a period of three months from the date of the order, to comply with a series of requirements with respect to his actions and whereabouts during that period (the 'action plan');
b   places the offender, for that three-month period, under the supervision of a probation officer, a social worker or a member of a YOT; and
c   requires the offender to comply with any directions given by his supervisor with a view to the implementation of the action plan.

An action plan order cannot be made if the offender is already the subject of such an order (s 69(5)(a)). Furthermore, an action plan order cannot be combined with a custodial sentence, a community order under s 177 of the CJA 2003, an attendance centre order, a supervision order or a referral order (s 69(5)(b)).

Under s 70 of the 2000 Act, the requirements under the action plan order itself, and the directions given by the supervisor, can require the offender to:

- participate in specified activities;
- attend at a particular place at a particular time;
- attend an attendance centre;
- stay away from a particular place or places;
- comply with arrangements for his education; and
- make reparation (otherwise than by payment of compensation) to the victim of the offence (or to someone affected by it), provided that person consents, or to the community at large.

Sections 70(4A)–(4H) enable a requirement for drug treatment (including testing) to be included in an action plan order where the court is satisfied that the offender is dependent on, or has a propensity to misuse, drugs and that his dependency or propensity is such as requires, and may be susceptible to, treatment. The testing element may only be included if the offender has attained the age of 14 and consents to the inclusion of that requirement.

Before an action plan order is made, the court must have a written report from the proposed supervisor setting out the requirements he thinks ought to be included in the order, the benefits to the offender that these requirements are designed to achieve, the attitude of the parent or guardian of the offender to those proposed requirements, and (where the offender is under the age of 16) information about the likely effect of the order on the offender's family circumstances (s 69(6)).

21.8 REPARATION ORDERS

Reparation Orders are designed to help young offenders understand the consequences of their offending and to take responsibility for their behaviour. They require the young person to repair the harm caused by their offence either directly to the victim (this can involve victim/offender mediation if both parties agree) or indirectly to the community. Examples of this include cleaning up graffiti or undertaking community work. The order is overseen by the youth offending team.

Under s 73(1) of the Powers of Criminal Courts (Sentencing) Act 2000, a reparation order may be made where a person aged under 18 has been convicted of an offence. The order requires the offender to make the form of reparation specified in the order (but not payment of compensation) either to the victim of the offence or someone otherwise affected by it (in either case, the person must be named in the order) or to the community at large.

A reparation order cannot require the offender to work for more than a total of 24 hours or to make reparation to any person without the consent of that person (s 74(1)). The form of reparation ordered must be commensurate with the seriousness of the offence(s) for which the offender is being dealt with (s 74(2)). The reparation has to be made under the supervision of a probation officer, a social worker or a member of a YOT specified in the order and has to be made within three months of the making of the order (s 74(8)).

Before making a reparation order, the court must obtain and consider a pre-sentence report indicating the type of work that is suitable for the offender and the attitude of the victim(s) to the requirements proposed to be included in the order (s 73(5)).

Section 73(8) requires the court to give reasons if it does not make a reparation order in any case where it has power to make such an order.

A reparation order cannot be made at the same time as a custodial sentence, a community order under s 177 of the CJA 2003, a supervision order which includes additional requirements under Sched 6 to the 2000 Act, an action plan order or a referral order (s 73(4)).

21.8.1 Breach of an action plan order and a reparation order

Schedule 8 to the Powers of Criminal Courts (Sentencing) Act 2000 deals with the enforcement of action plan orders and reparation orders.

If the youth court, on the application of the supervisor, finds that the offender has failed to comply with the requirements of the order, it may impose a fine of up to £1,000, or make a curfew order, or make an attendance centre order (para 2(2)(a) of Sched 8).

Where the original order was made by a magistrates' court, the magistrates may revoke the order and re-sentence the offender (para 2(2)(b)). If the order was made by a Crown Court, the magistrates may commit the offender (in custody or on bail) to be dealt with by the Crown Court, which may re-sentence the offender for the original offence (para 2(2)(c); para 2(4)).

Where the offender is re-sentenced, account must be taken of the extent to which he complied with the requirements of the order (para 2(7)).

Paragraph 5 of Sched 8 contains a general power to revoke or amend the order on the application of the supervisor or of the offender.

21.9 REFERRAL ORDERS

A referral order requires the offender to attend a youth offender panel. This is made up of two volunteers from the local community and a panel adviser from a Youth Offending Team. The panel, along with the young person, their parents/carers and the victim (where appropriate), agree a contract lasting between three and 12 months. The aim of the contract is to repair the harm caused by the offence and address the causes of the offending behaviour, with the aim of preventing reoffending by the offender. The power to make referral orders is contained in ss 16–28 of the Powers of Criminal Courts (Sentencing) Act 2000.

A referral order may be either compulsory or discretionary. The provisions apply where a youth court or adult magistrates' court is dealing with an offender under the age of 18 and the court is not minded to impose a custodial sentence, or to make a hospital order under the Mental Health Act 1983, or to grant an absolute discharge (s 16(1)).

Subject to the restrictions in s 16(1), under s 17(1), the court *must* make a referral order if:

- the offence is punishable with imprisonment;
- the offender pleads guilty to the offence and to any connected offence;
- the offender has never been convicted of any other offences; and
- the offender has never been bound over to keep the peace or to be of good behaviour.

Section 35 of the Criminal Justice and Immigration Act 2008 amends s 17(1) of the 2000 Act so as to remove the last of these, with the effect that the fact that the offender has previously been bound over to keep the peace would not be a bar on the making of a mandatory referral order.

Under s 17(1A), the court *may* make a referral order if the offence is not punishable with imprisonment but the other conditions in s 17(1) are met.

Under s 17(2), the court *may* also make a referral order if the offender is being dealt with for two or more connected offences and:

- he pleaded guilty to at least one offence, but also pleaded not guilty to at least one offence;
- he has never been convicted of any other offences; and
- he has never been bound over to keep the peace or to be of good behaviour.

Section 35 of the Criminal Justice and Immigration Act 2008 amends s 17(2) of the 2000 Act in order to modify the conditions that must be met before a discretionary referral order may be made. As with mandatory referral orders, the fact that the offender has previously been bound over to keep the peace would no longer be a bar to making a discretionary order. In addition, it would be possible to make a discretionary order where the offender had one previous conviction and where, in respect of that previous conviction, a referral order had not been made. Under the amended s 17(2), the discretionary referral conditions would be satisfied in relation to an offence if:

- the compulsory referral conditions are not satisfied;
- the offender pleaded guilty to the offence (or, if the offender is being dealt with for the offence and any connected offence, to at least one of those offences); and
- the offender:
  - has no previous convictions (s 17(2A)), or
  - has been dealt with for an offence on only one previous occasion but was not referred to a youth offender panel on that occasion (s 17(2B)), or
  - he has been referred to a youth offender panel on only one previous occasion, and an appropriate officer recommends that the offender is suitable for a second referral, and the court considers that there are exceptional circumstances which justify making a second referral order (s 17(2C)).

Section 35 of the 2008 Act also repeals s 17(5) of the 2000 Act. As a result, a conditional discharge would no longer be treated as a conviction for the purposes of s 17.

The court may specify the period for which any youth offender contract is to have effect (rather than leaving it to the discretion of the panel); that period must be between three and 12 months (s 18(1)). Where the court is dealing with the offender for more than one offence, separate periods may be specified (s 18(4)); those periods may be concurrent or consecutive, but, if they are consecutive, the total period may not exceed 12 months (s 18(6)).

Where the court makes a referral order in respect of an offence, the court is prohibited from imposing a community sentence, or a fine, or a reparation order, or granting a conditional discharge (s 19(4)). Where the court is dealing with the offender for two or more connected offences, and makes a referral order in respect of one of them, the court must either make a referral order or grant an absolute discharge in respect of the other offence(s) (s 19(3)(a)).

Unless the child is in the care of the local authority, a parent or guardian is required to attend meetings of the youth offender panel established for their child, unless (and to the extent that) it would be unreasonable so to require (s 20). Membership of the youth offender panel for an offender is governed by s 21 and will include a member of the YOT and two other appropriately qualified people. If the offender fails to attend a panel meeting, he may be referred back to the court (s 22(2)).

At the first meeting of the youth offender panel established for the offender, the panel seeks to reach agreement with the offender on 'a programme of behaviour the aim (or principal aim) of which is the prevention of reoffending by the offender' (s 23(1)).

Under s 23(2), the programme may include provision for:

(a) the offender to make financial or other reparation to any person who appears to the panel to be a victim of, or otherwise affected by, the offence, or any of the offences, for which the offender was referred to the panel;

(b) the offender to attend mediation sessions with any such victim or other person;

(c) the offender to carry out unpaid work or service in or for the community;

(d) the offender to be at home at times specified in or determined under the programme;

(e) attendance by the offender at a school or other educational establishment or at a place of work;

(f) the offender to participate in specified activities (such as those designed to address offending behaviour, those offering education or training or those assisting with the rehabilitation of persons dependent on, or having a propensity to misuse, alcohol or drugs);

(g) the offender to present himself to specified persons at times and places specified in or determined under the programme;

(h) the offender to stay away from specified places or persons (or both);

(i) enabling the offender's compliance with the programme to be supervised and recorded.

The programme cannot, however, provide for electronic monitoring of the offender's whereabouts, or for any physical restriction to be placed on his movements (s 23(3)). Where anyone else will be affected by a requirement in the programme, that person's consent must first be obtained (s 23(4)).

The programme is reduced into writing and is signed by the offender and a member of the panel (s 23(5) and (6)).

If the first meeting with the panel does not produce a contract with the offender, there may be a further meeting if the panel think it appropriate (s 25(1)). If it appears that there is no prospect of an agreement being reached within a reasonable period, the matter is referred back to the court (s 25(2)).

Section 26 provides for progress meetings to review the offender's progress in implementing the programme of behaviour contained in the contract. Progress meetings are also convened if the offender wishes the terms of the contract to be varied or if he wishes the order to be revoked because of a significant change in his circumstances (such that compliance with the contract is no longer practicable). A progress meeting is also appropriate if it appears to the panel that the offender is in breach of any of the terms of the contract (s 26(3)).

Section 27 deals with the final meeting, which is held when the compliance period of the contract is due to expire. At the final meeting, the panel reviews the offender's compliance with the contract and decides whether he has satisfactorily completed the contract (s 27(2)). If the panel decides that the offender has complied with the contract, this decision has the effect of discharging the referral order (s 27(3)). Otherwise, the panel refers the offender back to the court (s 27(4)).

Schedule 1 to the 2000 Act makes detailed provision for what happens where a youth offender panel refers the offender back to the court or where the offender is convicted of further offences during the currency of the order.

Under para 5 of Sched 1, if the court is satisfied that the offender has failed to comply with the requirements of the referral order, the court may revoke the order and re-sentence the offender for the original offence.

Under para 12 of Sched 1, where the offender reoffends during the period of a referral order, the court may extend his compliance period, but only if there is evidence of exceptional circumstances indicating that an extension of the compliance period is likely to help prevent further reoffending by him. Otherwise, under para 14, unless the court grants an absolute discharge for the subsequent offence, the court revokes the referral order and sentences the offender for the original offence as if the case were one where a referral order was not appropriate.

Section 36 of the Criminal Justice and Immigration Act 2008 inserts a new section, s 27A, into the 2000 Act. This section applies where, having regard to circumstances which have arisen since a youth offender contract took effect under s 23, it appears to the youth offender panel to be in the interests of justice for the referral order to be revoked. Under s 27A(3), the circumstances in which the panel may refer the offender back to the appropriate court include the fact that the offender is making good progress under the contract.

Section 37 of the 2008 Act inserts a further new section, s 27B, into the 2000 Act. This section applies where a youth offender contract has taken effect under s 23 for a period of less than twelve months, that period has not ended, and (having regard to circumstances which have arisen since the contract took effect), it appears to the youth offender panel to be in the interests of justice for the length of that period to be extended. In such a case, the panel may refer the offender back to the appropriate court, requesting it to extend the length of that period for up to 3 months. Under Pt 1ZA of Sched 1 to the 2000 Act (also inserted by s 37 of the 2008 Act), the court may extend the length of the period for which the contract has effect. Under para 9ZD, the extension must not exceed 3 months or cause the contract to last more than 12 months in total.

In the 1997 Consultation Paper issued by the *Home Office, No More Excuses – A New Approach to Tackling Youth Crime in England and Wales* (Cmnd 3809) (see <http://

www.homeoffice.gov.uk/documents/jou-no-more-excuses?view=Html>), the Government emphasises the underlying foundation of restorative justice on which the referral order is based (requiring as it does that the offender should make some sort of reparation, either to the victim – for example, through a letter of apology or a direct meeting with the victim; by putting right the damage caused by the offence; or through financial compensation – or, where the victim does not want direct reparation, making amends to the community as a whole). The Consultation Paper also emphasises the need for continued engagement with the offender (para 9.31):

> Although the formal referral would be for a fixed period of time, the youth panel would be encouraged to identify ways of supporting the young person at the end of the referral through community based schemes such as mentoring, to help prevent further offending.

This shows the importance of disposals such as referral orders in trying to nip youth offending in the bud.

21.10 A NEW SENTENCING REGIME FOR YOUNG OFFENDERS

Section 1 and Sched 1 of the Criminal Justice and Immigration Act 2008 create a new generic community order for children and young people, mirroring the generic community order for adults established by the Criminal Justice Act 2003 (see Chapter 18). The new orders (which were not in force at the time of writing) are to be known as 'youth rehabilitation orders'. Section 6 of the 2008 Act makes provision for the abolition of certain existing youth orders which can be made under the Powers of Criminal Courts (Sentencing) Act 2000, namely curfew orders, exclusion orders, attendance centre orders, supervision orders and action plan orders.

Section 1(1) of the 2008 Act provides as follows:

> Where a person aged under 18 is convicted of an offence, the court by or before which the person is convicted may in accordance with Schedule 1 make an order (in this Part referred to as a "youth rehabilitation order") imposing on the person any one or more of the following requirements—
>
> (a) an activity requirement (see paragraphs 6 to 8 of Schedule 1),
> (b) a supervision requirement (see paragraph 9 of that Schedule),
> (c) in a case where the offender is aged 16 or 17 at the time of the conviction, an unpaid work requirement (see paragraph 10 of that Schedule),
> (d) a programme requirement (see paragraph 11 of that Schedule),
> (e) an attendance centre requirement (see paragraph 12 of that Schedule),
> (f) a prohibited activity requirement (see paragraph 13 of that Schedule),
> (g) a curfew requirement (see paragraph 14 of that Schedule),
> (h) an exclusion requirement (see paragraph 15 of that Schedule),
> (i) a residence requirement (see paragraph 16 of that Schedule),
> (j) a local authority residence requirement (see paragraph 17 of that Schedule),
> (k) a mental health treatment requirement (see paragraph 20 of that Schedule),
> (l) a drug treatment requirement (see paragraph 22 of that Schedule),

    (m) a drug testing requirement (see paragraph 23 of that Schedule),

    (n) an intoxicating substance treatment requirement (see paragraph 24 of that Schedule), and

    (o) an education requirement (see paragraph 25 of that Schedule).

Section 1(6) of the 2008 Act makes it clear that the power to impose a youth rehabilitation order is subject to s 148 of the Criminal Justice Act 2003 (restrictions on community sentences), and so a youth rehabilitation order may be imposed only if the seriousness of the offence(s) merits it and the restrictions on liberty imposed by the order must be commensurate with the seriousness of the offence(s).

    Under s 5(5) of the 2008 Act, the offender is also required, while the youth rehabilitation order is in force, to keep in touch with the responsible officer (who supervises his performance of the requirements of the order) and to notify the responsible officer of any change of address. These obligations are enforceable as if they were requirements imposed by the order (sub-s (6)).

21.10.1 Requirements that may be imposed under a youth rehabilitation order

Detailed information about the various requirements that may be imposed is set out in Sched 1 to the 2008 Act.

21.10.1.1 Activity requirement

Under para 6(1) of Sched 1, this is a requirement that the offender must do any or all of the following:

    (a) participate, on such number of days as may be specified in the order, in activities at a place, or places, so specified;

    (b) participate in an activity, or activities, specified in the order on such number of days as may be so specified;

    (c) participate in one or more residential exercises for a continuous period or periods comprising such number or numbers of days as may be specified in the order;

    (d) ... engage in activities in accordance with instructions of the responsible officer on such number of days as may be specified in the order.

The number of days specified in the order must not exceed a total of more than 90 (para 6(2)). Participation in a residential exercise is limited to a period of 7 days (para 7(3)) and requires the consent of the offender's parent or guardian (para 7(4)(a)).

    Specified activities may consist of or include an activity whose purpose is reparation, 'such as an activity involving contact between an offender and persons affected by the offences in respect of which the order was made' (para 8(2)).

    The court may not include a requirement if compliance would involve the co-operation of a person other than the offender and the responsible officer, unless that other person consents to its inclusion (para 8(4)).

21.10.1.2 Supervision requirement

Under para 9 of Sched 1, this is a requirement that:

> during the period for which the order remains in force, the offender must attend appointments with the responsible officer or another person determined by the responsible officer, at such times and places as may be determined by the responsible officer.

21.10.1.3 Unpaid work requirement

Under para 10(1) of Sched 1, this is a requirement that the offender must perform unpaid work. The total number of hours unpaid work must be not less than 40, and not more than 240 (para 10(2)) Under para 10(3), the court may not impose an unpaid work requirement unless it is satisfied that the offender is a suitable person to perform work under such a requirement, and that appropriate work is available in the area where the offender resides.

Under para 10(6), the unpaid work must be performed during the period of 12 months from the making of the order. However, unless it is revoked, the order remains in force until the offender has completed the specified number of hours.

21.10.1.4 Programme requirement

Under para 11(1) of Sched 1, this is a requirement that the offender

> must participate in a systematic set of activities ('a programme') specified in the order at a place or places so specified on such number of days as may be so specified.

A programme requirement may also require the offender to reside at any place specified in the order, for any period so specified, if it is necessary for the offender to reside there for that period in order to participate in the programme (para 11(2)).

21.10.1.5 Attendance centre requirement

Under para 12(1) of Sched 1, this is defined as a requirement that:

> the offender must attend at an attendance centre specified in the order for such number of hours as may be so specified.

The total number of hours is governed by para 11(2), which stipulates that:

> The aggregate number of hours for which the offender may be required to attend at an attendance centre—
>
> (a) if the offender is aged 16 or over at the time of conviction, must be—
>   (i) not less than 12, and
>   (ii) not more than 36;
> (b) if the offender is aged 14 or over but under 16 at the time of conviction, must be—
>   (i) not less than 12, and

  (ii)   not more than 24;
(c)   if the offender is aged under 14 at the time of conviction, must not be more than 12.

The offender is required to 'engage in occupation, or receive instruction, under the supervision of and in accordance with instructions given by, or under the authority of, the officer in charge of the centre, whether at the centre or elsewhere' (para 11(7)).

Under para 11(6), the offender may not be required to attend at an attendance centre on more than one occasion on any day, or for more than three hours on any single occasion.

21.10.1.6 Prohibited activity requirement

Under para 13(1) of Sched 1, this is a requirement that the offender must refrain from participating in activities specified in the order (a) on a day or days so specified, or (b) during a period so specified.

21.10.1.7 Curfew requirement

Under para14 (1) of Sched 1, this is a requirement that the offender must remain, for periods specified in the order, at a place so specified.

The curfew requirement may specify different places or different periods for different days, but may not specify periods which amount to less than 2 hours or more than 12 hours in any one day (para 14(2)). Moreover, the curfew requirement may not specify periods which fall outside the period of 6 months beginning with the day on which the requirement first takes effect (para 14(3)). Before imposing a curfew requirement, the court must consider information about the place proposed to be specified in the order, including information as to the attitude of persons likely to be affected by the enforced presence there of the offender (para 14(4)).

21.10.1.8 Exclusion requirement

Under para 15(1) of Sched 1, this is 'a provision prohibiting the offender from entering a place specified in the order for a period so specified'. The period specified must not be more than 3 months (para 15(2)). Under para 15(3), the requirement may provide for the prohibition to operate only during the periods specified in the order, and may specify different places for different periods or days. The term 'place' includes ' an area' (para 15(4)).

21.10.1.9 Residence requirement

Under para 16(1) of Sched 1, this is a requirement that, during the period specified in the order, the offender must reside (a) with an individual specified in the order, or (b) at a place specified in the order ('a place of residence requirement'). The latter type of residence requirement may not be included unless the offender was aged 16 or over at the time of conviction (para 16(4)).

The court cannot impose a requirement that the offender reside with an individual unless that individual has consented to the requirement (para 16(2)).

If the order so provides, a place of residence requirement does not prohibit the offender from residing, with the prior approval of the responsible officer, at a place other than that specified in the order (para 16(5)).

Before making a youth rehabilitation order containing a place of residence requirement, the court must consider the home surroundings of the offender (para 16(6)).

21.10.1.10 Local authority residence requirement

Under para 17(1) of Sched 1, this is a requirement that, 'during the period specified in the order, the offender must reside in accommodation provided by or on behalf of a local authority specified in the order for the purposes of the requirement'.

The order may also stipulate that the offender is not to reside with a person specified in the order (para 17(2)).

The court may only include a local authority residence requirement in a youth rehabilitation order if it is satisfied:

(a) that the behaviour which constituted the offence was due to a significant extent to the circumstances in which the offender was living, and
(b) that the imposition of that requirement will assist in the offender's rehabilitation.

Before including a local authority residence requirement, the court must consult a parent or guardian of the offender (unless it is impracticable to consult such a person), and the local authority which is to receive the offender (para 17(4)).

The period for which the offender must reside in accommodation provided by or on behalf of a local authority must be no longer than 6 months, and must not include any period after the offender has reached the age of 18 (para 17(6)).

21.10.1.11 Mental health treatment requirement

Paragraph 20(1) of Sched 1 defines this as a requirement that the offender must

> submit, during a period or periods specified in the order, to treatment by or under the direction of a registered medical practitioner or a chartered psychologist (or both, for different periods) with a view to the improvement of the offender's mental condition.

The order may specify treatment as an in-patient or out-patient, but the order must not otherwise specify the nature of the treatment (para 20(2)).

Under para 20(3), the court may only include a mental health treatment requirement if the court is satisfied, on the evidence of a registered medical practitioner that the mental condition of the offender is such as requires and may be susceptible to treatment, but is not such as to warrant the making of a hospital order or guardianship order under the Mental Health Act 1983. Moreover, the offender must have expressed willingness to comply with the requirement.

21.10.1.12 Drug treatment requirement

Under para 22(1) of Sched 1, this is a requirement that the offender must submit, during a period or periods specified in the order, to treatment, by or under the direction of a person so specified having the necessary qualifications or experience ('the treatment provider'), with a view to the reduction or elimination of the offender's dependency on, or propensity to misuse, drugs.

Paragraph 22(2) stipulates that the court may impose a drug treatment requirement only if it is satisfied:

(a)   that the offender is dependent on, or has a propensity to misuse, drugs, and
(b)   that the offender's dependency or propensity is such as requires and may be susceptible to treatment.

The order may specify treatment as an in-patient or out-patient but the order must not otherwise specify the nature of the treatment (para 22(3)).

A drug treatment requirement may be included only if the requirement has been recommended to the court as suitable for the offender by a member of a youth offending team or a probation officer and the offender has expressed willingness to comply with the requirement (para 22(4)).

21.10.1.13 Drug testing requirement

Under para 23(1) of Sched 1, this is a requirement that:

for the purpose of ascertaining whether there is any drug in the offender's body during any treatment period, the offender must, during that period, provide samples in accordance with instructions given by the responsible officer or the treatment provider.

The court may include a drug testing requirement only if the order also imposes a drug treatment requirement, and the offender has expressed willingness to comply with the requirement (para 23(3)). The drug testing requirement must specify, for each month, the minimum number of occasions on which samples are to be provided, and may specify times at which, and circumstances in which, the offender may be required to provide samples and descriptions of the samples which may be so required (para 23(4)).

21.10.1.14 Intoxicating substance treatment requirement

Under para 24(1) of Sched 1, this is a requirement that:

the offender must submit, during a period or periods specified in the order, to treatment, by or under the direction of a person so specified having the necessary qualifications or experience, with a view to the reduction or elimination of the offender's dependency on or propensity to misuse intoxicating substances.

For these purposes, 'intoxicating substance' is defined in para 24(5) as meaning

(a)   alcohol, or
(b)   any other substance or product (other than a drug) which is, or the fumes of which are, capable of being inhaled or otherwise used for the purpose of causing intoxication.

Under para 24(2), the court may include an intoxicating substance treatment only if it is satisfied

(a) that the offender is dependent on, or has a propensity to misuse, intoxicating substances, and
(b) that the offender's dependency or propensity is such as requires and may be susceptible to treatment.

The order may specify treatment as an in-patient or out-patient but must not otherwise specify the nature of the treatment (para 24(3)). The court may include an intoxicating substance treatment requirement only if the requirement has been recommended by a member of a youth offending team or a probation officer, and the offender must have expressed willingness to comply with the requirement (para 24(4)).

21.10.1.15 Education requirement

Under para 25(1) of Sched 1, this is a requirement that the offender must comply, during a period(s) specified in the order, with approved education arrangements.

'Approved education arrangements' are arrangements for the offender's education made by the offender's parent or guardian, and approved by the local education authority for the area in which the offender resides (para 25(2) and (3)).

The court may include an education requirement only if it has consulted the local education authority and if it is satisfied that, having regard to the circumstances of the case, the inclusion of the education requirement is 'necessary for securing the good conduct of the offender or for preventing the commission of further offences' (para 25(4)).

An education requirement must not include any period after the offender has ceased to be of compulsory school age (para 25(5)).

21.10.1.16 Electronic monitoring

Under s 1(2)(a) of the 2008 Act, a youth rehabilitation order may impose an electronic monitoring requirement in addition to other requirements. Under s 1(2)(b), and para 2 of Sched 1, where the order imposes a curfew requirement or imposes an exclusion requirement, the order must also impose an electronic monitoring requirement unless (in the particular circumstances of the case), the court considers it inappropriate for the order to do so. These provisions are subject to the general restrictions on electronic monitoring contained in paragraph 26 of Sched 1.

Paragraph 26(1) defines such an 'electronic monitoring requirement' as

a requirement for securing the electronic monitoring of the offender's compliance with other requirements imposed by the order during a period specified in the order or determined by the responsible officer in accordance with the order.

Where there is a person (other than the offender) without whose cooperation it would not be practicable to secure that the monitoring takes place, the requirement may only be included in the order with that person's consent (para 26(3)).

21.10.1.17 Intensive supervision and surveillance

Section 1(3) of the Act makes provision for two specific types of youth rehabilitation order: (a) a 'youth rehabilitation order with intensive supervision and surveillance', or (b) a 'youth rehabilitation order with fostering' (see below). However, by virtue s 1(4), such orders may be made only if the offence for which the offender is being dealt with is punishable with imprisonment, the court is of the opinion that the offence was so serious that a custodial sentence would otherwise be appropriate (or, if the offender was aged under 12 at the time of conviction, and so not eligible for a detention and training order, would be appropriate if the offender had attained the age of 12) and, if the offender was aged under 15 at the time of conviction, the court is of the opinion that the offender is a persistent offender (and so eligible for a detention and training order).

Under para 3(2) of Sched 1, the court, if it makes a youth rehabilitation order which imposes an activity requirement, may specify in relation to that requirement a number of days, which must be more than 90 but not more than 180. Such an activity requirement is known as 'an extended activity requirement' and a youth rehabilitation order which imposes an extended activity requirement is known as 'a youth rehabilitation order with intensive supervision and surveillance' (paras 3(3) and 3(5)). Under para 3(4), a youth rehabilitation order which imposes an extended activity requirement must also impose a supervision requirement and a curfew requirement (together with an electronic monitoring requirement).

The minimum duration of a youth rehabilitation order with intensive supervision and surveillance is 6 months (para 32(3) of Sched 1).

21.10.1.18 Fostering requirement

If the conditions set out in s 1(4) are met (see above), the court may include a fostering requirement, provided that (under para 4(2) of Sched 1) it is satisfied that 'the behaviour which constituted the offence was due to a significant extent to the circumstances in which the offender was living', and that the imposition of a fostering requirement 'would assist in the offender's rehabilitation'. Before making what is known as 'a youth rehabilitation order with fostering', the court must first consult the offender's parents or guardians (unless it is impracticable to do so), and the local authority which is to place the offender with a local authority foster parent (para 4(3)). Under para 4(4), a youth rehabilitation order which imposes a fostering requirement must also impose a supervision requirement.

Paragraph 18(1) of Sched 1 defines a 'fostering requirement' as a requirement that, for a period specified in the order, the offender must reside with a local authority foster parent. Under para 18(2), this requirement must last for no more than 12 months and must not include any period after the offender has reached the age of 18.

Paragraph 19(1) of Sched 1 provides that the court may not include a local authority residence requirement or a fostering requirement in a youth rehabilitation order unless either (a) the offender was legally represented at the relevant time in court, or (b) the offender was granted legal aid but it was withdrawn because of his conduct, or he has refused to apply for legal aid.

A youth rehabilitation order with intensive supervision and surveillance may not impose a fostering requirement (para 5(1) of Sched 1), and so the two are mutually exclusive.

21.10.2 Choosing the requirements

Paragraph 29(5) of Sched 1 provides that:

> The court must ensure, as far as practicable, that any requirement imposed by a youth rehabilitation order is such as to avoid—
>
> (a) any conflict with the offender's religious beliefs,
> (b) any interference with the times, if any, at which the offender normally works or attends school or any other educational establishment, and
> (c) any conflict with the requirements of any other youth rehabilitation order to which the offender may be subject.

Section 5(3) imposes identical requirements on the responsible officer (who supervises the offender's performance of the requirements) when giving instructions to the offender pursuant to a youth rehabilitation order.

Paragraph 28 of Sched 1 requires that:

> Before making a youth rehabilitation order, the court must obtain and consider information about the offender's family circumstances and the likely effect of such an order on those circumstances.

Paragraph 29(1) also requires the court to consider the compatibility of the requirements imposed:

> Before making—
>
> (a) a youth rehabilitation order imposing two or more requirements, or
> (b) two or more youth rehabilitation orders in respect of associated offences,
>
> the court must consider whether, in the circumstances of the case, the requirements to be imposed by the order or orders are compatible with each other.

Paragraph 30(4) of Sched 1 provides that a court must not make a youth rehabilitation order in respect of an offender at a time when another youth rehabilitation order, or a reparation order (made under s 73(1) of the Powers of Criminal Courts (Sentencing) Act 2000) is in force in respect of the offender, unless when it makes the order it revokes the earlier order.

21.10.3 Concurrent and consecutive orders

Paragraph 31 of Sched 1 applies where the court is dealing with an offender who has been convicted of two or more associated offences. Under para 31(4), where the court includes requirements of the same kind in two or more youth rehabilitation orders, it must direct, in relation to each requirement of that kind, whether it is to be concurrent with, or consecutive to, the other requirement(s) of that kind. Where the court directs that two or more requirements of the same kind are to be consecutive, the aggregate number of hours, days or months specified must not exceed the maximum number which may be specified in respect of a single requirement (para 31(6)).

21.10.4 Duration of orders

Paragraph 32(1) of Sched 1 stipulates that a youth rehabilitation order must specify a date, not more than 3 years after the date on which the order takes effect, by which all the requirements in it must have been complied with. Where the order imposes two or more different requirements different dates may be specified (para 32(2)).

If a detention and training order is in force in respect of an offender, a court making a youth rehabilitation order may order that it is to take effect when the period of supervision under the DTO begins or on the expiry of the term of the detention and training order (para 30(2) of Sched 1).

21.10.5 Review of orders

Paragraph 35(1) of Sched 1 empowers the Secretary of State to make provision for youth rehabilitation orders to be reviewed periodically by the court.

21.10.6 Breach of youth rehabilitation orders

Breach of a requirement under a youth rehabilitation order is governed by Pt 2 of Sched 2 to the Criminal Justice and Immigration Act 2008. Paragraph 3(1) provides that if the responsible officer is of the opinion that the offender has failed without reasonable excuse to comply with a youth rehabilitation order, he must give the offender a warning or refer the matter back to the court. If a warning is given, it must state that the failure to comply is unacceptable and that the offender will be liable to be brought before the court if (in a case where the warning is given during the period of 12 months following a previous warning) the offender again fails to comply with the order, or (in any other case) if, during the next 12 months, the offender fails on more than one occasion to comply with the order (para 3(2)).

Under para 4(1) of Sched 2, if the responsible officer has given a warning ('the first warning') to the offender under para 3, and during the following 12 months has given a second warning to the offender, and during the period of 12 months following the date of the first warning the offender has again failed without reasonable excuse to comply with the order, the responsible officer must refer the matter back to the court. Paragraph 4(1) thus envisages two warnings before the case is referred back to the court.

The responsible officer may refrain from referring the matter back to the court if there are exceptional circumstances which justify not doing so (para 4(2)).

If the offender has not received a warning but fails without reasonable excuse to comply with the order, the responsible officer may refer the matter back to the court without going through the warning procedure set out in para 4(1) (para 4(3)). This might be appropriate where, for example, the breach is a very serious one or it is clear that the offender has no intention of complying with the order.

Where the offender is referred back to the court, this is done by the responsible officer laying an information, and the court then issuing a summons requiring the attendance of the offender, or issuing an arrest warrant if the information is in writing and on oath (para 5).

If the original order was made by the Crown Court and did not contain a direction (under para 36 of Sched 1) that further proceedings relating to the order should take place in a youth court or other magistrates' court, the offender will have to appear before the Crown Court. Otherwise, if he under 18, he will have to appear before the youth court for the area where he resides or, if he has attained the age, his local magistrates' court (para 5 of Sched 2).

Under para 6(1) and (2), where an offender appears before a youth court or other magistrates' court, and it is proved to the satisfaction of the court that the offender has failed without reasonable excuse to comply with the youth rehabilitation order, the court may

- impose a fine (up to £250, if the offender is aged under 14, or £1,000 in any other case);
- amend the terms of the youth rehabilitation order so as to impose any requirement which could have been included in the order when it was made, whether in addition to, or substitution for, any requirement(s) already imposed by the order; or
- deal with the offender for the original offence in any way in which the court could have dealt with him at the time.

When dealing with the offender, the court must take into account the extent to which he has complied with the youth rehabilitation order (para 6(4)).

Where the court re-sentences the offender for the original offence, it must also revoke the youth rehabilitation order, if it is still in force (para 6(11)). The offender may appeal to the Crown Court against the new sentence imposed by the magistrates (para 6(16)).

Under para 6(7), where the court imposes an additional unpaid work requirement and the original order does not contain an unpaid work requirement, the minimum number of hours is 20 .

Paragraph 6(8) stipulates that the court may not, if it imposing additional requirements, impose an extended activity requirement, or a fostering requirement, if the order does not already impose such a requirement.

Where the court re-sentences the offender for the original offence, and he has 'wilfully and persistently failed to comply' with a youth rehabilitation order, the court may impose a youth rehabilitation order with intensive supervision and surveillance under para 6(13) whether or not the offence is an imprisonable one and whether or not it crosses the custody threshold (and so the restrictions in s 1(4)(a) and (b) do not apply). If the offender subsequently breaches the youth rehabilitation order with intensive supervision and surveillance, the original offence was not punishable with imprisonment, and the court decides to re-sentence him for the original offence, para 6(15) provides that the court may deal with the offender for that offence by making a detention and training order for a term not exceeding 4 months.

If the order which has been breached is a youth rehabilitation order with intensive supervision and surveillance, and the original offence was punishable with imprisonment, the court may impose a custodial sentence notwithstanding the restrictions on imposing discretionary custodial sentences in s 152(2) of the Criminal Justice Act 2003 (para 6(14)).

Under para 7(1) and (2), where the youth rehabilitation order was made by the Crown Court and contains a direction (under para 36 of Schedule 1) that further proceedings should take place in a youth court or other magistrates' court, the youth court (or magistrates' court) may, instead of dealing with the offender themselves, commit him (in custody or on bail) to be dealt with by the Crown Court.

Where the offender appears before the Crown Court (either because the order was made by the Crown Court and did not contain a direction under para 36, or because the magistrates have committed the offender to the Crown Court under para 7(2)), and it is proved to the satisfaction of that court that the offender has failed without reasonable excuse to comply with the youth rehabilitation order, the Crown Court has the same options as the magistrates court, namely imposing a fine (limited to £250 if the offender is under 14, or £1,000 otherwise), or amending the youth rehabilitation order by imposing different requirements, or re-sentencing the offender for the original offence (paras 8(1) and (2)).

Paragraph 8(15) makes it clear that the question whether the offender has failed to comply with the youth rehabilitation order is to be determined by a judge sitting alone, not by the verdict of a jury.

Paragraph 9 provides that where the youth rehabilitation order imposed a mental health treatment requirement, a drug treatment requirement, or an intoxicating substance treatment requirement, the offender is not to be treated as having failed to comply with the order on the ground only that he has refused to undergo any surgical, electrical or other treatment required by that requirement if, in the opinion of the court, the refusal was reasonable having regard to all the circumstances.

21.10.7 Amendment of youth rehabilitation orders

Under paras 13 and 14 of Sched 2, the appropriate court may, on the application of the offender or the responsible officer, amend the youth rehabilitation order by cancelling any of the requirements of the order, or by replacing any of those requirements with a requirement of the same kind which could have been included in the order when it was made.

By virtue of para 16(3), the court may not impose a mental health treatment requirement, a drug treatment requirement, or a drug testing requirement, unless the offender has expressed willingness to comply with the requirement. However, if the offender fails to express willingness to comply with such a requirement, the court may revoke the youth rehabilitation order and re-sentence the offender for the original offence.

Under para 17, if it appears to the appropriate court that it would be in the interests of justice to do so, having regard to circumstances which have arisen since the order was made, the court may (on the application of the offender or the responsible officer) extend the period of 12 months in which an unpaid work requirement must be completed. This would be appropriate where, for example, ill health has prevented the offender from completing the order.

21.10.8 Commission of subsequent offences

Paragraphs 18 and 19 of Sched 2 to the 2008 Act deal with the situation where a youth rehabilitation order is in force in respect of an offender, and he is convicted of an offence (the 'further offence').

Where the offender is convicted of the further offence by a youth court or other magistrates' court ('the convicting court') and the youth rehabilitation order was made by a youth court or other magistrates' court, or was made by the Crown Court but contains a direction (under para 36 of Schedule 1) that further proceedings should be dealt with by a youth court or other magistrates' court, the convicting court may revoke the order (para 18(3)) and, if it does so, may also re-sentence the offender for the original offence (para 18(4)).

The convicting court may not revoke the order and re-sentence unless it considers that it would be in the interests of justice to do so, having regard to circumstances which have arisen since the youth rehabilitation order was made (para 18(5)). When re-sentencing the offender, the sentencing court must take into account the extent to which he has complied with the order (para 18(6)).

Where the youth court or magistrates' court re-sentences the offender for the original offence, he may appeal to the Crown Court against the sentence (para 18(7)).

If the youth rehabilitation order was made by the Crown Court and contains a direction under para 36 of Schedule 1, the convicting court may (instead of dealing with the offender themselves) commit him (in custody or on bail) to the Crown Court to be dealt with (paras 18(8) and (9)).

Where the youth rehabilitation order was made by the Crown court and does not contain a direction under para 36 of Schedule 1, the convicting court may commit the offender (in custody or on bail) to the Crown Court (paras 18(10) and (11)).

Under para 19(1)-(3), where a youth rehabilitation order is in force in respect of an offender, and he is convicted by the Crown Court of an offence (or has been committed to the Crown Court to be dealt with), the Crown Court may revoke the order and may also re-sentence the offender for the original offence. The Crown Court must not revoke the order or re-sentence unless it considers that it would be in the interests of justice to do so, having regard to circumstances which have arisen since the youth rehabilitation order was made (para 19(4)). When re-sentencing the offender, the Crown Court must take into account the extent to which the offender has complied with the order (para 19(5)).

Chapter 22

Ancillary orders

In this chapter, we consider the powers of the court to order an offender to pay compensation to the victim, to order forfeiture of articles used to commit crime and to confiscate the proceeds of crime. We also consider the special orders which can be made in respect of offenders who are mentally disordered and examine the power of the court to recommend that a person be deported. Finally, we look at Anti-Social Behaviour Orders and various orders involving exclusion and disqualification.

22.1 COMPENSATION ORDERS

Section 130(1) of the Powers of Criminal Courts (Sentencing) Act 2000 empowers a court which has convicted someone of an offence to require that person:

(a) to pay compensation for any personal injury, loss or damage resulting from that offence or any other offence which is taken into consideration by the court in determining sentence; or

(b) to make payments for funeral expenses or bereavement in respect of a death resulting from any such offence, other than a death due to an accident arising out of the presence of a motor vehicle on a road.

Under s 130(3), the court has to give reasons if it does not make a compensation order in a case where s 130 empowers it to do so. This effectively creates a presumption in favour of making a compensation order.

The victim should supply the police with accurate details of their losses and, where possible, documentary evidence (such as receipts). The police pass this information to the Crown Prosecution Service (CPS), who will inform the court that there is an application for a compensation order.

The term 'personal injury' in s 130 is not restricted to physical injury. It can include distress and anxiety (*Bond v Chief Constable of Kent* [1983] 1 WLR 40). The Sentencing Guidelines Council's guidance to magistrates' courts notes that the court should consider two types of loss:

- financial loss sustained as a result of the offence such as the cost of repairing damage or, in case of injury, any loss of earnings or medical expenses;

- pain and suffering caused by the injury (including terror, shock or distress) and any loss of facility. This should be assessed in light of all factors that appear to the court to be relevant, including any medical evidence, the victim's age and personal circumstances.

Where the personal injury, loss or damage arises from a road accident, a compensation order may be made only if there is a conviction for an offence under the Theft Act 1968 or Fraud Act 2006, or the offender is uninsured and the Motor Insurers' Bureau (see below) will not cover the loss (s 130(6)).

In *Holt v DPP* [1996] 2 Cr App R(S) 314, the Divisional Court held that there was no reason why a compensation order could not be made in favour of the victim's estate if the victim had died by the time the compensation order was made.

In *R v Donovan* (1981) 3 Cr App R(S) 192 at p 193, Eveleigh LJ said that:

> ... a compensation order is designed for the simple, straightforward case where the amount of the compensation can be readily and easily ascertained.

Similarly, in *R v Watson* (1990) 12 Cr App R(S) 508, it was held that no compensation order should be made unless the sum claimed has either been agreed or proved. Likewise, in *R v Horsham Justices ex p Richards* [1985] 1 WLR 986, it was held that the court has no jurisdiction to make a compensation order without receiving any evidence where there are real issues raised as to whether the claimants have suffered any, and if so what, loss. The same approach was followed in *R v White* [1996] 2 Cr App R(S) 58, where the Court of Appeal said that a compensation order should only be made where there is no question of a difficult or complex issue as to liability. However, in *R v James* [2003] EWCA Crim 811; [2003] 2 Cr App R (S) 97, Henriques J said (at para 15):

> where a court is of the opinion that a complete reconciliation as between the parties would present a complex and difficult task but that the calculation of the minimum loss arising is a comparatively simple task, and that it would be in the interests of justice to make a compensation order in a sum representing the minimum loss arising, it should make such an order rather than decline on grounds of complexity.

It is submitted that the appropriate approach is that the court should not refuse to award compensation simply because the full extent of the victim's loss is difficult to ascertain; in such cases, consideration should be given to making a compensation order for an amount representing the likely loss or the agreed minimum loss.

22.1.1 Causation

In *R v Corbett* (1993) 14 Cr App R(S) 101, Tuckey J (at p 102) said that:

> some causal connection between the offence and the personal injury, loss or damage must be established before compensation can be ordered ... The offence need not be the sole cause of the injury, loss or damage. Provided it can fairly be said that the loss, etc., has resulted from the offence, that will suffice ...

For example, in *R v Derby* (1990) 12 Cr App R(S) 502, the defendant pleaded guilty to a charge of affray. It was accepted by the prosecution that the offender was not the person who used violence against the victim. Although the defendant was part of the disturbance, he did not inflict any actual violence. It was therefore held that he could not be ordered to pay compensation to the victim of the violence, since the injury had been inflicted by someone else, albeit in the same incident. The court ruled that a compensation order should not be made unless there is some evidence of causation between the offence and the loss, damage or injury in respect of which the order is made. Similarly, in *R v Deary* (1993) 14 Cr App R(S) 648, the Court of Appeal quashed a compensation order because there was no proven causal link between the offender's part in an affray and the injury sustained by the victim.

However, other cases have placed less importance on the need to prove causation. In *R v Taylor* (1993) 14 Cr App R(S) 276, the defendant was convicted of affray following an incident in which a person had been kicked while on the ground. The offender was ordered to pay compensation to the person who was kicked. He appealed on the basis that it had not been proved that it was he who had kicked the victim. It was held that a compensation order may be made against someone who is involved in a fight in which someone is injured even if the injuries were not caused by that offender. In *Taylor*, it was seen as important that the defendant's behaviour was a factor leading to the start of the fighting in which the injury to the victim was inflicted. The court ruled that there was an adequate evidential foundation to justify the inference that the injuries to the victim were caused in part by the participation of the defendant in the affray. A similar approach was taken in *R v Denness* [1996] 1 Cr App R(S) 159, where there were three defendants. One of them was being arrested. There was a struggle as the other two tried to pull the first away from the police officer. Another officer intervened and a struggle ensued. One of the officers was injured. The defendants pleaded guilty to affray but were found not guilty of assault occasioning actual bodily harm. The Court of Appeal upheld the making of compensation orders against each of the defendants, on the basis that they were all involved in the incident in which the officer was injured.

22.1.2 Amount of compensation

If the court decides to make a compensation order, the offender is required to pay the money to the court, which then passes it on to the victim.

Under s 130(4), a compensation order should be for 'such amount as the court considers appropriate, having regard to any evidence and to any representations that are made by or on behalf of the accused or the prosecutor'. In other words, the amount of the damage should be proved if it is not agreed between the parties.

Section 131(1) of the 2000 Act sets a limit of £5,000 compensation for an offence where the order is made by a magistrates' court. There is, however, no limit on the aggregate amount of compensation where the court is dealing with the offender for more than one offence, so long as no more than £5,000 is ordered in respect of any one offence. Thus, if there are five offences, the maximum compensation is £25,000. There is no limit on the amount of compensation which can be awarded in respect of an offence by the Crown Court.

Where the offender asks for offences to be taken into consideration, compensation may be ordered in respect of offences taken into consideration but the total amount ordered must not exceed the maximum which could be ordered for the offence(s) of which the offender has actually been convicted (s 131(2)). Thus, if the offender is convicted of three offences and asks for six others to be taken into consideration, the maximum compensation order is £15,000.

The Sentencing Guidelines Council guidance to magistrates' courts includes suggested starting points for various injuries.

22.1.3 Means of the offender

Section 130(11) of the Powers of Criminal Courts (Sentencing) Act 2000 requires the court to take account of the offender's means in deciding whether to make a compensation order and, if so, the amount of the order. So, in *R v Ellis* (1994) 158 JP 386, a compensation order was quashed because the judge made it without there being any evidence that the defendant, who was unemployed, would be able to pay it. Such an order can only be made against an unemployed defendant if there is cogent evidence that he will be able to find employment. Similarly, in *R v Love and Tomkins* [1999] 1 Cr App R(S) 484, the Court of Appeal said that it is wrong to make a compensation order where the defendant has no assets and his means of earning income are being suspended or brought to an end by the imposition of a sentence of imprisonment. The court should also be very careful before making an order based on the defendant's capacity to earn money after release from prison. However, the court said that it is not necessarily wrong to combine a compensation order with a sentence of imprisonment. A compensation order may be appropriate in those cases where there is evidence that the defendant has sufficient assets or will have sufficient earning capacity after release from prison. The same approach was adopted in *R v Aitken* [2003] EWCA Crim 2587, where the Court of Appeal said that if an offender is sentenced to immediate imprisonment, a compensation order should not be made where it would subject the defendant, on release from prison, to a financial burden that could not be met. In the present case, the sentence of imprisonment necessarily led to the defendant's loss of employment; since he had no assets, the compensation order was wrong in principle (per Grigson J at para 6).

In *R v Harrison* (1980) 2 Cr App R(S) 313, it was said that a compensation order should not generally be made if its effect would be to require the offender to sell his home. However, in *R v McGuire* (1992) 13 Cr App R(S) 454, it was held that there is no general principle that a compensation order should not be made if it would force the defendant to sell the family home; a compensation order could properly be made, even though it would have the effect of forcing the offender to sell his home, at least if it appears that he will have sufficient money left over to buy a cheaper house. Indeed, in *R v Griffiths* [2001] EWCA Crim 2093; (2001) *The Times*, 17 October, whilst the court reaffirmed the general principle that a compensation order is not generally appropriate if the defendant's principal asset is the matrimonial home and the innocent spouse and children might suffer if a sale were to be forced, it went on to point out that a compensation order would be permissible in such a case if the husband and wife were both involved in the offending or where the sale of the home is almost inevitable anyway to satisfy a confiscation order made against the defendant or because the parties are divorcing.

In *R v Barney* (1989) 11 Cr App R(S) 448, it was pointed out that the court should avoid giving the impression that the offender will receive a more lenient sentence if he has sufficient funds to pay compensation; in other words, the impression should not be given that a person can buy their way out of prison. However, there is some tension between this laudable principle and the fact that willingness of the offender to pay compensation is relevant in mitigation to the extent that it indicates remorse.

It should be noted that if the offender misleads the court into thinking he can pay more compensation than he is in fact able to pay, the court will not subsequently vary the compensation order on the ground that he lacks the means to pay (*R v Hayes* (1992) 13 Cr App R(S) 454).

A compensation order should only be made if it is likely that the offender will be able to pay it (if necessary by instalments under s 75(1) of the Magistrates' Courts Act 1980) within a reasonable time. Ideally, compensation should be paid within a year; however, in *R v Olliver* (1989) 11 Cr App R(S) 10, it was said that a fine may be imposed if it can be paid within two or three years, and presumably the same principle applies to a compensation order.

The requirement to take the means of the defendant into account has the consequence that co-defendants may – and indeed should – be required to pay different sums under compensation orders if their capacity to pay is different (see *R v Beddow* (1987) 9 Cr App R(S) 235, where only one of three defendants was ordered to pay compensation, as he was the only one in employment).

22.1.4 Juveniles

Where an offender under the age of 18 is convicted of an offence, a compensation order may be made. However, where the offender is under 16, the court must order the parent or guardian to pay the compensation unless either the parent or guardian cannot be found or it would be unreasonable to require the parent or guardian to pay the compensation (s 137(1) of the Powers of Criminal Courts (Sentencing) Act 2000). Where the offender is aged 16 or 17, the court has a discretion to order the parent or guardian to pay the compensation (s 137(3) of the 2000 Act). Where the compensation is to be paid by a parent or guardian, it is their means (not the means of the offender) which are taken into account (s 136 of the 2000 Act). Under s 137(4), the parent or guardian must first be given an opportunity of being heard.

In *Bedfordshire County Council v DPP* [1996] 1 Cr App R(S) 322 it was held that, where the child is in local authority care and the court is minded to order the local authority to pay compensation, the court should normally find some causative link between any fault proved on the part of the local authority and the offence(s) committed before making a compensation order. If no such causative fault is shown, it is unreasonable to order compensation. In *R v JJB* [2004] EWCA Crim 14, [2004] 2 Cr App R (S) 41, the Court of Appeal applied the same principle in a case where a compensation order was made against a parent. This followed the approach taken in *R v Sheffield Crown Court ex p Clarkson* (1986) 8 Cr App R(S) 454, where it was held to be unreasonable to make a compensation order against a parent who has done what they can to keep the youngster from criminal ways.

22.1.5 Relationship between compensation orders and other penalties

Section 130(1) of the Powers of Criminal Courts (Sentencing) Act 2000 allows the court to make a compensation order as well as, or instead of, imposing a punishment on the offender. However, it should be noted that s 130(12) of the Act gives priority to compensation over fines. If the offender cannot afford to pay both compensation and a fine, no fine should be imposed (or else the amount of the fine should be reduced).

It must also be borne in mind (as we have already seen in the context of the offender's means) that a sentence of immediate custody may well have the effect that the offender will not be able to pay compensation (as it will have the effect of preventing him from earning the money with which to comply with the order) and, in such a case, the custodial sentence would preclude a compensation order (*R v Gill* (1992) 13 Cr App R(S) 36). This would not be the case if the offender had substantial savings or other realisable assets and so would be able to meet the order from his existing resources, or indeed if he had good prospects of finding employment on release from custody (*R v Townsend* (1980) 2 Cr App R(S) 328), or if the custodial sentence is relatively short and there is evidence that the offender's previous job will be open to him when he is released from custody (*R v Clark* (1992) 13 Cr App R(S) 124).

22.1.6 Enforcement of compensation orders

Essentially, compensation orders are enforced in the same way as fines (see Chapter 19). Enforcement is carried out by a magistrates' court, with a term of custody in default of payment. The maximum term of custody for non-payment of compensation is the same as the term for a fine of the same amount. Note, however, that the Crown Court does not have power to fix a term in default when making a compensation order (*R v Komsta* (1990) 12 Cr App R(S) 63).

22.1.7 Other methods of obtaining compensation

There are several other ways in which victims of crime may seek compensation, the detail of which is beyond the scope of the present work. The main ways are:

- compensation by the Criminal Injuries Compensation Scheme (set up by the Criminal Injuries Compensation Act 1995), administered by the Criminal Injuries Compensation Authority (see <http://www.cica.gov.uk>);
- for victims of road traffic accidents involving drivers who are uninsured or untraced, the Motor Insurers Bureau compensation scheme (see <http://www.mib.org.uk/MIB/en/Default.htm>);
- civil proceedings in the High Court or County Court.

Any amount paid by an offender under a compensation order will generally be deducted from a subsequent civil award or payment under the scheme to avoid double compensation.

22.2 SURCHARGES

Sections 161A of the Criminal Justice Act (CJA) 2003 provides that when a court is sentencing an offender for more than one offence it must also order him to pay a 'surcharge' (sub-s (1)) unless the court considers that it would be appropriate to make a compensation order, but the offender has insufficient means to pay both the surcharge and appropriate compensation, in which case the court must reduce the surcharge accordingly, if necessary to nil (sub-s (3)). This provision does not apply if the court grants an absolute discharge (sub-s (4)(a)).

Section 164(4A) of the 2003 Act makes it clear that a court must not reduce the amount of a fine on account of any surcharge it orders the offender to pay under s 161A, except to the extent that he has insufficient means to pay both.

Under Art 3 of the Criminal Justice Act 2003 (Surcharge)(No 2) Order 2007 (SI 2007/1079), the duty to order the offender to pay a surcharge applies only where he is ordered to pay a fine (whether or not any other penalty is also imposed). Under Art 4, the amount of the surcharge is £15.

The Government's intention (Hansard 20 April 2007: Column 827W, John Reid, then Home Secretary) is that money raised by the surcharge system will be spent on a range of services for victims of crime and witnesses, such as witness care units and services to victims of domestic violence and sexual violence (through the Victims' Fund, which supports the development of community-based services for victims of sexual offending).

22.3 RESTITUTION ORDERS

Section 148 of the Powers of Criminal Courts (Sentencing) Act 2000 applies where goods have been stolen and a person is convicted of theft (or asks for theft to be taken into consideration) in respect of those goods. Three orders are possible:

- The court may order anyone who has possession or control of the goods to restore them to the person who is entitled to have those goods (s 148(2)(a)).
- Where the stolen goods have been sold and the proceeds used to purchase other goods which are in the possession of the offender, the court may order the offender to hand over those goods to the person who was entitled to the stolen goods (s 148(2)(b)).
- Where the person who has possession or control of the goods is not the offender but an innocent purchaser who bought them in good faith, the court may order the offender to pay compensation to the purchaser out of any money in his possession at the time of his apprehension (s 148(2)(c)).

An order should only be made under s 148 where it is clear that the person benefiting under the order owned the goods; if there is any doubt, the matter is best left to the civil courts (*R v Calcutt* (1985) 7 Cr App R(S) 385).

22.4 FORFEITURE/DEPRIVATION ORDERS

Section 143 of the Powers of Criminal Courts (Sentencing) Act 2000 empowers the Crown Court or a magistrates' court to make a forfeiture order (sometimes called a 'deprivation order') in two situations.

- Under s 143(1), the court may make a forfeiture order in respect of property which has been lawfully seized from the offender, or which was in his possession or under his control at the time when he was apprehended for the offence. This power only applies if the property was used for the purpose of committing (or facilitating the commission of) an offence, or was intended by him to be used for that purpose.
- Under s 143(2), the court may make a forfeiture order where the offence consists of unlawful possession of property which has lawfully been seized from the offender or which was in his possession or under his control at the time he was apprehended for the offence.

In deciding whether or not to make a forfeiture order, the court must have regard to the value of the property and to the likely effect of the order on the offender (s 143(5)).

Under s 143(6) and (7), an offender convicted of an imprisonable offence under the Road Traffic Act 1988 may have their car seized.

An order is inappropriate if it would have a disproportionately severe impact on the offender because it inflicts too great a burden on him (*R v Highbury Corner Magistrates ex p Di Matteo* [1991] 1 WLR 1374, where the court quashed an order for forfeiture of the offender's car after he had been convicted of driving whilst disqualified and driving whilst uninsured)).

Goods seized under s 143 are usually sold, and the proceeds of sale retained by the Government. However, under s 145 of the Act, where goods have been seized under s 143 and the court would have made a compensation order but for the inadequacy of the offender's means, the court may order that a specified sum from the proceeds of sale should go to the victim of the offence.

22.4.1 Other powers of forfeiture

There are several specific statutory powers to make forfeiture orders, including the following:

- Section 27 of the Misuse of Drugs Act 1971 enables the court to order forfeiture (and destruction where appropriate) of property related to drugs offences or drug trafficking offences. It must be shown that the property is related to the offence of which the offender has been convicted. In *R v Cuthbertson* [1981] AC 470, it was held by the House of Lords that forfeiture orders under the 1971 Act apply to 'tangible' property such as the drugs, the equipment for making them, vehicles used for transporting them and cash handed over (or ready to be handed over) for them. Their Lordships expressed 'considerable regret' (p 479) that the power of forfeiture conferred by s 27 did not provide a means of stripping professional drug-traffickers of the whole of their ill-gotten gains or the total profits of their unlawful enterprises. This perceived deficiency was addressed by the enactment of a series of statutes directed at confiscation of the proceeds of criminal offending, culminating in the Proceeds of Crime Act 2002 (which is considered below).

- Section 52 of the Firearms Act 1968 provides that where a person is convicted of a firearms offence, or is convicted of a crime for which a custodial sentence is imposed, the court may order the forfeiture or disposal of any firearm or ammunition in his possession.
- Section 1(2) of the Prevention of Crime Act 1953 provides that where the offender is convicted of being in possession of an offensive weapon, the court may order the forfeiture or disposal of the weapon.
- Section 1(4) of the Obscene Publications Act 1964 states that where the offender is convicted of having obscene articles in his possession for gain (s 2 of that Act), the court shall order the forfeiture of those articles.
- Section 24(3) of the Forgery and Counterfeiting Act 1981 empowers the court to order the forfeiture (including the destruction) of anything related to the offence.

22.5 CONFISCATION ORDERS UNDER THE PROCEEDS OF CRIME ACT 2002

The Proceeds of Crime Act 2002 is a very complex piece of legislation, and what follows is merely a thumbnail sketch of some of its key provisions.

22.5.1 Making of a confiscation order

The basic procedure for making a confiscation order is set out in s 6 of the Act. The power to make a confiscation order only arises if the defendant is (sub-s (2)):

(a) convicted of one or more offences in the Crown Court; or
(b) committed to the Crown Court for sentence in respect of one or more offences under s 3, 3A, 3B, 3C, 4, 4A or 6 of the Powers of Criminal Courts (Sentencing) Act 2000; or
(c) committed to the Crown Court in respect of one or more offences under s 70 (which empowers a magistrates' court to commit a defendant to the Crown Court with a view to a confiscation order being considered).

A confiscation order can only be made if either (sub-s (3)):

(a) the prosecutor (or the Director of the Assets Recovery Agency) asks the court to proceed under s 6; or
(b) the court believes that it is appropriate for it to proceed under s 6.

Where s 6 is invoked, the court has to proceed as follows (sub-s (4)):

(a) it must decide whether the defendant has a criminal lifestyle;
(b) if it decides that he has a criminal lifestyle it must decide whether he has benefited from his general criminal conduct;
(c) if it decides that he does not have a criminal lifestyle it must decide whether he has benefited from his particular criminal conduct.

If the court decides that the defendant has benefited from such conduct it must (s 6(5)):

(a)   decide the recoverable amount, and
(b)   make an order (a confiscation order) requiring him to pay that amount.

In deciding whether the defendant has a criminal lifestyle, whether he has benefited from particular or general criminal conduct, and in determining the recoverable amount, the court must decide any question which arises on a balance of probabilities (s 6(7)).

The phrase 'criminal lifestyle' is defined comprehensively in s 75. Under s 75(2), a defendant has a criminal lifestyle if (and only if) the offence (or any of the offences) satisfies any of these tests:

(a)   it is specified in Schedule 2;
(b)   it constitutes conduct forming part of a course of criminal activity;
(c)   it is an offence committed over a period of at least six months and the defendant has benefited from the conduct which constitutes the offence.

The offences specified in Sched 2 include drug trafficking, money laundering, directing terrorism, people trafficking, arms trafficking, counterfeiting, intellectual property offences, and blackmail.

Under s 75(3), conduct forms part of a 'course of criminal activity' if the defendant has benefited from the conduct and:

(a)   in the proceedings in which he was convicted he was convicted of three or more other offences, each of three or more of them constituting conduct from which he has benefited, or
(b)   in the period of six years ending with the day when those proceedings were started (or, if there is more than one such day, the earliest day) he was convicted on at least two separate occasions of an offence constituting conduct from which he has benefited.

However, under s 75(4), an offence is disregarded for these purposes unless the defendant obtains benefit of not less than £5,000.

Section 75(5) defines relevant 'benefit' for the purposes of s 75(2)(b), as:

(a)   benefit from conduct which constitutes the offence;
(b)   benefit from any other conduct which forms part of the course of criminal activity and which constitutes an offence of which the defendant has been convicted;
(c)   benefit from conduct which constitutes an offence which has been or will be taken into consideration by the court in sentencing the defendant . . .

Section 75(6) defines relevant benefit for the purposes of s 75(2)(c) as:

(a)   benefit from conduct which constitutes the offence;
(b)   benefit from conduct which constitutes an offence which has been or will be taken into consideration by the court in sentencing the defendant . . .

The terms 'criminal conduct', 'general criminal conduct' and 'particular criminal conduct' are each defined in s 76:

(1) Criminal conduct is conduct which—

    (a) constitutes an offence in England and Wales,

    ...

(2) General criminal conduct of the defendant is all his criminal conduct, and it is immaterial—

    (a) whether conduct occurred before or after the passing of this Act;

    (b) whether property constituting a benefit from conduct was obtained before or after the passing of this Act.

(3) Particular criminal conduct of the defendant is all his criminal conduct which falls within the following paragraphs—

    (a) conduct which constitutes the offence or offences concerned;

    (b) conduct which constitutes offences of which he was convicted in the same proceedings as those in which he was convicted of the offence or offences concerned;

    (c) conduct which constitutes offences which the court will be taking into consideration in deciding his sentence for the offence or offences concerned.

In *R v May* [2008] UKHL 28, the House of Lords held that, in determining whether the defendant has obtained property or a pecuniary advantage and, if so, the value of any property or advantage so obtained, the court should (subject to any relevant statutory definitions) apply ordinary common law principles to the facts as found. The exercise of this jurisdiction involves no departure from the ordinary rules governing entitlement and ownership. The defendant ordinarily obtains property if in law he owns it, whether alone or jointly, which will ordinarily connote a power of disposition or control (as where a person directs a payment or conveyance of property to someone else). He ordinarily obtains a pecuniary advantage if (among other things) he evades a liability to which he is personally subject. Mere couriers or custodians, or other very minor contributors to an offence, rewarded by a specific fee and having no interest in the property or the proceeds of sale, are unlikely to be found to have obtained that property. It may, however, be otherwise with money launderers (see para 48). The House also held that there might be circumstances in which orders for the full amount against each of several defendants might be disproportionate, and so in such cases an apportionment approach might be adopted. However, a defendant who, jointly with others, is found to have obtained a benefit from his offending, should ordinarily have a confiscation order made against him for the total amount found to have been fraudulently obtained, provided that he has sufficient realisable assets to meet the order (paras 45 and 46). See also *R v Green* [2008] UKHL 30.

22.5.2 Criminal lifestyle: assumptions

Section 10 of the Act states that if the court decides that the defendant has a criminal lifestyle, it must make four assumptions for the purpose of deciding whether the defendant has benefited from general criminal conduct, and deciding the value of the benefit from that conduct. Those assumptions are as follows:

(2) The first assumption is that any property transferred to the defendant at any time after the relevant day was obtained by him—

  (a) as a result of his general criminal conduct, and
  (b) at the earliest time he appears to have held it.

(3) The second assumption is that any property held by the defendant at any time after the date of conviction was obtained by him—

  (a) as a result of his general criminal conduct, and
  (b) at the earliest time he appears to have held it.

(4) The third assumption is that any expenditure incurred by the defendant at any time after the relevant day was met from property obtained by him as a result of his general criminal conduct.

(5) The fourth assumption is that, for the purpose of valuing any property obtained (or assumed to have been obtained) by the defendant, he obtained it free of any other interests in it.

Under s 10(8), the 'relevant day' is the first day of the period of six years ending with the day when proceedings for the present offence were started against the defendant.

By virtue of s 10(6), the court must not make a required assumption in relation to particular property or expenditure if either:

(a) the assumption is shown to be incorrect, or
(b) there would be a serious risk of injustice if the assumption were made.

If the court does not make one or more of the required assumptions, it must state its reasons (s 10(7)).

In *R v Rezvi; R v Benjafield* [2002] UKHL 1; [2003] 1 AC 1099, the House of Lords held that similar assumptions to be made in confiscation proceedings under the Criminal Justice Act 1988 and the Drug Trafficking Act 1994 were not incompatible with the rights of a defendant under the European Convention on Human Rights. In *Phillips v UK* [2001] 11 BHRC 280, the European Court of Human Rights held that the statutory assumptions contained in the Drug Trafficking Act 1994 did not contravene Art 6 of the Convention, most importantly because the assumption could be rebutted if the offender was able to show, on the balance of probabilities, that the property had not been acquired by improper means. It seems likely, therefore, that the provisions of the Proceeds of Crime Act 2002, although draconian, are consistent with the Convention.

22.5.3 Recoverable amount

Section 7(1) of the Act defines the 'recoverable amount' for the purposes of s 6 as being 'an amount equal to the defendant's benefit from the conduct concerned'. However, under s 7(2), if the defendant shows that the available amount is less than that benefit, the recoverable amount is 'the available amount' or, if the available amount is nil, a nominal amount.

Section 8 of the Act provides that in deciding whether the defendant has benefited from conduct, and in deciding his benefit from the conduct, the court must take account of conduct occurring up to the time it makes its decision and must take account of property obtained up to that time.

Section 9 provides that for the purposes of deciding the recoverable amount, the 'available amount' is the aggregate of:

a   the total of the values (at the time the confiscation order is made) of all the 'free property' (that is, property that is not subject to a forfeiture order: see s 82) then held by the defendant, minus the total amount payable in pursuance of obligations which then have priority (namely a fine in respect of an earlier conviction or a preferential debt as defined by s 386 of the Insolvency Act 1986); and

b   the total of the values (at that time) of all 'tainted' gifts. Under s 77, if the court has decided that the defendant has a criminal lifestyle, a gift is to be regarded as tainted if either (i) it was made by the defendant at any time during the period of six years before the start of the proceedings for the present offence; or (ii) it was made by the defendant at any time and was of property obtained by the defendant as a result of, or in connection with, general criminal conduct. If the court has decided that the offender does not have a criminal lifestyle, a gift is to be regarded as tainted if it was made by the defendant at any time after the date on which the present offence was committed.

Under s 76(4), a person 'benefits' from conduct if he obtains property as a result of or in connection with the conduct. Under s 76(7), if a person benefits from conduct, his benefit is the value of the property obtained.

Valuation of property obtained by a defendant from criminal conduct is dealt with by s 80 of the Act. The material time for valuation is the time the court makes its decision (sub-s (1)).

Under s 97 of the Serious Organised Crime and Police Act 2005, a magistrates' court may make a confiscation order (but only up to a maximum amount of £10,000). Alternatively, it may commit the offender to the Crown Court where the prosecutor asks the court to commit for sentence with a view to a confiscation order being made (s 70 of the Proceeds of Crime Act 2002). The magistrates' court should indicate whether, apart from s 70, it would have committed the offender for sentence anyway (s 70(5)). If it would have so committed, the Crown Court may sentence the offender in any way in which it could have dealt with him if he had just been convicted before it; if the magistrates' court would not have committed the offender but for the provisions of s 70, the Crown Court is limited to the sentencing powers of the magistrates' court (s 71).

22.5.4 Time for payment

Section 11 of the Proceeds of Crime Act 2002 provides that the amount ordered to be paid under a confiscation order must normally be paid when the order is made. However, where the offender is unable to pay immediately, the court may make an order allowing payment to be made within a specified period; this time must not exceed six months from the date on which the confiscation order is made. The offender may, in exceptional circumstances, apply to the court for an extension of that period (up to a total of 12 months from the date of the confiscation order).

22.5.5 Effect of a confiscation order on the sentencing powers of the court

Under s 13 of the Proceeds of Crime Act 2002, the court must take account of the confiscation order before imposing a fine on the defendant, or (for example) a forfeiture order under s 27 of the Misuse of Drugs Act 1971. Apart from that, the court must leave the confiscation order out of account in deciding the appropriate sentence for the defendant (s 13(4)).

Under s 13(5) and (6), if the court makes both a confiscation order and a compensation order (under s 130 of the Powers of Criminal Courts (Sentencing) Act 2000), and the court believes that the offender does not have sufficient means to satisfy both orders in full, the court must direct that so much of the compensation as it specifies is to be paid out of any sums recovered under the confiscation order. The amount it specifies must be the amount it believes will not be recoverable because of the insufficiency of the offender's means.

22.5.6 Enforcement

Detailed provisions on the enforcement of confiscation orders are contained in ss 34–69 of the Proceeds of Crime Act 2002. Sections 34–37 enable the appointment by the court of the Director of the Assets Recovery Agency as enforcement authority for the order. Section 38 provides for the setting of a term of imprisonment in default of payment of the amount ordered to be paid under a confiscation order. The maximum terms to be served in default are the same as in relation to fines.

Where the defendant is ordered to serve a term of imprisonment in default of payment of a confiscation order, this term does not start to run until the defendant has served any prison sentence imposed for the offence(s) which led to the confiscation order being made (s 38(2)). If the defendant does serve a sentence in default of payment, that does 'not prevent the confiscation order from continuing to have effect so far as any other method of enforcement is concerned' (see s 38(5)).

In *R v Ahmed; R v Qureshi* [2004] EWCA Crim 2599; [2005] 1 WLR 122, the Court of Appeal said that, when assessing realisable assets for the purpose of making a confiscation order (under the Criminal Justice Act 1988), the court is bound to include the convicted person's share in the value of his house, irrespective of whether that might prejudice the interests of his wife or family. If the court is later asked to make an order for the sale of the matrimonial home, Art 8 of the European Convention on Human Rights is clearly engaged, and the court will have to consider whether or not it would be proportionate to make the order in the circumstances of the particular case. It is submitted that the same approach is applicable to confiscation orders made under the Proceeds of Crime Act 2002.

In *Crowther v UK* (App No 53741/00); (2005), *The Times*, 11 February 2005, the European Court of Human Rights held that Art 6(1) of the European Convention on Human Rights applies throughout the entirety of the proceedings for 'the determination of . . . any criminal charge', including proceedings whereby a sentence is fixed. Confiscation proceedings are analogous to the determination by a court of the amount of a fine or the length of a period of imprisonment to be imposed on a properly convicted offender. It follows that the authorities have to ensure that the proceedings are completed within a reasonable time. In the present case, a period of over four years had elapsed before any effective steps were taken to enforce the confiscation order. That inertia was both inexcusable and, given that somebody's liberty was involved, unconscionable. It followed that there had been a violation of Art 6(1).

In *R (Lloyd) v Bow Street Magistrates' Court* [2003] EWHC 2294 (Admin); [2004] 1 Cr App R 11, Dyson LJ (at para 27) said:

> in deciding what is a reasonable time, regard should be had to the efforts made to extract the money by other methods, for example . . . by the appointment of a receiver [under section 50 of the Proceeds of Crime Act 2002]. If a receiver has been appointed within a reasonable time and has proceeded with reasonable expedition, then the fact that all of this may have taken some time will not prevent the court from concluding that there has been no violation of the defendant's Article 6.1 rights if the unsuccessful attempts to recover the money have led to delay in the institution of proceedings to commit. Likewise, if the defendant has been evasive and has avoided diligent attempts to extract the money from him, he will be unable to rely on the resultant delay in support of an argument that his right to a determination within a reasonable time has been violated.

22.5.7 Postponement

The court should normally proceed under s 6 of the Proceeds of Crime Act 2002 before it sentences the offender for the offence(s) of which he has been convicted. However, s 14 enables the court to postpone proceedings under s 6 for a specified period. Such a period of postponement (which may be extended) should not, unless there are exceptional circumstances, be for more than two years from the date of conviction (s 14(2)–(5)). If the offender appeals against conviction, proceedings under s 6 may be postponed for a period of up to three months after the appeal is determined or disposed of (s 14(6)).

Section 15 provides that if proceedings under s 6 are postponed, the court may proceed to sentence the offender for the offence(s), but must not impose a fine or make a compensation order. When the postponement period comes to an end, the court may vary the sentence by imposing one or more of the financial orders, but it must do so within 28 days of the end of the postponement period (s 15(3), (4)).

22.5.8 Reconsideration

Sections 19–22 of the Proceeds of Crime Act 2002 enable questions relating to confiscation orders to be reopened. Section 19 provides that where the court did not proceed against the offender under s 6, and there is now evidence available to the prosecutor which was not then available, the prosecution or the Director of the Assets Recovery Agency may apply to the court for consideration of the evidence at any time prior to the end of the period of six years from the date of conviction.

Section 20 provides that where the court proceeded against the offender under s 6 but found that he had not benefited from general criminal conduct, or particular criminal conduct, and there is now evidence available to the prosecutor which was not then available, the prosecution or the Director of the Assets Recovery Agency may apply to the court for consideration of the evidence at any time prior to the end of the period of six years from the date of conviction.

Section 21 provides that where the court has made a confiscation order, and there is now evidence available to the prosecutor which was not then available, the prosecution or the Director of the Assets Recovery Agency may apply to the court (at any time prior to the end of the period of six years from the date of conviction) to make a new calculation of the offender's benefit from the conduct concerned.

Sections 22–25 allow for applications to be made to the court for reconsideration of the available amount, and for variation or discharge of the confiscation order in light of the inadequacy of the available amount.

In *Re Saggar* [2005] EWCA Civ 174; [2005] 1 WLR 2693, it was held that an application (made under the Drug Trafficking Act 1994) to increase the realisable amount ordered by way of confiscation engages the reasonable time requirement in Art 6(1) of the European Convention on Human Rights; on such an application, the length of time to be considered is the whole period of the drug trafficking offence proceedings and not only the period from the institution of the application to increase the amount. It is submitted that the same approach would be taken to similar applications under the Proceeds of Crime Act 2002.

22.5.9 Effect of the Proceeds of Crime Act 2002 on lawyers

Under s 328 (1) of the Proceeds of Crime Act 2002, a person commits an offence if he 'enters into or becomes concerned in an arrangement which he knows or suspects facilitates (by whatever means) the acquisition, retention, use or control of criminal property by or on behalf of another person'. However, under s 328(2), no offence is committed if that persons makes an 'authorised disclosure'. In essence, this requires the person to report the matter to the Serious Organised Crime Agency (<http://www.soca.gov.uk/index.html>) by making a 'suspicious activity report'. This provision raises obvious concerns about lawyers being involved unwittingly in transactions that involve property covered by the 2002 Act.

In *Bowman v Fels* [2005] EWCA Civ 226; [2005] 1 WLR 3083, the central issue was whether s 328 applies to the ordinary conduct of legal proceedings. The Court of Appeal held that ordinary conduct of litigation cannot be said to involve the carrying out of a transaction related to money laundering. This will remain the case even if assets which happen to be the proceeds of money laundering might be the subject of claims in the proceedings, or be retained or used to satisfy any liability according to the outcome of the proceedings (per Brooke LJ at para 62). At para 83, his Lordship said that:

> we conclude that the proper interpretation of s 328 is that it is not intended to cover or affect the ordinary conduct of litigation by legal professionals. That includes any step taken by them in litigation from the issue of proceedings and the securing of injunctive relief or a freezing order up to its final disposal by judgment.

The court went on to say that, if it was wrong on this central issue, the question would remain whether, on its true construction, s 328 has the effect of overriding legal professional privilege. The court noted that there is nothing in the language of s 328 to suggest that Parliament expressly intended to override legal professional privilege. It follows, said Brooke LJ (at para 90) that the court was:

> satisfied that even if, contrary to our primary view, s 328 is to be interpreted as including legal proceedings within its purview, it cannot be interpreted as meaning either that legal professional privilege is to be overridden or that a lawyer is to breach his duty to the court by disclosing to a third party external to the litigation documents revealed to him through the disclosure processes.

22.6 MENTALLY DISORDERED OFFENDERS

There are a number of different orders which may be made in respect of a mentally disordered offender. We have seen in Chapter 18 that a community order may contain a 'mental health treatment requirement', as defined by s 207 of the CJA 2003. For young offenders, a supervision order may contain a similar requirement under para 6 of Sched 6 to the Powers of Criminal Courts (Sentencing) Act 2000 (see Chapter 21).

Where the offender's condition is more serious, it may be necessary for the court to make an order under the Mental Health Act 1983. There are two main orders under this Act: the hospital order and the guardianship order.

22.6.1 Hospital orders

Section 37 of the Mental Health Act 1983 provides that, where a mentally disordered person is convicted of an offence which is punishable with imprisonment, the court may make an order for his admission to, and detention in, a mental hospital.

Under s 37(2) of the Mental Health Act 1983, a number of conditions have to be satisfied before a hospital order can be made. Those conditions are as follows:

- The court must be satisfied on the evidence of two duly qualified medical practitioners that the offender is suffering from 'mental disorder', that the mental disorder from which the offender is suffering is of a nature or degree which makes it appropriate for him to be detained in a hospital for medical treatment, and that appropriate medical treatment is available for him.
- The court must be of the opinion, having regard to all the circumstances including the nature of the offence and the character and antecedents of the offender, and to the other available methods of dealing with him, that the most suitable method of disposing of the case is by means of a hospital order.

It should be noted that the wording of s 37 does not require any causal link between the offender's mental disorder and the offence of which he has been convicted.

22.6.1.1 Restriction orders

Section 41 of the Mental Health Act 1983 empowers the Crown Court to make a 'restriction order' as well as a hospital order. The court may do so if:

> it appears to the court, having regard to the nature of the offence, the antecedents of the offender and the risk of his committing further offences if set at large, that it is necessary for the protection of the public from serious harm so to do.

The effect of the restriction order is that the offender cannot be discharged from the mental hospital without the permission of the Secretary of State or the Mental Health Review Tribunal.

Such an order can only be made where it is necessary to protect the public from serious harm: it cannot be made simply to reflect the gravity of the offence committed by the offender (see *R v Birch* (1990) 90 Cr App R 78).

22.6.1.2 Hospital orders and limitation directions

Section 45A of the Mental Health Act 1983 provides for the making of a hospital order coupled with a limitation direction. Before making such an order, the court must be satisfied, on the basis of evidence from two medical practitioners (one of whom must give oral evidence), that the offender is suffering from mental disorder, that the mental disorder from which the offender is suffering is of a nature or degree which makes it appropriate for him to be detained in a hospital for medical treatment, and that appropriate medical treatment is available for him. Such an order is made in addition to a sentence of imprisonment. When an order is made, the offender is conveyed to the hospital named in the direction. If the offender ceases to need treatment, he is returned to prison; if he is still in hospital when the sentence expires, he will cease to be subject to restriction and will remain in hospital as if detained under an ordinary hospital order made under s 37 of the 1983 Act.

22.6.2 Guardianship orders

Under s 37(1) of the Mental Health Act 1983, the court can make a 'guardianship' order in the same circumstances that it can make a hospital order. Under s 40(2) of the Mental Health Act 1983, a guardianship order confers the same powers as those given by a guardianship order made in the civil context (see Pt II of the Mental Health Act 1983). The powers include determining where the offender will reside and the power to require him to attend for treatment, occupational therapy, education or training.

22.7 ANTI-SOCIAL BEHAVIOUR ORDERS (ASBOs)

Section 1 of the Crime and Disorder Act 1998 makes provision for 'anti-social behaviour orders' (ASBOs). A relevant authority (the police, a local authority and certain other bodies (s 1(1A))) may apply to the local magistrates' court for such an order in respect of a person aged 10 or over.

a has 'acted in an anti-social manner' (i.e. 'in a manner that caused or was likely to cause harassment, alarm or distress to one or more persons not of the same household as himself'; and

b 'such an order is necessary to protect relevant persons from further anti-social acts by him'.

The ASBO is an order which prevents the person from doing anything described in the order (s 1(4)). The prohibitions imposed under the order can be anything the court considers necessary to protect people from further anti-social acts by the defendant (s 1(6)). It should be emphasised that an ASBO may include only *negative* prohibitions; there is no power to impose positive obligations.

The minimum period of such an order is two years (s 1(7)). No maximum period is specified by the Act. In *R (Lonergan) v Crown Court at Lewes* [2005] EWHC 457 (Admin); [2005] 1 WLR 2570, it was said that it does not follow from the fact that an ASBO must run for a minimum of two years, that each and every prohibition within a particular order must endure for the life of the order. For example, a curfew for two years in the life of a teenager is a very considerable restriction of freedom. In many cases it is likely that either the period of curfew could properly be set at less than the full life of the order or, in the light of behavioural progress, an application to vary the curfew might well succeed.

Section 4 of the Act provides for an appeal to the Crown Court against the making of an ASBO by a magistrates' court.

The same power to make an ASBO is available to the county court under s 1B of the Act.

In *R (McCann) v Crown Court at Manchester* [2002] UKHL 39; [2003] 1 AC 787, the House of Lords held that although proceedings under s 1 of the 1998 Act are civil in nature, given the seriousness of the matters involved, the court should be satisfied to the criminal standard of proof (beyond reasonable doubt) that a defendant had acted in an anti-social manner before making such an order.

Section 1(8) enables the applicant or the defendant to apply to the court which made the ASBO for it to be varied or discharged (although, unless both parties consent, it cannot be discharged before two years have elapsed (s 1(9)). The duration of an ASBO may be extended on an application to vary its terms under s 1(8), but an application to vary, if it imposes more stringent obligations (such as greater length), can only succeed if the applying authority can put before the court material which justifies the extension as necessary in order to achieve the statutory objective. The usual burden and standard of proof will apply to the determination of that question. Further, in an application to vary length, the applying authority will have to persuade the justices that it is appropriate to vary the length of the existing ASBO rather than make application for a new one (*Leeds City Council v RG* [2007] EWHC 1612 (Admin); [2007] 1 WLR 3025).

An ASBO can also be made where the defendant has been convicted of an offence. Under s 1C, where a magistrates' court or the Crown Court convicts an offender and it considers that the grounds for making an ASBO are made out, 'it may make an order which prohibits the offender from doing anything described in the order' (s 1C(2)). Under s 1C(3), the order can be made at the request of the prosecution or of the court's own motion. For the purpose of deciding whether to make an order under s 1C the court may consider evidence led by the prosecution and the defence (sub-s (3A)). Under sub-s (4), an ASBO may be imposed under s 1C only in addition to a sentence imposed in respect of the relevant offence or in addition to a conditional discharge (thus an ASBO under s 1C cannot be the only 'sentence' that is passed).

In *R (W) v Acton Youth Court* [2005] EWHC 954 (Admin); (2006) 170 JP 31, it was held that proceedings under s 1C are, despite their criminal context, civil proceedings. The machinery of the Civil Evidence Act 1995 and the Magistrates' Courts (Hearsay Evidence in Civil Proceedings) Rules 1999 is therefore applicable.

Section 1(10) provides that if, without reasonable excuse, a person does anything which he is prohibited from doing by an ASBO, he commits an offence (carrying up to six months' imprisonment and/or a fine of up to £5,000 following summary conviction or up to five years' imprisonment and an unlimited fine following conviction in the Crown Court). The meaning of the phrase 'reasonable excuse' in this context was considered by the Court of Appeal in *R v Nicholson* [2006] EWCA Crim 1518; [2006] 1 WLR 2857. The Court ruled that forgetfulness on the part of the accused, or a misunderstanding on his part of the terms of the ASBO, may be capable of constituting a defence of reasonable excuse (per Auld LJ at para 15). Where the accused appears before the Crown Court (the offence under s 1(10) is triable either way) and raises such a defence, it is a matter for the jury to resolve (at para 17).

Detailed procedural rules are set out in Pt 50 of the Criminal Procedure Rules, governing 'civil behaviour orders', including ASBOs under s 1C of the CDA 1998. The intended subject of the order must be given an opportunity to make representations at a hearing (r 50.2(1)(b)). Where the prosecution intend to seek an ASBO following conviction (under s 1C), written notice to that effect must be served on the court and the accused, and on any person on whom the order is likely to have a significant adverse effect (r 50.3(2)). The notice must summarise the relevant facts, identify the evidence on which the prosecutor relies in support, attach any written statement that the prosecutor has not already served, and specify the terms of the order sought (r 50.3(3)). The accused must then serve a written notice identifying any evidence on which he intends to rely and attaching any written statement that has not already been served (r 50.3(4)). Where the court indicates that it is minded to make an ASBO of its own initiative, a party who wants the court to take account of any particular evidence before making that decision must serve a written notice identifying that evidence and attaching any written statement that has not already been served (r 50.4).

22.7.1 The contents of an ASBO

General guidance in respect of the terms of any ASBO was provided by the Court of Appeal in *R v P (Shane Tony)* [2004] EWCA Crim 287; [2004] 2 Cr App R(S) 343. Giving the judgment of the court, which was presided over by Lord Woolf CJ, Henriques J said (at para 34):

(1) The test for making an order is one of necessity to protect the public from further anti-social acts by the offender.

(2) The terms of the order must be precise and capable of being understood by the offender.

(3) The findings of fact giving rise to the making of the order must be recorded.

(4) The order must be explained to the offender.

(5) The exact terms of the order must be pronounced in open court and the written order must accurately reflect the order as pronounced.

In *R v Boness* [2005] EWCA Crim 2395; [2006] 1 Cr App R (S) 120, Hooper LJ, said (at para 19):

> Because an ASBO must obviously be precise and capable of being understood by the offender, a court should ask itself before making an order: 'Are the terms of this order clear so that the offender will know precisely what it is that he is prohibited from doing?'

At para 28, his Lordship addressed the fact that the test for making an order that prohibits the offender from doing something is one of necessity:

> Following a finding that the offender has acted in an anti-social manner (whether or not the act constitutes a criminal offence), the test for making an order prohibiting the offender from doing something is one of necessity. Each separate order prohibiting a person from doing a specified thing must be necessary to protect persons from further anti-social acts by him. Any order should therefore be tailor-made for the individual offender, not designed on a word processor for use in every case. The court must ask itself when considering any specific order prohibiting the offender from doing something, 'Is this order necessary to protect persons in any place in England and Wales from further anti-social acts by him?'

At para 29, his Lordship said that:

> The purpose of an ASBO is not to punish an offender . . . This principle follows from the requirement that the order must be necessary to protect persons from further anti-social acts by him. The use of an ASBO to punish an offender is thus unlawful.

It follows that a court should not impose an ASBO as an alternative to prison or other sanction; rather, the court should decide the appropriate sentence and then move on to consider whether an ASBO should be made after sentence has been passed.

At para 30, his Lordship went on:

> It follows from the requirement that the order must be necessary to protect persons from further anti-social acts by him, that the court should not impose an order which prohibits an offender from committing a specified criminal offence if the sentence which could be passed following conviction for the offence should be a sufficient deterrent.

Thus, the court should not impose an order which prohibits a defendant from committing a specified criminal offence, if the sentence which can be passed following conviction for the offence should be a sufficient deterrent.

His Lordship added (at para 37) that:

> the terms of the order must be proportionate in the sense that they must be commensurate with the risk to be guarded against.

In *R v Wadmore* [2006] EWCA Crim 686; [2007] 1 WLR 339, Aikens J, giving the judgment of the court, said (at para 41):

(1) Proceedings under section 1C of the 1998 Act are civil in nature, so that hearsay evidence is admissible. But a court must be satisfied to a criminal standard that the defendant has acted in the anti-social manner alleged . . .

(2) The test of 'necessity' set out in section 1C(2)(b) of the 1998 Act requires the exercise of judgment or evaluation; it does not require proof beyond reasonable doubt that the order is 'necessary' . . .

(3) The findings of fact giving rise to the making of the order must be recorded by the court . . .

(4) The terms of the order made must be precise and capable of being understood by the offender . . .

(5) The conditions in the order must be enforceable in the sense that the conditions should allow a breach to be readily identified and capable of being proved. Therefore the conditions should not impose generic prohibitions, but should identify and prohibit the particular type of anti-social behaviour that gives rise to the necessity of an anti-social behaviour order . . .

. . .

(7) . . . each separate order [i.e. term] prohibiting a person from doing a specified thing must be necessary to protect persons from anti-social behaviour by the offender. Therefore each order [term] must be specifically fashioned to deal with the offender concerned. The court has to ask, 'is this order necessary to protect persons in any place in England and Wales from further anti-social acts by him?' . . .

(8) Not all conditions set out in an anti-social behaviour order have to run for the full term [i.e. duration] of the anti-social behaviour order itself. The test must always be what is necessary to deal with the particular anti-social behaviour of the offender and what is proportionate in the circumstances . . .

(9) The order is there to protect others from anti-social behaviour by the offender. Therefore the court should not impose an order which prohibits an offender from committing specified criminal offences if the sentence which could be passed following conviction (or a guilty plea) for the offence should be a sufficient deterrent . . .

(10) It is unlawful to make an anti-social behaviour order as if it were a further sentence or punishment. An anti-social behaviour order must therefore not be used merely to increase the sentence of imprisonment that the offender is to receive . . .

22.7.2 Where conduct prohibited is also an offence in its own right

In *R v Boness*, Hooper LJ also held (at para 32), following *R v Kirby* [2005] EWCA Crim 1228; [2006] 1 Cr App R(S) 26, that 'an ASBO should not be used merely to increase the sentence of imprisonment which an offender is liable to receive'. In *R v Morrison* [2005] EWCA Crim 2237; [2006] 1 Cr App R (S) 85, the Court of Appeal held that if the ASBO has the effect of prohibiting behaviour which would in any event be a criminal offence, the sentence for breach of that ASBO should not normally exceed the statutory maximum for the criminal offence. Hughes J, set out the following principles (at para 19):

(1) An anti-social behaviour order, though it may prohibit conduct which is also a distinct offence, must be justified by reference to the statutory requirements of section 1C(2)(a) and (b). Caution should be exercised in the making of an anti-social behaviour order if the behaviour in question would in any event be a criminal offence.

(2) An ASBO should not be made simply for the purpose of increasing the available sentence beyond the maximum which would otherwise be laid down by statute for the conduct which is prohibited.

(3) If a breach of an ASBO consists of no more than the commission of an offence for which a maximum penalty is prescribed by statute, it is wrong in principle to pass a sentence for that breach calculated by reference to the five year maximum for breach of an ASBO. Rather the tariff is determined by the statutory maximum for the offence in question.

(4) We draw attention, however, in that last proposition to the words 'no more than'. There may be exceptional cases in which it can properly be said that the vice of the breach of an ASBO, although it amounts to an offence, goes beyond that offence. We do not attempt to foresee circumstances in which that may occur but we have in mind, for example, repeated offences of criminal damage directed against a particular and perhaps vulnerable victim or group of victims. We have not, however, heard any argument about such an exceptional case. Argument about it must await the occurrence of appropriate events, if they occur. We are satisfied that, absent exceptional circumstances, the proposition which we have set out as number 3 must prevail.

In *R v Lamb* [2005] EWCA Crim 3000; [2006] 2 Cr App R (S) 11, however, the Court of Appeal disagreed with the view in *Morrison*, that if the breach of an ASBO amounts to the commission of an offence for which the maximum penalty is prescribed by statute, it is normally wrong in principle to pass a sentence for a breach calculated by reference to the maximum for breach of an ASBO. Leveson J (at para 16) said:

With respect, that appears to ignore the impact of anti-social behaviour on the wider public which was the purpose of the legislation in the first place; it also means that anti-social behaviour short of a criminal offence could be more heavily punished than anti-social behaviour that coincidentally was also a criminal offence.

At para 19, his Lordship added that:

Where breaches do not involve harassment, alarm or distress, community penalties should be considered in order to help the offender learn to live within the terms of the ASBO to which he or she is subject. In those cases when there is no available community penalty . . ., custodial sentences which are necessary to maintain the authority of the court can be kept as short as possible.

In *R v Stevens* [2006] EWCA Crim 255; [2006] 2 Cr App R (S) 68, Sir Igor Judge P said (at para 26) that any sentence:

must be proportionate or, to use the word with which all sentencers are familiar, 'commensurate'. Therefore, if the conduct which constitutes the breach of the antisocial behaviour order is also a distinct criminal offence, and the maximum sentence for the offence is limited to, say, six months' imprisonment, that is a feature to be borne in mind by the sentencing court in the interests of proportionality.

His Lordship emphasised that the court was not suggesting that an ASBO should be imposed as a device to circumvent maximum penalties which are believed to be too modest. However, it cannot be right for the court's power to be limited to the maximum sentence for the offence which mirrors the conduct prohibited by the ASBO, since breach of an ASBO is an offence in its own right. Accordingly, it is not wrong in principle for the judge to impose a custodial sentence for breach of an ASBO even if the maximum sentence for the offence is a fine (or to pass a prison sentence greater than the maximum for that offence). The court thus declined to follow *R v Morrison*.

It is submitted that the following principles can be derived from the case law:

i   it is permissible to include in an ASBO a clause which prohibits the offender from committing a specific criminal offence (or which prohibits the offender from engaging in conduct which also amounts to a specific criminal offence);

ii   however, this should not be done solely in order to increase the penalty which can be imposed on the offender if he commits that offence;

iii if the offender breaches that term of the ASBO, the court dealing with the breach should have regard to the maximum penalty applicable for the specific criminal offence but may, if it is just and proportionate to do so, impose a sentence for the breach of the ASBO which exceeds the maximum sentence for the specific criminal offence (subject of course to the maximum sentence available for breach of an ASBO).

22.7.3 Challenging the validity of an ASBO

What if the terms of an ASBO are drafted too widely? In *W v DPP* [2005] EWHC 1333 (Admin); (2005) 169 JP 435, the defendant had been made subject to an ASBO which contained a number of specific clauses and one which prohibited him from 'committing any criminal offence'. He committed an offence of theft during the currency of the order. It was held that the clause of the order restricting the defendant from committing any criminal offence was plainly too wide. It is, said the court, well established that a person subject to a restraining order is entitled to know what he can and cannot do (see *B v Chief Constable of Avon and Somerset Constabulary* [2001] 1 WLR 340). The court went on to hold that the clause in question was plainly invalid and, therefore, unenforceable.

However, the question of the raising arguments as to the validity in the context of proceedings for breach (rather than on appeal from the making of the order) was revisited in *DPP v T* [2006] EWHC 728 (Admin); [2007] 1 WLR 209. The court observed that the normal rule in relation to an order of the court is that it must be treated as valid and be obeyed unless and until it is set aside. Even if the order should not have been made in the first place, a person may be liable for any breach of it committed before it is set aside. The person against whom an ASBO is made has a full opportunity to challenge that order on appeal or to apply to vary it; accordingly, in so far as any question does arise as to the validity of such an order, there is no obvious reason why the person against whom the order was made should be allowed to raise that issue as a defence in subsequent breach proceedings rather than by way of appeal against the original order, or possibly an application for judicial review (per Richards LJ at paras 27 and 34). Therefore, there are strong arguments in favour of the view that the order must be treated as valid and must be obeyed unless and until it is set aside or varied on appeal or on an application to vary: during the intervening period it cannot be treated as a nullity and of no legal effect (ibid at para 33). At para 35, his Lordship went on to say that it is doubtful that the suggestion that a provision of the ASBO is unduly wide and uncertain and unnecessary for the purpose of protecting against further anti-social acts could be said to go to the validity of the order. If the order itself was within the court's jurisdiction, it would remain valid even if there were errors in it that were open to correction on appeal. His Lordship went on to suggest (at para 37) that it is open to the court dealing with the alleged breach to:

> consider whether the relevant provision lacked sufficient clarity to warrant a finding that the defendant's conduct amounted to a breach of the order; whether the lack of clarity provided a reasonable excuse for non-compliance with the order; and whether, if a breach was established, it was appropriate in the circumstances to impose any penalty for the breach.

It is submitted that the careful wording of the judgment of Richards J does not entirely rule out the possibility of arguing, in the course of proceedings for alleged breach of an ASBO, that the ASBO is invalid. The court does, however, appear to be suggesting that complaints about the wording of a particular clause – for example, that it is drafted too widely – are likely to be insufficient to render the clause invalid. It is very clear from this judgment that the Divisional Court wishes to discourage arguments on the validity of the ASBO, or particular clauses thereof, being put forward in proceedings for the breach of that ASBO (rather than on an appeal from the making of the order). It is significant that his Lordship suggests that a person subject to an ASBO may have a defence (of reasonable excuse for non-compliance) if a particular clause is not drafted with sufficient precision and clarity.

22.7.4 Reporting restrictions

Where proceedings are being brought under s 1(10) of the Crime and Disorder Act 1998, because the defendant is alleged to be in breach of the ASBO, and the defendant is under 18, the automatic reporting restrictions in s 49 of the Children and Young Persons Act 1933 do not apply, but the court has a discretion to impose reporting restrictions under s 39 of that Act (which is to be replaced by s 45 of the Youth Justice and Criminal Evidence Act 1999) (see s 1(10D)). The same applies where the defendant is alleged to be in breach of an ASBO imposed under s 1C (s 1C(9C)).

In *R (T) v St Albans Crown Court* [2002] EWHC 1129, Elias J said (at para 22):

> where an anti-social behaviour order has been imposed, that is a factor which reinforces, and in some cases may strongly reinforce, the general public interest in the public disclosure of court proceedings. There are two reasons for this. First, disclosure of the identity of the individuals may well assist in making an order efficacious. If persons in the community are aware that the order has been made against specified individuals, then it must improve the

prospect of that order being effectively enforced. Any subsequent breach is more likely to be reported back to the authorities. Second, the very purpose of these orders is to protect the public from individuals who have committed conduct or behaviour which is wholly unacceptable and of an anti-social nature. The public has a particular interest in knowing who in its midst has been responsible for such outrageous behaviour . . . In each case there will be a wide variety of factors which will have to be considered, and in each case the balance has to be struck between the desirability of public disclosure on the one hand and the need to protect the welfare of the individual at trial on the other after a full appreciation of the relevant considerations.

In *R (on the application of Stanley, Marshall and Kelly) v Metropolitan Police Commissioner* [2004] EWHC 2229 (Admin); (2004) 168 JP 623, the Divisional Court gave further guidance on publicity in connection with the making of ASBOs. When questions of publicity arise in such cases, the police and local authorities should recognise that those subject to the orders might have their rights under Art 8(1) of the European Convention on Human Rights infringed; they should therefore consider whether the publicity which is envisaged is necessary and proportionate to the authorities' legitimate aims. Whether publicity is intended to inform, to reassure, to assist in enforcing the existing orders by policing, to inhibit the behaviour of those against whom the orders have been made, or to deter others, it is unlikely to be effective unless it includes photographs, names and at least partial addresses. Those responsible for publicity have to leave no room for mis-identification. As to the remainder of the content of any publicity, that has to depend upon the facts of the case. If residents have been exposed to criminal behaviour for years, and orders have been obtained by reference to that behaviour, and in order to bring it to an end, there is no reason why publicity material should not say so. It must not assert that those against whom orders have been made have been convicted of any crime (since ASBO proceedings are civil, not criminal) (per Kennedy LJ at para 40).

22.7.5 Interim ASBOs

Section 1D of the Crime and Disorder Act enables the court to make an interim ASBO. Where an application is made for an ASBO under s 1, or a request is made by the prosecution for an order under s 1C, or the court is minded to make an order under s 1C of its own motion, the court may, if it considers that it is just to make an order pending the decision under s 1 or 1C, make an interim order. An interim ASBO has no effect unless the person to whom it is directed is present when it is made, or is handed a document recording the order not more than 7 days after it is made (r 50.2(3)).

Rule 5 of the Magistrates' Court (Anti-Social Behaviour Orders) Rules 2002 (SI 2002/2784) provides that:

(1) An application for an interim order under section 1D, may, with leave of the justices' clerk, be made without notice being given to the defendant.
(2) The justices' clerk shall only grant leave under paragraph (1) of this rule if he is satisfied that it is necessary for the application to be made without notice being given to the defendant.

In *R (M) v Secretary of State for Constitutional Affairs* [2004] EWCA Civ 312; [2004] 1 WLR 2298, Kennedy LJ said (at para 39):

(1) Although it is unusual for a court in this country to make an order against a person who has not been given notice of the proceedings that course is adopted when it is necessary to do so, and subject to safeguards which enable the person affected at an early stage to have the order reviewed or discharged.

(2) The more intrusive the order the more the court will require proof that it is necessary that it should be made, and made in the particular form sought, but there is nothing intrinsically objectionable about the power to grant an interim ASBO without notice.

(3) It is important to note that an interim ASBO made without notice is ineffective until served, and when made as required in the standard form it does make provision for all parties to attend at court, either on a return date or on a date fixed for the hearing of the full application . . .

(4) From the time that the order is served the person upon whom it is served can apply under rule 6 to have the order varied or discharged . . .

(5) Because an application for an interim order without notice can only be made when the justices' clerk is satisfied that it is necessary for the application to be made without notice, and because the order can only be made for a limited period, when the court considers that it is just to make it, and in circumstances where it can be reviewed or discharged . . . provided the interim order follows its normal course Article 6 of the European Convention will not be engaged.

. . .

(7) If Article 6 were engaged it would be appropriate to look at the process as a whole, bearing in mind that the application for an ASBO is a civil procedure to which an application for an interim order is ancillary, and if that approach were adopted no contravention of the requirements of Article 6 could be discerned.

(8) The test to be adopted by a magistrates' court when deciding whether or not to make an interim order must be the statutory test, whether it is just to make the order. That involves consideration of all relevant circumstances, including in a case such as this the fact that the application has been made without notice. Obviously the court must consider whether the application for the final order has been properly made, but there is no justification for requiring the magistrates' court, when considering whether to make an interim order, to decide whether the evidence in support of the full order discloses an extremely strong prima facie case.

In *R (Manchester City Council) v Manchester Justices* [2005] EWHC 253 (Admin), Henriques J said (at para 34) that a justices' clerk, when deciding if he is satisfied that it is necessary for the application to be made without notice pursuant to r 5(2), should have regard to the following factors:

(1) the likely response of the defendant upon receiving notice of such application;

(2) whether such response is liable to prejudice the complainant having regard to the complainant's vulnerability;

(3) the gravity of the conduct complained of within the scope of conduct tackled by ASBOs in general as opposed to the particular locality;

(4) the urgency of the matter;
(5) the nature of the prohibitions sought in the interim ASBO;
(6) the right of the defendant to know about proceedings against him;
(7) the counterbalancing protections for the rights of the defendant, namely:

  (a) the ineffectiveness of the order until served;
  (b) the limited period of time the order is effective;
  (c) the defendant's right of application to vary or discharge.

The r 5(2) test is substantially less stringent than the test applied by the justices following the granting of leave.

22.7.6 Reviews of ASBOs

Section 123 of the Criminal Justice and Immigration Act 2008 makes provision for the review of certain ASBOs. It adds a s 1J to the Crime and Disorder Act 1998, which applies where an ASBO is made (whether under s 1 or s 1C) in respect of a person under the age of 17 (s 1J(1)). Under s 1J(2), if the subject of the ASBO will be under the age of 18 at the 'review period' (defined in sub-s (3)) and the term of the ASBO runs until the end of that period or beyond, then before the end of that period a review of the operation of the order must be carried out. Under sub-s (3), the review periods are (a) the period of 12 months beginning with the date on which the ASBO was made (or the date when the ASBO is varied or an ISO made); (b) a period of 12 months beginning with the day after the end of the previous review period (or the date when the ASBO is varied or an ISO made). Under s 1J(6), the review must include consideration of:

  (a) the extent to which the person subject to the order has complied with it;
  (b) the adequacy of any support available to the person to help him comply with it;
  (c) any matters relevant to the question whether an application should be made for the order to be varied or discharged.

Under s 1K of the 1998 Act (also inserted by s 123 of the 2008 Act), reviews are to be carried out by the 'relevant authority' that applied for the order or (where the order was made under s 1C) by the police or by the 'relevant authority' specified in the order.

22.7.7 Criticisms of ASBOs

A number of criticisms have been made of ASBOs (see, for example, Alec Samuels, 'Anti-social Behaviour Order: their Legal and Jurisprudential Significance' (2005) 69 J Crim L 223):

- They blur the distinction between civil and criminal proceedings.
- The definition of anti-social behaviour is very broad.
- Behaviour which does not constitute a criminal offence effectively becomes criminal if that behaviour is prohibited by an ASBO (since breach of an ASBO is a criminal offence).
- The sanction for breach – up to 5 years' custody – is very severe.

• ASBOs seek to suppress anti-social behaviour but do nothing to address the causes of that behaviour.

22.7.8 Parenting orders

A parenting order is an order which requires the parent to comply, for a period not exceeding 12 months, with the requirements specified in the order and to attend a specified counselling or guidance programme for up to three months (s 8(4) of the Crime and Disorder Act 1998). The requirements that may be specified include (for example) conditions such as attending meetings with teachers at their child's school, ensuring their child does not visit a particular place unsupervised or ensuring their child is at home at particular times.

Under s 9(1B) of the Act, if an ASBO is made in respect of a person under the age of 16, the court must also make a 'parenting order' if it is satisfied that making the order would be desirable in the interests of preventing any repetition of the kind of behaviour which led to the ASBO being made. A parenting order may also be made (under s 8 of the Act) whenever someone under the age of 16 is convicted of an offence, and the court is satisfied that making the order would be desirable in the interests of preventing the commission of any further offence by the child or young person (s 8(6)).

Under s 9(7), failure without reasonable excuse fails to comply with any requirement included in the order, or specified in directions given by the responsible officer, is an offence punishable with a fine of up to £1,000 (level 3 on the standard scale).

22.7.9 Individual support orders

'Individual support orders' (ISOs) are aimed at preventing further anti-social behaviour where an ASBO has already been made against a person under the age of 18. The ISO may require the young person to undertake activities aimed at tackling the underlying causes of the behaviour that led to the ASBO. For example, the young person may be required to attend an anger management course.

Section 1AA(1) of the Crime and Disorder Act 1998 stipulates that where a court makes an ASBO in respect of a person aged between 10 and 17, it must also consider whether the individual support conditions are fulfilled. If the conditions are fulfilled, the court must (unless the juvenile is already subject to an ISO) make an ISO (s 1AA(2)). Before making an ISO, the court must be satisfied that the order 'would be desirable in the interests of preventing any repetition of the kind of behaviour which led to the making of the ASBO' (s 1AA (3)).

The maximum duration of an ISO is six months (s 1AA(2)(a)). Under s 1AA(5), the court may impose requirements under the order which the court considers desirable in the interests of preventing a repetition of the anti-social behaviour which led to the ASBO. Under sub-s (6), the offender may be required to participate in specified activities, to attend a specified place (or places), or to comply with specified arrangements for his education. The offender cannot be required to attend a place (or different places) on more than two days per week (sub-s (7)).

Under s 1AB(3), failure without reasonable excuse to comply with the requirements under the ISO is punishable with a fine of up to £1,000 for an offender aged 14–17, and £250 for an offender aged 10–14.

Under s 1AB(5), an ISO ceases to have effect (if it has not already expired) when the ASBO to which it is linked ceases to have effect. Section 1AB(6) allows the offender or the responsible officer to apply to the court for the order to be varied or discharged.

Section 4(2) of the Act makes provision for an appeal to the Crown Court against the making of an ISO by a magistrates' court.

Section 124 of the Criminal Justice and Immigration Act 2008 inserts new subsections (1A) and (1B) into s 1AA of the Crime and Disorder Act 1998, allowing ISOs to be made subsequent to the making of the original ASBO, provided that the court is satisfied that the other conditions for doing so have been met, namely that it is on application from the original applicant agency, that the subject is still under 18, that the associated ASBO is still in force, and that it will help prevent further anti-social behaviour on his part. Section 1AB(5A) of the 1998 Act provides that an ISO made subsequent to the original hearing cannot last beyond the lifetime of the ASBO. Section 1C(9AA) of the 1998 Act allows ISOs to be made alongside ASBOs made following conviction, provided that the other criteria for doing so are met.

22.8 OTHER ANCILLARY ORDERS

Finally, we consider a selection of orders which can be made when an offender is being sentenced.

22.8.1 Recommendation for deportation

Under s 3(6) of the Immigration Act 1971, a court which is dealing with someone who is not a British citizen, who has attained the age of 17, and who has been convicted of an imprisonable offence may make a recommendation to the Home Secretary that the person be deported. In *R v Nazari* [1980] 1 WLR 1366, Lawton LJ said that the seriousness of the offence and the extent of the offender's criminal record should be taken into account in deciding whether or not to make a recommendation for deportation.

Such a recommendation may be combined with any sentence, but is most common where the offender has received a custodial sentence; in such a case, the Home Secretary can order the offender's deportation once he is released from prison.

22.8.2 Exclusion orders

The courts have various statutory powers to exclude offenders from particular places, including the following:

22.8.2.1 Licensed premises/drinking banning orders

Section 1 of the Violent Crime Reduction Act 2006 empowers the court to make a 'drinking banning order' which prevents the person subject to it from entering licensed premises. Under s 2(1) of the 2006 Act, the order must have effect for between two months and two years. An order can be made on the application of a 'relevant authority' (i.e. the police or a local authority) where the individual has engaged in criminal or disorderly conduct while under the influence of alcohol, and the order is necessary to protect other persons from further conduct by him of that kind while he is under the influence of alcohol (s 3(2)). Under s 6(1), where an individual aged 16 or over is convicted of an offence and, at the time he committed the offence, he was under the influence of alcohol, the court must consider whether the conditions in s 3(2) are satisfied in relation to the offender; if the court decides that the conditions are satisfied in relation to the offender, it may make a drinking banning order against him (sub-s (3)). This provision (which was not in force at the time of writing) replaces s 1 of the Licensed Premises (Exclusion of Certain Persons) Act 1980.

22.8.2.2 Football matches: football banning orders

Under s 14(4) of the Football Spectators Act 1989, a 'banning order' is an order which (a) in relation to regulated football matches in England and Wales, prohibits the person who is subject to the order from entering any premises for the purpose of attending such matches, and (b) in relation to regulated football matches outside England and Wales, requires that person to report at a police station.

Section 14A of the Act requires the court to make a banning order where the offender is convicted of certain offences (listed in Sched 1 – offences involving use of violence etc. in relation to football matches) and the court is satisfied that there are reasonable grounds to believe that making a banning order would help to prevent violence or disorder at or in connection with regulated football matches (s 14A(2)). Unless there are exceptional circumstances, the offender is required to surrender his passport (s 14E(3)). If the order is made in addition to a sentence of immediate custody, the banning order must last for a specified period between six and 10 years; otherwise it must last for three to five years (s 14F).

In *R (White) v Crown Court at Blackfriars* [2008] EWHC 510 (Admin), it was held that a football banning order should only be imposed where there are strong grounds for concluding that the individual subject of the order has a propensity for taking part in football hooliganism. However, the court is entitled to take into account and to give great weight to deterrence; there are clear benefits in it being widely known that a person who assaults an official at a football match is liable to be made the subject of a football banning order even if the incident was, for that person, an isolated one.

22.8.3 Disqualifications

The courts also have a number of disqualification orders at their disposal. They include the following:

22.8.3.1 Road traffic offenders

Under s 34(1) of the Road Traffic Offenders Act 1988, where a person has been convicted of a road traffic offence involving obligatory disqualification, the court must order that he be disqualified from driving for at least 12 months unless the court finds that there are 'special reasons' for not disqualifying him or for disqualifying him for less than 12 months. A 'special reason' must be connected with the commission of the offence itself; mitigation which is personal to the offender is not a special reason (*Whittall v Kirby* [1947] KB 194).

Other road traffic offences carry discretionary disqualification (see Sched 2 to the Road Traffic Offenders Act 1988). In such cases, the punishment of disqualification should generally be restricted to cases involving bad driving, persistent motoring offences or the use of vehicles for the purposes of crime (per Morland J in *R v Callister* [1993] RTR 70).

Many road traffic offences carry a number of penalty points which have to be endorsed on the offender's driving licence in the event of conviction. The number of points to be endorsed is set out in Sched 2 to the Road Traffic Offenders Act 1988; sometimes, the number is fixed; sometimes, there is a range, with a minimum and a maximum number specified. If the offender is convicted of more than one offence, the points to be endorsed are those which relate to the offence which carries the highest number of points (s 28(4)); thus, if the offender is convicted on one occasion of careless driving (which carries three to nine points) and failing to comply with a traffic sign (three points), the maximum number of points which can be endorsed is nine. Section 28(5) empowers the court to dis-apply s 28(4) if it thinks fit.

Under s 35 of the Road Traffic Offenders Act 1988, where a person is convicted of an offence which carries discretionary disqualification and mandatory endorsement and the number of penalty points on the offender's driving licence (including those imposed for the present offence) number 12 or more, the court must disqualify the offender from driving for at least six months (if it is his first disqualification) or 12 months (if it is his second) or two years (if he has already been disqualified twice) unless the court takes the view that there are grounds for not doing so or for disqualifying for a shorter period. Penalty points are taken into account if they were imposed within the last three years (s 29(2)). This is known as a 'totting up' disqualification.

When the court is deciding whether there is mitigation to justify not disqualifying the offender (or shortening the disqualification), s 35(4) states that the court cannot take account of:

(a) any circumstances that are alleged to make the offence or any of the offences not a serious one,
(b) hardship, other than exceptional hardship, or
(c) any circumstances which, within the three years immediately preceding the conviction, have been taken into account under that sub-section in ordering the offender to be disqualified for a shorter period or not ordering him to be disqualified.

In *R v Thames Magistrates' Court ex p Levy* (1997) *The Times*, 17 July, the defendant had been disqualified from driving after being convicted of various driving offences. He appealed against these convictions but did not apply to have the disqualification suspended pending the appeal. The convictions were subsequently quashed following a successful appeal. Prior to the quashing of the convictions, he drove a motor vehicle. He was charged with driving while disqualified. The Divisional Court held, unsurprisingly, that he was guilty of driving while disqualified because he drove a motor vehicle while an order for disqualification was lawfully in force.

22.8.3.2 Disqualification under the Powers of Criminal Courts (Sentencing) Act 2000

Section 146 of the Powers of Criminal Courts (Sentencing) Act 2000 provides that, in addition to, or instead of, dealing with an offender in any other way, a court may disqualify him from holding or obtaining a driving licence for such period as it thinks fit. Thus, the penalty of disqualification from driving can be imposed for any offence, not just driving offences. When this power was debated in Parliament, it was said that (HC Official Report, SCA, 10 December 1996):

> ... it is important that the courts regard disqualification from driving as a heavy penalty, especially if someone is employed. There will therefore be occasions when they will not apply this penalty if it might result in a person losing his job, because that may seem disproportionate ... The important point ... is the idea that the use of the sentence should be appropriate to the nature of the offence, and that in most if not all cases there should be some relevance to the use of a vehicle.

In *R v Cliff* [2004] EWCA Crim 3139; [2005] 2 Cr App R (S) 22, it was held that it is not necessary for the offence to be connected to the use of the motor car. The section provides an additional punishment available to the court. However, the court added that it was not saying that a court can impose a period of disqualification arbitrarily. There must be a sufficient reason for the disqualification. The reasons will, of course, be open to scrutiny by an appellate court (per Gage LJ at para 15).

22.8.3.3 Company directors

Sections 1 and 2 of the Company Directors Disqualification Act 1986 apply where a court is dealing with a person who has been convicted of an indictable (including triable either way) offence connected with the formation, management, liquidation, or receivership of a company. The effect of the order is to prevent the offender from being a company director or being involved in the setting up or running of a company. The usual maximum period of disqualification is five years (magistrates' court) and 15 years (Crown Court).

Disqualification is usually appropriate where the offender has been guilty of conduct which is dishonest, or in breach of standards of commercial morality, or grossly incompetent, so that he would be a danger to the public if he were to be allowed to continue to be involved in the management of companies (per Hoffmann J in *Re Dawson Print Group Ltd* [1987] BCLC 601). In *Re Lo-Line Electric Motors Ltd* [1988] Ch 477 at 486, Sir Nicolas Browne-Wilkinson V-C said that ordinary commercial misjudgment is in itself not sufficient to justify disqualification. In the normal case, the conduct complained of must display a lack of commercial probity, although in an extreme case of gross negligence or total incompetence disqualification could be appropriate. These dicta were approved by the Court of Appeal in *Re Sevenoaks Stationers (Retail) Ltd* [1991] Ch 164.

22.8.3.4 Animals

Section 34 of the Animal Welfare Act 2006 enables a court to disqualify (for such period as it thinks fit) the offender from owning or keeping any animal where he has been convicted of certain offences under that Act, including causing unnecessary suffering to an animal (s 4) or failing to take such steps as are reasonable in all the circumstances to ensure that the needs of an animal for which he is responsible are met to the extent required by good practice (s 9)

22.8.4 Restraining orders

The court also enjoys a range of restraining orders (in addition to the anti-social behaviour orders considered earlier).

22.8.4.1 Sex offenders

Sections 80–92 of the Sexual Offences Act 2003 require those convicted of specified sexual offences (listed in Sched 3 to the Act) to notify certain personal details to the police. This process is popularly known as being put on the 'sex offenders' register'.

Section 104 of the Sexual Offences Act 2003 creates 'sexual offences prevention orders'. Where the court is dealing with an offender for a specified sexual offence (listed in Sched 3 or 5), the court may make a sexual offences prevention order if it is satisfied that 'it [is] necessary to make such an order, for the purpose of protecting the public or any particular members of the public from serious sexual harm from the defendant' (s 104(1)). Alternatively, where an offender has been dealt with for a specified sexual offence, the police may apply to a magistrates' court for a sexual offences prevention order if that person's behaviour gives rise to reasonable cause to believe that it is necessary for such an order to be made (s 104(5)).

Section 107 of the Act sets out the effect of the order: it prohibits the offender from doing anything specified in it; the only restriction on the prohibitions that may be contained in the order is that they must be 'necessary for the purpose of protecting the public or any particular members of the public from serious sexual harm from the defendant' (s 107(2)). The order must last for a specified period of not less than five years (s 107(1)). Section 108 enables applications to vary or discharge the order.

Under s 113, failure to comply with the order is an offence punishable with up to five years' imprisonment.

Section 114 of the Sexual Offences Act 2003 creates another preventative order, the 'foreign travel order'. The order prohibits offenders convicted of specified sexual offences (essentially, certain sexual offences against children under the age of 16) from travelling abroad where and insofar as it is necessary to do so to protect a child or children from serious sexual harm outside the UK. The order can prohibit travel to a named country or countries, to anywhere in the world other than a named country, or to anywhere outside the UK (s 117). Breach of the order is an offence under s 122 of the Act (again punishable with up to five years' imprisonment).

22.8.4.2 Protection from harassment

A court which is dealing with a person convicted of an offence under ss 2 or 4 of the Protection from Harassment Act 1997 (harassment or conduct causing fear of violence) may make a restraining order under s 5 of that Act. Under s 5(2), the order may, for the purpose of protecting the victim(s) of the offence, or any other person mentioned in the order, from further conduct which amounts to harassment, or which will cause a fear of violence, prohibit the defendant from doing anything described in the order. The order has effect for a specified period or until a further order (s 5(3)). The prosecutor, the defendant or any other person mentioned in the order may apply to the court which made the order for it to be varied or discharged (s 5(4)).

If, without reasonable excuse, the offender does anything which he is prohibited from doing under the order, he is guilty of an offence punishable with up to five years' imprisonment (s 5(6)).

Rather more controversial is s 5A of the 1997 Act (not in force at the time of writing). Section 5A(1) provides that a court before which a defendant is acquitted of an offence may, if it considers it necessary to do so to protect a person from harassment by him, make an order prohibiting him from doing anything described in the order.

22.8.4.3 Travel restrictions on drug traffickers

Under ss 33–37 of the Criminal Justice and Police Act 2001, the court may impose a travel restriction order on an offender who has been convicted of a drug trafficking offence and who has been sentenced by that court to a term of imprisonment for four years or more. The effect of the order is to restrict the offender's freedom to leave the UK for a period specified by the court, and (under s 33(4)) it may require him to surrender his passport. The minimum duration of a travel restriction order is two years, starting from the date of the offender's release from custody (s 33(3)). No maximum period is prescribed in the Act.

Breach of the order is an offence under s 36 of the Act (punishable with up to five years' imprisonment).

In *R v Mee* [2004] EWCA Crim 629; [2004] 2 Cr App R (S) 81, the court gave guidance on travel restriction orders. The power to make the order has to be exercised proportionately, and for the purpose for which it was granted, namely the prevention or reduction of the risk of reoffending after release from prison. The mere fact that a defendant has imported drugs does not necessarily give rise to the risk that, on release from prison, he will abuse his freedom to travel by engaging in that activity again. A distinction should be drawn between a one-off importation by a holidaymaker in a non-commercial quantity, and an established pattern of travel between one or more foreign drug sources, with the likelihood that a network of contracts in the trade had been established. Where such a risk has been identified, the length of an order should be that which is required to protect the public in the light of the degree of risk. Factors such as the offender's age, previous convictions, risk of reoffending, family contacts and employment prospects might be taken into account in that determination.

22.8.4.4 *Violent offender orders*

Sections 98–106 of the Criminal Justice and Immigration Act 2008 (not in force at the time of writing) make provision for 'violent offender orders' (VOOs). A VOO is designed to protect the public from the risk of future serious violent harm caused by the person subject to the order. In order to be eligible for a VOO, a person must come within s 99: he must have committed a specified offence (defined in s 98(3) – the list includes manslaughter, grievous bodily harm and wounding) and must have been sentenced to at least 12 months' custody in respect of that offence (s 99(2)). A VOO will contain such prohibitions as the court making the order considers necessary for the 'purpose of protecting the public from the risk of serious violent harm caused by the offender' (s 98(1)(a)). The minimum duration of the order is two years, unless it is discharged earlier and the maximum is 5 years (s 98(1)(b)). Applications for VOOs will be made by the police to a magistrates' court (s 100(1)) on the grounds that the person is a qualifying offender, and he has acted 'in such a way as to give reasonable cause to believe that it is necessary' for a VOO to be made (s 100(2)(b) and s 101(3)(b)).

Section 103 makes provision for variation, renewal or discharge of VOOs, and s 104 provides for interim VOOs. Section 106 provides that a person in respect of whom a VOO or Interim VOO has been made may appeal to the Crown Court against the making of the order.

Under s 113(1), a person who fails, without reasonable excuse, to comply with any prohibition, restriction or condition contained in VOO or interim VOO commits an offence punishable with up to five years' imprisonment.

Criminal justice glossary

Abscond Fail to surrender to custody after being released on bail (q.v.).

Accused Person charged with an offence. Also referred to as the 'defendant'. After conviction may be referred to as the 'offender'.

Acquittal Discharge of defendant following verdict of not guilty.

Adjournment The postponement of a hearing, usually because one of the parties is not ready to proceed. Where the court has to decide whether or not to grant the defendant bail (q.v.), the adjournment is called a remand (q.v.).

Advance information The entitlement of the defence to find out the essence of the prosecution case before mode of trial (q.v.) is determined.

Adversarial The system of criminal procedure used in England and Wales and other common law jurisdictions. The facts are ascertained by a process in which the two sides – prosecution and defence – present their evidence and challenging the evidence of the opposing side. The judge is neutral and acts as an umpire ensuring fair-play rather than someone who is investigating the matter himself.

Advocate General term for a lawyer appearing in court. In England and Wales the advocate will be a Barrister or a Solicitor.

Alibi A defence that someone accused of a crime was not there at the time and so could not have committed the offence.

Appellant Person who appeals to a higher court to review the decision of a lower court.

Arrest Lawful detention of a suspect, usually by a police officer.

Attorney General Government Minister responsible for prosecutions and the Crown Prosecution Service.

Autrefois acquit 'Previously acquitted': the general rule is that a person cannot be tried more than once for the same crime (see 'double jeopardy'), and so if a person has been previously acquitted he cannot be prosecuted again for the same offence. The Criminal Justice Act 2003 introduces a limited exception to this rule.

Autrefois convict 'Previously convicted': if a person has been previously convicted he cannot be prosecuted again for the same offence.

Bail Release of a defendant from custody, until their next court appearance. The bail may be subject to compliance with conditions specified by the court.

Bench Judges or magistrates sitting in court may be known collectively as 'the Bench'.

Bench warrant A warrant issued by a magistrate or judge for an absent defendant to be arrested and brought before the court.

Bill of indictment Old-fashioned term for a draft indictment (q.v.).

Caution

(a) An alternative to prosecution: can be either a 'simple caution' (a non-statutory warning given to adults by the police) or a 'conditional caution' (a warning given pursuant to the Criminal Justice Act 2003, with reparative, rehabilitative or punitive conditions attached); a caution can only be given if the suspect admits guilt; a caution does not count as a conviction but does form part of the person's criminal record.

(b) The warning given by police on arrest and immediately prior to an interview of a suspect: 'You do not have to say anything, but it may harm your defence if you do not mention when questioned something you later rely on in court. Anything you do say may be given in evidence.'

Chambers   Where a hearing is 'in chambers', the public are excluded.

Charge   A formal accusation against a person alleging s/he has committed a criminal offence.

Circuit   England and Wales is broken into six circuits for administrative and judicial purposes. Circuit judges will be assigned to a circuit and could be asked to sit in any court within the circuit. Each circuit is under the governance of a presiding judge. The six circuits are: Northern Circuit, North-Eastern Circuit, Midland and Oxford, Wales and Chester, South-Eastern and Western.

Circuit judge   Circuit judges are below High Court judges in 'rank'. They sit in County Courts and the Crown Court. Certain circuit judges are permitted to sit in the Court of Appeal. A Circuit judge is addressed as 'Your Honour' and is described as His/Her Honour Judge [Name] (abbreviated to HHJ [Name]).

Committal

(a) Committal for trial: the process of sending offences that are triable either way (q.v.) from the magistrates' court to the Crown Court for trial (this process is due to be abolished when the relevant provisions of the Criminal Justice Act 2003 come into force, at which point either-way offences will be sent to the Crown Court in the same way that indictable-only (q.v.) offences are).

(b) Committal for sentence: where the magistrates consider that an either-way offence justifies a sentence greater than they are empowered to impose, they may commit the defendant to the Crown Court for sentence (and that court may sentence the defendant as if he had just been convicted there).

Conditional caution   See **Caution**

Conviction   A formal finding of guilt. A defendant is convicted when he pleads guilty or is found guilty of an offence.

Counsel   A barrister.

Count   An individual offence set out in an indictment (q.v.). Each count includes a 'statement of offence', stating what crime has allegedly been committed, followed by 'particulars of offence', with such details as the date and place of the offence, property stolen, etc.

Court of Appeal   The Court of Appeal (Criminal Division) hears appeals from the Crown Court.

Criminal Cases Review Commission Public body responsible for investigating alleged miscarriages of justice.

Crown Court The Crown Court

(a) Sits as a court of trial for indictable-only offences, and for either-way offences where magistrates decline jurisdiction or defendant does not agree to summary trial (where the court is sitting as a trial court it comprises a judge (High Court judge, circuit judge or recorder (q.v.)) and a jury);

(b) Passes sentence where either-way offences are committed for sentence from the magistrates' court (the court comprises a judge (circuit judge or recorder))

(c) Hears appeals against conviction and/or sentence from magistrates' court (the court comprises a judge (circuit judge or recorder) and two lay justices (q.v.).

Crown Prosecution Service (CPS) The Crown Prosecution Service is responsible for prosecuting criminal cases investigated by the police in England and Wales. A Crown Prosecutor decides whether there is enough evidence to take the case to court, and whether it would be in the public interest to do so.

Defendant See 'accused'.

Director of Public Prosecutions (DPP) The head of the Crown Prosecution Service (q.v.).

Disclosure Revealing information to the other side. Often used in the context of the prosecution duty to reveal to the defence evidence that undermines the prosecution case or assists the defence case.

Discontinuance A decision by the Crown Prosecution Service not to continue with a case.

District judge (magistrates' courts) A legally qualified person who sits as a magistrate. A District judge may (and usually will) sit alone when trying cases. Previously known as a 'stipendiary magistrate'. Part-time District judges are known as Deputy District judges.

Divisional Court The Divisional Court of the Queen's Bench Division deals with appeals on points of law from magistrates' courts. It comprises two or more judges. It is not unusual for one of the judges to be a Lord Justice of Appeal.

Double jeopardy This rule precludes a person who has been acquitted of a criminal offence being tried for the same offence again. The Criminal Justice Act 2003 allows the prosecution the right to petition the Court of Appeal to quash certain acquittals and allow a retrial.

Dock Enclosure in criminal court for the defendant on trial.

Either-way offence An offence which may be tried in a magistrates' court or in the Crown Court. It may only be tried in a magistrates' court if the magistrates accept jurisdiction and the defendant consents to summary trial (q.v.). If the offence is not tried in the magistrates' court it will be sent to the Crown Court for trial by a judge and jury (see also **indictable offence, summary offence**).

Electronic monitoring A defendant who is on bail (q.v.), subject to a curfew order (q.v.) or Home Detention Curfew (q.v.) at the end of a prison sentence, has an electronic tag. The tag, worn on the ankle or wrist, notifies monitoring services if the offender is absent during the curfew hours.

Exhibit Item or document used as evidence during a trial.

Ex parte   A hearing where only one side is allowed to be present.

Fixed penalty notice   An alternative to prosecution. The offender is required to pay a fixed sum within a specified period or the case has to go to court.

Her Majesty's Courts Service   Her Majesty's Courts Service administers the civil, family and criminal courts in England and Wales, including the Crown Court and magistrates' courts.

High Court judge   High Court judges sit in the Crown Court to try more serious cases, and in the Divisional Court (q.v.) and in the Court of Appeal (q.v.).

Home Office   Government department responsible for all national issues such as crime and immigration.

In camera   In private. Used where a court is sitting but the public are excluded.

Indictable offence   An offence which may or must be tried in the Crown Court.

Indictable-only offence   An offence which must be tried in the Crown Court.

Indictment   A written statement of the charges against a defendant being tried in the Crown Court. Each offence is set out in a separate 'count' (q.v.). Two or more counts may appear in the same indictment if there is a close link between the offences.

Inquisitorial procedure   A system of criminal procedure in use in many European jurisdictions (but not England and Wales), in which there is an inquiry into the facts of the case conducted by the judge. In this system it is the judge who takes the initiative in conducting the case, rather than the prosecution; his role is to lead the investigation, examine the evidence, and interrogate the witnesses.

Juror   A person who has been summoned to be a member of the jury (q.v.).

Jury   Panel of 12 people randomly selected to try a case and reach a verdict according to the evidence heard in the Crown Court. The jury are the sole arbitrators of fact whilst the judge will decide matters of law. The Criminal Justice Act 2003 reformed the eligibility for jury service and effectively only those convicted of certain offences or who suffer from certain mental illnesses are now ineligible to serve on a jury.

Justice of the Peace   Another title for a lay magistrate (q.v.).

Juvenile   A person who is under the age of 18.

Lay justices   Another title for lay magistrates (q.v.).

Lord Chief Justice   Senior judge of the Court of Appeal (Criminal Division) who also heads the Queens Bench Division of the High Court of Justice). Under the Constitutional Reform Act 2005 the Lord Chief Justice became the head of the judiciary as President of the Courts of England and Wales. The title is abbreviated to either LCJ or Lord [Name] CJ.

Lord Justice of Appeal   Title given to certain judges sitting in the Court of Appeal.

Magistrate (lay magistrate)   A magistrate (also known as a justice of the peace) has no formal legal qualifications (hence the use of the phrase 'lay magistrate'). Magistrates receive no payment for their services but give their time voluntarily. For trials, they sit in groups of three (each group is called a 'bench'). See also **District judge**.

Magistrates' court   The court in which either magistrates or District judges (magistrates' courts) sit. It is the lowest of the criminal courts in England and Wales but deals with the vast majority of criminal cases. The magistrates' court can try any summary offence (q.v.) and may try either-way offences (q.v.) if the court accepts jurisdiction and the defendant consents to summary trial. The defendant always makes his first court appearance in a magistrates' court, however serious the offence might be.

Mode of trial   If an offence is 'triable either way', there has to be a hearing at which the magistrates decide whether or not their sentencing powers would be adequate and, if the magistrates accept jurisdiction, the defendant is asked whether he consents to summary trial or wishes to elect trial on indictment.

Offender   Someone who has been convicted of a crime.

PACE   Common abbreviation for the Police and Criminal Evidence Act 1984.

Plea   A defendant's reply to a charge put to him by a court, namely 'guilty' or 'not guilty'. If a defendant refuses to enter a plea, the case proceeds as though he has given a 'not guilty' plea.

Plea and Case Management Hearing (PCMH)   A preliminary hearing, before a judge at a Crown Court, where the accused will indicate whether he is pleading guilty or not guilty. Rulings may be given on points of law and the admissibility of evidence.

Plea before venue   Before mode of trial for an either-way offence (q.v.) is determined, the defendant is asked to indicate whether he intends to plead guilty or not guilty (if he indicates an intention to plead guilty, he is deemed to have pleaded guilty; if he indicates an intention to plead not guilty, or gives no indication, the court proceeds to determine where the case will be tried).

Quash   Annul, declare void.

Recorder   A barrister or solicitor who has been appointed to sit in a judicial capacity in the County Courts and Crown Court on a part time basis. A recorder has all the power of a circuit judge when exercising this role. A recorder is addressed as 'Your Honour'.

Remand   Where a case has to be adjourned (i.e. postponed) and the court has to decide whether or not to grant the defendant bail (q.v.), the adjournment is known as a 'remand'. The remand may be 'in custody', in which case the defendant is held in a prison until the next court appearance or it may be 'on bail', in which case the defendant is released pending the next court appearance.

Simple caution   See **Caution**.

Submission of no case to answer   At the close of the prosecution case (i.e. when the prosecution witnesses have all finished giving their evidence), the defence may make a submission that there is 'no case to answer'. The basis of the submission is that the prosecution have failed to adduce sufficient evidence on which a reasonable jury/ bench of magistrates could convict. If the submission is successful, the defendant is acquitted; if the submission fails, the defence case is presented to the court.

Summary offence   An offence which may only be tried in a magistrates' court (q.v.). See also **indictable offence, either-way offence**.

Summary trial   A trial that takes place in the magistrates' court (before three lay justices or a District Judge).

Summing-up   A review of the evidence and directions as to the relevant law by a Crown Court judge immediately before the jury retires to consider its verdict.

Summons   Court order requiring a person to attend court.

Surety   A person who 'enters into a recognisance' to guarantee the defendant's attendance at court. The surety promises to pay a specified sum of money to the court in the event of the defendant's non-attendance at court.

Trial on indictment   Trial in the Crown Court.

Verdict   Finding that the defendant is guilty or not guilty.

Young defendant   A defendant under the age of 18. Young defendants are sometimes referred to as 'juveniles' and may be sub-divided into 'children' and 'young persons'. A **child** is a person aged 10–13; a **young person** is someone aged 14–17.

Youth court   A magistrates' court which comprises either a district judge or a bench of three magistrates (at least one male and one female), with jurisdiction to deal with **young defendants** (sometimes called 'juveniles').

Youth Offending Team (YOT)   A Youth Offending Team is made up of local representatives from the police, probation service, social services, health, education, drugs and alcohol misuse and housing officers. The YOT identifies the needs of each young offender. It identifies the specific problems that make the young person offend as well as measuring the risk they pose to others. This enables the YOT to identify suitable programmes to address the needs of the young person with the intention of preventing further offending.

Sentencing glossary

Absolute discharge The court takes no further action against an offender, but the offender's discharge will appear on his or her criminal record.

Antecedents Information about the offender's background and personal circumstances.

Anti-social behaviour order (ASBO) A court order prohibiting the defendant from specific anti-social behaviour. An ASBO lasts for a minimum of two years. It is a civil order, but breaching an ASBO is a criminal offence punishable by a fine or up to five years in prison.

ASBO Abbreviation for **anti-social behaviour order**.

Attachment of earnings An order that directs an employer of a debtor to deduct regularly an amount, fixed by the court, from the debtor's earnings and pay that sum to the court.

Binding over A person may be 'bound over' to keep the peace. Failure to observe a binding order may result in a financial penalty.

Community order A non-custodial sentence – it may involve, for example, supervision by a probation officer or doing a number of hours unpaid work.

Compensation order An order requiring the offender to pay compensation to the victim in respect of damage to property or personal injury.

Concurrent sentence A direction by a court that a number of sentences of imprisonment should run at the same time.

Conditional discharge A discharge of a convicted defendant without sentence on condition that they do not reoffend within a specified period of time.

Consecutive sentence An order that two or more sentences should run one after the other, so that the second commences as soon as the first sentence has been served.

Curfew The subject of the order is required to remain at the address specified in the order during the curfew period. A tag, worn on the ankle or wrist, notifies monitoring services if the offender leaves the address during the curfew hours.

Custodial sentence A sentence of imprisonment (or, in the case of a young offender, detention).

Drug treatment and testing order (DTTO) A sentence for drug users who receive treatment for their drug use and have to give regular urine tests to make sure they are not using drugs.

Fine A sentence of the court which involves the offender paying money to the court as punishment for their crime.

Home detention curfew (HDC)   A prisoner serving a sentence of between three months and four years can be released between two weeks and four and a half months before their automatic release date, depending on the length of the sentence, under strict curfew arrangements and wearing an electronic tag.

Mitigation   The explanation given on behalf of an offender of the offence and of his personal circumstances, in an attempt to minimise the sentence.

Newton hearing   Where a defendant wishes to plead guilty but puts forward a different factual basis for the offence than that suggested by the prosecution, the court must (i) accept the defence version, or (ii) hear evidence about the commission of the offence and then make a finding of fact as to which version is to be believed (this is called a *Newton* hearing, as the procedure is based on *R v Newton* (1983) 77 Cr App R 13 and, in the Crown Court, is heard by a judge sitting without a jury), or (iii) where the difference between the two versions is, in effect, that the prosecution allege that the defendant committed an offence additional to that charged, bring a further charge against the defendant and try him for it in the usual way.

Offending behaviour programme (OBP)   A programme of work undertaken with an offender which is designed to tackle the reasons which led his offending.

Plea in mitigation   Statement on behalf of the offender when mitigation (q.v.) is presented to the court.

Restorative justice   This may involve a meeting between the offender and victim, with a mediator, where the victim can tell the offender how the offence has affected them, and the offender has the chance to make amends directly to the victim of the crime.

Suspended sentence   A custodial sentence which does not take effect unless the defendant commits a subsequent offence within a specified period which is known as the 'operational period'.

Young offender institution   A 'prison' for young people between the ages of 15 and 21. Young offenders have to be kept separately from adults (over 21s), and juveniles (under 18s) separate from 18–21-year-olds.

Index